Putin

Putin

PHILIP SHORT

HENRY HOLT AND COMPANY
NEW YORK

Henry Holt and Company
Publishers since 1866
120 Broadway
New York, New York 10271
www.henryholt.com

Henry Holt® and ⒣® are registered trademarks of Macmillan Publishing
Group, LLC.

Library of Congress Cataloging-in-Publication Data is available.

ISBN: 9781627793667

Our books may be purchased in bulk for promotional, educational, or
business use. Please contact your local bookseller or the Macmillan
Corporate and Premium Sales Department at (800) 221-7945, extension
5442, or by e-mail at MacmillanSpecialMarkets@macmillan.com.

Originally published by The Bodley Head (Penguin Random House UK)
in 2022
First US Edition 2022

Printed in the United States of America

10 9 8 7 6 5 4 3 2 1

For Romy, Ben and Sengan

Contents

Note on Spelling and Pronunciation

Almost every language in use in the world today has a generally accepted form of transliteration into English. Russian does not. Although various romanisations exist, none has yet established itself as a universal standard, partly, perhaps, because most require special characters and diacritical marks. The result is a hodgepodge in which names are spelt in a bewildering variety of ways.

This book uses transliterations which are as close as possible to the way Russian words should be pronounced while conserving the original orthography. Since the Cyrillic alphabet has no equivalent of the English letter 'x', the romanisation 'ks' is employed, as in Aleksandr, Aleksei, Ksenia, etc. Other letters not found in English include 'kh', pronounced as 'ch' in loch, and 'zh', as in rouge. When a name ends in -ii, like Georgii or Dmitrii, pronounced as a single syllable, the letter 'y' is usually substituted, thus Georgy and Dmitry. When -ii is pronounced as two syllables, as in Daniil, Gavriil or Mariinsky, it is written as such.

The trickiest letter of the Cyrillic alphabet is 'e', which can signify either 'ye' – as in Yeltsin, Yelena or Basayev – or 'yo', as in Gorbachev and Khrushchev. Unfortunately there is no hard and fast rule. In most cases, 'e' after 'ch' and 'shch' should be pronounced 'yo', except in words of Ukrainian origin, such as Chernenko, Chernobyl and names ending in -chenko (Kirichenko, Shevchenko, etc). There are exceptions, however, such as the playwright, Anton Chekhov. Other words where the pronunciation 'yo' applies are so spelt, for example, Kishinyov, Seleznyov and Snegiryov. Everywhere else, 'e' is pronounced 'ye', apart from a few place names, like Mount Elbrus, where in Russian a different form of letter 'e' is employed.

The system is not foolproof. Purists may object that, to be consistent, Belyaev should be written Belyayev, but that would be too much of a mouthful and in any case the second 'y' is elided. The other draw-back is that it does not indicate where the stress should come in a name, but for that there are no fixed rules. In theory, the surname Borodin could be pronounced Bórodin, Boródin or Borodín. In fact, the stress is on the last syllable, Borodín, but there is no way to guess that, you need to know.

Russian names always include the patronymic – thus, Vladimir Vladimirovich Putin; his father, Vladimir Spiridonovich; his grand-father, Spiridon Ivanovich, and so on, the middle name deriving from the father's given name. The combination of forename and patro-nymic is the polite form of address, 'Vladimir Vladimirovich' in Russian being the equivalent of 'Mr Putin' in English. For simplicity, patronymics are used here only when it is necessary to distinguish between individuals with the same first and family names, like Putin and his father, or when they appear in citations. For the same reason, the names of married women are given without a feminine ending: Lyudmila Putin rather than Putina, as would be written in Russian.

Prologue

Even in ordinary times, Moscow is a hive of rumour and speculation. In the spring and early summer of 1999, it was so humming with conspiracy theories and tales of dark intrigue that the Russian adage, 'lies have short legs', meaning that they cannot run very far, seemed no longer to apply.

The President, Boris Yeltsin, a massively built, larger-than-life figure in his late sixties with a broad, impassive face and a shock of silvery hair, was ailing. A quintuple bypass operation three years earlier had pulled him back from the brink, but his health had deteriorated again and there were doubts, even within his own entourage, that he would survive the coming winter. His enemies were circling. The man who seemed most likely to succeed him, Yevgeny Primakov, two years his senior, who had served as Prime Minister and, earlier, chief of foreign intelligence, had left no one under any illusion that, once in power, he would attack not only the corrupt business magnates who had flourished in Yeltsin's shadow but also those he considered to be their enablers in the Kremlin itself. Primakov, a bespectacled academic with jowls like a basset hound, was a tough, pragmatic conservative who had the support of the *nomenklatura*, the bureaucratic elite, and of the Communist Party. To the 'Family', the small group of intimates on whom Yeltsin increasingly relied – and who in turn relied on him – such an outcome would be, if not literally, then politically and materially, a death sentence. As the year progressed, it became more and more urgent for them to ensure that Primakov's rise was stopped.

The first hint of trouble brewing came at the end of May. Jan Blomgren, a veteran Swedish correspondent in Moscow, was told that the Kremlin was casting about for a pretext to postpone elections, due in December, for the lower house of parliament, the Duma, which were expected to result in a landslide for the Fatherland Party, whose members backed Primakov and his ally, the Mayor of Moscow, Yuri Luzhkov. Blomgren said later that he had two sources for the story, both with good access to the Presidential Administration. On June 6, 1999, he reported in the Swedish daily, *Svenska Dagbladet*, that several possibilities were being considered. Two involved changing the constitution, either to give greater independence to Russia's 89 constituent regions,[1] making the country a confederal rather than a federal state, or to consummate a long-discussed Union between Russia and Belarus, with Yeltsin as President and the Belarussian leader, Aleksandr Lukashenko, as Vice President. In either case, a new constitution would have to be written which would mean that the elections would be delayed.

The third possibility, Blomgren wrote, was to create a situation justifying the declaration of a state of emergency. That would be done through false-flag terrorist attacks that would be ascribed to militants from the autonomous republic of Chechnya, in the Caucasus, which had been in a state of insurrection for most of the previous decade.[2]

Ten days later, another report appeared, this time in a Russian newspaper, *Literaturnaya gazeta*. The writer, Giulietto Chiesa, had spent 20 years in Moscow as the correspondent of the Italian Communist Party newspaper, *l'Unità*, and later *La Stampa*. Chiesa also raised the possibility of terrorist attacks, which might be perpetrated by 'a secret service, either foreign or national' in order to create panic among the population.[3] The main Moscow city newspaper, *Moskovskaya pravda*, then followed up with an article entitled 'Storm in Moscow'. It quoted 'trustworthy sources in the Kremlin' as saying that the Presidential Administration had drafted a programme, which Yeltsin had approved, to discredit Luzhkov by launching provocations in Moscow, including 'terrorist acts (or attempts at terrorist acts)' directed at government buildings, designed to make Muscovites believe that 'Luzhkov had lost control of the situation in the city'.[4] The plan was dated June 29 and was said to have been leaked by Sergei Zverev, a deputy head of the Presidential Administration whom Yeltsin fired shortly afterwards.[5]

Hardly anyone took these reports seriously. They were just part of the cacophony of Moscow gossip. Eugene Rumer, then a young official at the State Department in Washington, did wonder about them.

He and a colleague at the Bureau of Research and Intelligence debated
whether to alert someone higher up. In the end, they decided not to.
'We thought it didn't quite rise to the level of writing a memo to anybody up the food chain,' Rumer remembered. 'Afterwards I rather
regretted that.'[6]

The explosions began two months later.

The first came during the evening rush hour at an underground shopping mall on Tverskaya Street, in the heart of Moscow, 200 yards from
Red Square. A small home-made bomb was left in an arcade lined with
slot machines near a fast-food restaurant. It exploded shortly after 8 p.m.
on August 31, killing one person and injuring more than 30 others.[7]

Thereafter, at intervals of three to five days, four other much larger
charges exploded. On the evening of Saturday, September 4, a truck
bomb detonated outside an apartment block housing border guards and
their families at Buinaksk, a town of 60,000 people in Dagestan, near the
Black Sea, 30 miles from the border with Chechnya. Fifty-eight people
were killed and a hundred injured. Another truck, packed with a far more
powerful charge containing two and a half tons of explosive – 'enough
to turn that part of the city into dust', as one newspaper put it – was
found an hour later, parked outside a military hospital. It was disarmed
with minutes to spare.[8] The following week, a nine-storey apartment
building was blown up in a working-class suburb of Moscow. The explosive, identified as hexogen, had been hidden in the basement. One
hundred and six people were killed and nearly 250 injured. On September 13, a similar blast in another Moscow suburb killed 119 people and
injured 200. Then, shortly before dawn on September 16, an explosion
destroyed an apartment building in Volgodonsk, a medium-sized city
600 miles south-east of Moscow. Nineteen people died and 69 were
injured.[9]

The authorities attributed the attacks to Chechen militants.

During the first week of August, a Chechen warlord, Shamil Basayev,
had taken more than a thousand fighters into neighbouring Dagestan
to support a group of Wahhabi Islamic fundamentalists who were trying to establish a Caliphate there. The invasion coincided with Yeltsin's
decision to fire his fourth Prime Minister in two years, Sergei Stepashin,
a high-ranking public servant who had been less than three months in
the job, and to appoint instead a man whom most Western diplomats

then regarded, if they knew of him at all, as a colourless functionary, noted for discretion but little else: 46-year-old Vladimir Putin.

Outside the Presidential Administration, Putin was an opaque figure. For the previous year he had served as Director of the FSB, which had succeeded the KGB as Russia's domestic intelligence service, and for the last few months had also been Secretary of the Security Council, Moscow's equivalent of the NSC, the National Security Council in the White House. But he preferred to remain out of public view, rarely giving interviews or appearing on television. After his appointment as Prime Minister, his deputy, Nikolai Patrushev, took over as head of the security service. A hard-bitten, granite-faced man, who swore like a trooper and took a dim view of the world outside Russia, Patrushev headed the investigation into the explosions.

The FSB had warned that the flare-up in Dagestan risked triggering terrorist attacks in Moscow and other cities,[10] and most Russians at first readily accepted that the explosions were the Chechens' doing. Disparaged as 'blacks', because of their darker skins, they had fought for centuries against integration into Russia and were reviled for trafficking in drugs and prostitution. They were feared for their stubborn clan loyalties and had a gruesome reputation for violence, which made even Russian organised-crime groups wary of confronting Chechen gangs. As the explosions continued, the Moscow police began aggressively rounding up and expelling from the city anyone with a Caucasian appearance who could not prove their bona fides. It was crude racial profiling, but in the panic after the bomb attacks, the authorities were desperate to be seen to be doing something to reassure the population.

Then, on September 22, an incident occurred which showed the government's actions in a very different light.[11]

Aleksei Kartofelnikov, a bus driver in the provincial city of Ryazan, 120 miles south-east of Moscow, had spent his day off, a Wednesday, working in the vegetable garden at his dacha. When he returned home, shortly after 8 p.m., it was already dusk. Outside his apartment block, on Novoselov Street, in a leafy, working-class suburb, he noticed a white Zhiguli car, with pieces of paper taped crudely over the number plates, which was parked by the entrance of the building and seemed to be waiting for something. A young woman stood nearby, looking around nervously. Kartofelnikov decided to telephone the police. After a certain amount of argument – no one at the station wanted to be bothered – a patrol eventually arrived. By then the car had gone, but Kartofelnikov's daughter insisted that the officers check the basement. There, ankle deep in water, they found in a raised alcove three 110-lb sacks, marked 'sugar', piled on top of each other, with an electrical device and a timer protruding from the top. The 12-storey building was hastily evacuated (apart from five bedridden invalids who were left to fend for themselves). As word spread, residents of nearby blocks poured out onto the streets as well. By midnight, almost all the 30,000 people living in that part of Ryazan were out of doors or in makeshift shelters in schools and cinemas. When bomb squad officers arrived and removed the detonator, they found the timer had been set for 5.30 a.m. A portable gas analyser showed that the 'sugar' was giving off fumes of hexogen, the same explosive that had been used in Moscow. After an exhaustive search, nothing more was found, the all-clear was given shortly after dawn and the residents allowed to return to their homes.

It seemed that a tragedy on the scale of the Moscow bombings or possibly worse had been narrowly averted. The Ryazan FSB announced that it was opening a criminal case against the presumed attackers, and 1,200 officers fanned out through the city, checking basements and cellars. The police issued identikit pictures of the young woman who had caught Kartofelnikov's attention and of two young men whom other eyewitnesses had reported seeing in the mysterious white Zhiguli. That evening Prime Minister Putin and his Interior Minister, Viktor Rushailo, praised the people of Ryazan for their vigilance.

By then, however, inconsistencies in the story were emerging.

The descriptions of the three occupants of the Zhiguli were not of Chechens but of European Russians. Then the police learnt of a suspicious phone call to Moscow. In those days, inter-city calls from the Russian provinces were connected by an operator, who on this occasion listened in. 'There are patrols everywhere,' she heard the caller say. 'Split up and each of you make your own way out,' the voice at the other end replied. The Moscow number turned out to be at the Lubyanka, the FSB's headquarters. Soon afterwards, an FSB general in the capital, Aleksandr Zdanovich, started to walk back the Ryazan FSB's account of the day's events, telling the Russian television channel, NTV, that it was not yet certain that there had been real explosives in the sacks. Another FSB official was quoted as saying that the whole affair might have been just 'a stupid joke'.

That night two of the three suspects were detained by the Ryazan police. To the officers' astonishment, both produced FSB identity papers and, on orders from Moscow, were quickly released.

Finally, at noon on Friday, more than 36 hours after the discovery in the basement at Novoselov Street, the FSB Director, Patrushev, emerged from a meeting in the Kremlin to announce that there had been no attack and no real explosives, it had been merely an FSB training exercise using a dummy device. The gas detector which had registered the presence of hexogen had allegedly 'malfunctioned'.

Under intense pressure from Moscow, those involved in the case in Ryazan reluctantly acquiesced in Patrushev's explanation. But the damage had been done.

The Ryazan incident cast a long shadow, which Vladimir Putin, soon to become Russia's President, would never be entirely able to throw off.

More and more Russians started believing that the Kremlin, not the Chechens, had organised the explosions.[12] Putin, it was thought, had taken office too recently and was too much in Yeltsin's shadow to have organised such an operation himself.[13] But the President and his inner circle, the Family, were a different matter. They might well have decided on a 'strategy of tension', as Giulietto Chiesa had called it, to justify a state of emergency and postpone the Duma elections.

Speculation about this lurid scenario began within hours of Patrushev's statement. *Moskovsky komsomolets,* a widely read if sensationalist Moscow tabloid which for days had been gleefully poking holes in the government's version of events, asserted bluntly that the Presidential Administration had planned an 'operation' to destabilise Russia and had given it the go-ahead after Putin's appointment as Prime Minister.[14]

Patrushev issued a denial, insisting that the perpetrators were 'not some mythical conspirators in the Kremlin but completely concrete international terrorists'.[15] But by then the floodgates had opened. Next day, *Nezavisimaya gazeta,* which was read by the Moscow intelligentsia and much of the liberal establishment, expanded on the tabloid's allegations. 'For the first time,' it said, 'responsibility for the bombings of the apartment buildings in Russia has been clearly [ascribed] to the presidential family and, personally, to the head of the government, Vladimir Putin, as the de facto sponsor and organiser of the explosions. This charge is too serious . . . to be ignored.'[16] A few days later,

Aleksandr Lebed, a retired general and former Secretary of the Security Council, told the French newspaper, *Le Figaro*, that he was 'almost certain' the regime was complicit in the bombings. 'In order to hold on to power,' he said, 'all means are good.'[17]

In a country where, over the centuries, people have learnt to expect the worst from their rulers, and where the news media, not long freed from the iron grip of Soviet censorship, had a pronounced tendency to confuse fiction with fact, Russians reacted to these claims more phlegmatically than might have been expected. The Kremlin remained silent. Talk of a state of emergency subsided.[18] Ten days later, the Russian army, whose forces had been massing along the Chechen border, launched a large-scale ground offensive.

Putin took charge of the war and the tough, no-nonsense manner in which he approached the conflict resonated with Russians. As his authority grew, the Kremlin's internal polling showed that the projected lead of Primakov's Fatherland Party in the Duma elections was melting away.

Yet at the same time evidence continued to accumulate of the government's complicity in the attacks.

On September 13, Gennady Seleznyov, the Speaker of the Duma, interrupted a closed session of parliament to announce that there had been an explosion in Volgodonsk. What was odd was that he spoke three days *before* the apartment block there was blown up.[19] The FSB, the opposition charged, must have alerted him prematurely. Then it was discovered that sacks identical to those found in Ryazan, also marked 'sugar' but containing what was thought to be hexogen, were being stocked at an army base near the city.[20] The Kremlin blocked an attempt to set up a parliamentary commission of inquiry[21] and ordered all official documents related to the Ryazan affair to remain sealed for 75 years.[22] By then, Yeltsin had resigned and Putin had become President. If he had nothing to hide, Russians asked, why was the dossier being kept secret?

Stripped of euphemisms, the Kremlin stood accused of organising mass murder, the killing of men, women and children, sleeping peacefully in their beds, for sordid political ends.

The allegation was breathtaking. Yet everything appeared to fit. In the summer, the Kremlin had been reported to be planning false-flag terrorist attacks which would be blamed on Chechen rebels. In

September, terrorist attacks did begin and were blamed on Chechen rebels. Then 'terrorists' were caught red-handed, planting explosives in Ryazan, and turned out not to be Chechens but Russian FSB officers. On the face of it, all the evidence pointed to a monstrous, cold-blooded conspiracy to seal Yeltsin's succession by sacrificing hundreds of innocent lives.

Or did it?

To try to answer that question, it is necessary to pick apart what happened, one piece at a time.

To anyone who had followed closely Yeltsin's presidency, the rumours that swept Moscow in the summer of 1999 were strangely familiar. Three years earlier, when he had faced another election which he was expected to lose, there had also been a debate in the Kremlin over whether to declare a state of emergency so that the vote could be postponed. Then, too, there was talk of false-flag attacks which could be blamed on the Chechens. Then, too, after explosions in the metro and on trolleybuses, there was immediate – and, as it transpired, unfounded – speculation that the authorities, not the Chechens, were responsible. 'Cui bono?' asked the investigative weekly, *Sobesednik*. Chechen militants had been in Moscow for years, it noted. Why would they wait to carry out explosions 'exactly when they were needed'? The authors of such attacks, it charged, would be found in the same department as was supposed to be investigating them – in other words, the FSB.[23]

When the same situation arose in 1999, the same arguments reappeared.

Among the journalists who had written about the rumours that summer, Jan Blomgren had come closest to describing what subsequently happened. Chiesa, whatever his merits as an observer of Russian affairs, was a notorious conspiracy theorist.[24] *Moskovskaya pravda*, which had reported Zverev's allegations, was controlled by the Moscow City Administration and, like its sister paper, *Moskovsky komsomolets*, was committed to supporting the election campaign of the mayor, Yuri Luzhkov, and his ally, Primakov, and to blackening by all means, fair or foul, the image of Yeltsin and his new Prime Minister.[25]

Blomgren had no axe to grind, which made his reporting more credible. The FSB evidently thought so, too. In November, after he published a follow-up article, casting further doubt on the Chechens' role in the attacks,[26] a drug was slipped into his drink at a Moscow discotheque where he went with a colleague one evening. He collapsed after returning to his apartment and woke up in hospital 48 hours later. When he was allowed to go home, he found that his computer had been tampered with and a videocassette was missing, but money and objects of value had not been touched.[27] Whoever was responsible appeared to be trying to discover his sources, an understandable subject of interest for the security services, though in other countries they might have used different methods.

But no matter how suggestive the sequence of events – rumours of bomb attacks, followed two months later by the bomb attacks themselves – there was no proof that the two were connected. In 1996, the rumours and subsequent explosions had turned out in the end to be unrelated.

'After' does not necessarily mean 'because'.

All five attacks in 1999 – from the bomb in the Moscow shopping mall on August 31 to the Volgodonsk explosion on September 16 – are viewed in the West and in Russia as a single series. The first may have been a trial run, to see how the authorities would react, or it may have been unrelated – the work of criminals rather than terrorists, shaking down local business interests.[28] But if the other four were connected, as most analysts believe, it raises an obvious question. The victims at Buinaksk were military families. It is one thing to accuse the FSB, or elements within it, of sacrificing civilian lives for political ends. There were ample precedents for that in Russia, not just under the Soviet dictator, Joseph Stalin, but also under tsarist rule. But would FSB officers murder in cold blood dozens of fellow soldiers and their dependants in order to manipulate a political succession?

In Stalin's time, perhaps. Not in the 1990s.

The explosion in Buinaksk had all the hallmarks of being the work of Islamic fundamentalists from Chechnya or, more likely, from Dagestan. When it occurred, Russian Army units were preparing to occupy a cluster of fundamentalist Dagestani villages, which had proclaimed sharia law. The radicals had warned that any attempt to do so would be met by bomb attacks 'all over Russia'.[29] Buinaksk was nearby and the border guards' living quarters and the military hospital were soft targets.

If the Buinaksk bombing was the work of Chechens or Dagestanis, is it plausible that only four days later, the FSB would have been able to launch a series of bombings in Moscow, which would have required weeks if not months of planning beforehand?

More than five tons of explosives, smuggled into Moscow, disguised as sacks of sugar, were discovered in the basements of other apartment buildings and disarmed by the security services before they could explode. If the security services were carrying out the attacks, would they also have been working to prevent them? It may be argued that that was a cover-up, to reassure a jittery population that the authorities were trying to protect them. But the more complex the planning, the more people would have had to be in the know and the greater the risk of leaks. Twenty years have passed and no leak has occurred.

Western intelligence officers based in Moscow in the late 1990s are categorical: if the FSB, or even elements within it, had participated in the bombings, it would have been impossible to maintain secrecy for so long. Mark Kelton was the CIA Station Chief in Moscow when the bombings occurred. 'One thing the Russians have learned, and the West has learned,' he said, 'is that no intelligence operation is going to stay secret for ever. That's one of the reasons I don't think they did it . . . When people talk about these large conspiracies, I don't buy it. Too many moving parts, too many things that can go wrong.'[30] Richard Dearlove, who headed MI6 in 1999, and his successor, John Scarlett, agree. As Scarlett put it, 'people would have started talking. And they haven't.'[31]

Kelton is adamant: 'I never saw any information that it was anything other than what it was portrayed to be, and that was that the Chechens were responsible.' Dearlove recalls that the British services had 'a lot of penetration' in Russia at that time. Had there been serious evidence of FSB participation, he says, MI6 would certainly have learnt of it.[32]

The announcement by the Speaker of the Duma, Gennady Seleznyov, on September 13, that a building had been blown up in Volgodonsk three days before it actually happened – a claim still regularly cited by Russian journalists and opposition politicians as proof of FSB intrigues[33] – turned out to have a simple explanation. On the evening of September 12, an explosive device did go off in Volgodonsk, killing one person and injuring two others. The first wire service newsflash landed at 10.38 the following morning.[34] At the time, the explosion was thought to be another in the same series. 'Buinaksk, twice Moscow, now Volgodonsk . . .' ran one newspaper headline.[35] It was on that basis that Seleznyov made his announcement. When the second, much larger explosion took place, on September 16, Seleznyov was briefly questioned about the earlier statement, but it was quickly forgotten. It became a major issue only two and a half years later, in March 2002, when his political opponents launched a campaign to unseat him.[36]

The incident at Ryazan is unlikely to be fully elucidated as long as the official papers are sealed. Yet, hiding in plain sight, there are revealing anomalies, the most striking being the sheer, bumbling incompetence of the FSB operatives charged with carrying it out.

The clumsy masking of the number plates of their car with crudely taped pieces of paper; the young woman nervously keeping watch at the entrance to the targeted building; the phone call afterwards on an open line to the FSB in Moscow; and finally the arrest within hours of two of the three members of the group, could be straight out of a film of the Three Stooges. The tradecraft was appalling.[37] If that was the best the FSB could do in a sleepy, mid-sized city in the provinces, was it credible that it could carry out, undetected, massive explosions in Moscow, where security was much tighter?

Gleb Pavlovsky, who was then in the Kremlin working as an electoral strategist but later broke with Putin, dismisses as ludicrous the idea that the FSB could have been responsible. 'The FSB of those days was not the FSB of today,' he argues. 'It was very weak, thin on the ground, most of its specialists had already long since left . . . There simply was no one there able to carry that out. I think it would have been impossible.'[38] Aleksandr Golts, a leading military analyst, concurs. The FSB in 1999, he says, was in 'a state of total degradation' as a result of budget cuts and repeated reorganisations. Even had it wished to, it lacked the capability to stage a clandestine bombing campaign.[39]

In that case, what was the purpose of the exercise at Ryazan? Patrushev's explanation that it was for training purposes, to test the vigilance of the population, was widely disbelieved. Yet it may have had a kernel of truth. If the bombings were not orchestrated by the Kremlin, the FSB would have been under intense pressure to find the perpetrators and bring the attacks to an end. Patrushev and his deputies would have been desperate to show that they were doing something, anything, to track down those responsible.[40]

To men whose outlook had been formed in the KGB in the 1970s, a simulated attack, using sacks marked 'sugar', identical to those filled with hexogen which had caused the Moscow explosions, would have been an obvious starting point. The counter-intelligence manuals used when Patrushev and others of his generation underwent basic training recommended 'operational experiments' to enable officers 'covertly to study . . . a situation or phenomenon of interest under specially created conditions. [These include] experiments to reproduce a specific situation [and those] carried out to check the effectiveness of counter-intelligence measures.'[41]

That is almost word for word what the FSB says it tried to do in Ryazan. The stupidity, 'the unbelievable stupidity', as one former senior KGB officer put it, was to carry out the exercise in a building where ordinary people were living, rather than in a government structure. 'We used to carry out exercises like that,' he said. 'I took part in them myself . . . The goal was to test systems of protection . . . But they were always against administrative sites, not residential buildings . . . People could have heart attacks, they could panic and throw themselves out of the windows. Whoever thought this up should be fired tomorrow. There are people at the head of the special services who are imbeciles. I say that as a professional, and I am not the only one to think so.'[42]

How much hexogen, if any, the sacks at Ryazan contained is unclear. If, for verisimilitude, empty sacks had been brought from the army base and filled with an inert substance, there might still have been enough traces of explosive to register on the gas detector. The detonator used was real, not a dummy. But when a sample of the substance was tested, it failed to explode.[43]

Most of the other arguments advanced to try to prove that the FSB was behind the bombings are equally questionable.

It was said that if Chechens had been responsible, they would have broadcast the fact. Yet it was a hallmark of Chechen terrorism that they almost never did so. In November 1996, 68 people had died in a similar explosion at an apartment building in Kaspiisk, on the Caspian Sea coast near the Dagestani capital, Makhachkala, which, like that in Buinaksk, housed border guards and their families. No one claimed responsibility. Others argued that Chechen fighters would have attacked army barracks, not civilian targets. But six months before the events in Moscow, Chechen terrorists had attacked a market at Vladi-kavkaz, in the nearby republic of North Ossetia, killing 52 people and injuring 168 others, almost all of them civilians. Army barracks were too well protected.[44]

Had the FSB really been behind the apartment bombings, it would have been logical for it to have issued a fake claim in the Chechens' name, in order to pin the blame on them more firmly in the public mind. It did not do so.

Shamil Basayev was quoted as saying after the first explosion in Moscow that it was 'not our work, but the work of the Dagestanis'.[45] That was probably true but it was a nuance. The two groups made common cause. Six weeks after the attacks, Putin told President Clinton during a meeting in Oslo that Russian intelligence had intercepted a message from Basayev's fellow commander, a Saudi Arabian jihadi named Khattab, to an associate in the Middle East, in which he said: 'In September, we hit Russia at its very core. The last time explosions like this were seen in Moscow was in World War II.'[46] Basayev had given due warning. The Chechens, he had announced some years earlier, were preparing a jihad that would 'engulf the world in blue flames', in which ordinary Russians would be as legitimate a target as their government.[47] Afterwards he taunted Putin, claiming that although his forces had 'no connection with the explosions, we can, in an appropriate form, accept responsibility for them'.[48]

What appeared to be a cast-iron case, built on seemingly incontrovertible evidence, showing that the Kremlin had organised a demonic scheme to murder its own citizens in order to bring a chosen candidate to power, on closer examination does not stand up.

It cannot be conclusively proved that no one from the FSB was involved. Although unlikely, it is possible that FSB explosives experts provided professional assistance for mercenary considerations, just as army officers must have been complicit when the hexogen was stolen from military warehouses and police officers paid to close their eyes to truckloads of 'sugar' passing through checkpoints.[49] That was how Russia worked in the 1990s.

But factual evidence of Russian state involvement is absent.

The story took on a life of its own for quite different reasons. *Kompromat* and 'Black PR' – damaging material used to create negative publicity – are a staple of Russian election campaigns. The explosions in Moscow were seized on by Putin's opponents as ammunition for electoral mudslinging. Initially, the press controlled by the Moscow City Administration tried to incriminate Yeltsin and Putin.[50] The following spring, when Putin stood for President, the accusations resumed. Then they were taken up by Boris Berezovsky, a business magnate who had become immensely wealthy after the collapse of the Soviet Union but had subsequently broken with Putin and was living in exile in London. Berezovsky financed a television documentary, 'The Assassination of Russia', and two books about the bombings, *Blowing Up Russia* and *Lubyanskaya prestupnaya gruppirovka* ['The Lubyanka Criminal Group'], co-authored by Aleksandr Litvinenko, a former FSB officer whose murder in London with radioactive polonium would later make worldwide headlines.

The claim that the Kremlin, and by implication Putin himself, had organised the apartment bombings found a receptive audience. Few in Russia believed the government's clumsy denials, and its subsequent efforts to suppress the story altogether, by silencing witnesses, blocking an official enquiry and ordering documents sealed, merely made matters worse.

Twenty years later, many Russian politicians, newspaper editors and political commentators, as well as their counterparts in the West, remain firmly convinced that the attacks were carried out by, or with the connivance of, the FSB.[51] Others are unsure but do not rule it out altogether. Yet it is almost certainly false.[52] Not because the Kremlin's strategists would necessarily have rejected such methods, but because the risks were too great. As Aleksandr Golts put it: 'There were people around Yeltsin who were extremely cynical. But they were not idiots. They understood that if something like that ever came out, it would be the end of everything.'[53]

The saga of the apartment bombings illustrates two of the main difficulties confronting anyone who seeks to penetrate the mysteries of Putin's Russia.

The first was described by the historian, Richard Hofstadter, at the height of the Cold War, when he wrote in *Harper's Magazine* of the American tendency to view every enemy as 'a perfect model of malice, a kind of amoral superman – sinister, ubiquitous, powerful, cruel . . . [who] profits from the misery he has produced.'[54]

Ronald Reagan's characterisation of the Soviet Union as 'the evil empire' and George W. Bush's denunciation of 'the axis of evil', referring to Iran, Iraq and North Korea, were in that mould. So was Senator John McCain's description of Putin as 'a thug, a murderer and a killer'.[55] To most Americans, Vladimir Putin is the embodiment of evil – 'a war criminal, a murderous dictator . . . a butcher', as President Biden put it – and that is all there is to be said. Should anyone doubt it, they need only look at the war which Putin unleashed against Ukraine to unseat a government whose crime, in his eyes, was to seek closer ties with the West. To suggest otherwise is to be an apologist or, at best, what in Germany is called disdainfully a *Putinversteher*, a 'Putin-understander'.

To Russia, the relationship with America is far more important than any other. For much of the time since the 1950s, America regarded Russia the same way, although now, in the light of China's rise, that is beginning to change. The two countries are antinomes, halves of a unique dyad which neither forms with any other nation. Both think of themselves as exceptional, which is a recipe for mutual incomprehension, if not animosity, no matter who occupies the Kremlin or the White House.

Europe follows America's lead, though in less polarised fashion. Geographically, Europe is closer and more conscious of the need to find ways to coexist with its giant neighbour. But even in Europe, Putin is seen as presiding over a corrupt, kleptocratic, authoritarian state, where those in power can have opponents assassinated or imprisoned at will, basic freedoms are curtailed, the media do the Kremlin's bidding and a small coterie of billionaires live off the fat of the land while the rest of the population struggles to survive.

Much of that is true. But it is not the whole story. Nor does it explain why Putin's regime is what it is. National leaders invariably reflect the societies from which they come, no matter how unpalatable that thought may be to the citizens of the countries concerned. Putin is no more an aberration in Russia than Donald Trump in America, Boris Johnson in Britain or Emmanuel Macron in France. He represents the hopes and fears, the aspirations and anguish, the conceits and resentments of a substantial part of the Russian population, who regularly support him.

To try to work out why Putin behaves as he does, why under his tutelage Russia has become the country it is and what may lie ahead, both while he remains its leader and under his successors, it is necessary to put aside stereotypes and examine each piece of evidence for what it is, soberly and without prejudgement.

Therein lies the second difficulty. Normally a biographer's task is to expound the 'why' and 'how' of his subject's life: the underlying facts are rarely in dispute. With Putin, that is often not the case. As with the apartment bombings, widely accepted assumptions turn out on closer scrutiny to be partial, misleading or downright wrong. That is part of a long tradition in Russia. Winston Churchill's famous definition of Kremlinology as watching 'a bulldog fight under a rug – an outsider only hears the growling, and when he sees the bones fly out from beneath it is obvious who won' – has been true of Russian governance since the sixteenth century or earlier. The Kremlin does not yield its secrets easily. The broad outline may be clear, but the devil is in the details and the details matter. If enough details change, the overall picture changes too.

Readers expecting to find a distillation of the turpitudes of the Russian regime will be disappointed by the account which follows, as will those who believe that everything written by Putin's critics must by definition be wrong. The purpose of this book is neither to demonise Putin – he is more than capable of doing that himself – nor to absolve him of his crimes, but to explore his personality, to understand what motivates him and how he has become the leader that he is. It has no agenda other than to establish as fully and accurately as possible the facts of his life and career, his truths and his lies, his successes and failures and the context in which he operates, and to set them out with sufficient clarity for readers to be able to make an informed judgement themselves. That is challenge enough.

I

Baskov Lane

Vladimir Putin was born on Tuesday, October 7, 1952, at Maternity Hospital No. 6, known locally as the Snegiryov hospital, five minutes' walk from his parents' home on Baskov Lane, which, despite its name, was a straight, wide street of what had once been elegant nineteenth-century apartment buildings, now shabby and dilapidated, just north of Leningrad's principal thoroughfare, Nevsky Prospekt, leading to the Winter Palace.[1]

The hospital, founded in 1771 by Catherine the Great, was the oldest in Russia and the largest and reputedly the best in Leningrad.[2] That was not saying a great deal. In Russian maternity clinics in those days, expectant mothers were crammed into filthy wards, infested with cockroaches, with blood and faeces on the floor and soiled bed-linen, where they were left to the mercy of nurses who, when they were not sadistic, were often callous. 'It doesn't hurt when you're screwing your husband, does it, but now you're having a baby, you're wailing,' one woman remembered a midwife telling her. Even at the Snegiryov, cleanliness was rudimentary and painkillers were unknown. Babies were separated from their mothers for 36 hours after birth. From the outset it was the survival of the fittest. One newborn in 50 died before leaving hospital.[3] Husbands were kept away, and Putin's father had to stand on the street outside with the other men, hoping to see his wife at one of the windows and to learn from her or another woman if the birth had gone well and whether he had a son or a daughter.[4]

Other traditions proved equally tenacious. In the cities, infants were no longer swaddled, as they were in the countryside; instead they were 'wrapped tight', so that they could not move, which amounted to the same thing. Otherwise, it was believed, their arms or legs would 'turn out crooked'.[5] Forty years later, a French medical team visiting the city was appalled to find that this 'medieval practice' continued and 'no one questions that it is correct.'[6]

Young Volodya, as his parents called him, spent the first weeks of his life in a wicker basket, suspended from the ceiling, as had been the custom in the countryside.[7] Both his father and mother had grown up near Tver, on the Volga River, 110 miles north-west of Moscow along the main highway to Leningrad. They lived in neighbouring hamlets which had once formed part of the domains of a Privy Councillor to Tsar Alexander the First, where Putin's great-grandfather, Ivan Petrovich, had been a serf. Ivan's son, Spiridon – Putin's grandfather – had moved to St Petersburg, then Russia's capital, in the 1890s, to train as a chef, eventually taking charge of the kitchens at the Astoria Hotel, the newest and most luxurious establishment in the city, built for the tercentenary of the Romanov dynasty in 1913. The family was comfortably off and lived in an apartment in nearby Gorokhovaya Street. It was there, two years earlier, that Putin's father, Vladimir, had been born. Among Spiridon's regular clients was Grigory Rasputin, the Siberian mystic whose hold over Tsar Nicholas II and his wife, the Tsarina Alexandra, helped bring about their downfall. According to family legend, when Spiridon cooked for him, the monk would tip him a ten-rouble gold coin.[8] But after the Revolution, the hotel closed and the rooms were taken over by Communist Party officials. The banks closed, too, and Spiridon, a frugal man, lost his considerable savings. As the White Russian armies, backed by the European powers, sought to strangle the new revolutionary regime at birth, civil war broke out. The Bolsheviks' leader, Lenin, unleashed a ferocious wave of terror against suspected counter-revolutionaries, conducted by the newly established Cheka, the ancestor of the KGB, which claimed at least a hundred thousand lives. Famine set in, killing five million more. In Leningrad two thirds of the population, recent immigrants from the countryside, fled back to the villages from which they had come. The city became a wasteland, with grass growing in the streets.[9]

Spiridon left, too, taking the family to his birthplace at Pominovo, a tiny settlement of crooked wooden houses straight out of a painting by Chagall, strung out along either side of a narrow dirt road, three hours on foot from Tver. It was there that his second son, Putin's father, Vladimir, met his future wife, Maria Ivanovna Shelomova, from the hamlet on the other side of the river. They married in 1928, when both were seventeen, and four years later moved to Peterhof, then a small garrison town that had grown up around Peter the Great's seafront palace on the Gulf of Finland, 20 miles west of Leningrad, where Maria's elder brother, Pyotr, who had wed Vladimir's younger sister, was living. At first the two couples shared a single room. But in 1934, after Vladimir had completed his military service as a submariner in the Baltic Fleet, he and Maria finally obtained a room of their own. Two children were born: Albert, who died of whooping cough in infancy, and Viktor, who succumbed to diphtheria when he was about two years old during the blockade of Leningrad in March 1942.[10]

Viktor's death has given rise to many unanswered questions.

As the Germans advanced on Peterhof at the end of August 1941, Maria and her baby son were alone: her husband was with the Red Army, no one knew where or even whether he was still alive. Another of her brothers, Ivan, a naval liaison officer attached to the Communist Party's Regional Committee, brought her to Leningrad and found her a place to stay with relatives.[11] But the city was already in the grip of famine and as a refugee from the suburbs, she had no ration book and no way of obtaining food for herself and her small son.[12] At first Ivan shared his own rations with them, but after he was transferred away from the city, their situation became desperate.[13]

There are conflicting accounts of what happened next. Putin remembered his parents saying that the authorities took his brother away, against his mother's wishes, and placed him in an orphanage on the grounds that he would have a better chance of surviving the winter there than if he stayed with her.[14] Another version, which may have come from Putin's mother herself, recounts that one day, when she was too weak to move, 'two young women came to her door. She asked them, "Take my son. Save him." And they took the boy away. A few days later she learnt that he had died.'[15]

Neither version is credible.

The city's orphanages did not accept children under three years old, and Viktor was not yet two. The 30,000 or so orphans rescued from the streets or from empty, freezing apartments in the winter of 1941–2, when the city was blockaded by the Germans and starvation was at its height, were all from families where the adults had died and there was no one left to take care of them. At least as many others were left to fend for themselves because there were not enough places.[16] Moreover conditions in the shelters were often appalling. The staff stole the children's food; the dormitories were unheated; in some establishments, one child in six died in the first weeks after admission.[17] Even in Moscow, which was far better provided for than Leningrad, the orphanages had a dreadful reputation. One mother, who had been warned by a friend that she would be well advised to bring her daughter home, found when she went to fetch her that the children's stomachs were swollen with hunger and they were all covered in lice.[18]

The story of the two mysterious young women is even less believable. At a time when the whole city – apart from the Party elite, which was well fed throughout the war – was maddened by hunger and everyone knew that there were cases of cannibalism, no parent, however desperate, would surrender their child to strangers.

One may legitimately wonder whether, behind Viktor's death, there lurked a family tragedy which no one would ever discuss. Putin himself did not learn until long afterwards that his brother had been buried in a mass grave in the Piskaryovskoe Cemetery, with some 470,000 others who had died during the blockade.[19]

Viktor's death, and perhaps remorse on his mother's part because of it,[20] may help to explain why she was obsessively protective of Volodya when he was a small boy, insisting on keeping him at home and working night shifts, first as a janitor and later in a bakery, in order to be with him during the day. Putin's father was by then a foreman at the Yegorov Railway Carriage Works, secretary of his workshop Party Committee and, from the spring of 1954, a member of the factory Party Committee, a position of some power.[21] Creche and kindergarten places were scarce and coveted, but, given his Party rank, he could have obtained one had he wished.[22] Evidently Maria Ivanovna did not want that. Volodya was the child of her old age – when he was born, she was a few days short of her 41st birthday – and she was taking no chances. Russian kindergartens in the early 1950s were not always the shining examples of proletarian care that Soviet propaganda made them out to be. In 1951, the year before Volodya was born, there had been a massive outbreak of diphtheria, the illness which had taken Viktor's life, in the city's preschools, and four years later an epidemic of dysentery.[23] So Volodya stayed home, apart from summer holidays with his mother's family near Pominovo, and visits to his grandfather,

Spiridon, who was then working as a chef at a Party sanatorium near Krasnogorsk, north-west of Moscow.[24]

The result was that Putin's early childhood was both cosseted and unusually free. Cosseted because, within the limits of what was possible for a working-class family in post-war Leningrad, his parents did everything they could for him; free because he was spared the discipline of Soviet preschool education, where play was combined with collective responsibility and the teachers instilled simple precepts of morality that would not have been out of place in a Victorian dame school. Even three-year-olds were expected to help clean up after lessons, clear the tables and, in winter, clear away snow.[25]

At home, there was none of that. His mother taught him to read and write and learn his numbers, but when he was done, he could go out and play in the inner courtyard, among piles of garbage, where the children found bits of broken crockery and beer-bottle tops and other intriguing objects, and stacks of winter firewood which their imaginations transformed into magical kingdoms. Four tall trees stood at the centre, their trunks protected from vandals by metal railings. To the parents, it was a safe space for children.

That was true only up to a point, for the older boys formed gangs and fought over territory, exciting the admiration of Vova, as his friends started calling him, and other younger children, who tried to emulate them. But as long as he stayed within the block – and, by his own account, he transgressed only once, at the age of five or six, when, attracted by the sounds of a May Day parade on nearby Vosstaniye Street, he sneaked out to watch, amazed and a little frightened at his own daring[26] – he was allowed to do as he wished.

Such was Putin's early childhood in his own telling and from the reminiscences of his contemporaries.

Another, very different, version exists, which is worth mentioning only because of its resemblance to the so-called 'birther' campaign in the mid 2000s to discredit President Obama, in which right-wing conspiracy theorists in America claimed that the certificate showing that Obama had been born in Hawaii was a forgery and that, in fact, he had been born in Kenya – or, in another version, was a citizen of Indonesia – and as a result had no right to be President. As late as 2010, two years after Obama's election, 25 per cent of Americans said they 'had doubts' about his place of birth.[27] Even after the President had authorised the release of his full, long-form birth certificate, a year later, 23 per cent of Republicans, including, notably, Donald Trump, and such luminaries as Joe Arpaio, Newt Gingrich, Sarah Palin and Michele Bachmann, clung to that fiction or pretended to do so.[28]

In Putin's case the conspiracy theory was woven more skilfully. It was alleged that Maria and Vladimir Spiridonovich were his adoptive parents, and that he had in fact been born in the small town of Ochyor, near Perm in the Urals, to a young single mother named Vera Nikolayevna Putin. Later, it was claimed, she had married a Georgian army officer, who resented the boy's presence and persuaded her to have him adopted by distant relatives in Leningrad.[29]

Like all good revisionist tales, this one contained grains of truth. A woman called Vera Nikolayevna Putin did marry a Georgian army officer and did have a child called Volodya, who was indeed given away for adoption.[30] As in Obama's case, it was alleged that the boy's birth certificate had been forged in order to disguise the fact that the Putins in Leningrad were not his real parents. Just as the 'birthers' had claimed that when Obama was 'growing up, no one knew him', Volodya, it was said, had suddenly appeared in Baskov Lane when he was already eight years old, and none of the Putins' neighbours remembered seeing him before that.[31] As in Obama's case, the allegations surfaced just when they might be most helpful to his political opponents.[32]

That it was a hoax should have been obvious from the start.

It had been concocted by Chechen intellectuals and later taken up by Yuri Felshtinsky, a Russian-American writer employed by Boris Berezovsky.[33] By the time Felshtinsky became involved, Putin's namesake from Georgia had been found working in a mining institute in Ochyor, where the couple who had actually adopted him lived. But Russians, like Americans, can be credulous when it comes to conspiracy theories. In both countries – America, founded on the notion of individual rights, limited federal power and the frontiersman's tradition of self-reliance; Russia, rendered cynical by centuries of official deceit – a significant part of the population regards government as inherently malign, to be suffered if need be but certainly not trusted. These are the people who are convinced that the Twin Towers were blown up by the CIA and the Moscow apartment blocks by the FSB. Even now, there are Russian opposition figures and Eastern European politicians who wonder aloud whether the adoption story might be true and, from time to time, that version is resuscitated in Western newspapers.[34]

The school year in Russia starts on September 1, unless it happens to be at a weekend. In 1960, it fell on a Thursday. School No. 193 was only two doors away from the building where the Putins lived. It had been founded by a progressive aristocrat, Princess Obolensky, to educate the daughters of gentlefolk – a Girls' Gymnasium, as it was called – and had numbered among its pupils Nadezhda Krupskaya, who afterwards married Lenin, as well as the daughters of Pyotr Stolypin, the Tsar's reformist Prime Minister who was assassinated in 1911. At the turn of the twentieth century, the school had moved from its original location, a few blocks further south, to a purpose-built five-storey building at No. 8, Baskov Lane. The brick façade, with inset panels of curlicued oak leaves and the Obolensky coat of arms, the high-ceilinged classrooms and imposing central staircase with wrought iron balusters, had survived, albeit in a state of chronic disrepair, both the Bolshevik Revolution and the Second World War, when it had been used as a staff headquarters for the Soviet air force.[35]

'First Bell Day', as it was called, was a rite of passage little changed since tsarist times. The new arrivals, immaculate in freshly pressed school uniforms – a grey jacket buttoned up to the collar, short trousers, a shirt and tie, and a peaked cap for the boys; a white blouse and grey skirt for the girls – gathered with their parents outside the main door, where the head teacher made a speech of welcome. Normally one of the children was then asked to ring a school bell, but at Putin's school that tradition was no longer observed. Instead they were ushered inside, each carrying a bouquet or a pot of flowers for their teacher, almost always for the younger children a woman.[36]

The junior classes resembled those in an old-fashioned elementary school in the West in the 1920s or '30s.[37] The children were taught to read fairy tales like 'The Three Bears' (in Leo Tolstoy's version, where the bears, not Goldilocks, are the heroes), and edifying accounts of students helping old people and caring for their comrades, illustrated by black-and-white sketches of radiant boys and girls.

There were also differences. The reading primer in first grade opened with a story about Lenin, the role model for Soviet children, depicted as a benign patriarchal figure, who spent his life delivering inspiring speeches, patting young children on the head, guiding the

Party wisely and gazing out pensively towards a bright, new communist future. Another chapter was devoted to the Red Army, which 'defeated the German fascists [who wanted] to conquer the whole world'. First graders learnt to sing, 'We are for peace! Let us rise as one! We will not allow war to be rekindled again.'

If that sounds heavy going for eight-year-olds (though perhaps no more so than 'Onward Christian Soldiers' and kindred Anglican hymns), there was lighter fare, including nature stories, jokes and poems. But the theme of all the lessons was the importance of patriotism, love of the Motherland, Soviet morality – held to be vastly superior to the bourgeois morality of the West – and collective values.

None of that greatly appealed to Volodya Putin. He drove his form mistress, Tamara Chizova, 26 years old and newly qualified, to despair. It was the first class she had taken on her own and it turned out to be an arduous assignment.[38] Dzerzhinsky district, where the school was located, was poor and run down. Putin's contemporary, Aleksandr Belyaev, who grew up there and would later become a prominent political leader in the city, remembered it as 'a criminal area', where the teenagers were all *shpana*, petty thugs and street hooligans. The best that they could hope for was to learn a technical skill and work in a factory all their lives.[39] The school itself provided only an 8-year, not a 10- or 11-year, course, which made it a dumping ground for those whose families could not hope for anything better. The historian, Lev Lurye, who taught at another 8-year school in Dzherzinsky district, explained:

> Those who graduated from 11-year schools generally were going to universities, as long as they passed the exams . . . And there were a lot of good 11-year schools in the Dzerzhinsky district. In fact, the best school in the country, School No. 239 . . . is just several blocks from where Putin lived . . . Those parents who cared always found a way to put their kids into a good school . . . As a schoolteacher I can say that you can divide parents into two groups: those who care and those who don't. [Putin's] school, School 193, was for kids from families which didn't care . . . I had 40 kids [in my class]. Only one was from a traditional family – only one girl, who had a mother and father together. All the others were from families where the parents were divorced or they had no father. Putin's school was like that.[40]

Even compared to his peers, young Volodya was a cross to bear. He was 'sneaky and disorganised', a child who would 'definitely cause problems', Tamara Chizova complained to a colleague.[41] He could not sit still for two seconds and, as soon as the bell rang for break, raced up and down the stairs to see if anything interesting was going on in the other classrooms.[42] An older teacher remembered:

> In the first classes [he] was very undisciplined, he lacked concentration, his studies hardly interested him at all. He had the habit of throwing his eraser, or his pen or pencil, on the floor, so that he could get up and fetch them – or simply to have an excuse to go and look out of the window. He always liked sitting by the window so that he could see out . . . He didn't care . . . what marks he got. It was of no importance to him.[43]

Part of the reason may have been that he had not attended kindergarten, where children learned 'to march in step with the collective', to fit in and behave like everyone else.[44] In Russian schools, a child who misbehaved was punished by emotional pressure – the teacher would act coldly and express disappointment – rather than by physical correction, which was forbidden.[45] The goal was to internalise obedience, so that the child would behave well not out of fear of retribution but to win the teacher's, and his peers', affection. To Putin, who had been brought up at home, that was all very new and strange:

> In the courtyard [he wrote later], the way a child asserts his identity is completely different . . . Growing up there is like living in the jungle . . . I was rebellious and so naturally I didn't follow the school rules. A school is a . . . structured community: there are clear norms of behaviour. But when someone is brought up in the jungle and then finds himself in a different context, he continues to live by the rules [he knew before]. In school he is put in a kind of cage. The cage is uncomfortable, and he begins to 'push back' against the 'walls' which hem him in. Naturally, such a rebellion, such a 'love of freedom', provokes a corresponding reaction on the part of the teachers. Already you don't like the way the teachers behave. So you start to resist. This, of course, produces more conflict. And on and on it goes.[46]

Such behaviour was all the more unacceptable in a system where moral upbringing lay at the core of political education. The school rules, which every child had to learn by heart, enjoined them 'not to arrive late for classes; to sit upright during the lesson, not leaning on the elbows or slouching; to listen attentively . . . and not to let [their] attention wander to other things; to be respectful to the school director and teachers and, when meeting them, to greet them with a polite bow – boys should also raise their caps; and to cherish the honour of school and defend it as their own.'[47]

Volodya honoured all that in the breach.

He was constantly late for lessons and ran home during breaks, which was forbidden. But his teachers were wrong to think that he did not care at all about his marks. He did the bare minimum to scrape through and avoid being held back for a year, a fate which befell one or two children in each class who got '2's for their work, marks being assigned out of a maximum of 5. Putin got '3's – unsatisfactory, but good enough not to fail.[48]

School for the junior classes was six days a week but only in the mornings. Volodya spent the afternoons making mayhem with his friends in the courtyard until it was time for his father to return from work, when he made his way up to the apartment and pretended to be doing his homework.

Vladimir Spiridonovich was master in his own home and his stern demeanour demanded respect. Short and solidly built, a cautious, thoughtful man, square-jawed, with close-cropped hair and a disquieting stare, he was a typical representative of the sturdy Russian peasantry who had flocked into the cities from the countryside in the 1930s to work in the factories during Stalin's industrialisation drive. Putin never openly defied him, and only on very rare occasions was he chastised with a belt: usually a look from his father was enough.[49] But there were times when his father clearly felt that dealing with his son was beyond him. 'What am I supposed to do? Kill him?', he asked plaintively when a teacher came to their home to complain yet again that Volodya was not working properly.[50]

This was partly a matter of education. Neither of Putin's parents had had more than a few years of primary school. After the war, his father attended night school to get a technical diploma, which he obtained at the age of 40, the year before Putin was born.[51] But he was not at ease talking to the teachers and rarely attended parents' meet-ings or other school activities.[52] Nor did Putin's mother, Maria, a handsome woman with long brown hair, a homebody who loved to cook and whose interests did not extend far beyond the family circle. As a result, Volodya was left largely to his own devices.

Under the school rules, consistent bad behaviour, which was noted in a child's personal file – a dossier that accompanied them throughout their school careers – was supposed to lead to expulsion, but schools were reluctant to take that step because it reflected badly on the teach-ers.[53] In Putin's case, moreover, his study marks were passable and it was felt that he had the potential to do better.[54] Only in one respect did his bad conduct hold him back. Like all children in the first and second grades, he was automatically enrolled as an *Oktyabryonok*, literally an 'October child', meaning a child of the Revolution. The movement had been created by Lenin's wife, Krupskaya, and was modelled on and designed to supplant Baden-Powell's Boy Scouts, which had attracted a following in Russia during the First World War.[55] The *Oktyabryata* were the equivalent of Wolf Cubs and Brownies and spent much of their time playing games. But there was also a more formal side. They wore red badges bearing an effigy of Lenin, sang patriotic songs and pledged to be 'diligent, to love school and respect their elders'.[56] Apparently young Volodya showed little enthusiasm for that part of their activ-ities, for when it came to joining the next level of the organisation, the Pioneers, to which children were usually admitted at the beginning of the third grade, he was rejected.[57]

That was highly unusual. Out of the 40 or 45 children in a class, one or two might be refused admission because of their bad marks.[58] Putin was rejected because of his bad behaviour – and not only in the third grade, when all his peers became Pioneers, but in the fourth and fifth grades as well.

In later life, Putin wrote that he had been a hooligan as a child.[59] Some of his contemporaries have argued that he was exaggerating to make it seem that his childhood had been tougher than it really was.[60] It is true that, in the Soviet Union at that time, a hooligan was a crimi-nal in the making and Putin did not take that road. But he was certainly a tearaway. The historian, Dmitry Travin, who also grew up in Lenin-grad in the 1960s, recounted: 'It wasn't so much that conflicts sought him out, it was he who was always looking for conflicts.'[61] Whenever a fight broke out, Putin was the first to pile in.[62] Viktor Borisenko, who became his best friend at school and for four years shared a desk with him, remembered:

> He could get into a fight with anyone. It still amazes me . . . He had no fear. He didn't seem to have an inner instinct for self-preservation. It never occurred to him that the other boy was stronger and might beat him up . . . If some hulking guy offended him, he would jump straight at him -- scratch him, bite him, pull out clumps of his hair . . . He wasn't the strongest in our class, but in a fight he could beat anyone, because he would get into a frenzy and fight to the end.[63]

It was partly a way of compensating for his small stature. He was thin and wiry, a child with a voracious appetite and a surfeit of nervous energy.[64] But he was also capable of thinking about what he was doing and attempting, if not always successfully, to exercise self-control. In Travin's words, he had 'both aggressiveness and common sense. At first glance, it seems they are total opposites . . . But in fact, they complement each other.'[65] Viktor Borisenko remembered one occasion when a teacher dragged him off by the scruff of the neck because a classroom which he was supposed to have cleaned was dirty. 'He was furious and sat silently for a long time . . . But then, when it seemed to be already over, he suddenly flared up and exploded. That happened several times.'[66] Although he showed little interest in his studies and was spurned by the Pioneers, his classmates respected him for his audacity and for the way he rushed to the defence of his friends.[67]

However, Volodya's misdeeds eventually caught up with him. When he was about 12 years old, the Housing Office of his apartment block ordered him to appear before a 'Comrades' Court', where he was given a solemn warning that, if he continued to make trouble, he would be sent to a reform school, at which children who had 'a negative and anti-social influence on other pupils' underwent re-education.[68] His father pleaded for leniency and the Court agreed to remand him to his parents' custody to see how he would behave.

Vladimir Putin grew up in a city more deeply scarred by the Second World War, or the Great Patriotic War, as Russians usually call it, than any outsider can begin to comprehend. For Americans in particular, whose country has never been invaded by a hostile power, and even for Western Europeans, who saw cities like Coventry, Dresden and Warsaw reduced to rubble, it is hard to grasp the enormity of what happened during the Leningrad blockade. After Hitler's troops surrounded the city in September 1941, with orders not to occupy it but to let the population starve, three quarters of a million Leningraders perished, most of them in the famine winter of 1941–2, when Putin's brother, Viktor, died, and the ration for dependants was reduced to a few ounces of ersatz bread a day. That was four times the death toll in Hiroshima and Nagasaki combined, and 35 times more than in the London Blitz. In this one Russian city, more people died than all the Americans who have died in every foreign war the United States has ever fought.[69]

By the time the Germans were beaten back, in January 1944, large parts of Leningrad were in ruins. Every sixth building had been destroyed by bombing or artillery fire, and many more were severely damaged. Oleg Kalugin, later a KGB general, who returned there that spring with his mother after spending the war years in Siberia, remembered: 'The city seemed deserted, the streets littered with tank traps and populated by emaciated figures who moved slowly to and fro . . . Not far from our old apartment, a German bomb had taken off the façade of a six-storey building, and on the top floor a grand piano stood in full view.'[70] The winter of 1941 had been one of the coldest on record with temperatures of minus 40 degrees, and many of the old wooden buildings had been torn down for firewood.

In terms of physical damage, Leningrad suffered less than cities like Stalingrad or Smolensk or Novgorod, where hardly a single building was left standing. But the physical scars of war can be repaired. By the time Putin was born, most of the centre of the city had been rebuilt. The psychological scars went far deeper.

Each person reacted differently. A few talked compulsively about what they had endured. But most, like Putin's parents, buried it deep inside.[71] As one blockade survivor put it, memories of that time were 'a minefield within the mind. You only have to step on them and you blow up. Everything flies to hell – quiet, comfort, present-day happiness.'[72] In Putin's family, the war was discussed only when relatives who had spent the war years elsewhere came to visit. From listening to those conversations, Volodya began to understand what his parents had endured.

Within 24 hours of the German invasion, at 4 a.m. on June 22, 1941, a hundred thousand Leningraders had signed up at recruitment centres.[73] Putin's father, like other skilled workers, was urged not to enlist, because they were needed in the factories, which were converted to arms manufacture.[74] Early in July, however, on Stalin's orders, the NKVD, the forerunner of the KGB, began recruiting trusted Party members to form partisan detachments to operate behind enemy lines. Those selected were chosen for political reliability by the *sekretnyi otdel* or 'Secret Department', the NKVD branch which existed in every factory and large enterprise.[75] Vladimir Spiridonovich, then 30 years old, was among them.

Between August and October, more than 6,000 Soviet partisans from Leningrad, under the command of the NKVD's 4th Directorate, responsible for border security, were infiltrated into German-occupied areas.[76] Putin's father's unit, comprising 28 men, was sent to the Estonian border near Lake Peipus, south of Kingisepp, in September.[77] They crossed successfully and blew up an arms depot. But then their hiding place was discovered by a company of Estonian scouts, working for the Germans, who called up reinforcements. They split up and headed back towards the front, 120 miles to the north-east. At one point, so the story went, Vladimir Spiridonovich hid underwater in a marshy pond, breathing through a hollow reed, to escape his pursuers. Only four of the group made it back, Putin's father among them, to be interrogated by the NKVD's fearsome Special Department – later renamed SMERSH, 'Death to Spies' – whose job was to stop German intelligence infiltrating the Red Army.[78]

He evidently passed the test for he was reassigned to a front-line unit on the *Nevsky pyatachok*, the 'Neva Patch', a small bridgehead on the left bank of the Neva River, eight miles south of Lake Ladoga.[79] The 'Patch' was a mile and a quarter long and 600 yards wide. Stalin hoped to use it as a wedge to open a land route to break the blockade, and in the closing months of 1941, ordered a series of suicidal attacks in which four Soviet divisions were annihilated, losing 95 per cent of their men. The fighting was among the fiercest anywhere on the North-Western Front. [80] A German officer wrote in his diary: 'One does not know what to marvel at more: the madness of those who gave the orders or the courage of those who carried them out.'[81] By the time it was over, 50,000 Russians and 10,000 Germans had died.

On November 17, 1941, Putin's father and another soldier were ordered to capture a 'tongue', a German soldier who was to be brought in alive for interrogation.[82] As they crawled towards an enemy foxhole, they were spotted and a soldier hurled a grenade at them. Apparently thinking them dead, he left the bodies where they lay. Vladimir Spiridonovich's left leg was shattered by shrapnel, but he was alive and under cover of darkness his comrades managed to get him back.[83] That in itself was almost miraculous. 'If you couldn't walk', another soldier wrote later, 'there was almost no hope of stretcher-bearers picking you up. Your only chance was if a friend helped you.'[84] Making matters worse, there was another, even more serious obstacle. The only way to get to a hospital was across the frozen river, which was under constant enemy fire. Again, fate smiled on him: out of the blue, a friend did appear. A soldier, who had been a neighbour years earlier, took him on his back and carried him 200 yards across the ice to the opposite bank. Both men survived the war. Putin's father spent several months in hospital and was then invalided out.[85]

Volodya learnt less about how his mother survived the blockade. In late 1941 or early 1942, her brother, Ivan, arranged for her to move to an apartment near the Ovodny Canal in the southern part of the city. Viktor was still with her then. [86] At some point that winter, she was apparently left for dead and laid out with the corpses of other starvation victims to await burial in a mass grave, when someone – in one version, Putin's father – found her and realised that she was still alive.

Putin told the story often, including to Hillary Clinton during a summit meeting in 2012. The details changed at almost every telling.[87] That does not make it untrue. Psychological research has shown that when traumatic events are recalled, recollections vary over time even when the person concerned was not a direct participant.[88] But it is also true that, like many politicians, Putin embellished his stories to fit his audience. His account of how his father, while being treated in hospital, gave his wife part of his rations until the doctors found out what he was doing and banned her from visiting him, likewise evolved over the years.

There were other wartime experiences which Putin's parents would certainly not have discussed, not least because in Soviet times they were officially off limits. Among them was cannibalism.

Volodya learnt about that from his schoolfriends, who gathered in

small groups to tell 'scary tales', the Soviet equivalent of the stories
found in Western horror comics at that time, daring each other to keep
their nerve at the terrors they related. Usually they were about gruesome murders, or ghosts, or other forbidden topics not found in the
books they were allowed to read.[89] In Leningrad, many of the stories
were about people who ate human flesh during the blockade – corpses
being cut up for food; amputated body parts being stolen from hospitals to be eaten; and people killing their own children and devouring
them.[90] It was all at the level of anecdote and rumour but it became
part of the folklore of the war. Half a century later, when Moscow
football fans wanted to insult St Petersburg supporters, they called
them 'blockade rats' whose 'grandpas were cannibals'.[91] In 2004, when
the city's police archives were opened, it was confirmed that most of the
stories were true. There had been cannibalism in the army, in the prisons and among the civilian population. Of the more than 2,000 people
arrested in 1941 and 1942 for consuming human flesh, many were young
women from suburbs like Peterhof, who had no ration books and no
relatives to help them, and who were desperate to find food of any
kind for their starving children.[92]

But those were merely fleeting glimpses of a blockade which had
lasted nearly 30 months. The rest, like the story of what happened to
little Viktor, had been obscured or forgotten.

After the overland link between Leningrad and the rest of Russia
was restored in 1943, Maria's brother, Ivan, who was helping to organise the evacuation convoys, arranged for the Putins to leave for Tver,
where they lived with Maria's family and worked on a collective farm
until the siege was lifted a year later. When they returned to Leningrad, Vladimir Spiridonovich was assigned to the Yegorov Railway
Carriage Works. For the first year they stayed with Ivan and his family
until, in 1945, the factory gave them their own room in a communal
apartment, a *kommunalka*, on Baskov Lane.[93] The city's population was
then barely a fifth of what it had been before the war. Among those
who had died were three of Putin's uncles, his maternal grandmother
and other relatives.[94]

The war might be over, but Leningrad's troubles were not. By 1946, the
wartime alliance with the Western Powers had mutated into the Cold
War. Stalin saw the city, historically Russia's gateway to the West, as a

weak link in the new Iron Curtain. Leningrad's artists and intellectuals were accused of 'cringing servility towards bourgeois culture'. A ferocious purge began, which coincided with renewed famine, as the Soviet grain harvest was hit by drought and a distribution system wrecked by war proved unable to cope with the vast population movements that followed the German defeat. Millions of Soviet soldiers were demobilised. Millions more civilians, who had fled eastward during the German advance, returned to their homes in western Russia – one and a half million to Leningrad alone. To speed recovery, Stalin ordered a new Stakhanovite movement, named after a model communist in the 1930s who had consistently overfulfilled his quota. At the Yegorov Works, Putin's father was among the movement's leaders, pledging in May 1946 that the welding shop which he headed would complete two years' production in one.

In the spring of 1948, the campaign against the intellectuals subsided and food supplies, though limited mainly to cabbage and bread, became more reliable. But that year another purge started. Leningrad's wartime leader, Andrei Zhdanov, who had been seen as Stalin's probable successor, died of a heart attack, triggering a covert power struggle between the KGB Chief, Lavrenty Beria, and his rival, Georgy Malenkov. In what later became known as the Leningrad Affair, Zhdanov's former colleagues were executed and some 2,000 other officials, reaching down to the level of factory Party Committees, were sent to labour camps.

It was not the best time to try to start a family. Russia, unlike Europe and America, had no post-war baby boom.

In the winter of 1951, the situation finally stabilised. A young woman doctor who arrived in Leningrad that year from the provinces remembered:

After the 400 grams [a day] of war-rationed bread [we had been getting], Leningrad seemed a gastronomic heaven. There were bread stores and milk stores and meat stores ... Sour black bread shared counter space with loaves of white ... There were even chocolate bars called Soviet Builder ... with a picture of a muscular man brandishing a hammer.[95]

Another recent arrival, a student from Brest, found Leningrad 'glorious'. Everywhere there was reconstruction, and 'life for [its] residents was slowly improving.'[96] People started to believe that, at long last, better times had arrived. Amid these newfound hopes, Volodya was born.

The following week, Stalin gave the closing speech at the 19th Party Congress, his last recorded public utterance. In it, he denounced the imperialist powers, 'the arsonists of war', and charged that the bourgeoisie, 'the arch-enemy of freedom', was becoming ever more reactionary and therefore weaker and easier to defeat.[97] By then he had come to believe that a new world war was imminent. A group of Jewish doctors had been accused of trying to kill the Soviet leadership in the so-called 'Doctors' Plot', which Stalin had concocted as justification for yet another massive purge.[98] But in March 1953, the old dictator died and it was acknowledged that the 'plot' had been a fabrication all along. In December, Beria was executed for treason and Nikita Sergeyevich Khrushchev – 'rumbustious, impetuous, loquacious, freewheeling, and alarmingly ignorant of foreign affairs, [like] a little bull who . . . would charge along . . . knocking down anything that was in his way', as one Western ambassador described him[99] – elbowed aside Malenkov to become Stalin's successor as General Secretary of the Communist Party and, later, Soviet Prime Minister.

The Putins' apartment, which they shared with two other families, was on the top floor of a grimy, run-down five-storey building which had not seen a coat of paint in many years.[100] The entrance, with a lavatory in a minuscule cubicle at one side, opened directly onto a dark, windowless kitchen, so narrow that if someone was preparing food no one else could get past. It had a gas burner and sink, and three shelves for the different families' utensils. Off the hallway were a small room occupied by an elderly couple, Grandma Anya and her husband, and the Putins' room, the largest in the apartment, which measured 215 square feet (20 square metres) and had two windows overlooking the courtyard. Beyond the kitchen were two smaller rooms, in which a Jewish tailor named Margolin, his wife and unmarried daughter lived. The rooms were divided by plywood partitions so everybody could always hear what everyone else was doing. Privacy was unknown. Until quite recent times, the Russian language had no word for it. Communal living was a long-established tradition.[101]

There was no central heating – each room had a wood-fired

stove – no hot water and no bathroom. The family went once a week to the *banya*, the public baths, around the corner in Nekrasov Street. In between they heated water in the shared kitchen and washed as best they could in the lavatory.

It was primitive. But Putin would say later that he 'never felt disadvantaged or miserable'.[102] It was the way everybody lived and the grown-ups had all known much worse. There was a leak in the roof, which, despite his father's entreaties, the Housing Office refused to repair. Putin's classmate, Borisenko, remembered the walls being always damp. But Borisenko's home was no different and, in his family, there were five people crammed into one room. In those days, if only two families shared an apartment, it was considered a luxury. More often there were four or five and sometimes as many as ten. There was no elevator in Putin's building, the staircase was filthy with missing steps, the metal handrail was coming adrift and most of the light bulbs were broken – replacing them being 'everybody's and therefore nobody's responsibility', as one *kommunalka* dweller observed.[103]

Like all Soviet apartment blocks at that time, the building was infested with cockroaches. Rats lived among the garbage in the yard. Putin and his friends used to chase after them with sticks, until one day a large rat, which he had cornered, turned and attacked him, giving him the fright of his life. The memory stayed with him, and years later he would draw the lesson: 'No one should be cornered. No one should be put in a situation where they have no way out.'[104]

As a foreman, Vladimir Spiridonovich earned a good wage. The family had a large black Bakelite telephone with a rotary dial and even a television set, which were the envy of Putin's friends. Both, particularly the telephone, were rarities in 1960s Russia. Volodya slept on a divan against one wall while his parents had a metal-frame bed in the corner, partly hidden by a screen. 'Each of us', he said later, 'encased himself in his own little cocoon.'[105] There was a writing table for his homework, a bookshelf with a complete set of the works of the nineteenth-century playwright, Anton Chekhov – another source of wonder to Putin's classmates, few of whom had anything like that in their own homes – a round dining table and a glass-fronted sideboard, known in Russian as a *servant*, where Maria Ivanovna displayed her crockery and other prized possessions.[106] The parents had two sets of clothes, one for everyday wear and the other for special occasions. In winter, food was kept in the space between the panes of the double windows until, when Putin was thirteen, his father bought a small refrigerator, which, compared with the other families, made them almost middle class.

When there was friction, as was inevitable in such a promiscuous setting, it was usually over the kitchen. Svetlana Boym, who also grew up in a communal apartment in Leningrad, remembered it as 'an area of frozen conflict'. In some apartments relations became so poisonous, she wrote, that 'neighbours peed into each other's teapots', and it was common for an alcoholic flat-dweller to be found, passed out, in a pool of urine in the corridor.[107] Putin's family was spared that. There were occasional quarrels – which young Volodya was told firmly to stay out of – but on the whole they got on well, and he spent almost as much time at the Margolins as he did in his own home. The tailor was religious, and it piqued the boy's curiosity to hear him chanting the Talmud on the Sabbath. But when the old man tried to explain its significance, Putin wrote later, 'I immediately lost interest.'[108]

Politics were not discussed in the Putin household. The kind of political debate that flourished in Moscow, where many people had individual apartments and trusted friends could gather round the kitchen table to discuss the events of the day, was rare in Leningrad. Most families either lived in a *kommunalka*, like the Putins, or shared a space in a dormitory in a hostel or a workers' barracks.[109] No one could ever be certain that a neighbour was not an informer, which some suspected was why Lenin had advocated communal apartments in the first place.[110]

Putin's father was a true believer, who read *Pravda* each day and edited the factory newspaper at the Yegorov Plant for several years. But he had a mind of his own – his defence of his fellow workers against what he considered unjust decisions by managers eventually led to his removal from the plant's Party Committee – and he followed closely the political situation after Stalin's death.[111] As a Party cadre, he would have been among those briefed on Khrushchev's Secret Speech – not officially published until more than 30 years later – in which, on February 25, 1956, the Soviet leader denounced his predecessor for 'a grave abuse of power . . . [authorising] cruel and inhuman tortures, . . . mass arrests and the deportation of thousands and thousands of people, executions without trial or normal investigation, [using] methods that were simple – to beat, beat and once again, beat.'[112]

Khrushchev's message was mixed: Lenin had been good but Stalin had been wicked; the system was correct but Stalin had betrayed it.[113] A year later, the last of the old guard – Malenkov; Stalin's long-time Foreign Minister, Vyacheslav Molotov; and the former Ukrainian leader, Lazar Kaganovich – were put out to pasture.[114]

The Secret Speech triggered unrest in Poland and an uprising in Hungary. At home, millions of prisoners were released from labour camps and hundreds of thousands of others who had been shot as counter-revolutionaries were posthumously rehabilitated.[115]

The 'Khrushchev Thaw', as it was called, reached its apogee with the removal in 1961 of Stalin's embalmed body from the mausoleum on Red Square, where he had lain in state beside Lenin, for reburial at the foot of the Kremlin Wall. A year later, the literary magazine, *Novy mir*, published Aleksandr Solzhenitsyn's short novel about life in Stalin's prison camps, *One Day in the Life of Ivan Denisovich*. Censorship eased; works which had previously been banned were revived; experimentation in the arts was permitted. It fell far short of the artistic freedom of the 1920s, but compared with what had gone before, it was, as a Soviet theatre critic put it, 'a great holiday of the soul'.[116] Criticism of abuses was permitted so long as it did not call into question the existing political order.[117] For the first time since the 1930s, Soviet musicians and ballet troupes were allowed to travel abroad. Russian cinemas began showing selected Western films and approved Western writers were published in translation. Khrushchev held that a new world war was no longer inevitable, as Stalin had believed, but East and West could practise peaceful coexistence.

How Putin's family viewed these changes is not recorded. But there is a clue in a story told by one of his schoolfriends.

After 1961, the portraits of Stalin which had hung in government and Party offices were removed and destroyed. Volodya, the friend said, found one intact in a pile of garbage, cleaned it and brought it home.[118] It would be wrong to read too much into that. He was eight or nine years old and it may have been no more than a childish prank. But given his parents' background – the family had not suffered either from collectivisation in the 1930s or from Stalin's purges; his father had started the war in an NKVD detachment; and his grandfather,

Spiridon, had served as a cook for high-ranking party officials – it is possible that the Putins, like many of their generation, had some sympathy with the late *Vozhd* and thought his successors were treating him too harshly.[119]

In Soviet schools in Stalin's time, children were expected to be docile and unquestioning. Under Khrushchev, that changed. There was no return to the years immediately after 1917, when rebelliousness was seen as a revolutionary virtue. But children were once again encouraged to be more independent and assertive.[120]

Whether for this reason, or because he was now older and starting to think about what he wanted to do with his life, in 1965, when Volodya was twelve, his behaviour began to improve. In the Soviet system, fifth grade marked the transition from elementary to junior high school. He had a different teacher for each subject and a new form mistress, Vera Dmitrievna Gurevich, who taught German. The previous spring, to his classmates' surprise, he had joined a German study circle which she had set up, a decision all the more unexpected because that year his marks had gone down. Instead of '3's, he had '2's in two subjects – drawing, which he hated, and singing. He had been allowed provisionally to proceed to fifth grade, but on probation.[121] Why he chose German rather than English, which was much more popular, he never explained: it may have been curiosity about the Soviet Union's enemies in the war, a desire to do something different from the majority of his classmates or simply because he liked his new teacher.[122]

Vera Gurevich was tough. She later worked with the police as a counsellor for young delinquents.[123] But she and Volodya got on well. He was quick and had an excellent memory and she decided that he was doing badly because he was bored.[124] She became his mentor. Under the Soviet system, teachers were expected to work closely with families, especially when a child proved difficult and in need of extra help. If the family did not pull its weight, considerable pressure could be brought to bear, including criticism at mass meetings at the parents' places of work.

The other change in Putin's life that autumn came from his discovery of *sambo*, a form of mixed martial arts based on judo which had been developed by the Red Army in the 1920s for use in hand-to-hand combat.[125] A year earlier he had started boxing, but his enthusiasm waned after his nose was broken in a fight and he had to stop train-ing.[126] Hanging around with nothing to do, one rainy October afternoon, he and his friend Borisenko decided to use his father's prized black telephone to call up the local *sambo* clubs and ask whether there were training sessions they could attend after school.[127]

Volodya's motives were mixed. He liked brawling and hanging out with the local toughs in the courtyard but he was beginning to realise that it would bring diminishing returns. 'The atmosphere was terrible,' Borisenko remembered. 'Unshaven, dirty guys with port wine and cigarettes. Booze, obscene language, fights. And Putin was in the midst of all these bums. He wasn't a hoodlum himself, but he was constantly hanging out with them.'[128] It was obvious that many of them would end up in prison. But what concerned Volodya more was his own sta-tus. 'To maintain the kind of leadership I had,' he explained later, 'it needed real physical strength and skills. I wanted to keep that kind of leadership . . . I knew that if I didn't start sport, then in the courtyard and at school, I would no longer have the position I was used to.'[129]

Most of the clubs they contacted turned them down, saying they were already full and they should come back next year. Finally, how-ever, Anatoly Semyonovich Rakhlin, the trainer at *Trud*, a club run by the Trades Union Federation, agreed to give them a hearing.[130] Volo-dya was so keen to be accepted that he initially claimed to be a year older. It turned out to be unnecessary. Rakhlin, who had spent his childhood during the Leningrad blockade in a house on Baskov Lane across the street from Putin's home, enrolled them both.

Sambo became Volodya's passion.

The club was in the western part of the city, near the Yusupov Pal-ace, where his grandfather's old customer, Rasputin, had been murdered half a century before. To his mother's dismay – she con-sidered *sambo* to be 'fooling about' and was terrified that he would break his neck – he took a tram there three evenings a week to spend two hours working out on the mat. For the first year, he trained wear-ing knitted woollen socks, having no wrestling shoes of his own or any other gear until Borisenko dropped out and bequeathed him his outfit. But most of the other boys were equally ragged.[131]

Putin stood out, Rakhlin remembered, for his single-mindedness and the determination with which he fought, as though each bout were his last. But his parents strongly disapproved. The sports clubs were frequented by criminals and former labour camp inmates. His father wanted him to play the accordion, which he himself had learnt in Tver when he was a boy. To please him, Putin mastered a few simple tunes, but his heart was not in it.[132] Eventually things reached a point where they forbade him to go to the club any more and Rakhlin had to intercede on his behalf.[133] This happened several times, and the *sambo* coach became a regular visitor to the Putins' home. From being Volodya's trainer, he became, like Vera Gurevich, his mentor.

Putin wrote later that Rakhlin's role was decisive. 'If I hadn't got involved in sports, I'm not sure how my life would have turned out. It was sports that got me off the streets.'[134]

In fact, it was a little more complicated. His relationship with Rakhlin, as with Vera Gurevich, was undoubtedly important. But Volodya himself was maturing. His efforts at self-control, which Borisenko had remarked upon a year earlier, had progressed. When he wrestled, Rakhlin noticed, the moment a bout was over, it would be as though the fight had never happened. The change was so sudden that it drew the coach's attention – an ability to switch instantly from aggression to friendliness was an unusual quality, he thought. He noticed, too, that whether Volodya won or lost, nothing showed in his face. 'He was very reserved . . . At such moments, it was impossible to tell what he was feeling.'[135] Not to show emotions was one of the key principles of both *sambo* and judo. The seventeenth-century Zen Master, Takuan Sōhō, held that 'internal "emptiness", the nihilation of consciousness, the absence of concentration and unshakable calm – these are the qualities which bring the adept of martial arts success. For emotions there is no place.'[136]

As a thirteen-year-old, Putin had never heard of Takuan. He was attracted by the ritual of *sambo* and the samurai traditions.[137] But intuitively he had somehow grasped the essence of the philosophy behind it.

Other facets of his personality also began to emerge. He was still, in his own words, a 'pretty haphazard student' and he finished fifth grade with, for the first time, some '4's but also some '3's. However there were no more '2's. And when a topic sparked his interest, he was capable of surprising those around him. That year he impressed Borisenko, who was of literary bent and would later become a theatre director, by his understanding of Gogol, not the easiest of nineteenth-century writers, whom they studied, along with Turgenev, Tolstoy and Dostoyevsky, in their literature class.[138]

Part of the change was due to the realisation that important choices were looming. In working-class districts of Soviet cities in those days, when a boy reached fourteen, a boundary was crossed.[139] Either he stayed with the other teenagers in the courtyard, where the older boys fought with bicycle chains, gambled and drank, and vied to become gang leaders, in which case he was on track for a criminal record, which the others would consider a badge of honour. Or he turned his back on that world and applied himself at school in the hope of gaining admission to a technical institute or, if he was really gifted, university.

Khrushchev's reforms had on the whole been extremely positive for children of Putin's generation, bringing new possibilities unimaginable to their parents, but increased access to higher education was not one of them. The death toll during the war – 20 million men and six million women – meant that, two decades later, there was still a crying shortage of blue-collar workers for industry. In the late 1960s, only three out of five secondary-school students were allowed to continue beyond eighth grade, a quota which would soon be cut back even further, and of these only a minuscule proportion went on to take a university degree.[140] No matter how much the Party might exalt the glorious role of the working class, the sight of older school friends being shunted off at sixteen to an apprenticeship or a vocational school, with the prospect of spending a lifetime in a dead-end job on a factory assembly line, was enough to concentrate the mind of even the most recalcitrant child.[141]

There was another factor, too. It was impossible to enter university without being a member of the Komsomol, the Communist Party Youth League. But to join the Komsomol, it was necessary first to have been a Pioneer.[142]

In the autumn of 1965, when Volodya entered sixth grade, all these elements came together. His marks improved dramatically and at long last – three years after his classmates – he was allowed to become a member of the Party's primary organisation.[143]

Normally at the induction ceremony, the new recruits, all nine- or ten-year-olds, lined up in formation, while the head teacher gave a speech and, as a bugle call rang out, children from the senior classes, usually Komsomol members, presented each of them with a red kerchief and the five-pointed Pioneer badge.[144] But Putin was thirteen, and to have asked him to line up with third graders would have been humiliating. So an exception was made and his class was taken on an excursion to the Lenin Museum at Ulyanovka, a village south-east of Leningrad where Lenin's brother-in-law had lived.[145] There the school's Pioneer banner was unfurled and Putin recited the Pioneer oath: 'In the presence of my comrades, I, Vladimir Vladimirovich Putin, solemnly promise to love my Motherland passionately, and to live, learn and struggle as the great Lenin bade us and as the Communist Party teaches us.'[146] To the sound of a drum roll, his friend, Borisenko, the head of the class's Pioneer detachment, placed the Pioneer kerchief round his neck.

It was a sea change. Until then, he had been an outsider, popular with his classmates but whose rebelliousness set him apart. Now he was one of them. His father, who for years had dutifully subscribed to the Pioneers' newspaper, *Pionerskaya pravda,* on his son's behalf, was delighted. The quarrels over *sambo* and Volodya's lack of enthusiasm for the accordion were quietly forgotten.

While Putin was working his way through the trials of childhood at the school on Baskov Lane, the Soviet leadership was in turmoil. In October 1962, the world had come closer than at any time before or since to all-out nuclear war. Khrushchev, reacting to the CIA's failed 'Bay of Pigs' invasion of Cuba by exiles in Florida and to the United States' decision to position nuclear-capable missiles in Turkey and Italy, agreed to a request from Fidel Castro to base Soviet nuclear forces on the island. Thanks to President Kennedy, who defied the Pentagon and his own advisers to urge a peaceful solution, and to a Soviet flotilla commander who countermanded an order to unleash a nuclear attack, war was narrowly averted. The United States withdrew its missiles from Europe. Khrushchev recalled the Soviet forces from Cuba. But because, at Kennedy's insistence, Washington's concessions were kept secret, the outcome was seen in Moscow as a humiliation. It looked as if the Soviet Union had backed down without getting anything in return. The economy was faltering, too. Far from catching up with America, as Khrushchev had promised, the Soviet Union was falling further behind. To his colleagues, his leadership had become impulsive and erratic. Two years later, he was removed from power by a conservative cabal headed by Leonid Brezhnev, a former protégé whom he had promoted to become his deputy.

For Volodya, Khrushchev's departure was both good and bad. The ousted leader's insistence on vocational training, which had meant that he and his classmates, starting in the primary classes, had had to learn carpentry and metalwork, was now quietly abandoned, to the relief of almost everyone concerned. But ideology, which until then had been largely ignored, came back with a vengeance.

To be a Pioneer, it was no longer enough to have an acceptable school record. Members also had to learn by heart the life stories of Pioneer heroes like Pavel Morozov, who, as a child during the collectivisation campaign in the 1930s, had denounced his father for hiding grain.[147] The old man had been imprisoned. Pavlik, as the boy was called, was afterwards murdered by villagers outraged by what he had done.[148] The story was controversial. On the one hand, Russian tradition and Party policy stressed the importance of the patriarchal family structure. On the other, it was a perfect example of a child who put his revolutionary duty first. Even Stalin had mixed feelings. 'What a little swine, denouncing his own father,' he was said to have commented privately. But as a symbol of self-sacrifice to further the communist cause, Comrade Pavlik was too good a model for Party propagandists to ignore. In the 1960s and '70s, he was *the* Pioneer hero, whose selfless courage all young people were expected to emulate. The paradox was that, by then, children of Putin's generation were becoming increasingly sceptical of the virtues which Morozov was supposed to embody. Schoolchildren everywhere loathe sneaks. 'I am not sure,' wrote Volodya's near contemporary, Yelena Gorokhova, 'that ratting on your father and having him shipped to Siberia is a heroic thing to do.'[149]

Putin probably felt the same way.[150] But neither he, nor any of his classmates, expressed their doubts openly. Under the Soviet system, conformity was the price of success. That was drummed into all of their heads from kindergarten up.[151] Even those like Putin, who rebelled, knew by heart the unwritten rules they were transgressing. In deciding to start working at his studies and, as a Pioneer, to take the first step on a ladder which might eventually lead to Communist Party membership, he had agreed to work within the system and, having done so, applied himself with the same single-mindedness that he gave to his training for *sambo*. He was not particularly keen on tidying up the school grounds, collecting waste paper and scrap metal, and all the other social chores for which Pioneers were expected to volunteer, but there was no point, as he would say later, in 'spitting against the wind'.[152]

Like the *Oktyabryata*, the Pioneers were modelled on the Boy Scouts, even down to their motto, 'Be Prepared'. But the organisation had very different goals. Scouts learnt to be self-reliant. Pioneers were taught that an individual thrives only as a member of a group.[153]

School, Pioneers and family were expected to work together to inculcate socialist values. Each class formed a Pioneer detachment, which was divided into 'links', each composed of five or six children, which competed among themselves. If a child failed to pull his weight, the whole link was criticised and the slacker denounced in the class's wall newspaper. Conversely, if he or she did particularly well, the link, not the individual, was praised. The lesson was that the judgement of the group was primordial, the individual was subordinate, and speaking out against the failings of one's comrades was not only morally correct but in a child's own interests, because otherwise he or she would be held jointly responsible for the others' mistakes. Starting in junior high school, each detachment elected a five-member council, which met once a month to discuss the pupils' work and behaviour, doling out criticism and praise and awarding a mark out of five which was entered into their school records and sent to their parents. The family, in turn, was expected to inform the school how the child behaved at home, whether he or she was obedient and helped with the household chores.

That, at least, was the joyless theory dreamt up by Soviet educationalists and Party bureaucrats. In practice, as with most things in the Soviet Union, theory and reality diverged.

Life for a schoolboy in Leningrad in the 1960s was much more fun than it was made to sound. Cinema seats cost next to nothing – there were foreign films like *The Three Musketeers* as well as Soviet productions – and the local puppet theatre put on performances of traditional folk tales.[154]

In winter, Volodya went with his classmates to practise cross-country skiing in the birch forests outside the city.[155] In summer, he spent the holidays with his mother at a dacha which his father had been allotted in the village of Pustomerzha, 60 miles from Leningrad, towards the Estonian border, near the area where he had fought as a partisan. It was little more than a simple log cabin with a vegetable garden and some fruit trees, but it got Volodya away from the city and from the young ruffians in the courtyard. His father came to join them at weekends, and he learnt to hunt for mushrooms in the woods and to ride a bicycle.

Later, the school organised a hiking trip to Lake Ladoga, to show the children the evacuation route used during the blockade. Over the objections of his mother, who was always terrified that some disaster would befall him, they camped out in tents in the forest. It was the first of many such expeditions. One winter, they stayed at a hunting lodge, arranged by one of the parents who was a member of the local hunters' association, and spent their days skiing and sledging.

Once the hurdle of joining the Pioneers was passed, other, longer trips followed. In the summer of 1967, Putin flew with his classmates to Nikolayev, on the Black Sea along the coast from Crimea, where they spent six weeks picking cherries at a collective farm and, on the return journey, visited Kiev. Another trip took them to Latvia, where they spent a month camping beside a lake and travelled to the capital, Riga, fascinated by the European architecture, quite different from a Russian city, and amazed by the cleanliness of the beaches.[156]

As is often the way with only children, especially the children of old age, Volodya's parents tried whenever they could to accommodate his wishes. He had pocket money to treat his friends to ice cream at the café along the street. He was allowed to keep two song birds, which, in a fifth-floor communal apartment, were realistically the only pets he could have. He took care of them himself, but refused to clean out their cage, holding that that was woman's work, so two of the girls in his class did it for him.[157] His mother, despite her opposition to Volodya practising *sambo*, nonetheless sewed him his first wrestling jacket.[158] To prepare him for the end-of-year school ball, his father paid for dancing lessons.[159] When, as a teenager, he was desperate to play the guitar, they gave him one, and on his sixteenth birthday, a record-player too.[160]

Meanwhile his career in the Pioneers prospered. After Borisenko was promoted to a higher post in the Pioneer organisation, his classmates chose Putin to succeed him.[161] It was a remarkable turnaround. Having spent years as the class troublemaker, Putin found himself, in seventh grade, head of its Pioneer Council.

Like the Scouts, the Pioneers exalted patriotism. The Pioneer Code, which they all had to learn by heart, declared: 'a Pioneer honours the memory of those who gave their lives in the struggle for freedom and for the flowering of the Soviet motherland.'[162]

To Volodya and his classmates, as to children throughout the Soviet Union, that was no abstract formula. All of them had lost relatives in the war. The school arranged visits to battlefields and to memorial sites, including Leningrad's Piskaryovskoe cemetery, where his brother, Viktor, was buried. Patriotism was coloured by Russian nationalism. Teachers emphasised the genius of Russian cultural figures – Chekhov, Dostoyevsky and Pushkin, and the composers, Mussorgsky and Tchaikovsky – and the role of Ivan the Terrible and Peter the Great in consolidating Muscovite power and the expansion of Russian territory.[163]

Putin evidently coped well with his new responsibilities in the Pioneers, for in 1967, at the start of his final year at the school, he was accepted into the Komsomol, the Party's youth movement, which bridged the transition between school and the start of a working career.[164]

It was not the only change in his life that year. The old couple who had lived across the corridor from the Putins – Grandma Anya and her husband – had moved to a new apartment in the suburbs after their room had been declared unfit for habitation. That left only two families sharing the apartment. Grandma Anya's room became the kitchen, where Volodya and his friends could now meet on their own, without being under his parents' feet.[165]

In the Soviet scheme of things, joining the Komsomol was a sign of maturity and a big step up in the world. But in many ways Putin remained the same incorrigible youth that he had always been. He still got into fights, though less often than before.[166] He still could not resist a challenge. There was a tradition in Baskov Lane, dating back to Stalin's time, of boys climbing along the cornices and window-ledges of a girls' school at the end of the street.[167] When another boy dared him to do the same at their school, he climbed out onto the iron balustrade of a fifth-floor window and, hanging onto the cornice above, pulled himself hand over hand across the façade of the building, unfazed by the 60-foot drop to the pavement below, until he reached the window of a neighbouring classroom and swung himself inside.

His classmates thought that he was 'attracted to risk'.[168] That was no doubt part of it. But there was also a part of Volodya which refused to be bound by the same rules as everyone else. His obstreperousness as a small boy was not simply, as he claimed, a rebellion against school discipline after the freedom of the courtyard: it reflected a desire to be different. When later his parents gave him a watch – in those days, an extravagant gift for a teenager: his cousin, Yevgeny, complained that he still did not have one, even though he was almost 20 years older[169] – he wore it ostentatiously on his right wrist, even though he was right-handed, claiming that he found it more comfortable there.[170] His father had given it to him in the hope that it would stop him being late. In that respect, it was not a great success. More than 50 years later, he still wore his watch on his right wrist and was still perpetually late.

The sense of being different showed in other ways, too. His coach, Anatoly Rakhlin, found him unusually independent-minded: 'He might agree or disagree with others, but it didn't change what he thought.'[171] Viktor Borisenko had the same impression. 'Making him do something by force was simply impossible. The only person who could really influence him was himself.'[172]

Yet if Volodya wanted to set himself apart, it was in his own mind as much as in the minds of others. Another part of his personality pulled in the opposite direction. Rakhlin noted that he was often self-effacing.[173] When not acting up as a hooligan, he seemed an introvert, keeping his distance and his thoughts to himself.[174]

In this, he resembled Vladimir Spiridonovich, who was equally taciturn and reluctant to show his feelings. Putin wrote later that his father was 'outwardly a surly man' with 'a very commanding personality'.[175] A schoolfriend remembered that he 'showed no special fatherly feelings'.[176] His teacher, Vera Gurevich, recalled that 'there were no kisses' in his family, 'none of that sentimental stuff in their house'.[177] But behind the stern exterior, his father, too, had another side, which he tried hard not to show.[178] 'I realised that he loved and cared about me,' Putin wrote. 'As for my mother, she fussed over me like a mother hen. Apart from me, she had no other goal in life.'[179]

Volodya often gave the same impression of coldness. He smiled rarely, one of his classmates remembered.[180] Even his closest friend, Borisenko, said later that there was an unspoken boundary in their relationship which he knew he should never cross.[181] 'With him it was like this,' Borisenko said, 'He seemed to be with the rest of us, but he stood a little bit aside. He would take part in an event, but even though he was taking part in it, he was looking at it from outside. He had his own point of view in everything.'[182]

Putin's decision in his final year to apply to a key school, specialising in chemistry, rather than the regular high school to which most of his classmates hoped to go, was a case in point. He had never shown any interest in natural sciences before, and Vera Gurevich, who, in Borisenko's words, was 'like a second mother to him', was dismayed. When she asked him the reason for his choice, he gently fobbed her off. He had decided, he said, and he would see when he got there.[183] It later emerged that a neighbour had told him that the school had an exceptionally gifted literature teacher, Mikhail Demenkov, who taught his students to 'think outside the box'.[184] But it was also, once again, a matter of being different. Key schools were new – they had just been introduced as part of a nationwide experiment to raise standards in science – and they were prestigious, accepting bright children from the whole city, not just from the immediate vicinity.[185] Putin had contracted meningitis in the winter and spent a month in hospital, which meant he was excused from the final exams. But he was given a place because during the year he had had straight '4's and '5's.[186]

The transition was not without difficulties. Putin and two other outsiders had to 'clarify matters' with their fists before their new classmates accepted them[187] and, as Vera Gurevich had feared, his enthusiasm for chemistry proved short-lived. But he did well in literature and history – as well as the Russian classics, he was entranced by the novels of Alexandre Dumas[188] – and in German, where she gave him extra coaching once a week.[189] He became smitten with a classmate, Lena Gryaznova, a sociable, outgoing girl with long, brown, wavy hair, whom he accompanied home after school and took out to dances in the evenings, until they decided that they were not meant for each other after all. With friends, he swopped tapes of the Beatles, then banned in the Soviet Union. On camping trips, they sang together the bitter-sweet songs of Vladimir Vysotsky and Bulat Okudzhava, two very different, immensely talented poets whose lyrics were at the limit of what the Soviet system could accept, but who both – especially Vysotsky, whose music even Brezhnev liked – had protection in high places.[190]

In short, Putin lived what for his generation in Leningrad was the life of a normal teenager.

Only in one respect did he differ from his contemporaries. He played almost no part in the school's extra-curricular activities. Whether it was social work, organised by the Komsomol, in which he did the strict minimum to avoid being reprimanded – though it helped that the Komsomol Secretary, a girl much admired by her schoolmates, had an unrequited crush on him – or amateur dramatics or school parties, Putin was absent.[191] All his spare time was devoted to *sambo*. Four evenings a week he went for two- or three-hour training sessions, and at weekends he travelled with Rakhlin and the other members of the *Trud* team to compete in other Russian cities. The effort paid off. In ninth grade, when he was sixteen, he took second place in the Leningrad Youth Championship and a year later was ranked as a sportsman at national level.[192]

The same singleness of purpose would soon lead him to make a much more important and more difficult decision than enrolling in a key school. But before that could happen, he had to get clear in his own mind what he wished to do with his life.

In the 1950s and early '60s, most Russians genuinely believed in the superiority of communism. It was true that the reality of their lives did not live up to the Party's promises. But both older people and the younger generation felt that Soviet society had a moral compass, in contrast to the capitalist West where the law of the jungle prevailed, and that, whatever the difficulties, the country was headed in the right direction.

After Khrushchev was ousted in 1964, that ceased to be the case. Party leaders closed their eyes to corrupt deals by lower-level officials in return for a share of the proceeds. Schoolteachers accepted favours to give children better marks; doctors to give patients better treatment; policemen to overlook offences. It did not happen all at once and it did not affect everyone. Some, including Putin's father, remained true believers all their lives. But gradually, over time, there was a creeping erosion of faith. To counter that, Brezhnev and his Politburo colleagues placed ever greater emphasis on ideological orthodoxy.

In February 1966, two writers, Andrei Sinyavsky and Yuli Daniel, were sentenced to seven and five years respectively in strict-regime

labour camps for anti-Soviet agitation and propaganda on the grounds
that they had published their works in the West. It was the first time
such a punishment had been meted out solely for literary output and
signalled the start of a two-decades-long campaign against dissidents,
or, as they were then called in Russia, *inakomyslyashchie*, 'those who think
differently'. Six weeks after their trial, in his address to the Soviet Communist Party's 23rd Congress, Brezhnev called for 'uncompromising . . .
struggle against bourgeois ideology, revisionism, dogmatism and
reformism [and against] the gigantic propaganda apparatus of imperi-
alism [which] corrupts the individual'. The correct response, he said,
was 'the creative development of Marxism–Leninism and its organic
combination with the revolutionary practice of the working class'.
He continued in that vein for a full four hours.[193] To contemporary
observers, both in Russia and the West, the Congress was 'grey and
monotonous . . . dull and indeterminate . . . the most boring Congress
in the whole of the Party's history'.[194] But that was exactly why Brezhnev had been appointed. He was a safe pair of hands who could be
relied on to restore stability and make life predictable again. The innovation and excitement of the Khrushchev era were over.

The new emphasis on ideological correctness made itself felt in the
Komsomol. Already as Pioneers, children had been exhorted to 'understand the superiority of the Soviet system over the bourgeois system'.
Now they were expected to 'raise their theoretical and ideological
level' by studying Marx and Lenin in order 'to produce a new type of
person'.[195]

To try to reconcile these high-flown aims with an increasingly recalcitrant Soviet reality, Brezhnev turned to Yuri Andropov, a Central
Committee apparatchik with no previous experience of security matters, whom he appointed in 1967 to head the KGB. Andropov, far from
being the closet liberal that Soviet propagandists pretended, was virulently anti-Western.[196] Oleg Kalugin, who worked under him as head
of the First Chief Directorate, wrote that 'he genuinely believed that
the United States and the West were working day and night to destroy
the Soviet Union.'[197] A year later, during what became known as the
Prague Spring, when Czechoslovak communists attempted to loosen
Soviet control and introduce a more democratic system, Andropov
was convinced that it was due to Western meddling and must be put
down by force.

Within Russia, he adopted a similar approach. There was little that he could do to stem the gangrene of corruption, with which members of the Politburo and Brezhnev's own family were tarred. Stamping out dissent was another matter. In July 1967, he established the KGB's Fifth Directorate, whose mission – officially described as 'ideological counter-intelligence'[198] – was to combat the political dissent supposedly being fomented by the Western powers. Dissidents were harassed and imprisoned or incarcerated in psychiatric hospitals on the grounds that anyone who opposed the Soviet system must by definition be mentally ill.

At the same time, Andropov attempted to restore lustre to the KGB's image, which had been catastrophically tarnished in the 1950s by Khrushchev's revelations of its crimes under Stalin.[199]

The one complemented the other. Stepped-up repression of dissent was camouflaged by insistence on noble aims. The security services were presented as heirs to the supposedly 'glorious traditions' of Dzerzhinsky's Cheka in the 1920s as though the Stalinist period had never existed. Television series like *The Shield and the Sword* and *Seventeen Moments of Spring*, which related the exploits of Soviet agents in Nazi Germany during the Second World War, depicted intelligence officers as selfless patriots and heroes, defending the homeland at the risk of their lives. The films were consciously designed to project an image of Soviet intelligence comparable to that created by the James Bond films in the West, which Russia had banned. Although the heavy hand of Soviet film censors made them 'clunky and schmaltzy', as one Western critic put it – 'no sex, no suspense, no ambiguities' – many Russians found them inspiring.[200]

The KGB, as Andropov conceived it, had a dual role: to defend Russians against 'corrupting influences' from abroad, by persuasion if possible – 'prophylactic work', as it was called – and by repression if not; and to use all possible means to weaken the ability of the Western powers to undermine the Soviet system.[201] For this a new generation of KGB officers was needed. A campaign was launched to recruit what was known as the 'Andropov levy', made up of gifted young graduates from universities and technical institutes with a solid Komsomol background, to replace the plodding Stalinist gumshoes who until then had dominated surveillance and counter-intelligence work at home.[202]

Putin was then in ninth grade and had decided that he wanted to become an airline pilot. The Civil Aviation Institute in Leningrad was the largest of the three faculties in the USSR where airline personnel were trained and, as an athlete, so long as his marks were acceptable, he would not have to take the entrance examination. 'I was hell-bent on getting in,' he wrote later. 'I read the literature and subscribed to an aviation journal.' He even enquired whether there was a preparatory course he could take but was told that there was not.[203]

But then something happened which made him change his mind. He explained later: 'Books and programmes about espionage like *The Shield and the Sword* took hold of my imagination. What amazed me most of all was how one man's effort could achieve what whole armies could not. One spy could decide the fate of thousands of people . . . The idea of the Civil Aviation Institute began to pall.'[204] The television series, *The Shield and the Sword*, was broadcast in August and September 1968. Shortly afterwards, Putin plucked up his courage and went to the *Bolshoi Dom*, the Big House, as the KGB headquarters in Leningrad was known. A monumental, eight-storey edifice in 1930s constructivist style, according to a local joke it was the tallest building in the city because even from the cellars you could see Siberia.

Putin found his way to the reception office, on a side street, and asked what he needed to do to be accepted as a recruit. He was not the only one: after every new spy film, a few bold youngsters would turn up at the office, asking how to join, and a counter-intelligence officer had been detailed to receive them. He took down Putin's particulars, explained to him that the KGB did not accept volunteers, and that in any case recruits had to have completed their military service or higher education. When Putin asked which kind of degree would be best, the officer recommended the Law Faculty.[205]

For most of the following year, he told no one what he had done. At one point, he made discreet enquiries about the recruitment procedure through a classmate, whose brother had a friend who was a KGB officer.[206] But to all outward appearances he was still set on becoming a pilot, a secure career for which he was virtually guaranteed a place. In contrast, the Leningrad Law Faculty, like that in Moscow, was among the most prestigious institutions in the country, as difficult to get into as Oxford or Cambridge or an Ivy League college in the United States. The annual intake was limited to a hundred students, of whom only a handful came direct from school, most of the places being earmarked for those who had already completed their military service.

There were 40 candidates for each place.[207] As Putin admitted later, 'it seemed about as likely as flying to Mars'.[208]

When finally he told his parents about his new plans, his father was adamantly opposed, not because he disapproved of a career in the KGB but because it seemed a hopeless gamble which was bound to end badly. Anatoly Rakhlin, his *sambo* coach, thought the same. If Putin concentrated on sport, he said, he might well become a national champion. If he tried to enter university and failed, he would have to do his military service instead. Bullying in the army was not as bad in the 1960s as it would become later and Putin no doubt felt that his skill at unarmed combat and the street smarts he had learnt in the court-yard would keep him out of harm's way. Nonetheless, compared to a cushy, all-but-certain place at the Aviation Institute, it was not a cheering prospect.[209] Nor did he get much support from his *sambo* partners. In the sports clubs, law enforcement was not looked upon kindly. Putin was infuriated when another of his coaches, Leonid Usvyatsov – who had recently completed a 10-year term in a prison camp – taunted him for wanting to go to law school 'to become a filthy cop'.[210]

It was, he said later, 'the first turning point of my life'.'[211]

Everyone he knew was against him. For the first time, he openly defied his father.[212] One of the few friends in whom he confided, Vasily Shestakov, remembered him brooding over what to do.[213] 'They put pressure on me every day,' Putin wrote later.[214] 'It was one of those moments when I had to go for broke. Either . . . I would have the next stage of my life the way I wanted, or I would lose everything.'[215] Finally, around March 1970, he told them he would not change his mind.[216] The Aviation Institute, he admitted, would have been 'a soft landing. Every-thing suited me there – I liked everything . . . But I decided to act differently.'[217] This time, however, it was not just a matter of being dif-ferent. He had found what he wanted to do with his life. It was a big risk. But that may have been part of the attraction.

Once he had taken his decision, he followed a principle that he had absorbed as a child in the courtyard: 'If you want to win a fight, you have to carry it through to the end, as if it were the most decisive battle of your life.'[218] He cut back on his *sambo* training, started skipping les-sons in science – where his marks went sharply down – and concentrated on the subjects he would need for the Law Faculty entrance exam: lit-erature, history, Russian language and German.

By then he had realised that he might after all stand a chance of winning a place. Soviet universities were required to take a certain quota
of students from working-class families. In that respect, Putin's background was impeccable: his father was a war veteran, a factory worker
and a Party member of 30 years' standing. His academic record was
good, if not exceptional: he finished tenth grade with '4's and '5's in the
humanities.[219] That spring he had become a Candidate Master of Sport.
Universities in the Soviet Union, as in America, set aside places for
promising athletes and Putin certainly fitted that description.

Whatever the precise combination of reasons, in July, when the list
of successful candidates was published, Putin's name was there.[220]
Afterwards he went to great lengths to deny that he had been admitted
on the strength of his sporting achievements. The Dean of the Law
Faculty, Nikolai Alekseyev, he claimed, had personally assured him that
'everyone gets into this university on equal terms, judged by their
knowledge, not by some list of athletes!', after which – Putin's account
continued – the Dean reached into his desk drawer, got out the list of
athletes which he had just said did not exist, and after glancing at it,
told him that his name was not on it.[221] It would not be the last time
that Putin would spin an incoherent tale while trying to elide an inconvenient aspect of his past.

Notwithstanding Putin's denials, his athletic prowess was clearly a
key factor.[222] According to one version, Rakhlin's colleague, Leonid
Usvyatsov, having failed to dissuade him from applying for a place,
used his influence with the head of the University Sports Department,
Mikhail Bobrov, to get him admitted.[223] The claim is plausible because
soon after his admission, Putin was told that he would have to leave his
old *sambo* club, *Trud*, and compete instead for the all-universities association, *Burevestnik*. When he refused, an unholy row broke out.
Bobrov felt he had been cheated and that Putin had been accepted
under false pretences.[224] They had, Vera Gurevich wrote, 'a very
strained relationship'.[225] By then, however, the die was cast. Putin had
his university place. It would prove to be the springboard for a most
improbable career.

2

Legal Niceties

The Law Faculty at Leningrad State University occupied an elegant eighteenth-century building with an imposing classical façade, surrounded by well-kept gardens, facing the River Neva, in what had once been the Smolny Convent, opposite the Cathedral of the same name, in the north-east of the city.[1] It was there that Lenin had proclaimed the Bolshevik Revolution in 1917 from a building which had formerly housed the Society for the Education of Noble Maidens, established by Catherine the Great in 1764, and afterwards became the Communist Party headquarters for the city and the surrounding region.

It was a far cry from the run-down communal apartment in Baskov Lane, with its leaking roof, rat-infested stairwell and piles of garbage in the courtyard. When he crossed the threshold for the first time in September 1970, Volodya Putin, then not quite eighteen years old, knew that he had entered a different world. Later he admitted: 'I tried not to advertise the fact that my parents were not just workers but my mother was even an unskilled worker. Naturally, I would have liked to be able to say, especially in the first year, that my father was a professor and my mother an associate professor.'[2] It was not 'a big issue', he added. But because he continued to live at home, sharing a room with his parents, rather than in a student hostel with his comrades, he was constantly reminded of the differences between the world in which he had grown up and where he had always belonged, and the new world he had just entered. Almost two thirds of the law students were from intellectual or bureaucrat families. Of those who had working-class backgrounds, most were older, having completed their military service. Very few had entered, as Putin had, directly from high school.[3]

He made friends, several of whom would remain close to him all his life.[4] llham Ragimov and Viktor Khmarin shared Putin's love of sport.

Khmarin would become a businessman, while Ragimov and another close friend, Nikolai Yegorov, would have high-flying legal careers. Aleksandr Bastrykin, who played bass in the Faculty's rock group, was also in their circle. But to the majority of his coursemates, Volodya Putin was 'not just inconspicuous, but invisible'.[5] The fact that he was 'from a family that was not well off', as one of them delicately put it, was clear to everyone. For the first time in his life, he felt intimidated.[6]

Being at university was an eye-opener in other ways. Law students learnt about crime statistics and such things as sex offences which were never reported by the Soviet media. 'We understood that not everything was as good as we were constantly told on television and in the newspapers,' one student remembered.[7]

Putin never openly called into question the prevailing orthodoxy. Unlike many of his fellow students, he did not listen to foreign radio stations. Events like the crushing of the Prague Spring in 1968 seem to have passed him by.[8] That was in part because he had been brought up in a conventional Soviet proletarian family where politics was rarely discussed. But it also reflected the way that most Russians accepted as a matter of course the disconnect between Soviet ideals and the realities of everyday life. Like Christianity, which exalts meekness and poverty, and Buddhism, whose teachings are based on the renunciation of earthly ties, Marxism as a secular religion was honoured in the breach. The difference was that, in the Soviet Union, the study of Marxism–Leninism was obligatory and everybody was required to pay lip service to it. Most students regarded it as a total waste of time and there is no reason to think that Putin felt differently. But without it, no one could graduate.

· The same was true of Komsomol work. Each year, at the end of September, the students had to help bring in the potato harvest from the collective farms in the surrounding region. In theory, participation was voluntary. But woe betide anyone who failed to turn up.

As at high school, Putin's priorities were study and sport. He rarely attended student parties. He did not smoke and drank little – his training regime ruled that out, apart from the occasional beer or a glass of sweet Georgian wine which he would nurse for hours.[9] One scorching hot day at a training camp in the provinces, he and his roommate bought a bottle of Moldavian wine. Having thought about the following day's competition, Putin decided to abstain and that evening his friend drank the whole bottle. Next morning, the friend, who had snored all night, awoke perfectly refreshed. Putin had been unable to sleep. It was a lesson, he said later. Being too strict was counterproductive.[10]

In the holidays, he invited friends to the family's new dacha at Tosno, 30 miles south-east of Leningrad, which his father had exchanged for the cottage near the Estonian border, having decided it was too far from the city. It was sorely lacking in amenities – water had to be brought from the well and the bathroom was spartan. Putin's parents were 'puritan, even ascetic', Borisenko said later, and the place was 'very modest'. They played records – bootleg copies of Western pop songs, engraved on home-made discs cut from plastic X-ray plates, known affectionately as 'rock-on-bones' – and in the winter went cross-country skiing in the surrounding forests.[11]

Putin had a student stipend of 35 roubles a month, roughly a quarter of the average worker's wage. During the summer vacation, he joined a construction crew, organised by the Komsomol, to work as an unskilled labourer. Later he would do other odd jobs, including working as an extra at the Leningrad Film Studios.[12] But in the first year, he went to the Komi Republic, on the Arctic Circle in the northern Urals, where Vorkuta, one of the harshest forced labour camps in the Stalinist prison system, had been located. There, six weeks chopping lumber and helping to repair houses earned him almost a thousand roubles, more money than he had ever seen in his life.[13] When he returned home, after giving presents to his family, he bought an overcoat. He wrote later that it was the first possession he had ever felt was truly his own.

The rest of his earnings he spent on a holiday to Gagra, on the Black Sea coast, an area which he would come to love. Then, as in later life, Putin adored the sun.[14] In Leningrad there rarely was any. The poet, Anna Akhmatova, wrote of its 'cold river, menacing sunsets and terrifying operatic moon', and those were the good days.[15] A foggy, grey, rain-soaked city, in winter it was sunk in gloom after three o'clock in the afternoon. By the time Putin's holiday was over, he had spent every kopek.[16] In the Soviet Union, that was what most people did. There was no point saving money because there was so little to spend it on.

That attitude helps to explain what happened when the family received an unexpected windfall soon after Volodya started his second year at university.[17] His mother, bored at home on her own, had started working at a local hospital, washing and sterilising laboratory equipment. One day in the canteen, the cashier ran out of change and gave her a ticket for the state lottery instead. A few weeks later, when everyone in the family had forgotten about it, it was found to be the winning number. She had won a Zaporozhets. It was the smallest and cheapest Soviet car, the equivalent of an early-model Fiat 500, but it still cost several years' wages and even then there was a long waiting list. To own any kind of car in the Soviet Union in the early '70s was reserved for the privileged few. The family debated what to do. 'We could have sold it for at least 3,500 roubles, which would have settled the family budget for a long time to come,' Putin wrote afterwards.[18] But Vladimir Spiridonovich, who did not know how to drive, decided that Volodya should have it, on condition that he took them to the dacha at weekends. It was an extravagant gift, but in keeping with the way his parents had indulged him ever since he had been a small child. At the age of nineteen, he may have been the only university student in the city to have a car of his own.

Learning to drive it was another matter. His friends remembered numerous scrapes and accidents narrowly avoided. Borisenko was with him when he was driving down the right-hand lane of a highway and suddenly decided to turn left, prompting a torrent of abuse from those behind who were forced to jam on their brakes.[19] On another occasion, he ran into a pedestrian, who was lucky to escape unharmed. 'He jumped in front of me or something,' Putin said lamely afterwards. '[He must have] decided to put an end to his life . . . What an idiot!'[20] His *sambo* coach, Anatoly Rakhlin, to whom he gave a lift, remembered telling him: 'Please steer properly! I don't want to be dead.'[21] But it didn't have much effect. Some months later, Putin recalled, when he drove Rakhlin to their training camp,

a truck with some hay was coming from the other direction. The hay smelled delicious. As I drove past the truck on a curve, I reached out to grab some . . . The car suddenly swerved . . . I turned the wheel sharply in the other direction, and [we] went up on two wheels. I almost lost control. We really should have ended up in the ditch . . . My coach sat there, frozen, speechless . . . When we arrived . . . he looked at me and said: 'You take risks!' Then he walked away.[22]

Putin might have matured since the days in the courtyard when he could never resist getting into a fight, but, as he later acknowledged, he still did 'stupid stuff'. He was 'a pretty wild driver' and he liked to drive fast.[23]

After Putin's first year at university, when he won the Leningrad *sambo* youth championship, he began training less obsessively.[24] He still competed in city and national competitions and, in addition to *sambo*, started to practise judo, which had recently undergone a renaissance in Russia, having been banned under Stalin.[25] Judo was an Olympic sport, which *sambo* was not, and while Putin himself had no Olympic ambitions, some of his teammates at *Trud* did.[26] Rakhlin felt Putin was better suited to judo, and claimed later that, had he continued, he could have become not just a Soviet but a European champion.[27]

Then, not long afterwards, he was confronted by a personal tragedy which might well have brought his sporting career to an abrupt end. He had become friendly with a young student from Ukraine, Vladimir Cheryomushkin. They had met during the entrance exams and had grown extremely close. Borisenko said that Putin had 'fallen under [Cheryomushkin's] spell'. The other students called them *Sherochka* and *Masherochka,* an expression for inseparable friends which dated back to the time of the Institute for Noble Maidens at Smolny, where the pupils, who were required to speak French, referred to each other as 'Chère' and 'Ma Chère' (*Sher* and *Masher,* 'Dear' and 'My Dear'). With Putin's encouragement, Cheryomushkin had taken up judo, and in March 1973, competed in the annual university championships. He was still a beginner, and when his adversary made a move which he had not been expecting, he responded awkwardly and landed on his neck, rupturing a ligament and dislocating his spine. The injury is rare, but when it occurs, usually fatal. Cheryomushkin died soon afterwards.[28]

Putin was devastated. Borisenko remembered him at the funeral ceremony, standing by the coffin, 'cold . . . and distant . . . Like a statue, not a single muscle moved on his face . . . He [seemed] alienated, completely closed.' He found Putin's lack of emotion shocking. Much later he learnt that afterwards, at the cemetery, when everyone else had left, and Putin and Cheryomushkin's mother and sister, and another close friend, Kolya Alekhov, watched the coffin being lowered into the grave, he had collapsed, weeping uncontrollably. 'He cried for so long,' Alekhov remembered, 'none of us could calm him down.'[29] The icy demeanour which had repelled Borisenko was a front, a protective shell, to stop himself breaking down in public. Borisenko was reminded of an incident in their childhood, when a woman had thrown a mother cat and the kittens to which she had just given birth into a garbage bin full of slops and closed the lid. Putin saved the cat and two of the kittens, but the others died. He was sickened by the woman's action, yet when they next met he behaved as though nothing had happened, afraid that if he let his anger show, he would not be able to control it.[30] 'There were moments,' Borisenko said, 'when Volodya became as if made of iron. I am talking about his inner attitude . . . He holds to the norms of behaviour . . . that have been instilled in him since childhood.'[31]

Putin did not give up sport after Cheryomushkin's death. He would have considered it weak, even disloyal, to have done so. He travelled all over the Soviet Union for competitions and, later that year, became a full Master of Sport at *sambo*, which meant he was ranked as a national champion. Two years later, he qualified as a Master of Sport in judo as well.[32]

The two sports are similar but with significant differences.

Judo was developed in the 1880s from ju-jutsu, a centuries-old form of hand-to-hand combat adopted by Japanese samurai on the battlefield, when they were at close quarters and could not use their long swords. The term can be translated as 'Yielding Path' – the Japanese character, *do*, being the same as the Chinese, *dao*, the path, or flow of nature, in the Daoist religion. Judo's founder, Kanō Jigorō, viewed it as a philosophy as much as a martial art. His guiding principles were 'maximum efficiency, minimum effort', and 'softness controls hardness': rather than resist a more powerful opponent, one should put him off balance and use his strength against him. 'This makes it possible', Kano wrote, 'for weaker opponents to beat significantly stronger ones.'[33] That appealed to Putin, as did the emphasis on respect. 'It's respect for your elders and for your opponent,' he said later. 'You come out onto the mat, you bow to one another, you follow a ritual.' With his time in the courtyard in mind, he reflected that it could be done differently: 'Instead of bowing, . . . you could jab him in the forehead.'[34]

Another key element in judo is surprise, at which Putin excelled. Anatoly Rakhlin wrote that he was equally good in throwing to the right and the left – an unusual ability in a judoka – which made it difficult for his opponents to predict what he would do next.[35] In judo, a single winning manoeuvre – an ippon – is enough to end the match.

Sambo combines judo with elements from Graeco-Roman wrestling. Matches are often won on points. Where judo relies on mobility and technique, *sambo* requires stamina and physical strength.

Putin would always esteem toughness and scorn those who were weak, a theme which recurs repeatedly in his memories of that time. He recalled an altercation between Leonid Usvyatsov, the coach who had just been released from prison, and another trainer whose class was overrunning its allotted time and who had ignored his request to finish. 'Without saying a word, Leonid flipped him, squeezed him lightly and dragged him off the mat. He had lost consciousness . . . That was our attitude.'[36] In another incident, a judo partner, Nikolai Vashchilin, was stopped by a gang of youths in a dark alley one night. 'Not only was he gigantic,' Putin recalled admiringly, 'but he had this incredible face. He had this massive jaw that jutted forward and a huge overhanging brow . . . He said, "Guys, calm down . . ." Then he took out a match, struck it, and held it up to his face. "Just look at me," he said. And that was the end of that.'[37]

Putin would no doubt have liked to produce the same effect himself. Sometimes, he did. One winter, when they were still at high school, his friend, Kolya Alekhov, was waiting with him at a tram stop when two drunks started bothering them. Putin asked him to hold his school bag. 'Suddenly I saw one of them go flying with his snout in a snowdrift,' Alekhov recounted. 'A couple of seconds later, the other one joined him.'[38]

The lessons of sport, and of the courtyard, would stay with Putin for the rest of his life. But after Cheryomushkin's death, his friends noticed that he 'closed up and withdrew into his studies'.[39]

Putin was attracted to law not merely as a vehicle towards a career in the KGB. It interested him for its own sake. As a schoolchild, he once said, he had never wanted others to recognise him as their chief. He preferred the role of arbitrator, 'an unspoken leader, [playing] the role of the judicial branch, not the executive'.[40] That memory was no doubt coloured by subsequent experiences: in the Soviet Union, arbitration did not have to be impartial. Nevertheless, the image is striking. His teacher remembered how, on a camping trip, the summer before Putin's final year at high school, the students had had to kill a duck to be cooked for supper. To justify the 'execution', Putin had organised a mock trial, at which the duck was condemned to die for 'impudently violating the rules of her existence, excessive eating and swimming, and then falling asleep,' in other words, in Soviet parlance, for antisocial behaviour.[41] It was a concept he understood well. As a twelve-year-old, he had been brought before the Comrades' Court on precisely those grounds and, later, some of the young toughs in the courtyard had been sent to reform school for the same reason. All Soviet citizens, even children, knew that anyone whose actions were seen as inimical to the Soviet social, economic and, above all, political order risked exemplary punishment.

At university, the theory on which this was based was expounded in Putin's classes on criminal law. The law, the students were told, was an instrument of the state, and its primary role was to protect state interests.[42] A crime was 'a socially dangerous act' – meaning that it was a danger to the social system instituted by the state. Crime was a class phenomenon, a relic of bourgeois behaviour, engendered by the capitalist system, which socialism had not yet been able to overcome. Article 70 of the Criminal Code, used principally to repress dissent, stated that 'anti-Soviet agitation and propaganda', in the form of preparing, keeping or circulating, verbally or in written form, 'slanderous falsifications which defame the Soviet political and social system', was an 'especially dangerous crime', punishable by up to 12 years of imprisonment and exile to a remote province.

Political crimes made up less than one per cent of the total. The students knew that, in those cases, the outcome was decided by the Party before they ever came to court, but that was not a subject the lecturers discussed.

Many non-political crimes also had a political subtext. A 'parasitic way of life' was illegal because earning money from activities other than those authorised by the state undermined the social system. 'Speculation', meaning buying and selling goods for a profit, was illegal because it undermined the economic system. Even such purely criminal offences as murder, rape and theft, had a political aspect, not only because they were socially disruptive but because they called into question the omnipotence of the state. For the same reason, fewer than one per cent of criminal trials ended in acquittal, because acquittals implied that the state, in the shape of the prosecutors, was mistaken. The primary purpose of Soviet law, one writer concluded, was not to protect the citizenry but to 'defend institutional authority by giving it an aura of legitimacy'.[43]

In the early days of the Bolshevik regime, jurisprudence had been even more politicised. Lenin had defined the 'dictatorship of the proletariat' as 'power limited by nothing, neither by laws nor by rules', a formula which recalled the absolutism of the tsars.[44]

By the time Putin was a student, the emphasis had shifted to what was termed 'socialist legality'. The presumption of innocence, which under Stalin had been decried as 'a worm-eaten dogma of bourgeois doctrine', was now grudgingly admitted. The courts ruled that legislation could not be applied retroactively, and Putin's lecturers criticised Khrushchev (a safe target, since he was long out of power) for a celebrated case in 1961, when two young currency speculators had been executed under a decree which had been issued long after their arrests. Putin found that scandalous. 'The state simply deceived them,' he told a friend. 'They knew that at most they would get ten years' imprisonment . . . If they had known that they risked capital punishment, they would probably not have gone into the business in the first place.'[45]

But cosmetic changes aside, the basic thrust of the law remained the same. When it was suggested that courts should have greater discretion over sentencing, Soviet legal scholars objected. The criminal code was precise and should be applied unconditionally, they said. Putin agreed. He often quoted a Latin tag from his classes in Roman law: *Dura lex, sed lex* – 'The law may be harsh, but it is the law.' If the law was bad, it should be corrected, which was the role of parliament. 'But what the law states must be followed. Otherwise it is all a mess.'[46] However, that did not rule out judicial subterfuge – 'legal niceties', as one of his lecturers called it – if the law as written was unable to accomplish the tasks which the Party laid down.[47]

Putin absorbed those principles. He often cited the lessons that he had learnt at law school. In later life, nothing he ever did suggested that he seriously questioned the premises on which Soviet criminal law was based.

Civil law was a different matter. In family disputes, state interests

were rarely involved, and the courts generally handed down judgements free of political considerations. Cases dealing with housing and
labour issues were more complicated, because local authorities or factory directors might intervene. But the outcome was not preordained,
as it was when the state was directly involved. Yet even here, there
were limits to what a Soviet-trained lawyer saw as his role. Kaj Hober,
who negotiated with Putin in the 1990s on legal matters involving
foreign investment, remembered: 'We had no lawyer-to-lawyer discussions, I mean, a sophisticated discussion on legal matters.' Rather than
debating legal points Putin simply carried out the instructions that he
had been given.[48]

This view of the law as a cog in an institutional machine was reinforced by the way it was taught. There was no attempt to instil critical
thinking or the ability to produce a reasoned argument, no Socratic
questions and answers to draw out the students' ideas. Instead, they
were expected to learn by rote, in order to produce 'the correct
answer, the answer that the teacher wants'.[49] An American exchange
student, who spent a year at the Leningrad Law Faculty shortly after
Putin left, said it reminded him of a US high school. 'We were told the
facts and during examinations we were expected to give the facts back,
not with analysis, not with differing interpretations.'[50]

That trend became more pronounced after the 24th Soviet Party
Congress in 1971, which approved Brezhnev's programme of détente
with the West but at the same time, to ward off potentially undesirable
side effects, called for an intensified campaign against the influence of
Western ideas. At the Law Faculty this had translated into a crusade
against 'bourgeois legal ideology'.[51] Students were required to lard
their essays with appropriate quotations from Lenin.[52] Those who
showed themselves insufficiently enthusiastic were reported to the
Dean or the Komsomol. Putin claimed afterwards that he had hardly
noticed Brezhnev's 'tightening of the screws'. Others remembered the
atmosphere as oppressive.[53]

Teaching was conducted mainly through lectures, not least because
it was almost impossible for students to buy textbooks, unless they
learnt in advance that a consignment was arriving at a bookshop and
got there before it sold out.[54] Most lecturers simply read out their notes
and did so slowly enough for the students to copy them down verbatim. A Fulbright lecturer, who visited the Law Faculty, wrote scathingly

that 'the professor's notes become the student's notes without passing through the minds of either.'[55] The relationship between professor and student, as in most Russian institutions, was rigidly hierarchical. Students stood when the professor arrived and, if they were late, had to wait outside – a particular trial for Putin, who seemed congenitally unable ever to be on time.[56] Very often they were treated as children, 'socially infantile', as one elderly professor put it.[57]

One of the few exceptions was Professor Olimpiad Ioffe, the university's – and the Soviet Union's – foremost authority on civil law. He had an entertaining, avuncular style, and lectured without notes. 'Students from the senior classes used to come back just to hear him speak,' one remembered. 'Everything was from memory, and his memory was brilliant.'[58] Putin liked him and, in his final two years, attended seminars conducted by one of his colleagues, an assistant lecturer named Anatoly Sobchak, who shared some of Ioffe's talent for giving interesting explanations of complicated legal issues.[59] Eventually, after Putin's graduation, Ioffe was banned from teaching, expelled from the Party, and emigrated to America. The ostensible reason was that his daughter and her Jewish husband had applied for exit visas to Israel. The truth was more complicated. His colleagues at the Faculty were jealous of his reputation and had persuaded the Leningrad Party Committee that he had violated Party guidelines.[60]

For the first three years at the Law Faculty, Putin heard nothing from the Big House, to which he had gone as a schoolboy to enquire about a KGB career. In the summer of 1973, the Faculty had moved from Smolny to much less elegant quarters – a decrepit building, which had formerly housed a secondary school and was now badly in need of repair, on a grimy street on Vasilevsky Island, in the west of the city, where the university's main campus was situated. A blue stencilled sign on the side of the building stated, 'Citizens! During artillery barrages this side of the street is more dangerous.' Beneath it was a white marble plaque, stating that the sign had been preserved to commemorate the heroism of Leningraders during the blockade.[61] It was actually a replica. Similar signs, warning that the northern side of streets should be avoided because the German batteries were to the south of the city, had been put up in several districts as a reminder to the younger generation of what their elders had been through during the war.

It was at Vasilevsky Island, in January 1974, that Putin received a message saying that he would be contacted about his future career.[62] He guessed, correctly, where it must have come from. It had been sent by Dmitry Gantserov, an amiable man in his late forties, who worked in the section responsible for universities at the personnel department of the Leningrad KGB. Every major Soviet university had a KGB 'curator', usually a colonel, whose job was to identify potential recruits. Gantserov had been observing Putin ever since he entered the Faculty.

The first step had been a background check. Anyone with Jewish antecedents was immediately rejected. Having relatives who lived abroad, or who had a criminal past, could also disqualify a candidate, although there were exceptions.[63] So could an unusually striking face, whether ugly or handsome. 'An operative must be inconspicuous, outwardly appearing as an ordinary person,' a KGB general wrote. 'I completely rejected those who were attracted to intelligence by romance or love of adventure. The best of those whom I selected looked the exact opposite of the image of an operative created in fiction.' The last thing the service needed was someone who resembled James Bond.[64]

On almost every count – except, perhaps, his romanticising of the profession, which he tried hard not to let show – Putin was an ideal candidate.

He was inconspicuous to a fault, the sort of person to whom no one, meeting him casually, would give a second glance. His family background was without blemish. His grandfather, Spiridon, had cooked for the Party elite. Putin would later claim that he had cooked for both Lenin and Stalin. That was gilding the lily. However, for more than a decade between the wars, Spiridon did work as a cook in the household of Lenin's widow, Nadezhda Krupskaya, and his sister, Maria, at their estate at Gorki, just outside Moscow. After their deaths, he had worked at a guest house for the Moscow City Party Committee, at Ilyinsky, a resort village a few miles further east.[65] To cook for senior Party officials in the last years of Stalin's life, when the leadership was paranoid about the risk of poisoning, let alone for Lenin's family, would have required an exceptional security clearance.

Other factors taken into consideration were psychological profile, academic work, sporting ability and patriotism, including work in the

Komsomol. Promiscuous behaviour or excessive drinking were both grounds for rejection. According to Gantserov, of the 100 or so students in each year at the Law Faculty, eight to ten passed the initial vetting, of whom only one or two would eventually be offered positions. Rigorous selection was possible because in the 1970s, working for the KGB, especially in foreign intelligence, was one of the most desirable jobs any young man could hope for. Students would choose unusual languages at college, like Spanish or Serbo-Croat, in the hope – not always fulfilled – that that would give them a head start.[66] Not only did KGB officers enjoy better material conditions than their colleagues in the police or the Prosecutor's Office, but if they entered the First Chief Directorate, considered to be the *crème de la crème*, they could expect to be posted abroad and paid partly in foreign currency, something of which most Soviet citizens could only dream. There were special rest homes and sanatoria for officers and their families, farms whose produce went exclusively to KGB administrations – no small advantage in a country where meat was often a luxury and most people subsisted on a diet of bread, cabbage, potatoes and dairy products – and an identity document with a red leather cover, embossed in gold with the Soviet crest and the letters, 'KGB, USSR', which commanded instant respect whenever it was shown. But most important of all, perhaps, was the sense of belonging to an elite, entrusted with forbidden knowledge denied to the rest of the population.

After Gantserov's initial meeting with Putin, the Personnel Department at the Big House dissected his biography. His relatives' histories were minutely verified to make sure that they were what they said. Gantserov met him once a month to 'work with him', as he put it, 'more intensively'.[67] Quite what that involved is unclear. It is often assumed that Putin was required to inform on other students. The Law Faculty, like most departments in Soviet universities, was a hive of *stukachi* – 'knockers', as they were called, because they 'knocked' on the KGB's door in order to denounce their comrades – and students watched what they said unless they were with trusted friends. Putin did not object in principle to the use of informers. 'The cooperation of normal citizens [is] an important tool for the state's viable activity,' he wrote later. '90 per cent of all intelligence information is obtained from . . . ordinary Soviet citizens.' If it was based on 'idealistic principles', and was carried out 'in the interests of the state', it was legitimate and necessary.[68] But he denied that he himself had acted as a *seksot*, a 'secret collaborator', and he was probably telling the truth. Even in Stalin's time, NKVD officers were rarely recruited from the ranks of informers – their job was to recruit others to inform, not to do so themselves – and by the 1970s, it had become extremely unusual for a *stukach* to be invited to join the KGB. However, Gantserov no doubt asked him, during his last two years at the Law Faculty, to carry out specific tasks, including making reports on his colleagues, in order to see how he dealt with them. That was common KGB practice and at least one of his university coursemates was convinced that he had done so.[69] A contemporary remembered: 'If you were too enthusiastic, it wasn't good, because it showed you had no character. But if you didn't report anything, that meant that you were lazy. The KGB never sought out the best or the brightest students, nor did it want the dumb or lazy ones. It wanted well-balanced prospects.'[70]

Whatever 'working intensively' meant in practice, Putin evidently did it satisfactorily. Gantserov concluded that he was able 'quickly to find the right way to approach people', one of the essential qualities any intelligence operative had to have, and, in January 1975, the KGB officially informed Vladimir Spiridonovich that it was considering recruiting his son. His father, convinced communist that he was, was wholly in favour and, in March, Putin was told that the KGB would offer him a position. He was overjoyed and invited Borisenko for a celebratory drink. But he was careful not to divulge what the celebration was about.[71]

After that, it was plain sailing. In the Soviet Union, students did not choose their future employment: they were told what their new posts would be when they graduated. When Putin appeared before the Assignment Commission three months later, there was a moment's uncertainty when he was initially informed that he would be called to the Leningrad bar as a lawyer. But then, as he later recounted, the KGB representative at the meeting 'suddenly woke up' and announced that that would not be the case as 'we are hiring Putin to work [with us]'.[72] The story is plausible. Department heads often did not know which students the KGB had recruited until the job assignments were announced.[73] It was part of the organisation's mystique, a demonstration of its power to take whomever it wanted, regardless of what anyone else might decide.

3

The Big House

On August 1, 1975, a Friday, Putin entered for the first time the Lenin-grad Regional Directorate of the KGB, the Big House on Liteiny Prospekt, in his new role as a junior lieutenant.[1] The induction cere-mony took place a week later, in the 'Red Hall' on the top floor of the building, where, in front of a huge, coloured bas-relief of Lenin, the Director, General Daniil Nosyrev, welcomed the new recruits, dressed in their service uniforms, used only on formal occasions.

Nosyrev was a martinet. An officer with his tie unknotted or a female employee wearing trousers could expect short shrift on his watch. But he had been appointed by Andropov and shared many of the latter's ideas, notably that, at a time of improved relations with the West, one of the biggest threats to the Soviet Union was subversion through an influx of bourgeois thinking.

By coincidence, the day that Putin started work, Brezhnev was in Finland with 34 other heads of state and government from Canada, the United States, and the whole of Europe (apart from Albania), to sign what would be called the Helsinki Final Act. The agreement was important to Brezhnev because it confirmed Europe's post-war bor-ders, effectively consolidating Moscow's gains in the Second World War. But in return he had had to accept the so-called 'third basket' of the accords, under which the Soviet Union pledged support for human rights and fundamental freedoms. Helsinki turned into a rallying cry for dissidents in the Soviet Union and throughout Eastern Europe.

Under Andropov, the struggle against bourgeois corruption of the Soviet body politic – 'attempts to take advantage of Helsinki to increase . . . ideological sabotage', as a KGB training manual put it – became the agency's *raison d'être*.[2]

Ever since its foundation by Peter the Great, Leningrad had been

Russia's window on the West. Nosyrev's task was to ensure that it remained firmly closed against the pollution of capitalist ideas. Of the 3,000 men and women who worked for the KGB in Leningrad and the surrounding region, 500 were officers, like Putin. About a thousand more, mainly women, worked full-time, recording and transcribing telephone calls and conversations from bugged apartments and hotel rooms. In another building, several hundred others opened, read and resealed foreign and domestic mail. Apart from the border troops and bodyguards for the Party elite, the great majority engaged in 'ideological counter-intelligence' for the Fifth Directorate, aimed at repressing dissent.[3]

Putin had hoped to be assigned to foreign intelligence, but, as he explained later, employing one of the vulgarisms which used to drive his old teacher, Vera Gurevich, to despair, 'You can't pick your nose and say, "I don't want this and I don't want that." '[4] So he followed orders. By his own account, he worked for the first five months as a dogsbody in the secretariat and then spent the first half of 1976 on a course at a KGB training institute, the 401 School at Okhta, in the suburbs across the river from Smolny.[5] At university he had attended a compulsory two-month army camp – 'much easier than athletics camps and we got really bored', he complained – and, in theory at least, he should also have spent two hours a week in military training at high school.[6] But the six months at Okhta were the first time he had been exposed to real military discipline.

The school was run like an army barracks. The students, who came from all over the Soviet Union, studied six days a week and were allowed outside only with special permission.[7] Putin evidently had a dispensation to continue his judo training, for in May 1976, he won the Leningrad regional championship, which earned him a mention in the evening newspaper.[8] But afterwards, Rakhlin wrote, 'it was as if the spark had gone out of him'. He took no further part in competitions.[9] Rakhlin thought it was because there was a conflict with his KGB career, but it seems more likely that he had decided that being Leningrad champion was as far as he wanted to go as a sportsman and he would now focus on something else.

The 401 School gave Putin his introduction to the KGB's fearsomely bureaucratic ways of working. The course itself was narrowly focused on techniques of external surveillance and was strictly limited to what the students needed to know. 'It would have cost far too much to indulge in the pleasure of teaching things which are not required for the job,' one of the instructors loftily explained.[10] External surveillance had many forms: covert, overt, combined (both covert and overt) and demonstrative, the last three being designed in varying degrees to confuse a target or to frighten them into giving themselves, and perhaps others, away.[11] Covert observation techniques included the 'chain' method, where members of a surveillance team followed a target successively; the 'fork', where several operatives observed a target from different sides, a method often used in a dense crowd; and 'parallel street observation', employed in a lightly populated area where a conventional 'tail' would be too obvious. Each method was minutely explained and the trainees were set practical exercises. A surveillance log had to be filled out for each target, and in especially important cases, when an individual 'posed a threat to the interests of the Soviet state', an operational surveillance file also had to be created, for which special authorisation was required. If a foreigner was involved, the file would be shared by the Fifth and Second Chief Directorates and archived by the KGB's Tenth Department.

The trainees were also instructed in counter-surveillance techniques, to ensure that they were not themselves observed, and in the recruitment of so-called 'Background Checking Agents' from among housing office employees, postal workers, doctors and others who, by the nature of their work, were in a position to provide information about potential targets, and specifically 'those who have suspicious contacts with foreigners'.

Putin claimed later that he found the 401 School disappointing, as well he may have done.[12] It had no connection with foreign intelligence. It had been established in the 1950s to train *toptuny*, the gumshoes who were sent out to undertake the time-consuming, wearisome business of external surveillance, where a team would stake out a building for hours and days on end without anything of note ever happening.[13] Putin, as an officer, would not be expected to perform that kind of task himself, but he needed to know how the system worked.

The course at the 401 School ended in June 1976. What Putin did for the next three years of his KGB career has been sedulously concealed ever since.

Putin himself claimed that he was transferred 'pretty quickly' to the

Leningrad Directorate's First Department dealing with foreign intelligence. In another version, he dated the transfer to a year or so later.[14] One of his former chiefs in Leningrad also maintained that, after 'a short time in another unit . . . I don't even remember which,' Putin was transferred to foreign intelligence in, 'it seems to me, 1976,' or perhaps 1977.[15]

In fact, as Putin himself later acknowledged, he transferred to foreign intelligence 'at the end of the 1970s'.[16] The unit which his former superior preferred not to remember was the Fifth Directorate – or the Fifth Department, as it was called in provincial KGB administrations like Leningrad – and the 'short time' Putin spent there lasted from July 1976 to late summer in 1979. Afterwards he spoke in general terms of working for 'counter-intelligence' – which was technically correct, since the Fifth Directorate's role was ideological counter-intelligence – but denied that he had ever dealt with dissidents. The recollections of his friends and KGB colleagues, as well as his own statements, leave no doubt that he did.

According to his former judo partner, Nikolai Vashchilin, he monitored sportsmen, religious figures and artists – all Fifth Department responsibilities.[17] His friend, Sergei Roldugin, a cellist whose elder brother was in the KGB, confirmed that he was involved in the surveillance of Orthodox believers. One Easter, probably in 1978, Roldugin accompanied him when he was assigned to keep watch on a church procession.[18] Sasha Nikolayev, another friend from his schooldays, knew that he worked 'in a department dealing with dissidents'.[19] A KGB colleague, Vladimir Agartanov, with whom Putin later shared an office, identified him as a Fifth Department operative and was struck by how knowledgeable he was about non-conformist artists and intellectuals and their ideas.[20]

Putin himself recalled a demonstration in Leningrad when a group of writers and artists gathered before the Bronze Horseman, a statue of Peter the Great, to commemorate the Decembrist Uprising, a failed attempt 150 years earlier to force the Tsar to introduce constitutional government. Rather than arrest them, Putin said, the KGB organised a counter-demonstration, complete with a brass band and patriotic laying of wreaths.[21] He recounted the incident to try to show that in those days the Fifth Department preferred to use indirect means rather than overt repression, which, by the second half of the 1970s, was largely true in cities like Leningrad and Moscow. Dissident activities were targeted only if they were seen as posing a direct threat to the state. Unofficial writers were permitted to circulate their works in *samizdat*, so long as they did not try to publish in the West. Non-conformist painters could hold exhibitions in private apartments.[22] General Nosyrev, old-school and straitlaced though he was, approved the establishment of an arts club, Klub 81, as 'a gathering place for the Leningrad counterculture', where they would be surrounded by 'a swarm of KGB agents* posing as hipsters'.[23] The goal was to bring the city's dissident movement as much as possible under KGB control.

When moderation failed, the bludgeon was still available. Most of the participants in the 1975 demonstration which Putin described were let off with warnings, but two poets, regarded as ringleaders, were sentenced to labour-camp terms. Nonetheless, where possible, the Leningrad KGB preferred 'prophylactic methods', using a combination of harassment, intimidation and social pressure to keep dissent within what it regarded as acceptable bounds. The historian, Lev Lurye, himself a member of the 1970s counterculture, wrote that so long as people followed certain rules – having a job (i.e., not being a parasite), not engaging overtly in politics or in illegal economic activities, and not using drugs – they were allowed considerable cultural freedom.[24]

It seemed at the time a sensible policy. But it would turn out to be a flawed compromise. The steady erosion of totalitarian rule, which had begun after the death of Stalin and accelerated under his successors, would culminate, 15 years later, in the system's collapse.

If Putin subsequently found it expedient to deny that he had ever worked in the Fifth Department, there is no reason to think that he had qualms about it at the time. On the contrary, he emphasised that, in general, he and his KGB colleagues operated strictly within the law, that what they did was usually 'not . . . so crude', and that in a country like the Soviet Union, a certain discipline, while perhaps regrettable, was necessary.[25]

Nor was he much bothered by the KGB's bloodstained past. 'To be honest, I didn't think about it at all. Not one bit,' he said later. 'I was a

---

* In Soviet terminology, an 'agent' was a Soviet citizen or a foreigner recruited by a KGB officer as a source of information. KGB officers, unlike their CIA counterparts, were not referred to as 'agents' but as 'operatives'.

pure and utterly successful product of Soviet patriotic education . . . I
knew about Stalin's cult of personality . . . I wasn't completely naïve.
[But] how deep was that cult of personality? How serious was it? My
friends and I didn't think about that.'[26] His former classmate, Viktor
Borisenko, took a similar view. 'We thought, "Yes, there were mistakes,
and that's bad. But mistakes happen, and they're being corrected."' It
was not until the arrival of Gorbachev in the mid 1980s that Borisenko
began to understand more.[27] Putin was reluctant even then to acknowledge the enormity of Stalin's crimes.

Vladimir Agartanov remembered a conversation with him, well
after Gorbachev came to power, about an incident which had occurred
in the Siberian town of Minusinsk, where there was a large Chinese
community, during the *Yezhovshchina*, the Great Purge of 1937 to 1938.
The local NKVD chief had received a cabled instruction to liquidate
400 Chinese spies. The order was sufficiently unusual to make him set
out for the provincial capital, Krasnoyarsk, to ask for an explanation.
His deputy telegraphed ahead of him, accusing him of trying to protect foreign agents. When he arrived, he was arrested and executed.
The deputy was promoted in his place and 400 Chinese were rounded
up arbitrarily and shot. Some months later, the newly promoted deputy was shot, too. Agartanov, who had himself served in the KGB
bureau in Krasnoyarsk, said the story had been told to him by old-
timers who had been junior NKVD officers there when these events
occurred. Putin refused point-blank to believe him. When Agartanov
insisted, pointing out that, at that time, the NKVD had issued execution quotas to many different localities, Putin did not believe that,
either. It was a fairy tale – it could not be true, he said.[28]

His reaction was all the more intriguing because he was well aware
that, under Stalin, 'enemies of the people' were summarily shot.

On his bedside table, at the dacha at Tosno, he kept a portrait of Jan
Berzin, who had been head of military intelligence from 1924 to 1935
and again briefly in 1937.[29] Berzin was an Old Bolshevik who had joined
the Party in 1905, taken part in the October Revolution, worked with
the founder of the Cheka, Feliks Dzerzhinsky, and served as chief
Soviet military adviser to the Republicans in the Spanish Civil War. In
the late 1920s, he had set up, in conditions of great secrecy, partisan
training schools where officers and men learnt how to carry out reconnaissance and sabotage, deep behind enemy lines.

Apart from Berzin's dazzling career as a spymaster – his agents included Richard Sorge, who later provided detailed advance warning of Hitler's Operation Barbarossa (only to have Stalin ignore it) – his role in founding the training schools would have struck a chord with Putin because his father had served as a partisan at the outset of the war. The schools had proved Berzin's undoing. He was accused falsely of creating 'bandit groups' for 'anti-Soviet terrorist activity' and in 1938 he was shot.

Putin apparently accepted that the execution of his hero was one of Stalin's occasional 'mistakes'.

The new orthodoxy under Brezhnev was that Stalin had made some errors, but the system itself had been good. Within the security services, that was an article of faith. In 1977, a committee, headed by Andropov's deputy, General Viktor Chebrikov, published an internal history of the KGB and its predecessor organisations, stamped 'Top Secret' and printed in individually numbered copies, which was issued as a teaching manual for use in regional directorates and KGB training institutes.[30] In this newly sanitised version, the actions of the security services from the foundation of the Cheka in 1918 until the early 1930s were irreproachable. Stalin's struggle against the rich peasants, the kulaks, was justified, because 'they came out against the Party's general line . . . and launched armed actions and terrorist attacks'. There was no mention of the fact that some ten million men, women and children had been deliberately starved to death. The show trials of Stalin's rivals were justified because they had been aimed at 'powerful counter-revolutionary organisations'. The fact that the evidence had been obtained through torture and that the grovelling confessions of the accused had been false was not mentioned either.

Chebrikov acknowledged that, for a brief period, 'there were certain complications, caused by subjective factors', notably from 1933 to 1941, when Stalin's 'mistaken formulation that class struggle was growing ever sharper caused much harm'. But this was only a temporary phenomenon, Chebrikov wrote, and in any case, there had been an imperative need for 'the final liquidation of capitalist elements in our country'. The main responsibility for these 'negative phenomena', he continued, belonged to 'the criminals at the head of the NKVD . . . political adventurists like Yagoda, Yezhov and others'.

That Stalin himself had appointed these 'adventurists' to head the

NKVD in the 1930s, just as he had later appointed the unnamed 'others' – Lavrenty Beria, Yezhov's successor, who was shot after the dictator's death in 1953, and his deputy, Viktor Abakumov, executed a year later – was also passed over in silence.

After the Second World War, Chebrikov admitted, there had again been 'violations of socialist legality' – apparently a veiled reference to the Leningrad Affair and the Doctors' Plot, neither of which he mentioned explicitly – but 'on the whole . . . these insufficiencies did not have a decisive influence on the overall positive results'. In other words, apart from a few regrettable lapses, the KGB and its predecessors had always acted honourably, continuing the Cheka's 'glorious traditions'.

The omissions and euphemisms were breathtaking. But that is what Putin was taught, and in the 1970s and '80s, that was evidently what he believed.

While Putin was working for the Fifth Department, his domestic circumstances changed. In 1977, his parents were at last able to move from the *kommunalka* in Baskov Lane to a two-room apartment in a newly built block of flats at Avtovo, in the southern suburbs, not far from the city's oil port. It did not provide much more living space than they had before, but, for the first time in his life, at the age of 25, Putin finally had a room of his own.[31]

He had acquired a steady girlfriend, Lyudmila Khmarina, a medical student, whose brother, Viktor, had been his close friend at the Law Faculty. They got on well and his parents strongly approved.[32] That year he became a senior lieutenant, a formality since promotion to that rank was automatic after two years' service, but nonetheless a sign that his career was progressing satisfactorily.[33] He had become a member of the Bureau of the KGB's Komsomol Committee, responsible for sports and personnel issues, and was described in an internal report as 'an observant, disciplined and conscientious colleague, who has earned the appreciation of the leadership of the Directorate for having organised his work effectively in his assigned sector . . . and enjoys well-deserved authority among his colleagues'. The language was boilerplate – 'he permanently raises his ideological-political level . . . actively participates in Party studies . . . is morally stable' and so on – and the document was drawn up so carelessly that the date when he joined the Komsomol was given incorrectly.[34] But it was what Putin needed in order to become a Party member, which he did that winter, thereby fulfilling another essential requirement to continue his service career.

If all this suggested that he was finally settling down, it did not prevent him continuing to do 'stupid stuff'. One evening, he met Sergei Roldugin, who had, as he put it, 'jumped over the fence and gone AWOL' from the barracks where he was doing his military service, and the two of them drove around Leningrad in Putin's Zaporozhets, backfiring furiously through a broken silencer, singing at the tops of their voices until the early hours of the morning.[35] On another occasion, again with Roldugin, when they were waiting at a bus stop, a group of youngsters came up and one of them asked for a cigarette. Putin refused, the situation degenerated, and the next thing Roldugin saw was 'someone's socks flashed before my eyes and the kid flew off somewhere.'[36] Old habits evidently died hard.

But his misdeeds, such as they were, evidently caused him no problems at work, for a year later he was sent to Moscow for further training.

Putin has offered contradictory explanations of how and when this occurred, none of them entirely truthful, in what appears to have been a further attempt to dissimulate the three years he spent with the Fifth Department.[37] In reality, he left Leningrad in the second half of 1978 for a course at the KGB's Dzerzhinsky Higher School pending a final decision on his next assignment.[38]

Luck was on his side. The same year that Putin had joined the KGB, Andropov had issued a decree, calling for the strengthening of foreign intelligence work within the Soviet Union.[39] By the late 1970s, a campaign was under way to recruit additional First Line officers in the regional directorates to staff the new departments being created or expanded. Putin would be one of the beneficiaries.

Whether he spent a full year at the Dzerzhinsky School, as he claimed, is doubtful. What were termed 'improvement courses' for serving officers normally lasted five months. But the syllabus was much broader, and more relevant to foreign intelligence, than anything he had learnt at the 401 School in Leningrad.

He was taught that, in dealing with foreigners, an intelligence officer should disguise his actions and identity by creating a 'legend' about himself – a studied mixture of fact and fiction which was close enough to reality to be credible while evading inconvenient truths.[40] It was a technique which Putin would use often in later life, although he did not always follow his instructors' advice that outright falsehoods should be employed only if they could not easily be disproved.

Above all, the lecturers stressed the overriding importance of recruiting agents. A KGB training manual explained:

> The tasks of departments carrying out political intelligence from the territory of the USSR are no different from those of KGB residencies abroad. The basic means of accomplishing them, as is the case in all foreign intelligence, is through agents. For this reason, the recruitment of agents among foreigners and Soviet citizens, the acquisition of reliable links and 'trusted persons' [the Russian equivalent of the 'honourable correspondents' used by western intelligence services], in order for these departments to create and consolidate their own agent networks . . . is the most important operational task of all ranks carrying out political intelligence work.[41]

At the Dzerzhinsky School, Putin was encouraged to take a broader view of intelligence work than he had in Leningrad. In the Fifth Department, his job had been to expose 'anti-Soviet elements' among the population. Now he was trained to seek information about Soviet émigré organisations and the activities of Western intelligence services. His main task would be to make contact with foreigners arriving in the Soviet Union who might be open to recruitment or ideological manipulation.

All foreigners were potential targets, but the trainees were urged to concentrate on those most likely to yield information of value. In Leningrad, these were consular officials and foreign students, airline representatives, visiting businessmen, cultural figures and scientists on exchange programmes, and the occasional journalist on an assignment from Moscow.[42] All such individuals, he was told, could have 'important secret information', and many could 'exert definite influence on the domestic and foreign policies of their governments'. Scientists were particularly important, because in their home countries, they might be asked to act as advisers to policy-making bodies. Journalists were also of special interest, as they could be manipulated to spread disinformation. Students from developing countries were targeted if they were thought likely to occupy important posts after graduating, especially if they were related to high government officials. Tourists were generally left alone – at that time, almost all non-official visitors to the Soviet Union were on package tours – unless they came privately to meet relatives, when family ties could be used as leverage to persuade them to 'cooperate' with the security services.

Since the KGB worked on the principle that Western intelligence services were a mirror image of themselves, it followed that their adversaries would 'do prophylactic work among their own citizens before they come to the Soviet Union . . . and, on their return, many of them will undergo questioning . . . to find out if they have been approached by Soviet intelligence.' A crude approach to a foreigner could allow the other side to manufacture a scandal, damaging Soviet relations with the country concerned. Contacts had to be painstakingly prepared. Counter-intelligence and the First Department were expected to work closely together. 'Counter-intelligence studies the behaviour and interests of the foreigner, the places he visits most, how he spends his days' in order to give the First Department the maximum of information to plan the initial pitch, which could be made by an intelligence officer using a cover story to hide his identity, or, more often by a Soviet citizen who had been recruited as an agent – a student, or journalist, or academic who could find a natural opening to strike up a conversation and lead it in the desired direction.

However it was done, the rule was that the foreigner had to be made to start the relationship so that he would feel that he was the one in control. The agent would then build on the initial contact to put the target at ease and establish a sense of trust – a lesson which Putin evidently took to heart, for he told one of his friends that he was now 'an expert in human relations'.[43] Only then would the case officer decide how to move forward: by persuasion or coercion, or playing on ideological affinity, or by the lure of material gain. It required the patience of a fisherman, for it might take as long as a year before the target could be reeled in.[44]

There were also lectures on sabotage by foreign special services and classes and practical work about secret inks, ciphers, disguises and 'mousetrap premises' to ensnare enemy agents, as well as such tried and tested methods as the use of 'swallows', attractive young women or men, to compromise a target.

Putin returned to Leningrad in the first half of 1979 and joined the
First Department in the autumn.[45] He would spend most of the next
five years there. The department was small, with only a few dozen
officers.[46] It was the job he had always wanted, or, to be more accurate,
it was a step in that direction. Working in the First Department of
a provincial directorate was not the same thing as working in the
First Chief Directorate itself.[47] FCD officers who had blotted their
copybooks were sent to the provinces as a demotion.[48] The First
Department answered not to Moscow but to the head of the Leningrad Directorate. The FCD's role vis-à-vis the provincial First
Departments was limited to approving their annual plans and coordinating their work with other directorates. FCD veterans liked to insist
that those, like Putin, who had worked in provincial directorates but
had never been employed by the Chief Directorate itself, had no right
to call themselves foreign intelligence operatives.[49]

Oleg Kalugin, who had headed the Counter-Intelligence Division of
the FCD and was sent as a punishment to be deputy head of the Leningrad Directorate, was scathing about the First Department's
achievements there, or rather, the lack of them.[50] 'I was shocked by . . .
the absence of real work and of any prospects for doing anything,' he
wrote.

> The level, in my opinion, was very low . . . It was a joke . . . They even
> worked on people that the Second Department, the counter-intelligence
> people, weren't remotely interested in. You must take into account that
> the peripheral organs have very limited possibilities for working with
> foreigners . . . So they dump on the so-called 'peripheral intelligence
> [departments]' the stuff that's of no interest to anyone or has abso-
> lutely no prospect of development or is already completely spent.[51]

Kalugin was prejudiced and his judgement should be read accordingly.
Nonetheless, there is no record of the Leningrad Directorate having
recruited any foreign agent in the early 1980s or having unmasked any
Western spy.

For Putin, however, the move to the First Department marked
another turning point.

He gave up judo entirely.[52] He broke off his engagement to Lyudmila Khmarina. By his own account, they had already applied for the

marriage licence and had bought the ring and the wedding dress. '[It] was one of the most difficult decisions of my life . . . I felt like a real creep. But I decided that it was better to suffer then than to have both of us suffer later.' Years later, asked why he had backed out, he was evasive, claiming that there had been 'some intrigue or other'. After deciding to call off the wedding, he said, he had told her 'the truth, [or] as much of it as I considered necessary'.[53]

The explanation rings hollow. Some of his friends suspected that he had come to feel that they were not really in love.[54] But they had known each other for years, and Putin was not the kind of man to have proposed marriage without having weighed up minutely the pros and cons. Moreover, in that case, why speak of an intrigue? Putin never mentioned the episode again and he remained close to Lyudmila's brother, Viktor.[55] One possible, and plausible, explanation is that, having finally attained his goal of working for the First Department, he learnt that there was something in her family background – perhaps a Jewish antecedent or a relative living abroad – which might prevent the KGB from giving him the overseas posting on which he had set his heart.[56] That would explain why he felt it was 'better to suffer then than . . . later', and why he spoke of telling her 'as much of [the truth] as I considered necessary'.

As the new year, 1980, began, Putin was unattached. He would not remain so for long. In March, his cellist friend, Sergei Roldugin, asked him if he could get four tickets for a performance by Arkady Raikin, Russia's equivalent of Charlie Chaplin, whose skits and impersonations gently skewered the idiocies of Soviet bureaucracy and the rudeness, inefficiency and shortages which made everyday life in Russia such a cross to bear.[57] Raikin's performances, at the Estrada Theatre, just off Nevsky Prospekt, were always sold out, but for someone of Putin's KGB rank –he had been promoted that year to captain – that posed no difficulty.

The outing was intended to impress Roldugin's new girlfriend, who brought with her another girl, a 22-year-old Aeroflot flight attendant from Kaliningrad named Lyudmila Shkrebneva.

Lyudmila's first impression of Volodya Putin was discouraging. 'He was poorly dressed,' she recalled. 'He looked very unprepossessing. I wouldn't have paid any attention to him on the street.'[58] However, the evening passed pleasantly, and the girls asked him if he could get them tickets for two more shows, which he did. By the time Lyudmila left, he had given her his telephone number, and from then on, whenever she flew to Leningrad they would meet.

The relationship did not go smoothly. Putin's parents could not understand why he had ditched his previous fiancée and were distinctly unwelcoming. The first time Lyudmila met them, she heard his mother say disapprovingly, 'But he has his Lyudmila already!'

Volodya's character did not help. 'There was a strange pattern,' Lyudmila remembered. 'For two months, everything would be fine, and then we would have a row. Afterwards everything would be fine, and then it would all start again.'

Like most of his male friends, the young Vladimir Putin had a very traditional view of the role that women should play. Lyudmila was an independent, modern young woman, for whom, as she put it, 'justice should prevail in a relationship'. Matters came to a head the following spring, when they went to a party together. Lyudmila enjoyed herself, dancing the evening away. Putin was furious. It may not have helped that he was not a great dancer himself. 'Apparently I was too uninhibited,' she said later. 'It was made quite clear to me that any further relationship was impossible.' She flew back to Kaliningrad, thinking it was all over. Two weeks later, he slipped a note under her door. He had found an excuse to come to Kaliningrad to see her and they made up.

There was no *coup de foudre*, she said later, but gradually she fell in love. Volodya was reliable, she decided, and she would be able to count on him if ever they made a life together. That summer, she left her job with Aeroflot and moved to Leningrad to be near him, taking a room in a communal apartment. To pay the rent, she found a job as a computer operator and took a preparatory course for Leningrad University, where she enrolled a year later in the philology department to study French and Spanish.

It was a not untypical story of a headstrong, self-centred young man, and an attractive girl who had decided that, come what may and 'with all faults', this was the husband she wanted.

The faults were there in abundance. Early on in the relationship, when Lyudmila paid a brief visit to Leningrad, Volodya spent the entire day repairing his Zaporozhets, because he was determined to drive her around the city. 'I just wanted to be with him, I couldn't have cared less about his car,' she recalled. 'But to him it mattered . . . so I spent the whole time at the hotel. It was infuriating.' Later, he insisted that they spend every weekend skiing. 'He did not ask my opinion. He just took it for granted that we would do so.' All their money went on the ski slopes, which Volodya loved, Lyudmila not so much. In 1981, when they and another couple went on holiday together at Sudak, on the Crimean coast – the men staying in one room, the two girls chastely in another – Lyudmila was left all afternoon being burnt to a frazzle on the beach, while Volodya tried, not very successfully, to hunt small fish with a spear-gun in the sea. 'There was always something I had to fight against,' she said, 'skis, mountains, sea.'

Worst of all was the fact that, whenever they went out on a date, he was late. She remembered waiting for him at a metro station. '15 minutes, you can accept. Even half an hour. But when it's been an hour and he's not there, you are just crying from the hurt. After an hour and a half, you feel nothing any more. All your emotions are spent . . . This happened all the time.' What made it still more galling was that he was punctual in everything related to his work.

It was not just a matter of being self-centred. Something more was at work. Towards Lyudmila, Putin was profoundly inconsiderate. It reached a point where she wondered whether he was doing it deliberately to see how much she would put up with.[59] Yet she stayed with him, always hoping that one day she would persuade him to mend his ways. Only much later did she realise that that was never going to happen.

In another important respect, their relationship was even more fraught.

Putin was exceedingly mistrustful. During their first year together, Lyudmila remembered, 'I had the feeling that he was watching me all the time, to see what decision I would make, whether it was correct or not, would I pass this or that test.'

For 18 months, he did not tell her that he was with the KGB, letting her believe that he was working for the Criminal Investigation Department of the police, which was his official cover. After all, he explained later, 'who knew how our relationship was going to turn out?'[60] When she found out that he had been deceiving her, she was mortified. 'If he had told me after six months, it would have seemed normal . . . But after a year and a half . . . It was a sign that I was still not trusted.' A

little earlier, there had been another incident, which in retrospect was
even more telling. There was no telephone in the communal apartment where she lived, so one evening she had gone out to call him
from a phone box. As she walked home afterwards, a young man came
running up and tried to start a conversation, asking for her phone
number. When she said that she had no telephone and in any case had
no intention of talking to him, he asked her to write down his own
number, 'in case you change your mind'. She refused and was finally
able to get rid of him. At the time, she assumed he was just another
young man, trying his luck. But after she learnt that Putin worked for
the KGB, she wondered whether it had been a test. When she questioned him, he would neither deny nor confirm it. 'I asked him many
times,' she said, 'and he always shied away from answering. So I still do
not know what it was: a test, or just an attempt by some young man to
meet me.'

Putin's refusal to give a clear answer was more revealing than the
incident itself. He could easily have reassured her that it was untrue, or
even, had he wished, acknowledged that he had indeed been testing
her. Yet he did neither. He deliberately left her in doubt. Like his persistent lateness, it was a perverse way of asserting himself as the
dominant partner in the relationship, laying down their limits as a
couple. During their courtship, there was always an undefined but
insurmountable distance between them.

It did not help that, even after he had told her that he was with the
KGB, he would not discuss his work – ostensibly because it was a rule
of the service, but no doubt also because he preferred it that way. To
Lyudmila, that was unacceptable. A couple, she believed, should share
everything. But Volodya, she was forced to recognise, had the same
'closed character' as his father and mother. She thought that was characteristic of Leningrad, where 'people show only what they consider
necessary, which is a way of emphasising that everything else is hidden.' But it was also characteristic of the *mir*, the traditional Russian
peasant community in which Putin's parents had been raised.

The most dramatic illustration of how far she and Volodya were
from a true meeting of minds came a year and a half later, in April
1983. Throughout the time they had been together, marriage had been
a taboo subject. Lyudmila had realised early on that 'Volodya could not
abide it if a girl began to press him,' so she never mentioned it. But

they both knew that at some point they would have to take a decision. Finally, as they were sitting talking one day, he suddenly put on a serious air and raised the issue that until then they had never discussed.

'I just froze inside,' she remembered. 'I realised that he had decided to break off our relationship.' Instead, he asked her to marry him and, when she agreed, immediately proposed a date for the ceremony, showing that he had prepared it all carefully beforehand.

That, after three years together, she could so completely have misread his intentions spoke volumes about Putin's personality. He did not simply play his cards close to his chest, mask his emotions, and send out ambiguous signals: he maintained an impenetrable shell, which prevented even those closest to him from divining his true intentions. One may legitimately wonder what prompted him to take the plunge. Putin himself said that his friends had urged him to get married and he realised that if he did not do so soon, he would stay a bachelor for ever, implying that it was a marriage of reason, rather than of love.[61] That may well have been the case, although perhaps for a different motive. That spring, he had learnt that he might be in line for further training which could open the way to a post abroad.[62] Married officers were preferred for foreign postings because a family was viewed as a source of stability.

As Lyudmila remarked later, whenever an important decision was to be taken, Volodya did not act spontaneously. 'Everything he did was always thought through.'[63]

They married on July 28, a Thursday, at the registry office, known as 'The Wedding Palace', on Pyotr Lavrov (now Furshtatskaya) Street, near the Tauride Gardens.[64] There were two receptions, one for family and friends, and another, the following day, for Putin's KGB colleagues. They honeymooned in Yalta, staying with another couple at a camping site in the mountains and driving down to the beach every day. Putin had sold the Zaporozhets and bought a second-hand Zhiguli,[65] a step up in the world of Soviet automobiles, but the radiator boiled, and their friends had to give them a tow until Putin was able to get it repaired. On the way back, they stopped off in Moscow, where he had to attend an interview. Characteristically, he did not tell Lyudmila what it was about.

Back in Leningrad, they moved in with Putin's parents in their two-room apartment at Avtovo. It was cramped and badly designed, with small windows so high up that it was impossible to see out. Their room was minuscule, barely big enough for a narrow bed, a divan, a table and two chairs.[66] But at least by then his parents had grudgingly accepted her. She was the girl their son had chosen, and for them he could do no wrong. He was, as Lyudmila put it, 'their sun, moon and stars'.[67]

She remembered their first year together as one of 'total harmony. There was a constant feeling of joy, as though we were on holiday.' He hurried home from work to be with her. It was as though the fact of being married and finally making a commitment to each other had erased his earlier doubts. The difficulties of their courtship seemed behind them. He was 'loving and romantic'.[68]

It was too good to last.

Volodya's old, bad habits gradually reappeared. He started coming home later on the pretext of extra work. 'I perfectly understood,' she said, 'that it was not [his superiors] who kept him working late. It was himself.' The worst of it was that he never called home to warn her that he was delayed. 'When he had promised to come back at 9 p.m., he came at midnight, and for the whole three hours I just waited.' Putin would no doubt have argued that, given the nature of his work, he could not be tied to his wife's apron strings. But it became oppressive. Being married to a KGB officer meant that she could not talk to her friends openly about the problems she faced. 'There was an implicit prohibition which depressed me,' she said. Over time, it left its mark. 'In a certain way, it crushed me.'[69]

The interview which Putin had attended on the way back from Yalta had been with the personnel department of the First Chief Director- ate. It had been arranged by his boss in Leningrad, General Feliks Karasev, a legendary figure in the service who had spent much of his career in Helsinki, first as a senior KGB officer, then as resident and finally, as Ambassador, becoming in the process a privileged interlocu- tor of successive Finnish presidents. Karasev acted as a mentor to both Putin and another young officer, Sergei Ivanov. Putin, he thought, was more a man of action, Ivanov more analytical. In 1981, he had sent Ivanov for further training at the FCD's Red Banner Institute in Mos- cow.[70] Two years later, he recommended Putin. At the time of the interview, Putin was already 30, the age limit for admission to the Insti- tute, and recently promoted to the rank of major. For an officer of his seniority to be given a place was unusual.[71] But luck was once again on his side and in March 1984, the Institute's selection board accepted him for a one-year course.[72]

It was the chance that he had been waiting for. He could now realistically hope for an assignment abroad. There was even a possibility that he might be transferred from the First Department to the FCD itself, becoming a ranking foreign intelligence operative, rather than just an officer in one of the 'peripheral services'.

The Institute's main campus, for recruits direct from university, was hidden in a birch forest about 12 miles north-east of Moscow, near the village of Nagorny. The woods nearby were reputed to contain mass graves, dating from the 1930s, where victims of the Great Purge had been buried. Officers who had already served in the KGB took a one-year course at a subsidiary site, also surrounded by forest, at Yurlovo, to the west of Moscow. It had no name and was identified only by a number. As far as the outside world was concerned, it was a research institute attached to the Ministry of Defence.[73]

Putin and the other trainees arrived at the beginning of July. On their first day, each was given an alias, starting with the first letter of his real name, which he would use throughout the year. Putin became Platov. They were allowed to keep their first names, but were told to say nothing which might indicate their real identities. If one of their number later defected, he would know little about his colleagues. Lest that seem far-fetched, Vladimir Piguzov, the Secretary of the Red Banner Institute's Party Committee while Putin was there, was shot as a spy in 1986. He had been recruited by the CIA in Indonesia in the 1970s and was betrayed by the American mole, Aldrich Ames.[74]

There were 60 students at Yurlovo, divided into sections of 20 men each in accordance with their language speciality.[75] Putin was appointed head of the German section. The Institute was no longer as elitist as it had been in the 1950s, when the students were served their meals by waitresses wearing starched white aprons and *kokoshniki*, the traditional Russian maids' caps, a relic of tsarist times.[76] But the accommodation was comfortable, with Finnish sofa-beds, individual work spaces, a wardrobe and washbasin, and there was a smoking room with a television where they could play chess. Putin shared a room with the secretary of the facility's Party bureau. It was more like a university hostel than a barracks, with a swimming pool and cinema.

Among themselves the trainees called it Yurmala, a pun on the name of a Soviet resort on the Latvian coast. But it was surrounded by a perimeter fence and barbed wire, and if an unwary villager searching for mushrooms came too close, he was quickly intercepted by an armed patrol with guard dogs.

The whole of the month of August they spent at a paratroop base near Odessa, where they were tested for willpower and physical endurance. There were drills on the parade ground, practice on a shooting range and a 30-mile forced march at night with full equipment. They were made to stand on a track and fall on their faces while a tank rolled over them, and to carry out parachute jumps, first from a 100-foot tower and then, at 3,000 feet, from an ageing, single-engined Antonov biplane.

On their return to Yurlovo, each section was divided into groups of five for language study, which occupied eight hours a week. For Putin's section, there were lectures and seminars on East and West Germany, Austria and Switzerland – social structure, political parties, local government and diplomacy, as well as etiquette and behaviour. The rest of the time was devoted to tradecraft.

Emphasis was placed on applied psychology. The books in the library included a Russian translation of Dale Carnegie's *How to Make Friends and Influence People* and, even more than at the Dzerzhinsky School four years earlier, the instructors stressed the importance of 'building interpersonal relationships', without which, they insisted, no intelligence work was possible.[77]

Another course focused on analysis: how to anticipate trends, how to prioritise information and how to write reports. There was an iron-clad rule: 'One cable, one topic.' If a message was intercepted and deciphered, only one topic would be compromised.[78]

They were taught how to recognise 'dangles', Western intelligence officers who turned up at Soviet embassies, posing as 'walk-ins' with important information to share. They learnt the different roles of 'neutral contacts' (people of no intelligence value whom an officer befriended in order to confuse an adverse counter-intelligence service); 'information contacts' (official sources whom he might meet in the course of his work, but with whom he had no intelligence relationship); 'trusted contacts' (persons whom the officer met publicly but with whom, secretly, he also had an intelligence relationship); and 'agents' (who spied on his behalf).[79] They practised 'brush contacts' (receiving a document from a source in a crowd without being seen), and the use of dead-letter drops, as well as of technical devices – tape recorders, concealed microphones and miniature cameras.

Being the section leader did not stop Putin bending the rules.[80] He usually skipped the compulsory morning run, preferring to swim laps of the pool instead. The old rebelliousness had not entirely disappeared. 'He did not kow-tow,' his boss in the First Department, Yuri Leshchev, said.[81] In the winter, he joined the others when they sneaked out on skis, beyond the perimeter fence, to buy wine at a village shop which they drank in a clearing on the way back because, within the institute grounds, alcohol was forbidden.

The instructors closed their eyes to such minor breaches if they did not actually encourage them, to see how the trainees behaved. All of them were under constant surveillance. Their conversations were monitored. Psychologists assessed their behaviour.[82] The director at Yurlovo, Colonel Aleksandr Kulkov, remembered Putin as being 'collected, very orderly and conscientious' – sometimes excessively so. He always wore a tie to lectures and during the final examinations, in the middle of an unusually hot summer, he appeared in a three-piece suit, which caused Kulkov to remark that even a German official would not have been as punctilious.[83] In cold weather he liked to wear a long overcoat with a wide-brimmed fedora hat, and carried a furled umbrella, which was regarded as somewhat eccentric. It was a way to affirm his difference within the limits of what the institute could accept.

During the summer, Lyudmila became pregnant with their first child.[84] She was about to start her fourth year of Spanish at the university and, at Putin's suggestion, was also taking a typing course. Having discovered the constraints of being married to a KGB officer, she had begun to figure out how to deal with him. 'Yes, Sir! I saluted for typing courses,' she told an interviewer, adding, tongue firmly in cheek: 'I always obeyed the wishes of Vladimir Vladimirovich.' That might be true up to a point, but she had no intention of giving up her independence. Putin's friend, Sergei Roldugin, had noticed early on that Lyudmila had a temper and was 'not afraid of speaking her mind'.[85]

She visited Volodya in Moscow from time to time at weekends and he was able occasionally to come to Leningrad. She had moved out of the parental home and rented a studio in the northern suburbs. Her relations with Putin's mother, Maria Ivanovna, were still difficult and she preferred to cope with the pregnancy on her own.[86] When the time came, she got a taxi to the hospital and gave birth four hours later. Putin was given leave of absence and flew to Leningrad the following day. But in the 1980s, as in the 1950s, fathers were not allowed inside Soviet maternity clinics, so he did not see his daughter until Lyudmila was allowed out, two or three days later. In the meantime he had chosen a name, Maria, after his mother. It was the last name Lyudmila would have wanted but she knew that it was pointless to argue. Her husband was Russian and believed that such things should be decided by the man of the family. The most he would accept was the diminutive, Masha.

Marriage had not changed Putin's view of a woman's role in the home. He thought like Roldugin, who admired the way that Lyudmila 'could stay up all night having a good time and still clean up the apartment and cook next morning'.[87] Even as a schoolboy at summer camp, Volodya had hated washing dishes and cleaning, and usually persuaded the girls to do it for him.[88] Since then, nothing had changed. 'Vladimir Vladimirovich had a principle,' Lyudmila remembered. 'The woman of the house should do everything by herself. So he never took any part in household chores.'[89] He stayed on three more days after she came home with the new baby, but she was not altogether sorry when it was time for him to go. 'Since he would have nothing to do with diapers or cooking . . . when he left, I no longer had to take care of the two of them, I just had Masha to look after.'[90]

In June, as the year's training course drew to a close, the instructors at Yurlovo wrote evaluations of the trainees in their charge. It was a moment everyone dreaded. Each student's appraisal had to be summarised on four sheets of foolscap – psychological portrait, strengths, weaknesses, skills and shortcomings – culminating in a recommendation about the trainee's future career.[91] Some were ruled unsuitable for intelligence work altogether; others were rated 'satisfactory', which meant they would be sent to second-ranking posts; those with a positive evaluation could expect to be promoted.[92]

Putin's report was mixed. Colonel Mikhail Frolov, who was responsible for his section, wrote that he had a number of negative characteristics. He was 'somewhat withdrawn and uncommunicative' and had 'a certain academic tendency'.[93] Another of his instructors, Colonel Prelin, found him pedantic.[94] Still worse, during a visit to Leningrad to see Lyudmila, he had got into a fight in the metro which had left him with a broken arm. Roldugin remembered him saying: 'They are not going to understand this in Moscow. I'm afraid there are going to be consequences.' He was right. His final report noted that he had 'a lowered sense of danger'.[95]

It was not a disastrous evaluation but nor was it the result he had hoped for.

Normally, by July, personnel officers from the different FCD departments would approach the trainees individually to sound them out on future postings, subject to formal approval by the Institute's graduation commission. It was a time for horse-trading, when departments competed to get the most promising graduates. But no one approached Putin. In the jargon of the trainees, he was an 'orphan', to whom nobody would offer a home.[96]

There are conflicting versions of what happened next.

Putin himself claimed that he could have gone to West Germany, but that any graduate wishing to do so had to spend a year or two working in Moscow at the FCD's Fourth Department, responsible for German-speaking states. He had decided, he said, that he would rather not wait but go straightaway to East Germany.[97]

That was transparently false.

First, the choice was not his to make. Graduates of the Red Banner Institute had no say over where they would work, they were ordered where to go. Second, there was no requirement to work at the Fourth Department before being posted to West Germany: others went there from the Institute directly. Third, it is highly unlikely that Putin was ever offered the possibility of transferring to the Fourth or any other department in the FCD. Had that happened, he would certainly have accepted, for he would then have become a fully fledged foreign intelligence officer, not just a First Department operative in the provinces.

The story was an invention, intended to divert attention from the fact that he had not been offered the post he had been hoping for in a prestigious Western capital like Bonn or Vienna. Instead he was sent back to the Leningrad Directorate to await secondment to East Germany when a position became free.[98] That was what usually happened to those who had not been chosen for assignments in the West. About a third of the 60 men who graduated from Yurlovo each year were posted to Warsaw Pact countries.[99]

The initial plan was for Putin to go to Karlshorst, the KGB

representation in East Berlin.[100] Colonel Kulkov had been promoted to head of the local arm of Directorate S in East Germany, dealing with 'illegals' – sleeper agents under deep cover using assumed identities and nationalities to acquire intelligence in the West. Kulkov planned to bring with him several of the young officers he had been training. Putin, he had hoped, would be one of them. Berlin was still a potential flashpoint in East–West relations and Karlshorst was the biggest KGB office outside the Soviet Union, with several hundred officers and support staff.[101] But the FCD's Personnel Department blocked the move, because it would have required transferring Putin to the central FCD establishment in Moscow, which would then have been responsible for his career after he returned. If he were seconded from Leningrad, he would return there from East Germany and Moscow would not need to become involved.[102]

Fortunately for Putin, he had a fallback position.

A fellow trainee at Yurlovo had told him that there would soon be a vacancy in Dresden, where another officer from Leningrad, Boris Mylnikov, whom Putin had known when they both worked at the Big House, was about to end his tour.[103] Mylnikov worked for Directorate S, which meant that Kulkov would have a say in who replaced him. In a country where the use of informal relationships to circumvent bureaucratic obstruction had been developed to a fine art, the situation was tailor-made for an arrangement. Mylnikov prepared the ground and when Putin arrived in Berlin at the end of August, along with a dozen other young seconded officers, the head of the Dresden office, a KGB veteran named Lazar Matveyev, was predisposed to give him a favourable hearing. After a meeting in Berlin at the beginning of September, Matveyev accepted Putin as Mylnikov's successor. A few days later, he arrived in Dresden to begin his new career.

It had taken Putin ten years in the service, almost to the day, to gain the position that he had dreamt of as a teenager, when his imagination had been caught by series like *The Shield and the Sword* and *Seventeen Moments of Spring*. It was not quite what he had hoped for all those years ago. Working in a provincial directorate had cured him of the romantic notions with which he had started out. From an intelligence-gathering standpoint, East Germany was a province, not much different from Leningrad.[104] He was not a high flier and he knew it.

On the other hand, given his modest background, the absence of influential connections and the fact that he had neither a brilliant academic record nor early fluency in foreign languages, he could tell himself that he had done quite well. The First Chief Directorate had 3,000 officers and the First Departments in the provinces only a few thousand more, out of a total KGB strength of more than half a million.[105] To be seconded to the FCD was not the same as being permanently assigned to it. But millions of Soviet citizens would have snatched at such a chance. Even secondment was an opportunity given to very few and still fewer could ever hope to have a post abroad.

By the time he left for Dresden, Putin's training as a KGB officer was complete. In the words of one of his instructors at Yurlovo, 'Putin had the manners and behaviour of a special services officer.'[106] The label would stick. Senator John McCain famously remarked: 'I looked in Putin's eyes and I saw three letters: a K, a G and a B.'[107] In 2013, Fiona Hill, a well-respected academic at Georgetown, who later became President Trump's Russia specialist in the National Security Council, co-authored a book entitled, *Mr. Putin: Operative in the Kremlin*, which sought to explain Putin's actions through the matrix of his experiences in the KGB.[108] Western newspaper articles invariably mention his KGB past, as though that in itself is enough to explain why he acts as he does.

But did the KGB form Putin? Or was he already, before he joined, in all important respects the person he would later become?

Putin himself is on record as saying that much of what he was taught in the KGB, he already knew long before.

> If something happens, you should proceed from the fact that there is no retreat [he said]. It is necessary to carry it through to the end. That's a well-known rule that was taught by the KGB, but I learnt it much earlier, scrapping with other kids. There was another rule the KGB taught. Don't reach for a weapon unless you are prepared to use it . . . It was the same on the street. [There] relations were clarified with fists. You didn't get involved unless you were prepared to see it through.[109]

From judo he had learnt how to use others' strengths against them and to exploit their vulnerabilities. At the Dzerzhinsky School he was taught that 'all else being equal, the side which goes onto the attack will achieve the best results', a principle the KGB called *nastupatelnost*, 'offensive posture'.[110] That, too, was familiar, both from judo and from his childhood fights.

Putin's character fitted the kind of work the KGB did. He liked to stay in the background and observe others, rather than to be the centre of attention himself. He was disciplined and pragmatic and able to concentrate his energies on the priority of the moment. He had been brought up not to show his emotions, which was another quality the KGB valued.

This is not to say that Putin gained nothing from his years with the KGB. But by the time he graduated from the Law Faculty, he was almost 23 years old and his personality was already formed. At the Dzerzhinsky School and the Red Banner Institute, he learnt new skills and techniques – how to manipulate an asset, how to analyse and evaluate information, how to distinguish the principal aspect of a problem from what was secondary.[111] He was taught how to appraise contacts. Were they likely to be useful? If not, why waste time on them?[112] Above all, he learnt never to take things at face value, to mistrust others' motives and intentions. Intelligence work is plagued by paranoia. Is a source what he or she claims to be, or are they working for another service, deliberately laying a false trail? But here, too, there was already a firm foundation on which his instructors could build. Even as a child, Volodya Putin had concealed his hand; as a young man, he did not vouchsafe information unless there was good reason.

Putin's time with the special services influenced his thinking and equipped him with new tools with which to view the world. But it did so by accretion. Putin was already Putin before he joined the KGB.

4

Quiet Days in Saxony

To say that Putin hibernated in Dresden would be an exaggeration, but not by very much.[1] He stopped taking part in sports, apart from an occasional game of soccer; he became a regular beer drinker, preferably the brew which the East Germans made for export in the nearby town of Radeberg (he tried to avoid the local beer after a colleague found a dead mouse in a bottle); he put on 25 pounds and had to buy suits three sizes bigger. His work was routine and not particularly demanding.[2] He took Masha to the crèche each morning and came home every day for lunch. It was, as Lyudmila said, a measured way of life, a time to lean back and take stock.

The KGB liaison office in Dresden was housed in a pleasant, three-storey villa, surrounded by a well-kept garden behind an eight-foot high wall, with a guard post at the entrance, at No. 4, Angelikastrasse, a quiet, tree-lined street, named for an eighteenth-century painter. It was one of a row of elegant turn-of-the-century homes, most of them divided into apartments for the city's Communist Party elite, fronted by flowerbeds which in spring and summer made a gentle haze of colour. One especially imposing villa, with two enormous old acacia trees and deer roaming in the grounds, where the local Soviet military commander lived, had formerly belonged to Field Marshal Paulus, whose forces had surrendered at Stalingrad.

The District Headquarters of the Stasi, the KGB's East German sister organisation, was a hundred yards away, a complex of administrative buildings spread over 15 acres along the bank of the River Elbe. Seven or eight minutes' walk in the other direction, Putin and four of his KGB colleagues had apartments in a huge apartment block, completed only two years earlier, whose square, concrete façade, imitating Le Corbusier, with twelve identical staircases at intervals along its length, stretched for more than a quarter of a mile. The KGB officers had three-roomed apartments on the right-hand side of the first staircase, Stasi officers had four-roomed apartments on the left. Putin inherited Mylnikov's apartment, on the sixth and top floor. Another group of officers from the GRU, Soviet military intelligence, lived nearby.[3]

Beyond lay the Dresden Heath, a vast expanse of park and woodland, seven times the size of Central Park in New York, which had once been a royal hunting estate and now contained the barracks of a Soviet Tank Regiment. It was the most exclusive and the most attractive district in Dresden and certainly the best protected.[4]

In the villa at Angelikastrasse, Putin shared a garret under the eaves with Vladimir Agartanov, an original spirit with a Ph.D. in nuclear physics, five years older than himself, to whom he took an immediate liking.[5] Agartanov had been destined to go to the KGB residency in Vienna, where his scientific background made him an obvious choice to keep tabs on the IAEA, the International Atomic Energy Agency. But during his training at the Red Banner Institute, he had seriously blotted his copybook by speaking disdainfully of the doddering leadership in the Politburo, and, as a punishment, had been packed off to a peripheral directorate in the provinces. Like Putin, he worked for Directorate S, dealing with 'illegals'.

The other two junior officers, who had separate offices on the first floor, were also from provincial directorates. Nikolai Tokarev, who had been transferred from the KGB district office in Leipzig, and worked for Directorate T, which conducted espionage in the field of science and technology, was a year or two older than Putin, and made a show of taking him under his wing.[6] Tokarev had a reputation as a lickspittle, concerned with advancing his career and currying favour with his bosses, but it evidently did him no harm, for he stayed for only a few months after Putin's arrival before being transferred again, this time to Karlshorst. His successor, Vladimir Bragin from the KGB directorate in Krasnodar, was more laid-back, except when it came to chess. Putin was not a chess player and in the evenings, while Agartanov and Bragin hunched over the chessboard, he drank beer with the other member of the quartet, Sergei Chemezov, who was from Irkutsk, in Siberia, and worked for Directorate K, responsible for counter-intelligence. Chemezov was the same age as Putin and they became close friends.

The fifth member of the liaison office, Matveyev's deputy, Colonel

Kalinin, was a dyed-in-the-wool Stalinist, whom all the others cordially detested.[7] He and Matveyev had a secretary, Lenchen, who came from a Baltic German family, was bilingual in German and Russian, and could act as an interpreter when the occasion required. There was also a German driver, Werner, who had been seconded from the Stasi, and, on the ground floor, a small detachment of Russian border guards, whose job was to protect the mission. In the basement, at Matveyev's request, a few months before Putin arrived, the Germans had installed a sauna to which the men repaired on Friday nights to drink beer and watch Soviet television.

Lyudmila came out with Masha to join him at the end of October. She immediately felt at home. Dresden reminded her of Kaliningrad, where she had grown up and which, before the Second World War, had been the Prussian city of Königsberg. There were the same bourgeois German mansions and the same, familiar smell of coke briquettes, used in stoves, which she remembered from her childhood. There were also, as in Leningrad, reminders everywhere of the savagery of the war. The ruins of the eighteenth-century Frauenkirche, one of the outstanding protestant churches of Europe, destroyed by Allied bombing raids in 1945, towered over the city centre as a grim memorial to the tens of thousands who had died. But Lyudmila liked Dresden because, as she put it, the move 'resolved certain material and domestic problems', a discreet allusion to the fact that, for the first time in their lives, she and Volodya had a home of their own, instead of being cooped up with her parents-in-law.

Like all Soviet visitors to East Germany, she was struck by the wealth of goods available in the shops, compared to what could be bought at home. So was Putin. 'We had come from a Russia,' he wrote later, 'where there were long lines and shortages, and in East Germany there was always plenty of everything.' Even bananas, which were unobtainable in the Soviet Union, could be bought in the army commissariat, to which, as a KGB officer, he had access.

It was the small details which Lyudmila noticed: the politeness of the shop assistants, who took time to find out what each customer wanted and to wrap each purchase individually, and then asked if they would like anything else, unlike their counterparts in Leningrad, who responded only to customers' shouts and then snarled that there was none left; the fact that there were no queues, that the streets were clean, that Germans cleaned the windows of their apartments every week; and the orderly way in which German housewives hung out their washing each morning on clothes lines in the courtyard.

Towards the end of the winter, Lyudmila, now pregnant with their second child, returned to Leningrad, taking Masha with her, to defend her final-year thesis for her university degree.

Putin was left a bachelor and his eye began to wander. One evening he attended a birthday party for Fritz Beissig, the Stasi chief in Grossenhain, a town 20 miles north-west of Dresden. Beissig's 26-year-old daughter, Doris, a spirited young woman with an engaging smile, had met Putin before. She found him attractive and he evidently felt the same way. That night, she remembered, he started drinking, which he rarely did in public, until, having got up his courage to kiss her, they engaged in some heavy petting. It was a brief lapse, which did not lead very far. Today she says that chapter of her life is closed: it was a youthful infatuation.[8] But Putin had taken a serious risk. Neither the Stasi nor the KGB permitted extramarital relations. He had still not completely overcome his old problem of a 'lowered sense of danger'.

Just how dangerous it might have been became clear a few months later, when Matveyev's deputy, the Stalinist colonel, was put on a plane back to Moscow. Officially his posting was terminated because he was bone idle, but while that was certainly true, it would not have been a reason, in the KGB in the late '80s, to send him home in disgrace. Later it emerged that the colonel had had an affair with the office secretary, Lenchen, whose opulent cleavage had gained her the nickname, *der Balkon*, 'the Balcony', and she had fallen pregnant. Much more serious, had Karlshorst known, was that Lenchen had been working for several years for the BND, the West German Foreign Intelligence Service. The BND spirited her out, arranged for her to have an abortion and set her up in a new life, running a small hotel in a provincial town in West Germany under a false identity.[9]

Lyudmila returned to Dresden in June after finishing her final exams.[10] During a pre-natal check-up, the German doctors found that she was suffering from anaemia and packed her off to hospital for five days of blood transfusions. Volodya was left in charge of Masha, then 14 months old.

It was, as Lyudmila had anticipated, a disaster, but also something of a revelation. She had given him detailed instructions how to prepare the little girl's food, but invariably by the time he started getting it ready, Masha was already hungry and venting her displeasure. On the other hand, having himself been brought up in a household where affection was rarely shown, he indulged Masha's every wish. When Lyudmila returned, she found the apartment a shambles, as she had expected, but her daughter a very happy little girl.

She told herself that it must have made him realise how difficult it was to be a mother. If so, he did a good job of concealing it.

At mealtimes, she remembered, 'he was capricious . . . If he did not think a dish was done properly, he would rather not eat it at all.' When she had made a particular effort to please him, and would wait, as she said, 'with a sinking heart' to hear his reaction, he would say, 'the meat is rather dry.' If it was really good he might say grudgingly, 'not bad'. She consoled herself with the thought that he was just applying the old Russian adage: 'Praise the woman, spoil the home.'[11]

In other respects, however, Putin was supportive, even when it meant defying the conventions by which a KGB officer was expected to live. By the time their second daughter, Katerina, was born at the end of August, Lyudmila had learnt passable German and began to make friends among the Stasi wives, which the KGB did not normally encourage.[12] The two girls, when they were old enough, went to the local nursery school and were soon chattering away in German at home, scandalising a visiting officer from Karlshorst who wanted to know why they were not speaking Russian.[13]

But there were limits to what was permitted, even in fraternal East Germany. When Putin found Lyudmila a job teaching Spanish at a local German school, she was ordered not to accept it.[14] When one of her German acquaintances was judged to be undesirable, she was instructed to break off the relationship.[15] She was not accustomed to that kind of discipline and chafed at the restrictions.[16]

Like most Soviet citizens posted abroad, the family lived frugally and saved as much as they could. Putin was paid 800 Ostmarks a month, which, although worthless outside East Germany, had notion-ally the same value as Deutschmarks and covered their living expenses, plus almost 100 US dollars a month in hard currency.[17] Lyudmila did not spend money on clothes but sewed them for herself and the chil-dren, and in the summer helped the local collective farm with the peach harvest, which brought in a little extra.[18]

It was a comfortable existence. They had the use of a dacha belonging to the Stasi, by a lake near the small town of Niesky, in a forest close to the Polish border, 50 miles east of Dresden.[19] In summer, they gazed wonderingly at East Germans practising *Freikörperkultur*, 'Free body culture' or beach nudism. In winter there was mulled wine at the month-long Dresden Christmas market – a fairyland of stalls and brightly coloured decorations, unlike anything that existed at home – and they went skiing in the hills above Königstein, in an area known as the Saxon Switzerland, only 20 miles away, towards Czechoslovakia.[20]

In 1987, Putin took them to Prague, a baroque, grey city whose architecture he adored, preferring it even to Leningrad.[21] They made trips to the theatre in East Berlin and bought a television and a video-recorder, both items for which there were waiting lists at home, from the diplomats' hard currency store. Their colleagues in Karlshorst sent them cassettes of American films, among them, *Blackbeard's Ghost*, starring Peter Ustinov. On Saturday nights they watched *Ein Kessel Buntes*, 'A Kettle of Colours', a popular variety show on East German television, which featured the singer, Wolfgang Lippert, whose lilting melodies Putin learnt by heart, and 'Big Helga' Hahnemann, who told scabrous comic tales in the coarse Berlin accent known affectionately as 'Berlin snout'. The only drawback was that they could not watch West German television, which was received everywhere in East Germany except in Dresden and on the Polish border, areas referred to dismissively as the 'Valley of the Unaware'.[22]

Dresden was East Germany's third-biggest city after East Berlin and Leipzig, with a population of more than half a million. It drew visits from foreign businessmen and tourists as well as West German relatives of local residents. The KGB office there was one of the largest in a country which, as Putin's superiors in Karlshorst never ceased to emphasise, was 'on the front line between Eastern Europe and the West' and therefore of primary importance for the security of the Soviet state.[23]

Whether the Dresden office ever produced intelligence of any real value is another matter.[24] Agartanov was scathing about its work. 'It was playing at intelligence,' he wrote. 'If any American spy had penetrated the operational staff, he would have been incredibly surprised: the formidable KGB was wasting its time on trifles.' The Dresden office was 'a personnel sedimentation tank . . . a most unprestigious place', which dealt with 'matters of a secondary nature' and had 'extremely modest' successes.[25]

Agartanov was jaundiced but his gripes rang true. The KGB Collegium, which determined policy, took its cue from the Party Central Committee, which believed that any problem could be solved by drawing up detailed monthly and yearly plans and throwing enough people at them to make sure that they were carried out.[26] Whether the plans were effective hardly mattered. The result was an overstaffed, bureaucratic swamp, in which all initiative was stifled. In Dresden, Putin answered to Colonel Matveyev, who had to sign off on every report he sent to Karlshorst. In Berlin, he reported to Colonel Kulkov, who was in charge of Directorate S. His immediate superior was another colonel, Yuri Leshchev, his former boss in Leningrad, who had now been transferred to East Germany to supervise and coordinate the KGB's 14 district offices there.[27]

As though that were not enough, there was a dispiriting lack of basic equipment. Putin and Chemezov had the use of one car, a modest Zhiguli, between them.[28] In the office which Putin shared with Agartanov, there was one telephone with a party line for each of them, and a single typewriter. At a time when in Western Europe, portable computers were already widely used in business and starting to make an appearance in private homes as well, the office had no word processor or printer. There was one thermal photocopier for the entire building, which produced copies in violet ink on beige paper that faded to nothing after a few months.

Reports for Berlin were sewn by hand between hard covers with a needle and thread, pressed tight with a special clamp, and sent by courier. Hence the saying, 'the Chekist's sharpest weapon is an awl', used to make holes in the papers that had to be sewn together. That procedure was almost unchanged since the days of the Okhrana, the secret service of Tsar Nicholas II, before the Revolution. The same was true of internal security. The metal boxes where classified papers were kept, and the doors to the offices when closed at night, were marked with a cachet of wax impressed with the personal seal of the officer responsible.[29]

But the main problem for Putin and his colleagues was that there was absolutely no way they could carry out the tasks which the Party set them. Chief among these was Operation RYaN – an acronym for *Raketno Yadernoe Napadenie*, 'Nuclear Missile Attack' – whose purpose was to collect intelligence on the supposed plans of the United States to launch a nuclear first strike against Russia.

The Politburo's concern had reached a peak in November 1983, when NATO carried out an exercise codenamed Able Archer, which culminated in a simulated nuclear strike. Moscow had suspected it to be a ruse to camouflage preparations for a real attack. Soviet nuclear forces were put on alert, and for five days, while Western leaders remained in blissful ignorance of the storm the exercise had kicked up, the world came closer to a nuclear conflagration than at any time since the Cuban missile crisis, 20 years before. Subsequently tensions eased, but the underlying fears did not. RYaN continued to be a Soviet obsession well into the second half of the 1980s. For KGB residencies in America and Western Europe, it was difficult enough to find evidence of a non-existent threat, but they, at least, could report that there was no sign of government ministries working late into the night, no indications of blood banks being readied, meat being put into cold storage or evacuation bunkers prepared, or any of the other three hundred or so clues they had been instructed to watch out for.[30] In a place like Dresden, even that was impossible.

The other major Soviet preoccupation was with NATO. The Dresden office was ordered to try to penetrate the three US army bases in West Germany where American special forces were located, because Moscow believed that one of the first signs of a coming conflict would be a state of heightened readiness by Green Beret detachments. But the bases, at Bad Tölz in Bavaria, home to the US 10th Special Forces Group, and at Wildflecken and Stelle, where there were smaller units, were hundreds of miles away, and there was no obvious way of obtaining information from them. Putin and Agartanov spent months going through thousands of *Anträge*, the application forms which East Germans had to submit when they invited West German relatives to visit them, to try to find those with family members living in those areas. Very few did so, Agartanov wrote, and none offered any realistic hope of recruitment. It was a total waste of time and in the end Putin decided they should give up.[31]

That left only what Agartanov called 'secondary matters'.

Formally both he and Putin belonged to Line N, which, confusingly, was the designation of officers working for Directorate S in the field.[32] Line N officers had two principal tasks: identifying potential recruits who might be trained as illegal agents, and assembling documents and other material which could be used to create 'legends' as cover stories for them. Western intelligence services almost never use illegals: the investment required to train and disguise an illegal agent is out of all proportion to the likely return. But in Russia, old traditions die hard. The Cheka started using illegals out of necessity, rather than choice, at a time when the Soviet Union had no diplomatic relations with the United States and tenuous ties with other Western countries, which made it impossible to set up legal residencies under diplomatic cover.[33]

Putin later claimed that 'all my work in foreign intelligence was connected . . . specifically with illegal intelligence'.[34] That was stretching the truth. He may have spent some of his time with the First Department in Leningrad on Line N matters, but it was certainly not his main task there.[35]

In East Germany, the search for potential illegals was a priority for Soviet intelligence because of the relative ease with which they could be infiltrated into West Germany. For that reason, the head of the Karlshorst representation, an officer of sufficient importance to have a seat on the KGB Collegium, was always from Directorate S.[36] But even in East Germany, identifying potential illegals was a soul-destroying task. Agartanov, being a physicist, compared it to extracting radium, which exists in a base mineral as one part in six million.[37]

Hopeful cases were referred to the FCD, which ran a trace on them. If they were approved, they would be cultivated in the same way as any other potential recruit, which might take a year or more.[38] Of those who passed that stage, all but a handful among every thousand candidates would fall by the wayside. Putin went through the motions, but he was only too well aware that any potential candidates he found were likely to end up stamped as rejects in some dusty file in the Tenth Department's archives.[39]

Assembling documentation for 'legends' was easier, but that was Agartanov's work, rather than Putin's, and it, too, was mind-numbingly routine.[40]

Putin's formal position in Line N did not absolve him from other intelligence tasks. Sergei Bezrukov, who succeeded Leshchev, said that like all Soviet intelligence officers in East Germany, Putin's first duty was to recruit agents, either directly or under a 'false flag', where the recruit was led to believe that he or she was cooperating not with the KGB but with some other organisation.[41]

In the first few months, Putin felt hamstrung by his poor command of German. Language lessons at the Red Banner Institute, he discovered to his dismay, were not at all the same as chatting informally to Stasi colleagues. Klaus Zuchold, who met him shortly after he arrived, remembered him preferring to speak Russian.[42] The KGB's language training was not one of its strengths. Oleg Kalugin, whose command of English was far better than Putin's German, was shocked to discover, when he first arrived in New York, that he, too, had difficulties.[43] Unlike many of his colleagues, Putin worked hard at his German and fairly soon achieved reasonable fluency, which improved further over time. Subsequent claims by Russian journalists that he was a brilliant linguist and had mastered different German dialects were pure fiction, but after a while he was at ease in the language and enjoyed speaking it.[44]

Even without fluent German, however, a KGB officer could work in East Germany, because much of the actual work of cultivating and recruiting agents was done by local intermediaries, seconded from the Criminal Investigation Department of the East German police.[45] Putin's predecessor, Boris Mylnikov, spoke abysmal German, but still managed to do his job.

The local men were paid by the Stasi, but worked full-time for the KGB, which supplemented their income. The Dresden office had four intermediaries at its disposal, of whom two, Rainer and Georg, were assigned to Line N.[46] Georg ran a number of auxiliary agents in West Germany, but according to Agartanov, the return from them was minimal.[47] Colonel Matveyev said Putin directly recruited other agents, including from among the students at the Technical University of Dresden.[48] One, from Colombia, put him in touch with a Colombian-born US Army sergeant in West Berlin, who sold him an unclassified army manual.[49] But that was about as far as his intelligence successes went.

The lack of results did no harm to Putin's career. In 1987, he received the rank of lieutenant-colonel. More importantly he was promoted to a higher grade. Ranks in the KGB depended solely on length of service. Grades were based on performance. Putin had come to Dresden with the grade of Senior Case Officer. He was promoted soon after to become Assistant Head of Department and later Senior Assistant. A higher rank brought only a modest pay increase, 10 roubles a month; a higher grade brought an extra 60 roubles a month, which would be factored into a final pension. By the end of his time in Dresden, Putin's notional salary was more than 600 roubles a month, three or four times the average Soviet wage.[50]

It was unusual for an officer to receive two promotions in quick succession, but Colonel Matveyev had insisted and the bureaucracy had agreed.[51] Despite his modest demeanour, the colonel was a figure to be reckoned with. He had worked for years in the office of the KGB Party Committee at the Lubyanka and had been a member of the same primary Party cell as Andropov.[52] In Dresden, he lived in a separate villa with a chauffeur-driven Volga sedan, and maintained contact with Hans Modrow, the head of the East German Party in the district, whom Moscow saw as a possible successor to the country's arch-conservative leader, Erich Honecker.[53]

It was at Matveyev's insistence that, soon after he arrived, Putin was appointed secretary of the KGB Dresden office Party cell.[54] This was a task which officers usually tried to avoid. The secretary had no real authority, and in the bigger residencies, the proceedings were purely formalistic. Each cell met once a month to consider a topic set by the Central Committee in Moscow. Usually there was no real discussion. In Dresden it was slightly freer, partly because, in the second half of the 1980s, the political climate was becoming more relaxed, and partly because they were only a small group. The KGB was officially designated 'the armed detachment of the Party', and taking on Party responsibilities could help one's later career. In Putin's case, moreover, it meant that he automatically became a member of the KGB Party Committee for East Germany, which was a more powerful body and put him in contact with high-ranking officers he would not otherwise have met.

Matveyev tried not to show favouritism, but he plainly regarded Putin as head and shoulders above the others, which caused some jealousy among his colleagues, who thought that he was no better than they were. Agartanov, who knew him best, called him 'an ordinary representative of our profession, . . . polite, affable, alert and unobtrusive, [but] not in any way outstanding'.[55] Viktor Adianov, who had replaced the disgraced Stalinist colonel, said he was 'hardly a superspy . . . not someone who stood out from his colleagues'.[56] Bragin said Putin was 'on a par with everyone else, without any special achievements'.[57] Both he and Adianov described him as a 'workaholic' and by comparison with them, he probably was, but to Agartanov he was 'conscientious and no more than that' and Matveyev concurred.[58]

On two points, however, Agartanov and Bragin agreed. Putin had a way of ingratiating himself with older people. As Agartanov put it: 'He was able to win over anyone he liked, but especially people his father's age.'[59] They also thought that he was not ambitious. In Bragin's words, 'he did not dream of a career.'[60] Agartanov felt that Putin might finish up as a colonel but he would go no higher. There was a ceiling for officers from the provinces which very few could break through. To attain the rank of general required approval at the level of the Party Central Committee and most senior posts, even in the provincial directorates, were held by officers parachuted in from Moscow.

Only Putin's wife, Lyudmila, thought that if he wanted to, he could rise further.[61] Perhaps she knew something that the others did not. But if Putin did aspire to higher things during his time in Dresden, he took good care to hide it.

When the family returned to Leningrad for their first home leave, in the summer of 1986, Putin's parents were at the dacha at Tosno, so he and Lyudmila had the apartment in Avtovo to themselves.[62] *Perestroika*, or 'restructuring', and *glasnost*, 'openness', the two signature programmes of the Soviet Union's new leader, Mikhail Gorbachev, were then still in their infancy. Most people thought that they would be just another failed attempt at reform which in the end would lead nowhere.

Gorbachev had taken power in March 1985, succeeding Brezhnev's long-time aide, Konstantin Chernenko, and the former KGB chief, Andropov, both of whom had been in chronic ill health and lasted less than 15 months in office. A year later his most visible achievement had been to launch a bitterly contested campaign against alcoholism. At the Red Banner Institute, the graduation ceremony for Putin's year, normally an uproarious, well-lubricated affair, had been dry. Colonel Kulkov had been disgusted. 'Imagine all these generals sitting around, raising a cup of tea or coffee,' he fumed. Putin and a group of friends defied the prohibition and celebrated in a restaurant, but well away from the institute lest more zealous colleagues denounce them.[63]

In Dresden, Lazar Matveyev also ignored the ban, arguing that they would look ridiculous in the eyes of their Stasi colleagues. But where Matveyev supported the campaign in principle, Putin did not. Alcoholism, he agreed, was a scourge, but the only effective means of fighting it was to raise the general cultural level of society. His reasons were strictly practical. Prohibition drove the problem underground, boosting illegal production of home-distilled liquor and poisonous surrogates and provoking a senseless mass movement to uproot valuable vineyards.[64] Three years earlier, in Leningrad, he told Agartanov, he had seen former colleagues from the Fifth Department posted outside cinemas and bathhouses to enforce a campaign which Andropov had launched to stop officials skiving off during working hours. That, too, he said, had been a mistake. It was an abuse of administrative measures and it did not solve the problem it was intended to address.[65]

Eventually the anti-alcohol campaign was curtailed, though not for the reasons Putin had adduced. It was wound up because the state could not do without the revenue from vodka sales.

When these topics arose at meetings of the Party cell, Putin was careful to say nothing to contradict Colonel Matveyev, who was an old-school communist in the same mould as his father. Arguing was pointless, he told Agartanov: it changed nothing and only put oneself and one's family at risk.[66] 'A person only has one life. Why waste it banging your head against a brick wall?'[67] He took the same approach to anti-Semitism, which was rife in the KGB. His predecessor, Boris Mylnikov, had been a rabid anti-Semite. Putin never gave any sign that he disagreed with Mylnikov's racist rants, even though his judo trainer, Anatoly Rakhlin, and many others in his immediate circle were Jews.[68] Similarly, when Matveyev complained, during a meeting of the Party cell, that the dissident physicist, Andrei Sakharov, whom Gorbachev had released from internal exile, was under Zionist influence through his Jewish wife, Yelena Bonner, Putin immediately supported him. In private, he maintained that Zionism had nothing to do with it, Sakharov's views were his own and no one influenced him.[69]

The disconnect between what one could say and what one could think, which Soviet citizens had factored into their behaviour since childhood without reflecting overmuch on the implications, became harder to ignore in the altered climate of the 1980s.

In the KGB, that was especially true. General Karasev, Putin's old mentor in Leningrad, wrote that young officers in the 1980s who 'knew much more about the flaws in the system than their compatriots, became critical of events and began to realise the need for change and renewal. They saw perfectly clearly that the system's own absurdities were causing as much damage to the country as all the foreign intelligence agencies put together.'[70] Putin had been struck by a conversation with a KGB colleague who had been with the Soviet army in Afghanistan. The man had told him that his main achievement there had been preventing pointless Soviet bombing raids. Putin had already realised that the war had been a mistake. Even so, he said, he was stunned. 'After discussions like that, you start to think and rethink things.'[71]

By the late 1980s, Putin was rethinking a great deal.

Vladimir Bragin concluded that Putin was no longer a communist.[72] His supervisor, Sergei Bezrukov, had a similar impression, while noting that the term, 'convinced communist', had by then lost most of its meaning.[73] Agartanov was amused by the contrast between Putin, the Party cell secretary, who, in front of Colonel Matveyev, was a true believer, and Putin the apostate, who in private considered communism an impossible dream.[74]

Putin had been deeply impressed by the private shops and small enterprises which the East German communists allowed to operate alongside the state sector. They were a different world from the grim, unwelcoming state stores at home with their empty shelves, bored shop hands and surly cashiers.[75] Private ownership, Putin concluded, was key. If people were to be motivated, they had to be allowed to accumulate property and to pass it on to their children. If the economy was to develop, there had to be competition.[76]

In Moscow, the Soviet Politburo was wrestling with the same issues. Party conservatives, led by Yegor Ligachev, Gorbachev's deputy, opposed radical change. Reluctantly they accepted the need for more flexibility in central planning, but the term, 'private property', was taboo. It was not until May, 1988, that Gorbachev was able to push through a law authorising what were euphemistically called 'cooperatives', which tentatively opened the door to private enterprise in the Soviet Union.

In the first years of *perestroika*, Putin, like many others, had grave doubts about Gorbachev's reforms. The problems, he argued, were systemic. Tinkering would achieve nothing.[77]

Moreover, seen from Dresden, the initial results were not encouraging. Corruption, which under Brezhnev had mainly been limited to the *nomenklatura*, the Party elite, was spreading to all levels of society. The exchange of favours, known as *blat*, had always been part of the Soviet system. But there was a difference between voluntarily giving preference to a friend; feeling obliged to give preference to a friend; and giving preference in return for a bribe. Putin held that the first was difficult to avoid. The second and third were inadmissible. In the summer of 1987, while on home leave, he travelled to Baku to visit Ilham Ragimov, his Azerbaijani classmate from the Law Faculty, and was dismayed to find that in the Caucasian republics, nothing could be accomplished without bribes.[78] In East Germany, officers in the Soviet armed forces started selling equipment and supplies on the black market. It became so bad that when Putin and his colleagues drove to Berlin, they were instructed to take their Makarov service pistols with them in case a rogue unit held them up and tried to steal their car.[79]

Another straw in the wind was the demand for Western fashions.

In the 1970s, Putin, like most young men of his age who could afford it, had splurged a good part of his wages on black-market Western jeans.[80] In the '80s, mail-order catalogues from West German fashion houses, from which a clever seamstress in Moscow or Leningrad could run up a good copy of a Western coat or dress, were a must-have item. Putin had friends in Directorate S at Karlshorst who got them for him from West Berlin. They were worth their weight in gold. Karlshorst might not be able to get much information about RYaN, Agartanov scoffed, but it overfulfilled its quota when it came to the latest creations of West German clothes designers.[81] Supplying fashion illustrations to the wives of the Moscow elite was profitable, but it was not why Putin had joined the KGB as an idealistic youngster a dozen years before.

When it became clear that Gorbachev was aiming at more than mere cosmetic change, Putin became more enthusiastic.[82]

Where previously he and his colleagues in Dresden had read the West German political magazine, *Der Spiegel*, to get the latest news, now there was a queue for the literary weekly, *Literaturnaya gazeta*, and *Ogonyok*, 'Small Fire', which had established itself as the standard-bearer for *perestroika* and was by far the most daring Soviet magazine of its time.[83] Another pathbreaking journal, *Novy mir*, serialised Boris Pasternak's *Doctor Zhivago*, George Orwell's *1984* and Solzhenitsyn's epic chronicle of Stalin's prison-camp system, *The Gulag Archipelago*, all of which had previously been banned.

For Russians, it was one of those extraordinary, uplifting, disconcerting times which a country experiences perhaps once or twice in a century. As in the 1960s in Western Europe, when the post-war generation rejected the cultural and social mores of their elders, so in the Soviet Union in the 1980s, previously unquestioned tenets of communist belief were cast aside and people allowed themselves to think and say things which had been unimaginable only a short time before.

For Putin's generation, it was exhilarating. For the East German leadership, and the leadership of the Stasi, it was terrifying. The underpinnings of the system they had built were being steadily hacked away.

Putin admired the Germans. They were orderly and diligent. They knew how to work and how to have fun without getting blind drunk as Russians did.[84] There was of course a more troubling side, too. Visiting Buchenwald and the sites of other Nazi concentration camps, Agartanov wrote, 'it was hard to believe that the satraps running these camps were the same Germans, brought up in the same way, with the same good manners, attending concerts of classical music . . . as those who accompanied us.'[85] But the 'real eye-opener', as Putin put it, was the backwardness of the East German political system. He had expected to be living in a European state. Instead he found himself in 'a harshly totalitarian country, similar to what the Soviet Union had been 30 years earlier . . . The entire population was under surveillance as though they were still living in Stalin's time.' *Perestroika* and *glasnost* were anathema.[86]

By 1987, the East German leaders, at meetings with their Soviet counterparts, were speaking out openly against Gorbachev's policies.

That September, at a meeting with a member of the KGB Collegium, the Security Minister, Erich Mielke, the most powerful Politburo member after Erich Honecker, charged that elements in the Soviet

Union were carrying out 'ideological subversion' against East Germany. He had been warning for months, he said, that 'hostile centres will immediately exploit *glasnost* and *perestroika* and use it as a cover for their operations ... The fundamental issue is capitalism or socialism. If [Moscow] goes towards capitalism, we can forget about socialism.'[87]

At the time, that sounded like panic-mongering, and Mielke's inter-locutor, the head of the KGB's Fifth Directorate, General Ivan Abramov, took it that way. But Mielke was not wrong. He saw, as Gor-bachev did not, where the logic of the Kremlin's policies would inevitably lead.

The first sign that *glasnost* might have unintended consequences came from Central Asia, where the veteran head of the Kazakh Com-munist Party, Dinmukhamed Kunayev, an ethnic Kazakh, had been forced to resign and replaced by a Russian, parachuted in from Mos-cow. The decision inflamed already smouldering resentment among the Kazakhs at Russian domination and triggered several days of eth-nic riots, repressed by the Soviet military, in which nearly two thousand people were injured. At the time, Gorbachev viewed it as an isolated incident. But before long, stirrings of nationalism were being felt elsewhere. With the Politburo fractured between reformers and hard-liners, the Kremlin was unable to develop a coherent response.

Three weeks after Mielke's meeting with Abramov, a thousand people staged a protest march in Yerevan, the capital of Soviet Armenia, calling for the annexation of Nagorno-Karabakh, an Armenian-populated enclave administered by neighbouring Azerbaijan. The police made a half-hearted effort to turn them back, but then allowed the demonstration to continue.[88] Four months later, in February 1988, hundreds of thousands of Armenians packed Yerevan's main square, demanding the territory's return.

Gorbachev belatedly recognised the danger of what he called 'nationalistic tendencies' and the problem was discussed in the Central Committee. But by then, the genie was out of the bottle. In the town of Sumgait, near Baku, dozens of Armenians – perhaps as many as 200 – were killed by Azeri mobs. In the late spring of that year, a nation-alist movement took wing in the Baltic republics. Gorbachev toyed with the idea of moving towards a confederal system, with greater powers devolved to the union republics.[89] In countries like Hungary and Poland, where pressure to throw off the Soviet yoke was never far below the surface, that was taken as a green light to push for greater independence.

Gorbachev's failure to stem the growth of nationalism was not the only sign that the Soviet system was beginning to flounder.

The nuclear power plant explosion at Chernobyl in April 1986, had been a major blow to Soviet pride. So was the exploit of Matthias Rust, a young West German who, on May 28, 1987, a few days short of his nineteenth birthday, flew a light aircraft from Helsinki to Moscow, making a mockery of Soviet air defences, and landed near Red Square.

For the reformers in the Soviet leadership, both events had a silver lining. The first provided a rationale for ending excessive secrecy and promoting *glasnost*. The second gave Gorbachev a pretext for purging the hardliners in the military opposed to *perestroika*. In June 1988, at the 19th Party conference, and at a subsequent Central Committee Plenum, he went further, winning approval for a sweeping programme of political reform, including the separation of state and Party organs, and competitive, multi-candidate elections, both at the local level and for a newly created Congress of People's Deputies, which would become the supreme organ of state power.

For the East German leaders, it seemed their worst fears were coming true. They became all the more determined to dig in their heels and resist.

The ideological conflict between East Berlin and Moscow was soon felt in Dresden. Horst Böhm, the young general in charge of the Stasi's district headquarters, was a hard-line Stalinist.[90] Putin, like the other members of the KGB office, had a pass giving him unrestricted access to the Stasi headquarters.[91] Böhm now ruled that in future, all contacts, other than formal celebrations of 'Soviet–German friendship', must be arranged through a designated Stasi liaison officer.[92] Colonel Matveyev's team found themselves having to arrange clandestine meetings with their sister service, as though they were operating in hostile territory, to obtain what was supposed to be shared information.[93]

Böhm's action was not just a result of ideological differences. In the 1970s, the KGB had launched a programme called *Luch*, 'Light beam', to monitor public opinion and gauge the degree to which Western influence was penetrating East German society.[94] Initially it was on a very small scale. But as relations frayed under Gorbachev, it acquired new significance. At the Dresden office, Sergei Chemezov found himself having to submit regular reports on the mood among East German Party members, Stasi officers and the population at large, which were collated with information from other district offices by a special unit at Karlshorst and sent back to Moscow. The decision to curtail contacts was the East German response.[95]

No one in Russia, at that point, expected serious ructions. It was obvious that there was a growing gulf between the East German leadership and the people but the Soviet Union had army bases there and the regime seemed firmly in control.[96] Yet before long there would be signs of fundamental change, which, with hindsight, should have given the Kremlin pause.

In November 1988, Estonia issued a declaration of sovereignty, asserting the supremacy of Estonian laws over those of the Soviet Union and ownership of the territory's land and natural resources. Three weeks later Gorbachev gave a speech to the United Nations General Assembly in which, between the lines, he made clear that Moscow would not use force to keep control of its East European satellites. In April 1989, the Polish government reached agreement with the main opposition movement, Solidarność, to hold free elections, leading to the formation of Poland's – and Eastern Europe's – first non-communist government. The same month, there were indications that the situation in the Soviet Union itself might be becoming unstable. A nationalist demonstration in the Georgian capital, Tbilisi, was dispersed brutally by soldiers who bludgeoned the crowd with sappers' shovels, leaving hundreds injured and 19 dead, most of them women.

For East Germany the turning point was the Hungarian government's decision in August to disconnect, and then dismantle altogether, the electric fence along its border with Austria, allowing Hungarians to travel freely to the West, the first breach in the Iron Curtain since before the Berlin Wall. As East Germans could visit Hungary without visas, they, too, were now able to cross into Austria and from there make their way to West Germany.

At a Warsaw Pact summit in Bucharest the previous month, Gorbachev had promised that all the member states could decide 'their own political line ... without external intervention'. Accordingly, when East Germany demanded that Moscow force the Hungarians to close the border with Austria, Gorbachev refused. In response, Honecker closed East Germany's own borders with its eastern neighbours, demanded that Prague and Warsaw prevent East Germans already on their territory from travelling to Hungary, and insisted that those who still wished to travel to the West be put aboard sealed East German trains, so that East Berlin could say that they were being deported as antisocial elements.

When the first train passed through Dresden on Thursday, October 5, 10,000 people converged on the railway station in the hope of being able to climb on board. They were driven back by police and troops using clubs and water cannon, and retaliated by hurling cobblestones. It was the biggest outbreak of civil disobedience in East Germany since an uprising against communist rule in 1953. More than a thousand people were detained.[97]

At that point, Putin understood that the East German leaders were losing control. But even then, he said later, 'I didn't imagine that the regime would collapse so quickly.'[98]

Nor did Mikhail Gorbachev, who arrived in East Berlin a day later to attend celebrations marking the 40th anniversary of the East German state. Honecker welcomed him at the airport with a 'fraternal embrace' and a kiss on the lips. That evening they stood together reviewing a torchlight parade. But in private the tension was palpable. 'Life punishes those who come too late,' the Soviet leader warned.[99] 'We will solve our problems ourselves, by socialist means,' Honecker replied. The East German was a 'scumbag', Gorbachev told his aides afterwards.[100]

Crowds lined Unter Den Linden, Berlin's equivalent of Fifth Avenue, chanting 'Gorby! Gorby!' and ignoring the East German leaders beside him. That night, near Alexanderplatz, police broke up anti-government demonstrations and made several hundred arrests. The 500,000 Soviet troops in East Germany were confined to barracks, under orders not to intervene should further disturbances occur.[101]

On Monday, October 9, 70,000 people staged a candlelight march in Leipzig, setting a pattern for demonstrations in other East German cities. Shortly afterwards, Honecker was replaced as General Secretary by the Party's nominal number two, Egon Krenz.

Throughout Eastern Europe, the pressure for change was becoming irresistible. Hungary approved multi-party elections and the Hungarian communists announced that they were reinventing themselves as social democrats. Then Krenz reopened the border with Czechoslovakia. Within days, more than 60,000 East Germans arrived in Prague heading for the West. The streets of the Czech capital were clogged with abandoned Trabants, the clunky East German version of the Volkswagen, the 'People's Car'. The Czech Party leaders were no less wary of Gorbachev's reforms than their allies in East Berlin, but confronted with an invasion of East German migrants, they urged Krenz to allow people to travel to the West directly. The following evening, an East German Politburo member inadvertently gave the impression that travel to West Berlin was now permitted. As the news spread, East Germans began massing at the crossing points. The border guards, vastly outnumbered and unwilling to use their weapons, gave way and let them pass. The Berlin Wall had fallen.[102]

In the dramatic weeks between the beginning of October, when demonstrators stormed the Dresden railway station, and the breaching of the Wall on November 9, Putin watched impotently as history unfolded before his eyes. He said later that he understood intellectually that the situation in East Germany was unnatural and that 'a position built on walls and divisions cannot last.'[103] But that was with hindsight. When it happened, he could only stand and stare.

Beyond East Germany's borders, the Kremlin's grip was weakening. In Ukraine, Rukh, a reformist-nationalist movement, was gaining strength with discreet support from Leonid Kravchuk, the wily Second Secretary of the Ukrainian Communist Party. In Kishinyov, the capital of Moldavia, anti-communist protesters burned down the Ministry of Internal Affairs. In Prague, after huge demonstrations and a general strike, the entire Communist Party leadership resigned and multi-party elections were called, as they had been earlier in Poland and Hungary, ending the Party's monopoly of power. Shortly afterwards, Bulgaria followed suit. By the time the year ended, Romania's communist regime, the last in the former Soviet bloc, had fallen and its leader, Nicolae Ceaușescu, and his wife had been executed.

On November 28, the West German Chancellor, Helmut Kohl, announced a ten-point programme for eventual reunification with the East. Shortly afterwards, Egon Krenz announced his resignation and the East German Party, too, agreed to hold elections.

Hans Modrow, the former Dresden Party chief whom Krenz had appointed Prime Minister, became East Germany's new leader. But he was not the liberal reformer that East Germans imagined and that

Gorbachev knew they needed. It was Modrow who had ordered troops to suppress the demonstrations at the Dresden railway station, describing them as 'terrorist riots'. Later he tried to protect the Stasi, proposing that it be renamed the 'Office for the Protection of the Constitution' – the same name that West Germany used for its domestic security service and almost identical to that recently given to the KGB's Fifth Directorate, which was now called Directorate Z, the Directorate for the Defence of the Constitutional Order.[104]

That move backfired badly. East Germans hated the secret police. On December 4, crowds ransacked the Stasi office at Erfurt in Thuringia. Next day it was the turn of Dresden. That afternoon, several thousand people gathered outside the Stasi headquarters. Horst Böhm ordered the guards not to resist. While Putin and two colleagues stood watching, the crowd surged through the gates and took possession of the buildings.[105]

General Vladimir Shirokov, who had replaced Matveyev the previous year, was then on leave in Moscow and Putin was in charge.[106] During the evening, a small group of demonstrators broke away and walked up Angelikastrasse to the KGB office, where they were stopped by a guard.

Accounts differ as to what happened next.

The demonstrators insisted later that there had only been 20 or 30 of them and they had never posed a threat.[107]

Putin remembered it differently. 'These people were in an aggressive mood,' he said; 'they were definitely going to storm the building.'[108] He ordered the guards to take up firing positions by the windows on the first floor, and then went out to talk to them:

> When I approached them, they asked me who I was and what this building was . . . I explained to them that it was a Soviet military organisation. Someone shouted from the crowd, 'Then why do you have cars with German licence plates in the parking lot? What are you doing here anyway?' . . . [I said] that we had an intergovernmental agreement, and I asked them to behave correctly and not to trespass on our land . . . I repeated that this had nothing to do with [the Stasi] or the East German army, it was a Soviet military facility and had extraterritoriality. Then I told the soldier [accompanying me] demonstratively to reload his weapon. I turned and slowly went back into the building.[109]

Once inside, he called the headquarters of the Soviet tank regiment, a couple of miles away, but was told, 'We cannot do anything without orders from Moscow. And Moscow is silent.' Eventually, 'after a few hours', the regimental commander sent a troop carrier with eight or ten soldiers, armed with AK-47s, who took up positions along the perimeter wall, at which point the crowd drifted away.[110]

This would later be depicted as a key formative memory, proving to Putin the overriding importance of maintaining a strong state and the dangers which an angry population could pose to what had previously seemed a solidly entrenched regime. Scholars have drawn a parallel with Andropov's experience in Budapest in 1956, when he saw Hungarian secret policemen hanged from the lamp posts beneath the windows of the Soviet Embassy and afterwards became obsessed by what he believed were Western attempts to foment dissent against the Soviet regime.

It is possible that that night in Dresden did play a formative role. Memories crystallise over time. 'That business of "Moscow is silent",' Putin said later. 'I got the feeling then that the country no longer existed . . . The [Soviet] Union was ailing. It had a terminal disease without a cure – a paralysis of power.'[111] But that was said more than a decade after, when he had different responsibilities and a very different agenda. In reality, it had been much less of a crisis than his memories made out. Far from having to wait several hours for military support, a patrol had been despatched to secure the building within thirty minutes.[112] His boss at Karlshorst, Sergei Bezrukov, to whom he reported next day, remembered it as a minor episode of no particular importance.[113]

But for Putin, it was the culmination of weeks of frustration, as East Germany – a country which he had come to regard as a second home – fell apart, while the mighty Soviet Union did nothing to stop it.[114]

A few days later, that impression was heightened when a hundred Stasi officers, locked out of their buildings by Neues Forum militants, came to plead with their Soviet colleagues for the KGB to use its influence on their behalf if, as seemed increasingly likely, the Stasi was disbanded and they lost their jobs.[115] Once again, there was nothing Putin and his colleagues could do. Years later, it still made him angry. 'The fact that we did not support [those who had worked for us] was lamentable,' he told an interviewer. 'Regardless of ideology, the special services should always take care of those who help them . . . It's the norm for any civilised state.'[116] Instead of that, he complained, those who had worked for the Stasi were 'persecuted for political reasons'.[117] He could understand that East Germans regarded their security service as a monstrous organisation, but it was the system which was wrong, not those who worked within it.

'The people I knew were decent people,' Putin insisted. 'They were my friends and I will not renounce them.' Some Stasi officers, he admitted, had 'probably' maltreated people, but he 'personally did not see it'.[118] It was the same reasoning that led him to minimise the horrors committed by the NKVD under Stalin. The state was a reflection of the society from which it came. So were its faults.

In the middle of December, the KGB group in Dresden was ordered to start burning its archives. 'We destroyed everything – all our communications, our lists of contacts and agent networks,' Putin remembered.[119] The office possessed an incinerator for that purpose, but the sheer volume of papers to be consumed was so great that it overheated and exploded. General Shirokov, who by then had returned from Moscow, arranged with the commander of the tank regiment to transport twelve carloads of files to the barracks to be burnt in a furnace. When that, too, blew up, they buried them in a hole in a landfill, intending to destroy them with napalm. But the engineering unit which was supposed to supervise the operation failed to arrive, so they used gasoline instead.[120]

The most important documents from KGB and Stasi district offices, as well as from the East German Defence Ministry and the Stasi headquarters in Berlin, were sent separately to Karlshorst and then flown to Moscow. According to Sergei Bezrukov, the operation lasted two to three months. All the most sensitive items were removed to the Russian archives.[121]

After the storming of the Stasi headquarters in Dresden, all work with agents ceased.[122] But in January 1990, Putin was instructed to start recruiting a new network, separate from those he had worked with before, so that they would not be compromised if the old networks were exposed.[123] He turned to Klaus Zuchold, the young Stasi officer he had met shortly after his arrival. It proved to be an unfortunate choice: later that year, after German reunification, Zuchold, like many others with KGB connections in East Germany, went to the West German security service and told them all he knew.

By then Putin had left Dresden. Sometime in mid January, he had been summoned to Berlin for a meeting with a KGB general from the newly renamed Directorate Z, who had just arrived from Moscow.[124] Exactly what was said is not known. Neither Bezrukov, his direct superior, nor anyone else from Karlshorst was allowed to attend. Bezrukov learnt that the meeting had concerned Putin's next assignment, but no one would tell him anything more. Immediately afterwards, Putin returned to Dresden and cleared his desk. He and his family returned to Leningrad on February 3, 1990.[125]

The suddenness of his departure would later give rise to many rumours.

The normal tour of duty for an officer seconded from a provincial directorate was five years. All Putin's predecessors had served their full terms. Vladimir Bragin, who had arrived a few months after him, stayed on until the autumn, when the office in Dresden was closed.[126] Putin left more than six months ahead of schedule. Stories began circulating that he had been withdrawn early because the Stasi had complained he was recruiting agents who were already compromised, which would put other networks at risk.[127] It was alleged that he had had unauthorised contacts with the West German foreign intelligence service, the BND, or with the CIA.[128] Another version, apparently encouraged by Putin himself, held that he had been recalled as part of a general reduction of KGB personnel in East Germany following the fall of the Berlin Wall.[129] But the timing did not fit. In mid January, the expectation in Moscow, as in London and Bonn, was that German reunification was still some way off. Dresden was of special interest to the Kremlin. It was Hans Modrow's political base and, in December, Helmut Kohl had chosen it for the first ever visit to East Germany by a West German Chancellor. It was the last place where the KGB would have started cutting back.

The truth was simpler. As Bezrukov suspected, Putin had been withdrawn to be given a new assignment – an assignment which would lay the groundwork for everything that followed.

In May 1989, the Congress of People's Deputies had held its opening session in Moscow. The debates, which were broadcast live, transfixed the

Soviet public. For two weeks, the whole country was at a standstill. Factories stopped work, the ministries were idle. People spent their days
glued to television sets and transistor radios, and the evenings discussing
what they had heard. The British Ambassador, Rodric Braithwaite, noted
in his diary:

> Not a single sacred cow has escaped assault. The leadership have been
> cross-examined about their private lives. The Party has been accused of
> narrowmindedness, privilege, and corruption. The government has
> been accused of gross mismanagement. The army has been accused of
> mounting punitive expeditions against the civil population, and its inva-
> sion of Afghanistan called a shameful crime. The KGB has been
> publicly assailed for murder and torture. Even Lenin has not escaped
> entirely: the proposal to remove him from his mausoleum, which so
> infuriated the Party in April, was publicly repeated . . . What has been
> said – about the mismanagement of the economy, the weaknesses of
> the leadership, the bankruptcy of the Party, the brutality of the army
> and police – cannot be unsaid.[130]

In the past, criticisms like this had been heard only from the most outspoken dissidents. Now they were coming from reformers within the
Communist Party itself.

The KGB took note. The new head of Directorate Z, General Filipp
Bobkov, was instructed to divert resources from suppressing traditional
dissent to surveillance of these new liberals who, far more than any
dissidents ever had, were threatening the established order of things.

One of the rising stars in the liberal firmament was Anatoly Sobchak, the Leningrad law professor who, as a junior lecturer, had taught
Putin in the 1970s. Richard Bridge, who was then with MI6 under
diplomatic cover in Moscow, remembered: 'When Sobchak stood up
to speak – and I used to attend those sessions – people listened. He
was scathing, critical, eloquent, brilliant . . . He was an orator and
he was very clever . . . he was an impressive guy.'[131]

Sobchak was a founding member of the Inter-Regional Deputies'
Group, the democratic opposition in the Congress, headed by Andrei
Sakharov and the former Moscow Party Secretary, Boris Yeltsin. Before
long he became a celebrity in his own right, a symbolic figure who
seemed to personify the changes that people were waiting for.[132] At a

time when most Soviet politicians still dressed drably, he came to debates wearing an elegantly cut beige-and-white plaid jacket which made him look, as Yeltsin's political strategist, Gleb Pavlovsky, put it, 'as though he'd just walked off the Champs Elysées after shopping in a designer boutique'.[133] It became such a trademark that in Soviet department stores, plaid jackets were referred to as 'sobchaks'. Alfred Kokh, a young economist who would go on to become one of Yeltsin's deputy Prime Ministers, thought 'he looked just the way a real politician should . . . Handsome, impressive. Bold. Smart. Educated. An aristocratic spirit . . . We adored him. There was nobody like him . . . He was one of a kind.'[134]

After a set-to in November 1989 with the hard-line Leningrad Party leader, Boris Gidaspov, whom Sobchak accused of trying to launch a Stalinist putsch, he became the uncontested leader of the democratic opposition in the city.[135]

The KGB had begun to take an interest in him when he headed a parliamentary commission into the suppression of the protests in Tbilisi the previous spring. Its report, issued in December, contained a devastating condemnation of the army's conduct and of Yegor Ligachev, who had chaired the meeting which had authorised the crackdown.[136] During the parliamentary debate, when the former KGB Chairman, Viktor Chebrikov, protested against the findings, he drew a tart rebuke from Sobchak: 'You should know that you are dealing with people who are not afraid of you.'[137]

The session was broadcast live. Anatoly Chubais, the future head of Yeltsin's privatisation programme, remembered thirty years later how he and his colleagues 'were all walking around with transistor radios pressed to our ears, in sheer disbelief'. The KGB was accustomed to being criticised for past misdeeds, but no one until then had dared attack its current role.

Nor did Sobchak stop there. He railed at the secrecy with which the 'Organs', as they were called, surrounded themselves, and in another jibe at Chebrikov, who until the previous year had been a member of the Politburo, he demanded that 'in future the leaders of the KGB no longer participate in the leadership of our country'. A colleague in the Inter-Regional Group, Sergei Stankevich, felt that at that moment, Sobchak and the KGB parted ways irrevocably. 'For the security services,' he said, 'he crossed a red line.'

Bobkov needed to find people who could get close to all the liberal leaders, not just Sobchak.[138] But Sobchak had become an especially high-profile target.

Thus far everything is well documented. What follows is unproven but fits all the known facts and is vouched for by several people who worked closely with Putin after his return from Dresden.

According to Sobchak's election assistant, Valery Pavlov, who had earlier been one of his students, the key role was played by Nikolai Yegorov, Putin's classmate at the Law Faculty who now headed the university's Civil Law Department and worked closely with the KGB's Leningrad Directorate. Yegorov, Pavlov said, was asked to provide the names of former students of Sobchak who might be able to attach themselves to his entourage. Yegorov proposed two of his close friends from that time: Putin and Aleksandr Bastrykin.[139] Bobkov's people chose Putin, perhaps on the advice of Colonel Matveyev, who had been impressed by Putin's legal background and whose years at the KGB Party Committee gave him influence beyond his rank.[140]

Pavlov's account is all the more credible because he and Bastrykin were close. After graduating, both worked for the Leningrad Regional Committee of the Komsomol and when, in 1988, Bastrykin was appointed head of the Leningrad University Party Committee, Pavlov followed him there.

There was then some discussion over whether Putin should be based in Moscow, where Sobchak and his colleagues now spent most of their time, or whether he should be in Leningrad.[141] The KGB was a military organisation and officers were not normally given a choice of where they would be posted. But in this case the mission was to cultivate a target who divided his time between Moscow and Leningrad and it was difficult to know which would be more productive.

Matveyev said later that he had advised Putin to stay in Leningrad on the practical grounds that the family had a flat there, whereas in Moscow it might take years before he was given an apartment.[142] Putin, too, spoke of the difficulty of finding accommodation in the capital.[143]

Left to his own devices, Putin's preferences would have been for Leningrad. Russians are territorial: Putin was a Leningrader through and through. His parents were nearly 80 years old and his mother was in poor health. Like other KGB officers at that time, he may also have had doubts about the future of the organisation. He had just seen his counterparts in the Stasi lose careers, which they had expected to last a lifetime, almost overnight. The Soviet Union had abandoned its positions throughout Eastern Europe. No one could say for sure what lay ahead in Russia either. If his career in the security services were to come to an abrupt end, it would be better to deal with that in Leningrad than in an unfamiliar city like Moscow.

Whether the difficulty of finding an apartment was really a factor – or whether that was just another false trail to divert attention from his assignment to Sobchak – is impossible to tell. In the end, the KGB opted for Leningrad.[144] The decision put paid to Putin's hopes of being transferred to a permanent post with the KGB Centre in Moscow. On the other hand, it was the safer choice. His new position, under cover of being an assistant to the Vice Rector in charge of International Affairs at Leningrad University, had been arranged on Moscow's instructions. It meant that he still had a link with the central bureaucracy, even as he returned to the 'peripheral organs' from which he had started out.

5

Back in the USSR

Soon after the train taking the Putins from Dresden to Leningrad had crossed the Soviet border, the family got out to stretch their legs on the platform at one of the stations along the way. While they were outside, Lyudmila's handbag, containing part of their savings, disappeared.[1]

It was the beginning of a rude awakening. After four years of *perestroika*, the crime rate in the Soviet Union was soaring and the economy was in free fall. Although they had returned to Leningrad on holiday each summer, the penury in the shops, after the plenty of Dresden, still came as a shock. To buy sugar, you needed a ration card and, starting on February 1, 1990, two days before they arrived, other basic foodstuffs could be purchased only with an identity card, proving residence in the city.[2]

'There were terrible lines [and] empty shelves,' Lyudmila remembered. 'For a while after we returned home, I was even afraid to go to the store . . . I wasn't able, like some people, to sniff out all the bargains . . . I would just . . . buy whatever was most necessary and go home. It was horrible.'[3] To make matters worse, because of the initial uncertainty over where Putin was to work, there was a dispute over which department should pay his salary. That took three months to resolve and they almost ran out of money.[4]

But the most striking change was in people's attitudes. Not only had living conditions, already bad in the mid 1980s, deteriorated further in the four and a half years the family had been away, but ordinary citizens now said openly, with all the grim melodrama which Russians affect at such times, exactly what they thought of their lives, their government and a future in which they saw nothing good. The words on everyone's lips were *razval* and *grazhdanskaya voina*, 'collapse' and 'civil war'.[5]

The French Foreign Ministry reported, in a confidential analysis of diplomatic despatches:

All the antagonisms which had earlier been contained [are] bursting out into the open: the desire for independence on the part of the border republics; the grumbling of those at the base of the political-economic pyramid against those in the upper echelons; the inevitable search for scapegoats – in which old-line Stalinists in the Party *apparat* join forces with right-wing nationalists against the Jews and the Judeo-masonic conspiracy . . . Add to that a generalised mistrust of the currency, fuelled by fears of economic and monetary reform; endemic food shortages in parts of the Russian Federation; increasingly open activity by all kinds of mafia organisations; accelerating disruption of the tissue of economic production and of all public services (transport, communications, health, justice); a vertiginous rise in criminality; the collapse of the family unit . . . and you have some idea of the moral disarray in which the population of the Soviet Union finds itself.[6]

'Russia has become the slum of the industrialised world,' another Western diplomat wrote. 'Its environment is devastated and its health system in crisis.'[7] Drunkenness was such a problem that in some parts of the Soviet Union, one child in six was born mentally retarded from an alcoholic mother.[8] In Leningrad, with its endless winters, half the streetlights did not work and the roads were full of potholes.[9] The most popular Soviet film that year – a comparison between life in Russia and life in the West – was entitled *Tak zhit nelzya*, 'We Can't Live like This'.[10]

For Putin and his family, as for millions of others, that pretty much summed it up.

The certitudes of the past were gone. Everything was in transition. Alongside articles extolling the Komsomol were photographs of long-haired Russian rock groups. Next to appeals to participate in the *subbotnik*, the April day when everyone was expected 'voluntarily' to join in community labour to mark Lenin's birthday, there was an earnest debate in the newspapers about whether Leningrad should have a Disneyland. Beside a gloomy headline about the plight of young graduates from the Philosophical Faculty – 'Today Scientific Socialism, Tomorrow Unemployment' – another headline, this time in English, promised advice on, 'How to Stay Younger, Longer!' A cartoon depicted a blind man with a white cane teetering on a tightrope, beneath a sign reading: 'This way to the market economy'.[11]

Having had an apartment to themselves in East Germany, the family was once again without a home of their own. As an invalid, Putin's mother had been given a one-room flat in a new building on Leninsky Prospekt. They had exchanged it and the flat at Avtovo for a three-roomed apartment on Sredneokhtinsky Avenue, across the river from Smolny, not far from the 401 School where Putin had begun his KGB training.[12] It was 'an old building, with very low ceilings – alright, but nothing luxurious', one visitor said tactfully, in 'an ordinary, slightly run-down area'.[13] Others were less diplomatic. Boris Fyodorov, a former Russian Finance Minister who was then working for the European Bank for Reconstruction and Development (EBRD), was appalled. 'It was awful,' he told a colleague. 'Those people are living very badly.'[14]

Lyudmila hated it. 'For three and a half years,' she said, 'we lived in a place where it was simply embarrassing to invite people . . . The apartment was in a terrible state and we had no money to repair it.'[15]

At first, they had no furniture. As there was no way they could buy any until Putin's salary came through, they lived for several months among packing cases, filled with their belongings from Dresden. These included a 20-year-old washing machine, a gift from their East German neighbours, which soldiered on for five more years. They did not have much else because Putin was still passionate about cars – in Dresden, the office driver, Werner, had nicknamed him 'Speed Freak' – and he had splurged most of their savings on an old Volga sedan, which he had bought on favourable terms from the Stasi car pool and driven back from Germany.[16]

Whether at Lyudmila's urging, or because, after four years of relative freedom, Putin also found it difficult to readjust to cramped, communal living, he reached an agreement with the East German consulate in Leningrad, which was to close after reunification, to take over the lease of their dacha at Zelenogorsk, an exclusive resort area set among pine forests on the Gulf of Finland, 35 miles north-west of Leningrad. The house, built of wood and with no running water, belonged to the Soviet Foreign Ministry and was intended for use only in summer. The Putins stayed there in winter, too, which made their neighbour, Vasily Golovko, a stern-faced, retired communist apparatchik from the regional Party committee, decide that they must be there to avoid living in their parents' apartment in the city.[17]

Lyudmila, frugal as ever, did the family's washing outside at a water pump on the street. But it was a step up from Tosno, where water had to be drawn in a bucket from a well. Lyudmila and the children had sledges and Putin went cross-country skiing. For the first time in his life, he had a dog, a shaggy Caucasian shepherd he named Malysh, 'Little One'.

As a member of the KGB's active reserve, a term used for officers working undercover in another state organisation, Putin was paid by the university as well as receiving his KGB salary. His new position as assistant to the Vice Rector for International Affairs at Leningrad University – on his English-language name card, he made it sound more imposing: deputy Director for International Affairs – was not particularly taxing.[18] The International Affairs Office vetted requests by foreign students and exchange scholars to travel within the Soviet Union. It distributed and, in some cases, monitored, incoming foreign mail. It had the final word on applications from teaching staff and students who hoped to travel abroad.[19]

The office had long had a reputation as corrupt and inefficient. But in 1990, the need to find new sources of income at a time of economic collapse forced it to branch out beyond its traditional functions of surveillance and control. That spring, Putin's boss, the Vice Rector, Yuri Molchanov, reached agreement with the US beauty products company, Procter and Gamble, to set up a joint venture. In return for a small share of equity, the university provided office accommodation and an entrée to the city's political and economic elite. Putin was not directly involved, but it opened his eyes to the possibilities that economic cooperation with Western companies might bring.[20]

Putin's duties at the university left him more than enough time to immerse himself in Leningrad politics and he evidently did so, for Lyudmila complained that after their return, 'he was simply never home. It was as though I had a husband who had fled.'[21]

There was a lot to keep up with.

If it was difficult to adjust to the social and economic upheaval, it was even harder to come to terms with the political transformation that Russia was undergoing. It had been one thing to sit in Dresden, reading liberal magazines like *Ogonyok* and *Novy mir* and watching Soviet television. It was quite another to be plunged into the midst of a city, and a country, in ebullition, where the rules today bore little relation to what they had been yesterday or what they might become tomorrow.

Leonid Polokhov, who had been Putin's classmate at the Law Faculty and happened to run into him that spring, remembered Putin peppering him with questions about the political situation, as if he was struggling to understand what was really going on.[22]

In February, less than a week after his return, the Central Committee, meeting in Moscow, voted to end the Party's 'leading role' and install presidential rule – momentous decisions which fundamentally changed the Soviet system and opened the way, in theory at least, to multi-party democracy. A month later, after the changes had been ratified by the Congress of People's Deputies, Anatoly Sobchak, whom Putin was following, as he put it, 'with great interest',[23] was nominated by the Inter-Regional Group of Deputies as its candidate to succeed Gorbachev as Chairman of the Supreme Soviet, the Congress's Executive Committee, when the latter became Head of State.[24] His chances of success were not great. Since the death of the group's spiritual mentor, Andrei Sakharov, from a heart attack in December, its membership had splintered into moderate and radical wings.[25] Sobchak was a free spirit, who tended to go his own way.[26] He had irritated the moderates by what they viewed as unduly harsh criticism of conservative positions, and on March 15, when the election took place, he lost by a wide margin to Gorbachev's candidate, Anatoly Lukyanov – a choice which Gorbachev would later bitterly regret.

In Leningrad the same month, voters went to the polls to elect the 400 members of the City Council, the Lensoviet. Sobchak was not a candidate. But after the setback in Moscow, he started wondering whether he should not retrench and make Leningrad his main political base.[27]

He did not have to wonder for long. The majority of the new Lensoviet were idealistic members of the democratic movement with no experience of politics and still less of how to conduct parliamentary debates. That was understandable. Until then, the Communists had had a monopoly of power. But the result was mayhem. The deputies were so fearful of allowing any of their number to attain a position of leadership, which they regarded as, by definition, undemocratic, that they appointed a different acting chairman each day to ensure that no one could concentrate power in their hands.[28] A dozen different factions formed, which coalesced into two main groups: one headed by Pyotr Filippov, a pragmatic economist representing the moderate wing of the democratic movement; the other around Marina Salye, an uncompromising radical whom the French Consul General, Marcel Roux, dubbed 'La Pasionara'.[29] Salye, a middle-aged research scientist with short-cropped grey hair, was in a sapphic relationship, which, at that time in the Soviet Union, was viewed as extraordinarily daring. She and Filippov both sought the Chairmanship of the Lensoviet, a role comparable to that of Speaker of the House but with broader powers. When neither would give way, it became clear that the only solution would be to bring in an outsider, an ancient tradition in Russia, going back to the time more than a thousand years before when the warring East Slav tribes invited Rurik, a Varangian chieftain, to rule them, so forming the basis of the first Russian state.[30]

There were three potential candidates for that role: Aleksandr Shchelkanov, a retired naval captain; Yury Boldyrev, a young economist; and Sobchak. Representatives of the two rival factions approached Shchelkanov first, but he made clear he did not wish to become involved. Boldyrev also refused, saying that he wanted to stay in Moscow, where, in addition to his role as a deputy, he was working as a parliamentary adviser to the Russian Federation government. That left Sobchak.

By then the deputies were desperate to find a way out of the impasse. A petition was drawn up, asking Sobchak to stand as a candidate in a constituency where no result had been declared because the minimum turnout had not been met. More than 100 deputies signed it, promising that if he did so, they would elect him Lensoviet Chairman.[31]

On April 9, Sobchak agreed.[32] He registered as a candidate in Vyborg District in the north-western suburbs of Leningrad, but refused to campaign and spent election day in Moscow attending a meeting of the Supreme Soviet. Even so, he won easily, thanks to what one of his supporters called 'blatant sins to which the Electoral Commission closed its eyes'.[33]

On May 23, 1990, Sobchak became Lensoviet Chairman, the effective head of the Soviet Union's second city, administering almost five million people. Not long afterwards, Vladimir Putin agreed to become his assistant.

Exactly how that happened is a matter of debate.

Putin said at first that Sobchak had met him by chance at the university, remembered him as a former student and suggested that they work together.[34] Both Sobchak and his wife, Lyudmila Narusova, later repeated that account, which was plausible and – despite the improbability of a university professor recognising, 15 years later, a student whom he had not known personally and who had merely attended some of his lectures[35] – might have gone unquestioned had Putin not subsequently given a totally different explanation. In this revised version, he claimed that a colleague at the Law Faculty had mentioned that Sobchak was looking for an assistant and had offered to put them in touch.

> I met Sobchak in his office at the Lensoviet [Putin said]. I remember the scene very well. I went in and introduced myself . . . He was an impulsive man, and he said to me right off: 'I'll speak to [the Rector] about it . . . Come to work starting Monday . . .' I felt I had to tell him: 'Anatoly Aleksandrovich, I would be happy to do that, [but] I must tell you that I am not just an assistant to the Vice Rector, I am also an officer of the KGB.' He was silent for a moment . . . He thought and thought, and then suddenly he said, 'Well, screw that!' . . . I told him that I would be happy to come and work for him, but that I would first have to tell my bosses at the KGB and resign from my university post.[36]

Not a word of that was true.[37] Sobchak had known all along that Putin was from the KGB. The post he occupied at the university was always held by a KGB officer.[38] Moreover the Law Faculty colleague who had introduced them – for that part of Putin's revised account was true – was the same Nikolai Yegorov who had originally suggested Putin's name to the KGB hierarchy as someone who could infiltrate Sobchak's entourage. Yegorov had already explained Putin's background to Sobchak and had been agreeably surprised to find that he was knocking at an open door.[39] It turned out that a KGB officer was exactly what Sobchak was looking for.

The Lensoviet Chairman was an academic, a liberal, a cultural dilettante, an idealist, frequently carried away by his own eloquence and with little inclination for the hard grind of practical politics, but he also understood that he needed competent people who could guide him through the maze of Soviet bureaucracy. As Putin would put it later, 'he needed [people] who knew which buttons to push to get things done'.[40] Sobchak's relations with the security services were execrable and he was desperate to find someone to liaise with them on his behalf. He had earlier asked Oleg Kalugin, the former deputy head of the Leningrad Directorate, to recommend to him a retired KGB officer who might be suitable. Kalugin had suggested two names, but Sobchak thought they were both too high-powered.[41] He wanted someone who would carry out his instructions without question and answer only to him.

Putin fitted the bill perfectly.

Mindful of his liberal credentials, Sobchak had no wish to let it be known that he had deliberately recruited a KGB officer as one of his principal advisers. Putin was equally keen to avoid any suggestion that he had joined Sobchak's team on the KGB's instructions. Their initial account of a chance meeting at the university was tailored accordingly.

But in that case, why did Putin change his story? He knew how to fabricate a credible 'legend'. That had been part of his basic KGB training. But he had also been taught that a legend need not last for ever. Once it had served its purpose, it could be discarded and replaced by something else. In this case, he put forward the new, more colourful version of how he came to work with Sobchak at a time, eight years later, when he was embarking on a political career and wanted to pique voters' curiosity about his background. It would not be the last time that Putin would fabricate a story, only to abandon it when it no longer served his purpose.

Sobchak found himself at odds with the Lensoviet deputies from the outset. No sooner had he been elected than he announced that he was leaving with his wife for a visit to the United States. On his return, he infuriated the members of the democratic movement who had voted for him by appointing neither Salye nor Filippov as Deputy Chairman, but instead choosing a prominent conservative, Vice Admiral Vyacheslav Shcherbakov, the candidate of the military–industrial complex. In

Leningrad, the defence sector accounted for 70 to 80 per cent of the city's industrial production.[42]

In retaliation, on June 18, the deputies elected Aleksandr Shchelkanov, the naval officer who had declined the offer to become the Lensoviet's Chairman, to head the Ispolkom, its Executive Committee, a post which made him in effect the city's Mayor.[43]

The inevitable result was a power struggle.

Sobchak argued that the Lensoviet should determine policy and the Ispolkom should carry it out. Shchelkanov held that the Ispolkom should govern while the Lensoviet should legislate. For the next two months, the City Council lurched from crisis to crisis, haemorrhaging public trust. Its meetings were televised, which meant that the deputies' endless wrangling, during which they accomplished nothing, was in full public view. 'We have 400 people who for eight hours a day have no idea what they are doing,' Sobchak fumed. But it was six of one and half a dozen of the other. 'The deputies are tearing their hair out,' the liberal newspaper, Smena, reported. 'They invited [Sobchak] to become their new "tsar" in the hope that he would be able to unite the different factions . . . And he has! Against himself. Now they would like to find a way to get rid of him. But they can't because he is more popular than they are.'[44]

The disarray of the newly elected representatives was palpable enough that many Leningraders started to wonder whether this strange thing called democracy, which had hardly yet even begun, was all that it was cracked up to be.

Matters came to a head at the beginning of August. Sobchak was in Estonia for the inaugural meeting of what would become known as the Tallinn Process, an attempt to open new channels for bartering essential supplies between Soviet republics, bypassing the government in Moscow, at a time when the old state planning mechanisms had broken down.[45] Today the initiative is long since forgotten, but at the time there were hopes that it might lead to the creation of a Baltic Economic Community with associate membership for Armenia, Georgia and Moldova as well as Czechoslovakia, Hungary and Poland. More realistically, it was a way for Leningrad and some of the Soviet republics to try to ensure food supplies at a time when there were not just empty shelves and ration books but real fears that the following winter the population would go hungry.

Sobchak's absence gave his opponents the chance they had been waiting for to vote his impeachment.[46] Vice Admiral Shcherbakov, who was also beginning to have doubts about Sobchak's suitability as Chairman, refused to intervene.

Putin at this point had not yet formally taken up his post and was working at the Lensoviet part-time as a volunteer. But Sobchak had two other aides.

One was Valery Pavlov, who had been with him since the spring of 1989 when he had helped run his campaign for the Soviet Congress of People's Deputies. When Sobchak became Lensoviet Chairman, Pavlov's background as a Komsomol official made him an ideal choice to liaise with the Communist Party Regional Committee at Smolny.[47]

The other, Yury Shutov, had been recommended by Bella Kurkova, the editor of 'The Fifth Wheel', a highbrow television programme about politics and the arts which had become compulsory viewing for Russian intellectuals.[48] Shutov was a controversial figure, an adventurer with a chequered past and a reputation for breaking the rules. He had been involved in a number of dubious ventures but managed to stay out of trouble until, in 1982, when he was working at Smolny, he was convicted of setting a fire to hide evidence of malversation and sentenced to five years in a labour camp. After he was freed under an amnesty, Kurkova, a close friend of Sobchak's wife, Lyudmila, took up the cudgels on his behalf, presenting him as an innocent victim of Communist Party persecution. At her urging, Sobchak engaged him in an unofficial capacity to work with foreign investors and to liaise with the semi-criminal entrepreneurs and gangsters who controlled the shadow economy.[49]

Shutov's ability to cut corners saved the day. He borrowed an air force helicopter, flew to Tallinn, called Sobchak out of the meeting and brought him back to Leningrad, whereupon the plot collapsed. Further attempts to oust him failed because Salye and Filippov were unable to agree who should have the leading role.

A month later, on September 14, Shchelkanov announced melodramatically that he was going to resign.[50] He had persuaded the main Leningrad television channel to interrupt live coverage of a football match to broadcast his announcement, in which he denounced Sobchak as a tyrant with whom no one could work. Behind him, as he spoke, sat a group of prominent supporters from the democratic movement. It was the first time any Soviet leader, even at municipal level, had ever appealed directly to the public. Leningraders, glued to their television sets, could hardly believe their eyes.

This time, Shutov found Sobchak a new ally.

Aleksandr Nevzorov presented a television show called '600 Seconds', which specialised in exposés of official misdeeds and was wildly popular all over Russia. A few days after Shchelkanov's broadcast, Nevzorov showed footage of the Soviet flag flying upside down above the Lensoviet building, an image sufficiently shocking to cause Gorbachev to telephone Sobchak the following morning to ask what on earth was going on. Nevzorov was an unabashed nationalist and his message was that the deputies were trampling on the Soviet Union's honour. The next night the programme showed hundreds of laboratory rats, reimagined as Lensoviet members, devouring a cake decorated with a statue of the city's founder, Peter the Great. Public opinion, which until then had backed Shchelkanov, turned in Sobchak's favour.

For the *coup de grâce*, Shutov organised truck drivers to blockade the Mariinsky Palace, where the Lensoviet met. They handed the frightened deputies leaflets warning: 'If you keep on making mischief, we'll throw your mandates under our trucks.' When Shchelkanov tried to reason with them, he was shouted down. To his supporters, it was a signal that the game had gone far enough. He and Sobchak declared a truce, and for the next nine months, there was an uneasy stand-off.

For Putin, a political education that would normally have taken years was being crammed into a few months.

When he had returned from Dresden in February, the Soviet Union was still a one-party state. In April, that already seemed another age. That month, he had watched tens of thousands of people gathering for protest rallies in front of the Winter Palace, the first to have been permitted since 1917.[51] Newspapers began to discuss previously forbidden topics: the execution of Tsar Nicholas II and his family at Yekaterinburg in 1918; the murder of the Leningrad leader, Sergei Kirov, on Stalin's orders in 1934, preceding the Great Purge; the assassination of Trotsky in 1940; and the massacre of 22,000 Polish officers at Katyn by the NKVD the same year. In June, within days of Putin agreeing to work for Sobchak, the authority of his new patron was being challenged, an experience which he found 'very unpleasant'.[52] Two months later, the same deputies who had begged Sobchak to become their Chairman were attempting to have him dismissed. To anyone who had grown up with the soporific predictability of Brezhnev-era Soviet politics, it was bewildering and a little frightening.

In these circumstances, Putin proceeded cautiously. When Sobchak said he would ask the President of Leningrad University, Stanislav Merkuriev, to release him from his post so that he could start work at once, he demurred.[53] There was no rush, he said. He spent the spring and early summer keeping his head down and observing what was happening around him. There was no way of telling what the next few months might bring or even whether Sobchak would be able to remain in power. As he put it later, 'It was risky to tie my future to his. Everything might unravel at a moment's notice.'[54] At one point, he started exploring other options. Galina Starovoitova, an anthropologist and leading member of the Inter-Regional Group, who was almost as prominent as Sobchak in the Leningrad democratic movement, decided to stand for the newly created Russian Congress of People's Deputies, representing the Sestroretsk–Zelenogorsk constituency.* Putin introduced himself and offered to act as her chauffeur during her campaign. According to her parliamentary assistant, Ruslan Linkov, for ten days in late May or early June, at about the same time that he was introduced to Sobchak, he drove her to campaign meetings.[55]

Starovoitova was elected on June 14 and soon afterwards moved to Moscow as an adviser to Boris Yeltsin, who, following his election that month as Chairman of the Russian Congress, was becoming a serious rival to Gorbachev.[56]

Putin did not finally commit to working for Sobchak until October, when it became clear that the Lensoviet Chairman had weathered the storm.[57] Dmitry Medvedev, another of Sobchak's former students, who was serving as a part-time adviser dealing with legal affairs and relations with the Lensoviet deputies, remembered Sobchak introducing them.

* The Soviet Congress of People's Deputies, which began meeting in 1989, included deputies from Russia and the 14 other Union Republics – Armenia, Azerbaijan, Belarus, the three Baltic republics Georgia, Moldova, the five Central Asian republics and Ukraine. The Russian Congress of People's Deputies was a separate body, formed a year later and composed of deputies only from Russia itself.

Putin, Sobchak told him, was older than the rest of them so he would be the senior assistant.[58] That made sense to Medvedev but it raised the prospect of conflict with Shutov, who was six years older than Putin and had started working with Sobchak nine months earlier.

It was not long in coming to a head.

By the middle of November, Putin had convinced Sobchak that Shutov should go. Exactly what arguments he used to undermine his rival, even Valery Pavlov did not know. 'I found Shutov a very strong, very bright person,' Pavlov recalled. 'He was very well prepared, good on questions of economic law, and of course literary matters . . . I respected both of them as people, as strong characters. When Putin first appeared, they had completely normal relations. But later on something happened between them. And Shutov walked away.'[59]

Sobchak claimed afterwards that Shutov had persuaded him to sign an agreement with a British businessman named Sherman Shah, who had made extravagant promises about developing Leningrad's foreign trade.[60] The arrangement prompted accusations that he was selling off the city's wealth to foreigners.[61] When the deal fell through, Sobchak said, he held Shutov responsible and fired him.[62]

With Pavlov, Putin adopted a different approach. Gradually he was marginalised.

To outward appearances, Putin was a minion who carried Sobchak's briefcase and remained discreetly in his shadow, never putting himself forward.[63] But, behind the scenes, Pavlov said, 'he took over personnel matters, issues relating to production, the reception and despatch of documents. It became like a puppet theatre.'[64]

Over time, that would indeed happen, but it did not occur all at once. At the end of 1990 and in the first half of 1991, Putin was still feeling his way.

Nevertheless, before the year was up, Pavlov already found Putin's methods sufficiently different from his own that he decided that he could not work with him any longer.[65] 'I didn't want – in fact I refused – to work in the system which Putin had set up. In terms of humanitarian ideas, ideas of justice, how to build up society and the state, my way was closer to Sobchak's ideas. But my system was weaker, it didn't have any people with epaulettes, there weren't any armed men . . . I was someone who could empathise, who could be close to people. Putin was the opposite. We had different paths.'[66]

Years later, Putin revealed his own feelings about Pavlov and Shutov. Sobchak had told him, he claimed, that when they were working for him, 'I was afraid to go out into the reception room. I didn't know who those people were'. Those two were 'harsh and rude,' Putin said, 'in the best traditions of the Komsomol and the Soviet school'.[67] It was a mind-boggling accusation. Pavlov had known Sobchak for years and remained one of his closest friends right up to his death. An accomplished musician who later became the director of the St Petersburg Capella, it would be hard to think of anyone to whom the words, 'harsh and rude' would less apply.[68] Even Shutov, although Sobchak came to hate him, was a cultivated man. That Putin, a decade later, would put into Sobchak's mouth words that he could not possibly have said in order to smear his one-time rivals was striking evidence of the animus he had borne against them at the time.

The only person he seems to have trusted completely was Dmitry Medvedev, with whom for the first few months he shared a desk in Sobchak's reception room at the Mariinsky Palace.[69] But Medvedev was only 25 years old, 13 years Putin's junior, and it may have done no harm that he was several inches shorter. Putin had been conscious of his slight build ever since he was a child – even in the KGB, he had been nicknamed 'Moth' – and he was often ill at ease with men who towered over him.

Putin's actions after joining Sobchak gave the lie to the claims of his colleagues in Dresden that he had 'absolutely no ambition'. On the contrary, they demonstrated a ruthless will to prevail, patient and well hidden, coupled with profound mistrust of the motives of those around him.

Putin's formal title was Adviser on International Relations. His job was to promote Sobchak's plans to build up Leningrad's links with the outside world and, in so doing, to affirm Leningrad's independence from its eternal rival, Moscow.

The city on the Neva – Northern Palmyra, as its inhabitants called it, after the great cultural centre of the ancient world in Syria – still saw itself as Russia's northern capital, as it had been before 1917. Anatoly Chubais, the young economist who had listened in disbelief to Sobchak's tirade against the KGB, was charged with drawing up a plan to establish a Free Enterprise Zone to promote foreign trade, similar to the special economic zones in China.[70] Under pressure from Moscow, it was shelved. But the Tallinn Process continued. At the end of September, Sobchak signed a cooperation agreement with the Estonian Prime Minister, Edgar Savisaar, and suggested that Leningrad and the surrounding region should be treated, for all practical purposes, as one of the Baltic republics.[71]

It soon became clear, however, that the two sides had very different goals. Sobchak might sympathise with the Balts' desire for sovereignty and the right to run their own affairs, but he rejected their demands for independence. The links between Leningrad and Estonia were historical and psychological as well as political and economic. At the beginning of the twentieth century, St Petersburg, as it was then, had had a larger Estonian population than Tallinn. Leningraders went for holidays on the Estonian coast and many had dachas there, especially in the northeast, around the ancient border fortress of Narva, where there had been massive Russian immigration after the Second World War. For Russians, the idea of a physical border at Narva was unimaginable. For Estonians, it was essential if sovereignty were to be restored.

As if that were not enough, there was a territorial dispute. After the war, some 750 square miles of Estonian borderlands had been transferred to Russia.[72] Estonian nationalists wanted them back. During the night of September 2, 1990, a commando group from the Estonian Defence League re-erected a number of border posts along the old frontier at the village of Komarovka, in Russian territory five miles east of Narva. Savisaar's government condemned the incident and tried to smooth things over. But the border issue remained 'a red rag to a bull'.[73] Although agreement was reached in October to establish what was termed an 'economic border' to prevent smuggling, the Russians adamantly rejected any suggestion of a political frontier.[74]

The incident made Putin realise for the first time that Moscow might have to relinquish control not only over Central and Eastern Europe, which were already to all intents and purposes lost, but over parts of Soviet territory as well – and not just any part, but Estonia, where his father had fought during the war. Mart Laar, one of Savisaar's successors, found that, when he met Putin in Moscow a dozen years later, the memory of the border incursion at Komarovka still rankled.[75] Estonia was part of the Soviet Union, Putin told a Western diplomat that winter. None of the Baltic republics should be thinking of leaving.[76]

For months, the Soviet Union had been threatening to break apart. But it was one thing to read about agitation far away in the Caucasus, quite another for Putin to find that it was happening on his own doorstep.

In the event, the tipping point came not in Estonia but in Lithuania, the southernmost Baltic republic, which Gorbachev had been pressuring to rescind what he called 'unconstitutional acts', meaning moves towards independence. After the Lithuanians refused to back down, in the early hours of Sunday, January 13, 1991, Soviet special forces stormed the television tower in the capital, Vilnius, scattering crowds of demonstrators who had gathered to defend it, killing 14 and wounding 160.[77]

The bloodshed provoked a crisis. Yeltsin flew to Tallinn, where, in the parliament building, ringed with barricades and defended by volunteers armed with shotguns and hunting rifles, he issued a joint statement with the Presidents of Estonia, Lithuania and Latvia, 'resolutely condemning acts of armed violence against the independence of the Baltic States'. Leningrad, but not Moscow, television broadcast film of the attack, showing black-uniformed officers from the Soviet Interior Ministry bludgeoning demonstrators with rifle butts.

Gorbachev waffled, claiming that what had happened was not his doing and that the military had staged a provocation to discredit him. No one in the Baltic republics, or in Leningrad, believed him. The Lensoviet met in emergency session to pass resolutions condemning his actions and, the following Sunday, thousands gathered for a protest demonstration on the square in front of the Winter Palace.[78]

Gorbachev's popularity had been waning ever since *perestroika* began. The more he was lionised abroad, the more he was detested at home. The previous twelve months had been his *annus horribilis*, the year when everything started to go wrong. On May Day, 1990, he had been booed by demonstrators in Red Square. In July, Yeltsin had resigned spectacularly from the Communist Party. Sobchak and the Chairman of the Moscow City Council, Gavriil Popov, had followed suit. During the autumn, Gorbachev embraced and then abandoned an ambitious programme of market reform, the so-called '500 Days' project. Finally, in December, his close ally, the Foreign Minister, Eduard Shevardnadze, announced that he, too, was resigning, warning melodramatically: 'A dictatorship is coming . . . No one knows what kind of dictatorship or who will be the dictator. [But] let this be my protest.'[79]

Until the Vilnius incident, Gorbachev had managed to hold off what was termed the 'Prague scenario', whereby agitation for freedom would be crushed by Soviet tanks. That was what had happened in Czechoslovakia in 1968 and it was what the hardliners in the Politburo and the military wanted.[80]

After January 1991, Putin concluded that Gorbachev was 'politically exhausted'.[81] Two months later, Yeltsin engineered a constitutional change enabling him to be elected Russia's President by popular vote, giving him a legitimacy which Gorbachev did not have. Shortly afterwards the Soviet leader made another fateful concession: the USSR would be replaced by a new, voluntary 'Union of Sovereign States', comprising Azerbaijan, Belarus, Russia, Ukraine and the five Central Asian republics.[82] The Baltic republics, Armenia, Georgia and Moldova refused to take part, but Gorbachev had recognised by then that they were going to become independent anyway and there was nothing he could do to stop them. Although no one would yet say so publicly, the Soviet Union's future was already hanging by a thread.

In Leningrad, even after the truce between Sobchak and Shchelkanov, the conflicts within the Lensoviet between the democratic majority and the communist minority and between the Lensoviet and the Ispolkom continued to make it almost impossible to administer the city rationally.

Sobchak sent Putin to negotiate on his behalf. It was the first time he had been given such a mission and he evidently acquitted himself well, holding meetings one on one with the deputies, winning the support of the heads of the district administrations and playing what one leading democrat, Dmitry Lenkov, described as 'a rather positive role'. Boris Vishnevsky, another prominent liberal, who would later become one of Putin's most vocal critics, remembered that 'he was polite, almost never raised his voice, and was always respectful to his interlocutor . . . He never set up anyone, even when it was detrimental to his own interests.'[83] By the spring of 1991, Putin had persuaded a majority of the deputies to accept Sobchak's key demand, which was that the city should have a mayor, elected by popular vote, who would head what would in effect be the City government. Moscow, which was facing the same kinds of problems, adopted a similar system. Elections would take place in both cities on June 12, the same day as for the Russian President.

Sobchak was so confident that he would win that he left Leningrad and, accompanied by Putin, spent a week campaigning for Yeltsin in the Stavropol region in southern Russia, where he had worked as a lawyer in the 1960s.[84] When the results came in, Sobchak had 66 per cent of the vote; in Moscow, Gavriil Popov was elected Mayor with 65 per cent; and Yeltsin won the presidency with 58 per cent.

Leningrad voters had to decide a second, much more contentious issue: whether the city should return to its pre-revolutionary name, St Petersburg. Sobchak had initially opposed the idea, as had Gorbachev, on the grounds that Leningrad was associated so closely with the heroism and tragedy of the war. Many veterans and their families, Putin among them, felt that changing the city's name would dishonour the 750,000 men, women and children who had died, as well as the survivors. There were demonstrations and counter-demonstrations. The exiled writer, Aleksandr Solzhenitsyn, proposed, not very helpfully, Holy Petrograd as an alternative. In the end, nearly 55 per cent voted for St Petersburg, and 42 per cent against. By then Sobchak had changed his mind and, when the result was announced, sought the credit for the decision.[85]

As was his wont, the moment the voting was over, the lure of foreign travel beckoned. Hoping to leave politics behind him for a few weeks, Sobchak set off for France and Germany, to make a speech at the French National Assembly and hold meetings with the Mayor of Paris, Jacques Chirac, and officials in Hamburg.

That turned out to be a mistake.

Sobchak had expected the Lensoviet to elect a Presidium which would serve as an advisory body, while the full Council would meet only once a year to approve the city's budget. He did not plan 'to share [his] power with anyone,' he said.[86] In his absence, however, the deputies persuaded the Russian Supreme Soviet to impose substantial new restrictions on his authority. Sobchak could organise the City Administration as he saw fit but he would have no control over the Lensoviet.[87] It was a compromise which satisfied no one.

Gorbachev had mixed feelings, too. Yeltsin's election victory in June had strengthened the position of his principal opponent. On the other hand, the path now seemed clear to a new Union Treaty, which would preserve the essence of the Soviet Union, albeit in diminished form. A draft of the treaty was approved on July 23, and Gorbachev and the leaders of the nine participating Union Republics agreed to hold a signing ceremony in the Kremlin on August 20.

There were hiccoughs along the way. Gorbachev's new Prime Minister, Valentin Pavlov, who had been appointed in January, asked the Supreme Soviet to approve the transfer of a wide range of presidential powers to the government on the grounds that Gorbachev was overworked. The three *siloviki*, the so-called 'power ministers' – Marshal Dmitry Yazov, at Defence; Boris Pugo, at Interior; and Vladimir Kryuchkov, the KGB Chairman – issued dark warnings that the United States was trying to undermine the Soviet state and that Gorbachev was not taking the threat seriously enough. Pavlov's proposal was resoundingly squashed a few days later, but not before the new Mayor of Moscow, Gavriil Popov, had informed the American Ambassador, Jack Matlock, that a coup was being prepared. The organisers, Popov said, were Pavlov, Kryuchkov, Yazov and the Supreme Soviet Chairman, Anatoly Lukyanov. On instructions from President George H. W. Bush, who was to visit Moscow the following month, Matlock sought an urgent meeting with Gorbachev to convey Washington's concern. The Soviet leader had burst out laughing, Matlock remembered. He appreciated Bush's warning, he said. 'But tell him not to worry. I have everything well in hand.' There might be a few hotheads in parliament, gossiping about a coup, but it was '100 percent unlikely'.[88]

Six weeks later, Bush's visit went off without a hitch. Even Popov began to wonder whether the coup rumours had been false.[89] Shortly afterwards, Gorbachev left for his villa at Foros, in Crimea, for two weeks' holiday, convinced that all was well.

In the early hours of Monday morning, August 19, Sobchak was awakened by a telephone call. He had arrived in Moscow the previous evening after spending the weekend in Lithuania, where he had signed an economic agreement between Leningrad and Vilnius. The caller was a journalist, who said he had just heard that the leadership in Kazakhstan, which was three hours ahead of Moscow, had been told that a state of emergency was about to be declared. Gorbachev was being relieved of his duties for health reasons, and a 'State Committee for the Emergency Situation' was assuming full powers.[90]

Confirmation was not long in coming. The radio was broadcasting the music of Swan Lake – a sure sign that something was wrong – and at 6 a.m., an announcer read out the State Committee's decree. It was signed by Gennady Yanayev, whom Gorbachev had appointed Vice President after Shevardnadze's resignation; the Prime Minister, Valentin Pavlov; and Oleg Baklanov, the Politburo member responsible for the defence industry. The remaining members were Boris Pugo and the three others Popov had named – Yazov, Kryuchkov and Lukyanov. The last two, it emerged later, were the prime movers of the putsch.

Sobchak summoned his bodyguard and driver and headed out to Yeltsin's dacha, at Arkhangelskoe, 12 miles west of Moscow, where he found the entire Russian cabinet had assembled, guarded by half a dozen men with automatic weapons. When he saw them, Sobchak gulped. If the putschists had been better organised, he thought, they could have taken out the whole of the opposition at a stroke. But they made no attempt to do so. Nor did the column of tanks, chewing up the tarmac on the Moscow ring road, try to stop Yeltsin's presidential convoy, when he drove later that morning to the House of Soviets, the seat of the Russian government, dubbed the 'White House', because of its white marble façade.

The telephone lines to Gorbachev's villa in Foros had been cut and he had been reduced to listening to the BBC World Service on an old-fashioned, short-wave radio to get news of what was happening. But international lines worked more or less normally as did inter-city communications. The lines to the White House and other government buildings also continued to function. Sobchak thought afterwards that the coup plotters had assumed that the population would accept Gorbachev's removal without question and that there would be no more than token opposition.

While Yeltsin set about organising the resistance in Moscow, famously climbing onto a tank in front of the White House and denouncing the putsch as 'a right-wing, reactionary, anti-constitutional coup', Sobchak took the first flight back to Leningrad, where he arrived in the middle of the afternoon.[91]

The Commander of the Leningrad Military District, General Samsonov, had received a phone call from Marshal Yazov at 4 a.m., instructing him to place the city under martial law.[92] After ordering his subordinates at Pskov, 200 miles to the south, to send 1,200 soldiers to Leningrad as reinforcements, he co-opted the regional KGB Chief, Anatoly Kurkov; the head of the Leningrad Communist Party Committee, Boris Gidaspov; Vice Admiral Viktor Khramtsov, representing the Lensoviet; and the generals commanding the region's Interior Ministry troops and Border Guards, to constitute the Leningrad branch of the State Emergency Committee. For good measure Samsonov added the names of Sobchak's deputy, Vice Admiral Shcherbakov and the Chairman of the Leningrad Region Soviet, Yury Yarov, neither of whom he was able to reach, on the assumption that they would have no objection.

At 10 a.m., Samsonov read out a statement on Leningrad television, warning that 'rampant crime and political speculation linked to the proposed Union Treaty posed a threat to the very existence of the Soviet state' and that the State Committee was acting to guarantee the security of the population.

It was the holiday season and many officials were away. Aleksandr Belyaev, Sobchak's successor as Chairman of the Lensoviet, heard the news on his car radio on the way to his dacha. He drove immediately to the Mariinsky Palace to summon all the deputies he could find to meet in emergency session. When it opened, Vice Admiral Khramtsov demanded the floor to make a statement on behalf of the Committee. He did not get very far. According to the verbatim record:

VITALY SKOIBEDA [a democrat]: I think it is high time to stop the statement by the illegal representative of the illegal committee. (*Applause*)

FROM THE FLOOR: Damn right!

SKOIBEDA: I declare that you be detained forthwith on the basis of your special dispositions!

Noise in the hall. A fight breaks out. Khramtsov is punched in the face. Skoibeda is pulled away . . .

BELYAEV: Comrades, I beg you, be calm! . . .

KHRAMTSOV [with a swelling bruise]: I was just trying to inform you . . . so that you understand the situation![93]

Such was the atmosphere when Sobchak returned. The democrats were seething, the communists unable to contain their delight.

By then Shcherbakov and Yarov were both back and had formally dissociated themselves from the Committee. The only person missing was Putin. He had left with his family the previous week to spend the holidays at a guest house on the Curonian Spit, a narrow tongue of sand dunes, bounded on both sides by the sea, which stretches for 60 miles from Kaliningrad to the Lithuanian coast. Their Volga had broken down on the way and they had had to go back to Leningrad to borrow another car from a friend. The announcement that Gorbachev had been deposed was broadcast the morning after they arrived.

Putin acknowledged later that 'when the putsch began, I had very complicated feelings. Very difficult!'[94] On the one hand, like many Russians, he was deeply dismayed by the thought that the Soviet Union might break apart and the State Committee seemed determined to stop that. On the other, he recognised that trying to turn the clock back would solve nothing and in any case was impossible. That afternoon, he drove to Vilnius, still uncertain what he should do. Only when Yanayev, flanked by the other members of the State Committee, gave a brief, televised news conference and the camera showed his hands shaking uncontrollably, did he realise that the putsch was doomed.[95] Later that evening he was able to reach Sobchak by phone and the following morning got a flight back via Moscow.[96]

Afterwards, it was claimed that Putin had organised bodyguards to go to the airport to protect Sobchak from possible arrest on the Mayor's return the previous day. That was another myth. For the first 36 hours, when the key decisions were taken, Putin had been, as he said himself, 'in the sticks', completely out of the loop.[97] A special forces unit had indeed been sent to escort the Mayor into the city, but it had been dispatched by Arkady Kramarev, the Chief of Police, who from the outset had opposed the putsch.[98] Sobchak had telephoned him to request that Interior Ministry troops guard the Leningrad television station, and Kramarev had decided off his own bat to make sure that he got back safely. Putin was not involved.

When Sobchak returned, he went directly to the Military District Headquarters to confront Samsonov, who was in conference with the other members of the Emergency Committee. 'I launched into a speech before they could get their mouths open,' he wrote later. 'I admonished them . . . Then I appealed to Samsonov: 'What are you doing getting mixed up with this bunch, this illegitimate gang?'[99] Decades later, his account comes across as theatrical. But it was genuinely a moment of high drama. Kramarev said afterwards that '[Sobchak] spoke to the general in a tone that no one had used to him before for many, many years. Samsonov did not know what to do.'[100]

That evening Sobchak reported to the Lensoviet:

> I reminded them of the decision of the Nuremberg tribunal, which judged the fascist criminals. It condemned not only those who issued the [criminal] laws, but also those who carried them out. That is why those who say that it is legitimate to carry out the orders of those who have usurped power are themselves criminally responsible. They cannot now try to repeat what happened in a different era when Khrushchev was removed from power.[101]

In the end, Samsonov agreed not to bring troops into the city. The detachments from Pskov, which were already on their way, were halted at Gatchina, 30 miles to the south.[102] Sobchak was not solely responsible for changing the general's mind. Vice Admiral Shcherbakov, as a fellow officer, influenced him as well.[103] The memory of the events at Tbilisi, two years earlier, also gave him pause.[104] On that occasion, Sobchak reminded him, Samsonov's refusal to associate himself with his superior's decision to send soldiers against the unarmed crowd had absolved him of responsibility for the bloodshed which followed.

Afterwards Sobchak went to the Mariinsky Palace, where he climbed onto the sill of one of the 12-foot-high ground-floor windows and read out to the crowd a decree from Yeltsin, branding the putschists state criminals, and warning that any official who carried out their orders would be subject to the full force of the law.[105]

In Moscow, the media were under the control of the Emergency Committee and subject to strict military censorship. But in Leningrad, Sobchak, Shcherbakov and Belyaev, together with Yury Yarov, were able to browbeat the manager of the local television station, Boris Petrov, not only into allowing them to broadcast but to have the programme transmitted by satellite, which meant that it could be viewed all over Russia. As Kramarev noted wryly, the fact that the station was surrounded by 60 men from the OMON special forces in full combat gear might have helped to persuade Petrov to cooperate. During the hour-long broadcast, Shcherbakov, speaking as a flag officer, urged the men of the Leningrad garrison not to allow themselves 'to be dragged into a fratricidal war'. Sobchak, wearing his law professor's hat, referred to

the putchists as 'former' officials, as if they were already on trial. Kryuchkov was furious and personally telephoned to demand that the
broadcast be stopped. The staff told him that, unfortunately, for technical reasons, that was not possible.[106]

Later that evening, Shcherbakov went to tell Samsonov that a mass
rally would be held next morning in the square in front of the Winter
Palace, which was also where the Military District Headquarters was
located.[107] Samsonov, who was still fuming after his confrontation with
Sobchak, warned that he had orders to open fire in the event of an
illegal gathering and that he would carry them out. Shcherbakov
observed that, if he did so, it would lead to a bloodbath far worse than
anything which had happened in Tbilisi.[108] Eventually a risible compromise
ise was reached: the pavement outside the Military Headquarters
would be treated as a restricted zone and anyone who dared to stand
on it would be shot. Otherwise the troops would hold their fire.

The agreement held. The following day, Tuesday, August 20, tens of
thousands of people gathered to hear speeches by Sobchak; Marina
Salye, the 'Pasionara' of the Left; Aleksandr Belyaev and Yury Yarov,
the chairmen of the City and Regional soviets; Yury Boldyrev and other
members of the Soviet Congress of People's Deputies; as well as intellectuals and church leaders – all proclaiming their defiance of the State
Emergency Committee's usurpation of power. An American businessman, travelling from Moscow to Helsinki in a small plane which flew
over Leningrad, remembered looking down to see the entire square
black with people, and marvelled at such numbers 'rallying on behalf
of freedom, of a better way of governing'.[109]

The next 12 hours were critical.

Putin got back that afternoon. Yuly Rybakov, a former dissident who
had become a leading democrat, remembered seeing him in the evening carrying a pistol, with a dozen armed guards, next door to Sobchak's
office:

Many of the deputies were also armed, with hunting rifles or shotguns
or whatever they could find, and people outside in the crowd also had
weapons . . . This was the time when we were expecting an assault. The
deputies were meeting almost continuously. During a break in the session, we received a telephone call from the White House in Moscow,
saying that there were tanks outside and an attack was imminent. The

last thing we heard him say was, 'Farewell!' . . . and then the line went
dead.[110]

At around midnight, the KGB chief, Anatoly Kurkov, arrived. Kurkov
had been named a member of Samsonov's Emergency Committee,
but he was against the putsch and thought the State Committee had
acted illegally. Belyaev saw him standing outside Sobchak's office
engaged in a long conversation with Putin. Afterwards it became
known that he had come to assure Sobchak that, in Leningrad at least,
the KGB would not intervene on the putschists' behalf.[111]

Then reports started coming in that a *spetsnaz* group from the army,
the equivalent of the US Delta Force or the British SAS, was on its way
to storm the building. Two independent radio stations, Radio Baltika
and Radio Open City, which had managed to stay on the air, broadcast
an appeal from Belyaev to the city's population to come to defend the
Lensoviet. Outside, crowds began erecting makeshift barricades. Three
hundred *afgantsy* – tough veterans of the war in Afghanistan, many of
them linked to organised crime – arrived to reinforce the police guarding
the building and Kramarev sent a group from OMON to protect Sobchak's and Belyaev's offices in case the outer defences were breached.

Sobchak and Shcherbakov agreed to split up and reconvene the Lensoviet at a site on Vasilevsky Island if the Mariinsky Palace was occupied.
Sobchak went with Putin to the Kirov machine-building plant, in the
south of the city, where they spent the rest of the night in a bunker.[112]

At 3.30 a.m. on Wednesday, August 21, Belyaev went out onto the
balcony of the Palace and told the crowd that he had received a message from Moscow that the troops which had been sent to storm the
White House had been ordered to stand down. At the Kronstadt Naval
Base, the commander of the Baltic Sea Fleet announced that he
opposed the coup. The Chairman of the KGB of the Russian Federation ordered regional KGB directorates to resist.

Although uncertainty continued until late in the afternoon, the
putsch was all but over.

It had not been entirely bloodless. In Moscow, on Tuesday night, three
young men had been shot and crushed under the treads of an advancing
tank. But they were the only victims. In Leningrad, no one died.

On Wednesday evening, Gorbachev was released from house arrest
at Foros and flown back to Moscow. Politically his career was over. By

trying to placate hardliners and liberals, conservatives and democrats, he had discredited himself in the eyes of both sides.

The Union Treaty was dead. After the putsch, Yeltsin saw no need for it. What mattered were the rights of the republics: the less power for the federal centre, the better. In the long battle with Yeltsin for pre-eminence, Gorbachev had lost. 'A tsar must conduct himself like a tsar,' he reflected bitterly afterwards. 'And that, I do not know how to do.'[113]

The Soviet Communist Party was dead, too. After Yeltsin suspended its activities in Russia, Gorbachev resigned as General Secretary, called for the Party's dissolution and decreed that all its property be placed under the control of city councils and republican parliaments.

The KGB survived, but for a time was severely weakened. On Thursday night, the 20-foot-high bronze statue of Feliks Dzerzhinsky, the founder of the Cheka, which stood in front of the Lubyanka, was toppled from its pedestal and taken away on a flat-bed truck. The KGB Chairman, Vladimir Kryuchkov, and six other members of the Emergency Committee were arrested. The eighth member, Boris Pugo, the Interior Minister, committed suicide.

Sobchak emerged from the crisis with his reputation enhanced. His denunciation of the plotters on television on the first day of the putsch had catapulted him back to national prominence. Aleksandr Yakovlev, the theorist of *perestroika*, thought he was now the most important Soviet politician after Gorbachev and Yeltsin.[114] Rodric Braithwaite, the British Ambassador, saw him as a possible successor to Gorbachev if the Union survived.[115]

Putin, as always, remained discreetly in the background. In these momentous days, which would soon bring seventy years of Soviet history to an ignominious end, his role had been negligible. Sobchak, in a lengthy account of the putsch, spread over two full pages of the newspaper, *Moskovskie novosti*, did not mention Putin's name once.[116]

But the year had not been wasted for him. Sobchak's daughter, Kseniya, and the Putins' children played together and the two families had become close. During the summer they went on holiday together to Turku in Finland, which was twinned with Leningrad, and went fishing in the archipelago with Juhani Leppä, the city's Mayor.[117] Putin might still be a neophyte, but he had won Sobchak's trust.

*

The political crisis in August briefly diverted attention from the economic crisis which had Russia by the throat and, equally briefly, made
City Hall and the Lensoviet bury their differences as they faced a common enemy in the shape of the State Emergency Committee. As soon
as the putsch was over, they both came roaring back.

The economic crisis came first. In the 18 months since Putin
had returned from Dresden, the decline in Soviet production had
accelerated.[118] Rationing of most basic foodstuffs had been imposed,
supposedly on a temporary basis, the previous winter, and had not
been lifted.[119] In September 1991, Sobchak and Belyaev wrote to Jacques
Delors, the President of the European Commission, expressing
'extreme concern' about food supplies. The Soviet distribution system
was broken, they told him, and since the Baltic States had declared full
independence in August, the Tallinn Process had stalled. St Petersburg,
as the city was once again called – the name change having taken effect
on September 6 – urgently needed 20,000 tons of butter and 50,000
tons of meat in humanitarian aid.[120]

Sobchak was mortified at having to make such a request – a feeling
shared by much of the city's population: an opinion poll found that
nearly half thought that asking for help from foreigners was humiliating.[121] But he had little choice. In November he called in the city's small
diplomatic corps for what the British Consul General, Barbara Hay,
called 'a begging bowl meeting'.[122] That month, even bread and potatoes, the ultimate staples in the Russian diet, were in short supply, and
there were long queues outside the few bakeries that were open. 'The
food situation is reaching breaking point,' the French Consul reported.
On November 10, the city had less than three days' supply of meat on
the basis of 1.5 kgs (3.3 lbs) per month per inhabitant. The ration of ten
eggs per person per month was cut to eight. Old people muttered
darkly about a repetition of the blockade winter of 1941. Businessmen
warned of 'a danger zone of potential social explosions where anything could happen'.[123]

Sobchak travelled to Britain, France, Germany and Spain to press
the city's case for help. Putin went with him. That summer, Sobchak
had named him Chairman of the city's Foreign Relations Committee,
responsible for visits by foreign dignitaries, relations with the diplomatic corps and joint ventures with foreign companies. Eventually a
trickle of foreign food aid did start arriving. But it was neither in the

quantities nor of the quality that the Russians had hoped for, and, to rub salt in the wound, the donors went to embarrassing lengths to vaunt their often parsimonious contributions. The French insisted that the medical supplies that they sent to St Petersburg be stamped with the French flag, and the words, 'French humanitarian aid', in Russian. 'This will make the French action particularly visible to the popula-tion,' the Foreign Ministry wrote.[124] When the Americans flew in food, mainly military rations from US bases in Germany, it was brought in by a convoy of Soviet army lorries which drove through the city centre, led by the US Consul General, Jack Gosnell, in a car flying the American flag.[125] When Britain sent livestock feed, a British minister demanded to be present when it was unloaded.[126]

It was not an edifying spectacle. 'The Western countries talk a lot more than they actually do in practice,' Sobchak said glumly. There were unfounded reports that Britain was trying to palm off on Russia unsaleable meat, infected with BSE, popularly known as Mad Cow Disease, and that Germany was sending food which was close to its expiry date. St Petersburg newspaper commentary was uniformly negative.[127]

The situation was made worse when Yeltsin and his Finance Minis-ter, Yegor Gaidar, decided that, with a few exceptions such as bread and fuel oil, price controls would be lifted in the New Year as part of what would later be known as 'shock therapy'. It was an attempt to do in weeks what Gorbachev had failed to do in years – to transform the Soviet planned economy into a free-market system, an endeavour which the American Ambassador, Jack Matlock, described as 'like try-ing to convert a submarine into an airplane while keeping it functioning with the same crew throughout'.[128]

As soon as the decision became known, supplies of almost every-thing dried up completely. What farm or factory in its right mind would send goods to the shops when, by waiting a few weeks longer, it could sell them for ten times more?

In this grim situation, Sobchak asked Putin in December 1991 to organise what amounted to an elaborate barter deal, whereby raw materials, including oil, timber and precious metals, would be exported to Western Europe and the proceeds used to purchase food for the population.

Barter trade had helped keep the wheels of the Soviet economy

turning for decades. In theory, the central planners took care of everything. In practice, there were always holes in the supply chain. All large
state enterprises employed fixers, known as *tolkachi*, literally 'pushers',
to barter excess production for raw materials which the planners had
failed to allocate. Never having known any other method, officials at
the St Petersburg City Hall had started earlier that year trying to use
the same approach with potential foreign partners. The first attempts
had been made by Georgy Khizha, the President of the St Petersburg
Association of Industrial Enterprises, which represented the military–
industrial complex in the city. A so-called 'Red director', who had been
appointed by the Soviet state, Khizha was intelligent, competent, wore
well-tailored suits and could have been mistaken for the CEO of a
Western company. But he had absolutely no idea how business was
conducted outside Russia. One of his proposals was for the Association
to send crude oil, or alternatively wood or copper, to Le Havre, in
return for machinery for making sausages and potato chips. Another
envisaged granting the French car makers, Renault and Citroën, free
sites for dealerships in the city centre in exchange for second-hand cars.
Yet another plan was to persuade a foreign company to build a brick
factory, to be paid for by ceding a lease on one of the city's hotels.[129]
Not surprisingly, none of these schemes came to fruition.

Putin's mission was more ambitious and potentially more realistic.
Instead of a direct barter arrangement, intermediaries would be used.
In normal times, that would have been impossible. Foreign trade was
the prerogative of the Soviet government in Moscow. But these were
not normal times. The Soviet Union was falling apart. The Baltic
States, Armenia, Georgia and Moldova had already left. On December 1,
Ukrainians voted for independence, effectively sounding the death
knell of the Union State. A week later, Yeltsin and the leaders of Belarus and Ukraine met at a hunting lodge in the Belovezha Forest, near
the Belarusian–Polish border, to sign an agreement creating the Commonwealth of Independent States, a voluntary association which
would eventually bring together most, though not all, of the former
Soviet republics. It was tantamount to a declaration that the USSR
had ceased to exist. For Yeltsin, it was a godsend: if the Soviet Union
was no more, his rival would no longer have a country to preside over
and his career would come to an end. Gorbachev bowed to the reality
on December 25 and announced his resignation as Soviet President.

The Hammer and Sickle flag flying over the Kremlin was lowered for the last time and the Russian tricolour raised in its place.

In these circumstances, the usual rules no longer applied. The Ministry of Foreign Economic Relations told Putin to go ahead on his own, which he did.

The trouble was that very little of the promised food imports ever materialised.

The licensing agreements between the Foreign Relations Committee (FRC) and the intermediary import–export companies, signed by Putin or his deputy, Aleksandr Anikin, were worth altogether 122 million US dollars.[130] The question that was raised when the food did not arrive, and which has been constantly raised ever since, was, what happened to the money?

It is worth examining the charges in detail, for it was later widely believed, both in Russia and in the West, that the episode very nearly brought Putin's career to an early end.

The agreements provided for the export of 1,000 tons of aluminium and the same amount of copper, 20,000 tons of cement, 120,000 tons of cotton, 150,000 tons of fuel oil, 30,000 tons of scrap metal, 750,000 cubic metres of timber and 14 tons of precious metals, in return for sugar, meat, cooking oil, potatoes, fresh fruit, cocoa, dried milk, baby food and livestock feed. All the contracts were riddled with drafting errors and violated multiple government decrees. The intermediaries were allowed to take an exceptionally generous commission of between 25 and 50 per cent of profits from the export sales. Eight of the thirteen agreements failed to stipulate penalties if the intermediaries reneged on their undertakings to use the money to import food. The companies chosen had no experience and at least some had privileged ties with Putin himself or other City Hall officials. In many cases, they paid rock-bottom prices in Russia for goods which they could sell in the West for tens or even hundreds of times more. One firm, Dzhikop, which was partly owned by the brother of Ilham Ragimov, Putin's former classmate at university, had contracted to buy the transitional metal, niobium, for seven times less than the world market price, yttrium for 20 times less, and scandium for nearly 2,000 times less.[131]

To Sobchak's opponents, the whole arrangement stank.

It looked as though Putin had farmed out lucrative contracts to his friends, who cynically broke their promises to bring back food to a hungry city and then pocketed the money. The assumption was that he and Anikin must have been rewarded with generous kickbacks.[132]

But appearances can be misleading.

It was true that the agreements were drafted so sloppily that a high-school student could have done better, and Anikin was eventually fired for having approved them.[133] But no one in St Petersburg had ever written a foreign trade contract before.[134] For the City Administration, it was unknown territory, as was shown by the earlier failure of even as savvy a businessman as Georgy Khizha to set up successful barter deals.[135] To complicate matters further, there was no established legal framework. That winter, as the Soviet Union collapsed and the new state of Russia emerged from the wreckage, no one knew for certain which laws applied.[136] Russian laws, when they existed, and Soviet laws, when they were still in force, were frequently in conflict. Officials made it up as they went along.

Moreover, Putin's FRC was not party to the export agreements. It issued licences on the basis of quotas, which had been approved beforehand in Moscow by Pyotr Aven, the Minister of Foreign Economic Relations; Yegor Gaidar, the Finance Minister; and Andrei Nechayev, the first deputy Minister for the Economy.[137] Large state companies were wary of engaging directly in transactions for which the legal basis was unclear, so Putin turned to friends, or friends of friends, to set up intermediary companies which could get the contracts fulfilled. That was how things worked in Russia at that time: informal networks were often the only way to get anything done, especially when, as in this case, official channels did not yet exist.[138]

In most countries, if a company registered precious metals for export at a tiny fraction of their world market price, it would send up multiple red flags. But Russia in 1992 was not like other countries. Since Soviet times, rare metals had been allocated by central planners, not traded. As there was no domestic market, there was no fixed domestic price. Andrei Illarionov, who later became Putin's economic adviser, has argued that the very concept of price was alien to Soviet economists: the state plan was based on 'material balances' in which price played no part.[139]

In any case, enterprises, like individuals, were so desperate for money during that winter that they were prepared to sell anything for whatever they could get. At a time when between 50 and 80 per cent of the population was living below the poverty line, and factories had stopped paying wages, any deal was better than nothing. Russian *babushki*, the eternal grandmothers who held families together, stood outside metro stations trying to sell bunches of violets or a few poor vegetables. Old men hawked family heirlooms or anything else that might bring in money.[140] A young Western banker was invited to a meeting with a man from the military–industrial complex, who pulled out a piece of paper covered with chemical formulae and said, 'I'm sure you know what this is.' It turned out that he was trying to sell enriched uranium. 'Everything was for sale,' the banker remembered. 'You could buy MiG fighters if you wanted.'[141]

In those circumstances, for a Russian metallurgical plant to sell scandium for one two-thousandth of the world market price was not as aberrant as it might sound, especially if the directors of the factory concerned were promised a share of the profits once the metal had been sold. There is no proof that that was the case – inexplicably, no one ever tried to discover the identities of the suppliers, and today, 30 years later, the trail has gone cold – but such kickbacks were common practice at that time and would provide a plausible explanation for why the price was so low.

The real problem, however, lay elsewhere. The agreements that Putin had approved were neither true barter deals nor normal commercial transactions. Once the companies had sold the exported commodities for foreign currency, even if the contracts stipulated penalties for failing to send back food, under Russian law there was no way to enforce them.[142] The entirely foreseeable result, as Putin later acknowledged, was that some of them violated their commitments.[143] One did not: Tamigo, a Russian–German joint venture, sent back two shiploads of cooking oil.[144] But others did as Russian companies usually did at that time if they were lucky enough to obtain export licences: they took advantage of the huge gap between the cost of raw materials in Russia and the selling price abroad, and stashed the profits in Western bank accounts.[145]

There was yet another twist to the story. As soon as the first shipment of cement and timber had left, the Customs Department blocked further exports, claiming that the documentation was not valid.[146] The head of the St Petersburg bureau of the Ministry for Foreign Economic

Relations, Anatoly Pakhomov, was furious that Moscow had gone behind his back and given licences directly to City Hall.

Unwisely, he told the customs officials that his minister's authorisation was insufficient. In March, Aven fired him and formally transferred to Putin's committee the right to license the city's foreign trade.[147] But the Customs Department then dug in its heels, insisting on the right to levy export duties.[148] The whole exercise degenerated into a massive bureaucratic turf fight. None of the rare earth metals left Russia.[149] Dzhikop was never heard of again.

That should have been the end of the matter. But by then, Sobchak's old adversary, Marina Salye, had got wind of the licensing agreements. Putin had been summoned to explain himself on January 14 before the Food Supply Commission of the Lensoviet – or Petrosoviet, as it had now been renamed – which she chaired.[150] He was unused to making formal presentations and the session did not go well. Boris Vishnevsky, who had been favourably impressed by Putin's attitude when Sobchak had sent him to negotiate with the deputies nine months earlier, said that this time he had come across as arrogant, rude and ill at ease.[151] Asked to provide further information, Putin refused on the pretext that commercial agreements were confidential.

Salye and her supporters, who had still not digested their failure to impeach Sobchak in 1990, sensed an opportunity.

A City Council working group was established to investigate. Its report, completed on March 23, recommended that Sobchak dismiss Putin and Anikin from their posts for 'incompetence verging on bad faith', accused them of being 'flagrantly and repeatedly in violation of the law', denounced what it termed 'criminal conditions' in the Dzhikop contract and called for a follow-up investigation to determine whether members of Putin's committee had engaged in corrupt practices.[152] At a press conference the same day, Salye went further, accusing Putin and Anikin of having a 'personal interest' in the 'oil-for-food' agreements and trying illegally to profit from them.[153] Belyaev ordered the report forwarded to the City Prosecutor's Office and to Yuri Boldyrev, whom Yeltsin had recently appointed to head the Main Control Directorate of the Presidential Administration, which was responsible, among other things, for investigating financial malfeasance.[154] When Sobchak rejected the group's findings, the deputies appealed to Yeltsin to remove him as well.[155]

Salye and her colleagues had done their best, but they had been unable to find a smoking gun. Alfred Kokh, who then worked in City Hall and later became one of Yeltsin's deputy Prime Ministers, explained why:

> Salye was a very good woman, but she understood absolutely nothing about the economy. So she wrote bullshit. She wrote in her report that Putin and Sobchak sent oil and other things abroad and promised that the money would be used to buy food . . . But . . . who owned the oil and the rare metals? Who did they belong to? They belonged to different companies [which] wanted to export. But they couldn't export without special permission. So they went to Sobchak and Putin, and they said: 'Get us authorisation. When we have sold the goods, we will bring back food.' They sold the goods, they got the money, and they didn't bring in food . . . Nobody stole anything from anybody! They were their goods, they sold them, and the money they got was theirs.[156]

Boldyrev was on bad terms with Sobchak and recused himself from the investigation. Nonetheless, he reached the same conclusion as Kokh. It was 'an absolutely run-of-the-mill affair', he remembered. There were 'significant violations', but no more serious than happened elsewhere in Russia. 'This kind of thing was very typical at that time – exporting strategic materials in exchange for food, which was then not supplied.'[157]

Contemporary reports bear that out. An almost identical episode occurred in Yeltsin's old fiefdom of Yekaterinburg, also in the spring of 1992. The regional Governor, Eduard Rossel, had been granted licences for the export of 110 million US dollars' worth of raw materials, exempted from customs duties, on condition that the proceeds be used to import 'foodstuffs, medicines and essential consumer goods'. As in St Petersburg, rare metals, including gallium and zirconium, were among the commodities exported. As in St Petersburg, the practical arrangements were entrusted to dubious local companies and joint ventures. And as in St Petersburg, the Customs Department rebelled and blocked part of the exports. The only difference was that the intermediary companies in Yekaterinburg were smarter than their St Petersburg counterparts and used a small part of the profits to buy cheap low-quality grain from Ukraine and Belarus to make it appear that they had fulfilled at least part of their commitments.[158]

Even if it was a 'run-of-the-mill affair', in Boldyrev's words, Sobchak was concerned enough to ask if he might bring Putin and several other members of the City Administration to Moscow to give their side of the story. There had been cases of provincial governors being dismissed on lesser grounds. It was not the offence which was important: it was whether Yeltsin or some other powerful figure wanted a pretext to get rid of a governor he found troublesome. The chemistry between Yeltsin and Sobchak had never been particularly good. Ever since Sobchak had emerged as a national leader during the putsch, Yeltsin had viewed him as a potential rival.[159] But Sobchak was loyal and that was enough. Putin gave evidence in writing, as did Sobchak and several others. Boldyrev recommended that he be given no additional responsibilities until the investigation was completed. But even that small slap on the wrist was countermanded by Pyotr Aven.[160]

By then, the food situation in St Petersburg had stabilised. Sobchak and Putin had negotiated a 500-million-dollar loan from a consortium of banks in Barcelona, 80 per cent of which was tied to the purchase of Spanish food products, and rationing had come to an end.[161]

Years later, when Putin rose to prominence in Moscow, the 'food scandal', as it became known, took on a new lease of life. It was claimed that he had come within an inch of being fired, that the amount of money involved was not 100 million but one billion US dollars, and there were veiled suggestions that a large part had ended up in Putin's and Sobchak's pockets.[162]

None of that was true.

Some of the businessmen involved certainly made big profits and certain officials in the Mayor's Office benefitted. But since the Customs Department had blocked all but the first shipment, the amount of money involved was far smaller than the sums originally reported. Even the St Petersburg press gave little space to the story. The liberal newspaper, *Smena*, focused not on Salye's allegations but on the turf fight between the City Hall, the Customs and the soon-to-be-dismissed Anatoly Pakhomov.[163] The business daily, *Kommersant*, in Moscow, accused the radical deputies of having raised a false alarm.[164] Even Marina Salye acknowledged that, at the time, 'our report did not interest anyone'.[165] Boldyrev went through the motions, sending a group of inspectors to examine the City Administration's files, but no proof of malfeasance was found. In July, the St Petersburg Prosecutor's Office ruled that there was no case for anyone to answer because there had been no crime.[166] And there the matter ended.

The attempted August 1991 putsch made Western governments and financial institutions uncomfortably aware that the gains of *perestroika* could be rolled back in the blink of an eye if a different kind of government came to power.

None of them wanted to pour in money for Gorbachev and still less for Yeltsin. Talk of a Marshall Plan for Russia never got off the ground. In retrospect their reluctance was understandable, although arguably short-sighted. Russia was a black hole, it was said. To give money to a government which lacked the infrastructure to use it constructively would be tantamount to throwing it away. With an election year looming in America, the George H. W. Bush administration was wary of anything that might make it look soft towards its former Cold War adversary. Absent an American lead, Western Europeans sat on their hands. But none of them wanted, either, to see a hard-line communist government in office, and, as the coup attempt had shown, given the right conditions, that could not be ruled out.

The answer, they decided, was to try to make the transition to a market economy irreversible as quickly as possible.

There had already been some progress in that direction. More joint ventures with foreign companies had been registered in Leningrad in the first eight months of 1991 than in the previous four years.[167] That summer the leaders of the G7, the Group of Seven industrialised countries, had discussed how to promote market reforms. It was agreed that the World Bank and the European Bank for Reconstruction and Development (EBRD) would divide up the major Soviet provincial centres between them with the goal, not explicitly acknowledged, of building 'a bulwark against communism'. The World Bank was assigned Nizhny Novgorod and Volgograd, the EBRD, Leningrad and Kiev.[168]

After the putsch, this programme went into overdrive.

Less than 48 hours after Gorbachev returned to Moscow from Foros, Jacques Attali, the EBRD Chairman, arrived in Leningrad and signed an agreement with Sobchak to launch a pilot scheme to privatise real estate.[169] The numbers of foreign businessmen coming to the city increased exponentially. In 1992, more than 3,000 joint ventures were registered by Putin's Foreign Relations Committee, ten times more than in 1991.[170] Russia became the new frontier for established Western companies wanting a foothold in what they hoped would be a vast potential market; for young start-ups which had launched businesses in Czechoslovakia, Hungary or Poland, and now sought fresh challenges further east; and for carpet-baggers and hucksters, who came to make a quick killing. St Petersburg, Russia's traditional gateway to the West, less than two hours' drive from the Finnish border, had its fair share of all three.[171]

For most of them, Putin's FRC was the first port of call. Sobchak had given him broad authority, and from the outset, Putin saw his role in expansive terms. As well as foreign trade and investment, he was in charge of hotel development and tourism, humanitarian aid, and liaison with foreign consulates in the city. Later he would also be given responsibility for the city's main airport at Pulkovo; the St Petersburg Oil Port; foreign television broadcasts re-transmitted in St Petersburg; and foreign financial institutions.

In December 1991, the French bank, Crédit Lyonnais, opened Russia's first foreign bank branch in St Petersburg, followed soon after by a Franco-German partnership between the Banque Nationale de Paris and the Dresdner Bank.[172] Six months later, the FRC helped to found the city's first – and Russia's second – foreign currency exchange.[173] Banking, along with the establishment of the Free Enterprise Zone, was among Sobchak's fetishes. He had visions of making St Petersburg the financial capital of Russia.

Even if some of Putin's obligations were more notional than real, it was a formidable list of responsibilities. He travelled widely, mainly within Europe but also to countries further afield, including Turkey, the US and Canada. When Sobchak received foreign visitors, Putin was a discreet presence sitting unobtrusively to one side. The US Secretary of State, James Baker, came in September 1991, followed, a month later, by the former British Prime Minister, Margaret Thatcher. Ex-President Nixon visited. Henry Kissinger and Sobchak co-chaired annual meetings of a commission set up by the Centre for Strategic and International Studies in Washington to promote development in the region. Prince Charles came, followed by Queen Elizabeth on the Royal Yacht *Britannia*, making the first visit to Russia by a British monarch since the murder of the Tsar in 1918. So did President Clinton,

Vice President Gore, Chancellor Kohl of Germany, and a host of lesser figures. In 1994, the EBRD held its annual conference in St Petersburg, with 5,000 attendees. On each occasion, Putin and his staff were responsible for arranging their programmes and security.

That was only the official part of his workload. Unofficially his primary task was liaison with the security services. Sobchak also used him as his point man for other, completely unrelated missions.

After the putsch and Yeltsin's decision to ban the Communist Party, Putin was made responsible for disposing of the property of the regional Party committee, which included office buildings, the Lenizdat printing works, a farm, dachas, summer camps and kindergartens, hotels, hospitals and a garage with more than a hundred official cars, as well as the Party archives and, reportedly, a 'black treasury' of secret Party funds.[174]

In October 1991, even before the FRC was properly up and running, he was given a further assignment: to control the gambling business in St Petersburg, including casinos and slot machines, the 'one-armed bandits' which were proliferating in the city.[175]

Later that month, the City Administration started relocating to the former Communist Party headquarters at Smolny, which had been vacated two months earlier.[176] There, Putin was finally given an office and a reception room of his own.

It was a modest enough place – 'a working office', as one visitor put it[177] – on the ground floor, in deference to Sobchak, who occupied the large suite previously used by the Communist Party First Secretary on the floor above. The waiting room had a desk for Putin's assistant, a couch, a couple of chairs, and a display cabinet with some dusty trinkets.[178] The inner sanctum was equally spartan: apart from a bookshelf containing a Soviet encyclopaedia, the only decoration was a plate of Dresden porcelain with a picture of a tram, a portrait of Yeltsin – replacing the portrait of Peter the Great which had graced the reception room at the Mariinsky – and a potted plant in the corner.[179]

Barbara Hay, the British Consul, who visited Putin shortly after he moved in, recorded in her diary that the place was 'a madhouse. People [are] queuing up to see him. It seems that no one can take a decision without referring to him or Sobchak. There's no organisation. His PA, a woman, [was] using two phones at once and managing at the same time to show a friend a [Western fashion] magazine.'[180]

The PA, Marina Yentaltseva, was joined soon afterwards by a private secretary, Igor Sechin, who had worked in the 1980s as a translator for the Soviet army in Angola and Mozambique under the aegis of the GRU, the military intelligence service.[181] Sechin, a stocky, muscular man in his early thirties, with dark, close-cropped hair, who could have been mistaken for a nightclub bouncer, served Putin with limpet-like devotion. Like his boss, he was from a working-class background and had grown up in a poor suburb of Leningrad. At Smolny, he took on the role of gatekeeper and tried to restore a semblance of order. But in the first few months, even Sechin was unable to instil any real sense of discipline. 'Putin's great weakness is his office,' sighed Sergei Pokrovsky, a fellow committee chairman. 'Disorganisation reigns and there are papers flying everywhere.'[182]

In one sense, that was in character. Putin's old teacher, Vera Gurevich, used to complain that, as a student, his desk was always a mess, until suddenly it was not and she learnt that he had joined the KGB.[183]

But something else was at work, too. Russian bosses usually rule with the knout.[184] That was not Putin's way. Marina Yentaltseva remembered that the first day he came to the office, she was in the middle of putting on lipstick. She assumed that she would be fired on the spot. Instead, he pretended not to notice. It was un-Russian, or at least, atypical. She did not know quite what to make of it.[185]

Many of Putin's Russian colleagues, including those who had little time for Sobchak and his administration, regarded him as an impressive operator. Pokrovsky, who later resigned from City Hall in disgust, said that he had 'a keen mind, he settles everything quickly and has a professional grasp of things'.[186] Aleksandr Belyaev, while stating frankly, 'I don't like Mr Putin', acknowledged that 'he understands how to cooperate with people, how to use them in his interest'.[187] Even Valery Pavlov, who, when they worked together, found him 'closed and secretive, never giving anything away', noted that he had quickly brought whole swathes of the administration under his control.[188]

Foreigners found him much harder to fathom.

The commonest reaction was not to notice that he was there at all. Western ambassadors visiting from Moscow would say later, 'I have absolutely no recollection of him. None whatsoever. I must have shaken hands with him – but absolutely no memory.'[189] Jaakko Kalela, who served as National Security Adviser to a succession of Finnish presidents, recalled that whenever Putin came with Sobchak to Helsinki, 'he somehow disappeared into the wallpaper'.[190]

Barbara Hay, who dealt with him extensively in 1991 and 1992, when she was trying to find premises for the British consulate in St Petersburg, wrote in her diary that he was alternately 'lugubrious' and looking 'tired and sick':

> [He was] nondescript, not tall, with thin, lank hair, pasty-faced . . . But I said to myself that no one looked good then, given the diet, the climate, their upbringing and so on . . . [He was] slightly built, quiet, he didn't put himself forward . . . No small talk. Gave nothing away. Not much finesse . . . Quite businesslike and to the point. Not social: he was purely focused on the business side of his work . . . He wore one of those shiny suits that Russian officials wore then – 'shiny suits and pointed toes' . . . And [on the rare occasions when he attended a diplomatic reception], he didn't circulate: he didn't work the room. He never appeared to really want to be there: it was a chore. Not even a duty, a chore.[191]

It was a chore because he regarded small talk and socialising as time-wasting, and he detested that. He did not suffer fools gladly. He could be impatient and did not mind if it showed.

Charles Ryan, a 25-year-old American who was Boris Fyodorov's deputy at EBRD, remembered going to Putin's office one morning in 1992 with a request for a tax waiver for Gillette, which wanted to renovate an old defence-industry plant and turn it into a joint venture making razor blades:

> He looked tired, he didn't seem in a very good mood, and he said, 'I saw your presentation. I get it. We don't need to go through it.' I was pretty grumpy because I'd worked hard on this, [so] I said, 'Really! Tell me, what do you get?' Then he got really annoyed, and he said – 'I'll tell you what I get. We're new to power. We want to stay in power. Staying in power means providing people with practical benefits from our period in power, which basically means jobs. Jobs require capital. We don't have any of that just now and foreigners do. So that requires foreigners. And foreigners require tax breaks. So tax breaks mean we stay in power.'

'Alright', Ryan conceded, suitably deflated: 'I guess you do get it.' Putin's approach, he thought afterwards, was totally pragmatic. The Gillette project went ahead and became one of the more successful joint ventures in the city.

If Putin looked perpetually tired, it was because he was. Most days he left the dacha early in the morning and did not return until midnight. His workload was crippling. As another young American official put it, 'he was the man who made the trains run on time for Sobchak.'[192] On summer weekends, the Putins would invite 15 or 20 guests, businessmen and city officials, for barbecued shashlik, to the exasperation of their straitlaced old communist neighbour, Vasily Golovko, who fumed about the big, foreign cars parked under his windows, whose drivers, 'muscular, well-fed young fellows, playing music or reading newspapers, paid not the slightest attention when I tried to reprimand them.'[193] But even at the dacha, Putin found it hard to let go. There was always some pressing business to discuss. Lyudmila remembered once they went mushrooming, and while everyone else was searching in the undergrowth, her husband stood nearby going through papers.[194]

To Sture Stiernlöf, the Swedish consul, he was 'quiet and evasive . . . correct and friendly in a cool, distant way. But he never entered into a dialogue. He listened but avoided taking a stand . . . As a lunch or dinner guest, he sat for the most part silently with an unfathomable little smile on his lips.'[195] Stiernlöf did not particularly like him and found him unpleasant to deal with. Putin, he remembered, always spoke so quietly that his interlocutor had to make an effort to hear what he was saying.[196] In one sense this was an aspect of his obsessive self-control. He almost never raised his voice, no matter how angry he was. But like his chronic lateness, it was also a way to put the other party psychologically at a disadvantage.

These were not techniques which Putin had learnt with the KGB. Forcing supplicants to wait was an old Russian bureaucratic tactic to assert superiority. Putin kept people waiting, unless there was an imperative reason to be punctual, because he could. Being on time brought no benefit and required effort which he could expend elsewhere.

Stiernlöf thought Putin's sympathies lay with Germany, 'in so far as any sympathies could be identified'. But he added pointedly: 'He is, I think, too calculating to be someone's friend . . . He is an operator and manipulator who sizes up his opportunities, coldly and soberly, and anticipates his own and others' actions well before he makes the first chess move. He is not spontaneous and he is least of all stupid. My experience of him is as a wily and, if necessary, a tough operator.' [197]

Jack Gosnell, Stiernlöf's American counterpart, also disliked Putin. He was 'a cold fish. Prussian. No sense of humour.'[198] The American Ambassador, Tom Pickering, agreed. 'He was totally closed,' Pickering remembered. 'Whatever he was going to say was based on a significant element of distrust.'[199]

Franz Sedelmayer, a young German businessman from Munich, came away from their first meeting with an equally unfavourable impression. Putin was 'like every typical German bureaucrat I'd ever met', he wrote, 'a mélange of implied power tinged with self-important arrogance'.[200]

But Sedelmayer, an expansive, outgoing man, ten years Putin's junior, who had come to Russia to sell counter-terrorism equipment and training programmes for the police, was the rare foreigner who managed to get beyond the unyielding façade, and over the next few years he and Putin developed an unusually warm relationship. Putin was fascinated by the state-of-the-art equipment which Sedelmayer was bringing in. He would drop by at Sedelmayer's villa on Kamenny Ostrov, where the city's elite had their mansions, and they would drink Bavarian beer and eat German sausages, which brought back memories of Dresden.[201] Eventually they had a serious falling out, but in the early 1990s Sedelmayer got closer to Putin than any other Westerner, although even he found there were limits:

> He was curious and of course, observant . . . And he was always in control, both of himself and the situation . . . He'd project himself differently to different people. He was chameleon-like. He'd give them back a mirror image of what he thought they'd like to see. He was . . . good at eliciting information from people, but reserved when talking about others . . . He was not a person who opened up. [He kept] his private life private . . . He continually kept a wall between people he knew and his family. [He] never talked about his parents, he never talked about his wife . . . I can't remember a single occasion when I had the feeling he was telling me anything revealing about his personal past.[202]

If he had to go to a reception, he would seek out a familiar face, usually either Sedelmayer himself or the German consul, Eberhard von Putt-kamer, an aristocrat who had married the daughter of a Finnish general and whose family tree stretched back to twelfth-century Pomerania.[203] If neither were present, he would stay the minimum time that etiquette required and then leave.

Von Puttkamer also found that Putin preferred to talk of practical things, never anything personal. There was 'a door that he never opened', he recalled. 'He is not a man to show his inner being.'

Putin was best with small groups, Sedelmayer said, 'one on one, or one on two or three'.[204] He was an individualist, not a team player.[205] When he had to make a speech or receive a large delegation, he was liable to become flustered and to muddle people's names.[206] Aleksandr Belyaev remembered Putin's first appearance before the Lensoviet, when he had presented a report on Sobchak's behalf. 'It was horrible. He could hardly get out a word. It was a total failure.'[207] Even his friend, Sergei Roldugin, was appalled by the way he gabbled and wondered why he did not express himself better.[208]

There was a simple answer. Along with the plethora of adjectives used by foreigners who tried to describe his character – 'quiet and non-descript; businesslike and pragmatic; cold, distant, reserved and evasive; calculating, not spontaneous; wily and tough' – Putin was shy. Most of his close Russian friends did not see it. But outside his own small circle, socialising did not come naturally to him. As Lyudmila put it, 'he had to work hard to seem at ease with people.'[209]

However, that was only one side of Putin.

Just as, when a schoolboy, he had always tried not to stand out, yet at the same time, by small signs, had asserted his difference – wearing his watch on his right wrist, playing the daredevil, choosing a different high school from his classmates – so, now, the city official who 'melted into the wallpaper' also had another face, which sat oddly with the rest. Where his colleagues wore standard grey suits, Putin wore a green suit and sported two-tone white and tan shoes.[210] At weekends he affected a raspberry-coloured blazer, emblematic of the so-called 'New Russians' – the young businessmen who had suddenly become rich, often by dubious means, and flaunted their new-found wealth with designer clothes and expensive foreign cars. Sometimes he paired the blazer bizarrely with a pair of blue Adidas track suit bottoms.[211]

If in St Petersburg Putin worked non-stop, on holiday he switched off completely. When a Swedish diplomat tracked him down one summer at a beach on the Black Sea coast, he was incensed that anyone should dare to disturb him while he was on leave.[212]

His private life, which he guarded jealously, was less conventional than it appeared. While he doted on his two small daughters, who went to the Piterschule, the German school in St Petersburg, and insisted that they have extra lessons in ballet and learn the violin, his relations with Lyudmila were erratic.[213] Like Sobchak, who was famously unfaithful, Putin's eye was still prone to wander. In 1992, Elizabeth Guigou, the urbane and stylish French Minister for European Affairs, led a delegation to St Petersburg to mark the opening of the European University there, a project launched jointly by Sobchak and Jacques Chirac. Putin hosted the welcoming banquet. It was a formal affair, for which the French side dressed in style, and he was unable to take his eyes off Guigou's décolleté, to the point where she found it necessary to ask her neighbour, the writer Marek Halter, to engage him in conversation in order to divert his attention.[214]

On another occasion, during a visit to Hamburg, he took Lyudmila and another couple to a strip club on the Reeperbahn in the city's redlight district. When the performers, 'a huge black man about two metres tall and a black woman, who was just a little girl', as Putin described them, began their routine, Lyudmila's friend fainted. No sooner had they revived her than she saw the two performers, by now naked, get down from the stage, and promptly fainted again. Putin claimed afterwards, somewhat improbably, that he had been sent to study the red-light district to see how to deal with similar establishments in St Petersburg. But he plainly enjoyed the experience, for on a subsequent visit to Hamburg he insisted on taking the Russian filmmaker, Igor Shadkhan, to the same club, and burst out laughing at the older man's shocked expression.[215]

He also made frequent trips on his own to Finland, telling Lyudmila, who apparently believed him, that it was the only place where he could talk and be sure that no one was listening in.[216] On one occasion, he took a football team from the Mayor's Office to play a Finnish team captained by the Mayor of Turku, Juhani Leppä, returning home with a broken collar-bone after a mid-air collision with John Vikström, the city's archbishop, who scored the home side's winning goal.[217] Altogether, he

visited Turku a dozen or so times and once, to celebrate his 40th birthday, travelled with Leppä and a group of Finnish friends to Lapland.

Leppä, who has remained close to Putin, pretends to be discreet
about those visits. 'I have so many stories that I cannot tell,' he says with
a mischievous smile, before adding, seemingly apropos of nothing: 'He
likes tall girls. They must also be slim . . . He is a very normal man.'[218]

It would be wrong to read too much into that. As Lyudmila put it,
'What sort of man would he be if he weren't attracted by beautiful
women?'[219] Nonetheless, it is a rather different image of Putin from
that of the faceless, puritanical, overworked bureaucrat who 'made the
trains run on time' and whom foreigners queued up to see when they
needed to get something done.

Ever since he had joined the Mayor's Office, Putin had been determined to bring all the city's foreign affairs work directly under his
personal control.

In his first published interview, in August 1991, he stressed that
responsibility for what he called 'the city's interests in the international
arena' should be centralised. St Petersburg got no benefit, he said,
when different individuals and departments dabbled in foreign affairs.[220]
The absence of a clear demarcation between the powers of the City
Administration and the Petrosoviet had created a situation where
Western companies did not know whom they were supposed to talk to
and in some cases simply gave up.[221] 'Anarchy in this field is impermis-
sible,' he said.[222] The Foreign Relations Committee should be the sole
interlocutor.

Putin would spend the next three years trying to bring that about.

The fact that he had Sobchak's trust gave him a head start. As Barbara Hay had noted, foreigners soon started to see Putin as the only
person, apart from the Mayor himself, capable of taking decisions.
That was not entirely true, but it was a view which Sobchak encouraged. When Boris Fyodorov arrived to open the EBRD office in St
Petersburg, Sobchak told him that the key members of his team were
Putin and Anatoly Chubais, whom he had appointed as his chief economic adviser.[223] In November 1991, Chubais left for Moscow to
become head of the State Property Committee.[224] He had never
shown much interest in foreign relations. There had been moments of
tension when foreign investors were involved in privatisation projects,

but Putin had not seen him as a rival.[225] That was not the case with Georgy Khizha, whom Sobchak appointed to head the city's Economic Development Committee, or of Sergei Belyaev, who became chief of the St Petersburg Property Committee.[226] Chubais would have preferred his own man in the St Petersburg post and, from his new power base in Moscow, named two young colleagues, Alfred Kokh and another economist, Mikhail Manevich, to serve as Belyaev's deputies. But it was Putin whom the appointments of Khizha and Belyaev bothered most. 'If he saw anybody else intruding onto what he regarded as his territory, he became very jealous,' Kokh remembered.[227] Charles Ryan, Fyodorov's young assistant in the EBRD, experienced that at first hand:

> It was a very tricky situation. On the one hand, our official interlocutor was Putin, and he was very thin-skinned, very touchy, about the fact that he and no one else was the point guy for us . . . And on the other hand, we had to talk to the Property Committee because they were doing the privatisation . . . Anyway, we went to meet Belyaev because we had a specific issue concerning one of our pilot projects. And we're sitting there, having lunch with Sergei, in the Hotel Grand Europa, and Putin walks in and sees us. You can just see this fury in his face. It was: 'You guys don't respect me' . . .[228]

After an awkward few weeks, Ryan managed to smooth things over. In due course, Belyaev, too, left for Moscow, where Chubais co-opted him as one of his deputies, and Mikhail Manevich, a swashbuckling figure with an instantly recognisable, booming voice, who became a good friend of Putin, was named as his successor.[229]

Khizha was a much more serious problem.

He ranked third in the Mayor's Office, after Sobchak himself and the Vice Mayor, Vyacheslav Shcherbakov, and was granted the right, not given to any other Committee Chairman, to sign financial documents on the Mayor's behalf. Soon after he was appointed, he ordered a structural review of the City Administration, which concluded, no doubt correctly, that there was a great deal of duplication, and recommended severe staff cuts, all of which turned out to be in departments which Khizha regarded as trespassing on his turf. It then transpired that he intended to increase his own committee's staff by 30 per cent on the grounds that every aspect of the City's work had an economic component. Shcherbakov objected violently, and in March, the liberal newspapers, *Smena* and *Chas pik*, accused Khizha of sidelining both Sobchak and the Vice Mayor in order to concentrate power in his own hands.[230] But Sobchak saw him as a useful counterweight to Shcherbakov and was reluctant to slap him down.

Khizha's expansionist tendencies exasperated Putin. He insisted on sitting in on Sobchak's meetings with foreign dignitaries and took an unwelcome interest in foreign trade, which left Putin, like the other committee chairmen, feeling left out in the cold.[231]

Salvation once again came from Moscow, where, in May 1992, Yeltsin summoned Khizha to become a deputy to Yegor Gaidar, whom he was about to appoint acting Prime Minister.[232] His departure left the way free for Putin to spread his wings. Earlier that year, in February, Sobchak had appointed him one of three deputy Mayors.[233] But the crucial step came four months later, when the Mayor signed a decree making it possible not only for Shcherbakov, as Vice Mayor, but for any of the three deputies to stand in for him when he was away.[234] On this occasion, perhaps on Putin's advice, Sobchak proceeded with unusual caution. The decree was presented as a standby arrangement, in case both he and the Vice Mayor should be absent at the same time. In August, when Sobchak went on holiday, Shcherbakov, as usual, became acting Mayor in his place. But in November 1992, when Sobchak next travelled abroad, he named Putin to act on his behalf.[235]

The City Council protested, arguing that Shcherbakov, as an elected official, could be named acting Mayor but Putin could not and his appointment was illegal, as was indeed the case.[236] Sobchak shrugged it off. Shcherbakov responded with a series of caustic newspaper articles, accusing Sobchak of trying to micro-manage the administration's work, taking credit for its successes and blaming his subordinates for its failures.[237]

The battle lines were drawn. But for Putin, it was already a triumph. In less than 30 months, he had gone from being a modest official in the Vice Rector's office at Leningrad University to acting head of the entire city. Two years earlier, he had seen off Sobchak's assistants, Valery Pavlov and Yuri Shutov. Now three other potential rivals – Anatoly Chubais, Georgy Khizha and Sergei Belyaev – had been removed to Moscow, while the status of the fourth, Vice Admiral Shcherbakov, was gradually being whittled away .[238] It was partly luck, partly being in the right place at the right time and partly skilled manoeuvring. Putin knew how to make himself indispensable, discreetly positioning himself so that if an opening arose, he was the obvious, indeed the only choice to fill it. It was a pattern which would repeat itself often in his career.

At the beginning of 1993, a political storm was brewing in Moscow. Yeltsin was at war with the Supreme Soviet of the Russian Congress of People's Deputies, which had refused to confirm Gaidar, his choice as Prime Minister and, since the previous summer, had systematically blocked his efforts at reform. It had started as an attempt by the opposition to capitalise on public discontent over 'shock therapy' but quickly degenerated into a bare-knuckled struggle for power. The Chairman of the Soviet, Ruslan Khasbulatov, an economics professor from Chechnya with a talent for political intrigue, was determined to wrest back from Yeltsin the powers which the Congress had conferred on him in the euphoria of Russian independence in 1991. Yeltsin was just as determined not to give them up.

In March, his Vice President, Aleksandr Rutskoi, a moustachioed air force general and decorated veteran of the Afghan War, threw in his lot with Khasbulatov and Yeltsin barely survived an impeachment attempt. Gaidar thought the country was edging towards civil war.[239]

In St Petersburg, the same scenario was playing out on a smaller scale. Having a directly elected Mayor had solved nothing. The Petrosoviet remained at loggerheads with City Hall. Each wanted to have the last word on the privatisation of real estate and foreign capital inflows because of the sums of money involved and the possibilities for enrichment.[240] Putin might have won control of the foreign affairs structures in the Mayor's Office but the Petrosoviet continued to do as it pleased. Its Chairman, Aleksandr Belyaev, told the new French Consul General, Roland Blatmann, that if foreign investors wanted their projects approved, it was not enough to get Putin's agreement. They must make sure that they had approval from the International Affairs Commission of the Petrosoviet as well. Blatmann protested that it was already time-consuming enough for foreign businessmen to navigate the various committees in the Mayor's Office. If they had to do the same at the City Council, they might give up altogether. Belyaev was unmoved. The Petrosoviet was there to oversee the Mayor's work, he said, and it intended to do so.[241]

In Moscow, after a summer spent bickering over proposals for a new constitution, Yeltsin reluctantly decided to act.

On September 21, he proclaimed the dissolution of both the Supreme Soviet and the Congress of People's Deputies and announced new elections for December. The decision, he acknowledged later, was illegal. But there was no choice. The alternative, he told Russians, was 'the disintegration of the Russian state, [and] chaos in a country which has an enormous arsenal of nuclear weapons'.[242]

That night, the Congress of People's Deputies, meeting in emergency session in the White House, voted to remove Yeltsin and appoint Rutskoi President in his place.

In St Petersburg, Sobchak and the City Administration, the Trades Unions and the Military District Command declared their support for Yeltsin. The Petrosoviet was split, with radical deputies arguing that the dissolution was illegal, others saying that Yeltsin and the Supreme Soviet were equally at fault and yet others supporting Sobchak. Shcherbakov appeared on television and accused both Sobchak and Yeltsin of acting like dictators – the next step, he said, would be civil war. Sobchak forbade him to enter Smolny and had his office sealed and placed under armed guard.[243]

For the next ten days, Putin held daily briefings for the consular corps at a guest house on Kamenny Ostrov.[244] There was not a great deal he could say. The action was all in Moscow and even there, until the beginning of October, very little happened. In St Petersburg, Blatmann reported, people watched events in the capital on their television sets 'as though it were a distant drama, being played out on a stage'.

On October 2, the denouement began. Khasbulatov had transformed the White House into an armed redoubt. Negotiations with the Kremlin, mediated by the Orthodox patriarchate, had broken down. That afternoon a pitched battle took place on Smolensk Square, in front of the Stalinist 'wedding-cake' tower which housed the Russian Foreign Ministry. On one side were the police, on the other, Rutskoi's supporters, who waved the yellow-and-black flags of Russian nationalists and hurled Molotov cocktails. One policeman was killed and 24 others injured.

Next morning, the demonstrators returned in greater numbers. The police, many of them youngsters, were soon overwhelmed and fled, looking to one observer 'like a flock of terrified penguins'.[245] The crowd, now 10,000 to 15,000 strong, some carrying portraits of Stalin, headed for the White House, where Rutskoi and Khasbulatov made fiery speeches, egging them on. While the demonstrators chanted slogans, calling for the restoration of the Soviet Union, the hard core of 150 deputies who had remained in the building, protected by an armed militia of Cossacks, Chechens, Afghan veterans and far-right nationalist thugs, began debating what to do with 'the fascist dictator, Yeltsin', after he had been arrested.

In Tverskaya Street, a mob commandeered two army trucks and smashed down the doors of the City Hall. Another group of heavily armed men occupied the Television Centre at Ostankino, in the north of the city.

It began to look like a repetition of 1917, when a few thousand Bolsheviks had overthrown the Kerensky government, installing a dictatorship which had lasted for 70 years. That night, Gaidar broadcast an emotional appeal to Muscovites to come to the square, outside the Mayor's Office, 'to stand together to defend our future and the future of our children, and not to allow our country to be turned once again into an enormous concentration camp for decades to come'.[246]

As they had during the putsch two years earlier, people responded. By midnight, 20,000 to 30,000 had gathered. Volunteer detachments formed, vowing to defend Yeltsin's government.

In the end, however, it was the army which saved the day. Not without difficulty, Yeltsin had persuaded the Defence Minister, Pavel Grachev, to bring in infantry, paratroops and men from a tank division to surround the White House. Soon after 7 a.m., armoured personnel carriers broke through the makeshift barricades which Khasbulatov's men had erected, and special forces troops, backed up by machine-gun fire, occupied the first and second floors. After further attempts at negotiation failed, a dozen heavy T-72 tanks were brought up and fired 12 shells at the upper storeys. Ten were blanks, two were live. With the top four floors on fire, groups of deputies and their aides, carrying white flags, walked out and were allowed to go free. Finally, at the end of the afternoon, Rutskoi and Khasbulatov surrendered and were taken to Lefortovo Prison.

Even then, it was not quite over. Armed extremists, who escaped with their weapons through underground passageways, continued to pick off soldiers and civilians seemingly at random. Sniper fire continued all night. Officially 187 people were killed in the conflict and up to a thousand wounded. Unofficial accounts suggested the figure may have been far higher.

In St Petersburg, there was no such drama. The city remained calm. Putin told the consuls that 'prophylactic measures' had been taken against armed extremists and OMON detachments had been assigned to protect the television station, the City Hall, and other sensitive locations. Asked about the authorities in the Leningrad Region, who had supported Khasbulatov's insurgency, he replied contemptuously that they were irrelevant. 'They have no money and no means of influencing the situation. At most they can get some collective farm to demonstrate.'

Stiernlöf, the Swedish Consul, was impressed despite himself. 'Here spoke a man . . . who knew how to exercise power,' he wrote to the Foreign Ministry in Stockholm. 'He showed . . . unequivocal support for Yeltsin and a slightly arrogant conviction that the coup makers did not stand a chance.'[247]

Unlike in 1991, Sobchak's role this time had been limited. Nonetheless, he was among the main beneficiaries. In appreciation of his support, Yeltsin named him Chairman of the Civic Chamber of the Constitutional Conference. In that capacity, he helped to draw up the new constitution, which was narrowly approved by a plebiscite in December. It gave the President greatly increased powers and relegated parliament to a secondary role. Of more direct relevance to St Petersburg, the Petrosoviet was dissolved. On Thursday, December 23, the deputies were given until 4 p.m. to remove their personal effects and leave, after which the Mariinsky Palace was sealed off by the police.[248] Its responsibilities were transferred to the Mayor's Office until new elections could be held the following spring.

The new division of powers between the Mayor and the Petrosoviet – which would henceforth be called the *ZakSobranie*, the Legislative Assembly – was heavily weighted in Sobchak's favour. The Assembly would have 50 members, as against 400 previously, and only the Chairman and his two deputies would work full-time. The other 47 would hold unpaid, part-time positions, supposedly to enable them to be closer to the concerns of their fellow citizens. If the Mayor rejected the

Assembly's decisions, it would require a two-thirds majority, in practice unattainable given St Petersburg's fractured politics, to override his veto.

The elections to the new assembly, which took place on March 20, 1994, did not go well. In half the electoral districts, the turnout was less than 25 per cent, which invalidated the results. But for Sobchak there was a silver lining. Since there were not enough members to constitute a quorum, he would be in sole charge of the city's affairs, with no legislative oversight, until fresh elections were held, which would not be until November.

Four days earlier, Putin had been appointed first deputy Mayor.

He shared that rank with two others: Aleksei Kudrin, a colleague of Chubais, responsible for Finance and Economic Development, and a relative newcomer, Vladimir Yakovlev, an engineer whom Sobchak had appointed the previous winter to take charge of Public Works.[249] But Putin was first among equals, serving as acting Mayor during Sobchak's frequent travels and placed immediately after the Mayor in diplomatic protocol lists.[250] Shcherbakov had finally accepted the inevitable and resigned. Khizha's successor, Dmitry Sergeyev, whose relations with Sobchak had also deteriorated, had left under a cloud.[251] Those whom Putin had perceived as rivals had all moved elsewhere. The rest of the city government were either allies or uncommitted.[252]

To all intents and purposes, Putin was now the second-ranking person in the city.[253] Only Vladimir Yakovlev was still something of an unknown quantity. But he was seen as a technocrat, without political ambitions.

6

The Grey Cardinal

Ever since Putin had joined Sobchak, there had been an unresolved conflict between his duty to the KGB and his loyalty to the Mayor. The Chairman of the Legislative Assembly, Aleksandr Belyaev, summed up: 'He came to Sobchak as a KGB minder and then, at some point, switched sides.'[1] But when and how he switched sides, and to what extent he really cut his ties with the security services, has been systematically obscured.

Putin's own explanations were contradictory and on several points patently false.

In November 1991, he told the newspaper, *Chas pik*, that when Sobchak had invited him to head the Foreign Relations Committee, in June that year, his resignation from the KGB was already 'signed and sealed'. He was no longer a member of the active reserve and had left with the rank of lieutenant-colonel. 'I don't work there,' he said, 'and I am not paid by them . . . I repeat, I have left the KGB.' If he had decided to address the issue publicly, which, as the interviewer noted, was extremely unusual – normally Putin shunned television appearances and avoided speaking to the press – it was because, he said, certain deputies in the Petrosoviet had 'tried to blackmail me for having belonged to the KGB'.[2]

The use of the word, 'blackmail', is intriguing.[3] It is true that some radical deputies bitterly reproached Sobchak for appointing an ex-KGB officer to the City Administration. Putin complained later that they made him feel 'as though I was wearing a pig's snout at a garden party'.[4] But Sobchak had recruited several other ex-KGB figures to high-profile posts and Putin had never made a secret of his past.[5] The only way there could be grounds for blackmail was if he had been lying about his role – if, for instance, he had deliberately attached himself to

Sobchak on the KGB's instructions; if he had worked for the hated Fifth Directorate, targeting political dissent; or if he had been a *stukach*, a KGB informer.

In the interview, Putin went out of his way to insist that none of that could be true. He had always worked for the KGB's 'elite' foreign intelligence service, he claimed, and had had 'no connection with domestic political problems', an area in which, he told *Chas pik*, the KGB had behaved 'monstrously'. Nor had he ever acted as an informer when he was a student. As for being a mole, 'how could the KGB attach me [to Sobchak] if I had already resigned?' He had transferred to the active reserve after returning from Germany, he said, rather than continuing to work as a full-time KGB officer, because he wanted to write a thesis on international trade law.

The first answer was a lie: he had spent several years working for the Fifth Department. The second answer may or may not have been true: accounts of his time as a student differed. The third was a dissimulation: he had agreed to work for Sobchak in June 1990, a year before his purported resignation, not after it.[6] The final assertion, about preparing a thesis, was a trope of a kind that Putin often used to obscure his real intentions. He had done so after leaving Dresden, telling colleagues that he thought he might have to find work as a taxi driver.[7] The thesis was a way to explain his presence at the university, lest anyone think that he had been sent there to infiltrate the democratic movement.[8]

It may be argued that these are matters of detail, which merely confirm that, early on in Putin's time at City Hall, there was much talk among the city's political elite about his KGB background as well as speculation that, through him, the special services might be manipulating Sobchak. As *Chas pik* put it: 'If Putin is not there, it is as though the Mayor has lost his right hand . . . Without Putin, he does not make a single decision.' That was an exaggeration. But it was what many democrats believed.

Ten years later, however, in the same way that he changed his story about how he had met Sobchak, he gave a completely different account of how he had left the KGB. No longer did he claim to have resigned in June 1991. On the contrary, he now said that when the putsch occurred in August of that year he was still a serving KGB officer, because his earlier letter – the one which he had told *Chas pik* was already 'signed and sealed' – had in fact 'stalled somewhere. Somebody, somewhere, apparently, just couldn't make a decision.' So on August 20, the same day that he flew back from Kaliningrad, he had written out a second resignation letter and, to ensure that this time it was acted upon, Sobchak had made a telephone call to the KGB chief, Vladimir Kryuchkov, in person. According to Putin, Kryuchkov obligingly spoke to the Leningrad Regional Directorate and 'the next day, they informed me that my resignation had been approved'.[9]

It is difficult to find a single word in that far-fetched tale which, even by the wildest stretch of imagination, could possibly be true.

The KGB bureaucracy, whatever its other failings, did not lose resignation letters. Equally implausible was the claim that Sobchak called Kryuchkov at the most critical moment of the putsch, when the plotters' fates were hanging by a thread, and that Kryuchkov made time to instruct his subordinates to accept the resignation of a not very senior active reserve officer in the provinces. Kryuchkov hated Sobchak and the feeling was mutual.

Long afterwards, Putin himself had the grace to acknowledge that it was all a bit hard to believe. 'I was a little surprised,' he said. 'Why would [Sobchak] call Kryuchkov?' Nevertheless, he continued to insist that the story was true, conceding only that his resignation was accepted not 'next day', as he had originally claimed, but 'within the next few days'.[10]

But if Putin knew in August 1991 that his supposed letter had not got through, why did he tell *Chas pik* three months later, in November, that it had been accepted? And why did he not mention in that interview his second resignation attempt, supposedly at the very height of the putsch? The story does not add up.

No less puzzling, Putin's original claim that he had resigned in June 1991, even if untrue, was difficult to disprove. Why call it into question?

It is tempting to speculate that, just as he had reworked his account of how he had become Sobchak's assistant, so now, on this issue, too, he felt the need for a more dramatic version that showed him taking the moral high ground. He hinted as much to Oleg Blotsky, an Izvestia correspondent who wrote his semi-official biography. 'My moral obligations [to Sobchak],' he said, 'were more important than my formal obligations [to the KGB]. That was my main reason for leaving . . . I made a choice in favour of my moral obligations.'[11]

But, beyond the discrepancy between the two versions, there is a larger question. If Putin really resigned from the KGB, why was it necessary to concoct an account at all? Why did he not simply say what had happened?

The most plausible explanation is that he never officially left.

Putin hinted at this himself, when he compared leaving the KGB to leaving the Communist Party.[12] He never resigned his Party membership. He simply put his membership card in a drawer and forgot about it.[13] Putin's purported departure from the KGB appears to have happened in a similar manner.[14] As he made clear when he spoke of 'moral obligations', his allegiance had switched to Sobchak, but in such a way as to avoid a rupture with his former service. Psychologically he had indeed left the KGB. Formally, he remained part of it.[15]

The ambiguity did not pass unnoticed.

After the siege of the White House in October 1993, Yeltsin, who deeply distrusted the KGB and its successors, toyed with the idea of disbanding it altogether and building a new security service from the bottom up. It was rumoured that, if that happened, Putin might be appointed to head a revamped regional directorate in St Petersburg.[16] When Franz Sedelmayer picked up echoes of this and ran them past his contacts at the Big House, he was met with a blank wall of incomprehension. 'No one here understands any more what Putin is,' they told him. 'We don't know who he's working for, we don't know whose side he's on.' Sedelmayer was intrigued. 'It was fascinating,' he said later. 'Putin was perfectly grey concerning his intentions.'[17]

There were good reasons for him to wish to conceal his hand.

Putin was working with Sobchak, a leading democrat, who had never hidden his hostility to the security services. It was one thing to announce for public consumption that he had resigned: that was part of his cover. It would have been quite another to have actually done so. His role as the liaison between City Hall and the Big House became more important than ever after his appointment as first deputy Mayor in 1994.[18] That year, Sobchak issued a decree setting out publicly Putin's responsibilities. In addition to chairing the FRC, they included:

Coordinating the activities of the Police Departments [GUVD] of St Petersburg and Leningrad Region with the Departments of Administrative Organs . . . Justice and . . . Public Relations [of the Mayor's Office].

> Heading the work of the Interprovincial Commission for coopera-
> tion with adjoining regions, the Supervisory Commission for the rights
> of detained persons . . . and the Commission on drug addiction and the
> narcotics trade.
>
> Ensuring teamwork among the territorial organs of the Defence
> Ministry, the Interior Ministry, the FSK [the successor organisation to
> the KGB] . . . the Prosecutor's Office, the Judiciary [and other bodies].[19]

These were not mere paper responsibilities. Putin delegated routine
work with the police to the Department of Administrative Organs at
City Hall, now headed by another ex-KGB officer, Viktor Ivanov, a
small, dapper, self-effacing man with a thin moustache, two years his
senior. But he personally supervised security for major events, including the Goodwill Games in the summer of 1994, which drew athletes
from some 50 countries and Sobchak hoped would be a prelude to St
Petersburg hosting the Olympics in 2004.[20]

Putin also coordinated the security arrangements for visiting statesmen, a tedious task which did not always turn out well. When Bill
Clinton made a stopover in St Petersburg in the spring of 1996, the
whole of the city centre was cleared of traffic for the 18 hours that he
was there. Clinton was furious that he was prevented from descending
from his motorcade and plunging into the crowd. Afterwards he threw
a temper tantrum, grumbling that it was 'one of the worst stops I've
ever had'. The Americans blamed Putin, who had supervised the security arrangements on the Russian side, although Clinton's advance team
may have been equally at fault.[21]

At a more cloak-and-dagger level, Putin represented Sobchak at
secret talks with Estonian separatists, which, significantly, were held
not at the Mayor's Office but at the Big House.[22] He also supervised
anti-terrorism training exercises and the purchase of hi-tech American
and German equipment for the special forces' anti-terrorist units and
SWAT teams.[23]

Finding a way to square the circle, to reconcile his loyalty to Sobchak with the need to keep channels open to the security services, had
not been easy. Lyudmila remembered him agonising over what to do.[24]
Putin himself said that 'it tore my life apart'. That was hyperbole, like
his claim that during the putsch, 'all the ideals, all the goals that I had
had when I went to work for the KGB, collapsed.'[25] Those illusions had

been lost much earlier. All the same, it had been a harrowing choice. He had discussed it with his cellist friend, Sergei Roldugin, who told him bluntly: 'You can stop working for this organisation, but its world view and way of thinking will remain stuck in your head.'[26] But in the end what mattered was that he had found a pragmatic compromise. If, in the process, he had spun tales which no thinking person could possibly believe, that was just too bad.

The years in the KGB were not the only baggage Putin carried from his past. Some of his childhood friends from the courtyard had gone on to a life of crime. In the judo clubs, he had been surrounded by criminals.[27] One of his mentors, Sergei Suslin, a five-times European Judo Champion, belonged to a gang led by Vyacheslav Ivankov, nicknamed Yaponchik ('Little Japanese') because of his Asian features. In 1982, Suslin had been given a nine-year sentence for armed robbery. The following year, Leonid Usvyatsov, the trainer whom Putin revered and who may have helped him get into university, was sentenced to a second ten-year term in a labour camp for currency speculation. Released ahead of time for good behaviour, he was shot dead at a gangland funeral in St Petersburg in 1994.

Some of these men, while prodigious sportsmen, were simply bandits. Others, like Suslin, were more complicated characters. Suslin died of a heart attack while taking a group of underprivileged children to visit Red Square in Moscow. Yet others, like Usvyatsov, were sentenced for crimes which, after communist rule ended, became legitimate business activities, but then, after their release, returned to the criminal brotherhoods from which they had come.

If the frontiers were blurred, it was because, in the Soviet Union, any form of private business was a criminal offence.

Every Russian businessman who rose to prominence in the early 1990s, including those who became billionaires, started by trading illegally. There was no other way. Even after Gorbachev allowed the formation of cooperatives, what was lawful and what was not depended on the whim of the local Party leader. In one city, old women were allowed to sell vegetables. In another, they were not.

The classic route to riches was to buy jeans, or rock 'n' roll records, from foreigners studying at Soviet universities, or from tourists or Third World diplomats, and sell them on the black market. With the capital thus accumulated, the bolder of the nascent entrepreneurs moved on to buying and selling computers and electronic equipment, also acquired initially from foreigners or through back-door deals with Soviet factories.[28] Others, with better connections, obtained seed money from the Komsomol or reached under-the-counter agreements with state-owned enterprises. Eventually, cooperatives and, later on, private individuals, were allowed to open bank accounts and to conduct foreign trade directly. Huge fortunes could then be made by playing on the difference between domestic and foreign commodity prices and exchange-rate differentials.

As street trading and small businesses proliferated, so did protection rackets. Even for quite modest firms, the racketeers' fees started at 300 to 400 US dollars a month, increasing to 25 or 30 per cent of net profits. If a businessman was recalcitrant, it was explained politely what could be done to him with a welding torch. Should he continue to resist, he would be taken into the forest and told to dig his grave, at which point even the most stubborn entrepreneur usually recognised that further argument was pointless.

Almost all Russian businesses in St Petersburg paid for protection in one form or another, either directly to organised crime groups or to private security companies with links to organised crime. The old Soviet-era underground, founded in the labour camps, with a strict code of conduct ruled by so-called *Vory v zakone*, 'Thieves in Law', who disdained any dealings with the authorities, was forced out by newer, more violent groups – the Chechen mafia and the Malyshev, Kazansky and Tambovsky gangs, 60 per cent of whose members came from boxing and judo clubs.[29]

Gangsters used rocket-propelled grenades, anti-tank mines and remote-controlled car bombs as well as Kalashnikovs and machine guns.[30] In 1995, the per capita murder rate in St Petersburg exceeded that in New York.[31] In Russia as a whole, it was between two and four times higher than in the United States.[32] The police estimated that 30 to 40 per cent of the killings in St Petersburg were the work of hitmen, often snipers, veterans of the Afghan war, the best of whom could shoot a man dead through the windscreen of a moving vehicle 100 metres away.[33]

The intensity of the gang warfare in St Petersburg, which reached a peak in 1994 and 1995, was the most dramatic manifestation of the breakdown of law and order which accompanied the transition to a market economy, but there were plenty of other signs that society had lost its moorings. Petty crime and street mugging were a daily hazard. Nearly 80 per cent of the adult population said they felt it was dangerous to walk in the streets, and 90 per cent said that the fight against crime should be the administration's first priority.[34] In the three years that the Putins spent at their dacha at Zelenogorsk, they were burgled twice.[35] Prostitution and drug abuse assumed epic proportions. At one high school, one in six of the girls in the senior classes said they wished to work as prostitutes after graduation. Half of the rest thought that was a legitimate choice but were deterred by the risk of AIDS or parental opposition.[36] With a population of five million, St Petersburg was officially stated to have one million alcoholics and 300,000 drug addicts – no doubt an exaggeration but perhaps not by very much.[37]

Not only was crime endemic, but the borderline between the criminal world and legitimate business was porous. Dmitry Potapenko, who started out as an 18-year-old *fartovshchik*, a black-marketeer trading in jeans, and went on to become Deputy CEO of the EN+ Group, owned by the multi-billionaire, Oleg Deripaska, said almost everyone in his generation could have gone one way or the other:

> I have friends, close friends, who went into crime . . . I saw how people who were close to me were killed. Business at that time was always absolutely on the edge – at the border between business and banditism. It was a choice . . . I don't know – and I will never know – if I made the right choice. I don't know what would have happened had I chosen the other route.[38]

It was a choice not only for businessmen but for officials. The temptations were immense. 'An honest policeman may soon become a rarity,' grumbled *Sankt-Peterburgskie vedomosti*.[39] 'Who's running the country?' asked the national newspaper, *Izvestia*. 'The government? Or clans of organised criminals?'[40] A corrupt mid-ranking police officer could make 20,000 US dollars a month at a time when a factory worker would be glad to earn a hundred dollars.[41] Government bureaucrats discovered previously undreamt-of sources of enrichment. Privatisation and the sale of municipal real estate offered ever more lucrative opportunities.

Mikhail Zolotonosov, the Political Editor of *Chas pik*, wrote that Russia was living through the same experiences as the United States, a century before:

> Any bureaucratic system has its own specific properties. One of them is the sale of decisions for money. Each person sells what he has. Bureaucrats sell decisions. In other words, they take bribes. This is not because of some moral deficiency on their part. It is an objective property of any system of power in which morality is absent.[42]

To understand St Petersburg, he added, one needed only to read Lincoln Steffens's essay, 'Tweed Days in St. Louis', describing municipal corruption in early twentieth-century Missouri.

Sobchak's administration was equally blasé. 'We are at the stage of the primary accumulation of capital,' said the head of the City's Property Fund, Valery Krasnyansky. 'The sources of capital have always been trade, robbery and bribes.'[43]

In a survey of 43 countries by the World Economic Forum in Davos, Russia came overall bottom for state sector bribery, bureaucratic obstruction and the financial and political risks of doing business.[44] In St Petersburg, bribery was no longer thought of as something criminal. It was 'part of the fabric of life – a fact that is taken for granted'. A cartoon in *Sankt Peterburgskie vedomosti* showed a company boss smiling appreciatively as an aide told him: 'The half-yearly results are quite encouraging, Sir. We took in 30 per cent more in bribes than we had to pay out.'[45] Bribes were paid 'in every imaginable form: roubles, dollars, apartments, motor cars, foreign holidays, or anything else. Just as varied is the range of services provided by the bribetakers – from long-term leases on property to licences to export raw materials to a favourable verdict in court.'[46]

This was the atmosphere in which Putin worked. The criminal world and the world of legitimate business – or business which hoped to become legitimate – were symbiotic, not merely linked but inextricably intertwined.

In 1992, Anatoly Smirnov, one of Putin's fellow students at the Law Faculty who was also ex-KGB and now worked for the Mayor's Office, was asked to set up a City Security Fund whose ostensible purpose was to fight against graft. It was to be financed by local businesses and joint ventures. Among those whom Putin invited to join the board was Franz Sedelmayer, the young German arms dealer he had befriended. When Smirnov gave him the list of founding members, Sedelmayer said, he was 'flabbergasted . . . This wasn't a security fund – it was a Cosa Nostra infiltration operation.' Most of the names on the list were gangsters or executives of companies controlled by Organised Crime groups.

When he raised his concerns with Putin, he remembered, the deputy Mayor 'said nothing. But he gave me a knowing look. Of course he did . . . Those things were around him all the time.'[47]

None of Sobchak's deputies could have done their jobs without channels to organised crime. Putin was particularly closely involved because he was responsible for security in the city. According to Dmitry Zapolsky, who was then a member of the Legislative Assembly, the policy of the Mayor's Office was to try to maintain a balance between the leading gangs to ensure that none became dominant. To that end, Putin procured the acquittal of Vladimir Malyshev, the head of the second largest gang in St Petersburg, who was on trial for organising a criminal enterprise. The plan was for Malyshev to act as a check on the rival Tambovsky gang, headed by Vladimir Kumarin, nicknamed the Night Governor because he ruled the city after darkness fell. The judge did as he was asked, freeing Malyshev on the original, if technically unassailable, grounds that, under Russian law at that time, organising a criminal group was not an offence.[48]

In the event, it changed nothing: the Tambovsky gang remained unchallenged and, because it was impossible to run St Petersburg without a working arrangement with at least one of the main crime groups, soon afterwards the Mayor's Office established a privileged relationship with Kumarin. The Tambovsky were seen as a lesser evil than the Kazansky, a particularly brutal gang from the Volga region. Malyshev's group was in decline and the Chechens were a law unto themselves.[49]

Whenever a foreign businessman had difficulties with Russian criminals, the consulates turned to Putin for help.

John Evans, the US Consul General who had succeeded Jack Gosnell, recalled seeking his intervention in 1995, when the Russian partner in a joint venture with the American sandwich firm, Subway, pushed out the US manager, pocketed the profits and renamed the franchise *Minutka*.

Putin told him that he would first check the terms of the contract, leading Evans to believe that he would try to resolve the conflict through the courts.[50] What he actually did was quite different. Subway's Russian partner, Vadim Bordyug, was alleged at that time to have links with the Tambovsky gang, which provided essential protection to many businesses in the city. Albert Stepanov, the head of the FRC's Joint Venture Department, who had good contacts with the Tambovsky group, was despatched to see him and try to sort out the mess. Bordyug refused to back down.[51] When it became clear that the Mayor's Office lacked the power – or was unwilling to expend the political capital – to force him to do so, the dispute went to arbitration in Stockholm.[52] In 1997, the Swedish court awarded Subway 1.2 million US dollars in damages and compensation. Bordyug refused to pay. Five years later, after a protracted legal battle, during which *Minutka* changed its name five more times, the City Property Committee succeeded in cancelling the restaurant's lease. Finally, in April 2003, the Russian Supreme Court ruled in Subway's favour and Bordyug was evicted.

He never paid back the money or the damages awarded in arbitration. But Subway were satisfied. They recovered their property, a prime site on Nevsky Prospekt, and their franchise was extended to the whole of Russia.

Cases like that were two a penny in Russia in the 1990s. The only unusual part on this occasion was that Subway eventually prevailed.

Malversation worked both ways. In 1994, the Mayor's Office transferred 4.5 million US dollars as an advance to the Finnish building company, Haka. Two days after receiving the money, the company declared bankruptcy. 'Did they really not know?' Putin exclaimed.[53] In another case, a Swiss-Israeli entrepreneur, Baruch Rappaport, whose name had been linked to machinations ranging from the Iran–Contra Affair to arms deals with the Medellín Cartel, swindled the Mayor's Office out of millions of dollars after reneging on a contract to equip a container port for St Petersburg. It emerged later that Rappaport had carried out similar scams in Odessa and Vladivostok.[54]

Putin's approach to the Subway affair, to try to seek a resolution by way of an informal compromise, rather than through the courts, was standard practice in Russia. It failed in this case because Bordyug had calculated, correctly, that the Mayor's Office would not risk a confrontation with the Tambovsky gang over such a minor issue. In other

cases, where both sides could find an interest, the City Administration
and organised crime cooperated more fruitfully. A classic example was
the distribution of gasoline to St Petersburg's petrol stations, which
was controlled by Surgutneftegaz, an oil company in western Siberia
whose refinery at Kirishi, 70 miles east of St Petersburg, was the main
supplier throughout the Russian north-west. Kumarin quickly realised
that there was money to be made from petrol stations. Yevgeny
Vyshenkov, who had been a member of the Brotherhood, as the St
Petersburg underworld was called, before reinventing himself as an
investigative journalist, explained what happened next:

> There was a very simple conversation. Kumarin said [to the Directors
> of Surgutneftegaz]: 'I have a suggestion. Let us own this property
> jointly – it will be useful, it will be a good thing. There are two possible
> answers: yes or no. If it's no, in a month or two, you will be killed.' He
> wasn't coming in just as a gangster, he was bringing his money, his con-
> nections, his services, to make a business. But for something that big,
> without the government, you couldn't do it. So you had to negotiate
> with the bureaucrats as well.[55]

Surgutneftegaz had recently cut fuel supplies to St Petersburg on the
pretext of unpaid bills in order to justify higher prices at the pump,
which had resulted in miles-long queues at petrol stations and widespread public dissatisfaction.[56] Sobchak was therefore predisposed to
view favourably any proposal which would force the oil company to be
more accommodating.

In September 1994, he announced that the City Property Committee had established what was to be known as the St Petersburg
Petroleum Fuel Company (PFC), which would have a monopoly on
fuel distribution in the city, as well as to the airport, the railways, the
merchant and river shipping fleets, and other large-scale consumers.
With the Tambovsky gang acting as enforcers, Surgutneftegaz was in
no position to object. The new company was as official as one could
wish. The well-respected former head of the Tax Inspectorate, Dmitry
Filippov, was named President. Kumarin became Vice President.[57]
There were no more queues at petrol stations and prices at the pump
were significantly reduced.

Kumarin's move from banditry to participation in legitimate, or quasi-legitimate, business, was part of a general trend in the second half of the 1990s.

Ilya Traber made a similar transition. He was nicknamed 'the Anti-quary', because that was how he had started his career. Like many others at that time, he straddled the borderline between legitimate business and the black market.[58] Sobchak and his wife, Lyudmila, who was fascinated by antiques, accepted him into their circle, and when Queen Elizabeth II visited St Petersburg in 1994, Traber arranged for her to be presented with a miniature iconostasis with finely painted likenesses of her grandfather, George V, and his cousin, Tsar Nicholas II, both in naval uniform.[59]

But there was another side to Traber which was less genteel. A young Western banker remembered attending a business meeting where the antiques dealer astounded the foreigners present by pulling out a pistol and telling them: 'This is how I resolve problems.'[60]

Kumarin and two other gang leaders, Sergei Vasiliev and Gennady Petrov, joined Traber to become the effective owners of the St Peters-burg Oil Port, which handled the bulk of Russia's seaborne oil exports until Primorsk, closer to the Finnish border, became operational in 2001.[61] Gigantic sums of money were at stake, which complicated rela-tions. Vasiliev was badly wounded and one of his bodyguards killed by a sniper after Kumarin accused him of breaking their agreement.[62]

Putin exercised oversight of all St Petersburg's ports for the Mayor's Office because of their role in foreign trade.

When a Dutch oil logistics company, Royal Pakhoed, expressed an interest in modernising the oil terminal facilities, Putin handled the negotiations. An agreement was initialled, and the CEO and several board members of the Dutch firm flew to St Petersburg for the signing ceremony. Putin kept them waiting. When eventually he arrived, he was stone-faced. 'We will not sign this,' he said. 'It is not in the interests of the Russian people.' Leaving the Dutchmen open-mouthed, he turned on his heel and left.[63]

No reason was given. The most plausible explanation is that Traber and Kumarin decided at the last minute that, whatever the practical advantages of modernising the terminal, they were outweighed by the disadvantage of having Western accountants nosing around, and Sob-chak and Putin were asked to quash the deal.[64] Afterwards, Royal

Pakhoed signed a contract with Estonia and set about modernising the port facilities at Tallinn.

Russians had had to learn to use informal networks to sort out problems among themselves because in Soviet, as in tsarist, times, the justice system, in so far as there was one, had been a political instrument. It was only when a problem involved foreigners, who, by definition, could not be part of Russian networks and did not understand the Russian way of doing things, that recourse would be had to the courts, and even then as a last resort.

Franz Sedelmayer experienced the process at first hand when his home on Kamenny Ostrov was expropriated without compensation in 1995 after the Kremlin decided that it would make a suitable residence for President Yeltsin when he visited St Petersburg. [65]

Putin initially told Sedelmayer that there must be a bureaucratic error and he could easily get it fixed. He persuaded the St Petersburg headquarters of the FSK to tell Moscow that the building was unsuitable on security grounds. However, the State Property Committee, which was behind the proposal, dug in its heels. Then Putin tried to negotiate with the head of the Kremlin's General Affairs Office, Pavel Borodin. On the basis of their discussions, he advised Sedelmayer to write Borodin a formal letter, agreeing to vacate the premises, but asking for the reimbursement of the 800,000 US dollars' worth of renovations that he had made and compensation for the expense of moving to new premises. To ensure that the appropriate forms were respected, Putin vetted the text before Sedelmayer sent the letter. But even before it arrived, Yeltsin had signed a decree, transferring ownership of the villa to the Presidential Administration. Three weeks later, Sedelmayer received Borodin's response. Sedelmayer's company had been established illegally, Borodin said. There would be no compensation and he was to vacate the property at once.

It was a flat-out lie. Putin himself had registered the company. It was completely legal.

In Sedelmayer's recollection, Putin told him: 'I'm your advocate, not your enemy. My name is on the registration papers. I know your company is legal . . . But I can't risk my career over this . . . I have to tread very carefully.' Sedelmayer said he understood that. There was no point blaming the messenger. '[Putin] knew precisely how the system worked,' he wrote later, 'and so did I.'

In Yeltsin's Russia, as in the Soviet Union and the tsarist empire before it, the Kremlin's word was law. A few months later, the building was sequestrated by special forces troops.

In this case, the Russian method of mediation and compromise had broken down because one side in the dispute was a foreigner and the other had overwhelming power. The only option was to go to court.

When Sedelmayer asked Putin what he should do, Putin replied: 'Sue them, Franz. If you don't like what they did to you, sue them.' So, like the owner of the Subway sandwiches franchise, Sedelmayer went to arbitration in Stockholm, where he was awarded 4.7 million US dollars in compensation and damages. In his case, however, the Russian Supreme Court refused to enforce the judgement. Sedelmayer's opponent was not a local entrepreneur like Bordyug but the Presidential Administration. Over the next 25 years, Putin's one-time friend, who was nothing if not persistent, obtained court orders for the seizure, by way of compensation, of Russian government buildings in Germany and Sweden which were not covered by diplomatic immunity and recovered almost all the 10 million dollars which, including interest, he was by then owed. In legal fees alone – not to mention the diplomatic fallout in terms of relations with Sweden, which Russia held responsible for the arbitration award – Moscow had spent tens of times more than the paltry 800,000 dollars which Sedelmayer had originally sought. But it had become a conflict involving the Russian state. Putin's assurance to Sedelmayer that 'whatever will take place from here on, it's not me,' no longer applied. Russia's 'face' was at stake.

That the Mayor's Office maintained relations with criminals is not in dispute.[66] As one of Sobchak's deputies put it: 'The head of the city has to deal with people he would much rather not know.'[67]

But association is not guilt. The more important question is whether and, if so, to what extent, Putin and his colleagues themselves were corrupt.

Some were indeed criminals. In October 1993, Lev Savenkov, the deputy Mayor responsible for Commerce and Food Supplies, was arrested on charges of having tried to export to Finland a few grams of Osmium-187, a rare isotope used for biomedical labelling.[68] The consignment was said to be worth nearly 500,000 US dollars. When the investigators searched Savenkov's apartment, they found 3.5 million roubles (35,000 dollars) plus a quantity of foreign currency. His official salary was about 80 dollars a month.[69]

The Mayor's Office initially defended him and allowed him to keep his job.[70] Putin told the press that it was not the first time that Savenkov had attempted a 'non-standard' deal to try to bring in revenue for the city and suggested that on this occasion he had been duped by tricksters.[71] Soon afterwards, the Chief Investigator in the Prosecutor's Office, Pyotr Kirosheyev, ruled that there was no case to answer. The whole affair, he said, had been fabricated by officers of the FSK. That was not quite as far-fetched as it might seem, for another recent high-profile case in St Petersburg, in which the shipping magnate, Viktor Kharchenko, had been accused of embezzlement, had indeed been fabricated by FSK officers as part of an intrigue initiated by the Ministry of the Merchant Marine in Moscow, which found it unacceptable that there should be a private shipping company in Russia outside its control.[72]

But then it was discovered that Savenkov had also been behind a botched attempt by the Tambovsky gang to smuggle seven and a half tons of caviar to Germany through Belarus.[73] After a lengthy trial, he was given a five-year term in a labour camp.[74]

The Mayor's Office had instinctively closed ranks to try to protect Savenkov because everyone knew they were potentially vulnerable.[75] That was why Sobchak had sent Putin to speak out in his defence lest the scandal spread and implicate others. Since the end of 1993, when the Petrosoviet had been dissolved, the City Administration had taken all the key decisions. Businessmen had learnt which officials had to be bribed in order to get things done.[76] As Yevgeny Vyshenkov put it, with only mild exaggeration: 'At that time, everybody took. It would be like saying that you fought in the Second World War for five years and did not kill anyone . . . Everyone took. But [they did so] to different degrees.'[77]

Prosecutions were rare because it was in no one's interest that cases come to court. In the six years that Sobchak was in power, apart from the Savenkov affair, only three officials were indicted. One was a legal adviser in the Registration Chamber of the FRC, who had accepted a bribe of 1,000 US dollars to register a fake joint venture. The other two were officials in the Property Committee who had been bribed to approve illegal privatisations.[78]

In reality that was just the tip of the iceberg.

The commonest form of corruption concerned real estate. Even in Soviet times, officials in resort towns like Sestroretsk had grown fat on bribes for authorising the construction of dachas. In St Petersburg, where two out of five families still lived in workers' hostels or communal apartments and people waited decades to obtain even a modest apartment of their own, the pressure on housing was intense. In 1993, 300,000 families were waiting for better accommodation. More than 13,000 received new apartments. But most of the lucky ones were not those in the housing queue. More than 90 per cent were people who 'knew someone', who 'had a relative who could help', who could offer a favour in return or who simply bribed the relevant officials. For the most part, this took place at the district level, but it reached up into the Mayor's Office as well. When the Legislative Assembly attempted to clean up the system, Sobchak was furious. It was far too useful an instrument of patronage for the administration to give up.[79]

Putin obtained an apartment on Vasilevsky Island that year by this means. The head of the district administration, Valery Golubev, had been his colleague in the KGB. After Putin joined the Mayor's Office, he had found Golubev a place in the secretariat. When the time came to return the favour, Golubev worked out a complicated arrangement whereby the residents of an apartment block were moved to inferior accommodation in the suburbs on the pretext that the building was to be renovated. Afterwards the newly refurbished apartments were allocated not to the long-suffering families who had been waiting in line for years, but to Golubev's friends and relations. The Putins received one apartment. Another went to Golubev's mother-in-law.[80]

The arrangement was corrupt, not because bribery was involved but because Putin had used his connections illegally to jump the queue. Afterwards, in an attempt to deflect criticism, he half acknowledged having done so while at the same time justifying it. He had acquired the new apartment, he said, in a three-way exchange with his parents' old flat on Sredneokhtinsky Avenue. 'Everything was done according to the rules. I paid for the extra square metres of floor space [since the new flat was bigger].' That said, he conceded that officials had 'possibilities' not available to ordinary citizens, thanks to their networks of relations, and the higher the official, the more 'possibilities' there were. 'I have to admit,' he went on, 'that as an ordinary citizen, and not deputy Mayor, to get better living conditions would have been much more complicated.'[81]

The statement was cleverly worded, very different from the blanket denials officials usually offered, and made it appear that Putin was trying to be honest, or at least more so than most of his colleagues.

The acquisition of the Vasilevsky Island apartment was not the only questionable real-estate deal in which he was involved. After giving up the rented summer house at Zelenogorsk at the end of 1993, he decided to build a dacha of his own. Initially Putin planned to renovate a tumbledown cottage on a small plot of land which he had acquired in Gdovsk district, near Lake Peipus on the border with Estonia, soon after his return from East Germany.[82] But then, thanks to 'networks of relations', he was offered for next to nothing a much more desirable piece of land bordering a lake in Karelia, three hours' drive north of St Petersburg. The dacha he built there cost about 60,000 US dollars. It has never been established with certainty who paid for it, but it cannot have been Putin himself.[83] With an official salary of at most a few hundred dollars a month, saving that amount in five years would have been beyond him.[84] It is possible that one of the big construction firms active in St Petersburg, which had benefitted from municipal contracts, financed it as an expression of thanks for services rendered, or the money may have come from other sources.[85]

In Russia, there is an important difference between an official who takes bribes, and one who accepts a recompense from a businessman he has helped. According to the St Petersburg historian, Dmitry Travin, it is a distinction which goes back to tsarist times:

> Many Russian officials, and not just then, but now, too, don't think that it is wrong to take kickbacks, they think it is just a legitimate return for the help they give to business. It's a moral question. In seventeenth-century Russia, there were two expressions for bribes: *mzdoimstvo* [donations] and *likhoimstvo* [extortion]. *Mzdoimstvo* was the proper sum of money for the official's help – it was accepted, and it was not subject to discussion, because officials never lived just on their salary. The expression is no longer used, but the idea [has survived]. It means that you can take your rightful due and that is fine. *Likhoimstvo* means asking much too much.[86]

Putin argued that bribe-taking was unacceptable, but on slightly different grounds. 'The person who gives a bribe,' he said, soon after becoming deputy Mayor, 'always humiliates the person who accepts it. Self-esteem, respect for one's own worth, is extremely important, in my view.'[87]

Respect was fundamental for Putin. Whether for himself as a boy in Baskov Lane or for Russia as a great power, the need to be respected was a constant principle all his life.

Most of the people who worked with Putin in St Petersburg have since maintained that he did not take bribes, at least not in the sense of *likhoimstvo*. That is probably true. Gifts were a different matter. But bribes involved a quid pro quo and made the bribe-taker dependent.

Savenkov's predecessor as head of the Commerce Committee, Sergei Pokrovsky, maintained that Putin was one of the few officials in the Mayor's Office who were clean.[88] So did Franz Sedelmayer, despite his bitterness at being expropriated. So did one of the most prominent of the 'new Russians', the future oligarch, Boris Berezovsky, who had opened a dealership selling foreign cars in St Petersburg.

Berezovsky's relationship with Putin had started badly. Soon after Sobchak became Mayor, Pyotr Aven brought Berezovsky to meet him.

> Putin was on Sobchak's right, Boris on his left [Aven remembered]. And Boris . . . fell asleep. Sobchak who was wrapped up in what he was saying, which lasted about 40 minutes, didn't notice. But Putin saw only too clearly. His face gradually reddened . . . He signalled to me, and, without Sobchak noticing, I started throwing balls of screwed up paper at Boris to try to wake him up. Berezovsky woke up, looked around . . . and fell asleep again . . . Putin was furious. [Afterwards] he did not shake hands with Boris, and took me aside . . . 'It's better that [that man] doesn't show his face again in our city,' he said. 'If I meet him, I'll break his legs.'[89]

Evidently matters were smoothed over. But when Berezovsky brought a brand new Zhiguli saloon to Putin's dacha, as a token of appreciation for his help in setting up the dealership, Putin thanked him but refused to accept it. Berezovsky was astonished. 'He was the first bureaucrat who did not take bribes,' he told the journalist, Masha Gessen, years later. 'Seriously. It made a huge impression on me.'[90]

Not long after that incident, Berezovsky's General Manager, Yuli Dubov, arranged to have lunch with Putin to discuss a business problem that had arisen. They met in his office at Smolny. Putin made a phone call, told Dubov that the question was resolved and then excused himself. 'I know we agreed to have lunch, ' he said, 'but then it turned out you had business to discuss. Let us not confuse different things.' In Moscow, Dubov thought, no official would lift a finger without being given lunch. 'Who is this weird fellow?' he asked Berezovsky when he got back. 'He's like that,' Berezovsky told him.[91]

These anecdotes can be read at several levels. Taken literally, they were the marks of an incorruptible public servant. Yet Putin's refusal of even a lunch invitation leaves the impression that he was protesting too much. Likewise his refusal to accept Berezovsky's offer of a car. What Berezovsky had proposed was not a bribe per se, but *mzdoimstvo*, a 'donation' – a distinction which Putin well understood. His reaction seemed rather to stem from distrust. He sensed, probably correctly, that if he accepted anything from the tycoon, he would be making himself vulnerable and it might later be used against him.

With people whom he trusted and who he could be sure would be discreet, Putin behaved differently. Natalya Gevorkyan, a journalist with *Kommersant*, remembered attending a dinner with friends at the *Train Bleu* restaurant in the Gare de Lyon in Paris, at which a St Petersburg businessman was present. He mentioned casually that he had recently met Putin, who was a good friend, and they had gone together to drink beer in a sauna. He had just secured a very lucrative contract, he said, and since Putin seemed not to have much money, he had given him 10,000 US dollars. There was no suggestion of any quid pro quo. Later in the evening, when one of the party mentioned that Gevorkyan was a journalist, the businessman blanched. 'You know what happens to people who talk too much,' he told her.[92]

Charles Ryan, the young banker who had set up the EBRD office in St Petersburg, divided Russian bureaucrats into three categories:

You had A's, B's and C's. The A's did not take money . . . They were chickenshit or it was just not their style. There was a very small group of them. The B's, who are the largest group, were generally speaking there for public service, but would have felt like idiots if they didn't at least create a pension for themselves. So they would do the odd deal to make sure that they had some kind of financial cushion, but they were largely speaking doing government service. The C's wouldn't lift a pen without getting paid. And I saw people make the transition. I saw people essentially start out as A minuses, and become B's. I saw people that were B's become C's.[93]

Putin was a solid 'B'. He 'took', as Yevgeny Vyshenkov put it, as did almost every official in St Petersburg, but as *mzdoimstvo* – gratuities, not bribes – discreetly and on a modest scale.[94]

Later it would be claimed that Putin had made large sums of money illegally from the Petersburg Fuel Company, from gambling establishments in the city and from a property development company registered in Frankfurt, the St Petersburg Real Estate Holding Company, known by its German acronym, SPAG.[95] On closer examination, none of those claims hold up.

Putin's only connection with the Fuel Company was that, in Sobchak's absence, he had signed the decree setting it up. The FRC did not own shares in it and Putin played no part in its management.

His role in the gambling business was slightly more consequential. When Sobchak appointed him to head the city's Gambling Commission at the end of 1991, the idea was that the Mayor's Office should not only license betting establishments but should acquire 51 per cent of their capital so that a corresponding share of the profits would go to the city budget.[96] Since the City Administration had no money to invest, in lieu of capital it provided premises rent-free, a scheme dreamt up by Sobchak's legal adviser, Dmitry Medvedev. In practice, it proved complicated. Federal and regional laws were in conflict, the Mayor's Office changed the form of its participation five times in four years and all the betting establishments in the city were controlled directly or indirectly by organised crime.[97] Putin claimed afterwards that the casino owners hid their profits and declared only losses.[98] In fact, the scheme worked better than he remembered. In 1994, the first year the Mayor's Office issued licences, the budget received 1.5 billion roubles (430,000 US dollars) in revenue and taxes from gambling establishments.[99] The actual profits were no doubt much larger. However, Putin was in charge only for the first ten months, after which he was replaced as Chairman by the head of the Finance Committee, Aleksei Kudrin, and the first licences were not issued until long after his departure.[100] While it is permissible to speculate that part of the proceeds ended up in the pockets of members of the Gambling Commission, there is no proof that that happened and still less is there any evidence into whose pockets it went.

Putin's links to SPAG were even more tenuous. He was an *ex officio* member of the Advisory Board, representing the FRC, along with German Gref from the Property Committee and Oleg Kharchenko, the City Architect. Through its local affiliate, the Znamenskaya Company, SPAG signed an agreement to redevelop property on Nevsky Prospekt. The company's problems began in the autumn of 1999, when the German Federal Intelligence Agency, the BND, started investigating suspected links between the company and the Tambovsky gang and the Cali cocaine cartel. In May, 2000, SPAG's Managing Director, a Liechtenstein-based lawyer named Rudolf Ritter, was arrested on charges of money laundering, of which he was later acquitted. By the time the case came to court, Putin had severed all contact with the company. His membership of the Advisory Board had been as a representative of the City Administration and there was nothing to suggest that he ever benefitted from the connection, any more than did Gref or Kharchenko.

The only basis for claiming that Putin enriched himself was that all the companies concerned were linked to well-known crime figures.

Kumarin, the leader of the Tambovsky group, controlled the Fuel Company and was a director of Znamenskaya, which was headed by Vladimir Smirnov. Putin had met Smirnov during a visit to Germany in 1991, and had given a licence to one of his companies to export raw materials during the food scandal that year. Later they had worked together to set up the St Petersburg Currency Exchange. Smirnov was one of the many indeterminate figures, emblematic of the mid 1990s in St Petersburg, who existed, like Ilya Traber, on the frontier between business, politics and crime.

Misha Mirilashvili, who controlled much of the gambling business in St Petersburg, was another. He and Kumarin financed Russkoe Video, a television production company which made promotional films for the Mayor's Office while serving as a front for more dubious activities. He was close to Sobchak, who made sure that the City government placed no obstacles in the way of his business activities, and to Galina Starovoitova, the democratic movement leader who had been an adviser to Yeltsin.[101]

It was a world in which all the barriers were fluid, where yesterday's criminal was tomorrow's business magnate and a politician today was a criminal tomorrow.

Putin understood that mindset. For some, he seemed to feel a sneaking admiration, just as he had admired men like his judo coach, Leonid Usyatov, and his one-time sparring partner, Nikolai Vashchilin, whose grim countenance alone would cause potential troublemakers to beat a hasty retreat. In Turku, St Petersburg's twin city in Finland where his friend, Juhani Leppä, was Mayor, Putin associated with Heikki Elia, reputed to be a figure in the Finnish underworld. In 1995, Leppä was forced to resign after a real-estate scandal. He was given a suspended sentence. Elia, 'a nice fellow, but with a criminal mind', as Leppä put it, was jailed. Sometime later, when a mutual acquaintance visited Russia, Putin, referring to Elia, asked how the 'Big Man' was doing.[102] Their association attracted the attention of the Finnish National Bureau of Investigation, which, having a rather different conception of the proper relationship between criminals and politicians from that prevailing in Russia, put Putin on a watchlist of suspect foreigners – an embarrassment which the Finnish authorities tried desperately to hush up when it emerged a few years later.[103]

'By their friends, ye shall know them,' goes the old saw. To be surrounded by shady characters is not in itself a crime and, in Putin's case, it was at a time when, in Russia, the distinction between politicians, businessmen and criminals was almost completely effaced. But it also reflected Putin's willingness to overlook deviant behaviour when it was in his interests to do so.

It went back to his rough-and-tumble childhood in Baskov Lane and his years in the judo clubs. At one level, he liked to portray himself as an intransigent guardian of the law. At a meeting in St Petersburg in 1991, he demanded that police officers respond 'instantly and harshly, and maybe even cruelly', if they found themselves under attack by gangsters. 'For every officer who is killed, ten criminals should be wiped out.'[104] Yet in everyday life, he behaved rather differently. While not a criminal or blatantly corrupt himself, he could live with those who were.

Putin's position as 'the second person in the city', as Lyudmila proudly put it, was now uncontested.[105] But he continued to shun the limelight, gaining a reputation as 'the most closed figure in the city government'.[106]

Most of the other leaders were accessible. 'Putin was totally different,' one journalist recalled. 'He would always try to escape the social part of an event. He tried to avoid all contact.'[107] On the rare occasions when he had to give a news conference, he usually contented himself with a short statement and then left, letting his deputy, Aleksei Miller, field the questions. It was not because he could not hold his own. If cornered, he was capable of talking animatedly and at length about the city's affairs while saying absolutely nothing that was newsworthy. 'He spoke extremely well,' the same journalist remembered. 'His diction was marvellous. Most of the leaders at that time mangled their words and spoke ungrammatically. Putin spoke like a member of the Leningrad intelligentsia. He used literary phrases, elegant constructions . . . But when you read it back, it was like a blank tape.'[108]

He was still famously thin-skinned. When the *Sankt-Peterburgskoe ekho*, an economic newspaper, mistakenly called him 'Valery Putin', he was furious at what he saw as a slight and demanded an apology.[109] But he had become a little more outgoing than in the early days. No longer did he evade questions about his future by speaking of becoming a taxi driver. If one day he left the Mayor's Office, he told an interviewer, 'I would like to do something which would give me moral satisfaction and material well-being and be on a large scale . . . Something comparable to the tasks I am dealing with today. For example, to work on some major project at the city or regional level.'[110]

Unlike many of his peers, Putin scrupulously avoided any hint of conspicuous consumption.

Apart from his official car, a medium-sized Nissan saloon, provided by the Mayor's Office, he had the second-hand Volga he had brought back from Germany while Lyudmila drove a Zhiguli, a far cry from the 'new Russians' in their BMWs and Mercedes. The apartment on Vasilevsky Island was certainly more comfortable than anything they had possessed before, with two bedrooms, a sitting room and, by Russian standards, a large kitchen.[111] But it was in a nondescript, five-storey block that was in no sense grand. Grubby middle-class would be a better description. Their dacha was not in one of the fashionable areas along the Gulf of Finland, but deep in the Karelian countryside. Far from being the 'palace' that some Western writers imagined,[112] it was a simple two-storey structure, built on the lakeshore on a one-hectare plot of land next to half a dozen other dachas of the same type. The owners later formed a cooperative, named Ozero ('Lake'), to manage the running costs of the estate, with one of their number, Vladimir Smirnov, as trustee.

The Ozero group would be accorded an exaggerated importance in the mythology of Putin's inner circle, although, with one exception, Vladimir Yakunin, none of its members would play a significant political role.

Viktor Myachin, Yuri Kovalchuk and Andrei Fursenko had been researchers at the Ioffe Institute of Physics and Technology in St Petersburg. Yakunin also had a scientific background. After spending three years at the Ioffe Institute as head of the International Relations Department, traditionally a KGB post, he had worked in New York for Line X in the KGB's First Chief Directorate, responsible for technical and scientific espionage. He, Kovalchuk and Fursenko were slightly older than Putin, Myachin eight years younger. After the collapse of the Soviet Union, the four of them went into private business, as did Fursenko's younger brother, Sergei, a radio engineer specialising in flight control mechanisms, and Vladimir Smirnov, who had started his career as an electrical engineer. The seventh member of the group, Nikolai Shamalov, was a dentist who became the St Petersburg representative of Siemens, importing medical equipment to Russia.

In the autumn of 1991, after the August putsch, five of the seven – Kovalchuk, Myachin, Yakunin and the Fursenko brothers – invested the profits from their joint ventures in Bank Rossiya, redeeming the shares formerly owned by the Leningrad Regional Committee of the Communist Party, which had founded the bank in June, 1990. The investment would make them all extremely wealthy. Kovalchuk became the principal shareholder, with more than 30 per cent of the capital, and Shamalov later acquired a 10 per cent stake.

Apart from Yakunin, whom Putin had encountered briefly when they both worked for the KGB, they had all met through the Foreign Relations Committee. Putin, a law graduate among scientists and a bureaucrat among entrepreneurs, was the odd man out.

His membership of the Ozero cooperative provided a rare insight into his financial situation as deputy Mayor of St Petersburg. He was not rich. His dacha had been built and paid for by others. The first summer the family spent there, when a fire broke out due to an electrical short-circuit, a briefcase with the family's savings went up in the flames. According to Lyudmila, it contained 5,000 US dollars.[113] Like many Russians in those days, Putin preferred cash, in foreign currency, to money in the bank. He tried desperately to recover it but was defeated by the smoke and heat. Part of the money must have come from 'donations': Putin could not have saved that much from his official salary. On the other hand, a wealthy man would not have risked his life for the sake of a few thousand dollars.[114]

Putin was comfortably off by the standards of the time. He had friends who were much wealthier than he was and who were ready to share their good fortune. He had no problem with that.

While Putin's career prospered, Lyudmila led a more cloistered life.

After their return from East Germany, she had found a job teaching Spanish four times a week at the university.[115] She also worked for a while at Delta Telecom, which had brought the first mobile phones to St Petersburg and had offices near the Astoria Hotel.[116] Official functions bored her to distraction and she almost never accompanied Putin to diplomatic receptions or other formal occasions. Sobchak used to hold her up as an ideal woman, telling his own wife, who was a social butterfly: 'Why can't you be like Lyudmila? She stays at home with the children and she doesn't need anything more.'[117]

So it was that, one Thursday morning towards the end of October 1993, she set out from the dacha at Zelenogorsk in the family Zhiguli to take her younger daughter, Katerina, then aged seven, to a rehearsal for the school pantomime in which she was playing Cinderella.[118] When they were close to Smolny, another vehicle jumped a red light and smashed into them. Katerina, who had been asleep on the back seat, suffered only minor injuries, but her mother was taken to the nearest hospital with suspected spinal fractures. Her memories of the place were Dickensian: 'It was full of people dying. There were gurneys in the hallways with dead bodies on them . . . They had no intention of operating on my spine, I don't think they even knew how. [But] my ear was torn and they decided to sew it up. They left me naked on the table in a freezing operating room . . . and went away.'[119]

By then, Putin's secretary, Marina, had reached Yuri Shevchenko, the chief surgeon at the military hospital in St Petersburg, who got

Lyudmila transferred to his own establishment. There, they performed an emergency operation on her spine and discovered that, rather more seriously, she also had a fractured skull.

Putin had been holding meetings that day with Ted Turner, the founder of CNN, and his film-star wife, Jane Fonda, to discuss the arrangements for the Goodwill Games, which Turner was sponsoring. When he learnt of the accident, he contacted the local hospital to which she had first been taken, but was assured that she was in no danger and had suffered only minor injuries. Turner urged him to go to his wife's side and leave his deputy, Aleksei Miller, to continue the discussions. Putin thanked him but insisted it was unnecessary. He spent the rest of the day with them as well as the following morning until their departure for Moscow.[120]

A normally concerned husband, on learning that his wife had just had a serious car accident, would drop everything and rush off to make sure that she was all right. Putin did not. He knew that she had been badly hurt because that evening Shevchenko had telephoned to tell him that Lyudmila's injuries were serious. Yet he stubbornly carried on with his work. It was not because he did not care. His daughter, whom he doted on, had also been in the car. But he did not break off the talks to go to her side either. The self-discipline that he had developed in his childhood had become a default position. His response to any untoward event was to suppress his emotions, wearing an impenetrable mask behind which everything was hidden.

Occasionally, for no obvious reason, his feelings would creep up on him and take him unawares. Then the mask would drop.

In the winter of 1994, when Yeltsin sent the Russian army, largely made up of untrained conscripts, to Chechnya to try to suppress the separatist rebellion there, Putin, as the deputy Mayor responsible for security affairs, was at the airport when the first body bags started coming back from the front. The German Consul, Eberhard von Puttkamer, who also happened to be there, was astonished to see that he was on the verge of tears.[121]

There would be other episodes of this kind, but they were extremely rare. More typical was his reaction when their sheepdog, Malysh, burrowed beneath the fence of the dacha and was hit by a passing car. His secretary went in to tell him that the dog had been killed. 'I looked at him, and there was zero emotion on his face,' she said. 'I was so surprised by the lack of any reaction that I couldn't contain myself and said, "Did someone already tell you about it?" He said calmly, "No, you're the first to tell me." And I knew I had made a blunder.'[122] For years after, he would not get another dog out of loyalty to Malysh.[123] But he refused to let it show. It was all bottled up inside.

Lyudmila had a second operation, this time to close the fracture at the base of her skull, followed by a week in intensive care and then six more weeks in hospital before she was allowed home, wearing a neck-brace, to spend the next two weeks, in her words, 'crawling round the apartment'.[124] In fact she got off remarkably lightly. In January 1994, she was well enough to attend a small, private dinner with von Putt-kamer's predecessor, Henning von Wistinghausen and his wife, on a visit from Estonia, where he was now Ambassador.[125] But she had memory lapses and worried that she had brain damage. At Putin's request, Matthias Warnig, who headed the Dresdner Bank in St Peters-burg, arranged for her to be examined at the bank's expense at a clinic in Bad Homburg, just outside Frankfurt, which gave her a clean bill of health.[126]

Warnig had worked as an informer, and later an officer, in the East German Stasi, retiring with the rank of major. By his own account, he first encountered Putin in St Petersburg in the early 1990s after being recruited by the Dresdner Bank following German reunification and sent to open a branch there.[127] Others insist that they not only knew each other but worked together in East Germany.[128] Wherever the truth lies, they evidently got on well. Warnig would become one of the very few foreigners admitted to Putin's inner circle and, for the next 30 years, would make his career in Putin's orbit.

Lyudmila's journey to Bad Homburg opened up for her a range of new possibilities. The following year, she and the children spent the summer in Hamburg as guests of the Russian Consul General, Dmitry Cherkashin. There she met a German novelist, Irene Pietsch, from an old patrician Hanseatic family, with whom she struck up an improb-able friendship. Pietsch wrote later that Lyudmila was emotional, unpunctual, easily hurt, given to floods of tears and bouts of pessi-mism where nothing in the world was right, but also an interesting companion and good friend.[129] It was clear, she thought, that Putin was the dominant partner in their marriage and that Lyudmila lived in his shadow.[130] But the relationship was complicated. On the one hand,

Lyudmila insisted that Vladimir was 'exactly the right man for me . . .
I cannot imagine a better one. He doesn't drink and he doesn't beat
me' – a remark which astonished her hostess but was evidently something which could not be said of all Russian husbands.[131] On the other
hand, Lyudmila, who, like many Russians, was a firm believer in astrology, told her that, 'unfortunately', Volodya must have been born under
the sign of the Vampire.[132]

She was direct and incapable of subterfuge; he was the opposite. At
times, Lyudmila said, when she tried to work out what he was thinking, 'Volodya's eyes were empty.'[133] But Lyudmila was not the easiest
person either. 'Anyone who can spend three weeks with that woman
deserves a monument,' Putin grumbled.[134]

While Putin, as first deputy Mayor, was careful to do nothing which
might leave traces that would cause future embarrassment, Anatoly
Sobchak had a cupboardful of skeletons.

Starting in 1992, the Mayor had gone each month to the Crédit
Lyonnais in St Petersburg with a briefcase full of foreign currency. The
expatriate staff were each allowed one weekend a month back in
France and, as foreigners, had the right to take with them up to 10,000
dollars. Marlène Julien, the bank's Chief Financial Officer in St Petersburg, estimated that 80 to 100,000 dollars a month were taken out in
this way and deposited in Sobchak's account at the bank's head office
in Paris. The bank staff assumed that the money came from bribes.[135]
But it turned out there was a more innocent explanation. The Baltic
Shipping Company, headed by Sobchak's friend, Viktor Kharchenko,
was still under pressure from the authorities in Moscow and its bank
accounts had been frozen. Sobchak was sending out the money on
Kharchenko's behalf to pay foreign port fees for his ships.[136] Technically it was illegal, but morally Sobchak had nothing to answer for.

Another, more serious, problem concerned his former assistant,
Yuri Shutov. After Sobchak fired him, Shutov started writing an exposé
of his one-time employer, whose title went through various iterations
but which was eventually published as *Sobchache serdtse*, literally 'Sobchak's Heart', an untranslatable play on words echoing Mikhail
Bulgakov's similarly titled novella, 'The Heart of a Dog' (*Sobache
serdtse*). On the evening of October 4, 1991, when Shutov returned to
his apartment, three men were waiting inside.[137] They beat him about

the head with hammers, fracturing his skull. The only thing taken was the manuscript of Shutov's book. Shutov claimed afterwards to have recognised his assailants as officers from RUBOP, the Regional Administration for Combatting Organised Crime, and afterwards evidence emerged that that may indeed have been the case.

Sobchak insisted that it was 'a purely criminal matter. There is nothing political about it,' and the police investigators followed his cue. But that looked like a cover-up. Although there was nothing to suggest that Sobchak himself had ordered the attack, somebody had plainly done so. Suspicion fell on Putin.

The evidence was circumstantial. By writing a tell-all book about Sobchak, Shutov had shown disrespect and disloyalty. Putin esteemed respect and loyalty above all else. His relationship with the security services meant it would have been easy for him to arrange for off-duty officers to intervene.[138] When aroused, he did not shy away from threatening violence: his promise to 'break Berezovsky's legs' was an example. Whether or not Sobchak was aware of his intentions, it would not have been out of character for Putin to have decided that Shutov needed to be stopped.[139]

Subsequent events lent weight to that idea. Six months afterwards, Shutov was arrested for allegedly heading a criminal organisation, an accusation which seemed to bolster Sobchak's claim that what had happened was between gangsters and not political. The charge was obviously fabricated and the court threw it out. But that was not the end of the matter. Seven years later, in February 1999, Shutov was re-arrested on charges of having organised the murders of two prominent politicians. When the court threw out those charges, too, masked special forces troops burst into the courtroom and re-arrested him. The investigation which followed lasted seven more years. Finally a new trial was held, not in a courthouse but, against all the normal rules of criminal procedure, in the prison where Shutov was being held. This time he was found guilty and sentenced to life imprisonment. He died in prison eight years later.

None of that constitutes proof that Putin was responsible. Shutov was no wide-eyed innocent and he may well have been guilty of crimes. But the attack on him in the spring of 1992, the relentlessness with which he was pursued by a justice system which invariably did the Kremlin's bidding, the circumstances of his repeated arrests and the fact that Putin personally loathed him constitute a prima facie case. No one has yet offered a better explanation for the way Shutov was hounded to death over more than 20 years.

If, in Shutov's case, Putin appears to have been the prime mover, there were other occasions where he and Sobchak engaged in a 'good cop, bad cop' routine.

In 1992, Sobchak had promised the Swedish Prime Minister, Carl Bildt, that the city would make available premises for a new Swedish consulate. Eventually they settled on a late nineteenth-century build-ing, just off Nevsky Prospekt, designed by the Swedish architect, Carl Andersson. Putin led the negotiations on the Russian side.[140] But, as the Swedish Consul, Sture Stiernlöf, recalled, the discussion did not work out as Stockholm had expected:

> At the start of the negotiations, the building was empty, deserted and unheated, with some squatters using stolen electricity and life-threatening fireplaces. Barely, however, had the negotiations begun than an energetic 'renovation' started . . . The ceilings and all original furnishings such as tile stoves, oak parquet and stucco were demolished and destroyed or, presumably, sold . . . Putin was politely evasive for months but then there was an unpleasant surprise. Suddenly there appeared at the negotiating table a so-called 'investor' demanding com-pensation for his 'improvement work' to the house.[141]

At that stage, Stiernlöf said, no one outside the Mayor's Office knew that Sweden was negotiating for a lease on the building and the so-called investor could only have learnt about it from Putin.[142] It cost the Swedish government one million kronor (about 130,000 US dollars) to buy him out.

Even then, the Swedes' problems were not over. They had wanted the lease to include an abandoned Lutheran Church adjoining the con-sulate building that had been taken over by a sports club. Out of nowhere, a Lutheran congregation suddenly appeared. In June, 1994, when the Swedish deputy Minister, Ulf Dinkenspiel, arrived for the signing ceremony, there was another contretemps. The draft had been initialled by both sides. But as they were about to open the champagne, Putin announced that it could not be signed as it stood – one of the clauses would have to be renegotiated in a sense more favourable to the Russian side. Three hours later, well after midnight, a compromise was reached. Stiernlof remembered looking at Putin afterwards and seeing on his face 'a faint glimmer of a Mona Lisa smile'.

It was the same scenario as Putin's last-minute rejection of the agreement with Royal Pakhoed to participate in the St Petersburg oil port. Sobchak was full of charm and good intentions, assuring Western partners that everything would be done as they wished. Putin was the hard man who haggled over the details and made things happen . . . or not.[143]

In the case of the Swedish consulate, most of the so-called compensation for the 'improvements' to the building went to the Mayor's Contingency Fund, Sobchak's reserve for off-the-books expenses. Like Putin, Sobchak was wary of outright bribes, but he accepted *blat* – 'donations' and other favours. One of the city's banks, as a 'token of appreciation', opened a special account for him, with an annual interest rate of more than 1,000 per cent so that any deposit he placed in it would double every month.[144] A certain amount of money was also skimmed off from the numerous renovation projects in the old city.[145] One of St Petersburg's top architects, Veniamin Fabritsky, remembered saying to Sobchak, as they inspected a refurbished building, 'Mr Mayor, you will see that the work is not complete, we still have to put in new window-frames,' to which Sobchak replied: 'But Veniamin, those *are* new window-frames.' The work had been paid for but the money had been siphoned off elsewhere.[146]

Sobchak was not greedy. He did not own a Mercedes or a BMW, any more than Putin did, and he avoided the ostentation associated with the 'new Russians'. But he loved foreign travel, he liked to live well and he had a succession of mistresses to support. His wife, Lyudmila Narusova, adored designer clothes, which, in Russia, cost as much as they did in the West. She told a German television station, 'Escada is my weakness', which no doubt pleased the Germans – Escada being a Munich-based luxury clothing line – but did not go down well in St Petersburg where millions of people had barely enough to eat.[147]

None of these things were affordable on Sobchak's official salary. But it was his apartment, filled with antiques, many of them provided by Ilya Traber, overlooking the Moika River in a fashionable area near the city centre, which would prove his biggest liability.

Sobchak had moved there from the suburbs shortly after his

appointment as Chairman of the Lensoviet in 1990.[148] Four years later, Narusova decided that it was too small and pressured the families in the communal apartment next door to move out to the suburbs, so that the two flats could be joined, making a sumptuous residence of some 3,200 square feet (300 square metres).

Many aspects of the transaction were dubious, but Narusova's biggest mistake was to ask the real estate company overseeing the deal, Renaissance Limited, to provide 54,000 US dollars towards the cost of the buy-out and refurbishment.[149] Sobchak had bent the rules to authorise projects for Renaissance, including the renovation of an apartment block on Ryleyeva Street, in the northern part of the city, so the refurbishment was in fact a disguised kickback. As in the case of the building where Putin lived, on Vasilevsky Island, most of the Ryleyeva Street apartments had been allocated not to those who had waited for years in the housing queue but to officials and their relations. The Legislative Assembly had protested, but since this kind of thing was happening all over Russia in the 1990s, it was not, in itself, a major scandal. Then it was learnt that one of them had been allotted to Sobchak's niece on the verbal understanding that she would repay the cost, some 25,000 dollars, by working as a cleaning lady in the building. Since she was never seen with so much as a mop in her hand, the story, once it leaked out, was met with derision. The favour for the niece plus the refurbishment of Sobchak's own apartment would come back to haunt him.

The six months from December 1995 to June 1996 were largely given over to elections, both at the national and the city level.

Sobchak had announced the previous spring that he intended to stand again as Mayor, or Governor, as the post would now be called.[150] Although he started as clear favourite, there were signs that he would face strong headwinds, many of his own making.

His strength was as an orator. But the novelty had worn off. Charles Ryan, the young banker from the EBRD, remembered: 'The first time you heard him speak, it almost brought tears to your eyes. And then the second time, you were like, wow, that's great, but very similar to the first time. And about the eighth or ninth time, you were thinking, "Give me a break!" '[151] Like a soufflé which collapses as it cools, there was a lot of hot air and little substance.

Sobchak charmed foreigners. But he had a remarkable ability to put his Russian colleagues' backs up. The Legislative Assembly deputy, Dmitry Zapolsky, remembered: 'He was able to do one thing to perfection: he made enemies out of people who would otherwise have been his friends. It took no more than five minutes . . . He treated everyone without exception as an underperforming student.'[152] Aleksandr Belyaev, the former Petrosoviet Chairman, thought it was because 'he regarded everyone as a rival . . . even his own allies.'[153] The ousted Vice Mayor, Vyacheslav Shcherbakov, grumbled: 'We have exchanged the dictatorship of the [Communist Party] for the dictatorship of Sobchak.'[154]

The result was not only trench warfare between the Mayor and the Legislative Assembly.[155] He alienated other constituencies as well.

The business community soon concluded that he was 'a hopeless manager. He makes promises and nothing gets done.'[156] Alfred Kokh, who had so admired him as a standard-bearer of democracy in Soviet times, found that, when it came to running a city, he was 'an awful Mayor'.[157] Sobchak adored hobnobbing with world leaders, being invited to Buckingham Palace, mediating in peace talks in Tajikistan or proposing ways to end the fighting in Chechnya.[158] But the nuts and bolts of administration bored him stiff and he did not try to hide it.

Even Putin, who made a fetish of loyalty to Sobchak, acknowledged that he needlessly antagonised others, especially the army and the security services. 'The generals really loathed him,' Putin said. Sobchak called them 'blockheads' and once, in order to attend a concert by a popular singer he liked, sent word that he was too ill to participate in a military conference, which did not go down well when he appeared on television that night, escorting the lady in question.[159]

The Mayor had grand visions of making St Petersburg the cultural capital of Russia. A film festival was launched, with the Italian actress, Gina Lollobrigida, presiding. The supermodel, Claudia Schiffer, came to judge a beauty contest.[160] The administration provided a generous subvention for the White Nights Festival, which was inaugurated with a series of rock concerts on midsummer evenings when, in northern latitudes, the light never completely fades.[161] But, at a time of economic and social collapse, that was not what people needed. *Chas pik*, which normally supported Sobchak, commented acidly: 'While thousands of fans weep with joy at seeing their idols in real life, hundreds of thousands of pensioners, who have just managed with immense difficulty to obtain their monthly pittance, are asking themselves whether Samantha Fox's breasts, which they were shown on television last night, are really the kind of foreign aid they need.'[162]

As 1995 drew to a close, 50,000 people in St Petersburg were homeless and a million others risked finding themselves on the street from one day to the next.[163] One family in 25 had what Russians considered a 'normal' standard of living; one in a hundred could take a holiday abroad. The rest were either poor, very poor or destitute.[164]

To compound the sense of despair, those who did have a little money frequently fell victim to Ponzi schemes. In St Petersburg and in Leningrad Region, tens of thousands were defrauded each year in swindles which netted the perpetrators millions of dollars.[165] The suicide rate in St Petersburg was among the highest in the world.[166] Tuberculosis, diphtheria and dysentery had reappeared.[167] Average life expectancy in the city had fallen from 72 in 1987 to 64 eight years later.[168] Basic services were collapsing, sometimes literally. In December 1995, a section of the metro line in the city centre caved in, unfortunately coinciding with the visit of a mission from the International Olympic Committee to inspect the facilities St Petersburg could offer if chosen to host the 2004 Games.[169] Of 4,000 buses in the city, 1,500 were beyond repair and another 900 were about to become so.[170] Half the public lavatories were out of order. There were power cuts even at Smolny. For the fourth year running, when the temperature fell far below freezing, the heating in apartment blocks broke down.[171] Snow piled up on the streets because the ploughs had stopped working.[172]

When Wassily Leontief, the émigré Nobel Prize winner whose work on economics had inspired Yeltsin's reforms, returned from Harvard for a visit, he felt the city was 'in ruins, . . . in a lamentable state'.[173]

In the early '90s, the slump in industrial production was steeper than during the Second World War.[174] Privatisation was widely seen as a gigantic swindle, like 'a drunkard in the street selling off his belongings for a pittance', as Yuri Luzhkov, Gavriil Popov's successor as Mayor of Moscow, put it.[175] Leontief and Anatoly Chubais had argued that it did not matter who bought privatised enterprises, they would eventually end up in the right hands – a proposition known as the Coase theorem. To that end, every Russian citizen was issued a privatisation voucher with a nominal value of 10,000 roubles. If the idea was to make Russia a nation of shareholders, it was a spectacular failure.

Inflation eroded the vouchers' value and most people sold them, for the equivalent of a bottle of vodka or less, to touts acting on behalf of factory directors or 'new Russian' businessmen.

Putin said afterwards that he could not remember what he had bought with his voucher but it was surely 'something stupid'.[176] That was true of many others. The result was asset-stripping, surging inequality and the emergence of a small group of billionaire entrepreneurs.

Chubais maintained later that there had been no alternative. Unlike in Eastern Europe, where communism had taken root only after World War II and elements of a market system had survived, in Russia, except among the criminal fraternity, every entrepreneurial instinct had been extirpated by 70 years of Bolshevik rule. Whether or not the reforms could have been conducted differently is beside the point. That was the way they were carried out and, in the mid 1990s, they were desperately unpopular.

By the beginning of 1996, as the city elections approached, the worst of the crisis had passed. Inflation that year was forecast at 55 per cent, still a scary figure but far more manageable than the 1,000 per cent or more in the earlier part of the decade.[177] But that was not how people saw it. 70 per cent of those questioned thought Russia was on the wrong road.[178]

To compound Sobchak's difficulties, his relationship with Yeltsin was deteriorating. He had been a persistent critic of 'shock therapy', quipping that 'first place should be given to therapy . . . From a shock, an organism dies.'[179] In December 1993, he had publicly blamed Yeltsin for the government's unexpected defeat in the Duma elections. The Communist Party, which had been reconstituted the previous February after the Constitutional Court had ruled that an outright ban was illegal, and a right-wing nationalist movement, the oddly named Liberal Democratic Party, headed by a populist demagogue named Vladimir Zhirinovsky, had between them won sufficient seats to produce what was in effect a hung parliament. The success of this 'red–brown coalition', as the democrats called it, was the result of Yeltsin's mistakes, Sobchak said. 'If we go on like this, Zhirinovsky and Co. will be in government.'[180]

With that speech, Sobchak had crossed a line, Chubais thought. 'He deliberately positioned himself as someone who had the right to speak negatively about the central government.'[181]

A year later, the rift widened when Sobchak denounced as 'insane'

Yeltsin's decision to send the army to Chechnya. It was 'a means of covering up the incompetence of the political, military and special services, . . . another outrage to the long-suffering Chechen people . . . and a threat to human rights everywhere in Russia.'[182]

Many Russians agreed.[183]

The Kremlin hawks – the Defence Minister, Pavel Grachev; the First Deputy Prime Minister, Oleg Soskovets; the head of the Kremlin Guard Service, Mikhail Barsukov, who subsequently became head of the FSB, as the FSK had been renamed; and the head of Yeltsin's personal bodyguard, Aleksandr Korzhakov – did not.

They decided that Sobchak had to be taught a lesson.

In May 1995, the St Petersburg Prosecutor's Office opened an investigation into Renaissance Limited – the company that had refurbished the Sobchaks' apartment – on suspicion of having given bribes to the Mayor's Office. In October, the pressure eased and it looked as though a behind-the-scenes agreement had been reached not to pursue the case.[184] But then Sobchak suggested that the Prime Minister, Viktor Chernomyrdin, would be a better candidate than Yeltsin in the 1996 presidential election.[185] He was not alone in that view. Yeltsin's popularity was at rock bottom: opinion polls gave him 10 per cent of voting intentions.[186] Russian democrats were horrified by his conduct of the Chechen War. Some felt that it had become morally impossible to support him, whatever the consequences. Yeltsin was drinking heavily. In Berlin, the previous autumn, he had grabbed the baton from the conductor of a brass band, playing outside the City Hall in his honour, and drunkenly led the ensemble for a few minutes before taking the microphone and singing some verses from a rousing Russian folksong. He had had two heart attacks in July and October 1995 and another unpublicised episode in December.[187]

Sobchak did not oppose Yeltsin on moral grounds. Rather he was concerned that Yeltsin would not survive the election campaign and that, if he did, he would lose. 'Mr President,' Sobchak asked, 'What if something happens to you . . . We would have to vote for the Communist [candidate]. Do you understand what position you are putting us in?'[188]

For the coterie around Yeltsin, if not for Yeltsin himself, that was the last straw. Sobchak would have to go.

A few months earlier, Korzhakov, a bull-like figure whose relationship with Yeltsin made him one of the most powerful men in the country, had appointed an ally, Yuri Skuratov, as the new Prosecutor General.[189] In December, Skuratov, Barsukov and the Interior Minister, Anatoly Kulikov, established a special investigation group to enquire into bribery and malfeasance by the St Petersburg City authorities. Sobchak was not named, but it was obvious to everyone that he was the target.[190]

Meanwhile, in the elections to the State Duma that month, the 'red–brown coalition' of Communists and Nationalists did even better than two years earlier, winning 208 seats out of 450, not far short of a majority.

That set off alarm bells not only in the Kremlin but in the United States, where President Clinton, who was also facing an election in 1996, had no desire to see a Communist-led government return to power in Russia. European leaders felt the same. So did the leading Russian business magnates.

All, in different ways, did what they could to prevent that happening. Clinton put pressure on the IMF to disburse aid which had been delayed. The French President, Jacques Chirac, provided a secret loan of 1.5 billion US dollars, and Germany 3.5 billion, to be used to pay pension arrears and finance other social needs.[191] The businessmen, meeting in February at the World Economic Forum in Davos, agreed to provide Yeltsin with all the media and financial resources they could muster.[192]

The campaign got off to a difficult start.

When Yeltsin announced his candidature in his old fiefdom of Yekaterinburg on February 15, 1996, he found himself with two competing election headquarters, putting forward conflicting strategies. One was led by Korzhakov, Barsukov and Soskovets; the other by Chubais and Yeltsin's daughter, Tatyana.

Korzhakov, who thought that Yeltsin was sure to lose, wanted the President to declare a State of Emergency, justified by the continuing war in Chechnya, and to postpone the elections for two years, so that he could step down at a moment of his choosing and name Soskovets or some other suitable candidate as his heir. To convince Yeltsin that this was the most sensible course, he proposed that the elections in St Petersburg, which were expected to mirror the national poll, be held earlier than originally planned. If, as Korzhakov anticipated, Sobchak lost, it would buttress the case for postponement.[193] Accordingly,

Sobchak was told that the city election must be held, not on June 16, the day of the presidential poll, but four weeks beforehand.[194]

Almost at once, however, these carefully laid plans were upended.

As often happened when Yeltsin had his back to the wall, he developed a new surge of energy and his poll numbers began to improve. Korzhakov and his allies were marginalised and then removed altogether. Chubais, working with Berezovsky and his fellow oligarch, Vladimir Gusinsky, who between them controlled the two main television channels, ORT and NTV, took over the campaign. At the national level, the President was drawing level with his main rival, the Communist leader, Gennady Zyuganov, and was well placed to surpass him. In May, a ceasefire in Chechnya removed the last major obstacle to Yeltsin's victory. But, in St Petersburg, the fuse that Korzhakov had lit continued to smoulder.

Vladimir Putin took a jaundiced view of politics. He saw himself as an administrator – a *chinovnik*, as he liked to say, using the old tsarist term for a bureaucrat – and his job was to keep the City government running. He explained why to Natalya Nikiforova, a journalist at *Chas pik* with whom he had struck up a rapport and who sometimes succeeded in getting him to speak more openly than he would to others:

PUTIN: I don't consider myself a politician and I don't deal with politics.

NIKIFOROVA: What does 'politics' mean to you?

PUTIN: It means creating an image and promoting oneself with a view to making oneself popular and, let's say, helping to find [oneself] further job opportunities. The main way to do that is to stand as a candidate in an election. I don't aspire to that.

NIKIFOROVA: Why?

PUTIN: If I'm completely honest, I don't want to be a puppet . . . In any market economy . . . money accumulates in the hands of specific groups. At the same time, the cost of election campaigns is growing and will keep on growing. In those circumstances, politicians at almost every level find themselves being controlled by those groups which have accumulated most wealth.

NIKIFOROVA: On principle, you don't like being dictated to?

PUTIN: Who does?[195]

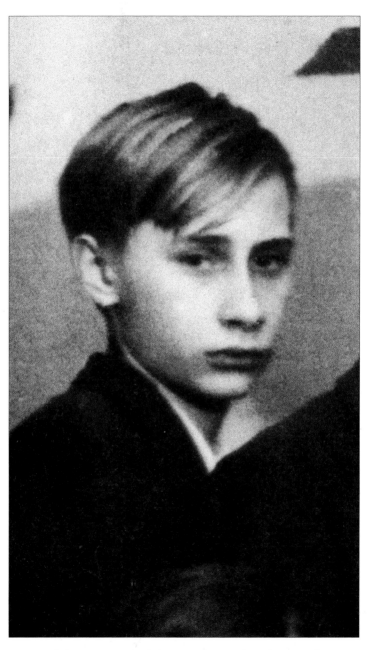

Vladimir Putin, aged about 13, from a class photograph
at his school in Leningrad.

With his parents,
Maria Ivanovna (*above*)
and Vladimir Spiridonovich
(*below*), as a six-year old in
the summer of 1959.

As President, more than 50 years later, he carried
a portrait of his father, wearing the uniform
of a submariner in the Soviet Baltic fleet,
in a procession to mark VE Day.

With his
parents in
1985, shortly
before he left
Leningrad to
join the KGB
liaison office
in Dresden.

A gauche 17-year-old, smitten with a classmate,
Yelena Gryaznova (*above*), in 1970, and (*below*),
judo training with a friend, Vasily Shestakov,
at the *Trud* club the same year.

At the Leningrad Law
Faculty, *c.* 1972.

With colleagues from the Leningrad KGB Directorate, *c.* 1977 (the man whose face is pixelated in the front row was the senior member of the group).

With Yuri Leshchev, Putin's boss in the First Department of the Leningrad Directorate, at the KGB dacha on the Baltic Sea coast in 1979. Note the watch on his right wrist and the street-smart image, with shirt open to the waist and Western black-market jeans.

In Dresden with his daughters, Katya (*left*) and Masha (*right*), *c.* 1987.

Putin and his colleagues, Nikolai Tokarev and Vladimir Agartanov, had passes issued by the East German Security Service, the Stasi. Tokarev (*left*) later became head of the Russian state oil pipeline company, Transneft. Agartanov (*right*) shared an office with Putin and, under a pseudonym, published an account of their work together.

The head of the Dresden KGB office, Lazar Matveyev,
pictured on his 90th birthday, helped advance Putin's career.

Deputy Mayor
of St Petersburg,
1993.

With Katya, Lyudmila, Masha and their Caucasian shepherd dog,
Malysh, in the birch forest near the family's dacha at Zelenogorsk, *c.* 1991.

Masha (*left*) and Katya (*right*), in Putin's library in the Kremlin,
shortly after he became President.

Putin's dress sense in the 1990s was decidedly eccentric. Here, alongside his mentor Anatoly Sobchak, the Mayor of St Petersburg, in 1993, he wears a raspberry-coloured blazer emblematic of the 'New Russians', paired with blue Adidas jogging pants.

Hosting Mikhail Gorbachev when he visited the city the following year. Putin never forgave Gorbachev for the disintegration of the USSR.

Three of Yeltsin's previous Prime Ministers: (*left to right*) Viktor Chernomyrdin, Sergei Stepashin and Sergei Kirilenko. The last two were considered potential successors before he fixed his choice on Putin.

A somewhat intimidated Vladimir Putin on New Year's Eve, 1999, shaking hands with Yeltsin after his appointment as acting President. Next to him is Aleksandr Voloshin, Yeltsin's – and later Putin's – Chief of Staff.

The first challenge Putin faced was the conflict in Chechnya, in which both sides violated all the rules of war. Here a group of Russian soldiers look at the bodies of three captured Chechen rebels whom they have stripped, bound and executed. Twenty years later the Russian army committed similar atrocities in Ukraine.

Ramzan Kadyrov, who, with Putin's backing, rules Chechnya as an independent fiefdom, pictured before a portrait of his father, Akhmad, assassinated by jihadist rebels in 2004.

A Russian soldier on patrol in the ruins of the Chechen capital, Grozny.
The city has since been entirely rebuilt.

When Islamic terrorists under the orders of the Chechen warlord, Shamil Basayev, seized a primary school in Beslan in 2004, 335 people died, many of them small children. Here a Russian special forces officer brings out an infant who survived the siege.

Volunteer stretcher-bearers rescue the wounded after the assault.

In happier times: with Tony Blair at a G8 summit (*left*), and riding to Buckingham Palace in the royal carriage with the Queen during a state visit to Britain in 2003 (*above righ*t).

Putin and Lyudmila with the Lord Mayor of London, Sir Gavyn Arthur, and Prince and Princess Michael of Kent, before a banquet in the Guildhall.

Putin complained afterwards that the pomp and circumstance of British royalty were excessive. But his own life in the Kremlin was scarcely less monarchical, surrounded by opulent displays of imperial magnificence.

While Russia's relations with Britain were already beginning to sour in the early 2000s, Putin remained on much better terms with President George W. Bush.

Despite his Munich speech in 2007 denouncing American hegemony, he was invited to the Bush family compound at Kennebunkport, Maine, where '41' and '43' took him fishing and the two sides agreed to make one more effort to put US–Russian relations back on track.

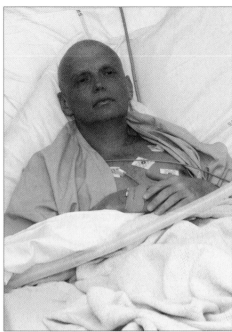

In 2005, Mikhail Khodorkovsky (*left*), an oil billionaire with democratic leanings whom Putin viewed as posing a political challenge, was given a long term of imprisonment. The following year, on Putin's orders, an FSB defector, Aleksandr Litvinenko (*right*), was poisoned with radioactive polonium in London.

In January 2007, when Putin received the new German Chancellor, Angela Merkel, in Sochi, he arranged for his black Labrador, Konni, to join them, knowing that she was afraid of dogs.

In 2008, Dmitry Medvedev succeeded Putin as President. Barack Obama thought he represented a new generation who would be Russia's future and, when he visited Washington, took him to his favourite burger joint, Ray's Hell Burger, in Arlington.

But Medvedev was Robin to Putin's Batman, and in 2012, after four years as Prime Minister, Putin returned to the presidency.

Aleksandr Solzhenitsyn, the dissident Soviet writer who won the Nobel Prize for literature, symbolised for Putin the tradition of Russian exceptionalism and the rejection of liberal, Western values, which became more pronounced after his second presidential term.

The feminist punk protest group, Pussy Riot, chant a blasphemous prayer
at the Church of Christ the Saviour in Moscow in 2012.

For Putin, visiting a monastery on Mount Athos (*left*) and attending a Christmas
service (*right*), the Orthodox Church had become a pillar of the regime.

To rally support
he approved
a clampdown on
'non-traditional
relations', which
triggered protest
demonstrations
in many European
countries, like this
one in Budapest
in 2015.

Barack Obama, pictured here at a G8 summit in Northern Ireland in 2013,
did not exactly hit it off with Putin.

Nor did the British Prime Minister, Theresa May. During Putin's third and fourth terms,
relations with the West went from bad to terrible.

Putin strengthened his ties with fellow autocrats like Xi Jinping in China, whom he taught to cook *blini*, Russian pancakes, at a summit in Vladivostok in 2018 (*above*), and Aleksandr Lukashenko, the dictator of Belarus, with whom he played ice hockey (*bottom left*).

At home he relied increasingly on the *siloviki*, the hawks from the security services, like Igor Sechin, the head of Rosneft (*playing pool*), Sergei Shoigu, the Defence Minister (*in uniform*) and Nikolai Patrushev, the Secretary of the Security Council (*next to him*).

In February 2015, Boris Nemtsov, a former deputy Prime Minister whom Yeltsin had considered as a possible successor, was shot dead by a hitman within sight of the Kremlin, triggering huge protest demonstrations.

Aleksei Navalny was arrested on his return to Moscow in January 2021 following a failed attempt by the FSB to poison him using Novichok, a chemical warfare agent.

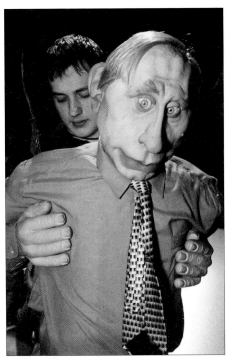

A lifesize puppet of Putin for the TV series, *Kukly*, a Russian version of Britain's *Spitting Image*.

When planning was underway for the war in Ukraine in October 2021.

The changing faces of a President:

After his inauguration in May 2000.

At a news conference in the White House in Washington in September 2005.

Looking considerably older at the start of his third term in July 2012.

Attending an investment forum in Moscow in October 2016.

Putin and his wife of 30 years, Lyudmila, attend a church service together in May 2012. A year later they divorced.

Putin had long been rumoured to be in a relationship with a young Russian gymnast, Alina Kabayeva.

Despite the resemblance, this drawing is not a caricature of Putin. It is a depiction of the Prince of Demons, Bael, by the French artist, Louis Le Breton, published in the *Dictionnaire Infernal* in 1863. A Russian editor, struck by the likeness, used it to illustrate an article about Putin in January 2022 – an early example of the Aesopian language to which the Russian media now resort to criticise the regime at a time of rigid press censorship.

Putin interrogates members of the Russian Security Council in the Kremlin's Catherine
Hall on the eve of the war in Ukraine. This meeting, like others which followed,
was intended to showcase his power as the ultimate decision-maker, but the imperious
mise-en-scène was also a masquerade, designed to create uncertainty in
the West about his state of mind.

His answers have the ring of truth.[196] Yet less than seven months later, in May 1995, Putin was elected acting Chairman of the St Petersburg regional chapter of Viktor Chernomyrdin's new party, Nash Dom Rossiya, 'Our Home is Russia', and confirmed in that post by the party's Second Congress, to which he led the St Petersburg delegation, not long afterwards.[197]

Why Putin changed his mind about entering the political fray is not entirely clear. Sobchak no doubt influenced him. His wife, Lyudmila Narusova, was standing as an independent candidate for the State Duma in December. As local party Chairman, Putin would be able to help her and, indeed, did so.[198] But he may also have decided that it would be valuable experience and allow him to make useful contacts among the political elite in Moscow.

Be that as it may, it soon became clear that he was not very good at it. He ordered the city's advertising hoardings to be plastered with Nash Dom Rossiya posters, provoking a backlash from voters who accused him of wasting money. Then he told a campaign rally that, once in power, the party would make it possible for every Russian to have their own motor car and not consider it a luxury.[199] 'Not a luxury!', one headline-writer expostulated, noting that even the cheapest Zhiguli cost the equivalent of five years of a worker's salary.[200]

Narusova was elected. But in a city regarded as a democratic stronghold, where 41.5 per cent of the vote went to pro-reform parties, twice the national average, Nash Dom Rossiya obtained only 12.8 per cent, not much more than in the rest of Russia.[201]

When the campaign for the municipal elections began the following spring, Sobchak decided he would run it himself, while Putin and the Finance Committee chief, Aleksei Kudrin, took care of the administration. Putin was given responsibility for budgetary allocations, the most delicate task in any administration and normally a jealously guarded prerogative of the Mayor himself.[202] Expenditure that year was estimated at 2.5 billion US dollars, revenue at 20 per cent less. To persuade the deputies to approve the deficit, Putin proposed that everyone who voted in favour be granted a million dollars in special funding to be spent on projects of their choice.[203] The budget passed.

Sobchak was convinced that he would cruise to an easy victory. The opinion polls appeared to bear that out. In mid March, he had 34 per cent of voting intentions against 23 per cent for his nearest rival, Yuri Boldyrev.[204]

But then, on March 27, less than eight weeks before the first round, Vladimir Yakovlev, the technocrat whom Sobchak had promoted to be the fourth-ranking member of the City government, announced that he, too, intended to stand.[205] It was a betrayal, Sobchak complained, a 'stab in the back' which he had not seen coming.[206]

In fact, his opponents had been manoeuvring in secret for months to find another candidate to stand against him.[207] Yuri Rydnik, the head of Soyuzkontrakt, at that time the biggest private company in Russia, who had made a fortune importing chicken legs from America – *nozhki Busha*, 'Bush's legs', as Russians called them, in a nod to the US President who had signed the original import agreement with Gorbachev – had decided that St Petersburg needed a Mayor who would give priority to the city's economic interests. Rydnik had sought advice from Aleksei Koshmarov-Trubetskoi, a flamboyant young electoral strategist who headed a Kremlin think tank. Initially they approached Valery Malyshev, the Head of Administration at the Mayor's Office, who, unknown to Sobchak, was also thinking of standing against him. But Malyshev got cold feet. By November 1995, Trubetskoi had concluded that Yakovlev would be the best candidate. Yakovlev, who was aware that Malyshev had been considering a run, had taken little persuading. 'It got me thinking,' he said later, 'why don't I give it a try?'

Trubetskoi then approached General Georgy Rogozin, Korzhakov's deputy. Known in the Kremlin as the 'Stargazer' and the 'Dark Magician', because of his fascination with astrology and the occult, Rogozin was the brains behind Korzhakov's brawn. He told Trubetskoi to go ahead.

Meanwhile Sobchak, having tired of organising his campaign himself, decided to appoint his wife, Lyudmila Narusova, to head his election headquarters.

Of all the mistakes he could have made, this was far and away the worst. Among the intellectuals and liberal democrats who made up the core of his support, Narusova was deeply unpopular. Most Russians took the view at that time – and many still do today – that politicians' wives should keep in the background. Narusova refused to remain, as she put it, 'in my husband's shadow', and like Raisa Gorbachev, she was hated for it.[208]

Putin said later that he had urged Sobchak to assemble a professional team. 'I told him right off: "You're on a completely different
playing field now. You need specialists."' But the Mayor ignored him –
partly, Putin surmised, because there was no money to pay for
professional advisers.[209] Apart from Sobchak's old friend, the shipping
magnate Viktor Kharchenko, almost no one from the city's business
community, which the Mayor had systematically antagonised over the
years, was willing to contribute. Rydnik, on the other hand, gave 12
million US dollars to Yakovlev's campaign, an astonishing amount for
a provincial contest when, in the presidential election, Yeltsin probably
spent only three or four times more.[210]

What little money Sobchak did have was not spent wisely. Narusova
made the same mistake as Putin had in the Duma elections, blanketing
the city with posters. This time they showed a smiling Sobchak against
the background of the city's tourist attractions, with the slogan, 'From
Mayor to Governor!' – a message of continuity which, to the millions
of Petersburgers living in poverty, was like a red rag to a bull. Dmitry
Yezhkov, who was a member of the campaign team, acknowledged
afterwards: 'You could not have come up with anything worse. It could
cause only one reaction: deep hatred of the candidate.'[211] The posters
proved so toxic that volunteers had to be sent out at night to take them
down.

Yakovlev's pitch was simpler and resonated far better: 'Vote for me,
and get Sobchak out!'

Sobchak had other problems too. Russkoe Video had made TV
commercials which, at Narusova's insistence, focused on Sobchak's
efforts to promote St Petersburg as a cultural and financial centre. That
just reminded people how little he had done to raise living standards.

Narusova became convinced that some of her assistants were
secretly informing Yakovlev's headquarters of Sobchak's strategy. She
was probably right.[212] But the result was to create a climate of paranoia
and mutual suspicion which left the team barely able to function.

On top of everything else, there loomed the spectre of the criminal
investigation into the Mayor's Office, which Skuratov had launched
the previous winter. Leonid Proshin, Skuratov's chief investigator,
remembered being summoned to Moscow at the beginning of March
for a meeting with Barsukov, Kulikov and Yeltsin's chief assistant, Viktor Ilyushin, who kept asking him: 'Why haven't you indicted [Sobchak]

yet?'[213] The indictment never came, but there were regular leaks to the press and Yakovlev's team distributed flyers, some of them scattered above the city streets from a helicopter, detailing Sobchak's alleged involvement in the scandal.[214]

Putin played no part in the election campaign until the end of April, by which time it was clear that Narusova's efforts were failing.[215] He, Kudrin and Manevich then set up an office in the Russkoe Video studios, where they commissioned TV commercials showing practical work like improvements to the city infrastructure, designed to appeal to working-class voters. On May 13, six days before the first round, all the members of the city government except Yakovlev signed a statement which Putin had drafted, expressing support for Sobchak and pledging to resign if he were not re-elected.[216]

'Putin went into overdrive,' Yezhkov remembered. He was exhausted, 'hardly knowing what day of the week it was or what was the time of day outside.'[217]

It was all a bit too late.

On May 19, Sobchak came first with 29 per cent of the vote and Yakovlev second with 21.6 per cent, which meant they would face each other in the run-off.[218]

Boldyrev, whom Sobchak had expected to be his opponent in the second round, was eliminated with 17.1 per cent, thanks partly to a crude manoeuvre orchestrated by Trubetskoi and his team. As election day approached, they had grown concerned that Boldyrev's support was rising and Yakovlev might not reach the second round. So they organised a fake Gay Pride demonstration, supposedly in support of Boldyrev's candidacy, in one of the city's parks.[219] Many Russians were then, and still are, ill at ease with homosexuality, and when reports of the demonstration were shown on television, tens of thousands of scandalised older people decided to vote for someone else.

Dirty tricks were the rule. Aleksandr Yuriev, a psychology professor who was working as an election strategist for Sobchak, opened his door one morning thinking it was a student who wanted to hand in an assignment. Instead, a man threw sulphuric acid in his face. He was not blinded, but needed extensive reconstructive surgery and was in hospital for the rest of the campaign.[220] Yakovlev's people accused Sobchak of putting out a contract on their candidate's life.[221] Sobchak's team spread rumours that Yakovlev had corruptly awarded contracts to a firm belonging to his wife.[222] Aleksandr Belyaev charged that some years previously British customs officers at Heathrow airport had found one million US dollars in cash in Sobchak's suitcase and detained him until the Russian Embassy intervened. The money had been used, Belyaev claimed, to buy villas for Sobchak and Putin on the French Atlantic coast. Sobchak ignored the attack. Putin sued but, after the election, the case fizzled out.[223] Neither accusation had any basis in fact. As Belyaev admitted years later: 'It was just politics.'[224]

Despite the factors stacking up against him, the election was still Sobchak's to lose.

He had the advantage of incumbency. His core constituency, the intellectuals, artists and liberal democrats, remained loyal, and many young people supported him. Yakovlev could count on the working class and the pensioners. Although the result would be close, most people in his own camp, and in Yakovlev's, thought Sobchak would scrape through.

Then, on the evening of May 31, two days before the second round, the two men faced off in a television debate. Sobchak was confident. In a similar debate seven years earlier, when he had stood for a seat in the Congress of People's Deputies, he had wiped the floor with his opponent. Yakovlev was not an orator. Even in technical discussions at the Mayor's Office, he often seemed tongue-tied. But this time was different. Sobchak appeared as usual in an elegant professorial suit and began reeling off statistics demonstrating his achievements. Yakovlev was in shirtsleeves and a tie, but no jacket, giving the appearance of a down-to-earth, practical man who would eschew high-sounding phrases and simply get things done. When he spoke, it was to ram that message home. Yakovlev's image maker, Aleksandr Yershov, who was in the studio with them, said that 'after about 20 minutes, I realised we would win.'[225] So did Anna Sharogradskaya, the head of the Russo-American Press Institute in St Petersburg. 'That debate was a disaster,' she said. 'As Mayor of the city, he didn't know the simplest things, and all his fine words were no help.'[226] Trubetskoi and Yershov had prepped Yakovlev for hours. Sobchak hardly looked at the briefing papers Putin and Kudrin had prepared for him.[227]

When the results were announced, Yakovlev came out ahead with 47.5 per cent of the vote. Sobchak received 45.8 per cent, a difference of 28,000 votes in an electorate of 3.7 million.[228] Later that month, Yeltsin came first in the opening round of the presidential election and, despite yet another heart attack, which was kept secret, won the run-off against Zyuganov by 54.4 per cent to 40.7 per cent.

The 1996 elections were a watershed, both for Putin and for Russia.

Had Sobchak won in St Petersburg, Putin would probably have remained at his side and, three and a half years later, Yeltsin would have chosen a different successor.[229]

For Russia, the means by which Yeltsin had achieved victory had consequences which were no less far-reaching.

In 1993, when Yeltsin had used the army to crush an insurgent but lawfully elected parliament, claiming that he had no choice because Russia was becoming ungovernable, Western governments had supported him, even though employing armed force to suppress political opposition was a flagrant violation of democratic principles. The new constitution, approved later that year, had provided a framework for authoritarian rule, a top-down system of government that would later be called the 'power vertical', in which, in theory at least, the President issued instructions and the machinery of state ensured that they were carried out.

The 1996 elections took that to a whole new level.

To ensure that there would be no return to communist rule, the United States and other Western governments aided Yeltsin's re-election campaign. In one sense, this was nothing new. Throughout the Cold War, both Russia and the US had tried to influence elections in states belonging to the opposite camp. But this was the first time that the West had tried directly to influence the outcome of voting in Russia itself. The methods employed were for the most part within the bounds of normal inter-state relations: secret loans, accelerated disbursement of IMF assistance, an official visit by President Clinton during the election campaign, and the sending, at the Russian side's request, of American electoral strategists to advise Yeltsin's campaign.[230] Nonetheless, a precedent had been created which, 20 years later, would come back to haunt Americans – or should have done, had anyone remembered it.

Meanwhile Yeltsin's campaign team undertook what Pyotr Aven, the former minister who has since become one of Russia's wealthiest bankers, called 'a gigantic manipulation of public opinion'.[231] The television channels, ORT and NTV, did not merely support Yeltsin. They blackened his communist opponents with every kind of calumny imaginable.

In an era when, in the West, 'fake news' has become the rallying cry of scoundrels of every stripe, that may sound quaint. But in Russia in the 1990s, journalists had been trying painfully, if not always successfully, to honour their newfound freedoms. That principled approach received a near-fatal blow in the 1996 election campaign. 'The age of innocence passed,' said Vladimir Pozner, one of the country's leading television journalists. 'Everything that has happened since had its roots there.'[232] Aven concurred. 'It laid down to a large extent the basis of the system which we have today,' he wrote in 2019. [233]

Russia's departure from what the West considered to be democratic norms did not start with Putin. It began in the 1990s, when America's friend, Boris Yeltsin, was in power.

7

The View from the Neva

Putin often said that he learnt far more from the six years he spent with Sobchak in St Petersburg than from anything he did afterwards in the Presidential Administration in Moscow.[1]

He had few illusions about the man he regarded as his mentor.[2] Sobchak was emotional, Putin said, and 'liked to be the centre of attention'.[3] He was complicated, unnecessarily blunt, did not care what people thought of him and was careless of the consequences of his actions.[4] Working with Sobchak had taught him not to give hostages to fortune; not needlessly to antagonise others; and, in politics as in life, not to 'spit against the wind'. Sobchak's campaign to try to get Lenin's body removed from the mausoleum on Red Square and reburied in St Petersburg, he thought, was a classic example of how not to do things. Although it was what Lenin himself had wished, it had been a political mistake because it had provoked the hostility of the communists and brought nothing in return. 'If only he had been a more nuanced politician,' Putin said, 'he would have kept silent on certain subjects or said things in a more roundabout way. But then he would not have been Anatoly Sobchak.'[5]

Putin's approach to politics was fashioned to a large extent by observing Sobchak's mistakes. He tried to avoid making enemies. With rare exceptions, he weighed each decision minutely and went ahead only when he had convinced himself that the balance of advantage was in his favour. Where possible, he avoided actions which would antagonise public opinion or his core supporters. This was not solely a result of his time at Smolny. Putin was also aware of the need to control his own riskier impulses. But the ex-Mayor's impetuousness and ability to rub others up the wrong way played an important part.

The years on the Neva were important in other ways. St Petersburg was a vantage point, a window not just onto the West but, as Putin put it, 'onto the outside world, [through which we can] strengthen Russia's economic and cultural links with all countries'.[6] He liked to say that he had first started thinking about foreign affairs when he was with the KGB and, to some extent, that was no doubt true.[7] But his convictions about foreign policy – and about the future of Russia – were shaped during the years he spent with Sobchak at Smolny.

The seminal event in the lives of most Russians at that time was the break-up of the Soviet Union. Putin was no exception. In a television interview in February 1992, six weeks after the Soviet flag had been lowered at the Kremlin for the last time, he set out his ideas:

> We need to see history as it was, and this [Soviet period] cannot be deleted from our history . . . [Communism was] harmful because the . . . attempt to put it into practice in our country caused enormous damage . . . [That is the root of] the tragedy that we are experiencing today, the tragedy of the collapse of our state . . . It was precisely those people in October 1917 who laid a time bomb under this edifice, the edifice of a unitary state, which was called Russia. They divided our homeland into separate territories, which previously did not even appear on the map of the globe. They endowed these territories with governments and parliaments. And now we have what we have . . . At the same time, they destroyed everything that brings together and rallies the peoples of civilised countries, namely they destroyed market relations . . . they destroyed nascent capitalism. The only thing they had to keep the country within common borders was barbed wire. And as soon as this barbed wire was removed, the country fell apart. I think this is largely the fault of those people [who made the Bolshevik Revolution]. Is that what they wanted? I don't think so. But objectively, that was the negative role that they played.[8]

Despite the careful phrasing – 'Is that what they wanted? I don't think so.' – the idea that the break-up of the Soviet Union had originated in the sins of the founding fathers was controversial and not widely shared. But many agreed with Putin that it was a tragedy.[9] Gorbachev himself described it as 'the greatest misfortune' and 'the cross I shall bear till the end of my life'.[10]

The lesson, Putin thought, was that Russia, or what was left of it, must remain united at all costs. He did not directly criticise Yeltsin's policy of allowing the constituent republics to 'take as much sovereignty as [they] can swallow',[11] but he made clear he disagreed. 'We should have one customs service, one legal and tax space, with a strong federal orientation' he said. 'Splitting up into separate princedoms will only bring utter confusion.'[12]

The corollary was to restore, to the extent possible, the links that had been broken between Russia and the other ex-Soviet states. But even at the level of policy – let alone its practical implementation – that posed insuperable problems.

What, for instance, was to be done about the free movement of peoples? In St Petersburg, in 1992, the surging crime rate was blamed – wrongly – on an influx of Georgians and Azerbaijanis, leading to calls for restrictions on immigration. Putin was in favour. 'Any limitation in the movement of people, goods and capital only complicates the task of restoring the lost links [between the former member states of the USSR],' he acknowledged, 'but unfortunately, the social and economic situation of today dictates otherwise. We are obliged to provide our citizens with the possibility to live normally and be masters in their own city.'[13] In other words, the interests of Russians, narrowly construed, must come first. The answer, he suggested, was to introduce residence permits for immigrants from other ex-Soviet states. But that was impracticable because it would trigger reciprocal restrictions on Russian expatriates in those countries.

Nowhere was this problem more acute than in regard to the Baltic States and above all, as far as Petersburgers were concerned, in neighbouring Estonia. Yeltsin had formally recognised their independence on August 24, 1991, immediately after the failure of the putsch. But it remained a neuralgic issue. For Putin, it was one of the few subjects capable of making him abandon his normally stoic self-control. Rodric Braithwaite, the British Ambassador, vividly remembered a conversation with him at Leningrad's Pulkovo Airport in November 1991, as they waited for the arrival of a visiting British minister. 'It was the most difficult thing I've ever experienced,' Braithwaite said. 'All I got was a rant about Estonia, which went on for about 20 minutes.' If Putin thought that was a way to impress on his Western interlocutor the importance of the issue to Russia, he was mistaken. Braithwaite made a mental note to give him a wide berth in future.[14] He recorded in his diary that night that Putin had spoken 'with great emotion' – which was the last thing Putin usually did – and had raised in particular two issues: Estonia's demands for the restitution of territory that 'had been part of Russia for decades', and proposals before the Estonian parliament which would lead to most of the Russian-speaking population being deprived of citizenship.[15]

The subject was much on Putin's mind because he had recently been in Narva to help negotiate a convention setting out the provisional arrangements for border crossings between Russia and Estonia.[16] The accord had been signed in September by Sobchak, whom Gorbachev had appointed to head the Soviet delegation, and Edgar Savisaar, the Estonian Prime Minister.[17] After further talks, agreement was reached on the *de jure* delineation of the border and a treaty was eventually signed, but objections from Estonian nationalists meant that, decades later, it had still not been ratified.[18]

If the border issue was mainly symbolic, practical matters loomed much larger. In the spring of 1993, Estonia had opened a consulate in St Petersburg, which soon became its biggest foreign mission, larger even than the Embassy in Washington, with 20 full-time officials.[19] The first acting Consul General had a nervous breakdown and was recalled. His successor, Märt Volmer, soon discovered why. Not only were there queues every day, hundreds of yards long, of frustrated Petersburgers, furious at having to obtain visas to visit their dachas across the border, but the city's criminal fraternity was also up in arms. Estonia was an important smuggling route for organised crime. 'That was our main issue,' Volmer remembered. 'We had to close the border to those guys . . . They all tried to keep a foothold in Estonia, so I had death threats on a daily basis. It's the only time in my life when I used to look under the car before driving off . . . [We would] tell them their visas were being refused. And they would say to your face, "You'll be dead tomorrow."'

In Volmer's recollection, Putin and his desk officer for the Baltic States, Vladimir Churov, were helpful and tried to solve problems pragmatically. But occasionally Putin's feelings about Estonia got the better of him. Eberhard von Puttkamer, the German Consul, remembered one such outburst:

In Putin's eyes, the fact that they'd established an independent state was absolutely ridiculous . . . It was absolutely outrageous. For him, Estonia

was still part of Russia. He was very emotional. My [Estonian] colleague was present – for him it must have been very, very difficult . . . It
didn't last long. But . . . it was very unusual. His idea was that Estonia
couldn't be an independent country.[20]

Sobchak was still more hostile, refusing to receive Volmer for the traditional farewell call at the end of his posting until Volmer shamed him
by informing the rest of the consular corps.[21]

The Estonians gave as good as they got. Volmer was under instructions to be intransigent, and the fact that he was only 27 years old and
in his first major post made him all the more determined to apply that
to the letter. 'If you are weak, you don't win in a negotiation,' he said.
'You put up a fight and see how it goes.'[22] The first test of this approach
came in December 1993, when the lease on the consulate's premises
was about to expire and Putin's Foreign Relations Committee dragged
its feet over finding alternative accommodation. Volmer announced
that on January 1, the mission would close, which it did, leaving irate
Petersburgers to travel to Kyiv or Moscow for visas. Six weeks later, the
grumbling had reached a point where Sobchak had to give in.[23] A suitable building was found on Petrogradsky Island and a 49-year-lease
hastily concluded – so hastily, in fact, that no one noticed until it was
too late that there was no provision for rent increases, making it by far
the best deal financially obtained by any foreign consulate.

'They were very unhappy,' Volmer remembered. 'They just wanted
to get it done and no one looked at it properly. Sometimes they could
be sloppy like that.'[24]

It was a textbook example of how not to conduct a negotiation.

Not only was the Mayor's Office forced to back down, but it got nothing in return. Putin's request for Russians owning property in Estonia
to be granted one-year multi-entry visas was rejected – the current rules,
he was told, under which they were limited to three-month visas, valid
for three visits, would remain in force.[25] Had he moved proactively, offering the building on Petrogradsky Island early on, instead of under
pressure, he would have had a much better chance of obtaining a quid
pro quo. It was a useful lesson and one which he would not forget.

But the biggest issue with which Putin had to deal concerned the
Russian diaspora in Estonia. The country's population was only 1.5 million, of whom 900,000 were Estonians, 74,000 were Russians, and

another 500,000, almost all of them Russian speakers, were stateless. Under Estonia's Law on Aliens, enacted in June 1993, non-citizens were required to apply for residence permits within a year. Permanent residents would be able to acquire citizenship by naturalisation, but only if they were proficient in the Estonian language, which most Russian-speakers were not, and if they had not served in a foreign army, which excluded military veterans who had settled in Estonia. Non-citizens were banned from joining political parties, membership of local councils and employment in the public service.

Apart from the provision concerning foreign military service, it was little different from comparable legislation in Western Europe. But Russia insisted that it was 'a grave violation of human rights' and announced that it was halting the withdrawal of Soviet troops from Estonia. The real problem was that the law was being applied to people who had previously shared Soviet citizenship, which they had lost, through no fault of their own, after the break-up of the Union State. Under pressure from the Council of Europe and the Organisation for Security and Cooperation in Europe (OSCE), the initial draft was amended to give it a less overtly nationalistic coloration. But the core provisions were maintained, and in the summer of 1993, in the heavily Russophone north-east, around Narva and Sillamäe, where separatist tendencies had already flared three years earlier, the city leaders announced a referendum on 'national–territorial autonomy', drawing instant condemnation from Tallinn, which denounced it as an attempt at secession.

With hindsight, the Narva Autonomy Campaign brings to mind the 1950s satire, *The Mouse that Roared*. Even in Estonia, 30 years later, it is largely forgotten. But at the time it looked very different. Carl Bildt, then the Swedish Prime Minister, remembered:

> We were extremely worried . . . There were substantial Soviet military assets and interests there and Russian minorities, some of [whom] were frightened and aggressive . . . So there was all of the potential for things to go very wrong, [with] substantial turmoil – violence probably, deaths, major refugee streams . . . You can make fairly sinister scenarios. And we did – we knew what could have happened.[26]

Bildt's concern was that, with Soviet troops still based in Estonia and no timetable for a final withdrawal, if Narva declared itself

autonomous, a frozen conflict would begin, similar to that in Transnistria, where the Russian-speaking minority had fought a brief war of
secession from Moldova a year earlier and founded an unrecognised
independent state with its capital at Tiraspol. He had been told by
Swedish intelligence that, as he put it, there were 'nasty types on the
other side . . . planning bad things'.[27] Lennart Meri, Estonia's President, worried about that, too. Some of the city leaders in Narva had
earlier served in Moldova and were in contact with the secessionists
there. There were reports of a militia force – or, by other accounts, a
regiment of Cossacks – gathering on the Russian border.[28]

At the beginning of July, the OSCE High Commissioner for Minor-
ities, Max van der Stoel, flew in to mediate. Bildt travelled to Tallinn.
The Ukrainian Prime Minister, Leonid Kuchma, came too, to show
solidarity with the Estonians against Moscow.[29]

A few days later, the Finnish President, Mauno Koivisto, invited
Meri and Sobchak to a secret meeting at Kultaranta, near Turku, where
he urged Meri to find common ground with the Russian-speaking
population.[30]

Putin made the arrangements but played no part in the talks.
According to Meri, when the three leaders repaired to the sauna, beat-
ing each other with birch twigs and drinking copiously, as they tried to
thrash out a strategy which would avoid civil war, Putin sat outside,
while Sobchak bellowed from time to time, 'More beer, Volodya!'[31]
After the referendum, which was held on July 16 and 17, Bildt sent a
message to Yeltsin urging him to calm things down.[32] In Moscow the
power struggle against Khasbulatov and Rutskoi was then at its height
and Yeltsin delegated the matter to Sobchak. He, in turn, delegated it
to Putin, who was told to make sure that the situation did not get out
of hand. The Russian-speaking population in the north-east had voted
for autonomy but in smaller numbers than expected. When Putin met
the Chairman of Narva City Council, Vladimir Chuikin, in St Petersburg, he urged caution, warning that if an armed conflict were to
develop, the separatists risked being crushed.[33] North-East Estonia, he
noted, was much smaller than Transnistria, and while Russia sympathised with the autonomists' aims, it had no intention of becoming
directly involved. The agitation faded as quickly as it had begun.

Putin would have one final run-in with Meri. Nine months later, in
March, 1994, the Estonian President was guest of honour at the annual

St Matthias banquet in Hamburg, a black-tie occasion hosted by the city's Mayor. Putin and the Russian Consul General were there representing St Petersburg. In his speech, Meri accused the West of appeasing Russia, which, he charged, was bent on carrying out a neo-imperialist policy towards the other former Soviet-bloc states. If the West continued to indulge in such wishful thinking, he warned, it would mean 'it cannot see an inch further than its nose'.[34] There was much more in the same vein. After Meri referred to the Soviet Union as an occupying power, Putin decided he had heard enough and, accompanied by the Consul General, stalked out, their footsteps echoing across the marble floor until the heavy iron door of the banqueting hall closed with a loud clang behind them.[35]

It turned out to be a last hurrah. In July, Meri met Yeltsin and it was agreed that all Russian troops would leave Estonia by the end of the following month. Visa problems continued, but in 1995, a new and more conciliatory government took office in Tallinn and relations slowly began to improve.[36]

At one level, it had been a storm in an egg cup. At another, the strategic consequences of a frozen conflict in Estonia – however remote the possibility – would have been potentially explosive. As it was, the Baltic States would remain an acute pressure point for both Russia and the West.

For Putin, however, the importance of the Narva affair lay elsewhere. For the first time in his life, he found himself dealing not merely with trade and joint ventures, his areas of responsibility at the Mayor's Office, but with foreign policy, in a region which, for a few months at least, was at the centre of diplomatic activity not only for St Petersburg and Moscow, but also for the Baltic States, their Scandinavian neighbours and countries further afield.

The experience started him thinking more deeply about the rest of the post-Soviet space,[37] for which Russian commentators were still trying to come up with an appropriate name. *Sankt-Peterburgskie vedomosti* had launched a rubric, entitled the 'Nearer Abroad'; *Chas pik* referred to the 'New Abroad' and then, the 'Nearest Abroad', before finally deciding: 'Other countries have neighbours, Russia has the Near Abroad.'[38]

The Near Abroad stuck. It covered an area extending from the Baltic States to Central Asia and from Ukraine to the Caspian Sea.[39] Putin knew that the former Soviet empire had been held together by brute force. But he preferred to think of the shared heritage of the post-Soviet states. 'We are all members of one economic community,' he said. 'Historically our peoples have a great deal in common – kinship, cultural links, a common history and common problems.'[40]

Ukraine lay at the heart of that shared history. The Russian state traced its origins to Kievan Rus, founded in the ninth century with its capital first in Novgorod, then in Kyiv. In 1991, Ukraine's insistence on independence precipitated the Soviet Union's collapse. Afterwards, throughout the 1990s, the flashpoint was Crimea. One bone of contention was the future of the Black Sea fleet, based at Sevastopol. Another was Crimea's political status, because two thirds of its 2.4 million inhabitants were Russians. 'Blood can flow there at any moment,' a Russian newspaper warned in 1992.[41] Crimea, wrote another, risked becoming 'a hotbed of danger and instability in the heart of Europe'.[42]

The territory, a peninsula almost the size of Belgium, jutting out into the Black Sea, had been part of Russia since 1783. It was transferred to Ukraine by Khrushchev in 1954, at a time when neither he nor anyone else imagined that the Soviet Union would ever break up. Formally the area was what was termed an 'autonomous republic'. In the early 1990s, the republic's administration tried repeatedly to organise an independence referendum, with support from the Mayor of Moscow, Yuri Luzhkov, and other sympathisers, drawing angry protests from Kyiv. When finally the referendum was held, in March 1994, it was ruled illegal by the Ukrainian Supreme Court. As a Russian commentator noted, two fundamental principles were in conflict: the right of peoples to self-determination and the inviolability of post-war frontiers.[43] The dispute was papered over, in the hope that the passage of time would permit a permanent solution, but the underlying problem festered.

'In the 1990s . . . the Russians were preoccupied with Ukraine,' one Western leader reflected, many years later. 'I don't think we sufficiently appreciated that at the time.'[44]

To Putin, Ukraine was a case study in the ingratitude of the former Soviet republics. 'Kiev owes us 4.5 billion US dollars for [subsidised Russian] energy supplies,' he complained in 1995. 'And of course, they can't pay . . . So why not, from tomorrow, sell [them] energy at world prices? But clearly no one wants that. They all want to get more and pay less. That's how it is.'[45]

What Russia wanted, Putin said, was 'a sensible balance of interests' with the states of the Near Abroad, not some supposed 'equal partnership'. Russia did not need that. 'We've had those kinds of loud slogans for decades, and we've swallowed enough of them . . . The [former] Soviet republics . . . were financed by Russia. Now what do we see there? Devastation, crises and wars . . . And what does Russia get out of it?'

The reference was to the frozen conflicts in Abkhazia and South Ossetia, which had seceded from Georgia, and Transnistria in Moldova; the stand-off between Armenia and Azerbaijan over the disputed enclave of Nagorno-Karabakh; and the civil war in Tajikistan, where Putin had accompanied Sobchak on a fruitless mediation mission in October 1991. All had erupted during the final years of *perestroika* and, to Putin, all had their roots in the Bolsheviks' mistaken nationalities policy back in the 1920s, which had led to the Soviet Union becoming a mosaic of ethnically defined republics and districts.

His frustration with the relations which Yeltsin had allowed to develop between Russia and the Near Abroad mirrored his unease at what he saw as the excessive freedom the President had accorded to Russia's own constituent territories. It evidently ran deep, for at a meeting with the consular corps in St Petersburg in December 1993, he abandoned his usual caution. No text of his remarks exists. The only record is a confidential telegram sent that evening by the French Consul General, Roland Blatmann, to the Foreign Ministry in Paris. It provides a succinct and unvarnished summary of Putin's views in a context where he could speak frankly, knowing that he would not be quoted in public:

In answer to one of my questions, [Putin launched into a diatribe] . . . against what he called the politics of dismemberment in Russia, which had lost 'Crimea, which we had won from the Turks, [as well as] Kazakhstan and so on', and the Baltic States, where the Russian and Russian-speaking population was ill-treated, not to mention the territorial pretensions of certain states like Estonia. Since 1991, he went on, Russia had lost too much, it had been too humiliated . . . The government's foreign policy did not conform to Russia's true interests.[46]

He sounded, Blatmann reported, as though he was defending the theses of a nationalist like Vladimir Zhirinovsky, and presented them
'with a vigour which for him was most unusual'.

To Putin in the mid 1990s, from his vantage point in St Petersburg, Russian unity was the first priority. The Near Abroad came second. In third
place were relations with the West.

Like most Russians, Putin initially had mixed feelings about Western investment. The idea of Western companies owning historic
buildings in the centre of St Petersburg made him uneasy, he said, until
he realised that in many Western cities, prime real estate was owned by
foreigners. Western aid, he thought, was acceptable in principle, but he
worried that Russia would become a dumping ground for 'second-rate
imports and outdated technology', which would do nothing for the
country's development.[47]

After decades of Cold War propaganda, in which the West had been
depicted as Russia's eternal and irreconcilable enemy, mistrust was
inevitable. In April 1992, an opinion survey found that more than half
of those questioned thought Russia should follow its own path, not the
Western, capitalist model.[48] Three years later, the same proportion
thought the West was trying to weaken Russia, while only a quarter
thought it was trying to help.[49] Many had had unrealistic hopes of what
relations with the West would bring. 'At the beginning of the 1990s,
there was euphoria,' one prominent Russian businessman recalled.
'We are going to join up with the West, we will now be friends for
ever.'[50] Putin, too, remembered how everyone, not only in Russia but
also in Eastern Europe, had imagined that the end of the Cold War
would bring instant prosperity, but it had turned out to be a mirage, 'a
bit like the Chinese Great Leap Forward'.[51]

Over time, he developed a pragmatic, down-to-earth approach
which distinguished him from most of his colleagues. Where Sobchak
complained that the IMF's conditions for helping Russia were too
strict and impossible to implement,[52] Putin argued, on the contrary:

The financial policy of the IMF, the European Community and the G7
countries is being carried out in a balanced and targeted way. It is aimed
at supporting Russia's reforms and its integration into the world economy, and in my view it is sincere and consistent ... The West's

philosophy is to create in Russia the nucleus of a future, effective market economy, to get things moving from a standing start, to help our enterprises to understand the philosophy of market relations . . . And that is all correct.[53]

Where Sobchak groused that the West was niggardly – 'They spent billions in the struggle against communism,' he said, 'and now they can't find any money to support a democracy that has overthrown communism'[54] – Putin accepted that Western aid would only ever be a drop in the ocean of Russia's needs. It was 'a real help in the process of transforming our economy', he argued, but it was not a panacea. What Russia needed most was not aid but 'a level playing field to work on'.[55] Under those circumstances, foreign investment could play a positive role. 'We need foreign resources, Western experience, new ecological technology. We don't need to be afraid of attracting large-scale Western capital. Business is egotistic by its very nature, but [we can] lay down strict legal limits.'[56]

Putin had no illusions about Russia's ability to sell its products abroad and he did not mince words about their poor quality. 'We must recognise honestly,' he said, 'that we don't have a single item of popular consumer goods that can compete on the world market. With us, everything is antediluvian, awful, ugly and unfashionable.' The only way to change that, he argued, was to open up the economy so that local manufacturers would be forced to compete with foreign imports. 'Otherwise we will just go back to where we started years ago.'[57]

These views qualified Putin as an economic liberal. He urged the repatriation of Russian capital from abroad; tax reform, to promote foreign investment as well as local manufacturing; a clear legal framework; and 'a fund to support foreign economic relations', which he did not define but may have intended as an embryonic form of sovereign wealth fund.[58] If he disagreed with Chubais and Gaidar over shock therapy, it was only because he felt it was asking too much of a population already in desperate straits.[59]

However he was notably less enthusiastic when it came to political democracy. 'Personally,' he said, 'I think that all political forces have the right to express their opinions' – the word 'personally' suggesting that, rather than being a fundamental democratic principle, this was a matter on which other views were also legitimate.[60] As for the division

of powers between the executive and the legislature, this was necessary, he said, because it was 'the most productive way'.[61] It sounded like
lip service to an idea which he could not, and perhaps did not wish to,
oppose, but for which he had no great sympathy.

Putin drew a similar distinction with regard to relations with the
West. Western investment and trade were advantageous to Russia.
Western foreign policy in the 1990s and the Russian response to it, in
his view, were not:

> Much of what was said publicly at that time by . . . the first persons in
> our city, region, and country, it seemed to me, was mistaken . . . It was
> absolutely clear to me that [Russia's] unilateral disarmament in all
> directions would not turn out to be good for us. Our fraternisation with
> recent geopolitical opponents was good in moderation. But those who
> at that time were in charge of this fraternisation did not know how far
> to go.[62]

Putin's criticism was directed primarily at Russia's Foreign Minister,
Andrei Kozyrev, who was widely regarded as pro-American. But he
had in mind Yeltsin and Sobchak, too. Americans were the largest
investors in St Petersburg, followed by Germany and Finland, and economic relations were good.[63] But politically there were hiccoughs. To
Putin, Russia was a great power and, even in its weakened state, it
should be treated as such.

A telling incident occurred when Vice President Al Gore came to
see Sobchak in December 1993. The Vice Consul, Andrew Goodman, a
large, burly man, who was part of the welcoming party, pushed past
the Russian military commander, Colonel-General Seleznyov, in his
haste to board the Vice President's plane. Putin was incensed. After
Gore's departure, with Sobchak's agreement, he summoned Goodman and informed him, in the presence of the local press, that in view
of his 'egregious conduct, blatantly violating protocol', he would be
banned from the City Hall and from any occasion at which officials
from the Mayor's Office were present.[64] The recently arrived American
Ambassador, Tom Pickering, flew down from Moscow to discuss what
was termed the 'misunderstanding' and an elegant diplomatic solution
was found. The man who had shoved aside the general, Sobchak and
the Ambassador agreed, 'bore a strong resemblance to Goodman' but

had in fact been one of the Vice President's bodyguards who was 'unfamiliar with Russian protocol'.[65] It is tempting to speculate that Putin came up with this ingenious formula, but in any event, he clearly remembered it, for a few years later he would use an almost identical phrase in another sensitive affair.[66]

The Goodman affair was a pinprick, of interest because it reflected Putin's obsession with respect – for Russia, no less than for himself – but of no lasting consequence. Much more important and much less easily finessed was his sense of Russia's place in the world.

Russia, he argued, should not be a buffer zone, 'a barrier between East and West, [but] first and foremost a connecting link between the two'.[67] The role of the Near Abroad was fundamental. Russia's influence there would remain dominant. Its neighbours in the post-Soviet space would serve as a go-between, linking Russia with Western Europe and Asia.[68]

The European Community was compatible with that vision: there was even talk in the early 1990s, both in Moscow and in some Western European capitals, of Russia eventually becoming a member.[69]

NATO was a different matter.

It had started well. US Secretary of State James Baker had told Gorbachev in February 1990, in the context of German reunification, that 'not an inch of NATO's present military jurisdiction will spread in an eastern direction'.[70] When Gorbachev doubled down and insisted that there should not be 'any extension of the zone of NATO', Baker assured him that that would be the case.[71] Although nothing was put in writing, from then on the State Department worked on the basis that there would be no eastward expansion of NATO and so did America's allies.[72] Helmut Kohl, François Mitterrand and Margaret Thatcher all reiterated Baker's assurances at meetings with Soviet leaders. In March 1991, when the Soviet Defence Minister, Marshal Yazov, expressed his concern to Thatcher's successor, John Major, about possible NATO enlargement, the British Prime Minister assured him that 'nothing of the sort will happen'.[73] Four months later, the NATO Secretary General, Manfred Wörner, told a Soviet delegation that he opposed NATO enlargement and so did most NATO members.[74]

The Pentagon, under Defense Secretary Dick Cheney, took a different view. He and his Under Secretary, Paul Wolfowitz, believed that, regardless of *perestroika*, Moscow was still America's main enemy and that Baker's assurances had been unwarranted. On the issue of NATO enlargement, it was better 'to leave the door ajar'.[75]

In Washington, the result was departmental warfare between State and Defense. Shaun Byrnes, who was responsible for Eastern Europe at State, remembered 'constant battles . . . Wolfowitz and his deputy, Scooter Libby, were looking for every way to move [NATO's borders] to the East, and we were constantly having to put out the fires they lit.'[76]

President George H. W. Bush was ambivalent. On the one hand, he wanted to reassure Gorbachev that nothing would be done which might threaten Soviet security. On the other, he viewed NATO as a vital instrument for projecting US power and influence and he had no intention of giving it up. When the new Czechoslovak leader, the former dissident playwright, Václav Havel, visited Washington and proposed that NATO be abolished as well as the Warsaw Pact, Bush demurred. NATO, he insisted, was an important source of stability in Europe.[77] Proposals by France and Italy that the two military blocs be replaced by an all-European defence structure were quietly squashed.

Until January 1993, when President Clinton took office, the State Department line prevailed. The message to Moscow was that NATO enlargement was not on the table.

But by then, Bush's insistence that the Atlantic alliance was a guarantor of stability, which had been strongly promoted by Wolfowitz, Paul Nitze and other Cold War hawks, had begun to make the East Europeans think again. The chaos in Russia, starting with the August 1991 putsch, followed by the collapse of the Soviet Union and the subsequent stand-off between Yeltsin and parliament, together with the civil war in Yugoslavia, focused minds on the need for military security. The change of guard in Washington helped, too. Clinton's National Security Adviser, Anthony Lake, was an enthusiastic supporter of enlargement, as were several other senior officials, on the well-intentioned but, as it turned out, spurious grounds that joining NATO would consolidate democratic reforms in the new member states.[78]

On the other hand, Cheney's successor at the Pentagon, Les Aspin, and his deputy, William Perry, had strong doubts. So did General John Shalikashvili, the US Commander in Europe. So did many of the old Russia hands – George Kennan, Richard Pipes, Jack Matlock and Strobe Talbott – who warned that any short-term gains from admitting the

Eastern and Central Europeans to NATO would be outweighed by the long-term damage it would do to the relationship with Russia.[79] The same message was conveyed to the White House by the CIA.[80]

Nevertheless, a year later, President Clinton announced: 'The question is no longer whether NATO will take on new members, but when and how.'[81] It took time for even some members of his own administration to realise that that was not just a way of kicking the can down the road but that Clinton's mind was made up. Moscow was also at first unsure how seriously to take Clinton's words. It was 'a hypothetical question', Yeltsin told an interviewer, but if it happened, 'it would be seen as damaging to Russia'.[82]

Clinton had tried to sweeten the pill, announcing that he was creating a 'Partnership for Peace' as a kind of halfway house leading to possible NATO membership. To avoid creating a new dividing line in Europe, he said, all the countries of the post-Soviet space, including Russia, would be welcome to join. Then, in September 1994, he promised Yeltsin that there would be no announcement of the names of the new members to be admitted to NATO, or of the timetable, until after the Russian presidential election two years later, to avoid providing ammunition to Yeltsin's opponents.

It all rang rather hollow.

That December, Yeltsin's patience snapped. In a blistering speech to an OSCE summit in Budapest, he warned that 'even before the legacy of the Cold War has been laid to rest, Europe risks encumbering itself with a Cold Peace'. The Americans, who had convinced themselves that the Russians would meekly accept the changes Washington had decreed, were stunned. But it turned out to be a one-off. Clinton had judged correctly. Russia was too weak, and too embroiled in its own problems, to be able to put up any serious resistance.

The one fly in the ointment was James Baker's promise to Gorbachev five years earlier that NATO would not move 'an inch' towards the East.

Eventually, a workaround was found. Baker's assurance, American officials claimed, had referred only to the stationing of NATO troops in East Germany. The question of what would happen further east had never been raised.[83] That was dishonest. Strobe Talbott, among others, has confirmed that Baker did indeed make an unconditional pledge that there would be no enlargement even if, in so doing, he may have gone beyond what President Bush intended.[84] But, as a get-out, it was the best that anyone in the State Department could come up with and it has remained the American position ever since.

The other argument the Clinton administration advanced to support enlargement was that, under the 1975 Helsinki agreement, any country was free to choose which alliance it wished to join, and no third country – in other words, Russia – had the right to veto that choice. In theory, this was unassailable. In a perfect world, the right of any country to determine its own future should outweigh commitments made by others on its behalf, such as that which Baker had made to Gorbachev. But that, too, was sophistry. Great powers, the United States foremost among them, act in their own interests, undeterred by the concerns of others. Clinton's predecessor, George H. W. Bush, took the view that, as Bob Gates, his CIA Director, put it, 'if you don't get it right with Russia and China, none of the rest matters'. Bush, Gates said, would have fobbed off the Eastern Europeans with half-measures and would not have allowed them to become full NATO members.[85] Clinton took the opposite tack. Partly for domestic political reasons – outflanking the Republican Party and gaining electoral support from immigrants from former Soviet-bloc countries – but above all because he had concluded that America's overriding interest was to lock Eastern and Central Europe firmly into the Western camp, Clinton put NATO enlargement first and Russia's sensitivities second.

Politically that seemed to make sense. As George H. W. Bush had said: 'We prevailed and they didn't.'[86] Clinton and his team thought the Russians, as the losers in the Cold War, 'had to eat their spinach' – which led even as pro-Western an official as Andrei Kozyrev to complain that the Americans were 'adding insult to injury by telling us that it's in our own interests to obey'.[87]

But militarily, as Shalikashvili had warned, it made no sense at all.

The Eastern European tail was wagging the American dog. There was no way that American security would be enhanced by taking on a commitment to defend the European states abutting Russia's borders. Francis Richards, who was at that time Under Secretary at the British Foreign Office, remembered: 'No one was going to pause and consider the wisdom of giving them an unconditional military guarantee, which . . . seemed to me lunacy.' It was a blank cheque that could never be honoured, and 'dishing out cheques that can't be honoured is . . . destroying the credibility of NATO as a defensive organisation.'[88] Lest that argument be dismissed as the pusillanimity of what Donald Rumsfeld liked to call 'Old Europe', it is necessary to ask whether any American President would risk a nuclear war with Russia in order to defend Latvia or Estonia. Even at the height of the Cold War, in the 1970s and early 1980s, France and Germany had doubts about America's willingness to come to their defence in the event of a Soviet invasion if doing so would entail an all-out nuclear conflict. From a European standpoint, such fears were well founded. The United States did not enter World War I until 1917, when it was already clear that Germany was losing, and remained aloof from World War II until it had itself been attacked in December 1941. There was no reason to think that in a new conflict, America would behave any differently.

Enlargement was a symbolic decision. The Russians thought that, if push came to shove, NATO would abandon its new members rather than risk a world war. But to both sides the symbolism was important. The Eastern Europeans felt protected and the Russians felt the West viewed them as an enemy.

Richards and a few others argued that the countries of Eastern and Central Europe should first join the European Community, an organisation which, in theory at least, was better suited to promoting political democracy than NATO, a military alliance. But NATO was under American leadership. The Community was not. To the Clinton administration, NATO membership was the appropriate response.

It would prove to be a fateful decision.

In public, at least, Yeltsin did not raise the matter of Baker's promise and the assurances which other Western leaders had given in the early 1990s, partly because he did not wish to base his case on commitments made to his old rival, Gorbachev, but also because accusing the United States of breaking its word would not make a solution any easier.

Putin, following these events from the Mayor's Office at Smolny, had no such qualms. John Guy, who later became British Consul General in St Petersburg, met him in November 1995 during a visit with a delegation from the British Defence College. 'He railed against the West and against NATO for breaking its pledge,' Guy remembered. 'He was willing to accept European Community membership [for the Eastern and Central Europeans], but NATO was a step too far. We argued that if you have democratically elected governments . . . and they choose of their own accord to join NATO, you shouldn't regard it as a hostile act. He wasn't prepared to accept that at all.'[89]

Not all of Putin's ideas about the world and the place which Russia should have in it were fashioned during the years he spent beside the Neva. But on the key issues – NATO, relations with the West, the importance of the Near Abroad, Russia's role as a bridge between Asia and Europe, and the need for strong, centralised government which would hold the country together – the basic strands of his thinking were already clearly laid down. Some of the ideas he espoused then would later be modified. Some would be discarded for a time, only to resurface later. But, in one way or another, the views he developed in St Petersburg would inform his decisions for the rest of his career.

8

Moscow Rules

When Putin awoke on Monday morning, June 3, 1996, he already knew that his days in St Petersburg were numbered.

His relations with Sobchak's successor, Vladimir Yakovlev, were not unfriendly.[1] During the campaign, they had vilified each other – Putin had accused Yakovlev of behaving like Judas Iscariot – but that was how elections were in Russia.[2] There were no lasting ill feelings.[3] All the members of the outgoing City government except Sobchak gathered afterwards for a farewell dinner, where, in Yakovlev's words, 'we talked, raised our glasses, joked, sat down and parted'.[4]

But when, a few days later, Yakovlev sent a message to Putin, asking him to stay on as Vice Governor responsible for foreign relations and liaison with the security services, Putin refused. 'I thought it would be impossible to work with him, and I made that clear,' he said later. The ostensible reason was that Putin had been too close to Sobchak and had announced publicly that he would resign if the Mayor was not re-elected. But that was true of others, too. The Chairman of the Property Committee, Mikhail Manevich, and the legal adviser, Dmitry Kozak, also felt duty bound to resign, but Putin persuaded both of them to stay on.[5]

The real reasons for his departure were more complicated.

In an interview, 18 months earlier, he had ruminated about the possibility of leaving Smolny. 'I love my work, but it won't go on for ever,' he had said. 'No one is irreplaceable.' At that time, he was adamant that, should he ever leave the City government, he would stay in St Petersburg. 'I know the city, I know its problems, I have a lot of relations. That's a good capital, which I . . . don't intend to waste.'[6]

Yet, when the time came, he did not try to find another position in the city.

That may have been because Yakovlev's attitude changed abruptly after Putin refused to serve under him. Boris Vishnevsky remembered standing talking to the new Governor, a week or so later, when an aide came up with a message and mentioned Putin's name. Yakovlev flushed and said furiously, 'Don't ever talk to me about that cunt again.'[7] Once the presidential election was over, Putin recalled, he was told 'rather harshly' to vacate his office at Smolny to make room for his successor.[8] The following month, when the Finnish Consul General, Osmo Lipponen, invited Yakovlev to a reception, one of the Governor's aides telephoned to enquire whether Putin would be present, 'because, in that case, the Governor will not attend'. Lipponen tartly reminded the caller that the Finnish government, not the Governor's Office, decided whom it wished to invite. Putin came, Yakovlev did not.[9]

But the rift between them may not have been the only factor. Putin appears to have started thinking of a possible move to Moscow several months earlier.

That spring, he had enrolled at the State Mining Institute in St Petersburg to begin preparing for a Candidate of Sciences degree, a level somewhere between a Western M.Sc. and a Ph.D.[10] Three preliminary papers were published in his name under the Institute's imprimatur a few months later. The following year, in June, he defended his dissertation.

The topic was 'Strategic Planning for the Rehabilitation of the Mineral Resources Base in St Petersburg and Leningrad Oblast'.[11] Parts were plagiarised from an American textbook on project management which had been translated many years earlier by a military-related department of the Soviet Academy of Sciences.[12] The speed with which it was completed and the technical complexity of the subject matter, replete with graphs and mathematical formulae far beyond the grasp of a man who had majored in humanities, left little doubt that it was largely if not entirely ghost-written. Later it emerged that it was the work of the Institute's Rector, Vladimir Litvinenko, who, a decade later, received several hundred million dollars' worth of shares in the country's largest phosphatic fertiliser company, PhosAgro, a windfall described euphemistically as a recompense for 'consulting services'.[13]

It was not the kind of subject to which Putin would naturally have been drawn.[14] As an undergraduate, he had written a dissertation on

Most Favoured Nation treatment in international trade and had later considered a thesis on German social democracy – topics with which he could have been expected to be more at ease than with the economics of natural resources.[15] But the importance of the thesis lay elsewhere. The acquisition of an academic qualification of this kind, while of little value to a provincial official, was a prized addition to the curriculum vitae of anyone with ambitions to climb the federal bureaucracy in Moscow.

The inference was that at some point that spring, Putin had decided that if Sobchak lost, he should consider doing what he had failed to do after his return from Dresden and seek a post in the capital.[16]

He had thought it through carefully. If he were no longer in the City government, he explained later, 'the world that I had had in St Petersburg [would be] gone. I understood this ... Everything [would] change ... It was the right moment to prove that it was possible, starting from scratch, to do something different.'[17]

As a consequence of Sobchak's difficult relations with Yeltsin, Putin had gained a reputation in the Kremlin as the 'go-to' person in St Petersburg when problems had to be solved.[18] His work for Yeltsin's campaign and for the Nash Dom Rossiya party had put him in touch with one of Russia's most influential figures, Prime Minister Viktor Chernomyrdin, and had reconnected him with another, Anatoly Chubais. Several other former colleagues from St Petersburg now held ministerial posts. Theoretically, therefore, there was no lack of highly placed bureaucrats who could help him find an interesting position.

At the end of June, while he was still working from Smolny for Yeltsin's campaign, the *Vertushka* – the high-frequency telephone link to the Kremlin – rang in Putin's office.[19] It was Pavel Borodin, the head of the General Affairs Office. Putin had kept in touch with Borodin after the Sedelmayer affair. When one of his daughters, who was at university in St Petersburg, fell ill, Putin arranged medical treatment for her. Whenever he visited the city, Putin made sure that he was suitably looked after.[20] Now Borodin enquired about his plans following Sobchak's defeat, and on being told that he had nothing fixed, suggested that he come to work in the Kremlin.

Ten days later, Putin flew to Moscow where the head of the Presidential Administration, Nikolai Yegorov – no relation to his namesake at the Law Faculty – offered to make him one his deputies, in charge of the Main Directorate for External and Internal Policy. It was exactly the kind of post Putin wanted and he gladly accepted. But on July 15, Yegorov was fired and replaced by Chubais, who launched a far-reaching reorganisation in which, among other things, all the Main Directorates dealing with policy were abolished.

For the next six weeks, Putin's career was in limbo.

Lyudmila had been away in Hamburg when the elections took place, officially the guest of the Russian Consul General, Dmitry Cherkashin, but in fact to see her German friend, Irene Pietsch. When she learnt that Sobchak had lost the election and that her husband was out of a job, she decided not to go back at once but to stay on for another week as she had originally planned. 'There isn't anything I can do,' she said, 'and I would just get in Volodya's way.'[21] It was the kind of problem that Putin preferred to deal with on his own. Even after she returned, 'he never talked about it,' Lyudmila remembered, 'but it was difficult . . . For a month and a half, it was completely unclear where he would work.'[22] To make matters worse, it was during this time that their dacha at the Ozero cooperative burnt down.[23]

In mid August, still without any firm commitment, Putin flew back to Moscow to see Aleksei Kudrin, his former colleague at the Finance Committee in St Petersburg, whom Chubais had called to the Kremlin to head the Main Control Directorate, keeping watch over the government's accounts. Chubais wanted Putin to join them, Kudrin told him, but the only post then available was as a department head in charge of public relations, working under Yeltsin's press spokesman, Sergei Yastrzhembsky.

Putin accepted because there was no other choice. But it was at a substantially lower rank than the post Yegorov had proposed and was not at all what he had been hoping for.[24]

This time, however, the fates were on his side. As he was driving out to the airport with Kudrin to return to St Petersburg, Chernomyrdin announced a government reshuffle. Another of Putin's St Petersburg colleagues, Aleksei Bolshakov, who had been Chairman of the Economic Development Committee under Sobchak in the autumn of 1991, was appointed first deputy Prime Minister. Kudrin suggested that they call him from the car phone to offer their congratulations. When Bolshakov heard about Putin's new post, he told him he could do better than that and asked him to delay his departure. Two days later,

Borodin offered to make him head of the Legal Department in the General Affairs Office, responsible for all Russian state property abroad – billions of dollars' worth of real estate, mainly embassy and trade mission buildings but also Communist Party properties in ex-Soviet bloc countries whose legal status was now in dispute. It was a position at almost at the same level as that which he had been offered by Yegorov and suited him far better.

On September 7, a Saturday, Putin left St Petersburg to take up his new post, accompanied by Igor Sechin, 'the adjutant', as the German Consul General, von Puttkamer, called him, who would serve as gatekeeper in his reception room in Moscow in the same way that he had done in Smolny.[25] The move to Moscow, Putin said later, had been 'the best solution . . . Inside myself, I was pleased that it had all turned out like that.'[26]

Putin's position in the General Affairs Office entitled him to a State dacha at Arkhangelskoe, in the western suburbs of Moscow. A gabled building in the traditional style with wooden balconies on the first floor, it had two spacious reception rooms and a large, old-fashioned kitchen downstairs, four bedrooms, and a garden on the edge of a birch forest.[27] Putin's old friend from Dresden, Sergei Chemezov, who was also now working for Borodin, lived nearby.[28]

Lyudmila found Moscow exhilarating and settled in almost at once.[29] Their daughters, then aged ten and eleven, had nightmares for weeks after the fire at the dacha, but they too adjusted quickly. At first, they went to a Russian primary school before transferring to the school at the German Embassy, where they gained a reputation as show-offs because they arrived every morning in a government car with a flashing blue light on the roof.[30] Of them all, Putin found it hardest to get used to Moscow. His whole life had revolved around St Petersburg. After the move, he often went back at weekends to see his parents and spend time with friends.[31] 'I wouldn't say that I didn't like Moscow,' he said later. 'It's just that I liked Petersburg more.'[32]

Putin worked with Borodin for just over six months. The property portfolio for which he was responsible was spread across 80 countries. Much of it had not even been inventoried and, especially in the ex-Soviet bloc states, there were innumerable dubious ownership claims, some of them so implausible that 'they made your hair stand on end'.[33]

During that time, Yeltsin underwent a quintuple bypass operation. Four months later, in March 1997, looking leaner and fitter than he had for years, he announced an ambitious second phase of the economic reform programme launched in 1992, which had stalled in the face of opposition from the 'red–brown coalition' of Communists and Nationalists in the Duma. It proposed tax reforms to spur economic growth; a reduction of the budget deficit; competitive bidding on government contracts; lower utilities tariffs; more direct investment in industry; measures to curb the powers of 'Red directors', who had seized control of former State enterprises during the privatisation campaign; and an end to the months-long backlog in pension payments and wages.

In the cabinet reshuffle which followed, Viktor Chernomyrdin was kept on as Prime Minister but, to push through the reforms, Yeltsin appointed two avowed liberals as his deputies: Anatoly Chubais, who relinquished his position as head of the Presidential Administration to become Minister of Finance; and Boris Nemtsov, the popular 37-year-old governor of Nizhny Novgorod, whose successes in his region made him a poster boy for market reform. Chubais appointed Aleksei Kudrin to act as first deputy Finance Minister, which meant that Kudrin's former post as head of the Main Control Directorate became vacant. His own position as head of the Presidential Administration went to Valentin Yumashev, who had been Editor-in-Chief of the liberal weekly, *Ogonyok*, and had co-authored two of Yeltsin's memoirs. At Chubais's suggestion, Yumashev named Putin as Kudrin's successor with the rank of deputy head of the Presidential Administration which he had narrowly missed the previous summer.[34]

He evidently acquitted himself well. Four months after his appointment, the Secretary of the Security Council, Ivan Rybkin, told an interviewer: 'Putin possesses systematic thinking and penetrates quickly to the heart of the matter.'[35] Another official a year later praised his 'behind-the-scenes problem-solving, phenomenal flair and extreme caution in making decisions'.[36] Yumashev remembered that 'from the very beginning, he stood out among the deputies. He formulated issues brilliantly.'[37]

Putin stood out in another way, too. Before leaving St Petersburg, he had made it clear that, when he arrived in Moscow, he intended to be his own man. 'It's hard for me to imagine what factions and cliques might exist there', he said. 'I'm not going to get involved in any of that.

They are bringing me to work, and that is what I am going to do.'[38] He tried to avoid becoming enmeshed in the intrigues which beset Yeltsin's court and apparently he succeeded. Lyudmila told her friend, Irene Pietsch: 'He is always trying to smooth out conflicts, and he manages to do it, even when I think he is wrong to try. He doesn't have any enemies, which is very unusual in Russia.'[39]

Putin showed himself determined in pursuing budgetary abuses and unafraid to offend powerful interests. In May 1997, he submitted a report on corruption in the military. A week later, Yeltsin dismissed the Defence Minister, General Igor Rodionov.[40] It was not quite cause and effect. Yeltsin was furious with Rodionov for blocking military reforms. But Putin's report came in handy. Shortly afterwards it was announced that 40 per cent of the Control Directorate's time would be devoted to inspections of the security forces. 'The Defence Ministry', Putin opined, 'will not be able to reform itself.'[41] Others would have to do it for them.[42]

Nonetheless, there were limits to how far he would go. When Rodionov's predecessor, Pavel Grachev – a man whose corruption was so notorious that he was nicknamed Pasha Mercedes – was accused of having illegally transferred a billion dollars' worth of arms to Armenia for its war with Azerbaijan over Nagorno-Karabakh, Putin announced with a straight face: 'We did not find any documents indicating that Grachev had given any direct orders or instructions about this matter.'[43] It was not that Grachev was untouchable but Yeltsin himself had approved the transaction.

Putin was equally prudent when the Control Directorate found financial abuses in a foundation set up by Anatoly Chubais, appending to his report the words: 'At your discretion'. When Chubais's colleague, Boris Nemtsov, asked Putin what that meant, he replied: 'You're the boss. You decide.'[44]

The Main Control Directorate had a broad remit. It dealt with public-sector pension and wage arrears, medical insurance, infrastructure expenditure, the creation of a unified legal space in Russia and even such seemingly abstruse problems as the rules for declassification of archives.[45] But its principal target was corruption and the misuse of government funds in the provinces. The main issues, Putin concluded, were 'sloth, mismanagement . . . and the poor quality of governance'.[46] In 1997, the Directorate found that nearly eight trillion roubles, or roughly 1.6 billion US dollars, of budgetary expenditure had been diverted to other purposes. Fifty criminal cases resulted, implicating several hundred officials.[47]

The next six months were the most intensive period of economic reform of Yeltsin's presidency.[48] State expenditures were cut by 20 per cent. Tax collection was sharply increased. Even the state-owned behemoths were unable to escape. The gas monopoly, Gazprom, alone paid 2.4 billion US dollars in back taxes. Almost 2,000 state enterprises were privatised, bringing the treasury another 2.4 billion dollars. Insider auctions were banned and, for the first time, foreign companies were allowed to take part.

To the oligarchs, as the leading business magnates were now called, that was going too far. Nine months earlier, Boris Berezovsky had told the *Financial Times* that he and six other businessmen, who would be dubbed the *semibankirshchina*, the seven bankers – a play on words on the *semiboyarshchina*, the seven boyars who ruled Russia after the overthrow of the Tsar in 1610 – effectively controlled the financial and political power of the state.[49] The time had come for him to prove that that was indeed the case.

The trigger was the auction in July 1997, of a 25 per cent stake in the state-owned telecommunications company, Svyazinvest. Chubais and Nemtsov had made it a point of honour that, unlike the earlier privatisations, this one would be transparent and clean. The winning bid came from a consortium of Vladimir Potanin's Oneksimbank, Deutsche Bank and George Soros's Quantum Fund. Berezovsky and Vladimir Gusinsky, the underbidders, were furious. Berezovsky had told Chubais beforehand that in future he could have as many open auctions as he liked, but they were entitled to a share of Svyazinvest as a recompense for having financed Yeltsin's 1996 election campaign. Chubais had turned him down flat.[50]

The same media groups, led by Berezovsky's ORT television channel and Gusinsky's NTV, which had vilified the communists to ensure Yeltsin's victory were now put to work to vilify his two first deputy Prime Ministers. At the beginning of November, Chubais and Nemtsov hit back. At their insistence, Yeltsin agreed to dismiss Berezovsky as deputy Secretary of the Security Council, a post to which he had been appointed a year earlier to oversee the implementation of the

Khasavyurt peace agreement, which, in August 1996, had ended the war in Chechnya. But by then, Berezovsky's sleuths had discovered that, two months before the Svyazinvest auction, a publishing company controlled by Oneksimbank had paid Chubais and four others an advance of 450,000 US dollars to write a book on the history of privatisation. For the media, the implication was clear: the 'advance' was in fact a bribe, and, in return, Chubais had arranged corruptly for Oneksimbank and its allies to win the Svyazinvest shares.

It was partly true and partly false. No Russian book on privatisation merited an advance remotely that size. But it had not been a bribe. The Svyazinvest auction had been straightforward. The advance had been *mzdoimstvo*, a manner of expressing appreciation without a direct quid pro quo, whereby Oneksimbank hoped to ingratiate itself with some of the key decision-makers in Yeltsin's administration. After the scandal broke, Chubais announced that he was giving the greater part of his royalties to charity. But it was too late. His four co-authors, all senior officials in the government or the Presidential Administration, were dismissed. Chubais resigned as Finance Minister in November 1997, and he and Nemtsov lost their posts as first deputy Prime Ministers in a reshuffle four months later. Berezovsky and Gusinsky had had their revenge.

For Putin, it was a salutary lesson. Two of the leading oligarchs, through their wealth and control of the media, had been able to evict some of the most powerful men in the government and Presidential Administration on essentially specious grounds. Yeltsin was well aware the charges were baseless. But he had allowed it to happen, because it was not a battle he wanted to fight.

With her husband in a senior position in the Kremlin, Lyudmila was able to indulge her love of foreign travel, which had begun with her visits to Germany after the car accident in St Petersburg. In the autumn of 1996, soon after the move to Moscow, she took the children for a half-term visit to Hamburg on the pretext that they needed to keep up their German.[51] That winter the whole family went skiing in Davos, where they stayed as the guests of Nikolai Shamalov, the Putins' neighbour at the Ozero cooperative in Karelia. Next spring, Lyudmila went on holiday to Eilat, in Israel. In May, she and the children were in Hamburg again. Shortly afterwards, her German friend, Irene Pietsch, and her husband, Matthias, visited the Putins at Arkhangelskoe. Then there was a beach holiday for the whole family on the Côte d'Azur, a few days in Finland, another skiing holiday with the Shamalovs in Davos that winter, and in the spring of 1998, a trip with the children to Hamburg, Vienna and Mauritius.

How Putin was able to afford all that is a mystery. Wealthy friends like Shamalov certainly helped. But, at a time when even Yeltsin earned officially only a few hundred dollars a month, Putin plainly had other sources of income.[52] As head of the Legal Department at the General Affairs Office and then of the Kremlin's Control Directorate, he would have had no shortage of supplicants, seeking ways to express gratitude for favourable findings or appreciation of what might be done for them in the future. There is an obvious parallel with the lobby system in Washington, D.C. All countries are to some extent corrupt but there are differences of degree. Whereas in the West, illicit exchanges of favours are seen as reprehensible, in Russia, as a patrimonial state, they are an intrinsic part of the system, without which it could not function.

Even so, for Putin, there were limits not to be transgressed. Lyudmila, who had been a model of frugality in Dresden and even after their return to St Petersburg, was fast becoming a 'new Russian'.[53] When she returned from her travels, her suitcases were so overweight with purchases she had been unable to resist that, on one occasion, the airline refused to accept them. 'Her Russian soul could not withstand the turmoil of Western temptations,' Irene Pietsch wrote. Putin did not appreciate that and refused to allow her a credit card.[54]

Lyudmila's expensive tastes were not the only problem he had to deal with. Anatoly Sobchak had stayed on in St Petersburg, where he occupied a sinecure at a cultural association, financed by the casino magnate, Misha Mirilashvili, whose business activities in St Petersburg he had favoured when he was Mayor.[55] For the first year after the election, the prosecutors had left him in peace. Korzhakov, who had initiated the apartment case, had been dismissed, and so long as Chubais remained head of the Presidential Administration, Sobchak was protected. But after Chubais left the Kremlin, the investigation quietly resumed, encouraged by the Mayor of Moscow, Yuri Luzhkov, who had become Skuratov's new patron. Luzhkov was close to Vladimir Yakovlev, his counterpart in St Petersburg, who hated Sobchak almost as much as he hated Putin.[56]

In August, 1997, the head of the Renaissance Company, which had refurbished Sobchak's apartment, was brought in for questioning. Two months later, as Sobchak left his office, he was surrounded by Interior Ministry troops who took him to the Prosecutor's Office. He was able to telephone his wife, who immediately called Putin, who got a message to Boris Nemtsov, the young reformist first deputy Prime Minister, who was with Yeltsin at Zavidovo, a hunting estate, 80 miles north-west of Moscow, where the President was engaged in his favourite pastime of duck-shooting.

Berezovsky's campaign against Chubais and Nemtsov was then still in its early stages and Nemtsov was able to persuade Yeltsin that the persecution of Sobchak was being carried too far. The former Mayor, he argued, had always been an ally whenever there was a critical moment. He had done nothing worse than many other provincial leaders, yet now he was being hounded by his opponents at a time when he had serious heart problems and the strain of prosecution might kill him.

The mention of heart problems evidently got Yeltsin's attention for, after at first dismissing Nemtsov's concerns, he asked to speak to Skuratov. 'Don't touch Sobchak,' he told him. 'You don't kick a man when he's down. His heart is bad.' When Skuratov tried to object, he repeated, 'Don't touch him,' and put down the phone.[57]

In St Petersburg, Sobchak's wife, Lyudmila Narusova, insisted that he was dangerously ill and demanded that he be examined by a doctor before the investigators questioned him. He spent the next five weeks in hospital. But time was not on his side. Chubais's position was becoming increasingly precarious. Narusova toyed with the idea of making a dash across the border to Estonia, where the former Justice Minister, Jüri Raidla, was a friend.[58] Then, at the end of October, Skuratov asked the Health Ministry to send a team of cardiologists from Moscow to verify whether Sobchak's condition was really too serious to prevent him answering the investigators' questions. They were to arrive on November 10, after the long holiday weekend marking what used to be the anniversary of the Bolshevik Revolution and was now called 'Reconciliation Day'.[59]

Putin told Yumashev that he would need to take a few days off.[60] It seemed that Sobchak would be arrested very shortly, he said. 'I'm going there to try to help . . . If it doesn't work out, please tell Yeltsin that . . . I felt I had no choice.' Yumashev said it was up to him, but if anything went wrong, 'you won't be able to work here any more. I'll have to fire you.'

Sobchak was permitted to go home for the holiday, ostensibly to celebrate his daughter's sixteenth birthday. Instead, he flew to Paris on a medical evacuation plane chartered by Gennady Timchenko, a wealthy oil trader who had built a flourishing career when Sobchak had been Mayor and had close ties to Putin.[61] The moment had been well chosen. Moscow was preoccupied with the storm brewing over the 'book scandal', and the holiday meant that, in the services which should have been keeping watch on Sobchak, only a skeleton staff was on duty. An ambulance took him to the airport. He went through customs and immigration in the normal way and, on arrival at Le Bourget, was driven to the American hospital in the Paris suburb of Neuilly.

When Putin reappeared as usual in his Kremlin office on Monday morning, Yumashev remembered breathing 'a huge sigh of relief'. It meant that he would not have to have a difficult conversation with Yeltsin, who, had the venture failed, would certainly have condemned it. Instead, when eventually he did tell the President what had happened, Yeltsin said nothing. Yumashev got the impression that 'deep down, he sympathised with what Putin . . . had done'. Others were impressed, too. He had not been afraid to take a risk which, if it had gone wrong, would have ended his career.[62] As Gleb Pavlovsky, Yeltsin's political strategist, put it: 'The stakes were extremely high for Putin. It was at this point that the people in the Kremlin started noticing him . . . There were a lot of windbags around, who were incapable of carrying out an actual project. And here was Putin – look at the logistics of what he did! He didn't just declare his loyalty, he did [it] and he succeeded. It was a success . . . And to be honest, success was pretty rare in the Kremlin then.'[63]

It was not the only display of loyalty on Putin's part that autumn. A month after his return from St Petersburg, another incident occurred which did him rather less credit.[64] He was travelling along the Minsk Highway in his official car, a Jeep Cherokee, one evening, when Boris Zykov, his driver, pulled out to overtake a truck. There was a second truck in front of it and he was unable to get back into his lane. After hitting one oncoming car, the Jeep swerved and crashed into a second car, killing a five-year-old boy. When the family demanded justice,

Putin protected Zykov, who had been his driver since he arrived in Moscow, and 18 months later arranged for him to be amnestied before the case could come to trial. It was the same code that he had learnt as a child in the courtyard in Leningrad: even if your friend was a criminal, you defended him because he was your friend.

Putin's part in getting Sobchak to Paris would later play a crucial role in determining his future career. But before that could happen, Yeltsin sprang a surprise.

On March 23, 1998, he announced on television that he had dismissed the government, which had been headed for the previous five years by Viktor Chernomyrdin, and was nominating in his place 35-year-old Sergei Kiriyenko, who had become a minister only six months earlier. There were several reasons. The Prime Minister had started to see himself as a future candidate for the presidency and Yeltsin had decided his wings needed to be clipped. It was also a generational change. Chernomyrdin was an old-school 'Red director', a man who had risen through the ranks of the Communist Party to become the first Chairman of Gazprom. He was an habitué of smoke-filled rooms, unenthusiastic about economic reform but able to cut deals with the 'red–brown coalition' in the Duma. Kiriyenko, the youngest Prime Minister Russia had ever had, was a successful private businessman with a completely different approach.

One of Kiriyenko's first challenges was to reassert Moscow's control over the regions, which had taken to heart Yeltsin's directive to 'take as much sovereignty as [they] can swallow' and were increasingly charting their own paths.

Until November, regional policy had been the responsibility of a veteran official named Aleksandr Kazakov, but he had been fired in the Oneksimport book scandal. Yumashev had wanted Putin to succeed him.[65] But the timing was not right. Putin was too closely identified with Chubais's St Petersburg clan. After some hesitation, Yeltsin had appointed Viktoria Mitina, a loyalist from one of the Moscow districts who had worked on his election campaigns and was close to his daughter, Tatyana. Yumashev thought the appointment a mistake and by the spring it was clear that he was right.[66] Mitina was out of her depth.

In May, General Aleksandr Lebed, once Yeltsin's ally but now a potential rival, was elected Governor of Krasnoyarsk, defeating the

Kremlin's candidate. It was one of a series of 'misfires' that it was Miti-na's job to prevent. Russia was then in the grip of a nationwide strike by miners protesting against unpaid wages, who blocked railway lines and camped out in front of the White House, demanding that Yeltsin resign. Instead of clamping down on the unrest, numerous governors stood aside, arguing that it was not their problem. There were scat-tered calls from regional assemblies for the President's impeachment, and the Federation Council, the upper house of parliament, in which the governors had a dominant voice, rejected Yeltsin's attempts to limit budgetary expenditures.

On May 25, Mitina was fired. Putin was named her successor, retain-ing his position as head of the Control Directorate and becoming one of two first deputy heads of the Presidential Administration.[67]

It was a substantial promotion and, according to Putin himself, came not a moment too soon. Yumashev recalled that when he offered him the post, Putin replied: 'If you hadn't asked me to become first deputy head, I would have left, because [this work I'm doing now] doesn't interest me.'[68]

That should probably be taken with a generous pinch of salt.

Putin had complained earlier to Aleksei Kudrin that working at the General Affairs Office under Borodin had been boring. 'It was not my thing,' he grumbled. 'It wasn't a very lively job compared to what I did in St Petersburg.'[69] That might have been true, but the Control Direc-torate had been different: during the 15 months he spent there, he had had his finger on the pulse of everything going on in Russia and the reports that he issued put fear into army generals, government minis-ters and governors alike.

It was true that he could only make recommendations. The deci-sions were taken higher up. And the atmosphere was depressing. Aleksandr Voloshin, who had started working as an assistant to Yuma-shev that winter, found the Kremlin 'an unpleasant place – silent, with people speaking in whispers . . . Everything annoyed me: the way people talked to each other; the empty corridors, the long carpets, the [high frequency secure] telephones that gave you electric shocks . . .'[70] As Control Directorate chief, Putin spent most of his time in his office on the fifth floor of the Presidential Administration building in Old Square, *Staraya Ploshchad*, which had once housed the Communist Party Central Committee, rather than in the Kremlin itself. But the ambiance was similar, and there was the same, pervasive climate of back-stabbing and petty intrigue which Putin tried to avoid.

Yet it is difficult to believe that he would willingly have given up a career in public service to move to the private sector when his name was constantly being mentioned in the press as a man destined for higher things. He was a *gosudarstvennik*, a statist, through and through. He might occasionally wonder aloud about life as a lawyer or a businessman, but in reality, as he said himself, entrepreneurship was 'not [his] thing at all'.[71] The griping about being bored was a front. He preferred public service and would leave only if he had no choice.[72]

As first deputy head of the Presidential Administration, Putin had a position of real power. He was listed as one of the hundred most influential figures in Russia.[73] He stood in for Yumashev when the latter was away, and, for the first time, had direct access to Yeltsin, being responsible for the President's schedule when he travelled within Russia.[74] His main task – relations with the regions – was a job for which he was well prepared. As *Novoe vremya* observed, after 15 months heading the Control Directorate, 'no one in the government knows as much as Putin does about the governors' activities. They will soon feel the difference.'[75]

Shortly after his appointment, Putin brought in Nikolai Patrushev, the unsmiling, hawk-faced ex-KGB officer who had been his colleague in St Petersburg in the 1980s, to succeed him at the Control Directorate.[76] Patrushev's task, it was announced, was 'to accustom the regions to financial discipline'.[77] Putin himself said he did not intend to 'tighten the screws' but it was necessary to install a 'federal vertical' chain of command.[78] He saw his own role as being to confront recalcitrant governors, in regions where there was social unrest, with evidence of their malfeasance, and to propose that they use the funds that they had misappropriated to pay wage arrears. 'Conversations with the governors,' he explained, 'are much more effective when one has operational data to hand.'[79]

The only place where that did not work was Chechnya, for which Putin shared responsibility with the Interior Minister, Sergei Stepashin. Moscow could regulate the flow of money to the Chechen capital, Grozny, but there was no way it could control what happened to it afterwards.[80]

That summer, Putin travelled constantly. One of his assistants, asked

by a British diplomat what he thought of his new boss, told her: 'I
don't know. He's never here.'[81] In July, Yeltsin also put him in charge of
the State Committee which negotiated the division of powers between
Moscow and the regions. His predecessor in this post, Sergei Shakhrai,
obedient to Yeltsin's directive about sharing sovereignty, had negotiated agreements giving substantial independence to more than half
the country's territories. Putin put a stop to that. He was 'a hardliner
regarding the regions', the newspaper, *Kommersant*, said approvingly.[82]

However, little more than a week later, the governors breathed a
sigh of relief. They would still have to deal with Patrushev. But Putin
was to be promoted again, for the second time in as many months.

Ever since the putsch in August 1991, if not earlier, Yeltsin had been
wary of the security services. He had restructured the FSB four times
since taking power and had tried out five different directors, an average
of one a year.

The first, General Viktor Barannikov, a police officer by training,
was fired for corruption. His successor, Nikolai Golushko, was a stop-
gap, tainted by the failure of the special services to support the Kremlin
during the White House siege in October 1993. Yeltsin decided that he
was incapable of carrying out the necessary reforms.[83] Stepashin then
held the post for a year. He was more successful, but resigned in June
1995, after Chechen terrorists staged a spectacular hostage-taking at a
hospital in Budyonnovsk, in southern Russia, leaving more than 140
dead. In his place, Yeltsin appointed Mikhail Barsukov, the head of the
Federal Protection Service and a close friend of his chief bodyguard,
Andrei Korzhakov. Barsukov was fired together with Korzhakov and
the first deputy Prime Minister, Oleg Soskovets, during the 1996 election campaign. His deputy, Nikolai Kovalyov, succeeded him and set a
record by lasting two years in the job. But by the summer of 1998 he,
too, was found wanting and Yeltsin began looking for a replacement.
There was going to be a 'hot autumn' politically, leading up to parliamentary elections a year later.[84] It was time to bring the security
services directly under the Kremlin's control.

Rumours that Kovalyov was about to be sacked and that Putin was
among the candidates to succeed him had begun circulating as early as
June 1997, not long after Putin became head of the Control Directorate.[85] After Yeltsin issued a formal denial, they died down, only to

resume the following spring.[86] When Lyudmila questioned him, he promised her that, even if it were offered, he would not accept the post. 'You don't enter the same river twice,' he said, 'and, to be honest, I thought it was a dead end.'[87]

Coming from a man who liked to portray himself as a disinterested state functionary with no political ambitions, that remark is revealing. To be named FSB Director would be a substantial promotion. Yet Putin was more concerned that, if he returned to the special services, he would be typecast and the possibility of further advancement would be closed off.

Nonetheless, three months later, on July 25, 1998, Yeltsin summoned Kiriyenko to the State guest house in Karelia, where he was vacationing, and handed him a decree naming Putin FSB chief. The Prime Minister flew back to Moscow and the same evening Putin took up his new functions.[88]

Kovalyov's downfall triggered endless speculation.

Yeltsin told the press enigmatically: 'You journalists think that if a minister shaves every morning, he's a good minister. But you do not know as much as I know.'[89] There were rumours that it was because Kovalyov had become too close to Yeltsin's long-time adversary, the Mayor of Moscow, Yuri Luzhkov, or, alternatively, that the President had been angered by a series of botched FSB operations.[90] Others claimed that it was connected with the murder of General Lev Rokhlin, the former head of the Duma Defence Committee who had been organising an opposition movement in the army. Rokhlin had been shot dead in mysterious circumstances three weeks earlier.[91]

The truth was more prosaic. Kovalyov was dismissed not so much for having failed but because, as Kiriyenko put it, two days later, 'when conditions change, people change.'[92] The miners' strike had taken the Kremlin unawares and Yeltsin wrote later that Kovalyov had been 'almost panicking . . . This situation was new to him and he didn't know how to handle it.'[93] Yumashev and Kiriyenko both thought that Putin would be a safer pair of hands.[94] Yeltsin reached the same conclusion.

Putin had been on holiday with Lyudmila and the children on the Côte d'Azur while this was brewing and was summoned back posthaste to Moscow.[95] When Yumashev telephoned him to tell him of Yeltsin's decision, Putin claimed to be 'not overjoyed'.[96] Lyudmila was distraught. For her, 'it would mean a return to a closed life . . . Don't

go there, don't say that. Talk to that person, don't talk to this person.'
When she called her German friend, Irene Pietsch, to tell her what had
happened, she was in tears. 'It's terrible,' she said. 'Why does he only
pursue his own interests and show no consideration for me and the
children?'[97]

Putin told her that he had had no choice but to accept – which was
no doubt true – and that, in any case, it would not be for more than
two years, as Yeltsin's term would end in 2000 and he would not stay
on in the FSB afterwards.[98] But Lyudmila's fears were well founded.
Her relations with the Pietschs were severed, never to be resumed, and
within Russia, her circle of friends and acquaintances became more
circumscribed.

If Putin had reservations about his new position, he did not let them
show. When Kiriyenko took him to the Lubyanka to present him to the
FSB generals as Kovalyov's successor, he told them that 'returning
here is like returning home'.[99]

The generals were not so sure.[100] They did not like having to answer
to a mere colonel who had served in a regional, not even a central,
directorate. Putin was associated with men like Sobchak and Chubais,
whom most of them regarded as traitors, and they assumed that his
arrival heralded a purge. Three weeks earlier, Yeltsin had called for a
wholesale reorganisation, including cuts in the central staff working at
the Lubyanka to not more than 4,000 officers, and the establishment of
a new Constitutional Security Directorate to conduct political surveillance of extremist groups and the labour movement.[101] Putin, they
surmised, was the hatchet-man who was to carry this out.

That proved to be the case. Several directorates were merged and
nearly 2,000 officers were dismissed.[102] 'The situation in the FSB was
very bad at that time,' Gleb Pavlovsky remembered. 'Putin was given
the task of carrying out a purge and he applied himself to that very
actively. He fired a lot of people. That was something no one else had
done before. People were afraid. And that pleased Yeltsin.'[103]

He also brought in loyalists from St Petersburg to fill a number of
key posts. Viktor Cherkesov, who had headed the regional FSB office
there, was promoted to become one of two first deputy Directors.
Nikolai Patrushev was moved from the Control Directorate to become
head of Economic Security. Another former colleague, Sergei Ivanov,
became head of Analysis and Strategy.[104] Putin himself refused

promotion to the rank of general, preferring to become the FSB's first civilian director.[105]

The day after his appointment, he announced the new priorities. The FSB would combat political extremism and nationalism. It would step up the fight against terrorism; protect essential military and technological secrets, with the proviso that it was 'important to define what should be protected, and what not'; and it would establish a mechanism for surveillance of the internet.[106] The new Constitutional Security Directorate, he promised, would not engage in the kind of social snooping that had caused the KGB to be so hated. It had been 'justified at the time', he maintained, 'because it had contributed to the stable functioning of society' – a statement which dismayed Russian liberals but no doubt reassured Putin's wary FSB colleagues – but 'nowadays it is not needed'.

The main priority, however, on which both Kiriyenko and Yeltsin had insisted when he was appointed, was economic security.[107] This covered privatisation and relations with the oligarchs; control of financial flows through private and state-owned banks; and the repatriation of illegally exported capital.[108]

The reason soon became clear. Russia was on the verge of financial meltdown. It stemmed from the Asian financial crisis a year earlier, which had led to a sharp fall in the price of oil and gas and non-ferrous metals, then, as now, Russia's biggest exports. The situation had been made worse by the government's insistence on maintaining the exchange rate of the rouble, which quickly drained the country's foreign reserves. In July, the IMF and the World Bank agreed a 22.6-billion-dollar rescue package, designed to support the Russian currency by converting high-interest short-term loans into longer-term Eurobonds. But far from being reassured, money managers took fright. On August 17, 1998, Russia defaulted on domestic debt, announced a moratorium on foreign debt repayments and abandoned the floating peg for the rouble, which over the following month lost two thirds of its dollar value.

Six days later, Kiriyenko resigned.

Putin had known what was coming. Earlier that month, he had been introduced by Aleksei Kudrin to a radical young economist named Andrei Illarionov, who ran a small think tank which had infuriated the government by insisting that a devaluation was inevitable.

Illarionov remembered that it had been a strange encounter. Putin had asked him to explain his reasoning. 'I told him that a crisis was coming, it's impossible to avoid, no matter how much money you borrow abroad . . . I spoke for maybe five or six minutes. Putin said nothing. Absolutely nothing. He did not change his expression; his eyes did not move . . . In the end, Kudrin thanked me and I left.'[109]

The crisis left Yeltsin severely weakened. His first reaction was to call on Chernomyrdin to return as Prime Minister, but the Duma refused to confirm him. In mid September, he proposed the Foreign Minister, Yevgeny Primakov, as a compromise candidate acceptable to all the main parliamentary groups. In his youth, Primakov had been a correspondent for the Communist Party newspaper, *Pravda*; then a senior researcher and later director of a prestigious research institute under the Academy of Sciences; and most recently, before joining the government, head of the SVR, the successor to the KGB's First Chief Directorate.

A solid, well-respected, avuncular character, he quickly won parliamentary approval and over the next eight months showed himself to be the reassuring figure that Russia needed. The devalued rouble, by making imports more expensive, sparked a recovery in domestic manufactures, oil prices rose and sovereign debt was restructured. By the end of the year, instead of collapsing as many had feared, the economy was beginning to rebound. 'Primakov . . . had a confident ease about him that was able to quell and subdue the almost panic-stricken people in September and October,' Yeltsin wrote later. '[He] achieved the kind of stable position that no other Russian Prime Minister had been able to achieve before.'[110]

Soon after becoming FSB Director, Putin was confronted with a scandal involving Chubais's nemesis, Boris Berezovsky. In April, 1998, five FSB officers working for URPO, the Department for Investigating Organised Crime groups, had reported to Kovalyov that their boss, General Yevgeny Khokholkov, had given them secret orders to assassinate Berezovsky and several other prominent figures. The story was not implausible. It was an open secret that certain senior FSB officers were in the pay of mafia figures. When Kovalyov failed to take action, they made a formal complaint to the Presidential Administration, at which point they were suspended while the Military Prosecutor's Office carried out an investigation.

After Putin's appointment, Berezovsky took the group's leader, Aleksandr Litvinenko, to meet him at his office in the Lubyanka and make a full report. Putin heard him out, but the meeting did not go well. He had shown no interest, Litvinenko told his wife afterwards. 'He was cold and formal.'[111] It could hardly have been otherwise. Putin despised FSB officers who made their grievances public. But Litvinenko was wrong to think that the new director did not take his complaints seriously. Putin usually heard out his interlocutors in silence – as did Yeltsin – and decided only later how to respond.

Two months later, Putin disbanded URPO. But he did not dismiss Khokholkov outright. Instead the URPO commander was transferred to a sinecure in the Tax Inspectorate. That was intended partly as reassurance to the FSB hierarchy that the new director had their backs. But it was also typical of Putin's manner of dealing with opponents. He tried to give them a way out and, by doing so, to win them over.

However, that was not the end of the matter. In November, Berezovsky published an open letter, claiming that the FSB was riddled with corrupt officers and demanding that Putin act more forcefully to 'establish the constitutional order'.[112] Berezovsky was interfering, Putin retorted. Did he want a return to the Stalinist repression of the 1930s? Berezovsky had proposed nothing of the sort, but Putin was furious that he had dared, as he put it, 'to wash our dirty linen in public'. If the charges against Khokholkov and his subordinates proved unfounded, he warned, the FSB would take to court both Berezovsky himself and the officers who had 'knowingly given false testimony'.[113]

The same day, Litvinenko and his colleagues, some of them wearing ski masks to hide their faces, gave a surreal press conference, at which they repeated their charges.[114] If it was an attempt to force Putin's hand, it backfired badly. The FSB Director appeared two days later on the main television evening current affairs programme to say there was no independent evidence that anyone had ever tried to kill Berezovsky and that the officers who had appeared masked – 'like Alisa the Fox and Basilio the Cat', two swindlers from the Russian version of Pinocchio – were themselves under investigation for criminal activities. Berezovsky, whom Yeltsin had recently appointed Executive Secretary of the CIS, the Commonwealth of Independent States, had made 'a big mistake', he said. He would do better to apply himself to his new job instead of making wild allegations against the security services.[115]

Next day, Yeltsin summoned Putin to Gorki-9, his country residence, surrounded by birch forests near the Moscow River, about 20 miles west of the city, setting off a frenzy of speculation that he was about to be fired. Yeltsin, it was assumed, was angry about the Litvinenko scandal. But Putin stood his ground and the President declared himself satisfied.[116] Shortly afterwards Litvinenko was dismissed from the FSB and arrested. It was the start of a long journey which would eventually lead him to an agonising death in London.

Putin had had reservations about Berezovsky ever since their first encounters in St Petersburg. Lyudmila told friends that they regarded the oligarch as 'Enemy Number One'.[117] Apart from the spat during the Litvinenko affair, however, Putin was careful not to criticise him. Only once, at a private meeting with the Finnish Ambassador, Markus Lyra, not long after Litvinenko's press conference, did he let down his guard.

The circumstances were unusual. Lyra had been Consul General in St Petersburg and he and Putin had struck up something approaching a friendship. After they met again in Moscow, when Putin was working for the Presidential Administration, he would visit Lyra from time to time to relax and drink beer in the Finnish Embassy sauna.[118] They talked about how his children were doing at the German school, his old friends in Turku, his holidays in Lapland – the sorts of everyday subjects that he never discussed with other foreigners. In the sauna, naked, he looked incredibly fit, Lyra remembered, with not an ounce of fat on his body.[119]

After Putin became FSB chief, the visits stopped, but in the winter of 1998, Lyra went to the Lubyanka to arrange a meeting between Putin and Seppo Nevala, the new head of SUPO, the Finnish intelligence service. To his surprise, Putin launched into a tirade against Berezovsky. 'He's the worst criminal you can think of,' Putin told him. 'He's going to damage Russia and he will damage your country, too.'[120]

The outburst was all the more striking because, less than three months later, Putin arrived, uninvited, with an enormous bouquet of roses, at a birthday party for Berezovsky's wife, Lena.[121] It was a seemingly incomprehensible gesture. Primakov hated Berezovsky. Skuratov, the Prosecutor General, had launched an investigation into his affairs and it was widely expected that he would soon be arrested. Putin was the only high-ranking official to attend.

The explanation emerged gradually over the following months.

Putin was not a chess player but he could still think several moves ahead. Not long after he took office, his relations with Primakov had soured. The Prime Minister had asked him to wiretap the liberal leader, Grigory Yavlinsky, whose Yabloko party had 45 seats in the Duma. Putin had refused and informed Yeltsin, who approved of his decision. Two months later, Primakov had asked Yeltsin to fire Putin on the grounds that he had purged a number of veteran FSB generals and brought in 'non-professionals' from St Petersburg to replace them. Again, Yeltsin refused.[122] By the time the birthday party took place in late February 1999, Putin sensed that the Prime Minister's days were numbered.

Whatever Putin's private feelings about Berezovsky, he was a powerful figure and would become more so if, as Putin now expected, he came through Primakov's attacks unscathed. Birthdays in Russia have an importance of which it is difficult for Westerners to conceive. To attend a birthday party for Berezovsky's wife at a time when the oligarch was at his most vulnerable would earn his undying support. The ruse succeeded. Berezovsky was convinced from then on that Putin was a true and loyal friend, and he continued to think so long afterwards, even after they had fallen out.

The seeds of Primakov's downfall had been sown the previous autumn, when the Prosecutor General, Yuri Skuratov, had launched an investigation into reports that a Swiss construction company, Mabetex, had paid a substantial kickback to Putin's former boss at the General Affairs Office, Pavel Borodin, in return for contracts worth several hundred million dollars for restoration work in the Kremlin.[123] As the investigation developed, Swiss prosecutors claimed to have evidence that Mabetex had also made payments and settled credit card bills for Yeltsin and his daughters.

Borodin was subsequently arrested in New York and extradited to Switzerland where a court fined him 300,000 Swiss francs for money laundering, no more than a rap over the knuckles given the sums involved.

Whether there was any truth in the charges against Yeltsin and his family is harder to judge. In the case of the President, it is highly unlikely. Concerning his daughters, it is less clear, but even if Mabetex did settle bills for them, given the way that things were done in Russia, it was a very minor offence.[124]

Nevertheless, a financial scandal was the last thing the Kremlin wanted.

Yeltsin's political opponents had already begun referring to his immediate entourage as the Family, with a capital 'F', claiming that the President was being manipulated by a corrupt cabal, whose core members were his daughter, Tatyana, Yumashev and Voloshin. Russian newspapers speculated endlessly about who else should be included. To those named it was a badge of honour, or dishonour, depending on one's point of view. Berezovsky was invariably declared to be a member, which flattered him, even if it was not strictly true. So was his business associate, Roman Abramovich, a young oligarch who, although he had an entrée to the Kremlin, had little political influence. For a time, Sergei Pugachev, the co-founder of Mezhprombank, which had a privileged role in the Kremlin's financial operations during Yeltsin's last years in power, was also said to be a member.[125]

For the opposition, the malign influence of the Family was a useful fiction, a vehicle for smear campaigns which were impossible to disprove. The Mabetex investigation was grist to their mill.[126] The Kremlin needed to find a way to bring it rapidly to an end.

On February 1, Nikolai Bordyuzha, who had succeeded Yumashev as head of the Presidential Administration, summoned Skuratov and showed him a grainy video of what would later be termed 'a man resembling the Prosecutor-General' – a phrase curiously reminiscent of that applied to the American diplomat with whom Putin had had a run-in in St Petersburg, five years earlier – frolicking in bed with two naked girls. It had been filmed with a hidden camera in a Moscow apartment, once used as a KGB safe house, which was now owned by a businessman, Suren Yegiazaryan, who had reportedly arranged the services of young women for Skuratov on a number of previous occasions.[127] Yegiazaryan's brother, Ashot, a banker who was then under investigation for fraud, had decided that it would be foolish to pass up the opportunity to obtain compromising material which might come in handy if the Prosecutor General decided to take him to court. One of Ashot's friends who had a grudge against Skuratov obtained a copy of the tape and passed it to Pugachev, who gave it to Bordyuzha.[128]

Initially Skuratov did not deny that he was the man shown. He agreed to resign on health grounds and a letter to that effect was given to Yeltsin the same day. But after the President's opponents in parliament refused to approve his resignation, Skuratov changed his mind and claimed that the film had been faked.[129] Putin visited him several times in hospital, where he was supposedly being treated for ulcers, and tried to persuade him to leave quietly. For two months, there was a stand-off. Then, on March 17, extracts from the video were shown on the evening news by the state-owned RTR television channel. Putin was said to have been present in the gallery when the broadcast went out and afterwards vouched for its authenticity.[130] Finally, on April 2, a criminal investigation was launched and the Prosecutor General was suspended.[131]

The Skuratov affair damaged Primakov, not because he supported the Prosecutor General openly but because Yeltsin suspected complicity between them.[132] By then, he had started to have doubts on other scores as well.

The Prime Minister was an intelligent, thoughtful man, but he was also, in the President's view, an old-school apparatchik, a 'real dinosaur . . . hostage to Soviet stereotypes',[133] as had been shown by his reaction – or the lack of it – when a wave of anti-Semitism, whipped up by ultra-nationalist members of Zhirinovsky's party in the Duma, had swept over Russia the previous winter.

In November 1998, the standard-bearer of the St Petersburg democrats, Galina Starovoitova, who was Jewish, had been shot dead at the entrance to her apartment block. Yeltsin, for whom she had once worked as an adviser, was incensed and sent Putin and Stepashin, the Interior Minister, post-haste to St Petersburg to head the investigation. It was later established that her murder had been ordered by three members of the Duma from Zhirinovsky's party, all leading figures in the Tambovsky organised crime group, who had convinced themselves that she was part of a Jewish conspiracy to bring Russia to its knees.[134] A few weeks earlier, a retired general, Albert Makashov, had told a rally in Moscow that he wanted to 'take a dozen Yids with me into the next world'.[135] The Duma had refused to lift his parliamentary immunity. Putin, on behalf of the FSB, had demanded that Makashov be prosecuted for inciting inter-ethnic hatred and urged the Duma to decide accordingly.[136] Yeltsin, too, strongly condemned Makashov. But Primakov's Justice Ministry and the Prosecutor General's office held that there was no case for him to answer.

'We will go on being anti-Semites and we will prevail,' Makashov exulted.[137]

In the end, the anti-Jewish tumult died down. But Yeltsin was not pleased. By then, he was also growing concerned that Primakov, like Chernomyrdin, was developing presidential ambitions. 'I gradually began to sense the danger of the situation,' Yeltsin wrote later. 'I realized that he was becoming a serious political alternative to my course and my plan for the country's development . . . [He] threatened to roll back reforms, collapse the embryonic economic freedoms and trample [on] democratic liberties . . . freedom of speech and the preservation of a system of normal political competition.'[138]

By mid April, 1999, the President had decided that Primakov would have to go. It was a delicate moment because the Duma, which had been threatening for almost a year to impeach Yeltsin, was finally preparing to put the issue to a vote. Yeltsin was accused on five counts: responsibility for the collapse of the Soviet Union in 1991; using armed force to disperse the Congress of People's Deputies during the White House siege in 1993; launching an illegal war in Chechnya; weakening Russian military power by ill-considered budget cuts; and genocide against the peoples of Russia through economic reforms which had caused demographic decline.

On May 12, three days before the Duma was due to vote, the President dismissed Primakov and nominated Stepashin to take his place. Should the impeachment succeed, it would mean that Stepashin rather than Primakov would become acting President pending fresh elections. Yeltsin recognised that it might make the opposition close ranks against him, but he discounted that. 'A sharp, unexpected, aggressive move always throws your opponent off balance,' he explained, 'especially if it is unpredictable and seems absolutely illogical.'[139] It was a lesson from a master tactician which Putin would take to heart. When the vote came, Zhirinovsky's nationalists refused to participate and some members of Yabloko abstained. None of the impeachment charges obtained the two-thirds majority needed to pass. A week later, parliament confirmed Stepashin as Russia's new Prime Minister.

Ever since the 1996 presidential election, Yeltsin had been preoccupied, if not obsessed, with how to safeguard his legacy. Gleb Pavlovsky, his political strategist, remembered how, in August that year, Chubais, who had just been appointed head of the Presidential Administration, had called a meeting of the President's closest aides. Yeltsin would not stand again, he said. The main challenge of his second term would be to find a suitable successor.[140]

Yeltsin had initially seen Boris Nemtsov as a possible candidate. During his first term, he had visited Nizhny Novgorod, where Nemtsov was Governor, and had been impressed by his energy. He had mentioned him to Bill Clinton and Helmut Kohl as a young man with a future.[141] But after persuading him to come to Moscow in the spring of 1997, Yeltsin had been disappointed. Nemtsov, he decided, was like Chubais – 'a technologist, a manager, a specialist, [not] a national figure capable of consolidating whole segments of society'.[142] Chernomyrdin and Primakov were of another generation, reticent about reform and incapable of leading Russia in the new century that was about to dawn. Kiriyenko's government had been 'managerial, technocratic . . . and had no political backing – no credibility and no influence over the public'.[143] Yeltsin had considered others, too, but had quickly ruled them out. The leader of Yabloko, Grigory Yavlinsky, was 'a good, strong figure' but sectarian and too much obliged to his own political faction.[144] Igor Ivanov, the Foreign Minister, was an ally of Primakov.[145]

A more serious contender was Nikolai Aksyonenko, the Railways Minister. Yeltsin considered him an excellent economic planner and a possible alternative to both Kiriyenko and Stepashin. But the majority of the Duma disliked him and Yeltsin concluded that he was better kept in reserve. He remained a potential successor who never quite made the grade.[146]

That left Vladimir Putin.

Yeltsin had begun thinking of Putin as a possible Prime Minister in the summer of 1998, when it had become clear that Kiriyenko was not up to the task.[147] He had thought hard about Putin's role in Sobchak's departure. 'I had mixed feelings [about it],' he wrote later. 'Yet I profoundly admired his actions.'[148] Yumashev was convinced that that episode, more than any other, persuaded Yeltsin that Putin had the stuff to become President.[149] He had already been effectively in charge of Russia's second city, St Petersburg. After he was given responsibility for the regions, he impressed Yeltsin by the tough, no-nonsense approach he took towards the governors. As FSB chief, he had refused to kowtow to Primakov. He did not 'allow himself to be manipulated

in political games', Yeltsin wrote, and his 'very tough remarks condemning political extremism' had prevented troubles spilling over into
the streets after the government's tepid response to Makashov's anti-
Semitic speeches.[150]

Then came the Mabetex affair. There, too, he had shown himself
sure-footed. Yeltsin thought Skuratov was merely 'a pawn in the game
of bigger political people'. He was being manipulated by Luzhkov
who wanted to trigger a political crisis. The way Putin had dealt with
the Prosecutor General had convinced him, he wrote later, that he had
the 'tough character traits . . . needed in a fierce political battle'.[151]

Yeltsin claimed afterwards that he had never intended Stepashin as
anything more than a stop-gap Prime Minister and that he had been
planning all along to appoint Putin when the time was right:

> Putin . . . had the will and the resolve. I knew he did. But intuition told
> me that it would be premature to bring Putin into the political ring at
> that moment [in May, 1999]. He had to appear later . . . I didn't want the
> public to get too used to Putin in those lazy summer months . . . The
> surprise factor had to remain intact . . . I needed someone to serve as a
> decoy. There was no alternative. This role had to be entrusted to the
> nice, decent Sergei Stepashin. Of course, I would try to explain to him
> that the question of the future, of the presidential elections, was still
> open. And he, too, would have a chance to show himself.[152]

But those lines were written a year later, when the drama had already
played out. At the time, it was not as clear-cut. Yeltsin felt that Putin
would make a strong candidate. But that did not mean that he had
taken a final decision. Both Yumashev and Aleksandr Voloshin, who
had replaced Bordyuzha as head of the Presidential Administration in
March 1999, thought that he had not yet made up his mind.[153] When
Stepashin was appointed, the intention was still to hold the presidential elections as planned in June 2000. He had a full year to prove
himself. Had he done so, Yeltsin might have made Stepashin, rather
than Putin, his preferred successor.

There was another consideration, too.

Yeltsin had won re-election in 1996 thanks to the support of the oligarchs. They had now become too powerful, as had been shown by the
ease with which Berezovsky and Gusinsky had brought down Chubais

and Nemtsov after the Svyazinvest auction. Berezovsky, in particular, was a thorn in Yeltsin's side. He was 'sick and tired of even the mention of Berezovsky's name', he wrote. 'But I always tried to keep him on my team . . . We are at times compelled to use people for whom we don't have particularly warm feelings. [He] was unquestionably an ally. But he was a difficult ally.'[154]

The only group in Russia capable of cutting the oligarchs down to size were the *siloviki*, the men – and, in Russia, they were all men – in senior posts in the 'power ministries': Defence, the Interior, the FSB, the Border Troops, the GRU, which ran military intelligence, and the SVR, foreign intelligence. Kiriyenko had been Yeltsin's last purely civilian Prime Minister. Primakov had headed the SVR; Stepashin, as well as being Interior Minister, had headed the FSB. Putin's elevation to become first deputy to Yumashev and then FSB chief in 1998 had been one of a number of changes designed, in the words of Yeltsin's spokesman, Sergei Yastrzhembsky, to make the Presidential Administration more 'muscular'. Patrushev, at the Control Directorate, was also from the FSB, as were two other senior officials newly appointed to high-ranking posts.[155]

Yeltsin framed the recourse to the *siloviki* not as an attempt to curb the oligarchs but as a response to a changing mood in society. In fact, the two were linked. 'For some time,' Yeltsin wrote, 'I had been sensing the need for a new quality in the state, for a steel backbone that would strengthen the whole government. We needed a person who was intellectual, democratic, [but also] firm in the military manner.'[156]

Putin, Yeltsin thought, answered that description. So, to a certain extent, did Stepashin.[157]

As FSB Director, Putin was more in the public eye than in any of his previous Moscow posts. To deal with that, he tried to assemble a small coterie of trusted journalists to whom he would give coveted interviews, much as he had done when he was deputy Mayor in St Petersburg. His efforts did not always produce the results he hoped for. Yelena Tregubova, a tousle-haired blonde in her twenties from *Izvestia*, with a sharp mind and a gift for satire, later wrote a hilarious account of Putin's attempt to charm her at a flirtatious tête-à-tête dinner in an empty sushi restaurant, from which other clients had been banished. He told her, in terms strikingly similar to those he had used five years earlier to Natalya Nikiforova, when he had mused about quitting the

Mayor's Office in St Petersburg, that he would not remain FSB chief for ever. It was 'an interesting and honourable page in my life which will one day be turned', he said. Tregubova took that as a sign that he had no higher ambitions, which was no doubt the message he wished to convey.[158]

It was not only that Putin was more at ease working behind the scenes. It also gave him more freedom. The French counter-intelligence agency, the DST, was shocked to discover, some considerable time afterwards, that in 1999, Putin, while FSB chief, had visited southern France incognito for a family holiday. The French security services had been unaware of it. On another occasion, he telephoned the Finnish Ambassador, Markus Lyra, to ask for visas so that the family could go skiing there. Instead of sending an aide to collect them, as anyone else in his position would have done, he turned up in person, arriving at the Embassy, apparently alone, in a jeep which he drove himself. Lyra noticed that as he left, an escort car pulled out discreetly behind him. Nonetheless, it was such unconventional behaviour that a former CIA officer who had served in Moscow, when told of the incident, rolled his eyes and burst out in disbelieving laughter. Yet what seemed inconceivable to an experienced US intelligence agent was exactly what Putin had done.[159]

Stepashin was a much more orthodox figure. Apart from four years with the FSB and its predecessors in the early 1990s, he had spent almost his entire career in the Interior Ministry, doing what Putin considered, rather disdainfully, to be police work. The FSB, Putin argued, had kept 'a certain purity' because it did not have to deal with criminals all the time.[160]

Where Stepashin was a conciliator, a product of the bureaucratic machine, Putin was willing to strike out on his own and act outside the box. As the summer of 1999 wore on, it was left to Yeltsin to determine not only which of the two would make the better successor but, equally important at a time when his own popularity was in the single digits, who would stand a better chance of being elected.

While serving as FSB chief, Putin was concurrently Secretary of the Security Council, a post he had taken over from Bordyuzha when the latter had been dismissed in March. In that capacity, Putin had to deal with foreign policy no longer as an intermediary or as an interested observer but as a decision-maker. For the Yeltsin administration, the key issues remained what they had been in Soviet times: relations with the United States and the role of NATO.

When Putin had arrived in Moscow in the autumn of 1996, it was already clear that NATO was determined to take in new members from Eastern and Central Europe, but as yet there had been no public announcement. The following March, Yeltsin met President Clinton in Helsinki and warned again that enlargement risked leading to renewed East–West confrontation. The Americans responded by offering to make Russia a full member of the Group of Seven, which would then become the G8. Other cosmetic gestures followed and in May 1997, Yeltsin travelled to Paris to sign what was known as 'The Founding Act on Mutual Relations, Cooperation and Security between NATO and the Russian Federation', setting up a formal structure for consultations. But it was acquiescence in the face of *force majeure*, and when, in July, NATO officially extended membership invitations to the Czech Republic, Hungary and Poland, Russian opposition was undimmed.

Putin at that time echoed the official Russian position that NATO posed 'no direct strategic threat to Russia'. But he added that the government should seize the opportunity to modernise the armed forces, focusing in particular on research and development.[161] The implication was that he did not think NATO would necessarily remain non-threatening for ever.

In March 1999, when he took charge of the Security Council, the situation evolved further. That month, the three former Warsaw Pact states became NATO members, bringing the American-led alliance to the border, if not of the Russian mainland, at least of the enclave of Kaliningrad. At the same time, the war in Yugoslavia, that had seemed on the way to resolution with the signing of the Dayton accords which ended the conflict in Bosnia, suddenly entered a more dangerous phase. Kosovo, a semi-autonomous region of southern Serbia, bordering Albania and with a majority Albanian population, became the new flashpoint.

Armed clashes had broken out the previous year between the Serbian army and Kosovar insurgents demanding independence. Both sides committed atrocities but the Serbs engaged in systematic rape and pillage. Western sympathies were with the Kosovars, of whom a quarter of a million, nearly a sixth of the population, had fled their homes to escape the depredations of the Serbian soldiery. Peace talks at Rambouillet, outside Paris, broke down on March 18 when the Russians and Yugoslavs rejected a proposal to send in a NATO peacekeeping contingent. Six days later, without UN authorisation, NATO forces began airstrikes against Serbian army positions, including targets in Belgrade and other Yugoslav cities, to try to force the Serbian troops to withdraw.

Up till then, Yeltsin had offered cautious support to the Serbian leader, Slobodan Milošević, but had avoided doing anything which might cause Russia to be dragged into the conflict. The United States had been equally wary. The bombing raids changed that. To Russians, the Serbs were fellow Slavs who, all through history, had been their allies. Moscow was outraged at what was seen as Western aggression, all the more humiliating because it was powerless to intervene.

Two and a half months later, Yeltsin succeeded in brokering a compromise. The airstrikes would be suspended; Serbian forces would withdraw; and a 30,000-man peacekeeping force of NATO and Russian troops would be deployed to Kosovo under UN auspices. But the most dangerous moment was still to come. The Russian General Staff was incensed that the Americans seemed to be taking Moscow's cooperation for granted. Instead of waiting to start moving in simultaneously with NATO forces on the morning of June 12, as had been agreed, they had despatched a column of 30 armoured vehicles the previous evening to secure the country's one airport, outside the capital, Priština. When the NATO contingent arrived, it found the airport already in Russian hands.

Putin would later claim that, in his role as Secretary of the Security Council, he had authorised the Russian operation. The Chief of the General Staff, Anatoly Kvashnin, had proposed it, he said, and 'I told him: "If you consider it appropriate, do it."'[162]

His account is plausible.[163] General Mike Jackson, the British Commander of the NATO force, wrote afterwards: '[It] was a reminder that the Russians were still players on the world stage, that they still needed to be treated with respect.'[164] Those were precisely Putin's feelings. It was the kind of gesture that both he and Yeltsin favoured – an unpredictable move which would take the adversary by surprise – but hedged with a certain caution. Putin had made clear to Kvashnin that it was up to him to take the final decision.

Gleb Pavlovsky, who worked with Putin for 12 years, saw that as one of the hallmarks of his style of governance. As a general rule, Pavlovsky said, 'he doesn't like to answer in a definite way . . . He can give an emotional impression; he can show the direction. But not be definite. That way, his own responsibility is not engaged. It's your fault for understanding it like that.'[165]

To the Americans, Putin presented things rather differently. Strobe Talbott, the Deputy Secretary of State, had flown to Moscow on June 11 for talks on coordinating the peacekeeping operation. It was the first time he had met Putin. Talbott was struck by 'his ability to convey self-control and confidence in a low-key, soft-spoken manner. He . . . radiated executive competence, the ability to get things done.' There were no histrionics or bombast, but rather 'a menacing, or at least, a commanding, undertone; softness with a hard edge'.[166] On that occasion, Putin gently led his visitor up the garden path. When Talbott expressed concern about threats by General Leonid Ivashov, the hawkish Defence Ministry representative at the Kosovo talks, to send in Russian troops unilaterally if NATO did not agree to the terms of Russian participation, Putin, he wrote afterwards, 'adopted the bedside manner of an experienced physician with a hypochondriac for a patient'. It was probably just an emotional outburst, he assured Talbott. Nothing on the Russian side had changed and a statement to that effect would be issued shortly. Anyway, Putin asked, 'who is this Ivashov?' – as though the General, whose face had been on Russian television almost daily for the previous six weeks, was a complete nonentity.

The statement was never issued. Even as Talbott and Putin were meeting, orders had already been given for Russian troops to enter Kosovo. The critical point came the following day, when the American Supreme Commander in Europe, General Wesley Clark, ordered the runways at Priština blocked to prevent the Russians resupplying their soldiers, raising the prospect of a direct clash between Russian and NATO forces. 'Sir, I'm not going to start World War III for you,' Jackson famously replied.[167] Clark backed off and a compromise was eventually found: the Russians would play a supporting role in Kosovo, much as they had in Bosnia under the Dayton accords. When Putin next saw Talbott, he explained glibly that there were hawks and doves in Russia, as in the United States, and that the hawks had been behind the pre-emptive sprint to Priština. But there had been no loss of life and at least no one could now call Yeltsin a NATO puppet.[168] It was a deft performance, Talbott thought.

Clinton said afterwards that he had never believed that Kosovo would trigger a full-scale nuclear showdown because, unlike Khrushchev during the Cuban missile crisis in 1962, Yeltsin had not been testing American resolve. Nonetheless, for 24 hours, the Cuban crisis had been on everyone's minds.[169] Although the circumstances this time were very different, there was a similar sense that a line had been crossed. Clinton had felt it during a telephone call to Yeltsin the day the airstrikes began. 'Something pretty basic is broken, and it will take a lot of fixing,' he told Talbott afterwards.[170]

It would be wrong to focus on NATO enlargement and the Kosovo affair as the origin of all America's subsequent problems with Russia. But the combination was devastating.

As Moscow saw it, less than three weeks after NATO had admitted its first Eastern European members, it had begun bombarding Serbia, a traditional Russian ally. It was the first sustained combat operation the alliance had conducted since its founding, 50 years before, and it had been undertaken without UN authorisation and in disregard of Yeltsin's entreaties to find a diplomatic solution. Without the bombing raids, Milošević would no doubt have bludgeoned the Kosovars into submission. But under international law, Kosovo was part of Serbia. To Russia, NATO's intervention was a crude attempt to modify a post-war European border by armed force.

At a time when Russia itself was facing a separatist rebellion in the Caucasus, Yeltsin's government felt particularly vulnerable. The Foreign Minister, Igor Ivanov, told his American counterpart, Madeleine Albright: 'Madeleine, don't you understand, we have many Kosovos in Russia.'[171] Nor was Russia alone in having reservations. Greece and Spain faced secessionist pressures in Macedonia, the Basque country and Catalonia. For them, too, Kosovo created a disturbing precedent.

Yet the real problem, as Talbott wrote, was that, 'from the Russian standpoint . . . the US was acting as though it had the right to impose its view on the world'.[172] Many Russians thought that the US had been acting that way since the end of the Second World War. Kosovo brought the point home.

★

Putin and the new Prime Minister, Sergei Stepashin, were close. When, early in 1999, Primakov had wanted Putin fired, Stepashin had sprung to his defence.[173] It was all the more awkward, therefore, when Putin learnt that Yeltsin might have appointed his friend merely as a stand-in and that he himself, while enjoined to the strictest secrecy, was a candidate to take his place. Gleb Pavlovsky remembered going with Voloshin for shashlik at Putin's dacha, one weekend in May, soon after Stepashin's appointment, when it was clear from the discussion that Voloshin and Putin both knew that the new Prime Minister's days might be numbered and that, if so, Putin would be his successor.[174]

The secret was well kept. Stepashin believed that his main rival was the Railways Minister, Nikolai Aksyonenko, whom Yeltsin had considered as a possible candidate when Kiriyenko was dismissed.[175] Putin's name was not mentioned publicly until the beginning of August, when a report appeared in *Kommersant*, speculating about Stepashin's possible replacement.[176] American specialists on Russian affairs were even more in the dark.[177]

Yet by the first half of July, if not earlier, Yeltsin had made up his mind.[178]

Stepashin had proved himself competent and workmanlike, but the President had decided that he was not the right man to lead the fight against Primakov and Luzhkov in the Duma elections in December.[179] Berezovsky picked up echoes of this and, ever anxious to ingratiate himself with the politically powerful, immediately hurried off to see Putin, who was on holiday with his family, hoping to be the first to tell him the good news.[180]

Two weeks later Yeltsin himself told the Tatarstan President, Mintimer Shaimiev, in confidence: 'Between ourselves, in a while I shall dismiss the government of Stepashin and appoint Putin as Prime Minister. After that he will become President.' As Shaimiev sat, looking stunned, Yeltsin said, 'That's what I wanted to tell you, Mintimer Sharipovich,' and then stood up, shook hands and left. Voloshin, who had been present, remembered that Shaimiev had come up to him afterwards, visibly shaken, and said: 'But nobody knows him! It can't be. I have very good relations with Putin, but that simply cannot be!'[181]

Yeltsin had still not decided at that point exactly when to announce Putin's nomination. But events forced his hand. The situation in Chechnya had been steadily deteriorating. The Chechen President,

Aslan Maskhadov, had lost control of the local warlords, the 'field commanders', as they were known, who demanded the installation of an Islamic Republic under sharia law. Order had broken down completely. The only gainful activities were the embezzlement of government funds, kidnapping for ransom and dealing in narcotics.

In March 1999, Stepashin's representative in Chechnya, General Gennady Shpigun, had been seized by insurgents at Grozny airport. When the government refused to pay 15 million US dollars for his release, he was killed. Two weeks after his abduction, the market at Vladikavkaz, in neighbouring North Ossetia, was blown up by Chechen terrorists, leaving dozens dead.

That spring, contingency plans were drawn up for the Russian army to occupy the northern third of Chechnya, as far as the Terek River, 15 miles north of the Chechen capital, Grozny. Yeltsin hesitated. The experience of the First Chechen War was not one he wished to repeat. But at the end of July, he found himself with little choice. Two villages just over the border in neighbouring Dagestan, which had embraced the radical Wahhabi strain of Islam, announced the establishment of a shura, or consultative assembly, independent of the local authorities. When Interior Ministry troops were sent in to restore order, the villagers fought back. 1,400 armed militants, led by Shamil Basayev, the most feared of the Chechen field commanders, gathered at the border, preparing to come to their aid. Basayev may have been tricked into entering Dagestan in order to justify what followed. The Russian General Staff was itching for revenge after its humiliation in the first Chechen War. But whether contrived or not, the resumption of hostilities meant that Yeltsin could no longer delay.

On Thursday, August 5, the President summoned Putin from St Petersburg, where his father, who had been ill with cancer, had died three days earlier.[182] In Yeltsin's recollection, their conversation went as follows:

> 'I've made a decision . . . I would like to offer you the post of Prime Minister,' I told Putin . . .
> 'I will work wherever you assign me,' [he] replied with military terseness.
> 'And in the very highest post?'

Putin hesitated. I sensed that for the first time, he truly realized what the conversation was about.

'I had not thought about that. I don't know if I am prepared for that,' said Putin.

'Think about it. I have faith in you,' I said.

Yeltsin then received Stepashin for what turned out to be an excruciating discussion. Everyone else seemed to know what was afoot, but to the Prime Minister, the news of his impending dismissal came as a bolt from the blue. He flushed and stammered, Yeltsin remembered, and asked to speak to him in private. Then he launched into an anguished self-justification which made Yeltsin, already unhappy at having to fire him, feel even worse. Finally the President lost patience and told him to go, saying that he would 'think about it'. As Stepashin went out, Yeltsin heard him say to Voloshin: 'Have you gone mad?'[183]

The following day Chubais, Yumashev, Voloshin and Yeltsin's daughter, Tatyana, met for four hours for what Yumashev described as 'a heated, difficult conversation'.[184] Chubais argued that, while Putin might be a good candidate, the Duma would refuse to confirm him, triggering early elections, which would be a disaster as Yeltsin's opponents would sweep the board. Yumashev held the contrary view. As far as the deputies were concerned, he said, Putin was a nobody. Most of them would welcome his appointment, believing that the pro-government faction in the Duma would then lack an effective leader for the parliamentary elections that winter.

Voloshin summed up the discussion for Yeltsin afterwards, adding that, in his view, it was worth taking the risk. The President agreed.

Chubais was not done, however. On Sunday, he called a meeting of the leading oligarchs. They agreed to make a joint appeal to Yeltsin to keep Stepashin in his post and deputed Aven to see Putin and urge him to refuse if Yeltsin tried to appoint him. Aven drove to Putin's dacha, where they had arranged to meet at 5 p.m. 'He was late, as usual,' Aven recalled, '[and when] he got out of the car, he called out as he was walking towards me: "I've already agreed!"'

Next morning, Yeltsin received Putin, Voloshin and Stepashin at his home at Gorki-9.[185] The Prime Minister was agitated. He shook hands with the President, but not with any of the others, and when Yeltsin asked him to countersign the decree appointing Putin first deputy Prime Minister, a necessary formality for the transfer of powers, he became flustered and objected. Aksyonenko, the other first deputy, whom Yeltsin had asked to be present so that he could sign in Stepashin's place if the Prime Minister refused, started to remonstrate with him. Putin stopped him. 'It's hard enough for Stepashin,' he said. 'Let's not make it worse.' Stepashin signed. Shortly afterwards, announcing his departure on television, he described Putin as 'a decent and worthy man', but added, unable to hide his bitterness: 'I wish him good luck, really good luck, because he has everything else.'[186]

From the start, Putin struck a different tone from his predecessors. Yeltsin had given him a mandate to be tough and it seemed to fit him like a glove. In his first television interview, a few hours after his appointment, he was asked what he would do if strikers decided to 'go out and sit on the railway tracks', as the miners had done during the summer. 'If they sit?', he asked, and then answered his own question: 'They'll sit in the slammer. Anyone who destabilises the situation will be put away.'[187] That was not how government ministers usually talked. Asked how he felt, he replied: 'combative'.[188]

Putin ordered airstrikes against the bases of the militants in Chechnya and pay rises for troops fighting in the Caucasus.[189] It was announced that the Chief of the General Staff, General Kvashnin, would in future report to him, not to Yeltsin.[190] So would Nikolai Patrushev, who had succeeded him at the FSB.

'We are dealing with international terrorist gangs,' Putin warned. 'The abscess will remain, [until] our relations with Chechnya are settled.'

The following day, August 16, he was confirmed as Prime Minister by the Duma by a narrow but sufficient margin, as Yumashev had predicted. Two weeks later, it was announced that the first phase of the campaign in Dagestan had been completed. Basayev's forces had been driven out.[191] The fighting had caused massive destruction of civilian life and property. Nonetheless, it was hailed as a victory. 'Putin has won his first battle,' wrote the newspaper, *Kommersant*. 'His debut was successful.'[192]

It turned out to be just the prologue.

Within days of Basayev's withdrawal, Russian special forces, backed by airstrikes, attacked three villages in the mountains south of Buinaksk, in central Dagestan, which, two years earlier, had proclaimed themselves an Islamic djamaat, or self-governing community. The whole area had been heavily fortified and the Djamaat's leaders had warned that, if the Russian army intervened, there would be reprisals. These were not long in coming. On September 4, a block of flats in Buinaksk housing border guards and their families was blown up, killing 58 people and injuring a hundred others. It was the first of the so-called apartment bombings which, in the next two weeks, would claim more than 300 lives. Putin had told the troops during a visit to Dagestan a few days earlier: 'We have no right to allow ourselves to be weak.'[193] After the Buinaksk explosion, he ordered the three villages razed.

Five days later, a second explosion occurred, killing 106 people in Moscow. At first it was thought to have been caused by a gas leak. But on the morning of September 10, it was officially confirmed that it was a terrorist attack.[194] Putin was due to leave that day for a summit meeting of APEC, the Asia–Pacific Economic Cooperation forum, in Auckland, New Zealand, almost 24 hours' flying time from Moscow. With Yeltsin's agreement, he decided that the visit should go ahead. The day after he arrived, he told President Clinton that the apartment bombings were linked to the situation in Dagestan and that he had 'every reason to believe' that the perpetrators were from the movement led by Osama bin Laden which had also been attacking US targets.[195] Clinton let the reference to al-Qaeda pass but assured him that 'so long as you use appropriate means to fight terrorists and separatists, the United States will stand by you.'[196] As would become clear over the next year, when allegations flew back and forth about the excesses of the Russian military, the word 'appropriate' was an important qualification.

Yeltsin had originally planned to attend the Auckland summit himself, but a few days earlier had called Clinton to tell him that Putin would go instead, adding, almost as an afterthought, that he would be 'the next Russian President in the year 2000'.[197]

The officials listening in at the White House were 'blindsided', one of them said later.[198] When Yeltsin had announced Putin's appointment, he had described him as 'a person who is able . . . to consolidate society and . . . ensure the continuation of reforms in Russia'.[199] But he had not said directly that Putin was the heir apparent. Many in Washington had assumed that he would be just another in the seemingly endless series of prime ministers whom Yeltsin tried out for a few months and then discarded. It gave his meeting with Clinton in New Zealand an entirely different significance.

The two men spent more than an hour together. The transcript shows them both probing, trying to get the measure of each other without giving much away.[200]

Putin began by referring to Clinton's early association with Senator Fulbright, a Democrat from his home state of Arkansas, who in the 1960s had championed détente with the Soviet Union. It was a characteristic flourish, intended to show his interlocutor that he was exhaustively briefed. He had done something similar when he first met Strobe Talbott, mentioning in passing the Russian constructivist poets Talbott had studied at Oxford. But this time it fell flat. Clinton had worked only briefly for Fulbright, as an intern one summer.[201] Moreover, it was through Fulbright that he had met Jim McDougal, with whom he had later become embroiled in a failed real-estate venture, the so-called Whitewater affair, which had poisoned his first term. It was not a happy memory.

Putin's reference to Clinton's visit to St Petersburg in 1996 was equally ill-advised. Clinton had hated that visit, when, as he told Talbott, he had felt that the security measures which Putin had organised had 'kept [him] in a goddamn cocoon'.[202]

Nonetheless, the US President came away feeling that the new Russian Prime Minister was 'very smart and thoughtful' and had 'enormous potential'.[203] He appeared flexible on Strategic Arms Reduction, genuinely concerned about nuclear proliferation and the risk of nuclear terrorism, and willing to discuss export limits to Iran so long as there was a level playing field for Russian companies dealing with Tehran. However, it was when the conversation turned to election strategy, a subject close to Clinton's heart, that the President got the clearest sense of where his interlocutor was coming from. Some of Yeltsin's actions domestically, Putin told Clinton, might seem hard to understand, but they made sense in a Russian context. Americans needed to remember that 'Russia does not have an established political system. People don't read [party] programmes. They look at the faces of the leaders, regardless of party affiliation . . . Most of the population thinks like that. They are not very sophisticated. That's the reality we have to deal with.'[204]

Elections were much on Putin's mind because he would face two in quick succession in the coming months: first, the Duma elections in December and then the presidential election which was to take place the following summer. He had never liked elections – an aversion aggravated by his experience with Sobchak in St Petersburg – and did not try to hide it. Yeltsin had reassured him: 'You won't have to run the campaign. The main thing is your will, your confidence, your actions. Everything will depend on that.'[205]

So it turned out. For the Duma elections, Gleb Pavlovsky worked on strategy – a subject in which, he said, Putin showed no interest whatever. They had had a meeting with Voloshin at the end of August, at which Pavlovsky had given a brief explanation of the concept for the campaign. 'I finished my presentation,' he remembered, 'and Putin was silent. He said nothing. So Voloshin asked him: "What's the matter? Are you against it?" And Putin said, "I'm not against it." That was all he said. And that's how we started the campaign.'[206] Boris Berezovsky created from scratch a new party, Yedinstvo, 'Unity', whose emblem was a bear, and persuaded a number of governors and leading oligarchs to give it their support, arguing that, if elected, Primakov would strip them of their powers and confiscate their wealth.[207] It was not a difficult case to make. Primakov, when Prime Minister, had threatened to 'empty the prisons to make room for those who commit economic crimes'.[208]

Meanwhile Putin cultivated the image of a tough, determined, young leader, valiantly defending the Russian people against cowardly terrorist attacks. After another explosion in Moscow on September 13, which killed 119 people, he denounced those responsible as 'rabid beasts'.[209] Chechnya had become 'an enormous terrorist camp', he warned, where banditry was the normal way of life.[210]

But behind the tough rhetoric, Pavlovsky had the impression that Putin was still trying to decide how to respond:[211]

For the first few days after the apartment bombings, there was a mood of utter prostration. No one knew what to do . . . Then Putin said to us. 'You do as you like. I am going to fight. If I lose, I lose. But I am going to make war . . .' I remember the day when he took that position[212] – he simply felt that this was his moment and this was what he had to do . . . We had hoped that he would distance himself from all that. Because, without exception, all the politicians who have taken on Chechen wars have bitten the dust. It's a cemetery, a political graveyard. No one comes out of a Chechen war looking good.

In electoral terms, Pavlovsky was convinced that it was a terrible idea. Putin was undeterred. He started systematically preparing public opinion for a protracted conflict. The Khasavyurt agreement, which Yeltsin had signed to end the first Chechen war, had been a mistake, he said. 'We've looked on helplessly for too long. We should not whimper and whine . . . We must stamp out the vermin. If we do not do it today, it will be worse tomorrow.'

Those responsible for policy in the past, he went on, had been cowards.[213] After Khasavyurt, the Chechens had created a criminal economy in their republic. 'What did Russia do? Nothing . . . That was sheer defeatism . . . If you begin to retreat, it leads to more aggression and the number of victims goes up and up.'[214]

This was fighting talk. No Prime Minister before had criticised Yeltsin so bluntly. None had spelt out so defiantly the need to resist. But Putin felt it necessary to distance himself from the President and make clear that he was his own man, not least because Yeltsin's ratings were close to zero.

By the last week in September, some 50,000 Russian troops were massed along the Chechen border.[215] There were daily air-raids on militant bases, ammunition dumps, fuel supplies and communications lines. After the airport at Grozny was bombed, Putin was asked by a reporter what areas were being targeted. 'Wherever the bandits are,' he replied. 'If they are at an airport, we'll hit them at the airport.'[216] Next day, asked the same question again, he came out with a one-liner which would stay with him for the rest of his career: 'If we catch them in the shithouse, we'll wipe them out in the shithouse.'[217]

Western Russia experts argued for months whether the outburst had been planned by Putin's spin doctors to strike public opinion or whether it had come naturally. His colleagues knew better. It was the language of the streets, which would erupt spontaneously when Putin felt provoked.

Pavlovsky was struck by the dissonance. He had noted, like the journalists who had known Putin earlier in St Petersburg, his 'very distinctive style, a very unusual, literary way of speaking', totally unlike Yeltsin or any of the Soviet leaders. Yet he could also be crude and vulgar. That autumn, when Pavlovsky grew concerned at the numbers of casualties among the civilian population in Chechnya and urged Putin to rein in the generals, he shot back: 'If I send them to war, I can't order them to chew snot!'[218]

Putin tried to reassure Russians that there would be no repetition of what he called the 'ill-fated Chechen campaign' of the mid 1990s.[219] Any operations would be carried out in 'a very measured and careful way'.[220] There would be 'no frontal assaults. We will patiently and methodically destroy them from the air.'[221] As late as September 28, he insisted that 'we are not talking about a ground operation'.[222]

Two days later, Russian ground forces crossed the border.

By October 5, they had occupied the plains north of the Terek River and had started creating what was termed 'a security zone around the Chechen Republic' to prevent terrorist incursions into the rest of Russia.[223] The plan at that point was to pound the insurgents' positions with air and artillery strikes and delay a general offensive until the winter. But General Kvashnin argued that the troops would become demoralised by prolonged inaction and it would be better to press on before the resistance had time to organise. Putin agreed. On October 15, the offensive resumed.[224]

Putin then promised 'no tank attacks or raids on towns' and 'no extreme measures like carpet bombing', in order to minimise civilian casualties.[225] Soon afterwards, tank attacks and carpet bombing began.

The Russian army was a blunt instrument. Much of the officer corps was primitive and corrupt. The rank and file were brutalised. The generals did not, in Putin's words, 'chew snot'. They smashed everything in their path. Civilian casualties were not their problem. The first of many barbaric attacks to make headlines in the West was a missile strike on Grozny on October 21, in which at least 140 people, including many women and children, died when the city's market, a mosque and a maternity hospital were hit. Putin, who had just arrived in Helsinki for an EU–Russia summit, denied that Russian forces were responsible and surmised that it might have been the result of 'a fire-fight between rival bandit groups'.[226] That was a bare-faced lie. The missile strikes were part of a systematic campaign to terrorise the civilian population and show that resistance was useless. Nearly 180,000 refugees had already fled to neighbouring republics. Putin's assurances that 'we are not putting an equals sign between the bandits and the Chechen people' convinced no one.[227]

The Russian military were incapable of waging a sophisticated counter-insurgency campaign. They understood only violence. But they were the only army Putin had. On the Chechen side, Maskhadov's government was no better. Its writ did not run outside Grozny. Elsewhere, local warlords held sway. Chechnya was a failed state, not much different from Somalia except that it was part of Russia.

Putin was well aware that in the end there would have to be a political solution, but for that to happen he had to have a partner to negotiate with. In the winter of 1999, there was none. The alternatives were either to beat the insurgents to a bloody pulp, regardless of the civilian death toll, or to allow the territory to secede and become a hotbed of Islamic fundamentalism, a precursor to the Caliphate which would be proclaimed by ISIS, the so-called Islamic State, in Syria and Iraq, a dozen years later. To Putin, the brutality of the war was the price to be paid to prevent still worse tragedies, and those who refused to see that were hypocrites.

The Grozny attacks drew condemnation from many Western leaders. The new German Chancellor, Gerhard Schröder, spoke of a massacre. Jacques Chirac said Europe was 'deeply shocked by Russian behaviour'. Clinton was more cautious, speaking only of the need to minimise civilian casualties. But when he met Putin in Oslo, where they were both attending a conference on the Middle East, at the beginning of November, he urged him to start negotiations:

CLINTON: It's important to protect your sovereignty and territorial integrity and to stand against terrorism. But if the price is to incur major civilian casualties, that's too high a price to pay . . . You need to combine a political with a military strategy . . .

PUTIN: I think you will agree with me that it is not in the United States' interest to have an extremist state between the Black Sea and the Caspian . . . The question is how we crush this base of terrorism but take minimal losses. What will be done will be done . . . How can we negotiate with terrorists? . . .

SECRETARY OF STATE MADELEINE ALBRIGHT: We would be very upset as well if we had experienced terrorist bombings in our country . . . But you need . . . to get a political dialogue going.

PUTIN: I agree that we need to find a partner, but I don't know how we are
    going to do this . . . Can we say that we have commonality in strategy?
CLINTON: You put me in a difficult position. What if there is another attack
    where you shell civilians? How can I say I agree with that?[228]

John Beyrle, who was there from the State Department, remembered
that, throughout the meeting, Putin pushed back hard.[229] It was very
different from their first, rather tentative encounter in Auckland. On
other contentious issues – the presence of Russian troops in Georgia
and Transnistria, and the revised treaty on Conventional Armed Forces
in Europe which was to be signed in Istanbul later that month – Putin
did not give an inch.

That was partly because he found Clinton's arguments on Chechnya
unconvincing and partly because, as the US President acknowledged,
the conflict was 'playing well for [Putin] at home'.[230] The newspaper,
Izvestia, wrote that week: 'His tough stance on Chechnya has endeared
him to virtually all Russians . . . The more the West pressures [him],
the more attractive he appears to Russian voters.'[231]

The opinion polls bore that out. In August, fewer than 2 per cent of
those questioned said they would vote for Putin as President. By late
September, after his promise to 'wipe out the bandits in the shithouse',
his support jumped to 8 per cent and then, despite Pavlovsky's misgivings about the wisdom of waging war in Chechnya, to around 15 per
cent in mid October. At the end of that month, Putin was the front-
runner, ahead of both the Communist Party leader, Gennady
Zyuganov, and Primakov, with more than 20 per cent of voting intentions, a figure which increased to 30 per cent in November and over 40
per cent in December.[232]

But if Putin was riding high, Yedinstvo, the party on which the Kremlin was counting for the Duma elections, was not. Given that it had
been founded only at the beginning of October, that was hardly a surprise. Sergei Shoigu, the long-serving Minister for Emergency Situations,
whom Putin had asked to be its leader, was a popular and well-respected
figure from the Siberian republic of Tuva, but he had no political track
record. Some of the provincial governors whom Berezovsky had roped
in to support the new party had dubious reputations – 'deadbeats who
depend on federal subsidies', as the pro-Luzhkov *Moscow Times* put

it[233] – and Berezovsky himself was scarcely an asset in terms of public opinion. Ordinary Russians loathed him, as they did the other oligarchs. Yumashev had tried to persuade him to keep a low profile during the campaign, but with little success.[234] Even Putin, who tried to conciliate everyone, was wary of Berezovsky's endorsement. Asked about his relations with the oligarch, he quoted the Latin tag: '*Timeo Danaos et dona ferentes.*'*

Six weeks after its foundation, Yedinstvo had 7 per cent of voting intentions, no match for the Communists with 33 per cent, the Luzhkov–Primakov bloc with 22 per cent or even Yabloko with 16 per cent.[235]

The Duma elections were important, not just as a springboard for Putin's expected presidential bid the following June, but because, if elected, he would need a majority in parliament in order to carry out his programme. Otherwise he would be hobbled, just as Yeltsin had been, by a Duma dominated by his opponents.[236] Yumashev and Voloshin thought the answer was for Putin formally to endorse Yedinstvo, so that some of his personal popularity would rub off on the party. German Gref, Putin's colleague from St Petersburg, who now headed a Moscow think tank, the Centre for Strategic Research, disagreed. If Putin openly supported Yedinstvo, he said, not only would the party's ratings not rise but, because it was associated with Berezovsky, Putin's own ratings would fall.[237]

Pavlovsky came up with a compromise.[238] At his urging, in the last week of November, Putin announced that, although as Prime Minister he did not wish to express a political preference, 'as a private citizen I will vote for Yedinstvo'.[239] Its leader, Sergei Shoigu, he added, was one of his closest friends.

It proved to be a winning move. Over the following three weeks, voting intentions for the party tripled.

On election day, December 19, nearly two thirds of registered voters went to the polls. The Communists, as expected, did best, winning 113 seats in the 450-seat assembly. Yedinstvo came a surprise second, with 73 seats, and the Luzhkov-Primakov bloc, third, with 67 seats. The proportion of votes going to party lists, as against single-party constituencies, was even more striking: the Communists scored 24 per cent; Yedinstvo, 23 per cent. With support from the two main

* 'I fear the Greeks, even when they bring gifts' is a line from Virgil's *Aeneid*, in which the priest Laocoön warns the people of Troy of the dangers of the Trojan Horse.

democratic parties, the Union of Right Forces, led by Sergei Kiriyenko, and Yabloko, as well as from independents, Putin would have a working majority.

Primakov complained that the election had been fraudulent, that ORT, Berezovsky's channel, the most widely watched TV station in the country, had poured out 'streams of lies',[240] and that Putin and Shoigu had taken advantage of their government posts to promote Yedinstvo's cause.

It was all true.

Even by the standards of 1990s Russia, it had been a filthy campaign. ORT's star presenter, Sergei Dorenko, had charged that Luzhkov was implicated in the murder of an American businessman; that he and his wife, Yelena Baturina, were mired in corruption and that Primakov, who was awaiting a hip replacement operation, was too old and sick to govern.[241] To make his point, Dorenko had shown gruesome footage from an operating theatre, warning viewers that this was what their new leader would look like if they voted for Primakov's party. But even without the torrent of calumny from ORT and the other state-owned channel, RTR, Yedinstvo, with Putin's backing, had been poised to do well. As he had told Clinton, most Russians voted for a personality, not a programme. Many people, particularly in the provinces, found Putin more attractive than Primakov, a *nomenklatura* apparatchik, or Luzhkov, who was popular in Moscow but not outside the capital.

Five days prior to election day, Yeltsin had summoned Putin to Gorki-9, where he told him that he intended to resign and make him acting President.

Putin was taken aback.[242] 'I'm not ready for that decision,' he said. 'You see, it's a rather difficult destiny . . . Maybe it would be better if you left at the end of your term.' But Yeltsin's mind was made up. Instead of waiting until June 2000, it would be better to resign now, take his opponents by surprise and give Russia a new President for the new millennium. 'You haven't answered,' he pressed Putin. 'I agree,' the Prime Minister replied.[243]

He did not really have a choice. As he put it: 'My fate was allowing me to work at the highest level . . . It would be stupid to say, "No, I'd rather sell sunflower seeds," or "No, I'm going into private law practice . . ." So I decided to do it.'[244] On December 27, with the Duma elections behind them, he and Yeltsin met again, this time in the Kremlin, to iron out the details of what would be Russia's first constitutional transfer of power.

Meanwhile, the war in Chechnya ground on.

At the beginning of December, Russian aircraft had dropped leaflets into what remained of Grozny, warning that anyone who did not leave the city within five days would be 'considered a terrorist and destroyed'. An estimated 40,000 civilians were living in basements and cellars and the army wanted them gone before it launched a final assault.

Under Western pressure, the ultimatum was withdrawn. But Grozny was already in ruins. The insurgents who remained, estimated to number between five and seven thousand, had established a network of interconnecting trenches, minefields, booby-trapped buildings and sniper nests in high-rise apartment blocks. In the countryside beyond, discipline in some Russian units had broken down completely. Interior Ministry troops massacred Chechen villagers. There was widespread rape and looting. On Christmas Day, the General Staff gave the order to start tightening the noose around the blockaded city, heralding the start of weeks of house-to-house fighting in which thousands of civilians died and combatants on both sides suffered heavy losses.

Western criticism, from the US and from Britain, France, Germany and other EU states, was ratcheted up another notch. There was talk of suspending aid unless the fighting stopped. Ominous comparisons were drawn between Putin's invasion of Chechnya and Milošević's attempts to subdue the rebellious Kosovars, which had prompted NATO intervention. Although the Russians angrily denied it, there was an obvious parallel. But it was one thing for the West to go to war against a small Balkan state like Serbia, quite another to risk war with Russia, a nuclear-armed former superpower which, if it were to begin to disintegrate, would pose unimaginable security concerns. In practice, Western governments went no further than verbal condemnation.

Putin was unmoved. 'Russia has the right to defend itself,' he said. 'If we don't complete this operation, everything will start all over again.'[245]

The day after he met Putin in the Kremlin, Yeltsin summoned Voloshin and Yumashev and told them of his decision. At Yumashev's insistence, he also informed his daughter, Tatyana. But he kept it secret from his wife, Naina, until a few hours before he made the announcement, which was broadcast at noon on New Year's Eve. Putin's wife,

Lyudmila, was even more in the dark. She learnt that Volodya had become acting President when a girlfriend who had heard Yeltsin's speech telephoned to congratulate her.[246]

For Yeltsin, it was an emotional farewell. Speaking slowly, a few words at a time, his face like a leather mask, he apologised for all that he had failed to do and said that Russia needed 'new politicians, new faces, new, strong, intelligent and energetic people':

> We, who have been in power for many years, must go . . . Many of our hopes were not realised. What we thought was easy has proved pain-fully difficult. I would like to ask forgiveness from those of you who hoped that we would be able to make a leap in just one go from the grey, stagnant totalitarian past to a bright, prosperous and civilised future. I myself believed in this. But it was not possible . . . In some respects, I was naïve . . . I did everything I could.[247]

As he left the Kremlin for the last time – an immense, monolithic, bear-like figure, in a heavy coat and fur shapka – he turned to Putin, who was standing beside him, looking small and rather awkward, as if daunted by the burden that had fallen on his shoulders, and said quietly: 'Take care of Russia!'[248]

9

The Cap of Monomakh

The first decree which Putin signed as acting President, using the same pen that Yeltsin had used to name him his successor, granted the former President 'immunity [from] criminal or administrative investigation, detention or arrest' for actions while in office; ordered the protection of his archives, his residence and his possessions; and laid out in general terms the benefits he would have in retirement. Voloshin had argued that a decree was necessary to avoid a legal vacuum. Since no Russian leader had stepped down voluntarily before, there was no legislation to cover it.[1]

It was not a good idea.

Although the decree applied only to Yeltsin himself, not his family or aides, his political opponents and a large section of the Russian media immediately speculated that he and Putin had come to an arrangement: in exchange for making Putin acting President, Yeltsin would be protected from prosecution over the Mabetex affair and other supposedly corrupt dealings.

Yeltsin was mortified. He was not a man who made deals of that sort. Nor did he need to. As Russia's 'First President' – his official title after retirement – he continued to enjoy the perquisites he had had when he was in power: the presidential dacha, the bodyguards, the servants, the official limousine, a practically unlimited allowance. He had no need of money from Mabetex or anyone else. Gleb Pavlovsky, his campaign strategist, maintained that the immunity issue was an artificial problem. 'No one would have touched Yeltsin', he said. 'But we Russians like to struggle in a Gothic atmosphere as if it is Armageddon. We need that.'[2] Yeltsin himself wrote later that the move to grant him immunity was 'a rather questionable decision'.[3]

Putin's second decree confirmed Voloshin as head of the Presidential

Administration, one of several appointments intended to emphasise continuity. Putin himself remained Prime Minister as well as acting President. He appointed the liberal Finance Minister, Mikhail Kasyanov, as his first deputy, with a mandate to run the government while he dealt with the war in Chechnya, on the understanding that, if and when he became President, Kasyanov would become Prime Minister and Aleksei Kudrin would take over at the Finance Ministry. Most of the rest of the cabinet, many of whom had served under Stepashin, kept their posts, although Putin's supposed one-time rival, the Railways Minister, Nikolai Aksyonenko, lost his position as a first deputy Prime Minister. Pavel Borodin, tarnished by Mabetex, was also moved aside, departing the General Affairs Office to take up the prestigious but essentially fictive post of State Secretary of the Union of Belarus and Russia, a proposed federal state which existed mainly on paper.

Among those who had been closest to Yeltsin, his daughter, Tatyana, stepped down as a deputy head of the Administration. But Yumashev kept his office in the Kremlin, continuing to serve as an unofficial adviser.

There were new appointments, too, many of them from St Petersburg. Viktor Ivanov, Dmitry Medvedev and Igor Sechin were appointed deputy heads of the Presidential Administration. Ivanov, who had handled security issues at the St Petersburg Mayor's Office, took charge of personnel matters in the Kremlin. Sergei Ivanov – no relation – became Secretary of the Security Council. Medvedev, the young lawyer who had advised the Foreign Relations Committee in St Petersburg, was named head of Putin's Election Committee. Sechin kept his former post as head of Putin's secretariat, while Dmitry Kozak, who had headed the Legal department at City Hall, became head of the Prime Minister's Office.

Yuri Shevchenko, the St Petersburg doctor who had helped arrange Sobchak's flight to Paris, was appointed Health Minister. Leonid Reiman, another old St Petersburg friend, who for a couple of years in the late 1990s had given Lyudmila an honorary but well-paid post as Moscow representative of his telecommunications company, Telecominvest Inc., took over as Communications Minister. After the presidential election, German Gref became Minister for Economic Development.

It was not unusual for Russian leaders to bring with them former colleagues from the provinces. Brezhnev had surrounded himself with

officials who had worked with him in Ukraine, the so-called Dnepro-
petrovsk mafia. On a smaller scale, Gorbachev had a Stavropol clan and
Yeltsin brought with him a number of key aides from Yekaterinburg.

Nonetheless, as Dmitry Kozak noted, Putin put a premium on working with people 'he had been personally acquainted with and known for
a long time'.[4] Colleagues from the St Petersburg Mayor's Office, businessmen he had known there and men he had worked with in the KGB
predominated. Most, though not all, of those he promoted were experienced, competent people. But ability took second place to trust. So did
probity. Several of the senior ministers he appointed were notoriously
corrupt. But that had also been true of members of Yeltsin's governments. Provided their work was satisfactory, Putin did not see that as a
problem. It was in the nature of the system, something that any Russian
leader had to live with and, provided they kept their greed within limits,
it had the advantage of rendering them vulnerable.

In his choice of government ministers and members of the administration, Putin combined continuity and change in carefully measured
doses. Enough of the first to reassure the establishment; enough of the
second to show that the chaos of the 1990s was at an end and that the
new millennium would be characterised, in his words, by 'a stable
political system and a strong state'.[5]

He adopted the same pragmatic, calculating, not to say cynical,
approach to the Duma. Instead of building a partnership with Yabloko
and the Union of Right Forces, which were Yedinstvo's natural allies,
the party reached agreement with the Communists to allow Zyuganov's colleague, Gennady Seleznyov, to remain Speaker of the
Duma, and to divide up between them the chairmanships of the parliamentary committees, shutting out not only the liberals and
democrats but also, more importantly, the Luzhkov-Primakov bloc. It
was a classic Putin manoeuvre: co-opt your adversary. The democrats
were furious but they had nowhere else to go. Afterwards Putin bro-
kered a reconciliation with the Union of Right Forces leader, Sergei
Kiriyenko. It gave him the compliant parliament he needed and marked
the first step in a process which would eventually lead to both the
Communists and Zhirinovsky's nationalists, the two principal alternatives to Yedinstvo, becoming what would be known as the 'systemic
opposition' – an opposition in name only, operating within narrow
limits that the Kremlin laid down.

In his public appearances, Putin continued subtly to distance himself from his predecessor. The US Ambassador, Jim Collins, remembered: 'It was the imagery of "not Yeltsin" . . . On New Year's Eve, you had a President who was ill, unable to do his job, and suddenly you've got this young guy, vigorous, athletic . . . It was that contrast that he was trying to create.'[6]

Putin said things that Russians liked to hear. 'Anyone who insults Russia won't be long for this world,' he told an interviewer.[7]

He did things which struck people's imagination. A few hours after Yeltsin had named him acting President, he flew to Dagestan, accompanied by Nikolai Patrushev and both their wives, to celebrate New Year's Eve with the troops in Chechnya.[8] They boarded helicopters to Gudermes, the interim Chechen capital, 25 miles east of Grozny, but were prevented from landing by thick fog. As midnight struck, they shared a bottle of champagne, flying back to the Dagestan capital, Makhachkala. Motor transport was organised and they set out by road to drive the 100 miles to Gudermes, arriving soon after 5 a.m. Russian television cut out of its New Year's Night programme to go live to the barracks, where Putin was shown presenting awards to a group of soldiers and giving each one a hunting knife. After the ceremony, they drove back and flew to Moscow, where Putin and his wife paid a courtesy call on the Yeltsins at Gorki-9 to wish them a Happy New Year.

Two months later, Putin flew to Grozny, where the airport had by then been secured, not in a presidential aircraft but in the co-pilot's seat of a Sukhoi Su-27 jet fighter. He said afterwards that the pilot had allowed him to take the controls for a few minutes and they had executed a roll, which left him 'close to ecstasy'.[9] However one cares to read that, it was a performance which none of his political opponents could have matched.

While Putin tried to give Russians hope, he was brutally frank about the tasks ahead. Soon after being appointed Prime Minister, he had asked German Gref and his colleagues at the Centre for Strategic Research to prepare a blueprint for the first decades of the twenty-first century. Entitled, 'Russia on the Threshold of the New Millennium', it was published on December 28, three days before Yeltsin's resignation, as a personal statement by Putin about what needed to be done. From a man who had told Bill Clinton that most Russians had no interest in political programmes, it was a revealing document and uncompromisingly bleak.

Putin denounced the 'historic futility of the Bolshevik social experiment', for which Russians had had to pay 'an outrageous price'. Communism, he said, had been 'a blind alley, far away from the mainstream of civilisation', which had doomed Russia to lag behind the advanced countries.

> Russia's GNP is ten times smaller than the US and five times smaller than China ... Labour productivity and real wages are extremely low ... Over 70 per cent of our machinery and equipment is over ten years old ... Only five per cent of Russian enterprises are engaged in innovative production. [This] is the price we have to pay for the economy we inherited from the Soviet Union. But then, what else could we inherit? ... Today we are reaping the bitter fruit, material and intellectual, of the past decades.[10]

The 1990s, he said, had shown the direction that Russia must take, but the country had spent that decade 'groping in the dark'. It would take another 15 years to reach the per capita GNP even of countries like Portugal and Spain, 'not among the world's industrialised leaders', and then only if Russia could achieve an annual growth rate of 8 per cent. Trying to replicate foreign models did not work. Russia had to find its own path, 'combining the principles of a market economy and democracy with Russian realities'. What was needed was not a state ideology but 'an organic unification of universal human values with the traditional values of Russia', first and foremost patriotism and belief in the country's greatness:

> Russia will not become a second edition of, say, the US or Britain, where liberal values have deep historic traditions. Our state and its institutions and structures have always played an exceptionally important role in the life of the country and its people. For Russians a strong state is not an anomaly to be got rid of. Quite the contrary, it is a source of order and the main driving force of any change. [People] look forward to a certain restoration of the guiding and regulating role of the state ... [In Russia], a striving for corporative forms of

activity has always prevailed over individualism. Paternalistic sentiments have deep roots . . . It will take a long time for this habit to
die . . . Russia needs a strong state power . . . To determine the extent
and mechanism of state regulation, we should be guided by the principle: 'The state must be there as much as is necessary, freedom should
be there as much as is required.'

Putin qualified that statement by insisting on the need for 'a full-blooded
civil society to monitor and act as a counterweight to the authorities'
and emphasising that 'all authoritarian forms of government are tran-
sient; only democratic systems are lasting'. Nonetheless, the warning
was clearly spelt out. Russia was part of Europe but that did not make it
part of the West. It had a different understanding of democracy. Freedom would exist only 'as much as is required'. Putin's wife, Lyudmila,
liked to say that in Russia, one had to 'read between the lines and listen
between the words'.[11] In this case, no such subtlety was needed. But who
would determine how much freedom was 'required' was left unsaid.

Putin's core theme was that Russia must regain the global status
that it had had before the Soviet Union collapsed. 'It is too early to
bury Russia as a great power,' he said. But recovering what had been
lost would not be easy:

Russia is in the midst of one of the most difficult periods in its history.
For the first time in the past 200 to 300 years, it is facing a real danger of
sliding to the second, and possibly even third, echelon of world states.
We are running out of time . . . Nobody will do it for us. Everything
depends on us and us alone . . .

Another document, the National Security Concept, which Putin
approved two weeks later, also spoke of the need to 'strengthen [Rus-
sia's] interests as a great power and an influential centre of a multipolar
world'. It went on to denounce 'attempts [at] domination by developed
Western countries . . . under US leadership, designed to bring about
unilateral solutions (primarily by the use of military force) to key issues
in world politics'. The reference was to NATO's actions in
Yugoslavia.

These programmatic texts, aimed at the Russian elite and at foreign
chancelleries, were accompanied by efforts to make the new acting

President better known to the population at large, answering the question which Trudy Rubin of the *Philadelphia Inquirer* had posed that January at the World Economic Forum at Davos: 'Who is Mr. Putin?'

Here, too, the goal was to underline the contrast with his predecessor.

To those around him, Yeltsin behaved as a tsar. He was remote, intimidating and imperious. Boris Nemtsov related how, shortly after he had moved to Moscow, Yeltsin had asked him how he was settling in. Nemtsov mentioned that the Mayor's Office was dragging its feet over issuing his family's residence papers. Without a word, Yeltsin picked up the phone, pushed the button for his direct line to Luzhkov and, addressing him by his name and patronymic, said, 'Yuri Mikhailovich! Petty and unworthy conduct!', and hung up. Seeing Nemtsov's puzzled expression, he said: 'Now he'll spend the next two hours finding out who was with me. Then he'll understand.'[12] Except with those he considered his equals, like Clinton, he would rarely engage in discussion.[13] With his advisers, he would listen in silence to what they said and then announce his decision, which from that moment on was irrevocable and had to be carried out at once. Georgy Khizha, Sobchak's former colleague whom Yeltsin had called to Moscow to become a deputy Prime Minister, heard a newsflash on his car radio one day that he had been fired in a cabinet reshuffle. When he picked up the car phone to call the Kremlin, it had already been disconnected.[14]

Putin was not a tsar in that sense. He could make his subordinates tremble. He kept a certain, almost indefinable distance, which he tried to wear lightly but which those around him took care to respect. But he was not imperious and did not wish to be seen as such. Mikhail Kozhukhov, a TV talk-show host who served briefly as his press secretary, found him to be 'a new type of politician, completely unpretentious, who does not get stroppy or throw his weight around [or] play the big boss'.[15] His assistant in St Petersburg, Marina Yentaltseva, had had the same impression when she first met him eight years earlier. Journalists discovered to their surprise that he not only had a gift for repartee but a sense of humour. When an interviewer mentioned that the imminently expected six billionth inhabitant of the planet might be a Russian baby and asked Putin whether he was awaiting this happy event, he deadpanned: 'You mean, me personally?'[16]

Gleb Pavlovsky had wanted him to do a book of interviews about his life in time for the Duma election in December. It was not that he was the complete unknown that most Western writers pretended. Months before he had become Prime Minister, *Nezavisimaya gazeta* had rated him among the 20 most influential figures in Russia. But the general public, which would have to be persuaded to vote for him, knew little about his personality or his past.

Putin had been too busy during the autumn. But the following spring he sat down for six four-hour interviews with three journalists from *Kommersant*, which resulted in a book entitled *Ot pervogo litsa*, 'First Person', a play on words signifying that it was both a personal account and by the 'First Person of the State'.

By the time it was published in March, two weeks before the presidential election, it was clear that Putin would win.[17] Pavlovsky's main concern was about turnout. Accordingly, the book was designed to get out the vote, so that Putin would be elected in the first round and there would be no need for a run-off. It included interviews with close friends, former colleagues in the KGB and in St Petersburg, and even Putin's two teenage daughters, of whom he was normally fiercely protective. Because it was brought out in record time, the editing was cursory. Afterwards analysts from the CIA and other Western intelligence agencies painstakingly deconstructed the text to try to tease out the signals they thought Putin wished to convey.[18] The assumption was that every word had been carefully weighed to send appropriate messages to different groups of voters, as would have happened in an American election. That was not the case. Pavlovsky's team had simply been trying to make Putin sound sufficiently interesting to persuade people to make the effort to go to the polling station and vote.

Much as Madison Avenue used to hold that 'all publicity is good publicity', they included whatever they thought most likely to pique readers' curiosity, whether or not it showed Putin in a favourable light. His childhood as a young hooligan; his love of taking risks; his KGB instructor's description of him as 'withdrawn and uncommunicative'; his wife's comment that the first time she saw him, she found him 'very unprepossessing'; and much more in the same vein, were very far from the hagiographic portraits of politicians to which Russians were accustomed. They conveyed the image of a tough, determined young political outsider from a background which most readers could relate to, who thought and talked in ways which ordinary people could understand.

Parts of *First Person,* dealing with Putin's time in the KGB and the manner in which he started working for Sobchak, were pure invention. But those episodes aside, it was an unvarnished portrait on the principle of 'what you see is what you get'. Nothing published since has been as revealing.

The Chechen capital, Grozny, fell to Russian troops on February 6 after six weeks of urban combat in which the insurgents were slowly driven back, one city block at a time. Both sides tortured prisoners to death, there was indiscriminate killing of civilians and, to the Defence Ministry's embarrassment, some 2,000 Chechen fighters managed to break out of the government encirclement and escape.

Putin announced on television that 90 per cent of the territory was in government hands and warned that there must be no let-up. 'This is not just about Chechnya,' he said. Similar battles with Islamic extremism were being fought in Tajikistan and other Central Asian states. 'Chechnya is merely one fragment of a broader struggle to change the world.' If the jihadists succeeded, it would lead to the Balkanisation of Russia and its eventual disintegration.[19] For the first time, he criticised the West directly for its refusal to understand what was at stake in the Caucasus. 'Not only are we disappointed with the Western position,' he said, 'but we consider that it is in the national interest of the Western countries to support Russia in its struggle with international terrorism.'[20]

Only two weeks earlier, Putin had said that if Western leaders did not understand the situation in Chechnya, it was 'clearly our own fault' for not having explained it well enough.[21] The change of tone reflected his growing confidence, both about the war and about his own position.

Western attitudes were changing, too. As it became increasingly clear that Putin would be elected in March and might lead Russia for years to come, the United States and Britain toned down their criticisms. The Kremlin took note. When the US Secretary of State, Madeleine Albright, visited Moscow at the beginning of February, Putin told the press before the talks began: 'The United States is conducting a policy of pressure against us in Chechnya.' Then, after the reporters had left, he turned to her with a smile and added: 'I said that so your domestic critics will not attack you for being soft.'[22]

They talked for almost three hours, three times longer than planned. She found him, she said afterwards, confident, candid and very well informed – a leader who pushed aside his briefing notes when the meeting began and engaged with her as 'a problem-solving Russian patriot'. The headline next day in the British newspaper, the *Guardian*, read: 'Albright warms to Putin despite war'.[23] Her British counterpart, Robin Cook, was still more enthusiastic, declaring himself 'amazed by his openness and readiness for frank dialogue'. Putting pressure on Russia over Chechnya was 'unproductive', he said. 'It is important that we keep good relations.'[24] His Prime Minister, Tony Blair, would write later: 'I understood the criticism, [but] this was a vicious secessionist movement with Islamic extremism at its core, so I understood the Russian perspective as well.'[25] Hubert Vedrine, the French Foreign Minister, whose country was much more exercised over Chechnya than either Britain or America, also found Putin impressive – 'very intelligent, very precise [and] cool-headed, . . . patriotic, not nationalistic'. He, too, said afterwards that France did not contest Russia's right to pacify Chechnya but was 'shocked by the cruel [and] disproportionate methods' being used.[26]

As Western governments started playing down the horrors being inflicted on the Chechens, media and human rights organisations stepped up to take their place. For Putin and the Russian Defence Ministry, this created a dilemma. The Kremlin had no interest in allowing independent journalists to report freely and expose atrocities by its troops. On the other hand, if it restricted media access, it would play into the hands of those who maintained that the Russian army was massacring the civilian population and wanted the press kept well away in order to hide what it was doing.

The issue burst out into the open with the disappearance of Andrei Babitsky, a young reporter for Radio Liberty, a US government-funded radio station established during the Cold War, which Yeltsin had allowed to broadcast in Russia following the 1991 putsch. The army command hated Babitsky for his exposés of military abuses and accused him of siding with the Chechens. On January 18, he was detained by Russian soldiers as he was trying to leave Grozny. At first the Russian government denied any knowledge of his whereabouts, but after Madeleine Albright had raised the issue with Putin, it was announced that he had been handed over to a Chechen insurgent group, supposedly at his own request, in exchange for five Russian soldiers. When Babitsky was eventually freed, almost a month later, it turned out that the handover had been faked.

His detention in Grozny had been a local initiative. But Putin himself had then taken charge of the case, authorising a convoluted rigmarole designed to show that journalists who criticised the Russian army were actually working for the insurgents and should be treated as such.[27] In an icy exchange in February with the journalists who interviewed him for *First Person*, Putin insisted that Babitsky was a traitor:

> He was working directly for the enemy. He was not a neutral source of information. He was working for the bandits. [They] wouldn't do anything to Babitsky because they thought of him as one of their own . . . [He] was justifying the decapitation of [our] people . . . What authority did he have to stick his nose in there without official accreditation? . . . [I'll tell you] some other time what happens to people who fight on the side of the enemy. What Babitsky did is much more dangerous than firing a machine-gun.[28]

Those arguments would have seemed threadbare even if the handover had been real. The government would then have had to explain why it surrendered a Russian citizen to the enemy in the middle of a war. Once it became clear that the supposed prisoner exchange had been faked, they made even less sense.

But the episode offered a foretaste of the tactics which Putin and his administration would use towards journalists and others whom they considered to have crossed a red line. Criticism, even opposition, was acceptable, but only within limits which the state would define. Putin argued that this was not contrary to the principle of freedom of the press, which, he said, had never been intended to cover 'direct complicity in crimes'.[29] Russian journalists were not reassured.

By mid March, the situation in Chechnya had evolved further. 'Organised resistance has been crushed,' Putin declared. 'Large-scale military operations are coming to an end.'[30] That was spin, geared more to the imminent presidential election than to realities on the ground. The surge of popular enthusiasm that had accompanied the army's initial successes had waned. Resistance in the form of terrorist attacks, hostage-taking and guerrilla actions was continuing. But it was true that, in most of Chechnya, large-scale clashes had ended and, for the first time, Putin started speaking of the possibility of peace talks.

The only Chechen leader in whom Putin had even minimal confidence was the Chief Mufti, Akhmad Kadyrov. He had been born in Kazakhstan, where Stalin had exiled the Chechens during World War II. After restrictions on religious freedom were relaxed under Gorbachev, he had studied at a madrasa in Bukhara and afterwards in Tashkent and Amman, returning to Chechnya in 1991 when its then leader, Dzhokhar Dudayev, declared independence. As well as acting as a spiritual guide, Kadyrov was an influential figure in one of the most powerful *teips*, or clans, the Benoy. As Chief Mufti, he had proclaimed a jihad against Russia and fought in the first Chechen War alongside Shamil Basayev. But under Dudayev's successor, Maskhadov, he had become increasingly concerned by the inroads of Wahhabism and the internationalisation of the conflict and had spoken out publicly against Basayev's expedition to Dagestan and the insurgency that followed.

After their first meeting, the previous November, Putin had described Kadyrov as 'not a very easy partner' but a man who deserved respect.[31] But to commit to any Chechen leader was a gamble and Putin proceeded cautiously. That spring he declared direct presidential rule in Chechnya and appointed Kadyrov head of administration. It was made clear that it was an interim position. There would be no final decision on the territory's future for another two years.

The expectation that Putin would be in office for some considerable time had implications for both Moscow and Washington. While the US administration tried to size up the new occupant of the Kremlin, Putin was pondering how best to develop relations with America, long the only partner that really mattered to Russia.

The task was made more difficult because it was an election year in the United States and nobody could be sure whether Clinton's successor would be a Democrat or a Republican. The ill-feeling generated by Kosovo and NATO's bombing campaign in Yugoslavia had not dissipated. NATO enlargement remained a running sore and the Americans seemed determined to develop a National Missile Defense system which Russia feared would undermine strategic arms control.

For all these reasons, Putin sought a back-channel to Washington which would remain operational whoever won the US election. The obvious choice, given Britain's much vaunted 'special relationship' with the United States, was the British Prime Minister, Tony Blair. The

Kremlin started putting out feelers in January. Richard Dearlove, then the head of MI6, recalled an FSB emissary suggesting that Blair might like to pay an unofficial visit to Russia as Putin's guest before the presidential election. Similar proposals were conveyed to other senior officials, and, against the advice of the Foreign Office, Blair decided that if a formal invitation were made, he would accept.[32] On March 10, the Prime Minister and his wife, Cherie, flew to St Petersburg for a two-day informal visit hosted by Putin and Lyudmila.

Blair's initial impression was favourable: 'Putin wanted Russia to orient towards Europe,' he wrote later. 'He admired America and wanted a strong relationship with it. He wanted to pursue democratic and economic reform . . . We were the same age and, it seemed, shared the same outlook.'[33]

Alastair Campbell, Blair's confidant and press spokesman, who accompanied him, found Putin 'bright and very focused . . . physically very fit, sharp-eyed but [with] a nice smile . . . Definitely not a pushover'. Most of the first round of talks, with officials present, was devoted to Chechnya, where Putin was 'pretty fired up' in defence of the Russian position but conceded that 'at least we [British] were more balanced in our views than France'.[34] As with Madeleine Albright, Putin conducted the whole meeting without briefing notes, which astonished the British delegation. Blair's Chief of Staff, Jonathan Powell, remarked afterwards that 'even leaders as bright as Al Gore used to depend on clutch cards to remind them of key questions'.[35] At a second session, one on one with only interpreters present, Putin opened up further, telling Blair that the Soviet version of socialism had so poisoned the minds of the people that reforms were going to be difficult. Tony Bishop, who had interpreted for British prime ministers in their meetings with Russian leaders going back to Khrushchev, pronounced it 'a very good first encounter'.[36]

There were other signs, too, that Putin's interest in a better relationship with America was genuine and not just presentational. Already in January, he had spoken of 'a certain positive trend in relations between Russia and NATO'.[37] The following month, Lord Robertson, the NATO Secretary General, visited Moscow, signifying a resumption of contacts which had been effectively frozen since the clash over Kosovo. Robertson spoke of opening a new chapter in relations.[38] Putin was more cautious. 'Since the events in Yugoslavia', he said, 'these issues will not be resolved easily in Russia.'[39] A few weeks later, he was asked by a BBC interviewer, David Frost, how he envisaged future relations with NATO:

PUTIN: Russia is part of European culture. I cannot imagine my country in isolation from Europe and from the so-called, as we often say, civilised world. So I find it difficult to imagine NATO as an enemy. It seems to me that . . . even posing the question this way can be damaging . . .

FROST: Is it possible that at some point Russia could join NATO?

PUTIN: Why not? Why not? I would not rule [it] out . . . But [only] if Russia's interests are taken into account and if Russia is treated as a partner with equal rights. I want especially to emphasise this . . . When we speak out against NATO's expansion to the east, . . . we are thinking first and foremost about our country's place in the world . . . If there are attempts to exclude us from the process of decision-making, this naturally causes us concern and irritation.[40]

Putin's response – 'Why not?' – was widely reported. Western governments listened politely, but did not take it too seriously. In practice, full Russian membership was never going to happen. Russian critics pooh-poohed the idea. 'Russia will not now be able to object to NATO's further expansion,' complained *Nezavisimaya gazeta*. 'We have lost our trump card.'[41] The Eastern Europeans were quick to follow. 'If NATO is not Russia's enemy,' said the Latvian Foreign Minister, Indulis Berzins, 'why shouldn't the Baltic countries become members?'[42]

The all-important qualification, that Russia could have normal relations with NATO if, and only if, it were treated as an equal partner, was largely ignored.

So was an earlier segment of the interview, in which Putin talked about the persistence of Cold War attitudes in the West. 'Unfortunately', he said, 'I have the impression that our partners . . . all too often remain prisoners of their previous views and continue to regard Russia as a potential aggressor. That is an absolutely wrong picture of our country. It is untrue, and it prevents the development of normal relations in Europe and in the world as a whole.'[43]

That was not only the case in the West, however. On both sides of the former Iron Curtain, political and military leaders found it difficult to throw off Cold War thinking. It could scarcely have been otherwise.

Attitudes which have become entrenched over decades do not disappear overnight.

The interview was Putin's first extended conversation with a Western journalist and he used it to convey a message. First, that, under his leadership, Russia would insist on equal treatment. Second, that it expected 'full-fledged participation in decision-making',[44] or, as Tony Blair would say later, to have a seat at the top table.[45] Third, that the legacy of the Cold War would not go away on its own: real efforts would be needed on both sides if it were to be surmounted. For the next twenty years or more, these would be the three key principles driving Russian policy towards the West and, above all, towards the former 'main adversary', the United States.

The British Prime Minister's visit to St Petersburg was not only a means for Putin to open a new, indirect communications route to Washington. It was also a way of showing his domestic opponents, two weeks before election day, that the West already accepted him as Russia's future leader.

Putin had played almost no part in the election campaign. He did not need to. As acting President, he was given adulatory wall-to-wall coverage on television every night. Viewers saw him 'awkwardly bending over an Irkutsk orphan in an effort to bestow a kiss on the girl's cheek, . . . shaking hands with babushkas enveloped in woolly scarves and, at an official function, giving that special smile to the Canadian Foreign Minister, who happens to be a woman,' a Russian analyst reported. 'They watched a squabble between two elderly ladies in the street: "If he worked for intelligence, he must be clever," one shouted to the other. "Our intelligence services don't employ fools." '[46] Another study found that Putin had as much airtime as his three main rivals put together.[47] Berezovsky's channel, ORT, which made no pretence of being neutral, savaged his opponents.

His refusal to campaign was also intended to show that he was above that kind of thing. Electioneering was dishonest, he declared. 'It involves looking into the eyes of millions of people and making promises you know are impossible to fulfil. I cannot bring myself to do that.'[48] He would not hold election rallies or take part in television debates, and still less would he broadcast political campaign spots.

'That is advertising,' he told a journalist in disgust. He did not intend to stoop to the same level as 'selling Tampax or Snickers'.[49]

That was disingenuous. It did not prevent him making crowd-pleasing gestures, raising pensions and promising to pay off wage arrears, which were in practice little different from the 'electioneering' he condemned.

It also raised questions about how much Putin really understood about the way a democratic system worked. Ruling Russia and governing a Western country had always been very different things. Yeltsin wrote later that when he decided to nominate Putin as Prime Minister, 'I wasn't just offering him a promotion. I wanted to hand him the cap of Monomakh' – a reference to the fourteenth-century gold filigree crown which had been used at the coronation of Ivan the Terrible and had been part of the regalia of the Russian tsars ever since.[50] Whatever Putin's own feelings about the pomp and ceremony of the Kremlin, he was part of that tradition. Blair had noticed, when Putin accompanied him to the Mariinsky Theatre for a performance of War and Peace during his visit to St Petersburg, that 'people fell back as he approached, not in fear . . . but a little in awe and with reverence. It was a tsar-like moment. I thought: Hmm, their politics really isn't like ours at all.'[51]

Yeltsin had gone out on the campaign trail in 1996 because he had no choice. He had to show that he was still physically capable of assuming a second term. Putin had no need to do that. His one concession to the exigencies of the election was an 'Open Letter to Voters', published at the end of February, which was full of zinging one-liners calculated to appeal to his electoral base:

> The stronger the state, the freer the individual . . .
> We are a rich country full of poor people . . .
> We have high taxes but collect them poorly. We should have low
>   taxes but collect them well . . .
> Bureaucrats are pushing paper but are not doing any real work . . .
>   what's the use of such a government?[52]

The 'Letter' was less bleak than the Millennium Declaration issued two months earlier. Despite the current difficulties, Putin declared, Russia was 'a confident power with a great future and a great people'.

If he had to choose a campaign slogan, it would be: 'A Decent Life!' Later that week, at a congress of Yedinstvo, he tried to walk back his comment that electioneering was dishonest. 'It is people who make it dirty,' he said. 'Politics is only as clean or as dirty as the people who make it so.'[53]

While Putin concentrated on the war in Chechnya, his election headquarters sent proxies, known as *doverennye litsa,* literally 'trusted persons', to campaign in the regions on his behalf.

Among them was Anatoly Sobchak, who had returned to Russia from Paris in July 1999, after his tormentor, the Prosecutor General, Yuri Skuratov, had been suspended. The investigation into the apartment scandal, which even Skuratov had admitted by then was 'trivial',[54] was closed. But Sobchak was no longer the same man as he had been when Mayor of St Petersburg. Alfred Kokh, who had visited him in Paris, had found him metamorphosed into 'a deadly weary, middle-aged professor'.[55] In December 1999, he stood for a seat in the Duma and was soundly defeated.

On February 19, Sobchak was in Kaliningrad to campaign for Putin.[56] Next morning he was found dead in his hotel room having suffered a heart attack. His funeral, at the Aleksandr Nevsky Monastery in St Petersburg, was a tense, unhappy affair. His widow, Lyudmila Narusova, on learning that her husband's nemesis, the Governor, Vladimir Yakovlev, planned to be present, said that if he came, she would insist that he be thrown out. Yakovlev did not attend.[57]

In an interview before the ceremony, Putin charged that Sobchak had been 'hounded to death by those who persecuted him'.[58] Conspiracy theorists alleged that the Kremlin had had him killed to silence him because he 'knew too much'. Neither was true. Sobchak had a history of heart trouble. There was no credible evidence of foul play.[59] Putin's true feelings were laid bare during the small, private ceremony at the graveside, where he was to deliver the eulogy as the coffin was being lowered into the ground. Hans Olsson, the Swedish Consul General, who was the only Westerner present, watched as he began his speech and then stopped, unable to go on. 'His voice just broke,' Olsson said. 'There were tears running down his face.'[60] It was an explosion of suppressed grief like that thirty years earlier, when his best friend at university had died after an accident at judo.

*

Putin's only serious competitor in the election was the Communist Party leader, Gennady Zyuganov. Primakov, who, a few months earlier, had been regarded as the favourite, had withdrawn in February. Luzhkov had dropped out even before that. The two other main contenders, Grigory Yavlinsky of Yabloko and the nationalist leader, Vladimir Zhirinovsky, were both in single digits. The opinion polls gave Putin between 54 and 58 per cent in the first round, which turned out to be accurate. When election day, Sunday, March 26, finally arrived, he received 53.4 per cent of the vote with a turnout of nearly 70 per cent. Zyuganov, with 29.5 per cent, did better than the polls had predicted, probably because some of those questioned had been unwilling to admit that they intended to vote for the Communist Party candidate. There were the usual accusations of ballot-stuffing, but on the whole, the election was fair, certainly much more so than the 1996 presidential election or the Duma elections the previous winter. Had there been no fraud at all, Putin would still have won, if not in the first round then by a large margin in the run-off.

Yeltsin and his family watched as the results came in on television at their home at Gorki-9.[61] Yumashev was at Putin's election headquarters, together with Chubais, Medvedev, Kasyanov, Voloshin, Pavlovsky and the rest of the campaign team. Putin was relaxed, casually dressed in a turtleneck sweater. Only his wife, Lyudmila, seemed ill at ease, looking as though she felt she did not really belong.

When the initial projections showed that he was certain to get more than 50 per cent, Putin stood up to speak, reprising his dislike of elections and all their works. 'Never in my worst nightmares,' he told them, 'did I imagine myself taking part in an election. Don't laugh! I'm serious . . . But at least, the way it was organised, I did not have to mislead vast numbers of people.' Then he thanked those present, raised a glass of red wine, drained it and left, telling them to drink up and go to bed as there would be work to do tomorrow. Yumashev telephoned Yeltsin to tell him that the campaign's internal polling showed that Putin had definitely won, although there had not yet been an official announcement. As the family toasted the victory with champagne, Yeltsin picked up the telephone to congratulate his successor. Putin was not available, he was told, but he would call back shortly. Yeltsin waited an hour and a half. When there was still no word from Putin, he retired grumpily to bed.

Next morning Putin came in person to Gorki-9 to celebrate the victory with the former first family. His failure to return Yeltsin's call had been deliberate. Yeltsin himself had done the same thing three months earlier when, a few minutes after his resignation, Bill Clinton had telephoned and he had told him to call back later. As he explained in his memoirs, '[He was] the President of the United States . . . [But] now I could indulge a little. I was retired.'[62]

Yeltsin's refusal to take the call had signalled that his official duties were over, Putin's that his were just beginning. The cap of Monomakh, which Yeltsin had worn for eight years, was now borne by another.

Power Vertical

The six weeks between Putin's election and his inauguration were a hiatus, a time for reflection, for planning and, above all, for trying to come to terms with the awesome responsibilities that now rested on his shoulders.

There was a hint of that in an interview he gave shortly after Yeltsin's resignation. 'I never strove for this,' he said. 'There are people here, so-called professional politicians, who wait for decades – it's in their blood. I never set myself those goals.'[1] As far as it went, that was true. Vladimir Putin had never been the small boy in a blurry black-and-white photograph standing with his parents in front of the Spassky Tower at the Kremlin, as others had stood outside 10, Downing Street, or the White House. He was not an 'accidental president' either, as some claimed.[2] His rise to power had been the unintended but logical consequence of his career in St Petersburg and Moscow. But the realisation that he was no longer merely a candidate for the presidency, but the ruler of a huge, nuclear-armed, almost ungovernable country, emerging from a period of extraordinary social, political and economic turmoil, heavily indebted to its Western creditors and embroiled in a civil war in Chechnya, would have daunted even the boldest spirit.

The first 100 days would produce 'enough change for an entire four-year term', one Russian commentator wrote later.[3] But while there were clues as to what those changes would be – Putin spoke of 'equal rules for all market players' and 'a more rigid, vertically structured system of administration' – nothing could begin until the inauguration was behind him.[4]

Russians value ceremonial as much as, if not more than, the British or the French, and Putin's consecration in the Grand Kremlin Palace was designed to underline the continuity with Russia's past. He arrived in a black stretched Mercedes limousine with a motorcycle escort, through streets emptied of traffic and pedestrians, a diminutive, solitary figure, made to look smaller still by the massive architecture of the long galleries through which he walked, his right arm hanging stiffly by his side – an affectation rather than the result of an accident – applauded by some 1,500 church and state dignitaries and foreign envoys.

Yelena Pamfilova, who would later head the Kremlin's Human Rights Commission, thought he looked tense and nervous,[5] as well he might, for, from that day on, everything in Russia would revolve about his person.

An escort from the Kremlin Guard Regiment preceded him, in dress uniforms replicating those of 1812, when the Russian army had repulsed the *Grande Armée* of Napoleon. Like clockwork soldiers, executing a meticulous, goose-stepping slow march, they carried the Russian flag, the Presidential standard, a copy of the constitution and the emblem of office, through the Georgievsky and Aleksandrovsky Halls into the St Andrew's Hall, resplendent in white and gold, with an immense, vaulted Gothic ceiling, resembling that of a great cathedral. The wall at the western end is embellished with a bas-relief of a giant, striated sun, having at its centre an eye – the 'All Powerful Eye' of the Tsar – whose golden rays shine down towards the imperial throne below. When Putin took the oath of office, the throne was discreetly hidden behind a blue silk curtain. But the underlying message was clear. Russia's new ruler was heir to an imperial tradition.

In his speech, Putin said he was assuming a 'sacred duty' to preserve the unity of Russia. Afterwards the Orthodox Patriarch, Aleksei II, pronounced a solemn blessing.[6] It was more like a coronation than taking an oath of office.

These were the atmospherics which Tony Blair had sensed in St Petersburg, two months earlier. It was a role that Putin had to play, although not one which, in the beginning, he particularly liked or that came naturally to him. To rule Russia, it was necessary, if not to act as a tsar, at least to be perceived as one, because that was what the country expected.

There was a telling example a year or so later, when Putin paid an official visit to Helsinki, during which he was to visit the Finnish parliament. The usual protocol was for visiting dignitaries, including heads

of state, to ascend the stone stairs leading up to the parliament building, where the Secretary General and the Speaker would wait to greet
them. The only exception was for the Kings and Queens of Denmark,
Norway and Sweden, whom the Secretary General greeted at the foot
of the steps. The Secretary General at that time was Seppo Tiitinen,
who happened to be a former head of the Finnish secret service,
SUPO. 'Putin's protocol people somehow learnt about this,' he
recalled, 'and they absolutely insisted that the same procedure should
be followed as for Nordic royalty.' The Finns acquiesced – there was no
point in making an issue of it, however ridiculous it might seem – and
Tiitinen greeted Putin at the foot of the steps as though he were a
reigning Nordic monarch.[7]

Putin knew nothing of that and probably knows nothing about it to
this day. It was the work of his entourage. In Russia, the legacy of
Prince Potemkin who, in the eighteenth century, beautified the villages, or by some accounts built fake ones, along the route taken by
Catherine the Great, is still alive and well.

When it was learnt that Putin was to visit Kaliningrad, where Lyudmila's mother lived, shortly after he became President, the City
authorities sent building crews post-haste to renovate her home, in an
old pre-war building whose roof had been leaking for decades and
which had not seen a lick of paint since 1945.[8] It was the same whenever
Lyudmila came to stay in the Putins' apartment on Vasilevsky Island,
which usually happened at election time. The façades of the buildings
along the route she would take to the polling station were freshly
painted, but only half-way up – as high as she would see from the windows of a moving car. The local joke had it that when the painters
arrived, it meant an election must be coming.[9]

Wherever Putin travelled in the provinces, the local authorities
spruced up the areas he would visit. It was such a standard procedure
that normally no one paid any attention, although a television correspondent in one small northern town, finding little else to say, thought
it worth reporting: 'The townsfolk will vividly remember the president's stay on account of 200 metres of newly laid tarmac, freshly
decorated façades and one or two ornate fences painted the day before
his arrival.'[10]

Some went to even greater lengths. Diana Kachalova, a St Petersburg journalist with *Novaya gazeta*, was driving along a potholed

country road in the pine forests, north of the city, when she came across a gang of Tajik labourers painting a white line down the middle. 'They were even painting it across the potholes,' she remembered . 'So I stopped and asked the foreman, "Why are you doing that?" He said, "We've been told that Putin is flying to Igora [a ski resort]. He'll be in his helicopter above this road, so he'll see that it looks nice." . . . You really couldn't make that up. But in Russia it's normal.'[11]

Putin adapted gradually to his new eminence. After his election, he decided to move from the Prime Minister's residence in Gorki, not far from Yeltsin's mansion, to Novo-Ogaryovo, in the same elite area west of Moscow but a few miles closer to the city. It had been built in the 1950s in a vast area of parkland beside the Moscow River and in the 1980s and '90s had been used as a state guest house.[12] According to Sergei Pugachev, who accompanied Putin to visit the house shortly after his election, he was enraptured by the Olympic-sized swimming pool.[13] The building was extensively remodelled before the family moved in,[14] and when Tony Blair visited, a year later, he was struck by the opulence of the place. 'Vladimir Putin, when we first met him, was modest and unassuming,' Blair's Chief of Staff, Jonathan Powell, wrote later. 'But each time Tony visited him, he had acquired more grooms for his horses and lived in greater luxury . . . He became hubristic. Each time we saw him there was more this, more that . . . more pomp. In the end, we just couldn't take it any more.'[15]

Yet alongside this 'folie de grandeur', as Powell's colleague, Alastair Campbell, called it,[16] Putin could also show a quite different side.

During his state visit to Finland, the same visit for which his entourage had demanded that he be treated as visiting royalty, he and Lyudmila were guests of honour at a banquet in the former Governor General's residence in Helsinki. As they were about to leave, Jaakko Kalela, the Finnish President's National Security Adviser, found himself on the staircase leading down to the entrance hall and ducked discreetly into an alcove, hoping not to be noticed. Kalela had known Putin since the early '90s, when they both attended meetings between Sobchak and the Finnish President, and he had always had the impression of an unspoken sympathy between them, as they each sat silently, listening to the great men converse about affairs of state. As Putin walked past, he caught sight of Kalela out of the corner of his eye. When he was halfway down, he stopped, leaving Lyudmila to continue on her own, and ran back up the stairs to greet him. 'I couldn't imagine any other head of state,' Kalela said, 'turning round to come back up as he did, no matter who I was.'[17]

It was not an isolated instance. A year later, when Putin attended a reception in the Berlin City Hall during an official visit to Germany, he noticed among the crowd Eberhard von Puttkamer, the former Consul General in St Petersburg, now long since retired. To the astonishment of his German hosts, he left the official party, walked across the room and embraced him. Shortly afterwards von Puttkamer and his wife received an invitation to the Kremlin, where Putin had them to lunch in his private apartments and personally showed them around.[18]

He treated those with whom he worked, including foreigners, as people whose views should be listened to and taken seriously, regardless of their difference in status.

The US Ambassador, Jim Collins, found him 'a huge contrast to Yeltsin. If you went in to see Yeltsin, you would state your business and he would then make a pronouncement in response. [I] never had a discussion with Yeltsin . . . With Putin, it was different . . . You engaged with him. If I went in and said something, he would respond to that. We'd have a back and forth. He talked to you as a person.'[19]

Andrei Illarionov, the libertarian economist who had briefed Putin on the inevitability of a devaluation, shortly before the default in August 1998, picked up the telephone one February afternoon to hear a voice at the other end tell him that the acting President wished to see him. They met at his dacha at Gorki that evening. Illarionov was impressed despite himself when Putin began the conversation by asking: 'Assuming we win the election, what do you think should be my first decisions?' It was restrained and down to earth, he thought. They talked for about three hours, in the course of which Putin indicated that he was considering appointing Illarionov his economic adviser. Towards the end of the discussion, a staff officer came in and handed Putin a note announcing that Russian soldiers had captured an important district centre in Chechnya. Illarionov, who was not a man to mince words, told Putin to his face that what Russia was doing there was a crime:

For about 15 minutes, we had an interesting exchange. But, as you know, when people have – to put it mildly – slightly different views on a subject, the tone mounts . . . He did not raise his voice. It was different. His voice became colder and steelier . . . Like steel, absolutely cold, with icy eyes . . . We both knew that if we went on – because neither of us would compromise – it would be finished forever. And because he is a good psychologist, not academically but intuitively, he said: 'Stop. In future we will not talk about Chechnya.' For 30 or 40 seconds he remained silent, forcing himself to calm down . . . maybe it lasted a minute. Then he said: 'Let's talk about the economy.'[20]

As he was leaving, Putin suggested to Illarionov's surprise that they meet again the following day, February 29. Illarionov apologised but said he was not available – it was the anniversary of his wife's arrival in Russia and since that date occurred only once every four years, he had promised to spend the day with her. His wife, he added, happened to be American.

Putin shook hands and said goodbye, and Illarionov went home convinced that he would never hear from him again. To refuse a meeting with the Head of State was unheard of in Russia. The idea that a Russian President – a former KGB officer to boot – would appoint an assistant with an American wife was even more so.

But a couple of days later, the telephone rang again and the same voice invited him to another meeting with Putin. More discussions followed. Illarionov accompanied Putin on trips to the provinces, where he noticed that the economic ideas which he had been promoting began to crop up in impromptu speeches. After a while, Putin's speechwriters asked him to meet them and explain his thinking so that they could include it in what they wrote. Then, on March 30, Putin asked him to take part in a restricted meeting at the White House. Only six others were present: Putin himself, the Prime Minister-designate, Mikhail Kasyanov, their respective chiefs of staff and the Ministers of Finance and Economic Affairs.

As the meeting ended, Putin turned to the others and said: 'I should have explained why Andrei Nikolayevich [Illarionov] is here. He is going to be my economic adviser.' It was insoluble, Illarionov wrote later. To contradict the President-elect was unthinkable; to remain silent, impossible. After thanking Putin for inviting him, he added, feeling that he was walking on eggshells: 'Unfortunately, and I do apologise, I have not yet taken that decision.'

Once again, Illarionov assumed that their relationship was over. But, ten days later, he was invited to yet another meeting to discuss Putin's future economic programme, and there, for the first time, he had the impression that Putin was testing him. Was he just a windbag full of clever ideas, or did he want to do the hard work of trying to put them into practice? Afterwards, Putin asked him again: 'Are you sure you don't want to be my assistant?' This time, Illarionov said, he agreed. 'He had outsmarted me.'

The story is all the more striking because, by the time Illarionov related it, he had become one of Putin's sternest critics. Even allowing that he may at certain points have embellished his account, what came across most starkly was Putin's refusal to take no for an answer.[21] Eighteen months earlier, Illarionov had been right about the default where everyone else had been wrong. Putin wanted him as his adviser and was not going to be deterred by disagreements over Chechnya, Illarionov's repeated rejection of his overtures – even in front of members of his cabinet – or anything else. Lèse-majesté was secondary; what mattered was achieving his goal.

Vitaly Mansky, who was making a documentary about Putin during the election campaign, filmed a similarly contentious discussion with him, in which they repeatedly disagreed on camera. When Mansky continued to hold to his own opinion, Putin said: 'You can't persuade everyone, unfortunately . . . Though it seems to me I'd be able to if I could talk to each one individually. Only that's impossible.'[22]

Afterwards he would attempt to do just that with an annual phone-in programme, 'Direct Line with Vladimir Putin', often lasting more than four hours, where, in theory, viewers, or those lucky enough to be put through, could ask anything they wished. The first programme, in March 2001, was moderated by the BBC's Moscow correspondent, Bridget Kendall, and was totally unscripted.[23] Over time, that changed. Questions were filtered. Whether at the insistence of his entourage or because his own conception of his role evolved, the exercise became more formal and less informative. The same happened with meetings of the Valdai Club, which started as an informal discussion group where Putin would meet small groups of Western scholars for no-holds-barred conversations, only to metamorphose over time into an institutionalised propaganda forum with hundreds of attendees.

There was a delicate balance to be struck between Russian tradition,

which viewed the President as a modern autocrat, in a direct line from
imperial times, and the exigencies of a modern European state, on the
cusp of the twenty-first century, which saw itself as a nascent democracy, even if on Russian, rather than Western, terms. Putin was the
symbol of that state. At the same time he had to appear approachable
to those who formed his electoral base. It was not a unique dilemma:
Western royalty also struggled to find a way to reconcile the mystique
of monarchy with popular curiosity about their private lives. Putin's
ability to straddle that divide enabled him to end his first year in office
with a more than 70 per cent approval rate. *Izvestia* wrote that autumn
that as well as appearing presidential, he had managed to make ordinary Russians feel, 'he's just like me', with the result that 'changing
one's good opinion of Putin would require changing one's good opinion of oneself, which is very hard to do.'[24]

The political programme which Putin and his advisers had worked out
that spring was launched as soon as the inauguration was over.

He had three main targets: the media, the oligarchs and the regional
governors. Common to all three was the need for greater centralised
control – the 'power vertical' which Yeltsin had spoken of but had
never seriously tried to install. Putin intended to change that, if not in
absolute then at least in relative terms.

In practice, the different strands overlapped.

The media felt the heat first. Even while Yeltsin was in power, his
entourage, the so-called Family – particularly his daughter, Tatyana,
Yumashev and Voloshin – had been gunning for NTV, the independent
channel owned by Vladimir Gusinsky's Media-Most Group.[25] When
Stepashin was Prime Minister, he had given Gusinsky a measure of
cover.[26] But during the Duma elections in December 1999, NTV had
backed the Luzhkov-Primakov bloc. Voloshin and his colleagues had
decided that the channel would have to be brought to heel.[27]

At the end of February 2000, Mikhail Lesin, the Press Minister,
announced that broadcasting licences for television stations would no
longer be automatically renewed.[28] Then, in March, the Kremlin learnt
that NTV was preparing a programme on the previous autumn's
apartment bombings which would suggest that the buildings had been
blown up by the FSB to bolster Putin's election chances. Yumashev
warned the station's Director General, Yevgeny Kiselyov, that if NTV

went ahead, a red line would be crossed with unpleasant consequences. The message was ignored. The programme was broadcast the night before Election Day.

Four days after Putin's inauguration, armed men, wearing black ski-masks and camouflage uniforms, raided Media-Most's offices. They identified themselves first as members of the Tax Police and then as special forces from the Interior Ministry, investigating charges that Media-Most's security service had been conducting illegal surveillance operations. In reality it was straightforward intimidation – a warning to Gusinsky that the Kremlin's patience had run out.

Putin claimed afterwards that he 'had not liked' the use of force, but compared it to a recent case in Florida, in which more than a hundred armed and helmeted US border patrol agents had been sent to seize a six-year old Cuban boy, Elián González, who was the subject of a custody battle.[29] From then on it would become standard practice, whenever Russian law enforcement was criticised, for Putin to draw attention to excesses by its American counterpart.

There was speculation that the raid was in retaliation for NTV's most popular weekly show, 'Kukly' ('Marionettes'), a Russian version of the British political satire, *Spitting Image*, in which Russia's leaders were caricatured, often viciously, as deformed rubber puppets. One episode in particular, in which Putin was depicted as Little Zaches, a deformed, evil dwarf from an old German fairy tale, who appears to others as a handsome youth, was said to have irritated him.[30]

That may have been partly true. His wife, Lyudmila, was said to have been outraged and several of his aides wrote to *Sankt-Peterburgskie vedomosti*, demanding that those responsible be prosecuted. However Putin himself insisted that he had not been particularly offended by it.[31]

In fact, there was no single proximate cause. Putin had concluded that the principal privately owned media – which, in those days, when most Russians got their news from television, meant the national TV channels – must be brought under state control and NTV, the most hard-hitting of them, was the logical place to start.[32] In public, Putin maintained that 'a free press is one of the most important instruments guaranteeing the health of society' and without it, Russia would have no future.[33] In private, he took the view that the media everywhere were the instruments of those who controlled them, and that, if he did not do so, someone else would.[34]

He had a point. NTV might be independent, but that did not stop Gusinsky using it to advance his own political and economic agenda. He did so no more, and in some senses less, than media barons in the West. But that was more than Putin was willing to accept.

Gleb Pavlovsky, the election strategist, thought he had been influenced by watching the spin doctors at work during the Duma campaign. 'We had meetings every day,' Pavlovsky said. 'It was decided which television channels should show what news, what kind of articles would be published in different newspapers . . . There was a strict plan and it was implemented precisely . . . Putin witnessed that. He began to think that . . . any kind of press, any TV programme, is manipulated. It's all paid for by someone.'[35]

That may have been part of it. But Putin's view of the media dated from his time in St Petersburg, when he had decided that its practitioners could never be anything but prisoners of those who financed them. He considered it beneath his dignity to dictate personally to journalists how they were supposed to work. In 1992, when he gave his first extended television interview, he astonished the director, Igor Shadkhan, by telling him to edit it as he liked: he did not want to be involved.[36] Ten years later he told Vitaly Mansky: 'I won't interfere in the creative process. You'll make it the way you see fit . . . I just want to state my point of view and you decide if you use it or not.'[37] Bridget Kendall remembered how he had 'seemed to enjoy to have someone to spar with' in the phone-ins she moderated, when unexpected questions were thrown at him and he had to think on his feet.[38] But that did not make him any less determined to ensure that the national media served as instruments of state power, and that any criticisms they might voice were within limits which the state laid down.[39]

A month after the raid on Media-Most, on June 13, Gusinsky was arrested and taken to the Butyrka, a red-brick nineteenth-century remand prison in central Moscow, about three miles north of the Kremlin, notorious for its overcrowding and primitive cells, where the poet, Vladimir Mayakovsky and, later, Aleksandr Solzhenitsyn, had once been held. He was accused of having embezzled 10 million US dollars in government funds during NTV's takeover of Russkoe Video, the St Petersburg company which had earlier produced Sobchak's election publicity.[40] The charge was not implausible. Russkoe Video's founder, Dmitry Rozhdestvensky, had been in prison since September

1998, accused of money laundering and other crimes, and the conditions under which NTV had acquired the company and Channel 11, a local television station it owned, were, to say the least, ambiguous.

Putin was then in Madrid, on an official visit to Spain, and denied all knowledge of what had happened. It had come as a surprise to him, he said. He hoped that 'whoever was responsible' had sufficient justification for the arrest.[41] His personal view, he went on, was that there had been no need to detain the oligarch, whom he described as 'a very talented man', but the Prosecutor's Office evidently thought differently and, since it was 'totally independent', it would be wrong for him to interfere.[42] In Russia, he repeated, 'it is absolutely impossible to influence prosecutors . . . They are not answerable to anyone.'[43]

If that did not strain credulity sufficiently, he added that he had been unable to reach the Prosecutor General, Vladimir Ustinov, to find out further details – as though it were normal for a Head of State not to be able to contact a member of his government for several days.

When Putin returned to Moscow, three days later, Gusinsky was released on condition that he did not leave the country. Mikhail Lesin, the Press Minister, then made him an offer he could not refuse. Media-Most had large debts, including 200 million US dollars owed to Gazprom.[44] The solution, Lesin told him, would be for him to sell his shares to Gazprom, which meant in practice to the state, after which the debt would be written off and all would be forgiven. If he refused, he would return to prison. At Gusinsky's request, Lesin added a protocol to the agreement, which the two of them and the Chairman of Gazprom-Media, Alfred Kokh, then signed, guaranteeing 'an end to [his] criminal prosecution, . . . the right to freedom of movement, to choose his place of residence and to travel freely within and outside Russia'.

It was an astute move on Gusinsky's part, for it enabled him to claim later that the agreement had been extorted in exchange for his freedom and that he had signed under duress. It also blew a huge hole in Putin's claim that the Prosecutor's Office in Russia acted independently.

Putin was furious that Lesin had failed to foresee that such a crude attempt at blackmail – 'racketeering', as *Nezavisimaya gazeta* called it – was bound to backfire.[45] The minister kept his job but was in the doghouse for several months. Gusinsky left Russia in July, never to return. His attempts to repudiate the agreement came to nothing. No one else was willing to take the risk of purchasing his shares. After months of legal argument, Gazprom foreclosed the following spring. NTV continued broadcasting, but under state ownership.

Gusinsky's arrest and exile drew less condemnation inside Russia than might have been expected. The liberal elite and the journalists were up in arms. But no one was sure how much of it was Putin's doing, how much was the work of Voloshin, who detested Gusinsky, and what influence had been exerted by *siloviki* like Patrushev and Yuri Zaostrovtsev, the head of the FSB's Economic Counter-Intelligence Directorate, whom Gusinsky's newspaper, *Segodnya*, had been investigating for corruption.[46]

Western leaders, too, tended to give him the benefit of the doubt.[47] Putin was new to office and it was still uncertain how much he was really in control. Moreover, in those more innocent times, they were reluctant to believe that the new Russian President was simply lying when he claimed not to have known in advance of Gusinsky's arrest.

The Russian public was largely indifferent.[48] Gusinsky was perceived as an oligarch – a class of person whom most people loathed – who was getting his comeuppance. 'Putting an oligarch in prison has been an almost universal dream,' wrote *Nezavisimaya gazeta*. 'Why? In order to show that a struggle against corruption has begun in this country.'[49] Putin emphasised that, too. 'The accusations levelled [against Gusinsky] were not as a journalist', he said. 'He's a businessman, an entrepreneur.'[50] It was a useful way to distract attention from concerns about press freedom.[51]

The raid on Media-Most in May and Gusinsky's arrest showed that the oligarchs were no longer untouchable. The era of Wild West capitalism which had flourished under Yeltsin was over.

There had been a hint of that during the presidential campaign, when Putin's election headquarters had systematically refused offers of financing from the business magnates who were queuing up to provide it. 'It is not an oligarchy but a monopsony,' *Izvestia* commented. 'The sellers are all competing for a single buyer, but Putin doesn't need help from anyone at all.'[52]

Other signals followed.

That summer, three of Russia's biggest companies – Lukoil, Norilsk Nickel and the automobile manufacturer, Avtovaz – joined Media-Most in the sights of the Prosecutor's Office. 'There are fishermen who have caught a lot and are keen to keep doing so,' Putin said in July. 'I doubt this suits either the Russian people or our partners abroad . . . [That] does not mean that the punishment must be severe, harsh or even brutal. But it must be inexorable.'[53] By then, even the most obtuse businessman understood that the wind had changed.

Later that month, Putin summoned 21 of the leading business magnates – including Mikhail Khodorkovsky of Yukos; Pyotr Aven, who now headed Alfa Bank; and Rem Vakhirev of Gazprom – to a meeting in the Kremlin to hear the new rules of the game.[54] The period of 'initial capital accumulation' in Russia was over, he told them. If they did not like the results, they had only themselves to blame. 'You yourselves have created this situation, to a large extent through political and quasi-political structures which you control. The last thing you should do is blame the mirror.'[55] There would be no attempt to reverse the results of privatisation, he assured them. They could keep what they had, no matter how it had been obtained. But from now on, they should stay at arm's length from the state and they would not be permitted to involve themselves in politics. If they followed those rules, law enforcement would keep its distance too.

The one significant absentee from that meeting was Boris Berezovsky.[56]

For Putin, Berezovsky posed a problem. He was an ally but, as Yeltsin had said years earlier, 'a difficult ally'. Voloshin and Yumashev had persuaded him to stay away from Russia during the presidential campaign because his reputation was so toxic that, if he were seen to be associated with it, he would cost Putin votes. Accordingly he had spent most of the winter on his yacht in the Caribbean.[57]

When Putin was elected, Berezovsky was convinced that his hour had come. 'Everything's fine now,' he exulted. 'Our man is in power.'[58] It was typical Berezovsky. A mathematician by training, he was a gadfly, an eccentric, a formidable wellspring of ideas, 'emotionally deaf . . . totally amoral, but with great ambitions and strengths,'[59] in the words of his friend, Pyotr Aven. 'His ultimate goal', Aven wrote, 'was to control Russia.' In his relationship with Putin, 'he really thought he had God by the beard and could walk on water,' commented his business partner at the time, the billionaire investor, Leonid Boguslavsky.[60]

As would soon become clear, Berezovsky had totally misjudged the situation.

His first mis-step was in April, when he told Putin, even before his inauguration, that he should hold office only for one term. After that, he said, Russia would need a 'normal President', elected through a 'normal party system'. Putin shrugged it off as just another of Berezovsky's eccentricities, but when the oligarch told Sergei Dorenko, the charismatic chief news anchor on ORT, about the conversation, Dorenko was horrified. "You fool!", he told him. 'You complete fool! You're not talking to 'Volodya' any more. You're speaking before the throne of the Russian empire! You ought to be on your knees when you go there . . . You're an idiot if you don't understand that.'[61]

But Berezovsky listened only to himself. Shortly afterwards, he doubled down on his error by opposing Putin's drive to restore to Moscow the powers which Yeltsin had devolved to the regions.

Putin had kicked off his campaign in Bashkiria and Tatarstan, two predominantly Turkic, Muslim republics in central Russia, which had been refusing to remit locally collected taxes to the federal government. He received the republics' leaders in April, after which it was announced that payments would resume. How he had persuaded them was not disclosed. 'I just made them understand that the situation had changed,' he said cryptically.[62] The next step was to create seven federal districts, each comprising a dozen or more regions, headed by a presidential representative, a system similar to that which had existed under Peter the Great.[63] The plenipotentiaries, as they were called, most of whom were from the army and security services, were there to ensure that Russian laws were applied uniformly throughout the country. The regional constitutions, Putin complained, contained 'all sorts of stuff, from sow's ears to purses. The only thing they don't mention is that they are parts of Russia.'[64] It was as though the country were still living in the Middle Ages, he went on. 3,500 regional laws were in conflict with federal legislation. The governors had resorted to 'every trick in the book to dodge compliance' with Moscow's directives. Now that the 'good life' was ending for them and order was being restored, they were 'screaming about a threat to democracy'.

The governors would continue to be elected, rather than appointed, as had been the case in tsarist times, lest it make them feel less responsible for their work.[65] But they would no longer be *ex officio* members of the Federation Council, the upper house of parliament, which meant that they would lose their immunity from prosecution. Their ability to lobby for their regional or personal interests would be much reduced and the federal authorities would have the power to dismiss them.[66]

Berezovsky opposed the new measures because, the previous autumn, when he had created Yedinstvo to fight the Duma elections, he had won the governors' support by promising them that Putin, unlike Primakov, would do nothing to limit their powers. Those assurances were now being shown to be hollow.[67]

In an open letter, published at the end of May in the business daily, *Kommersant*, which Berezovsky owned, he attacked the changes as 'inappropriate [and] anti-democratic', a regression towards Soviet-style practices which would produce 'closed, corrupt, monolithic local bureaucracies'. In a democracy, unlike a dictatorship, he reminded Putin tartly, it was necessary 'to persuade citizens that you are right, not order them what to do'.[68] Publicly Putin welcomed the intervention. Berezovsky had drawn attention to potential weaknesses, he said, and it was 'not a bad thing' to have another point of view.[69] In private, he told him that he disagreed entirely.[70] It did not help that the personal copy of the letter that Berezovsky had sent to him, though not the published version, was addressed to 'Dear Volodya' and used the familiar *ty*, instead of the formal *vy*. To Putin, the lack of respect – if not towards himself then towards his position as Head of State – was unforgivable. Aven thought the letter was the point of no return. When they met, Berezovsky made matters worse by telling Putin : 'If it's like that, I shall publicly oppose you', to which the President replied drily: 'As you like. That's your affair.'

Dorenko thought he had taken leave of his senses. Berezovsky refused to understand, he said, that there was a difference between the nature of power in Russia and in Europe. 'There the rulers are leaders. In Russia, we have a priest-king.' Berezovsky's mistake had been to think that Putin was his creation and that he could treat him accordingly.

The oligarch made good on his threat to go into opposition. He resigned his seat in the Duma, where he represented the small Caucasian republic of Karachay-Cherkessia – a post that he had wangled through money and connections – and tried to set up a 'party of governors' to oppose Putin's reforms, which he now denounced publicly as 'a path towards dictatorship'.[71] It never got off the ground. The governors, having been burnt once by trusting Berezovsky, were not about to make the same mistake again. For a while, he maintained tenuous contacts with the Kremlin, but sometime in the first half of July, Putin told his aides he would not meet him again.[72]

A month later, Putin was confronted by the first major crisis of his presidency. On the afternoon of August 12, he had flown to Sochi to join Lyudmila and the children for the summer holidays.[73] At 7 a.m. next morning, which was Sunday, he was awakened by a telephone call from the Defence Minister, Marshal Igor Sergeyev, who told him that communication had been lost with an Antey-class nuclear submarine, the *Kursk*, which had been taking part in a training exercise with the Northern Fleet in the Barents Sea. Built in 1994, the vessel was the world's biggest nuclear attack submarine and the pride of the fleet. One and a half times the length of a football pitch, it had a double hull, coated with rubber to confuse radar detection and reputedly was able to withstand a direct hit from a torpedo. A crew of 118 men were aboard and it had a full complement of conventional weapons: 18 SS-N-16 anti-submarine missiles and 24 SS-N-19 cruise missiles.[74]

After enquiring about the nuclear reactors and being assured that they were safe, Putin asked whether he should fly to the scene. Sergeyev told him that a search was already under way and his presence was not necessary.[75] Gleb Pavlovsky, his political strategist, whom he also consulted, gave the same advice. 'I was wrong,' Pavlovsky acknowledged later, 'but I really thought he didn't need to go there. There was nothing he could have done.'[76]

The following day the navy issued a bland communiqué saying that the *Kursk* had suffered 'a malfunction' and was resting on the sea floor.[77] The crew was believed to be alive – 'acoustic signals' had been detected – and had sufficient oxygen to last for two weeks.[78] Sergeyev and other officials suggested that it might have collided with a foreign submarine that had supposedly been shadowing it.[79] When Britain and Norway offered help, they were told that Russia had everything necessary for the rescue effort, but it was being hampered by bad weather.[80] Not until Wednesday, August 16, after President Clinton had telephoned to express concern about the length of time that the rescue operation was taking, did Putin order the navy commander, Admiral Kuroyedov, to 'accept any assistance, wherever it may come from'.[81]

Even then the military were reluctant to allow Western experts access to the stricken vessel and continued to drag their feet.

Throughout that week, Putin remained on the Black Sea coast, taking care of routine business – holding meetings, appointing ambassadors, sending greetings to a well-known actress on her 70th birthday. It was exactly how officials would have reacted in Soviet times. Accidents were hushed up or, if that was impossible, minimised; the media kept silent; and the country's leaders carried on as if nothing had happened.

But these were not Soviet times. The media did not keep silent. Day after day, the plight of the crew dominated the newspaper headlines and television screens. Russians were transfixed. 'The whole country was in tears', one of Pavlovsky's young assistants, Marina Litvinovich, remembered. 'It was a national tragedy. Everyone was very emotional. And people could not understand why Putin was so remote and distant.'[82]

What was most damaging was not just that he remained silent, seeming not to care, but the contrast between the images of the President, relaxed and smiling, in shirt sleeves, at a sunlit beach resort, and the pictures of the sailors' distraught families with haggard faces – unable even to learn whether their sons or husbands were on board the sunken ship, because the navy, 'on security grounds', kept the crew list secret[83] – waiting desperately for news in their cold, grimy apartment blocks, with peeling paint and dilapidated façades, at the Kursk's home port, Vidyaevo, on an inlet from the Arctic Ocean, north of Murmansk.

For a leader who prided himself on being 'an expert in human relations', as Putin had told his friend, Roldugin, in St Petersburg, many years earlier, it was a catastrophic misjudgement.

After the call from Clinton, Putin finally issued a statement, acknowledging that the situation was 'difficult' and promising that everything possible would be done to try to save the crew.[84] It was far too little, too late. A snap poll conducted by the liberal radio station, Ekho Moskvy, found that three quarters of those questioned thought Putin should have been at the scene, supervising the rescue operation in person.[85] Next day, August 17, Nezavisimaya gazeta wrote: 'Everyone in the leadership of Navy and the Defence Ministry . . . covered up the truth. They lulled themselves and the country's leaders with honeyed lies.' But Putin was to blame, too. 'He did not support the sailors in their hour of need,' it charged. 'He could not bring himself to interrupt his vacation, if only for an hour.'[86]

It was the beginning of a tidal wave of criticism which would continue for weeks. Mikhail Gorbachev said Putin had let the military make a fool of him.[87] Boris Nemtsov, the leader of the liberal Union of Right Forces in the Duma, said his behaviour was amoral.[88]

Even then, the bureaucrats in the Kremlin were reluctant to ask him to return. At the regular Friday morning meeting with Voloshin and Oleg Dobrodeyev, the chief editor of RTR, to discuss media strategy, Marina Litvinovich insisted that they call him. Voloshin thought it was unnecessary.[89] Eventually, after a heated argument, he telephoned the President and summed up the different views.

Putin flew back that night.

By then six days had passed since contact had been lost. The following day, it was admitted for the first time that all the crew members were almost certainly dead. Any remaining doubt was removed on Monday, when a Norwegian diving team succeeded in opening the escape hatch, and found the stern compartment, where it had been hoped there might be survivors, flooded.

After his return to Moscow, Putin started to understand how seriously his public image had been damaged.[90]

During his first 100 days in power, the end of which had coincided, almost to the day, with the sinking of the *Kursk*, everything had gone like clockwork. The media had been uniformly supportive, muting their criticisms of the war in Chechnya and even letting him off lightly for the ousting of Gusinsky.

Now much of the written press and the two TV channels controlled by private interests, Berezovsky's ORT and NTV, whose ownership remained in dispute between Gusinsky and Gazprom, had turned violently against him. Many Russians blamed him personally for mishandling the rescue operation. The country had looked to him for strong leadership and he had failed to provide it.

The only way he could hope to turn the situation round, Putin decided, was by getting out in front and meeting the families of the crewmen at Vidyaevo.

It was a high-risk undertaking. That weekend, Ilya Klebanov, the deputy Prime Minister responsible for the military–industrial complex, had been savaged in front of the television cameras when he and

Admiral Kuroyedov had received the family members. Klebanov was a holdover from the Yeltsin administration, a former 'Red director' who had headed an optical works in St Petersburg. Instead of trying to engage the increasingly frantic and overwrought crowd, he infuriated them by regurgitating official claims that the *Kursk* had been sunk in a collision. The worst moment had come when a middle-aged woman, Nadezhda Tylik, whose son, a senior lieutenant, was among the dead, broke down, shouting at Klebanov: 'You swine! Did I bring up my son for this? You sit there getting fat and we have nothing. My husband was in the navy for 25 years and now my son is buried down there.' Turning to Kuroyedov, she told him, her voice rising to a scream: 'Go tear off your epaulettes and shoot yourself.'[91] As a staff officer tried to calm her, a navy nurse came up from behind and injected her with a powerful sedative. She collapsed and was carried out.

In the West, the scene, which was broadcast live, provoked a horrified reaction. Russia, it was said, was returning to the methods which the Soviet Union had used to quell dissent. To most Russians, it was simply an attempt to calm a terribly distressed woman. The family members in Vidyaevo were on the brink of mass hysteria. For several days many had been heavily sedated by naval doctors sent to the port for that purpose.

Making matters still more difficult for Putin, Klebanov announced on Tuesday morning – the day Putin was to go there – that the authorities had known for a full week, ever since August 14, that none of the crew had survived.[92] That was true. Klebanov's admission was a misguided attempt to show that, even if foreign help had arrived sooner, it would have made no difference. But the message to the families was that everyone, from the Head of State down, had been lying to them. Klebanov then compounded his error by telling them, 'almost casually', as one reporter recalled, that to recover the bodies would take 'maybe a few months, maybe a year'. In the pandemonium that followed, 'a short woman in a mohair sweater and a long skirt ran up to him, grabbed him and began to shake him. "You bastard! Go there and save them!" ' As she was dragged away, she shrieked: 'You are scum. Scum!'[93]

That afternoon, Putin flew to Murmansk for what would prove the toughest meeting of his career. He had told Vitaly Mansky six months earlier that if he could talk to people, one on one, he knew that he could convince them that he was right. Now he had to make good on that boast or risk becoming discredited, less than four months into his first term.

He arrived at Vidyaevo just before 9 p.m., wearing a black suit and black shirt without a tie, and went straight to the Garrison Officers' Hall, where some five hundred family members were waiting. Apart from the state-owned TV channel, RTR, which was afterwards allowed to broadcast only a brief segment lasting less than 30 seconds, journalists were excluded.

'He's committing suicide,' one elderly woman whispered to her companion as Putin passed. 'They'll tear him to pieces.'[94]

He began by announcing that next day would be a National Day of Mourning. That produced a furore. No one wanted mourning ceremonies until the bodies had been recovered, and many families still hoped that there might be survivors, trapped in air pockets:

PUTIN: I, too, have been hoping – and, honestly, I will hope from the bottom of my heart to the very last – that there will be a miracle . . . But it's a clearly established fact that people have died . . . That doesn't mean we should stop hoping . . .

SHOUT FROM THE HALL: Shut up!

WOMAN: Why weren't foreign specialists invited right away?

PUTIN: Sergeyev called me on Sunday at 7 o'clock in the morning . . .

MAN: The ship was missing on Saturday, and they only called you on Sunday?

PUTIN: Wait . . . The navy believed that we had the necessary means to carry out the rescue ourselves. But as soon as foreign aid was offered, on the 15th, Kuroyedov immediately agreed . . .

SHOUTS, NOISE IN THE HALL: That's a lie . . .

PUTIN: It's true! It's true! . . . Even if we'd asked the Norwegians to come on the 13th, it would still have taken them until the 19th to get here and dock with the submarine. But to come back to the rescue craft . . . Our own craft are no good. We don't have anything in this country. Nothing! That's how it is.

SHOUTS: But do we have our own means or not? You just said . . .

PUTIN: No . . . We don't have the diving equipment that we needed. (Noise in the hall).

WOMAN: When will we get them out? Whether they are dead or alive. Answer me like a President should!

PUTIN: I'll tell you what I know . . .

A SHOUT FROM THE HALL: Will it take a year?

PUTIN: No, not a year . . .

ANOTHER MAN: They're deceiving us. They're deceiving us again.

WOMEN (WAILING): Where's my son? How much longer before I can see my
son? And now we have no money left . . .

PUTIN: As regards money . . .

SCREAMS FROM THE HALL: It's not about money, it's about our families!
When will they give us our children back? Don't you talk about money.
Who decided to stop the search? . . .

PUTIN: No one can reach the 8th compartment of the hull. If I could, I'd
climb down there myself . . .

A WOMAN (SOBBING): Tell us truthfully! We don't need money. We need
them alive. Then we'd have everything. Children would have their fathers,
wives their husbands. They trusted the government to save them. How
can't you understand that?

A MAN SHOUTS: Can't you save at least five of them? You bastards![95]

No Russian leader, before or since, had ever experienced a public
tongue-lashing like that. It lasted for nearly three hours. Andrei Kolesnikov, a reporter who had managed to get in, posing as a representative
of a Russian NGO, said later he feared that Putin would not get out
alive. 'There was such a heavy atmosphere – hatred, despair, pain, all
clotted together . . . I never felt anything like it in my entire life.'[96]

Despite the angry protestations that money was not the issue, in the
end it was all Putin could offer and all the bereaved families could hope
for. He told them that they would each receive ten years of an officer's
salary, equivalent to 26,000 US dollars, a large sum at that time, and
that they would be given new apartments in Moscow or St Petersburg –
which were regarded as the best places to live in Russia – or anywhere
else they wished, and free university education for their children. Much
of the remaining discussion was taken up with assurances that the aid
would not be held up by bureaucratic red tape, that unmarried women
whose partners had died would benefit like everyone else, and other
practical issues. Putin also promised that, contrary to the usual practice when ships were lost at sea, the wreck would be brought to the
surface and all the bodies recovered. It took a year and cost 130 million
dollars, but it was done.

When the meeting ended, shortly before midnight, the abscess had been lanced. More than what Putin had said, it was the simple fact that he had come to face them that helped. Western writers afterwards reproached him for failing to show empathy during the crisis, and it was true that he held his emotions in check, though not, as they claimed, because of his KGB training, but because that was the kind of person he was. Russians gave him credit for having belatedly done the right thing and by the end of the year his approval rating was back at the same level as it had been before the disaster.[97]

Nonetheless, it left scars. When the American journalist, Larry King, began an interview in September by asking, 'What happened with the submarine?', it took all Putin's self-control not to get up and walk out. 'One could read on his face at that moment the complete works of Dostoyevsky,' a Russian journalist said.[98]

'It sank,' he replied.[99]

The cause would not finally be confirmed until two years later.[100] It had nothing to do with a collision or a mine or a test of a new ultra-high-speed torpedo or any of the other theories that had been circulating. Hydrogen peroxide fuel – which most navies had abandoned because it is unstable – had leaked from a faulty seal on a dummy torpedo as it was being loaded for a test firing. The resulting explosion had killed everyone in the forward part of the submarine instantly. Two minutes and 14 seconds later, after the submarine had come to rest on the seafloor, seven more torpedoes exploded, triggering a shock wave measuring 4.2 on the Richter scale and felt as far away as Alaska. Twenty-three sailors in the rear compartments of the submarine survived for six or seven hours. But even before the navy realised that the Kursk was in difficulties and launched a search, everyone on board was dead.

To Putin, the whole episode had been a huge shock. He had trusted the military and they had lied to him.

He refused a rush to judgement. 'Firing someone . . . is the easiest thing to do,' he told the families at Vidyaevo. 'Maybe it would make people happy and they'd think I did the right thing. [But] if really someone is to blame, we should make the decision clear-sightedly on the basis of reliable information.'[101] The following March, Putin replaced the Defence Minister, Marshal Sergeyev, with his old colleague from St Petersburg, Sergei Ivanov, then serving as Secretary of the Security

Council.[102] In December, the Commander of the Northern Fleet, Admiral Vyacheslav Popov, his Chief of Staff and 12 other flag officers were fired.[103] Officially their departures had nothing to do with the *Kursk* disaster and most of them were found civilian sinecures to see them through to retirement. That was one of Putin's principles. Those he dismissed were moved sideways to an equivalent or lesser post. Nonetheless, it was the first time for many years that the armed forces' top brass had been punished for a fatal accident or, indeed, anything at all. Soon afterwards Klebanov was also demoted.

Putin learnt his lesson. Russia had indeed changed. So had people's expectations of the President. Public relations, as he had called it dismissively, were part of the job description.[104] For several years after the tragedy of the *Kursk*, whenever disaster struck – a heating shortage in the Russian Far East, a blizzard which killed four people in Sakhalin, floods in Siberia, the hijacking of a Russian plane in Turkey or bomb attacks in the Caucasus, all normally matters which the Prime Minister, not the President, would handle – he would take personal charge, setting up an Emergency Headquarters or flying out to the affected area himself.

The other major consequence of the sinking of the *Kursk* was the downfall of Boris Berezovsky.

Putin had been outraged by the media coverage. When some of the families at Vidyaevo had accused him of falsehoods, saying that they had seen television reports which showed that he was lying, he had flared up, launching a furious tirade against the broadcasters.[105] Certain people, he said, were 'trying to profit from this tragedy . . . [They] are trying to get political dividends.' These people had amassed fortunes; they had villas in France and Spain, registered under false names. Where had all that money come from? Although he mentioned no names, it was clear who he meant.

Berezovsky, Putin decided, was not just an enemy but a traitor.

He had explained the difference to Aleksei Venediktov, the editor of *Ekho Moskvy*, shortly after his return from Vidyaevo. He was in a black mood, Venediktov remembered. 'With enemies you fight,' Putin said. 'Then you conclude a truce, then a peace, and they become allies in another war . . . Then perhaps you fight them again. But always face to face. A traitor is a man who is always near you, but at the moment you are weak, or he thinks you are weak . . . he stabs you in the back. To them – no mercy!'[106]

A few days after that conversation, Putin attempted to persuade ORT's star presenter, Sergei Dorenko, who, a year earlier, had savaged Primakov and Luzhkov during the Duma elections, to break with Berezovsky and become 'part of [our] team'.[107] Dorenko refused and, that weekend, in his trademark attack-dog style, used his regular Saturday evening programme to broadcast images of the President, bronzed and smiling, relaxing at Sochi, alongside film of the harrowing search for survivors. Putin's claims that bad weather had held up the operation were juxtaposed with weather maps showing calm seas. Putin's explanation to the families at Vidyaevo, Dorenko said, had been a tissue of lies.[108]

The gloves were off.

Once again, Berezovsky had miscalculated. His error, Yumashev said later, was to think that he could use ORT to blackmail Putin.[109] He had failed to recognise that he was vulnerable because, although he decided the channel's editorial policy, he held only 49 per cent of the shares. The state held the rest.

After ORT's reports on the *Kursk*, Voloshin summoned Berezovsky to the Kremlin and told him that his control of the station had been terminated. 'We are telling [the staff] to take no further instructions from you. If they do so, they will be fired.'[110] Berezovsky said he wanted to hear that from Putin himself. The following morning, the President agreed to see him in Voloshin's office and told him: 'The show is over'.[111] They never met again.

A week later, Berezovsky announced that he had decided to divest himself of his shares in ORT. He would not sell to the state, he said – 'I will not submit to dictatorship' – but instead they would be offered to 'representatives of the creative intelligentsia'.[112] He then left on his private jet for his villa in Antibes. There he learnt that the Prosecutor General had revived a case against him – first launched when Primakov was Prime Minister, but afterwards abandoned – for allegedly defrauding the Russian airline, Aeroflot, of tens of millions of dollars through a network of Swiss companies which had creamed off its foreign currency revenue. In November, he moved to Britain and applied for political asylum. Like Gusinsky, he would never return.

ORT soldiered on for a few months more while Berezovsky tried unsuccessfully to set up a journalists' consortium to take over. In February 2001, he sold his ORT shares for 175 million US dollars to Sibneft, an oil company owned by his erstwhile business associate, Roman Abramovich.[113] The shareholding would undergo further mutations, but from the spring of 2001, ORT, or Channel One as it would later be called, was effectively under state control.[114]

Despite Putin's admonition to Berezovsky, the show was not quite over.

The oligarch still had majority ownership of another station, TV6, which focused on providing family entertainment. When Gazprom foreclosed on NTV in April 2001, Yevgeny Kiselyov and a number of other leading NTV journalists migrated to TV6, which, with Berezovsky's support, was transformed into an opposition channel. By the end of the year, TV6's ratings had doubled to 16 per cent of the national audience. That was more than Putin was willing to accept. This time, retribution was exacted not through Gazprom but through the oil company, Lukoil, owned by another pro-Kremlin oligarch, Vagit Alekperov. Lukoil, with 15 per cent of TV6's shares, used an obscure law, which was abrogated as soon as the case ended, to argue that the channel had been operating illegally because it lacked sufficient authorised capital. The liberal establishment, including not only Gorbachev but also Yeltsin, who normally kept silent about such matters, protested vigorously and in several Russian cities there were protest demonstrations.[115] But shortly after midnight on January 21, 2002, in the middle of a programme, the plug was pulled and TV6 was taken off the air.

That was still not the end of the story. The protests within Russia coupled with a wave of criticism abroad persuaded Putin to compromise. TV6 would close, but the journalists were allowed to start a new channel, financed by 12 business magnates who were close to the Kremlin, among them Abramovich; Oleg Deripaska, the Chairman of Rusal, the world's biggest aluminium producer; and Anatoly Chubais, who now headed the state electricity monopoly, UES. TVS, as the new station was called, went on the air in June 2002. Differences among the journalists, arguments among the sponsors and, above all, financial difficulties caused by the paucity of advertising revenue, doomed the project and, just over a year later, TVS stopped broadcasting.

That left the three main channels – RTR (renamed Rossiya), Channel One and NTV – all now owned by the state, with between 50 and 60 per cent of the national audience and a near monopoly on social and political reporting. For a time, TV Ren, another station partly owned by UES, continued to broadcast critical political reports, but in 2005, it too, fell into line.[116]

Putin was unrepentant. When students at Columbia University, during a visit to New York, took issue with him over infringements on freedom of speech in Russia, he shot back: 'We've never had freedom of speech in Russia, so I don't quite understand what there is to be infringed.'[117] That was an exaggeration, but not by very much. Even under Yeltsin, when there were fewer constraints than at any time before or since, there were limits which journalists knew they could not or did not dare to transgress. Apart from that brief period in the 1990s, the rest of Russian history, Soviet and tsarist, had been characterised by censorship so rigid as to make the restrictions Putin imposed seem mild.

That is not to minimise the backsliding that occurred in Putin's first term. It marked a significant step back from the free-wheeling anarchy of the early 1990s. But it needs to be seen in context.

To many in the West, it seemed that Russia was reverting to its totalitarian past. Yet such words must be used with care. In a totalitarian state, the government exercises *total* control over what its citizens may say or write or, in extreme cases, even think. Putin's Russia had become more authoritarian, less pluralistic, than Yeltsin's. As Voloshin put it, 'the degree of freedom was smaller . . . the degree of order, larger'.[118] But there was no comparison with Soviet practice in the 1970s and early '80s, let alone to a genuinely totalitarian state like China, where the media must follow to the letter the guidelines of the Central Committee's Propaganda Department about what must as well as what cannot be said.

That would slowly change. But at this stage of Putin's presidency, the liberal radio station, *Ekho Moskvy*, continued to broadcast stinging attacks on government policy. There were few restrictions on the print media and no attempt to control internet sites, which, unlike in China, were uncensored and became more and more popular among the young.

Aleksei Venediktov, the *Ekho Moskvy* editor, once said that if Putin so wished, 'he could close us down with his little finger'.[119] If he chose not to, it was partly because he recognised that Russian society needed safety valves and partly to reassure his Western partners of his democratic intentions. But more importantly it was because a degree of freedom – a degree which would change over the years and which Putin alone would determine – corresponded to the system he wished to build. The meaning of that enigmatic phrase in the Millennium Declaration, three and a half years earlier – 'The state must be there as much as is necessary, freedom should be there as much as is required' – was now clear. In Putin's view, the truly 'mass' media, the national TV channels, had to be in the state's hands. Other sources of information would be enough to provide the degree of freedom which, in his judgement, Russian society could reasonably be allowed to enjoy.

Four days before the *Kursk* sank, an explosion outside a stall in a pedestrian underpass in central Moscow, in which eight people died and more than 50 were injured, provided an unwelcome reminder that the war in faraway Chechnya was not yet over.[120]

Since military operations in the territory had been scaled down the previous April, the conflict had settled into a pattern of small-scale guerrilla attacks, punctuated by suicide bombings, mainly in Chechnya itself and the neighbouring republics. In that sense, the Moscow explosion was an outlier. Federal forces were in control of virtually the whole of Chechnya. The FSB chief, Nikolai Patrushev, estimated that only about 1,500 insurgents were still active, mainly in the mountainous regions in the South. In January 2001, Putin felt sufficiently confident to announce that regular army units, numbering some 40,000 men, would begin a phased withdrawal. Future operations would be carried out by Interior Ministry troops and the special services.

The ultimate goal was to make the Chechens themselves responsible for the territory's security. To that end, Kadyrov's position was strengthened and Putin pushed for a greater role for the Chechen police.[121] But there were enormous problems. The republic's institutions had been destroyed and much of the economy, or what was left of it, was in the hands of criminals. The whole of Chechnya's oil production, potentially well over a million tons a year – enough to finance the entire reconstruction effort – was either going up in smoke in oil well fires or being stolen and sold on the black market. It was Catch-22. Without peace and security, reconstruction was impossible. And until there was reconstruction, disaffected young men would continue to engage in banditry and smuggling and there would be no peace.

Each new atrocity committed by Russian troops, of which there were many, generated a fresh wave of hatred against the occupying forces and against Chechens perceived to be collaborating with them. Putin might insist till he was blue in the face that it was wrong to blame the Chechens as a nation for the jihad in their republic – 'Terrorists,' he said, 'have neither nationality nor religion'[122] – but that did not change the behaviour of the troops on the ground. Putin's own envoy, Abdul-Khakim Sultygov, reported: 'Nothing can control the military's actions . . . Nothing has changed the way the notorious "sweeps" [search and destroy operations] are being carried out. Robberies take place openly and people disappear without trace. Horrific things are still happening in Chechnya.'[123]

There were occasional glimmers of hope.

Putin approved exploratory talks with Akhmed Zakayev, representing the ousted Chechen President, Aslan Maskhadov – the first serious attempt at negotiations since the conflict began. After al-Qaeda's attacks on the World Trade Center and the Pentagon on September 11, 2001, Western governments' criticisms of Russian operations in Chechnya largely ceased. In April 2002, Khattab, the Saudi jihadi who was Basayev's second-in-command, died after opening a letter which the FSB had coated with a powerful neurotoxin.

But the mood was grim. According to one opinion poll, only 20 per cent of Russians thought Putin would succeed in Chechnya – a far cry from the overwhelming approval he had had when the war started.[124] It had become a different kind of war, one commentator said, 'a war that can go on for years, a war that everyone is tired of'.'[125]

A month after Khattab's poisoning, Basayev struck back with a car-bomb attack during a military parade at Kaspiisk, in Dagestan, in which 44 people died and more than 130 were injured. It was the first major attack outside Chechnya since a series of explosions at markets in the Stavropol region had killed more than 20 people a year earlier.

But the biggest blow was yet to come.

On the evening of October 23, 2002, a performance of *Nord-Ost*, 'North-East', a Russian musical about a love story between two orphaned children, whom fate brings together in the search for a doomed expedition to the Arctic, was under way at the Dubrovka Theatre, a late-Soviet modernist building in Moscow's southern suburbs. Billed as 'the first world-class Russian musical', with a budget of four million US dollars, it was said to be the most expensive theatre production in the country's history. It had been inspired by the Broadway productions of Andrew Lloyd-Webber's *Cats* and *The Phantom of the Opera* and had been playing to packed houses for more than a year.

Shortly after the intermission, as the hero, newly qualified as an air force pilot, was celebrating with his comrades, a masked man entered from stage left.[126] Even when he let off a volley from his Kalashnikov, most of the audience assumed it was part of the plot. Moments later, however, the theatre was swarming with armed men. There were young women, too, wearing black hijabs, with suicide belts round their waists – 'black widows', as they were called, who had taken a vow of vengeance after their husbands or siblings had died at the hands of Russian troops. They fixed explosives to the columns around the hall and attached Chechen flags to the stage curtain and a balcony, along with a black banner, proclaiming in Arabic: 'There is no God but Allah, and Mohammed is his Prophet'.

Russia must end the war in Chechnya, they said. Otherwise they would blow up the theatre and everyone in it would die.

Putin announced that he was cancelling visits to Germany, Portugal and Mexico, on which he was to have set out the following morning, and promised that the authorities' first priority would be to free the hostages and to assure their safety 'as much as possible'.[127] At the time, that qualification was not widely noted. Its meaning would become clear later.

The hostage-takers, 22 men and 19 women, were led by a 25-year-old jihadi, Movsar Barayev, whose uncle, one of the most feared of the Chechen rebel commanders, had been killed that summer. 'I swear to God,' Barayev said in an interview released shortly after the siege began, 'we love death more than you love life'.[128] No compromise was possible, he maintained. 'Our aim is not to stay alive. It is to force Russian troops out of Chechnya.'[129]

Nonetheless, nearly 200 of the 900 or so hostages, including children, Muslims and some of the foreigners present, were eventually released or managed to escape, and Barayev and his deputies agreed to receive a succession of intermediaries who promised to convey messages to the Kremlin. One of the leaders of the liberal Union of Right Forces, Irina Khakamada, a tall, slim woman who was a fixture on the covers of Russian glamour magazines, was among the first to be allowed through. She told Voloshin afterwards that she found Barayev's men less fanatical and less determined to blow themselves up than they had made out. An eclectic assortment of Russian politicians and celebrities followed, some of whom had a similar impression. They included Grigory Yavlinsky of Yabloko; Iosif Kobzon, a crooner whom Russians compared to Frank Sinatra, both for his singing style and his suspected ties to organised crime; and Anna Politkovskaya, a *Novaya gazeta* correspondent whose sympathetic reporting of the Chechens' struggle had made her one of the Kremlin's bêtes noires.

Conditions in the theatre were deteriorating. There was little food or drink. After two hostages escaped, the remainder were barred from using the lavatories and told instead to relieve themselves in the orchestra pit, men on one side, women on the other. By the evening of the third day, it was clear that a denouement of some kind was approaching.

At that point, the Kremlin sent a message that Putin's plenipoten-tiary in the Caucasus, General Viktor Kazantsev, was flying to Moscow and would open negotiations next morning. 'Everything is going to be alright,' Barayev told the hostages. 'We are not going to kill you if you stay quiet.'[130]

It was all an elaborate charade.

Putin's assurance that the top priority was to save the hostages, the endless succession of intermediaries, the message that Kazantsev was on his way to start talks, were a ploy to make the hostage-takers believe that the Kremlin might eventually agree to some of their demands and thus gain time to prepare an assault. Putin had never, for an instant, intended to negotiate. To compromise, he argued, would simply encourage further outrages. What was happening at the Dubrovka Theatre was the consequence of 'the weakness of the state and the inconsistency of its actions' in the past – a reference to the events at the hospital in Budyonnovsk in 1995, when Yeltsin had allowed the terror-ists to go free to save the lives of the surviving hostages. There would be no repetition of that on Putin's watch. 'I want to stress,' he told the cabinet, 'that Russia will not enter into any agreement with terrorists and will not yield to any blackmail.'[131]

At 5 a.m. the following day, Russian special forces began pumping a powerful anaesthetic into the theatre's air-conditioning system. Minutes later, they stormed the building. The hostage-takers were systemati-cally killed, some in shoot-outs but most in cold blood. 'When a woman is wearing two kilograms of plastic explosives,' one officer explained, 'there is no other way to disarm her.'[132] But it also sent a message. 'The only good signal to terrorists,' Putin had said after the massacre at Kaspiisk, 'is a bullet in the head.'[133]

From the standpoint of the Kremlin, the military operation went flawlessly. It had been meticulously planned. But luck was also on the authorities' side. Several minutes elapsed before the gas took effect, more than enough time for the terrorists to detonate the high explosives with which the building was packed. Apparently taken by surprise, they made no attempt to do so.[134]

Once the terrorists had been neutralised, however, the rescue effort descended into chaos. No one had given any thought to what should happen next. The *Washington Post*'s Moscow correspondents, Peter Baker and Susan Glasser, watched from across the street:

> Unsure what to do, [the] commandos . . . began picking up the unconscious bodies of the hostages and hauling them out of the building into the damp early-morning air. Medical personnel were nowhere to be found . . . We could see bodies being stacked up like so much cordwood. Finally, around 7 a.m., [two hours after the operation had started], the first of dozens of ambulances raced up to the theatre. [The] authorities commandeered buses and began piling bodies on board . . . Many were still unconscious or dying, choking on their own tongues or vomit . . . All the faces of the hostages looked alike, bluish with distorted features and strangely bared teeth . . . Medics and rescue workers showed up at the scene . . . without being informed what chemical had been used, without being given instructions how to revive people before they succumbed . . .[135]

Six people had been killed by the terrorists during the siege. One hundred and twenty-five lost their lives during the rescue. Not only had the authorities refused to reveal the nature of the anaesthetic gas, which was a derivative of fentanyl, but there had been a total lack of coordination between the FSB and the rescue services. Almost all those who died could have been saved had medics been on hand immediately after the assault, properly briefed on how to treat them and equipped with breathing tubes to stop them choking to death.

In Russia, for centuries, the interests of the state have come first, the lives of the people second.[136] But the way the Dubrovka siege was handled also reflected Putin's priorities. His goal was to show the insurgents – not only their leader, Shamil Basayev, but also the rank and file who served as cannon fodder – that such attacks would achieve nothing. If, in the process, there was collateral damage, that was unfortunate but secondary. 'We could not save everyone. Please forgive us,' Putin told the Russian people in a broadcast that night. 'But we proved that Russia cannot be brought to its knees.' The terrorists were fighting a losing battle, he said. 'They must be defeated and they will be defeated . . . They have no future. We do.'[137]

The bloodshed at the Dubrovka theatre marked a turning point for both sides.

To Basayev and his jihadist supporters, it was the beginning of a Chechen version of the Palestinian intifada. The Dubrovka had not been targeted by chance. The audience for *Nord-Ost* was largely made up of the nascent middle classes, comfortably off and indifferent to the horrors being perpetrated by Russian troops in the Caucasus. Basayev's goal was to make them realise that they would not be safe as long as the war continued, just as the intifada was an attempt to make Israelis understand the desperation of the Palestinians.

To Putin, it was proof that the army's strategy in Chechnya was failing. It was 'behaving like a bull in a china shop', he admitted, and the security 'sweeps' against which Sultygov had railed were 'harmful and inadmissible'.[138] Far from rooting out the insurgents, the violence against peaceable villagers was winning the jihadis new recruits. Large-scale operations must stop in favour of 'pinpoint, targeted attacks'. The troop withdrawals, which he had announced in January, would be halted, but the army must remain in its barracks instead of marauding through the countryside.[139] There would be a renewed drive for Chechenisation, with the Chechen police encouraged to play the leading role in efforts to provide security in the villages and towns.

It was a long overdue recognition of realities. The difficulty was that the generals, who were to implement this new approach, had neither the trained professionals, nor the specialised weaponry, nor, above all, the mindset to understand how 'pinpoint, targeted attacks' might be carried out. The Russian High Command had spent their careers thinking about large-scale conventional conflicts with the West, fighting war games and conducting military exercises because actual fighting never took place. Very few had ever led troops in combat and even fewer had any inkling of what effective anti-guerrilla tactics might look like.

The new strategy was accompanied by a much tougher attitude towards the ousted Chechen government and its sympathisers in the West. The talks with Zakayev had hit a dead end and would not be resumed. 'Those who choose Maskhadov, choose war,' Putin declared. 'All such people, wherever they are, inside Russia or outside, will be treated as accomplices of terrorists.' As for people who, 'following the tenacious European tradition of appeasement', urged Russia to negotiate with murderers, 'I would like to suggest that they set us an example and sit down to negotiate with bin Laden and Mullah Omar.'[140]

The harshness of the rebuke was telling. Putin had earlier cancelled a visit to Denmark because Zakayev and other Chechen separatists had been invited to a conference there, and he had insisted that the annual European Union–Russia summit be moved from Copenhagen to Brussels. The summit itself produced a bland statement pledging joint action against international terrorism, but at a news conference afterwards, Putin's continuing frustration with the West's refusal to understand what Russia was up against in Chechnya finally boiled over.

The trigger was a question from a correspondent from the French newspaper, *Le Monde*, who condemned the Russian army's tactics. Putin responded that the jihad in Chechnya was part of a global threat which put everyone in danger:

> Even if you decide to become a Muslim, it won't save you, because in their view traditional Islam is also hostile to their goals. If you want to become an Islamic radical and are ready to be circumcised, I will invite you to Moscow. We are a multi-faith country and we have specialists who can do that. I will recommend that you have the operation done in such a way that nothing will ever grow again.[141]

As the interpreter stopped in embarrassment, the Russian delegation sniggered and the room fell silent.

Amid the shocked headlines prompted by that sally, two much more significant moves, which would guide Russian policy in Chechnya for the next decade or more, passed almost unnoticed. The first was a

decision to speed up political reform in the republic and give full backing to Akhmad Kadyrov as the best, perhaps the only, hope of restoring
stability there.[142] The second was an internal directive, authorising
the security services to hunt down suspected terrorists not only inside
Russia but also abroad.[143]

In March 2003, a referendum was held to decide Chechnya's future
status. Almost 90 per cent of eligible voters were said to have taken
part – a near miraculous figure in a territory where a war was in progress, which showed, if nothing else, that Kadyrov was able to get out
the vote, or at least make it appear that he had – of whom 96 per cent
voted in favour of Chechnya remaining part of Russia. After the results
were ratified, Kadyrov was named acting President, pending elections
that autumn, and the Kremlin launched a public relations offensive to
convince Chechens that life in the republic would soon start returning
to normal.

There were a few, largely symbolic, troop withdrawals. The number
of roadblocks and checkpoints, which served mainly to allow Russian
soldiers to extort bribes, was reduced. 280,000 people whose homes
had been destroyed in the fighting were promised compensation.

It was time, Putin declared, for the people of Chechnya 'to cease to
live in fear, to cease to fear a knock at the door in the night and to hide
from so-called mopping up operations'.[144] However, it was one thing to
call for the situation to be 'normalised', quite another to make it happen. Sweeps or 'cleansing operations', as the army now called them,
when soldiers surrounded a village and took away the young men for
interrogation, became less common. Instead, men wearing camouflage uniform, using armoured personnel carriers, made targeted raids,
usually at night, on the homes of suspects, who were never seen again.

It was not a great improvement. According to official figures, some
2,000 young men had 'disappeared' in this way – tortured to death for
information they did not have and buried in mass graves – but the real
number was far higher.[145] At first it was thought that the army was
responsible but later there were strong indications that Chechen death
squads were involved.[146] Kadyrov's thuggish younger son, Ramzan,
had assembled a personal security force of a thousand men, made up
largely of rebels who had surrendered, who quickly acquired a horrific
reputation for sadistic violence.[147]

As the Kadyrovs consolidated their authority in Chechnya, Basayev and his followers responded asymmetrically, taking their struggle to other parts of Russia.

In July, 2003, two 'black widows', wearing suicide belts blew themselves up at a rock concert at Tushino, in the north-western suburbs of Moscow, killing 15 people. Another attack in the capital was foiled when a young woman who claimed she had been forced by male relatives to carry out a suicide bombing decided not to go through with it.[148]

Meanwhile the Kremlin tried to implement the other strand of Putin's strategy, by putting pressure on Chechen leaders in exile. Requests to Western countries to extradite Zakayev and other members of Maskhadov's government were rebuffed and there was little that Moscow could do about it. But when a request to Qatar to extradite the former Chechen President, Zelimkhan Yandarbiyev, a close ally of Shamil Basayev, was also rejected, Putin decided to act. On February 13, 2004, as Yandarbiyev was returning from Friday prayers in the Qatari capital, Doha, a bomb attached to the chassis of his jeep exploded, killing him and his two bodyguards and critically injuring his thirteen-year-old son. Qatari investigators said that two GRU officers had carried out the attack, acting on instructions from the Defence Minister, Sergei Ivanov. They were initially sentenced to life imprisonment but, a few months later, following discreet contacts between Putin and the Emir of Qatar, were released into Russian custody and flown to Moscow, where they received a red-carpet welcome. It was the first time on Putin's watch that the security services had been ordered to carry out an assassination abroad. It would not be the last.

Normalcy, when applied to Chechnya, was a relative term.

Putin insisted that progress was being made. 'The changes,' he maintained, 'are invisible only to those who do not wish to see them.'[149] Up to a point that was true: basic services in many parts of Chechnya were slowly being restored.[150] But when he flew in a helicopter over the bombed-out ruins of Grozny, even he was shocked to see how much remained to be done. The city, he admitted, still looked like a war zone.[151]

Seven candidates stood in the election for the Chechen presidency, which took place on Sunday, October 5, 2003. Campaigning was minimal. A Russian journalist reported: 'It's not a matter of how many campaign staff a candidate can field, but of how many armed men he can deploy to protect them.' At the few rallies which were held, bodyguards often outnumbered participants. The election headquarters of one of Kadyrov's rivals was 'like a besieged fortress, surrounded by concrete blocks. The windows are protected with sandbags and a guard with a machine gun is standing at the gate.'[152]

Like the referendum, six months earlier, the election was a masquerade. The three candidates who could have posed a challenge to Kadyrov were either pressured to withdraw or had their registration invalidated by compliant judges.[153] *Ekho Moskvy* said it would announce the results on the eve of Election Day since there was clearly no need to wait for people actually to cast their votes.[154] With much help from the stuffing of ballot boxes, the turnout this time reached 87 per cent, and Akhmad Kadyrov was proclaimed the winner with 81 per cent of the vote.[155]

However, the violence continued unabated.

Two months later, 80 people died when a suicide bomber drove a truck packed with a ton of high explosive into the government headquarters in Grozny, reducing the building to a smouldering ruin.[156] The following February, an explosion on board a metro train in southern Moscow killed 40 people.[157]

Then, on May 9, 2004, as Kadyrov was attending an open-air concert in the public stadium at Grozny on Victory Day, commemorating the end of the Second World War, a huge explosion demolished part of the VIP stand where he was seated, killing him and five others. It was discovered later that a mine had been hidden by building workers, probably months before, inside one of the ferro-concrete supporting pillars. That Kadyrov was present that day was pure chance. He had been expected to review a military parade outside the city and had changed his plans at the last moment.[158]

For Putin, it was a devastating blow. Kadyrov had been the one man capable of getting the republic under control.

The Russian press was uniformly pessimistic. *Moskovsky komsomolets* called it 'the final collapse of any hope that a settlement can be reached' and 'a terrible blow to Putin's pride'.[159] *Novye izvestia* wrote that four years of effort had been buried.[160] To the Western media, the assassination was proof that Putin's policy had been wrong all along, a purely military solution would never succeed and negotiations with the separatists were the only possible way forward.

Instead, Putin doubled down on his existing strategy. In the short term, Kadyrov had no obvious replacement. His son, Ramzan, was 27, and under the Chechen constitution would not be eligible for the presidency until he reached the age of 30. Putin could have changed that, but chose not to, partly because the jurist in him, no matter how the law might be twisted in practice, was reluctant to bring in special legislation, and partly to see how the young man would act. Ramzan was in Moscow when his father was killed and the President received him a few hours later. Evidently Putin decided that he had the stuff to become a leader, for the following day it was announced that he had been appointed Chechnya's first deputy Prime Minister. For the next two years, the republic would be ruled by an uneasy duumvirate consisting of Kadyrov's former Interior Minister, Alu Alkhanov, who was elected President at the end of August, and Ramzan, who answered only to Putin and acted as de facto Prime Minister, a post to which he was formally promoted 18 months later.

After the assassination of Akhmad Kadyrov, the insurgents changed their tactics. In neighbouring Ingushetia, one night towards the end of June, some 200 Ingush and Chechen combatants staged coordinated attacks on police stations, border guard barracks and munitions depots in the capital, Nazran, and several other towns, killing 90 people and seizing 1,500 pieces of weaponry.[161] The following month, insurgents attacked Avtury, 15 miles south-west of Grozny, leaving 20 people dead. In August, the same scenario played out in Grozny itself. At nightfall, several hundred militants in camouflage uniform set up checkpoints, executing anyone they suspected of being linked to the security forces. Fifty-eight people were killed.

On the evening of August 24, the 'black widows' struck again. Two women boarded internal flights at Moscow's Domodedovo Airport. The ground staff were bribed not to check their IDs. Both planes exploded in mid air and 89 passengers and crew were killed. It was the first time Chechen rebels had targeted passenger aircraft.

The following week, another suicide bomber killed ten people by blowing herself up at a metro station in the northern suburbs of Moscow.

But those attacks paled into insignificance beside the tragedy which unfolded at Beslan, a sleepy provincial town with tree-lined streets, home to some 35,000 people, 60 miles east of Grozny in the republic of North Ossetia.

Wednesday, September 1st, was the beginning of the school year, known as 'First Bell Day' when Putin was a child, but now called more prosaically the 'Day of Knowledge'. Nearly 800 children, their teachers and hundreds of parents gathered at School No. 1, a complex of one- and two-storey nineteenth-century red-brick buildings on the town's main street.[162] Shortly after 9 a.m., as the opening ceremony was about to begin, there was a loud popping noise. The gym teacher, Aleksandr Tsagolov, thought at first that some of the balloons, decorating the courtyard, had burst. But then the sound resumed, much closer, and he realised it was gunfire. Masked men in camouflage uniform appeared from nowhere and, firing volleys into the air, began pushing everybody inside. A military truck sped up with another group, armed with AK-47s. In the confusion, about fifty people, most of them children, managed to escape. But more than a thousand others were herded into the school gymnasium.

Several parents had been killed during the initial attack. The terrorists dragged in one of the bodies and dumped it on the floor, leaving a trail of blood, to dispel any doubt that they were in earnest. One of their number then called for silence and announced that the hostages would be held prisoner until Putin agreed to withdraw the Russian army from Chechnya. In the hubbub that followed, one of the parents stood up and tried to calm the children, speaking in the local language, Ossetian. 'Speak Russian,' he was told. When he continued, a gunman put a pistol to his head and shot him dead, leaving his body where it fell, in front of his two young sons.

The attack on the school, like the hostage-taking at Dubrovka, had been masterminded by Shamil Basayev.[163] Beslan had been chosen because it was a soft target – the terrorists had been able to bribe their way through police checkpoints, pretending to be smugglers – and because North Ossetia and its neighbour, Ingushetia, had a long-standing territorial dispute, in which, 12 years earlier, several hundred people had died.[164] The Ossetians were Christians, not Muslims, and Basayev may have hoped to ignite ethnic and religious strife which would fuel a wider conflict.[165]

Putin was in Sochi when the news broke. That morning he had told a group of Turkish journalists that the situation in Chechnya was 'getting back to normal'.[166]

He flew immediately to Moscow. Patrushev and the Interior

Minister met him at the airport. The mood was grim. It was the Dubrovka scenario playing out all over again, but this time with children as hostages. As before, Putin announced publicly that the first priority was to save the lives of the hostages.[167] In private, he ruled out any compromise. That night, units of the FSB's elite Alpha force were flown to Beslan to prepare to storm the building.

The terrorists at Beslan were far more ruthless than those who had seized the theatre in Moscow. On the first day they ordered 20 or so of the strongest looking male hostages to help them build barricades. When the work was completed, they were taken to a second-floor classroom, where they were executed and the bodies thrown out of a window. The hostages had no food or water and were reduced to drinking urine – their own or each other's – to relieve their thirst. Among their captors were two women, draped in black, with explosives belts around their waists. The gym coach, Tsagolov, remembered one of them looking like 'death walking round with a scythe'. Whenever the small children cried, she put a pistol to their heads. On the second day, one of the terrorists' wives was brought to the school and called her husband on his mobile phone. When she pleaded with him to spare the children, he asked to speak to the FSB officer with her. 'Kill her,' he said, 'and kill my three kids, too.'

The only negotiator the hostage-takers would talk to was the former Ingushetian President, Ruslan Aushev, a hero of the Afghan war, who was widely respected in the region. He was allowed to bring out twelve nursing mothers and their babies. A thirteenth refused to leave her other children behind, so Aushev brought out her infant himself. By then, conditions were deteriorating fast. The gym was 'like a steam bath,' he said later. 'The children were almost naked . . . They had had nothing to eat for two days.' All that night negotiations continued to allow the delivery of food and water, but no agreement was reached.

The denouement came without warning shortly after 1 p.m. on the third day. The terrorists had agreed to let a team of medics approach the building to retrieve the bodies of hostages who had been killed. As they began work, shooting broke out, followed by two loud explosions in the gymnasium, the second of which blew a huge hole in one of the walls. Scores of children were killed instantly and many others severely injured.

It was never established exactly what had caused the blasts. The building had been wired with explosives, some attached to a 'dead man switch' which, if released, would detonate them. It is equally possible that a Russian army unit opened fire. The military had brought in weapons that had no place in a counter-terrorist operation, including T-72 tanks and 'Shmel' rocket-assisted flamethrowers, which produced a blast as powerful as that of a 155 mm artillery shell. Both were used in the ensuing firefight. But, if the initial explosions were caused by the government side, the special forces were as much taken by surprise as everyone else. Amid the pandemonium that followed, Alpha unit commandos charged forward without even having time to put on their bulletproof vests, protecting the children with their bodies as they helped them out of the burning building, often at the cost of their own lives. Ten special forces officers died, including all three unit commanders, and 30 were seriously wounded.[168]

The firefight lasted almost six hours, with an intensity which even veterans of the Afghan war had not seen before. By the time it ended, 32 terrorists had been killed. Another was beaten to death by an enraged mob of parents. One man was captured alive and later sentenced to life imprisonment. Others almost certainly escaped.

The government had learnt from what had happened at Dubrovka and had flown in field hospitals, which saved many lives. Nonetheless, 335 hostages died, including 186 children, killed either by the hostage-takers or when the building was stormed. Given the disorganisation of the final assault, it was something of a miracle that the toll was not still higher.

In the early hours of the following morning, Putin flew to North Ossetia to visit the injured. He promised later to receive the members of the special forces who had participated in the operation. But there would be no meeting with the victims' families.[169] None of them knew he had even been there until after he had left. Partly it was to avoid a repetition of what had happened at Vidyaevo after the sinking of the *Kursk*. But it was also because, for the government, the tragedy at Beslan was a monumental failure. The less publicity it was given, the better.

That evening, for the first time since the crisis began, Putin appeared on television to address the Russian people.[170]

The key section was quite brief. 'We showed weakness,' he said, 'and the weak get beaten.' It was the same argument that he had made after Dubrovka. Russia was paying the price for the concessions made to Chechen fighters by Yeltsin's government in the 1990s, which had made them believe that if they were ruthless enough, Moscow would always buckle and compromise.

The root cause of the present troubles, Putin insisted, had been the break-up of the Soviet Union, which had unleashed ethnic tensions previously held in check by what he described as 'the ruling ideology' – a notably more euphemistic formulation than he had used ten years earlier, when he had spoken of the country being held together by barbed wire. Those divisions, he went on, were being exploited by international terrorism, which had declared war on Russia. Nowhere in his speech did he mention Chechnya or show any sign of recognition that the spiral of violence had been fuelled by his own aggressive tactics.

In the event, the massacre of the children at Beslan turned out to be Basayev's swansong. The outpouring of revulsion, both in the West and in the Muslim world, persuaded the Chechen leaders that such actions harmed their cause. 'A bigger blow could not have been dealt to us,' one rebel official said. 'People around the world will think that Chechens are beasts and monsters if they could attack children.'[171] No less damaging, it cost them public support in Chechnya as well. In the spring of 2005, after the separatist President, Aslan Maskhadov, was killed, his successor, Abdul-Halim Sadulayev, called for an end to suicide bombings, hostage-taking and attacks on civilians. It was more important, he said, for the peoples of Chechnya and the other Muslim republics in the North Caucasus to direct their energies against military targets. A year later, Basayev died in Ingushetia when a mine exploded as he was checking a consignment of weapons. It was never established whether the explosion was an accident or whether, as the FSB claimed, it was triggered by the special services by remote control.

The attacks at the Dubrovka Theatre and at Beslan led directly to a further clampdown on the media.

During the stand-off at the theatre, journalists had been allowed considerable latitude. They were permitted to cross police lines, interview the hostage-takers and broadcast live as the crisis developed. After Gusinsky's departure from NTV, Gazprom had appointed a Russian-American financier, Boris Jordan, as the station's managing director, who had tried to maintain a degree of independence. It had been a delicate balancing act. Jordan was American enough to know what a free press should look like, but not quite Russian enough to know the limits of what he could do. As a colleague put it, he 'didn't fully understand that in Russia, if you don't listen to the Kremlin, you won't be allowed to work.'[172]

The crunch came when the theatre was stormed. The Press Minister, Mikhail Lesin, had asked NTV and the other channels to shut down their transmissions temporarily for 'national security reasons'. At 5.45 a.m., a young NTV reporter at the theatre saw special forces arriving and sent word that he wanted to go live. The engineer in the control room, who had not been told of the ban, switched him through and he began broadcasting his report.

Putin, who was monitoring the operation from the Kremlin, was furious. 'It could have caused a huge tragedy,' he told a conference of media executives later. 'Why was that done? It's clear and you know it full well. To boost the channel's rating, to raise its capitalisation and ultimately to earn money. Making money is fine. But it can't be done . . . with the blood of our citizens.'[173]

That was unfair. It had not been a deliberate breach and no one had died because of it. But three months later, Jordan was fired, officially because of a change of 'economic strategy', and a more compliant leadership installed.[174]

His departure was typical of the way Putin dealt with the media. Publicly he insisted that 'a free press is the most important guarantor of our country's democratic course'.[175] If the government brought pressure to bear, it was never for their reporting. There were always 'technical' or 'economic' reasons, or the Prosecutor's Office, which was 'completely independent', believed that they had broken the law.[176] Yevgeny Kiselyov, the former NTV presenter, wrote perceptively: 'His style is to unleash a war and then step aside . . . Putin unleashed the war against NTV and now he pretends to have nothing to do with it.'[177]

It was not just a matter of leaving no fingerprints. Remaining aloof meant that he could intervene and accuse others of having gone too far, playing the traditional role of the good tsar surrounded by bad boyars, a staple of Russian folk tales since the days of Ivan the Terrible. He did so that autumn, when the Duma proposed a sweeping new media law which would give the authorities discretion to censor almost any reporting and ban any publication which disseminated 'extremist views' during public emergencies. Putin himself had floated the idea.[178] But after an outcry, he vetoed it and a watered-down version was approved.

The Dubrovka siege had been a pretext for a crackdown that would have come anyway. Putin's spokesman, Sergei Yastrzhembsky, had warned weeks earlier that what he called 'the bacchanalia of press freedom in Russia' was coming to an end.[179]

By the time the Beslan tragedy occurred, the media were already on a much tighter leash. The last of the privately owned national TV channels, TVS, had ceased broadcasting. In Chechnya, independent reporting, without a military escort, had been banned.[180] When Anna Politkovskaya and Andrei Babitsky, the two journalists who had most strongly resisted Kremlin control, set out for Beslan, both were stopped en route. Babitsky was detained by police for 'hooliganism' as he was about to leave Moscow. Politkovskaya was taken ill during her flight to the Caucasus, apparently after drinking poisoned tea, and spent the siege in hospital.[181] In both cases, the FSB had acted pre-emptively. Not because Putin had ordered it to do so: he did not need to. The use of extra-judicial measures to restrain overly inquisitive reporters had become standard operating procedure.

There had been other changes, too. At Dubrovka, the Kremlin had lied after the siege was over, claiming that most of the dead were victims not of the fentanyl derivative which had been pumped into the building but of heart attacks and pre-existing conditions. At Beslan, officials lied from the outset, claiming for days that there were only a hundred hostages when the true figure was over a thousand,[182] and insisting that the hostage-takers included Arabs and, in one version, an African, in order to bolster the official narrative that the attack was the work not of Chechens but of international terrorists linked to al-Qaeda.[183]

Even more striking than the lies themselves was the way the media kept broadcasting them although the journalists on the spot knew that they were untrue. Self-censorship of that kind was new in Putin's Russia. When the final assault began, BBC World and CNN broke into their normal programmes and went over to Beslan live. Russian television did not.[184]

For the first time, the restrictive new climate was felt by the printed

press, too. After *Izvestia* published on its front page harrowing photographs of distraught parents clutching injured children, the editor,
Raf Shakirov, was fired.[185] Officially that had nothing to do with Putin.
Izvestia was owned by a pro-Kremlin oligarch. Unofficially it was
explained that by publishing graphic images of the horrors that the
terrorists had inflicted, Shakirov, whether intentionally or not, had
abetted their cause.[186] Other newspapers had given the authorities a
far harder time than *Izvestia* without suffering retribution. But they
did not publish pictures. Verbal criticism was tolerated. Photographs
of martyred children whom the government had failed to protect
were not.

In one sense, the Russian press coverage of Beslan was a reminder
that the rules were still very different from what they had been in
Soviet times. *Novaya gazeta* accused the security services of being 'ineffective, unprofessional, demoralised and thoroughly corrupt'.[187] They
lie to us, fumed *Moskovsky komsomolets*. 'They lie so much it makes
your head spin. The last five terrorist attacks have been one long unin-
terrupted stream of lies.' Yet, in important ways, after Beslan, the
media were cowed. Editors now knew that there were no-go areas,
which, if touched, might get them fired or their newspapers closed
down. What those areas were was never formally set out. It was left
to each newspaper to judge what Putin would accept and what he
would not.

The attack at Beslan had other far-reaching consequences.

The day after the siege ended, Putin said it had shown that Russia's
political system required adjustment. 'Measures must be taken to
strengthen the country's unity.'[188] A week later, he spelt out what that
meant at a meeting with the heads of all the regions and republics.[189]
To strengthen the 'executive power vertical', he told them, governors
would no longer be elected but appointed. He would nominate candidates and the regional parliaments would be asked to confirm them.

On the face of it, the change made little difference. It was rare for a
governor to be elected against the Kremlin's wishes. But now they
were directly dependent on the President, rather than the electorate in
their regions, which eroded their legitimacy and the autonomy they
had previously enjoyed.

It was not a total surprise. 'Governors should be professionals,'

Putin had complained that summer, 'not just people who have a loud voice'.[190] But he had promised so often that the system of gubernatorial elections would not be altered that he needed a convincing reason to go back on his word. Beslan gave him the pretext he was looking for.

The other change he announced was even more far-reaching.

The Duma had until then consisted of 225 members from single-member constituencies and an equal number elected from party lists by proportional representation. Starting from the next election, Putin said, the single-member constituencies would be abolished and all 450 deputies elected from party lists. This would strengthen the role of the national parties, which should become 'one of the mechanisms ensuring dialogue and cooperation between society and the state'. That was something Putin had been pressing for ever since he had complained to Bill Clinton in 1999 that, in Russia, people voted for personalities, not for programmes or ideas.[191] But his concept of the role that a political party should play was not quite the same as in a Western democracy. In Putin's scheme of things, a party was a transmission belt – an idea derived from his courses in Marxism–Leninism when he had been a student – which marshalled its supporters behind a political programme within parameters set by the state.[192] Abolishing single-member constituencies, which might elect maverick deputies, impervious to party rules, would make parliamentary democracy easier to control.

Russian liberals had no doubt that control was Putin's objective. Olga Kryshtanovskaya, a leading sociologist at the Academy of Sciences, warned: 'On the one hand, . . . there is talk of the importance of a multiparty system, but under cover of this story, the bureaucratic hierarchy is being strengthened and the numbers of state overseers are growing.'[193] Putin himself acknowledged: 'we cannot and must not live in as carefree a manner as we did before.'[194]

The result was there for all to see. By the end of 2004, both the media and the regional administrations had, to all intents and purposes, been subdued. But there remained one potential source of opposition which was not yet fully under the Kremlin's control. Putin was in the process of dealing with that, too.

The new rules governing the relations between business and politics in Russia, which Putin had set out in July 2000, had in the main been observed. If any of the magnates had been tempted to circumvent them, the persecution of Gusinsky and Berezovsky had made them think again. Some of the lesser fry – those who were seriously wealthy but not quite billionaires – moved their money and families abroad. But the bigger players all knuckled under.

All, that is, except one.

Mikhail Khodorkovsky was the richest man in Russia, with an estimated net worth of 15 billion US dollars. Short and solidly built, ten years younger than Putin, he had close-cropped black hair beginning to grey and, behind rimless spectacles, a gaze whose intensity gave him the appearance of a youthful nineteenth-century anarchist. He had started in business during *perestroika* in the 1980s, ostensibly on behalf of the Komsomol, of which he was a junior official, to raise funds to make up for the shortfall in dues as young people lost interest and the membership declined. An import–export cooperative followed, then a bank. Finally, in 1995, Khodorkovsky acquired a 78 per cent stake in Yukos, then the country's second-largest oil producer, in one of the so-called 'loans-for-shares' auctions, in which Yeltsin had pledged state-owned enterprises as collateral for cash advances to plug the budget deficit and pay wages arrears before the 1996 presidential election.

Like all the 'loans-for-shares' deals, Khodorkovsky's acquisition was controversial. He paid 309 million US dollars for a firm which not long after was worth several billion. It was also true, however, that, given the political and economic uncertainties of Russia in the mid 1990s, any investment was a huge gamble. Had Yeltsin lost the election six months later, the company might have been declared forfeit. But Yeltsin won and Yukos prospered because Khodorkovsky, an iron-willed workaholic, reinvested the company's profits in new technology and infrastructure and hired Western consultants, including McKinsey and Price Waterhouse, to reform the management structure and introduce modern accounting practices. Habitual drunkards were fired – an unheard-of measure in the Russian oil business – and production costs were reduced by two thirds.

Yukos soon acquired a reputation as a well-run company espousing Western principles of business practice. But there was another side, too. Although there was never any proof of who was responsible, a number of businessmen and officials who tried to block Yukos's expansion in the 1990s ended up dead.[195] Khodorkovsky later described those years as being a time of 'primary capital accumulation . . . If you conducted yourself too much in a western manner, you were simply torn to pieces and forgotten.'[196] It was the same justification that officials in St Petersburg had used to explain the financial chicanery in the city when Sobchak had been mayor.

After the financial crash in 1998, Khodorkovsky's foreign partners discovered what 'not conducting yourself in a Western manner' meant. He defaulted on 236 million US dollars of loans from British, German and Japanese banks and impudently thumbed his nose at them when they tried to seize the Yukos shares which he had pledged as collateral.

By 2001, oil prices had risen, Yukos was once again flourishing and the dispute with his creditors had been smoothed over. That year, Khodorkovsky established the Open Russia Foundation, modelled on George Soros's Open Society Institute, with Henry Kissinger and Lord (Jacob) Rothschild among its board members, to promote the development of civil society in Russia. Although philanthropy was the Foundation's stated goal and Khodorkovsky spent millions of dollars funding educational and youth projects across Russia, he also had political ambitions and began holding regular meetings with the leaders of the parliamentary factions in the Duma. He did not say so publicly, but he was growing increasingly concerned at the way that the *siloviki* – men like Patrushev, Igor Sechin and Viktor Ivanov – who were ill at ease with a free-market system and wished to reassert the leading role of the state, were beginning to dominate Putin's inner circle.

Putin's preference for working with colleagues from the security services was hardly new. Valery Pavlov had complained that, at Smolny, he had surrounded himself with 'people with epaulettes'. But the Kremlin was a much bigger pond, and Sechin, in particular, had acquired formidable powers. The film director, Vitaly Mansky, who was then seeing Putin regularly, remembered that when Sechin first arrived, 'he wouldn't go into a room where the bosses were meeting. He'd wait outside with the document case. Half a year later, he'd be sitting there with his feet on the table. It was a fantastic difference . . . He started talking as though he was running the country.'[197]

Over this period, Sechin and Putin became extremely close. 'He'd spend hours in Putin's office', Mansky said. Others in the Presidential Administration took note and behaved accordingly. When Dmitry Yezhkov, a journalist who had known Sechin in St Petersburg, came to ask him for help finding a job, Sechin summoned Putin's press secretary, Aleksei Gromov, who stood stiffly in front of Sechin's desk while the other two remained seated. 'I thought my career as a political correspondent was over,' Yezhkov wrote later. 'No one from the corridors of power could accept such a humiliation.' But Sechin merely said, 'Take this man!', and Gromov found him a place in the Kremlin reporters' pool.[198]

Khodorkovsky was no fool. He knew that there was no way he could influence the power balance in the Kremlin. But he thought it might be possible gradually to increase the influence of the Duma so that Russia would evolve into a parliamentary, rather than a presidential, republic. Accordingly, he offered financial support not only to the two democratic parties, Yabloko and the Union of Right Forces, but also to the Communists and the pro-government party, United Russia, which had been formed by a merger between Yedinstvo and the Luzhkov–Primakov Fatherland–All Russia bloc, in return for the right to place his own candidates in eligible positions on their party lists.

In principle, this was acceptable. Notwithstanding the agreement in July 2000, that businessmen should stay out of politics, there was a tacit understanding that they could make contributions to the parties' election campaigns to ensure that their interests would be taken into account in future legislation.

What made Khodorkovsky's approach different was the scale of what he was attempting and the openness with which he went about it. 'He was going around Moscow saying that he wanted to buy one third of the Duma [seats]', Pyotr Aven remembered. 'He behaved as though nothing had changed and Yeltsin was still the President.'[199] Rumour had it that Khodorkovsky wanted to become Prime Minister and reduce the presidency to a figurehead. He denied that. But true or not, the Kremlin – or at least, Igor Sechin – took it seriously.

Putin's Chief of Staff, the head of the Presidential Administration, Aleksandr Voloshin, looking back years later, said Khodorkovsky had been naïve. Even if, in reality, he did not pose any significant political threat, he had not understood how it would be viewed by 'the conservative part of the establishment'.[200]

In the winter of 2002, on Sechin's instructions, the Economic Counter-Intelligence Directorate of the FSB, headed by Yuri Zaostrovtsev, the same man who had led the charge against Gusinsky and Berezovsky, began discreetly investigating Yukos.[201] Years later, Khodorkovsky came to the conclusion that Sechin's interest had been essentially financial. He wanted to find a way for the state oil company, Rosneft, of which he would subsequently become Chairman, to take over Yukos's assets.[202] For that to happen, he needed to persuade Putin that Khodorkovsky's political ambitions made him a potential danger and that, as long as he remained at the helm of Yukos, he would pose a threat.

Putin was in two minds. He needed no convincing that businessmen must be kept on a short leash. Khodorkovsky, in particular, he viewed with suspicion. They had much in common – the same iron self-control, the same obsessive sense of commitment, the same desire to play a key role in Russia's future development. But Putin agreed with Voloshin that Khodorkovsky posed no immediate threat. If he were to act against him, or any of the other leading business magnates, there would be an immediate outcry in the West and Russia's ability to attract foreign investment would be compromised. It was better, Putin thought, to keep them on their toes, aware that any false step on their part could bring down retribution in the form of tax demands or a re-examination of the way they had acquired their enterprises during the questionable privatisations in the 1990s.[203]

In December 2002, the businessmen tried to find a way out of this predicament by proposing one-off payments to the state as compensation for the sums they had underpaid during the privatisations. The Prime Minister, Mikhail Kasyanov, who thought it was an excellent idea, calculated that it would bring in between 15 and 20 billion US dollars. Putin would have none of it. 'I told him it would be good for stability, for attracting foreign capital and promoting investors' trust,' Kasyanov said.[204] 'But for him, it was more important not to let them off the hook. So long as they had no guarantee of their property, they could be manipulated.'[205]

There matters might have remained, had it not been for a routine meeting in the Kremlin on February 19, 2003, between Putin and the leading members of the Russian Union of Industrialists and Entrepreneurs.

It started with a discussion of administrative reform which quickly developed into criticism of the state bureaucracy.[206] One speaker recounted the experience of a friend who had abandoned an attempt to open a new store in Moscow because it required approval from 137 different officials. 'Could we not reduce that to 10 or 12?' he asked. To everyone's relief, Putin agreed. When it was Khodorkovsky's turn, he raised the subject of corruption, which he said had grown by 25 per cent in recent years and now amounted to some 30 billion US dollars a year, 12 per cent of the country's GDP. Corruption, he complained, was becoming systemic. University graduates competed to join the tax directorate because of the opportunities it offered for enrichment. Business decisions were being taken not on their own merits but for the kickbacks they might generate. For approving large contracts, officials had started demanding multi-million-dollar bribes, which went not into some carefully disguised slush fund but straight into their own pockets.

Khodorkovsky was sailing close to the wind, as was his habit, but he would probably have got away with it had he not cited as an example the recent purchase of a small Siberian oil company, Severnaya Neft (Northern Oil), by Rosneft, for 600 million dollars. Yukos had wanted to buy it, but the price had been much more than the company was worth. 'Everyone believes,' Khodorkovsky said, 'that this deal had, let us say, an extra dimension . . . The President of Rosneft [Sergei Bogdanchikov] is present today. Perhaps he can confirm that?'

Bogdanchikov, a former 'Red director' with close ties to the *siloviki*, 'turned to stone,' wrote a journalist who was present. It had been widely rumoured that there had been a kickback of at least 100 million dollars, possibly two or three times that much. The acquisition had been overseen by Sechin, evidently with Putin's knowledge, for when the Prime Minister, Mikhail Kasyanov, enquired about it afterwards, he found that the President knew much more than he did about the details of the arrangement.[207] Afterwards it was reported that the money was for a war chest for the forthcoming Duma elections and Putin's own re-election campaign the following year.[208]

Khodorkovsky had made a huge misjudgement. In attacking Sechin, he had appeared to be implicitly attacking Putin as well.[209]

When the President spoke, it was in the icy tones that meant he was seriously angry. He said he would ask German Gref, Rosneft's Chairman, for a report on the acquisition.[210] His understanding was that

Rosneft wanted to expand its available reserves, which he thought was normal. Yukos, he added pointedly, had immense reserves. If Khodorkovsky was going to question other companies' expansion plans, it was legitimate to ask how Yukos had managed to acquire such vast assets. Afterwards, according to the banker, Sergei Pugachev, who was also at the meeting, he was still seething. 'Who does he think he is?' he asked. 'He's got some nerve, preaching to me in front of everyone.'[211]

It would later be claimed that this meeting sealed Khodorkovsky's fate.[212] In fact, its importance lay elsewhere. It gave Sechin an opening to start building a case against him. From February onwards, Zaostrovtsev's FSB team redoubled their efforts to find incriminating material, both against Yukos and against Khodorkovsky personally. But Putin had not yet taken a decision. Yukos continued to negotiate a merger with Sibneft, the country's fifth largest oil producer, whose owner, Roman Abramovich, had privileged contacts with the Presidential Administration and would have pulled out if he had sensed serious trouble.[213]

At the end of April, Putin met Khodorkovsky and Yevgeny Shvidler, one of Abramovich's closest colleagues, at his residence at Novo-Ogaryovo to discuss the merger plan, which had been made public a few days earlier, as well as Khodorkovsky's proposal to form an alliance with the American company, Chevron, which, if it were realised, would make the group the world's largest oil company.[214] According to Voloshin, Putin liked the idea, provided the American company had no more than a 25 per cent stake. Sechin, who believed the oil and gas sector should be in the hands of the state, did not. Concerning some of Khodorkovsky's other plans, Putin had reservations. Yukos had been pressing for an oil pipeline from eastern Siberia to China as a geopolitical counterbalance to a pipeline it planned to build to Murmansk to export to the United States.[215] Rosneft preferred the route to the Pacific port of Nakhodka to export to Japan. To Putin, these were matters for the state to decide, not private enterprise. He also told Khodorkovsky to stop giving money to the Communist Party, a demand to which he readily acceded. If Putin told him that he could finance Yabloko and the Union of Right Forces, but not the Communists, he was not going to argue about it. Overall, Khodorkovsky felt the meeting had gone well and left reassured that Putin saw Yukos as playing an important role in Russia's integration into the world economy.

Sechin, however, had not been idle. In May, at his instigation, a Moscow think tank headed by Stanislav Belkovsky, an eccentric young political commentator with a bushy beard, an absurdist sense of humour and a penchant for conspiracy theories, issued a report with the striking title, 'An Oligarchic Coup is being Prepared in Russia'.[216] It argued that the leading business magnates were planning to install a system like that in fourteenth-century Venice, where the Council of Ten ruled the principality and the nominal leader, the Doge – a transparent allusion to Putin – became a figurehead. Khodorkovsky, the report insinuated, was the moving spirit behind this supposed plan.[217] When Putin was asked about it at a news conference, four weeks later, he warned that Russia 'would not allow individual businesspeople to influence the political life of the country in their own corporate interests'.[218] The magnates, he said, must keep 'equidistance from state bodies . . . As for those who disagree with that principle – you know what they used to say in the past: some are gone forever and others are far away.' The line was from the final stanza of Pushkin's *Eugene Onegin*, evoking the fate of the Decembrists who had been exiled to Siberia after rebelling against Nicholas I.

That week, the head of Yukos's security service, Aleksei Pichugin, was arrested on murder charges. It turned out to be the first of a succession of warning shots. On July 2, Platon Lebedev, the Chairman of Yukos's parent company, Menatep, was also detained. Two days later, Khodorkovsky and his partner, Leonid Nevzlin, were summoned for questioning at the Prosecutor's Office. On July 16, it was announced that Yukos would be subject to a tax audit.

In fact, even at this stage, Putin had still not taken a final decision.

Sechin and his allies were pressing for exemplary punishment on the grounds that, if Khodorkovsky's ambitions were not curbed, others would follow his example and the state would find itself disarmed against the power of money. But the damage to the Russian economy from capital flight and the drying up of foreign investment which would follow a full-scale crackdown on Yukos were not to be dismissed lightly. The Union of Industrialists and Entrepreneurs was sufficiently alarmed to draft a letter to Putin, warning that 'gangsters wearing uniforms' were trying to 'undermine stability [and] revise the results of privatisation'. Who the 'gangsters' were was left unsaid, but the press, which had obtained an advance copy, pointed the finger at Sechin, Patrushev and Viktor Ivanov. In the end, the Union's courage failed and it delivered an edulcorated version instead.[219] 'Oligarchic solidarity is not working,' the influential weekly, *Argumenty i Fakty*, commented. 'Everyone is terrified.'[220]

Khodorkovsky was more forthright. What was happening to Yukos was 'a nightmare, a monstrous process'. He had no intention of backing down, he said. 'I don't think I have ever been more under threat of arrest than I am now, but I am trying to support my comrades who have found themselves in prison. This is my country and I have nowhere else to go.'[221] His colleagues thought he was courting martyrdom. That summer, his business partner, Leonid Nevzlin, left quietly for Israel. But while Khodorkovsky was resigned to the possibility of arrest, he did not think it was inevitable. When word came down indirectly from the Kremlin that it might be better if he left the country, he ignored it. After Platon Lebedev's arrest, he travelled overseas 17 times. Each time he came back.

Khodorkovsky's stubbornness was his downfall. Putin had hesitated. As late as August, the government had formally approved the merger of Yukos with Sibneft.[222] But the Duma elections were approaching. Putin had promised that the oligarchs would 'cease to exist as a class'.[223] Most Russian voters hated them. To let Khodorkovsky's challenge pass would be to show weakness, both to the *siloviki* who formed a key part of his base and to the country at large. By September, he had made up his mind. That month he told John Browne, the Chairman of BP: 'I have eaten more dirt than I need to from that man.'[224] It was one of those occasions when he told a foreigner something which he was not yet quite ready to say publicly to his own people. A few weeks later, Khodorkovsky was detained by the FSB when his plane landed at Novosibirsk, in Siberia.

After an inordinately long trial, he was sentenced to nine years in a labour camp for fraud. Lebedev received the same sentence for tax evasion, embezzlement and money laundering; Pichugin was given a life term for murder; and Yukos was broken up and sold off.

Western investors fled and Western governments began to revise their earlier optimistic view of Putin as a free-marketeer whose economic instincts were basically sound. Russians saw it differently.

Mikhail Fridman, the founder of Alfa-Bank and one of the country's most versatile and successful business magnates, had warned Khodorkovsky in August: 'Putin will act decisively . . . It's dangerous for us, as well as for you . . . Putin has [to] show who is the boss.'[225] He explained years later what he had meant:

> It's a basic law: you don't fight the system in Russia . . . The machinery of state power in Russia is old, and pretty rusty, but it turns, maybe not so effectively, but it turns nonetheless . . . To break that machine is unrealistic, because it's the expression of ideological elements that have been built up over hundreds of years. The origin of that power is sacral, divine . . . Berezovsky and Gusinsky and Khodorkovsky all broke their teeth on that machine. They didn't understand that the image of the nature of power, which has a sacral, mystic character, is lodged in the head of the whole of society – both the bureaucrats and ordinary citizens . . . Up to a certain point, that power can be bent and pushed around. But at a certain point, when the situation becomes dangerous for the power itself, it snaps back like a spring.[226]

Khodorkovsky's arrest and imprisonment, and the destruction of Yukos, were a watershed.

If the choice was between, on the one hand, a pluralistic system, in which entrepreneurs could build business empires independent of the state, lobby to influence government policy and have political ambitions of their own and, on the other, the preservation of state power, the interests of the state would always win out. The damage to the economy, to Russia's ability to attract investment and its image in the West were secondary. Maintaining the 'power vertical', which Putin had created and was the core of his regime, outweighed everything else.

After Khodorkovsky's imprisonment, the businessmen did not raise their heads again. They could do business as they wished, but only as long as it did not infringe on the state's prerogatives. It was the same principle that had been applied earlier to the media and the regions. With rare exceptions, the written press could criticise as much as it liked, so long as the truly 'mass' media, the national television channels, were firmly under state control. The governors were free to rule their regions as they wished, so long as they acted within the parameters which the Kremlin set out. It was more than cosmetic free-dom. Throughout the first decade that Putin was in power, Russia had a genuine multiplicity of voices and of economic and political actors. But the limits within which they could operate were decreed from above.

11

A Bonfire of Illusions

When Bill Clinton telephoned Vladimir Putin on New Year's Day, 2000, to congratulate him on his appointment as acting President, Putin told him: 'There are certain issues on which we do not agree. However, I believe that on the core themes we will always be together.' Clinton was equally upbeat. Putin, he said, was 'off to a very good start' and they had much in common that they needed to get done.[1]

There were grounds for optimism on both sides. Clinton, like Tony Blair in Britain, believed that Russia under Putin could become a reliable partner for the West. 'His intentions are generally honourable and straightforward,' he told Blair. He was concerned, he added, that Russia might get 'squishy on democracy', an allusion to the war in Chechnya, which was a major issue for the Democratic Party, and to the treatment of Gusinsky, who had influential friends in Washington, but he felt Putin had 'a lot of ability and ambitions for the Russians . . . He wants to do a good job. He works at it every day. He's intelligent and disciplined.'[2] Not only was the American President impressed by the young Russian leader but he wanted him to succeed and fretted about the inequities of the Russian tax system, which discouraged foreign investment, and the country's declining life expectancy. 'My gut tells me it could do wonders for his popularity,' Clinton said, 'if he could make some progress on healthcare.'[3]

The Russian economy was improving, thanks to rising oil prices and the rouble devaluation in 1998 which had made local manufactures more competitive. Moscow and Washington were working together on restructuring the debt that had built up under Yeltsin and getting Russia off the international money-laundering black list, where it appeared alongside Israel and Ukraine and a host of small, mainly British tropical, fiscal paradises. In June 2000, a joint working group was set up by the CIA, the FSB and the Russian foreign intelligence service, the SVR, to exchange information about the terrorist threat from Afghanistan.[4]

The two countries shared concerns about nuclear proliferation. Putin told Clinton that his talks with Kim Jong-Il in Pyongyang in July had convinced him that the United States was 'to a large extent correct' in its assessment of North Korea's behaviour. 'I'm worried about it myself,' he said. 'We don't want any rogue states to acquire these weapons.'[5] The same applied to Iraq, which was denying access to UN weapons inspectors. Publicly, Putin called for the lifting of sanctions against Saddam Hussein's government, arguing that diplomatic and political means, not military or economic pressure, should be used to resolve the dispute.[6] But 'entirely off the record' he told Clinton that he supported US bombing raids against Iraqi military bases. 'I would have done the same in your shoes,' he said.[7]

Iran was a different matter. Russia would not help Tehran with its nuclear weapons programme, Putin said, but Russian companies would work with the Iranians on civilian nuclear power projects just as Western companies did.[8] In the Middle East, where the Second Intifada was getting under way in Israel and the Palestinian territories, they agreed to press their respective clients, Yasser Arafat and Ehud Barak, to resume peace negotiations.[9] Putin also promised to try to persuade the Serbian leader, Slobodan Milošević, to concede defeat after the disputed presidential election in September 2000.[10]

Points of friction remained. NATO enlargement was a continuing affront, but Putin had concluded that there was nothing to be gained by making an issue of it. 'We don't like NATO,' the Foreign Minister, Igor Ivanov, explained. 'But we can't pretend that it doesn't exist.'[11] The Defence Minister, Marshal Sergeyev, compared the relationship to 'the slow thawing of the permafrost'.[12]

More irritating, though little was said about it, was the way the United States appeared to think it had a *droit de regard* over Russia's Near Abroad. America's interest, Clinton told Putin, was to see that Russia had 'good, stable relations with its neighbours'. Russians of all political persuasions found that exasperating. It came across as patronising, reflecting America's self-image as the undisputed leader of a unipolar world. In response, Putin mentioned casually that he had just visited Cuba, intending it as a delicate reminder that America's own relations with its neighbours were not always either good or stable. But Clinton did not, or chose not to, notice.[13] Later, the United States' interest in Russia's relations with its neighbours would become a neuralgic issue. For the moment, it was merely an annoyance.

The one real cloud on the horizon was America's proposed National Missile Defense system, which the Republicans had been urging ever since Ronald Reagan's Strategic Defence Initiative (SDI), the so-called Star Wars programme, had been abandoned as unworkable in 1993. Unlike Reagan's concept, which envisaged a space-based anti-missile shield capable of intercepting an all-out Soviet nuclear attack, the defence system the Clinton administration proposed was on a much more modest scale, designed to stop a small number of incoming missiles, carrying either nuclear or non-nuclear warheads, launched by rogue states or even, in theory, non-state actors. The downside was that it would violate the Anti-Ballistic Missile (ABM) Treaty, which Russia regarded as the foundation of the entire edifice of nuclear arms control that had been painstakingly erected, treaty by treaty, since the first agreements had been signed in Moscow by Brezhnev and Richard Nixon 30 years before.

The ABM Treaty allowed each country to install missile defences to protect only one designated site – for the United States, a nuclear missile base in North Dakota; for Russia, the capital city, Moscow. Clinton maintained that that need not be an obstacle because, if it were modified, America would share with Russia the new anti-missile technology which it planned to develop, just as Reagan had promised Gorbachev that he would give Russia access to Star Wars technology once it had been perfected.

'This is good for both of us,' Clinton had assured Yeltsin in 1999. 'The system we are looking at would operate against just 20 missiles.'[14] It would be ineffective against Russia. Yeltsin had not been convinced. In Moscow's view, the moment the door was opened to nuclear missile defence, even if in the first instance it was limited to preventing small-scale attacks by rogue actors, there would be no way to stop its further development and the logic of deterrence would collapse.

In public, Putin tried to put a good face on it. Russia, he said, was ready to contribute to building a non-strategic defence system, that would be able to deal with the medium-range missiles which were all that countries like Iran, Iraq and North Korea would have for the foreseeable future.[15] If Russia and the US pooled their efforts, they could protect both their own territories and Western Europe.[16] 'We hope,' he said, 'that we will be able to find a mutually acceptable solution.'[17]

In private, he was much blunter. The US position was 'a major strategic miscalculation',' he told Clinton. 'It amounts to cutting off your nose to spite your face.'[18]

That spring, Putin had persuaded the Duma to ratify START II, the Strategic Arms Reduction Treaty signed by Yeltsin and George H. W. Bush in 1993, which banned multiple independently targetable warheads on intercontinental ballistic missiles.[19] It had been languishing in the Russian parliament for seven years and Clinton hailed its ratification as 'a great accomplishment' for the security of the United States.[20] Putin also held out the possibility of Russian agreement to a START III Treaty, under which both countries would reduce their nuclear stockpiles to 1,500 warheads or, he suggested in November, an even lower level, from the 3,000 to 3,500 permitted under START II.[21]

But it was carrot and stick. Russian adherence to START was conditional on US adherence to the ABM treaty, Putin said. The United States had a choice: 'Either to be a globally condemned wrecker of the underpinnings of strategic security embodied in the treaty-based system, . . . or to refrain from deploying a national missile defence system.'[22]

Putin laid out the Russian position formally in a joint declaration with the Chinese leader, Jiang Zemin, in July 2000. America's justification for breaking the ABM Treaty was 'totally groundless', they said. The United States was 'striving for unilateral superiority in the military field'. It was a step backwards and would lead to a new spiral in the arms race.[23]

By then, Clinton was also beginning to have doubts. If the missile defence system being proposed went into a second phase, he told Blair, it could stop 50 or 60 warheads, which would be enough to destabilise the nuclear balance with China. Then they would be into a whole different ball game. It would be better if they could 'get rid of these damn offensive weapons altogether'.[24]

On September 1, two months before Election Day in America, Clinton announced that, given the substantial international opposition and the technical uncertainties surrounding the project – at least two and arguably all three test firings had failed – he would leave to his successor the decision on whether or not the system should be deployed.

It was a classic case of kicking the can down the road. Clinton had hoped to do a deal with Putin to forestall a possibly more sweeping initiative by a future Republican administration. But he had left it too late. No one knew whether his Vice President, Al Gore, or the Republican challenger, George W. Bush, would succeed him. It was not a time for Russia to make commitments to America on arms control or anything else.[25] Putin had used his first year in office to probe Western intentions, to set out Russian objections – notably on missile defence – and to delineate the contours of Russia's foreign policy priorities. What happened next would depend on what America's convoluted and archaic electoral system would deliver.

On December 14, 2000, the United States Electoral College voted by the narrowest of margins, 271 votes to 266, to elect George W. Bush as the next US President. It was always going to be a close race and the result itself was not a surprise. But the way it came about left many Russians shaking their heads in disbelief. Here was a country, which prided itself on being the most advanced democracy in the world and a technological powerhouse, using old-fashioned voting machines which generated 'hanging chads' that a Russian bus conductor would have been ashamed of – a country which, weeks after Election Day, was still struggling to count the votes that had been cast and had eventually been forced to turn to the Supreme Court to determine an outcome in which, for the first time in more than a century, the winner of the popular vote was declared the loser.

Russian liberals were appalled. Hardliners saw it as proof of what they had been saying all along: the American system was a fraud. Even Putin could not resist a jibe. Perhaps, he suggested, the Chairman of the Russian Election Commission, Aleksandr Veshnyakov, who happened to be in Washington, 'might be able to advise his American colleagues on what to do'.[26]

For the first six months after Bush's election, Moscow sent mixed messages.

On the one hand, Putin noted that under Republican presidents, relations with Washington often flourished or at least did not wilt.[27] As a goodwill gesture, he pardoned Edmond Pope, an American businessman who had been convicted of spying.[28] He insisted that Russia no longer 'viewed America as an enemy or even as an opponent. The United States is Russia's partner.'[29] When Bush made a similar statement, he welcomed it as 'a good basis for a dialogue'.[30]

On the other hand, Putin started pushing much harder on their points of discord. There were forces in the West, he said, that continued to view Russia as 'the main geopolitical enemy'.[31] The Warsaw Pact had been dissolved and the Soviet Union no longer existed. 'But NATO still exists. What for?' How could Russia feel at ease with NATO expansion, when it was itself excluded?[32] It was a fair question. He told a group of Italian journalists a few months after Bush took office: 'We all say – I hear it all the time from my [Western] colleagues and the mass media in the West talk about it constantly – we say: "We don't want Europe to be divided, we don't want new borders and barriers, new 'Berlin Walls' dividing the continent." But when NATO expands, the border doesn't go away. It simply moves closer to Russia.'[33]

NATO liked to claim that it was becoming more of a political than a military organisation, Putin added. 'But if it's a political organisation, why did it bomb Yugoslavia?'[34]

Part of the problem was that the Kremlin was unable to get a sense of the new administration's priorities. Condoleezza Rice, Bush's National Security Adviser, was in charge of policy towards Russia. A talented, highly intelligent but somewhat blinkered academic, she had worked earlier as an adviser on Soviet Affairs for Bush's father. The Russians found her difficult to get through to and eventually asked Tony Blair to act as an intermediary to Bush, as he had done to Clinton a year earlier.[35] But Blair was also trying to figure out where Bush was coming from and this time was less able to help.

The upshot was that when Putin and the new US President finally met face to face at Brdo, a sixteenth-century estate near Ljubljana, in Slovenia, on June 16, nobody on either side was quite sure what to expect. The encounter had been carefully choreographed, starting with a private meeting, with only national security advisers present, followed by a walk in the grounds and an enlarged session attended by the foreign ministers. Bush's aides thought he was nervous.[36] Putin appeared nervous, too.[37] Bush would be in power for at least the next four, probably eight, years. It was important that they get off to a good start.

They did. 'Rarely have the two nations' leaders so surpassed the

limited expectations of their meeting,' the *New York Times* wrote afterwards.[38] The private talks lasted an hour and 40 minutes, three times
longer than planned. It was not a negotiating session – none of the
outstanding issues was resolved – but the chemistry was good and
Bush told a news conference afterwards that he felt Russia could be 'a
strong partner and friend, more so than people could imagine'. Putin
spoke of having established 'a high level of trust', and although he
later backed away from that phrase, talking instead of 'an element of
trust emerging', he agreed that they had what he called 'a good basis
on which to start building'.[39] On their personal relationship, Bush was
even more fulsome:

> I looked the man in the eye. I found him to be very straightforward and
> trustworthy. We had a very good dialogue. I was able to get a sense of
> his soul: a man deeply committed to his country and to the best inter-
> ests of his country.[40]

Condoleezza Rice winced at that. 'I visibly stiffened,' she wrote later.
'We were never able to escape the perception that the President had
naively trusted Putin and then been betrayed.'[41] The Russia specialists
at the CIA were aghast. How could an American leader be so gullible,
they wondered.[42] The hawks in Congress and the foreign policy community pounced. 'I don't trust Mr Putin', declared Senator Joe Biden.
'This is a man trained to lie', said Michael McFaul, later US Ambassador in Moscow.[43] John McCain let rip with one of his trademark
one-liners: 'I looked into Mr Putin's eyes and I saw three letters, a K, a
G and a B.'[44]

   Afterwards there was much speculation about where Bush had got
that idea. Had someone been talking to the President about the mysteries of the Russian soul? Not so, it turned out.[45] Bush himself, looking
for a way to ease the tension which both men felt, had remembered
during the meeting being briefed about Putin wearing a cross and had
asked him about it.[46]

   Putin had explained that his mother had had him baptised as an
infant without telling his communist father, a common practice during
the years when Stalin was in power. Officially the Soviet Union was
atheist, but mothers often took their babies surreptitiously to an orthodox priest. Many of Putin's KGB colleagues – not to mention the

Soviet leaders, including both Gorbachev and Yeltsin – had been baptised as infants. In Gorbachev's case, it had been done secretly. In Yeltsin's, the village priest had been so drunk that the future President had nearly drowned after being left unattended in the font.

While he was deputy Mayor of St Petersburg, Putin told Bush, he had visited Jerusalem. His mother had given him his baptismal cross to have it sanctified at the Church of the Holy Sepulchre. A few years later, when his dacha had burnt down, the workmen had found the cross in the rubble. He had worn it ever since.[47]

Rice thought it 'a rather syrupy story'.[48] But George Bush was a devout born-again Christian. Putin had embellished the tale, telling Bush that, after the fire, 'all he cared about was the cross', and dramatically recounting the moment when a workman brought it to him, miraculously saved from the flames, 'as if it were meant to be'. The American President was moved. 'Vladimir,' he told him. 'That's the story of the cross. Things *are* meant to be.'[49]

For Putin, it had been the perfect opening. One of the things he had learnt in the KGB, he told an American journalist afterwards, was the importance of establishing a dialogue with an opposite number. 'You should make that person feel that there is something that unites you, that you have some common goals,' he said.[50] In this case, that something had been his baptismal cross. It was all the more important because a close relationship with Bush, he felt, would be the only way to penetrate what was otherwise, from the Russian standpoint, a distinctly rebarbative administration. The Vice President, Dick Cheney; the deputy Defense Secretary, Paul Wolfowitz; and Scooter Libby, Cheney's National Security Assistant, had all been leading proponents of NATO enlargement during George H. W. Bush's presidency. Wolfowitz's boss, Donald Rumsfeld, was an avowed hawk, and Condoleezza Rice was on record as saying Russia only respected toughness. Over the next few days, 'the retinue', as Putin called them,[51] appeared on US talk shows to insist that, notwithstanding the warm atmosphere at Ljubljana, nothing of substance had changed. Condoleezza Rice declared that the United States would proceed with National Missile Defense 'with or without Russia'.[52] Colin Powell, the Secretary of State, told Fox News: 'We can't allow ourselves to be stopped by the constraints of a treaty that is almost thirty years old and was designed for . . . a different world.'[53]

In response, Putin said it was up to America to decide what it wanted. 'We offer cooperation. If that's accepted, we'll do it. If not, we will go it alone.' Russia could replace the existing warheads on its inter-continental ballistic missiles with MIRVs – multiple independently targetable re-entry vehicles – quintupling their nuclear firepower, and it would cost next to nothing, he said. 'But I don't think the US and Russia, or for that matter humanity as a whole, stand to gain by that.'[54]

During the summer, nothing moved. Putin wondered aloud who was making policy in the White House, Bush or his entourage.[55] On a visit to Finland in September, he was asked about NATO's plans to admit the Baltic States. It was a wrong step, he said. There was no point getting hysterical over it, but it would solve nothing. It required 'a sick, fevered imagination' to think that Russia would attack its neigh-bours. Yet that was what 'some people' evidently wished to believe.[56]

There were much graver threats to worry about, Putin went on, but the United States refused to take them seriously. 'It is important not to bury our heads in the sand, ostrich-like, and pretend that those threats do not exist.'[57] Yet it seemed that that was what the West was doing.

Eight days later, two hijacked American airliners smashed into the 110-storey twin towers of the World Trade Center in New York, 17 minutes apart, causing both to collapse. A third aircraft hit the Pentagon. A fourth, apparently heading for the Capitol, crashed in a field in Penn-sylvania after the passengers tried to overpower the hijackers. It was the first foreign attack on American soil since Japan had bombed Pearl Harbor, 60 years earlier – the act which brought the United States into the Second World War. Nearly 3,000 people died, making it the deadli-est terrorist incident of modern times.

Putin was alerted by a telephone call from the FSB chief, Nikolai Patrushev, within minutes of the first tower being hit. It was 5 p.m., Moscow time. As he watched – not on Russian television but on CNN – first one tower, then the second, collapsed.[58]

His first reaction was to telephone George Bush, but the President was on board Airforce One and out of reach, so he spoke instead to Condoleezza Rice at the Emergency Operations Centre in a bunker beneath the White House, asking her to convey to Bush Russia's total support. He told her that Russia was cancelling all military exercises, that he understood America's decision to put its forces on heightened alert and that there would be no corresponding action on Russia's part.[59] In a telegram to Bush afterwards, he again expressed Russian solidarity, describing the attacks as an act of barbarism which must not go unpunished.[60]

It was claimed afterwards that Putin had ignored the advice of his colleagues, who had argued that it would be best to wait and see how the situation developed before deciding how to react. The chronology makes clear that that was not so. Men like Nikolai Patrushev and Igor Sechin certainly had doubts about the wisdom of backing America so strongly. But by the time Putin called them to a meeting with the other intelligence chiefs and the Interior and Defence ministers later that evening, Russia's course was already set.[61] It was a golden opportunity, an unlooked-for chance, Putin thought, to prove to the hardliners in Bush's entourage that Russia was – as the American President had put it at Ljubljana – a genuine 'partner and friend' on whom America could rely in its hour of need. That was why he had telephoned the White House even before the dust from the explosions had settled, the first foreign leader to do so, a gesture which Bush appreciated and did not forget, and why, over the following days, he surprised the American President by offering fuller cooperation than anyone in the White House had thought possible.[62]

In a statement on Russian television that night, Putin said he wanted the American people to know: 'We are with you. We share and feel your anguish totally and completely. We support you.'[63] The message was not only for Americans. It was also to tell the Russian people, the armed forces and the security services, that at least for the purposes of the struggle against terrorism, Russia and the United States would be allies.

Next morning, he called Bush and told him, in suitably biblical terms: 'Good will triumph over evil. I want you to know that in this struggle, we will stand together.'[64] It was a bit like Tony Blair's assurance nine months later, during the planning for the invasion of Iraq: 'I will be with you, whatever.' But coming from Russia, which had for so long been America's Cold War adversary, American officials were staggered.

Putin was as good as his word. The following week, to facilitate the US invasion of Afghanistan to neutralise al-Qaeda, which the Americans now knew had organised the attacks, he told Bush that Russia would open its airspace to American military aircraft and use its influence with Kyrgyzstan and Uzbekistan to persuade them to allow the United States to lease military bases there. 'It was an amazing conversation,' Bush wrote afterwards. He had thought that Putin would be worried about Russia being encircled if the US acquired facilities in Central Asia in addition to those in Europe. Instead, he found the Russian leader completely focused on the terrorist threat. 'He even ordered Russian generals to brief their American counterparts on their experience during their Afghanistan invasion in the 1980s . . . I told Vladimir I appreciated his willingness to move beyond the suspicions of the past.'[65]

Had Bush reflected further, he would have seen the logic of the Russian position. As Putin himself said later, 'I acted not on impulse. I must be honest about it, I acted from pragmatic considerations.'[66]

For two years, he had been warning the West about terrorism, only to have his words fall on deaf ears. Condoleezza Rice admitted later that he had pressed Bush about it at Ljubljana. 'Putin suddenly raised the problem of Pakistan, . . . its support of extremists and [its] connexions with . . . the Taliban and al-Qaeda,' she recalled. 'Those extremists were all being funded by Saudi Arabia, he said, and it was only a matter of time until it resulted in a major catastrophe.' She was struck by his alarm and vehemence, she wrote, but put it down to Russian bitterness about Pakistan's support for the Afghan mujahidin during the Soviet occupation in the 1980s.[67] It was a strange reaction. Putin's concern was with the present, not with a war that he regarded as mistaken and which had taken place 15 years earlier. But neither Rice nor anyone else in the White House had been in a mood to listen.

It was not that the Bush administration did not know that al-Qaeda might be planning an attack. It did. But it had no idea when, where, how or on what scale. Not only were its intelligence agencies constrained by bureaucratic and legal firewalls but they suffered from the kind of inward-looking America-centric tunnel vision that drove both the Russians and America's own allies to despair. Two years before the 9/11 attacks, Putin had told Clinton that a message had been intercepted in which Khattab, the Saudi deputy to Shamil Basayev, had boasted about the Moscow apartment bombings.[68] Yet when the FBI found that Zacarias Moussaoui, a French associate of the future hijackers, had been in contact with Khattab, it concluded that the Saudi was 'not sufficiently associated with a terrorist organisation' to justify seeking an authorisation to wiretap Moussaoui[69] – a decision of mind-boggling incompetence. It was as if information that did not come from America's own sources, or from other 'Five Eyes' countries or from Mossad, was not worth bothering with. Had the FBI followed up on Moussaoui, the attacks might well have been averted.

That was not the only link between 9/11 and the Chechen war. It was later discovered that a number of the hijackers had originally planned to fight in Chechnya but had been diverted to Afghanistan instead.[70]

Putin was careful to absolve Bush personally for America's failure to take his warnings seriously. It was the Clinton administration, he claimed, that had been most at fault. 'I alerted them to the bin Laden problem,' Putin said. 'They simply shrugged helplessly and said, "What can we do?" . . . That was the kind of America that Bush inherited.'[71] Apart from being highly undiplomatic, the accusation was untrue but, like everything Putin did after 9/11, it was designed to create a sense of complicity with Bush, showing that, whatever might have gone wrong in the past, Russia and America were now in this together. He drew a parallel with World War II, when they had fought shoulder to shoulder against the Axis powers. The 9/11 attacks, he said, had opened 'broad opportunities for acting together, for . . . creating a single front',[72] an alliance against terrorism like the heroic days of the fight against fascism. It was a wake-up call to get rid of Cold War attitudes.[73] Russia and America would show once again what could be achieved when civilised nations joined together.[74]

Russia provided intelligence as well as tens of millions of dollars' worth of arms to America's allies in the anti-Taliban Northern Alliance. But Putin felt the United States was ignoring at its peril the lessons of earlier wars in Afghanistan. 'The USSR's error,' he said, 'had been to install a pro-Soviet government . . . Afghanistan is not a country that can be privatised.'[75] America should not make the same mistake. A pro-American government would not be able to bring peace. That would require a government with broad international support, backed by all the country's social and ethnic groups. It was sound advice from a country which had paid for its knowledge with 15,000 dead in nine years of war. But as so often, Washington knew better.

*

The first canker on this blossoming partnership appeared in December 2001, when Bush announced that the United States was giving the statutory six months' notice to withdraw unilaterally from the ABM Treaty. Putin had realised after 9/11 that the Americans' minds were made up and he had given up warning that the abrogation of the treaty would risk up-ending the whole structure of strategic arms control. But he still hoped for a compromise. Russia had been willing to discuss possible amendments to bring the treaty into line with what the Americans wanted to do, he said later. 'But nothing specific was given to us . . . We just kept getting insistent requests that we should withdraw together. To this day, I fail to understand that, especially since our position was quite flexible.'[76]

Condoleezza Rice wrote later that the 'real issue' for the Russians was not the substance of the treaty but its symbolic value as proof that Russia had inherited the superpower status of the USSR and could deal with America as an equal.[77] It is hard to know whether she believed that or whether it was simply spin. In any case, it was wrong. The United States never produced a credible reason for abrogating the ABM Treaty. Bush claimed that America needed a missile defence system to guard against 'terrorists who might acquire weapons of mass destruction to be delivered by ballistic missiles'.[78] The Russians found that risible. 'Neither terrorists nor rogue states have strategic ballistic missiles,' Putin exclaimed, 'and they are unlikely ever to get them.' The truth, as the Russians quickly realised, was that the Pentagon still hoped to develop a missile defence system which, like Star Wars, would protect America from a Russian second strike, making a nuclear war winnable. The United States insisted it had no such intention. That was flat-out dishonest. If, as Clinton had told Blair, America knew that the missile defence system would upset the nuclear balance with China, it followed that further development would upset the balance with Russia. In any case, as Putin kept pointing out, intentions did not matter. What counted was the capability the system would confer.

Putin thought the United States was wasting its money.[79] Even if the new missile defence system worked, which was far from certain, it would serve no useful purpose. Russia had more than enough missiles to penetrate American defences and would respond by developing more.[80]

But he wondered, not for the first time, who was actually making the decisions in Washington. Were the neoconservative hawks who had risen to prominence under Bush driving policy in directions which, left to his own devices, he might not otherwise take? 'If that is the case,' he observed, 'it's not a team but a rag-tag band. I would not want to be surrounded by such people.'[81]

On other fronts, the relationship continued to make progress, although less than met the eye.

Amid great fanfare, the two countries concluded the Strategic Offensive Reductions Treaty (SORT), which Bush and Putin signed in Moscow in May 2002, whereby both sides pledged to reduce their strategic arsenals to between 1,700 and 2,200 nuclear warheads by the end of 2012. For once, the devil was not in the details, of which there were very few. The weakness of the agreement was that, at America's insistence, the provisions were vaguely worded to allow maximal flexibility and minimal constraints. The reductions made spectacular headlines but were no more than both countries had been planning all along.

The same was true of Russia's relationship with NATO.

Four weeks after the 9/11 attacks, Putin had met the NATO Secretary General, George Robertson, in Brussels, and proposed the setting up of a working body to examine how the two sides might cooperate more closely. 'There is far more that unites NATO and Russia than divides us,' he said. Although Russia remained opposed to NATO enlargement, 'we might change our position if we didn't feel sidelined.'[82]

The following day, Tony Blair visited Moscow. That evening, at Putin's estate at Novo-Ogaryovo, he proposed a mechanism to address Russia's concerns. On certain issues, he suggested, notably the fight against terrorism and nuclear non-proliferation, Russia and the 19 members of NATO, instead of meeting bilaterally as '19 plus one', as had been the case until then, should form a unified 'Group of 20', which would have the power to agree joint policies.[83] Putin leapt at the idea. 'We are ready to go as far as the North Atlantic bloc is ready to go', he said.[84] 'If the format of our relationship changes, NATO enlargement will cease to be an issue.'[85] Either they could list areas such as defence policy, from which Russia would be excluded, which would be 'a more serious and radical approach' – Russia would be a fully fledged participant in all the others – or they could list the issues on which Russia would take part.[86] Unsurprisingly, NATO opted for the more modest variant, and it was on that basis that the NATO–Russia Council was established in Rome in the spring of 2002.

It sounded wonderful. 'Each nation will have one vote,' Putin jubilated, 'and all the issues will be resolved without any prior decisions being taken within the bloc.'[87] A few days later, George W. Bush, visiting Moscow for the signing of the SORT agreement, declared: 'For decades, Russia and NATO were adversaries. Those days are gone.'[88] If Estonia wanted to join NATO, Putin said, 'Let it do so if it thinks it will be happier that way. I see no tragedy there . . . The choice of any nation must be respected.'[89] The same applied to Ukraine.[90]

How much of this either of them believed is a different matter.

It was partly theatrics, for Putin to show his domestic critics – the Communists, the nationalists in Zhirinovsky's Liberal Democratic Party, and others who held yet more extreme views, as well as all those in the military and the security services who remained deeply suspicious of the West – that the partnership was bringing appreciable dividends.

In NATO, as Putin knew full well, not every nation had equal weight. The alliance's worst-kept secret was that the Quad, an unacknowledged, informal group, consisting of the United States, Britain, France and Germany, 'pre-cooked' NATO decisions, which the rest then had to endorse.[91] When Condoleezza Rice asked Sergei Ivanov, then Security Council Secretary, how far Russia wanted to go in integration with NATO, he rolled his eyes and told her: 'Condi, forget it. We're not going to join an alliance where our vote is the same as a country like Latvia. You needn't ask me that again.'[92]

For Russia, a closer relationship with NATO made sense only if there was at least an element of joint decision-making. But that was not something the United States could ever bring itself to accept.

America's attitude had not changed since the days when Bush's father said of the Cold War, 'We won, they didn't!', and Clinton concluded that Yeltsin would just have to 'eat his spinach'. It was true: Russia did lose the Cold War. But, as Putin ruefully observed, it seemed that the West was determined never to let Russians forget it. 'Russia has changed radically, the West hardly at all,' he told an interviewer in 2003. 'Stick-in-the-mud thinking and behaviour are very strong there.'[93]

Putin's Western partners begged to disagree. The entrenched attitudes, they claimed, were all in Russia. Richard Dearlove, then head of

MI6, insisted: 'We did try, but they didn't pick up the ball . . . We would propose advancing on a particular issue, but then we never got anything back from them.'[94]

The bureaucracy on both sides had a lot to answer for. The Pentagon, under Donald Rumsfeld, was allergic to anything which might constrain America's freedom to act as it wished. The Russian General Staff was obsessed with the idea that NATO was planning to deploy troops along Russia's borders.[95] Putin himself acknowledged that 'many things that seem fine in negotiations often end up bogged down in practice.'[96] But even if the blame were shared, the West often gave the impression of deliberately dragging its feet. Francis Richards, who at that time headed GCHQ – the British equivalent of the US National Security Agency – remembered: 'We were quite grateful for Putin's support after 9/11, but we didn't show it very much. I used to spend a great deal of time trying to persuade people that we needed to give as well as take . . . I think the Russians felt throughout that [on NATO issues] they were being fobbed off. And they were.'[97]

There were other disappointments, too.

In the autumn of 2001, Putin announced that Russia's radar station at Lourdes, in Cuba, which monitored American missile and space launches, and its naval base at Cam Ranh Bay, in Vietnam, would be closed, on the grounds that the country's defence priorities had changed. The Russian military saw that as an unnecessary, unilateral concession with no quid pro quo. The security services complained that, while they provided their American colleagues with valuable intelligence about Afghanistan, they got nothing in return. The Jackson–Vanik amendment, which President Ford had approved in 1975 to pressure the Soviet Union to allow the emigration of Soviet Jews by denying the USSR Most Favoured Nation status in trade, remained in force a decade after all restrictions on emigration had been lifted. Congress refused to exempt Russia to signal displeasure over human rights issues and to mollify the US farm lobby, which wanted concessions for American agricultural exports.

The result was a growing feeling among the Russian elite that Putin was being played – the Americans were saying all the right things, but when it came to matters of substance, they were bringing nothing to the table.

Vladimir Lukin, who had been Yeltsin's first ambassador to the

United States, protested: 'One sided steps cannot be taken forever . . . Decisions should go both ways. They should not end just in smiles and encouragement.'[98] Others asked whether Russia was returning to the era of Andrei Kozyrev, who, as Foreign Minister in the 1990s, had been pilloried for what were seen as his pro-American policies. There was grumbling, not only in the army and navy but also within the Presidential Administration, at what was termed 'a policy of concessions' which brought Russia no tangible benefit.[99]

Putin held firm. Russia had made 'a strategic choice',[100] he said:

> People ask me whether things may go the same way as under Gorbachev. He too sought to mend fences with the West, but it did not go down very well with the population . . . This is different. Russia today is cooperating with the West not because it wants to be liked or to get something in exchange. We are not standing there with an outstretched hand and we are not begging anyone for anything. The only reason that I pursue this policy is that I believe it fully meets [our] national interests . . . A rapprochement with the West is not Putin's policy, it is the policy of Russia.[101]

There were sound reasons for that. Well over half of Russia's foreign trade was with Western countries. Russia's future growth depended on its integration into the world economy, which, in the early 2000s, was still dominated by the United States, the European Union and Japan. The United States was its principal strategic interlocutor. And, as Putin constantly emphasised during his first years in power, although Russia was geographically in both Asia and Europe – the national emblem, the double-headed imperial eagle, he noted, faced both East and West – 'in terms of culture and mentality it is . . . an inalienable part of Europe.'[102] Russia's policy was 'directed primarily towards Europe and to the formation of a common European space . . . We rightfully consider ourselves Europeans. The culture of Russia and its essential traditions were formed precisely by European civilisation.'[103]

That said, he recognised that Russia would have to be patient. 'The processes of estrangement have their own inertia,' he told the *Financial Times* in December, 2001. 'It is quite hard to reverse them.'[104]

By then, another problem was looming which threatened to try Russia's relations with the Bush Administration more severely than any of the disagreements before. Within days of the 9/11 attacks, Dick Cheney had started pushing a story that one of the hijackers, Mohamed Atta, had had a meeting in Prague earlier that year with an Iraqi intelligence officer. The CIA investigated and reported that it did not stand up.[105] But Cheney was undeterred. In November, Bush asked the Pentagon to review contingency plans for military action to topple Saddam Hussein. The following month, as the White House started to believe that the war in Afghanistan was nearing a successful conclusion, Cheney declared that it was 'pretty well confirmed' that Atta had indeed met with Iraqi intelligence. 'Given the increasing linkage between terrorists and weapons of mass destruction,' he went on, 'the President will ultimately have to make a decision about what kind of policy we want to pursue with respect to Iraq.'[106]

Not a word of that was true. But it became an important element in the Bush Administration's false claims that the Iraqi government was supporting al-Qaeda. In his State of the Union address in January 2003, President Bush denounced Iraq, Iran and North Korea as 'an axis of evil' and warned that there would be consequences. These countries, he said, 'pose a grave and growing danger . . . The price of indifference could be catastrophic . . . I will not wait on events . . . The United States of America will not permit the world's most dangerous regimes to threaten us with the world's most destructive weapons.'[107]

Putin had had no problem supporting retaliation against Afghanistan, whose regime posed no less a threat to Russia than to the United States. Iraq was a different matter.

It was not merely, as Bush's advisers claimed, that Russia had extensive and long-standing economic interests in Iraq and was reluctant to jeopardise its oil contracts there.[108] Decades of close relations meant that Moscow had much better intelligence about the Iraqi regime than was available to the CIA. Putin knew that Saddam Hussein had no nuclear weapons and no means of obtaining them. He also knew that the Iraqis had no connection with al-Qaeda. Saddam's regime was 'liked by no one but himself',[109] he said. But the pretexts which Bush invoked to justify his overthrow were phoney.

In his public comments, Putin walked a fine line between opposing military action against Iraq and expressing sympathy with America's concerns. Bush's speech, he said, had been 'very emotional'. That was understandable – America was moved by 'wounded pride after 9/11, and the need to assert itself' – but it was not a reason to draw up 'black-lists' of so-called rogue states. Moscow supported measures to compel Saddam to admit United Nations inspectors to verify whether Iraq had weapons of mass destruction. However the use of force must be a last resort and only then if approved by the UN Security Council.[110]

Over the next 12 months, Putin reiterated that in increasingly forth-right terms. In April 2002, he warned that any unilateral action would be 'counterproductive';[111] in January 2003, that it would be 'controver-sial';[112] in February, that it would be 'a great mistake'.[113] If America acted on its own, the result would be 'Iraq's [probable] disintegration with unforeseeable consequences for all its neighbours, the radicalisa-tion of the Islamic world and a new wave of terrorist acts'.[114] He accused Bush's colleagues, though not the President himself, of lying about Iraq's supposed links with al-Qaeda. When it came to concoct-ing fables, Putin said, 'those of us [who worked] in the KGB were children compared to [American] politicians'.[115] It was time for 'fewer emotional statements and more common sense'. Nothing in the UN charter authorised regime change.[116]

The Soviet Union, Putin recalled, had once tried to export its ver-sion of socialism. If others now started trying to export 'capitalist democracy, the world will have embarked on a very perilous, slippery road'.[117]

In March 2003, the United States and its allies, Australia, Britain and, symbolically, Poland – the 'coalition of the willing', as Bush called it – invaded Iraq.

'Some did some shooting, some did some looting, and now some-one has to pick up the tab,' Putin commented acidly.[118]

Both the United States and Russia avoided criticising each other directly. Moscow aimed its sharpest barbs at Bush's chief European ally, Britain. Washington denounced the Western European countries that had opposed the invasion. 'Punish France, ignore Germany and forgive Russia!' Condoleezza Rice allegedly said,[119] and Congress duly obliged, declaring that henceforth, French fries would be called 'Free-dom fries'.

Putin's sense of ridicule was somewhat better developed. At the end of April, with Prime Minister Tony Blair standing beside him at a news conference in Moscow, he asked sarcastically: 'Those weapons [of mass destruction] have still not been found. So where is Saddam? . . . Is he hiding somewhere in a bunker, sitting on cases full of them, preparing to blow the whole place up?' It was an awkward moment. Blair could only double down on what was beginning to appear to be a tissue of lies. 'One thing is sure,' he said defiantly. 'Saddam did have weapons of mass destruction . . . It's an established fact. I am sure the evidence will be there.'[120] In reality, as the evidence piled up, it showed something quite different – that both Blair and Bush had justified the invasion by cherry-picking the intelligence and ignoring anything which might cast doubt on the course they had already decided.

The relationship between the United States and Russia survived. Putin said afterwards that what brought them together had 'proved stronger than the differences'.[121] But there was important collateral damage.

On several occasions just before the invasion, Bush had assured Putin that he did not want war.[122] The problem was not so much that that was untrue. Putin himself often had a tenuous relationship with the truth. The former US Ambassador, Jim Collins, put it most charitably when he said that Putin lied 'only if he was put in a position where he felt he couldn't tell you the truth', by which he meant that Putin, like most human beings, was a pragmatic, rather than a compulsive, liar.[123] What disturbed Putin was that Bush appeared deliberately to have misled him when there had been no need to do so. He did not allow it to change their relationship, but it raised questions about Bush's intentions.

There was another problem, too. When Putin warned that the joint fight against terrorism – a key element in the relationship between Russia and the US, where they saw themselves as not merely partners but allies – was being put at risk by American unilateralism, he was not thinking only of Iraq. There had always been a lurking suspicion in Moscow that the West had ulterior motives in the conflict in Chechnya. Even as Putin proclaimed that the United States was a friend and that NATO was not an opponent, he would occasionally come out with a remark which gave a very different impression. 'The dream of our geopolitical enemies,' he told a meeting of Russian generals in an unguarded moment in November 2000, 'is to see Russia bogged down in bloody, inter-ethnic conflict.'[124] That was what many of the *siloviki* believed and what men like Sechin and Patrushev were constantly whispering in Putin's ear. If the West was sincere about fighting jointly against terrorism, he wondered, why did it not support Russia in Chechnya, 'on the front where we are fighting alone'?[125] Why did America and Britain give political asylum to ministers in Maskhadov's rebel government?[126] Why did the West's special services maintain discreet contacts with leaders of the Chechen jihad, both inside Chechnya and in Dubai, supposedly to keep themselves informed?[127] Why, even after the suicide bombings and the hostage-taking at the Dubrovka theatre, were there still people in the West who urged negotiations with the terrorists? 'Russia does not talk to terrorists, it destroys them,' Putin said.[128]

These suspicions and the frustration they engendered boiled over after the massacre of the children at Beslan. In a televised address the night after the school was stormed, Putin placed the blame not only on Russia's own failings, but on aggressive forces in the West that were trying to exploit them:

> Certain people would like to tear from us a succulent morsel. Others help them. They help, reasoning that Russia, as one of the world's major nuclear powers, still poses a certain threat to somebody. So that threat must be removed. Terrorism is naturally just an instrument for achieving these aims.[129]

To those who had been listening carefully to what Putin had been saying, it was not a total surprise. To most, it came as a shock. Western diplomats and journalists suddenly took notice.

A few days later, at a meeting with Western scholars, Putin was asked to explain what he meant. It was 'a replay of the mentality of the Cold War', he said. He was not accusing Western governments or their leaders of supporting terrorism. 'I didn't say it was policy. But . . . there are certain people who want us to be focused on internal problems, and they pull strings here so that we don't raise our heads internationally.'[130] He returned to that idea repeatedly in the weeks that followed. 'Too many people in the West still . . . look on Russia as they used to look at the Soviet Union, as some wild, frightful, untamed animal . . . [It's] like a lion that fell into a trap, and jackals run around and bark, maybe from fear or maybe for joy . . . They must get rid of the idea that international terrorists can be used against their supposed geopolitical opponents.'[131]

In the West, few understood where all this was coming from.

Many assumed that Putin was reacting emotionally to the carnage at Beslan, in the same way that he himself had interpreted the invasion of Iraq as an emotional reaction to 9/11, and that the moment would pass.

That was a misreading.

Looking back over the four years of his first presidential term, from 2000 to 2004, Putin felt, with some justification, that he had put himself out on a limb to help the United States after the terrorist attacks. Russia had done everything Bush had asked for and more: it had shared intelligence, given the Americans overflight rights and encouraged its allies to provide base facilities. But what had it got in return? The SORT agreement and the NATO–Russia Council were hardly great American concessions. Neither was Russia's membership of the Group of 8 leading industrialised nations, which had been accorded in 2002. Russia already attended G8 meetings anyway. All that changed was that it became a member by right. It was not a very important difference. Meanwhile, America had insisted on abrogating the ABM Treaty, rather than modifying it as the Russians had suggested; it had gone ahead with plans for a national missile defence programme over Russian objections; NATO enlargement was continuing apace and would soon reach Russia's borders; and Russia's concerns about America's invasion of Iraq, which were shared by many of America's own allies, had been summarily dismissed.

Whatever Putin might say about the rapprochement with the West being in 'Russia's national interests', it was difficult to argue that any of these developments had been to Russia's advantage.

American officials saw things differently. They focused instead on Russian backsliding over human rights and democracy issues. Putin's construction of a 'power vertical' had made Russia by 2004 a more authoritarian country than four years earlier. But few Russians thought that that was any of America's business. Even liberals who excoriated Putin's regime jibbed at heavy-handed foreign criticism. Putin spoke for a wide segment of Russian society when, commenting on American criticisms of the Russian elections, he said: 'we are none too happy about everything that happens in the United States either. Do you think that the electoral system of the USA is perfect?'[132] If America tried to dictate to others how they should behave, treating them, as he put it, as raw recruits in the barracks of a unipolar world, then 'no matter how this dictatorship is packaged in a pretty wrapping of pseudo-democratic phrases', no one would want to accept it.[133]

On the surface, the relationship remained correct. But there were worrying undercurrents. Putin continued to describe Bush as 'a very decent and consistent man',[134] but he did not forget what he saw as his attempts to dissimulate America's aims in Iraq. For all its fine words, Bush's administration, he felt, wanted to keep Russia down and was prepared to go to almost any lengths to do so. Whether, or to what extent, that was true was almost beside the point. What mattered was perception, and the leaders' perceptions of each other's goals were starting to diverge. Then, as the year drew to a close, a new conflict arose, much closer to home for Russia, which would reinforce Putin's misgivings about America's intentions, adding yet another dimension to the matrix of cross purposes that was pushing them apart.

For Russia, relations with the Near Abroad – the Baltic and the CIS states – were the bedrock of its foreign policy. It is true that it did not always seem that way. Much of the time Moscow appeared fixated on its relations with the United States and the European Union. But the Near Abroad had fundamental importance, not just because the countries concerned were Russia's neighbours, but because, for centuries, most of them had been part of the Russian empire and later the Soviet Union. Like Gorbachev, Putin regarded the break-up of the USSR as a tragedy which could never be undone. A few weeks before his election as President in March 2000, he had said: 'He who does not regret the destruction of the Soviet Union has no heart, he who wants to see it recreated in its former shape has no brain.'[135]

Yet precisely because of that accumulated history, when, by Putin's own admission, the Soviet Union had been 'held together with barbed wire', the Kremlin's relations with the Near Abroad were mind-numbingly complicated and difficult to manage. Like siblings in a dysfunctional family, suddenly freed from an abusive parent, they were condemned to go on living alongside each other amid rancours and injustices, rivalries and hatreds, inherited from the past.

On one issue or another, almost everyone felt unfairly treated.

Putin grumbled that Russia had had to assume the whole of the Soviet Union's foreign debt, including that incurred by its CIS partners, and more than a decade later was still paying it off. The supply of gas, oil and electric power to Russia's neighbours at preferential prices, which had irritated him ever since he had been deputy Mayor in St Petersburg, was another sore point, threatening to poison relations with Belarus, Ukraine and Georgia.

Belarus's President, Aleksandr Lukashenko, a burly, combative, populist, former collective-farm head whose autocratic rule had alienated the majority of his neighbours, had an ability to get under Putin's skin to which the master of the Kremlin never found an adequate response. The key to the relationship was that Russia needed Belarus as a buffer on its western flank. When Putin demanded that Minsk repay 200 million US dollars in gas debts, the Belarusian leader retorted that his country's contribution to Russian security was worth 900 million dollars a year. 'That's why there's no point nagging us for 200 million dollars of gas . . . Who owes whom?'[136] They bickered over who was to blame for the lack of progress towards a Russia–Belarus Union, each accusing the other of refusing to make up his mind. Lukashenko, Putin said in exasperation, did not seem to understand that he should 'keep the meat and the flies apart', in other words, go to the core of the issue and stop poisoning it with trivia.[137] But Belarus's role as a pro-Russian Slav state on the border with Eastern Europe was too important for Putin to put at risk, so he had little choice but to tolerate Lukashenko's needling.

Ukraine, the most consequential of all Russia's neighbours, by virtue both of its size – in 2000, it had a population of nearly 50 million – and of their shared history, posed fewer problems in Putin's first term. Kyiv owed Moscow two billion dollars for gas, ten times more than Belarus. But Putin found Leonid Kuchma, the former Communist apparatchik who had become Ukraine's second President in 1994, easier to deal with than Lukashenko. In October 2000, he agreed to defer Ukraine's debts for ten years at a favourable interest rate, and progress followed on two other key issues – the extension of the lease on the Russian naval base at Sevastopol, and the delineation of the land and sea borders.

Georgia was another story entirely.

After a period of extreme nationalism in the early 1990s, when the country descended into civil war and two Georgian provinces – Abkhazia and South Ossetia – declared de facto independence, a measure of stability returned when Gorbachev's former Foreign Minister, Eduard Shevardnadze, who had earlier been Georgia's Communist Party First Secretary, became President in 1995. But his regime turned out to be repressive, deeply corrupt and either unable or unwilling to prevent Chechen rebels establishing sanctuaries near their common border or to stop Arab jihadists travelling to Chechnya through Georgian territory. In reprisal, in the autumn of 2000, Putin ended visa-free travel for Georgians who came to Russia. When President Clinton, in a year-end telephone call, warned him against putting pressure on the Georgians, pointing out that they had significant bipartisan support in Washington, Putin was outraged, lecturing the US President like a schoolmaster berating a particularly dim pupil. 'I would like you to try to listen to what I am saying to you now,' he began, prompting the White House note-taker to write in the margin: 'Putin's voice becomes increasingly emotional and insistent as he discusses Georgia.' The burden of his response was that the Georgians were ingrates. More than 600,000 Georgians were working illegally in Russia, he said. Their remittances helped to keep the Georgian economy afloat and Russia, despite its own difficulties, continued to provide the country with gas and electric power at well below market rates. 'Georgia exists at our expense,' Putin complained. It owed Russia tens of millions of dollars which would have to be paid back.[138]

The relationship fluctuated between bad and terrible. Occasionally Putin acknowledged that Russia's problems with Georgia, like those which bedevilled its relations with all the other former Soviet republics, stemmed from Russia's long history of imperial domination. 'The blame is not all on Georgia's side,' he said. 'Georgia fears Russia's imperial ambitions.'[139] More often, however, he lashed out at the Georgians for sympathising with the Chechens, comparing them with the Taliban in Afghanistan who had protected al-Qaeda.[140]

It was in Georgia, in November 2003, that the first of what became known as the 'colour revolutions' occurred. The term referred to popular uprisings in former Soviet states, often triggered by disputed elections, which overthrew established governments, in most cases without violence. In Georgia, exit polls during the parliamentary elections on November 2 showed the main opposition party, led by She-vardnadze's former Justice Minister, Mikheil Saakashvili, comfortably ahead. But when the results were announced, the ruling party was declared the winner. Massive street protests followed and, when Shevard-nadze attempted to open the new session of parliament three weeks later, Saakashvili burst into the chamber at the head of hundreds of opposition supporters, holding red roses in their hands. The incident gave its name to what would be called the Rose Revolution. The follow-ing day, Shevardnadze resigned after the Georgian military refused to support him and Russia made clear that it would not intervene.

Mikheil Saakashvili, who, at the age of 36, was elected President in January 2004, had studied at Columbia and George Washington uni-versities in the United States and was strongly pro-Western. To Putin, that was not necessarily a problem. Shevardnadze had also tilted towards Washington. The Bush administration viewed Georgia as a US bridgehead in the Caucasus, counteracting Russian influence in the region. Under Shevardnadze, America had given Georgia economic aid and a military training programme and had supported the con-struction of the Baku–Tbilisi–Ceyhan oil pipeline, which would reduce the country's dependence on Russian energy supplies. Georgia, in turn, had sent troops to fight with the coalition in Iraq. Putin under-stood that Saakashvili would continue those policies but hoped that his election might make possible a new start in a relationship which, under Shevardnadze, had come to a dead end.

For a time, that seemed to be happening. After talks in Moscow in February, Saakashvili declared that 'for the first time in ten years, a positive trend has been created in Georgian – Russian relations'.[141] The two countries agreed to carry out joint patrols and special operations to prevent infiltration across the border with Chechnya, which Putin said might make possible the resumption of visa-free travel.[142] On the crucial issue of separatism, he reiterated Russia's support for Georgia's territorial integrity. It was up to Tbilisi, he said, to resolve its differ-ences with the breakaway provinces of Abkhazia and South Ossetia, as well as with Adjara on the Black Sea coast, the country's most prosper-ous region, which had also become largely autonomous. Russia would not interfere, he added, but he hoped that it would be done 'in such a way that the interests of the [non-Georgian] population in those terri-tories will not be harmed'.[143]

In practice, things were a little more complicated. Russia had 3,000 peacekeepers in Abkhazia, and the South Ossetian government was heavily dependent on Russian support. But at least Putin's statement of principle was what the Georgians wanted to hear. On another sensitive issue, the presence of two Russian military bases in Georgia, which had been there since Soviet times, Putin also undertook to be flexible in return for an assurance that, as Saakashvili put it, no 'third party' – in other words, the United States – would take Russia's place.[144]

It was too good to last.

In May, Saakashvili regained control of Adjara, the most populous of the breakaway provinces. It was done peacefully, the Georgians promised to respect Adjarian autonomy and Putin acquiesced. But then the Georgian President turned his attention to Abkhazia and South Ossetia, announcing at a military parade in Tbilisi that he intended to end what he called 'the disintegration of Georgia' and restore a unified state, the implication being that if negotiations failed, he reserved the right to use force.[145] That led Putin to warn that any attempt to do so would be 'unproductive, . . . long and exhausting'.[146]

Relations with Georgia were particularly sensitive during Putin's first years in power because of its proximity to Chechnya. But almost everywhere in the post-Soviet space caused problems of one kind or another.

Even the Central Asian republics, which Putin and the President of Kazakhstan, Nursultan Nazarbayev, had hoped would join Belarus, Russia and Ukraine in a newly established Eurasian Economic Community, were wary of Moscow's imperial reach. The President of Tajikistan, Emomali Rahmon, was a 'difficult, complex fellow', Putin complained.[147] So was the Uzbek leader, Islam Karimov, who sympathised with the Taliban, wanted to do arms deals with Israel and shied away from any kind of joint action with his Central Asian neighbours. But worst of all was Saparmurat Niyazov, the megalomaniac President of Turkmenistan, who had taken the title, Turkmenbashi, 'Father of the Turkmen', and appointed himself President for life. Niyazov had renamed the days of the week and the months after members of his family, and in the main square of the capital, Ashgabat, he had erected a triumphal arch, almost as tall as the Statue of Liberty, surmounted by a 40-foot-high gold-plated statue of himself, which rotated so that it always faced the sun.

Putin's memories of his first visit to Turkmenistan, a few months after his election, were deeply unpleasant. Niyazov treated him as a novice, instructing him when to sit down and stand up. Putin was 'green with fury', the *Kommersant* correspondent, Yelena Tregubova, reported. On one occasion, when the beefy Turkmen leader tried to give him a Soviet-style kiss on the lips, his training as a judoka got the better of him and he forcibly pushed him away.[148] But Turkmenistan was of vital interest to Russia and Niyazov had to be humoured, however obnoxious he might be. With a population of less than 5 million, it possessed some of the world's biggest gas and oil reserves and occupied a strategic corridor stretching westward from Afghanistan along the northern border of Iran.

Niyazov had banned Russian newspapers and television, prohibited Russian teaching in schools and universities, abolished dual citizenship, forbidden Russians to own property and made them obtain exit visas if they wished to leave the country. Putin uttered not a word of protest. While the 120,000 Russian expatriates endured relentless discrimination at the hands of the Turkmen government, the Russian Embassy in Ashgabat was under strict orders not to intervene. It was cynical, ruthless and pragmatic. 'We kick up a storm when there is any slight to a Russian in Latvia or Estonia,' the newspaper, *Vremya novostei*, observed, 'but in Turkmenistan it is ten times worse and we don't say a word.'[149]

Problems of ethnicity and nationalism abounded in the post-Soviet space. Some were so intractable that they became 'frozen conflicts', like those in Abkhazia and South Ossetia, which, despite Putin's claims of neutrality, gave the Kremlin leverage against the country whose integrity had been compromised. Others, like the conflict between Armenia and Azerbaijan over Nagorno-Karabakh, allowed Russia to play the honest broker, gaining influence with both sides. Yet others, such as the Russian separatist enclave of Transnistria, brought little direct benefit to the Kremlin but proved impossible to resolve.

However, the biggest challenge of all came from a totally unexpected quarter.

In the summer of 2004, Leonid Kuchma, the Ukrainian leader, was nearing the end of his second term and could not stand again. His chosen successor, the Prime Minister, Viktor Yanukovych, represented the predominantly Russian-speaking, heavily industrialised, eastern region of Ukraine. Yanukovych, like Putin, was from a working-class family. He had lost both parents while still a child and had been jailed twice as a teenager for assault and robbery. Afterwards he had made a career as a transport manager, entering politics only in his mid 40s and then making an even more rapid ascent than Putin, being appointed head of government just six years later. Yanukovych's principal rival, Viktor Yushchenko, who had also served as Prime Minister, was supported by the Ukrainian-speaking areas in the centre and west of the country. Unlike Yanukovych, he was from an intellectual family and had had a distinguished career as a banker. Yushchenko stood on a liberal programme and advocated closer relations with the West, including membership of NATO and the European Union.

In the early stages of the campaign, Yushchenko was consistently ahead.[150] But at the beginning of September, after attending a dinner hosted by Volodymyr Satsyuk, the deputy head of the Ukrainian security service, the SBU, he fell ill. It was later established that he had been poisoned with a compound of dioxin, dissolved in his soup, which left him severely disfigured. It was never proved who was responsible, but Satsyuk, an ally of Yanukovych, later fled to Russia, which granted him citizenship, preventing his extradition. Given the very high degree of purity of the dioxin which was used, it could only have come from a laboratory in Russia.

That did not necessarily mean that the SBU's sister service, the FSB, was behind the operation or that the Kremlin had approved it. Kuchma and Yanukovych were quite capable of having organised it themselves. Even within Yushchenko's own camp, there were enough intrigues and rivalries to provide a motive for eliminating, or at least incapacitating, him.

Whatever the truth of Yushchenko's poisoning, Putin left no doubt that he was solidly behind Yanukovych. In October, he invited him to Moscow to attend his birthday celebrations, an important symbolic gesture in the Russian-speaking world,[151] and on the eve of the first round of the election, he paid a three-day visit to Kyiv, ostensibly to mark the 60th anniversary of the city's liberation from the Germans in 1944 (the date having been brought forward by ten days to fit the electoral calendar) but actually to support his campaign. Russian businessmen were 'encouraged' to contribute to Yanukovych's election fund – by one account, they raised 200 million US dollars[152] – and

Putin praised Yanukovych's government for what he called the 'positive, sustainable development [of] the Ukrainian economy'.[153] Ukrainian voters, he said, must now decide whether to continue on this promising course or to take a leap into the unknown.[154]

As a sweetener, Putin pledged to maintain passport-free travel for Ukrainians visiting Russia, and to examine the possibility of dual nationality, both of which were among Yanukovych's campaign promises.[155] Other Russians, including the Mayor of Moscow, Yuri Luzhkov, Russian rock stars and the crooner, Iosif Kobzon, campaigned on Yanukovych's behalf, and the Kremlin's political strategist, Gleb Pavlovsky, moved to Kyiv to advise his election headquarters.[156]

The results of the first round were a disappointment to Moscow. Despite having had a near monopoly of television coverage, Yanukovych, with 39.32 per cent of the vote, finished slightly behind Yushchenko, who had 39.87 per cent. Both sides cried fraud, each accusing the other of every dirty trick in the book, and the Election Commission delayed announcing the official results for more than a week, apparently to prevent Yushchenko capitalising on his advantage. 'With every passing day,' wrote the non-partisan *Zerkalo nedeli*, the country's most influential weekly, 'Ukraine reminds one more and more of Orwell's world turned upside down, where black is white and white is black, lies are presented as unvarnished truth and truth is tarnished with filth.'[157]

On November 12, nine days before the second round, Putin intervened again, paying an unscheduled visit to Crimea, where he was shown wishing Yanukovych good luck.[158]

Ukrainian pollsters had calculated that Putin's support would add two or three per cent to Yanukovych's vote,[159] and when the results started coming in, it looked as though they were right. With more than 90 per cent of the votes counted, the Election Commission reported that he had a lead of 3 per cent. Putin, who was in Latin America for an APEC summit, was delighted and telephoned his congratulations even before the count was completed.

By then, the government's scenario was starting to unravel.

It emerged late that evening that the Ukrainian TV channels had falsified the exit polls to show that Yanukovych was winning when in fact Yushchenko had been ahead. At 2 a.m., Yushchenko declared that the Election Commission's figures were fake. Next day he told a crowd of several hundred thousand people who had gathered on Maidan, Kyiv's Independence Square, that the results were not believable and the election must be annulled.

Throughout the following week, the evidence of fraud piled up.

OSCE monitors reported that in eastern Ukraine, some pro-Yanukovych districts had reported turnouts of more than 100 per cent. Ukrainian intelligence officers sympathetic to Yushchenko leaked wiretaps of the Prime Minister's supporters discussing how to falsify the result. In areas which supported Yushchenko, it was claimed that pro-Yanukovych officials had put special pens in the voting booths whose ink faded and disappeared, leaving the ballot papers blank.

On Maidan, the crowds of demonstrators, wearing orange scarves and waving orange flags, the colour of Yushchenko's coalition, grew larger day by day. As the protests spread to other cities, the Ukrainian Supreme Court announced on December 3 that the results of the second round were being annulled on the grounds of widespread fraud. A new vote would be held on the last Sunday of the year.

Putin was livid.

He accused the OSCE, which had first raised the alarm about election irregularities, of allowing itself to be used by 'someone' as 'a political tool to achieve tactical goals'.[160] Who the 'someone' was, he did not say, but nor did he need to. That year, a string of high-ranking Americans, including George H. W. Bush, Henry Kissinger and John McCain, had come to Ukraine to demonstrate Washington's interest in the outcome of the elections. Bush had sent the Chairman of the Senate Foreign Relations Committee, Richard Lugar, to Kyiv as his personal emissary. President Carter's former National Security Advisor, Zbigniew Brzezinski, had spoken of the importance of prising Ukraine away from Russia's embrace.[161]

The Orange Revolution, as it would be called, had developed into a trial of strength by proxy – political rather than military, but a trial of strength nonetheless – between Russia and the United States.

What was most galling to Putin was that it was a battle which he was losing. In public, he insisted that Russia would work with whomever the Ukrainians chose as their President and that any differences between Moscow and Washington were 'inconsequential, fleeting . . . things of a tactical nature'.[162] But other, less guarded comments indicated a much more bitter reaction. Shortly after the Ukrainian Supreme

Court's decision to cancel the second-round results, Putin groused to a small group of Russian journalists that the United States was behaving in Europe the way the colonial powers had in Africa:

> I wouldn't like Europe to be divided . . . into first- and second-class citizens, . . . where first-class citizens are able to live according to stable and democratic laws, while second-class citizens are told by well-intentioned persons in pith helmets what political course to follow. And if the ungrateful natives object, they will be punished by having bombs dropped on their heads, as happened in Belgrade.[163]

That was dishonest. Putin had intervened in the Ukrainian elections far more blatantly than the Americans had. Yanukovych, as even some Russian commentators acknowledged, had been a weak candidate, unable to gain broad support outside his own fiefdoms in Donetsk and Luhansk.[164]

But this was not how Putin saw it. In his view, America had tried to suborn the most important of Russia's post-Soviet neighbours. It was 'a stab in the back,' he was quoted as saying. 'They are stealing Ukraine from under me.'[165]

When the results of the restaged second round were announced, Yushchenko had won 52 per cent of the vote, Yanukovych 44.2 per cent. Putin swallowed his anger and relations between Russia and Ukraine settled back into their former pattern of outward cordiality masking wariness and mistrust.

Nevertheless, the episode left deep wounds.

The historical divisions between western and central Ukraine, formerly part of the Polish–Lithuanian Commonwealth and then the Austrian empire, which looked to Europe, and eastern Ukraine, formerly part of the Russian empire and oriented towards Moscow, had initially been masked by shared enthusiasm for Ukrainian independence.

No longer. 'The gloomiest predictions are coming true,' wrote *Komsomolskaya pravda*. 'Ukraine has again been split in two.'[166] For a time the two halves would continue to co-exist, but ten years later, the underlying strains would produce an eruption of far greater violence, with malign consequences for everyone concerned.

Putin had been badly burned by the events in Kyiv not only because Russia had suffered a geopolitical defeat, but because, abandoning his usual caution, he had personally thrown his support behind the losing candidate. It hardly dented his popularity at home. But Putin did not easily forgive his own errors, and when he looked for an explanation, he became convinced that the main blame for Yanukovych's defeat lay with the neoconservatives in the Bush administration, who were obsessed with expanding America's influence up to Russia's borders.

He was wrong. A majority of Ukrainians voted for Yushchenko not because of American support but because they were fed up with the corruption of the Kuchma–Yanukovych tandem and were looking for change. But he was right about the growing influence of the neoconservatives at the start of the American President's second term.

On January 20, 2005, three weeks after Yushchenko was officially proclaimed the victor in Kyiv, Bush declared in his inaugural address, at the start of his second term, that henceforward it would be 'the policy of the United States to seek and support the growth of democratic movements in every nation and culture'. America's freedom, he said, was intimately linked to freedom in other lands. 'We will persistently clarify the choice before every ruler and every nation: the moral choice between oppression . . . and freedom . . . [and] we will encourage reform in other governments . . . Today, America speaks to the peoples of the world: . . . When you stand for your liberty, we will stand with you.'[167]

To many Americans, it was an uplifting speech, albeit marked by a certain tunnel vision. To declare that 'from the day of our founding, we have proclaimed that every man and woman on this earth has rights . . . No one is fit to be a master and no one deserves to be a slave', without mentioning America's long history of slavery or the systemic racism ingrained in American society, required singular blindness to America's faults. But Bush's call for the United States to take the lead in fighting against tyranny, wherever it might be found, resonated with a nation which had grown up with the idea of American exceptionalism as a force for good in the world.

To most Russians, Putin among them, the speech conveyed hubris and hypocrisy.

Hubris because, in this new, ideological iteration, the Bush doctrine, as it was called, sought to formalise the right of the United States to intervene in other countries' affairs and 'clarify the choice' for their rulers by pressuring them to follow the political advice that America would provide.[168] Ronald Reagan's image of a shining city on the hill, attracting others by example, had morphed into 'men in pith helmets' instructing the natives how to behave. Bush's attempted disclaimer that America would not 'impose our own style of government on the unwilling' did not carry much weight in Moscow.

Hypocrisy because the United States had a long record of consorting with tyrants – from Videla in Argentina to Pinochet in Chile, Somoza in Nicaragua and Stroessner in Paraguay – as long as they backed American interests. Under George W. Bush, it would continue to support undemocratic regimes in the Middle East, notably in Saudi Arabia and the Gulf states, whose propagation of Wahhabite fundamentalism was one of the wellsprings of Islamic terrorism.

The Soviet Union, of course, had done exactly the same. For decades, Moscow had imposed its will on its satellites in Eastern Europe and had supported singularly vile third-world dictatorships. But as far as Putin was concerned that was not his problem.

It was a classic case of two powerful countries talking past each other and refusing to look in the mirror. That had been so throughout the Cold War. The antagonisms which came into focus in the winter of 2004 were an enantiomorph of the problems of the 1960s and '70s. Russia was no longer trying to export its ideology and value system. Instead, America was.

Bush's State of the Union address, coupled with the Rose Revolution in Georgia, the Orange Revolution in Ukraine and, a few months later, the Tulip Revolution in Kyrgyzstan, where the government was overthrown in March 2005, convinced Putin that genuine partnership with the United States, let alone an alliance, was going to be a challenge.

NATO enlargement, from the Kremlin's standpoint, had been provocative enough. But that had started when Yeltsin was in power and there was little that Putin could do about it. Iraq had been an irritant, but Putin's reaction, as one American official put it, had been 'more in sorrow than in anger'.[169] The colour revolutions posed a threat of a different order. They risked jeopardising Moscow's position on its own turf, inside the post-Soviet space. It did not require a great stretch of imagination on Putin's part to suspect that behind Bush's professions of friendship, the US government, or at least a powerful element within it, was playing a double game. Up to then, both sides had been at pains to play down their differences: Bush, because he assumed that, in the end, Moscow would accept Washington's choices; Putin, because he remained convinced that good relations with the United States were one of the keys to Russia's future. But now it was clear to the Kremlin, if not yet to the White House, that much more difficult times lay ahead.

The gradual erosion of Russia's relationship with Washington was mirrored by changes in its relations with the main Western European powers, Britain, France and Germany.

Britain's Tony Blair had initially been closest to Putin, providing a valued channel to the White House during the first year of his presidency.

Afterwards, Gerhard Schröder, who had succeeded Helmut Kohl as German Chancellor, inherited that mantle. He and Putin developed a close political relationship and became good personal friends. Putin's affection for Germany and his fluency in the language helped. Both men came from modest backgrounds. Schröder had left school at fourteen, studied at night school and eventually, like Putin, obtained a law degree. In January 2001, he and his wife stayed at Novo-Ogaryovo for the Orthodox Christmas holiday. Later Putin helped them adopt a three-year-old Russian girl from an orphanage in St Petersburg.[170]

Relations with France were at first more distant because of French criticisms of Russian policy in Chechnya and the peculiar complexity of French politics at a time when a right-wing President, Jacques Chirac, shared power with Lionel Jospin, a left-wing Prime Minister. Putin had grown used to dealing with European sniping over Chechnya. To begin with, he admitted, Russia had responded to criticisms 'by looking at its partners with sad eyes or mooing something incoherently as though it had mad cow disease'.[171] Now, he took them in his stride. He found the relationship between Chirac and Jospin much harder to fathom. Hubert Vedrine, the French Foreign Minister, remembered Putin asking him, during a visit to Paris, who had the final say: the President, who determined foreign policy, or the Prime Minister, who headed the government? The only thing that interested Putin, Vedrine said, was where power lay – a tricky question, to which there was not always a simple answer. [172]

18 months later, in June 2002, after Chirac's re-election, his party regained control of parliament and power-sharing came to an end. By then France's relationship with Russia was on a different level. Chirac, Schröder and Putin all opposed the invasion of Iraq and started holding tripartite summits to coordinate their positions. Blair, who had sided with Bush, was excluded.

The 'schism', as British officials called the European divide over Iraq, had lingering effects. It was 'difficult to put the pieces back together again after the conflict', Blair's foreign policy adviser, Nigel Sheinwald, remembered.[173] Years later, it would be seen as one of the cracks in the façade of European unity which would culminate in Brexit.

Putin nursed a grudge against Blair, who he thought, like Bush, had lied to him about preparations for the Iraq invasion. For the most part he kept it hidden, but occasionally a glimmer of irritation would break through. His taunting of Blair over Saddam's non-existent weapons of mass destruction had been one such instance. Another occurred when he paid a state visit to Britain in the summer of 2003 and grumbled about the pomp and ceremony and having to wear tails – 'I can't say that I liked it, it's very uncomfortable', he said.[174] It was intentionally churlish – an oblique jab at the fading grandeur of a nation that he was beginning to find even more annoying than its American cousins – and stood in marked contrast to his first visit three years earlier, when he had met the Queen for tea at Windsor Castle and had been agreeably surprised by her interest in Russia.[175]

By now, other problems were intruding. Boris Berezovsky and the Chechen foreign minister, Akhmed Zakayev, had both applied to Britain for political asylum. In September, the Home Office granted Berezovsky's request. Zakayev's application was approved two months later. Russia had been seeking their extradition – Berezovsky to face trial for embezzlement and fraud, for which he was later sentenced in absentia to two terms of imprisonment, and Zakayev for alleged terrorist offences. In Berezovsky's case, extradition proceedings were abandoned because he had been granted refugee status. In Zakayev's, the judge had ruled that the accusations were politically motivated and that there was a risk that he would be tortured if he was returned to Moscow.

Britain insisted that the government had no control over the courts. Tony Brenton, who arrived in Moscow as British Ambassador a year later, found that whenever he talked to Russian officials, the first thing they brought up was the two men's extradition. 'I used to tell them,' Brenton said, 'I can't do that. Tony Blair can't do that. You need to persuade a British judge to send them back.'[176]

That was being economical with the truth.

The reason that they could not be extradited was that the British government, through the Home Office, had granted them asylum. Blair might claim that he had had no choice because both men risked persecution for their political views if they returned to Russia, but that was a harder case to argue than just saying that the courts were responsible.

Putin did not buy it. From Moscow's standpoint, Zakayev was the spokesman for a Chechen jihadi movement whose members committed terrorist acts, and Berezovsky, even if he had done no more than other Russian oligarchs, had used dubious if not criminal methods to build his business empire. By granting them asylum – in Zakayev's case, shortly after the Beslan massacre – the British government had made clear that it did not trust the Russian justice system to deal with them fairly. On that score, the British were correct. What in Soviet times had been called 'telephone justice' was as much part of Putin's repertoire as it had been of his Soviet predecessors. There was now a new name for it, 'Basmanny justice', after the court in the Basmanny District of Moscow, north-east of the Lubyanka, to which the Kremlin confided politically sensitive proceedings. But it worked in exactly the same way. Judges handed down the sentences the authorities had determined in advance.

Putin's disillusionment with Blair was reciprocated. Within the British government, there was, as Sheinwald put it, 'an increasing realisation of the degree of oppression in Russia and of Putin's character and methods. [Blair] felt let down by the Putin who was emerging, a more overtly brutal and autocratic Putin than the one he'd hoped for.'[177]

Over the next few years, that view became more widely shared in Europe. Gerhard Schröder, who had argued that it was wrong 'to place excessive demands on Russia when it comes to the rate of domestic political reform',[178] was replaced by Angela Merkel, who had grown up in East Germany and had far fewer illusions about Russia. In Italy, the ebullient Silvio Berlusconi, with whom Putin had developed a warm relationship, sending his daughters to spend holidays with the Prime Minister's children at the family villa in Sardinia,[179] was succeeded by the cerebral Romano Prodi. In France, Nicolas Sarkozy, an impulsive right-winger who was an unknown quantity in Moscow, took over from Jacques Chirac.

Despite the changes, Russia's relations with the European Union continued to make progress. Areas of cooperation known as 'common spaces' were established covering economic relations, security and legal affairs, external security and science, education and culture, and there was renewed talk – though only talk – of easing visa requirements. But the political climate in Europe was distinctly cooler than during Putin's first years in power.

For Moscow, Britain became a touchstone, a place to probe America's intentions and reactions to Russian initiatives without endangering the core relationship with the United States itself.

The chill that had set in after the invasion of Iraq was felt across the board. When Richard Dearlove visited Moscow in 2004 for talks with Patrushev, his opposite number in the FSB, he found that 'the shutters were coming down.'[180] Blair's contacts with Putin became less frequent. Sheinwald spoke of 'a slow burn'.[181] Russian commentators wrote that relations were deteriorating.[182]

Ambassador Brenton tried to put a good face on it. 'They were doing things that we didn't like,' he said, 'but fundamentally these were the problems of a country which was still finding its feet after the collapse of communism . . . The expectation was that we would work our way through this and Russia would become a normal member of the international community.'[183]

With hindsight, that appears naïve. But it was a view widely shared in the West at that time. Outwardly, relations were correct.[184] When Blair visited Moscow in June 2005, Putin received him at Novo-Ogaryovo, rather than in the Kremlin, which was seen as a positive gesture, and he appeared to take pleasure in showing Blair around the grounds.[185] In July, during the Gleneagles G8 Summit, when Islamist terrorists killed more than 50 people in suicide bombings in London, the British found Putin 'magnanimous and supportive and everything you would expect a leader to be'.[186] Three months later, when he visited Britain again for a Russia–EU Summit, Russian journalists noted appreciatively that Blair had invited Putin to his home, where they talked 'in a room cluttered with children's toys'.[187]

But alongside these superficial courtesies, Putin was becoming deeply impatient with what he saw as British hypocrisy.

Wealthy Russians with dubious backgrounds were granted residence and invested their fortunes in Britain. Putin's opponents were granted asylum. Blair seemed not to want to understand that he could not be both with Russia and against it. The Russian leader's frustration showed through again when he was taken to see COBRA, the secure briefing room beneath the Cabinet Office building where crisis meetings are held, to hear a briefing on British counter-terrorism tactics in the wake of the London bombings. He listened for a while and then said quietly: 'You know how we deal with Islamic terrorists? We kill them.'[188]

Even in the Foreign Office, where imperturbable optimism did duty as the diplomatic equivalent of the stiff upper lip, there was a growing recognition that all was not well. At the formal talks in Downing Street, when the subject of Berezovsky and Zakayev came up, the Foreign Secretary, Jack Straw, told Putin directly: 'I wish I could get rid of these people. They are damaging our relations.'[189]

From there on, it was all downhill.

A row broke out over foreign – and specifically British – support of Russian NGOs, a subject which had been troubling Putin since the Rose Revolution in Georgia two years earlier, in which American financed NGOs had played a prominent role. 'Not all NGOs are oriented to standing up for people's real interests,' Putin grumbled in the spring of 2004. 'For some of them, the priority is to receive funding from influential foreign foundations [and] they can't bite the hand that feeds them.'[190]

The following year, the FSB discovered an unusual dead letter drop in one of Moscow's garden squares. Disguised as a small rock near some bushes, it contained a device which was capable of receiving and storing electronic messages from specially equipped mobile phones carried by Russian informants. Their controllers, four MI6 officers under diplomatic cover at the British Embassy, retrieved the messages electronically on a pocket-sized computer as they walked past.[191]

For several months, the story was kept under wraps. Then, as though pulling a rabbit out of the hat, in January 2006, it was made public with great fanfare in a special programme on the state-owned TV channel, Rossiya 1.

Espionage, however, was not the only accusation. The Russians claimed that the diplomats had also provided illegal financing to Russian human rights organisations, a charge which the British government strongly denied. The accusation was designed to justify a bill imposing new restrictions on NGOs which the Duma had passed a week earlier.[192] The timing was such that some Russians suspected the whole story was a fabrication and that no rock had ever existed, fake or otherwise. That was not so. Blair's Chief of Staff, Jonathan Powell, acknowledged later that the rock, which was made of grey plastic, had been real enough and that MI6 had been caught with its pants down.[193]

Putin dismissed the episode as petty squabbling between intelligence services, adding mischievously that the diplomats concerned would not be expelled because, if they were replaced, their successors might turn out to be more skilful.[194] What was regrettable, he said, was the covert financing of non-governmental organisations. 'That money has a bad smell,' he declared. 'We do not want [our NGOs] to be run by puppet-masters from abroad . . . States cannot use NGOs as an instrument of foreign policy on the territory of others.'[195]

Much as he had done when the Duma had passed harsh new restrictions on the media after the Dubrovka attack, Putin watered down the NGO legislation, playing the now familiar role of the 'good tsar reproving bad boyars', but the new laws remained sufficiently vague to give the authorities wide latitude to crack down if and when they wished.[196]

A few days later, the Prosecutor's Office announced that it was proceeding with a criminal investigation into the British Council office in St Petersburg for 'illegal commercial activities', which turned out to mean organising English language classes.[197] The accusation was left hanging, a muffled threat which could be put into effect whenever the political situation required. In July 2006, when Russia was to host the G8 in St Petersburg, Tony Blair announced that he planned to attend the opening of the Council's new offices on Nevsky Prospekt. Not possible, he was told: the Fire Department had refused to certify the building. In that case, Blair said, he would conduct the opening ceremony on the pavement outside. Faced with a scandal on the eve of the summit, the Russians backed down.[198] But the investigation into 'illegal language teaching' continued. The British Council's difficulties were not over.

Nor were Ambassador Brenton's.

A few days before the G8 meeting, he had addressed what was termed an 'alternative summit' in Moscow organised by the leaders of several small opposition parties and human rights groups to discuss political freedoms.[199] The Kremlin youth movement, Nashi – meaning 'Ours', a name designed to underline the difference between what was Russian (*nash*), and what was not Russian or foreign (*ne nash*) – promptly demanded that he apologise for attending a 'fascist' event.[200]

Nashi had been created by the Kremlin ideologist, Vladislav Surkov, a talented, unconformable young man, half-Chechen and half-Russian, who was as much at home writing rock songs and novels as devising Machiavellian political strategies. His formal position was first deputy head of the Presidential Administration. He had established Nashi to act as a shock force to support Putin should there be any attempt to launch an Orange Revolution in Russia.

When no apology was forthcoming, Nashi members, waving banners and chanting demands for Brenton's recall, picketed the British Embassy, housed in a palatial nineteenth-century merchant's home on the bank of the Moscow River, opposite the Kremlin. It seemed to be straight out of the playbook of the Maoist Red Guards, 40 years earlier, although far less violent – a sort of 'Cultural Revolution lite'.

The harassment continued intermittently for 18 months. After one young man, who had vowed to make Brenton his 'personal affair', came to blows with an Embassy guard, the Russian Foreign Minister, Sergei Lavrov, called in the movement's leaders and reminded them of Russia's obligations under the Vienna Convention. It made little difference. The police were under orders not to intervene.

The campaign against the British Council and the harassment of the British Ambassador had Putin's authorisation. But Britain was a surrogate target. The Kremlin was much more concerned about the United States' democracy promotion initiatives and support for human rights groups through congressionally funded organisations like the National Endowment for Democracy.

Putin was not yet ready to confront Washington directly and

perhaps hoped that he would not have to. Instead, he adopted the Chinese adage, 'pointing at the mulberry to curse the locust tree'. The British Council's misfortunes, the Kremlin hoped, might make the Americans think again.

Brenton himself was a stalking horse, too.

American officials like Dan Fried, the Assistant Secretary of State for European and Eurasian Affairs, who had attended the same 'alternative summit', incurred none of the wrath that fell on their British colleague.[201] When Alexander Vershbow, the American Ambassador in Moscow for most of Putin's first term, was summoned to the Foreign Ministry for a dressing down after attending an opposition conference on freedom of the press, he informed them: 'I am here to defend American values.'[202] He, too, was spared the kind of harassment which Brenton had to endure.

By then, another incident had occurred whose significance was not recognised at the time but whose effect was to make Putin even more jaundiced about the United States' role in the world.

The Russian government had announced in the summer of 2004 that the main production complex of Mikhail Khodorkovsky's Yukos oil company, Yugveskneftegaz, would be sold at auction to pay off the 27.5 billion US dollars in back taxes which it claimed the company owed. Putin decided that Gazprom should buy it as part of a diversification programme. A consortium of Western banks, headed by Deutsche Bank, had put together a loan package of some 18 billion dollars – the company's estimated market value – to finance the acquisition.

Khodorkovsky's nemesis, Igor Sechin, now Rosneft Chairman, had strongly opposed the arrangement, supposedly on the grounds that Western banks could not be trusted to finance a strategic asset, but in reality to defend his own turf. Gazprom, in Sechin's view, had no business involving itself in oil production. That was Rosneft's domain.

Putin then decided that Gazprom and Rosneft should merge.

This was partly a sop to the West, to mitigate the negative fallout from the arrest of Khodorkovsky and the break-up of Yukos. It would create a behemoth, five times bigger than ExxonMobil, and restrictions on foreign participation – which had limited foreign ownership in Gazprom – would be lifted. It would also serve to reinforce Putin's control over the energy sector as a whole.

Sechin liked that idea even less.

Early in December, Putin called a meeting to discuss the takeover. Sechin dug in his heels and the discussion degenerated until the President, finally losing patience, told him that the decision had been taken and if he did not wish to accept it, he could go – a reprimand which left him shaken.[203]

Three days later, in Texas, a judge in a district court in Houston granted Yukos and its American subsidiary an injunction barring Gazprom or any of the other prospective bidders from participating in the auction for Yuganskneftegaz pending Chapter 11 bankruptcy hearings.[204]

The Deutsche Bank consortium suspended the loan package for fear of US sanctions.

The auction went ahead nonetheless on December 19. A previously unknown company, Baikalfinansgrup, which had been hastily registered not long before at a building housing a vodka bar and a mobile phone shop in Putin's ancestral hometown of Tver, was the only bidder.[205] Yuganskneftegas changed hands for 9.3 billion US dollars, half its real value. Four days later, Rosneft bought Baikalfinansgrup, becoming the biggest oil company not only in Russia but the world.

Sechin had won game, set and match.

Not only had he gained control of Yuganskneftegaz, the crown jewel in Yukos's portfolio, but he had been proved right where Putin had been wrong. Western banks could not be relied upon, not because they were untrustworthy but because the international financial system was under American control.

That a district judge in Texas could block a financial transaction by the Russian state, carried out inside Russia, showed in stark terms how far America's arm could reach.

A few months later, the case was dismissed on the grounds that the Texas court had no jurisdiction. But by then, the damage had been done. Publicly Putin grouched about 'imperial' extra-territorial judgements and asked whether the judge 'even knew where Russia is on the map'.[206] Privately, he was shocked. It had brought home to him the extent to which the United States was still the global hegemon.

When Putin next met Bush in Bratislava, the Slovak capital, in February 2005, he blithely maintained that the two countries' 'fundamental relations . . . have probably never been at such a high level as they are now'.[207] It sounded very strained.

The drumbeat of accusations from Western human rights organisations, protesting against atrocities in Chechnya; the clampdown on the Russian media; the arrest of Mikhail Khodorkovsky; the failure to curb corruption at every level, from the traffic cop on a street corner to government ministers and members of Putin's inner circle; the evidence that the Kremlin was imposing an ever more authoritarian and arbitrary regime – all had combined to make Western public opinion and Western politicians, many of whom had initially been willing to give Putin the benefit of the doubt, redouble their criticisms.

Even as Putin was extolling his personal relationship with Bush, the Russian press was writing that relations with the West were reverting to what they had been during the Cold War.[208] The Chinese media, normally wary of commenting on the affairs of Beijing's partners, called the relationship 'an alliance of convenience'.[209] A German commentator wrote that, behind the façade of amity, 'a kind of proxy war is being waged'.[210]

That came out most clearly over the US democracy promotion campaign.

At the start of his second term, Bush had promoted Condoleezza Rice to be Secretary of State, replacing Colin Powell, whom Putin later described as 'one of the few genuinely very agreeable partners among the US officials we dealt with'.[211] If that sounded like a jab at Rice, it was intended as such. The 'Iron Magnolia', as the Russian press dubbed her, had taken up her new post with guns blazing.[212] Shortly before visiting Moscow, in April, she called on Putin not to stand again as President when his second term ended in 2008, and then followed up with an interview with *Ekho Moskvy* in which she complained that Russia needed more democracy and that Putin had concentrated too much power in his own hands.[213]

Democracy, he retorted, 'is not a commodity that can simply be exported from one country to another . . . It is a product of society's internal development.'[214] Russia had no future without democracy but it had to be governed 'using methods best suited to its conditions and not in the same way as in some European countries or the United States'.[215]

President Bush had some sympathy with that. He would never

expect Russia to look like America, he said. Instead, it would have 'a Russian-style democracy'.[216] The neocons in his entourage, Rice among them, took a different view.

⌐ The issue kept coming up and kept hitting a raw nerve. When a British journalist suggested a parallel between the human rights situation in Russia and in Africa, Putin responded coldly: 'We know that in some African countries until quite recently it was the practice to eat one's political opponents. We do not have this practice, so I consider any comparison in this area to be tactless.'[217] The reference was to Jean-Bedel Bokassa, the self-proclaimed Emperor of the former Central African Republic, who was widely believed to have engaged in political cannibalism in the 1970s. The retort went down well in Russia but, like many of Putin's off-colour sallies, produced a shocked silence among the Westerners present.

There were other irritants. America was planning to open military bases in Bulgaria and Romania. There had been no progress towards a compromise on the US National Missile Defense system and no progress on nuclear disarmament. The days when Putin had called for closer relations with NATO were in the distant past. Now he complained about the alliance's double standards. On the one hand, the West urged recognition of the independence of Kosovo, which was legally a part of Serbia, threatening the inviolability of Europe's post-war frontiers.[218] On the other, it closed its eyes when Latvia classed nearly half a million Russian residents as 'non-citizens' and denied them political rights.[219]

It was with the problems of the Russian diaspora in mind – the 25 million Russians who, almost from one day to the next, had found themselves expatriates in newly independent post-Soviet states – that, in an address to the two houses of the Russian parliament in April, Putin asserted that the collapse of the Soviet Union was 'the greatest geopolitical catastrophe of the century'.[220]

The phrase was unfortunate. It made him look like an unreconstructed Soviet apologist whose aim in life was to restore the USSR as it had been before. In fact, he had already stated on multiple occasions that, while the Soviet period was 'a complicated page of our history, heroic, constructive yet also tragic, it's a page that has been turned. That ship has sailed.'[221] All he had meant by calling it a catastrophe, he maintained later, was that it was a humanitarian disaster.

In fact there was more to it than that. The word 'geopolitical' was key. He had inadvertently opened a window onto what he really believed. For Putin, as for most Russians of his generation, the end of the USSR had been an earth-shattering event. Asked many years later what had influenced him most and what he would most like to be able to undo, he replied: 'The Soviet Union's collapse'.[222]

At the end of 2005, another of the consequences of the Soviet break-up came home to roost. Ukraine still paid for Russian gas supplies by an arcane system of barter. Ever since Putin had been in charge of foreign trade in St Petersburg, he had favoured moving to market relations, under which Ukraine and the other post-Soviet states which benefitted from what had been called 'friendship prices', often three or four times lower than those practised elsewhere, would start paying at the same rate as Western Europe. Russia had been for too long 'a milch-cow for all and sundry', he said, subsiding oil and gas supplies to the other CIS members to the tune of several billion dollars a year.[223]

Putin's relations with the Ukrainian leader, Viktor Yushchenko, had improved markedly since his election the previous winter, but on the gas issue there had been no progress. Ukraine's Prime Minister, Yulia Tymoshenko, a businesswoman turned charismatic symbol of the Orange Revolution, whose trademark blonde braids and elfin looks concealed a ruthless aptitude for political manoeuvre, was reluctant to grasp the nettle. In September, Yushchenko fired Tymoshenko, and took control of the gas dossier himself. But there was still no resolution. 80 per cent of Gazprom's exports to Western Europe transited through Ukraine and, as Yushchenko later admitted, the Ukrainians had been illegally siphoning off a sizeable portion for years for their own domestic use. Even for the part that was paid for, Ukraine was charged 50 US dollars per thousand cubic metres instead of the European price of more than 200 dollars.

On December 13, Gazprom warned that if the issue was not resolved, it would halt supplies at the end of the month. Two weeks later, when there was still no agreement, Putin offered Ukraine a loan to cover the difference between the 'friendship' and the market price, but emphasised that it would have to be guaranteed by an international bank and eventually reimbursed. Yushchenko refused. Finally, on December 31,

Putin suggested a compromise: Russia would continue to supply gas in the first quarter of 2006 at the present price, provided Ukraine agreed to transition to market rates thereafter. Again, Yushchenko refused. Accordingly, on January 1, 2006, Gazprom shut off the supply. Three days later, the Ukrainian President capitulated, an agreement was signed providing for a gradual transition to market prices and supplies resumed.

It was not the first time Russia had shut off the gas. Two years earlier, Gazprom had cut supplies to Belarus during a similar dispute. But on that occasion the only other countries affected were Poland and Lithuania. This time, Austria, France and Italy, as well as much of Eastern Europe, found their gas supply cut off.

The effects were twofold. Although European governments had some sympathy for Putin's position – the Ukrainians were behaving badly; there was no reason at all for them not to pay the market rate[224] – most of the Western news media, which had little interest in the technicalities of long-term gas contracts, saw it as crude Russian bullying. Public opinion, already disenchanted with Putin and his regime, became further disabused. Equally if not more important, the issue of energy security, and the vexed question of whether Europe was becoming too dependent on Russian oil and gas, was put firmly back on the agenda. That had been an American hobby horse ever since the Reagan administration had tried to block the construction of a Russian gas pipeline to Western Europe in the 1980s. But now it took on additional significance because, apart from geopolitical considerations, Washington was seeking European markets for US exports of Liquefied Natural Gas.

The US Ambassador in Moscow, Bill Burns, counselled caution. 'It's important to take a step back when considering the current angst,' he wrote in a cable to Condoleezza Rice in February. 'Russia's energy relations with its former Soviet neighbours are like an awful divorce process. [But] moving to cold hard contracts may mark the end of the heavy-handed use of energy as a political bludgeon, not the beginning, [and] we are all likely to be better off in the end.'[225]

That was not how the administration hawks saw it.

In May, Vice President Dick Cheney travelled to the Lithuanian capital, Vilnius, to speak at a conference on democracy, attended by the heads of state of nine pro-Western or Western-leaning countries along

Russia's periphery, including Ukraine and Georgia. After a diatribe against the Belarus President, Aleksandr Lukashenko, whom he accused of heading 'the last dictatorship in Europe', Cheney directed his attention to Russia:

> In Russia today, opponents of reform are seeking to reverse the gains of the last decade . . . The government has unfairly and improperly restricted the rights of her people. Other actions by the Russian government have been counterproductive and could begin to affect relations with other countries. No legitimate interest is served when oil and gas become tools of intimidation or blackmail . . . Russia has a choice to make . . . None of us believes that Russia is fated to become an enemy.[226]

The implication was that if Russia did not change its ways, it would indeed become an enemy. A Western diplomat in Moscow called it 'the most abrasive speech against Russia' since Reagan had spoken at the Brandenburg Gate in 1987 and urged Gorbachev to tear down the Berlin Wall.[227]

Putin's response came six days later in his annual address to the two houses of parliament, the Russian equivalent of the US State of the Union address. He added an extra sentence which had not been in the prepared text. 'The wolf knows who to eat,' he said. 'How quickly the pathetic utterances about human rights and democracy are laid aside when one's own interests come to the fore!'[228] In plain English, Cheney was a hypocrite and America a predator whose default reaction was not to try to work out differences but to resort to force.[229] Asked later to comment directly about the Vice President's statement, he compared it to 'an unfortunate shot while out hunting' – a reference to an incident earlier that year when Cheney had accidentally shot and injured a companion during a quail shoot in Texas. It was 'a relic of Cold War thinking', Putin said, on the part of a person 'who does not understand the geopolitical changes taking place in the world today'.[230]

The gas dispute marked the beginning of a profound change in Russia's attitude both to its neighbours and to the West.

The days when Putin would lean over backwards to avoid unnecessarily antagonising the United States and its European allies were long gone. The Russian economy seemed strong. Oil prices were at record highs. The country had paid off its foreign debts, depriving the West of an important source of leverage. Putin's popularity was consistently above 70 per cent.

For the first time, Russia had begun to flex its muscles, demonstrating its newfound power. It had not done so very skilfully. Putin admitted that Russia had explained its case poorly[231] – a failing which he sought to remedy by signing up an American public relations firm, Ketchum, to burnish Moscow's image. But he had shown that he was prepared to be tough in defence of what he saw as Russia's interests, even if it led to problems with the West, and that went down well with Russians.

By the summer of 2006, Putin had concluded that he had nothing further to lose by giving Britain a hard time. Russia's most important partner was the EU and, in his view, its leading members were 'Germany, France, Italy and Spain', in that order. Britain, which three years earlier he had described as the key to Russia's integration with the European economy, no longer even got a mention.[232] Blair's government was seen as so subservient to the United States that it would never act independently. Whatever happened to Moscow's relationship with Washington, for better or worse, Putin thought, Britain would follow meekly behind.

His next move took the conflict to a new level.

On November 23, 2006, Aleksandr Litvinenko, the FSB whistle-blower who had infuriated Putin eight years earlier by making public allegations of criminal behaviour against his service chief, died an excruciating death in a hospital in London, having fallen ill three weeks earlier with what at first had been thought to be food poisoning.

After Litvinenko had arrived in Britain, MI6 had paid him a retainer for a time for information about the Russian leadership, but he was regarded as something of a loose cannon and the relationship was discontinued. He remained close to Boris Berezovsky, who gave him a generous stipend to work for his quixotic campaign to bring down Putin's regime. He also became friendly with Akhmed Zakayev, the Kremlin's other bête noire in Britain, who was a neighbour in the North London suburb of Muswell Hill, where Litvinenko lived with his wife and son. Litvinenko had served in Chechnya during the first Chechen War and in London took up the Chechens' cause and converted to Islam. He was one of those charming, mercurial individuals who are often a cross to bear for those around them. Alan Cowell, the *New York Times* London correspondent, wrote in his book, *The Terminal Spy*, that he was 'prone to obsessions and crusades . . . He was undiscerning of the truth. He relished campaigns, reached wild conclusions. He was a zealot. He was flaky. He saw connections where no one else did.'[233] A month before his death, he became a naturalised British citizen, of which he was immensely proud.

Through his connection to Berezovsky, in October 2004, Litvinenko resumed contact with a former KGB colleague, Andrei Lugovoi, who had been head of security at ORT, the television station which Berezovsky had controlled in the late 1990s.[234] Lugovoi claimed to have been arrested in 2001 and detained for 15 months for trying to help one of Berezovsky's associates to escape from a Russian prison. Whether that was actually so is uncertain. What is sure is that shortly afterwards, with the FSB's encouragement, he re-established contact with Berezovsky, who saw his alleged imprisonment as proof of his bona fides. Litvinenko, who had known him when they had both been in Moscow, also trusted him and they started working together as consultants, doing due diligence for British companies considering investments in Russia. Lugovoi portrayed himself as a successful businessman who came to London with his family from time to time to watch football matches.

During one of these visits, on November 1, 2006, Litvinenko joined him for a drink at the Millennium Hotel in Mayfair. That evening, he fell ill. His symptoms mystified the British doctors treating him. Suspicion quickly fell on Russia, and after food poisoning was ruled out, tests were conducted for thallium, a radioactive heavy metal element which the Soviet KGB had used for assassinations. But gamma radiation tests came up negative. One of the specialists treating him was quoted as saying it was quite possible that the cause would never be known.[235] An FSB spokesman in Moscow, dismissing the idea of Russian involvement, said the agency was sorry for what had happened to him and wished him a speedy recovery. Those responsible, he added, were probably to be found among the Russian exile community in London.[236]

For Moscow, that would have been the ideal outcome. One of Putin's most virulent critics, who had thought himself safe in the West, had suffered a mysterious, agonising and very public death. To Russian political émigrés, the message would have been clear. This was what would happen to those regarded as traitors. The fact that Moscow could eliminate adversaries undetected thousands of miles away made it even more frightening.

Litvinenko himself, in a final testament, accused Putin of being responsible. Asked to comment at a news conference in Helsinki, the Russian leader offered his condolences, saying that 'the death of any person is always a tragedy', before adding with undisguised malice: 'Mr Litvinenko, unfortunately, is not Lazarus.' Officially the British police described his illness as 'unexplained'.

The FSB very nearly got away with it.

Almost by chance, a few hours before Litvinenko died, a sample of his urine which had been sent to the British Atomic Weapons Establishment at Porton Down was found to contain another radioactive element, polonium-210. One of the most lethal substances known, it emits alpha, not gamma, radiation which does not register on standard detectors.

After that, the pieces began to fall into place. The British police announced that traces of polonium had been found in high concentration at the bar of the Millennium Hotel, where Litvinenko had met Lugovoi and another Russian, Dmitry Kovtun, the day that he fell ill. While there, he had drunk half a cup of tea poured from a teapot which afterwards showed a high level of primary polonium contamination. The subsequent investigation revealed a radioactive trail in Britain and Germany, wherever one or other of the two suspects had passed, and on the aircraft in which they had been passengers. There was also evidence that a third Russian, who was never publicly identified, had come to Britain to supervise the operation. After their return to Moscow, both Lugovoi and Kovtun, who evidently had little idea of the dangers of the material they were handling, were also found to have mild symptoms of radioactive contamination, which the Russians argued showed that they, too, were victims of whatever had caused Litvinenko's death. In May 2007, Britain demanded Lugovoi's extradition, which Russia predictably refused, triggering the expulsion of four Russian diplomats from London and, by reciprocity, four British diplomats from Moscow. Later that year, Lugovoi was elected to the Duma, which gave him immunity from prosecution.

Blair's government was in a quandary. On the one hand, as his Chief of Staff, Jonathan Powell, put it, 'we cannot do nothing when they go around killing people on the streets of London.'[237] On the other hand, relations were bad enough already; the British oil company, BP, had major investments in Russia; and no one wanted a complete rupture. Accordingly London spoke gingerly of 'state involvement' but did not accuse the Kremlin directly. The government resisted calls for a public inquiry and the inquest into Litvinenko's death was suspended without reaching a verdict.

To Putin that was just another sign of British weakness.

But Blair knew something which Putin did not. The CIA had a source in the Kremlin with regular access to the Russian President. At some point – it has not been disclosed exactly when – the source reported that the FSB chief, Nikolai Patrushev, had organised Litvinenko's murder on Putin's instructions.[238] Under the 'Five Eyes' intelligence-sharing agreement between Britain and America, the MI6 chief, John Scarlett, was informed. Raw intelligence is not proof, which was one of the reasons why, some years later, when the British did convene an official inquiry, the Chairman, Robert Owen, concluded that Putin had 'probably', rather than certainly, ordered Litvinenko's murder.[239] But it was prima facie evidence that the decision had been taken by Putin himself.

Why did he do it?

Litvinenko was a has-been as far as Moscow was concerned. From time to time, he came out with outlandish claims like Putin being a paedophile, which he based on an incident in which the President had kissed the tummy of a small boy he encountered among a group of tourists visiting the Kremlin. In the West, that would be regarded as very odd, but in Russia, where grown-ups frequently cuddle other people's children, it elicited little surprise.[240] In any case, the story made no sense. Just as alcoholics try to hide their addiction, the last thing a genuine paedophile would do is fondle a child in public. The rest of the time, Litvinenko contributed articles to obscure Chechen websites. There were other exiles in London whom the Kremlin regarded as a much greater threat.

Yet that may have been the point. Litvinenko was not a high-profile opponent. His murder was symbolic and, had the British police not discovered the polonium trail, Moscow would not have suffered any adverse consequences.

His killing followed the passage of a new law by the Duma giving the security services increased powers to act against 'terrorists' and 'extremists' abroad. It was an odd piece of legislation. The Russian special services had never previously required legal authority to murder exiled opponents – the killing of the Chechen leader, Zelimkhan Yandarbiyev, in Qatar by the GRU in 2004 was a recent example. But the law and Litvinenko's murder had the same purpose: they were a warning to Russian expatriates not to get out of line.

The Litvinenko affair finally convinced Blair that he had to confront Putin.

Ever since Russia had begun putting pressure on the British Council, his aides had been urging him to have it out with the Russian leader, but each time, as Nigel Sheinwald put it, they had the feeling that 'he pulled his punches'.[241] In June 2007, three weeks before Blair was to step down as Prime Minister, he and Putin met, each with only an interpreter and one close aide present, on the margins of the G8 summit at Heiligendamm, on the Baltic Sea coast in former East Germany. Blair did not raise directly the question of who had ordered Litvinenko's killing lest he inadvertently let slip something which would alert Putin to the existence of an informant inside the Kremlin. Instead, he vented a long list of grievances that had built up since the Iraq War and told Putin bluntly that people in the West were becoming fearful of the direction Russia was taking. 'Putin gave it back in spades,' Jonathan Powell, the notetaker on the British side, remembered. The atmosphere was glacial.[242]

The arrival of Gordon Brown as Blair's successor did nothing to halt the slide in relations. BP's huge investments in the Russian oil and gas business kept running into trouble, or hitting 'bumps in the road', as the chief executive, Tony Hayward, preferred to put it,[243] and six months later, the British Council's regional branches outside Moscow were all ordered to close on the grounds that there was 'no legal basis' for their activities in Russia.[244]

At the time, the assassination of Litvinenko was seen as essentially a bilateral issue between Russia and Britain. That was a mistake. It had much broader significance. Putin rarely acted without thinking through the possible consequences. He had known that there was a chance – probably a good chance, given the tendency of all secret services to screw up – that Litvinenko's murder would be traced back to

Russia. If he had decided to go ahead, it was not merely because, by the summer of 2006, he had largely given up on Britain, but more importantly because he was beginning to have serious doubts about Russia's future relationship with America. Ever since Putin had become President, six years earlier, his goal had been to forge a close relationship with the West. Now he was beginning to wonder whether that was even possible.

In October 2006, a few months after the spat with Cheney over Ukraine, Putin received Condoleezza Rice in Moscow. This time the problem was Georgia. It was an issue, she said later, on which she found him completely intransigent.[245]

'If Saakashvili uses force in South Ossetia, which we are convinced he is preparing to do,' Putin told her, 'the Georgian people will suffer most . . . If Georgia causes bloodshed in Ossetia, I will have no alternative to recognising South Ossetia and Abkhazia and responding with force.'

Putin had been arguing for months that there was no difference between Kosovo and the two breakaway Georgian regions, and that if the United States recognised the independence of the one, Russia would feel free to recognise the independence of the others.[246] But this was the first time he had threatened to respond militarily if Saakashvili intervened.

Rice responded that if Russia did so, relations with the United States would take a hit. That set off another tirade. Georgia was a US puppet, Putin told her. First, Washington had acted through Shevardnadze, now through Saakashvili. It was time that the United States yanked back the strings. 'I understand that there will be problems in US–Russian relations if we act in South Ossetia,' he added melodramatically, 'but what good is a strong Russian–US relationship to me if I lose Russia?' Rice assured him that the United States was 'doing everything it could to restrain the Georgian leadership' – a significant remark, because it showed that the State Department, at least, understood that Saakashvili could turn out to be a loose cannon – but urged Russia to 'use its head too'.

Whether because of US pressure or because, shortly afterwards, Putin confirmed the withdrawal of the last Russian troops from the old Soviet-era bases in Georgia, or for some other reason, the tensions

over South Ossetia temporarily eased. But there were deeper grievances. Ambassador Burns listed them. They included 'the sense that
we didn't show as much concern for [Putin's] interests as he did for
ours after 9/11 by facilitating Central Asian basing; that we don't understand how hard for him it has been to restore order in Russia (such as
it is) after Yeltsin's chaos; and that we are fundamentally uncomfortable with Russia's return as a Great Power and seek to constrain it'. It
was 'not a pretty picture', Burns thought. The US–Russian relationship was 'drifting into very rough waters' which would be difficult to
navigate for at least the next 18 months and probably much longer.[247]

Just how rough would become clear two and a half months later,
when Putin addressed the Munich Security Conference, a privately
organised annual get-together of world leaders, political figures, diplomats and military experts to discuss global security with particular
reference to transatlantic and European defence issues.

He prefaced his remarks with a deceptively light-hearted warning
that he would avoid 'excessive politeness [and] pleasant, but empty, diplomatic formulae, and say what I really think', adding that he hoped the
Chairman would not cut him off if he gave offence. Then he let rip:

> Today we are witnessing an almost totally unconstrained, hypertro-
> phied use of force – military force – in international affairs, force that is
> plunging the world into an abyss of successive conflicts one after
> another. As a result we do not have sufficient strength to find a compre-
> hensive solution to any of them. Their political settlement also becomes
> impossible. We are seeing an ever greater disregard of the fundamental
> principles of international law . . . What's more, individual laws, in fact,
> virtually the whole legal system, of one particular country, the United
> States, have transgressed that country's national boundaries in every
> sphere – the economy, politics and humanitarian affairs – and have been
> imposed on other nations. And who likes this? Who likes it?[248]

Attempts were being made, he said, to impose a unipolar system, in
which there would be 'one centre of authority, one centre of force,
one centre of decision-making, . . . a world in which there is one master, one sovereign'. That was unacceptable and undemocratic. Russia,
Putin said, was 'constantly being lectured about democracy. But for
some reason, those who teach us do not want to learn themselves.'

Unipolarity was pernicious 'not only for those within the system, but also for the sovereign [power] because it destroys itself from within'. In a world where the combined economies of China, India and other rising powers would soon be larger than that of America, it was inevitable that, sooner or later, whether the United States wished it or not, a multipolar system would develop.

After the Cold War, Putin went on, ideological stereotypes and relics of bloc thinking had been left lying around 'like live ammunition'. The United States and its allies had transformed the OSCE, which had been established as a multilateral organisation, into 'a vulgar instrument to promote [their] foreign policy interests'. The Treaty on Conventional Armed Forces in Europe was in 'a pitiable state' as a result of arguments about the presence of Russian troops in Georgia and Transnistria and the United States' decision to build forward bases in Bulgaria and Romania. The US National Missile Defense system would not only spark a new arms race, which no one in Europe needed, but, should it ever be developed to a point where it could neutralise Russia's strategic systems, the nuclear balance which had kept the peace for the previous half-century would be totally destroyed.

Russia was ready to pursue disarmament negotiations with America, Putin said, but he hoped that the United States would not hide 'a couple of hundred extra warheads . . . under the blanket, as it were . . . for a rainy day'. If the new American Defense Secretary, he added – addressing Robert Gates, who was in the audience – would promise not to do so, he would invite everyone to stand up and applaud. Mr Gates, stone-faced, did not respond.

Putin's message was less memorable than that delivered by Churchill in the 'Iron Curtain' speech at Fulton, 61 years earlier, but the theme was the same:

> The stones and concrete blocks of the Berlin Wall have long since been distributed as souvenirs . . . Now they are trying to impose on us new walls and new dividing lines. This time the walls are virtual, but none-theless they divide . . . Will it once again take us decades . . . before they are dismantled?

Like Boris Yeltsin's angry diatribe in Budapest 12 years earlier, warning that NATO expansion would usher in a 'cold peace', Putin's speech caught American officials wrong-footed. 'Most of the audience was stunned,' the *Financial Times* reported. Senator John McCain, who attended the conference each year, called it 'the most aggressive remarks by a Russian leader since the end of the Cold War'.[249] The White House said it was 'surprised and disappointed'.[250]

Bill Burns in Moscow captured it best when he told Condoleezza Rice that it was 'pure Putin – the attraction of swaggering into a den full of security policy wonks, sticking out his chin and letting them have it with both barrels'.[251]

In fact, Putin said little that he had not said before. The one new element was the emphasis he attached to building a multipolar world.[252] Even that was not really new. It had been a core principle of Russian foreign policy ever since the late 1990s, when Yevgeny Primakov had been Prime Minister. But until the Munich speech, American officials had tended to dismiss it as empty posturing.[253]

What had changed was the tone. What Putin liked to call the 'false bottom' to US–Russian relations[254] – the pretence that all was well and that Russia and America were solid, strategic partners with just a few trifling tactical problems – had been discarded. In simple terms, Ambassador Burns wrote, the message was: 'We're back, and you'd better get used to it!'[255]

The speech was the culmination of frustrations and grievances that had built up over more than a decade, coupled with a growing conviction on Putin's part that America was not listening to Russia's concerns and would not do so until given a salutary shock. No single event triggered it. Rather, as Putin told a group of Russian journalists a few days later, he had 'come to the conclusion that it doesn't matter what we do – speak out or keep silent – there'll always be some pretext for attacking Russia. In this situation, it is better to be frank.'[256]

The Bush administration had just lost both the Senate and the House to the Democrats in the mid-term elections. Iraq was a mess. Europe was distracted by leadership transitions. The Munich conference, an informal, non-governmental gathering – the security equivalent of the World Economic Forum at Davos – was the right place at the right time for Russia to put its message across.

Unlike Yeltsin, who hastily backtracked after the Budapest speech, Putin doubled down on what Burns called Russia's 'pugnacious and swaggering behaviour'.[257] The West, he charged, was using 'the dirtiest techniques to try to ignite inter-ethnic and inter-religious hatred' in Russia.[258] It claimed to be 'shining white, clean and pure', while Russia was 'some kind of monster that has only just crawled out of the forest, with hooves and horns'.[259] Certain countries – by which he meant the United States – were trying to impose an imperialist dictatorship: 'We need to say this straight out and call a spade a spade.'[260]

There was an old Soviet joke, Putin told a group of foreign journalists that summer, about the telephones on the desks of the Warsaw Pact leaders. 'How do you tell which one goes to Moscow? It's the one which has a receiver, no mouthpiece. The same goes for NATO, only the line is to Washington.'[261] What do we want? he asked. 'We want to be heard. We want our position to be understood . . . Some people have the illusion that they can do everything just as they like, regardless of the interests of others.'[262]

Not everything was black. The two countries agreed terms for Russia's application to join the World Trade Organisation to proceed. Discussions continued on how to work together in Afghanistan and on counter-terrorism issues. They had similar views on nuclear non-proliferation, notably concerning Iran, which the United States suspected of running a covert nuclear weapons programme, and North Korea, which had recently carried out its first successful underground nuclear test. In June, in the margins of the G8 summit in Germany, Putin had what he called 'a very encouraging conversation' with Bush, during which he proposed that US missile defences be based not in Eastern Europe but in Turkey or even perhaps Iraq. 'What was the war for, after all?' he asked. 'At least some benefit could be gained from it.' Another suggestion was for America to use an existing Russian station in Azerbaijan, rather than building a new one in the Czech Republic. It was agreed that talks would begin in a '2 + 2' format between the two sides' Defence and Foreign ministers to explore these ideas.[263]

The following month, Putin visited the Bushes at their summer retreat at Kennebunkport, on the Atlantic coast in Maine, where they went fishing together and agreed to start talks on a successor agreement to the Strategic Offensive Reductions Treaty (SORT), which would expire in 2011.[264]

The chemistry between the two men was genuinely good. Putin would insist right up to the end of Bush's presidency that he was 'a very reliable partner and a decent person' who was honestly defending what he saw as America's interests.[265] Bush, too, even if Putin had disappointed him on many issues, continued to describe the Russian leader as a friend, and when he came to write his memoirs some years later, largely abstained from criticising him. Even Condoleezza Rice, not Putin's greatest admirer, wrote that their relationship helped to 'calm the waters'.[266]

But having good personal relations was one thing, the imperatives of national security were another. As Putin had put it at Munich, when discussing the nuclear balance: 'There's nothing personal here – it's all a matter of calculation.'[267]

The '2 + 2' talks sputtered along but Putin's proposals went nowhere. The US national security establishment wanted bases in the Czech Republic and Poland in order to strengthen America's footprint in the region, even though, in terms of intercepting missiles from Iran and North Korea, it did not make much sense. Neither country had missiles capable of reaching Eastern Europe, let alone the United States. Even if Iran one day acquired them, Turkey and Azerbaijan were better locations geographically for an anti-missile shield, while a putative North Korean missile attack on America would pass over the Arctic, going nowhere near Europe.

The only other thing which might have reconciled Putin to the missile defence system – permanently stationing Russian military observers at the key sites – was ruled out because neither the Czechs nor the Poles were prepared to have Russian officers based on their territory.

As the prospect of agreement receded, Putin ordered Russian strategic nuclear bombers to resume regular patrols for the first time since the 1980s[268] and, in December 2007, Moscow suspended its participation in the Treaty on Conventional Armed Forces in Europe.

The torrent of angry words from the Kremlin, which had never entirely abated, resumed with redoubled intensity. If the United States went ahead with its plans for missile defence facilities in the Czech Republic and Poland, Putin warned, Russia would have no alternative but to target those installations with its own missiles. Soviet brinkmanship had caused the Cuban missile crisis in 1962. Now, even though Moscow and Washington were no longer adversaries, America was making the same kind of error.[269] 'I would not say that NATO is the stinking corpse of the Cold War,' Putin told *Time* magazine that winter, 'but it is certainly a holdover from the past.' He sometimes had the impression, he added, that 'America does not need friends. It needs vassals it can command. We cannot build our relations with other countries on such principles.'[270]

In the opening months of 2008, further sources of strain appeared.

On February 17, Kosovo declared independence and was recognised by the United States, Britain, France, Germany and most, though not all, of the other members of the European Union. Negotiations with Serbia, of which Kosovo was officially part, were at a stalemate and the majority view in the West was that there was no other way forward. Putin denounced the move as 'unlawful and immoral' and angrily dismissed as 'bullshit' Western claims that Kosovo was a special case but indicated that, for the moment, he would not make good on his threat to recognise the breakaway Georgian provinces in response.[271]

The mildness of his reaction was deceptive.

Kosovo had been the first major conflict Putin had dealt with as Secretary of the Security Council in 1999. He had watched then as NATO bombed the Belgrade government into submission, justifying its intervention on humanitarian grounds, while Russia stood by impotently. By recognising the government in Priština, the West was demonstrating yet again that it could use its power unilaterally to decide the fate of other states. Once more, there was nothing Russia could do to prevent it. But he was not going to take it lying down.

Four days later, he had a meeting with Saakashvili on the margins of a CIS summit in Moscow. 'You know we have to answer the West on Kosovo,' he said. 'We are very sorry, but you are going to be part of that answer.'[272] It was not Georgia's fault, Putin went on, but 'your geography is what it is'. Russia's response would not be a mirror image of what had happened in Kosovo, he said, but it would expand its economic, political and legal ties with Abkhazia and South Ossetia. Saakashvili then made a sweeping proposal for a settlement of all outstanding issues. 'Let's sit down and talk about how to respect each other's sovereignty and territorial integrity', he said, '[taking] into account the vital strategic interests of both sides, including those questions you are worried about.' It was a hint of a possible trade-off: a solution to the problems of Abkhazia and South Ossetia in return for Tbilisi reconsidering its NATO aspirations. Putin did not take the bait. In a referendum the previous month, 70 per cent of Georgians had voted in favour of joining NATO and Saakashvili had afterwards made a formal application for Georgia to accede to NATO's Membership Action Plan (MAP), a programme to help aspiring candidates prepare for membership negotiations.[273] To suggest that the Georgians might change their minds at this late stage was not convincing. 'You shouldn't worry,' Putin responded. 'What we will do will not be directed against you, it will be our response to [the West]'. He then explained why Russia opposed Georgian membership of NATO:

> [If] Georgia is a member of the organisation, you will have to follow the discipline of the bloc and will therefore be a threat to our nuclear and military capacity. Nobody will bother to ask your opinion [when decisions are taken] . . . NATO's purpose is aimed against the sovereignty of Russia . . . After joining NATO your sovereignty will be limited, and Georgia, too, will be a threat to Russia.[274]

As the meeting ended, he warned again that NATO membership would be counterproductive at a time when, he said, tensions between Russia and Georgia were easing.[275] 'You think you can trust the Americans,' he told Saakashvili. 'Nobody can be trusted! Except me. I will do what I promise.'[276]

Georgia had not been alone in applying to join NATO's Membership Action Plan at the beginning of 2008. Ukraine had also done so. France and Germany had immediately objected, arguing that neither country was ready. The prospect of Ukrainian membership worried Putin even more. Russia had been hoping to negotiate a Strategic Partnership Declaration with Kyiv. 'Can you imagine Sevastopol [the home port of the Russian Black Sea Fleet] with a NATO base there?' he asked. 'Just think of the impact that would have!'[277] In private, he made clear that any such move would be totally unacceptable. Ambassador Burns had written to Condoleezza Rice earlier that month:

> Ukrainian entry into NATO is the brightest of all red lines for the Russian elite (not just Putin). In my more than two-and-a-half years of conversations with key Russian players, from knuckle-draggers in the dark recesses of the Kremlin to Putin's sharpest liberal critics, I have yet to find anyone who views Ukraine in NATO as anything other than a direct challenge to Russia's interests. At this stage a MAP offer would

be seen not as a technical step . . . but as throwing down the strategic gauntlet. Today's Russia will respond.[278]

Even in the case of Georgia, he added presciently, an offer of eventual NATO membership would probably lead Russia to recognise Abkhazia and 'the prospects of subsequent Russian–Georgian armed conflict would be high'.

But Burns was a voice in the wilderness. The neoconservatives in the White House had very different ideas.

Matters came to a head at the NATO summit in Bucharest at the beginning of April. George Bush arrived in high spirits, direct from a visit to Ukraine where he had been given a hero's welcome, and called on his colleagues to 'send a signal through the region . . . [and] welcome Georgia and Ukraine into the Membership Action Plan'.[279] After Angela Merkel and the French President, Nicolas Sarkozy, had signalled disagreement, the Secretary General, Jaap de Hoop Scheffer, called an adjournment, whereupon the foreign ministers from the new member states, led by Poland, which were all in favour of the two countries' admission, went into a huddle at the back of the hall with Merkel and Rice to try to find a compromise.

'There were all these old guys in grey suits,' Bush's National Security Adviser, Steve Hadley, remembered, 'Merkel in a lime-green jacket, and Condi Rice, a black Secretary of State, all talking Russian together.'[280]

That may have been the problem.

They spoke Russian because it was the one language the East Europeans, Merkel and Rice had in common. But Angela Merkel's Russian was rusty and Condoleezza Rice was less fluent than she liked to pretend. *Komsomolskaya pravda* had sniffed disparagingly. 'The hard and tough Condi . . . has largely forgotten her Russian and only rarely ventures a few heavily accented words out of politeness.'[281] Whether or not that was a factor, there was none of the usual haggling over commas and semicolons and unintended consequences which professional diplomats are trained to engage in, and the result showed.

When the summit reconvened next morning, Scheffer read out the text of the communiqué that they had agreed. It proved, as Hadley put it with some understatement, to be 'very forward-leaning'.[282] After welcoming Ukraine's and Georgia's 'Euro-Atlantic aspirations', the document stated baldly: 'We agreed today that these countries will become members of NATO.'[283] As that sentence was read out, the British Prime Minister, Gordon Brown, turned to Bush and said quietly: 'George, I know we didn't give them MAP, but I'm not sure we didn't just let them in!'[284]

That was not at all what Merkel and Sarkozy had intended. They had argued that Ukrainians were too divided over NATO membership to be granted MAP status and that Georgia's admission was rendered problematic by the Saakashvili government's repression of opposition movements and the frozen conflicts in Abkhazia and South Ossetia.[285] How Merkel let the new language pass has never been adequately explained. One can only assume that she was so focused on preventing MAP that she failed to see that an undefined commitment, which Rice and the East Europeans presented as a major concession on their part, risked causing yet bigger problems down the road.

Once the details were revealed, it turned out that neither Georgia nor Ukraine had got everything they wanted, and nor had Bush. There was to be a 'progress review' by the alliance's foreign ministers at the end of the year and further moves towards MAP status were by no means automatic.

But it was enough for both countries to portray the outcome as a triumph. Saakashvili exulted: 'We received more than we hoped for.'[286] Yushchenko spoke of 'an exceptional victory [which] exceeded all expectations'.[287]

For Putin, who arrived that evening to attend the Russia–NATO Council meeting which was to follow – the first such gathering at heads of state level for six years – it was, in Hadley's words, 'like a cold fish slapping him across the face'.[288] But his speech was restrained and, at a news conference afterwards, he emphasised the positive side of the relationship. Later it emerged that Bush had phoned him ten days earlier to warn that he intended to push for MAP at Bucharest and to express the hope that there would not be 'a dust-up', which would make it difficult for him to accept Putin's invitation to pay a farewell call on him in Sochi, after the conference, when both their presidential terms would be coming to an end. Putin had promised to avoid a confrontation and he had kept his word.[289]

Once again, the mildness of his reaction was deceptive.

Bill Burns had been right to warn Condoleezza Rice that if the

United States persisted in its plans for NATO enlargement, Putin would respond. At Bucharest, he had hinted at his concerns in diplomatic terms. 'Ukraine, in its current form, was created in Soviet times,' he had said. A third of the population was Russian. In Crimea, 90 per cent of the population was Russian. It was 'a very complicated state formation', and introducing a NATO dimension risked complicating it still further.[290] At Sochi, that weekend, he was much blunter. Why, he asked Bush, was America willing to put at risk its relations with Russia for marginal gains? 'What is Ukraine?', he said. 'Ukraine isn't even a country. Part of its territory is in Eastern Europe, while the rest was a gift from Russia'.[291] As for Georgia, it was not part of Europe, so what was its place in a Euro-Atlantic alliance? 'You and I,' he went on, 'are the only two people in our respective administrations that want good relations between the United States and Russia. We are the only ones . . . If you only knew the kind of proposals that come to me for systems I'm supposed to deploy against the United States, you wouldn't believe it.'[292]

That was no doubt true. Putin was surrounded by people who were much more sceptical than he was of the benefits of close relations with Washington. But it was also a warning. The personal link with Bush had become one of the few remaining threads holding the relationship together.

The meeting in Sochi was not quite the end of the story. Russian–American relations often moved two steps forward, one step sideways, one step back, or vice versa, rarely in coherent straight lines. The two men discussed what Hadley called 'the Checklist', a plan to get Russian ministers and their US counterparts from different branches of government to work together on areas where the two countries could cooperate and report to the two Presidents every six months. Putin liked the idea. He then reverted to the proposal he had made at Heiligendamm for a joint approach to missile defence, on which Russia and the United States would work together. They had discussed it again at Kennebunkport, but afterwards it had become lost in the bureaucracy.[293] Putin declared himself 'cautiously optimistic . . . If we can agree on a missile defence system for Europe and then start working on a global missile defence system, that would be the biggest and most important result of all the work we have done so far.' But he added prudently, 'the devil will be in the details'.[294]

Hadley and his Russian opposite number, Sergei Prikhodko, worked through the summer and, by the beginning of August, Hadley thought they had reached an understanding which both sides could accept.[295]

But the time bomb of NATO enlargement continued to tick away. Sergei Lavrov, the Foreign Minister, had warned after Bucharest that Russia would do 'everything possible' to prevent Georgia and Ukraine gaining membership.[296] A few months later, the bomb would explode and make agreement impossible.

Reflecting, a decade after these events, on the steady, seemingly inexorable deterioration of relations between the United States and Russia after Putin came to power, Bill Burns concluded that both countries had been deluding themselves all along. 'The Russian illusion,' he thought, '[was] that somehow they were going to be accepted, even though the power realities had changed enormously, as a peer, as a full partner.' The American illusion was that 'we could always manoeuvre over or around Russia. There was bound to be a time when they were going to push back . . . A certain amount of friction and a certain number of collisions were built into the equation.'[297]

In retrospect, what is surprising is not that Russia's relations with America finished up as a train wreck, but that it took so long to happen.

Putin was not a natural liberal any more than he was a natural democrat. But he was a realist and, contemplating the available alternatives after the collapse of the Soviet Union, he concluded that cooperation with the West was the only sensible policy. It was the same logic that led him to advocate at least a measure of democracy, not as an end in itself but because, without it, economic reform would be impossible and without economic reform, Russia would never become strong enough to regain what he saw as its proper place in the world.

In the centuries-old divide which had separated Russian intellectuals into Slavophiles, who harked back to Russia's Orthodox roots in the East, and Westernisers, who looked towards Europe, Putin was a Westerniser. But it was a pragmatic rather than an ideological choice.

He held to that view after he came to power, even though his natural allies, the *siloviki*, the military and the state bureaucracy, were much more mistrustful of the West's intentions. The first setbacks – the Bush administration's withdrawal from the ABM Treaty; the second round of NATO enlargement to admit the Baltic States; and then the US-led invasion of Iraq – were mistakes in Putin's view but not fatal to the relationship. America's support of what it regarded as pro-Western elements during the Orange Revolution in Ukraine, coinciding with the intervention of an American judge in the Yukos case, hit closer to home and was viewed more seriously. The final straw was the decision to base American missile defence units in Eastern Europe and install NATO forward bases in Bulgaria and Romania. America's reluctance to give up what were supposed to have been temporary facilities in Central Asia providing logistical support for its forces in Afghanistan, which it had obtained largely through Putin's good offices, did not help either.[298]

The United States was equally disappointed. The belief that Moscow would become a partner, if not an ally, espousing Western values in an American-led world, which had animated US policy towards Russia since the early 1990s, had proved vain. American exceptionalism found to its surprise that it was facing a Russian exceptionalism which was no less tenacious. The ideological convictions of the Bush administration, shared not just by Cheney and Rumsfeld and Wolfowitz but also by Bush himself, made agreement all but impossible. The fundamental problem, Putin decided, was the Americans' unshakeable belief that their way was best and their decisions optimal for everyone else.[299]

That he waited so long before finally losing patience and drawing back the curtain to reveal the raw tangle of contradictions that the relationship had become was partly because there was no obvious Plan B. Culturally, spiritually and, in part, geographically, Russia belonged with Europe. It had nowhere else to go. The Russian elite did not send their children to study in Beijing or Shanghai. They sent them to British or American schools and universities. Russian oligarchs did not park their ill-gotten gains in Seoul or Bangkok, they invested in London or New York and bought property in Knightsbridge or Chelsea, Manhattan or Miami.

There was another more personal reason for Putin's reluctance to abandon the rapprochement with the West. In trying to promote cooperation with Russia's former adversaries, he had overridden the reservations of many of his closest colleagues. Hardliners like Sechin and Patrushev had been dubious from the outset about the wisdom of trusting Western governments to engage with Russia as genuine partners. Putin was in no hurry to admit that their misgivings had been justified.

Could it have been done differently? In theory, at least, the answer must be yes. Were there missed opportunities, which, had they been taken, might have set relations on a different road? No doubt. Would the outcome then have been different? Perhaps, but not necessarily; there is no way to be sure. But it was not done differently and by 2008, as Putin ended his second four-year term as Russia's leader, the rift had become too deep to heal.

12

The Russian Idea

The collapse of the Soviet Union left a spiritual vacuum.[1]

'We find ourselves in a kind of void,' Putin said.[2] For as long as most Russians could remember, Marxism–Leninism, even if honoured in the breach, had provided a moral framework, which, whether accepted, ignored or resisted, gave meaning to people's lives. It had been 'a beautiful song, but a false one', Putin declared.[3] Now that it had been rejected, the question was, what should replace it? Russia was 'not a chip off the Soviet block'.[4] It would have different beliefs, a different identity and a different sense of its role in the world.

Yeltsin had tried to address this issue after his re-election in 1996. 'In Russia, we have had various periods: tsarism, totalitarianism, *perestroika*,' he told a meeting of his supporters. 'Each stage had its ideology, its national idea. But now we have none and that's too bad.'[5] A committee was set up to discuss what could be done. The government newspaper, *Rossiiskaya gazeta*, under a banner headline – 'Who are we? Where are we going?' – launched a competition with a prize worth 2,000 US dollars for the best essay on the subject.[6] But that was as far as it went. A year later, Yeltsin lost interest, the committee was disbanded and the competition was wound up without the prize being awarded.[7]

Putin was then in Moscow, working in the Presidential Administration, and was apparently struck by the futility of the whole exercise, for when the issue next came up, during his own election campaign in February 2000, he was adamant: 'We should not start all over again looking for an elusive national idea. It's a subject which people talk about frequently and generally quite pointlessly.'[8] After the election, however, he was less dogmatic. 'Many lances have been broken over this issue,' he told an interviewer from *Izvestia*. 'A national idea is not something that can be invented. [To try to do so] is vain and meaningless. [But] people are changing and their understanding of life is changing. I am convinced that the outline of a new nationwide ideology is already taking shape.'[9]

It was an odd choice of words. Putin did not like ideologies. He was pragmatic. He told the Polish historian, Adam Michnik, in 2002, that 'the only correct approach to politics in general is [to be] neither left nor right, neither pro-Western nor anti.'[10] What was important was for Russia to have a moral compass and to cherish the achievements of the past.[11] The key elements, he said, were 'patriotism [and] religious and cultural values – everything that . . . makes us a people with our own originality, different from others'.[12] These were the fundaments of Russian identity. They shaped each individual and it was essential that they be preserved.[13]

At one level these were platitudes of the 'motherhood and apple pie' variety. But they offered clues to Putin's thinking. Patriotism, religion and 'cherishing what we have' – in other words, Russia's past – were all conservative signboards. In the autumn of 2000, four months after his inauguration, he and Lyudmila spent an evening with Aleksandr Solzhenitsyn, the bearded chronicler of Stalin's prison camps, whom Putin claimed to have admired ever since his time with the KGB in Dresden.[14] The writer, now in his 80s, radiating the aura of an Old Testament prophet, had returned to Russia to a triumphal welcome after Yeltsin came to power. He shared Putin's view that the country needed a strong presidential system but thought it should be offset by the kind of grass-roots democracy he had seen in rural communities in America during his exile in Vermont, which had reminded him of the traditional Russian practice of *sobornost*, or 'gathering together' to resolve problems.[15] He urged the restoration of the religious and cultural values which the Bolshevik Revolution had sought to destroy and declared that under Putin's leadership, 'the nation was rediscovering what it was to be Russian'.[16]

Putin's first moves after their meeting were not entirely to Solzhenitsyn's liking.[17] In 1990, as the Soviet Union was beginning to come apart, Yeltsin had chosen a piece of music by the nineteenth-century composer, Mikhail Glinka, entitled 'Patriotic Song', to be Russia's new national anthem, replacing the Soviet anthem which had extolled 'the great Lenin' and 'the triumph of communism'. But Glinka's composition had no lyrics. Attempts to commission words to the music went nowhere and every time the issue was debated in the Duma, the Communists demanded that the Soviet anthem be restored.

Yeltsin's choice was not popular: the melody was uninspiring and, because there were no words, it could not be sung at football matches and other public events. In October 2000, Putin used that as a pretext to have the issue re-examined. Later it became clear that he had decided from the outset what the result would be. But, to cover himself, he went through the motions of popular consultation. New music was commissioned – no fewer than eight new compositions were presented[18] – and Sergei Mikhalkov, who had written the lyrics both for the wartime Stalinist anthem and for the revised version introduced by Brezhnev in the 1970s, was dragged out of retirement to write new words, in which references to communism and Lenin were replaced by 'sacred Russia' and God.

At the beginning of December, the State Council, a consultative body which had been established as a consolation for the regional governors when they had lost their seats in the upper house of parliament, rendered its verdict. First it approved the adoption of the pre-revolutionary white, blue and red national flag and the imperial coat of arms with a double-headed eagle on a red heraldic shield, both of which had been introduced provisionally by Yeltsin. Then, more controversially, it announced that the music of the Soviet anthem would be restored.

The choice was presented as a carefully weighed compromise: the communists welcomed the Soviet-era music but loathed the pre-revolutionary flag and emblem; the liberals loathed the music, which they associated with Stalin's purges and the persecution of dissidents, but welcomed the restoration of the imperial symbols.[19]

The restoration of the anthem caused a hullabaloo.

Yeltsin, who until then had refrained from criticising his successor in public, declared that he was 'categorically against it'.[20] The cellist, Mstislav Rostropovich, said he would remain seated when the new anthem was played.[21] So did a pleiad of Russian cultural figures – actors, artists, ballet dancers, composers, film directors, historians and writers – who signed a petition warning that 'the wounds of history are still bleeding' and that reviving the Soviet-era music would be 'an emblem of revenge . . . insulting the memory of the victims of Soviet repression'.[22]

Putin was unmoved. Three weeks later, he signed the measures into law.

Both sides, he acknowledged, had legitimate objections. During World War II, Soviet deserters who had fought alongside the Germans had used the white, blue and red flag. The tsarist coat of arms had been the emblem of a country which 'not for nothing was called the prison of the peoples'. In the case of the Soviet anthem, there were 'people, still alive, who personally experienced the horrors of Stalin's prison camps'.

But it was a mistake, Putin argued, to associate these symbols only with 'the darker sides of our history':[23]

> If we are guided by this logic, . . . where are we going to place Pushkin, Dostoyevsky, Tolstoy or Tchaikovsky? . . . Their names and achievements were related to these symbols, too. And is there nothing good to remember about the Soviet period? Was there nothing but Stalin's prison camps and repression? . . . I cannot agree to this . . . [Yes,] we can concoct a new anthem, flag and coat of arms. But then we will become a people with no memory of where we came from.[24]

The restoration of the old anthem with new words, he said, had 'finally overcome the disparity between past and present . . . One cannot be permanently in contradiction with one's own history.'[25]

The idea that Russia should assume its past, while focusing on its achievements rather than its failings, would be a guiding principle throughout Putin's presidency.[26] 'Why can't we, when we listen to the anthem, think about the victory in World War II rather than the Gulag?', he asked. 'Why do we have to associate it with the worst aspects of Soviet life?' There was a political rationale for restoring the old anthem, he admitted, because many Russians felt 'a certain nostalgia' for it, and gaining their support would enable him to realise other, more important parts of his agenda. 'But there is also a moral aspect . . . You must not deprive people of everything [they value]. I think about this when I remember my parents. This was part of their life. Should we dump it all in the scrap heap of history? As if they hadn't lived at all?'[27]

For similar reasons, Putin rejected the entreaties of the liberals to remove Lenin's mummified body from the mausoleum on Red Square.

Anatoly Chubais and others had argued that if he insisted on restoring the music to the Soviet anthem, which they considered a mistake, the least he could do was have the founder of the Bolshevik regime laid to rest. Putin disagreed. Public opinion was divided. At least 40 per cent believed that the Bolshevik Revolution had been mainly positive.[28] Removing the symbol of that revolution, he said, would mean to many older people that 'they had worshipped false values . . . and their lives had been wasted. I think the main achievement of the recent period is a measure of consensus in society. I will not do anything to upset that.'[29] The presence of the mausoleum on Red Square was inappropriate, he agreed, and at some point the issue would have to be resolved. But it should be left for another day.[30]

Accordingly, the music of the Soviet anthem resounded once again on state occasions and at sporting competitions. Lenin remained in Red Square, entombed in his secular shrine of red granite, maintained by a team of embalmers who periodically provided cosmetic attentions to his corpse. And Putin continued in his attempts to reconcile the seemingly irreconcilable – the loyalties of the majority, who regretted the passing of the Soviet Union and were rooted in the past, and the aspirations of younger, more emancipated Russians, who represented the future.

In 2005, to the fury of the communists, he announced that the November 7 anniversary of the Bolshevik Revolution, which had been renamed by Yeltsin, more in hope than expectation, the 'Day of Accord and Reconciliation', would be replaced by a new holiday, three days earlier, called Unity Day. It commemorated the expulsion of the Polish army from Moscow by Russian volunteers in 1612. He arranged for the remains of General Anton Denikin, who had led one of the anti-Bolshevik 'White' armies during the civil war of 1918–20, to be brought back from America, where he had died, and reinterred in the Donskoi Monastery in Moscow.[31] That proved less controversial: although Denikin had been anti-communist and, like most of the White officer corps, a virulent anti-Semite, many Russians regarded him as an honest patriot. Then, in 2007, Putin succeeded in brokering the reconciliation of the Russian Orthodox Church with its estranged sister church, the Russian Orthodox Church Outside Russia, which had been founded by White Russian émigré clergy, ending a schism which had lasted 80 years.[32]

But dealing with the conflicts which had set Whites against Reds almost a century before was easier than achieving consensus on more recent history.

The touchiest issue was Stalin: murderous tyrant to some, heroic wartime leader to others. For most of his first two terms, Putin tacked first one way, then the other. Stalin, he said, had been 'greatly to blame for the failures of the first year or year and a half of the war',[33] refusing to believe warnings that Hitler was preparing to invade. He also bore responsibility for 'the tragedy of deportation', when entire nations, mainly in the Caucasus, were uprooted from their homes and exiled to Central Asia, because he feared they might collaborate with the Germans.[34] But those criticisms were offset by the unveiling of a huge bronze plaque in the Kremlin's Palace of Congresses, glorifying Stalin's wartime role.

When it came to the Molotov–Ribbentrop pact, under which, in 1939, Russia and Nazi Germany had agreed to divide up Eastern Europe between them, Putin tried to satisfy both sides. On the one hand, it had been a 'personal decision by Stalin', not in the interests of the Soviet people, he declared.[35] On the other, it had been necessary as a response to the Munich agreement, which Britain and France had signed with Hitler the previous year, hoping to sit out the war while Germany and the Soviet Union destroyed each other.[36]

To find a middle course in a debate where passions were even more inflamed than over Lenin was impossible. It was one thing to argue over essentially symbolic issues – quite another when Stalin's iron rule had affected every Russian family and was seared into every memory. Everyone had a friend, or a brother or sister, or a cousin or a father or an uncle or a grandparent, who had been sent to a labour camp from which they either had or had not returned.

Putin finally made up his mind to address that issue in October 2007, during a visit to the Butovo execution site, 15 miles South of Moscow. There, at the height of Stalin's Great Purge in 1937 and 1938, more than 20,000 people had been killed and buried in mass graves.

We are gathered here, [Putin said,] to honour the memory of the victims of political repression . . . 1937 is considered to be the year that the repression peaked, but it had been well prepared by the brutality of the previous years. It is sufficient to recall the shooting of hostages during the civil war, the destruction of entire social classes, of the clergy, the dekulakisation of the peasants, the destruction of the Cossacks. Such tragedies . . . happened when ideals which were attractive at first glance but which proved in the end to be empty, were placed higher than fundamental values of human life, human rights and freedoms. Millions of people were destroyed, sent to labour camps, shot and tortured to death. As a rule they were people who had their own views, who were not afraid to speak out. They were the most capable people, the flower of the nation . . . Much must be done to ensure that this is never forgotten.[37]

Russian liberals seized on his words as a significant clarification of his position on Stalinism. But he went on to imply that the victims had died in 'political struggle'. The memory of their deaths, he declared, was a warning that 'political arguments and disagreements' must never again take such a destructive form.[38]

That was dishonest, and Putin seemed ill at ease as he said it – 'unusually distracted', as a reporter from *Kommersant* put it.[39] Most of those murdered at Butovo had played no part in political struggle. They included more than 900 Russian Orthodox clergy, executed solely for their beliefs, and countless thousands of loyal citizens, arrested by the NKVD because they had quotas to fill, regardless of supposed guilt or innocence.

Putin used an equally specious argument to exculpate the NKVD officers who had carried out the executions. The security services, he said, 'did not instigate those mass repressions. Rather they were an instrument in the hands of the Communist Party.'[40]

It was like exonerating the SS on the grounds that it was merely an instrument of the Nazis.

Fence-sitting was uncomfortable and deceitful, but Putin evidently felt that it was the least bad option. Opinion polls in 2001 had shown that 60 per cent of Russians believed that Stalin's record was globally positive, while 25 per cent thought the opposite.[41] Among Putin's main support base – the security forces, the bureaucracy and the older generation – nostalgia for the *Vozhd*, the Leader, was even stronger. Six years later, almost 40 per cent of the population still believed that Stalin's role had been positive.[42]

Attitudes were slowly changing, but the question remained deeply divisive, as was shown by the tribulations of Zurab Tsereteli, a sculptor who had risen to prominence in Soviet times. In 2004, he created a monumental bronze statue of Stalin, Roosevelt and Churchill, which he wanted to erect in front of the Livadia Palace in Yalta, where the three leaders had met in 1945. After weeks of angry debate, the Crimean parliament rejected his proposal.[43] Volgograd, the former Stalingrad, also turned him down.[44] So did Sakhalin, in the Russian Far East. 'We are being asked to install a monument that no one else in Russia wants,' the region's Governor complained.[45] 'Russians today have an extremely contradictory attitude to this historical figure.' A statue of Stalin would only cause 'unwanted tension, senseless arguments and tension within the Sakhalin community'.[46]

Putin's concern was not with statues but with Stalin's place in history and, more particularly, in the history books used in Russian schools.

'Some of the things in Russian textbooks . . . make one's hair stand on end', he grumbled.[47] 'While keeping in memory the tragedies of the past, we should base ourselves on the best things that our people have accomplished.'[48] Putin had been complaining about the way history was being taught since the early days of his presidency. In the summer of 2007, soon after his speech at Butovo, he finally got round to doing something about it. A teachers' manual was produced under the watchful eye of Vladislav Surkov, the Kremlin ideologist, followed by a textbook for high-school students. The guiding principles were that the history of the tsarist empire, the Soviet Union and post-Soviet Russia should be treated as a single, continuous whole, and that the positive aspects of Russian history should be emphasised, rather than 'the black pages'.[49]

Putin called it 'objective and thorough'. Others saw it as a 'lacquering' of history.[50] 'In Russia, only the past is unpredictable', one commentator wrote wryly, reprising an old Soviet joke.

In Putin's new authorised version, Stalin's despotism was depicted as having created the necessary conditions for modernising the country's economy. 'The Bolsheviks were able to fulfil this task only by violence,' the textbook explained. 'They had no other instruments for modernising Russia, so violence was inevitable.'[51] It criticised Khrushchev for 'hare-brained schemes'; praised Brezhnev for having, like Putin, brought stability; accused Gorbachev of having brought about the break-up of the Soviet Union, but also grudgingly gave him credit for, as Putin put it, 'destroying a system which Russians could endure no longer'. Yeltsin was criticised for his 'crisis-ridden governance' but praised for 'giving Russians freedom, indisputably the great achievement of the Yeltsin era'.[52] Putin's own presidency was described as a time of efficient government and democracy.

Amid all his conflicting statements, it is hard to pin down what Putin really thought of Stalin.

He probably came closest to revealing his own opinion when he said: 'Stalin was certainly a tyrant, many call him a criminal, but he was not a Nazi.'[53] It was hardly a glowing assessment. While the new textbook played down Stalin's crimes, a tendency which would become more pronounced in Putin's later years, it did not omit them altogether, and books like Solzhenitsyn's *Gulag Archipelago*, which recounted in unflinching detail the ghastliness of Stalin's prison camps, remained on the high-school history reading list. Russia was rewriting its own past, as many other countries had, but it was not the complete whitewash that human rights organisations had feared.[54]

Putin's emphasis on what he saw as the correct teaching of Russian history, in particular about Russia's role in World War II, reflected the importance he attached to patriotism as an essential part of the ideological glue needed to hold the peoples of post-communist Russia together.

Americans, with help from the mythmakers of Hollywood, like to believe that the United States, aided by the plucky British, played the main role in defeating Hitler's Germany. Winston Churchill, addressing the House of Commons in August 1944, was more lucid. 'The obvious, essential fact,' he declared, '[is] that it is the Russian armies who have done the main work in tearing the guts out of the German army ... No force in the world which could have been called into being ... would have been able to maul and break [the Nazi regime] unless it had been subjected to the terrible slaughter that has fallen to it through the strength of the Soviet Russian armies.'[55]

Russia lost 27 million people, 15 per cent of the population, during the war, a gargantuan blood-letting from which the country has still not recovered. For Russians, it was the defining event of the twentieth century, overshadowing the Bolshevik Revolution, the Civil War, the horrors of Stalin's purges and the collapse of communism. The memory of those who fought in it was capable as nothing else of uniting the nation in homage. Each year on Victory Day, May 9, a military parade is held on Red Square, including, since 2008, armoured vehicles and

ICBMs, and a flypast by the Russian air force. It is followed by a march of the 'Immortal Regiment', in which participants, including Putin and other leaders, carry photographs of relatives who fought in the war. More than 75 years after its end, it is a way to keep the memory alive when there are ever fewer surviving veterans.

Patriotism, epitomised by the heroism of Russian soldiers in World War II, was to Putin one of two key elements of what he called 'Russia's moral foundation'.[56] The other was religious belief, which in practice – although Russia is a multi-confessional state, whose population includes Buddhists and Jews as well as 25 million Muslims – meant Russian Orthodoxy.

Traditionally the Church was such a fundamental part of Russian identity that in the eighteenth and nineteenth centuries, when countryfolk were asked what nation they belonged to, they would answer: 'Orthodox'. The principles of tsarist rule were 'Orthodoxy, Autocracy and National Essence', the last of which signified that Russia should cleave to its own traditions and eschew foreign influences. In Soviet times, the Church was repressed. But, during *perestroika* and especially after 1991, it re-emerged, in Putin's words, 'like grass in a big city which grows up through the asphalt'.[57] As deputy Mayor of St Petersburg in the mid 1990s, he had attended Easter services. So did Sobchak and Yeltsin, who were both confirmed atheists. It was a political gesture by elected officials to show respect towards the faithful. Notwithstanding his baptism, and the cross which he had shown to George W. Bush, there was nothing to suggest that in the 1990s he himself was a believer.[58]

Putin's first pronouncements as President confirmed that impression. He spoke of Christianity as 'an ideology' rather than a faith.[59] Asked whether he was a believer, he replied that he was 'a believer in human beings'. A person's beliefs were 'inside a man's heart', not to be flaunted on the public stage.[60]

Gradually that changed. He began saying that the Russian Orthodox Church gave him 'a kind of inner peace'.[61] By the middle of 2001, he was speaking of himself as 'a Christian, an Orthodox believer'.[62] A chapel had been consecrated in the Kremlin, in the building housing the President's office, when Yeltsin was in power. It had stood empty until Putin arrived. Now he started taking foreign guests to see it.[63] His spin doctor, Gleb Pavlovsky, thought that, like the story of his cross, he was using it to create an emotional rapport with them by lifting a corner of the veil on his private life.[64] The ruined church at Novo-Ogaryovo was also restored.

The banker, Sergei Pugachev, who had close ties to the Orthodox Patriarch, Aleksei, felt that Putin's embrace of the Church was for pragmatic reasons.[65] At first, Pugachev said, he did not know how to how to hold a candle, how to cross himself with the right number of fingers or how to conduct himself during a service.[66] But then, he thought, Putin realised that 'Orthodoxy was the embodiment of the national idea, with a greater capacity to unify the people than any political party.'[67] Upwards of 80 per cent of Russians, even if they had never read the Bible and knew nothing of Christian teaching, considered themselves Orthodox. The Church could fill the ideological void that had been left by communism.[68]

Given that Putin placed himself in a tradition going back to tsarist times, an intimate relationship with Orthodoxy, whether simulated or real, was an essential attribute of the presidency. But what appears to have started as a political manoeuvre may have developed over time into something deeper.

He began visiting Orthodox monasteries and religious sites more often than was strictly necessary for public relations purposes. In off-the-cuff remarks, he started to make religious allusions. 'All nations are equal before God,' he would say. 'God gave me the good fortune to work for the good of my country.'[69] The death penalty is 'a matter for the Almighty'. On long flights, Putin confided – admittedly in an interview destined for an American readership – he often read the Bible.[70]

He acquired the habit of crossing himself when the Devil was mentioned, a custom among Orthodox monks but not normally among laypersons.[71] The Kremlin let it be known that Archimandrite Tikhon, the Abbott of the Sretensky Monastery, not far from the Lubyanka, had become Putin's confessor. Tikhon, ten years younger than the President, with a rusty brown beard and long hair tied into a ponytail, declined to confirm the relationship, but Pugachev, who had introduced them in the late 1990s, when Putin was FSB chief, said he clearly had unusual access.[72]

Whether it was all an elaborate charade or whether Putin was really a convert was never clear. Orthodox believers at church services he attended said he appeared completely immersed in the ritual like a true member of the faith.[73] It is possible that, like many others who 'found God' by a circuitous path, he initially embraced the Church for political reasons and then became a believer. It is also possible that, like the majority of Russians who consider themselves Orthodox, he assumed the mantle of Christianity but little else.

Only Putin himself knows what he really believes. Some of his immediate circle, like Vladimir Yakunin, a fellow member of the Ozero cooperative who afterwards became Railways Minister, and reputedly – if surprisingly – Nikolai Patrushev, Putin's successor as FSB chief, were said to be genuinely devout. Others, like Viktor Ivanov and Sechin, and a host of lower-level officials, embraced Orthodoxy less from personal conviction than because in Putin's Russia it was politically correct to do so. None of them, devout or not, conducted themselves in a particularly Christian fashion. But that is true of leaders – and people – everywhere, whatever faith they profess.

A unified view of Russian history, the exaltation of patriotism and a commitment to traditional Orthodox values formed the bedrock of what Putin saw as Russia's national identity. The fact that more than a sixth of Russia's population was Muslim made no difference. Samuel Huntington's thesis, which the Bush administration had embraced, that the world was headed for a clash of civilisations, was pernicious, Putin thought. 'We are first and foremost human beings,' he said, 'and only afterwards representatives of different religions and creeds.'[74] Muslims and Christians had coexisted in Russia for centuries and, despite the war in Chechnya, there was no reason they should not continue to do so.

Putin's stated goal during his first term as President was to make Russia 'a normal, democratic society with a market economy and democratic politics',[75] that would become part of what he called 'the civilised world',[76] by which he meant the West. But as relations with the United States soured and the prospect of Russia being fully accepted into that civilised world receded, he began to look at alternatives.

There were plenty of voices urging him to do so. The *siloviki*, although fractured into different clans which fought amongst themselves, were united in their suspicion of Western motives. Archimandrite

Tikhon, even if his influence on Putin was less than was made out, spoke for the Orthodox hierarchy, which feared that Russia would be undermined by the West in the same way that, in the Middle Ages, Byzantium had been weakened by the assaults of the Crusaders, economic concessions to Venice and Genoa, and demands that Orthodox clergy submit to the primacy of Rome. But the decisive voice was that of the film director, Nikita Mikhalkov, whose father, Sergei, had written the lyrics to the Russian anthem.

An imposing figure among Russia's cultural elite, Mikhalkov was known for a ready wit, a bushy moustache, and a willingness to play court to power. His film, *Burnt by the Sun*, which told the story of a Red Army officer executed during the Stalinist terror in the 1930s, had won the Grand Prix at Cannes and an Oscar for best foreign-language film in 1995. Mikhalkov had developed a close relationship with Putin in his first term, inviting him to his home to meet Jack Nicholson and other Hollywood stars.[77] They had discussed the importance of inculcating traditional Russian values into the country's youth, who, Putin said, had 'lost touch with their cultural roots [after] being bombarded with surrogate products from abroad'.[78]

Mikhalkov was a conspiracy theorist, a fervent Orthodox believer and a Slavophile who thought that Russia should follow its own path, rather than kowtow to liberal Western ways. One of his heroes was the White Russian émigré philosopher, Ivan Ilyin, who had died in Switzerland after the Second World War. Sometime in 2004, he introduced Putin to Ilyin's writings.

Like many White Russian exiles, Ilyin was profoundly anti-Semitic and had initially welcomed the rise of Hitler and Mussolini, believing that they would save Europe from Bolshevism. He became less enthusiastic after the new Nazi authorities fired him from his teaching post at a government institute in Berlin in 1934 and put him under surveillance.[79] Nonetheless, he insisted that, despite 'deep and serious mistakes', fascism proceeded in principle from 'a healthy national-patriotic feeling'.[80] To Mikhalkov, that had to be seen in the context of the time and was of little importance. What mattered were Ilyin's ideas about Russia.

A convinced monarchist, he had advocated an autocratic regime with strong centralised power, necessary to manage a country with vast territories. He had predicted that, after the inevitable collapse of

communism, Russia would follow a special path, rejecting both Western democracy and totalitarianism. 'Democracy is a dead end,' he
wrote.[81] Abraham Lincoln's idea of 'government of the people, by the
people and for the people', which had been regarded for 150 years as a
political panacea, had led to 'the greatest difficulties and disasters'.
States were either corporate, made up of equal actors who came
together voluntarily and decided their future by the ballot box, or institutional, built on the principle of guardianship, in which the people
were governed from above. The first, if taken to an extreme, would
lead to anarchy; the second would extinguish all human freedom and
initiative.

Russia, Ilyin concluded, should aim for a judicious combination of
the two. How that should be done, Russia itself would decide. 'There
is no single yardstick,' he wrote. 'Russia will have to find for itself its
own, original state form . . . which will correspond to [its] national
history.'[82]

Putin was intrigued.

At a time when America was bogged down in Iraq and relations
with the West were becoming increasingly strained, Ilyin appeared to
offer a different political path.

During this period, he also started reading the works of Nikolai
Berdyaev, an Orthodox Christian philosopher who had settled in Paris
in the 1920s after being banished by Lenin. Berdyaev's ideas about the
Russian people were more down to earth than Ilyin's. Russians were 'a
conglomeration of contradictions,' he wrote, '[who] can inspire both
intense love and violent hatred [and] have a disturbing effect on the
peoples of the West'.[83] In some respects for Putin, Berdyaev was a curious choice. He was often called the philosopher of freedom, of
creativity and of the individual, which sat oddly with the principles of
a statist regime. But as part of individual freedom, he defended inequality, and Putin's Russia, as a result of the privatisations of the 1990s,
was one of the most unequal places on earth. In 2005, the ten richest
Russians had a net worth equal to 10 per cent of the country's GDP,
twice as large a share as that of the ten richest Americans.[84]

Berdyaev wrote at length about Russia's role at the confluence of
East and West: 'In Russia, two streams of world history jostle and
influence each other. The Russian people is not purely European and it
is not purely Asiatic. Russia . . . unites two worlds, and within the

Russian soul, two principles are always engaged in strife – the Eastern and the Western.'[85] Ilyin had written in similar terms. That resonated with Putin's own thinking about Russia's place in the world. Russia, he sometimes argued, was both European and Asian, combining 'European pragmatism and Oriental wisdom'.[86] It had common European roots with the West, but they had put forth different branches.[87]

Another nineteenth-century philosopher whose work began to interest him was Vladimir Solovyov, an other-worldly, mystical thinker who had been a friend of Dostoyevsky and was said to have been the inspiration for the character of Alyosha, the hero of *The Brothers Karamazov*. Solovyov had devoted his life to the ideal of a Universal Church in the Russian tradition of *sobornost*, which accorded with Putin's conception of the oneness of Russia, wherein different nationalities and ethnic groups – by no means all of them European – would live in harmony.

Vasily Klyuchevsky, the pre-eminent historian of Russia in the nineteenth century, was yet another influence.[88] Klyuchevsky held that the state represented a covenant between the authorities and the different social classes, and argued, as Putin did, that Russia should progress by evolutionary change, rather than by revolutionary leaps.

But Ilyin was the key figure. From 2005 onwards, Putin began citing Ilyin's writings in his speeches. Others quickly followed suit.[89] One senior official commented, only slightly tongue in cheek, that 'the demand for his ideas in today's Russia is so strong that sometimes there is a feeling that Ivan Ilyin is our contemporary.'[90] Putin arranged for Ilyin's remains to be brought back from Switzerland and buried at the Donskoi Monastery, next to General Denikin.[91] His collected works were published. The following year, the Russian billionaire, Viktor Vekselberg, acquired Ilyin's archive for the state from the University of Michigan.[92]

At one level, the rehabilitation of men like Ilyin, whose works had been banned during the Soviet period, was a means of linking Russia with its pre-revolutionary past. At another, it provided an ideological foundation for Putin's attempts to shape the new post-Soviet polity. This new–old Russia would reject the 'formal democracy' of the West, proclaim a Eurasian identity, gather together its multiple faiths and ethnicities under the banner of Russian culture and Orthodoxy and be guided by a strong centralised power.

What to call this new democracy, and what it should consist of, was a more difficult question. Vitaly Tretyakov, the editor of *Nezavisimaya gazeta*, proposed 'managed democracy', but Putin disliked the term, arguing – not very convincingly – that it would give the impression that Russian democracy was 'controlled from the outside', on a par with countries like Georgia which were under the sway of the United States.[93] In fact, it seems that he was more concerned at the implication that democracy would be restricted, which was not the image he wanted to convey either to Russian liberals or to Russia's partners in the West.

The Kremlin's ideologist, Vladislav Surkov, then came up with the idea of 'sovereign democracy', which Putin liked much better. 'Not many countries in the world today are sovereign,' Putin declared. 'Apart from Russia, China, India and a few others, all the rest are either dependent on others or on the leaders of their blocs.' Indeed, he added mischievously, the European Union and some of its member states would do well to think more about sovereign democracy. Then Russia would be able to deal with an independent EU that defended its own interests instead of deferring to Washington all the time.[94]

Exactly what 'sovereign democracy' should consist of was left deliberately vague. Putin repeated endlessly that 'the principles of democracy must be adapted to the realities of Russian life today, to our traditions and history'[95] and that no one else could tell Russia what kind of system it should have. Yet at the same time he rejected the idea of 'inventing some kind of local, home-grown democracy'.[96] That may have been partly because he was addressing different audiences: patriotic Russians on the one hand, Western liberals on the other. But he seemed genuinely uncertain how in practice Russia should proceed. Eurasianism was fine in theory. But Russia's culture and beliefs were fundamentally European.

The key points to which Putin returned again and again were the need for developed political parties, a thriving civil society and a strong middle class, 'the standard-bearer of [democratic] ideology', which would defend social stability.[97] They would not be the same as in the West. In Russia, Putin said, political parties were accountable to the state as well as society. Centralised power and democracy did not contradict each other and to suggest otherwise was to create 'a false conflict'.[98]

It was the same principle that applied to the media and big business: political parties and civil society were free but only within the limits which the state laid down. One day that might change, Putin said, but at this stage, Russia was still taking its first steps along the path to democracy.[99] In Europe and North America, democratic systems had developed over hundreds of years.[100] 'Creating fully fledged, functioning institutions [in Russia]', he went on, 'is not something which can be achieved overnight.'[101] The country had gone directly from tsarism to communism. Then, under Yeltsin, freedom and democracy had been handed down from above. 'There was no chance for an evolutionary development, [where we could] spread out reforms over decades and wait for people's minds to change.'[102]

Those in the West who refused to recognise that Russia had become a more democratic state were 'not quite honest', Putin maintained. However, genuine parliamentary democracy was for future generations. For the moment, what Russia needed was 'strong presidential power'.[103]

As his second term drew to a close, Putin had become reconciled to the need for a national idea. Searching for it was 'an old tradition, a favourite pastime . . . something akin to looking for the meaning of life', a task that was never-ending, but also 'useful and interesting'. If Russia was to achieve its goals, he told parliament, it needed 'a common system of moral guidelines'.[104] It had taken him nearly eight years to reach that conclusion, yet in retrospect there was a kind of inevitability about it. The singularity of Russian culture and history is such that, whoever had succeeded Yeltsin, sooner or later Russia would have sought its own path. But the way in which it came about meant that the search for that path was undertaken in opposition to the West. That was not predetermined.

13

Body Politic

When Putin took office in 2000, he announced that his administration would devote itself primarily to domestic, not foreign, policy.[1] That was easier said than done. The key domestic tasks, after establishing the 'power vertical' with its apex in the Kremlin, were administrative and economic reform.[2] Reining in the regions, the media and the oligarchs had been the easy part. The next stage would be much more difficult.

What needed to be done was clear enough. The problem was how to do it.

In speech after speech, Putin listed the obstacles to economic growth: high taxes, capital flight, the 'offshorisation' of profits, the arbitrariness of the bureaucracy, corruption in the state monopolies, rampant crime, uncompetitive industry, inadequate guarantees for property rights, restrictions on the buying and selling of land, a still primitive banking system, the burden of foreign debt, the failings of the judicial system and demographic decline.

There were some bright spots. The rouble devaluation after the financial crash of 1998 had given the economy a shot in the arm and Putin was lucky in that oil prices nearly doubled during his first year in office. They would continue to rise almost without interruption throughout his first two terms.

It would have been easy to squander those advantages. Putin did not. His experience as deputy Mayor of St Petersburg, where Sobchak had run constant budget deficits, had made him a fiscal conservative. 'Rehabilitate the economy first, and only then raise living standards,' he said. 'You can't put the cart before the horse or it will fall into the ditch.'[3] His principal economic advisers – the Finance Minister, Aleksei Kudrin, who had drawn similar lessons from his time at Smolny, and Andrei Illarionov – concurred. Illarionov urged him to repay ahead of schedule the 130 billion US dollars of foreign loans that Russia had taken out under Yeltsin, mainly from the IMF and the World Bank, which he did.[4] Kudrin proposed the establishment of a stabilisation fund to serve as a strategic reserve, financed by taxing windfall profits reaped by the oil companies, defined as net revenue accruing when the price of crude oil exceeded a certain benchmark, set initially at 20 dollars a barrel. That was done, too, giving Russia a financial cushion which soon exceeded 100 billion dollars. A flat-rate income tax of 13 per cent, the lowest in Europe, was introduced, replacing higher taxes which in practice were rarely collected.

Reaching agreement on the buying and selling of land was harder. Apart from a brief interlude after the 1905 Revolution, when the reformist Prime Minister, Pyotr Stolypin, had authorised individual land ownership by peasants as an alternative to communal land tenure, almost all the land in Russia had been owned by the state, and before that, the imperial family, the nobility or, in the late nineteenth century, wealthy merchants with aristocratic pretensions. The notion that land could be bought and sold, like any other commodity, was so alien that when it was debated in the Duma, in 2001, the Communists swarmed the tribune and a fist fight broke out. By the time calm was restored, the Speaker, Gennady Seleznyov, had been taken to hospital complaining of high blood pressure and one deputy had a broken nose.[5] A law permitting private ownership of non-agricultural land was eventually passed, but it was not extended to farmland until several years later.

There was progress in reducing crime. The banditry of the 1990s, when, in the larger cities, people were often afraid to go out onto the streets lest they be mugged or caught in a firefight between rival gangs, became a thing of the past. The murder rate began declining in 2002 and, by the end of Putin's second term, had halved, halving again over the following decade. In Moscow and St Petersburg, there were fewer killings in proportion to the population than in most American cities. Street crime and burglaries came down to levels comparable to those in Paris or London. Organised crime was a bigger problem because it was frequently linked to powerful figures in the security forces and in local governments.[6] 'It's not always clear who people fear most,' Putin grumbled in 2004, 'the criminals or the police.'[7] Part of the problem, he admitted, was 'endemic corruption' in the power bodies and the law enforcement agencies.[8] But from the standpoint of the local authorities, a dominant crime group could maintain order and keep lesser criminals in line, help to bring in votes at election time and undertake sensitive tasks, unofficially, which the administration did not wish to do itself. It was the same logic that had led the Mayor's Office in St Petersburg to forge a relationship with the Tambovsky gang. The same applied at national level. There were tasks which the FSB preferred to contract out rather than undertake itself.

Putin was well aware of all that. But he either saw it as unavoidable or as an acceptable trade-off or, more likely, both. Whatever the rationale, Russia's cities became less violent.

The dividing lines between organised crime, the political establishment and legitimate business, already blurred in the second half of the 1990s, dissolved altogether. When a gang leader wanted to seize the assets of a legitimate company, he would now send in lawyers, armed with fake depositions, rather than thugs with AK-47s. Mark Galeotti wrote in his book about the Russian underworld, *The Vory* ('The Thieves'): 'Little by little, things are changing . . . As Russia acquires branches of HSBC and Starbucks, as Russians watch *The Simpsons* and *The Sopranos* [and] travel and study abroad, as their financial systems become more interconnected with others, . . . bit by bit their criminals will increasingly come to resemble ours.'[9]

Putin was blunt about the failings of the system he had inherited. 'The people who strive to cosy up to power are precisely those who should not be allowed within cannon range of it,' he said. 'It's always been like that, it is now and it always will be.'[10] Russia must try to build the kind of society where 'state officials and assorted phrasemongers cannot use state interests and democratic rhetoric as cover for filling their own pockets'.[11]

That was fine in principle but difficult to accomplish. It had indeed 'always been like that' in Russia. The great officials in tsarist times had plundered the state. On a much more modest scale, they had done the same when Brezhnev was in power. Only under Stalin had fear kept greed at bay. Putin came to power vowing to extirpate such practices. 'There cannot be any kind of positive development in this country until this problem [of corruption] is resolved,' he told a television audience in 2000 during the election campaign. 'I am convinced of that. Absolutely convinced! Otherwise it will eat everything from inside. It will devour everything.'[12]

He was right. But his admission that 'it always will be' like that, was not reassuring.

Moreover Putin's actions told a very different story. Pavel Borodin had been caught red-handed taking kickbacks amounting to tens of millions of dollars from Mabetex for the renovation of the Kremlin. Far from punishing him, Putin appointed him to a lucrative sinecure. A few months later, the Energy Minister, Viktor Kalyuzhny, who likewise had a chequered past, was fired. After a short interval, he was named Special Envoy for the Caspian Sea and, later, Ambassador to Latvia.[13]

The following year, 2001, Putin forced the resignation of Yevgeny Nazdratenko, the Governor of Primorye in the Russian Far East.[14] Nazdratenko's malfeasance had left the territory without heating in one of the coldest winters in recent memory, when temperatures fell to minus 50 degrees or below. In his eight years as Governor, he had bled Primorye dry.[15] Yeltsin had tried repeatedly to dislodge him without success. Putin did so by promising him a more senior post. Over the objections of the Prime Minister, Mikhail Kasyanov, Nazdratenko was appointed head of the State Fisheries Committee. Two years later, he was fired again. After being transferred to a post on the Security Council, he was dismissed for a third time but still obtained another position.

Vladimir Yakovlev, Sobchak's successor in St Petersburg, whom Putin had denounced as a Judas, was ousted in much the same way. In June 2003, Putin offered him a specially created post as deputy Prime Minister in charge of housing, communal services, public works and transport development.[16] Once he had been detached from his provincial power base, he was moved to a less prominent position but allowed to serve out his time in a succession of junior posts.

'I do not bear grudges,' Putin said. 'I am not inclined to believe that yesterday's opponents are one's enemies for the rest of one's life.'[17] It was easy enough to fire people, he added, but how could one be sure that those who replaced them would be any better?

There were exceptions.

One was Nikolai Aksyonenko, his putative rival for the Prime Ministership in 1999. Within days of becoming acting President, Putin demoted him. That was followed, in the autumn of 2001, by the opening of a criminal investigation against him for misappropriating funds. Whether Aksyonenko was any more guilty of that than other members of the government was debatable. Kasyanov thought not and argued that he should stay.[18] But Putin wanted him out. He resigned in January 2002, having been promised that if he did so, the case against him would be dropped.[19] It was not. He was suffering from leukaemia and eventually was allowed to leave Russia for medical treatment in Germany, where he died three years later at the age of 56.

Putin's reluctance to fire people outright, as Yeltsin used to do, might be explained by his being newly elected and engaged in a brutal war in Chechnya. The last thing he needed was to make enemies if it could be avoided. That had been one of Sobchak's great mistakes. Even Aksyonenko had been persuaded to resign, rather than being summarily dismissed. Putin's friend, Sergei Stepashin, thought he had made it a principle 'not to discard people' unless exceptional factors were at work.[20]

In fact, there was a deeper reason.

The system of power that Putin was building was intrinsically corrupt. It was not merely patrimonial, as had been the case in imperial times. Under the tsars, high officials who had risen to the pinnacle of power and amassed immense fortunes through the favour of the throne could find themselves out of office and stripped of their wealth from one day to the next. In Putin's Russia, that happened only in the most unusual circumstances. The higher levels of power were structured as a matrix of interlocking pieces, configured as informal networks, each of which protected its own. They competed among themselves for influence but provided Putin, the linchpin of the system, with a solid base of support. As in a stack of tumble timber, individual pieces could be shifted from one place to another. But, if they were removed altogether, the structure would become unstable. Putin could talk as much as he liked about the need to fight corruption. But, above a certain level in the power structure, actually doing something about it would involve risks that he was not prepared to take.

Similar considerations applied lower down the scale.

Addressing a meeting of businessmen shortly before he was elected, Putin had complained of the 'unquenchable' desire of officials to extort profits from the private sector. 'It is so strong,' he said, 'that I have no idea how to fight it!'[21] It was a strange admission. Putin knew perfectly well what the problem was and what needed to be done, and the businessmen did, too.

They had become accustomed to the police demanding that bars be put on the windows to prevent burglaries and, as soon as that had been done, the fire inspector insisting that they be removed for safety reasons. After that, the health inspector would arrive.[22] Each inspection involved the payment of a bribe. One business was reported to have been inspected by different agencies 300 times in a single year.[23] Then there were the difficulties in obtaining licences. Small and medium companies were being strangled,[24] Putin admitted, by 'red tape and "gratuities" paid to local officials for authorisations and signatures'.[25] Dozens, sometimes more than a hundred, different permissions had to be collected to open a new business. 'People rightly say', he went on, 'that you can't resolve even an insignificant little problem without paying a bribe.'[26]

The remedies were not complicated: licensing procedures should be simplified; the role of the state reduced; civil society strengthened; and the rule of law enforced.

Putin said all the right things.[27] He proposed a 'one-stop shop' for licensing and inspections and called for 'a dictatorship of the law, the only dictatorship we can agree to be governed by'[28] – a phrase which shocked many in the West, where it was taken as a sign that Putin was backing away from democracy. In fact, it had been coined by Gorbachev, who had declared, ten years earlier, 'We should have one dictatorship for all, the dictatorship of the law.'[29]

However, words were one thing, putting them into practice was another.

When Putin took office, the Russian bureaucracy, consisting of public servants, members of the security forces and employees of state-owned enterprises, numbered 25 million people, more than a third of the total workforce. In March 2004, he launched an ambitious programme to streamline the state apparatus, which, he said, had become 'a bureaucratic quagmire of formalities and incompetence'.[30] The idea was to create a three-tiered structure, in which the ministries would draw up policies, federal agencies would carry them out and an intermediate layer of officials would control their implementation.[31] No minister was to have more than two deputies, staffing levels were to be reduced by 15 to 20 per cent and comparable cuts were to be made in the Presidential Administration.[32]

It looked good on paper but the result, as the business newspaper *Vedomosti* wrote, was that 'the situation worsened on all fronts. Instead

of increasing the effectiveness of the state apparatus, the reform paralysed it.'[33] Putin himself admitted as much. Russia still had 'a
super-bureaucratised economy', he said, 'and a super-bureaucratised
state where officials appropriate the right to decide everything'.[34] An
estimated 60 per cent of his orders were ignored or implemented only
in part.[35] In 2008, after repeated attempts at reform, the country had
more civil servants than the Soviet Union, with twice the population,
had had 20 years earlier.[36] Far from declining, public-sector employment during Putin's first two terms increased by three million to reach
40 per cent of the workforce, almost twice the level in developed market economies.[37]

The bureaucracy was a Hydra. Short of arrest and imprisonment, it
was almost impossible to remove a well-entrenched official. When
posts were closed, those who were ousted moved sideways, new
departments were opened and new posts created. 'The state cannot
support and does not need such an enormous public sector,' Putin
complained. '[It] is weighed down by bureaucracy and does not have
the motivation for positive change, let alone dynamic development.'[38]

That had always been the case in Russia. But if nothing changed, it
was because Putin refused to act. The same bureaucracy which he
excoriated – 'an exclusive and often arrogant caste, regarding state service as an alternative form of business'[39] – formed the core of his
political base. Antagonising it was not a risk he was ready to take.

Occasionally an official would be selected as a sacrificial lamb, to
show the Russian public, the main victims of bureaucratic avarice, that
the authorities were not totally inert. When a power cut blacked out
most of Moscow in May 2005, Putin accused the leadership of the
city's electricity utility, Mosenergo, of using the company's substantial
profits – nearly 200 million US dollars the previous year – to buy prime
real estate through shell companies in Cyprus instead of replacing
obsolete equipment.[40] The company head, Arkady Yevstafiev, a former
KGB officer, resigned. But he was not prosecuted and afterwards
embarked on a successful business career. Even Putin had to admit that
progress in tackling corruption had been minimal.[41] As his second term
drew to a close, Russia's place in Transparency International's Corruption Perceptions Index was near the bottom, better than Cambodia but
not as good as Egypt.

★

The toxic combination of bureaucracy and corruption, was the principal, but not the only, cause of the failure of Russia's economy to develop to its full potential. Inadequate protection of property rights and legal abuses deterred foreign investors and persuaded Russians who were able to do so to park their gains offshore.

Even so, GDP growth averaged 6.6 per cent annually over Putin's first two terms. Productivity increased by more than 5 per cent a year, inflation remained modest, each year saw a substantial trade surplus and by 2008, the Central Bank had the world's third-largest foreign reserves, totalling 570 billion US dollars. Real incomes rose across the board, 10 per cent a year on average for the bottom quintile, 12 per cent for the top and many times more for the richest 0.001 per cent.[42]

Oil and gas accounted for roughly half of Russia's export earnings. Putin had decided early on that he should bring them under his personal control.

The hardest nut to crack was the gas monopoly, Gazprom.

Rem Vyakhirev, the CEO and Chairman of the Management Board, was a protégé of the former Prime Minister, Viktor Chernomyrdin, who, during his time in government, had granted Gazprom extraordinary privileges.[43] As a result, both men had become immensely wealthy. Charles Ryan, the young banker who had been with EBRD in St Petersburg, estimated that the sums being stripped out of Gazprom and finding their way into the pockets of board members were of the order of 2 to 3 billion US dollars a year.[44]

Putin was determined to push Vyakhirev out.

The problem was that Chernomyrdin had set up the board in such a way that Vyakhirev and his allies had six seats and the government, despite being the principal shareholder, only five. Even after Putin had appointed Dmitry Medvedev as Board Chairman, Vyakhirev retained effective control.[45]

A solution was proposed by Yeltsin's former Finance Minister, Boris Fyodorov, who now headed an investment company in Moscow, UFG Asset Management, of which Ryan was Chief Financial Officer. UFG had built up a stake of almost 10 per cent in Gazprom, entitling it to a seat on the board. Together with another minority shareholder, Hermitage Capital Management, founded by Bill Browder, an American-born British financier who was the grandson of Earl Browder, the long-time head of the American Communist Party, UFG wanted to force Gazprom to divest itself of its non-core interests and pay shareholders dividends which would reflect the company's true value.[46] If the board change was approved, Fyodorov told Putin, the UFG representative would vote with Medvedev and the other government-appointed directors and Vyakhirev's stranglehold on the company would be broken.

According to Ryan, Putin accepted Fyodorov's proposal, but on one condition, the significance of which would become clear only much later: the agreement must remain secret. 'They will attack you,' he warned, 'but when they do so, I want you to know that you have my complete guarantee for your personal safety, your clients' property and your business.'

The attacks were not long in coming. In a scene out of *The Godfather*, Fyodorov's dog was killed. Ryan was detained by men who claimed to be from the security services, and interrogated in a cellar. Gazprom and UFG obtained court orders, freezing each other's shares. At that point Medvedev called in the two sides and told them to back off. UFG did so. Gazprom refused. A few hours later, its Finance Director was arrested.

Only then, it seems, did Vyakhirev realise that his problems were not the work of a group of pesky Western investors but came from much higher up.

In October 2000, Fyodorov joined the management board. Eight months later, as the members were about to meet to discuss an extension to Vyakhirev's contract, Putin summoned Gazprom's management to the Kremlin.[47] He had no intention of interfering in the affairs of a private company, he said, but Gazprom played an exceptional role in Russia's economy and, if nobody objected, he would like a few words with Rem Vyakhirev before the meeting took place. They spent about an hour together. When Vyakhirev emerged, he told his colleagues that he had decided to step down.

Neither Putin nor Vyakhirev ever divulged what had been said, but it appears that Putin presented him with a choice. Either he could be voted out ignominiously by a split board decision in which Fyodorov would have the casting vote, in which case a criminal investigation for corruption might well follow; or he could retire gracefully, keeping all his perquisites and a seat on the board for a decent interval thereafter. Either way he would have to leave.

All 11 board members, Vyakhirev included, then voted for Putin's one-time deputy at the Mayor's Office in St Petersburg, Aleksei Miller, to become CEO and Chairman in his place. That day, Gazprom's shares on the London Stock Exchange shot up 134 per cent.[48]

Ryan thought it was a very clever move. Fyodorov's appointment to the board had made it possible to remove Vyakhirev, but Putin had manoeuvred in such a way that he was not beholden to UFG, as he would have been if Fyodorov had had to cast the deciding vote. As it was, it was merely Gazprom's board voting to replace one CEO by another.

Miller was out of his depth in his new post and in the first year there were rumours that he would be fired.[49] Putin shrugged it off. He took the strategic decisions for the company himself and would continue to do so throughout his presidency, often surprising his foreign counterparts with his detailed knowledge of the industry. Miller was loyal and that was what counted.

Once Gazprom had been reeled in, other moves followed.

Putin gave Igor Sechin, the Chairman of Rosneft, wearing his other hat as deputy head of the Presidential Administration, an unofficial mandate to oversee the oil industry as a whole.[50] Nikolai Tokarev, who had served with Putin in the KGB at Dresden, became head of Transneft, the state oil pipeline company, which also owned the country's biggest oil ports. Vladimir Yakunin, Putin's former neighbour in the Ozero cooperative in Karelia, was put in charge of Russian Railways, another major revenue earner.

It was blatant cronyism. But it meant that Putin had men he trusted in charge of the state enterprises which generated the biggest financial flows.

Putin had moved quickly to bring Gazprom to heel because of its importance to the economy and as an instrument of foreign policy. Normally his style was more deliberate. 'You need haste only when catching fleas,' he liked to say.[51] For everything else, caution was preferable.

In the West, this was interpreted as a sign that he was not yet in complete control. That was a misjudgement. Voloshin, who knew better than anyone what really went on in the Kremlin, was categorical: 'From the moment he became President, he held all the power in his hands.'[52]

Change in the upper ranks of the administration often came in two stages. Those whom Putin wanted to put into top positions, like Miller and Dmitry Medvedev, were moved into lower-level posts from which, when the time was right, they could be promoted. The second stage often took much longer. Voloshin remained head of the Presidential Administration under Putin for almost four years. He was replaced by in October 2003, having unsuccessfully opposed Khodorkovsky's arrest, which he feared correctly would scare off foreign investors.[53]

The departure of men like Voloshin and Aksyonenko and their replacement by loyalists who had worked with Putin in St Petersburg was seen by many Russian commentators as a purge of those associated with the Family, the inner circle of Yeltsin's entourage. In fact, it was not that simple. Putin did not set much stock on guilt by association. Others who had been even closer to the Family, like Valentin Yumashev, continued to act as advisers. So did Vladislav Surkov, who had worked for Khodorkovsky.

Putin's ultimate goal was to refashion the body politic, to control the regional satrapies and the main political parties and, above all, the central apparatus of power.

To achieve that, he could call on his former associates in St Petersburg, who were often but not always synonymous with the liberal reformers; the business magnates who had thrown in their lot with the Kremlin, like Berezovsky's former business associate, Roman Abramovich, and the aluminium billionaire, Oleg Deripaska; the *siloviki*; and a few young technocrats brought in from the provinces.

None of these groups was homogeneous. Igor Sechin, Nikolai Patrushev, Viktor Ivanov, Viktor Cherkesov at the Narcotics Commission and Putin's chief bodyguard, Viktor Zolotov, all had their own interests and allies, and the latent conflicts between them frequently degenerated into what Cherkesov called 'clan warfare'.[54] The same was true of the liberals, where men like Kudrin, Gref, Medvedev and Chubais, while all sharing broadly the same philosophy, had different goals and ambitions.

From Putin's standpoint, this was not necessarily a bad thing. It was not a matter of divide and rule, in the crude sense that Yeltsin had practised it, but rather of keeping a balance of interests within the ruling elite.

Kasyanov remembered attending a buffet dinner in the Kremlin in

December 2000, to mark Chekists' Day, the anniversary of the founding of the Cheka in 1918. Addressing the assembled FSB brass, Putin
deadpanned: 'I wish to report that the group of FSB colleagues whom
you assigned to work undercover in the government have accomplished the first stage of their mission.'[55] The generals applauded
furiously. But he went on to issue a pointed and no doubt unwelcome
reminder that times had changed. They had to learn the bitter lessons
of the KGB's past, he said. 'The days are long gone when the security
services had the job of suppressing and – I want to stress this – did suppress human rights and freedoms.' Their job now, he said, was to
protect citizens' constitutional rights and freedoms.[56]

Putin's message – even if in practice it would be honoured in the
breach – was that they should not assume that because a former KGB
officer was in power, the security services would have free rein.

In the same way, when Sechin, an abrasive bulldozer of a man,
started spreading his wings a little too wide for Putin's liking, early in
his first term, he was moved sideways, surrendering control of the
President's agenda to his liberal counterpart, Dmitry Medvedev.[57] It
was not exactly a demotion. Sechin remained head of Putin's private
office and controlled the flow of documents to the President's desk.
But control of Putin's daily schedule meant control of what in Russia
is called 'access to the body'. In a system where all the key decisions
flow down from the one man at the top, it gave Medvedev enormous
power, marking the beginning of his ascent to higher things.

Putin's goal was to create a unified team capable of implementing his
vision of Russia's future. To a large extent he succeeded. But because
he retained ultimate power – and, in consequence, nothing would happen unless he personally signed off on it – he ended up with an
intolerable workload. Where an American President or a British Prime
Minister, or almost any other European leader, would devote his
energy to the relatively few key issues which required a top-level decision, Putin spent much of his time on matters which, in other countries,
would have been dealt with at ministerial level or below.

One typical three-month period saw him attending conferences and
giving speeches on such mundane topics as the modernisation of
regional health services, ways to improve road safety, education and
vocational training, financial support for Russia's Olympic team, state

aid to charities and measures to develop gold-mining – all important in themselves, no doubt, but which, in a democratic system, would not have required the President to intervene.[58]

This was in addition to regular government meetings, which took place three times a week. At 10 a.m. every Monday, Putin chaired a meeting of the inner cabinet, consisting of up to a dozen senior ministers and advisers; on Wednesday mornings, he received the Prime Minister, tête-à-tête; and on Saturdays, he chaired the Security Council.[59] Outside those fixed points, there was a constant stream of visitors which kept his appointment book full from morning till late at night.

Over the same three months, Putin had meetings in Moscow with more than 20 visiting foreign leaders and senior officials. He hosted two international conferences and travelled abroad five times, first to Britain and Belgium; then for a State Visit to the Netherlands; to Turkey; to Japan and South Korea; and to Malaysia. Jetlag did not figure. When Putin flew back from the Far East or from America, he would arrive in Moscow in the morning, hold a full day of meetings in the Kremlin and often go on to attend a function in the evening.[60]

When he was not travelling, Putin's day started at Novo-Ogaryovo with a work-out for half an hour followed by 20 or 30 laps of the Olympic-sized pool. Whenever possible, he would exercise for another hour – either at home after breakfast, which was usually *kasha*, a Russian porridge; or in the gym adjoining his office in the Kremlin after lunch, which was often just *kefir*, a yoghurt drink, and fruit.[61] No matter where he was, he said, he tried to exercise for an hour and a half to two hours a day.[62] Swimming was an obsession. Vladimir Bragin, his former colleague from the KGB in Dresden, recalled how, during a visit to Sochi, he tried to persuade him to stop and come and have a beer. Putin insisted on completing the 50 laps he had set himself. 'I have to,' Bragin quoted him as saying. 'If I don't keep fit, I won't be able to do my work, I won't be able to keep up.'[63]

He usually arrived at the Kremlin soon after 9 a.m. and began by going through the documents and briefing notes that Sechin had laid out on his desk. Among them was a daily intelligence summary from the FSB. When there was a topic of special interest, Putin might ask to see the raw intelligence files from which it was drawn.[64] Meetings started at 10 a.m., unless he extended the morning workout at Novo-Ogaryovo, in which case they began at noon.[65] He tried to skim through the main newspapers himself, rather than have them summarised by officials, and he watched as much as he could of the TV news bulletins, usually on videocassettes in his car as he was driven to and from work.[66]

During Putin's first two terms, the highway into Moscow was closed to other traffic whenever his motorcade passed, causing monster traffic jams. Later a helipad was built for his use inside the Kremlin walls.

The working day normally ended at 10 or 11 p.m., though sometimes it went on as late as 1 a.m., after which he spent an hour with a tutor trying to improve his English.[67] He understood the language. When he was working at the Mayor's Office in St Petersburg, he used to correct his interpreter when he felt that she had not conveyed his meaning properly.[68] He had started studying again after his first encounter with Tony Blair, which left him feeling frustrated that, while understanding much of what Blair said, he was unable to respond.[69]

This workaholic image might be dismissed as public relations spin – and it is true that he was able to get away for a day's skiing in the winter or a week at Sochi in the summer, breaks which became more extended as his presidency perdured. Nonetheless, the schedule was crushing. His Chief of Staff, Aleksandr Voloshin, said later: 'I simply put a line through five years of my private life . . . I would see the unhappy faces of my children, "Papa, when are you going to play with me?" "On Sunday". And on Sunday, something would happen. And it was like that, month after month after month.'[70] For Putin, it was worse, especially in the first two terms when he took off hardly any time at all.[71] Asked what novels he liked to read, the only authors he could cite were those he had read as a child or earlier in his career.[72] He rarely listened to music – when he did, it was Liszt or Tchaikovsky – and almost never watched films.[73] The one exception was Russian history, which fascinated him.[74] If he had no time to read himself, he listened to audiobooks while travelling.[75]

Sometimes, even for him, it all became too much. 'I feel like a workhorse heaving along a cart filled with a heavy load,' he grumbled.[76] What did he do to cheer himself up, he was asked. 'I work,' came the gruff reply.[77]

One of the hallmarks of Putin's first years in office was his tolerance of public disputes over policy.

Andrei Illarionov, the enfant terrible of the Presidential Administration, engaged in barely concealed warfare with German Gref, the
Economic Development Minister. Kasyanov and Stepashin, who had
been appointed head of the Accounts Chamber of the Duma, bickered
over the Chamber's oversight role.[78] Gleb Pavlovsky denounced Sechin
for his role in the Yukos affair.[79] Even in the military, where disagreements over policy were normally treated as state secrets, there was a
blazing, public row between Marshal Sergeyev, the Defence Minister,
and General Anatoly Kvashnin, the Chief of the General Staff, over the
status of the Strategic Missile Troops, responsible for Russia's nuclear
strike force. Kvashnin wanted the missile troops, who answered to Sergeyev, subordinated to the same chain of command as other combat
arms. He was crazy, Sergeyev fumed. It was 'a crime against Russia'.[80]
Putin dismissed the quarrel as a discussion between professionals.[81]
'You only find total calm in a cemetery,' he told a journalist. 'Where
there are living people, there are clashes of opinion and different views.
There is nothing strange about that.'[82]

But while Putin was willing to allow his senior officials unusual latitude to express contrary views, there were limits to what he would
accept.

Illarionov, who was incapable of mincing words, was the first to
overstep the mark. The sale to Rosneft of Yukos's main oilfield was
'the scam of the year', he declared.[83] It represented the deliberate
expropriation of private property and had been carried out 'in a monstrously unprofessional and incompetent way', which would cause
colossal economic damage.[84] After that philippic, he was removed as
Russia's sherpa to the G8. But even then, Putin asked him to stay on as
his economic adviser.[85]

Within the Kremlin, a similar degree of openness obtained. Mikhail
Kasyanov, the Prime Minister, remembered meetings of the Security
Council so tense that, although no one raised his voice, it felt as if 'we
were shouting at each other'.[86]

A certain etiquette was observed. Only the Prime Minister and the
head of the Presidential Administration could confront Putin directly.[87]
But other officials were expected to argue their case.

'He liked bright people with unusual ideas,' Voloshin said.[88] That
was one reason that he had wanted to employ Illarionov and kept him
on despite his public diatribes against government policies. The

ideologist, Vladislav Surkov, was another whom Putin valued for his ability to think outside the box. 'People who really say what they think are few and far between,' he said. 'They are the true objective spirits, those who have a bit of a dissident streak.'[89]

Unlike Yeltsin, who would not tolerate anyone disagreeing with him to his face and still less in front of others, Putin appreciated those who pushed back. If his interlocutor agreed all the time and had nothing original to contribute, he quickly lost interest.[90] At the Munich Security Conference, after his combative speech which had so shocked the Americans, his first words, when the audience started firing back questions, were: 'It's a shame we have so little time. I'd like to be able to talk to each of you individually. I love this!'[91]

Putin was also able to think outside the box. He surprised his hosts on a visit to Japan not long after he became President by suggesting that they build a rail tunnel from Hokkaido to the island of Sakhalin, which in turn would be linked by a bridge to the Russian mainland.[92] Technically, it was feasible; economically, it was questionable; but the importance of the gesture lay elsewhere: it was an attempt to persuade the Japanese to view the relationship in a different light, circumventing the two countries' territorial dispute over the Kuril Islands, which, 60 years after the end of World War II, continued to block Japanese investment in Russia. The same logic led him to propose to South and North Korea that they link their rail systems with the Trans-Siberian, providing an overland route to markets in Europe – an unrealisable idea at the time but intended to make the two sides think about the possibility of a different kind of future.[93]

He had an agile mind and a gift for repartee. Asked how he had changed during his first year as President, he replied laconically: 'I am three years older.'[94] How would he describe the relationship between the state and the media? 'There is a saying, a decent man should always try and a decent woman should always resist.'[95] On the brain drain from Russia: 'If brains are leaving, at least it means there were brains to begin with.'[96]

He did not win every argument. Johan Molander, the Swedish Ambassador, remembered a small, private lunch in the Kremlin, which Putin gave for King Carl XVI Gustaf. Putin wanted to get the King to discuss the first Nord Stream pipeline under the Baltic Sea, which was then in the planning stages and would provide Russian natural gas to

Germany. The King, who had an engineering degree but was also an ardent ecologist, refused to be drawn. 'He ducked,' Molander remembered.[97] 'What he did was to give an extremely knowledgeable, extremely detailed and very boring lecture on the ecology of the Baltic Sea. He started with the algae, then the herring and the cod, all the way up the food chain. Putin was sitting there, obviously thinking: "Why do I have to put up with this idiot? But he's the King and there's nothing I can do." So he started making a pyramid out of breadcrumbs. After a while he started to eat them, until, finally, the King came to a conclusion.' At that point, Molander thought, the King had finished. But then he launched into a new theme: the need for double-hulled ships to transport oil in order to protect the ecology of the Baltic. 'It was a memorable meal,' Molander chuckled afterwards. They never did discuss Nord Stream. As the lunch drew to a close, Putin's gaze alternated between the King and what was left of the pile of breadcrumbs.

Putin's mastery of a brief, which had impressed Madeleine Albright and Tony Blair when he was acting President, only grew with time. Tony Brenton, who could hardly be suspected of sympathy for Putin, given the harassment to which he was subjected, said the only other leader he had ever met who was as well briefed was Margaret Thatcher.[98]

It was not that Putin never used briefing notes: occasionally he did, as at his meeting in Ljubljana with George W. Bush. But he rarely needed them. Molander's predecessor, Sven Hirdman, remembered attending an EU–Russia meeting in Moscow during Putin's first term, with the Swedish Prime Minister, Göran Persson, the President of the EU Commission, Romano Prodi, and the EU's Foreign Policy Representative, Javier Solana. 'He knew all the facts . . . about visas, about overflights in Siberia, about free trade . . . you name it,' Hirdman said. 'The EU lot, my Prime Minister and the others, they knew the nice words, democracy, human rights, strategic partnerships and so on, but they didn't know anything of the substance . . . It was two different worlds talking to each other.'[99] Persson, understandably, put it rather differently. But he, too, remembered Putin, at the same meeting, speaking for half an hour without notes in a minutely detailed exposition of each separate terrorist group which might threaten Russia along the thousands of miles of its southern border, from the Caucasus to China.[100] Angela Merkel later had a similar experience.

Hirdman's contemporary, the German Ambassador, Hans-Friedrich von Ploetz, was struck by Putin's unusually retentive memory. 'That was a constant,' he said. 'We used to talk a lot, one on one. He never made a note. But when he said he would do something, it would be done.'[101]

It was still true that he was best with small groups. Persson attended the St Petersburg tercentenary celebrations in 2003, along with some 40 other heads of state and government from all over the world, including China, India, Japan, the United States and most of Europe. Putin addressed the assembled dignitaries before a crowd of several hundred thousand people. 'It made me realise the difference between a politician elected in a free election in the West and a leader elected in Russia,' Persson said. 'This was a once in a lifetime event and he gave a terrible speech. It was meaningless . . . The rhetoric was a catastrophe . . . It was because he wasn't raised as a politician who had had to learn to express his feelings to an audience.'[102]

Over time, that would change. Persson wrote that later he found him more mature as a politician and his shyness became less visible.[103] But it did not come naturally. Putin remained an introvert who, as his wife, Lyudmila, had said years earlier, needed to work hard to appear at ease. Brenton, watching him with Tony Blair, thought he never relaxed. Unlike other statesmen, he never switched off – he was always looking for a way to advance his agenda.[104]

In the autumn of 2003, elections beckoned. First for the Duma, in December, then, the following spring, for the presidency. Putin's dislike of elections was unchanged. They were among 'the unavoidable costs of democracy', he complained, forcing leaders to think about the political tactics needed to win rather than solving their country's problems.[105]

Four years earlier, during the Duma elections of 1999, he had tried to stay above the fray. This time he publicly backed United Russia. Its main task, he said, was to form 'a powerful centrist bloc' in parliament which would provide reliable support for the government's policies.[106] But his willingness to indulge in party politicking still had certain limits. When he stood for re-election as President, the following spring, it was as an independent, not a party candidate.[107]

In the parliamentary election, United Russia won the largest share of the vote, gaining 223 seats out of 450 in the Duma, which, with support from independents, gave it an ironclad majority and the chairmanship of all the parliamentary committees. The Communists came second, with 52 seats, a big drop from the 90 they had had in the previous parliament, followed by two nationalist parties, the Liberal Democrats, headed by Vladimir Zhirinovsky, and a newly formed movement, Rodina, 'Motherland', led by Dmitry Rogozin, a solidly built right-wing firebrand whose rhetoric attracted malcontents both from the far left and from extreme far-right groups. It was widely suspected but never proved that Rogozin had received covert encouragement from the Kremlin in order to weaken the other opposition parties.

Observers from the OSCE and the Council of Europe concluded that the voting itself had been conducted with relatively few 'irregularities', but there had been massive use of what were termed 'administrative resources' and systematic bias on the part of the state media in favour of United Russia. Overall, they concluded, there had been a 'regression of democracy'. The election 'fell far short of European standards'.[108]

Putin disagreed. If some Russian deputies had tried to use 'dirty election techniques', he said cheekily, it was because they had learnt these bad habits from the West.[109] In any case, the results really showed 'a reinforcement of democracy'.[110]

The riposte was jocoserious. Russian politicians did not need anyone to teach them how to game the system. But it was not completely untrue. Gerrymandering, voting restrictions, ballot-stuffing and all the other techniques for falsifying election results were not invented in Russia. They had flourished for decades in the United States and parts of Western Europe and continued to do so in so-called 'illiberal democracies' like Hungary and Poland.

Ten days after the Duma results were announced, Putin confirmed that, as expected, he would stand for a second term. The only question was who would oppose him. No opposition would mean no interest, which would translate into a low turnout.

There was a brief flurry of excitement when Ivan Rybkin, a former Duma Chairman, who was standing for a small opposition party, disappeared for several days and claimed to have been kidnapped by FSB agents in Kyiv.[111] His captors, he said, had drugged him and, when he regained consciousness, showed him a 'revolting videotape' in which he was seen performing sex acts which he preferred not to describe. The episode was never properly explained. Rybkin had fewer than one per cent of voting intentions and posed no conceivable threat to Putin. It is tempting to speculate that the whole episode was concocted by the Kremlin to generate interest in the campaign, which, for a week or so, it did. Afterwards Rybkin fled to London and dropped out of the race.

More serious and much more intriguing was Putin's sudden decision on February 24, less than three weeks before election day, to dismiss the government of Prime Minister Mikhail Kasyanov. At the time it was widely viewed as another ploy to liven up what, even after the Rybkin affair, remained a rather dull campaign.[112] Kasyanov had been expected to leave once the election was over. He was the last major figure associated with the Family still in a key post. Putin had not hidden his irritation at what he saw as the government's foot-dragging over tax and other reforms, and he and Kasyanov were increasingly out of sync.[113] Firing the Prime Minister when it was least expected would be the kind of unpredictable move, throwing everybody off balance, at which Yeltsin had excelled.

The only problem with that interpretation was that the decision showed every sign of having been taken in a great hurry.

When Putin summoned him to inform him of his decision, Kasyanov recalled, he seemed nervous and avoided eye contact. Neither he nor any of his ministers nor, apparently, Putin's aides in the Presidential Administration, had had any inkling of what was about to happen. At first, Putin told him that he had decided to dismiss the Prime Minister but to keep the government in place. Kasyanov reminded him that that was not possible. Under the constitution, if the Prime Minister resigned, the government automatically resigned as well. It was not the kind of mistake that Putin would normally make. Nor was it the only anomaly. The usual rule was that the outgoing Prime Minister would stay on in an acting capacity until his successor was named. But Putin did not want that. Kasyanov then suggested that he name one of his deputies, Viktor Khristenko, to act as Prime Minister until the Duma approved a permanent replacement, a suggestion which the President accepted.

Something, it seemed, had happened out of the blue which had persuaded Putin that Kasyanov must be removed immediately. The President offered no explanation. But Kasyanov remembered having seen him at a reception in the Kremlin the previous evening, deep in conversation with the FSB chief, Patrushev. Later he learnt that a rumour had been circulating that he and the liberal leader, Boris Nemtsov, had come up with an ingenious plan to prevent Putin winning a second term.

Under the Russian constitution, if the turnout was less than 50 per cent – which was a possibility, since the turnout for the Duma election had been only 55.7 per cent – the election would be annulled. The entire process would then start again from scratch: the candidates would have to re-register and campaign all over again, and the Prime Minister would become acting President until the new election took place. If Kasyanov were in that post, so the story went, and if he stood as a candidate with all the resources of the state behind him, as Putin had done four years earlier, he might well win the election.

In fact there was no such plan and, even if there had been, Putin's popularity was such that it was hard to imagine any circumstances in which Kasyanov would have beaten him. However, to a conspiratorial mind, it might not seem totally far-fetched. The Kremlin was seriously worried about the turnout. Local officials had been ordered to do whatever was necessary to get out the vote. In the Russian Far East, hospitals refused to admit patients unless they could show absentee ballots. Workers at state enterprises were warned that they would be fired if they failed to vote. Free concerts were held at polling stations and, in some places, free medical check-ups were offered.[114]

Patrushev, like many intelligence chiefs, and not only in Russia – James Jesus Angleton at the CIA comes to mind – was paranoid. It would be entirely in character for him to have warned Putin that a plot was afoot. Whether Putin believed him is another matter, but he evidently decided that it was better to be on the safe side, with the added advantage that firing the Prime Minister would put the election back on the front pages during the run-up to the vote.

Ten days later, on March 5, Putin named Mikhail Fradkov, a competent, colourless bureaucrat with no obvious political ambitions, as head of a slimmed-down cabinet in which almost half the ministers were newcomers. Fradkov's appointment, like Kasyanov's dismissal, took everyone by surprise. The speculation had been that a senior minister like Sergei Ivanov or Kudrin would be named. Instead Putin chose a man whom most Russians had never heard of. Fradkov's background was in foreign trade. When Putin appointed him, he was serving as Russian Ambassador to the EU in Brussels. A short, tubby man with a puckish face and slightly pointed ears, the press nicknamed him Winnie the Pooh.[115]

Putin's reasoning became clear later. He was thinking four years ahead to when his second term would end. Unless the constitution were amended, he would then step down. Installing a faceless, neutral figure with no presidential ambitions as head of government would give him a free hand to test other, more substantial candidates for the eventual succession.

As was his custom, Putin tried to move Kasyanov into another post, proposing that he become Secretary of the Security Council or head of the Intergovernmental Bank for the CIS states. Kasyanov hesitated but in the end, to the President's annoyance, decided to go into opposition.[116]

On March 14, 2004, Putin was re-elected with 72 per cent of the vote. The Communist Party's candidate came second with nearly 14 per cent. None of the others got more than 4 per cent. The turnout, more by crook than by hook, was officially recorded as 64 per cent. As usual there was ballot stuffing, biased coverage by the state media and flagrant abuse of official resources.[117] But even without that, Putin would still have won handsomely.

As Putin settled in for another four-year stint, the economy was growing strongly and the goal that he had set a year earlier, of doubling GDP in the next decade, looked to be within reach.[118] Social issues, which, in his first term, he had insisted should be deferred until the economic situation improved, were now declared to be the main domestic priority, and four so-called 'national projects' were unveiled: to build affordable housing; to develop health and education; and to improve life in the rural areas in order to promote agriculture.[119]

First, however, Putin wanted Fradkov to deal with the practice, inherited from Soviet times, of providing free bus passes and other social benefits to retirees, war veterans and various other groups. It was expensive and wasteful and Putin argued that the money would be better spent raising pensions, which were still pitifully small.[120] On the other hand, free universal benefits had been considered one of the triumphs of the Soviet system. Kasyanov, recognising that any change would be fiercely resisted, had refused to touch it.

Putin knew that it would be a delicate exercise. At a news conference on the night of his election, he had said that modernising the social sector was essential 'but we have to do it carefully, so as not to . . . undermine the public's trust, [otherwise] it will be impossible to do anything in the future'.[121] Shock therapy was out.[122] Instead the government must find 'the golden mean between the necessary and the possible'.[123]

The monetisation of social benefits, as it was called, ran into trouble from the very start.

In April 2004, Yuri Luzhkov, who had been re-elected Mayor of Moscow, said that according to City Hall's calculations, pensioners in the city would lose up to 80 per cent of their benefits.[124] Sergei Shoigu, the Emergencies Minister and longest-serving member of the cabinet, told his colleagues: 'No normal person would ever agree to this, because it's several times less than they are getting now.'[125] The Governor of Yaroslavl, Anatoly Lisitsyn, warned of growing social tension.[126] The Communist Party denounced the plan as 'odious and antisocial'.[127]

In August, after Fradkov had made substantial concessions, increasing the compensatory payments and allowing people to opt out and retain certain benefits in kind, the Duma passed the enabling legislation.[128] Nearly 13 million people would be affected.[129] Opinion surveys showed that two thirds opposed the measures and half were prepared to demonstrate against them.[130]

During the summer, there were scattered protests.[131] But the trouble began in earnest in January 2005, when the legislation took effect and millions of people suddenly discovered that they no longer enjoyed free public transport. Crowds of angry pensioners blocked roads. Ticket collectors were beaten up. Policemen, who had also lost their travel concessions, stormed buses and trams. At metro stations, soldiers broke the ticket barriers.[132]

It was one thing for the authorities to arrest an oligarch like Mikhail Khodorkovsky, commented *Moskovsky komsomolets*, but 'quite another to fight a whole army of outraged benefit recipients'. The business newspaper, *Tribuna*, wrote of 'a tsunami of social dissent'.[133] In region after region, the local authorities modified or rescinded the most contentious provisions.

When the protests started, Putin kept his head down, deflecting criticism onto the government and the Duma.[134] He had promoted the reform partly because of his own experience as deputy Mayor in St Petersburg, where the cost of subsidising transport had been a major burden on the city budget.[135] But he admitted that it had been a miscalculation.[136] One of his guiding principles was that 'it is impossible to reform the economy without popular support'.[137] He had ruled out shock measures because they risked undermining the social contract which kept him in power. But if gradualism did not work and shock therapy was not possible, it was hard to see how social and economic reform could continue.

The consequences of the 'transport war', as it was called,[138] turned out to be out of all proportion to the issue which had caused it.

For the first time since Putin had come to power, significant sections of the Russian population had come out onto the streets to oppose the government's policies. The Kremlin was already nervous because of the Orange Revolution in Ukraine, which it saw as a stark warning of where popular dissension could lead if allowed to get out of hand. No one seriously imagined that anything on that scale would happen in Russia. But Putin was taking no chances.[139] The example of Gorbachev, whose attempts to reform the Soviet system had brought about its collapse, was never far from his mind.

One of Putin's early goals had been to reform the main state monopolies. Even before the 'transport war', he had hesitated. Kasyanov had suggested that Gazprom should be split into two companies, one handling gas production, the other, distribution, to introduce more competition.[140] Putin had decided that Gazprom was too important as a cash cow for the state budget and an instrument of foreign policy for normal economic considerations to apply. The same arguments precluded any change in the monopoly status of the Russian arms export corporation, Rosoboroneksport. There was tinkering with the electricity monopoly and Russian Railways but the promised reduction in the role of the state faltered, and after the 'transport war', stopped altogether.

The only area in which real progress was made was currency liberalisation. By 2007, the rouble was fully convertible.

The backsliding on economic reform was not solely due to the backlash against the change in social benefits, though, by feeding into Putin's aversion to political risk, it was certainly a major factor. But the rise in oil prices did not help either. It made businessmen reluctant to invest in other, less profitable sectors and, when money was pouring into the state coffers, the pressure on the government to make painful but necessary changes eased.

Putin had known that that might happen. The Soviet economy had failed to develop, he said, because, since the 1960s, it had been able to live off oil exports.[141] If oil prices became 'excessively high', it would 'boomerang against us'.[142] He would not let that happen, he said. 'We are not going to curl up under a warm blanket of petrodollars.' [143]

Yet that was exactly what Russia then did. The price of Urals crude, which had fallen below 10 US dollars a barrel in the winter of 1998, reached 40 dollars in 2004, 60 dollars a year later, 70 dollars in 2007 and a peak of nearly 130 dollars in 2008. Putin continued to talk from time to time about the need to diversify and carry out reforms. But it no longer seemed such a priority. To all intents and purposes, after 2007, structural economic reform was abandoned.

Russia's newfound oil wealth affected the regime in multiple ways. The elite and those with access to it found new opportunities for enrichment. Western officials noticed that their Russian counterparts acquired a certain swagger.[144] George W. Bush, who regarded Putin as a wily operator, 'sometimes cocky, sometimes charming, always tough', complained that he had now become 'aggressive abroad and more defensive about his record at home'.[145] That was in part a reaction to Putin's Munich speech, when he had made clear that Russia was no longer prepared meekly to accept America's view of how the world should be run. But Bush was not wrong about the linkage: Russia was more assertive because its oil wealth allowed it to be.

More money meant more corruption, not only among low-level officials but in the highest reaches of the state. The law enforcement agencies had taken note of the impunity Putin had accorded to men like Borodin and Nazdratenko and acted accordingly. 'Despite having reliable information about corruption among high-ranking personages,' the Prosecutor General, Vladimir Ustinov, complained, '[the agencies] do not even attempt to act upon it.'[146]

High-level corruption became institutionalised. The widely reported kickbacks from Rosneft's purchase of Northern Oil in 2003, which had contributed to Mikhail Khodorkovsky's downfall, had been a foretaste of what was to come. In Putin's second term, for the political elite to accept 'donations', *mzdoimstvo*, for state contracts they authorised, was standard practice. Illarionov found that unacceptable and, in December 2005, resigned as Putin's economic adviser, citing 'the emergence of a corporativist model of the state'.[147] But Fradkov's government was compliant and no one else in the Presidential Administration objected.

Some of the money was parked in offshore accounts in Panama and the British Virgin Islands, but the principal depository was Bank Rossiya, run by Putin's neighbours from the Ozero cooperative, Yuri Kovalchuk and Nikolai Shamalov. Both men had become multi-billionaires, along with others among Putin's old friends from St Petersburg, including the oil trader, Gennady Timchenko, and the brothers Arkady and Boris Rotenberg, who had been his judo partners at Anatoly Rakhlin's club when they had all been teenagers. They were often described as a new caste of oligarchs, but that was a misnomer. They were businessmen who became rich through their proximity to power, but unlike Berezovsky and the oligarchs of the 1990s, they neither sought nor played any political role.

By the end of Putin's second term, the assets of Bank Rossiya had increased a hundredfold. It had taken control of one of the country's largest insurance companies, had started developing a media empire and had a stake in the management of the Gazprom pension fund. Timchenko's Swiss-based Gunvor company had become the world's third-biggest oil trading concern, with an annual turnover of 75 billion US dollars, largely on the strength of its access to Russian oil accounts.

But it was the Rotenbergs who provided the clearest illustration of how the new system worked.[148] After Putin gained control of Gazprom in 2001, the brothers began investing, often with loans provided by Bank Rossiya, in construction and pipeline companies which were given inflated Gazprom contracts. A 1,500-mile-long pipeline which the Rotenbergs built from a new gas field in northern Russia came in at 44 billion US dollars, three times more than a pipeline of equivalent length in Europe. Gazprom sold the brothers five construction and maintenance companies, all at a knockdown price, which they merged and transformed into one of Russia's largest building firms. That was followed by highway construction, urban development and even educational publishing.

The simple explanation was that the authorities gave lucrative contracts to companies run by members of Putin's inner circle, allowing them to make inordinate profits at the state's expense. As one gas industry analyst put it, 'Gazprom switched from a principle of maximising shareholder profits to one of maximising contractor profits.'[149] There was actually a little more to it than that. Men like Arkady Rotenberg were canny organisers whose success owed much to their relationships with Putin and other members of the political elite but was also due to their own business acumen. As well as providing the Kremlin with a pool of money for unrecorded expenditures, they could be relied on to undertake major, prestige projects and get them done.[150] They were rewarded accordingly.

In America, that would be called crony capitalism which, indeed, it was. To Russians, it increasingly resembled the imperial court of pre-Bolshevik times.

One prominent business magnate offered Putin a 57-metre yacht.[151] A fund, financed by donations from the super-rich, was set up to buy medical equipment for Russian hospitals and to promote other hi-tech projects, but 25 per cent of every contract was creamed off to finance the building of a palatial residence for the President near Gelendzhik on the Black Sea coast.[152] In return for their support, the new aristocracy were granted not serfs and land, as would have been the case under the tsars, but the opportunity to make their fortunes through government largesse. Cronyism was an imprecise description. It was closer to a feudal regime, in which oil wealth took the place of landed estates – a system less arbitrary than in earlier times but built on similar principles.

Whether Putin himself was amassing personal wealth from the opportunities granted to those around him was a more complicated issue.

Stanislav Belkovsky, the outspoken, conspiracy-minded political analyst who had claimed in 2003 that the oligarchs were planning a coup, told the *Guardian* in 2007 that Putin had a personal fortune of 40 billion US dollars and controlled, through a network of offshore companies, 75 per cent of Gunvor, 37 per cent of Surgutneftegaz and 4.5 per cent of Gazprom.[153] Gunvor issued a denial and Putin, questioned about the claims at a news conference, shot back one of his trademark vulgarisms: 'Of course! I'm the richest man in the world . . . They picked all this out of their noses and smeared it over their papers.'[154]

Belkovsky was known for colourful but not always well-founded allegations, and his track record for accuracy where Putin is concerned has been spotty, to say the least.[155] Nonetheless, in the West, those figures stuck in people's minds. Then it was reported that the CIA had drawn up a secret report in 2007 which had reached similar conclusions.[156] A decade later, to justify sanctions against the aluminium billionaire, Oleg Deripaska, the US Treasury said he had 'reportedly been identified as . . . holding assets and laundering funds' on Putin's behalf.[157] But it was all at the level of uncorroborated allegations. Not only was there no proof, there was not even any hard evidence.

Michael Morell, who had been Director of Intelligence at the CIA, then Deputy Director and Acting Director, and who could hardly be accused of being soft on Russia, was categorical that, up to the time he retired from the agency in 2013, he never saw anything to indicate that Putin had accumulated great wealth. That did not mean it was not true, he added. But why would he need it? 'I mean, where is he going to go?'[158]

It is a fair point. Putin is not Mobutu, the Congolese leader who, when reminded that his country was tens of millions of dollars in arrears on debt repayments, pulled out a personal Union Bank of Switzerland chequebook and asked, 'Who shall I make it out to?'[159] If and when Putin leaves office, he will stay in Russia. His future will be assured, as Yeltsin's was, not by money but by the protection of those who come after him.

There are other reasons to doubt that Putin has great private wealth. As President, he has access to anything he could wish for. If he gives away a 20,000-dollar Blancpain watch to a schoolboy, it is because he can.[160] In his position, such sums are of no consequence. His daughters are well provided for. Both married wealthy businessmen. In St Petersburg, while accepting 'expressions of gratitude' from trusted friends, he consistently refused to do anything which might make him beholden to those who sought his help. It is possible that he has behaved differently as President, but it appears highly unlikely. As Russia's ruler, manipulating the elite clans and interest groups which form the basis of his support, Putin could not allow himself to behave as they did, even if he wished to. He had to operate on a higher plane, because if he abased himself to their level he would risk losing control. The much-quoted Panama Papers showed that many of his personal friends had millions or billions of dollars stashed away in fiscal paradises and that, like most of the ultra-rich, they tried to hide their wealth. But there was nothing in the Panama Papers to suggest that Putin himself had illicit riches concealed in offshore accounts.

'My personal view,' said Morell, 'is that money doesn't matter to him very much. Not personally. Money matters to him to buy the support he needs from the elite. Giving it away – giving out the ability to make money . . . that's the key.'[161] Without being more specific, Morell made clear that that judgement was based in part on the classified information available to him at the CIA.[162]

As President, Putin claimed, he never lost his temper.[163] 'I have learned to restrain myself,' he said. 'I think I have become quite good at it . . . I may fly off the handle on occasions, but it is extremely rare, and I get very angry with myself when it happens because I see it as a sign of weakness.'[164]

That did not stop him tearing a strip off officials who displeased him. Andrei Illarionov said it was a game, which Putin played for effect. But those who had to endure it found it frightening. It was a sign that Putin was changing – 'behaving more like a tsar', in Illarionov's words – and that the 'kid gloves' approach of the first term was giving way to something harder.[165]

In Siberia, in January 2005, he berated a group of local administrators for failing to move ahead with plans to build an IT technopark in the science city of Akademgorodok in Novosibirsk.

PUTIN: I know what we agreed. I haven't gone mad yet. But we have to move more quickly . . .
[LOCAL OFFICIAL]: Vladimir Vladimirovich, I . . .
PUTIN: When did I telephone you? Three weeks ago. And now you ask what you are supposed to be doing about it. You should have taken the [documents] and read them. Then you wouldn't be asking these questions. Why do you think we are meeting here? To drink tea? . . . Why do you think I phoned you? . . . This is why these things drag on for years.[166]

Exchanges like that were shown on television as a warning to others. 'It takes months and even years to take even the most elementary decisions,' Putin groused to the State Council.[167] Legislation languished in the ministries 'even though all they have to do is amend one word in one clause'.[168]

At cabinet meetings, ministers found themselves subjected to a presidential inquisition.[169] It was a way to show that the good Tsar was looking after his people's interests even when the boyars were negligent.

Putin's frustration at the unwieldiness of the Russian system was genuine. 'Everyone is used to waiting for the boss to decide,' he complained.[170] But if that was so, it was partly his own doing. He had failed to reform the bureaucracy, curtailed democratic freedoms and imposed top-down control.

Nonetheless, the way he treated those around him was changing. One minister remembered being summoned to his office. 'Putin was writing at his desk,' he recalled. 'He didn't even look up when I came in. He just told me what he wanted and said, "you may go."' It was a bit like the way Stalin had behaved.[171]

Foreigners also noticed it. During Putin's visit to London for an EU–Russia summit in October 2005, he and Blair had a private dinner, one on one, in Downing Street. The normal procedure was for their advisers to leave them on their own with just interpreters present, and then, towards the end of the evening, to go in to see how they were getting on. When Blair's foreign policy aide, Nigel Sheinwald, suggested to his counterpart, Sergei Prikhodko, who had been working as an adviser to Putin for years, that it was time to interrupt the tête-à-tête, he and his Russian colleagues went pale. 'They were terrified,' Sheinwald recalled. 'It was imperial. They were worried about going into the presence and interrupting . . . Eventually we did, but they kept well in the background.'[172]

There were other changes, too.

The annual phone-in, which initially had been a free-wheeling affair in which Putin would answer whatever questions were thrown at him, became a carefully choreographed ritual. In December 2003, no one asked about the two burning issues of the day – the arrest of Mikhail Khodorkovsky, which had occurred two months earlier, and the situation in Chechnya.[173] The participants were screened beforehand, awkward issues weeded out and only softball questions permitted.[174]

The tough-guy attitude, which Bill Burns and others had remarked upon, became more pronounced. Before the German Chancellor, Angela Merkel, paid her visit to Moscow in January 2006, her foreign policy adviser, Christoph Heusgen, warned his Russian counterparts that the Chancellor did not like dogs, having once been badly bitten.[175]

By way of welcome, Putin presented her with a small black and white toy dog.[176] A year later, when they met in Sochi, before the press corps were ushered out, Konni, his large and rather overweight black Labrador, joined them, and came and sniffed at the Chancellor's shoes. 'I don't think the dog frightens you, does it?' Putin said archly, sitting with his legs wide apart. 'She's a nice dog, we needn't worry that she'll do anything bad.' Merkel, who had stiffened at the dog's approach, had the presence of mind to turn it to derision, responding in Russian: 'At least she doesn't eat journalists, it seems!'[177] It was churlish and, above all, counter-productive. Of all the Western Europeans, the Germans were the biggest investors in Russia and the keenest to maintain correct relations. Merkel was tough enough not to let it bother her, Heusgen said. 'But she noticed. Those are KGB tactics, to make the other side look weak.'[178] Afterwards she told a German journalist: 'I understand why he thinks he needs to do this – it's to prove his virility.'[179]

In fact, it was a mixture: the crass behaviour of a street yob, which had percolated down from Putin's childhood, and the attitudes inculcated by a Soviet upbringing and a decade in the Big House. In a revealing incident when he was President-elect, in April 2000, he came to the defence of the Foreign Minister, Igor Ivanov, who had been attacked by Communist deputies in the Duma for allegedly inappropriate contacts with his Western counterparts. Ivanov, Putin told them, had done nothing wrong. But then he added that if any minister, or indeed 'any Russian citizen', had contacts with foreign officials 'outside the framework of their official duties', then naturally, 'they will be subject to certain procedures under the criminal code'.[180]

Any Russian citizen? The remark caused consternation.

'It appears that he was just trying to say that everyone is equal before the law,' wrote the newspaper *Segodnya*, 'but it came out that if you have contacts with a foreigner, you can end up in prison.'[181] It was dismissed as a slip of the tongue, but it offered a glimpse of a mindset from a different age. In Brezhnev's day, when Putin had been working in the Fifth Department in Leningrad, Russian citizens could indeed be arrested for unauthorised contacts with the West.

In Putin's second term, such glimpses became more frequent.

Whether out of frustration at Russia's deteriorating relationship with the United States or a broader disenchantment with the West, or because, in consequence, he was listening more and more to the *siloviki* in his entourage, he began to make far-fetched claims which were clearly not just slips of the tongue.

Asked about measures to prevent opposition candidates from standing in regional elections in Russia, he retorted: 'Go and talk to the opposition parties in any of your own countries . . . Exactly the same thing [happens there].'[182] If Russia had a bad image in the West, it was because Western journalists 'continue blindly repeating what they have been paid to say'.[183] In America, journalists who refused to toe the government line were sacked[184] . . . and much more in the same vein.

It was the way Soviet officials had talked, 30 or 40 years earlier. In his first term, Putin had avoided that kind of crude falsification. In his second term, that changed.

Putin's reaction to a rumour about the former US Secretary of State, Madeleine Albright, that had been started two years earlier by a Russian internet troll, was equally revealing.

She had been quoted as saying that Siberia was much too large and well endowed with natural resources to belong to Russia alone and should be placed under American management to benefit all mankind.[185] The story had been picked up by the government mouthpiece, *Rossiiskaya gazeta*, which had interviewed an eccentric retired FSB general named Boris Ratnikov. He and his colleagues, he claimed, had worked for a secret FSB unit conducting psychic research. They had 'connected to Secretary Albright's subconscious', where they had found that she did indeed have such thoughts.[186]

In Russia, where belief in extra-terrestrials and parapsychology is widespread, that did not strain credulity in the same way as it would have done in the West. Even so, it was plainly drivel. Yet when Putin was asked about it during his annual phone-in in October 2007, he replied in all seriousness: 'I understand that this cannot fail to worry us. I am not familiar with this statement by Mrs Albright, but I know that ideas like this are brewing in the heads of certain politicians . . . Such statements . . . confirm that everything we are doing to heighten our country's defence capability is correct.'[187]

After that, the 'Albright Declaration', as it became known, established itself as a staple of Russian newspaper commentary[188] and was repeated as incontrovertible fact by Patrushev and others in Putin's entourage.[189]

It was another sign that the ground was shifting. When, after Beslan,

Putin accused 'certain people' in the West of wanting to see Russia bogged down in internal conflicts, there was a certain logic to it. The United States had supported proxy wars to destabilise its adversaries in the past. So had Russia.[190] Putin's attitude towards the 'Albright Declaration' was different. He deliberately lent credibility to a claim which he knew to be totally false.

During Putin's second term, his view of his status and role as Head of State had altered. When a journalist asked him whether he trusted other leaders, he replied: 'You can't ask a question like that to someone at my level. How can I trust or not trust someone else? I trust only myself.'[191] It was the loneliness of a monarch. 'He trusts no one, not even his own people,' said his old acquaintance, the filmmaker, Igor Shadkhan, who felt that he was becoming estranged even from those who had formerly been close to him.[192]

Early on, a personality cult had started to build. A factory in Chelyabinsk, in the Urals, which used to make watches with a portrait of Stalin, began manufacturing Putin watches and reported a huge demand. Busts and badges appeared.[193] Putin's portrait was painted on Easter eggs and printed on the T-shirts worn by members of the Kremlin youth movement. An annual calendar was issued, with a different picture of Putin for each month.[194] In 2002, an all-girl electro-dance band, *Poyushchie vmeste*, 'Singing Together', recorded 'A Man like Putin', which topped the Russian charts for months:

> I want a man like Putin,
> A man like Putin, full of strength,
> A man like Putin, who won't get drunk,
> A man like Putin, who won't hurt me,
> A man like Putin, who won't run away.[195]

Initially, Putin claimed to see the cult as a regrettable but unavoidable consequence of the job. 'In our country, unfortunately,' he said, 'this reflects the general cultural level. There's nothing you can do about it. That's just how it is.'[196] By the end of his second term, that reticence was gone. He was posing, bare-chested on horseback in the taiga or swimming across Siberian rivers, for macho pin-ups which made those early calendars look very modest indeed.

Another factor added to his isolation. Most leaders have a family to help them keep their feet on the ground. In Putin's case, by the middle of his second term, if not earlier, that was no longer so. Already in 2003, there were rumours that his marriage was on the rocks.[197] Two years later, Lyudmila stopped accompanying him on visits abroad.[198] They were seen in public together only twice in the next three years: for Yeltsin's funeral, in 2007, and to vote in the presidential election in March 2008. By then, their daughters had grown up and were leading lives of their own.

It had never been a particularly happy marriage, but the rigours of the presidency had killed it. Lyudmila had hated being First Lady. A Russian journalist who watched her during the Blairs' visit to St Petersburg, even before Putin's election, had been struck by 'her endlessly sad eyes'.[199]

In 2005, the Moscow rumour mill started linking Putin's name romantically with Alina Kabayeva, a 22-year-old Olympic gold medallist in rhythmic gymnastics. When, three years later, a Moscow tabloid, *Moskovsky korrespondent*, finally dared to publish a story to that effect, adding incorrectly that Putin was planning to marry her, it was shut down within days.[200] There was 'not a word of truth in it', Putin insisted. The names of a number of 'successful and beautiful young women' had been linked to his, he said. 'I like them all, just as I like all Russian women.' As an attempt to deflect attention from Kabayeva, it was rather lame, for hers was the only name that had been mentioned in the press. He then denounced 'those who, with their snotty noses and erotic fantasies, meddle in other people's lives', before adding, plaintively: 'I know that politicians live in a glasshouse . . . But all the same, there are certain limits. There is such a thing as a private life.'[201]

Many Russians would sympathise with that. But public and private lives can never be completely dissociated for they are different sides of the same person. After 2005, for whatever reason, Putin's behaviour subtly changed. At news conferences, he flirted with the young female journalists. 'Greetings to you and to all blonde women,' he told one questioner. 'What's that picture you've got?' he asked another. 'Some sort of jolly picture. And you're a blonde, too . . .' It was hardly sparkling repartee but it was not something he had done before[202] and it was consistent with the attitude of a middle-aged man who, fleeing a wearisome marriage, had entered into a relationship with a much younger woman and felt his spirits lifted. The psychological boost that such a change can produce is not limited to private life.[203] Was that one of the factors which helped to produce what appeared, from a Russian standpoint, to be a more self-confident and forceful approach in foreign policy, but in the West was seen as more aggressive? It is possible but, given Putin's determination to conceal his private life, there is no way of knowing.

Putin worked mainly in the Kremlin and from his home at Novo-Ogaryovo but, during his second term, he began spending more time at Bocharov Ruchei, the presidential retreat in Sochi, a squat, square two-storey building in 'Stalinist classical' style, constructed in the 1950s for Marshal Kliment Voroshilov when he became Head of State after Stalin's death. It was hidden in a wooded park, in the centre of the city, overlooking the Black Sea, with a helipad, staff accommodation, a separate residence for the head of the Presidential Administration and a guest cottage for the Prime Minister.

Security was assured by a double enclosure of concrete and steel mesh fence, patrolled by guards and, when Putin was in residence, a naval frigate offshore. At dinners with visiting dignitaries, even if there were only three or four people present, both in the Kremlin and at Sochi, Putin's food and wine were each brought by a waiter who served him alone.[204] When he travelled abroad, he took with him two doctors, a nurse and sometimes a food-taster and a chambermaid with his personal bed linen. His advance team would give prior approval for each dish on the banquet menu.[205]

The threat of assassination was not to be taken lightly.

A report compiled by the German Federal Intelligence Service, the BND, listed five attempts on Putin's life after he became President.[206] The first allegedly occurred during Sobchak's funeral in St Petersburg in February 2000.[207] The second was at Yalta, in Crimea, where Putin attended a CIS summit in August of that year. The Ukrainians announced that they had expelled four Chechens, whom they suspected of being involved.[208] A third attempt, also involving Chechens, was said to have been thwarted in Azerbaijan. They had allegedly planned to set off an explosion under Putin's motorcade when he visited Baku in January 2001.[209] Britain deported two Russians suspected of planning to assassinate Putin during his State Visit in June

2003,[210] and another plot was supposedly uncovered shortly before he visited Iran in 2007.[211]

How serious these alleged plots were is another matter. *Nezavisimaya gazeta* said that the purported assassination plan in St Petersburg was probably a PR ploy to boost interest in the forthcoming election.[212] The two Russians who were deported from Britain had visa violations and were sent home as a precautionary measure. The supposed assassination planned in Tehran may have been a rumour put about by Mossad to try to persuade Putin to call off a visit to a state which had demanded that Israel be wiped off the face of the earth.[213]

Nevertheless, the continuing violence in the Caucasus, the massacres at Dubrovka and Beslan, and other terrorist attacks showed that the risk was real.

Political assassination has a long history in Russia. The tsars lived in constant fear of attempts on their lives. Between 1760 and 1801, three Romanov monarchs were killed: Ivan VI, Peter III and Paul I. Later in the nineteenth century, Aleksandr II was assassinated, along with dozens of ministers and provincial governors. In 1911, it was the turn of the reformist Prime Minister, Pyotr Stolypin, followed in 1934 by Stalin's rival for power, the Leningrad leader, Sergei Kirov.

Putin shrugged off such concerns, quoting the Russian proverb, 'those who are destined to be hanged are not going to drown', meaning that assassination was probably not his fate.[214] But his security services were taking no chances.

If the President was well protected, others were not so fortunate.

In the 1990s, there had been nearly a dozen high-profile political murders, most of which remained unsolved.

After Putin took office, the series continued.[215] In 2003, Yuri Shchekochikhin, the deputy editor of *Novaya gazeta* who was also a liberal member of the Duma, died after a short illness, officially due to a rare allergy but almost certainly the result of radioactive poisoning. The following year, Roman Tsepov, the head of the Baltik Eskort security company in St Petersburg, died in almost identical circumstances. Tsepov had organised bodyguards for Sobchak and Putin in the 1990s and had also acted as a discreet intermediary between the Mayor's Office and organised crime. Viktor Zolotov, who went on to become Putin's chief bodyguard at the Kremlin, had been Tsepov's deputy. His funeral, in the Serafimovskoe cemetery in St Petersburg, at which Zolotov pronounced the eulogy, was attended by the elite from both sides of the criminal divide – crime bosses like Vladimir Kumarin, the head of the Tambovsky gang, and the FSB and Interior Ministry generals whose task was to fight against them.

Shchekochikhin's medical records were sealed. Tsepov's death was attributed to an overdose of a drug used against leukaemia, an illness from which he did not suffer. Radioactive poisoning was the signature of the FSB. In neither case was any serious effort made to find out who was responsible.

No charges were brought, either, against those who organised the murder of Anna Politkovskaya, the *Novaya gazeta* journalist who was shot dead in the entrance hall of her apartment block in the autumn of 2006. Five Chechens were eventually convicted of the crime. But they were foot soldiers. Those who ordered her death were never troubled. When she died, Politkovskaya had been working on an article about the Kadyrovtsy, the sadistic paramilitary units loyal to Chechnya's 29-year-old leader, Ramzan Kadyrov, who had recently been appointed the republic's Prime Minister.[216] Putin remained silent for three days. When he did speak, not in Moscow but during a visit to Germany, he denounced her murder as 'a horribly cruel crime [against] a woman and a mother' but gave the impression that the government would investigate only because it had to. The perpetrators, 'whatever their motives', would 'naturally' be punished, Putin said. However, people should realise that the dead woman's influence in Russia was 'extremely insignificant, minimal', and that 'her murder had caused much more harm and damage . . . than her articles ever did.'[217]

That was tone-deaf – insensitive, inappropriate and unhelpful in terms of Russia's image abroad – even if it was true. Anna Politkovskaya was courageous and headstrong, an avowed opponent of Putin's regime and an indefatigable defender of human rights, in Chechnya and elsewhere, but had she not been brutally murdered, which made her a household name, her influence would have been far less.

The day that she was killed, October 7, was Putin's 54th birthday. Some wondered whether that date had been chosen deliberately to point the finger of suspicion at the Kremlin – to 'create a wave of anti-Russian sentiment in the world', as Putin himself put it.[218] In reality there was a simpler explanation. Ramzan Kadyrov had offered Politkovskaya's death to Putin as a birthday present. In Chechnya, gestures of that kind were immediately understood. Naturally there was no proof that the murder was organised by Kadyrov's entourage. There never is in such cases in Russia.[219] But, as one of his aides said later, 'if she had trod more cautiously, she would still be alive.'[220]

Afterwards Putin was at pains to exculpate the young Chechen leader. It was 'not possible' that he had had anything to do with her murder, he said. Politkovskaya's writings might well have caused 'a certain discontent, but I cannot imagine that anyone in authority would go so far as to organise such a horrible crime'.[221]

Keeping control of Chechnya was far more important than the murder of a journalistic gadfly in Moscow.

It was not that the Kremlin issued orders for the murders of political opponents – at least, not in Putin's first two terms. Liquidating those considered to be traitors, who had fled abroad, like Litvinenko and Yandarbiyev, was a different matter. But at home, Putin's responsibility was passive. By failing to punish those who ordered the killing of people like Anna Politkovskaya and Yuri Shchekochikhin, he allowed a climate to develop in which powerful, well-connected individuals knew that they could, literally, get away with murder if they chose. Morally, that made him as guilty as if he had authorised the killings himself. Contrary to widespread belief in the West, he did not. But the outcome was the same.

The same cynical, pragmatic reasoning protected highly placed officials implicated in large-scale corruption cases.

In November 2005, the financier, Bill Browder, was declared 'a threat to Russian national security' and deported to Britain. His offence was to have exposed ongoing corruption in Gazprom and other state-owned enterprises.[222] Eighteen months later, Browder's Hermitage Fund was the object of an elaborate scam, involving senior officials of the Interior Ministry and the Tax Inspectorate, corrupt judges and an organised crime group, which netted 230 million US dollars in faked tax rebates.[223] The money was never recovered and none of those involved were punished.

The other major corruption scandal of Putin's second term, the so-called 'Three Whales' case, was equally revealing. It had begun in 2000 when the Customs Directorate accused a Moscow company of that name of evading 5 million US dollars in duty by understating the value of Italian furniture which it imported. The Interior Ministry launched an investigation. But two months later, it emerged that one of the company's backers was Yevgeny Zaostrovtsev, a retired Major General who, earlier in his career, had mentored the FSB chief, Nikolai Patrushev. Zaostrovtsev's son, Yuri, had become Patrushev's first deputy. The case was immediately closed and, for the next five years, the Prosecutor General, Vladimir Ustinov, and the FSB went to extraordinary lengths to ensure that it was not reopened. The original investigators were fired and charged with abuse of office. A judge who acquitted them received death threats. Another judge in the same case was removed by the Supreme Court. A key witness was murdered and two others shot and wounded. The death of Yuri Shchekochikhin, the Duma deputy who had been poisoned in 2003, also appeared to be connected. After he had launched a parliamentary inquiry into the case, friends in the FSB had warned him that his life was in danger.

In June 2006, Ustinov was fired. His successor, Yuri Chaika, reopened the investigation and ordered the arrests of the head of the Three Whales company, Sergei Zuyev, and four of his assistants. Rumours began to circulate that the affair concerned not only unpaid duties on furniture but money laundering and large-scale smuggling from China, which generated revenue streams tens or hundreds of times greater.

At first it was assumed that Putin had decided that the Three Whales case had become an embarrassment and could not be allowed to continue. The truth turned out to be more complicated. It was not so much the corruption that was a problem but the rift that it had created among the President's closest allies in the security services. What had started as a fight between Customs and the Interior Ministry on one side and the Prosecutor's Office and the FSB on the other had drawn in other figures. Chaika's investigation was supported by Viktor Cherkesov, the head of the Narcotics Commission; Putin's chief bodyguard, Viktor Zolotov; and General Yevgeny Murov, the influential head of the FSO, the 50,000-strong Federal Guard Service. Arrayed against them were Ustinov, whose disgrace proved to be short-lived: five weeks after his dismissal, he was appointed Minister of Justice; Igor Sechin, whose daughter, Inga, was married to Ustinov's son; and Nikolai Patrushev.

To untangle these rivalries, Putin insisted on bringing in an outside prosecutor, ostensibly to ensure that, as he put it, 'the investigators have no connection with the Moscow law enforcement bodies',[224] but in reality because he needed a political rather than a legal resolution. For that purpose, he chose a former classmate from the Leningrad Law Faculty, Vladimir Loskutov, to orchestrate the outcome.

Three months later, it was announced that 19 senior officials in the FSB had been dismissed for their role in the case, including two Colonels-General and a Lieutenant-General.[225] As so often in Russia, however, things were not what they seemed. Many of those who had supposedly been fired never left. In some cases, Patrushev had been able to defend them, in others their defenestration had been a fiction all along.[226] Afterwards the FSB chief took his revenge. He could not touch Zolotov or Murov, who were under Putin's personal protection, but Cherkesov was another matter. Patrushev first ordered the detention of Cherkesov's deputy at the Narcotics Commission on the pretext of having carried out illegal wiretaps. Then he launched investigations against several of Cherkesov's assistants.[227] Finally, in 2008, Cherkesov himself was moved to a less important post and, two years later, left the administration altogether.

It was a price Putin was willing to pay to restore harmony among a key section of the elite. The senior officials who had concealed the scandal, profited from it and resorted to intimidation and murder to keep it under wraps, did not incur even token punishment. Sergei Zuyev, after a term of imprisonment, was able to return and resume running the Three Whales company as before.[228]

By the end of Putin's second term, impunity had become one of the hallmarks of his regime. Men like Patrushev, Sechin and Ustinov protected those of their subordinates who were caught with their hands in the till because that was the role of a *krysha*, a 'roof'. The beneficiaries of that protection responded by giving them their loyalty, providing a reliable support base to buttress their power. Putin, the ultimate *krysha*, protected the elite on whom his own power depended.

The two years from the spring of 2006 to March 2008, were dominated by the issue of Putin's succession. Would he ask the Duma to change the constitution to enable him to stay for a third term, as many of his inner circle wished? Or would he step down, in which case, who would succeed him and what would his own future hold?

Putin himself had stated repeatedly that he would step down as planned. Yeltsin had relinquished power voluntarily. Not to do the same would be humiliating. It was a matter of self-respect. If he were seen to be manipulating the system simply in order to stay in office, he would be lowering himself in his own and others' estimation and it would be a betrayal of the ideals to which he continued to pay lip service and in which, to a certain extent, he continued to believe. Moreover, being President was hard work. He had complained privately more than once, even in his first term, that he was tired of it.[229] That was to be taken with a grain of salt, like his stories in St Petersburg about giving everything up to become a taxi driver, or to write a university thesis, or his gripes to Yumashev that he was bored by his work in the Presidential Administration. But leaving the presidency would give him an opportunity to stand back and to see whether the person he proposed as his successor was capable of governing the country in his place.

He made his first move in November 2005, nominating Dmitry Medvedev, then his Chief of Staff, as first deputy Prime Minister under Mikhail Fradkov. The same day, Sergei Ivanov, the Defence Minister, was appointed a deputy Prime Minister.[230]

They were regarded as the two front-runners.

Medvedev was loyal and hard-working but, in Bill Burns's view, 'too mild-mannered for Russian tastes in leadership'. He was viewed with deep suspicion by the *siloviki*, who mistrusted his liberal views. Ivanov was a more forceful character but had no political base other than Putin's personal support and, in Burns's words, had 'an albatross round his neck in the shape of the unreformable Russian military'.[231]

That was shown dramatically at the end of December when a particularly ghastly case of a conscript being tortured occurred at an army camp in the Urals. Bullying exists in most armies, including that of the United States, where it is known as hazing. But in Russia it was infinitely worse. Discipline had deteriorated since the collapse of the Soviet Union, when defence spending was cut and material conditions for the troops worsened. Each year, between 1,200 and 2,000 soldiers died as a result of abuse – many by committing suicide – and another 1,600 or so deserted to escape maltreatment.[232] The root of the problem was that there were no professional NCOs. Conscripts were brutalised by their older comrades. The system was known as the *dedovshchina*, 'the rule of grandfather'. The army denied that there was any problem or, to the extent that it did admit it, blamed it on a few bad apples.

On New Year's Eve, a drunken sergeant and four of his colleagues in a tank regiment at Chelyabinsk took umbrage at a young conscript named Andrei Sychev, beat him savagely and left him hanging from a beam for hours. His wounds were not treated for several days, gangrene set in and, when he was finally transferred to hospital, his legs and genitals had to be amputated.[233]

The incident was by no means exceptional. Two years earlier, more than 100 conscripts on their way to the Russian Far East were left standing outside for hours in summer uniforms in temperatures well below zero while their officers caroused in a military mess hall. One died and the others were hospitalised with pneumonia.[234]

That incident caused outrage but was eventually forgotten. Sychev's case was different.

When Sergei Ivanov was asked about it, he at first denied all knowledge. 'If it had been something serious, it would have been reported to me,' he said.[235] That set off a firestorm of protests. In Moscow and St Petersburg, demonstrators carried banners declaring, 'Ivanov's legs should be cut off', and called for his dismissal.[236] The media accused him of not being tough enough with the generals, resorting to half-measures and being more interested in protecting the army's esprit de corps than rooting out abuses – much of which was true.[237]

Ivanov had handled it poorly and, when the storm eventually subsided, emerged weakened. But the media onslaught had not been spontaneous. Behind the scenes, the Prosecutor General's Office, then still headed by Vladimir Ustinov, had been quietly pouring fuel on the flames.

Like the Three Whales case, the martyrdom of young Andrei Sychev became a weapon for Kremlin infighting. Igor Sechin detested Ivanov almost as much as he disliked Medvedev. He and Ustinov were close. Not only did they have family ties, but they shared a conservative outlook, mistrust of the West and a common attraction to Russian nationalism and the Orthodox Church.[238] Sechin saw in the Sychev affair a chance to strike a blow at Ivanov's presidential ambitions.

That was not in Putin's plan. Formally, at least, he had not yet made his choice and would not do so for another 18 months. Keeping the uncertainty alive was necessary to prevent him becoming a lame duck.

Ustinov's campaign against Ivanov, and the public outcry it had helped to ignite, risked upsetting that. He had another concern as well. Ustinov and Sechin had started meeting privately with the Prime Minister, Mikhail Fradkov, and the Mayor of Moscow, Yuri Luzhkov. It was Luzhkov's presence that aroused Putin's suspicions. Although outwardly their relations were correct, Putin had always regarded him as a snake in the grass, too strongly entrenched in his Moscow fiefdom for it to be worth a head-on conflict, but fundamentally untrustworthy. That Sechin, his closest aide, the Prosecutor General and the Prime Minister were consorting with Luzhkov gave him pause. When he wondered aloud what they could be discussing, his chief bodyguard, Viktor Zolotov, and Viktor Cherkesov – who were at daggers drawn with Ustinov over the Three Whales affair – were happy to oblige. The tapes they provided of the four men's eavesdropped conversations confirmed Putin's suspicions. Sechin was looking for a way to find another, more malleable candidate for the succession, who would be neither Ivanov nor Medvedev, and his eye had fallen on Fradkov.

It was not very serious. Mikhail Zygar, in his book, *All the Kremlin's Men*, wrote that they were 'just letting off steam'.[239] Fradkov was not remotely presidential material. But Ustinov was getting above himself and Sechin needed to be brought back into line. This, rather than the Three Whales affair, had brought about Ustinov's sudden fall. It was 'classic Putin', Zygar wrote. He made his move when it was least expected. His quarry was caught off guard and given no time to react.[240]

Ustinov's temporary removal was a warning to Sechin and to the rest of the elite. If they thought that, just because Putin might step down, they could conspire behind his back, they were mistaken.

Nine months later, Putin appointed Ivanov first deputy Prime Minister, giving him the same rank as Medvedev. It was a way to keep him in play and show that the succession was still open. Then, in September 2007, in another move that came out of the blue, Putin asked Fradkov to resign. In his place, he appointed Viktor Zubkov, who had been one of his deputies in the Foreign Relations Committee in St Petersburg and had afterwards worked in the tax inspectorate and the finance ministry.

No one could work out what Putin was up to. There was speculation that the new Prime Minister might be a compromise candidate for the presidency to enable him to avoid choosing between representatives of the two dominant clans. Zubkov himself encouraged that idea, refusing to rule out the possibility that he would stand the following spring.[241]

In fact, it was a precautionary measure, to clear the decks before the transition began in earnest. If Putin was going to step down, he was leaving nothing to chance. Fradkov had ties to other power-holders, as his conclaves with Sechin had shown. It was safer to move him aside. Zubkov had no such links. He was a Putin loyalist who would keep a low profile and do as he was told. The sudden change of government was also a way for Putin to keep the initiative, throwing everyone else off balance. That had been Yeltsin's preferred method and Putin had learnt the lesson well. For those able to decipher it, Zubkov's appointment was a sign that Putin had made his choice. Although he would not make a formal announcement until December, he had decided that Dmitry Medvedev would be his successor.[242] It was not only that he trusted Medvedev.[243] He had confidence in Ivanov, too. But, if differences arose, he could be sure that Medvedev would defer to his wishes. In the words of one observer who had watched them working together over the years: 'There's no daylight between them.'[244]

With hindsight, it is legitimate to ask whether Sergei Ivanov was ever anything more than a foil whose role was to maintain the suspense, in the same way that Yeltsin had played with Stepashin before appointing Putin.

That was not how it looked at the time. Most of the Russian political elite, not to mention Western observers, thought he had a better chance than Medvedev of coming out on top. However, Putin was a past master at disguising his intentions. Ivanov would remain one of the inner circle. But his appointment as Defence Minister would mark the high point of his career. He had been set the task of reforming the military and he had failed. For all his hawkish reputation, he had not been tough enough. The far-right leader, Vladimir Zhirinovsky, summed it up: 'A defence minister should be . . . a martinet, a beast, so that everyone's knees are shaking . . . He should tear off the generals' shoulder boards.'[245] Ivanov had not done that and the generals had been able to carry on as they pleased.

The consummation of Putins' plans came in several stages.

On December 2, 2007, a new Duma was elected by proportional representation from party lists with, for the first time, no single-seat constituencies, under the new, more restrictive legislation enacted after the Beslan massacre.

Putin had put aside his stated aversion to election campaigns and had agreed to head the United Russia list, though not to become a Party member – a curious attempt to square the circle, intended to reconcile support for the ruling party with his insistence on being the President of all Russians, regardless of party affiliation.[246] It was necessary, he explained, to have a solid majority in the Duma to work with the new administration.[247] That meant 'persuading people to vote for this party', which he duly did, delivering an electoral address that showed that, when the situation required, he was as capable of shameless demagoguery as anybody else:

We have no right to allow the Duma to become a mob of populists, paralysed by corruption . . . We have to prevent what happened before in our country from happening again . . . Our opponents [abroad] . . . need a weak nation, a sick nation, . . . a disoriented and divided society . . . And we still have people in this country . . . who count on the support of foreign money and foreign governments, rather than the support of their own people . . .

Who is responsible [for the difficulties we have been facing]? Those who guided Russia for decades, [who] left people without the most basic services and goods – no sugar, no meat, no salt, no matches – [and who] were responsible for the collapse of the Soviet Union . . . Those who occupied high positions in the 1990s, who bargained away our national wealth, [who] made bribery the principal means of economic and political competition . . . In short, they are all those who at the end of the last century brought mass poverty and an epidemic of corruption to Russia, which we have been fighting ever since.

Do not harbour any illusions! These people have not left the scene . . . They want to take revenge . . . If they are returned to power, they will rob millions of people again.[248]

When the election results came in, United Russia had won a more than two-thirds majority, with 315 of the 450 seats; another, newly formed pro-Putin party, Just Russia, had 38 seats, with the remainder being divided between the Communists and Zhirinovsky's right-wing nationalists. Just Russia had been created by Putin's strategist, Surkov, as a left-of-centre, social-democratic counterpart to United Russia, which was centre-right. The idea was to drain away votes from the liberals.[249] It worked. For the first time since the early 1990s, Yabloko and the Union of Right Forces had no parliamentary representation.

There was widespread fraud and ballot-stuffing, especially in the Caucasus, where Chechnya claimed a 99.5 per cent turnout, of which 99.36 per cent voted for Putin's party, not far off the 100 per cent support which Ramzan Kadyrov had pledged to deliver. However, as had been the case four years earlier, even if the elections had been scrupulously fair, United Russia would have had a comfortable majority. At the end of his second term, Putin had an approval rating of nearly 80 per cent.

Two weeks later, Medvedev was proclaimed the party's presidential candidate. In his acceptance speech, he announced what until then had only been hinted at, namely that, if he was elected, Putin would become Prime Minister.[250] The Head of the Presidential Administration, Sergei Sobyanin, who had replaced Medvedev in that position three years earlier, would move with Putin to the White House, while the head of the government apparatus, Sergei Naryshkin, would accompany the new President to the Kremlin.[251]

On March 2, 2008, Medvedev was elected with 71.2 per cent of the vote, fractionally less than Putin four years earlier. Zyuganov, for the Communists, came second with 18 per cent, followed by Zhirinovsky with nearly 10 per cent. Two months later, Medvedev took the oath of office in the Kremlin's Grand Palace, at a ceremony identical to Putin's inauguration, becoming, at the age of 42, the youngest Russian Head of State since Nicholas II.

Observers from the Council of Europe pronounced that election, too, 'neither free nor fair'.[252] *Novaya gazeta* called it 'an apparent election to elect an apparent President'. *Kommersant* grumbled: 'It's like a third marriage. Feelings are not as strong.'[253]

Exactly how the tandem, as it would be called, would function, was a matter of intense speculation. Putin himself called it a 'curious' situation.[254] He would not hang Medvedev's official portrait in his office, he said, because 'given the nature of our relations, it would be unnecessary'.[255] Yet Putin's own portrait had always hung on Medvedev's office wall. Nor, he promised, would he try to enlarge the powers of the Prime Minister at the President's expense.[256] However, he 'wanted to work' and that would 'no doubt be a factor which the future President will have to take into account'.[257]

In April, Putin announced that he had agreed to become Chairman of United Russia. Membership of a political party, he said, although inappropriate for the Head of State, was 'a civilised, natural and traditional practice' for a Prime Minister.[258] Becoming head of the ruling party as well as head of government were hardly the actions of a man who intended to withdraw from the political fray. It raised the question, which Medvedev was never able to lay to rest, of whether he would be a President in the full sense of the term or merely a placeholder, keeping the position open while Putin decided what to do next.

14

Tandemocracy

On the evening of Friday, August 8, 2008, Prime Minister Vladimir Putin joined more than a hundred other heads of state and government to watch the grandiose opening ceremony of the Beijing Olympic Games, a spellbinding four-hour extravaganza of Chinese culture and history, conceived by the film director Zhang Yimou and staged by 15,000 performers in the spectacular new Bird's Nest Stadium, designed by Chinese and Swiss architects.

Putin's mind was not entirely on the pageant playing out before him. Since that morning, Russia and Georgia had been at war.

It was the culmination of months of meticulous planning that had intensified after the Bucharest summit. Throughout the late spring and early summer, the Russians had steadily reinforced their units in Abkhazia. Saakashvili was convinced that Putin was preparing an attack to drive out the breakaway province's remaining Georgian population and recognise Abkhazian independence in retaliation for Western recognition of Kosovo. Russian diplomats assured their US counterparts that nothing of the kind was contemplated. Moscow had intelligence, they said, that Saakashvili had been discussing the possibility of a lightning campaign to reoccupy former Georgian-populated areas along the Abkhazian border and then dig in while awaiting Western diplomatic support. Russia was merely bolstering its forces there to dissuade him from doing anything rash.

It was not implausible. The Georgian leaders were emotional and hot-headed, and the US and the Europeans were constantly warning them not get into sucked into a conflict with Russia that they could not possibly win. Saakashvili was obsessed by fears that Abkhazia and South Ossetia would slowly slip from Georgia's grasp if the status quo persisted and they would then be definitely lost. He was wrong. So long as the conflict remained frozen, nothing would change. But Saakashvili's government and its Western backers talked past each other – the Georgians desperate to recover their territory, their allies insistent that they do nothing which might provoke the Russian military to respond.

In that breach, Putin laid his trap.

By mid July, to everyone's surprise, the tension over Abkhazia eased. Saakashvili left for two weeks' holiday at a health spa in Italy, planning to travel on to Beijing. Soon afterwards, skirmishes broke out on the South Ossetian border, but it had become almost a tradition that, in late July and August each year, there were exchanges of mortar fire between South Ossetian paramilitary units and Georgian border troops, and at first no one paid much attention. But then, for the first time, the Ossetians started using heavy weapons. There were reports that Russian troops were massing north of the Caucasus mountains. Saakashvili raced back to Tbilisi. On August 7, as Putin was airborne, on his way to Beijing, the Georgians received what they believed was reliable information that, in the early hours of the morning, 500 Russian soldiers, allegedly bringing heavy armour, had traversed the Roki Tunnel, the only road access from North Ossetia. It was never completely clear whether these were combat units or a regular rotation of Russian peacekeepers, but Georgian units began preparing a counterattack. That afternoon, at 3 p.m., OSCE observers saw large numbers of Georgian artillery units and GRAD rocket-launchers heading north towards the South Ossetian border.[1]

Meanwhile, the intermittent exchanges of mortar fire between the Ossetians and Georgian border forces, which had been going on all week, continued.

At 6.40 p.m., in what the Georgians said was an attempt to prevent the situation deteriorating further, Saakashvili announced a unilateral ceasefire. South Ossetian villagers, assuming that the clashes had ended for the night, emerged from their bunkers and returned home to supper and bed. But then, five hours later, at 11.35 p.m. Georgian time, 3.35 a.m. on August 8 in Beijing, the Georgian President ordered an all-out attack on the South Ossetian capital, Tskhinvali.

What happened during those five hours to make Saakashvili change his mind is a matter of dispute. The Georgians claimed that, soon after 8 p.m., the Ossetians resumed shelling Georgian villages. According to

OSCE monitors on the ground, that was untrue: in villages the Georgians named as targets, no further shelling occurred.[2] Was Saakashvili fed false intelligence? Did he abruptly decide that, unless he acted at once, South Ossetia would be lost? Or was the ceasefire, as the Russians later alleged, a trick to give the Georgians time to move heavy artillery into place?

It is unlikely that there will ever be a clear answer. But what is not in doubt is that Saakashvili ordered a massive Georgian artillery barrage against Tskhinvali – with hundreds of rounds landing indiscriminately on residential areas as well as supposed military targets – well before any Russian attack.[3]

The war, which the Western media – and Western governments – would afterwards describe as a Russian invasion, was launched not by Russia but by Georgia. Putin would later marvel at the way the story was spun to present Russia as the aggressor. 'It's terrific, amazing . . . simply mind-boggling', he said.[4] No matter how much the Kremlin spent on PR agencies like Ketchum, it would never be able to compete with that.

The conflict would indeed trigger a Russian invasion – an invasion totally disproportionate to the original offence – but that was not how it began. It began as a carefully laid Russian trap into which Mikheil Saakashvili walked with both feet. That he did so, given Russia's military superiority, is almost inexplicable.

Later it would be alleged that the Americans had sent mixed messages about the extent of their support. That may well have been true. Condoleezza Rice, in private, told the Georgian leader that, if he launched a war, America would certainly not come to his aid. In public, she was more ambiguous. 'We always fight for our friends,' she declared at a news conference, with Saakashvili standing beside her. It was said in the context of America's efforts to help Georgia join NATO but it came across as much more sweeping.[5] There were also conflicting signals from the White House. Dick Cheney's deputy National Security Adviser, Joseph Wood, had opened a direct channel to Saakashvili. According to John Beyrle, who had succeeded Burns that summer as US Ambassador, the Georgian leader was hearing one thing from the State Department, 'warning him to be careful, . . . and a second set of messages, from the Vice President's Office, urging him to stand firm and implying that he had America's support.'[6]

Whether or not that played a role, it appears that in the end Saakashvili came to the conclusion that the Russians were determined to pick
a fight and that his best course was to try to seize the initiative, even if
he had no realistic hope of success.[7]

Tactically, that might have made sense. The Georgian offensive took
the Russians by surprise. Next morning, Saakashvili's ground forces
occupied the South Ossetian capital, now in ruins after the Georgian
bombardment. The Russians scrambled to bring in extra units, in many
cases staffed by conscripts who had no idea what they were supposed
to be doing.[8] It took them until the following day to drive the Georgians out.

But in the broader scheme of things, it was a fatal error.

The Russians had begun contingency planning for a conflict with
Georgia as early as 2006.[9] That Saakashvili should have struck first was
an unlooked-for stroke of luck. Had he not done so, it would have
been far more difficult for Moscow to have found a pretext to attack.
Moreover, the timing was perfect. Most of the world's leaders, including Putin himself, were in Beijing, where a small war in the Caucasus
was viewed as an annoying distraction from the Olympic festivities.
Europe was on holiday. Saakashvili had allowed his hand to be forced
in a place where he had not expected it – South Ossetia, rather than
Abkhazia – at a time when many of his officers were on leave and one
of Georgia's four combat brigades was abroad, serving with the US-
led coalition in Iraq.

The first, fragmentary reports reached Beijing late in the morning
of August 8. George W. Bush spoke briefly to Putin as they arrived at
the Great Hall of the People for a welcoming luncheon, hosted by the
Chinese President, Hu Jintao. They agreed, Putin said afterwards, that
'no one wants a war'.[10] For Russia, that was not true at all. Moscow did
want a war, ideally to remove Saakashvili from power and end Georgia's dalliance with the West, or, if that were not possible, to create
sufficient instability in the region to block any move towards Georgian
or Ukrainian NATO membership when the alliance's foreign ministers
met in December.

Later Bush called Medvedev, who told him that Saakashvili had
launched an unprovoked attack in which 1,500 people had died. He was
a war criminal, Medvedev said, like Saddam Hussein in Iraq. Bush
wrote afterwards that he had urged him to de-escalate the conflict as

quickly as possible, a point he also made to Putin at the opening ceremony that night. Saakashvili was hot-blooded, Bush said, and Russia
had made a mistake.

'I'm hot-blooded too,' Putin retorted. 'No, Vladimir,' Bush replied.
'You are cold-blooded.'[11]

Putin flew back from Beijing to the North Ossetian capital, Vladi-
kavkaz, where he arrived late on the afternoon of Saturday, August 9,
to take personal command of the operation. Bush was in no hurry to
leave and remained in Beijing three days more. Whatever the American press and the State Department spinmeisters might be saying,
Bush had no illusions about Saakashvili's role. On his return to Washington, his first words to his aides were: 'Who started it?'[12]

For the Americans, there were no good options. Military intervention was ruled out. 'Are we prepared to go to war with Russia over
Georgia?', Bush's National Security Adviser, Steve Hadley, asked. Short
of that, Washington's leverage was negligible.

Initially the White House hoped that the Russians might stop after
expelling the Georgians from South Ossetia. But in a telephone call
that weekend, Condoleezza Rice's opposite number, Sergei Lavrov,
told her that that would not be enough. 'Saakashvili has to go,' he said.
Rice feigned indignation and, violating diplomatic protocol, made the
exchange public. 'The Secretary of State of the United States does not
have a conversation with the Russian Foreign Minister about overthrowing a democratically elected President,' she declared.[13] Lavrov
thought that was a bit rich coming from a government which had just
waged war to effect regime change in Iraq. To Rice, the parallel was
false. Saddam Hussein had been an unelected dictator.

By then, Russian units were heading south towards Tbilisi, while
others advanced from the West, across the border with Abkhazia.
Altogether it was estimated that some 40,000 Russian troops were
deployed. Bombers and helicopter gunships pounded Georgian positions
across the whole of the northern third of the country. By Monday evening,
August 11, it looked as though Tbilisi would fall. The Georgian government was on the brink of collapse and a panicky exodus of civilians began.

Asked why Russian forces had continued their advance into Georgia
long after South Ossetia had been secured, Putin was unapologetic.
The Americans, he said, had 'egged on the Georgian side to take
aggressive actions'.

Why did we act as we did? Because the infrastructure [the Georgians] used to attack Tskhinvali, . . . the control centres, radars and arms dumps . . . [were in Georgia itself] . . . I hear about disproportionate use of force . . . When they use tanks, rockets and heavy artillery against us, should we respond by using catapults?

Let us remember how the Second World War started. On September 1, 1939, Nazi Germany attacked Poland. Then they attacked the Soviet Union. [When we succeeded in driving them back,] were we supposed to stop the moment we reached our own border? No. The aggressor had to be punished.

Some people are so fond of shooting and bombing that they think [it's the only answer]. Why did they think that they would succeed here when they had failed in Afghanistan, Iraq and the Middle East? . . . Those who believe that [military force] is the most effective instrument of foreign policy in the modern world will fail again and again . . . One cannot behave in the world like a Roman emperor.[14]

Bush feared that if America tried to mediate, the Russo-Georgian war would become a US–Russian confrontation. Instead he urged the French President, Nicolas Sarkozy, who held the rotating presidency of the EU, to take the lead in bringing the war to an end.

Sarkozy hesitated. He had talked to Putin in Beijing and had found the Russian Prime Minister in a 'Roman emperor' mood himself, determined to teach Saakashvili a lesson. But he agreed to telephone Medvedev and, after a day of hectic negotiations, flew to Moscow, on the understanding that the advance towards Tbilisi would end before his plane landed. Otherwise, he said, he would instruct the pilot to turn round and fly straight back to France.[15]

The Russians kept their word. A few minutes before his plane touched down, a ceasefire was announced.

When Sarkozy arrived at the Kremlin, Medvedev told him that Putin would like to join them for lunch. The Prime Minister's cheek was swollen. He had just come from the dentist, he said. 'I have a raging toothache and I'm in a foul mood.'

There were better ways of starting a meeting, Sarkozy thought, and he was not wrong. 'Putin was furious,' Sarkozy wrote later. 'He let rip with a 15-minute monologue, a violent diatribe against Saakashvili, his methods, his policies, his personality.' Whenever he pronounced the

Georgian leader's name, he crossed himself, as though he were mentioning the Devil. While Medvedev sat, as quiet as a mouse, Putin
launched into a new philippic. 'After all the crimes [Saakashvili] has
committed,' he began, 'he cannot stay in power . . .'

At that, Sarkozy lost patience. 'I haven't come all this way to listen
to your insults and threats towards another head of state,' he told
Putin. 'I came to try to help you find a way out of a situation in which
everyone will end up the loser. But you don't want to listen to anything. I've had enough. I'm going.' With that he got up, picked up his
jacket, which he had left over the back of his chair, and headed for the
door. To his relief, Putin stood up, too, and asked him to come back
and continue the discussion. 'There hasn't been any discussion yet',
Sarkozy retorted acidly. Nonetheless, he sat down, and they began to
talk more calmly. But Putin had not quite finished. He looked hard at
Sarkozy. 'I want to hang that man by the balls,' he said.[16] The French
President was startled, not so much by the remark itself but because,
as Putin obviously knew, he had made a very similar statement about
a political rival two years earlier, threatening to 'hang him from a
butcher's hook'.[17] When Bush had hanged Saddam Hussein, Putin continued, Sarkozy had not protested. So why complain now, when Russia
wanted to get rid of Saakashvili? Sarkozy had a ready answer. 'So your
dream is to end up like Bush,' he said, 'detested by two thirds of the
planet! I didn't realise that he was your model.' Putin burst out laughing. 'You scored a point there', he said.

After that, the negotiation began. The draft agreement that resulted
called for a permanent ceasefire, mutual troop withdrawals and renunciation of the use of force by both sides, all of which was acceptable.
But, for the Georgians, two other points caused problems. The agreement failed to reaffirm their country's territorial integrity and it called
for 'an international debate on the future status of South Ossetia and
Abkhazia'.[18] At Saakashvili's insistence, the Russians removed the latter
reference. It turned out to be a mistake. Two weeks later, Medvedev
announced that Russia would recognise the independence of the two
provinces, citing as a precedent the West's recognition of Kosovo the
previous spring.[19]

Kosovo was a constant reference throughout the Georgian war and
the settlement that followed. One of the US government's best specialists on the Caucasus, Ron Asmus, wrote: 'Moscow's terminology and

rhetorical line of defense were almost a mirror image of the West's rationale on Kosovo . . . It was payback time for a grievance that Russia had borne against the West for nearly a decade.'[20] Putin accused the Georgians of ethnic cleansing in Ossetia, the same argument that NATO had used to justify taking action against the Serbs.[21] Russia portrayed Saakashvili as a latter day Milošević, and the Ossetians as oppressed by Tbilisi in the same way as the Kosovars had been oppressed by Belgrade. Most of that was a stretch. But the West's hypocrisy in pretending that Kosovo was a 'special case' – an argument rejected by Cyprus, Greece and Spain and other states facing separatist movements, including Georgia itself – had finally come home to roost.

Kosovo was not the proximate cause of the war with Georgia. It became inevitable only after the American overreach at Bucharest, when Bush and Condoleezza Rice had pushed through an ill-considered commitment to grant Ukraine and Georgia NATO membership. The Bush administration had assumed that Russia would accept a fourth round of NATO enlargement after the Visegrád states in 1999, the Baltic States and East and Central Europeans in 2004, and the accession of Albania and Croatia, which would take place the following spring. Ambassador Burns and others had warned that this time Putin would dig in his heels. The White House had not listened.

That was compounded by another error. When Sergei Lavrov declared after Bucharest that Russia would do everything in its power to ensure that Georgia and Ukraine did not join NATO – a warning repeated a month later during a visit to NATO headquarters by the Russian Chief of Staff, General Baluyevsky[22] – the White House did not take that seriously either.

The result was that a lame duck American President, who had alienated many of his European colleagues, found himself powerless to protect an ally whose adventurism had been abetted by the political, military and economic support his administration had provided.

For Georgia the war was a disaster. The two territories Saakashvili had wished to recover were irretrievably lost. He managed to serve out the remainder of his term but his position was increasingly contested.

For the United States, the consequences were more nuanced. Bush would shortly be succeeded by a Democrat, Barack Obama, who would try a new approach to Russia. But Bush had left a troubling legacy. The spectacle of American forces bogged down in Afghanistan and Iraq had shown that the United States, even if it had become the world's sole superpower, was not the all-powerful hegemon it had imagined itself to be. The Georgian war convinced Putin that, in a battle of wills with Russia, America was not invincible either.

The reform of Russia's armed forces had been one of Putin's priorities ever since he came to power. The need for change had become painfully evident, he said, when, as Prime Minister in the autumn of 1999, Yeltsin had given him charge of the war in Chechnya. Out of 1.4 million men in the armed forces, only 55,000 were in combat-ready units and they were dispersed all over the country. 'That is how we ended up sending into battle kids untested by fire to be butchered', Putin said. 'I will not forget that ever.'[23] The following year he approved plans gradually to transition to a fully professional army.[24]

The generals were appalled and commenced a series of rearguard actions. Putin wanted a pilot programme to transform the 76th Airborne Division based at Pskov, south of St Petersburg, into an all-volunteer unit.[25] The Defence Ministry tried to delay it by several years. When that failed, it produced figures showing that the cost would be prohibitive. To sabotage the recruitment of volunteers, no enlistment centres were opened, and in order to hide the deception, conscripts with six months' training were offered volunteer contracts instead.

By 2008, instead of a claimed professional force of more than 200,000 men, there were actually no more than 50,000, most of whom, as was later admitted, were not much better than draftees.[26]

The root of the problem was the mindset of the General Staff and their allies in the political elite. The Soviet army, like the tsarist army before it, had been based on the idea of mass mobilisation. The Russian military followed the same model. From the standpoint of the officer corps, the system had distinct advantages. In the early 2000s, the Russian army had more colonels than lieutenants and one officer for every two ordinary ranks. The huge officer corps was needed, it was claimed, in case one day the civilian population had to be drafted in time of war. On top of that, an estimated 350 million US dollars changed hands in bribes each year to obtain conscripts' deferments. But as well as being the foundation of the system, conscription was its Achilles' heel. The falling birth rate since the 1980s meant that there were no longer enough draftees to go round, and since wealthier and better educated students usually managed to avoid serving, the quality of the recruits was lamentable.[27]

The reforms were not blocked completely. The armed forces were reduced by more than 300,000 men, bringing the total number down to one million; the defence budget was increased by an average of 20 per cent each year to finance the procurement of modern equipment; and it was announced that conscripts would no longer be sent to Chechnya or other war zones.

On paper, it looked like a great success.

The Georgian war showed that in practice it had been a total failure.

When Putin flew back to Vladikavkaz from China on August 9, he found the operation in chaos. The supposedly modern communications equipment worked so poorly that General Khrulyov, the commander of the force leading the assault, had to borrow a mobile phone from a journalist to give orders to his subordinates. Half the tanks and armoured vehicles never reached Tskhinvali because they broke down. What the Defence Ministry claimed were fully professional units turned out to have been cobbled together with 30 per cent of draftees. For lack of training, the Russian air force had only half a dozen pilots capable of combat missions. Most of the ground force commanders were desk officers who had spent their entire careers pushing paper. 'They were simply not capable of making combat decisions,' a senior general admitted later. 'When [they] were given people and equipment, they were at a loss. Some of them even refused to carry out orders.'[28]

Despite all the money that had been poured into the defence budget, the army's performance in Georgia had been not much better than in Chechnya, nine years earlier. Indeed, the government concluded that had the Georgians been better equipped and had fielded a slightly larger force, the outcome might have been different.

The failure of the modernisation programme was blamed on the Defence Minister, Sergei Ivanov. But Putin was also responsible. Having initially embraced the concept of a fully professional army, he had got cold feet.[29] It would require structural change and the dismissal of large numbers of officers, which would alienate an important segment of his political base. In the end, he chose a bastard compromise. Conscription would be maintained, but reduced from two years to twelve months, which allowed the General Staff to maintain the cherished principle of a Soviet-style army but, beyond that, satisfied no one. Even the generals understood that one year's training was too little to produce a soldier equipped to wage war under modern conditions.

In the spring of 2007, Putin finally decided that he could delay no longer. Ivanov was replaced by Anatoly Serdyukov, who had proved his worth as head of the Federal Tax Service, where he had led the campaign against Yukos. A massively built bear of a man, Serdyukov was a martinet. Russians compared him to Count Aleksei Arakcheyev, the eccentric, uncouth and much hated eighteenth-century war minister, who had reorganised the tsarist army under Paul I and whose name became a byword for ruthlessness and repression. Serdyukov was married to the daughter of Prime Minister Viktor Zubkov and had the backing of Putin's powerful personnel chief, Viktor Ivanov. He was the right man to 'tear off the generals' shoulder-boards', as the nationalist leader, Vladimir Zhirinovsky, had urged a year earlier.

His appointment had come too late to make any difference to the conflict with Georgia, but at least now the reforms began in earnest. Within nine months, Serdyukov had fired the heads of the air force and the navy and several of their deputies. A Russian military commentator wrote of 'convulsions that have not been seen in the Defence Ministry for decades'.[30] In June 2008, the Chief of the General Staff, Yuri Baluyevsky, was dismissed. But that was merely a foretaste of what would happen after the fiasco in South Ossetia. That autumn, Putin approved a plan to reduce by more than ten times the number of ground force formations and halve the number of air force and naval units. The officer corps would be cut from 355,000 to 150,000: 220 generals, 16,000 colonels, 74,000 majors and 50,000 captains would be discharged, and, for the first time, a training system would be introduced for professional NCOs.

In his usual 'good tsar, bad boyars' fashion, Putin promised to intervene if 'instances of overreach appear, or things surface that had not been planned'.[31] But if, for political reasons, he was prepared to show sympathy for the military's tribulations, in practice he and Medvedev gave Serdyukov unqualified support. Generals were forced to submit to performance reviews and lower ranking officers to fitness tests, which many of them failed. The head of the GRU, the military intelligence directorate, and other top generals resigned in protest.

Serdyukov and General Nikolai Makarov, Baluyevsky's successor as Chief of the General Staff, who helped him force through the reforms, were universally loathed.

The crunch came in 2010, when, against a background of global recession, Serdyukov was unable to persuade the Finance Ministry to continue providing funds for severance pay and other benefits, to which the discharged officers were legally entitled. 70,000 of those whose posts were to have been abolished were granted a last-minute reprieve.

Even so, the officer corps had been cut by almost a third. The procurement system had been streamlined. The vast sums spent on defence finally started producing modern, functional equipment, comparable to that in Western armies. Serdyukov dealt with bullying by the simple but brutal expedient of dismissing the entire chain of command, from the commanding general down, of any unit where there was significant abuse.[32] That was language the army understood. Bullying did not end but it was significantly reduced.

By 2011, the army command had been forced to accept that, no matter what it did, demographic considerations made a conscript army impossible. In any case, hi-tech weaponry needed skilled professionals, not cannon fodder. The General Staff announced that the transition to a fully professional force would continue and that the draft might end completely in 2017. That did not happen, but from 2012 onwards, the makeup of the armed forces stabilised at some 450,000 contract soldiers and 250,000 conscripts, which, with the officer corps and support personnel, brought the total contingent to nearly one million. Financial constraints were partly responsible: contract personnel cost much more than conscripts. But Putin and others in the political elite also saw the draft as promoting patriotism and maintaining the link between the military and the civilian population. In Western countries where conscription had been abolished, civilians' readiness to fight in defence of the homeland had notably declined.[33]

The reaction to the Georgian war in the West was tepid. America, having sat on its hands while the fighting was under way, tried to make up for its inaction by offering Georgia a one billion-dollar programme of humanitarian and economic aid.[34] The European Union fudged the issue with what Angela Merkel called 'an excellent compromise. Not business as usual [with Russia], but making clear that we want to maintain contact.'[35] The strongest reaction came from the Poles, who, after hesitating for 18 months whether to provide a forward base for America's National Missile Defense (NMD) system, now eagerly signed up.[36]

If the response was generally restrained, it was partly due to an uncomfortable awareness that Saakashvili, by his recklessness, bore much of the blame himself, and partly due to reservations about the wisdom of the decisions that had been made at Bucharest.

In any case, other, much more threatening problems were absorbing Western governments' attention. The collapse of the housing bubble in the United States, fuelled by risky bank lending – the so-called sub-prime mortgage crisis – was about to trigger what would become known as the Great Recession. In September, the US investment bank, Lehmann Brothers, failed. A cascade of even bigger failures was prevented only by huge taxpayer-funded bailouts. Between a fifth and a quarter of American household wealth was wiped out. Consumption fell precipitously, credit dried up and investment ground to a halt. The old adage, 'when America sneezes, Europe catches a cold', showed its truth yet again. But in the new, globalised world of the twenty-first century, it was not just Europe that suffered. Every country was affected.

Putin tried to see a positive side to the crisis. The problems in the United States, he said, were 'a further step towards strengthening a multipolar world'.[37] The American system had shown itself incapable of resolving the problems it created.[38] 'Faith in the United States as leader of the free world and the free market . . . has been undermined, I think forever,' he said, in an access of wishful thinking. 'It will never return to what it was before.'[39]

By October, the Russian stock market had fallen 75 per cent from its May highs and trading was suspended so frequently that Russians joked it was like a cuckoo clock.[40] The price of oil, which touched an all-time high of 129 US dollars a barrel for Urals crude in July, was down to 40 dollars a barrel nine months later, before recovering to 70 dollars by the end of 2009. Russia's 25 wealthiest men saw their assets slashed by 230 billion dollars over the course of a few months.[41] But, initially at least, ordinary people were not affected. Only one per cent of the population owned shares and one in three had no bank account. Russia had 600 billion dollars in foreign-exchange reserves, which supported the value of the rouble, and the Stabilisation Fund made up for the shortfall in budget revenue. Despite price hikes, growing arrears of unpaid wages and rising unemployment, protests remained limited. Memories of the 1990s, when shock therapy had caused much greater economic pain, were sufficiently recent for people to think twice before going out onto the streets and, in the second half of 2009, once oil prices had started to recover, the recession began to ease.

Nonetheless, it was a turning point. For the next decade or more, the Russian economy essentially stagnated. Putin's hopes of transitioning to a skills-based economic model, which he had unveiled with great fanfare during the 2008 election campaign, were quietly abandoned. Even in the best of circumstances, that would have been a stretch. He had proposed that by 2020, labour productivity would quadruple, Russia would become one of the top five nations in terms of GDP after the US, China, Japan and Germany, the middle class would make up 60 to 70 per cent of the population and average life expectancy – still only 68 years in 2008 – would increase to 75.[42] The last target was almost met: in 2020, Russian life expectancy reached 73 years, eight and a half years more than in the mid 1990s, though that was still not enough to arrest the country's long-term demographic decline. But the other goals were unattainable. By 2020, nominal GDP had fallen back to the level of 2007. Far from becoming one of the top five global economies, Russia slipped from tenth to eleventh place.

On November 4, 2008, when Barack Obama was elected President of the United States, there were mixed feelings in Moscow. On the one hand, it was a relief. The Republican candidate, John McCain, was a hawk who would have continued the policies of the Bush administration. The arrival of a new man in the White House was an opportunity for a new start. On the other hand, historically, the Kremlin had always found Republicans easier to deal with than Democrats, who tended to focus on human rights issues and were chary of bold initiatives lest they be accused of being soft on America's enemies.

The following day, in his annual address to the Federal Assembly, Medvedev staked out a conspicuously tough position towards the United States, as if to show the incoming administration that, notwithstanding his liberal reputation, he was not going to be a pushover.[43] America, through its hubris, Medvedev said, had encouraged Georgia's 'barbaric attack' on South Ossetia. Its arrogance had blinded it to the failings of its financial system, which had plunged the world into recession. Its decision to build a National Missile Defense system in the Czech Republic and Poland would compel Russia to deploy electronic jamming equipment and Iskander short-range ballistic missile batteries, capable of neutralising the US system, should that become necessary. They would be based in Kaliningrad, just across the Polish border.

Americans grumbled that the speech was bellicose. But it provided the basis for a quid pro quo, which Obama set out in a letter to Medvedev in mid February 2009. If Russia would help to ensure that Iran did not develop a nuclear weapons capability, he wrote, there would be no need for America to install a missile defence system in Eastern Europe and Russia would not then need to install a countervailing force in Kaliningrad. After much diplomatic jiggery-pokery, that was what eventually happened. NMD and the Russian response were both put on hold. Developments in North Korea, which had been part of the original justification for the US programme, were not mentioned any more. Even the Pentagon had recognised by then that touting a Europe-based defence system as protection against missiles from Pyongyang which, if they ever existed, would fly round the other side of the world, was not very convincing.

The only people who were unhappy were the Czechs and the Poles, who had gone out on a limb to back the American missile system in the belief that it would help protect them against Russian aggression. Now it turned out that they had irritated the Russians and got nothing in return.

There was movement in other areas, too. In a keynote speech at the Munich Security Conference, the same forum where, two years earlier, Putin had lambasted the Bush administration for trying to rule the world, Vice President Joe Biden promised to 'press the reset button' on the two countries' relations.[44] The metaphor did not work out quite as the Americans had hoped. When, in March, Hillary Clinton, whom Obama had named as his Secretary of State, met her Russian counterpart, Sergei Lavrov, in Geneva, she presented him with a small yellow box with a red button, marked 'RESET' in English and 'PEREGRUZKA' in Russian. Unfortunately, *peregruzka* meant not 'reset' but 'overload'.

The Russians laughed off the incident but they might have been forgiven for wondering why the world's pre-eminent power, when proposing a fresh beginning to their relationship, could not take the trouble to get a simple translation right. Was it a Freudian slip or casualness to the point of disrespect?

Nonetheless, when Medvedev met Obama for the first time at a G20 summit in London in April, the two men got on well. They agreed to press ahead with a new Strategic Arms Reduction Treaty to replace START II, which – still unratified by the US Congress – was due to expire in December. New START, as it was called, reduced the number of missile launchers that each side was allowed from 2,200, the figure agreed by Bush and Putin under the Strategic Offensive Reductions Treaty in 2002, to fewer than 1,500. It was signed by Obama and Medvedev in Prague in April 2010. Putin had first proposed a cap of 1,500 missiles more than eight years earlier, but the proposal had gone nowhere amid the rancour caused by the Bush administration's decision to abrogate the ABM Treaty.

The two countries cooperated in the UN Security Council to impose economic and military sanctions on Iran, leading, four years later, to the Joint Comprehensive Plan of Action (JCPOA), under which Tehran reluctantly agreed to dismantle much of its nuclear programme and allow international inspections. Previously Putin had argued that Iran had the same right as any other country to develop civil nuclear power. But as evidence accumulated that Tehran was evading its obligations under the non-proliferation accords, he took a harder line.[45] The final straw came when the Americans produced photographs of the then secret Iranian nuclear enrichment facility near Qom, of which the Russians had been unaware.[46]

Other issues which had caused ructions with the Bush administration were also quietly despatched.

Obama acknowledged that neither Georgia nor Ukraine would join NATO for the foreseeable future. Medvedev approved overflight rights for the US to supply its forces in Afghanistan. America, in turn, supported Russia's long-standing efforts to gain admission to the World Trade Organisation, which finally came to fruition, after 18 years of negotiations, in December 2011.

Obama saw Medvedev as 'a poster child for the new Russia, young, trim and clothed in hip, European-tailored suits'. The Russian President was affable, he wrote later, 'with a slightly formal, almost self-deprecating manner, more international management consultant than politician or party apparatchik'.[47] The two men had a lot in common. Both had studied and taught law, they were of similar age and both had young families.

But the question which bothered the White House and to which it struggled to find an answer in the first years of Obama's presidency was how much leeway Medvedev had to make policy on his own and to what extent he was constrained by the need to respect the views of his predecessor, now Prime Minister. In his memoir, *A Promised Land*, Obama depicted an administration torn between wanting to believe that Medvedev could put relations with America on a new footing and fearing that Putin would not allow him to do so. But that was with hindsight. Initially, wanting to believe predominated.

During his first visit to Moscow in July 2009, Obama met both men.[48] Spending the evening privately with Medvedev and his wife, Svetlana, at their residence at Gorki, he found himself discussing Silicon Valley and IT, which fascinated the Russian leader, the problems of being Head of State and bringing up teenage children, and politics hardly at all. It made him think that, but for the interpreters, they could be 'attending a dinner party in any well-to-do American suburb'. Next morning, when he met Putin, the atmosphere was very different. There was 'a casualness to his movements,' Obama wrote, 'a practiced disinterest in his voice, that indicated someone who'd grown used to power.' Putin subjected him to a 40-minute monologue, recapitulating all the grievances against America that Russia had accumulated over the previous eight years. The meeting ran on for two hours, twice as long as planned, but by the end of it Obama felt that the Russian leader was at least open to the reset effort, if not enthusiastic.

As he left, Putin noted that in future, the discussions would be with Medvedev. 'These are now his decisions,' he said. Obama said later that he had doubted that last statement. But, on the surface, that was how it appeared. Medvedev became Obama's sole interlocutor. Putin made clear that, as Prime Minister, he did not see it as his role to receive visiting heads of state. 'In the division of powers in Russia,' he said, 'the President has the last word, and the President today is Mr Medvedev.'[49] It was a matter of respect for the function.

Later that year, Obama told a reporter that he thought Medvedev was more 'forward-looking' than Putin.[50] Given the White House's uncertainty over where power really lay, that was probably unwise. But

Medvedev consistently showed himself more cooperative than the Americans had anticipated and they concluded that, as Obama wrote later, Medvedev was 'willing to stake his presidency on a closer relationship with the United States'.[51] Obama's advisers continued to puzzle over his ties with his predecessor, but the assumption was that he must be confident of Putin's support.[52]

There was plenty to puzzle over.

At one level, Putin seemed to be relieved to be spared the daily grind of the presidency. Officially his role as Prime Minister was to focus on the nuts and bolts of economic and social issues and they dominated his agenda. He attended endless meetings about the finer points of the high-school syllabus, the pricing of pharmaceutical products, maternity care in the provinces, the problems of company towns, where entire communities depended on a single employer, and much else of the same kind. During his annual phone-in, which he continued after leaving the Kremlin, the questions, more carefully vetted than ever, were all about housing, health care, education and farming – the issues covered by the so-called national projects, which he had launched midway through his second term – as well as the perennial subject of pensions.

There were advantages to Putin in no longer being on the front line. He could stand back and let his successor do the dirty work, confronting powerful interest groups and taking unpopular decisions. The generals, even if they knew that Putin was backing Anatoly Serdyukov's hated reforms, directed their anger at Medvedev. It was Medvedev who had to deal with the discontent of the middle classes, who could no longer afford to go on holiday each summer to disport themselves on Turkish beaches. It was Medvedev, too, who was charged with the messy business of replacing the 'barons', the old generation of regional leaders who had held sway ever since Yeltsin had told them to take 'as much sovereignty as you can swallow'.

Men like Mintimer Shaimiev in Tatarstan and Eduard Rossel in Sverdlovsk, who had been in office for nearly 20 years, agreed to go quietly. But some dug in their heels and had to be compelled to leave, which proved more difficult than the Kremlin had expected.

In theory, the new system of gubernatorial appointments, which Putin had introduced after Beslan in 2004, had put the regions firmly under Moscow's control. In practice, the newspaper, *Yezhednevny zhurnal*, stated, relations with the regions remained 'absolutely medieval'. The governors were vassals. 'They swear an oath of loyalty to the suzerain, and then they feel entitled to do whatever they want in their own territories. The illusion of presidential authority becomes obvious when the Kremlin tries to remove them from office and the vassals revolt.'[53]

The two principal hold-outs were Kirsan Ilyumzhinov, the President of Kalmykia, a Buddhist, largely agricultural region in southern Russia, populated by people of Mongol descent, and Yuri Luzhkov, the Mayor of Moscow.

Ilyumzhinov was an illuminé, who claimed to have been kidnapped by aliens and taken in their spaceship to visit another planet, and to be able to give his people subconscious instructions by creating an extra-sensory field around the republic. But he was an astute businessman as well as a gifted chess player, serving for 23 years as President of the International Chess Federation, FIDE. In the end, Medvedev managed to persuade him not to seek what would have been an unprecedented fifth term.

Luzhkov was another matter. He had irritated Putin for years, just as he had Yeltsin, but he was popular and it had always seemed more trouble than it was worth to make the effort to unseat him. However, by 2010, his approval rating was falling. Moscow was paralysed by traffic jams and Luzhkov was widely criticised for plans to demolish public housing along the Moscow River on what he claimed were environmental grounds. His wife, Yelena Baturina, had made a fortune from city construction contracts, becoming Russia's first and, for a long time, only female billionaire, and Luzhkov himself was reputed to have ties to organised crime.

The issue came to a head that summer, when Moscow was choked by smog from peat fires in the surrounding countryside.[54] In August, as the crisis was its height, Luzhkov went on holiday to the Austrian Alps and was in no hurry to return. Medvedev publicly reprimanded him and, shortly afterwards, suspended one of Luzhkov's pet projects, a highway through a protected forest north of the city which had become a cause célèbre for Russian environmental groups[55]. Luzhkov hit back, accusing unnamed figures in the Kremlin of trying to cause bad blood between himself and Putin.[56] That was the signal for a barrage of attacks against him by the three state television channels. Luzhkov insisted that he had no intention of resigning and returned to Austria to continue his vacation. But by then the die was cast.[57] When he came back at the end of September, Medvedev announced that he had been fired.

Putin publicly endorsed his dismissal. 'The Mayor's relations with the President did not work out,' he said. 'The Mayor is the President's subordinate, not the other way round, so steps had to be taken to resolve the situation.' But where Medvedev said simply that he had lost trust in Luzhkov, Putin spoke of him more flatteringly as 'a significant figure in modern Russia'.[58]

No one was quite sure what to make of that. Was there a split in the tandem? Had Luzhkov tried to drive a wedge between the duumvirs, as sources in the Kremlin charged? Was Medvedev, for the first time, striking out on his own? If so, what did that say about his prospects for staying on in 2012? Or was it simply, 'good cop, bad cop', with Putin, for once, in the 'good cop' role?

There was similar confusion when Medvedev announced that the constitution would be amended to extend the presidential term from four to six years. Putin had made clear on several occasions that he thought a four-year term was too short, so the change itself was not a surprise.[59] It would take effect after the next election. To some, that suggested that Putin planned to return as soon as Medvedev's four years were up. Others saw it as a signal that Medvedev might be given a second term.

Even more puzzling was Medvedev's decision in March 2011, to bar members of the government from serving as directors of state companies. Officially that was intended to improve the investment climate, but it was clear to everyone that the real target was Igor Sechin, who was forced to step down as Chairman of Rosneft.[60] The mutual antipathy between Sechin and Medvedev was not exactly a secret. What was intriguing was that Putin had raised no objection.

Was that, too, a portent? Or was Putin delivering a warning?

Sechin had an annoying tendency to freelance on his own account. Andrei Illarionov remembered an incident in 2005, when Putin had called a meeting to discuss plans to float part of Rosneft's shares on the New York Stock Exchange. Sechin had failed to mention that he intended to use a percentage of the proceeds, amounting to 1.5 billion

US dollars, for 'material incentives for the company's management', in other words, bonuses for top executives and board members, including himself. When Illarionov pointed out the discrepancy, 'Sechin turned crimson', he recalled. 'He jumped up from his seat like a schoolboy caught by the teacher . . . Putin exploded. Sechin was so frightened that he went rigid and couldn't get out a single word.'[61]

Putin had not forgotten that Sechin had joined Ustinov and Luzhkov to try to promote Fradkov as a possible successor. The dismissal, first of Ustinov in 2006, then of Fradkov a year later, had been shots across Sechin's bows. The firing of Luzhkov, with whom Sechin had had close relations, was another. His separation from Rosneft, his stronghold – and, what was worse, at the hands of his hated rival, Medvedev – was a still more serious blow. It was not that Putin intended to dispense with Sechin's services. He was already planning to have him leave the government the following spring and become Rosneft's CEO, a much more hands-on position than Chairman of the Board.[62] What mattered was to prevent him, or anyone else in the inner circle, becoming too powerful. With Medvedev as President, Putin could manoeuvre unobserved behind the scenes.

During the first years of 'tandemocracy', as Russian newspapers called the duumvirate's rule, Putin appeared to give Medvedev considerable latitude. Medvedev, in turn, was careful not to overstep the limits of what he thought Putin could accept.

Much of the head-scratching in the West about their relationship was because people were looking for conflicts which did not exist. It was assumed that the two men were constantly jockeying for position and that, sooner or later, Medvedev would try to push Putin aside. That was never the case. On matters of human rights and social and economic policy, there were important differences of style, but much less in terms of substance. Medvedev made a fetish of modernisation. He gave interviews to liberal newspapers which Putin would have disdained. But the media were, if anything, less free during his presidency than they had been under Putin,[63] and while there was much talk of innovation, of economic reform and of the struggle against corruption, it was no more than talk. In practice, little changed.

It was on Medvedev's watch that Bill Browder's lawyer, Sergei Magnitsky, was detained after he had named some of the senior officials implicated in the scam involving Browder's Hermitage Fund, in which 230 million US dollars had been embezzled through falsified tax- rebate claims. While Magnitsky was detained in Moscow's Butyrka prison, the investigators, acting on behalf of those he accused, tried to force him to recant. When he refused, he was repeatedly beaten and denied medical treatment, dying a painful death in November 2009, at the age of 37, from pancreatitis, untreated gallstones and other ailments. A post-mortem found extensive bruising caused by beatings with a blunt instrument. A number of prison officials were fired but the medical staff who refused to treat him were either not charged or acquitted. To add insult to injury, in 2012, shortly before Medvedev's term was due to end, the Kremlin approved a posthumous trial, the first in modern Russian history, at which, in a macabre twist, the dead man was convicted of tax evasion.

It was never formally established who, in the topmost reaches of the administration, had protected those involved in the scam, but suspicion fell on Putin himself and his immediate entourage. One of those implicated was Aleksei Anichin, the deputy Interior Minister in charge of the investigation, who had been Putin's classmate at the Leningrad Law Faculty.[64] Anichin was subsequently sanctioned by the United States for his role. But in Russia, above a certain level, impunity was absolute. The *Financial Times* wrote that the case typified 'the darker side of Putinism'.[65] That was an understatement.

It was during Medvedev's presidency, too, that fresh accusations – even more far-fetched than at their original trial – were made against Mikhail Khodorkovsky and his co-defendant, Platon Lebedev, who were about to become eligible for parole. They were now charged with stealing 350 million tons of oil, equivalent to the total production of Yukos from 1998 to 2003. When the case ended, in December 2010, both were sentenced to 14 years' imprisonment, to run concurrently with their earlier sentences. One of the judge's assistants confirmed afterwards that the verdict had been handed down by the political authorities.

In neither case did Medvedev attempt to intervene.

He had the right, as President, to pardon Khodorkovsky and Lebedev, whose imprisonment was a strong disincentive to Western investment in Russia. He did not. The trial had been stage-managed by

Sechin. Putin had commented, shortly before the verdict, 'I believe that a thief belongs in prison.'[66]

Nor did Medvedev press for exemplary punishment of those responsible for Magnitsky's death. It was not that he lacked the power to do so. It was not even that he was a prisoner of the machinery of state which Putin had constructed. It went much deeper. The banker, Mikhail Fridman, had spoken of a system 'built up over hundreds of years [and] lodged in the heads of the whole of society'. That system was not completely frozen. But the pace of change was glacial. To expect that Medvedev could suddenly transform it, as many liberally inclined Russians and the Obama administration hoped, was simply naïve.

Putin's role as Prime Minister did not mean that he kept a low profile. Although much of his time was spent on run-of-the-mill government business, he injected a sense of drama which caught the imagination of the Russian public.

At a meeting in Nizhny Novgorod in July 2008, three months after he became head of government, he accused Mechel, one of Russia's biggest mining and steel companies, of manipulating the price of coal in order to evade taxes. The CEO, Igor Zyuzin, a stubborn, reclusive man, had refused to attend on the pretext of an indisposition. 'I think he should get better as soon as possible,' Putin said menacingly, 'otherwise we will send him a doctor.' He would ask the Anti-Monopoly Commission and the Prosecutor's Office to provide a suitable physician.[67] Next day, Mechel's shares on the New York Stock Exchange lost 40 per cent of their value.[68] The company had been exporting coal at heavily discounted prices to a wholly owned Swiss subsidiary, which then sold it for six times more on the world market and banked the profits in a tax haven. The crackdown on Mechel marked the start of a drive against tax evasion by Russia's ultra-rich, which, in the midst of a recession, was a very popular move. It also provided an opportunity for well-informed members of Putin's entourage to make a killing buying Mechel shares at rock-bottom prices.[69]

The following year it was the turn of Oleg Deripaska, the head of the aluminium giant, Rusal, to be humiliated in front of the television cameras. Deripaska, who had married the daughter of Yeltsin's former Chief of Staff, Valentin Yumashev, was in good odour at the Kremlin.

But the recession had caused demand for non-ferrous metals to plummet and he had closed one of his plants at Pikalyvo, a small town in the Leningrad region. It was the only large employer in the area and the workforce had not been paid for months. In June 2009, several hundred laid-off workers blocked the main highway to Moscow, causing a traffic jam which stretched more than a hundred miles. Unless the government intervened, they said, they would block the railway too.[70]

Two days later, Putin helicoptered in to confront Deripaska and two of his colleagues. 'Why did you start running around like cockroaches the moment you heard I was coming,' he asked them angrily.[71] 'You have made thousands of people hostages to your ambition and incompetence and perhaps also to your greed.' He ordered Deripaska to restart production immediately and pay the workers what was owed. Then, pointing to a copy of an agreement they had drafted, he threw his pen across the table and told him to sign. As a further humiliation, once the magnate had complied, Putin snapped: 'Now give me back my pen.' Within hours, the accumulated back wages – the equivalent of 1.5 million US dollars – were transferred to the workers' accounts, and Russian television showed long lines of people waiting to withdraw money from cashpoints.

It would later be claimed that the whole thing had been staged.

On Putin's side, it was. The display of prime ministerial wrath was to show Russians that Putin was there to defend them against predatory tycoons and, as Putin himself later acknowledged, 'to send a message to leaders at all levels . . . that they would be held accountable for developments in their areas'.[72] It was also, as both Russian and Western commentators noted at the time, not something which Dmitry Medvedev would have been able to do.

On Deripaska's side, it was not staged at all. Douglas Lund, a veteran British civil engineer who headed the magnate's construction division, watched the sweat running down his face as Putin gave him a tongue-lashing. 'I had never seen Oleg like that,' he said. 'He was belittled, made to feel like he wanted to crawl under a rock. Oleg's face and the faces of the people around him said it all. It was like a mass execution. It was the first time I had been close enough to see Putin in action and see what he was prepared to do.'[73]

Alongside these moments of political drama, a steady stream of tabloid-fodder events, carefully crafted by Putin's advisers, kept him firmly in the public eye.

He was filmed in a camouflage outfit and desert boots, firing a tranquilliser dart at an Amur tiger in Siberia, so that it could be fitted with a satellite transmitter as part of a research programme.[74] The Russian television crew embellished the story by claiming that the animal was about to attack when Putin anaesthetised it.[75] The tale of his heroics was somewhat spoiled when it emerged that the unfortunate beast was not a wild tiger at all but had been brought to the forest from a zoo, heavily sedated, for the sequence to be filmed. Afterwards Russians were invited to follow the animal's progress on the Prime Minister's website, but that, too, turned out to be fake. The tiger in the forest had different markings from the one to which Putin had fitted the satellite collar.[76] Something similar happened when he was filmed recovering two ancient Greek amphora fragments from the bed of the Black Sea. It was later admitted that local archaeologists had put them there in advance.[77]

The liberal intelligentsia sniggered. But it did no harm to Putin's image with the Russian man or woman in the street.

Nor did the other publicity stunts he engaged in. On his birthday in 2008, he was presented with a tiger cub.[78] After that came photo-shoots showing him bare-chested on horseback in Siberia and doing the butterfly, the most aggressive of swimming strokes, in an icy river.[79] In 2010, he co-piloted a firefighting plane combating the peat fires around Moscow. He went one mile down in a bathyscaphe to the floor of Lake Baikal, took a skin sample from a grey whale in Kamchatka using a specially equipped crossbow and presided over a festival of rap and break-dance.[80] He was filmed with members of the Night Wolves, a nationalistic Moscow motorcycle club modelled on the Hells Angels, wearing dark glasses and black leather like a diminutive Arnold Schwarzenegger in a scene from a Russian *Terminator* movie.[81] At a star-studded charity concert in St Petersburg, attended by hundreds of Western celebrities, including Sharon Stone, Ornella Muti, Alain Delon and Gérard Depardieu, he performed the song, 'Blueberry Hill', to raise money for cancer treatment – though not without breathing an audible sigh of relief after managing to play the piano introduction.

In that case, too, there was an unfortunate scandal afterwards, for

part of the funds that were supposed to have been raised to treat seriously ill children mysteriously disappeared.[82]

The anti-Kremlin media had a field day. One popular website
commented: 'The police are hated by the people, corruption is omni-
present, the economy is backward, one third of the housing stock is in
ruins, one third of the population has taken to drink, . . . while the top
man is catching tigers, kissing a fish to which he has taken a fancy, diving to the bottom of Lake Baikal, inviting pop stars to have fun and
relaxing with a friend . . . And all this rubbish is shown endlessly on
television!'[83]

It was true but it was not the point.

For Putin, it was a way to remain relevant. To the great mass of Russians in provincial towns and rural villages, he was there every night on
the TV screen, doing something inspiring or intriguing or simply
different – a presence, as one commentator wrote, more familiar than
their own parents.[84] Whether Putin intended Medvedev to have a second term or to return to the presidency himself, one thing was clear:
he was not contemplating early retirement.

Although foreign policy was Medvedev's responsibility Putin was in
charge of relations with the Near Abroad, particularly Georgia and
Ukraine, and anything touching on oil and gas exports.

When yet another gas dispute blew up with Ukraine in the closing
months of 2008, it was Putin who negotiated a settlement with his
counterpart from Kyiv, Yulia Tymoshenko. The political situation in
Ukraine had changed dramatically since the previous gas crisis two
years earlier. Tymoshenko was back in Yushchenko's government as
Prime Minister but their relations had again deteriorated and by September 2008, she had forged a tactical alliance with her pro-Russian
opponent, Viktor Yanukovych. The gas issue became embroiled in
Ukrainian domestic politics and, on New Year's Day, 2009, Russia
turned off the supply, not only to Ukraine but also to the rest of
Europe. After two weeks of inconclusive discussions, Tymoshenko
and Putin held a late-night meeting in Moscow which became famous
not for the resulting accord but for the little black dress the Ukrainian
Premier wore, which, as one Ukrainian commentator delicately put it,
merited a place in the Museum of Ukrainian Diplomacy.[85] The Russian
media, less given to subtlety, guffawed that it had a zip all the way

down the back, which meant it was 'able to be removed in a single movement'.[86]

The substance of the agreement was that the gas price would rise incrementally over the next ten years to reach European prices. No less important, Gazprom would deal directly with the Ukrainian state gas company, cutting out RosUkrEnergo, a dubious Swiss-registered intermediary, allegedly controlled by Semyon Mogilevich, a mafia kingpin with high-level protection in Moscow. RosUkrEnergo had taken a substantial commission which had been used to finance Yushchenko's election campaigns and also reportedly served as a source of funding managed by Putin's friends, the Rotenberg brothers.[87]

The gas flow was restored on January 20. This time the Europeans grumbled less about the dangers of energy dependence on Russia. Ukraine had clearly broken its earlier agreement with Moscow and it was difficult to see what else the Russians could have done.

Putin hoped that the gas agreement would lay the groundwork for a permanent alliance between Tymoshenko and Yanukovych, but that did not happen. Yanukovych, who had once said of his putative partner, 'she's so vile, I don't think I could fuck her even if I wanted to,' decided that he stood a better chance of regaining power without her. He was right. In February 2010, thanks to massive vote-rigging, he won back from Yushchenko the presidency which he had lost during the Orange Revolution in 2004. Tymoshenko went into opposition and, after a series of politically motivated court cases, was convicted of abuse of power – ironically, in connection with the gas deal which she had signed with Putin – and sentenced to seven years' imprisonment. She was later amnestied, but her political career never recovered.

In relations with the West, formally at least, Medvedev was in the driving seat.

But uncertainty continued over how much authority he really possessed. Tarja Halonen, the Finnish President, remembered meeting him to discuss efforts by the Baltic countries to reduce marine pollution. Medvedev had been 'very, very positive', she said, but even on such an anodyne subject as that, 'he could not commit himself without agreement from Putin'. Watching Medvedev and Obama at the UN General Assembly in September 2009, she had noticed how similar their body language was. 'Medvedev could work with Obama,' she said, 'but he hadn't enough power. So that made it more difficult.'[88]

It took time for the US administration to realise that its assumption that Medvedev and Putin were essentially on the same wavelength on foreign policy issues was not necessarily correct. 'What became clear, but wasn't clear to us initially,' Obama's Deputy National Security Adviser, Ben Rhodes, said later, 'was that Medvedev was pushing out in front of Putin and trying to create his own political identity as some-one who could work with the West.'[89] The problem was that neither the Americans nor Medvedev himself could be sure how far he could push before he exceeded the limits which Putin would accept. Ideally, Rhodes acknowledged, the White House should have tried harder to keep lines to Putin open, but in practice that was all but impossible because of the Prime Minister's insistence that, in matters of US–Russian relations, Medvedev was in charge.

It did not help that some of Obama's key foreign policy appointments rubbed the Russians up the wrong way.

Hillary Clinton, who had become Secretary of State, was a Russia hawk and surrounded herself with people who held similar views. During the primary campaign, she had asserted that, since Putin had been a KGB agent, 'by definition he does not have a soul'.[90] It was a riff on Bush's statement at Ljubljana that he had looked into Putin's eyes and 'got a sense of his soul'. Putin had taken note. 'I think, as a mini-mum,' he said acidly, 'a state official needs to have a head.'[91]

Clinton's distrust of Russia, which she wore as a badge of honour, was not the best basis on which to seek a fresh beginning.

She met Putin for formal talks while she was Secretary of State only once, in March 2010, at Novo-Ogaryovo. By her own account, it did not start well.[92] The main issue was relations with Iran.[93] Putin gave a pro forma defence of Russia's position, as he had done many times before, but he was clearly bored. To change the subject, she asked him about his conservation efforts for Siberian tigers. His demeanour changed instantly, she wrote, and he got up and took her down a long corridor and through an armoured door to his private office, where he launched into an animated discussion – in English, which he never normally spoke during negotiations with foreign visitors – about tigers and polar bears and other endangered species. He was going to Franz Josef Land in the Russian Arctic later that spring to tag polar bears, he said. Would her husband like to come with him?

It could have been an opening. She did not follow up. For whatever reason, an opportunity to break the ice had been missed.[94]

The replacement of the US Ambassador, John Beyrle, by Clinton's adviser, Michael McFaul, was another badly thought-out move. Beyrle's father, Joseph, had parachuted into France during the Normandy landings, been captured by the Germans and sent to a prison camp in the East, from which he escaped and joined a Soviet tank regiment, becoming, it was said, the only American to serve both with US forces and the Red Army during World War II. In Russia, where the war is seen as the defining moment of the country's modern history, such things have immense importance. Ambassador Beyrle had the respect of the Kremlin not merely because of his position but because of his family history. McFaul was an academic who described himself as a 'specialist in democracy, movements against dictatorship and revolutions', an ardent supporter of the Orange Revolution in Ukraine and a severe critic of Putin and his regime.[95] To Moscow, it was the kind of appointment that a foreign government would make if it wished to implement a strategy of tension. It had apparently never occurred to anyone in the White House that Putin might not take kindly to the nomination of someone with McFaul's views and antecedents.[96]

Whether it would have made any difference if Beyrle had stayed on or if Hillary Clinton had been more empathetic to Russian concerns is another matter. Personal chemistry is important and its absence can be a drawback. But it does not change underlying realities.

Two years before Medvedev's election, in a supposedly off-the-record conversation with a group of German journalists, Putin had acknowledged that it was 'theoretically possible' for him to 'take a break for a certain length of time' and return to the presidency afterwards.[97] At the time, it was assumed that he wanted to maintain the suspense about his future intentions. But Putin did not make such statements lightly. By the beginning of 2011, the question of whether or not Medvedev would stand for a second term was becoming more urgent.

No one, apart from the two men themselves, knew exactly what they had agreed when Putin had proposed four years earlier that

Medvedev stand for the presidency. However, it appeared that what was to follow had been left deliberately vague. It would have made no sense for Putin to commit himself one way or the other until he saw how Medvedev performed. Part of the point of the exercise was to find out whether the younger man was a possible long-term successor. Putin had no desire to stay in power for life, as was the case of some of his fellow leaders in Central Asia, and given the nature of the system he presided over, the succession was a matter of vital concern.[98]

Sometime in 2010, around the midpoint of his presidency, Medvedev started to believe that Putin was open to the idea of him standing for a second term. The spin doctor, Gleb Pavlovsky, thought the same. So did Vladislav Surkov, the Kremlin ideologist, who started looking for ways to build up Medvedev's political support. When Medvedev met Obama in Prague in April that year and later, when he came to the United States in the summer to visit Silicon Valley and to sample, with his host, the delights of American cuisine at Ray's Hell Burger in Arlington, the Americans also had the impression that he was beginning to see himself as a statesman in his own right.[99] CIA analysts concluded that he was 'making a play to stay on'.[100]

But then Medvedev began pushing a little bit too hard.

In February 2011, Pavlovsky launched a trial balloon, predicting in an interview that Medvedev, with Putin's acquiescence, would stand again in 2012. Shortly afterwards, Medvedev gave a speech in St Petersburg to mark the 150th anniversary of the abolition of serfdom. Ostensibly about Russian history, it was widely viewed as a coded appeal to Russian liberals. 'Freedom cannot be postponed,' Medvedev said. 'The nation . . . cannot be kept together by tightened screws . . . Excessively harsh policies [lead] not to the elimination of corruption but to its growth, not to the evolution of governance but to its degradation.'[101] The idea that Russia should follow some kind of special way was a fantasy, he said. Russia should look to the example of the Tsar Liberator, Aleksandr II, who had freed the serfs and sought to install 'a normal, humane order', not 'Nicholas I or Stalin' – a line which many in the audience took to refer to Putin.[102]

Medvedev presumably thought the historical allusion sufficiently obscure for Putin to let it pass. But he was venturing onto dangerous ground. Moreover, he had recently lost an important source of insights into the way Putin's mind was working. The Prime Minister's Chief of Staff, Sergei Sobyanin, had left to replace Yuri Luzhkov as Mayor of Moscow and his own chief aide, Sergei Naryshkin, was barely on speaking terms with Sobyanin's successor. High-level communication between the Presidential Administration and the Prime Minister's office had broken down. [103]

Whether for that reason or because Medvedev had grown overconfident, in March he committed a fatal error.

That winter a wave of unrest had swept across the Arab world. It had started in Tunisia, where the death of a fruit-seller, who set himself on fire after a municipal inspector had confiscated his wares, triggered protests which, a month later, brought down the corrupt regime of President Ben Ali. Shortly afterwards, the Egyptian President, Hosni Mubarak, was deposed. Then the protests spread to Libya and, a month later, to Syria. In each country, there were specific causes, but economic inequalities, exacerbated by the global recession, and the corruption of the ruling elites, formed a common thread. The overthrow of Saddam Hussein, four years earlier, had proved to the Arab street that it was possible to bring down a seemingly immovable tyrant, and the spread of social networks, which the authorities were unable to control, gave the opposition a way to organise.

The West hailed the Arab Spring as a movement bringing democracy to the region. Putin saw it differently. He agreed that the ousted leaders had brought their troubles on themselves by refusing to recognise the need for change. But no one could foresee what the results of the upheaval would be.[104] 'One cannot simply transfer a familiar template to other regions of the world. We need to let other peoples determine their fate and their future in their own way,' he said.[105] After Egypt and Tunisia, the Libyan regime was now teetering. If Colonel Gaddafi were overthrown, Putin warned, it might have 'negative consequences for . . . Europe'[106] – cautionary words which European leaders preferred to forget when Libya became a failed state and 650,000 economic migrants from sub-Saharan Africa poured across its borders to be trafficked by smugglers to Italy.

Medvedev shared Putin's pessimism. If the North African states disintegrated, he thought, fanatics might come to power, bringing further conflagrations and the rise of extremism.[107]

In Europe, however, pressure for intervention in Libya mounted.

Public opinion was outraged by television coverage of civilians being slaughtered as Gaddafi's forces, backed by mercenaries, fired indiscriminately at unarmed protesters. France urged the imposition of a no-fly zone. Obama was reluctant to see America become involved in yet another Middle Eastern conflict when it was still looking for a way out of Iraq and Afghanistan. But in the end, he agreed that the US Air Force would neutralise Gaddafi's air defences, so long as the Europeans then took the lead. On March 17, 2011, the UN Security Council voted not only to impose a no-fly zone but 'to take all necessary measures . . . to protect civilians and civilian populated areas under threat of attack'. Russia, China, Brazil, Germany and India abstained. Lavrov had urged Medvedev to veto the resolution, but the Americans had persuaded him that intervention was necessary because a long civil war in Libya might turn it into a base for international terrorism.[108]

Two days later, a coalition of Western countries, led by Britain, France and Italy, joined by Qatar and, later, Turkey, with air support from the United States, launched sustained attacks on Libyan government military formations.

It became clear almost at once that it was not an operation to restore peace or even to protect the civilian population, but a coordinated attack led by NATO to overthrow Gaddafi's regime, little different from George W. Bush's invasion of Iraq, but this time with UN cover. Obama acknowledged later that he had had grave reservations. 'Why Libya and not the Congo, for example, where a series of civil conflicts had resulted in millions of civilian deaths?' he asked.[109] He left the question unanswered. Libya was a small, oil-rich Arab state, strategically placed across the Mediterranean from Southern Europe. The Congo was neither oil rich nor strategically located. As in most wars of choice, the moral justification for intervention cloaked a decision taken for political reasons.

Putin, who was visiting the Soviet Far East when the assault began, was furious with Medvedev for not using Russia's veto. The UN resolution, he said, was 'defective and flawed . . . It allows them to do what they like, to undertake any manner of actions against a sovereign state. It reminds me of a medieval crusade.' The West used force in international affairs with no thought for the consequences. America had done so in the Balkans, in Afghanistan, in Iraq, 'and now it's Libya's turn'.[110]

He was careful to add that he was merely giving his 'personal opinion', leaving the door open for Medvedev to accuse NATO of having gone beyond its UN mandate, as was indeed the case. Instead the President dug himself deeper into the hole he had made for himself. He had personally ordered the Foreign Ministry not to veto the resolution, he said. 'It is entirely unacceptable,' he went on, 'to use expressions which indicate a clash of civilisations. The word, "crusade", for instance. We must all remember that such language could make the situation even worse.'[111]

It was a direct rebuttal of everything Putin had said.

The state-owned television channels, which had been prominently featuring Putin's remarks, were at a loss to know what to do. It had never happened before that the President and the Prime Minister had directly contradicted each other. Eventually word came from Putin's aides that, since the President was responsible for foreign affairs, 'Prime Minister Putin's statement should be forgotten'.[112] That evening, only Medvedev's comment was broadcast.

It looked as though he had come out on top. In fact, he had committed political suicide.

Had Medvedev dissociated himself from the decision to abstain, Putin might conceivably have pardoned his misjudgement. Doubling down on it sealed his fate. Nothing more was said publicly, but in private, Putin was quoted as saying: 'Don't worry . . . Come September, we'll do what we have to do and everyone will breathe a sigh of relief.'[113]

Even without the Libyan imbroglio, Putin would have had reservations about Medvedev staying on for a second term. He was bright, modern, loyal – all the things that Obama saw in him. But he lacked gravitas. The US Ambassador, John Beyrle, described him in a cable to the State Department as 'Robin to Putin's Batman'.[114] A commentator on *Ekho Moskvy* mocked him as 'just an adjective that goes with the noun, Putin'.[115] Medvedev was blamed for being soft on terror[116] after bomb attacks in Moscow and St Petersburg killed more than a hundred people and injured several hundred more. During Putin's second term, there had been no large-scale attacks. The *siloviki* detested Medvedev's liberal, market-oriented policies. Apart from Pavlovsky, Surkov, the former head of the Presidential Administration, Aleksandr Voloshin, and a small coterie of like-minded officials, he had little personal support among the elite. Despite having all the resources of the Kremlin behind him, their attempts to build a new party to serve as his support base had come to nothing.[117]

Medvedev was President because Putin wished him to be. Without Putin's backing, he would be President no more.

In August, the two men went fishing together for three days on the River Volga near Astrakhan. There Putin informed him that he had decided to stand for election as President in the spring. To soften the blow and to ensure that Medvedev's fealty did not waver, he proposed that they exchange places and the younger man take over as Prime Minister.[118] They emerged before the cameras looking relaxed and apparently in good spirits. Russian commentators concluded, a little too quickly, that the conflict between them over Libya had been laid to rest.

A few days later, that country's capital, Tripoli, fell to anti-government forces after an uprising coordinated with NATO airstrikes. Gaddafi escaped and made his way to his hometown of Sirte, 230 miles to the East, on the Mediterranean coast. In October, Sirte, too, was overrun. As the Libyan leader fled, his convoy was attacked by NATO aircraft and he and a few bodyguards took refuge in a culvert. There, the insurgents found him, bleeding and dazed. Videos, which Gaddafi's captors took on their cell phones and posted on the internet, showed him being beaten violently and sodomised with a bayonet before being stripped naked and killed.

Putin declared himself revolted. First Saddam Hussein had been condemned to an ignominious death after the Americans delivered him to his enemies in Iraq. Then, the moment it served their interests, they had abandoned their long-time ally, the Egyptian leader, Hosni Mubarak. Now Gaddafi, who had been Putin's guest in the Kremlin, had been murdered by American-backed forces.

Western intelligence officials alleged afterwards that Putin had watched the images of Gaddafi's death not once but several times and kept a copy of the video in his office as a reminder of the Libyan leader's fate.[119] That appears implausible. But it fed into a narrative, widely accepted in the West, that Putin was terrified that something similar might one day happen to him. In fact, his outrage, while real, had a different purpose. He emphasised Gaddafi's sordid end – 'horrible and repulsive scenes of [his] murder, with footage of his bloody body broadcast all over the world' – in order to pin the responsibility more firmly on the United States, whose special forces, he claimed – falsely – had been present at his death.[120]

The United States had shown itself once again – at least in Putin's mind – to be ruthless and untrustworthy. To justify invading Iraq, a Republican administration under George W. Bush had promoted a fabricated story about non-existent weapons of mass destruction. To justify overthrowing Gaddafi, a Democratic administration headed by Barack Obama had misled the United Nations by concocting a story about protecting Libyan civilians. There would be consequences.

On September 23, 2011, 10,000 delegates from United Russia, now the undisputed, but increasingly unpopular, ruling party, gathered in Gostiny Dvor, a vast, nineteenth-century covered market behind the Kremlin which had been transformed into an exhibition centre, to choose their candidates for the Duma elections in December. Putin, as party leader, proposed that Medvedev head the party list, as he himself had done four years earlier.

That should have given a clue of what was about to unfold. When Putin had agreed to head the party list in 2008, it was because he was about to leave the presidency. But no one grasped the significance until Medvedev, in his acceptance speech, mentioned, almost in passing, that if he was going to concentrate on party affairs, it was only right that Putin should return to the presidency. After several minutes of thunderous applause from the massed ranks of party faithful, he went on:

> Sometimes people would ask Vladimir Putin and me: 'Have you been quarrelling with each other?' I want to confirm [that] what we are suggesting to the Congress is a carefully thought-out decision . . . We actually discussed this scenario back at the time when we first decided to form [the tandem] . . . We waited a long time to reveal [this] publicly . . . I hope that you and all our citizens will understand that this was a matter of political expediency.[121]

Putin then took the stage to announce that, if elected, he would ask Medvedev to serve as his Prime Minister, an alternation of roles which Russians call *rokirovka* or 'castling', after a chess manoeuvre in which the king and a rook are moved at the same time.

Up to the last moment, no one had been sure of Putin's intentions.

Some prominent liberals had concluded even before the announcement that Medvedev was a broken reed. Earlier that month, Vladimir

Ryzhkov, a leader of what was termed the 'non-system opposition' – the small grassroots democratic parties excluded from parliament – had complained that those who continued to believe in Medvedev's promises of reform were 'first-class fools'. Medvedev was Putin's 'useful idiot,' he said, 'a loyal subordinate and junior partner, [providing] a false ray of hope'. [122] But now that the exchange of roles was official, those who had trusted Medvedev were infuriated by his assertion that he and Putin had been in agreement all along that he would serve only one term. Putin had insisted that Medvedev say it to reassure the party faithful that the leadership was united. But it was also a not-so-subtle way of putting the younger man in his place, of showing that, in the final analysis, he was just a puppet. Medvedev was paying the price for having dared to go beyond what his patron was prepared to accept. He sat glumly, listening to Putin's closing address, humiliation written all over his face.

The unintended consequence was that all those who had hoped for a more liberal, democratic Russia felt profoundly cheated. If Putin and Medvedev had been planning to swap places all along, what was the election for? The whole thing was a charade.

Four years earlier, that might not have mattered. Most people then got their news from television and all the main TV channels were firmly under the Kremlin's control. Putin had co-opted the mainstream opposition, the Communists and Vladimir Zhirinovsky's nationalists, who understood that it was in their interests to act as though the elections were real. The liberal parties formed in the 1990s, Yabloko and the Union of Right Forces (subsequently 'Right Cause'), were a spent force. Their successors, Drugaya Rossiya ('The Other Russia') and Solidarnost, headed by Boris Nemtsov and the former world chess champion, Garry Kasparov, had been marginalised. Political technology, as it was euphemistically called, and the use of 'administrative resources', had taken care of the rest.

In 2011, the situation was very different.

The internet had taken off. Russia had 51 million users, more than any other European country. A quarter of them, mainly professional people and students, got most of their news online.[123] Unlike China, Russia had no 'Great Firewall'. What was on the internet was beyond the government's control. This was a conscious decision on Putin's part. Like the freedom allowed to Russian newspapers and privately owned radio stations, it was thought to be a necessary safety valve. Chinese-style censorship would be 'technologically difficult and wrong politically', he said.[124] But the result was that the social media networks, which had had little influence a few years earlier, now gave the regime's critics a means of organising that the Kremlin had not had to deal with before.

A little-known anti-corruption activist called Aleksei Navalny started to make a name for himself with a blog denouncing United Russia as 'the party of crooks and thieves'.[125] He posted photographs of the palatial residence being built for Putin at Gelendzhik and details of the excesses of other members of the political elite. The government had failed to tackle corruption during Putin's first two terms, he said, and it had not done so under Medvedev either.

So long as the economy was growing, the young professionals, who had seen their lives transformed under Putin's stewardship, were ready to close their eyes to the failings of the regime. After the 2008 financial crisis, that was no longer the case. The influential weekly, *Argumenty i Fakty*, had warned, years earlier, that 'the bar of public expectations has risen.'[126] The nascent middle classes, especially in Moscow and St Petersburg, wanted to see the country become a modern, democratic state, where people's rights were protected and the rule of law applied.

Opinion surveys indicated that United Russia would have difficulty getting 50 per cent of the vote. Putin's personal popularity was sharply lower at 61 per cent, down from 80 per cent, 18 months earlier.[127] For the first time ever, he was jeered in public when he attended a Mixed Martial Arts contest in Moscow.[128] At a concert in Siberia, a popular rock group was booed after it was announced that United Russia was sponsoring their performance.[129]

In this febrile atmosphere, Russians went to the polls on December 4.

United Russia won 49.3 per cent, which gave it a narrow majority in the 450-seat chamber. However, turnout was down and the party's 238 seats were 77 fewer than in the outgoing assembly. Just Russia, the centre-left pro-Kremlin party; the Communists; and Zhirinovsky's nationalists all improved their scores. As always, there was widespread ballot-stuffing and fraud. But whereas, in previous elections, that would not have affected the final result, this time the margin was close enough that, had it been a clean contest, United Russia would likely have lost its majority. It would still have had a plurality and, with Just

Russia, would have had more than enough deputies to support the government's policies. Nevertheless, the results were a warning. The middle class had become disenchanted. Reciting the same old mantras of modernisation and reform while failing to put them into practice did not work any more.

Protests began even before the outcome was officially announced.

On Monday, December 5, Navalny called on his supporters to come out onto the streets and voice their disgust. That night in Moscow, 5,000 people did so.[130] It was another first. Where previous protests had been directed against unpopular measures like changes in the system of social benefits or factory closures and layoffs, this time the target was Putin himself.

Navalny was hauled away by the police and sentenced to 15 days' imprisonment for having allegedly resisted arrest. But the movement he had launched grew stronger. The elections were widely seen as fraudulent and the level of public dissatisfaction was to match. For the first time since Putin had come to power, a leader had emerged in Russia who was able to channel that anger into defiance of his regime.

Navalny was 35 years old, a tall, slim man with Nordic good looks – dark hair and piercing blue eyes – who embraced controversy, had a knack of skewering the elite with pungent phrases that lodged in people's minds, and was refreshingly direct. He was not a saint. Four years earlier, he had been expelled from the liberal party, Yabloko, for what was euphemistically described as 'nationalist activity', after he had issued a video describing immigrants as 'cockroaches' infesting Russia and urging that they be shot.[131] Later he had distanced himself from the far right and built up a strong online following.

Five days after the first demonstration, some 30,000 people – twice that number by an unofficial count – gathered in Bolotnaya Square, on the south bank of the Moscow River, opposite the Kremlin, to call for fresh elections; the resignation of Vladimir Churov, Putin's one-time desk officer at the Mayor's Office in St Petersburg, who now headed the Election Commission; and new laws to stop the authorities barring opposition candidates from standing.

It was the biggest protest Moscow had seen since at least the mid 1990s.

Two weeks later, an even larger crowd, perhaps as many as 80,000 people, braved temperatures well below freezing to attend a rally on

Andrei Sakharov Prospekt, a few blocks north of the Lubyanka. The list of speakers was a roll call of everyone, from the left and the right, who had ever had reason to oppose the regime. They included prominent liberals, including Grigory Yavlinsky and Boris Nemtsov; the far-left National Bolshevik leader, Eduard Limonov; the Eurasianist philosopher, Aleksandr Dugin; the former Prime Minister, Mikhail Kasyanov; musicians, rappers, writers and actors; and Anatoly Sobchak's daughter, Kseniya, who had become a vampy, young television star, the 'it girl' of the political elite.

Putin's long-standing colleague, the former Finance Minister, Aleksei Kudrin, who was greeted with a mixture of boos and cheers, told the protesters that he supported many of their demands. Mikhail Gorbachev sent a message of support and called on Putin to resign.

But it was Navalny, released from prison three days before the second rally, who electrified the crowd. The leaders hiding in the Kremlin were not the 'big scary beasts' that they pretended to be, he said to thunderous roars of applause. 'They are sneaky little jackals.'[132]

Many of those who took part, then and in the succeeding weeks, were well dressed, obviously well off and had clearly never participated in a demonstration in their lives before. When one left-wing speaker insisted that it was not a middle-class revolt, proclaiming, 'we are not revolutionaries in mink coats', a middle-aged woman in the crowd, swathed in mink, shouted back: 'Well I am!'[133] The atmosphere was *bon enfant*. But there was an undercurrent of rage. 'We have been living like rats and toads, like mute cattle,' one speaker said.[134] Banners proclaimed: 'Putin is a thief'.[135] His announcement that he was returning to power was perceived as a humiliation, a way of telling people that their choices counted for nothing and that everything would be decided for them by the ruling elite.

It was a situation which Putin had not encountered before. The very people who had benefitted most from his regime – the up-and-coming middle classes who lived so much better than their parents could have dreamed of, who dressed like their peers in Western Europe, who bought their groceries in supermarkets no different from those in London or Paris and went on holiday to Turkey or Cyprus – these were the people who had now turned against him. And not only in Moscow: tens of thousands turned out for protest rallies in St Petersburg, Yekaterinburg, Novosibirsk, Rostov-na-Donu and other large provincial cities. As Kudrin noted, these were people who valued stability and had a lot to lose. But the way the Kremlin had played fast and loose with the rules, falsifying the elections, was more than they were prepared to accept.[136]

Putin was uncertain how to react, and it showed.

His first instinct was to sneer, just as he had sneered that the murdered Anatoly Litvinenko was 'unfortunately' not Lazarus and that Anna Politkovskaya had had virtually no influence in Russia until she was killed. The white ribbons which the protesters wore looked like condoms, he said. The students who took part had been paid to attend. The organisers were trying to destabilise Russia, in the same way that the Orange Revolution had destabilised Ukraine.[137] He gave the impression of flailing about, trying to find a convincing explanation for something that had not been supposed to happen. But at another level he evidently recognised that he had to reach out to the protesters. He was still far and away the most popular leader in Russia and the demonstrators were a tiny minority, less than one per cent of the population as a whole. However, they were an important part, they had numerous sympathisers and there was a danger that the unrest could spread. By 2011, one in four Russians identified themselves as middle class.

Accordingly, in his annual phone-in the following week, he went out of his way to sound conciliatory, insisting that people had the right to speak out, 'so long as they abide by the law'. Many of the young protesters, he said, had made their case 'in a clear and lucid manner . . . If this is the result of "Putin's rule", it's all to the good . . . I'm truly pleased that we have such people in our country now.' Discontent was normal, he added, especially at a time of economic recession.[138]

As Putin struggled to find the right note, Hillary Clinton inadvertently threw him a lifeline. The United States had 'serious concerns' about the conduct of the Duma elections, she told an OSCE conference in Vilnius, and she wanted 'a full investigation of electoral fraud and manipulation'.[139] It was the cue for Putin to claim that the demonstrations were being fomented by the Americans. 'The first thing the Secretary of State did was to say that the elections were not honest and fair,' he charged. 'She sent a signal to some of the militants in our country, and as soon as they heard it, they started active work with the support of the State Department.'[140]

He had hinted at Western meddling in Duma elections before[141] but this time he was much blunter. 'When foreign money is brought in to influence political activities inside our country, that makes us think,' he said, 'and when it is poured in to affect our electoral processes, it is particularly unacceptable.'[142]

The accusation was false, no more true than his claims, years earlier, that the rebellion in Chechnya was all the work of al-Qaeda. But it allowed him to reconcile conflicting imperatives: to express understanding for the protesters while suggesting that, without their realising it, they were being manipulated by cynical puppet-masters overseas. It did not cut much ice with the demonstrators, who asked mischievously when they were going to see the colour of Hillary's money. But for Putin's supporters in the provinces, it apparently made sense. Some such explanation had become necessary because, after an initial blackout, Putin had authorised the national TV channels to broadcast reports of the protests lest the government give the impression that it was running scared. Demonstrators were shown holding banners saying, 'Putin must go' and 'Churov must stand trial'. NTV, the boldest channel, repeated Navalny's description of United Russia as 'the party of crooks and thieves' and openly suggested that the elections had been rigged.[143] For most people in the countryside and in small towns, the pictures had come as a shock. If the deceitful Americans were behind it all, it became more understandable.

Putin had not enjoyed having to make concessions to the protesters and he tried as much as possible to shift the responsibility onto Medvedev. When the first demonstrations occurred, he had not been consulted, he said. He had been out with friends, 'trying to learn to play ice-hockey'. Indeed, he had 'not been in the Kremlin for quite a while'.[144]

However disagreeable he found it, the tactic worked. There was one more big protest meeting in Moscow in February 2012. Then the young middle-class professionals who had been the core of the movement began to drift away, yielding place to left-wing radicals and black-clad nationalists who disagreed about everything and fought among themselves.

Nonetheless, it enlivened what in other respects was a rather dreary presidential campaign. Convoys of cars, decorated with competing slogans by Putin's supporters and opponents, careered around Moscow's Garden Ring, until the police, while waving on the pro-Putin brigade, flagged down the opposition vehicles and gave them traffic tickets. One long, black limousine, with its windows rolled down, contained a bevy of girls in bikinis, who, shivering in the freezing temperatures, urged voters to give Putin a third term. 'For a real man, three times is normal', was emblazoned along the side.[145] Worse was to come. Hacked emails were posted on the internet containing titillating messages between the head of the pro-Putin youth movement, Nashi, and an aide. In retaliation, the FSB uploaded intimate videos of an opposition leader *in flagrante*, prompting the liberal newspaper, *Novaya gazeta*, to ask: 'What charge are they going to level against him? Are they jealous of his big dick?'[146]

Another pro-Putin video imagined what Russia would be like without him. There would be famine and civil war and the country would disintegrate, it warned. China would invade the Russian Far East, Japanese peacekeepers would land at Vladivostok, NATO would take over the western borderlands, and an Islamic Emirate would be proclaimed in the Caucasus. Navalny would seek asylum in America and would be awarded the Nobel Peace Prize. Four million people watched online, and pundits from government-backed think tanks opined that such a scenario was by no means improbable.[147]

As usual, Putin barely campaigned. He did not need to. Protests or no protests, most Russians could not imagine any other leader. For the first time, his electoral headquarters bought TV commercials, in which popular celebrities proclaimed their support. He signed a series of articles, full of crowd-pleasing promises – higher wages for teachers, bigger child allowances – but otherwise offered little that was new. At the one mass rally he held, in a sports stadium in Moscow on February 23, he compared American meddling in Russia to the Napoleonic invasion, 200 years earlier, and urged his supporters to join together to defend the country, as the *bogatyri*, the knights-errant of old, had done, against those who 'look abroad, scuttle to one side and betray the motherland'.

'We will not let anybody interfere in our domestic affairs,' Putin declared. 'We will not let anyone impose their will on us. We are a nation of winners, it's in our genetic code.' As if to counter the fiery oratory of Navalny, he abandoned his usual reserve and tried to build an emotional bond with the crowd. 'Do we love Russia?' he asked. 'Will we win? . . . I'll ask you again: Do we love Russia?'[148] The assembled multitude, many of whom had been bussed in by their employers, dutifully responded: 'Yes!' But it did not come naturally and fell rather flat.

It was enough, however.

The following weekend, when Election Day arrived, Putin won 63 per cent of the vote, with more than 50 per cent in every one of Russia's regions except Moscow, where 46.95 per cent was recorded. The eternal Communist candidate, Gennady Zyuganov, came second with 17 per cent, followed by the billionaire, Mikhail Prokhorov, who had been persuaded to stand to make the contest seem a little less predictable, Vladimir Zhirinovsky, and the leader of Just Russia, Sergei Mironov. The result had never been in doubt. The OSCE observers reported ballot-stuffing and 'carousel voting', where the same voters cast their ballots at several different polling stations, but even if 10 per cent of the votes had been falsified – the most the observer teams thought possible – it would not have changed the outcome.[149]

That night, Putin savoured his victory before a crowd of supporters in Manezhnaya Square, just across from the Kremlin. 'It was an emphatic victory,' he declared. Russia had shown that 'political provocations whose sole objective . . . is to usurp power' would not succeed.[150]

As he spoke, tears rolled down his cheeks. He claimed afterwards that it was due to the bitterly cold wind.[151] It was not. It was one of those rare moments, like the funeral of his best friend at university, Vladimir Cheryomushkin, or the return of the first body bags from Chechnya, when everything he had bottled up inside suddenly overwhelmed him and his normally stoic self-control broke down. After 12 years in power, Putin had come to see himself as the incarnation of the state. He felt 'one with the Russian soil,' he said. 'Russia is my life . . . Not for a second can I imagine myself without her . . . It's not just love that I feel . . . I feel part of our people.'[152] It was not a president but a priest-king speaking.

15

The Straitjacket Tightens

Putin's inauguration on May 7, 2012, marked the beginning of a period of deepening change which would make the years that followed very different from his first two terms.

In domestic, as in foreign policy, Putin had concluded that there was nothing to be gained by trying to accommodate his opponents. It was what he had told his teacher, Vera Gurevich, as a boy at primary school, when he was reprimanded for getting into a fight: 'There are people who can't or won't understand, no matter how you try to explain to them. The only thing they understand is strength.'[1]

The disaffection of the middle class had come as a shock. Rationally, Putin might recognise that, as a British colonial civil servant once said of the natives he administered, 'their very discontent is a measure of their progress.'[2] But the aspirations of this new bourgeoisie that he had helped to bring into being now threatened to undermine his rule. Accordingly, the 'cubicle dwellers' of the big cities – 'the street cleaners, car drivers, office plankton, journalists and bloggers who don't produce anything,' as Putin's long-time colleague, Sergei Ivanov, described them – would in future be excluded from calculations of where the regime's political interests lay.[3] They would be kept in order, by force if necessary. Even more than in the past, he would rely instead on the 'authentic Russians' of the small towns and the countryside.

The change found symbolic expression in the sudden and meteoric promotion of one such authentic Russian, a humble assembly-line foreman at a tank factory at Nizhny Tagil, in the Urals, to become the equivalent of deputy Prime Minister.

Igor Kholmanskikh had had his 15 minutes of fame during the anti-government protests in December, when he had told Putin, during his annual phone-in, that 'if the police can't handle the situation, me and the lads will come up and sort things out to defend stability,' adding hastily, 'within the limits of the law, of course.'[4] It was music to Putin's ears and the Kremlin kept in touch. 'You showed who the Russian people are,' Putin told him. 'You showed that you are a head taller than any of these good-for-nothings and loudmouths.'[5] Two months later, in one of the first appointments after his inauguration, Putin named Kholmanskikh presidential plenipotentiary in the Urals Federal District, a post with senior cabinet rank.

The appointment generated much ironic comment. 'The biggest mystery now,' quipped one liberal deputy, 'is who will be named to the vacant position of head of the assembly line.'[6] *Nezavisimaya gazeta* compared it to the Emperor Caligula appointing his favourite horse, Incitatus, to the Roman Senate.[7] But no one was in any doubt of the meaning of Putin's message. It was a gesture of thanks to the blue-collar workers at state-owned factories all over Russia, whose support had assured his election victory, and a shot across the bows of the ungrateful 'cubicle dwellers', the new gentry in the cities who had gone into opposition. It also showed in no uncertain terms that, having returned to power, Putin would rule unconstrained by political conventions or by what others might think.

The symbolism was backed up by substance. On the eve of the inauguration and on the day itself, there had been renewed anti-government protests in Bolotnaya Square. This time, the young professionals who had come out to demonstrate during the winter stayed away. The riot police were out in force and cracked down hard. The protesters responded in kind. In the ensuing brawl, dozens of people on both sides were injured, some seriously, hundreds were detained and a number charged with criminal offences.[8] The following month, Putin signed legislation making participation in unauthorised demonstrations punishable by a fine of up to 300,000 roubles (about 9,000 US dollars), three hundred times more than before, and twice that amount or more for those who organised unsanctioned protests.[9] Demonstrators who were unable to pay their fines would be ordered to perform 200 hours of community service instead.[10]

Liberal deputies in the Duma complained that this was a violation of constitutional guarantees of freedom of assembly, which indeed it was. Putin maintained that the right to demonstrate was not being infringed and that the only constraint was that protesters must not break the law.[11]

A few days later, on June 11, the police staged early-morning raids on the homes of leading opposition figures, including Navalny, Boris Nemtsov and Kseniya Sobchak, who were then summoned to the Prosecutor's Office to prevent them taking part in another protest rally, planned for the following day. State media reported falsely that Sobchak had opened the door to the police wearing only a pair of panties.[12] The goal was to paint her as an airhead, not to be taken seriously, while at the same time distracting attention from the crackdown on the demonstrations, which many Russians thought was unjustified.[13] In the same vein, it was announced that more than 1.5 million US dollars in cash had been found in a safe in her apartment.[14] It was money which she had earned legitimately from celebrity shows on Russian television but it gave the tax authorities a pretext to launch an investigation.

The decision to target her was deliberate. Given Putin's close relationship with her father, she had been thought untouchable. Her presence at the demonstrations had been taken as a sign that participation was acceptable. The raid was 'a warning to everyone', wrote the popular tabloid, *Moskovsky komsomolets*. If Kseniya could be punished, it meant that, from now on, any form of opposition was unsafe.[15]

Other measures followed. In July, Putin signed a law requiring every Russian NGO which accepted financial contributions from abroad to register as a 'foreign agent', a term which to Russians is synonymous with spy.[16] He insisted that it would apply only to organisations which engaged in 'political activity' and compared it to the US Foreign Agents Registration Act. That was disingenuous. The American legislation concerns only lobbyists for foreign governments and political parties. Activities of a religious, educational, scientific or cultural nature, as well as human rights matters, are specifically excluded. The Russian definition of 'political activities' was so vague that it could be stretched to cover almost anything. Even when NGOs refused foreign funding, the regulations could be manipulated. There would be cases of Russian NGOs receiving unsolicited money transfers from foreign bank accounts operated by the FSB, which was afterwards cited as evidence justifying 'foreign agent' status.

Ten days after the NGO bill became law, on July 30, three young women appeared in court in Moscow charged with hooliganism.[17]

Nadezhda Tolonnikova, 23, Maria Alyokhina, 24, and Yekaterina Samutsevich, 29, were members of an avant-garde performance art collective called Pussy Riot. Shortly before the presidential election, wearing brightly coloured leggings, long pullovers and balaclavas, they had gone to the Cathedral of Christ the Saviour on the bank of the Moscow River, a quarter of a mile from the Kremlin, where, gyrating frenetically to a recorded soundtrack, they chanted a blasphemous punk prayer in front of the high altar:

> Virgin Mary, Mother of God, cast Putin out,
> Cast Putin out, Cast Putin out . . .
> Shit, shit, holy shit!
> Shit, shit, holy shit! . . .
> The Church sings the praises of rotten dictators,
> Black limousines form the procession of the Cross.

A security guard radioed for the police. The three young women and two other members of the group who had participated in the protest got away before they arrived. That evening, they posted a video of the performance online.

The Kremlin's initial reaction was not to take it too seriously. Putin derided the group for supposedly uploading pictures of orgies to the internet. 'Some fans of group sex say it's better than one-on-one,' he said, 'because, as in any teamwork, you don't have to hit the ball all the time.'[18] It was the same kind of toe-curling putdown that the Kremlin had used against Kseniya Sobchak.

But Patriarch Kirill, who had succeeded Aleksei when the latter died in 2008, was not amused at all. A highly intelligent, unscrupulous, manipulative man, Kirill had made a Faustian bargain to subordinate the Church to Putin in order to further his personal ambitions. He had backed him in the elections, calling him 'a miracle of God', and given the regime his blessings. Kirill owned a 40,000-dollar Swiss watch and a 1.5 million-dollar apartment in the House on the Embankment, a huge residential complex on the Moscow River, built in Stalin's time, which was home to government ministers and other members of the political elite. Both, he insisted, had been given to him by wealthy parishioners.

The Patriarch saw himself as an Orthodox Pope with temporal as well as spiritual power, playing a role like that of the Princes of the

Church in seventeenth-century France. Such was his status that when a fellow tenant, the former Health Minister, Yuri Shevchenko, had his apartment refurbished, causing dust to settle on the Patriarch's valuable library upstairs, the courts immediately awarded Kirill almost 700,000 US dollars in damages.[19] Shevchenko had been close to Putin. He had headed the Military Hospital in St Petersburg in the 1990s when Lyudmila had had her near-fatal car accident and had later been instrumental in preventing Anatoly Sobchak's arrest until Putin could arrange his flight to France. But the loyalty which Putin extolled as the greatest of human virtues was not always a two-way street.

Kirill denounced Pussy Riot's performance as 'a devil's scheme' and raged against those who treated it as an affair of no importance.[20] That left Putin little choice but to order the women's arrests.[21] It was not the best solution. They posed no political threat. Two of them – Nadezhda Tolonnikova and Maria Alyokhina – had small children, and putting them on trial risked turning them into martyrs.[22] But the Church was too important as a spiritual prop for the regime for Putin to risk antagonising its leader.

In August, the three young women were sentenced to two years' imprisonment, a year less than the prosecution had sought and far less than the maximum of seven years provided for by the law. Putin had said earlier that they should not be judged 'too harshly'.[23] On appeal, Samutsevich, who had been present in the cathedral but had not taken part, had her sentence commuted to probation, but the other two were sent to serve out their prison terms in labour camps in Mordovia and the Urals.[24]

The trial caused an outpouring of indignation.

In the West, Björk, Radiohead, Paul McCartney, Bruce Springsteen, Sting, U2 and other celebrities issued statements of support for the women. When Madonna performed in Moscow that summer, she made an onstage appeal for the group's release, donned a balaclava and pulled off her jacket to show the words, 'Pussy Riot', emblazoned on her back.[25] Politicians in America and all over Europe protested that the punishment was disproportionate to the offence. *Moskovsky komsomolets* called it 'a huge moral and political defeat for the Russian authorities'. The *Moscow Times* wrote that Russia had returned to the Dark Ages and could no longer be considered a civilised nation.[26]

But there were advantages in having the Western media focus on the plight of the three young punks, for it distracted attention from another case which, from the Kremlin's point of view, was infinitely more important.

On July 31, the day after the Pussy Riot trial began, Aleksei Navalny was charged with large-scale fraud.[27] The affair dated back to 2009, when he had been working as an unpaid adviser to Nikita Belykh, the liberal Governor of Kirov province, 500 miles east of Moscow.[28] In that capacity, he had arranged a contract between the region's timber company, KirovLes, and a brokerage firm called VLK, which was headed by an acquaintance. The contract did not work out as planned but a subsequent investigation found no evidence of wrongdoing. Two years later, however, the Investigative Committee, headed by Aleksandr Bastrykin, Putin's former classmate at the Leningrad Law Faculty, which had recently been formed to deal with particularly sensitive cases previously handled by the Prosecutor's Office, ordered the case reopened. In April 2012, that investigation, too, was terminated, having failed to find any evidence of criminal conduct. Bastrykin, who by then had been personally targeted by Navalny's anti-corruption campaign, was not pleased. Two weeks later, a third investigation was launched. This time, Navalny was charged with conspiring with the head of VLK to embezzle 16 million roubles, or about 500,000 US dollars, by deliberately under-pricing the timber that had been sold.

The political motivation for the charges was transparent. Navalny had become Putin's bête noire. For the first time since Khodorkovsky's imprisonment, Putin sensed a political challenge. 'Wherever this gentleman appears,' he commented later, 'he always brings trouble with him.'[29] Over the next 12 months, three more spurious cases were opened, each on the basis of fabricated or non-existent evidence.[30] In January 2013, Navalny was placed under house arrest for allegedly violating bail and six months later was sentenced by the Kirov district court to five years' imprisonment for his role in the KirovLes case.

But then came a *coup de théâtre*. At the request of the prosecution, Navalny was freed pending appeal.[31]

The decision was unprecedented.

When the full story emerged, it became clear that it was part of an elaborate *mise en scène*. Russia was gearing up for the Winter Olympics, which were to be held in Sochi in February 2014. Relations with the

West were testy. Putin wanted to avoid any repetition of what had happened to the Soviet Union in 1980, when the United States and most of its allies had boycotted the Moscow Olympics in protest against the Soviet invasion of Afghanistan. Freeing Navalny was a goodwill gesture to those concerned about human rights in Russia. But that was merely the prelude. An even bigger surprise would follow. The Mayor of Moscow, Sergei Sobyanin, was to stand for re-election that autumn.[32] Putin had decided that Navalny would be allowed to stand against him.[33] Holding a genuinely competitive election in Moscow, he thought, would show that, despite the crackdown on protest demonstrations and NGOs, Russia was much more democratic than it was given credit for. On the President's instructions, Sobyanin worked behind the scenes[34] to ensure that Navalny obtained the requisite number of signatures to take part and, on the last day before the lists closed, he was registered as a candidate.

It was a gamble, but the Kremlin's internal polling had shown that Navalny was unlikely to get more than 10 per cent of the vote, which would demonstrate his lack of popular support.[35] If he had posed a real threat, Putin acknowledged later, 'we wouldn't have let him participate.'[36] In the event, it was much closer than he had anticipated. Navalny came within a whisker of forcing Sobyanin into a run-off. The incumbent won 51.37 per cent of the vote. Navalny came second with just over 27 per cent.[37]

'You see, the elections were free and fair,' Putin told a group of Western scholars afterwards. 'People expected that Sobyanin would win . . . by a large margin. But . . . his main rival had almost half as many votes . . . I can't even imagine what we could do to make [the elections] more transparent.'[38] It was true. The mayoral elections in Moscow in September 2013, were the freest in Russia for 20 years.[39] Nor was it an isolated case. In Yekaterinburg, another opposition figure, Yevgeny Roizman, who had waged a national campaign against drug addiction, defeated the Kremlin's candidate, leading the liberal newspaper, *Yezhednevny zhurnal*, to exclaim, 'politics has come back!'[40] In Petrozavodsk, the provincial capital of Karelia, an independent was elected.[41]

Other conciliatory gestures followed, also with the Olympics in view.

In October, the Constitutional Court ruled that a criminal conviction would no longer entail a lifetime ban on standing for public office.

Navalny's five-year suspended prison term, if confirmed on appeal, would therefore disqualify him from taking part in the presidential election in 2018 but afterwards, in theory, his ineligibility would end.[42]

Two months later, on December 18, the Duma approved an amnesty for the two imprisoned members of Pussy Riot, who were nearing the end of their terms. Thirty members of Greenpeace, who had been detained that autumn for protesting against Russian oil exploration in the Barents Sea, were also freed and their ship, the *Arctic Sunrise*, which had been impounded, was released. Next day Putin announced that he would pardon the former oligarch, Mikhail Khodorkovsky, who by then had spent more than ten years in prison. He had served 'a serious length of time', Putin acknowledged, and since his mother was dying of cancer, he would be freed on humanitarian grounds. A few hours later, Khodorkovsky was whisked away from his labour camp in northern Russia and flown to Germany, where Angela Merkel and the former Foreign Minister, Hans-Dietrich Genscher, had been discreetly urging his release.[43]

Putin had gone to great lengths to secure the Winter Olympics for Sochi. He had flown to Guatemala to meet the International Olympic Committee and, when presenting Russia's candidature, had addressed them in English, something he had never done before and would not do again.[44] It would be a unique opportunity, he thought, to show the world how Russia had changed. Fifteen years earlier, the Goodwill Games in St Petersburg, even with the limited means then available, had opened the eyes of Western visitors to the new Russia emerging under Yeltsin. The Beijing Olympics, a decade and a half later, with a television audience of hundreds of millions, had transformed China's image internationally. Putin hoped that the Sochi Games would do something similar. They would be Russia's coming-out party – a national celebration of its coming of age as a post-Soviet power.

The Games, however, proved no more than a fleeting interlude.

On Monday, February 24, 2014, the day after the closing ceremony, seven of the demonstrators detained at Bolotnaya Square on the eve of Putin's inauguration, almost two years earlier, were sentenced to between two and a half and four years in labour camps for rioting and assaulting police officers. The sentences had been delayed to avoid casting a shadow over the festivities in Sochi. Another defendant was given a suspended term. All eight had been excluded from the December amnesty, as had two of the organisers of the Bolotnaya protests, who were later sentenced to four and a half years' imprisonment.[45]

The trials recalled the persecution of dissent in Soviet times. More than a quarter of a century had passed since Russians had last been condemned to labour camp terms for the simple act of demonstrating against government policies. Putin maintained that they had got off lightly. 'In some countries,' he said, evidently with the United States in mind, 'raising your hand against a police officer is enough to get you shot between the eyes without a second thought.'[46]

More than 400 people were detained outside the court building for protesting against the sentences of the 'Bolotnaya Eight'. Most were quickly released but four opposition leaders, including the former deputy Prime Minister, Boris Nemtsov, received ten-day jail terms.

Navalny, who had been present, was also detained and, shortly afterwards, placed under house arrest.[47] The pretext was a case involving the French cosmetics company, Yves Rocher, which had signed a distribution contract with a company owned by Navalny and his younger brother, Oleg.[48] They were accused of having fraudulently extorted 30 million roubles, or about 600,000 US dollars. The evidence was non-existent. The amount allegedly stolen had been earned over the previous three years for services the Navalnys' company had provided. But on December 30, 2014, Oleg was sentenced to three and a half years in a labour camp. Aleksei Navalny received the same sentence but, as in the KirovLes trial, it was suspended.[49]

It was a cruel game of cat and mouse.

Putin was concerned that if Navalny were imprisoned, he would become a martyr. Far better to attack him where he was most vulnerable, through his family. That was confirmed a few days later when Navalny announced that, in view of his brother's imprisonment, he was removing his electronic bracelet and would no longer respect the conditions of his house arrest. The Prosecutor's Office was told to ignore it.[50] The suspended sentences were kept in reserve, ready to be enforced when Putin decided the time was ripe.

The wave of repression that had commenced with his re-election in 2012 had resumed as though the Games had never happened.

Defamation and libel, which Medvedev had ordered to be treated as civil matters, were returned to the criminal courts, giving the regime a potent weapon against political opponents. The power to open cases

for tax evasion, a favourite tool of the *siloviki* for squeezing uncoopera-
tive businesses, was transferred from the tax authorities to Bastrykin's
Investigative Committee, which answered directly to the Kremlin.[51]
Dozhd, an independent TV channel which Medvedev had allowed to
start broadcasting in 2010, was banned from Russian cable and satellite
services, meaning that it could only be received via the internet, which
was itself no longer quite as free as before.[52] Following the protests at
Bolotnaya at the end of 2011, new regulations had given the authorities
the power to close websites with what was termed 'dangerous content'. Officially that was limited to child pornography, the promotion
of illegal drugtaking and encouragement to suicide, but those categories could be interpreted very broadly.[53]

The internet, Putin claimed, had originated as 'a special project of
the CIA'.[54] He was wrong: it had been a US Defense Department project. But the charge provided justification for treating it as suspect and
insisting on rigorous supervision. Government officials with access to
sensitive information were henceforth required by law to use encryp-
tion approved by the FSB. From May 2014, websites with more than
3,000 daily visitors were treated as news media and held responsible for
their content. Bloggers had to register with the government and use
their real names when online. Social networks and search engines had
to keep records of everything posted for six months.[55] Foreign ownership of media companies was banned and, at the beginning of 2015,
internet companies which collected data on Russian citizens were
required to hold it on servers located physically within Russia.[56]

It was death by a thousand cuts.

However, there were limits to how far, at that stage, Putin was willing
to go. The historian, Simon Sebag Montefiore, noted that Putin's Russia
was still very different from the Soviet Union. Nicholas I, who had exiled
the Decembrists, had been called 'Genghis Khan with a telegraph', he
wrote, and Stalin had been called 'Genghis Khan with a telephone', but
Putin was not 'Genghis Khan with a Blackberry . . . Today's Russia is
authoritarian, but still freer.'[57] At the midpoint of Putin's third presidential term, in 2015, that remained largely true but it was becoming less so.
The space for political freedom was steadily shrinking.

The clampdown on the opposition did not occur in isolation.

The liberals around Putin, who had played a prominent role in his first two terms and had dared to believe that, when Medvedev became President, their hour might have come, only to find that it had been a false dawn, were pushed aside and, for the most part, discredited. Only five ministers out of 22 in the previous cabinet kept their posts, most of them Putin's allies from the so-called power ministries.[58] The new men were conservatives whose distinguishing trait was loyalty to Putin.[59] Gleb Pavlovsky, Putin's long-serving political strategist, and Vladislav Surkov, the Kremlin ideologist, who had encouraged Medvedev to seek a second term, were both fired.[60]

It was as though Medvedev's humiliation in the *rokirovka* had not been enough. Putin seemed determined to condemn him to servility. He railed at the ministers during cabinet meetings: 'I want to ask you, are you going to get to work or not? . . . If we decide something, we need to get it done.'[61] While not criticising Medvedev directly himself, he encouraged others to do so.[62] In August 2012, a video was posted on the internet in which the former Chief of the General Staff, Yuri Baluyevsky, and other retired officers accused Medvedev of indecisiveness and cowardice in the run-up to the Georgian war four years earlier. He had hesitated for a whole day, Baluyevsky claimed, and hundreds of lives had been lost as a result. Only when Putin telephoned from Beijing and 'kicked him in the backside', did he summon up his courage and order the Russian army to counter-attack.

The identities of those responsible for the 45-minute documentary, entitled 'A Lost Day', were not disclosed, but it was a highly professional production and had evidently been made with the support of senior figures in the Presidential Administration.[63]

Medvedev had always maintained that, as President and Commander-in-Chief, he alone had taken the decision to send in Russian troops. Baluyevsky hated him and the charges in the film were false. But when Putin was asked to comment, he gave a carefully worded reply. No time had been wasted, he said, but Baluyevsky was correct in saying that he had twice telephoned Medvedev from Beijing at the start of the crisis to discuss how to proceed.[64] Medvedev, speaking to journalists during a visit to South Ossetia earlier that day, had offered a very different version. 'Decisions of this kind are taken by one person only and I was that person,' he said. 'Those who say otherwise are either ignorant or deliberately distorting the facts.'[65]

There the matter rested. Neither Putin nor Medvedev wished to take it further. But their relations remained frosty.

Bastrykin's Investigative Committee, with Putin's agreement, started looking into the hi-tech site at Skolkovo, near Moscow, which had been one of Medvedev's pet projects. Putin needled him with public praise of Aleksei Kudrin, who had refused to serve as Finance Minister in Medvedev's government because, Putin said witheringly, Kudrin had not wanted to be associated with 'half-measures and half-reforms'.[66]

Pavlovsky thought that Putin suspected Medvedev of having plotted against him in the final year of the tandem, much as Kasyanov and Nemtsov had been suspected of conspiring against him at the end of his first term.[67] Making Medvedev Prime Minister had been a way to neutralise him. By the autumn of 2013, Pavlovsky said, Putin realised that his suspicions were unwarranted, the chill ended and Surkov returned to the Kremlin as a presidential adviser. But by then, Medvedev had become a political eunuch. He would continue as Putin's Prime Minister for several years more and would remain a member of the inner circle. But the President had crushed him. Whatever credibility he might once have had, and with it the chance of becoming Putin's eventual successor, had been irremediably compromised.

Alongside the marginalisation of the liberals and the curbing of political freedoms, Putin began to think more deeply in his third term about the philosophical underpinnings of his regime. Terms like 'sovereign democracy' disappeared from his vocabulary. The goal became to find an overarching narrative behind which the whole country could unite – a way to affirm Russia's difference, the unique identity which set it apart from other nations.

In this latest iteration of 'the Russian idea', the key concept was tradition. Russia, Putin said, was 'a civilisational state, bonded together by the Russian people, Russian language and Russian culture, native for all of us, which unites us and prevents us dissolving into this diverse world'. Russia's spirituality had been in decline and renewed efforts were needed to reverse that. 'We must be and remain Russian . . . We must wholeheartedly support those institutions which are the bearers of traditional values.'[68]

That meant ever greater emphasis on the role of the Orthodox Church, coupled with a new stress on family values and 'patriotic education'.

The church, under Patriarch Kirill, had become a pillar of the state and a political force to be reckoned with. Family values were more of a problem.

Most Russians were extremely conservative in their view of the relations between men and women. The family, in their view, was composed of a husband, a wife and children. Extra-marital affairs were normal. Same-sex relationships were not. To the vast majority of Russians, homosexuality was a perversion promoted by the decadent West to erode healthy Russian values. Yuri Luzhkov, when he was Mayor of Moscow, had banned Gay Pride parades, which he denounced as 'satanic' events.[69]

Putin himself, initially, had been much more broadminded. When he had been deputy Mayor of St Petersburg, an American concert promoter named Richard Torrence had joined the Mayor's Office as a cultural events adviser. Torrence was wealthy, talented and artistic, with a list of celebrity clients that extended from Elizabeth Taylor, Eartha Kitt and Madonna to Leonard Bernstein and Mstislav Rostropovich. He was also flamboyantly gay. Sobchak found that hard to stomach. Putin defended him. Torrence did his work well, he said. His private life was his own affair. When Torrence left, in 1996, Putin gave a lunch in his honour and toasted him as 'a member of our family', a gesture which the American found surprising and touching. It went far beyond the obligatory minimum for a departing adviser.[70]

A decade and a half later, the situation had changed. Patriarch Kirill was fiercely opposed to homosexuality, which he denounced as a disease and a sin.[71] In the Duma, a hard core of conservatives wanted homosexual relations criminalised.[72] After the Bolotnaya demonstrations, tarring the opposition as supporters of homosexual rights had been a sure way to discredit them.[73] Opinion polls showed that 75 per cent of Russian voters thought homosexuals were either immoral or had psychological problems; the same proportion said homosexuality was unnatural; and 40 per cent thought they should be required to undergo medical treatment.[74] Amid a groundswell of popular support for restrictions on homosexual behaviour, the Duma approved a bill banning 'propaganda of paedophilia and homosexuality to minors' – an amalgam which suggested that it regarded them as one and the same.[75]

For more than a year, Putin remained silent. When he did finally address the issue, his first instinct, as with Pussy Riot, was not to take it too seriously. Russia was in demographic decline, he said, and 'let's face it, gay marriages don't produce children!'[76] A few months later he recalled that Tchaikovsky had been homosexual. 'We don't love him for that . . . but we all love his music. And so what?'[77]

In time, however, Putin realised that he could turn the campaign to his advantage. At that point, his language underwent an abrupt change.

Addressing a gathering of Western scholars and politicians, broadcast live on Russian television in September 2013, he accused the United States and Western Europe of abandoning the Christian values on which Western civilisation was based.[78] 'They are implementing policies that equate large families with same-sex partnerships, belief in God with belief in Satan,' he said. 'The excesses of political correctness have reached a point where people are seriously talking about registering political parties whose aim is to promote paedophilia' – a reference to a fringe Dutch party which advocated legalising child pornography and bestiality (and whose right to do so, bizarrely, had been affirmed by the Dutch courts).[79] In certain countries, Putin went on – meaning the United States, where some cities refused to put up Christmas decorations lest people of other faiths be offended – people were afraid even to call Christmas and Easter by their proper names. 'They are aggressively trying to export this model all over the world,' Putin charged. Russia would not follow that path. 'The rights of the minority must be respected, but the rights of the majority are paramount.'

Homosexuality and Christian values, however, took up only part of his speech. Putin's main concern was with the kind of country Russia was going to become:

Today we need new strategies to preserve our identity in a rapidly changing world . . . [This] question is . . . really fundamental . . . A new national idea doesn't simply appear. [It] cannot be imposed from above . . . We need a synthesis of . . . our cultural, spiritual and political traditions, and we [must] understand that identity is not a rigid thing that will last forever but rather a living organism . . . All of us, so-called neo-Slavophiles and neo-Westernisers, must work together . . . Questions about how to assess certain historical events still divide [us]. We need to heal these wounds and repair the tissue of our historic fabric . . . We must be proud of our history, and we have things to be proud of. Russia's sovereignty, independence and territorial integrity . . . are red lines which no one is allowed to cross . . . Debates about identity and about the future of our nation are only possible if the participants are patriotic.

It was the ideological equivalent of his Munich speech on security six years earlier. At the time it passed largely unnoticed,[80] but it marked the start of a nationwide campaign to promote traditional values, which drew the attention of the far right in Europe – parties like Jobbik and Fidesz in Hungary, the Freedom Party in Austria, the National Front in France and UKIP in Britain – as well as some Christian conservative groups and the right wing of the Republican Party in the United States.

'So-called conservative values are acquiring a new significance,' Putin declared.[81] 'More and more people in the world support our position. [In] many countries, . . . strange as it may seem, society is now required to accept without question the equality of good and evil.' That was music to the ears of the religious right in the West. 'Of course,' Putin added, 'this is a conservative position.' He then quoted Nikolai Berdyaev, whose philosophical writings he took as a reference, as saying that the merit of conservatism was that it did not stop progress but prevented a descent into chaos and darkness.[82]

Soon after that speech, Putin sent copies of Berdyaev's book, *The Philosophy of Inequality*, together with Vladimir Solovyov's *The Justification of the Good* and Ilyin's selected essays, published under the title, *Our Tasks*, to all of Russia's regional governors with instructions to read them during the winter holidays.[83] All three works exalt Russian exceptionalism, the country's unique role in the world and its singular culture and history, and warn that the West tries constantly to undermine its spiritual purity. In Ilyin's words: 'Western peoples . . . cannot abide the originality of Russia . . . They need to dismember Russia . . . in order to destroy her. [theirs is] a plan of hatred and lust for power.'[84]

Putin had said something similar after the school massacre at Beslan, when he had accused the West of wanting to tear 'a succulent morsel' from Russia. But for all his frustration with the West, Putin was not an ultra-nationalist, imbued with hatred, as Ilyin was. He still believed that Russia and Europe belonged to 'the same civilisation [with] the same ingrained values'.[85] They were different, he said, because the Russian mentality had developed under serfdom and was rooted in a sense of community, whereas Europeans had had to fend for themselves in a competitive, market-based environment.[86] That was both good and bad, he thought. Good because Russians were 'more spiritual . . . We have bigger hearts [and] a more generous spirit.' On the other hand, 'not so good because there is no individual responsibility'.[87]

That image of big-hearted Russians, contrasted with mean-spirited Westerners for whom, as Putin put it, 'the only yardstick is personal success',[88] might cause eyerolls outside Russia, but most of his generation thought the same.

Putin had tried to explain it to Joe Biden when the latter visited Moscow in March, 2011. 'Don't be under any illusion,' he had told the US Vice President. 'We only look like you . . . Russians and Americans resemble each other physically. But inside we have very different values.'[89] Medvedev was then President and Putin may have been trying to warn the Administration not to assume that the personable young Russian leader, who appeared so Westernised, thought in the same way as they did. Nonetheless, it was a revealing comment. In Soviet times, many Russians did indeed seem to inhabit a different mental universe from the Westerners with whom they dealt.[90] But that was becoming a thing of the past. For men like Medvedev, who had grown up under *perestroika*, it had already begun to change, and for the post-Soviet cohort, it was hardly so at all.

Differences between the generations were more pronounced in Russia than in Western Europe or America because the change of system after the collapse of communist rule in 1991 had been total. Putin's concern, however, was less with the behaviour of younger people – a tolerance which may have stemmed from his memories of his own truculent youth – than with their lack of a sense of national identity. He complained of their 'appalling' ignorance of their country's past and quoted his favourite historian, Vasily Klyuchevsky: ' "History doesn't teach anything, but it punishes those who haven't learnt their lessons" . . . We cannot build a nation without it.'[91]

Accordingly, in 2013, Putin ordered the elaboration of a new 'history-teaching concept', to complement the teaching manual he had approved six years earlier.[92] Despite his previous efforts, he complained, far too much 'ideological garbage' was still being taught. The goal was 'to re-establish the unbroken flow of our history',[93] showing how Russia's identity was forged by the efforts of many generations over the course of a thousand years.[94] The foundations of patriotism, Putin said, were laid down during childhood and youth, and it was on that basis that Russia's future would be built.[95]

The 'concept' went much further than the manual which had preceded it. The 'black pages' of Russia's history were no longer merely lacquered, but whitewashed or written out altogether. Stalin's purges were still mentioned but paired with glowing accounts of the country's industrialisation. One critic wrote, with only slight exaggeration: 'It's as though German history books featured . . . the murder of six million Jews on the same page as the building of high-speed autobahns'.[96] Researchers who challenged the new interpretation risked losing their jobs or worse.[97] The new guidelines exalted military glory, especially in 1812, the first 'Great Patriotic War' when Napoleon was repulsed; and 1945, the second, when Nazi Germany was defeated.[98] Tsarist Russia was presented as a multi-ethnic state, fundamentally different from the colonial empires of Britain and France. Controversial events in the post-Soviet period were glossed over or omitted. Khodorkovsky was not mentioned and, still less, Navalny.

The 'concept' extolled Russia's unique role in the world – Moscow, it reminded the country's teachers, had been the Third Rome of the Orthodox Church – and its impact on global history. In short, it was a *vade mecum* for the Kremlin's new worldview. Under Putin, Russia took pride in its past and would forge its own future.

16

Payback

For the Obama administration, the crackdown on dissent in Russia and the curtailment of political freedoms following Putin's return to power, coupled with the declining influence of liberal figures in the leadership, brought a sinking feeling of déjà vu. It was a reprise of the end of George W. Bush's presidency, when Putin's speech at Munich had finally dashed hopes that the two countries could be partners and signalled a shift to an adversarial relationship. This time, however, there was an added complication. Not only was Russia growing more refractory towards the American-led world order but it was gradually developing an ability to resist.

The warning signs had been there even before Medvedev stepped down. In March 2011, large-scale protests had broken out in Syria, which was experiencing massive crop failures caused by an unusually prolonged drought. Bashar al-Assad's government had responded, as it usually did, with violence, sending in troops to open fire on the demonstrators. When that failed, Assad offered concessions. That did not work either. In July, armed clashes broke out and the conflict started to develop into civil war. The following month, the United States, Britain, France, Germany and a number of Arab countries called on Assad to step down. When he refused, they took their case to the UN Security Council, where they circulated a draft resolution threatening sanctions if the repression continued.

Putin had already been burnt once when Russia had abstained on the Libyan resolution. This time he told Medvedev to veto it. A second Russian veto followed in February 2012 and a third in July.[1] By then the CIA had launched a covert operation to provide weaponry and training to what Putin dismissively called 'the so-called armed opposition'.

Russia's position, he said, was that there must first be a ceasefire and an end to the violence and only then negotiations on a possible change of government. If it were done the other way round and Assad stepped down before a political settlement was achieved, as the Western powers seemed to want, the result would be chaos.[2] The Americans naïvely believed that if they brought democracy, peace and stability would follow. 'That's not how it works,' Putin said. 'you can't ignore history, traditions, religious beliefs.'[3] Look at what happened in Libya. 'Ethnic, clan and tribal conflicts, . . . the murder of the US Ambassador [in Benghazi] . . . Do you want us to repeat these mistakes indefinitely in other countries?'[4]

Even worse was the precedent of Afghanistan, where the United States had used the mujahidin against the Soviet Union, only to find that they morphed into the Taliban. It was a 'dangerous and very short-sighted policy', Putin said.[5] He hoped no one was thinking of doing anything similar in Syria.

The analogy was stretched but Putin had touched a nerve. America knew full well that it could not support Assad's Islamist adversaries, however tempting it might be. Over the next three years, Washington would spend billions of dollars trying to train and arm a moderate Syrian opposition force, only to find that it was ineffective. After that, the United States backed the Kurds, which enraged Turkey. Then it made unsuccessful attempts to train independent paramilitary units before finally having to acknowledge that the main forces fighting against Assad, the radical Jabhat al-Nusra and other al-Qaeda affiliates, were no less unpalatable than the Damascus regime itself.

By the autumn of 2012, at least 30,000 Syrians had been killed and three quarters of a million were refugees. Putin, like Obama, was wary of getting dragged into a conflict which both men realised would not easily be ended. Russia was 'not that bothered about the fate of Assad's regime,' he insisted. 'Without a doubt, change is required.'[6]

That was deliberately misleading. Moscow had a long history of supporting Syria. Medvedev had recently paid an official visit to Damascus. Russian investments there amounted to some 20 billion US dollars and the Russian navy maintained a support base at Tartus, its only such facility in the Mediterranean. Whatever Putin might say in public, he had no interest in seeing a pro-Western government come to power. Russia had resumed arms supplies – to 'the legitimate government', Putin stressed, not the opposition, whom he described as terrorists.[7]

'Members of the armed Syrian opposition take out the internal organs of their dead enemies and eat them,' he claimed, adding mischievously and, as often, not in the best of taste: 'I hope we will not see such negotiators at the [peace talks] in Geneva, otherwise it will be difficult for me to guarantee the safety of the Russian delegation.'[8]

Nonetheless he was cautious. Delivery of the S-300 anti-aircraft missile system, which Syria had ordered, was put on hold.[9] Officially Russia insisted that it was 'not an advocate of the incumbent Syrian government or of the incumbent President, Bashar al-Assad'.[10]

That position of pretended neutrality began to crumble after the G8 Summit in Northern Ireland in June 2013, where Obama told Putin and the other leaders that American intelligence was convinced that Syria had used chemical weapons against opposition strongholds on at least three occasions that year. Obama had warned earlier that the use of such arms would cross 'a red line' for Washington. At a news conference afterwards, Putin described the American allegations as 'unsubstantiated'.[11] But then, in August, Assad's forces fired rockets carrying warheads filled with the nerve agent, sarin, into two densely populated, opposition-controlled suburbs on the outskirts of Damascus. Hundreds of people, many of them children, died in their sleep. Others suffered an agonising death, convulsing, foaming at the mouth and unable to breathe. The death toll may have exceeded a thousand.

Television pictures of the massacre caused a wave of revulsion in the West. François Hollande, who had succeeded Sarkozy as French President, vowed to punish the Syrian government for what he called 'this vile attack'. Obama ordered his National Security Council to prepare military options. In London, Prime Minister David Cameron sought parliamentary authorisation for British forces to take part in what he called a 'proportionate' military response. But then, suddenly, the West's plans for punitive strikes fell apart. The British public had little appetite to be dragged into yet another Middle Eastern adventure by their reckless American cousins and, in a stunning rebuke to Cameron, parliament voted against participation. In the United States, Congress was equally reticent.[12] Obama found himself out on a limb. The red line had been crossed but neither America's allies, with the sole exception of France, nor its elected representatives were prepared to back him up.

In the end, it was Putin who helped him find a way out.

They met on September 5 in the margins of the G20 which took place that year in St Petersburg. Putin said afterwards that they had 'agreed to disagree' on Syria but that a dialogue had been established.[13] In fact, they had sketched out the beginnings of a quid pro quo. Putin would persuade Assad to surrender his chemical-weapons stockpile – which the Russians maintained Syria had only developed as a counterweight to Israel's nuclear arsenal – and, in return, the United States would forgo military action.[14]

The deal was in everyone's interests and was approved within days. It let Obama off the hook. He could tell the American people that he had achieved a diplomatic solution.

For Assad, it removed the threat of further escalation.

For Moscow, it was a chance to act as a mediator and to present the Syrian leadership, which increasingly appeared as a potential long-term partner for expanding Russian influence in the region, as a responsible interlocutor.

In addition, it had given Putin an opportunity to gauge the American President's resolve. Obama had told the world that the use of chemical weapons was a red line that Assad must not cross. But when confronted with the reality of a chemical attack and offered a diplomatic way out, he had backed off, just as George W. Bush had done when Russian troops had punished Georgia for Saakashvili's attempt to occupy South Ossetia.

The lesson was that Russia stood by its allies in their hour of need. America did not. It was a sign of weakness which Putin would not forget.

After Obama's announcement, Putin set out Russia's position in an op-ed article for the *New York Times*. He presented himself as a voice of reason. Reprisals by the United States, should they take place, he wrote, risked creating yet more victims and spreading the conflict far beyond Syria's borders:

> There are few champions of democracy in Syria. But there are more than enough al-Qaeda fighters and extremists of all stripes, battling the government . . . Mercenaries from Arab countries fighting there, and hundreds of militants from Western countries and even Russia, are an issue of our deep concern. Might they not return to our countries with experience acquired in Syria? After all, after fighting in Libya, extremists moved on to Mali. This threatens us all . . .

Military intervention in internal conflicts in foreign countries has become commonplace for the United States. Is it in America's long-term interests? I doubt it . . . [To] America . . . 'you're either with us or against us'. [But] force has proved ineffective and pointless . . . Afghanistan is reeling, . . . Libya is divided into tribes and clans [and] in Iraq, the civil war continues . . . We must . . . return to the path of civilised diplomatic and political settlement.[15]

Putin took issue with Obama's vaunting of American exceptionalism. 'It is extremely dangerous to encourage people to see themselves as exceptional,' he wrote, adding sanctimoniously: 'We are all different, but when we ask for the Lord's blessings, we must not forget that God created us equal.' Years later he would admit that Obama's bragging that America was an exceptional nation with, as he put it, 'special, exclusive rights over practically the whole world', had got under his skin. 'I cannot go along with that,' he said. 'It's absolutely unfounded.'[16]

But the tone of the article was more of sorrow than of anger and Putin welcomed Obama's decision to exercise restraint in Syria. 'I don't think this was an easy situation for him,' he said later. 'But I am very pleased that [he] took such a position.'[17]

Putin could afford to be magnanimous. This time, he felt, he had been the one calling the shots.

The agreement to eliminate Syria's chemical-weapons stockpile was a striking demonstration of both countries' recognition that they needed to compartmentalise their relations, working together on issues where they had a mutual interest and against each other when they did not. It was all the more remarkable because, since the Libyan episode, Russia had been much less accommodating.

An early intimation of the changed climate in Moscow was the reception accorded to Michael McFaul, the new US Ambassador, who was harassed by groups of young Russians claiming to be journalists. It was not as tough as the treatment meted out to the British Ambassador, Tony Brenton, by the Kremlin youth movement, Nashi, six years earlier, but the State Department was outraged.[18]

Then the US Agency for International Development was accused of giving grants to NGOs to try to influence Russia's domestic politics and ordered to cease operations.[19] A month later, in November 2012, the Russians informed the US government-funded broadcasting station, Radio Liberty, that its licence to transmit locally, which it had been granted by Yeltsin in the 1990s, was being cancelled. In fact that merely brought Russia into line with American practice: it, too, barred foreigners from owning broadcasting licences. But, in Washington, it was seen not as reciprocity but as yet another sign of Russian ill will.[20]

The picture was not totally black. That summer, Putin and Obama had met on the margins of an international conference in Mexico. Putin was 40 minutes late, as was now often the case when he had to meet Western leaders. Nonetheless, they had a substantial discussion which covered, as well as Syria, strategic arms issues and shared concerns over the Iranian nuclear programme. Russian rockets, launched from Baikonur, carried American astronauts to the International Space Station, and Russia continued to give transit rights for the resupply of US troops in Afghanistan through what was known as the Northern Distribution Network, without which it would have been much more difficult, if not impossible, for the US to launch the raid which killed Osama bin Laden at his safe house in Pakistan.[21]

However, there were plenty of small irritants, and the core problems – missile defence and Russia's vexed relationship with NATO – remained unresolved.

America had put on hold its plans for an anti-missile shield in Europe but it had not shelved them altogether. Putin wanted any such system placed under joint American–Russian–European control. For Washington, that was out of the question.[22] Notwithstanding American claims to the contrary, the shield was defensive in name only. In reality it was an integral part of America's offensive capability.[23] When Moscow sought 'military and technological guarantees fixed in legally binding documents' that it would not be directed against Russia, the Americans offered only verbal assurances. 'Statements like "Don't worry, we promise nothing will happen" are not sufficient,' Putin complained. 'That's childish.' Russia had heard promises before that NATO would not expand, yet now 'military bases are springing up all around us like mushrooms.'[24] Having been cheated once, Moscow would not be cheated again.[25]

Obama might well be sincere in wanting to reach agreement on these issues, Putin said. 'But will they let him do it?' – 'they' being 'the so-called deep state', whose principal representatives were the military–industrial lobby and the conservatives in the State Department.[26] Even if Obama did sign an accord on missile defence – which he had hinted to Medvedev might be possible after the US presidential election in November 2012[27] – how long would it last? Obama's Republican challenger, Mitt Romney, had described Russia as America's 'No. 1 geopolitical foe'.[28] 'In four years' time,' Putin noted, 'Romney or someone like him could come to power.' Russia might hope for the best, but it had to prepare for the worst.[29]

By then, another, even older problem had raised its head again.

The Jackson–Vanik amendment to the US Trade Act, denying Russia Most Favoured Nation status, had still not been repealed. For 17 years, successive US Presidents had granted a yearly waiver. However, Russia's accession to the World Trade Organisation, which by 2011 was virtually a done deal, made that untenable. Under WTO rules, if Jackson–Vanik remained in force, American companies exporting to Russia would face higher tariffs.

Bill Browder, who had been trying to persuade Congress to sanction the Russian officials responsible for Magnitsky's death, saw an opportunity. Instead of allowing the Jackson–Vanik amendment simply to lapse, he suggested that it should be replaced by a new law, to be known as the 'Sergei Magnitsky Rule of Law Accountability Act', under which Russian officials suspected of corruption or human rights abuses could be denied entrance to the United States and any assets they had in America frozen.

The Obama administration opposed the measure, arguing that it would have little practical effect beyond antagonising Moscow and making it harder to work together on issues like Afghanistan, Iran and North Korea, on which the United States needed Russian cooperation.[30] But Congress was adamant. The Magnitsky Act came into force on December 14, 2012. Obama tried to limit its scope, naming only 18 relatively minor officials who would be barred from obtaining American visas, but was unable to block it altogether.

The Russians were furious. Jackson–Vanik had been a sore point for decades. To replace it, now that at long last it was being repealed, with an equally offensive piece of legislation, was rubbing salt into the wound.

One anti-Soviet, anti-Russian law is being substituted for another [Putin fumed]. They can't seem to do without it! . . . They talk about human rights in Russian prisons and places of detention. That's all well and good, but they have plenty of problems of that kind themselves. [Look at] Abu Ghraib – or Guantanamo, where people are kept jailed for years without being charged. Not only [that], the prisoners walk around shackled, like in the Middle Ages. They have [even] legalised torture. Can you imagine if we had done anything like that? They would have eaten us alive . . . It would have been a global scandal. But in their country, everyone keeps quiet about it . . . Those so-called secret CIA prisons: who has been punished for that? . . . They are up to the ears in shitty stuff, they're drowning in it, and they still insist on criticising us.[31]

'I am probably a bad Christian,' he added, 'because as a Christian you are supposed to turn the other cheek. I am not yet morally ready for that. If they slap our face, we have to retaliate. Otherwise they'll go on slapping us for ever.'

Putin's outrage was partly feigned. He knew very well why the Magnitsky affair had caused such dismay in the West. It was not just that Magnitsky had died in prison in gruesome circumstances. The real issue was that the Kremlin – and ultimately Putin himself – had protected the officials, at deputy minister level and higher, who had profited from the tax scam which Magnitsky had exposed. It was a topic he refused to discuss. Whenever journalists tried to question him about the higher-ups who had been responsible for Magnitsky's death, he clammed up.

Yet his diatribe about Abu Ghraib and Guantanamo, cynical though it was, could not simply be dismissed out of hand. The International Red Cross had been warning for months of a pattern of abuse in American detention facilities in Iraq. When the Abu Ghraib scandal broke, the soldiers who had carried out torture, rape, sodomy and murder and then circulated photographs and videos of their acts, were given relatively brief prison terms and their officers reprimanded. But those higher up the chain of command were not punished at all and in a number of cases were promoted. At Guantanamo, indefinite detention of suspects without charge or trial was by definition an abuse of human rights. After 9/11, rulings by the Department of Justice, authorising torture, opened the way not only to what happened at Abu Ghraib but to systematic abuses at CIA 'black sites'. None of those who approved the so-called torture memos or the euphemistically named 'enhanced inter-rogation techniques' was ever held responsible.

Some, though not all, Americans might argue that exceptional cir-cumstances required exceptional measures. Most of the rest of the world was revolted.

Over the years, Putin's view of the United States had changed. He now saw it as a deeply flawed, hypocritical, violent country, which, while preaching to others, had spent decades during the Cold War sup-porting Latin American dictatorships which had imprisoned and tortured to death tens of thousands of their citizens. 'The develop-ment of the American continent began with large-scale ethnic cleansing that has no equal in the history of mankind,' he declared. 'The indi-genous people were destroyed. After that [came] slavery ... That remains until now in the souls and hearts of the people.'[32]

Putin's philippic was one-sided and ignored the horrific violence in Russia after the Bolshevik Revolution as well as the grislier episodes of tsarist rule. Americans like to dismiss such arguments as 'whata-boutism'. That is a feeble response. When the pot calls the kettle black, it is not because either is white but because both are noxious.

The retaliation for the Magnitsky Act which Putin had promised came in two stages. Symmetrically, the Kremlin issued a list of US officials who would be banned from Russia. Asymmetrically, the Duma passed legislation forbidding the adoption of Russian children by American families.

The 'Dima Yakovlev Law' was named after a toddler who died of heatstroke in 2008 after his American adoptive father forgot to drop him off at day care, leaving him locked in a car for nine hours. The case, and the man's subsequent acquittal by a court which ruled that it was a tragic accident, caused outrage in Russia. But it did not prevent Moscow signing an agreement on adoptions with the US government three years later. Since the collapse of the Soviet Union, 60,000 Russian orphans had been adopted by American families, many of them chil-dren with handicaps whom Russian foster-parents would not accept. Out of that number, 19 had died at the hands of abusive American parents. Hundreds of times more had died from abuse in Russia.[33] Even Rossiya 1, the main state TV channel, acknowledged that the plight of many Russian children was dreadful: 'Every day more than 200 kids are taken away from alcoholic or sadistic parents,' it reported. 'Altogether we have a total of 700,000 orphans. And God knows how many homeless children there are.'[34]

That the Yakovlev case should have been exhumed to justify additional measures against the Magnitsky law was pure sophistry. Not only Russian liberals but members of Putin's government, including the Foreign Minister, Sergei Lavrov – a consummate diplomat who rarely ventured onto sensitive political terrain – and the Education Minister, Dmitry Livanov, spoke out publicly against the proposal.[35] The Kremlin's Human Rights Commissioner, Vladimir Lukin, a scholarly man who had served as Yeltsin's Ambassador in Washington, denounced it as 'a monstrous thing which disgraces our country'. To use children as pawns in a political dispute was 'absolutely cynical and shameless', he said.[36]

Putin thought otherwise. Although formally the ban on adoptions had been proposed by a rank-and-file member of the Duma, which allowed him to pretend that it was a parliamentary initiative, it had in fact been his idea.[37] The ban, he said, was not aimed at American parents, most of whom were 'good, decent people'. It was necessary because the American justice system failed to prosecute when children were abused and denied Russian consular officials access to the proceedings. That was a humiliation which Russia would not accept. Other nations could continue to adopt Russian children, but not Americans.[38]

It was a singularly unconvincing excuse.

The real reason lay elsewhere. Foreign adoptions had been controversial in Russia ever since the 1990s. At one point Yeltsin had wanted to ban them altogether. Putin calculated that blocking adoptions by Americans would be popular with a sizeable part of his electorate,[39] just as the jailing of Pussy Riot had gained him support among Orthodox believers. Moreover, it allowed him to hit back at the United States in a way which Congress had not anticipated and which, as far as the Russian government was concerned, was essentially cost-free.

For several hundred small children, who had already met their adoptive parents and begun to develop a relationship with them and then suddenly found their hopes of being accepted into a family brutally snatched away, it was not cost-free. Tens of thousands more were condemned to remain in Russian orphanages, which, while no longer Dickensian, gave them little chance of growing up to lead normal lives, let alone if they were severely disabled.

Congressmen, members of the Senate and American celebrities urged Putin to allow at least those orphans whose adoption had already been agreed to depart. Their appeals went unanswered.[40]

Like the Jackson–Vanik amendment which preceded it, the Magnitsky Act had been a way for Congress to demonstrate its power. Most US Congressmen were breathtakingly ignorant of foreign affairs. It was a classic example of a symbolic initiative which, far from bringing any improvement, ended up making matters far worse.

The next twist in this infernal, downward spiral came six months later.

In May 2013, Edward Snowden, a young contractor for the US National Security Agency who had become a whistle blower, arrived in Hong Kong. In the first half of June, he contacted the Russian consulate about the possibility of obtaining asylum.[41] By then, newspapers in the West, including the Guardian and the Washington Post, had begun publishing his revelations about the NSA's global surveillance programme, which scooped up indiscriminately the communications of adversaries and allies alike, including personal cell-phone calls by the German Chancellor, Angela Merkel.

When Snowden landed at Moscow's Sheremetyevo Airport on June 23, ostensibly heading for Latin America, Putin insisted that the young man's arrival had been 'completely unexpected'. Any suggestion that the Russian special services had been involved was 'complete nonsense', he said. 'He came as a transit passenger [and] as a transit passenger, he has the right to buy a ticket and fly where he wants . . . The sooner he chooses his final destination, the better it is both for us and for him.' He hoped, he added, tongue in cheek, that it would not affect 'the businesslike nature of our relations with the United States'. He would leave it to the FBI and the FSB to sort it out between them. 'I would rather not deal with such questions myself. It's like shearing a piglet: there's a lot of squealing, but not much wool.'[42]

It was quintessential Putin. No fingerprints.

In fact, he had followed closely every step of Snowden's progress since the American had first made contact in Hong Kong. Publicly, Putin minimised the significance of his disclosures, claiming that 'he told us nothing that we did not know before.'[43] But he was keenly aware of the anger the leaks had caused in Washington and took a malicious pleasure in taunting the Obama administration. Snowden was a fighter for human rights and democracy like the great Soviet dissident, Andrei Sakharov, he declared. If he wanted to stay in Russia, he could, although naturally he would have to 'stop . . . harming our American partners'.[44] Extradition was not possible because, although Russia had proposed a treaty covering such cases the year before, 'unfortunately' the United States had not replied.[45]

For six weeks, while Snowden's whereabouts remained a mystery to everyone else,[46] Putin twisted the knife in the wound. Finally he announced that the American would be granted temporary asylum.

Obama came under intense criticism for failing to take a tougher line. Republicans accused him of spinelessness. Democrats condemned his 'broken commitment to human rights in Russia'. Putin had no ideology, wrote the *Washington Post*, 'only a noxious mixture of personal aggrandisement, xenophobia, homophobia and primitive anti-Americanism'.[47]

At the beginning of August, Obama announced that he was cancelling a meeting with Putin which was to have taken place ahead of the G20 in St Petersburg the following month. It was the first time since the U-2 spy plane incident in 1960 that a Russian–American summit had been called off. Afterwards, the US President said he intended to 'take a pause and reassess where Russia is going'. The problem, Obama insisted, was not his personal relationship with Putin. 'The press likes to focus on body language and he's got that kind of slouch, looking like the bored kid at the back of the classroom. But the truth is that, when we're in conversation together, oftentimes it's very productive.'[48]

Understandably, the headlines next morning were all about the 'bored kid at the back of the classroom'. It was a sound-bite no journalist could resist. Moreover, it was true. After 14 years in power as President or Prime Minister, Putin did often look bored. Obama's main point – that, appearances notwithstanding, their talks were often 'candid [and] constructive'[49] – was forgotten.

The cancellation of the summit – 'not a catastrophe', Putin said[50] – was in fact the least Obama could have done, given the pressure on him at home to be tough. He had rejected calls for an Olympic boycott and had maintained his trip to Russia for the G20 in September. The two countries had concluded a Cybersecurity Pact during the summer

and their counterterrorism services continued to exchange information. When two young Chechens, whose presence in America the
Russians had already signalled to the FBI, detonated home-made
bombs during the Boston Marathon, Putin ordered the FSB to give
American investigators whatever help they could. Other initiatives
were stillborn. When Obama wrote to Putin in April, proposing further nuclear arms cuts, the Kremlin insisted that there must first be
progress on missile defence. But the agreement they reached in the
autumn on the destruction of Syria's chemical-weapons stockpile
showed that, where the two countries had shared interests, it was still
possible to work together.

Nevertheless, Putin's conviction that Russia and the United
States were on fundamentally different and incompatible paths was
deepening.

'Today we have practically no ideological contradictions,' he told
a Russian journalist during the row over Edward Snowden. 'We
have basic differences in terms of cultural norms. The foundation of
the American identity is individualist. The basis of Russian identity is
collective . . . It's a somewhat different philosophy of life. That's why
it's difficult for us to understand one another.' America, he went on,
needed enemies – external threats – to unite its own people and to
justify its position as 'leader of the Free World', protecting and, at the
same time, dominating its allies.[51] It did not greatly matter who the
enemy was. 'It could be Iran, . . . China, . . . or Russia.'[52] Whichever
was the adversary, America would not treat it as an equal, because, as
an imperialist power, to do so would denote weakness.

One day, Putin thought, Americans would realise that negotiation
and compromise were more profitable than unilateral diktat, but it
would not be any time soon.

Those reflections should have sounded an alarm. Obama had said a
few weeks earlier that the key question facing the United States in its
relations with Russia was where the country was headed.[53] Putin's
musings suggested an answer. Russia's belief that its future lay with
the West, which had guided the Kremlin's policies for the last two decades, ever since Yeltsin had come to power, had stretched to breaking
point. Putin was about to embark on a much less amenable course.

To policy-makers in Washington, heaving a sigh of relief that the
crisis over Syria's chemical weapons had been defused, it seemed that

the worst was over. After a rocky 12 months, relations with Moscow appeared to have stabilised and the Olympic Games promised to provide a much-needed respite. The release of Mikhail Khodorkovsky and the young women from Pussy Riot, as well as other gestures, pointed in the same direction. The American media continued to fulminate against Russia's restrictions on homosexual rights and there was much sour commentary about the inflated cost of the Games. It was said that contracts had been padded to provide billions of dollars in illicit profits to Putin's 'cronies', as the American press now called them – which was true – and that the total expenditure would exceed 50 billion dollars – which was not. Terrorist attacks, which Western journalists had predicted would disrupt the competition, failed to materialise. The weather stayed fine, the snow was adequate, the hotels and other facilities more or less worked.

By the time the Games ended, on Sunday, February 23, 2014, all but the most inveterate Western critics admitted that it had gone a lot better than they had expected. The closing ceremony, wrote the *Washington Post*, had 'all the elegance of a Fabergé egg, a glittering evening tucked full of tributes to the Russian arts'.[54] In what appeared to be a discreet hint of friendlier times, one of the Russian tableaux was staged to the theme song of the film, *It's a Wonderful Life*, an old American Christmas time favourite, starring James Stewart. The music had been composed by Dimitri Tiomkin, a Russian émigré who had worked in Hollywood in the 1930s.

Russia had come top of the medals table, with 33 medals, including 13 gold, America second with 28 and nine gold. The President of the International Olympic Committee, Thomas Bach, in his closing address, said Russia had delivered all that it had promised.

It was the calm before the storm.

After the Bucharest summit in April 2008, Russia's relations with Georgia had been 'clarified', as Putin might have put it, by the five-day war that summer which had culminated in Moscow's recognition of the breakaway regions of Abkhazia and South Ossetia. But Georgia had not been the only problem at Bucharest. A much bigger issue was Russia's relationship with Ukraine.

Putin's grievances against Ukraine went back to the 1990s. The country's role in the break-up of the Soviet Union; the status of

Crimea; squabbles over the lease of port facilities at Sevastopol for Russia's Black Sea fleet, arguments over the demarcation of the two countries' borders; disputes over culture, language, history and even between rival branches of the Orthodox Church – all ensured that Ukraine would be Russia's prickliest partner, no matter who was in power in Moscow or in Kyiv. The Orange Revolution had been a nightmare for Putin, who continued to have great difficulty navigating the country's constantly shifting political alliances. Nevertheless, after returning to the presidency in 2012, he decided to make one more attempt to bring Ukraine back into the Russian fold where he was convinced it rightly belonged.

One of Putin's key priorities – 'the core of our foreign policy and our strategic objective', as he put it – was to strengthen integration among the post-Soviet republics in the Commonwealth of Independent States.[55] This was in part to compensate for Russia's deteriorating relationship with the West. The three largest CIS states, Russia, Ukraine and Kazakhstan, together with Belarus, had signed a treaty ten years earlier to set up a Common Economic Space as the nucleus of a future Eurasian Economic Union, which Putin envisaged as a Russian-led alternative to the EU. But after the Orange Revolution, the next step, the establishment of a Customs Union, had stalled. Putin argued that going ahead with the union would create a powerful economic bloc of 210 million people, which would be in all their interests.[56] Viktor Yanukovych, now back as Ukraine's President, was torn. In March 2012, he had initialled an Association Agreement with the European Union, a possible first step to eventual EU membership. But the European Commission insisted that, before it could be signed, Kyiv would have to take significant steps to reduce corruption, strengthen democracy and improve the rule of law. Yanukovych, who was corrupt to the core, realised that that might be difficult.

At this point, it might still have been possible to find a compromise. But Russia's attitude to the EU had changed. Initially Putin had seen it as a positive force, an independent power centre which, unlike NATO, was not always condemned to follow America's lead. The refusal of France and Germany to join the US-led invasion of Iraq had appeared to bear that out. So had the EU's rejection of American concerns about excessive dependence on Russian energy supplies. But gradually the relationship had soured. By the time that Ukraine's Association

Agreement came under discussion, Putin was starting to regard the EU as a stalking horse for NATO. He told Angela Merkel: 'When I look at the membership of the EU and I look at the membership of NATO, I see basically the same thing. So when I hear about an Association Agreement for Ukraine, I know that NATO will follow.'[57]

The deterioration in Russia's relations with the EU had coincided with the appointment of José Manuel Barroso as President of the EU Commission. Barroso had been Portuguese Prime Minister at the head of a centre-right government which had strongly supported George W. Bush's invasion of Iraq. He had little time for Russia and made sure that it showed. At one of his first meetings with Putin, he began the conversation by saying: 'I'm sorry, I can only give you an hour. I have another appointment which I can't cancel.'[58] Putin found him antipathetic, arrogant and self-important. Barroso's attitude was not the only factor. By 2012, Russia and the EU were at odds over a range of economic issues as well.[59] But the lack of empathy did not help.

Barroso's message to Ukraine was that it could not have both an Association Agreement with the EU and be a member of Russia's Eurasian Economic Union. Yanukovych had to choose. It was one or the other.

The Germans disagreed and Angela Merkel urged the Commission to seek an accommodation.[60] Romano Prodi, the former Italian Prime Minister who had been Barroso's predecessor, thought that 'with goodwill [and] a very few changes', membership of the two organisations could easily be made compatible.[61] Barroso agreed reluctantly to initiate talks but at too low a level to make any difference. Part of the problem was the nature of EU decision-making. An organisation in which officials from 27 different countries have to haggle over the fine print before a consensus can be reached has little scope for flexibility. But it was also arrogance – 'the arrogance of the bureaucrats', as Merkel's Chief Foreign Policy Adviser, Christoph Heusgen, put it. The EU's attitude was 'take it or leave it'.[62]

Merkel was almost the only EU leader to foresee that this might end badly. She talked to Putin more often and had a clearer understanding of his thinking than any of her colleagues. Almost half of Ukraine's exports went to Russia, she reminded Yanukovych. Unless a compromise was reached, Kyiv would lose that market. That was not in either country's interest and it was not clear how Putin would react.[63] There were other reasons not to rush ahead. The EU was suffering from enlargement fatigue and France and Germany both wanted to call a halt until the new members from Eastern Europe had settled in and the union was functioning better. But, above all, Merkel was concerned that no one seemed to have thought through the implications of Ukrainian partnership.

In public, Putin insisted that Russia would respect whatever decision Ukraine made.[64] In private he offered Yanukovych a choice. If he signed with the EU, Russia would retaliate; if he did not, Moscow would provide substantial aid, including preferential prices for gas and a 15 billion US dollar credit.

All through the summer of 2013, the Ukrainian leader dithered.

Even with hindsight, it is hard to understand why no one in the European Commission realised that they were playing with fire. Ronald McIntosh, who had held a succession of posts at the top of the British civil service, wrote in disbelief:

> Did the European policy-makers in Brussels (the capital of a country whose ethnic, linguistic and religious differences are uncannily similar to those of Ukraine) not know that any Russian government [would] resist with the utmost vigour any attempt to bring the strategically located state of Ukraine, through which all Russia's invaders in the last century have passed, into the orbit of the European Union and therefore, by extension, of NATO? For anyone with a knowledge of history, this was not difficult to foresee.[65]

Putin had made clear at Bucharest that any move towards Ukrainian membership of NATO would have grave consequences. The Georgian war had been a warning, and had been intended as such, of how Russia was likely to react if that were ever to happen. The Europeans insisted that the EU was quite separate from NATO and blithely assumed that Ukraine's association would not pose any particular problem. It was not merely short-sighted, it was wilfully blind.

The Americans were equally blinkered. Vice President Joe Biden, whom Obama had put in charge of Ukrainian matters, had immense experience of American politics but knew little of the sensitivities at work in Kyiv and Moscow. Victoria Nuland, the State Department's point person on Ukraine, was a Russia hawk whose abrasive intelligence disconcerted friends and foes alike. It was Nuland who, when discussing America's plans for Ukraine, famously declared: 'Fuck the EU!'[66]

The remark was unintentionally revealing.

For all the high-minded talk out of Washington about promoting human rights and freedoms, neither the United States nor Russia had any real concern for Ukrainian interests and it was hypocritical to pretend otherwise. Washington's goal was to expand American influence into the areas along Russia's borders. Paul Wolfowitz was no longer in government but his ideas lived on. Carl Gershman, the long-time President of the National Endowment for Democracy, called Ukraine 'the biggest prize' for America to pluck from Russia's grasp.[67] Aleksandr Vindman, who was responsible for policy towards Ukraine in the White House some years later, characterised it as a buffer state – 'a bulwark against Russian aggression in Eastern Europe, . . . crucial to US and NATO interests'.[68]

That this was how the US viewed Ukraine should have been a surprise to no-one and it certainly was not to Putin. It is what dominant powers do. The two principal protagonists were engaged in a geopolitical zero-sum game in which America's gain was Russia's loss. It was no longer just a matter of it ending badly, as Angela Merkel had feared. Everything was in place for a catastrophic train wreck.

On November 28, 2013, Yanukovych flew to the Lithuanian capital, Vilnius, for a two-day summit of the Eastern Partnership, a forum linking the EU with six former Soviet republics. Kyiv had announced a week earlier that it was putting the Association Agreement on hold. But Barroso still believed that an accord was possible, even offering to waive the EU's insistence that the Ukrainian President first release from prison his rival, Yulia Tymoshenko, if that was all that prevented him signing.

Yanukovych refused.

He was then asked whether he would commit to signing at a subsequent EU summit.

Again, he refused.

Instead Yanukovych proposed trilateral talks with the EU and Russia to examine the economic consequences, in particular the cost of upgrading the Ukrainian economy to meet European quality standards and to compensate for the loss of Russian markets – a suggestion which was angrily rejected by Barroso and Herman Van Rompuy, the former Belgian Prime Minister who presided over the European Council, the assembly of EU Heads of State, and who had been chosen for that post precisely because he was colourless and no threat to his peers. Barroso harrumphed that 'the time for limited sovereignty was over' and Van Rompuy declared that Europe would not countenance external interference, 'least of all from Russia'.

It was not the EU's finest hour.

Brussels, however, was no longer the main player. That role now fell to the people of Ukraine. Thousands and, soon, tens of thousands, gathered in the main squares of Kyiv and other cities to demand that Yanukovych reverse course and sign the Association Agreement. As ever, the country was split between the pro-European West and the pro-Russian East but there was also a generational divide. For a majority of young Ukrainians, who had grown up after independence, the EU was a beacon of hope, holding out the prospect of an end to the ubiquitous corruption which poisoned everyone's lives and respect for the rule of law and democratic values. Older people were more reticent.

Yanukovych blew hot and cold. On his return from Vilnius, he insisted that talks with the EU would continue and that the Association Agreement would be signed 'in the near future'.[69] But the same evening, he sent in riot police and the hated Berkut, Ukraine's special forces, to disperse the protesters who had gathered in Kyiv's Independence Square, which they did with characteristic vigour. Dozens were injured and ended up in hospital.

It turned out to have been a serious mistake. Two days later, on December 1, two hundred thousand people, defying a ban on further demonstrations, descended on the city centre in protest. It was a repetition of the Orange Revolution, ten years earlier, and on a similar scale. All that month, the 'Euromaidan', as the movement was known, continued. In mid January, Yanukovych pushed through parliament harsh new restrictions on free speech and assembly which provoked more giant demonstrations. This time the police fired live rounds at the crowd, killing four protesters and injuring many others. When that failed to quell the protests, Yanukovych offered concessions. That had no effect either.

In private, Putin tried to strengthen the Ukrainian leader's resolve. In public, he sent mixed messages.[70] On the one hand, he wanted

Yanukovych to stand firm. On the other, he was increasingly concerned that the unrest would overshadow the Sochi Olympics, which opened on February 7. He telephoned Yanukovych almost every day to try to ensure that he did nothing foolish.[71] But the situation continued to degenerate. Radical groups and extreme right-wing nationalist organisations formed self-defence detachments which did battle with the riot police. The Ukrainian leader's support haemorrhaged away and his parliamentary majority fractured. He was out of his depth and did not know how to respond.

Matters came to a head as the Olympics drew to a close. All that week, downtown Kyiv had been in a state of insurrection. The protesters threw Molotov cocktails and cobble stones, and invaded Yanukovych's party headquarters, which they set on fire. The Berkut responded with water cannon, tear gas and flash and stun grenades. Interior Ministry troops, armed with AK-47s, opened fire on the crowds. Members of an ultranationalist paramilitary group, Pravyi Sektor, 'Right Sector', fired back. On Tuesday and Wednesday, February 18 and 19, at least 28 people died. On Thursday, a ceasefire was declared. Then sniper fire rang out. At first, it was assumed that the special forces were responsible. When riot police as well as civilians were wounded, some suspected that extremists were firing indiscriminately to ratchet up the tension and make compromise impossible. Others, perhaps more logically, thought marksmen on both sides were at work.

On Thursday, February 20, by which time 90 people had died, the French, German and Polish Foreign Ministers arrived to mediate.

Yanukovych at first dug in his heels, refusing to give ground. But after a telephone call from Putin, who told him bluntly that he had to negotiate to save what he could, he agreed to form a government of national unity and call early elections, which had been the opposition's main demands.[72] The agreement, which Yanukovych believed would keep him in power for at least a few more months, was signed with much ceremony the following day and the mediators left for home, content that their work was done.

But by then the President's allies in the power ministries had seen the writing on the wall. His concessions told them that his fate was sealed. The police and Berkut units which had been guarding government buildings started to melt away. At Yanukovych's garish 300-acre estate on the outskirts of Kyiv, complete with a private zoo, faux-Greek statuary and a full-scale replica of a Spanish galleon, aides began frantically burning documents and dumping sacks full of files into a nearby river.[73]

Only Yanukovych himself seemed oblivious of the forces bearing down on him. When Putin telephoned him that evening, he insisted that the situation was under control.[74] He was about to leave for Kharkiv, in eastern Ukraine, he said, to attend a regional party conference. Putin urged him to stay, telling him it was not the moment to leave Kyiv.[75] Yanukovych said he would think about it.

Whether he was really 'living in an illusion', as some of his colleagues believed,[76] or whether, deep down, he understood that the battle was lost, he left for Kharkiv by car in the early hours of Saturday morning with some of his closest aides. From there he travelled on to Donetsk, intending to fly to Russia, but border guards prevented him boarding his plane. Putin, who had remained in telephone contact, told him to head towards the coast. Eventually, in the early hours of Sunday morning, Russian special forces helicopters located the convoy and flew the party to Crimea.[77] Yanukovych reached Moscow the following Tuesday, February 25.[78]

In public, Putin refused to comment on the Ukrainian leader's flight, but when a journalist asked him whether he sympathised with Yanukovych's predicament, he replied tersely, 'No. I have very different feelings.'[79] In private, he was quoted as saying: 'I never imagined that he was such a cowardly piece of shit.'[80] However, Yanukovych still had value as a figurehead. In the Kremlin's narrative, he remained Ukraine's legitimate President and his authority would frequently be invoked to justify future Russian actions.

On the night of Saturday, February 22, while Yanukovych's motorcade was still somewhere in southern Ukraine – no one knew exactly where – Putin summoned the heads of the special services, the Security Council, the Presidential Administration and the Defence Ministry to Novo-Ogaryovo. The developments in Kyiv, he told them, meant that a decision could no longer be delayed. There was a narrow window of opportunity, while Ukraine was without a government and its authorities were in disarray, for Russia to take back control of Crimea, which Khrushchev had transferred to Ukraine 60 years earlier.[81]

The discussion lasted all night. The future of Crimea had been on

Putin's mind for months. In December, he had been asked whether he would consider sending troops there if the situation deteriorated. 'That's just nonsense,' he replied. 'There's nothing like that now and never will be.'[82]

But 'never' is a mutable term. By the time the meeting broke up, Putin had 'set specific tasks. I said what we should do and how we should do it.' The Security Council Secretary, Nikolai Patrushev, and Aleksandr Bortnikov, a contemporary from the Leningrad KGB who had succeeded him as head of the FSB, were enthusiastic. The Defence Minister, Sergei Shoigu, who would be responsible for the operation, much less so. No contingency plans existed; the operation would have to be played by ear;[83] it was unclear how the West would react; and if the Ukrainian troops there resisted, it would become a bloody mess.

Shoigu had been appointed a year earlier after his predecessor, Anatoly Serdyukov, had been entrapped in a Kremlin intrigue concocted by Sechin and Sergei Ivanov. Serdyukov had been cleared of the accusations against him but Putin felt that the military reforms which he had been appointed to carry out had gone far enough. The generals hated him and it was time to replace him with a less contentious figure.

That morning, Sunday, February 23, Shoigu's objections were overruled. While Putin flew to Sochi, to attend the Olympic closing ceremony, the Defence Minister made his dispositions. Paratroops from the elite Pskov 76th Guards Division were flown in to support Russian special forces units at Sevastopol, and 150,000 troops were moved to western Russia, close to the Ukrainian border, for a surprise military exercise, supposedly to 'check preparedness'.[84] The latter was a diversionary move, but it meant that there would be forces nearby if the Crimean operation ran into trouble and the Ukrainian army resisted.[85] The paratroops wore unmarked green uniforms, leading local journalists to dub them 'little green men', or more circumspectly, 'polite armed men'.[86] But there was no attempt to hide where they came from. They spoke Russian and drove military vehicles with Russian number plates.

Three days later they seized control of government offices and the Crimean Supreme Council building, where the regional parliament met. The following morning the deputies voted to dismiss the region's pro-Ukrainian Prime Minister. In his place, they named 41-year old Sergei Aksyonov, a local right-wing politician with the build of a heavyweight boxer, a dubious reputation and allegedly a long history of links to organised crime.[87]

The appointment was confirmed by Yanukovych – 'the lawful incumbent', as Putin called him – which the Russians insisted made it 'legally watertight'.

The takeover went more smoothly than Shoigu had feared.

Thanks to his predecessor's reforms, the 'little green men' were well equipped, well trained and highly motivated. The veteran *New York Times* correspondent, C. J. Chivers, noted the contrast with the down-at-heel conscripts who had been sent to fight in Chechnya and Georgia. These men were lean, fit and sober, he wrote. Even soldiers on guard duty had push-to-talk encrypted radios and flak jackets. The military vehicles were in excellent repair and they had state-of-the-art electronic warfare platforms to jam GPS and satellite communications. The 22,000 Ukrainian troops based in Crimea made no attempt to resist, and by the weekend, the intruders, still officially unidentified, controlled the whole peninsula.[88]

No one in the West was yet sure of Putin's intentions. He had told Angela Merkel that the lives of Russian citizens in Crimea were being threatened by the 'Ukrainian ultranationalists' who had taken power in Kyiv and that Russia had a duty to protect them.[89] Afterwards Merkel told Obama that she was 'not sure he was in touch with reality – [he seemed to be] in another world'.[90] The only certainty was that neither the United States nor any other Western government was contemplating a military response. Putin's instincts had been correct. There would be symbolic protests against the takeover of Crimea and, no doubt, economic sanctions. But no one would actually try to stop it.

For ten days after Yanukovych fled from Kyiv, Putin made no public comment. Finally, on March 4, he summoned the press to Novo-Ogaryovo for what turned out to be a strangely disjointed news conference.[91] The Ukrainian President, he said, had been overthrown in a coup d'état organised by the United States, which had trained 'combat detachments' in Lithuania and Poland for 'an armed seizure of power'. Yet at the same time he expressed sympathy for the demonstrators on Maidan. Corruption in Ukraine, he said, was 'beyond anything we can imagine'. People were fed up with seeing 'one set of thieves replaced by another'. They wanted 'radical change, not just some cosmetic remodelling of power'.

Putin was trying to square the circle, to reach out to the Ukrainian people while denouncing the reactionaries, 'the people wearing arm-bands with signs like swastikas', who had allegedly done the West's dirty work. Outside Russia, few found that credible.

Russia's long-term goal for Ukraine, Putin indicated, would be some form of federal system under which the country's Russian-speaking East would have constitutional guarantees giving it – and hence the Kremlin – a voice in Ukraine's future geopolitical orientation. In the meantime, he went on, Russia had the right to intervene militarily because Yanukovych, the 'legitimate President', had requested him 'to use our armed forces to protect the lives, freedom and health of Ukrainian citizens' and the Federation Council had granted him emer-gency powers to do so. Russia would act, he added, only if chaos spread to eastern Ukraine and the Russophone population there asked for help. It would be 'a humanitarian mission' and would be undertaken only as 'a very last resort'. So far, he said, 'there is no need for that. But the possibility is there.'

The one subject on which Putin refused to be drawn was the future of Crimea. The 'little green men', he insisted, were just 'local self-defence units'. If their uniforms resembled those of Russian soldiers, it was because 'anyone can go into a store and buy all kinds of uniforms.' As for the possibility of Crimea seeking to join Russia, 'we will in no way . . . encourage such sentiments'.

In fact, plans were already well under way for a referendum on that very subject. Less than two weeks later, on Sunday, March 16, 82 per cent of the electorate – a figure which coincided exactly with the pro-portion of Russian speakers in the territory[92] – lined up to cast their votes and 96 per cent of them voted to rejoin Russia. Not long after-wards, Putin finally admitted that the 'little green men' were indeed Russian troops.[93] The takeover, he stressed, had been bloodless, which he seemed to think made it alright. But it did not change the fact that a region of Ukraine had been occupied by the Russian army.

At a joint session of the two houses of parliament the following Tuesday, Putin set out the reasons for what he called the decision to 'return Crimea to be part of Russia'.[94]

The first was cultural, historical and sentimental – 'sacral', as he later put it. Crimea had always been 'an inseparable part of Russia'. In the tenth century, Prince Vladimir had been baptised into the Orthodox faith at Chersonesus, on the outskirts of present-day Sevastopol. The territory's history was a saga of 'Russian military glory and outstanding valour'. When Khrushchev had given it to Ukraine, 'Russia was not simply robbed, it was plundered.'

The second, more urgent, reason was to prevent Ukraine joining NATO. 'If we hadn't done anything,' Putin said, 'Ukraine would have been drawn into NATO at some point in the future, and we'd have been told, "This isn't your business."'[95] As long as Ukraine was embroiled in a territorial dispute with its neighbours, NATO membership was ruled out.[96]

Then he turned to those who he claimed were really responsible for what had happened in Ukraine. The Maidan demonstrations, he repeated, had been understandable: Yanukovych and his cabal had been 'milking the country, fighting among themselves for power and cash flows'. But behind the protesters stood people who had a very different agenda – 'nationalists, anti-Semites, neo-Nazis and Russophobes . . . ideological heirs of Bandera,* Hitler's accomplice during World War II'. This motley band of fascists 'set the tone in Ukraine to this day', he charged. They controlled the country's new provisional administration. Behind them stood the United States, 'the foreign sponsor of these so-called politicians'. America's complaints that Russia had violated international law by annexing Crimea were 'amazing, primitive, blunt cynicism':

> The Crimean authorities followed the well-known Kosovo precedent – a precedent our Western colleagues created with their own hands in a very similar situation, when they agreed [to] the unilateral separation of Kosovo from Serbia, exactly what Crimea is doing now . . . One should not call the same thing white today and black tomorrow . . . Our Western partners, led by the United States, . . . have come to believe that they can decide the destinies of the world, that only they can ever be right . . . They have lied to us many times, made decisions behind our backs, placed us before a fait accompli. This happened with NATO's

---

* Stepan Bandera was the head of the OUN, the Organisation of Ukrainian Nationalists, which was responsible for wartime pogroms and massacres of tens of thousands of Jews and Poles in western Ukraine. He had been a Nazi collaborator since the early 1930s and after the war was protected by the German BND. He was assassinated by the KGB in Munich in 1959.

expansion to the East [and] with the deployment of a missile defence
system . . . In short, we have every reason to assume that the infamous
policy of containment, carried out in the eighteenth, nineteeth and
twentieth centuries, continues today. They are constantly trying to
sweep us into a corner because we have an independent position . . .
But there is a limit to everything. And with Ukraine, our Western partners have crossed the line . . . They must really have lacked . . . common
sense not to foresee the consequences of their actions. They put Russia
in a position which left it with no way out. If you compress a spring all
the way to its limit, it will snap back hard.

The key reference was to 'containment'. It was the first time that Putin
had raised directly what would become a major theme of his later
years in power – that Russia was being encircled by a ring of hostile
states and would shape its foreign policy accordingly.

In Russia, the Crimean operation was regarded as a triumph, a
demonstration of the country's newfound strength. Putin's ratings
shot up above 80 per cent. The *fronde* which had marked the beginning
of his third presidential term was largely forgotten.

In the West, it was portrayed as naked aggression. But the accusation of double standards was not easy to rebut. In July 2010, the
International Court in the Hague had ruled that Kosovo's declaration
of independence from Serbia, of which it had been part, did not violate international law. If the Kosovars had the right to secede, it was
hard to argue that the people of Crimea did not. In both cases, secession had been made possible by foreign military intervention. There
were differences – Crimea, at the time of the referendum, was occupied by Russian troops; in Kosovo, independence was proclaimed
after NATO troops had left – but, nuances aside, there were obvious
parallels.

The United States struggled to coordinate an appropriate response.
Words were easy. The US Secretary of State, John Kerry, accused Putin
of 'behaving in nineteenth-century fashion by invading another country'.[97] Obama said derisively that Russia was just 'a regional power',
which was threatening its neighbours 'not out of strength but weakness'.[98] But Putin had caught the West off guard and, beyond verbal
outrage, it was far from clear what Western governments could do.
America and Britain announced that they would not send official

delegations to the Paralympics in Sochi later that month. As punishment for the occupation of Crimea, it seemed a little inadequate.

Over the next few months, the United States imposed further sanctions on members of Putin's inner circle. The OECD suspended Russia's membership application. NATO broke off its few remaining contacts with Russia. The US–Russia liaison commissions, set up by Putin and George W. Bush, ceased meeting. Russia was expelled from the G8 and, the following year, Western leaders boycotted celebrations marking the 70th anniversary of victory in the Second World War, a symbolic move which, while perhaps unavoidable politically, angered many ordinary Russians, who took it as a gratuitous insult to the tens of millions of their fellow citizens who had sacrificed their lives to defeat Hitler's armies.

But none of that inflicted real costs. Even at the level of symbolism, there were limits to what could be done. NASA had planned to halt cooperation with the Russian space programme but found it could not because, after the demise of the US Space Shuttle, Russian rockets launched from Baikonur were the only way to get US astronauts to the International Space Station. The Americans swallowed their pride and Putin was happy to let them do so.

Another unpleasant surprise for Washington was the discovery that the Ukrainian economy was in a far worse state than anyone had realised. The United States, having cheered on the opposition, was less enthusiastic about investing the tens of billions of dollars needed to nurse the country back to economic health. Likewise the EU. The level of corruption was, as one expert put it, 'insane'. There was no functioning government and the country was culturally and linguistically divided. Ukraine, like Iraq, began to look like a poisoned chalice which the West would have done better to leave alone.

There is a broad consensus among Western scholars and diplomats that Putin's annexation of Crimea was a huge mistake, condemning Russia to international isolation, alienating the Ukrainian people and ensuring for the foreseeable future a hostile state on its south-western flank. That argument can certainly be made. It is more than possible that, even if Russia had not intervened, Ukraine would not have been accepted as a full member of the Western camp. In that case, the outcome that Putin feared – Ukrainian membership of NATO – would never have been on the table and all Russia's subsequent travails, not to mention the suffering in Ukraine, would have been avoided.

It was a risk that he was not willing to take.[99]

At first, it appeared that Putin's calculations had been correct. In the summer of 2014, NATO let it be known that further enlargement would be put on hold.[100] The view in the Kremlin was: 'Oh, they [the Ukrainians] will cry for a year or two, but there are so many connexions, people have personal ties, it will work itself out.'[101] Putin himself had stated repeatedly, before the annexation of Crimea, that Russians and Ukrainians were 'fraternal nations, . . . fundamentally a single people' and that 'no matter what may happen, . . . regardless of the paths we take, we will come together in the end'.[102]

There was a certain logic to that. Geography condemns Ukraine and Russia to be neighbours and ultimately neighbouring countries have to find a way to coexist. The war between Russia and Georgia had had no lasting consequences. Turkey had occupied northern Cyprus since 1974 but had suffered only token condemnation.[103] Putin initially assumed that the annexation of Crimea would be the same.[104]

Within days, however, clashes broke out in eastern Ukraine between the Russian-speaking population and Ukrainian nationalists. The United States accused Moscow of being behind the unrest. That may have been true. But it is equally likely that the initial outbreaks were spontaneous.

Putin's behaviour was difficult to read. In mid April, he seemed to be pouring fuel on the flames, threatening to 'do everything we can to help these people [the Russian-speaking population] to defend their rights and determine their fate on their own'. In the West it was assumed that he had been carried away by the success of the Crimean operation and was itching to do something similar in Novorossiya, a vast swathe of land stretching from Donetsk in the east to Odessa in the west, which, in tsarist times, had been Russian territory. That was not the case. Militarily it was impracticable[105] and, in any case, it was unnecessary. If the goal was to keep Ukraine out of NATO, the annexation of Crimea was sufficient. The alliance did not accept new members embroiled in territorial disputes. But a local insurgency in eastern Ukraine might pressure Kyiv to install the kind of federal system that Putin regarded as the best long-term solution to Russia's concerns. He therefore approved limited aid to the separatist militias.

The problem, as he soon discovered, was that a popular resistance movement, even if stiffened by Russian volunteers and advised by the Russian military, was almost impossible to control. In May, the Kremlin instructed the insurgent leaders in Donetsk and Luhansk to scrap plans to hold referenda on declaring their self-proclaimed republics independent.[106] The separatists went ahead anyway.

That month, Moscow began signalling that it was ready to explore a political solution. Russian troop concentrations near the Ukrainian border were withdrawn.[107] Putin backed proposals by Angela Merkel and the OSCE for direct talks between the separatists and the authorities in Kyiv.[108] At the beginning of June, when he travelled to France to attend ceremonies marking the 70th anniversary of the D-day landings, he had a meeting with Merkel, Hollande, and Petr Poroshenko, a billionaire industrialist who had been elected Ukraine's President ten days earlier.[109] The Normandy format, as the four-way framework was afterwards called, became the vehicle for peace negotiations.[110]

However, it was carrot and stick. Alongside the conciliatory gestures, there was no let-up in Russian rhetoric. The insurgency developed from isolated clashes into the beginnings of civil war. By mid June, the separatists controlled an area of about 500 square miles. The Russian 'volunteers' supporting them included army veterans, soldiers from the 76th Pskov Division who had been in Crimea and were supposedly on leave, and fighters from Chechnya and other Caucasian republics despatched by Ramzan Kadyrov. Russian arms crossed the frontier and the Russian Defence Ministry provided tactical advice.

The mission had originally been conceived as a black operation, to provide guidance, weapons and deniable volunteer support, and let the separatists fight it out by themselves. But Russia found itself being sucked in to a much greater extent than Putin had intended. He continued to insist publicly that 'there are no Russian units in eastern Ukraine, no special services, no advisers. All this is being done by local residents.'[111] But deniability had been lost. Putin was about to discover the perils of supporting a war which he did not fully control.

On the afternoon of July 17, a Thursday, a separatist spokesman in Donetsk announced that a Ukrainian An-26 military transport plane had been shot down by what he called 'a mobile anti-aircraft missile system' about 40 miles east of the city. The announcement appeared credible. The separatists had shot down another Ukrainian air force plane, also an An-26, three days earlier. The story was given prominent coverage by Russian state news media.

However, other reports then started coming in, quoting Ukrainian aviation officials as saying that the plane which had been brought down was not an An-26 at all, but a Malaysian airliner with 298 passengers and crew on board.

The plane, a Boeing 777 on a scheduled flight from Amsterdam to Kuala Lumpur, had mysteriously disappeared from the radar screens in the same area, two hours before the separatists' announcement.[112] It was later established that it had disintegrated at 33,000 feet, scattering bodies and debris over an area of 20 square miles. They included 193 Dutch citizens, 43 Malaysians, 27 Australians and 10 Britons. There were no survivors.

That morning, a Buk mobile surface-to-air missile launcher from Russia's 53rd Anti-Aircraft Missile Brigade based in Kursk, 100 miles to the north, had been set up in a wheat field near the separatist-controlled village of Pervomaisky. Later that day, when the unit returned to Russia, satellite photographs showed that one of its four missiles was missing.

The provision of anti-aircraft weapons to the insurgents had been authorised a few days earlier by the Russian General Staff, which had become concerned that Ukraine's domination of the air would turn the tide against them.[113] The Ukrainian army had launched a large-scale pincer movement to cut the supply routes from the border. The Russians had deployed Grad multiple rocket launchers but they had failed to halt the Ukrainian troops' advance.[114] The decision to provide the Buk launcher, had been taken by a top FSB officer, Colonel-General Andrei Burlaka, the first deputy head of the Border Guards.[115]

The political fallout from the shooting down of Flight MH17 was disastrous. Not only had Putin's denials that Russian troops were waging war against Ukraine been exposed for the lies they were, but the Russians had been caught providing their protégés in the Donbas with advanced weaponry without taking even basic precautions to control how it would be used. The liberal commentator, Yulia Latynina, wrote in *Novaya gazeta*: 'The blame rests entirely with those who put matches in the hands of the patients in the Luhansk–Donetsk asylum.'[116]

The incident marked a turning point in Russia's relations with the West.

Seven years earlier, Putin had acknowledged at Munich that whatever hopes Russia might have had of becoming an equal partner in a Western-dominated world had been an illusion. At the end of Medvedev's presidency, the Libyan fiasco had convinced the Kremlin that America and its allies were fundamentally untrustworthy and that Russia could only work with them if it had binding guarantees. The annexation of Crimea had brought further intractable problems. But after the shooting down of the Malaysian airliner, a door slammed shut. It was one of those pivotal moments that influence everything that follows. For the foreseeable future, any hope of a lasting improvement in relations with the West was foreclosed.

The immediate reaction in Moscow was to brazen it out. Andropov had done the same when a Soviet fighter pilot shot down a South Korean airliner which had gone off course over the Soviet Far East. But that was in 1983, at a particularly tense moment of the Cold War, and Andropov, after initial denials, had eventually acknowledged Russian culpability.

Putin denied to the end that Russia had been involved.

In his first public comment, a brief televised address three days later, he said only that no one must attempt to exploit the tragedy politically and that it was essential that hostilities end.[117] His delivery was stilted and unnatural, he had dark circles under his eyes and his face showed a waxen pallor. One Russian commentator said he 'looked as though he had not slept for several days and was nervous and floundering'.[118] Russians compared his situation to the chess position called zugzwang, where a player is obliged to make a move but whatever he does will leave him worse off.[119]

Putin had concluded that the shooting down of MH17 had caused such outrage in the West that Russia would gain nothing by admitting it and, by denying it, had nothing to lose.

The Russian Defence Ministry issued a stream of far-fetched allegations whose only common point was that the Ukrainians were responsible. Why Ukraine should have been targeting aircraft when the separatists did not possess any was not explained. But, according to opinion polls, that was what 80 per cent of the Russian population wished to believe. In November, when Putin flew to Australia for a summit of the G20, he was ostracised and left early. The United States and Europe imposed a second and then a third round of financial sanctions. Russia banned European agricultural imports. US–Russian agreements on security and disarmament matters, which had resisted earlier crises, began to unravel.

But the main effect was in Ukraine itself. Putin had initially hoped that a mix of irregular forces, Russian volunteers using conventional weaponry and disguised Russian regular units would be enough to ward off Ukrainian government attacks. But in the late summer of 2014, it became clear that that would not be enough. The insurgents were being mauled by a large-scale Ukrainian offensive. Russia had no choice, he decided, but to take charge directly.

On the morning of August 24, Russian armoured columns crossed the border moving west, towards Luhansk, and south towards the Azov Sea coast. Since the MH17 disaster had exposed the fiction that it was merely a local insurrection, there was no longer any need for sub-terfuge. In less than a week, most of the areas which the separatist forces had yielded were back in Russian hands and 7,000 Ukrainian sol-diers were surrounded. Putin savoured Poroshenko's humiliation, proposing that they open a humanitarian corridor to allow the Ukrain-ian troops to withdraw.

To all intents and purposes, the insurgency had become a conven-tional conflict between Russia and Ukraine. That had not been the original plan. But the Ukrainians had put up stiffer resistance and the separatists had been more undisciplined than the Russians had expected.

The entry of the Russian army forced Kyiv to recognise that a mili-tary solution was no longer possible. The West would not fight for Ukraine or even provide offensive weapons. In September, talks between the two sides were held in Minsk and a ceasefire was declared, which, like all the ceasefires which would follow, lasted only a matter of days before fighting resumed.

A second meeting in Minsk, in February 2015, this time between Poroshenko, Putin, François Hollande and Angela Merkel, made more substantial progress. Hollande wrote later that they talked through the night, breaking up at 7 a.m. Putin, he thought, was the most difficult foreign leader he had ever had to deal with. 'Muscular, enigmatic, as warm and solicitous as he could be glacial and brutal,' Hollande wrote, 'he looked directly at his interlocutor with blue eyes which were by turns seductive and disturbing, reasoning cynically, expansively bursting into laughter, uttering placidly the harshest words.'[120] Merkel wrote out the articles of agreement by hand on a notepad as the discussion progressed.

The main point of contention was over the timing of a new cease-fire. Putin wanted it delayed to give the separatists time to occupy more territory, in particular the town of Debaltsevo, a rail and road junction midway between Donetsk and Luhansk, where 6,000 Ukrainian soldiers had been surrounded. Hollande and Merkel refused. By then nearly 10,000 people had lost their lives in the conflict. The European Union insisted that hostilities end at once. Later in the morning, Putin backed down. But it turned out to be a feint. Although the cease-fire along most of the frontline took effect at midnight that night, the battle for Debaltsevo raged on. The Ukrainians broke out, with heavy casualties, three days later, and the separatists took possession.

The agreement, known as Minsk II, signed by representatives of Russia, Ukraine and the separatists, called for an exchange of hostages, an amnesty for the insurgents, a pull-back of heavy weapons by both sides, the restoration of economic links and the holding of local elections in the separatist areas, which were to have substantial autonomy. The key provision, however, was for constitutional reform to give the Russian-speaking regions a voice in national policy.[121] Poroshenko said later he had agreed because it was the only way to stop the fighting, but he had known that it would never be implemented because neither the political establishment nor public opinion in Ukraine would accept it.

And so it turned out. Minsk II remained unrealised. The conflict remained frozen. There were sporadic outbreaks of renewed fighting, but the frontline remained largely unchanged. The separatists controlled about 6,000 square miles, 2.5 per cent of Ukraine's territory, an area larger than Connecticut but smaller than Wales. More people would die, though far fewer than in the early days of the war. Russia would have to live with yet another hostile state on its western border. On the other hand, Ukraine could not join NATO, which, to Putin, was what mattered most, and the Russians had a means of pressure which he hoped would eventually force Kyiv to begin negotiating a permanent solution.

As the conflict in Ukraine stabilised, a new threat – and, for Putin, a new opportunity – arose.

ISIS, the Islamic fundamentalist group also known as Daesh, and the Islamic State of Iraq and the Levant, which had originally been affiliated to al-Qaeda, had been gathering strength in northern Iraq and Syria. In the spring of 2014, it seized control of Iraq's Fallujah province and drove the Iraqi army out of the country's second-largest city, Mosul. That got the attention of the Obama administration, which in August authorised targeted attacks on ISIS formations, first in Iraq and then, a month later, in Syria.[122] Until then the United States, having failed to create an effective moderate Syrian opposition force, had adopted a hands-off policy towards the jihadist groups which had been bearing the brunt of the fighting against Assad's army. Washington could not support them but it had not attacked them either. After ISIS captured Mosul, that policy was no longer tenable.

Washington found itself with no good options. Attacking Assad strengthened ISIS and attacking ISIS would strengthen Assad.

To Putin, America's difficulties offered an opening. The United States, he said, was behaving as though there were 'good terrorists and bad terrorists'. But in what way were they different? 'Is it that the so-called moderates behead people more delicately or in more limited numbers?'[123] The only realistic policy, he argued, was to support Assad's government, because without the participation of the Syrian army, it was not possible to eliminate the jihadist threat.[124] Airstrikes on their own were not enough. They had to be coordinated with forces on the ground.[125]

By this stage – early in 2015 – the conflict had become a full-scale civil war. Almost five million Syrians had fled, most of them to neighbouring Turkey, Lebanon and Jordan. Hundreds of thousands of desperate families had set out in rickety boats to try to reach Greece, the nearest EU state. The awfulness of their plight was brought home to Europeans, who until then had paid little attention, sitting comfortably in their living rooms watching the news on television, by a single heart-wrenching image of a dead toddler, whose body had washed up on a Turkish beach, lying doubled up, face down on the sand.

Facing a humanitarian crisis of unprecedented proportions, both Russia and the United States called for an international coalition to fight ISIS. But they were talking about different things. Putin sought an alliance 'similar to the anti-Hitler coalition, willing to stand firm against those who, like the Nazis, sow evil and hatred'.[126] He looked to the Syrian government, the Kurdish militias in northern Syria and Iraq, and the regional powers, Egypt, Iran and its protégé, Hezbollah.[127] The United States looked to its traditional allies – Australia, Britain, France and the Sunni states along the Gulf, Saudi Arabia, the Arab Emirates and Qatar – all of which continued to demand Assad's departure.

Putin set out Russia's position in a speech to the UN General Assembly at the end of September 2015. The refugee crisis, he said, was the result of the recklessness with which the US and its allies had destroyed government institutions in Iraq and Libya without any thought of what to put in their place.

> Instead of bringing democracy and progress, there is violence, poverty, social disasters and total disregard for human rights . . . I want to ask those who brought about this situation? Do you finally realise now what you have done? But I am afraid this question will be left hanging in the air, unanswered, because they refuse to abandon this policy, which is based on arrogance, exceptionalism and impunity.[128]

It was 'a great mistake' to refuse to cooperate with the Syrian authorities, Putin said, because the Syrian army and the Kurds were the only ones really fighting ISIS. The jihadists were 'not stupid', he said. 'They are as smart as you [Americans].' They sought Assad's overthrow in order to create the same kind of chaos that allowed them to flourish in Libya and Iraq. Supporting the moderate armed opposition was no answer because it lacked the strength to act independently and, in many areas, worked so closely with the radicals that they were almost indistinguishable.[129]

The following day, Putin met Obama. It was their first extended encounter for more than two years. He said afterwards that they had reached an understanding to create 'appropriate mechanisms' to coordinate their policies in Syria, and that there were 'many points, strange as it may seem, on which our opinions coincide'.[130] The American readout was more cautious. The United States was bogged down in its interminable war in Afghanistan and Obama was still bruised by what he now acknowledged to have been his error in endorsing the French-led attack on Libya.[131] No one in the administration or in Congress had much appetite for getting entangled in yet another unpopular Middle Eastern war.

The meeting gave Putin the confirmation he needed. Obama would not authorise more than limited intervention.

Back in Moscow, on September 30, he announced that Russia would begin attacking ISIS positions, but there would be no involvement of ground forces and the operation would be limited in time.[132]

The same day, the Russian General Staff launched a simulacrum of George W. Bush's 'shock and awe'. Fighter-bombers based at Khmeimim, on the Syrian coast near Latakia, carried out airstrikes. Strategic bombers were sent from as far away as Murmansk, in the Russian far north and, in a studied demonstration of 'great power' technical prowess, 3M14T cruise missiles, travelling at a height of between 150 and 650 feet across Iran and Iraq, were fired at ISIS bases from Russian warships in the Caspian Sea, nearly a thousand miles away to the east.[133] Others were launched from a Russian submarine in the Mediterranean.[134]

The Russian intervention did not quite measure up to the hi-tech wizardry the Americans had deployed against Saddam Hussein, 12 years earlier. The ageing Russian aircraft carrier, the *Kuznetsov*, limped down from the Barents Sea, belching black smoke like a warship in a grainy old movie of World War I and suffering the indignity of being refused port facilities by Malta and Spain.[135] Nonetheless, for the first time since the collapse of the Soviet Union, Moscow had shown that it was able to project power to regions far from its own borders.

In the West, there was outrage at the systematic destruction of Aleppo and other insurgent-held cities, large parts of which the Russians flattened, killing thousands of civilians, in much the same way as they had destroyed Grozny during the Chechen war, 15 years earlier. To Putin, that was hypocrisy. 'Attempts to spare terrorists under the pretext of protecting civilians are unacceptable,' he said.[136] 'We keep hearing, Aleppo, Aleppo, Aleppo. But what is the issue here? Do we leave the terrorists in place, or do we squeeze them out? . . . Look at Israel's example. Israel never steps back but fights to the end and that is how it survives. There is no alternative. We need to fight. If we keep retreating, we will always lose.'[137] War was by definition brutal and it was naïve to think otherwise.

It was not the only complaint against the Russians' tactics. The Americans accused them of targeting the moderate Western-backed opposition rather than the jihadist groups. But the situation was more complicated than either side wished to admit. The American-led coalition targeted ISIS but left Jabhat al-Nusra and other radical groups alone because they were often inseparable from the moderate opposition. The Russians attacked all the jihadist groups indiscriminately and provided air cover for Syrian ground forces. If Western-backed units opposing Assad suffered collateral damage, the Russians were not going to shed tears. The Americans, understandably, saw things differently.

Another, even trickier, issue was Russia's relationship with Turkey.

The whole of Syria's northern border, almost 600 miles long, adjoined Turkish territory. Putin had developed good relations with Recep Tayyip Erdoğan, Turkey's President and earlier long-time Prime Minister. Six million Russian tourists visited Turkey each year, Russia was building a nuclear power station at Akkuyu, on the Mediterranean coast, and the two countries had recently reached agreement on a pipeline project under the Black Sea – a substitute for an earlier scheme known as South Stream, which had been rejected by the European Commission when José Barroso was President – to provide Russian natural gas to Turkey and South-East and Central Europe. On the other hand, Turkey was a member of NATO and Erdoğan, like the rest of the alliance, wanted Assad out of power. To that end, the Turks had been providing military support to the Syrian Turkmens, an ethnically related group opposed to the Syrian government, who lived along the border.[138]

That divergence was compounded by Ankara's sensitivity towards anything remotely connected with the Kurds. To Erdoğan, Kurdish separatism was an existential threat and the Kurdish People's Defense Units, the YPG, as much an enemy as al-Qaeda and ISIS.[139] To Putin, the Kurds were 'the most combat-ready group opposing ISIS'[140] and were making 'a large and significant contribution . . . to the fight against terrorism'.[141]

The tension between those two positions was unsustainable.

On November 24, 2015, a Russian Sukhoi attack aircraft, returning from a raid against positions held by the Turkmens and Jabhat al-Nusra, was shot down by a Turkish air force fighter. The pilot and navigator ejected. One was shot and killed as he parachuted down – a violation of the Geneva Convention – the other survived and was helicoptered out, though not before the Turkmens had fatally wounded one of the rescue team. Ankara claimed that the Russian plane had violated Turkish airspace, which the Russians denied. Exactly where the fault lay is unclear. The whole border was on a hair-trigger.[142] Erdoğan immediately appealed to his NATO partners for protection, earning Putin's enduring contempt. He was 'brown-nosing the Americans', he said, 'running to [NATO], shouting "Help!"' instead of picking up the phone and trying to straighten things out.[143]

To Putin, it was 'a stab in the back', a deliberate betrayal by Erdoğan's 'ruling clique', which, he charged, had long acted as the terrorists' accomplices and now bore 'direct responsibility' for the Russian servicemen's deaths.[144] Russian pilots, Putin said, had reported seeing miles-long convoys of thousands of oil tankers, driving from ISIS-controlled areas into Turkey, where their cargos were sent on to Turkish ports for export.[145] 'We know who are stuffing their pockets in Turkey and letting the terrorists prosper from the oil they are stealing,' he told the Russian parliament. 'The jihadists used the money to recruit mercenaries and buy weapons and plan inhuman attacks against people in France, Lebanon, Mali and other places.'[146]

In the West, there was a deafening silence. It was a dirty little secret which everyone knew was true. No matter how much Erdoğan might deny it, the bulk of ISIS's revenue came from smuggling oil across the Turkish border.[147] From Turkey's standpoint, ISIS was both a barrier against the Kurds and the most potent force opposing Assad's army. Covert support for the jihadists made sense, just as it had made sense for Pakistan – another nominal American ally – to provide refuge for bin Laden while backing the Taliban in Afghanistan.

The Russians dragged up other old grievances. Turkey, Putin said, had given safe-conduct and material support to Islamic fundamentalists who had been active in Chechnya.[148] Erdoğan had been following a policy of Islamisation in Turkey that would have made Kemal Atatürk, the country's secular founder, turn in his grave.[149]

But it was one part anger and three parts calculation.

The Foreign Minister, Sergei Lavrov, had informed his Turkish counterpart almost at once that Russia would not go to war over the incident.[150] That prompted sighs of relief in Washington, which, in the event of hostilities, would have been faced with an impossible choice between honouring its Article 5 commitments at the risk of uncontrolled escalation, which might end in nuclear war, and leaving its

Turkish allies to hang out to dry. Instead, Putin announced economic reprisals: a ban on Russian tourists travelling to Turkey which would cause a loss to the Turkish exchequer of nearly 6 billion US dollars a year; draconian restrictions on trade; and the suspension of the gas pipeline and nuclear power projects.

Ankara was too important for Russia to allow the conflict to drag on. Turkey was the odd man out, a potential weak link in NATO – a Muslim state ruled by a corrupt autocrat with dreams of restoring the glory of the Ottoman Empire. The country played a key role in Gazprom's plans to expand gas exports to Europe and, without Ankara's cooperation, a lasting settlement in Syria would be impossible. Alongside the cold fury, there were hints that Moscow was looking for ways for the relationship to be repaired.[151]

First, however, Erdoğan would have to come on bended knee to seek forgiveness for his offence. For Putin, it was a matter of respect. Before relations could be mended, Turkey had to acknowledge its error.

Throughout the first half of 2016, the Turkish leader stubbornly refused. At the end of May, Putin told journalists during a visit to Athens: 'We are awaiting concrete steps from Turkey. We have seen none so far.' But a month later, Erdoğan abruptly backed down, writing to Putin: 'We never had the desire nor the deliberate intention to shoot down the Russian plane . . . I wish to express my deepest condolences and to say [that I am] sorry.'[152]

The probable reason for his change of heart became clear three weeks later, when a coup attempt took place in Turkey. There were strong indications that Erdoğan had known of it and had allowed it to proceed in order to have a pretext to crack down on the opposition. Resolving the dispute with Russia beforehand left him free to concentrate on the more important business of purging his enemies at home. In any event, his apology was what Putin had been waiting for. 'Do we want the full restoration of relations? Yes, we do,' he declared, adding, apparently without irony, 'Life moves on very quickly.'[153]

Within a year, relations were back to something close to normal. They were not quite as before. For Russia, as for the United States, Erdoğan was not an easy partner. Over the next few years, there were renewed clashes between Russian- and Turkish-backed forces in Syria. Erdoğan infuriated Putin by inserting himself into what Russia regarded as its back yard, supporting Azerbaijan against Armenia during a flare-up over the disputed enclave of Nagorno-Karabakh. He provoked Putin again by voicing support for the Ukrainians over Crimea and supplying them with Bayraktar drones for use against the separatists in the Donbas. But both sides were careful not to cross each other's red lines. The relationship settled into what one commentator called 'cooperative rivalry'.[154] Erdoğan threw down the gauntlet to the Americans by purchasing the Russian S-400 air defence system, an unheard-of gesture of independence by a NATO member state. Putin continued to hope that Turkey would remain such a thorn in the side of the alliance that it would make the relationship worthwhile.

In Syria, Putin had played a weak hand with considerable skill. Obama had entered the conflict reluctantly and, when the Russians had jumped in afterwards, had expected them to bog down in the same kind of quagmire that the United States had experienced in Iraq. That had not happened.

By the spring of 2016, the situation had stabilised and Syrian government forces were back on the offensive. The Russians began regular troop rotations through their air base at Khmeimim and the naval facility at Tartus. For combat operations, they deployed special forces and mercenaries from the Wagner Group, the Russian equivalent of Erik Prince's ill-famed Blackwater Group, which provided security for the US State Department in Iraq and elsewhere. Wagner was allegedly linked to an equally controversial figure, a Russian criminal-turned-businessman named Yevgeny Prigozhin, known in the West as 'Putin's chef'. He had made a fortune providing catering services to the Kremlin and to Russian schools and army units, and owned a number of upscale restaurants, where Putin had dined with foreign leaders, including George W. Bush. Like Blackwater, Wagner worked closely with the authorities, in this case the GRU and the Russian Defence Ministry. It provided the Kremlin with plausible deniability in the case of Russian losses.

Two years after Putin had come to Assad's aid, the bulk of the fighting was over. The Russians continued to provide air support, but, in December 2017, Putin was confident enough to order the main contingent of the expeditionary force to begin returning home. There were 'loose ends',[155] as Putin put it: ISIS was still active in a few places along the Iraqi border. But what was left of the opposition was being slowly hemmed into the area around Idlib, while Assad's forces consolidated their control over most of the rest of the country.

Putin had no illusions about the nature of Assad's regime. It was as cruel and violent as that of Saddam Hussein. But that was not the point. If Assad had been removed, Syria would have become a seeding ground for terrorism that would have spread its tentacles into Europe and America as well as the post-Soviet space.[156]

From Moscow's standpoint, the operation had been a success because, first and foremost, the Syrian state had been preserved. Secondly, thousands of foreign volunteers from the Caucasus and Central Asia who had flocked to the Islamic State, and who might otherwise have returned to Russia to carry out terrorist attacks, had either been killed or detained in camps in Iraq. Thirdly, it had given Russia's armed forces what Putin called 'a unique tool, a unique opportunity', to test the command structure and the country's new weaponry, not just in exercises or simulated war games but in real combat conditions. More than 50,000 officers and men had been rotated through Syria. Inevitably there had been casualties, but it had been, in Putin's words, 'an important and noble mission'.[157]

There were other tangible gains, too. The American military had agreed on deconfliction measures. At first, Putin said, Washington had insisted that this was not to be seen as a normalisation of military relations, which had been frozen after Crimea.[158] But before long the simple fact that the two countries were the main players in Syria forced them to work together. Russia and the US became Co-Chairs of the International Syria Support Group, whose role was to organise political contacts between Damascus and the 'moderate' opposition.

'It seems that our efforts to combat international terrorism have gone some way to improve our relations,' Putin noted drily.[159] The fact that John Kerry had replaced Hillary Clinton as Secretary of State also helped.[160] In April 2016, ambassadorial meetings of the NATO–Russia Council resumed after being suspended for two years. The following year, after the centrist, Emmanuel Macron, had replaced François Hollande as France's President and invited Putin to a summit at Versailles, French policy towards Russia also became more accommodating. Macron was no pushover but he was pragmatic and, like Angela Merkel, he understood that, whatever view the Americans might take, an isolated, hostile Russia was not in Europe's long-term interests.

More important than anything else, however, was that Russia had re-emerged as a major and, in some ways, indispensable power. Twenty-five years after the collapse of the Soviet Union, Moscow could no longer be dismissed, in Obama's words, as a mere regional player. Putin had grasped the opportunity that America's difficulties in the Middle East had created. He had taken a gamble and the gamble had paid off.

By the time the tide had turned in Syria, it was once again election season in the United States. Putin thought that was one of the weaknesses of American democracy. 'Everyone lives from election to election. There is a very limited planning horizon, which doesn't allow anyone to take a long-term view and that's bad.'[161]

It was a fair point. Short-termism is ingrained in the American way of life. But more disturbing from Putin's standpoint was the possibility that, in 2016, Hillary Clinton would become Obama's successor. Since her comment, eight years earlier, that, as a KGB man, by definition he could have no soul, their relations had not improved. After he had accused her of encouraging the street protests which had followed his decision to return to the presidency, she had warned, in a valedictory memorandum when she stepped down as Secretary of State, that relations would deteriorate under Putin and the administration should push back hard.[162]

Later she had compared his decision to annexe Crimea to Hitler's annexation of the Sudetenland in 1938. 'Mrs Clinton has never been too gracious in her statements,' Putin said caustically. 'When people cross certain boundaries of propriety . . . it's because they are weak. But perhaps weakness is not the worst quality in a woman.'[163]

In those circumstances, it was hardly surprising that the Kremlin would try, if not to prevent her election outright, at least to muddy the waters. Initially Moscow's goal was simply to sow distrust, so that whoever emerged as Obama's successor would lack a solid mandate. But after Mrs Clinton confirmed that she would run, in April 2015, Russia redoubled its efforts to influence the outcome.

It did not exactly come out of the blue.

Putin had established a Cybersecurity Department in the FSB as early as 1998.[164] At first, the focus had been on defending Russian government sites from attack by Western special services. But its brief quickly expanded. In 2007, a Russian Denial-of-Service attack knocked out government and financial websites in Estonia. A year later, during the war over South Ossetia, Georgian government and military communications were targeted. The first known case of election interference occurred in 2014, when Russian hackers intervened in Poroshenko's presidential campaign in Kyiv. That year, the Internet Research Agency in St Petersburg, a troll factory owned by Yevgeny Prigozhin, the Wagner Group's reputed founder, created a specialised unit, which would eventually have 80 staff members and a budget of a million dollars a month, to plan the American operation.[165]

Putin had recognised that, given the deteriorating relationship with the West, Russia needed to spend much more on promoting its soft power. Funding for the Russian government's international TV service, RT, sharply increased, and a news agency, Sputnik, was established to issue Russia-friendly radio, wire service and internet reports. Officially, their purpose was 'to break the Anglo-Saxon monopoly on global information streams . . . and reflect the Russian government's official position'.[166] In practice, they purveyed Russian disinformation.

America's intelligence services had tracked the build-up of RT and Sputnik, and Russia's increasing presence on social networks. In 2014, they had also identified two state-sponsored hacking groups, APT28, nicknamed Fancy Bear and linked to the GRU, and APT29, Cozy Bear, believed to be controlled by the SVR. They had noted Putin's statement in April of that year that 'a kind of informational confrontation' was brewing with the US. 'It's taking on new forms,' he had said. 'Our special services are working on this.'[167]

Yet when, two years later, it was discovered that the Democratic National Committee (DNC) had been hacked, the Obama administration seemed perplexed and uncertain how to respond. The hackers, later identified as Cozy Bear, had penetrated the DNC's computers shortly after Mrs Clinton had launched her campaign and had downloaded thousands of emails and documents, including campaign analysis and strategy memos, which were released by Wikileaks. Other documents had been obtained from the email account of her campaign Chairman, John Podesta. But it was several months before the US intelligence community was prepared to make a formal assessment that the Russian government was behind it.

Others had had less difficulty reaching that conclusion.

Asked what the Russians were up to, James Dobbins, a veteran State

Department official who had served as Assistant Secretary of State under George W. Bush, had a one-word answer: 'Payback!'

Dobbins had overseen a year-long 40 million dollar campaign, run by the US State Department, to unite the Serbian opposition against Slobodan Milošević, which resulted in the Yugoslav leader's downfall in October 2000.[168] America had been doing similar things for decades. As the *New York Times* put it, 'trying to manipulate elections is a well-honed American art form.'[169]

However, that was not the message that most Americans wanted to hear. 'The assumption', wrote the historian, Marc Trachtenberg, 'is that while we have the right to intervene in the internal political affairs of all kinds of countries around the world, it is outrageous if any of them try to do the same thing to us.'[170] There was no possible moral equivalence, declared the CIA veteran, John Sipher, because America acted from 'noble intentions and a desire to do good in the world', whereas Russia sought 'to undermine our democracy'.[171] Among the tens of thousands of articles published in mainstream US newspapers about Russian election interference over the next four years, the number which suggested, however timidly, that perhaps the United States had done the same, could be counted on the fingers of one hand.[172]

At first, it appeared that Putin had badly misjudged America's mood. The Kremlin had expected the press and the political elite to focus on the DNC's efforts to ensure that Hillary Clinton, rather than her rival, Bernie Sanders, won the primary campaign.[173] Instead, Putin complained, the US media had concentrated on the source of the leaked documents, making 'hysterical accusations' against Russia, as though that was 'the number one problem in the entire election campaign'. The Democrats were 'freaking out', he said, trying to portray the Republican candidate, Donald Trump, as some kind of Russian puppet in order to persuade people not to vote for him.[174]

Initially, Putin, like most of the Russian political elite, thought Clinton was almost certain to win and avoided criticising her by name. Only in the last two weeks of the campaign did he indicate that he was starting to rate Trump's chances more highly.

He behaves extravagantly, of course, we all see this. But I think there is some sense in his actions. I say this because in my view, he represents the interests of a sizeable part of American society that is tired of the elites that have been in power for decades now . . . He portrays himself as an ordinary guy who . . . does not like to see power handed down by inheritance . . . He operates in this niche. The elections will soon show whether this is an effective strategy or not.[175]

On the morning of November 9, when Russians discovered that Trump had been elected, there was little jubilation. He was seen as the lesser evil, but nothing more. The fact that Trump had said he wanted to restore normal relations with Russia was welcomed.[176] Putin congratulated him, flattering him for his 'convincing victory'.[177] But he had few illusions that Trump would be able to reverse or even halt the downward spiral in the two countries' relations. As he explained to a French journalist:

> I have already dealt with four American presidents. They come and go. But the politics remain the same. Do you know why? Because of the power of the bureaucracy. When a person is elected, they may have some new ideas. But then the people with briefcases arrive . . . And instantly, everything changes. It happens with every administration.[178]

It was a conviction that had been growing on him throughout his third presidential term. The American foreign policy consensus was unbreakable. The White House had 'an inexplicable, irrational desire,' he said, 'to keep stepping on the same rake, making the same mistakes over and over'.[179] If that had been so under Obama, there was no reason to think it would be different under Trump.

For Russia, Trump's election was a windfall, but for other reasons.

He would prove one of the most disruptive presidents in American history. For the United States' allies in NATO, the European Union and the G7, trust in America as a reliable partner was irremediably damaged. America itself was arguably more divided than at any time since the Civil War. The political system was dysfunctional, Congress so polarised that Democrats and Republicans were unable to work together on even the most anodyne subjects and society so divided that each camp was convinced that the other was bent on the country's destruction. Conspiracy theories, running unchecked on social media, undermined the very institutions which were supposed to hold the nation together. Trump's election was the culmination, not the cause, of these problems, which had been accumulating in plain sight since Reagan's presidency in the 1980s. But Trump exacerbated them to a degree which no American, whatever their political persuasion, could any longer ignore.

To Putin, these were the marks of an imperial power which had passed its apogee, kicking and screaming in protest as it began its slow decline.

From that standpoint, far from being a misjudgement, the campaign against Hillary Clinton had brought immense, if unanticipated, dividends. General Michael Hayden, who had headed the National Security Agency and the CIA under George W. Bush, called it 'the most successful covert operation in history'.[180]

That assumed, however, that the Russian campaign had been instrumental in Trump's victory, which was debatable. The issue was not whether Russia had *tried* to influence the vote in Trump's favour. Despite Putin's pro forma denials, there was no question that it had. What was and remains unknowable is the *effect*, if any, that the Russians' meddling had. It is plausible that in some of the key swing states, like Wisconsin, where Trump won by fewer than 23,000 votes, and Pennsylvania, where the margin was 44,000, Russian trolling moved the needle in Trump's favour. But it is equally possible that the Democrats' constant labelling of Trump as 'the Russian candidate' had a contrary effect. In any case, far more important than anything the Russians could have done were the Clinton campaign's errors and the amplifier effect of the Electoral College, which may have been appropriate when it was created in 1787 but made little sense 200 years later.

To Trump, the idea that the Russians had aided his victory was anathema. If true, it raised questions about the legitimacy of his election. After his one and only formal summit with Putin in Helsinki, in July 2018, he said the Russian leader had given him an 'extremely strong and powerful' assurance that Moscow had not had anything to do with it. He saw no reason to disbelieve him, he added.[181]

That was a disavowal of the conclusions of his own intelligence services, and when he returned to Washington, he was forced to walk it back, claiming that he had misspoken.[182] But he continued to maintain that the cyberattacks on Clinton's campaign could have been the work not of Russia but of 'somebody sitting on their bed that weighs

400 pounds', a line that seemed straight out of Stieg Larsson's *Millennium* novels.[183] Putin, who had been through something similar himself, when the FSB was accused of staging the Moscow apartment bombings to help him become President, was happy to back him up. 'There are a lot of hackers today, you know, and they cover up their activity,' he told an American correspondent.[184]

The hacking was not the only Russia-linked scandal in which Trump became embroiled. There was evidence that members of his entourage had colluded illegally with Russian officials to try to compromise the Clinton campaign. Even seamier accusations surfaced in January 2017, ten days before Trump's inauguration, when the internet news site, Buzz-feed, published a 35-page dossier compiled by a former British intelligence agent, Christopher Steele, for a Washington, D.C. research company, Fusion GPS.[185] Much of the dossier merely corroborated evidence of Russia's election interference which was already available from other sources. But the most sensational parts claimed that during a visit to Moscow in November 2013, Trump had engaged in behaviour which made him vulnerable to Russian blackmail. Specifically it alleged that, while attending a Miss Universe pageant in the Russian capital, sponsored by the Trump Organization, he had hired the presidential suite where the Obamas had stayed in the Ritz-Carlton Hotel, near Red Square, and paid Russian prostitutes to urinate on the bed they had slept in, an exploit which was said to have been filmed surreptitiously by the FSB.

Given that Trump had earlier been caught on tape, boasting about 'grabbing [women] by the pussy',[186] the story was not inherently implausible. On the other hand, if Trump's electoral base was prepared to close its eyes to the pussy-grabbing episode, it was unlikely to be overly concerned at claims that he had arranged for the defilement of a bed used by a man most of them hated. The potential for blackmail appeared limited. Trump, naturally, denied the charges, but so clumsily as to make them seem more credible.[187] Putin once again came to his aid, arguing – with barely concealed glee at the American President's discomfiture – that Trump was surrounded by beautiful women and therefore would have had no need for 'Russian girls of limited social responsibility, even though ours, of course, are the best in the world'. Those who concocted such stories, he added sententiously, were 'worse than prostitutes themselves'.[188]

Steele's dossier was based on raw, unverified intelligence, meaning that it included unsubstantiated rumours and anecdotes, and had not been intended for publication. Parts, apparently including the allegations about the prostitutes, were later discredited.

But the importance of the dossier lay elsewhere. The suggestion that Putin had some kind of hold over Trump took on a life of its own. The American President's refusal to acknowledge Russian meddling in the election; his sensitivity over the hacking episodes; his reluctance to criticise Putin, exemplified by his behaviour at Helsinki – 'abject', 'humiliating', 'disgraceful', 'nothing short of treasonous', fulminated Republicans and Democrats in rare unison[189] – his refusal to divulge his tax records, which, many suspected, might contain details of dubious dealings with Russian financiers, all combined to give the impression that he had much to hide. Whether that was true or not, it created a climate in Washington in which any improvement in relations with Russia was impossible. 'Our relationship has become hostage to the domestic situation in the United States,' Putin said. 'We are patiently waiting for this period in US politics to end.'[190]

Russia's election interference had been the political equivalent of 9/11. One, the first foreign attack on US soil since Pearl Harbor, had wounded America in the flesh; the other had struck at the heart of American democracy. The country was in the grip of Russophobia on a scale not seen since the days of Senator McCarthy.[191]

'It reminds me of anti-Semitism,' Putin said. 'The Jews are to blame for everything.' Only now, for Jews, read Russians.[192]

The American media en masse painted Russia a monotone shade of black. Newspapers like the *Chicago Tribune*, the *Washington Post* and the *Wall Street Journal* seemed unable to mention the country without attaching the adjective 'aggressive'. Putin's regime was depicted as a kleptocracy on a par with Equatorial Guinea, where those in power made obscene fortunes and the mass of the citizenry struggled to survive, a prey to corrupt police, arbitrary officials and a venal judiciary. Even Ambassador McFaul, the last person to be soft on Putin, complained that the US press gave a 'cartoonized' view of Russia.[193]

To Americans who thought of themselves as the liberal resistance, the right-thinking people who opposed the crazies of Trumpland, the battle against Putin and the war against Trump were two sides of the same coin. In their view, wrote the *New York Times* columnist, Ross Douthat,

Putin was a figure of extraordinary menace, the leader of an authoritarian renaissance whose tentacles extended everywhere, from Brexit to the NRA. He had hacked American democracy, placed a Manchurian candidate in the White House, sowed the internet with misinformation, placed bounties on our soldiers in Afghanistan, extended Russian power across the Middle East and threatened Eastern Europe with invasion or subversion. In this atmosphere, every rumour about Russian perfidy was pre-emptively believed.[194]

The handful of diplomats and scholars who argued otherwise, most of them old Russia hands like Jack Matlock and Stephen Cohen, often went overboard trying to explain Putin's actions and ended up discrediting themselves.

Between these two extremes – those who loathed Putin and everything he stood for and the contrarians who tried to understand what made him act as he did – there was no middle ground. To propose a balanced account of Russia during the years that Trump was in power was like trying to argue that Hitler had redeeming features.

In this context, unsurprisingly, the gulf of incomprehension between the two countries widened still further.

Shortly before Trump took office, the Obama administration had expelled 35 Russian intelligence officers, operating under diplomatic cover; ordered the closure of two country estates used by the Russian Embassy for recreation; and announced an umpteenth round of sanctions.[195] It was announced that it was in retaliation for Russia's hacking of the DNC and Clinton's campaign headquarters.

Putin waited six months before unveiling an asymmetrical response. The 1,200-plus staff at America's diplomatic missions in Russia must be reduced to the same level as those at Russia's missions in America, he said. Altogether, 755 posts would go. Two American consulates were closed altogether, which, under reciprocity rules, entailed the closure of two Russian consulates, and the US Embassy's operations were very sharply cut back. As one CIA veteran noted grimly, America had finished up in a much worse place than if Obama had taken no action at all.[196]

Seven months later, in March 2018, the GRU attempted to assassinate a former double agent, Sergei Skripal, who had been freed as part of a spy exchange and was living in the sleepy cathedral city of

Salisbury, in the South of England. The Russian operatives had smeared Novichok, a prohibited chemical warfare agent, on the door handle of Skripal's house. He and his daughter recovered but another person died.

The Trump administration accused Putin of being behind the attempt, announced yet more sanctions and expelled another 60 Russian diplomats. Putin noted the contrast with Trump's reaction to the murder of Jamal Khashoggi, a journalist for the *Washington Post* and US resident, who had been killed at the behest of the Saudi Crown Prince, Mohamed bin Salman. Not a single Saudi diplomat had been expelled, he pointed out, and bin Salman himself had been treated with kid gloves.[197] But the Crown Prince was an American ally. Putin was not.

He continued to refrain from criticising the American President by name, on the grounds, as he explained later, that when everything else was going wrong, personal relationships between leaders were often the only thing left.[198] But his denials that Russia had interfered in the American election campaign became more nuanced. Perhaps, he said, 'patriotic hackers', angered by Western criticisms of Russia, had decided to intervene.[199] To every action there was 'an appropriate counter-action', he told the NBC presenter, Megyn Kelly. 'The United States constantly interfered in other countries' election campaigns . . . So if someone, and I'm not saying it's us, does [the same to you,] you should not be offended. You do it yourselves all the time.'[200] Russia, for its part, he added, would in future leave the US elections alone, because 'it was not worth the effort'.[201]

On that point, at least, he was as good as his word. In the 2020 presidential election, there was no Russian hacking and only limited indirect interference, though that may have been because Americans were generating so much fake news on their own that there was little point trying to add to it.

Despite hints to Medvedev that America might be flexible on missile defence, Obama had in the end gone ahead with the planned NMD installations in Romania and Poland. To the Kremlin, it was Reagan's 'Star Wars' programme all over again. It risked giving America the illusion of invulnerability from a second strike, enhancing its offensive capability and compelling Russia to take counter-measures which would make arms control more difficult.[202]

By then, Russia had further reduced its participation in the Conventional Forces in Europe [CFE] Treaty, which it had suspended in 2007 because of a dispute over troop levels in Moldova and the Baltic States.[203] A number of civil nuclear power agreements had lapsed or been suspended. America had withdrawn from an agreement to dispose of weapons-grade plutonium and had delayed compliance with its commitment to destroy its chemical-weapons stockpile.[204] The key strategic arms agreements remained intact, but after the missile defence system became operational in May 2016, they, too, were under strain. Each side accused the other of violating the 1987 INF Treaty, signed by Reagan and Gorbachev, which banned the deployment of ground-launched medium-range nuclear missiles.[205]

After Trump took office, the breakdown of the mechanisms ensuring the military balance accelerated. The paradox was that under a President who spoke constantly of the need for America and Russia to get on better together, relations deteriorated faster than under any of his predecessors.[206]

By the end of Trump's first year, Putin was speaking of 'a critical mass of problems building up in global security'.[207] Ever since the US withdrawal from the ABM Treaty in 2002, he said, he had been warning that Russia would be forced to take retaliatory measures but the Americans had ignored him.[208] They were shooting themselves not in the foot but 'somewhere higher up'.[209]

In March 2018, in an address to the two houses of parliament, Putin set out in detail what those measures would involve.[210] Illustrating his remarks with videos, he described six new weapon systems which he said Russia had developed. The 200-ton ultra-heavy Sarmat ICBM was capable of carrying up to 15 independently targetable warheads and had a reported range of more than 20,000 miles, enough to reach North America by a trajectory over the South Pole, which would render it invulnerable to any anti-missile system yet devised. The Sarmat was to go into service in 2021 and would replace Russia's existing heavy missiles, codenamed 'Satan' by NATO, by 2027. As well as normal nuclear warheads, it could carry the Avangard, a hypersonic glide vehicle, already in serial production, which had been tested at speeds up to Mach 27, more than 15,000 miles an hour. Another hypersonic weapon, the air-launched Kinzhal ballistic missile, was already deployed. There had also been 'significant progress' in laser weapons as well as two futuristic systems still under development: a nuclear-powered cruise missile, later named the Burevestnik, and a massive nuclear-powered torpedo, the Poseidon, which could be used to attack coastal cities.[211] Whether these last two weapons would ever become operational was uncertain, but that work on them was ongoing was confirmed 18 months later when five scientists died in an explosion linked to a nuclear power source for a rocket engine.[212]

None of the weapons Putin mentioned would give Russia a decisive strategic advantage.[213] Nor were they quite as new and awe-inspiring as he made it appear. But they would maintain strategic parity.[214] It was a message, he said, 'to those who live in the past and are unable to look to the future, to stop rocking the boat in which we all find ourselves and which is called "Planet Earth" '.[215]

Six months later, Trump announced that he had decided to pull out of the INF Treaty, ostensibly because of Russia's alleged violations but in reality because the US no longer wished to be bound by its restrictions.[216]

He then despatched to Moscow his National Security Adviser, John Bolton, an avowed opponent of any form of arms control, to convey the decision to Putin. Bolton, of whom it was said that 'he never met a war he didn't like',[217] was a hawk even by Republican standards. Receiving him, Putin noted that the US seal depicted a bald eagle holding an olive branch and a quiver of arrows. 'The question is', he asked quizzically, 'has your eagle already eaten all the olives, leaving only the arrows?' Bolton confessed that he had brought no olives.[218]

America's European allies found themselves back in the situation they had been in during the 1970s, when Soviet SS-20s faced off against American Pershings and cruise missiles with only eight minutes' warning in the event of an attack.

In November 2020, Trump announced that he was also withdrawing from the 1989 Open Skies Treaty, which allowed Russia and the United States to conduct reconnaissance flights over each other's territory as a confidence-building measure.

The arms-control regime, which had been built up painstakingly, over decades, one small step at a time, and had kept the peace in Europe since the end of the Second World War, was hanging by a thread. Each country accused the other of being responsible for its demise.

In fact, both had demonstrated bad faith. But the two key agreements – the ABM and INF treaties – had been terminated not by Russia but by the United States, which had come to view them as irksome constraints. Of all the nuclear accords, both civil and military, that had been signed earlier, only the New START treaty, concluded by Obama and Medvedev in 2011, remained in force. It, too, would expire in 2021 and the Trump administration showed little interest in extending it. Once that went, there would be nothing at all to prevent uncontrolled nuclear competition.

It had been a very bleak four years.

Not long after Trump had been elected, he and Putin had agreed that their countries' relations could hardly be worse.[219] They had been wrong. By the time Trump left office, the fabric of ties had become so frayed that it was barely holding together. It was far, far worse than when he had come to power.

The term, 'payback', can be applied to much of what Putin did during his third term.

Russia's annexation of Crimea was payback for Kosovo, 'the place where it all started',[220] which he viewed as the first of the West's three cardinal sins – the others being NATO enlargement and America's withdrawal from the ABM Treaty – that had destroyed both sides' hopes of building a better, more peaceful world after the collapse of the Soviet Union.

Russia's intervention in Syria was payback for Libya and Iraq.

Snowden's asylum and the adoption ban were payback for the Magnitsky Act.

Russia's interference in the US election was payback for America's efforts to spread – or 'impose', as Putin preferred to say – its own, supposedly universal, system of values to other nations.

But payback was not an end in itself. It was part of a broader response to the economic and military pressures which the United States and its allies were exerting to punish what they termed Russia's bad behaviour and what Putin depicted as his country's refusal to submit to American diktat.[221] Above all, it was an attempt to assert Russia's place as an independent actor in an increasingly multipolar world in which, in Putin's view, the United States was destined to lose its role as a hegemonic power.

Over the course of his third term, his thinking about Russia's relationship with the West crystallised, forming, in his mind at least, a coherent picture of all that had happened in the 25 years – the 'wasted years', as he now put it – since the Soviet Union's demise.[222]

The relationship had started going wrong from the very beginning, Putin said.[223] The United States, 'having declared itself the victor in the Cold War, [behaved] the way nouveaux riches always behave when they come into a great fortune . . . Far from managing their wealth wisely, they committed many follies.'[224] Instead of establishing a new balance of power in Europe, new divisions had been created. The West's argument that NATO had no choice but to accept new members from Central and Eastern Europe was false. It was true that other countries had the right to apply, but that did not mean that the existing members were obliged to accept them if they thought it was contrary to their own interests. 'They could have said: "we are pleased that you want to join us, but we are not going to expand our organisation because we see the future of Europe differently" . . . If they had wanted to, they could have [refused]. But they didn't want to.'[225]

Putin was not wrong. The NATO Charter says only that the member states 'may invite any other European state in a position to . . . contribute to the security of the area'. There is no obligation to do so.[226]

For Washington, NATO enlargement was a means of consolidating America's hold over its European allies, even though it implied obligations which, were war ever to break out, the United States might be reluctant to fulfil. For countries like France and Germany, the advantages were less obvious. It was hard to see how their security would be enhanced by a commitment to defend the Baltic States, let alone Georgia or Ukraine, from possible Russian aggression, which was why Sarkozy and Merkel had opposed their accession to the Membership Action Plan at the Bucharest Summit in 2008. But in the early days, amid the euphoria which marked the end of the Cold War, when the West assumed that Russia was destined to become part of the American-led world and Moscow was far too weak to resist, none of America's partners thought it worthwhile to object. The result was that NATO's military infrastructure arrived at Russia's borders.

What would America have done, Putin wondered, if it had been the other way round – 'if Russia had placed missile systems on the US–Mexico border or the US–Canadian border?'[227] The answer was self-evident. When Khrushchev had attempted to install Soviet missiles in Cuba in 1962, the world had been brought to the brink of nuclear destruction and the issue remained so fraught that, 60 years later, the United States continued to subject the island to an economic blockade.

American officials reject such comparisons. The United States, they say, supported NATO enlargement not to threaten Russia but to reassure America's European allies. The reality was more galling and more prosaic. The United States acted as it did because it could.

At one level, Putin acknowledged with some bitterness, Russia had been at fault for failing to foresee that. 'Our biggest mistake,' he told an American scholar, 'was to trust you too much. Your mistake was to take that trust as weakness and abuse it.'[228] It was a lesson, he said. If a bear stops defending its territory, 'someone will always try to chain him up. As soon as he is chained, they will tear out his teeth and claws . . . When that happens, . . . they will take over his territory . . . and then, perhaps, they will stuff him . . . We must decide whether we want to keep going and fight . . . Or do we want our skin to hang on the wall?'[229]

In Putin's metaphor, the bear's teeth and claws were Russia's nuclear arsenal. But it was also intended in a wider sense. Other countries, he said, were afraid of Russia's size, its hugeness.[230] All through history, they had tried to contain her. 'The more we give ground,' Putin warned, 'the more brazen, cynical and aggressive [their] demeanour becomes.'[231] It had been the same in the nineteenth and early twentieth centuries.[232] 'Whenever we try to raise our head, someone else tries to push us down and put us in our place.'[233]

As he looked back over the previous two decades, Putin saw – or claimed to see – an America which, from the outset, had set out to dupe Russia. Its withdrawal from the ABM Treaty, supposedly to counter Iran and North Korea, had all along been designed to give the United States a strategic advantage.[234] Globalisation, which had been held out to Russia as a panacea for its economic ills, had turned out to be a lure, whose true purpose was to advance America's own economic interests.[235] The United States had been deceitful over missile defence and NATO expansion. It had backed Ukraine against Russia, not from solicitude for the Ukrainian people's welfare, but to expand its empire and, above all, to give NATO an identifiable enemy, which it had lacked since the end of the Cold War.[236]

As Putin's view of the state of the world grew more bleak, the accusations he levelled became increasingly outlandish. The West, he charged, had backed 'an international terrorist invasion of Russia'[237] giving 'direct support' to the Islamic fundamentalists who had tried to dismember the country in the 1990s. 'This is an established fact and everybody knows it.'[238]

It was the language of *Pravda* editorials of the 1960s and '70s, which used to open with the words, *'Kak izvestno'* – 'As is well-known' – before launching into some far-fetched horror story about the iniquities of the Western world. The mindset was that of the *siloviki*, men like Patrushev and Sechin – the mirror image of US Russia hawks like John Bolton – who increasingly had Putin's ear. They believed to the core of their being that the West was on a mission to bring Russia to its knees. To Putin, it no longer mattered whether that was true or not. It fitted the narrative of a hostile Western world headed by a waning hegemonic power, which was trying by fair means or foul to tear Russia apart as it struggled to fight off its own inexorable decline.[239]

In the 1990s, the Western countries had been the undisputed leaders of the global economy and the rest of the world had to follow behind.[240] That was no longer so. 'Western hegemony is ending,'[241] Putin declared. Russia's ejection from the rich nations' club, the G7, scarcely mattered because no international organisation could be effective without India and China.[242] The G7's share of global GDP had dropped from 70 per cent, in the early 1990s, to 45 per cent two decades later. China would soon become the world's leading economic power.[243] It was Russia's 'strategic partner in every sense of the word' – unlike the United States, with which relations were 'getting worse by the hour'.[244]

On the face of it, it was a staggering turnaround from the policies Putin had espoused when he first took office. But there were hints that it might be less clear-cut than he made it appear.

An unstated problem in Russia's relationship with China – the elephant in the room – was that its Asian neighbour's economic strength, dynamism and demographic weight would inevitably make it the senior partner in any future alliance. To Putin, that would be no more acceptable than being under the sway of the United States. Another major impediment was that Russia was, as he kept repeating, 'a country of European culture ... Russia and Europe share the same civilisational code.'[245] Despite everything that had happened, Russia's ideal remained a 'common economic and humanitarian space with the European Union, extending from the Atlantic to the Pacific'.[246]

Whichever way Putin looked as his third term drew to a close, there seemed no straightforward path ahead. Relations with both the world's major powers were treacherous although in different ways. Perhaps, Putin thought, Russia should act like 'a clever monkey', sitting to one side, watching to see how the battle between America and China would work out.[247] In any case, he said, 'Russia is not going anywhere. We have a vast territory and we can manage on our own.'[248] Sooner or later the moment would come when the situation would change.[249]

He paraphrased Pushkin: 'It will pass. Everything passes, and this will pass as well.'[250]

17

Nemtsov, Wild Boar Sausages and the End of Liberalism

On a cold, misty winter evening, early in 2015, Boris Nemtsov and his girlfriend, Anna Durytska, a Ukrainian fashion model, left the restaurant, just off Red Square, where they had been having dinner, and decided to go home on foot, rather than take a taxi. As they walked, hand in hand, across the Bolshoi Moskovoretsky bridge, which starts by the Kremlin wall, Nemtsov's girlfriend heard a popping sound. She felt his hand go limp and he slumped to the ground. The assassin had shot Nemtsov from behind, using a silenced pistol. He died almost instantly.

The immediate reaction in the West, and among Russian liberals, was to assume that the security services had killed him to remove one of Putin's most persistent critics. Nemtsov had changed little since he had burst onto the political scene as a dashing young idealist in the early 1990s. Handsome, curly-haired, witty and gregarious, at the time of his death he was a member of the regional Duma in Yaroslavl, 150 miles north-east of Moscow, and one of the leaders of a small liberal party. He had been working on a report showing that Russian troops were supporting the separatists in eastern Ukraine, which at that point the Kremlin still denied, and had unearthed evidence that businessmen with links to Putin and other high-ranking officials had skimmed off billions of US dollars from contracts for the Sochi Olympics. For almost a year, the pro-government Russian media had been denouncing 'national traitors' and 'fifth columnists'.[1] Nemtsov could well be seen as fitting that description.

The problem with this theory was that Putin had no conceivable reason for wanting Nemtsov killed.[2] Like the other liberal leaders who had come to the fore under Yeltsin, his time had passed. He posed no political threat.[3]

As had been the case when the journalist, Anna Politkovskaya, had been murdered eight years earlier, Nemtsov acquired a symbolic importance after his death which was disproportionate to his role before he died. Politkovskaya had been assassinated on Putin's birthday. Nemtsov had been killed 150 yards from the Kremlin, where Putin worked. In both cases, once the fog of conspiracy theories cleared, responsibility was traced back to the entourage of the Chechen leader, Ramzan Kadyrov.

Putin himself had been certain from the moment he was informed of Nemtsov's murder that night that it had been Kadyrov's doing. The difficulty was what to do about it.

After previous political murders in which the Chechens had been implicated, including those of Politkovskaya and Ruslan Yamadayev, another of Kadyrov's opponents, who had been shot dead when his car stopped at a traffic light in central Moscow in 2008, the killers themselves had been arrested and sentenced to long prison terms but the investigators had made no attempt to question those suspected of ordering the murders. Putin regarded Politkovskaya's murder as politically inept, but she had been a fierce critic of his regime and he cannot have been sorry to see her silenced, even if he would have preferred it to happen in a different way. Yamadayev's killing had been an intra-Chechen affair, and in such matters he made it a principle not to get involved.

Nemtsov's case was different. He was a former first deputy Prime Minister, once seen as a possible successor to Yeltsin, and, even though he had joined the opposition, he remained an accredited member of the political elite. It was the first time a leader at that level had been killed in Russia, and his death stunned the Moscow establishment.

A week after the murder, on March 6, Putin disappeared from view, supposedly because he had flu but in reality to ponder his next move. The following day, the first arrests were made, including that of the presumed assassin, a member of Kadyrov's Sever battalion named Zaur Dadayev. That produced an immediate protest from Kadyrov himself, who posted a message on Instagram, describing Zaur as 'a true patriot of Russia, . . . one of the bravest men in the regiment . . . prepared to give his life for the Motherland'.[4] If Zaur had indeed been involved in the murder, Kadyrov said, it might be linked to the *Charlie Hebdo* affair – when eight journalists had been murdered by Islamic terrorists in Paris after the French satirical magazine had published what Muslims regarded as blasphemous caricatures of the prophet, Mohammed. The claim did not add up. Nemtsov had never defended the publication of the caricatures.[5] In any case, the timing did not fit. Zaur's group had been conducting discreet surveillance of him since October 2014, three months before the *Charlie Hebdo* attack.[6]

Zaur was only a foot soldier. The orders had come from much higher up. Both before and after the murder, he and his associates had been in frequent telephone contact with Adam Delimkhanov, a Chechen member of the Russian Duma who acted as Kadyrov's pro-consul in Moscow, and Suleiman Geremeyev, a senator representing Chechnya in the Federation Council, who had been suspected of organising Yamadayev's murder in 2008. The implication was that the decision to have Nemtsov killed had come from Kadyrov himself.[7]

Putin's response came in stages.

On March 9, the day after Kadyrov's public defence of Zaur, it was announced that the Chechen leader had been awarded a state award for 'active public service'.[8] Officially, it was a coincidence – Andrei Lugovoi, who had poisoned Litvinenko in London seven years earlier, received the same award that day[9] – but it was widely viewed as a signal that, regardless of where the investigation into Nemtsov's death might lead, Putin had Kadyrov's back. However, the President refused to take Kadyrov's calls.[10] After Nemtsov's murder, whenever he tried to reach him, he was told that Putin was unavailable. Instead, he was summoned to a meeting with Patrushev, the Security Council Secretary, who let him understand that Putin was aware of all the details of the murder and suggested that if he wished to learn more, he should look to his own inner circle.

After the President reappeared in public on March 16, he continued to refuse Kadyrov's calls. But the Chechen leader could play that game, too. Ten days later, he flew to Dubai, accompanied by a large delegation, ostensibly to go to the races, in which some of his horses were running. While there, he openly taunted Moscow. 'Some media have even produced headlines, "Is the Kremlin afraid of Chechnya?"' he wrote. 'This is a provocation . . . The Kremlin has nothing to fear.'[11] That hit very close to the bone. The liberal newspaper, *Novaya gazeta*, had written earlier that month: 'Power means the right to commit violence without punishment. The one whose violence goes unpunished is the ruler. The murder of Boris Nemtsov suggests that Putin is no longer the strongest man in Russia.'[12]

When Kadyrov returned, Putin made clear that he regarded the affair as closed.[13] Zaur Dadayev and four others were sentenced to long terms of imprisonment but no one higher up was troubled. Ruslan Geremeyev, Senator Geremeyev's nephew, and two other men who had helped organise the killing, were living openly in the Delimkhanovs' fiefdom of Dzhalka, some 15 miles east of Grozny on the road to Gudermes. The Russian investigators sent to question them reported that they could not be found.[14] When Aleksei Venediktov, the Editor-in-Chief of *Ekho Moskvy*, asked Putin during his annual phone-in whether the Russian state had become so weak that 'the interrogators are unable to question an army major . . . who is hiding in a Russian region' – meaning Ruslan Geremeyev – the President changed the subject and did not answer.[15] Two years later, asked at another news conference why Geremeyev had never been questioned, he again dodged the question.[16]

The tail had started wagging the dog.

Until Nemtsov's death, Putin's reluctance to bring Kadyrov to heel was purely pragmatic. Chechnya was unmanageable. Kadyrov's excesses were tolerated because his iron-fisted rule kept the region under control.

After Nemtsov's murder, that changed. The conventional explanations – that Putin was afraid to confront Kadyrov for fear of what might happen if he did, as the Chechen leader himself had impishly implied; or that the regime was too weak and the *siloviki* too divided to risk reining him in – did not really add up. Rather, it seemed, Putin was no longer willing to expend the time and energy required to force key allies and subordinates to do his bidding. But whatever the reasons, the facts spoke for themselves: a leading Russian politician, a member of the establishment of more than 25 years' standing, had been murdered in front of the Kremlin and the President had not lifted a finger to punish the man everyone knew was responsible.

It marked the inflection point of a tendency that had been developing since his re-election in 2012 and which, after Nemtsov's murder, would become steadily more pronounced. Putin's once iron grip on the levers of control was flagging.

A few weeks later, after a shooting incident in Grozny involving police from neighbouring Stavropol, Kadyrov ordered his security forces to open fire if a police unit entered Chechnya again without explicit authorisation. Putin said nothing. The Interior Ministry complained weakly that Kadyrov's remarks were 'unacceptable'. It was hardly even a slap on the wrist.[17] The following year, Kadyrov lashed out at the liberal opposition, describing them as 'vile cowards' and 'enemies of the people', a phrase evoking Stalin's blood purges in the 1930s. To make his point, he posted a video of the former Prime Minister, Mikhail Kasyanov, seen through the cross hairs of a gunsight.[18] Putin said later he had raised these matters at a private meeting with Kadyrov, explaining to him that such comments were 'detrimental to stability. Once that is understood, and I am sure it will be, there will be no more statements of that kind.'[19] It was a gentle remonstrance, far removed from his usual style of laying down the law.

Putin did express reservations over the increasing use of sharia law in Chechnya, under which polygamy and honour killings – illegal in Russia – were encouraged, women were expected to wear headscarves and men to grow beards.[20] 'You must ensure compliance with Russian law in all areas of life,' he told Kadyrov. 'I stress this point,' Putin added, 'in *all* areas of life.' Yet, even on that occasion, according to the published account, most of their meeting was devoted to praise of Kadyrov's stewardship of Chechnya and Putin's request that he stay on as head of the region for another five-year term.[21]

It was starting to resemble a game of chicken in which the same side always won. Kadyrov pushed the envelope to see how far he could go. Putin invariably backed down.

When Angela Merkel complained in 2017 about the repression of Chechen homosexuals, Putin promised to 'monitor the situation'.[22] He did not. Chechens suspected of homosexuality continued to be tortured and killed in secret prisons. Nor did he complain when Kadyrov protested against what he called the genocide of Rohingya Muslims in Myanmar, accusing the Kremlin of failing to take a stand against it – an intervention in foreign policy which would have cost any other provincial leader his post.[23] It was merely Kadyrov's personal opinion, Putin said, 'not a rebellion by the Chechen leadership. Everything is fine, no need to worry.'[24]

It was a very complicated relationship.

Putin had always admired toughness. Kadyrov exuded the same aura of controlled menace as had his old judo partner, Nikolai Vashchilin, whose face was so intimidating that others instinctively recoiled. Putin's bodyguard, Viktor Zolotov, and the head of the FSO, the Presidential Protection Service, Yevgeny Murov – 'dangerous men', as a former SVR colleague put it[25] – were in that mould. So was Steven Seagal, the American martial arts specialist and action-movie hero, whom Putin esteemed for his skill at aikido, a style of unarmed combat similar to judo.

Kadyrov, in Putin's eyes, was 'a young wolf in need of shelter', for whom he was a father figure.[26] Anna Politkovskaya had been more lucid. The Kremlin, she said, had raised a little dragon. 'Now they need to feed it, otherwise it will spit fire.'[27]

Feed it, Putin did. More than 80 per cent of Chechnya's budget came from Moscow.[28] As much as a third of that went for Kadyrov's personal use, financing not only his praetorian guard but, among other things, a stable of exotic cars including a two million dollar Lamborghini Reventon, and a large private zoo.

Putin's reaction to Nemtsov's murder, or the lack of it, did not go unnoticed within his inner circle. The first to draw the lesson was Igor Sechin, who, as CEO of the oil behemoth, Rosneft, had been trying to win Putin's agreement for an expansion programme to disguise the company's parlous bottom line. Sechin, like the head of Gazprom, Aleksei Miller, had been appointed for loyalty rather than competence. Neither was an especially good manager and neither company had been doing particularly well.

Sechin's latest venture had been an attempt to buy Bashneft, a flourishing regional oil company based at Ufa, in the flatlands west of the Urals. Bashneft's owner, Vladimir Yevtushenkov, a telecommunications billionaire, had rejected Sechin's offer. In September 2014, he was accused of money laundering and placed under house arrest. It was a replay of Sechin's efforts, ten years earlier, to take down Mikhail Khodorkovsky and seize control of Yukos. But where Khodorkovsky had dug in his heels, Yevtushenkov, a down-to-earth, scholarly-looking man in his mid 60s, was philosophical. 'In games with the state, you always lose,' he had once said. 'The weakest state is always stronger than the strongest businessman.'[29]

Yevtushenkov's holding company, Sistema, instead of resisting, negotiated a compromise. In December, Bashneft was taken over by the state on the spurious grounds that its privatisation in the 1990s had been illegal. A few days later, Yevtushenkov was released from house arrest. Sistema was granted minimal compensation, most of which was later gouged back and, after a decent interval, the case against Yevtushenkov was dismissed.

In retrospect, the episode can be seen as another early sign that Putin was beginning to tire of keeping the 'boyars' in line. He had no personal quarrel with Yevtushenkov. But when Sechin had argued that renationalising Bashneft would help Rosneft and strengthen the state control over a strategic sector of the economy, he had made no objection.

That, however, was far from the end of the matter.

In 2016, Russia's economy was hit by a combination of sanctions and slumping oil prices. Facing a projected 36 billion-dollar budget deficit, Putin decided that shares in some of Russia's state-owned assets would have to be sold off, because, as he frankly admitted, 'we need the money'. Bashneft was among them. Western investors showed no interest. The way that Yevtushenkov had been stripped of his assets had been even more damaging to foreign confidence than the Yukos affair. Sechin announced that Rosneft intended to bid, after which potential Russian investors also backed away.

The Economy Minister, Aleksei Ulyukayev, who was among the last holdovers from Yeltsin's team in the 1990s, expressed reservations on the grounds that Rosneft was majority state-owned, so it would be a fake privatisation with Bashneft being transferred from one government-owned entity to another.[30] But Putin argued that it would create a 'synergy effect', because 19.5 per cent of Rosneft's shares would be sold off afterwards and the merger would make the sale more profitable. The deal went ahead[31] and, later that year, the Rosneft shares were bought for 10.7 billion dollars by a joint venture between Glencore, a huge multinational commodities conglomerate with a history of controversial deals, and the Qatar Investment Authority.[32]

Igor Sechin, however, was not a man to forgive a slight. He and Ulyukayev had been at daggers drawn since the summer. The FSB had bugged Ulyukayev's phone and Sechin had sent the President transcripts, purporting to show that the minister was obstructing policies which Putin had approved.[33]

In November, a month after the Bashneft acquisition was completed,

Sechin invited Ulyukayev to his office and, in an apparent gesture of reconciliation, presented him with an enormous basket, containing a bottle of rare wine and a selection of home-made wild boar sausages. The minister knew that he was in the habit of making such gifts to close friends after returning from hunting trips. But as his driver was stowing it in the trunk of his car, they were surrounded by FSB officers, who found, hidden at the bottom of the basket, two million US dollars in cash. Ulyukayev, Sechin claimed, had demanded that sum as a bribe to drop his opposition to the Rosneft deal, so he had set up a sting operation to expose the minister's behaviour. Putin fired Ulyukayev next day and he was placed under house arrest.

The whole story stank. Aleksandr Shokhin, the head of the main business lobby, the Russian Union of Industrialists and Entrepreneurs, was openly incredulous. 'You'd have to be insane to do that,' he said. 'To threaten Rosneft? To extort two million dollars? From Igor Sechin of all people? . . . If that had really happened, Ulyukayev should not have been detained by the Investigative Committee but sent to a lunatic asylum.'[34]

The absurdity of the charges did not appear to trouble Putin, or the Prime Minister, Dmitry Medvedev, or most of Ulyukayev's colleagues. When the case came to trial, a year later, Sechin was more truculent and imperious than ever. The judge, he complained, had acted like a 'professional cretin' by allowing discussion of such trivia as the basket of sausages instead of focusing on the seriousness of Ulyukayev's alleged offence.[35] When summoned to be cross-examined, Sechin refused to attend.

'Some citizens are more equal than others,' commented *Novaya gazeta*. 'But then, at this level of power, equality is inconceivable. It's like the old days, when a nobleman would not fight a duel with a commoner – he'd order him flogged in the courtyard.'[36] Even Putin agreed that Sechin should have appeared in court, though he added, illogically, that he did not think he had broken the law.[37] The Russian Criminal Code is categorical: the defence has an absolute right to cross-examine prosecution witnesses and failure to allow it to do so is a ground for dismissing the case. Needless to say, that did not happen.

In December 2017, Ulyukayev was found guilty of bribery on a particularly large scale and sentenced to eight years in a strict-regime labour camp.

The trial, coming in the wake of Putin's decision not to confront Kadyrov over Nemtsov's murder, was confirmation that the rules of the game in the Kremlin were changing, not for the better. There had been no rational basis for Ulyukayev's imprisonment. He was a conscientious, capable minister who had merely been doing his job. His only offence – or so it seemed to most observers – had been to fall foul of Igor Sechin, a vengeful man who was determined to make him pay for having dared to oppose him.

The state media had spun his conviction as a warning that no one, however highly placed, would escape prosecution if engaged in corrupt practices. In reality, the message conveyed was the exact opposite. As a Russian journalist complained to Putin a few weeks later, it showed that 'there are two different legal realities in our country' – one for those who enjoyed the Kremlin's protection, another for those who did not.[38] By letting Sechin have his way and by failing to rein in Kadyrov, Putin had signalled to those around him that that so long as their loyalty was unquestioned, they, too, could do as they wished, and he would cover up for them if the need arose.

Putin's decision to cease micromanaging the system had other consequences, among them the botched attempt to murder the former GRU agent, Sergei Skripal, in Britain. After being recruited by MI6, Skripal had blown the identities of several hundred of his colleagues before he was arrested in 2004. He had been freed as part of an exchange with a group of Russian sleeper agents in America. There was an honour code that those exchanged in spy swaps should not be harmed. But the *siloviki* had never digested the decision to release him. In the winter of 2017, when the GRU found itself with greater latitude to act as it saw fit, it seized the opportunity.

In Skripal's case, unlike that of Litvinenko, there was nothing to suggest that Putin had ordered the attack or even that he had approved it. The Kremlin had nothing to gain from his death and relations with the West, already dire, would get even worse if Russia were shown to be involved. Afterwards, however, he covered up for those responsible. The men the British accused of being GRU operatives were civilians, he insisted[39] – ordinary Russian tourists visiting an English provincial town. In any case, Skripal had deserved everything he got. He was 'not worth five kopeks',[40] 'a traitor to the motherland, . . . just scum'.[41]

When other scandals arose, Putin reacted the same way.

After it emerged that many of the Russian athletes at the Sochi Olympics had been taking prohibited drugs, the minister responsible, Vitaly Mutko, an old friend from his St Petersburg days, was promoted to become a deputy Prime Minister. Putin accused WADA, the World Anti-Doping Agency, of carrying out a 'politically tainted investigation' under pressure from the United States.[42] Later he admitted that Russia 'was partly to blame because we gave cause . . . We must turn over a new leaf and learn the lesson.'[43] But that turned out to be merely a feint to ensure that Russia would be allowed to host the soccer World Cup in 2018.

When the cellist, Sergei Roldugin, who was godfather to one of Putin's daughters, was found to have stashed away a large fortune in offshore tax havens, the Kremlin denounced it as a smear campaign.[44] Roldugin, Putin insisted, was a philanthropist, buying instruments abroad to help less fortunate Russian musicians. 'I am proud of him,' he added, 'and proud to count him among my friends.'[45]

This was not just a matter of personal loyalty. To Putin it was essential to defend the Russian state – and the small group of people who exercised power within it or who were close to those who did – at all times.

It was the same logic that had led the acquittal rate in Russian criminal trials to fall from one per cent, when Putin had been a student in the 1970s, to 0.25 per cent in 2018.[46] Michael Calvey, an American businessman who was one of the biggest foreign investors in Russia, fell victim to that. In 2019, he was arrested on trumped-up charges inspired by a Russian competitor with close ties to the Kremlin. The initial dispute was eventually resolved. But, to show that the arrest had been justified, the court, ignoring the evidence, gave him a five-and-a-half-year suspended sentence.

The Kremlin's response to corruption allegations against Dmitry Medvedev was in the same mould. As Putin's third term was nearing an end, Medvedev was approaching his sell-by date. He had lost all credibility not only with the liberal intelligentsia but with the population at large. But when Aleksei Navalny's Anti-Corruption Foundation posted a 50-minute documentary on YouTube, alleging that he had received 1.2 billion US dollars in bribes from Russian business magnates, disguised as donations to a charitable foundation, Putin immediately went out of his way to show his support. Whatever thoughts he might have had of replacing Medvedev were shelved.

The documentary drew millions of views and provoked widespread demonstrations. But Navalny was struck by the fact that no one seemed to find the revelations surprising. 'You make a case that someone has taken more than a billion dollars in bribes, and what's the reaction? Everyone says: "What's so interesting about that?".'[47]

Russians had long since lost any illusions about the regime's failure to rein in corruption.

Putin could deny as much as he liked that his inner circle was corrupt. He could lash out at the government, standing by 'like a bearded peasant, idly picking at bits of cabbage in his beard, watching as the state became a swamp [plundered] by oligarchs'.[48] But the old saw about the good tsar and bad boyars had worn thin. People had heard Putin making the same complaints for 20 years while corrupt practices spread ever more widely. The fine words were a smokescreen to persuade them that their ruler meant well and had their interests at heart, while his courtiers continued to amass wealth on a scale of which most Russians could not even dream.

At the highest levels of the state, outright bribery was rare. Money was made from kickbacks, unspecified 'commissions' and consulting fees, arcane financial transactions, transfers of state-owned real estate at knockdown prices and grossly inflated infrastructure contracts. The sons and daughters of Putin's colleagues, and their nieces and nephews and cousins, moved effortlessly into positions on the boards of state-owned companies, banks and construction firms, where they parlayed their networks of relations into multi-million-dollar fortunes. In the provinces, the same scenario played out on a more modest scale.

The effects were felt at the grassroots as well.

'Under Yeltsin,' one woman complained, 'if a traffic policeman flagged you down, you would hand over your driving licence with the equivalent of a few dollars tucked inside and he'd wave you on. Now they play with you. They can hold you for hours to see how much they can make you pay. And it isn't a few dollars any more.'[49]

The experience of an émigré Russian businessman on a visit from Germany, who was driving a brand-new black Porsche Panamera, was typical. One day in the summer of 2019, he was flagged down by a traffic cop who asked him how much he would pay. He had a thousand dollars with him, he said. 'Not enough,' said the officer. 'It looks as though I shall have to detain you . . . Speeding and resisting arrest.' After some discussion, the businessman asked if he could make a phone call to ask a friend to bring some extra cash, to which the policeman agreed. Having explained the situation – 'He wants more money. Can you help?' – he handed the officer the phone. The man went pale. At the other end was an irate general in the Interior Ministry. The policeman saluted, returned the thousand dollars, which he had already pocketed, and apologised profusely.[50] The businessman had a *krysha*, a 'roof'. Most Russians did not.

None of this was new. It had been a feature of Russian life since at least the early 1990s. Attitudes to the police – other than traffic cops – had actually improved during Putin's third term.[51] But the bad apples were more numerous, more conspicuous and more confident that they would not be punished. Graft had become the glue that held the system together.

In the decade since the Great Recession, Russia had seen zero growth and real incomes had fallen. Yet the opinion polls indicated that, despite the economic woes and Putin's failure to tackle corruption, his approval rating remained above 80 per cent.[52] In elections for the Duma in September 2016, the ruling party, United Russia, won more than three quarters of the 450 seats, its best performance ever.

There were several reasons for this. Most Russians were still cock-a-hoop over the return of Crimea. To older people, Putin, for all his faults, was seen as a guarantor that there would be no return to the chaos of the 1990s. Moreover, there was no real alternative. Putin himself admitted that the available choices were 'a little bit boring'. The Communist leader, Gennady Zyuganov, and the head of the nationalist Liberal Democratic Party, Vladimir Zhirinovsky, were both in their seventies and had been leading their parties for a quarter of a century. They formed a tame opposition, 'hand-fed', as one Russian journalist put it, and financed from the state budget.[53] It was in their interests to see that challengers were kept out. Even with the restoration of single-seat constituencies for half of the Duma's 450 seats, which theoretically opened the door to independents, only three deputies were elected who did not belong to the main parties.

Those who were genuinely critical of the regime faced multiple obstacles. Navalny's Party of Progress attempted nine times to register for elections. Each time its application was rejected by the Ministry of Justice, preventing it putting up candidates.[54] The rules were constantly bent. Between 2003 and 2016, the regulations for State Duma elections were amended no fewer than 40 times.[55] Both the Central Election Commission and its regional counterparts were packed with establishment figures. Candidates from minor parties who wished to stand had to produce signatures of support from thousands of registered voters, which were often declared invalid. In practice, no candidate whom the authorities decided to exclude was able to take part.

At the same time, the government stepped up efforts to control the internet and restrict the activities of those NGOs which could be painted as 'foreign agents'. The new target was 'extremist ideology', a term so vague that it could cover almost anything. Extremism was corrupting the nation's youth, Putin said and, unless stopped, would pose 'a threat to national security'.[56] Laws against extremism had existed in Russia since the 1990s but had been directed mainly against neo-Nazi groups.[57] Now they would be used against any political movement of which the Kremlin disapproved.

The same blurring of boundaries occurred in other fields.

In May 2017, masked police staged a dawn raid on the home of one of Russia's leading theatre directors, Kirill Serebrennikov, who was led away for questioning, supposedly on suspicion of embezzlement.[58] To many Russians, it recalled the arrest by the NKVD in 1939 of Vsevolod Meyerhold, the greatest Soviet theatre director of his day, who was executed for 'formalism' during the final spasm of Stalin's Great Purge.

Putin was not pleased. 'What fools!', he exclaimed. It was 'simply preposterous' to carry out a police raid in a case like that. 'In our country the security forces are used at the drop of a hat, even when it is completely uncalled for. It makes no sense, and it made no sense in this case.'[59]

Serebrennikov did not suffer the same fate as Meyerhold: times had changed. But the Bolshoi was forced at the last minute to cancel a ballet which he had directed and, three months later, he was placed under house arrest charged with stealing a million dollars in public funds.

'The "fools" strike back,' wrote *Novaya gazeta* the morning after his arrest. Serebrennikov's travails, it noted, followed those of Yevtushenkov and Ulyukayev. 'The system of the law enforcers' lawlessness, which was built to strengthen the President's power, has finally become deranged . . . Putin either does not want or is not able to intervene.'[60] Other newspapers commented in the same vein. 'Something has gone wrong in this country', wrote *Moskovsky komsomolets*. 'Now the "fools" are showing that they, not the President, are in charge.'[61]

That was certainly what it looked like. Putin's criticisms had been very publicly ignored. Like his failure to punish Kadyrov, it raised questions about who held the real power in Russia.

As it turned out, there was a deeper explanation.

Putin's decision to delegate authority – to play a more 'hands off' role, except in regard to strategic and foreign policy issues, the traditional prerogatives of the presidency – was one factor. The growing influence of the *siloviki* was another. But they were merely facets of a much broader shift, both in the Kremlin and in the country at large, towards conservative values.

With hindsight, the crackdown on Pussy Riot in 2012 had been an augury. Putin had not been enthusiastic about punishing the punk performance art group but had found it expedient to do so. Four years later, suppressing 'non-traditional' culture had become the norm. Conservative deputies in the Duma and officials in the Ministry of Culture condemned plays and films and even, in one particularly absurd case, a performance of Wagner's classic opera, *Tannhäuser*, as repugnant to traditional Russian values or offensive to Orthodox believers. As in Serebrennikov's case, they used the security services to put pressure on those they targeted.[62]

Not only were liberal values in retreat. The very concept of democracy was being questioned. Throughout his first two terms, Putin had insisted that Russia's future was as a democratic state, albeit in a form which would take due account of its history and traditions. Now, he suggested, Russians might not yet be quite ready for that. 'It's a very complex process and there are certain stages that cannot be skipped,' he said. 'Our citizens have to get used to it.'[63]

The message between the lines was that, given Russia's economic difficulties and the hostility of the United States and its European allies, it was time to return to a more autocratic style of rule. For that, the *siloviki* and the conservatives who now dominated the elite would form an indispensable political base.

Putin explained his thinking in an interview with the *Financial Times*, two years after the Serebrennikov affair:

The so-called liberal idea . . . has outlived its purpose . . . [It] has become obsolete. It has come into conflict with the interests of the overwhelming majority of the population. Take traditional values . . . We have no problem with LGBT persons, let them live as they wish . . . But this must not be allowed to overshadow the culture, traditions and traditional family values of millions of people making up the core population . . . Have we forgotten that we all live in a world based on Biblical values? Even atheists live in that world . . . We do not have to [be] devout . . . but, deep inside there must be some fundamental rules . . . Traditional values are more stable and more important than this liberal idea. [Of course], it has the right to exist. But it should not be seen as being as of right the dominant idea.[64]

When Putin spoke of 'liberalism', he meant liberal democracy. Russian commentators saw in his statement an echo of Soviet times, when communist propagandists spent their lives denouncing 'bourgeois democracy'.[65] In fact, he was reverting to a much older tradition, dating back to the beginning of the sixteenth century, when Philotheus, the Elder of Eleazar Monastery at Pskov, declared that, after the decadence of Rome, attested by the Great Schism between Eastern and Western Christianity in 1054 and the fall of Orthodox Constantinople in 1453, Muscovite Russia would be the centre of the Christian world, 'and there will be no other'.

If Russia had fallen behind in its efforts to become a great economic power, Putin seemed to be saying, it would become a moral beacon, radiating out to the rest of the world illiberal, conservative values. Other countries could adopt the liberal model if they wished. Russia would not.[66]

That position was set out in greater detail two years later in a new National Security Doctrine, which reaffirmed 'the crisis of the Western liberal model' and continued:

The freedom of the individual is being made absolute; permissiveness, immorality and selfishness are being actively propagated; the cult of violence, consumption and pleasure is being implanted; the use of drugs is legalised and [LGBT] communities are formed which deny the natural continuation of life . . . The imposition of alien ideas and values . . . leads to disunity and the polarisation of national societies . . .

> Traditional Russian spiritual, moral, cultural and historical values are being actively attacked by the United States and its allies [through] information and psychological sabotage and "Westernisation" . . . [These] values . . . have been formed over centuries of Russian history [and constitute] the basis of Russian society . . .[67]

Whether Putin was really as convinced of the imminent demise of Western liberal thought as those statements suggested is open to question. Dmitry Trenin, the head of the Carnegie Moscow Center, wrote that the document marked 'an important milestone in the country's official abandonment of the liberal phraseology of the 1990s'.[68] But phraseology and underlying beliefs do not always coincide. It was true that the West's share of the global economy was declining, and anyone with a Marxist education would infer that Western influence in the realm of ideas – the 'superstructure', as Marx called it – would decline as well. On the other hand, liberal ideas had always proved remarkably resilient.

Regardless of whether Putin believed it, it was smart politics.

The principles he now espoused were shared by many conservatives in Europe and the United States and they resonated deeply in Russia, especially among those who lived outside the big cities and formed the critical mass of Putin's political base.

The new emphasis on traditional values was accompanied by another, less explicit shift. It was not merely the collapse of the Soviet Union that was to be regretted, Putin said, but the passing of the Russian empire. In the early 1990s he had accused the Bolsheviks of sowing the seeds of the country's destruction by dividing it into autonomous regions, each of which, in theory at least, had the right of secession. In December 2019, he repeated the same words he had used a quarter of a century before: 'They put a time bomb under Russia.'[69] This time, however, he blamed Lenin by name. One of the journalists present remembered 'something close to rage on his face' as he spoke. By breaking up a centralised empire that had existed for hundreds of years, the Bolshevik leader, he charged, had made 'an absolute, pivotal, fundamental error'.[70]

That was harsher than anything he had said before about the founder of the communist state. It was another sign that times were changing. Two years earlier, the only ceremony which Putin had attended, linked to the centenary of the Bolshevik Revolution, was the opening in central Moscow of a 'Wall of Sorrow' as a memorial to the victims of Stalin's purges. 'It is important,' he said, 'that future generations . . . remember this tragic period of our history, when . . . absolutely absurd charges could be brought against anybody, [and] millions of people were declared "enemies of the people", shot, mutilated, or suffered in prisons, labour camps or exile. This terrifying past cannot be deleted from our national memory and [can never be] justified.'[71] In another speech, he accused the Bolsheviks of having practised 'complete and total deception' after they seized power.[72] People had been promised a brave new world, he said, and instead they got mass graves.[73]

Putin could afford to take a tougher line with the communists. Their ranks were thinning. The older generation, which had formed the core of their support, would soon be no more. The Soviet period had not been all bad, Putin acknowledged. But it had been a parenthesis in the great sweep of Russian history, a time when the country had taken a wrong turn, which fortunately had now been corrected.

Putin might claim to reject liberalism, and, by implication, democratic rules, but elections continued to play an important part in the system he had created. They were not window-dressing, he insisted.[74] They served as a plebiscite, a ritual reaffirmation of the contract with the Russian people which enabled him to rule.

The presidential election in March 2018 posed a familiar problem: how to generate sufficient interest to ensure an acceptable turnout when the outcome was a foregone conclusion.

The Kremlin's target was 70/70, meaning 70 per cent of the vote for Putin in the first round and a 70 per cent turnout. A sure-fire way to ensure a high turnout would have been to allow Aleksei Navalny to stand. But, having been burnt once by his unexpectedly strong performance against Sobyanin in the mayoral elections in Moscow in 2013, Putin decided the risk was too great.

Throughout the presidential campaign, Navalny was harassed. Three times he was jailed for holding unauthorised rallies. An unidentified attacker threw green dye at him which had been mixed with a caustic substance, partially blinding him in one eye. The Supreme Court ordered a retrial of the KirovLes case, the first judgement having been overturned by the European Court of Human Rights. To no one's surprise, he was again found guilty and his five-year suspended sentence reimposed, which meant that he could not register as a candidate. In December 2017, when the Electoral Commission confirmed that he would not be allowed to run, he called on his supporters to boycott the election. But nationally they accounted for only about five per cent of the electorate[75] and since they would not have voted for Putin anyway, it made little different to the outcome.

To inject a little more interest into the proceedings, Putin persuaded Kseniy Sobchak to stand on behalf of the non-system opposition. But her candidature never took off. She was dismissed, perhaps a little unfairly, as 'a project of the Kremlin'. Her pro-Western, pro-democracy stance appealed to younger, better-off voters in the big cities, but most of the electorate regarded her as a self-centred socialite and television personality with a somewhat chequered past. The Kremlin's efforts six years earlier to depict her as a mindless bimbo, opening the door to the police half-naked, had not helped. Where Mikhail Prokhorov, the businessman who had played a similar role in the 2012 elections, had ended up with 8 per cent of the vote, Sobchak's projected score never exceeded 2 per cent.

Putin, as usual, did not officially campaign. He announced a rise in pensions and social security benefits, increased maternity capital on the birth of a second child and higher salaries for state employees – offers crafted to appeal to key parts of his base – and, in his speeches at the beginning of the year, he reiterated his determination to reduce the poverty rate, raise real wages, and improve health, education and housing. He had made the same promises many times before but they were still what people wanted to hear. When the results were announced on March 18, 2018, Putin obtained nearly 77 per cent of the vote, 13 per cent more than in 2012, and the turnout of 67 per cent was also higher. Four years after the annexation of Crimea, the gale of nationalist fervour that had enveloped Russia had still not blown itself out. In any case, who else was there to vote for? The Communists received 12 per cent and Zhirinovsky, the eternal, now ageing rabble-rouser, six per cent, which represented the protest vote.

On May 7, Putin took the oath of office in the Grand Kremlin Palace at the commencement of what was expected to be his fourth and last presidential term.

18

The Endgame

In February 2000, a few weeks after Putin became acting President, he was asked to comment on the misfortunes of Helmut Kohl, then embroiled in a financial scandal after having been the longest-serving German Chancellor since Bismarck. 'After 16 years,' Putin said, 'any people – including the stable Germans – get tired of a leader, even a leader as strong as Kohl. It just took them a while to realise it.'[1]

When Putin's fourth term commenced, he had been in power for almost 20 years.

Russia was not Germany. Notions of political alternance were far less well established than in Western Europe. Many Russians were tired of Putin, but even more found it hard to imagine anyone else in charge. Rather, there was a deepening sense of ennui, of drift, of being stuck in a rut, which recalled the stagnation that had marked Brezhnev's final years.

There were important differences. The Brezhnev era had signalled ineluctable decline with little hope that anything would change for the better. The boredom that marked the start of Putin's fourth term was not hopeless. But more and more Russians started to feel that change would not come until, and unless, he decided to step down. Putin liked to claim that he had been thinking about an eventual successor from the day he first took office.[2] He certainly found himself from the outset having to answer questions about his long-term intentions. In May 2000, only ten days after his inauguration, he told an interviewer: 'I am not going to be here forever . . . Sooner or later, we all leave our posts.'[3] The following year he said that he always thought twice before taking decisions, because the day would come when, as an ordinary citizen, 'you will be confronted with what you have done.'[4] In 2003, he reflected anew. 'When a person stays in power too long, no matter how good he is, his drive is blunted, he doesn't have the same "fire in his belly" as at the start of the journey. And secondly, he comes to be surrounded by [a] sort of . . . camarilla.'[5]

In one sense, such remarks were predictable and largely meaningless. But they demonstrated concern with an issue which Western politicians rarely had to bother with.[6] In the West, elections were won or lost and, if term limits intervened, even a successful leader would be obliged to retire. For Putin, it would be a choice. Barring a putsch, he could remain President for as long as he wanted. If he left, it would be because he had decided that the time had come for him to go.

After the *rokirovka* with Medvedev, when Putin returned for his third term, the questions about his future became more pressing. Most times he fobbed them off. He would leave 'sooner or later', he said.[7] Perhaps he would sever all links with the political administration, as Yeltsin had done. Or perhaps not.[8] Occasionally, he said something which gave an insight into the way his mind was working. He cited the example of the Rurikid dynasty, which had ended in 1598 with numerous usurpers and impostors claiming the title of Tsar.[9] It was important to have clarity regarding the succession, he said. A dual power structure, in which he continued to exercise authority after ostensibly stepping down, would be 'absolutely ruinous for Russia'.[10] On the other hand, he did not wish to leave politics altogether because, he admitted, 'I feel responsible for what is going on and what will happen in the future.'[11]

It was a conundrum to which he struggled to find an answer.

The one thing which was absolutely clear was that – regardless of when and how, or even whether, in the foreseeable future, he would relinquish power – whatever decision he eventually reached would need to be minutely prepared. From the beginning of his fourth term in May 2018, the issue of the succession was never far from his mind.

Putin's first major initiative appeared totally unrelated to the succession issue. It concerned the age at which Russians could retire.

For years, he had insisted that the pensionable age, 55 for women and 60 for men, would not change as long as he was in power.[12] His economic advisers had warned repeatedly that, in the long term, that was unsustainable. The Pension Fund would go bankrupt, and the longer he waited, the harder it would be to put right. Putin had resisted because any change would be hugely unpopular. In the highly personalised system over which he presided, the source of his legitimacy was public approval. Since the violent backlash against the monetisation of social benefits in 2005, he had been careful to do nothing which might antagonise his political base. Raising the retirement age would cause even fiercer protests. But by 2015, it was clear that, sooner or later, it would have to be done.[13]

In the chaos of the 1990s, Russia's birth rate had collapsed, producing a demographic black hole a generation later. Not only would far fewer young people enter the labour market from 2015 to 2025, but the number of women of child-bearing age was expected to fall by a third, producing a knock-on effect which would continue for decades after.[14] As the economy had improved, the birth rate had increased, the death rate had fallen and life expectancy had risen to 68 years for men and 78 for women, not far behind the United States. But the hole in the pension fund kept stubbornly growing.[15]

Even so, Putin was wary. First, he delayed the decision until the presidential election was behind him and the country's attention was focused on the 2018 FIFA World Cup. Then he left it to Dmitry Medvedev, whom he had reappointed as Prime Minister, to shepherd the legislation through the Duma.[16] The retirement age would be increased by stages – an extra six months each year – until it reached 65 for men in 2028 and 63 for women six years later. At a time when most of Western Europe had agreed to raise the pension age to 67 or even 68 for both men and women, that was relatively modest. Russians found it totally unacceptable. Opinion surveys showed that more than 90 per cent were categorically opposed.[17] At protest demonstrations, people held up home-made signs reading: 'Pay your taxes and DIE before you reap any benefit!', 'Pay and CROAK!', and 'Pensions for Living People, not the DEAD!'

In fact, the headline figures were misleading. As Putin tried to explain, male life expectancy in Russia was lower than in Western Europe because there was a higher death rate among younger men due to alcoholism and drugs, accidents and a rickety health system.[18] Men who reached the age of 65 were likely to live, on average, another 14 years, only four years less than the OECD average.[19] But that was not an argument which Russians wanted to hear.

In August, to soften the impact, Putin announced that the retirement age for women would be capped at 60, not 63, and that a number of special categories, including mothers of large families and miners – later expanded to include teachers, military and law enforcement personnel – would continue to retire earlier.[20] That did not stop his approval rating plummeting from 83 to 65 per cent.[21] But it did bring an end to the demonstrations. After Putin had spoken, people understood that the decision was final and further protests were pointless.[22] At his annual news conference in December, he made what sounded like an apology. 'It's unpleasant, it's not fun,' he said. 'If I were not convinced that we had to do it, I would never have allowed it to happen.'[23]

But there was evidently more to it than that. Putin himself had admitted a few months earlier that the state could have continued to finance the Pension Fund deficit for 'another seven to ten years' before the strain became intolerable.[24] In that case, why was it so essential to act in 2018?

Officially the government was being far-sighted, biting the bullet early and taking a difficult choice for the common good. But some suspected that there might be another reason. Leonid Bershidsky, the founding editor of *Vedomosti*, wondered if Putin was not 'doing his potential chosen successor a favour by taking the heat for an extremely unpopular but necessary move'.[25]

Putin seemed to be clearing the decks to smooth the path for a possible transition while at the same time keeping his options open, taking advantage of the momentum from his re-election to push through an unavoidable measure which would be far more difficult later on, whether he continued as President or not.

Putin's next move was easier to decipher. In December 2018, the Speaker of the Duma, Vyacheslav Volodin, proposed a review of the constitution.[26]

Volodin, a solidly built man in his mid fifties with short, greying hair, had earlier served as first deputy Head of the Presidential Administration. The Americans regarded him as one of Putin's protégés. Shrewd, ambitious and sycophantic, he had coined the slogan, 'No Putin – No Russia'.[27]

At first no one paid much attention to Volodin's proposal. It was known that Putin was devoted, as one Russian journalist archly commented, 'to the letter of the law, if not quite as much to the spirit',[28] and that he had repeatedly ruled out amending the constitution to retain power beyond his current term. Six months later, however, Volo-din returned to the charge with a long article in which he suggested 'targeted adjustments' to improve the 'balance between the legislative and executive branches', by which he meant that parliament should have a bigger say in ministerial appointments.[29]

Whether or not Putin directly inspired Volodin's initiatives or simply made use of them, the question of amending the constitution was now clearly on the agenda. In December, at his annual news conference, a planted question from a member of the Kremlin press pool gave him an opportunity to express his views.[30] The underlying principles of the constitution should not be changed, Putin said, but other provisions could perhaps be amended, including those relating to the separation of powers. That was suitably vague – a former aide noted drily that Putin was, as usual, 'giving himself the widest possible latitude for future moves on the political chess board'[31] – and in the end it turned out to be a red herring. But another remark was more revealing. The word 'consecutive', in the clause stating that the President should not serve 'more than two consecutive terms', might be removed, he suggested.[32] He himself would not be affected because the change would apply only from the time it was enacted. But it would mean that, after he stepped down, future presidents would be limited to two six-year terms.

It was the first clue that the constitutional changes under discussion were being made with the post-Putin period in mind.

On January 15, 2020, in an address to a joint session of parliament, Putin put forward additional proposals. The President, he said, should have the right to dismiss federal and Supreme Court judges. The Russian constitution should take precedence over international law, which would mean that Russians could no longer appeal to the European Court of Human Rights. No one could stand as a candidate for the presidency if they had ever held foreign citizenship or a foreign residency permit, which would bar émigrés like Mikhail Khodorkovsky.[33]

Since most of this was of scant interest to the Russian man or woman in the street, three further provisions were added to ensure that, when the time came to ask them to approve the reforms, people would come out and vote. The minimum wage would be guaranteed by the constitution at not less than subsistence level; pensions would be indexed for inflation; and marriage was reaffirmed as the traditional union of one man and one woman.

The same day, at Putin's request, Dmitry Medvedev resigned. Having served a total of eight years as Prime Minister, he was moved sideways into a specially created honorific post as Deputy Chairman of the Security Council. To succeed him, Putin named Mikhail Mishustin, a technocrat with an engineering background who had previously been head of the Tax Service. Mishustin, a large, expansive man, was bright, competent and highly professional. He had digitised tax collection, using state-of-the-art software to allow real-time oversight, reducing evasion on VAT payments from 20 per cent to almost nothing. The *Financial Times* had called him 'the tax man of the future'.[34] Outside the Presidential Administration, he was virtually unknown. Putin told journalists afterwards that his staff had drawn up a list of three or four potential candidates for the premiership, but he had rejected them all and chosen Mishustin instead.[35] The implication was that the new Prime Minister was his personal protégé and it was noted afterwards that, unlike earlier incumbents, Mishustin was given a virtually free hand to select his cabinet.

When the new government was announced on January 21, the key ministers – Defence, Finance, Foreign Affairs and the Interior – were unchanged, but more than half the others were new faces. The time had come, Putin said, 'to train a new generation of managers, who will be able to take responsibility for Russia'.[36]

The same processes were at work in the provinces, where Putin had started promoting younger men – though no women – as regional governors.[37] With a handful of exceptions – among them, Kudrin, Sergei Ivanov, Patrushev and Sechin – almost all those who had held key posts during his first and second terms had been put out to pasture.

The constitutional reforms which Putin announced at the beginning of 2019 were rushed through at breakneck speed. The 'non-system' opposition cried foul. 'History is being written quick and dirty,' complained *Moskovsky komsomolets*.[38] *Novaya gazeta* spoke of 'a constitutional coup and usurpation of power'.[39] The working group set up to draft the amendments said it would take at least a year to complete the necessary legislation. They were told they had two months.[40] That may have been partly because the Covid-19 pandemic was looming and nobody, at that point, knew how serious a problem it would become.[41] But it seemed that Putin had other reasons for wanting to move fast.

As it turned out, the real *coup de théâtre* was still to come.

In mid March, as the Russian media buzzed with speculation that Putin was laying the groundwork to take an elder-statesman role after his term ended in 2024, the Duma met for what was expected to be a routine second reading. But the doyenne of the chamber, Valentina Tereshkova, who, in the 1960s, had been the world's first woman cosmonaut and was now an octogenarian deputy for United Russia, proposed a surprise amendment. When the constitutional reform took effect, she said, the clock should be reset to zero and previous presidential terms not taken into account. If approved, that would mean that Putin could stand again in 2024 and in theory, if he wished, in 2030 as well.

The whole exercise was carried out with balletic precision.[42] Tereshkova was a legendary figure, a Hero of the Soviet Union and holder of the Order of Lenin, the country's highest decorations. No sooner had she ended her speech than it was announced that Putin would address parliament later that afternoon.[43] When he did so, he opined somewhat diffidently, as though discovering the proposal for the first time, that it seemed 'in principle, possible', and that, given the need for stability, it might prove a wise solution. 'I have no doubt,' he added, 'that the day will come when presidential power in Russia will not be so personalised – not so connected to a specific individual – but that is how it has been all through our history and we cannot but take that into account.'[44]

The amendment was immediately passed *nem. con.*, with only the Communists abstaining. Within a matter of hours, the prospects for political change in Russia had been turned arsy-versy.

Even the Russian press, inured to the ways of Russian politics, was stunned by the sleight of hand with which Putin had moved the goalposts when no one was paying attention.[45] All the talk about enhancing the powers of parliament turned out to have been a smokescreen, a pretext to allow him to sneak in undetected the one change that really mattered.[46]

By law, constitutional amendments approved by the Duma and the Federation Council must be sent to Russia's 85 regional assemblies, which each have up to a year to debate and vote on them. This time all the regions approved them within 48 hours.[47] Four days after Tereshkova's proposal, Putin signed the reforms into law.

There was one further stage before the revised constitution came into force. Putin had insisted on a nationwide vote – not technically a referendum, more in the nature of a plebiscite – to give 'the Putin Con-stitution', as it was now called, the seal of popular approval. It was originally planned for April, but as the pandemic took hold, it was postponed until the end of June. When the results were announced, two thirds of registered voters had taken part and 78 per cent had approved. The vote was a sham. State employees were bused in to cast their ballots and, where all else failed, the ballot boxes were stuffed to make up the numbers. But even had there been no skulduggery and no administrative pressure, the measures would probably still have scraped through.[48]

The assumption in the West was that Putin would now remain in power for at least one and probably two more terms, up to 2036, when he would be 83 years old, and perhaps even longer.[49] Much of the Rus-sian press thought the same.

That was a misreading.

As Putin himself later acknowledged, the primary purpose of the amendment had not been to prolong his time in power – although that remained a possibility – but to prevent him becoming a lame duck.[50] Without it, the remaining four years of his term would have been con-sumed by factional intrigues among the political elite, jockeying for the succession, and speculation about what role, if any, Putin would play after stepping down. The moment he was able to stand again, what would happen in 2024 ceased to be an issue and the problem disappeared.

Later that year another constitutional amendment was passed, whose significance at the time was largely overlooked but provided a further clue to Putin's intentions. Former presidents could in future, when retired, become *ex officio* members for life of the Federation Council, the upper house of parliament. This would confer immunity from prosecution, not only for anything they might have done during their time in office but also before and after.[51] Putin later dismissed that airily as just 'a third-tier issue'.[52] It was much more than that. Another piece of the jigsaw had slipped into place.

In terms of legislation, the preparations were now complete. Putin could step down in 2024, or earlier if that seemed desirable, or he could embark on a fifth presidential term. It would be up to him to decide.

⋆

The next step was to emasculate the 'non-system' opposition.

After Putin's re-election in 2018, the squeeze on anything resembling politically contentious activities intensified.

The designation of organisations as 'foreign agents', initially limited to NGOs which received foreign funding, was extended first to foreign-backed media and internet channels and then to individual journalists.[53] Designated organisations had by law to identify themselves as such, signalling pariah status. Media outlets found that advertising dried up. Individuals became unemployable. Increasing use was also made of another designation, 'undesirable organisation', which had been introduced in 2015 to allow the banning of the National Endowment for Democracy and other foreign associations promoting human rights and democracy.[54] In 2021, the number of undesirable organisations more than tripled.

The authorities began cracking down much harder on unauthorised demonstrations. Putin was unrepentant. If the police did not keep order, he said, 'cars will be set on fire, shop windows will be smashed, people will be harmed . . . If you protest without authorisation, be ready [to sit in prison] for as long as the court rules.' When a journalist pointed out that the only time cars had been set on fire in Moscow was after a football match which Russia lost to Japan, he pretended not to hear.[55]

In October 2019, Aleksei Navalny's Anti-Corruption Foundation was declared a foreign agent. Navalny had come up with a new tactic, which he called 'smart voting'. If no 'non-system' candidate was allowed to stand, his supporters would vote for whoever had the best chance of defeating the candidate of United Russia, Putin's party. It might be a Communist or a member of Zhirinovsky's Liberal Democratic Party or a candidate from Just Russia, all of whom, if elected, would in practice support the government. But that was not the point. The fewer votes went to the ruling party, the more Putin's legitimacy was undermined.

The combination of 'smart voting' and the steady drip of sensational exposés of corruption by highly placed officials exasperated Putin. Sometime towards the end of 2019 or early in 2020, he decided that, one way or another, Navalny would have to go.

The following summer, the opposition leader travelled across Russia, mobilising his supporters for the regional elections which were to take place in September. On the morning of Thursday, August 20, he was in

Tomsk, in Siberia, where he boarded a plane of the domestic Russian airline, S7, to fly back to Moscow. Half an hour after take-off, he began to experience a strange feeling which he had difficulty describing – not so much pain, he said later, but 'as if the life were being sucked out of me'. He managed to walk to the lavatory before collapsing, groaning uncontrollably. The pilot diverted to Omsk and radioed ahead for an ambulance. By the time they landed, Navalny was in a coma. He was later flown to Berlin, where it was found that he had been poisoned with a cholinesterase inhibitor, subsequently identified as a nerve agent of the Novichok group, similar to that used against Sergei Skripal in Salisbury.

Navalny remained in a coma for a month. The German doctors said afterwards that the good sense of the ambulance crew at Omsk, who gave him atropine, an anticholinergic drug used as an antidote against certain forms of poisoning, coupled with the quick reaction of the pilot, had almost certainly saved his life.

Navalny had been attacked before by FSB agents or people acting on their behalf. This time was different.

The complexity of the planning, the number of people involved and the sophistication of the substance used, all indicated that it had been authorised at a very high level. A team of FSB agents had been tracking Navalny's movements since the beginning of the year.[56] In Tomsk, they had entered his hotel room while he was out and smeared Novichok on articles of clothing. An FSB chemical-weapons specialist had afterwards been sent to recover the contaminated items.[57]

The use of the nerve agent was confirmed by German, French and Swedish laboratories and by the Organisation for the Prohibition of Chemical Weapons, which found that the type of Novichok which had been used was a novel variant, apparently developed more recently than the poison used against Skripal.

The Russian Foreign Ministry and Putin's spokesman, Dmitry Peskov, both issued blanket denials that the Russian State had had anything to do with Navalny's illness.[58] Putin himself remained silent.

On September 14, however, he took a call from the French President, Emmanuel Macron, which resulted in what the Elysée Palace called 'a dialogue of the deaf'. Macron insisted that what he termed this 'criminal act' could only have been perpetrated with the complicity of the Russian authorities. Putin was dismissive: Navalny was 'a troublemaker'; the allegations were 'unfounded'; anyone could have poisoned him, he might even have staged the poisoning himself to enhance his own importance. Macron was sufficiently exasperated by Putin's obvious bad faith to authorise the leaking of the conversation to the newspaper *Le Monde*, which published a detailed summary a week later.[59]

When eventually Putin was forced to address the issue publicly, at his annual news conference in mid December, he claimed that Navalny had been working for the CIA – a traditional Russian smear against those who opposed the Kremlin – and that therefore it was only natural that the FSB had been keeping him under surveillance. 'Of course, that's not to say,' he added with a grin, 'that he ought to have been poisoned. Who needs that? If they'd wanted to [kill him], they would probably have finished the job.'[60]

It was the same kind of *capo mafioso* sneer with which he had treated Litvinenko's death ('unfortunately [he] is not Lazarus') and the killing of Anna Politkovskaya ('her death caused more damage than her writings'). But this time it caught him out. If the FSB had been monitoring Navalny's movements so carefully, a reporter asked Dmitry Peskov afterwards, how was it that they had not been able to prevent him being poisoned? 'That is not a question for me,' snapped a plainly discomfited Peskov, bringing the briefing to an abrupt end.[61]

The issue, however, was not whether Putin was lying. He was. The question was whether he himself had ordered Navalny killed or whether, given the 'hands off' mode in which he had been running Russia since the middle of his third term, the final decision had been taken by *siloviki* in his inner circle who assumed that he would be only too glad to see his long-time adversary removed.

Even among Russians opposed to the regime, many thought the latter was more likely. Yet there are good grounds for thinking that Putin himself took the decision. His antipathy towards Navalny was personal. He refused to utter Navalny's name, speaking instead of 'the Berlin patient', 'this person' or 'this gentleman'. Putin compared him to the former Georgian leader, Mikheil Saakashvili, whom he despised. Navalny was a clown, he said, who had nothing to offer and manipulated those credulous enough to follow him.[62] That Western leaders should regard this upstart as a possible challenger to Putin, putting them on the same level, he found absolutely intolerable.

For that reason alone, it is very difficult to believe that anyone in the upper echelons of power would have dared to initiate an attack on Navalny without Putin's explicit agreement.

Whether he signed off on the method used is a different matter. It would have been far easier to stage, for instance, a fatal car accident. But old habits die hard. The use of obscure poisons had been a favoured technique of the FSB and its Soviet predecessors ever since the 1920s. Even though, over the years, it had proved less reliable and more complicated in execution than more orthodox methods, the Russian services remained wedded to it.

The timing of the attack also suggested an awareness of possible foreign policy repercussions which the *siloviki*, had they been in charge, would have been unlikely to take into account. In August 2020, the United States was in the midst of a presidential election and Europe was consumed by the Covid-19 pandemic. The world's attention was elsewhere, and even if the FSB's role became known, in all probability there would be little that Western governments would wish or be able to do about it. That proved to be the case. In Germany, there were calls to cancel the Nord Stream 2 gas pipeline, but they were quickly squashed. The EU imposed sanctions on the FSB chief, Aleksandr Bortnikov, and four other Russian officials. The Trump administration did nothing. It was not even a rap over the knuckles.

But there is another, more compelling, reason to think that Putin personally approved the attack on Navalny. It crossed a line.

Many in the United States and Europe are convinced that Putin has been behind every high-profile killing in Russia for the last 20 years. The case for that was made directly in a lengthy interview with him in June 2021, by Keir Simmons of NBC. When Putin demurred, Simmons persisted: 'Let me give you some names. Anna Politkovskaya, shot dead. Aleksandr Litvinenko, poisoned by polonium. Sergei Magnitsky, allegedly beaten and died in prison. Boris Nemtsov, shot moments from the Kremlin . . . Mikhail Lesin died of blunt trauma in Washington, D.C. Are all of these a coincidence, Mr President?'[63] The problem with that list, to which at least another dozen names could easily be added, was that, with the exception of Litvinenko, none had been killed at Putin's behest.[64] In a number of cases, he had been complicit in the cover-up that followed and he bore indirect responsibility by permitting a climate of impunity in which powerful figures could do as they wished. But that was not the same as directly ordering the death of a political opponent.[65]

The attempted murder of Navalny was the first time since Stalin's day that a Russian ruler had organised the assassination of a rival.[66] It was too strong a taboo to have been broken without Putin's authorisation.

A few years earlier, Putin had been asked by a group of students whether he believed that the end justified the means. 'No,' he said. 'If you use some appalling means to reach your goal, you actually destroy the very goal you live for.' Then he paused and added a qualification: 'Not always.'[67] There might be exceptions. The need to eliminate Navalny from the political arena, to clear the way for the Duma elections due the following autumn and for whatever political transition might follow, was evidently in the 'not always' category.

Putin had been hoping that Navalny would stay in the West, as Khodorkovsky and Berezovsky had done, in which case, as an émigré, his appeal to Russians would fade. Instead, he decided to follow the path traced by Nelson Mandela, hoping that a sojourn in prison would enhance his status and make him the undisputed standard-bearer of all who opposed the regime.

The result was a political fight in which neither side gave quarter. When Navalny flew back to Moscow in January 2021, he was arrested on arrival.

Two days later, a two-hour documentary was uploaded to his YouTube channel, showing the palatial residence at Gelendzhik which had been built for Putin ten years earlier at a reputed cost of 1.3 billion dollars. The story was not new. Navalny himself had posted photographs of the complex, spread over 68 hectares, overlooking the Black Sea, during the Duma election campaign in 2011. However, this was a more sophisticated production, made by a German television studio using state-of-the-art software and animation techniques. Parts were pure invention: images of a violet-lit hookah bar with an area for pole-dancing owed more to Navalny's imagination and computer enhancement than to reality. But the picture of opulent decadence which Navalny had conjured up struck a chord with Russians, whose incomes had been stagnating or declining for the last ten years, and it had soon attracted more than 100 million views.

Putin denied any connection with the Gelendzhik 'palace'. Shortly afterwards, the building magnate, Arkady Rotenberg, announced that he was the owner and intended to turn it into a luxury hotel. But the scandal, coupled with Navalny's arrest, triggered demonstrations all over Russia, in which more than 5,000 people were detained.

In February, the suspension of Navalny's jail sentence in the Yves Rocher case was revoked and he was sent to a penal colony, 60 miles east of Moscow. Political prisoners were isolated, woken every hour during the night, forbidden eye contact with guards and made to do repetitive, meaningless tasks. After a month, Navalny went on hunger strike in protest against the authorities' refusal to let him have medical treatment. Three weeks later, on Putin's instructions, they backed down. So long as he was in prison, there was nothing to be gained by pushing the situation to extremes. His suspended five-year sentence in the KirovLes case was still pending. As Khodorkovsky had discovered, a prisoner who crossed Putin could be detained for as long as the authorities desired.

After Navalny ended his hunger strike, the West largely lost interest. So did most Russians. Opinion surveys found that more than half of those questioned did not believe that he had been poisoned, fewer than 20 per cent approved of his activities and only four per cent thought he was trustworthy.[68] Despite all he had been through, Navalny remained more a gadfly than a national leader. But he was the only opposition figure with the charisma to bring large crowds of protesters out onto the streets and he had the potential to develop into a bigger threat. Putin's popularity had taken a hit from the pension reform and although he still had a 60 per cent approval rating, his position was weaker than it had been before. If he was considering, even as a theoretical possibility, stepping down in the next few years, he intended to leave nothing to chance. That meant not only keeping Navalny out of circulation but limiting as much as possible the ability of the opposition to use 'smart voting' in the Duma elections which were to take place in September.

With that in mind, while Navalny had been in Berlin, parliament had approved a raft of new restrictions.[69] The Foreign Agent designation was extended to include any individual who had links with an organisation receiving funding from abroad, a definition so broad that it covered all of Navalny's supporters. Political activities were redefined to include 'taking part in public debates and discussions'. Demonstrators who obstructed traffic, even unintentionally, or who disobeyed the orders of the police, could be charged with 'group hooliganism'. Since 2016, the only form of unauthorised demonstration officially permitted had been so-called 'single-picket protests', in which individuals waited in line to take turns staging a one-person demonstration, usually outside official buildings. That, too, was now banned. Facial recognition technology meant that anyone who took part in a demonstration could be identified and tracked down. Moscow alone had more than 200,000 CCTV cameras.[70]

But the biggest blow was yet to come.

In June 2021, Navalny's Anti-Corruption Foundation was declared to be an extremist organisation and therefore illegal. Anyone continuing to work for it faced up to six years in prison and anyone who donated money to it up to ten years. Those who had been 'involved' in its activities, which could mean simply having attended a rally several years earlier, were barred from standing for election. Moreover, the 'extremist' designation was retroactive. Anyone who had associated with Navalny's organisation in the three years before it had been declared illegal was also banned from standing as a candidate.

Novaya gazeta accused Putin of 'legalising despotism'.[71] Andrei Pertsev, of the Carnegie Moscow Center, concluded: 'Any form of politics that is not controlled by the Kremlin . . . is essentially outlawed.'[72]

Navalny's websites were closed down on the pretext that they carried 'extremist propaganda'. His closest colleagues were prosecuted or forced into exile. Government employees and workers in state-owned enterprises who had contacted his organisation were tracked down, called in by their bosses and reprimanded or, in some cases, fired.

Russia was still a far cry from the Soviet Union, let alone China, where, the same year that Navalny was jailed, the penalty for political protest was life imprisonment.[73] But the difference was being steadily eroded. During the summer, *Dozhd*, the one remaining independent television news network in Russia, and the popular website, Meduza. ru, were designated foreign agents. In December, the country's oldest human rights organisation, Memorial, which had been founded by Andrei Sakharov, was ordered to close. Only *Ekho Moskvy* continued to function as an independent broadcaster and it, too, became more

cautious about what it felt able to say. The printed press retained considerable latitude. The previous year, Russia's three heavyweight
newspapers – *Kommersant*, *Vedomosti* and *RBK* – published identical
front pages protesting against the arrest of a prominent investigative
journalist, Ivan Golunov, on whom the police had planted drugs.[74] On
that occasion, the charges were dropped and two police generals dismissed. But it was the exception which proved the rule. Media freedoms
were being rapidly and inexorably whittled away.

So was the space for dissent. Russia, one commentator wrote, had
become 'a country of appearances and fictitious political institutions'.[75]
It was a Potemkin village of democracy. By the summer of 2021, an
estimated nine million people – nearly 10 per cent of the electorate –
had been barred from standing in elections on one pretext or another.[76]
That year saw the biggest exodus of journalists, human rights activists
and opposition politicians, seeking refuge abroad, since late Soviet
times.[77] The 'non-system opposition' had virtually ceased to exist.

Moscow's relations with the Biden administration began warily. Putin
waited almost six weeks after the November 2020 election, twice as
long as even the Chinese, before congratulating Biden on his victory.
Four years earlier, he had sent a warm message to Trump the following
morning. It was a signal that Russia was in no hurry to seek an
accommodation.

Asked in mid December how he envisaged relations with the new
President, Putin said, 'I don't know . . . It all depends who makes up his
team.'[78] By then, it had been announced that Anthony Blinken would
become Secretary of State with Victoria Nuland as his deputy. In Moscow, both were viewed as Russia hawks. Nuland was an experienced
Russia hand but with very set ideas. The Kremlin saw her, not without
reason, as the Democrats' version of John Bolton, absent only the
flamboyant moustache.

Two months later, during an interview for ABC's 'Good Morning
America', Biden was asked whether he thought Putin was a killer. 'I
do,' he replied.[79] It was a way to underline his difference from Trump,
who, when asked the same question, had answered: 'There are a lot of
killers . . . You think our country is so innocent?' – an acknowledge-
ment of moral equivalence which had infuriated many Americans.[80]
Biden went on to recall that, when he had met Putin as Vice President,

ten years earlier, he had referred to George W. Bush's much maligned remark about having looked into Putin's eyes and 'got a sense of his soul'. Biden said he had told him: 'When I look into your eyes, I don't think you have a soul.' Putin, he said, had responded: 'We understand each other.' He then recounted how, in a telephone conversation in January, a few days after his inauguration, he had told Putin that, if it were proved that Russia had interfered in the 2020 election, he would pay a price. 'I said, "I know you and you know me. If I establish that this occurred, then be prepared." '[81]

It was fighting talk and the Russians responded in kind.

The Russian Ambassador in Washington was recalled for 'consultations'. Soon afterwards, so was his American colleague. The Russian government mouthpiece, *Rossiiskaya gazeta*, said the American President was suffering from 'irreversible dementia'. *Komsomolskaya pravda* accused him of 'unprecedented boorishness' and said he had crossed 'a very red line'.[82]

Putin shrugged it off. 'When we evaluate other people,' he said, 'it's always as though we are looking into a mirror . . . and seeing ourselves.' The time had come for them to talk directly, rather than 'sparring at a distance'.[83]

In reality, behind the macho rhetoric and public grandstanding, the relationship had got off to a much less rocky start than it had been made to appear. Four days after Biden's inauguration, on January 25, 2021, the two countries had agreed to a five-year extension of New START, the only arms control agreement still in force after the cascade of unilateral American withdrawals during the George W. Bush and Trump presidencies.[84] For the Russians, and for America, that was of vital importance. The following day Biden had telephoned Putin, and although they spent much of their time rehearsing their disagreements, the fact that he had taken the initiative was seen in Moscow as a positive sign.[85] In March, when the White House finally got round to imposing sanctions on Russia for Navalny's poisoning, they were the strict minimum. Two months later, Biden announced that the United States would waive threatened countermeasures against companies involved in the Nord Stream 2 gas pipeline to Germany, a project which had been fiercely opposed by both the Obama and Trump administrations. It was made clear that the United States had not abandoned its reservations but that it would no longer try to enforce them.

For the Western Europeans, this was a major concession. Since the days of the Reagan administration, in the 1980s, they had bridled at America's insistence that Washington, D.C. knew better than they did what was best for their own security. Here at last was an American President who, on this issue at least, was willing to heed European priorities. For a White House desperate to repair the damage done to the transatlantic alliance by the Trump administration, it was an astute move. For Putin, it cut both ways. The completion of Nord Stream 2 would be a good thing. Restored amity between the United States and Western Europe, rather less so.

While Putin avoided criticising Trump in public – no one, after all, could be sure that he would not return to power in 2024 – the key consideration from the Kremlin's standpoint was that Moscow now had a more rational, less impulsive partner in Washington. 'Predictability and stability are the most important values in international affairs,' Putin told an American journalist in June. He hoped, he added, that there would be no more 'knee-jerk reactions' and that relations from now on would be based on 'defined rules of engagement'.[86]

Another telling clue to his attitude came when he was asked whether it was true that Biden had once told him that he had no soul. Putin was nothing if not thorough. He had certainly reviewed the transcript of their March 2011 conversation and knew exactly what had been said. But instead of giving a straight answer, he played with the question like a cat with a mouse. 'I'm not sure,' he said. 'One has to think what a soul is. To be honest with you, I just don't remember that particular bit of the conversation . . . There must be something wrong with my memory.'[87] It read like a coded message: 'I know exactly what was said, but I won't let on. It will remain between us. On that basis, if you wish, we can do business together.'[88]

There was only one thing which did not quite fit. In early February, US intelligence had begun reporting a build-up of Russian forces on the Ukrainian border. By April, it became clear that it was the biggest concentration of Russian ground troops in the area since 2015. Russian officials, including Dmitry Kozak, the deputy head of the Presidential Administration who had taken over responsibility for Ukraine from Vladislav Surkov, began issuing ominous warnings that Moscow would not stand idly by if Kyiv moved against the separatists in the Donbas.[89]

The consensus in Western chancelleries was that it was essentially

Russian muscle-flexing. The fact that the build-up had been carried out so openly suggested that the Kremlin's goal was to get the Americans' attention, rather than to prepare an invasion. But no one could be sure.

If that was Putin's aim, he succeeded, Biden was already wrestling with problems at home and the withdrawal of US troops from Afghanistan. The last thing he needed was a crisis in Ukraine. In April, the White House proposed that they meet earlier than had originally been envisaged and hold talks in Europe, which the US President was to visit that summer for summits of the G7 and NATO on the first overseas trip since his election.

When they met in Geneva on June 16, Biden opened by saying that he expected the two countries to conduct themselves as befitted 'two great powers' – a way of dissociating himself from Obama's caustic dismissal of Russia as just 'a regional power'. 'We will try to determine where we have mutual interests and we can cooperate,' he went on, 'and where we don't, [we will] establish a predictable and rational way [to deal with the issues] on which we disagree.'[90]

Putin described their two hours of talks as 'very constructive', 'fruitful' and, at times, marked by 'flashes of trust'[91] which, while positive, implied that for most of the discussion trust had been in short supply. Each side set out its red lines: for the United States, an end to Russian election interference; for Russia, no move by NATO to extend its influence further to the East. It was agreed that the two ambassadors should return to their posts and that a 'Strategic Stability Dialogue' should begin at ministerial level to 'lay the groundwork for future arms control and risk reduction measures'.[92] There was even tentative discussion of renewed cooperation to contain the fallout from the United States' withdrawal from Afghanistan, a distant echo of the days when the two countries had worked together after 9/11.

Over the next few months, a succession of senior US officials made their way to Moscow and, in October, Putin declared that, despite setbacks on some issues, the two countries were 'on the right track'.[93] Journalists on both sides wrote of a return to the way relations had been conducted during the Cold War, when Moscow and Washington had kept national security matters separate from other issues. It seemed that the relationship with the new administration in Washington had got off to a better start than anyone had expected.

★

Midway through Putin's third presidential term, in 2015, he had told an American interviewer: 'How long I remain in power will depend . . . on the specific situation in the world, in the country, and my own feelings about it.'[94]

In the summer of 2021, the situation in the world, seen from Moscow, was more favourable than for a long time past. Under Biden, the United States had started to take seriously Russian concerns which until then it had refused to discuss, notably in the field of arms control. Moscow's relations with China were stronger that they had ever been. In the Middle East, in Africa and the Arctic, Russia had reasserted itself as a power the United States had to reckon with. In Western Europe, Ukraine fatigue had set in. The main European powers – France, Germany, Italy and Spain – were reluctant to see their ties with Russia held indefinitely hostage to Crimea and the situation in the Donbas, and were open to discreet moves towards a more normal relationship. Britain was an outlier. Putin compared London's subservience to Washington to that of Tabaqui, the jackal in Kipling's *Jungle Book*, who 'ran around . . . and howled to make his lord happy'.[95] But since leaving the European Union, London's usefulness to America and its importance to Moscow had diminished. Moreover, with the West wanting to focus attention on China, the Kremlin might hope that European solidarity against Russia would gradually erode. During the Cold War, the threat of nuclear conflict had kept the United States and Western Europe on the same page. That time seemed to be past.

Within Russia, the 'non-system opposition' had been broken. In the Duma elections that year, 'smart voting' had had only a marginal effect. United Russia won 324 of the 450 seats. This time the usual panoply of electoral dirty tricks had been expanded by the addition of electronic voting, which gave the authorities practically limitless opportunities for falsifying the results. Even more blatantly than in 2016, the outcome was a travesty. Had the election been conducted fairly, United Russia would have lost its majority. It was a warning sign. The mood of the country was changing. But for the moment, the regime was in complete control.

In short, if Putin were to judge by the criteria that he himself had set, the situation in the world and in Russia that summer was as good as it was likely to get.

That left the decisive factor: Putin's own feelings about his future role.

As ever, he kept his cards extremely close to his chest. But his age was clearly beginning to tell. The macho photographs for his annual calendar were long gone, along with the Botox that had hidden his wrinkles. The steepest ski slopes were now beyond him. For his Easter greetings in 2021, he was shown sitting by a wood fire with a *kulich*, a Russian Easter cake, and teacups on a low table beside him. It was the traditional image of a Russian father figure. Only the samovar was missing.

He started talking more about his children and grandchildren, previously a taboo subject, complaining that he had no time to see them.[96] Eight years earlier, after nearly 30 years of marriage, he and Lyudmila had divorced. They had long been living separate lives, so it made little practical difference. She remarried. He did not. But the rumours of his romantic entanglement with the gymnast, Alina Kabayeva, continued. Asked point-blank when he was going to get married again, he acknowledged that 'at some point, as a gentleman, I shall probably have to,'[97] which, if not quite a confirmation, was hardly a denial.

Moscow intellectuals noticed that Putin's speeches were beginning to acquire a philosophical bent. 'I can see that you are reassessing things,' the commentator, Fyodor Lukyanov, told him. 'It's not everyone who now speaks about trust, harmony, the meaning of life and our mission on Earth, and you didn't use to before, either.'[98] He published long articles on historical issues such as the respective roles of the Soviet Union and the West in the build-up to World War II[99] – matters on which scholars might ruminate but very far from the concerns of the Russian man or woman in the street. Instead of focusing on Russia's future, he spent more and more time thinking about the past.

The 'power vertical' that Putin had so painstakingly constructed during his first two terms was no longer enforced as rigidly as it had been before. Not only did men like Sechin and Kadyrov feel that they could act as they wished, but so did minor officials. 'There is no single internal policy,' wrote the Republic.ru editor, Ivan Davydov. 'There is the petty vindictiveness of local republican bosses . . . They don't need "instructions from above" because there are no special instructions. [Instead of] a single policy, there is chaos.'[100] The Covid-19 pandemic was a good example. First Putin allowed the regions to decide what policy to follow. Then he gave responsibility to the government. Finally, in November 2021, by which time Russia's death rate was among the highest in Europe and only a third of the population had been fully vaccinated, he reluctantly reversed course and ordered the measures that he had refused to approve 18 months earlier.[101]

It was not that Putin had lost his grip. But, except in foreign policy, he seemed to have no appetite to exert it.

By the summer of 2021 he had watched the leaders of three other former Soviet states wrestle with the problem of whether and how to leave office. Saparmurat Niyazov in Turkmenistan had died not long after declaring himself President for Life. Aleksandr Lukashenko, in Belarus, had been kept in power by the security services after an election which he would otherwise have lost. Putin had backed Lukashenko for pragmatic, geopolitical reasons. In theory, he could do the same thing himself – staying in office indefinitely by resorting to ever harsher repression. But that was not a long-term solution. Unless he died in harness, he would still have to step down at some point. The longer he left it, the more difficult it would be.

More interesting was the approach adopted by the President of Kazakhstan, Nursultan Nazarbayev, who, after 27 years in power, had retired in 2019 to make way for a younger man. Nazarbayev had not withdrawn completely, remaining head of the ruling party and Chairman of the Kazakh Security Council, which laid down policy guidelines for the government. But he had stepped back.

For Putin, that was a possible model. Nazarbayev's retirement had been only partly successful. He had held on to his residual powers for too long and his children and fellow clansmen, who had amassed obscene fortunes during his years in power, refused to accept the leadership of his successor. Putin would not have that problem. If he stayed on as Chairman of the Russian Security Council, a deliberative body which had come to resemble the old Soviet Politburo, it would give him oversight over Russian policy without responsibility for the day-to-day grind of having to run the country.[102] Being President was wearisome work. 'Sometimes,' Putin complained, 'you have the feeling that you're ceasing to be a human being and turning into just a function.'[103]

A move to a less front-line role would be a logical continuation of the gradual disengagement that had begun after his re-election in 2018. There were hints that he was thinking along those lines.[104] Yet he seemed genuinely torn. When he had said that a dual system of rule would be 'absolutely ruinous' for Russia, he meant it. He had not enjoyed the four years that he had spent ruling in tandem with Medvedev. But retiring altogether as Yeltsin had done did not appeal to him either. If he stayed on after stepping down as President, he had told an interviewer, 'the question is: in what capacity? Right now, I have no answer.'[105]

Until August 2021, the possibility of initiating the transition to a new generation of leaders remained uppermost in Putin's mind. He had still not reached a final decision. But preparations continued. Age restrictions, which would have forced some of his closest colleagues to step down, were lifted. Term limits for regional governors were abolished. The emphasis on maintaining the status quo became so marked that one Russian analyst concluded: 'he must be planning something'.[106]

There was just one piece of unfinished business: Ukraine. Whatever hopes Putin had had of an improvement in relations under the new Ukrainian President, Volodymyr Zelensky, who had succeeded Poroshenko in 2019, had proved vain. For Moscow, progress needed to come through the implementation of the Minsk accords. For Kyiv that was politically impossible. As long as the frozen conflict in the East continued, Ukrainian membership of NATO was ruled out. But it did not prevent Ukrainian territory becoming, for all practical purposes, an extension of the Western alliance. For Putin, that situation was untenable.

Less than a week after his meeting with Biden, the British Prime Minister, Boris Johnson, keen to show that post-Brexit Britain was still a force to be reckoned with, sent a destroyer through Crimean waters to demonstrate the West's refusal to recognise Russian sovereignty. What would the West have done, Putin mused afterwards, if Russia had sunk the British ship? Not much, he thought. No one would risk all-out war, because such a war could not be won.[107]

In hindsight, it was a revealing remark. At the time, the prospect of a wider conflict over Ukraine appeared remote. Yet here was Putin saying that, were one to occur, the West would be unable to respond militarily for fear of provoking a nuclear riposte.

Three weeks later, he published a long article entitled, 'On the Historical Unity of Russians and Ukrainians'.[108] Much of it restated well-worn themes. Ukrainians and Russians were in reality one people; Ukrainians' sense of national identity stemmed mainly from the errors of the Bolsheviks, who, by introducing a federal system, had 'chopped

Russia into pieces'; the West was now exploiting this 'to undermine our unity' – and more in the same vein. But Putin then went on to deliver a message which went significantly further than anything he had said before. Ukraine, he declared, had become 'a willing hostage to someone else's geopolitical will'. It was being turned into a 'springboard against Russia', an 'aggressive state' whose armed forces were supervised by Western advisers and whose territory was being used for the deployment of NATO infrastructure. Russia would never accept that, Putin warned. 'We will never allow our historical territories . . . to be used against [us]. To those who will undertake such an attempt, I would like to say that this way they will destroy their own country.'

The phrasing was deliberately vague. What was meant by Russia's 'historical territories'? Who would 'destroy their own country' – the Ukrainians, or those Putin called the 'Western authors of the anti-Russia project' – in other words, the United States? Asked directly what he meant, he declined to elaborate.[109] But his words were plainly addressed to the White House. What America was doing in Ukraine, Putin warned, was comparable to 'using weapons of mass destruction against us'.[110] It was not a problem between Moscow and Kyiv, it was a problem between Russia and America and it would be up to Moscow and Washington to resolve it.

Although few realised it at the time, the article signalled a change in Putin's thinking. Ukraine's separation from Russia had rankled ever since the early 1990s, when he had astonished the French Consul General by the vehemence with which he had denounced the loss of Crimea. It was now becoming an obsession. Had Trump remained in office, Putin might well have been more cautious. Trump was already undermining NATO without Moscow's help. Moreover, he was unpredictable and, for all his vaunted admiration of Putin, was capable, if challenged, of lashing out recklessly with disastrous consequences. Biden was a much steadier pair of hands. Ukraine was a useful pressure point, as had been shown by the administration's decision to hold early talks in Geneva. Putin's takeaway from that meeting had been that America would seek to avoid needless conflict with Russia. The challenge of the future was China; Russia was not exactly a distraction but it was no longer America's main foe. If a different president were elected in 2024, that might change.

As Putin weighed his options that summer, there appeared to be a window of opportunity for one last push to bring Ukraine to heel. It would be a gamble. But if he could carry it off, correcting what he viewed as one of the cardinal sins of his predecessors, it would be the crowning achievement of his career – the last box to check before embarking on a political transition at home, allowing him to leave office on a high note.

Then, in the second half of August, came the debacle of America's chaotic withdrawal from Afghanistan. To the Kremlin, it signalled chronic weakness. In Kabul, as in Saigon 50 years earlier, faced with fierce resistance, the Americans had cut and run, leaving their one-time allies to their fate. Georgia had had a similar experience when it took on Russian forces in 2008. President Bush's National Security Adviser, Steve Hadley, had asked then: 'Are we prepared to go to war with Russia over Georgia?' The answer was obvious. In Putin's estimation, the same would be true of Ukraine.

In October, the build-up of Russian troops on the Ukrainian border resumed. The following month, Putin called for 'serious long-term guarantees to ensure Russia's security'.[111] At the beginning of December, he spelt out what these would entail. He wanted 'concrete agreements that rule out any further eastward expansion of NATO and the deployment of weapons systems posing a threat to us in close proximity to Russia's territory'. Given the West's failure to honour its earlier commitments in this regard, he added – a reference to James Baker's promise in 1990 that NATO would move 'not an inch' to the east – there would need to be 'precise, legal, juridical guarantees'.[112] Verbal assurances would not be enough.

When, as Putin had anticipated, the United States declined to negotiate on that basis, the pressure on Kyiv intensified. The Biden administration began warning publicly of the likelihood of a Russian invasion and promised that, if that happened, it would arm Ukrainian insurgents to turn the country into a 'porcupine' which Moscow would be unable to swallow.[113] However the US President also said that he would not send troops to defend Ukraine since it was not a NATO member. At one level, that was simple prudence. But to Putin it confirmed that his instincts had been correct. There would be no risk of direct Western military intervention. At most, NATO would provide weapons and encourage the Ukrainians to fight Russia in its stead. There would be economic sanctions, too, but the Kremlin had been living with sanctions for eight years, ever since the annexation of Crimea.

At the beginning of February 2022, Putin travelled to Beijing, making only his third trip abroad in more than two years, to assure himself of Chinese support. In a joint communiqué, he and Xi Jinping called for an end to NATO expansion and declared that their countries' friendship had 'no limit'.[114]

Just over two weeks later, in an address to the Russian people on the evening of February 21 and at a news conference the following day, Putin rehearsed a litany of grievances against the Ukrainian government.[115] Much of it was familiar but the tone was angrier and more violent. Ukraine was 'historically Russian land' which had now become 'a puppet regime' controlled by America. It was 'like a knife at our throat', Putin said. Eventually Ukraine would join NATO and its territory would become 'an advanced bridgehead for a [pre-emptive] strike' against Russia. There was no longer any point in hoping for a peaceful settlement through the Minsk accords – those agreements were dead. He had therefore decided to recognise the independence of the separatist statelets of Donetsk and Luhansk to protect the Russian-speaking population against 'horror and genocide' at the hands of a goverment in Kyiv which had elevated 'Neanderthal and aggressive nationalism and neo-Nazi ideology . . . to the level of national policy'.

The speech was for domestic consumption. The claim of 'genocide' against Russian-speakers in Donetsk and Luhansk, while transparently false, was designed to echo NATO's argument 20 years earlier that it had been forced to intervene in Kosovo to stop ethnic cleansing by the Serbs. Putin's charge that the government of Ukraine's President, Volodymyr Zelensky followed a 'neo-Nazi policy' reprised a theme that Russian propagandists had been promoting since the Maidan demonstrations in 2014, which, they alleged, had been fomented by followers of Stepan Bandera, the virulently anti-Semitic Ukrainian leader who had cooperated with the Nazis during the Second World War and whom many Ukrainian nationalists continued to regard as a hero. That claim, too, was equally false. After independence, Bandera had been rehabilitated and neo-Nazi paramilitary groups had gained a foothold in mainstream Ukrainian political life. But to pretend that the Ukrainian government was run by Nazis was absurd. Zelensky was a Russian-speaking Jew – hardly the man to lead what Putin termed dismissively 'a junta . . . of neo-Nazis and drug addicts'.[116]

For Russians, particularly of the older generation, Putin's allegations resonated. In the West, they appeared malign and surreal.

Even more revealing than the address itself was the meeting of the
Russian Security Council which preceded it. Normally a secretive body,
this time its proceedings, in the immense, domed, circular, blue and
white Catherine Hall of the Kremlin, were televised in their entirety.
Putin was shown sitting at a desk on one side, interrogating his top
officials, ranged before him in a semicircle, twenty yards away. One by
one, they assured him of their support, like frightened boyars pledging
allegiance. It was the *mise-en-scène* of a monarch, a display of raw
power, designed to show that the leadership was united but in reality
making clear that the decisions were all taken by one man. The liberal
newspaper, *Novaya gazeta*, reported afterwards that the most powerful
men in Russia had been shown like zombies, 'with gloomy, tense
faces . . . afraid to look at each other, paralysed with fear'.[117]

Two days later, at dawn on February 24, Putin announced the invasion, describing it tendentiously as a 'special military operation' to
protect the Donbas. Russia had no choice but to defend itself, he said,
because 'irresponsible Western politicians' had 'rudely and uncere-
moniously' pushed NATO's military infrastructure up to its borders:[118]

> Where did this insolent manner of talking down to us from the height
> of their exceptionalism . . . come from? What is the explanation for
> their contemptuous, disdainful attitude? . . . The answer is simple . . .
> In the late 1980s, the Soviet Union grew weaker and subsequently broke
> apart. [In the West] there was a state of euphoria, a feeling of absolute
> superiority . . . They deceived us, or, to put it simply, they duped us
> [like] a con artist . . . The whole so-called Western bloc, formed by the
> United States in its own image, is . . . an 'empire of lies'.

The speech, delivered in a deceptively quiet monotone, pulsated with
anger and resentment. For more than 30 years, Putin had seethed at
what he saw as Russia's humiliation following the break-up of the
Soviet Union. Now he had decided to do something about it. That
morning, the almost 200,000 Russian soldiers who had gathered on the
border launched a multi-pronged attack on Kharkiv, Kyiv and Ukraine's
ports along the Black Sea coast.

In the West and in Russia, the war was met with disbelief. Most

Europeans – and much of the Russian intelligentsia – thought Putin had taken leave of his senses. There was speculation that his long isolation during the pandemic had affected his judgement. Since March 2020, he had rarely moved outside his residences at Novo-Ogaryovo and Bocharov Ruchei in Sochi, where identical offices were said to have been built, so that when he held video-link meetings, no one would know where he was.[119] Even more than before, he lived in a bubble and there were times when it seemed to show. In June 2021, he had astonished a group of Western news agency heads by declaring that, in the West, opposition groups like those of Aleksei Navalny were 'speedily disposed of . . . by the security services' and that Russia was merely doing the same. There was a silence. The remark was unhinged. So was his claim that the Russian media, which that year had been subjected to an unprecedented clampdown, were far more critical of his regime than media were allowed to be in the West. It brought to mind Angela Merkel's comment, years earlier, that he was living on a different planet.

The staging of the Security Council meeting at which he had publicly cross-examined his subordinates had overtones of megalomania. So, too, did subsequent meetings where Putin was pictured sitting at one end of a long table with his defence chiefs huddled at the other end, 20 feet away.

The theatricality was a giveaway. It was Putin's version of Richard Nixon's 'madman' theory, intended to make him appear so irrational and unpredictable that adversaries would hesitate before testing his resolve.[120] To ram the message home, he warned that any attempt to intervene would bring 'consequences such as you have never seen in your entire history' and announced that Russia's nuclear forces had been placed on full alert. That turned out to be untrue: the Americans said later there had been no change in Russia's nuclear force posture.[121]

Stripped of the angry rhetoric, it was typical of the way Putin operated. Almost everyone had been blindsided. The United States, which was monitoring Russian military communications, had concluded, correctly, that an invasion was being planned. But until a week or so beforehand, the CIA believed that Putin had not taken a final decision.[122] Everyone else, including European governments as well as most Russians, had assumed that he was bluffing – which was why, in the days immediately following, some of Russia's richest men,

including members of Putin's entourage, found their assets sequestrated and their mega-yachts impounded in European ports. To them,
the idea that Russia would launch a full-scale land war against Ukraine
had seemed unthinkable. To Putin, it made perfect sense. For centuries in Europe, war had been an extension of diplomacy. After World
War II, Europeans had assumed a little too readily that all that was
behind them. Putin surmised that, even in the interconnected world
of the twenty-first century, the supposedly obsolete methods of the
past could still prove their worth. As a young deputy Mayor, he had
wept when bodybags started arriving in St Petersburg during the First
Chechen War. Three decades later, he was ready to send thousands of
Russian soldiers to their deaths and to wreak untold suffering on millions of Ukrainian civilians. He had often warned against using
military means as an instrument of foreign policy, but that was in the
context of America's wars in Vietnam, Afghanistan and Iraq. Russia's
use of force, he thought, was different. It was justified because it was
the only way to make the United States take Moscow's concerns
seriously.[123]

Western governments and their advisers struggled to understand
Putin's reasoning. Fiona Hill, who had served as an adviser to George
W. Bush and Obama, as well as Trump, thought it was 'essentially a
post-colonial land grab'.[124] But Russia already had more territory than
it knew what to do with. Grabbing more land for its own sake served
no purpose. The State Department insisted that the war had nothing
to do with NATO enlargement and everything to do with Putin's
refusal to accept Ukraine's existence as an independent state, which
may have been good spin but was poor history. East European leaders
warned grimly that the invasion was the first step in a broader scheme
of Russian expansionism. That was not convincing either. The Russians had enough on their hands without contemplating a wider
offensive. Others speculated that Putin was unable to stomach the
thought of a democratic government in Kyiv which might lead Russians to reject his own, autocratic form of rule. But that was tantamount
to saying that all that prevented Russia from becoming a Western-style
democracy was Putin and the kleptocrats supporting him. Much as the
West might wish that to be true, it was not the case.

The decision to invade, far from being aberrant, was consistent
with the way he had acted before. Throughout Putin's time in office,

whenever he was faced with what he saw as an existential choice between antagonising the West and preserving his own power and Russia's position in the world, the latter always prevailed. In 2003, he had ordered the arrest of Mikhail Khodorkovsky because nipping in the bud the political ambitions of the business elite was more important than the loss of Western investment. In 2014, he occupied Crimea and backed the creation of rump protectorates in Donetsk and Luhansk because safeguarding the Black Sea Fleet's base at Sevastopol and keeping Ukraine out of NATO were more important than Western sanctions. In each case, Putin accepted the economic damage to Russia as a price that had to be paid.

In 2022, the invasion of Ukraine followed the same pattern.

Whereas eight years earlier, the Russian General Staff had advised against trying to occupy Novorossiya – the swathe of land in eastern and southern Ukraine stretching from Donetsk to Odessa – on the grounds that it would be difficult to conquer and even more difficult to hold, this time Putin insisted. Even the Pentagon believed that Kyiv would fall in a matter of days. Putin assumed that Zelensky would then flee, the Kremlin would be able to install a puppet government and Ukraine would be politically and militarily neutralised.

But that was not the only goal. In addition to returning Ukraine to Moscow's sphere of influence, Putin wanted to show that the United States was powerless to prevent it.

As the Russian Foreign Minister, Sergei Lavrov, put it: 'This is not actually, or at least, not primarily, about Ukraine at all. . . It reflects the battle over what the [future] world order will look like. Will it be a world in which the West will lead everyone with impunity and without question or will it be something different?'[125]

This was partly spin. Portraying the conflict as a proxy war in which Russia was fighting on behalf of the non-aligned nations of the world to end American hegemony made it a much easier sell to Russian public opinion as well as to countries like China and India which favoured a multipolar global system. In this reading, Ukraine was merely the theatre for a larger struggle. That was a deceit. Moscow's aim had always been to bring Kyiv back into the Russian fold. But it contained a nub of truth. Putin believed that if Russia succeeded, it would fatally undermine the structures of European security which had been built up under American leadership since the end of the Cold War. Biden might insist that Ukraine was a special case because it was not a member of the alliance and that, were any NATO state attacked, America would rush to its defence. But how much reliance could countries like Poland and the Baltic States place on such assurances when NATO was so risk-averse that it refused to establish a no-fly zone to protect Ukrainian cities for fear of nuclear escalation? Putin's charge that the West was happy to fight to the last Ukrainian was dismissed as shallow propaganda in America but it gave pause to leaders in Eastern Europe.[126] Would America really risk nuclear annihilation to defend Warsaw or Tallinn? The question was not new but the invasion of Ukraine put it in a harshly different light.[127] To Putin, even if Russia had failed to prevent NATO enlargement, it might yet sow doubt about the alliance's reliability, undermining faith in America's support for other states on Russia's borders, NATO members or not.

The Biden administration recognised the danger. America's goal, said the National Security Adviser, Jake Sullivan, was 'a free and independent Ukraine, a weakened and isolated Russia and a stronger, more unified West'.[128] The deputy Secretary of State, Wendy Sherman, put it more succinctly. America, she said, wanted to inflict on Putin a 'strategic failure'.[129]

It was déjà vu all over again. The West was returning to the old policies of containment that it had practised during the Cold War, but this time with a more radical objective: not merely to contain Russia but to leave it so diminished that it could never threaten its neighbours again.[130]

No war works out as planned and Putin's was no exception.

From the outset, things started to go wrong. It was not that the Russians had expected to be 'welcomed with open arms', as Western commentators claimed. They had known from their experience in the Donbas over the previous eight years that the Ukrainian army would fight back. But they had not anticipated such fierce resistance. The US, Britain and Canada had been training Ukrainian forces since 2015 for just this kind of eventuality and it showed. Nor did the Russian General Staff expect the civilian population to come out as they did in support of the Ukrainian army. Instead of remaining passive, Ukrainians of all ages volunteered to join home defence detachments. Others acted as scouts and sent back information on the Russians' positions. President Zelensky, far from fleeing the country as Putin had expected, proved an inspirational wartime leader. The close ties between the two peoples – more than 40 per cent of Ukrainians have relatives in Russia[131] – also played a part, though not in the sense that Moscow had hoped. The conflict was fratricidal – not quite a civil war, but close – with all the emotional intensity that characterises such conflicts. In the regions bearing the brunt of the fighting, bordering the Donbas in eastern and south-eastern Ukraine, which before the war had been largely sympathetic to Russia, much of the population went over to supporting Kyiv.

Putin's biggest mistake was his refusal to accept that Ukrainians and Russians, although closely related, are not one people but distinct Slav nations, each of which cleaves to its own national identity. His second, scarcely less serious, miscalculation was to overestimate the capabilities of his armed forces. Instead of securing the Ukrainian capital within days, the Russian offensive rapidly stalled. The troops were dispersed across too many different fronts. There was no unified command. The secrecy surrounding the operation meant that many units were ill-prepared. Some believed until the last moment that they were taking part in a training exercise, others had to enrol conscripts to bring them up to strength.

In war, people defending their homeland have an innate advantage over those seeking to deprive them of it. Putin knew that from the Soviet experience in Afghanistan as well as America's failures in its foreign wars, yet he chose to ignore it.

Initially the Russian forces were under strict orders to spare the civilian population, which led to bizarre scenes as miles-long Russian armoured columns halted at traffic lights to allow Ukrainian motorists to pass. But after the first few days, discipline began to unravel. Because it had been assumed that the operation would be over quickly, many units ran out of rations and began pillaging and looting. Command and control broke down. As Ukrainian resistance intensified, the local population became the enemy. Russian soldiers stole whatever they could lay hands on. Those with access to military field mail sent hundreds of tons of plundered goods, including heavy items like washing machines and television sets, back to their families in Russia. Ukrainian civilians were tortured and killed, women were raped. There were missile and artillery attacks on hospitals, on social centres where families had taken refuge and on evacuation convoys. The atrocities that marked the opening months of the war were not on the same scale as in Yugoslavia, where, thirty years earlier, 150,000 people had been killed, many of them dying in spasms of ethnic cleansing that bore the hallmarks of genocide, nor were they as systematic as in Chechnya or Syria.[132] Cities like Kyiv and Kharkiv were not reduced to rubble, as Grozny and Aleppo had been, a degree of restraint which puzzled Western military analysts as well as many Russians, who wondered why their army was being asked to fight 'with one hand tied behind its back'.[133] Mariupol was an exception because it controlled the land bridge between the Donbas and Crimea and the Russians were determined to take it no matter what the cost. But the war crimes committed by Russian forces were too widespread to be attributable to targeting errors or the actions of rogue units. In Crimea in 2014, the special forces, better equipped and better trained than regular troops, had impressed Western observers by their discipline. But they had met no resistance. Eight years later, the war in Ukraine showed that, despite a modernisation programme costing billions of dollars, the Russian army was still a blunt instrument, parts of which would revert to savagery when faced with serious opposition.

That should not have come as a total surprise. Ten years earlier, Putin had halted efforts by the then Defence Minister, Anatoly Serdyukov, to promote independent thinking in the military lest the army become politically unreliable. Junior officers were discouraged from showing initiative. The NCOs – the corporals and sergeants who form the backbone of Western armies – lacked proper training. Instead of transitioning to a fully professional force, conscription had been maintained, also for political reasons, albeit on a reduced scale. Under Serdyukov's successor, Sergei Shoigu, corruption had resumed and spread unchecked.

In the first two-and-a-half months, the Russian expeditionary force was said to have lost up to 15,000 soldiers killed and perhaps 30,000 to 40,000 wounded – more than all the American casualties in 20 years' fighting in Afghanistan. Thousands of Ukrainians died, a quarter of the population was displaced and more than five million fled the country as refugees.

Ukraine writhed in torment but fought back.

The West responded not with half-measures as in 2014 after the annexation of Crimea but by pouring in arms supplies and imposing unprecedented economic sanctions. Western public opinion, appalled by images of the horrors inflicted on the civilian population by Russian troops, captured by ordinary citizens on smartphones and relayed instantly by social media, damned Putin as a monster.

Within Russia, dissent was crushed. When a few business magnates dared to express reservations, Putin delivered a furious tirade against what he called a 'fifth column of national traitors [and] scum' who had grown rich on the country's natural resources but mentally were slaves to the West.[134] Demonstrations were banned. Any form of protest was ruthlessly suppressed. One man was detained for standing in Red Square holding a copy of Tolstoy's *War and Peace*. Another was arrested for spilling blue and yellow paint – the colours of the Ukrainian flag – near the entrance to the Mayor's office in Novosibirsk. Schoolchildren were encouraged to denounce their teachers if they spoke out in class against the war, bringing back chilling memories of Stalinist repression in the 1930s. The Kremlin introduced what amounted to military censorship. The Russian media became an echo chamber of lies. The last bastions of independent journalism – the radio station *Ekho Moskvy* and the television channel *Dozhd* – were closed. Liberal newspapers like *Novaya gazeta* ceased reporting the war entirely or resorted to Aesopian language and historical analogies. Even the word 'war' was forbidden – the fighting had to be described as a 'special military operation'. Journalists who refused to toe the line were liable to up to fifteen years' imprisonment. The internet, which had been largely free of controls throughout Putin's years in power, was subjected to draconian restrictions. Russian-language sites critical of the government were blocked, along with the BBC, the Voice of America and Radio Liberty, Facebook and Instagram. Most sites remained accessible to those who had proxy servers, but it marked a giant step back towards the totalitarian controls that had existed in Soviet times.

In the West, there was a broad consensus that Putin had made a fatal error. The progress of the war seemed to confirm that. After six weeks, the Russians withdrew from Kyiv, apparently abandoning hopes of regime change and regrouping for the more limited objective of securing the Donbas and the land bridge to Crimea. Western governments steadily increased the amounts of heavy weaponry they were sending and discussed ending purchases of Russian oil. President Zelensky, who, earlier in the conflict, had proposed, in return for a peace agreement, Ukrainian neutrality and an end to the country's NATO ambitions, now pledged never to give up an inch of Ukrainian territory and spoke of driving out the Russians altogether.

However the situation was more complicated than those optimistic readouts made it appear.

British and American commentators initially sought to portray the conflict as 'the world against Russia'. It soon became clear that in fact it was 'the West against Russia'. Among the ten largest countries, only one – the United States – unequivocally supported Ukraine. The others, representing between them more than half the world's population, either supported Moscow or sat on the fence. So did notional US partners like Saudi Arabia and the Gulf States. Even Israel was reticent.

Had the Biden administration focused on the violation of Ukraine's territorial integrity – a principle on which all countries could agree – the tally might have been different. By framing it as a struggle between democracy and autocracy, the White House rebuffed countries with autocratic regimes which might otherwise have been supportive. The contrast between the outpouring of sympathy for Ukrainian refugees and Europe's cold rejection of Afghans and Syrians and anyone from sub-Saharan Africa did not help either. From the standpoint of the developing world, it seemed that, if you were white and Christian, you would be welcomed with open arms. If not, the West's borders were closed.

Even within NATO, where at first sight the war created a renewed sense of unity and common purpose and Finland and Sweden announced that they envisaged membership, there were fissures beneath the surface. 'Old Europe' and 'New Europe', as Donald Rumsfeld had called them, had very different agendas. Poland, the Baltic States, the Czech Republic and Slovakia took a maximalist position, holding that Russia only understood the language of force and Europe would not be safe until it had been decisively defeated. Britain played the role of cheerleader. France, Germany, Italy and Spain looked more soberly to the day when peace would be restored and relations would have somehow to be repaired.

Producing fractures of this kind, globally and within Europe, had been one of Putin's aims. As the economic fallout from the conflict mounted, such divisions, he thought, would become more pronounced. How would Europeans react, Russian officials gloated, when faced with sharply higher inflation, shortages of energy and basic foodstuffs? How long would Europe's welcome last if millions of Ukrainian refugees stayed on indefinitely? What would happen if hunger in Africa and the Middle East brought fresh waves of migrants towards Europe's shores? When the war eventually ended, who would pay the half trillion US dollars or more that Ukraine's reconstruction would need?

If Western leaders had hoped that economic pressure would turn Russians against Putin's regime, they were disappointed. Sanctions are a double-edged sword. In the first months, most Russians saw little change in their everyday lives. The rich resigned themselves to holidaying in Dubai rather than on the Côte d'Azur. The poor had their income protected by government subsidies. The rouble kept its value. The Russian economy did not collapse. Everyone understood that more difficult times lay ahead. One leading Russian economist described the state support measures as 'putting cosmetics on a corpse'.[135] But sanctions reinforced the Kremlin's narrative that the West was determined to bring Russia to its knees and every patriotic citizen was duty bound to resist. Private Western initiatives to condemn the Russian invasion had a similar effect. Banning Russian tennis players from Wimbledon, renaming Degas's 'Russian Dancers' as 'Ukrainian Dancers', suspending Russian opera singers and cancelling concerts of Russian music, however virtuous such decisions might seem to those responsible, gave Russians the impression that all of them, even those most opposed to their government's actions, were irrevocably tarred with collective guilt.

Unsurprisingly, in these circumstances, except in Russia's biggest cities, where liberal views predominate, the government's portrayal of the war as a battle against Ukrainian fascists, manipulated by NATO, was widely believed. Putin's ratings improved, not by as much as the opinion polls claimed but still enough to register a substantial gain.

While the war continued, Putin's plans for a transfer of power in Russia were put on hold, to be revived or not, depending on the outcome, once the conflict had played out.

However it eventuated, there was a palpable sense that an era had ended. The three decades since the Cold War in which the United States had been the uncontested superpower were over. Beijing was challenging American supremacy in the South China Sea. Russia, with Chinese backing, was contesting American power in Europe. What would follow was uncertain. A new geopolitical reality would emerge, but what form it would take, no one could predict.

Afterword

Anyone, Russian or foreigner, who reflects on Russia's situation after more than 20 years of Putin's rule, is bound to wonder: Did it have to be this way? Was the drift towards authoritarianism preordained? Were Russia's relations with the West fated from the outset to decline into mutual hostility and conflict or could that have been avoided?

The temptation to pontificate on how things might have been if only the principal actors had behaved differently is hard to resist. Counterfactuals, as they are now called, a term conferring a veneer of academic respectability on idle speculation, are inherently beguiling. Unfortunately, they generate much heat and very little light. Russia today is what it is and its relations with the West are what they are, not what others might wish them to be.

A common view, especially in the United States but in much of Europe as well, is that 'Russia is under the thumb of a brutal dictator no different from the communists'. Until the war in Ukraine, that was a gross oversimplification. For most Russians, even after the crackdown on the opposition in 2021, life was far less bleak than it was painted in the West. Despite glaring inequalities, living standards had risen across the board. Crony capitalism and corruption were rampant and growth had stalled after the recession of 2008. Nonetheless, the economy had doubled in size under Putin's stewardship and the population as a whole lived better than at any time in the past. The share of oil and gas in GDP had been significantly reduced. Agriculture, which Mikhail Gorbachev used to say had been a disaster ever since 1917, was booming. Where in Soviet times, Russia imported food, farm exports were bringing in more money than arms sales.

Since the war in Ukraine, much of that has since changed for the worse. Many of the achievements of Putin's first three terms risk being lost. Yet even amid war and economic reprisals by the West, the quality of life for most Russians bears little resemblance to what it was in the early 1990s, let alone under communist rule. The modernisation of Russia's armed forces, which had been touted as one of Putin's great achievements, has turned out to be far less impressive than had been claimed. Nonetheless, by fair means and foul, Russia has reasserted itself as a major actor in international affairs whose voice cannot be ignored.

The question is not whether Russia *could* have taken a different path. It is *why* Russia – and Putin – took the path they did and where the country will go from here.

The seminal decisions, which have helped to determine Russia's course ever since, were taken in the 1990s. The Yeltsin constitution established a presidential republic in which parliament played a secondary role. The privatisation of state-owned industry and natural resources to well-connected insiders at fire-sale prices – a programme inspired by the doctrines of the Chicago school and enthusiastically supported by American advisers – created an economic base not that different from that built by Henry Ford, Carnegie, Vanderbilt, Rockefeller and Pierpoint Morgan in America a century earlier.

In both cases – the creation of a powerful presidency and of an oligarchy detested by the general population as much as the US robber barons ever were – Yeltsin and his advisers believed there was no alternative. They may well have been right. But whether right or wrong, those were the choices they made.

The Clinton administration and its European allies also took two key decisions which had a lasting effect on developments within Russia and on its relations with the West. The first was to hold off from providing large-scale financial aid after the collapse of the Soviet Union. The second was to offer NATO membership to the former Warsaw Pact states of Central and Eastern Europe.

To policy-makers in Washington, those choices seemed entirely logical.

Yeltsin's Russia was so dysfunctional, they argued, that giving Moscow economic aid would amount to pouring it down a black hole. The Russian state had first to get itself in order. Only then could economic assistance make any real difference. Accordingly, the West gave far more aid to Poland, a country with a quarter of Russia's population, than it did to Moscow. In the light of the trillions of dollars which America subsequently poured into unsuccessful wars in Iraq and Afghanistan, it is permissible to wonder whether that was a wise decision. But it was the decision that was made. In the same way, NATO expansion was seen as necessary to bind the newly liberated Eastern European states to the West and ensure that Russia would never subjugate them again. That, too, can be questioned, but it was what was decided.

Russians saw things very differently.

From their perspective, they had abandoned communism, embraced what until then they had disparaged as 'bourgeois democracy', begun the painful transition to a market economy and accepted such un-Russian ideas as individual property ownership and a multiparty political system, yet instead of welcoming them back like the prodigal sons they were, the United States and its allies had kept them at arm's length. They felt cheated. America, far from being the role model and strategic partner that they had hoped, seemed bent on keeping Russia down. NATO enlargement was incomprehensible. Russian leaders throughout history had feared invasion from the West. Both Napoleon and Hitler had sent their armies that way. If the West meant well, why was it moving its troops closer and closer to Russia's borders?

Americans could not see that. The Cold War was over, they said. A new era had been born, a new world order in which everyone was on the same side. What was there for Russia to worry about?

To the Kremlin, that was hypocrisy. Politics the American way had always been a zero-sum game. The Cold War had indeed ended. Russia had lost. The West had won.

It is not difficult to make a case that the West, as the stronger partner, bears most of the responsibility for the failure to establish normal relations after the Soviet Union's collapse. At a time when Russia was on its knees, many Western leaders, not only in the United States, concluded myopically that it was finished and would never again be a major power. It was for the West to set the rules, they argued. Russian sensitivities could be ignored. Until the Ukraine crisis in 2014 and Putin's intervention in Syria, the following year, the United States was proactive, Russia reactive. Even the war in South Ossetia in 2008 was launched by Georgia under the mis-apprehension that it had US support. America intervened in Kosovo, Iraq and Libya. It dismantled arms-control agreements which it saw as limiting its strategic forces and it launched a democracy promotion campaign to spread its values and political beliefs to Russia and the rest of the world.

None of that should have been a surprise. The United States was merely doing what great powers always do. Strong countries lay down the law and demand that defeated opponents follow. After World War II, former enemies like Germany and Japan became America's allies. Russia was expected to do something similar.

For a number of reasons, that did not happen.

Russia was too huge to fit into the Western alliance. It had been the West's main adversary for half a century, whereas Germany and Japan had only briefly been America's enemies. Unlike the Axis powers, Russia had not been defeated in war and retained a formidable nuclear arsenal. Military establishments do not turn on a dime: deeply entrenched attitudes take generations to change. NATO enlargement was an insurance policy as well as a way to project American power.

When Putin took office, he was an outsider, a realist about Russia's future who did not share the reticence of much of the Moscow establishment towards closer relations with the West. He believed that Russia's destiny was as a European state. Culturally, economically and politically, Europe was where it belonged.

George W. Bush welcomed that. But, like Clinton, Bush saw Russia's future as part of an American-led world.

Putin did not.

Even had there been no NATO expansion, no bitterness over the parsimony of Western aid, no arguments over missile defence and arms control, this would always have been a fundamental stumbling block to the establishment of normal ties. In that sense there was an inevitability about the way the relationship developed. It was largely the result of a series of Western, essentially American, decisions. But for the United States to have acted differently would have required an effort of statesmanship and far-sightedness, calling into question basic assumptions about America's role in the world, of which no American leader was capable. The chain of cause and effect, starting in the 1990s, that has led to the present state of affairs, could doubtless have taken other forms. But it is unlikely that the end result would have been significantly different, because the historical forces driving it would have remained the same.

America, the dominant global power, believes that its role is to lead. Russia refuses to be led.

The United States' belief in its own exceptionalism has not helped. If a nation regards itself as exceptional, it cannot, by definition, accept others as equals. Russia demanded equality and its corollary, respect.

Since World War II, the United States has sought to impose its will on allies and adversaries alike. That, too, is in the nature of things. It is what dominant powers do. That Russia, the loser in a 70-year-long struggle to set the world's ideological agenda, should seek to challenge the post-Cold War order which America had built was not something the United States would ever willingly accept.

The consequences of this dissonance on the part of the world's two leading nuclear powers were not limited to foreign affairs. As relations with the West worsened, pro-Western liberals in Russia were excluded from decision-making. Those advocating democratic values were marginalised. That, too, might well have happened irrespective of the state of US – Russian relations. Liberal democracy has shallow roots in Russia. In some ways, the most remarkable thing about the early 2000s was not that Putin sought to restrict it but that it survived at all. However, the result has been a vicious circle. As relations with the West have deteriorated, the influence of the *siloviki* and other conservatives has increased, further eroding democratic freedoms and making relations with the West still worse.

If it is relatively straightforward to see how the present state of affairs in Russia has arisen, it is far harder to describe what may happen next. Anyone who tries to peer into the future, in Russia or anywhere else, is on a hiding to nothing. But history – the history which failed to 'end' after the Soviet Union's collapse but instead came roaring back – offers a few clues.

There is no reason to think that when Putin leaves the scene, the West's problems will be over. A different leader might well have stopped short of waging war against Ukraine. But whoever succeeds Putin – whether an individual or a collective leadership – is unlikely to put Russia on a fundamentally different course, either at home or abroad. As yet, the sense of hopelessness and frustration that allowed Gorbachev to build a constituency for radical change in the 1980s is absent. Russians grumble because their expectations are not being met. But the majority have too much to lose to want to risk another tectonic upheaval. If the conflict with Ukraine perdures and sanctions intensify, that could change. The longer Putin remains in office, the more deeply Russia will become mired in stagnation and economic decline and the sharper will be the social tensions festering beneath the surface. But a transfer of power cannot be avoided indefinitely and the transition to a new leader may be the *sine qua non* for tensions with the West to abate.

Whatever happens in the short term, within the next 10 to 15 years power will pass to a generation of Russians who grew up after the Soviet Union ceased to exist. Their attitudes and their sense of Russia's place in the world are very different from those of their parents' generation. They will be faced with the tasks that Putin has left undone. His principal achievements have been the reassertion of Russia's military power and political cohesion. In the coming decades, Russia's international status will depend less on its military and its diplomats and more on the success or failure of its domestic transformation. For his successors, the key challenges will be structural reform, technological innovation and diversification away from oil and gas exports to take account of climate change, which could force a radical reshaping of the Russian economy as early as the 2030s.[1]

External factors may also play an important part.

In most countries, foreign policy is driven by domestic considerations, not the other way round. In Russia for most of the past century, the opposite has been true.[2] Under Stalin, Khrushchev and Brezhnev, as well as their successors, Russian domestic policy has been heavily influenced by ties with the West. In the years ahead, the shifting relations between the world's 'Big Three' – America, China and Russia – will be a crucial variable. It would be foolish to expect anything comparable to Nixon's China opening in 1971, when Beijing and Washington found common cause against the Soviet Union. The times are not the same. China is a rising power. America, in Moscow's view, is in relative decline. But a degree of realignment is possible. America's insistence on pressing ahead with a missile defence shield – originally to steal a march on Russia – is coming back to haunt it as Bill Clinton feared it might. China has embarked on a massive expansion of its ICBM launch facilities and the development of hypersonic weapons which, within the next decade or so, may give it a nuclear arsenal comparable to that of the United States.[3] Even if this is not directly a matter of cause and effect – sooner or later Xi Jinping's China would have sought nuclear parity whatever America did – it will alter fundamentally the contours of the great power triangle.

A shift in American policy to focus on China's growing strength will affect the West's relations with Russia which in turn will influence Russian domestic policies. It has been a constant of Russian politics for at least the last century that a less adversarial relationship with the West translates into greater freedoms at home.

Other global challenges may also intervene. Apart from climate change, they include greatly increased economic migration and, possibly, a new and deadlier zoonotic pandemic. If any of these were to become critical, the present divisions between the world's great powers might become less relevant. As Putin himself put it, 'in such conditions, geopolitical [and] ideological rivalry loses its meaning'.[4] It has happened before. During the Second World War, Russia and the Western powers cast aside their political and ideological differences to join forces against the common threat from Nazi Germany. It may be argued that that is a long shot: the alliance in World War II was the exception that proves the rule. The Covid-19 pandemic, far from promoting unity, exacerbated existing divisions. Even if something of this kind does occur, its effects may well be marginal. But it cannot be ruled out altogether.

A Russian journalist once remarked to Putin that Saudi Arabia would always be a US ally. 'Always?', Putin wondered. 'Always doesn't exist.'

Russia is used to playing a long game. Just as Putin is convinced that one day, despite the war, Moscow and Kyiv will overcome their differences, he believes that America and Russia will eventually settle into a less contentious relationship. In the long term, he is no doubt right, the only uncertainty being how long it will take. The maxim that countries have permanent interests, but no permanent friends or enemies, remains as true today as when Lord Palmerston coined it in 1848.

It would be wrong, therefore, to regard the current hostility between Russia and the West as for ever fixed. But in the meantime, Russia will remain an awkward bedfellow. An unimaginably vast country, suspended across the top of the world between Europe and Asia, its history is profoundly different from that of its European cousins, yet its people are formed in exactly the same mould. That is part of the problem. Family quarrels are often the most intractable. Russians not only look like Europeans, they *are* Europeans and are expected to behave as the rest of the family does. Unaccountably, stubbornly, they refuse to do so. That will not soon change.

Acknowledgements

Writing is a solitary pursuit. The research that precedes it is not.

Over the eight years that this book has been in gestation, I have accumulated an immense debt of gratitude to people in many different countries who have helped me try to tease out the reality of the man behind the public persona of Vladimir Putin. They include Western heads of state and government, ministers, senior advisers and ambassadors who dealt with Putin as part of their official duties; Russians who worked with him in St Petersburg and in the Kremlin; former heads of Western secret services, intelligence analysts and officers under diplomatic cover in Moscow; Russian academics, analysts, journalists and politicians; and bankers and businessmen who interacted either with Putin himself or members of his inner circle. Their reminiscences and insights have put flesh on what might otherwise have been a cerebral, bare-bones account drawn from written texts alone. Not all those whose names appear in the list of interviewees that follows are cited directly in this book, but all helped immeasurably to illuminate Putin's character through personal anecdotes, analysis and context. I cannot thank them enough for their generosity and patience in answering questions not only about matters of state but also, no less importantly, about the minutiae which bring a character to life.

Others opened doors for me which might have otherwise have remained shut. Måns Lönnroth, Sweden's State Secretary for the Environment in the government of Göran Persson, put me in contact with politicians and diplomats in Scandinavia and the Baltic States. Sir David Manning, Britain's Ambassador to the United States under Tony Blair, and David Muir, Director of Political Strategy under Blair's successor, Gordon Brown, provided introductions to their colleagues in Britain and America. Daniel Benjamin, Counter-terrorism Coordinator in the Obama Administration, not only gave me a home during the fall and winter of 2018 as a visiting fellow at Dartmouth, where he heads the Dickey Center, but was unfailingly generous in helping me through the revolving door that is Washington, D.C., as well as places further afield. Jake Sullivan, my colleague at Dartmouth at that time, now President Biden's National Security Adviser, put me in touch with former officials from the Obama and Clinton administrations. My thanks also to Professor Linda Fowler, who first brought me to Dartmouth, many years ago, and to others there who helped smooth my way: Stuart Finkel and Sean Griffin at the Department of Russian Studies; Tom Candon at the Dickey Center; Mark Boettcher and Richard Brittain at Computer Research; and John DeSantis and Todd Minsk at the Baker-Berry Library.

In Russia, I am indebted to Irina Rodina for opening doors and to Irina Solareva of *Ekho Moskvy*, Inna Iskratova in St Petersburg and Ilya Khorkov for their help in arranging interviews; in Germany, to Wilhelm Dietl, Jens Kreutzfeldt, Michael Renz and Katharina Schwan; in France, to Chantal Cardin and Jean-Pierre Rodrigues at the Bibliothèque des Fenouillères at the University of Aix-Marseille; and in Britain to Chris Westcott, Steve Herrman and Markus Ickstadt for providing access to the BBC Monitoring Service's translations from the Russian media. In addition, I owe a special word of thanks to Jean-Michel Carré of Les Films Grain de Sable in Paris, who generously allowed me to consult and quote from the transcripts of hundreds of interviews made by his team in Moscow and St Petersburg in 2005 and 2006 for a series of television documentaries for *France 2*.

If writing – the proverbial struggle with a blank sheet of paper or, more prosaically these days, with a blank computer screen – is a monachal occupation, transforming the results into a book is very much a collective endeavour. This book represents the efforts of many people: my editors, Stuart Williams, Jörg Hensgen and Lauren Howard at Bodley Head and Jack Macrae, Tim Duggan and Conor Mintzer at Henry Holt; my agents, Veronique Baxter at David Higham in London and Emma Sweeney and Margaret Sutherland Brown at Folio Literary Management in New York; Henry Howard, copy editor hors pair, who succeeded, against all odds, in imposing a corset of rigour on my idiosyncrasies, and Anthony Hippisley, whose eagle eye lighted infallibly on transliteration errors and repetitions. To all of them, my thanks.

Moscow – La Garde Freinet, April 26, 2022

Illustration Credits

Aged 13: Laski Diffusion / Contributor via Getty Images • *with parents at age seven:* Kremlin.ru, CC BY 4.0 • *with portrait on VE day:* AFP / Stringer via Getty Images • *with parents in 1985:* Laski Diffusion / Contributor via Getty Images • *with girlfriend 1970:* Laski Diffusion / Contributor via Getty Images • *wrestling:* Laski Diffusion / Contributor via Getty Images • *at Law Faculty:* Zuma Press • *with KGB colleagues:* private collection • *with Yuri Leshchev:* private collection • *with daughters in Dresden:* Zuma Press • *Stasi passes:* courtesy Stasi Archives, Dresden • *with Lazar Matveyev:* Kremlin.ru, CC BY 4.0 • *as Deputy Mayor, 1993:* Ullstein Bild / Contributor via Getty Images • *with Lyudmila and daughters, c. 1991:* Zuma Press • *Masha and Katya:* website of Sergei Pugachev • *with Sobchak:* Dmitri Lovetsky / AP / Shutterstock • *with Gorbachev:* Zuma Press, Inc. / Alamy Stock Photo • *Chernomyrdin, Stepashin, Kiriyenko:* Rossiya Segodnya • *as Acting President:* Itar-Tass News Agency / Alamy Stock Photo • *executed Chechen prisoners:* Laski Diffusion / Contributor via Getty Images • *Kadyrov and father:* Rossiya Segodnya • *Grosny ruins:* Oleg Nikishin / Contributor via Getty Images • *infant rescued at Beslan:* Reuters / Alamy Stock Photo • *volunteer stretcher bearers:* Reuters / Alamy Stock Photo • *embracing Blair:* Gilles Blassignac / Contributor via Getty Images • *in royal carriage:* Tim Graham / Contributor via Getty Images • *with Lord Mayor:* Itar-Tass News Agency / Alamy Stock Photo • *in the Kremlin's gilded halls:* Rossiya Segodnya • *with George W. Bush, 2001:* Ronald Martinez / Stringer via Getty Images • *fishing at Kennebunkport:* Bloomberg / Contributor via Getty Images • *Khodorkovsky:* Tatyana Makeyeva / Stringer via Getty Images • *Litvinenko:* Natasja Weitz / Contributor via Getty Images • *with Merkel:* Imago / CommonLens • *Obama and Medvedev:* US Government work, 2010 • *Batman and Robin:* Oleg Nikishin / Stringer via

Getty Images • *with Solzhenitsyn:* Rossiya Segodnya • *Pussy Riot:* Zuma Press • *at Mount Athos:* AKG / Picture Alliance / dpa • *Christmas service:* Rossiya Segodnya • *LGBT Demonstration:* Sean Gallup / Staff via Getty Images • *with Obama:* Reuters / Alamy Stock Photo • *with Theresa May:* Carl Court / Staff via Getty Images • *with Xi Jinping:* Kremlin Pool / Alamy Stock Photo • *ice hockey with Lukashenko:* Mikhail Klimentyev / Tass • *Sechin:* Mikhail Svetlov • *Shoigu and Patrushev:* Mikhail Metzel / Tass via Getty Images • *Nemtsov demonstration:* Alexander Aksyakov / Stringer via Getty Images • *Aleksei Navalny:* Mstislav Cherny / AP / Shutterstock • *Kukly puppet:* Wojtek Laski / Contributor via Getty Images • *Putin, 2000:* Laski Diffusion / Newsmakers • *Putin, 2003:* Brooks Kraft / Contributor via Getty Images • *Putin, 2007:* Ullstein Bild / Contributor via Getty Images • *Putin, 2013:* Mikhail Svetlov / Contributor via Getty Images • *Putin, 2021:* Mikhail Svetlov / Contributor via Getty Images • *with Lyudmila:* Alexei Nikolsky / RIA-Novosti / AFP via Getty Images • *with Alina Kabayeva:* Sergei Chirikov / Staff via Getty Images • *Louis LeBreton caricature:* Republic.ru • *meeting Security Council:* Kremlin.ru.

Note on Sources

It is a sound rule of thumb to keep source notes to a strict minimum or, if possible, to avoid them altogether. They are often seen as rebarbative rather than illuminating and, to many readers, they make a book appear excessively academic. But to every rule, there is an exception and, for better or worse, this book is one. Even the most basic facts about Putin's life and ideas are so open to dispute, so controversial and so hemmed about with half-truths and speculation, that it is crucial that every affirmation be anchored in a credible source which readers can consult in order to draw their own conclusions.

That said, there are limits to the light which such notes can shed. Some information derives from interviews which are not publicly accessible. Many of the sources cited are in Russian – either from contemporary newspaper reports or, in a few cases, memoirs – or in Estonian, Finnish, French, German, Swedish and other European languages. Some are taken from diplomatic despatches to and from the French missions in Moscow and St Petersburg in the 1990s, which may be viewed at the Diplomatic Archives in Nantes – in marked contrast to the situation in Britain and the United States where, notwithstanding Freedom of Information laws, such material is systematically withheld on national security grounds. For most readers, accessing the originals will be difficult.

Despite those limitations, the notes do make it possible to see exactly where each statement or citation has come from. They also provide supporting arguments to buttress the text, which, if incorporated into the main body of the book would make it unwieldy and unreadably verbose.

For those who wish to search further, more and more sources, including archives of the main Russian newspapers, are now available on the internet. Non-Russian speakers can get a sense of their content by using online translation services which, while still imperfect, offer possibilities unimaginable even a few years ago. In addition, the Kremlin website, www.kremlin.ru, contains Russian transcripts and English translations of many, though not all, of Putin's public speeches, news conferences and interviews, as well as accounts of meetings. The translations , which have the same URL as the Russian originals, at www. en.kremlin.ru, are generally adequate although in some cases the renderings are rather free. For that reason, the original Russian texts are cited in the notes and where appropriate have been retranslated.

Another key resource is the BBC Monitoring Service and its US partner, Open Source Enterprise (formerly the Foreign Broadcast Information Service, FBIS), which provide translated texts, often verbatim, of Russian radio and television broadcasts, news agency and newspaper articles and, more recently, links to blogs and social network comments. Virtually all Russian newspaper articles from the mid 1990s onward are also available online through www.integrum.ru. Earlier editions of Leningrad/St Petersburg newspapers are found only in the Russian State Library in Moscow and the Russian National Library in St Petersburg but no doubt they, too, will eventually be digitalised.

Because so little of the source material is in English, a detailed bibliography would serve little purpose. In any case, the vast majority of the thousands of books which have been published about Putin's time in office deal with Russian politics rather than the man himself. The only biography, in the traditional sense of the term, to have appeared in English until now has been Steven Lee Myers's pioneering work, *The New Tsar* (Simon and Schuster, 2015), which takes the story up to the annexation of Crimea. Previous to that, Fiona Hill and Clifford Gaddy had published *Mr. Putin: Operative in the Kremlin* (Brookings Institution, 2012, with an expanded and much improved edition in 2015), which views Putin's life schematically through the prism of his service in the KGB.

Three other relatively recent accounts are Masha Gessen's *The Man Without a Face: The Unlikely Rise of Vladimir Putin* (Riverside Books, 2012), Karen Dawisha's *Putin's Kleptocracy* (Simon and Schuster, 2014) and Catherine Belton's *Putin's People: How the KGB Took Back Russia and then Took On The West* (William Collins, 2020). All three offer interesting insights. Gessen focuses on Putin's psychology. Dawisha's book, while unfortunately marred by numerous errors of fact, was significant as the first in-depth attempt by a Western writer to examine Putin's time in St Petersburg. Belton is particularly strong on the financial machinations of the Russian elite and the pervasive corruption of Putin's regime. But all three need to be read with care, for they set out the case for the prosecution and, like all prosecutors, the authors select their evidence accordingly.

Mikhail Zygar offers a different perspective. His book, *All the Kremlin's Men: Inside the Court of Vladimir Putin* (Public Affairs, 2016), gives an intimate, carefully weighed and so far unequalled account of life among the Russian elite based on years of unattributable conversations with key decision-makers in Moscow. The French philosopher, Michel Eltchaninoff, explores Putin's thinking and his debt to Russia's nineteenth-century writers in an invaluable study, now translated into English, *Inside the Mind of Vladimir Putin* (Hurst, 2018). Angela Stent's *Putin's World: Russia against the West and with the Rest* (Twelve Books, 2019), while focused on foreign policy, is good on Putin's character and modus operandi. Daniel Treisman, in *The Return* (Free Press, 2011) and *The New Autocracy* (Brookings, 2018), provides context and attempts with considerable skill to draw up a balanced assessment of Putin's regime.

These books are not, strictly speaking, biographies, but rather chronicles of Putin's regime or investigations into particular aspects of his rule. That is also the case of Richard Sakwa's *Putin: Russia's Choice* (Routledge, 2003, revised edition in 2007) and *The Putin Paradox* (I.B. Tauris, 2020), and Angus Roxburgh's *The Strongman: Vladimir Putin and the Struggle for Russia* (I.B. Tauris, 2011, 2013 and 2021), although the latest expanded edition of the latter work develops a stronger biographical narrative. Taken together, while the list is far from exhaustive, they provide a variety of views of Putin's personality and rule among which readers must decide for themselves what is plausible, what sounds false, what rings true and what does not.

Yet of all the books about Putin published in English, the most intriguing is perhaps the earliest, *First Person* (Public Affairs, 2001), drawn from a series of interviews he gave during his first presidential campaign – a time when, with certain exceptions, he was far more open about his life and ambitions than he would ever be again. For anyone who wishes to get a sense of how Putin saw himself as he prepared to rule Russia, it remains essential reading.

Interviews

Tom **Adshead**, Director of Research, Macro-Advisory, Moscow (May 21, 2019).

Christopher **Andrew**, Historian (Cambridge, May 14, 2017).

Sergei **Baluyev**, Editor-in-Chief, *Smena*, 1994–1998 (St Petersburg, May 29, 2019).

Dirk **Banse**, *Die Welt* (Berlin, June 13, 2017).

Aleksandr **Belyaev**, Chairman, Lensoviet, 1991–1993, member Federation Council, 1993–6 (St Petersburg, June 3, 2019).

Örjan **Berner**, Swedish Ambassador, Moscow, 1989–1994 (Stockholm, Feb. 26, 2017).

Tomas **Bertelman**, Swedish Ambassador, Moscow, 2008–2012 (Stockholm, Oct. 12, 2017).

John **Beyrle**, US Ambassador, Moscow, 2008–2012 (Washington, D.C., March 12, 2019).

Carl **Bildt**, Prime Minister of Sweden, 1991–1994 (Stockholm, Oct. 13, 2017).

Hans **Blix**, Head of the IAEA, 1981–1997, and Head of UNMOVIC, 2002–2003 (Stockholm, Oct. 12, 2017).

Anders **Blom**, Finnish businessman, Adviser to the St Petersburg Foreign Relations Committee, 1993–2016 (Turku, March 5, 2017).

Jan **Blomgren**, Moscow correspondent for *Svenska Dagbladet*, 1993–2001 (Ronninge, Sweden, Oct. 13, 2017).

Yuri **Boldyrev**, Member, Soviet Congress of People's Deputies, 1989–1991, Head, Main Control Directorate of the Presidential Administration, 1992–1993, Member of the Federation Council, 1993–1995 (Moscow, Nov. 20, 2019).

Yves **Bonnet**, Director, DST (Direction de la surveillance du territoire), French Counter-Intelligence, 1982–1985 (Rouen, March 29, 2016).

Sir Rodric **Braithwaite**, British Ambassador, Moscow, 1988–1992 (London, Sept. 27, 2016).

Sir Anthony **Brenton**, Counsellor, British Embassy, Moscow, 1994–1998, Ambassador, 2004–2008 (Cambridge, May 14, 2017).

Richard **Bridge**, British Embassy, Moscow, 1989–1993 (London, May 12, 2017).

Philipp **Burger**, Bonn University (June 7, 2017).

Shaun **Byrnes**, US State Department, 1975–2004 (Arlington, Va., March 11, 2019).

Igor **Chubais**, Russian philosopher (Moscow, Nov. 28, 2019).

Jean-François **Clair**, DST (Direction de la surveillance du territoire), French Counter-Intelligence (Paris, June 23, 2016).

Peter **Clement**, Russia analyst, later deputy assistant Director for Europe and Eurasia, CIA, currently Adjunct Professor at Columbia University (New York, Feb. 7, 2019).

Jim **Collins**, US Ambassador, Moscow, 1997–2001 (Feb. 20, telephone interview and Washington, D.C., March 12, 2019).

David **Crawford**, CORRECT!V (Berlin, May 5, 2017).

Mikhail **Delyagin**, Adviser to the Presidential Administration, 1994–1999, Adviser to the Prime Minister, 2002–2003 (Moscow, Nov. 28, 2019).

Vyacheslav **Dolinin**, Human rights activist (St Petersburg, June 6, 2019).

Sir Richard **Dearlove**, Head of MI6, 1999–2004 (Paris, June 24, 2016 and Cambridge, May 14, 2017).

John **Evans**, US Consul General in St Petersburg, 1994–1997 (Washington, D.C., March 10, 2017).

Sir Brian **Fall**, British Ambassador, Moscow, 1992–1995 (London, Sept. 29, 2016).

William **Flemming**, Tashkent-based British economist, banker (April 13, 2019, telephone interview).

Lyudmila **Fomicheva**, Press Secretary to Anatoly Sobchak, 1994–1996 (St Petersburg, May 28, 2019).

Lars **Freden**, Baltic Affairs Adviser to Swedish Prime Minister Carl Bildt, 1992–1994 (Cannes, Dec. 15, 2016 and Stockholm, Oct. 12, 2017).

Daniel **Fried**, Assistant Secretary of State for European and Eurasian Affairs, 2005–2009 (Washington, D.C., Dec. 10, 2018).

Svetlana **Gavrilina**, *Smena*, 1993–1995 (Skype interview from Israel, Nov. 25, 2019).

Natalya **Gevorkyan**, Russian journalist, formerly with *Kommersant*, co-author of *First Person* (Paris, March 31, 2016).

Aleksandr **Golts**, Military historian, analyst (Moscow, Nov. 20, 2019).

Aleksandr **Gorshkov**, Editor-in-Chief, Fontanka.ru (St Petersburg, Nov. 27, 2019).

Jack **Gosnell**, US Consul General, Leningrad/St Petersburg, 1991–1994 (Falls Church, Va., Oct. 30–31, 2018).

Nigel **Gould-Davies**, British Ambassador, Minsk 2007–2009, Senior Fellow, International Institute of Strategic Studies, London (Bangkok, Feb. 14, 2019).

Tom **Graham**, Director for Russia at the National Security Council, 2004–2007 (New York, March 7, 2017 and Feb. 7, 2019).

William **Green**, CIA Directorate of Operations, 1986–1996 (Washington, D.C., Dec. 11, 2018).

Elizabeth **Guigou**, French Minister for European Affairs, 1990–1993 (Paris, Oct. 14, 2016).

Sergei **Gulyaev**, *600 Seconds*, 1991–1993, Member of the St Petersburg Legislative Assembly, 2002–2006 (May 28, 2019).

John **Guy**, British Consul General in St Petersburg, 1996–2000 (Skype call to London, Jan. 16, 2020).

Steven **Hadley**, National Security Adviser to George W. Bush, 2005–2009 (Washington, D.C., March 11, 2019).

Tarja **Halonen**, President of Finland, 2000–2012 (Helsinki, March 6, 2017).

Marek **Halter**, French writer and journalist (Paris, June 24, 2016).

George **Handy**, St Petersburg Programme Director, Centre for International and Strategic Studies, 1992–2006 (Nov. 30, 2018, telephone interview).

August **Hanning**, Head of the BND (German Foreign Intelligence), 1998–2005 (Berlin, June 12, 2017).

Dame Barbara **Hay**, British Consul General in Leningrad/St Petersburg, 1991–1992 (London, Sept. 21 and 25, 2016).

Harry **Helenius**, Finnish Ambassador, Moscow, 2004–2008 (Helsinki, March 5, 2017).

Christoph **Heusgen**, Foreign Policy Adviser to Angela Merkel, 2005–2017 (New York, March 14, 2019).

Toomas **Hiio**, Military Historian (Tallinn, May 22, 2017).

Sven **Hirdman**, Swedish Ambassador, Moscow, 1994–2004 (Stockholm, Feb. 26, 2017).

Kaj **Hober**, Uppsala University (Stockholm, Oct. 12, 2017).

Kate **Horner**, British Embassy, Moscow, 1997–2000 (Richmond, Surrey, Sept. 28, 2016).

Andrei **Illarionov**, Economic Adviser to Vladimir Putin, 2000–2005 (Washington, D.C., Feb. 16 and March 13, 2019).

Nate **Jones**, National Security Archive, George Washington University (Washington, D.C., March 9, 2017).

Marlène **Julien**, Operations Manager, Credit Lyonnais, St Petersburg, 1992–1995 (Dana Point, Calif., Feb. 22, 2019).

Vladimir **Juškin**, Adviser to the Estonian Prime Minister, 1990–1992 (Tallinn, May 23, 2017).

Diana **Kachalova**, *Nevskoe Vremya*, 1990–1992 (St Petersburg, June 3, 2019).

Jaako **Kalela**, National Security Adviser to the President of Finland, 1972–2005 (Helsinki, March 2, 2017).

Oleg **Kalugin**, Deputy Head of the Leningrad KGB Directorate, 1980–1987 (Rockville, Md., Oct. 30, 2018).

Mikhail **Kasyanov**, Prime Minister of Russia, 2001–2004 (Moscow, Nov. 19, 2019).

Seppo **Kauppila**, Finnish Consul General, St Petersburg, 1993–1995 (Helsinki, March 3, 2017).

Mark **Kelton**, CIA Station Chief, Moscow, 1999–2001 (Washington, D.C., Oct. 31, 2018).

Bridget **Kendall**, BBC Moscow Correspondent, 1989–1994 (Cambridge, May 17, 2017).

Toomas **Kiho**, Adviser to Estonian President Lennart Meri, 1997–2001 (Tallinn, May 25, 2017).

Alfred **Kokh**, St Petersburg Mayor's Office, 1991–1993, Chairman, State Property Committee, 1996–1997, Deputy Prime Minister, 1997 (Rosenheim, Germany, Oct. 9, 2019).

Paul **Kolbe**, CIA Moscow station, 1993–1996 (Washington, D.C., March 11, 2019).

Andrei **Kolesnikov**, Carnegie Moscow Center, (June 13, 2019).

Pyotr **Kotov**, *Vechernii Leningrad*, *Vechernii Peterburg*, 1991–1996 (St Petersburg, May 28 and Nov. 27, 2019).

Daniil **Kotsyubinsky**, *Smena*, *Chas pik*, 1990–1999, Historian (St Petersburg, May 30, 2019).

Mark **Kramer**, Director, Cold War Studies Project, Davis Center, Harvard University (Cambridge, Mass., March 11, 2017).

Eerik-Niiles **Kross**, Estonian Government Intelligence Coordinator, 1995–2000 (Tallinn, Feb. 28, 2017).

Mart **Laar**, Prime Minister of Estonia, 1992–1994 and 1999–2002 (Tallinn, May 27, 2017).

Ivan **Lavrantjev**, Historian (Tallinn, May 25, 2017).

Juhani **Leppä**, Mayor of Turku, Finland, 1989–1995 (Turku, March 4, 2017).

Mats **Liljefors**, Guest Conductor, Hermitage Symphony Orchestra, St Petersburg, 1993–2014 (Stockholm, Oct. 12, 2017).

Ruslan **Linkov**, Assistant to Galina Starovoitova, 1990–1998 (St Petersburg, June 2, 2019).

Osmo **Lipponen**, Finnish Consul General, St Petersburg, 1995–1999 (Helsinki, May 30, 2017).

Marina **Litvinovich**, *Fond effektivnoi politiki* (Foundation for Effective Policy), 1996–2002, later a leader of the democratic opposition (Moscow, Nov. 18, 2019).

Anders **Ljunggren**, Swedish Ambassador to Estonia, 2013–2018 (Tallinn, Feb. 27, 2017).

Jüri **Luik**, Estonian Ambassador in Moscow, 2013–2015, former Defence Minister and Foreign Minister (Tallinn, Feb. 28, 2017).

Douglas **Lund**, British engineer, Head of Construction for Oleg Deripaska, 2006–2011 (Dec. 27, 2018, telephone interview from Prague).

Gunnar **Lund**, Swedish negotiator with St Petersburg Mayor's Office, 1992–1994, later Ambassador in Washington and Paris (Stockholm, Feb. 26, 2017).

Lev **Lurye**, Historian (St Petersburg, May 27, 2019).

Sir Roderic **Lyne**, British Ambassador, Moscow, 2000–2004 (London, Sept. 27, 2016).

Markus **Lyra**, Finnish Consul General, Leningrad/St Petersburg, 1990–1993, Ambassador, Moscow, 1996–2000 (Helsinki, March 2, 2017).

Ekaterina **Makhotina**, Bonn University (June 7, 2017).

Sir Christopher **Mallaby**, Head of Chancery, British Embassy, Moscow, 1975–1977, later British Ambassador to Germany and France (London, March 8, 2017).

Vitaly **Mansky**, Filmmaker (Moscow, Nov. 29, 2019).

Suzanne **Massie**, Adviser to Ronald Reagan, long-time resident of St Petersburg (Nov. 24, 2019).

Sir Simon **McDonald**, Foreign Policy Adviser to Gordon Brown, 2007–2010, later Head of the British Diplomatic Service (London, Sept. 29, 2016).

Alex **Meerovich**, US Consulate General, St. Petersburg, 1995–1998 (Feb. 15, 2019, telephone interview).

Richard **Miles**, US Consul General, Leningrad, 1988–1991 and Deputy Chief of Mission, Moscow, 1993–1996 (Fort Hunt, Va., Dec. 11, 2018).

Pablo **Miller**, Russia Specialist, MI6 (London, Sept. 22, 2016 and Salisbury, May 13, 2017).

Johan **Molander**, Swedish Ambassador, Moscow, 2004–2008 (Stockholm, Oct. 10, 2017).

Michael **Morell**, CIA Deputy Director, 2010–2013, Acting Director, 2011 and 2012–2013 (McLean, Va., March 11, 2019).

Michael **Morgan**, CIA Central Eurasia Division, 1999–2002 (New London, Dec. 29, 2018 and Hanover, New Hampshire, Feb. 20, 2019).

Uwe **Müller**, *Die Welt* (Berlin, June 13, 2017)

Rein **Mullerson**, First Deputy Foreign Minister, Estonia, 1991–1992 (Tallinn, May 25, 2017).

Raymond **Nart**, Deputy Director, DST (Direction de la surveillance du territoire), French Counter-Intelligence, 1989–1998 (Paris, March 30, 2016 and telephone interview, June 10, 2016).

Lyudmila **Narusova**, widow of Anatoly Sobchak (Moscow, Nov. 21 and St Petersburg, Nov. 26, 2019).

Andrei **Nechayev**, First deputy Minister, then Minister of Economic Affairs, 1991–1993 (Moscow, Nov. 18, 2019).

Martin **Nicholson**, British Embassy, Moscow, 1994–1997 (London, May 15, 2017).

Natalya **Nikiforova**, *Vechernii Sankt-Peterburg*, *Chas pik*, 1991–1996 (Moscow, June 13, 2019).

Mart **Nutt**, Member of the Estonian parliament, 1992–2019 (Tallinn, March 1, 2017).

Hans **Olsson**, Swedish Consul General, St Petersburg, 1996–2000 (Stockholm, Oct. 13, 2017).

Sir Robert **Owen**, Chairman, Inquiry into the Death of Alexander Litvinenko (London, Sept. 26, 2016).

Valery **Pavlov**, Assistant to Anatoly Sobchak, 1989–91 (Skype interview from Turkey, Nov. 27, 2019).

Gleb **Pavlovsky**, Adviser to the Presidential Administration, 1996–2011, President, *Fond effektivnoi politiki* (Moscow, Nov. 21, 2019).

David **Pepper**, St Petersburg Programme, Center for Strategic and International Studies, 1993–1995 (Jan. 28, 2019, telephone interview).

John **Pepper**, CEO, later Chairman of the Board, Procter and Gamble, 1995–2002 (Jan. 24, 2019, telephone interview).

Göran **Persson**, Prime Minister of Sweden, 1996–2006 (Stockholm, Feb. 27, 2017).

Tom **Pickering**, US Ambassador, Moscow, 1993–1996 (Washington, D.C., Feb. 15, 2019).

Jüri **Pihl**, Head of Domestic Intelligence, Estonia, 1991–2003 (Tallinn, May 24, 2017).

Mart **Piiskop**, Estonian Consul General, St Petersburg, 1996–1999 (Tallinn, May 22, 2017).

James **Platt**, Dartmouth Medical School – Psychiatry (Hanover, N.H., Feb. 19, 2019).

Dmitry **Potapenko**, Deputy CEO, En+ Group (Moscow, Nov. 22, 2019).

Jonathan **Powell**, Chief of Staff to Tony Blair, 1997–2007 (London, Sept. 22, 2016).

Gerald **Praschl**, German journalist (Berlin, June 12, 2017).

Manfred **Quiring**, Moscow correspondent for *Berliner Zeitung*, 1982–1987 and 1991–1995, and *Die Welt*, 1998–2010 (Birkenwerder, June 11, 2017).

Jüri **Raidla**, Estonian Justice Minister, 1990–1992 (Tallinn, May 23, 2017).

Ben **Rhodes**, Deputy National Security Advisor to President Obama, 2009–2017 (Venice Beach, Calif., Feb. 22, 2019).

Sir Francis **Richards**, Deputy Chief of Mission, British Embassy, Moscow, 1992–1995, later head of GCHQ (Stanton St Quintin, May 12, 2017).

Eugene **Rumer**, US National Intelligence Council, 2010–2014, afterwards Carnegie Endowment (Washington, D.C., Dec. 10, 2018 and March 13, 2019).

Charles **Ryan**, EBRD St Petersburg, 1991–1994, afterwards UFG Asset Management, Moscow (Jan. 9, telephone interview and Conshohocken, Pa., March 14, 2019).

Yuli **Rybakov**, member of the Lensoviet, 1990–1993 and the State Duma, 1993–2003, human rights activist (St Petersburg, June 3, 2019).

Patrick **Salmon**, Historian, British Foreign Office (London, Sept. 26, 2016).

Robert **Sasson**, EBRD, St Petersburg, 1992–2005 (Moscow, June 13, 2019).

Svetlana **Savranskaya**, George Washington University (Washington, D.C., March 10, 2017).

Sir John **Scarlett**, Moscow Station Chief, 1991–1994 and Head of MI6, 2004–2009 (London, Sept. 26, 2016).

Karl **Schlögel**, Historian (Berlin, May 6, 2017).

Serge **Schmemann**, *New York Times* (Paris, Oct 13, 2016).

Erich **Schmidt-Eenboom**, German writer and journalist (Weilheim, June 9, 2017).

Franz **Sedelmayer**, German arms dealer in Leningrad/St Petersburg, 1989–1996 (Spotsylvania, Va., Oct. 30 and Dec. 12, 2018).

Stephen **Sestanovich**, Adviser to the US Secretary of State on Russian affairs, 1997–2001, currently Columbia University and the Council on Foreign Relations (New York, Feb. 8, 2019).

Natalya **Shadkhan**, Filmmaker (St Petersburg, May 31, 2019).

Anna **Sharogradskaya**, Regional Press Institute, St Petersburg (May 27, 2019).

Sir Nigel **Sheinwald**, Foreign Policy Adviser to Tony Blair, 2003–2007 (London, May 17, 2017).

Sergei **Shelin**, *Chas pik*, 1991–1992, *Sankt-Peterburgskoe ekho*, 1992–1993 (St Petersburg, May 29, 2019).

Michael **Sohlman**, Under Secretary, Swedish Foreign Trade Ministry, 1989–1991 (Stockholm, Feb. 26, 2017).

Mike **Sulick**, CIA Station Chief, Moscow, 1994–1996, later Head of the CIA's Clandestine Service (Raleigh, N.C., March 8, 2017).

Strobe **Talbott**, US Deputy Secretary of State, 1994–2001 (Washington, D.C., Feb. 15, 2019).

Indrek **Tarand**, Estonian government representative in Narva, 1993–1994 (Brussels, May 3, 2017).

Seppo **Tiitinen**, Head of SuPo (Finnish Intelligence), 1978–1990, Secretary General, Finnish parliament, 1992–2015 (Helsinki, May 29, 2017).

Dmitry **Travin**, Historian (St Petersburg, June 4, 2019).

Dmitry **Trenin**, Director, Carnegie Moscow Center (June 11, 2019).

Erkki **Tuomioja**, Finnish Foreign Minister, 2000–2007 and 2011–2015 (Helsinki, March 3, 2017).

Arnold **Vaatz**, 'Neues Forum', Dresden, 1989–1990, later a Christian Democrat member of the Bundestag (Berlin, June 12, 2017).

Raivo **Vare**, Estonian Transport Minister, 1996–1999 (Tallinn, March 1, 2017).

Hubert **Védrine**, French Foreign Minister, 1997–2002 (Paris, Sept. 28, 2015).

Alexander **Vershbow**, US Ambassador, Moscow, 2001–2005 (Washington, D.C., Dec. 10, 2018).

Carl-Henrik **Victorin**, former CEO, Reso Hotels (Stockholm, Oct. 11, 2017).

Boris **Vishnevsky**, St Petersburg opposition politician (May 31 and Nov. 25, 2019).

Mart **Vollmer**, Estonian Consul General, St Petersburg, 1993–1996 (Copenhagen, Oct. 10, 2017).

Hans-Friedrich **von Ploetz**, German Ambassador, Moscow, 2002–2005 (Berlin, May 5, 2017)

Eberhard **von Puttkamer**, German Consul General, St Petersburg, 1991–1996 (Potsdam, May 6, 2017).

Ernst-Joerg **von Studnitz**, German Ambassador, Moscow, 1995–2002 (Bonn, June 7, 2017).

Vladimir **Voronov**, Journalist (Moscow, Nov. 22, 2019).

Yevgeny **Vyshenkov**, Fontanka.ru (St Petersburg, June 1, 2019).

Andrew **Weiss**, Carnegie Endowment (Washington, D.C., March 13, 2019).

Hans-Georg **Wieck**, Head of the BND (German Foreign Intelligence), 1985–1990 (Berlin, June 13, 2017).

Sir Andrew **Wood**, British Ambassador, Moscow, 1995–2000 (London, Sept. 23, 2016).

Grigory **Yavlinsky**, Chairman, Yabloko, 1993–2008 (Moscow, Nov. 19, 2019).

Viktor **Yerofeyev**, Writer (Moscow, Nov. 20, 2019).

Aleksandr **Yershov**, Image-maker for Vladimir Yakovlev, 1996 (St Petersburg, Nov. 26, 2019).

Dmitry **Yezhkov**, *Smena* (St Petersburg, May 30, 2019).

Dmitry **Zapolsky**, Journalist, member of the Lensoviet, 1990–1993 (Skype interview from Helsinki, Nov. 26, 2019).

Mikhail **Zygar**, Journalist, author, *All the Kremlin's Men* (Moscow, Nov. 21, 2019).

Notes

In the following pages, CADN denotes the *Centre des Archives Diplomatiques* in Nantes, France. Interviews undertaken in Russia in 2005 and 2006 on behalf of Les Films Grain de Sable for French television are referenced as 'interviews for Jean-Michel Carré'. Publication details of books cited are given in full at first reference, thereafter by author and short title followed, where apposite, by *supra* or ibid. The one exception is the two-volume Russian language biography of Putin by Oleg Blotsky which, after the first reference, is given simply as *Blotsky*, Vol. 1 or 2. Blotsky's book, like the reminiscences of Putin's teacher, Vera Gurevich, is more laudatory than the extracts from Putin's interviews published in *First Person* but provides a wealth of information not available elsewhere, including extracts from unpublished interviews with Putin himself, his wife, Lyudmila, childhood friends, and colleagues in the KGB. After Putin's first term as President, he authorised no further accounts of his life and a planned third volume of Blotsky's biography was abandoned.

All websites cited were most recently accessed Dec. 2021–April. 2022

Prologue

1. The number of regions in Russia has changed as a result of mergers, from 89 in the 1990s to 83 in 2014 and 85 – including Sevastopol and Crimea – in 2022.

2. Blomgren, Jan, *Moskva tror inte på tårar: en tidsresa i det nya Ryssland*, Ersatz, Stockholm, 2009, pp. 108–9; and author's interview, Rönninge, near Stockholm, Oct. 13, 2017.

3. 'Terroristy tozhe raznye' ['Terrorists also come in different forms'] in *Literaturnaya gazeta*, June 16, 1999; see also Chiesa, Giulietto, *Russkaya ruletka: chto sluchitsya v mire, esli Rossiya raspadetsya*, Prava Cheloveka, Moscow, 2000, pp. 207–8. In the *Literaturnaya gazeta* article, which Chiesa described as 'a veiled warning', he wrote in general terms and did not link possible terrorist acts to the forthcoming elections. In a follow-up piece in June, he

speculated that the Kremlin might engineer a breakdown of public order in the capital to show that Luzhkov was no longer in control, and then went on to suggest, as Blomgren had done earlier, that a Union State with Belarus might be concluded in order to delay the elections (*30Giorni*, No. 6, 1999). The following month he wrote of the possibility of 'explosions in the metro' which might be blamed on Chechens as part of a 'strategy of tension' (*Russkaya ruletka*, p. 208).

4.   *Moskovskaya pravda*, July 22, 1999.

5.   Ibid., Sept. 15, and *Novaya gazeta*, Nov. 18, 1999. Zverev was fired on August 3, 1999 after less than three months in the post.

6.   Eugene Rumer, author's interview, Washington, D.C., Dec. 10, 2018.

7.   *Kommersant*, Sept. 1, 1999; Satter, David, *Darkness at Dawn*, Yale University Press, New Haven and London, 2003, p. 64.

8.   *Komsomolskaya pravda*, Sept. 22, 1999.

9.   These were the figures cited at the time. Later the Russian Procurator General's office issued different totals: 100 dead and 690 injured on September 9; 124 dead and seven injured on September 13; 19 dead and 88 seriously injured (with more than 1,200 others having slight injuries) on September 16.

10.   *Kommersant*, Sept. 1, 1999.

11.   The following account of the incident at Ryazan draws on information compiled by John B. Dunlop in *The Moscow Bombings of September 1999*, ibidem-Verlag , Stuttgart, 2012, pp. 167–215, and David Satter in *Darkness at Dawn*, pp. 67–71.

12.   After the explosions in Moscow, several newspapers criticised the security services for incompetence and failing to follow up leads. *Novaya gazeta* reported on September 13 that it had received detailed information about plans for the explosions and had passed them on to the Interior Ministry but had been ignored. *Obshchaya gazeta*, three days later, quoted a member of the Duma, Konstantin Borovoi, as saying that he, too, had tried to pass information to the Security Council but had been rebuffed. *Moskovsky komsomolets* went still further, asking sarcastically on September 15 whether the law enforcement agencies 'had simply been bought by the bandits'. In an article the following day headlined, 'Bombs put together in the Kremlin?', it suggested that 'former employees' of the special services 'might' have carried out the attacks. After the Ryazan incident, Russian newspapers started directly accusing the Kremlin of responsibility for the explosions.

13.   An opinion poll taken from September 17 to 20, after the Volgodonsk bombing but before the incident at Ryazan, indicated that in mid September, 47 per cent of those questioned blamed Yeltsin for failing to prevent the attacks. Only 5 per cent held Putin responsible (Interfax, Sept. 25, 1999).

14.   *Moskovsky komsomolets*, Sept. 24, 1999.

15.   Ibid., Sept. 25, 1999.

16.   *Nezavisimaya gazeta*, Sept. 25, 1999.

17.   *Le Figaro*, Sept. 28, 1999.

18.   Putin told parliament on September 14, after the second of the two Moscow explosions, that a state of emergency was not needed (Interfax, Sept. 14, 1999).

19.   *Moskovsky komsomolets*, March 16, 2002.

20.   *Novaya gazeta*, March 13 & 27 and April 3, 2000; *Moscow Times*, March 16 & 21, 2000; Satter, *Darkness at Dawn*, pp. 30–32. Whether in fact the sacks contained hexogen is not certain. Their existence was revealed by two soldiers, who, thinking that they contained sugar, took some to sweeten their tea and were repelled by the bad taste. The problem with this

account is that hexogen does not dissolve in water and in any case is tasteless. It might have been mixed with ammonium nitrate, which does indeed resemble sugar, or it might not have been hexogen at all.

21. Lev Levinson in 'Grani vremeni', *Radio Liberty*, Sept. 5, 2017, transcript at www.svoboda. org/a/28718520.html

22. Grigory Yavlinsky, author's interview, Nov. 19, 2019.

23. *Sobesednik*, No. 41, 1996. The article, by Vladimir Voronov, one of the best-informed Russian journalists reporting on the security services, is reprinted in his book, *Sluzhba*, Tsentr Gumanitarnogo Obrazovaniya, Moscow, 2004, pp. 120–26 esp. pp. 124–5. In the 1990s and early 2000s, *Sobesednik* was often a trailblazer, publishing hard-hitting political reports on sensitive topics. More recently it has focused on safer subjects.

24. Chiesa later became a member of the European Parliament, in which capacity he promoted the theory that the Twin Towers in New York had been blown up by explosives rather than demolished by aircraft hijacked by al-Qaeda. He has also championed the idea that the vapour trails of aircraft are seeding the atmosphere with toxic chemicals as part of a secret plan to slow global warming.

25. See Orttung, Robert W., *The Republics and Regions of the Russian Federation: A Guide to the Politics, Policies and Leaders*, Routledge, Abingdon and New York, 2019.

26. Blomgren's editor at *Svenska Dagbladet* was so appalled by his suggestion that the Kremlin might have had a hand in the bombings that he initially refused to publish the article. He relented only after protests from Blomgren's colleagues (Blomgren, interview, *supra*).

27. Ibid. and *Moskva tror inte på tårar*, pp. 106–8. The only other thing missing from the apartment was some snuff, which was a rarity in Russia. The investigators may have suspected that it was a drug.

28. Almost a year later, no definite conclusion had been reached as to the nature of the shopping mall explosion (Rossiya TV, Aug. 12, 2000).

29. Cited in Reddaway, Peter, and Glinski, Dmitri, *The Tragedy of Russia's Reforms: Market Bolshevism Against Democracy*, United States Institute of Peace Press, Washington, D.C., 2001, pp. 615–16, n. 288. See also Ware, Robert Bruce, and Kisriev, Enver, *Dagestan*, Routledge, New York, 2010, pp. 121–55.

30. Mark Kelton, author's interview, Washington, D.C., Oct. 31, 2018.

31. John Scarlett, author's interview, London, Sept. 26, 2016; Richard Dearlove, author's interview, Paris, June 24, 2016. Sceptics may wonder why in that case there were no leaks after the FSB's Ryazan operation. But that involved only a small team of operatives and a handful of support staff, which would have made it relatively easy to control information. In Moscow, where several tons of explosives were found at half a dozen different sites, many more people would have had to take part. Colonel Igor Prelin, a 30-year veteran of the KGB, was categorical: 'Leave aside the moral aspect, the fact that it would be the murder of our own people . . . I am speaking simply as a professional. To blow up those buildings . . . would have to be planned and organised and carried out. That would have involved a very large number of people. It would have been impossible to keep it secret, especially in our country, where everything always leaks' (interview with Jean-Michel Carré, 2006). The Chechens, bound by family, clan and religious loyalties, were much better at maintaining secrecy. During the first and second Chechen wars, the FSB had virtually no success in penetrating Chechen networks.

32. Kelton and Dearlove, *supra*.

33. For instance, Mikhail Zygar, the former editor-in-chief of Dozhd TV, one of the

best-connected journalists in Moscow, continued as late as 2019 to cite Seleznyov's announcement as evidence of FSB involvement (author's interview, Moscow, Nov. 21, 2019). So did Marina Litvinovich, who worked as an adviser to Putin's first presidential election campaign (author's interview, Moscow, Nov. 18, 2019).

34. *Khronika kriminalnykh sobytii (PSF)*, Sept. 13, 1999.

35. *Sobesednik*, Sept. 14, 1999.

36. *Nezavisimaya gazeta*, March 22 and Olga Pashkova, 'Dumskoe bolshinstvo vs Seleznev', *Politkom.ru*, March 27, 2002.

37. Mark Kelton points out that there is 'an assumption sometimes in the West that when the Russians are conducting operations, things always go according to plan ... But often [that's not so]. Something went wrong or someone screwed up, they didn't plan, it was badly conceived, badly thought through' (author's interview, Oct. 31, 2019). In fairness, it should be added that western intelligence services also commit egregious blunders. In 1986, two French agents who had been sent to New Zealand to prepare the blowing up of a Greenpeace vessel, the *Rainbow Warrior*, were identified and arrested after making a call on an open line to the Defence Ministry in Paris. The FSB later claimed that the operatives sent to Ryazan were under orders to act in a way which would attract attention to themselves because the goal of the operation was to test the vigilance of the local police and population (*Sovershenno sekretno*, No. 6, 2002). That sounds like post-hoc justification, but if they had been trying to be caught, they would hardly have acted differently.

38. Gleb Pavlovsky, author's interview, Moscow, Nov. 21, 2019.

39. Aleksandr Golts, author's interview, Moscow, Nov. 20, 2019.

40. If the exercise was authorised by an officer below Patrushev's level, it might explain why it took more than 36 hours for the FSB to work out what had happened and issue a public statement. Some reports have claimed that the operation was conceived by General Aleksandr Tikhonov, who later became the head of the FSB's Special Forces Centre.

41. 'The Counter-Intelligence Lexicon', translated in Mitrokhin, Vasiliy, *KGB Lexicon*, Routledge, 2002, pp. 155 & 413–15. The manual, which was issued in the early 1970s, was used at the Higher KGB School in Minsk where Patrushev studied from 1974 to 1975.

42. Colonel Igor Prelin, who had been one of Putin's instructors at the KGB's Red Banner Institute (interview with Jean-Michel Carré, 2006).

43. 'Otvet Genprokuratory na deputatskii vopros o vzryvakh v Moskve', May 14, 2002, archived at web.archive.org/web/20120210221753/http://vip.lenta.ru/doc/2002/05/14/prosecutors and *Segodnya*, Sept. 24, 1999. According to the prosecutors' report, the sample that failed to detonate weighed 3 kg. *Moskovsky komsomolets*, which by then was openly accusing the FSB of responsibility for the blasts, argued that this was too small an amount for the tests to be conclusive (Sept. 25, 1999). However, even a few hundred grams of hexogen are sufficient for a car bomb.

44. The first large-scale terrorist attack by Basayev's forces, at Budyonnovsk in 1995, was also aimed at civilians. So were almost all the high-profile attacks by Chechen insurgents which followed the apartment bombings. Chechen attacks on military installations were the exception, rather than the rule, and even then were usually directed at soft targets, such as military hospitals or housing, or poorly guarded police stations and arms depots. In January, 1996, Chechen guerrillas raided a military airbase at Kizlyar, in Dagestan, but there is no recorded instance of a direct attack on an army barracks.

45. Basayev, interview with *Lidové noviny*, Prague, Sept. 9, 1999, cited by BBC Monitoring on Sept. 30, 1999. After the second apartment block explosion in Moscow, a caller told TASS

on Sept. 15 that the attacks were in reprisal for the Russian bombardment of the Dagestani village of Karamakhi. When the FSB eventually released a list of suspects, all were from Dagestan and other Muslim republics, and none from Chechnya (*Moscow Times*, Feb. 19, 2000).

46. Memorandum of Conversation, 'Meeting with Russian Prime Minister Putin', Oslo, Nov. 2, 1999, Clinton Presidential Library, Doc. 9908099, Box 2578.

47. See Pokalova, Elena, *Chechnya's Terrorist Network: The Evolution of Terrorism in the North Caucasus*, Praeger, New York, 2015.

48. Handwritten note, addressed to Putin by Basayev, dated August 30, 2004, found at Beslan after the hostage-taking that year and included in court documents at the trial of Nurpasha Kulaev in 2006 (www.pravdabeslana.ru/zapiska.htm).

49. Some years earlier, the commander of an army engineering battalion was arrested in St Petersburg with over 650 lb of hexogen in his apartment which he was preparing to sell to an organised crime group (*Sankt-Peterburgskie vedomosti*, March 7, 1995).

50. The Chechen website *Kavkaz-Tsentr* began posting similar claims on September 23.

51. Among them Grigory Yavlinsky, Andrei Illarionov, Mikhail Zygar and many others. In the West, such long-term observers of Russian affairs as David Satter and Amy Knight also believe that the Kremlin's responsibility has been established beyond reasonable doubt.

52. The qualification, 'almost certainly', is necessary because, as long as the case documents remain sealed, it is impossible to prove that the FSB played no part. All that can be said is that, other than circumstantial evidence, no proof that it did so has yet been found.

53. Golts, interview, *supra*.

54. 'The Paranoid Style in American Politics', in *Harper's Magazine*, Nov. 1964.

55. *Face the Nation*, CBS, Dec. 11, 2016.

1: *Baskov Lane*

1. Blotsky, Oleg, *Vladimir Putin: Istoriya zhizni*, Izdatelstvo Mezhdunarodnye Otnosheniya, Moscow, 2001 [hereafter Blotsky, Vol. 1], p. 24.

2. *Akusherstvo, Ginekologiya, Reproduktsiya*, Vol. 11, No. 2, 2017, pp. 69–74.

3. Kelly, Catriona, *Children's World: Growing up in Russia, 1890–1991*, Yale University Press, New Haven and London, 2007, pp. 319–23 & 646 n. 218.

4. Ibid., p. 322.

5. Ibid., pp. 331, 337 & 648 n. 285.

6. French Diplomatic Archives, Nantes [hereafter CADN]: MAE, Division médicale, 92/297/DV/CP, Dinah Vernant, March 4, 1992. Curiously, in recent years, swaddling has come back into fashion in America.

7. This and the following section are drawn from Blotsky, Vol. 1, pp. 24, 29, 31–2 & 36–8; and Putin, Vladimir, *First Person*, Pulic Affairs, New York, 2000, pp. 3–10.

8. According to his grandson, Aleksandr, Spiridon himself recounted that on at least one occasion Rasputin gave him a *chervonets*, a gold coin then worth 10 roubles (*Moskovsky komsomolets*, Oct. 6, 2017).

9. Reid, Anna, *Leningrad: The Epic Siege of World War II, 1941–1944*, Walker and Co., New York, 2011, p. 160.

10. Gurevich, Vera Dmitrievna, *Vladimir Putin: Roditeli, Druzya, Uchitelya*, Izdatelstvo Yuridich-eskogo Instituta, St. Petersburg, 2004, p. 9; Tuominen, Arvo, *Vladimir Putin: Koko Tarina*,

readme.fi, Helsinki, 2019, p. 75. Tuominen writes that Putin's eldest brother, who died in 1936, was named Oleg rather than Albert. Putin's father was born in what was then still St Petersburg on February 23, 1911, his mother near Pominovo on October 17 the same year (Blotsky, Vol. 1, p. 24). For Vladimir Spiridonovich's service with the Baltic Fleet from 1933 to 1934, see *Nagradnoi list*, June 22, 1945, at podvignaroda.ru/filter/filterimage?path=VS/188/033-0686196-4369%2b040-4378/00000454.jpg&id=26750331&id1=87476b083ad2293651c13 2549300220f. In 2014, after the annexation of Crimea, Putin, who rarely let the facts get in the way of a good story which might bring him political advantage, told a meeting that his father had served in the submarine fleet at Sevastopol from 1938 to 1939 and 'carried the photographs from that period throughout his entire life' ('Meeting with the Russian Popular Front', April 10, 2014, www.kremlin.ru/events/president/transcripts/20753). That was pure invention. In 2011, a St Petersburg memorial group found a record of an infant named Viktor Vladimirovich Putin, the only child with that family name and patronymic, who had been born in 1940, had died in 1942 and been buried at Piskaryovskoe cemetery (*New York Times*, Jan. 27, 2012). Several sources, including Blotsky, state that Viktor was five years old when he died, but that is clearly incorrect (Vol. 1, pp. 84 & 97, and Hutchins, Chris, *Putin*, Matador Books, Leicester, 2012, p. 16). See also Stone, Oliver, *The Putin Interviews*, Skyhorse Publishing, New York, 2017, p. 6.

11.   Gurevich, ibid. The historian, Lev Lurye, wrote in *Kommersant* (Oct. 1, 2012) that she initially stayed with her brother at his apartment on Radishchev Street, not far from Baskov Lane.

12.   Rationing was introduced throughout the Soviet Union on July 18, 1941. In Leningrad, six weeks later, the ration for dependants and children was cut to 300 grams of bread a day and was further reduced during the course of the winter (Bidlack, Richard, and Lomagin, Nikolai, *The Leningrad Blockade, 1941–1944*, Yale University Press, New Haven and London, 2012, p. xxvii).

13.   Putin, *First Person*, pp. 5–6.

14.   Ibid., p. 5. On another occasion, Putin said that he believed that Viktor had been placed in the orphanage to await evacuation by the ice road across Lake Ladoga (*Pionerskaya pravda*, April 30, 2015). However, children as young as Viktor were not accepted for evacuation unless accompanied by their mothers.

15.   Gurevich, *Putin*, p. 10.

16.   In December 1941, there were 17 orphanages in the city. Between January and May 1942, 85 more were opened, but that was still only enough to accommodate half those who needed places (Bidlack and Lomagin, *The Leningrad Blockade*, pp. 274–5). In late June and July 1941, an evacuation drive was started and parents were encouraged to send their children out of the city to safety in the interior of Russia. 395,000 children left, including 100,000 of pre-school age. But the effort was botched: convoys were sent directly towards the German lines, evacuation trains were strafed by German fighters and epidemics of cholera and typhoid broke out among the evacuees. By the end of August, 175,000 children had been brought back to Leningrad. Many starved to death the following winter (ibid., pp. 42 & 285; and Reid, *Leningrad*, p. 98).

17.   Reid, pp. 262–3 & 364–5.

18.   Albats, Yevgenia, *The State within a State*, Farrar, Straus, Giroux, New York, 1994, p. 104.

19.   *New York Times*, Jan. 27, 2012.

20.   There may be a faint echo of this in a remark which Putin made to Oliver Stone in an interview on July 2, 2015, when he explained that his mother had stayed at home with him

when he was small because she 'didn't want to give me up to an orphanage' (Stone, *The Putin Interviews*, p. 5). He presumably meant that she didn't want 'to let me go to a kindergarten', but it was an interesting Freudian slip.

21. Blotsky, Vol. 1, pp. 276–7.
22. On the scarcity of places, see Kelly, *Children's World*, p. 405.
23. Ibid., pp. 344–5 & 348–9. Thirty years later, the poor reputation of Soviet kindergartens still deterred many mothers from using them (Atwood, Lynne, 'Gender and Soviet Pedagogy', in Avis, George [ed.], *The Making of the Soviet Citizen*, Croom Helm, London, 1987, p. 130).
24. Blotsky, Vol. 1, pp. 42 & 49; Gurevich, *Putin*, p. 20; Putin, *First Person*, p. 3; Stone, *The Putin Interviews*, p. 7.
25. Bronfenbrenner, Urie, *Two Worlds of Childhood*, Penguin, Harmondsworth, 1974, pp. 22–3.
26. Blotsky, *supra*, p. 49 and Putin, *First Person*, p. 15.
27. A Harris poll published on March 24, 2010 found that 25 per cent of Americans did not believe that Barack Obama had been born in the USA; a CNN poll on April 4 the same year found that 27 per cent had doubts or were certain that he had been born abroad.
28. Donald Trump, the most prominent promoter of the 'birther' claims, refused to concede until September 2016, when the presidential campaign was already in full swing, that Obama was US-born. Joe Arpaio, a disgraced sheriff from Arizona and darling of the Republican right, continued even after that to maintain that Obama's birth certificate was a forgery. Newt Gingrich, Sarah Palin and Michele Bachmann expressed doubts in 2009 about Obama's birth and never issued a retraction.
29. These claims are detailed in Ibragimov, Vakha, *Tainaya biografiya Presidenta Rossii*, Vagrius, Moscow, 2000; Felshtinsky, Yuri, and Pribylovsky, Vladimir, *The Corporation*, Encounter Books, New York, 2008, pp. 29–38; and Kurczab-Redlich, Krystyna, *Wowa, Wołodia, Władimir*, Wydawnicza W.A.B, Warsaw, 2016, pp. 13–36.
30. The story derived added credibility from the fact that Putin's mother was almost 41 years old when he was born. In Russia, as in the West, this was unusual at that time. But it was less exceptional than was later made out, especially among peasant families – and the Putins were of peasant stock. Volodya's grandmother had given birth to a daughter, his father's sister, when she was past 40, and three generations earlier his great-great-great-grandmother bore her youngest child at the age of 41 (Gurevich, *Putin*, p. 7).
31. The quote about Obama is from Donald Trump, speaking on *Good Morning America* (cited in *Politico*, March 17, 2011). In Putin's case, it later emerged that some of his neighbours did in fact remember him as a small child. Moreover, the Volodya Putin in Leningrad had no Georgian accent. According to a teacher at the village school in Georgia where Vera Nikolayevna's son studied, he was fluent in Georgian but spoke Russian badly.
32. The charge that Obama was foreign born was first raised during his 2004 Senate campaign. It resurfaced in March 2008, when it became clear that he was likely to become the Democratic presidential candidate. The rumours about Putin started circulating in 1999, shortly after he became Prime Minister. Within days of Yeltsin's resignation, a Chechen delegation went to Georgia to meet Vera Nikolayevna, then already an elderly lady, and convinced her that Russia's new acting President was indeed her son. To forestall embarrassing questions, they confiscated all the photographs of the boy that they could find on the excuse of taking them into safe-keeping. It was a wise precaution, for the one photograph she managed to hold on to showed a small boy who bore little resemblance to the Volodya Putin in Leningrad.
33. Felshtinsky's co-author Vladimir Pribylovsky acknowledged later, rather shamefacedly,

that the story of Putin's adoption was 'apocryphal' (Pribylovsky, *Pereklichka Vladimira Putina*, Algoritm, Moscow, 2013, p. 4).

34.   See, for example, *Die Zeit*, May 7, 2015, and *Daily Telegraph*, Dec. 5, 2008. Among those who refuse to rule out the possibility of Putin having been adopted are Andrei Illarionov, his former economic adviser, and Eerik-Niiles Kross, a former head of Estonian intelligence (Illarionov, author's interview, Washington, D.C., March 13, 2019; Kross, author's interview, Tallinn, May 22, 2017).

35.   *Arkhtekturnyi sait Sankt-Peterburga* at www.citywalls.ru/house6155.html?s=9qlm5fbtlsgoqo oq9licm1e907

36.   Blotsky, Vol. 1, p. 50; Gurevich, *Putin*, p. 21; Grant, Nigel, *Soviet Education*, Penguin, Baltimore, 1964, p. 85; Kelly, *Children's World*, pp. 511 & 514; Bronfenbrenner, p. 23.

37.   The following is drawn from the first grade reading primer, *Rodnaya rech*, by E. E. Solovyova, L. A. Karpinskaya and N. N. Shchepetova (Gosudarstvennoe Uchebno-Pedagogicheskoe Izdatelstvo, Moscow 1957), esp. pp. 4, 48–62 & 105–8. See also Kelly, *Children's World*, pp. 530–31.

38.   Blotsky, Vol. 1, p. 55.

39.   Aleksandr Belyaev, author's interview, St Petersburg, June 3, 2019. He was a year younger than Putin.

40.   Lev Lurye, author's interview, St Petersburg, May 27, 2019. See also *Kommersant*, Oct. 1, 2012.

41.   Putin, *First Person*, p. 17.

42.   Vera Gurevich, interview for Jean-Michel Carré, 2006. Viktor Borisenko also remembered that during breaks he 'ran around constantly to and fro . . . in the school corridors. He wore the stairs smooth' (cited in Blotsky, Vol. 1, p. 67).

43.   Gurevich, Vera Dmitrievna, *Vospominaniya o budushchem prezidente*, Izdatelstvo Mezhdunarodniye Otnosheniye, Moscow, 2001, p. 8, and interview, *supra*.

44.   Gorokhova, Elena, *A Mountain of Crumbs*, Simon and Schuster, New York, 2010, p. 31, and Zajda, Joseph I., *Education in the USSR*, Pergamon Press, New York, 1980, pp. 63 & 65.

45.   Bronfenbrenner, pp. 10–14.

46.   Cited in Blotsky, Vol. 1, p. 59.

47.   Grant, *Soviet Education*, pp. 48–9.

48.   Putin, *First Person*, p. 18. See also Blotsky, *supra*, p. 110, and Grant, p. 44. In the Russian school system, the pre-revolutionary system of marking had been reintroduced by Stalin and still remains in force. '1' (almost never given), was for work that was considered awful; '2', bad; '3', tolerable, but disappointing; '4', good; and '5', excellent.

49.   The only time Putin mentioned being beaten was when he and some friends played truant and took a train ride out of the city (*First Person*, p. 16). See also Blotsky, Vol. 1, p. 90, and *Moskovsky komsomolets*, Oct. 7, 2010.

50.   Putin, *First Person*, p. 18.

51.   Gurevich, *Putin*, p. 8; and Borisenko, interview for Jean-Michel Carré.

52.   Blotsky, *supra*, p. 106.

53.   Kelly, *Children's World*, p. 517; Grant, *Soviet Education*, p. 57; Zajda, *Education in the USSR*, p. 81.

54.   Putin, *First Person*, p. 17.

55.   Putin never mentioned having been an *Oktyabryonok* but membership was automatic unless the parents objected, which almost never happened.

56.   Zajda, *Education in the USSR*, pp. 148 & 153; Bronfenbrenner, *Two Worlds of Childhood*, pp. 36–7.

57.   Zajda, p. 154, and Blotsky, Vol. 1, p. 16.

58. Travin, Dmitry, *Prosushchestvuyet li putinskaya sistema do 2042?*, Norma Press, St Petersburg, 2016, pp. 65–6; Blotsky, Vol. 1, p 105.

59. Putin, *First Person*, p. 18.

60. Yevgeny Vyshenkov, author's interview, St Petersburg, June 1, 2019. Vyshenkov, who joined a street gang and later served a prison term for extortion before becoming a highly regarded journalist for Fontanka.ru, argues that Putin was never 'a real hooligan', though he could have become one had his life worked out differently.

61. Travin, *supra*, p. 66.

62. Putin, *First Person*, pp. 15–16; Gurevich, interview for Jean-Michel Carré.

63. Quoted in Blotsky, Vol. 1, pp. 68–9.

64. Both Borisenko (cited in ibid., p. 67) and Gurevich (interview, *supra*) recalled his 'overflowing energy'. Gurevich remembered that he was 'always eating': patisseries, milk, scrambled eggs two or three times a day and sweetmeats such as nougat.

65. Travin, p. 64.

66. Cited in Blotsky, *supra*, p. 67.

67. Ibid., pp. 72, 108–9 & 163; Putin, *First Person*, pp. 16–17.

68. Blotsky, Vol. 1, p. 71, and Zajda, *Education in the USSR*, pp. 90–91. The special schools were for delinquents aged between 11 and 18: it appears that this episode occurred when Putin was in Grade 4.

69. There were 116,000 US war deaths in the First World War, 405,000 in the Second World War, 54,000 in the Korean War, 58,000 in Vietnam, 2,400 in Afghanistan and 4,500 in Iraq. If other, smaller-scale foreign conflicts are included, the total is 662,000.

70. Kalugin, Oleg, *Spymaster*, Basic Books, New York, 2009, pp. 3–4.

71. 'They didn't talk about it to their kids. There are experiences like that . . . which people don't want to remember' (Lev Lurye, author's interview, St Petersburg, May 27, 2019).

72. Reid, *Leningrad*, p. 409.

73. Bidlack and Lomagin, *The Leningrad Blockade*, pp. 333–4.

74. There is uncertainty over exactly what Putin's father was doing before the Germans invaded. He was probably working in a factory in Peterhof, since, according to his war record, that is where he enlisted (*Nagradnoi list, supra*).

75. Bidlack and Lomagin, pp 42 & 116; Reid, *Leningrad*, pp. 39-40.

76. The fullest account of the NKVD's role in recruiting and organising the partisan detachments is given in Kutuzov, V. A., and Stepanov, O. N., 'Organy gosbezopasnosti na zashchite Leningrada', in *Narod i voina: 50 let velikoi pobedy*, Petropolis, St Petersburg, 1995, esp. p. 226, which states that 6,344 men were sent behind enemy lines from Leningrad between August and October 1941. Bidlack and Lomagin, relying on different documents in the KGB archives, put the figure at 8,613, including seven large units and 66 small detachments of around 30 men each (*The Leningrad Blockade*, p. 187). Blotsky, who provides no source, writes of 300 detachments of 35 to 50 men each (Vol. 1, p. 79). See also Kokurin, A. I., and Petrov, N. V., *Lubyanka: Organy VChK–OGPU–NKVD–NKGB–MGB–MVD–KGB, 1917–1991*, Mezhdunarodny fond 'Demokratiya', Moscow, 2003, pp. 32–3.

77. The following draws on Blotsky, Vol. 1, p. 80–81; Putin, *First Person*, p. 6; and author's interview with the Estonian military historian, Toomas Hiio, Tallinn, May 22, 2017.

78. Some Russian researchers, notably Sergei Gulyaev, a deputy in the St Petersburg Duma, claim that the wartime exploits of Putin's father are 'fairytales' (author's interview, St Petersburg, May 28, 2019). It is true that the only source for his participation in the partisan detachment is Putin himself. However, his account matches everything that is known from

Russian and Estonian sources about partisan actions on the North-Eastern Front in the first months of the war and there is no reason to disbelieve it. Sputnik News reported, without citing a source, that Putin's father's unit was 'Guerrilla Detachment No. 80' (sput niknews.com/onlinenews/2004012739906137). That no original documentary evidence of his unit has been found is unsurprising. In the weeks immediately after the invasion, the first partisan detachments were improvised on the fly.

79. Vladimir Spiridonovich's war record (*Nagradnoi list*, June 22, 1945, *supra*) states that he was assigned to the 330th Rifle Regiment, part of the 86th Infantry Division, which began arriving at the Nevsky Patch on October 20, 1941. Blotsky (Vol. 1, p. 82) says Putin's father was with the NKVD 20th Division, which was mobilised to cross to the bridgehead six days later, 'having been replenished with personnel from partisan . . . detachments'. The two units fought alongside each other from the end of October, and there were cases of men being transferred on the battlefield from one regiment to another as individual units were decimated (see, for instance, Mikhail Andreevich Pavlov's article in 'Ya pomnyu: vospominaniya veteranov VOV', at iremember.ru/memoirs/pekhotintsi/pavlov-mikhail-andreevich/). It would be logical that, having served in a partisan detachment, Putin's father should have been assigned to the 20th Division. The official record on this point may well be incorrect.

80. The Russian word *pyatachok* can mean a small coin, a pig's nose or a 'pocket', in the sense of a small area of land. There are many accounts of the fighting in the 'Neva Patch'. I have relied principally on Volkovsky, N. L., *Blokada Leningrada v dokumentakh rassekrechennykh arkhivov*, Izdatelstvo Poligon, St Petersburg, 2005, and Lebedev, Yu. M., *Po obe storony blokadnogo koltsa*, Izdatelskii Dom 'Neva', St Petersburg, 2005.

81. Buff, Wolfgang, *Vor Leningrad: Kriegstagebuch Ost, 29 September 1941–1 September 1942*, Volksbund Deutsche Kriegsgräberfürsorge, Kassel, 2000.

82. This account is drawn from Blotsky, Vol. 1, pp. 82–4, and Putin, *First Person*, pp. 7–8.

83. According to his war record, Vladimir Spiridonovich had 'serious injuries' to the lower part of his left leg and foot. For his conduct that day, he was awarded the Medal of Military Merit. At the end of the war, he was also awarded the Medal for the Defence of Leningrad (*Nagradnoi list*, *supra*).

84. Reid, *Leningrad*, p. 89.

85. He was formally discharged in April 1942 (*Nagradnoi list*, *supra*).

86. See Gurevich, *Putin*, pp. 10–11; *Pionerskaya pravda*, April 30, 2015.

87. In *First Person* (p. 6), Putin wrote that his mother fainted from hunger and was about to be taken off for burial, when it was realised that she was still alive. In the version he recounted to Clinton, he claimed that his father had returned to Leningrad on leave from the front and, recognising her in a pile of bodies on the pavement near their apartment, was able to save her (Clinton, Hillary, *Hard Choices*, Simon and Schuster, New York, 2015, pp. 214–15). In yet another version, he said his father found her when he came home from the hospital where he was being treated for his wounds (*Pionerskaya pravda*, *supra*).

88. Dr James Platt, author's interview, Hanover, NH, Feb. 19, 2019. Such discrepancies led the historian, Ben McIntyre, writing in the London *Times* (June 13, 2014), to argue that nothing in Putin's accounts of his parents' actions during the war should be taken at face value. That is a misreading. A survey of more than 3,000 people after the September 11, 2001, attacks in the United States found that, three years later, almost 50 per cent of the details they claimed to remember had changed since they were originally interviewed (*Scientific American*, Sept. 6, 2011).

89. Kelly, *Children's World*, p. 493.

90. A sober description of the extent of cannibalism in Leningrad during the blockade may be found in Reid, *Leningrad*, pp. 286–7, 318, 444 n. 27 & 445 n. 39. Harrison Salisbury's pioneering work, *The 900 Days* (Harper and Row, New York, 1969) published long before the Soviet archives were opened, is a good deal less accurate.

91. Kelly, *Children's World*, p. 4.

92. Reid, p. 287, and Bidlack and Lomagin, *The Leningrad Blockade*, p. 53.

93. Gurevich, *Putin*, p. 13; *Pionerskaya pravda*, April 30, 2015. Blotsky writes that Vladimir Spiridonovich joined the Yegorov plant, which had been converted to making shells and mines, and repairing tanks, in 1942, immediately after he was discharged from the military hospital (Vol. 1, pp. 96 & 99–100), but that appears to be incorrect.

94. Blotsky, Vol. 1, pp. 39 & 49.

95. Gorokhova, *Mountain of Crumbs*, p. 25.

96. Cherkashin, Victor, *Spy Handler*, Basic Books, New York, 2005, pp. 41–3.

97. J. V. Stalin, *Speech to the 19th Congress of the CPSU*, October 14, 1952 (www.marxists.org/reference/archive/stalin/works/1952/10/14.htm).

98. Bidlack and Lomagin, *The Leningrad Blockade*, pp. 67–76.

99. The British Ambassador, William Hayter, cited in Taubman, William, *Khrushchev: The Man and his Era*, W. W. Norton, New York, 2003, pp. 334–5.

100. The following description is taken from Gurevich, *Putin*, p. 15 and *Vospominaniya*, pp. 13–16; Putin, *First Person*, pp. 10–11; Blotsky, Vol. 1, pp. 88–9; Borisenko, interview for Jean-Michel Carré; and *Moscow Times*, Nov 18, 2004. See also Boym, Svetlana, *Common Places: Mythologies of Everyday Life in Russia*, Harvard University Press, Cambridge, Mass., 1994, pp. 140–41 & 145.

101. Privacy was disdained in Russia even in pre-revolutionary times. Nineteenth-century Russian travellers remarked condescendingly on the excessive individualism of life in western Europe, where people were isolated from each other. The nearest Russian expression, *chastnaya zhizn*, means literally 'particular (or partial) life', implying that no one can live fully unless integrated within a community. See Boym, pp. 3, 73–6 & 78–80 and Gorokhova, *Mountain of Crumbs*, pp. 90–92.

102. 'Interview with ABC', Nov. 7, 2001, www.kremlin.ru/events/president/transcripts/21392

103. The phrase is Svetlana Boym's. It sums up perfectly the problems of communal living (*Common Places*, p. 141).

104. Ibid. and Stone, *The Putin Interviews*, p. 24 (translation amended).

105. Cited in Seipel, Hubert, *Poutine: Une Vision du Pouvoir*, Edition des Syrtes, Geneva, 2016, pp. 120–21.

106. Gurevich, *Putin*, p. 16.

107. Boym, *Common Places*, pp. 121 & 123.

108. Putin, *First Person*, p. 11.

109. In 1970, 40 per cent of Leningraders were still housed in communal flats, including most of the population in the central districts of the city. In a hostel, a married couple was supposed to be allotted half a room, shared with another family. But a couple with a child might find that the only space available was 30 or 40 square feet (3 or 4 sq. metres) in a dormitory, screened off by a cupboard. That year, a further 5 per cent of the city's population lived in hostels or barracks (Kelly, Catriona, *St Petersburg: Shadows of the Past*, Yale University Press, New Haven and London, 2014, pp. 65–7 & 70).

110. Boym, *Common Places*, pp. 123 & 146–7.

111. Blotsky, Vol. 1, pp. 277–80.

112. 'On the Cult of Personality and its Consequences', February 25, 1956, digitalarchive. wilsoncenter.org/document/115995

113. Taubman, *Khrushchev*, p. 272.

114. Ibid., pp. 310–24.

115. Zemskov, Viktor Nikolayevich, *Gulag*, Khronos, 2001, available at www.hrono.ru/statii/2001/zemskov.php

116. Maya Turovskaya, cited in Taubman, p. 306.

117. Vaksberg, Arkady, *The Soviet Mafia*, Weidenfeld and Nicolson, London, 1991, p. 80.

118. The story is related by Putin's childhood friend, Sergei Bogdanov (*Moskovsky komsomolets*, Oct. 7, 2010).

119. Putin himself confirmed that the family had not been 'dekulakised' in the 1930s (Blotsky, Vol. 1, p. 49).

120. Kelly, *Children's World*, pp. 142 & 153.

121. Gurevich, *Putin*, p. 24.

122. Borisenko, whose father had been captured and had learned German in a PoW camp, was also intrigued by the Germans (ibid.)

123. *Kommersant*, Oct 1, 2012.

124. Gurevich, *Vospominaniya*, p. 9.

125. *New York Times*, July 19, 2008. The word 'sambo' is an acronym for *samozashchita bez oruzhiya*, literally 'unarmed self-defence'.

126. Putin, *First Person*, p. 19; Blotsky, Vol. 1, p. 133.

127. Unless otherwise indicated, the following account is drawn from Blotsky, Vol. 1, pp. 125–9 & 139–43.

128. Ibid, p. 68.

129. Ibid., pp. 133–4.

130. Rakhlin's patronymic was Solomonovich but he adopted the non-Jewish Semyonovich instead, supposedly on the grounds that it was easier to pronounce (ibid., p. 122).

131. Ibid., p. 134.

132. Ibid., pp. 75, 134 & 159–60.

133. Ibid., pp. 134–5.

134. Putin, *First Person*, p. 19. Years later, in a judo handbook, he and his co-authors wrote: 'Overcoming on the tatami our weaknesses and insufficiencies, we come to know ourselves, we change ourselves for the better and we change for the better the world around us' (Putin, Vladimir, Shestakov, Vasily and Levitsky, Aleksei, *Uchimsya dzyudo s Vladimirom Putinym*, Olma Press, Moscow, 2002, p. 5).

135. Cited in Blotsky, Vol. 1, pp. 141–2.

136. Putin, Shestakov and Levitsky, *supra*, p. 17.

137. Putin, *First Person*, p. 19.

138. Blotsky, Vol. 1, p. 71.

139. Kelly, *Children's World*, pp. 434–5.

140. Vasil'eva, Evelina Karlovna, *The Young People of Leningrad*, International Arts and Sciences Press, White Plains, N.Y., 1976, pp. xv–xvi & 44. In 1968, 61 per cent of secondary school students entered 9th grade; by 1974, the proportion had fallen to 45 per cent.

141. Kelly, *Children's World*, pp. 568–9.

142. Gurevich, *Vospominaniya*, pp. 28–9; Gorokhova, *Mountain of Crumbs*, pp. 174–5.

143. Putin, *First Person*, p. 18.

144. Gorokhova, *supra*, p. 60.

145. Gurevich, *Putin*, pp. 43–4.

146. Grant, *Soviet Education*, p. 65.

147. Kelly, *Children's World*, p. 560.

148. Kelly, Catriona, *Comrade Pavlik: The Rise and Fall of a Soviet Boy Hero*, Granta, London, 2005, p. 207. For the account which follows, see esp. pp. xxiii–xxv, 146–7 & 212.

149. Gorokhova, *supra*, p. 58.

150. There is no contemporary account of how Putin reacted, but the importance he attached to loyalty, which dated from his schooldays, makes it unlikely that he would have had any sympathy with the way Morozov behaved.

151. As Gorokhova put it: 'You pretend . . . just as in nursery school we pretended to chew the bread with rancid butter' (ibid.).

152. Usoltsev, Vladimir, *Sosluzhivets*, Eksmo, Moscow, 2004, p. 186.

153. See Bronfenbrenner, *Two Worlds of Childhood*, pp. 36, 49–51, 55 & 58–65; Grant, *Soviet Education*, pp. 27, 58–61 & 69; and Zajda, *Education in the USSR*, pp. 157–8 & 161–3.

154. Blotsky, Vol. 1, pp. 67–8 & 74–5.

155. Ibid., p. 55.

156. Gurevich, *Putin*, pp. 32–6, 41, 55–9 & 70–73.

157. Ibid., pp. 26 & 162.

158. Blotsky, Vol. 1, p. 128.

159. Gurevich, *Putin*, pp. 64–5.

160. Ibid., p. 87.

161. This and the following are drawn from Gurevich, *Vospominaniya*, pp. 30–31.

162. Grant, *Soviet Education*, p. 68.

163. Ibid., p. 29.

164. Blotsky, Vol. 1, p. 112.

165. Ibid., p. 91.

166. Ibid., pp. 61 & 70.

167. Kelly, *Children's World*, pp. 667–8 n. 82.

168. Blotsky, Vol. 1, p. 113.

169. Ibid., p. 46.

170. The earliest known photograph of Putin wearing a watch on his right wrist dates from the summer of 1979, when he was 26.

171. Blotsky, Vol. 1, p. 140.

172. Ibid., p. 110. Borisenko and Putin were close from 1961 until about 1980, when their paths diverged. He added that Putin 'made himself what he became'. Rakhlin used a very similar phrase. 'He made himself, not only as a sportsman but as a person' (ibid., p. 144).

173. Ibid., p. 142. He added: 'This restraint had been his since he was a child.'

174. Ibid., p. 76.

175. Ibid., p. 215; Putin, *First Person*, p. 23.

176. Blotsky, Vol. 1, p. 70.

177. Putin, *First Person*, pp. 17–18 (translation amended to conform to the Russian text).

178. Viktor Borisenko remembered one occasion when, as he was leaving the Putins' dacha, he saw Vladimir Spiridonovich waving goodbye with tears running down his cheeks (ibid., p. 210).

179. Blotsky, Vol. 1, p. 215.

180. Ibid., p. 151.

181. Ibid., p. 288.

182. Ibid., p. 76.

183. Ibid., p. 147; Borisenko, interview for Jean-Michel Carré.

184. Gurevich, *Putin*, pp. 68 & 74; Blotsky, Vol. 1, pp. 151–2 & 206. One of the essay subjects Demenkov set them was, 'What do telegraph poles think when they remember that they were trees?'

185. *Nezavisimaya gazeta*, March 28, 2000.

186. Gurevich, *supra*, pp. 66–7; Blotsky, Vol. 1, p. 147.

187. Blotsky, Vol. 1, p. 176, see also p. 62.

188. 'Meeting with Finalists of the Student Essay Competition', June 5, 2003, www.kremlin.ru/events/president/transcripts/22021

189. Blotsky, Vol. 1, p. 152; Gurevich, *supra*, p. 75.

190. Gurevich, ibid., pp. 36 & 70–72. See also Yurchak, Alexei, *Everything was Forever, Until it was No More*, Princeton University Press, Princeton, 2005, pp. 123–4.

191. *Nezavisimaya gazeta*, March 28, 2000; Blotsky, Vol. 1, pp. 150–51, 155 & 207.

192. Blotsky, Vol. 1, pp. 144 & 161.

193. *Pravda*, March 30, 1966.

194. Marcus Wheeler, 'Political Aspects of the 23rd Congress of the CPSU', *The World Today* (RIIA), Vol. 22, No. 7, July 1966, p. 307; Ernest Germain, 'The 23rd Congress of the CPSU', *International Socialist Review*, Vol. 27, No 4, Fall 1966, p. 145; and Roy Medvedev, quoted in Bacon, Edwin, and Sandle, Mark [eds], *Brezhnev Reconsidered*, Palgrave Macmillan, Basingstoke, 2002, p. 26.

195. Grant, *Soviet Education*, pp. 53 & 55, and Avis, *The Making of the Soviet Citizen*, p. 1.

196. Andrew, Christopher and Mitrokhin, Vasily, *The Mitrokhin Archive: The KGB in Europe and the West*, Allen Lane, the Penguin Press, London, 1999, pp. 405–38.

197. Kalugin, *Spymaster*, pp. 293 & 298.

198. Bobkov, Filipp, *Poslednie dvadtsat let*, Russkoe Slovo, Moscow, 2006, p. 66.

199. Fedor, Julie, *Russia and the Cult of State Security*, Routledge, London, 2011, p. 49.

200. Ibid., pp. 59, 87, 104, 114–15; Ben McIntyre in *The Times*, Feb. 20, 2020.

201. Fedor, p. 56; Kalugin, *supra*, p. 298.

202. Hill, Fiona and Gaddy, Clifford G., *Mr. Putin: Operative in the Kremlin*, Brookings Institution Press, Washington, D.C., 2015, pp. 109–10 & 172.

203. Gurevich, *Putin*, pp. 78–9; Putin, *First Person*, p. 22.

204. Ibid. (translation amended). Putin called it the 'Academy of Civil Aviation', but it did not acquire that name until later.

205. Ibid., p 23; Blotsky, Vol. 1, pp. 169–74. Putin remembered visiting the Big House at the start of 9th grade. According to Vera Gurevich, he told his family in the middle of 10th grade (*Putin*, pp. 78–9).

206. Blotsky, Vol. 1, pp. 210–11.

207. According to *Kommersant*, Oct. 1, 2012, in 1970 only 10 students were admitted to the Leningrad University Law Faculty direct from high school. The other 90 had already completed their military service.

208. Putin, *First Person*, p. 22.

209. Ibid., pp. 22–4; Gurevich, *Putin*, pp. 78–9; Blotsky, Vol. 1, pp. 201–2.

210. Putin, *First Person*, p. 23. On Usvyatsov's career, see 'Soratniki po borbe', Dec. 21, 2015, at putinism.wordpress.com/2015/12/21/soratniki. The article is unsigned, but the author is clearly well informed about the world of *sambo* in Leningrad and its criminal ramifications from the 1960s onward. See also antimonstrs.livejournal.com/80016.html

211. Blotsky, *supra*, p. 218.

212. Putin, *First Person*, p. 23. He wrote: 'My father had a commanding personality, but I dug in my heels and said I had made up my mind.' His parents' opposition to his joining the *sambo* club had been different because Rakhlin had interceded on his behalf before his father forbade it. This time there was no mediator.

213. Blotsky, Vol. 1, pp. 79–80. Shestakov dates the conversation to May or June 1970, but it was probably earlier.

214. Putin, *First Person*, p. 23.

215. Blotsky, Vol. 1, p. 218.

216. Gurevich, *Putin*, p. 78. She dated his decision to the middle of 10th grade, but wrongly assumed that he had visited the Big House only a short time before.

217. Quoted in Blotsky, *supra*, p. 202.

218. Ibid., p. 61.

219. Ibid., pp. 155–6.

220. According to Blotsky, in the entrance exam he got '4' for his composition – the set topic being Lenin, whose centenary was celebrated that year – and '5's in all the other subjects (ibid., pp. 221–2).

221. Putin, *First Person*, p. 24.

222. Lev Lurye cites other examples of students being admitted to Leningrad State University on the basis of sporting achievements (author's interview, May 27, 2019).

223. 'Soratniki po borbe', *supra*.

224. Ibid. and Putin, *First Person*, p. 24; see also Blotsky, Vol. 1, p. 225. If sport had not been a factor in his admission, it is difficult to see why the University's Sports Department should, in Rakhlin's words, have tried to 'force him' to join *Burevestnik* or why Bobrov should have claimed to have 'helped [him], as an athlete, to get into the university'.

225. Gurevich, *Putin*, p. 80. See also Putin, pp. 24–5; Blotsky, *supra*, p. 225.

2: *Legal Niceties*

1. The Law Faculty shared the building, at 3 ulitsa Smolnogo, with two other faculties – Geography and Philosophy (Igor Chubais, author's interview, Nov. 28, 2019; and Lempert, David H., *Daily Life in a Crumbling Empire*, East European Monographs, Boulder, 1996, Vol. 1, p. 543).

2. Blotsky, Vol. 1, p. 216.

3. Lempert, *supra*, p. 358. Before 1968, students were not admitted to the Law Faculty unless they had completed their military service.

4. The following is taken from Anatoly Rakhlin's recollections in *Zhizn*, April 4, 2001, and from the biographies of Bastrykin, Khmarin, Ragimov and Yegorov, published by Vladimir Pribylovsky on anticompromat.panchul.com. Each year's intake of freshmen was divided into four groups. Bastrykin and Ragimov were each, at different times, the *starosta*, or 'elder', heading Putin's group.

5. Lev Lurye, writing in *Kommersant*, Oct. 1, 2012.

6. Blotsky, *supra*, p. 223.

7. Ibid., p. 254.

8. As he wrote later: 'For better or for worse, I was never a dissident' (Putin, *First Person*, p. 49).

9. Blotsky, *supra*, p. 209.

10. Ibid., p. 237, and Putin, *First Person*, pp. 34–5.

11. Blotsky, *supra*, pp. 209–10 & 305 and *Vladimir Putin: Doroga k vlasti*, Osmos Press, Moscow [hereafter Blotsky, Vol. 2], p. 129; Yurchak, *Everything was Forever*, pp. 181–7.

12. 'Soratniki po borbe', Dec. 21, 2015, *supra*. See also Tuominen, *Putin*, p. 84.

13. Blotsky, *supra*, pp. 225–7, and Putin, *First Person*, pp. 30 & 36. Putin remembered it as 'a packet of money, probably about 1,000 roubles' (see also 'Live with President Vladimir Putin', Dec. 24, 2001, www.kremlin.ru/events/president/transcripts/21457). On another occasion, he said 'about 800 roubles' ('Interview with Abkhazian media', Aug. 12, 2009, archive.premier.gov.ru/events/news/4722/). Borisenko thought he earned 500 roubles.

14. Blotsky, *supra*, p. 206.

15. Akhmatova's poem is cited in Reid, *Leningrad*, p. 12.

16. Putin, *First Person*, p. 30.

17. Gurevich dates this episode to Putin's first or second year. His own account is contradictory. At one point, he says that it happened later, in the autumn of 1972, at the beginning of his third year. Elsewhere he says that it occurred shortly after he spent the summer working in the Komi Republic, which was in 1971. His mother became seriously ill in 1972 and afterwards stopped working, so it must have been before then. It seems most likely that it took place at the beginning of his second year, in the autumn of 1971 (Gurevich, *Putin*, pp. 81–2; Putin, *First Person*, pp. 30 & 36). There have been allegations that the whole story of the lottery ticket was an invention and that his father was given the car by the KGB for unspecified 'services', but there is no evidence to support that and it appears implausible.

18. Putin, *First Person*, p. 36 (translation amended).

19. Blotsky, *supra*, pp. 229–30.

20. Putin, p. 36 (translation amended).

21. Blotsky, *supra*, pp. 227–8.

22. Putin, *First Person*, pp. 206–7.

23. Ibid., p. 36; Blotsky, *supra*, p. 229.

24. Putin, *First Person*, p. 32.

25. Judo had been introduced into Russia early in the 20th century by Vasily Oshchepkov. During Stalin's Great Terror in 1937, he was declared an 'enemy of the people' and shot, after which *sambo* became the only officially tolerated martial art.

26. Blotsky, Vol. 1, p. 240. In 1969, Rakhlin moved to the Leningrad Metal Works (LMZ), where his new club was called *Turbostroitel*. Putin and the others followed him there, but continued to refer to themselves as members of *Trud*.

27. Ibid., pp. 241, 302 & 308.

28. Ibid., pp. 222 & 245–7; Putin, *First Person*, pp. 33–4.

29. Gurevich, *Putin*, pp. 137–40.

30. Ibid., pp. 96–7.

31. Blotsky, *supra*, p. 307.

32. Ibid., pp. 299–301.

33. Kano, Jigoro, *Mind over Muscle: Writings from the Founder of Judo*, Kodansha, Tokyo, 2005, pp. 39–40.

34. Putin, *First Person*, p. 19.

35. Blotsky, *supra*, p. 302.

36. Putin, *First Person*, p. 20.

37. Ibid., p. 35. Putin names the protagonist only as 'Kolya', but an annotation by Vashchilin, published at www.chitalnya.ru/work/1739267/ confirms the story and makes clear that he is the person concerned.

38. Blotsky, *supra*, p. 161.

39. Ibid., p. 253.

40. Putin, *First Person*, p. 16.

41. Gurevich, *Putin*, p. 72. If, as seems likely, the 'trial' was Putin's idea, the anecdote is doubly revealing as he was then trying to make up his mind whether to apply to the Law Faculty.

42. Except where otherwise indicated, the following account draws on Feldbrugge, F.J.M. [ed.], *The Distinctiveness of Soviet Law*, Martinus Nijhoff, Dordrecht, 1987, pp. 68–9, 199–216, 227 & 231–68.

43. Lempert, *Daily Life in a Crumbling Empire*, p. 756.

44. Cited by Richard Pipes in 'Putins Diktatur des Rechts', *Die Welt*, June 6, 2000.

45. Usoltsev, *Sosluzhivets*, p. 129.

46. Ibid., p. 128.

47. See Ioffe, O. S. and Maggs, P. B., *Soviet Law in Theory and Practice*, Oceana, London, 1983.

48. Kaj Hober, author's interview, Stockholm, Oct. 12, 2017.

49. Lempert, *supra*, p. 722 and Robinson, Logan, *An American in Leningrad*, W. W. Norton, New York, 1982, pp. 45–6.

50. Ibid.

51. Lempert, *supra*, p. 531.

52. Putin's friends remembered him writing essays with Lenin's selected works on his desk (Blotsky, Vol. I, p. 224). Rein Mullerson, later Estonia's first deputy Foreign Minister, had to rewrite his Ph.D. thesis at the Moscow Law Faculty in 1978 because it did not have enough Leninist citations (author's interview, Tallinn, May 25, 2017).

53. Putin, *First Person*, p. 48, and Lempert, *supra*.

54. Robinson, *supra*, pp. 36–8.

55. William Burnham, quoted in Lempert, *supra*, p. 718. The comment dates from 1991, but 20 years earlier the teaching methods would, if anything, have been even more rigid.

56. Lempert, *supra*, pp. 719 & 754.

57. Ibid., p. 755.

58. Robinson, *supra*, pp. 43–5, and Blotsky, Vol. I, p. 253.

59. Sobchak was then teaching in Ioffe's Civil Law Department (Smolyak, Pavel, *Sobchak*, Izdatelskie resheniya, St Petersburg, 2018), p. 18. See also Svanidze, Marina and Nikolai, *Medvedev*, Amfora, St Petersburg, 2008, pp. 135–6, and Lyudmila Narusova, author's interview, Moscow, Nov. 21, 2019. Putin himself mentioned attending lectures, rather than seminars (*First Person*, p. 88).

60. Lempert, *supra*, pp. 535–9.

61. Robinson, *supra*, pp. 23 & 40–41.

62. Except where otherwise indicated, the following section is taken from Blotsky, Vol. I, pp. 263–6 & 284–7; and Putin, *First Person*, pp. 40–44.

63. At least one Jew worked for the KGB: Samuel Meyerovich Kvastel was an information analyst in the First Chief Directorate with the rank of colonel. However, he did not travel abroad (Leonov, Nikolai, *Likholet'e*, Mezhdunarodnye otnosheniya, Moscow, 1994, p. 249). The grandfather of Putin's colleague, Vladimir Agartanov, had been shot in 1942 as an enemy of the people, but that did not prevent him being recruited to the KGB in Krasnoyarsk (Usoltsev, *Sosluzhivets*, pp. 67 & 129; see also the record for his grandfather, Mikhail

Fyodorovich Agartanov, posted by the Russian Association for the Victims of Illegal Political Repression at www.rosagr.natm.ru/card.php?person+573806).

64. Kostromin, Lev Petrovich, *Moya zhizn – razvedka*, DetektivPress, Moscow, 2011, pp. 7–8.

65. Blotsky, Vol. 1, pp. 38 & 42. For Putin's claims that his grandfather cooked for Lenin and Stalin, see *First Person*, p. 3; Stone, *The Putin Interviews*, pp. 7–8; Reuters, March 11, 2018. Vera Gurevich wrote that Putin's father also told her that Spiridon had cooked 'several times' at one of Stalin's dachas (Gurevich, *Vospominaniya*, p. 26). Evidently it was a family legend, not to be taken literally.

66. *New York Times*, May 26, 2017.

67. Blotsky, *supra*, pp. 286–7.

68. Putin, *First Person*, pp. 39–40.

69. The fellow student, who did not wish to be named, told the Swedish Ambassador, Örjan Berner, that she had no doubt that, at the Law Faculty, Putin was working for the KGB (Örjan Berner, author's interview, Stockholm, Feb. 26, 2017).

70. Earley, Pete, *Comrade J*, G. P. Putnam's Sons, New York, 2007, p. 35. Oleg Kalugin made the same point (Voronov, *Sluzhba*, p. 273).

71. Blotsky, Vol. 1, pp. 287–8.

72. Putin, *First Person*, p. 42.

73. See, for instance, Kuzichkin, Vladimir, *Inside the KGB: Myth and Reality*, Andre Deutsch, London, 1990, p. 40.

3: *The Big House*

1. This account is based on a memoir by Pavel Koshelev, who attended the Law Faculty with Putin and joined the KGB a year earlier, on August 1, 1974 (veteran-fsb.ru/biblio/knigi/sledstvie-prodolzhaetsya-kniga-5/nosyrev-daniil-pavlovich).

2. Chebrikov, Viktor, et al. [eds], *Istoriya sovetskikh organov gosudarstvennoi bezopasnosti*, Red Banner Institute, Moscow, 1977, p. 588.

3. The figures are from Oleg Kalugin, who was Nosyrev's deputy in Leningrad in the 1980s (Kalugin, *Spymaster*, pp. 335–6 & 347–8, and author's interview, Rockville, Md., Oct. 30, 2018). The bodyguards were from the KGB's 9th Department, which was responsible for security for senior political figures, including the First Secretary of the Leningrad Regional Party Committee, Grigory Romanov, 'a tiny conceited man with a Napoleon complex', as Kalugin described him, who alone had 100 men assigned to him.

4. Putin, *First Person*, p. 43.

5. Ibid., pp. 47–8. His training lasted five months, from February to June 1976 (Usoltsev, *Sosluzhivets*, p. 267). The school, at 27, Prospekt Energetikov in Leningrad, has since been rebuilt and substantially enlarged.

6. Putin, *First Person*, p. 37; TASS, Feb. 8, 2000; Zajda, Joseph, *Education in the USSR*, pp. 206, 208 & 213; and Weaver, Kitty, *Russia's Future: The Communist Education of Soviet Youth*, Praeger, New York, 1981, pp. 97–8.

7. Blotsky, Vol. 2, pp. 104–5.

8. *Vechernii Leningrad*, May 4, 1976. Angela Stent, in her excellent book, *Putin's World* (Twelve Books, New York, 2019, p. 4) writes that the article predicted that although Putin was 'not well known for the moment among the broad circle of specialists and fans', this would soon change. Puzzlingly, that does not appear in the original article.

9.	Blotsky, Vol. 1, pp. 302 & 308.

10.	Blotsky, Vol. 2, p. 105.

11.	The following is drawn from Mitrokhin, Vasily, *KGB Lexicon: The Soviet Intelligence Officer's Handbook*, Routledge, Abingdon, 2002, esp. pp. 22, 54, 122, 159, 161–2, 180, 194–6, 206–7, 255–8, 260 & 320–21. The book comprises translations of two training manuals, on intelligence and counter-intelligence, issued to KGB higher schools in the 1970s.

12.	Interviewed 15 years later, he remembered the school as 'not too exceptional' (*First Person*, p. 48).

13.	Albats, *The State within a State*, p. 50. An American diplomat, who was allowed, after the collapse of the Soviet Union, to see the dossier which Bulgarian intelligence had compiled on him when he had been based in Sofia, discovered that his apartment had been under observation 24 hours a day. The entries recorded such banalities as his departure for work in the morning, a light being turned on during the night and the sound of a lavatory flushing. An immense investment in manpower had yielded nothing of intelligence value.

14.	*Vlast'*, broadcast by Leningrad TV in February, 1992, and Putin, *First Person*, pp. 52–3.

15.	Blotsky, Vol. 2, pp. 117–18.

16.	Putin, *First Person*, p. 48.

17.	www.proza.ru/2016/03/30/1296

18.	Putin, *First Person*, p. 52. The procession can be dated to 1978 because Putin met Roldugin in 1977 and in the spring of 1979 he was not in Leningrad.

19.	*Komsomolskaya pravda*, May 7, 2004.

20.	Usoltsev, *Sosluzhivets*, pp. 184–6.

21.	Putin, *First Person*, p. 50. When asked whether he had taken part himself, he replied 'not especially', a curiously weak denial. See also the account of Yuli Rybakov, who was one of the participants (*Moi vek*, Part 1, DEAN, St Petersburg, 2010, p. 214; and author's interview, St Petersburg, June 3, 2019). Rybakov and another demonstrator, Vyacheslav Dolinin, believe that Putin was present at the police post to which they were taken, but acknowledge that they cannot be sure. The story is hard to believe as Putin did not become a recognisable figure, even in Leningrad, until more than 15 years later. Putin himself said he heard about the incident from other KGB officers, who 'chatted about it openly' in the canteen, but that does not ring true either, for there was a strict rule that officers should not discuss their work with colleagues. In the published *First Person* interviews, it was the only specific incident from his KGB career in Leningrad that he mentioned.

22.	Robinson, *American in Leningrad*, pp. 208–9 & 214.

23.	Pavel Koshelev in veteran-fsb.ru/biblio/knigi/sledstvie-prodolzhaetsya-kniga-5/131-nosyrev-daniil-pavlovich.html (no longer accessible online).

24.	*Zvezda*, No. 8, 1998, pp. 210–13.

25.	See Putin, *First Person*, pp. 47 & 49–50.

26.	Ibid, pp. 41–2.

27.	Viktor Borisenko, interview for Jean-Michel Carré.

28.	Usoltsev, pp. 116–18. This discussion took place in 1986 or 1987. The KGB started opening its archives only in 1989.

29.	Blotsky, Vol. 1, pp. 180–88, and Aleksandr Gurin, *Yan Berzin. Latysh, sozdavshii sovetskuyu razvedku*, Baltnews, Nov. 25, 2019, at www.lv.baltnews.com/Russia_West/20191125/1023521856/Yan-Berzin-Latysh-sozdavshiy-sovetskuyu-razvedku.html

30.	*Istoriya gosudarstvennykh organov bezopasnosti*, published by the Higher Red Banner School of the KGB [Vysshaya Krasnoznamennaya Shkola KGB, imeni F. E. Dzerzhinskogo],

Moscow, 1977. The citations below appear on pp. 228–9, 271–2, 283, 286, 291 & 489. Dr Mark Kramer, of the Davis Center at Harvard University, discovered an almost complete copy in the KGB archives in Riga after Latvian independence. I am grateful to him for making it available to me.

31. Gurevich, *Putin*, pp. 93 & 95, and Putin, *First Person*, p. 61.

32. Blotsky, Vol. 2, pp. 16–17, and Putin, *First Person*, p. 39. The relationship apparently started when Putin was still at the Law Faculty or shortly afterwards.

33. On promotions, see Kuzichkin, *Inside the KGB*, pp. 90–91.

34. *Kharakteristika-Rekomendatsiya*, signed by the secretaries of the KGB Komsomol Committee and the Dzerzhinsky District Committee, exhibited at the Leningrad Communist Party Archives in November 2019. A manuscript note at the top of the document bears the date, October 10 1977. The document states erroneously that Putin joined the Komsomol in 1972. In fact he joined in 1966. Had he not been a Komsomol member, he would not have been able to attend university.

35. Putin, *First Person*, p. 35.

36. Ibid., p. 52.

37. In one version, Putin said that after his training at the 401 School, his superiors decided that he needed more field preparation, so 'I studied in Moscow and then came back to [Leningrad] for half a year in the counter-intelligence division' – implying that he went to Moscow immediately after the 401 course. In another version, he said that he was 'sent for special training in Moscow' to prepare him for a transfer to the First Department in Leningrad, the territorial adjunct of the First Chief Directorate (FCD), which dealt with foreign intelligence, which was closer to the truth but still misleading because, at that stage, his transfer to the First Department had not yet been decided (Putin, *First Person*, pp. 48 & 53).

38. Vladimir Pribylovsky wrote that Putin attended the higher KGB school in Varsonofevsky Lane, just behind the Lubyanka, in 1979 (*Pereklichka*, p. 5). However by then the school had moved to Leningradsky Prospekt, near the Belorussky Station. Because Putin was sent there for short-term training, and did not complete the full two- or three-year course, his name does not appear on any Soviet lists of graduates from the school. Nor has anyone come forward to say that they remember studying with him there. Nonetheless, there is no obvious reason why he should have invented it and one must assume, absent evidence to the contrary, that it is broadly correct.

39. *Politicheskaya razvedka s territorii SSSR*, Red Banner Institute, Moscow, 1989, p. 10. The manual was published on Dec. 27, 2017, at www.thedailybeast.com/the-kgb-papers-here-are-the-originals. It is possible that some sections have been doctored – it seems tailor-made to buttress Western grievances about Russia's use of disinformation and agents of influence – but the historical information it contains appears to be accurate.

40. Unless otherwise indicated, the following section is drawn from *Politicheskaya razvedka*, pp. 4–40, and Mitrokhin, 'The Counter-Intelligence Lexicon', in *KGB Lexicon*, pp. 151–374. This section of Mitrokhin's book contains the translation of a training manual issued by the Dzerzhinsky School. *Politicheskaya razvedka* was written 10 years after Putin attended the school, but the principles it described were long-established.

41. *Politicheskaya razvedka*, p. 5.

42. The only Western journalist based in Leningrad in the 1970s was Emil Sveilis of United Press International. He and his wife lived there in 1976 and 1977, but the KGB made their lives so difficult by constant harassment that after two years they were withdrawn and not replaced.

43. Putin, *First Person*, p. 44.

44. Earley, *Comrade J*, p. 48.

45. Putin himself said he spent a further six months in counter-intelligence after returning to Leningrad (*First Person*, p. 48). That is plausible. A photograph taken that summer, probably in July or August 1979, at the KGB dacha on the Gulf of Finland, showed him walking with Yuri Leshchev, his immediate superior in the First Department. By Putin's own account, he joined the First Department 'about four and a half years' before going back to Moscow in mid 1984, which would make it at the latest in the winter of 1979 (ibid., p. 53). Sergei Ivanov said later that he spent two years with Putin in the First Department and left in the late summer of 1981 (*Izvestia*, Nov. 9, 2000).

46. Sergei Ivanov (ibid.) wrote that they both served in 'one very small unit of a rather large organisation'.

47. Dmitry Yezhkov, author's interview, St Petersburg, May 30, 2019.

48. See, for example, Kostromin, *Moya zhizn – razvedka*, p. 65, and Usoltsev, *Sosluzhivets*, p. 115.

49. Voronov, *Sluzhba*, pp. 274–5. Putin was never registered as an FCD operative (*Argumenty i Fakty*, July 29, 1998). The First Departments were supervised and coordinated by the FCD's 12th Department, which in 1980 was renamed Directorate RT. Andropov attached increasing importance to foreign intelligence work within the USSR as the Soviet Union's ideological attraction waned and it became more and more difficult for the FCD to recruit agents in the West (*Politicheskaya razvedka, supra*, pp. 10–11).

50. Kalugin, Oleg, *Proshchai, Lubyanka!*, PIK-Olimp, Moscow, 1995, p. 266.

51. Quoted in Voronov, *Sluzhba*, p. 274.

52. Blotsky, Vol. 1, p. 308.

53. Putin, *First Person*, pp. 37–8.

54. Ibid., p. 39. Sergei Roldugin remembered her as 'a pretty girl . . . with a strong character. She was a friend to him, a woman who would take care of him. But did she love him? I don't know.'

55. Viktor Khmarin was the witness, equivalent to the best man, when Putin married four years later ('*Lena, kotoraya nravilas Vove*', June 7, 2017, at www.anews.com/p/72058686-lena-kotoraya-nravilas-vove-kem-vyrosli-odnokashniki-putina/).

56. Lev Lurye is among those who advance this hypothesis, while admitting that there is no proof (author's interview, May 27, 2019). See also Putin, *First Person*, p. 58, where Putin spoke of the importance of keeping his KGB employment secret, otherwise 'you would not be allowed abroad'.

57. Except where otherwise indicated, the following account is drawn from Blotsky, Vol. 2, esp. pp. 13–18, 22–5, 30–36, 39–41, 49–55 & 58–60. Putin himself gave a slightly different version of the first evening, saying that his friend obtained the tickets (*First Person*, p. 56). Lyudmila's comments date from 2001 and 2002, a time when her relationship with Putin was stable and as nearly normal as it ever became.

58. Putin, *First Person*, p. 57.

59. She told Blotsky: 'That was the way Vladimir Vladimirovich took the measure of me' (Vol. 2, p. 25).

60. Putin, *First Person*, p. 58.

61. Ibid., p. 56.

62. See note 70 below.

63. Blotsky, Vol. 2, p. 15.

64. www.putinforever.wordpress.com/2010/10/14/дружочек-и-лапуля-растет-ли-у-путина-си/

65. *Argumenty i Fakty*, Oct. 23, 2006.

66. Blotsky, Vol. 1, p. 92; Putin, *First Person*, pp. 60–61. The room measured about 130 square feet (12 sq. metres).

67. Putin, *First Person*, p. 61.

68. Ibid.; Blotsky, Vol. 2, p. 53.

69. Ibid., pp. 61–2.

70. Tuominen, *Vladimir Putin*, pp. 86–9; Anders Blom, r's interview, Turku, Finland, March 5 2017; *Izvestia*, Nov. 9, 2000. Karasev was an alias, which he used throughout his diplomatic career. His real name was Syrtoev. If, as seems likely, he told Putin in the spring of 1983 that he intended to recommend him to the 'Credentials Committee' of the Red Banner Institute, that may well have been the trigger for his proposal to Lyudmila. It would also explain why, even before she had agreed, he had already worked out a date for the wedding: if the ceremony were at the end of July, it would allow time for the honeymoon before the FCD interview, towards the end of August. For a man who 'always thought out everything in advance', as Lyudmila put it, that is all too plausible.

71. Colonel Igor Prelin, interview for Jean-Michel Carré.

72. Blotsky, Vol. 2, pp. 166–7.

73. Except where otherwise specified, this and the following section are drawn from Blotsky, Vol. 2, pp. 150–62, 167–210.

74. Earley, *Comrade J*, pp. 55 & 70–72. Piguzov stopped working with the CIA after his return to Moscow in 1979 and provided no information about his time at the Institute.

75. Blotsky, Vol 2, p. 170. Kuzichkin, who studied at Yurlovo some years earlier, remembered 120 students divided into groups of 30 (*Inside the KGB*, p. 49).

76. Kostromin, *Moya zhizn*, p. 61. *Kokoshniki* were worn by women of all classes, by the aristocracy and the imperial family no less than by the wives of peasants and artisans. They could be simple or extremely elaborate family heirlooms, brought out only on special occasions.

77. Kuzichkin, *supra*, pp. 61–2.

78. This and the following passage are drawn from Earley, *supra*, p. 52. His source, Sergei Tretyakov, a KGB defector, studied at the main campus of the Red Banner Institute near Nagorny from 1984 to 1985, the same year that Putin was studying at Yurlovo.

79. Ibid., pp. 47–8.

80. The following is drawn from Blotsky, Vol. 2, pp. 184–7.

81. Ibid., p. 211.

82. Kuzichkin, *supra*, p. 48. Putin recalled that at Yurlovo, psychologists observed the students 'secretly and over a long period of time' (*Kommersant*, March 10, 2000).

83. For a different take on his wearing a three-piece suit in midsummer, see Putin, *First Person*, p. 53.

84. The following is drawn from ibid., pp. 125–30.

85. Putin, *First Person*, p. 62.

86. She told a friend later that their relations had been 'extremely strained' – there had been times when she had hated her mother-in-law. When Maria Ivanovna died in 1998, Lyudmila was in France and refused to return for her funeral, although afterwards she attended the memorial meeting (Irene Pietsch, *Heikle Freundschaften*, Molden, Vienna, 2001, p. 387).

87. Putin, *First Person*, p. 61.

88. Gurevich, *Vospominaniya*, pp. 42–4.

89.   Blotsky, Vol. 2, pp. 241–2.

90.   Ibid., p. 129.

91.   Putin, *First Person*, p. 54.

92.   Ibid., pp. 54–5 and Blotsky, Vol. 2, pp. 161–2.

93.   Putin, *First Person*, p. 55.

94.   Prelin, interview for Jean-Michel Carré.

95.   Putin, *First Person*, pp. 36–7 & 62; *Kommersant*, March 10, 2000.

96.   Putin, *First Person*, p. 55; Blotsky, Vol. 2, pp. 195–7. On horse-trading, see also Kuzichkin, *Inside the KGB*, pp. 76–7.

97.   Putin, ibid. He did not name the Fourth Department, calling it 'the appropriate department'.

98.   Prelin, interview for Jean-Michel Carré. See also Voronov, *Sluzhba*, p. 275.

99.   Blotsky quotes Lazar Matveyev as saying 15 of the new graduates from the Institute had been assigned to Karlshorst (Vol. 2, p. 230); see also Usoltsev, *Sosluzhivets*, p. 62. It would be logical to assume that some of the others were sent elsewhere in the socialist bloc and that a number would have been deemed inapt for intelligence work and returned to their original departments. It is probable that fewer than half of those who graduated were accepted into the FCD and sent to countries outside the Soviet bloc.

100. Putin, *First Person*, p. 62.

101. In the 1980s, there was a bigger KGB contingent in Afghanistan, but that was a temporary situation resulting from the Soviet occupation.

102. Blotsky, Vol. 2, pp. 209–10; Pribylovsky, *Pereklichka*, p. 18.

103. Pribylovsky, ibid. The following also draws on Blotsky, who refers to Mylnikov by the pseudonym, Malyutin (Vol. 2., pp. 212, 228 & 230–32).

104. Putin, *First Person*, p. 67.

105. According to *Politicheskaya razvedka*, *supra*, p. 10, by the mid 1980s, there were First Departments in more than a hundred KGB provincial directorates, three times more than a decade earlier, although most of them were very small.

106. Prelin, interview for Jean-Michel Carré.

107. www.youtube.com/watch?v=lAVlaIJWP-Q, July 18, 2007 and Reuters, Sept. 27, 2008.

108. Hill and Gaddy, *Mr. Putin: Operative in the Kremlin*.

109. Blotsky, Vol. 1, p. 61.

110. Mitrokhin, 'The Counter-Intelligence Lexicon', in *KGB Lexicon*, p. 261.

111. 'Discussion with Representatives of leading US media organisations', June 18, 2001, www.kremlin.ru/events/president/transcripts/21269

112. Much of this is common to all intelligence services, not just the KGB. Michael Morgan, formerly of the CIA's Moscow station, described what he called 'an intelligence officer's approach to life' as follows: 'How can I turn this to my advantage? You meet someone on the street or at a cocktail party and if, after 20 minutes, you find you can't figure out how this person could be useful to you, you're not going to call that person again. You just move on' (author's interview, New London, N.H., Dec. 29, 2018).

4: Quiet Days in Saxony

1.   The following is drawn from Blotsky, Vol. 2, pp. 219 & 255–6, Usoltsev, *Sosluzhivets*, p. 84, Putin, *First Person*, pp. 70–71, Vladimir Bragin, '*Rabotali kogda-to v Drezdene dva Volodi i dve*

Lyudy', Strana.ru, March 9, 2004, at www.flb.ru/info/26023.html, and CORRECT!V, July 30, 2015.

2. Many of the more persistent rumours about the nature of Putin's posting to East Germany are untrue. It is often asserted that he was in East Germany under cover of being director of the Soviet–German Friendship Association in Leipzig (or alternatively, in Dresden). Leipzig had its own KGB district office, so it would have made no sense for Putin, serving in an office 80 miles away, to occupy such a post. In any case, Soviet–German Friendship Associations, which existed within all East German state organisations, including the Stasi, were always headed by Germans, not Russians. Since East Germany was a Soviet bloc state, the KGB operated there openly. No KGB officer needed a cover story. The story of the Friendship Association, which is still widely believed in Russia, is a myth. Equally baseless are claims that, in the early 1980s, Putin was posted under an assumed name to the Soviet consulate in Leipzig or, alternatively, that he was sent on an assignment as a TASS correspondent to West Germany.

3. Unless otherwise indicated, the following section is derived from Blotsky and Usoltsev, *supra*, and Putin, *First Person*.

4. Arnold Vaatz, author's interview, Berlin, June 12, 2017. Vaatz, who has represented Saxony in the Bundestag since 1998, was a member of the *Neues Forum* opposition movement in Dresden in 1989.

5. Agartanov's account of the two years he spent with Putin in Dresden, *Sosluzhivets* (Eksmo, Moscow, 2004), written under the pen-name, Vladimir Usoltsev, was first published in German in 2003. It was unauthorised and, after its publication, Agartanov went to ground in the Czech Republic. He elided certain issues and used pseudonyms for his colleagues. The chronology is not always correct and his recollections of conversations are sometimes too detailed to be wholly believable. Nonetheless, if read with care, the book is an invaluable source on Putin's time in Dresden. For the most part, it rings true.

6. *Vedomosti*, Feb. 11, 2013.

7. Usoltsev refers to Kalinin by the pseudonym, Polkash, military slang for colonel. His real name is given in a 1985 Stasi telephone list for the KGB liaison office. The same document identifies Usoltsev as Agartanov (twitter.com/KevinRothrock/status/1351540663813353472/photo/2).

8. Michael Renz (author's interview, Wiesbaden, June 8, 2017); Wilhelm Dietl and Katharina Schwann, private communications.

9. Erich Schmidt-Eenboom, 'Wladimir Putin im Visier des BND', Jan. 5, 2014, at www.geheimdienste.info/texte/beutezug.pdf and author's interview, Weilheim, June 9, 2017; Dr Hans-Georg Wieck, author's interview, Berlin, June 13, 2017. Dr Wieck was head of the BND from 1985 to 1990. On Colonel Kalinin's premature departure, see Usoltsev, *Sosluzhivets*, pp. 176–7. The novel, *Illegal Action*, by the former head of MI5, Stella Rimington (Vintage, London, 2009), alludes indirectly to this episode.

10. Blotsky, Vol. 2, pp. 241–4.

11. Ibid., pp. 250–51.

12. Katerina took the name of Lyudmila's mother.

13. Sergei Bezrukov, interview for ZDF (2016).

14. Blotsky, Vol. 2, p. 222.

15. Putin, *First Person*, p. 70.

16. Usoltsev, *Sosluzhivets*, p. 151.

17. Ibid., pp. 36 & 158; Blotsky, Vol. 2, p. 220.

18.   Ibid., pp. 220 & 223–4.

19.   Blotsky, Vol. 1, p. 41; Usoltsev, *Sosluzhivets*, p. 41.

20.   Ibid., pp. 93–9, 157–8 & 207.

21.   Ibid., p. 203; Blotsky, Vol. 2, p. 225.

22.   Usoltsev, *Sosluzhivets*, pp. 90–91; Blotsky, Vol. 2, p. 212; *Der Tagesspiegel*, Nov. 17, 2003; Bragin, NTV interview, Jan. 25, 2004.

23.   Only the offices in Karlshorst and Leipzig were bigger.

24.   Catherine Belton, in her book, *Putin's People: How the KGB Took Back Russia and then Took On The West* (William Collins, London, 2020, pp. 38–42), quotes a former member of the West German terrorist group, the Red Army Faction (RAF), as saying that the group's members visited Dresden half a dozen times in the 1980s for training sessions and discussions with Stasi and KGB officials. Putin allegedly played a leading role in these meetings, discussing possible targets for terrorist attacks, arranging for weapons and explosives to be made available to the RAF at secret locations in West Germany and giving orders to the Stasi general who accompanied him. These and other details – like the alleged use of a Zil limousine, a model reserved for the exclusive use of the Politburo, to transport the group – would be hard to credit even if there were no other reasons for doubting them and Belton herself acknowledges that the story is 'near-impossible to verify'. According to the leading German specialist on the RAF, Tobias Wunschik of Humboldt University in Berlin, by 1984 – a year before Putin arrived in Dresden – the East Germans had put their relations with the RAF on ice (Wunschik, 'Panzerfaust-Training und DDR-Unterricht', Oct. 19, 2013, www.focus.de/politik/deutschland/raf/die-raf-stasi-connection-terrorismus_id_1921528.html and private communication, Sept. 26, 2021). Ten 'drop-outs' from the group had been given refuge in East Germany, among them, apparently, Belton's source. When Masha Gessen interviewed the same person in 2011, nothing was said about Putin's alleged role in planning RAF attacks. On that occasion, the interviewee claimed to have given Putin a Grundig Satellit shortwave radio and a Blaupunkt car stereo and grumbled that Putin had not offered to pay for them. That story, too, is unverifiable. Gessen concluded that while 'assassinations and terrorist attacks [were] exactly the sort of work that Putin had once dreamed of, there is no evidence that he was directly connected to it' (Gessen, Masha, *The Man Without A Face: The Unlikely Rise of Vladimir Putin*, Riverhead Books, New York, 2012, p. 65).

25.   Usoltsev, *Sosluzhivets*, pp. 31, 34 & 265.

26.   *Politicheskaya razvedka*, *supra*, p. 17.

27.   Blotsky, Vol. 2, pp. 210–11.

28.   Usoltsev, *supra*, pp. 56 & 72 and *Argumenty i Fakty*, Oct. 23, 2006.

29.   Usoltsev, *supra*, pp. 105–8; Kuzichkin, *Inside the KGB*, p. 109. A similar system was used when offices in the Kremlin and in government ministries were closed overnight or at weekends.

30.   Bernd Schafer, Nate Jones and Benjamin B. Fisher, 'Forecasting Nuclear War', at www.wilsoncenter.org/publication/forecasting-nuclear-war

31.   Usoltsev, *supra*, p. 110.

32.   Kuzichkin, *Inside the KGB*, p. 119. In the same way, officers working for Directorate T (technical and scientific intelligence) in KGB residencies and representations, or in provincial directorates, were described as belonging to Line X.

33.   Ibid., p. 78.

34.   Vladimir Putin, interview with RT, June 24, 2017, extracts at www.rt.com/news/393981-putin-KGB-illegal-intelligence. Earlier he had claimed that 'my speciality [in the KGB] was

political intelligence. I was basically engaged in research into international politics' ('Interview with NPR', Nov. 16, 2001, www.kremlin.ru/events/president/transcripts/21402; see also Putin, *First Person*, pp. 69–70). That was not true either.

35. According to *Politicheskaya razvedka*, pp. 12–13, the work of the First Department of the Leningrad Directorate did include some Line N responsibilities.

36. Kuzichkin, *supra*, p. 79.

37. Usoltsev, *Sosluzhivets*, p. 70.

38. Kuzichkin, *supra*, pp. 187–91.

39. Usoltsev, *supra*, pp. 69–71. According to Pablo Miller, a former MI6 station chief in Estonia, Russian illegals destined for the West were trained at a base north of Tallinn. Out of every hundred candidates, between two and five completed the course, of whom even fewer went abroad (author's interview, Salisbury, May 12, 2017).

40. Documentation and recruitment of illegals were handled respectively by the 2nd and 3rd Departments of Directorate S in Moscow (Kuzichkin, *supra*, pp. 79–80). Agartanov wrote at length of Putin's efforts to cultivate potential illegals, but nowhere does he mention documentation or 'legends'. Given his discretion about his own responsibilities, it is a plausible assumption that those tasks were his.

41. Bezrukov, interview with ZDF (2016). Leshchev said the same. 'In principle,' he told Oleg Blotsky, 'Vladimir Vladimirovich was engaged in Dresden in the same work as in Leningrad, only from the territory of East Germany' (Blotsky, Vol. 2, p. 211).

42. CORRECT!V, July 30, 2015. Zuchold's comments need to be treated with caution. His recollection of Putin's language abilities is corroborated by Agartanov, but elsewhere he has exaggerated his own importance and recounted anecdotes which are implausible and in some cases have turned out to be untrue.

43. Kalugin, author's interview, Oct. 30, 2018.

44. Usoltsev, *Sosluzhivets*, pp. 64–5; Bragin, Strana.ru, March 9, 2004, at www.flb.ru/info/26023.html. The German Consul General in St Petersburg, Eberhard von Puttkamer, said he spoke fluently when they met in 1991 (author's interview, Potsdam, May 6, 2017).

45. According to Putin, 'a large part of our work was done through [East German] citizens' (*First Person*, p. 74).

46. Usoltsev, *supra*, pp. 73–4 & 212. Agartanov described Rainer as a full-time salaried CID officer. According to *Der Spiegel* (June 10, 1991), he was 'an unofficial employee of the Criminal Investigation Department'. David Crawford and Marcus Bensman (CORRECT!V, July 30, 2015) identify him as Rainer Sonntag, who was deported to West Germany in 1987, and speculate, apparently on the basis of statements by Zuchold, that he was expelled from Dresden with Putin's agreement in order to infiltrate the extreme Right in West Germany. Sonntag became a prominent neo-Nazi and remained so after German reunification until his murder in Dresden on June 1, 1991.

47. Usoltsev, *supra*, p. 250.

48. Blotsky, Vol. 2, p. 229. According to Viktor Adianov, the office also cultivated technicians at Robotron, a subsidiary of Siemens, and at Manfred von Ardenne's research institute in Dresden, not because they were of interest in themselves but in the hope that they might provide a link to colleagues in the West (Quiring, Manfred, *Russland*, Christoph Links Verlag, Berlin, 2008, p. 120, and *Die Welt*, Dec. 21, 2004). Allegations by Klaus Zuchold that Putin tried to entrap an East German scientist by using pornography to blackmail him (CORRECT!V, July 30, 2015) appear to be pure fiction. That would have been a task not for

Putin but for the Science and Technology case officer, Vladimir Bragin, and in any case there would have been no need for it: East Germany was a Soviet satellite and did Moscow's bidding in such matters.

49. Sergei Bezrukov cited in Gessen, *Man without a Face*, p. 66.

50. Kuzichkin, *Inside the KGB*, pp. 90–91. The grades were Junior Case Officer (with a rank of lieutenant); Case Officer (captain); Senior Case Officer (major); Assistant Head of Department (lieutenant-colonel); Senior Assistant (lieutenant-colonel or colonel). Putin's rouble salary was notional because in Dresden he was paid in Ostmarks and US dollars. The average Soviet wage at that time was between 150 and 200 roubles, though many people earned less.

51. Putin was promoted to Assistant Department Head in 1987 and Senior Assistant two years later (Blotsky, Vol. 2, p. 234). The dates are significant because Matveyev returned to Moscow in January 1988. That he was instrumental in Putin's promotion the following year confirms that, after his departure, he continued to have influence over Putin's career. The importance of that would become apparent when Putin returned to Russia just over a year later.

52. Usoltsev, *Sosluzhivets*, pp. 56–7.

53. According to Agartanov, however, the relationship was limited to 'official contacts', and Matveyev found out nothing about Modrow's fraught relations with Honecker which was not already public knowledge (ibid., p. 208). Putin said simply that contacts with Modrow were above his rank (*First Person*, p. 73).

54. The following section draws on Kuzichkin, who describes the workings of the Party cell at the Tehran residency in the late 1970s (*Inside the KGB*, pp. 173–6), Usoltsev, *supra*, pp. 169–71 and *Die Welt*, Dec. 21, 2004.

55. Usoltsev, *supra*, pp. 20 n. & 172.

56. *Die Welt*, Dec. 21, 2004. Adianov's situation was anomalous. He held the lowly rank of lieutenant, later rising to become a captain, but because he was from the First Chief Directorate, he outranked Putin, who was from a provincial service, until the latter was promoted to Senior Assistant Head of Department (Quiring, *Russland*, p. 120).

57. Bragin, quoted in Strana.ru, March 9, 2004, at www.flb.ru/info/26023.html

58. *Die Welt*, Dec. 21, 2004 (Adianov); Strana.ru, March 9, 2004 (Bragin); Usoltsev, *supra*, p. 225 (Agartanov) and Blotsky, Vol. 2, p. 234 (Matveyev). On Adianov's work habits, see Usoltsev, p. 177. It may be pertinent to note here that among his former colleagues at Dresden, Putin has remained close only to Tokarev and Chemezov, both of whom have been extremely discreet about their relationship with him.

59. Usoltsev, *supra*, p. 172. Bragin said 'he especially attracted people of the older generation' (Strana.ru, March 9, 2004).

60. NTV interview transcript, Jan. 25, 2004.

61. Usoltsev, *supra*, p. 151.

62. Blotsky, Vol. 2, p. 241. It is difficult to pinpoint exactly when this was. It was probably in July, a month or so before Katerina was born.

63. Ibid., pp. 200–202.

64. Usoltsev, *supra*, p. 114. Putin claimed that it had also led to increased crime. In fact, violent crime and hooliganism, which were often fuelled by excessive alcohol consumption, sharply decreased. The campaign succeeded in reducing the number of alcohol-related deaths by an estimated 1.5 million over three years.

65. Ibid., pp. 131–2.

66. Ibid., p. 116.

67. Bragin, NTV interview, Jan. 25, 2004.

68. Usoltsev, *supra*, pp. 121–2.

69. Ibid., pp. 184–6.

70. Karasev, Felix, *Naapurinpojan muistelmat*, Kustannusosakeyhtiö Otava, Helsinki, 1998, p. 161.

71. Usoltsev, *supra*, p. 130 and Putin, *First Person*, p. 68.

72. Bragin, NTV interview, Jan. 25, 2004.

73. Bezrukov, interview with ZDF (2016).

74. Usoltsev, *supra*, pp. 118–19, 172 & 189. Putin said later that he realised that the communist system was not working 'in the mid or late 1980s' ('Interview for BBC *Breakfast with Frost*', March 5, 2000, Russian text at www.kremlin.ru/events/president/transcripts/24194).

75. Putin was not alone in finding that a revelation. In 1990, Lieutenant-General Anatoly Kurkov, who by then had succeeded General Nosyrev as the head of the Leningrad KGB, paid an official visit to Finland as the guest of Seppo Tiitinen, the head of the Finnish security police, SUPO. On the return journey, Tiitinen accompanied him as far as the border. At Kurkov's request, they stopped at a supermarket in a small town on the way. When they passed the meat counter, 'Kurkov stopped', Tiitinen remembered. 'He stood there for minutes. And minutes. When we got back to the car, he said: "We will never have anything like that in the Soviet Union. Never." (author's interview, Helsinki, May 29, 2017). Boris Yeltsin had a similar experience when he first visited America in September 1989.

76. Usoltsev, *supra*, pp. 166–8 & 188–9.

77. Ibid., p. 189.

78. Ibid., pp. 87, 177 & 181–3.

79. Ibid., pp. 50 & 159–60.

80. In a photograph with Leshchev at the KGB dacha outside Leningrad in 1979, Putin is wearing tight-fitting western jeans with a heavy belt and shirt unbuttoned to the waist, looking more like a bad boy off the street than a KGB officer.

81. Usoltsev, *supra*, pp. 209–11.

82. Bezrukov, interview with ZDF (2016).

83. Usoltsev, *supra*, pp. 144 & 184.

84. Ibid., pp. 88 & 201.

85. Ibid., pp. 195–6.

86. Putin, *First Person*, pp. 77–8 and Blotsky, Vol. 2, p. 263.

87. 'Note regarding the Meeting of Comrade Minister [Erich Mielke] with the Head of the 5th Directorate of the KGB of the USSR, Comrade Lieutenant General Abramov, Sept. 26, 1987, Berlin', in CWIHP e-Dossier No. 37, digitalarchive.wilsoncenter.org/document/115722

88. *Boston Globe*, Oct. 19, 1987.

89. The Diary of Anatoly S. Chernyaev, Dec. 4, 1988, at nsarchive2.gwu.edu/NSAEBB/NSAEBB250/Chernyaev_Diary_1988.pdf

90. After German reunification, Böhm, the youngest general in the Stasi, committed suicide, one of three officials at that level to do so.

91. *Bild*, Dec. 12, 2018.

92. The East Germans tried to compensate for the lack of substantive exchanges by redoubling the numbers of formal meetings. Putin was awarded the gold medal of the Stasi branch of the German–Soviet Friendship Association in November 1987 and a bronze

medal for 'outstanding services to the National People's Army' a year later. Neither award had any significance.

93. Usoltsev, *Sosluzhivets*, pp. 42–4.

94. Andrew and Mitrokhin, *The Mitrokhin Archive*, p. 354, and Pablo Miller, author's interview, May 12, 2017. According to Agartanov, *Luch* was launched after Brezhnev became concerned that Honecker's conservative policies were at variance with the Soviet Party's position (Usoltsev, *supra*, p. 252).

95. Usoltsev, *supra*, pp. 36–7, 44, 208, 252, 255–6 & 259. According to Agartanov, the Karlshorst unit dealing with *Luch* was 'a tiny, insignificant little group' staffed by only one or two people. Andrew and Mitrokhin state that it was elevated to the status of a full directorate in 1974, but that appears to be an error. Putin had no connection with *Luch*, which was Chemezov's responsibility, since he was in charge of counter-intelligence in Dresden. Many years later, Chemezov included a mischievous allusion to this episode in his official biography, claiming that in the 1980s he was 'head of the *Luch* Association representative office in East Germany' (www.rostec.ru/about/controls/sergey_chemezov/). *Luch* is frequently confused with a sister programme named *Progress*, which was designed to set up networks of agents in eastern Europe who would work against the West after the end of communist rule. Böhm's deputy, Horst Jemlich, maintained that the Stasi had not known about *Luch* and that the Russians had 'cheated and lied to us' (Myers, Steven Lee, *The New Tsar*, Simon and Schuster, London, 2015, p. 53; Usoltsev, p. 255). That was untrue. The Stasi leadership was well aware of what its Soviet allies were up to.

96. According to Agartanov, no one in the Dresden bureau realised that the East German leaders might be in trouble until the second half of 1989 (Usoltsev, *supra*, p. 207). Putin claimed that he had 'begun to suspect that the regime would not last long' (*First Person*, p. 78), but that was later.

97. *New York Times*, Oct. 6, 1989. The demonstrations took place on October 4 and 5. Altogether 14 trains, carrying 12,000 people, crossed East Germany between October 1 and 8. Those from Prague and Wrocław went through Dresden, those from Warsaw through Berlin.

98. Blotsky, Vol. 2, p. 259.

99. Gorbachev himself, in public, put it more tactfully, saying, 'Dangers await only those who do not react to life.' The much-quoted phrase, 'Life punishes those who come too late', was coined by the Soviet press spokesman, Gennady Gerasimov, as a summary of what Gorbachev had told Honecker. His exact words to the East German leader have not been preserved (*Frankfurter Allgemeine*, Oct. 6, 2004).

100. Chernyaev Diary, Oct. 11, 1989, at nsarchive2.gwu.edu/NSAEBB/NSAEBB275/1989%20for%20posting.pdf

101. *Frankfurter Allgemeine*, *supra*, and *New York Times*, Oct. 7, 1989.

102. Vilém Prečan and Thomas Blanton, 'Prague Communists Called for Wall to Open on November 8, 1989', Nov. 8, 2009, at nsarchive2.gwu.edu/NSAEBB/NSAEBB294/index.htm

103. Putin, *First Person*, p. 80.

104. Z for *Zashchita* (Defence). In Russian the new name was *Upravleniye zashchity konstitutsionnogo poryadka*.

105. Putin, *First Person*, pp. 76–7. According to Agartanov, Putin had earlier arranged with General Böhm's liaison officer, Thomas Müller, for the Stasi files relating to the KGB to be transferred to Angelikastrasse for safekeeping. However Agartanov had already left Dresden, and it is not

clear how reliable his information was (Usoltsev, *Sosluzhivets*, p. 241). Peter Schröter of *Neues Forum* said later that he saw three KGB officers – apparently Putin and two colleagues – watching as the protesters overran the site (Stasi archives, Dresden).

106. Matveyev had returned to Moscow in January 1988. Shirokov arrived later that year (*Voenno-promyshlenny kurer*, Dec. 14, 2005). Blotsky (Vol. 2, p. 260) quoted Putin as saying that Shirokov had left town that evening and could not be found, but that appears to be a misunderstanding.

107. Siegfried Dannath, quoted in Myers, *New Tsar*, pp. 50–51, and Peter Schröter, *supra*.

108. Putin, *First Person*, p. 79, and Blotsky, Vol. 2, p. 263.

109. Blotsky, Vol. 2, p. 264. Subsequent Russian and Western accounts, depicting Putin with a drawn pistol, single-handedly warding off an angry mob, were fiction.

110. Putin, *First Person*, p. 79; Bezrukov, interview with ZDF (2016). Peter Schröter (*supra*) said the soldiers were carrying Kalashnikovs; Putin, sub-machine guns; Bezrukov, machine pistols. Putin's phrase, 'Moscow is silent', echoed, no doubt consciously, the closing words of Pushkin's *Boris Godunov*: 'The people are silent.'

111. Putin, ibid.

112. Bezrukov, *supra*, said simply, 'I don't think that he waited very long. He got what he requested.'

113. Ibid.

114. Blotsky, Vol. 2, p. 262 ('second homeland').

115. Peter Schröter, *supra*.

116. Blotsky, Vol. 2, p. 266.

117. Putin, *First Person*, p. 75.

118. Ibid., p. 77.

119. Ibid., p. 76. It is not certain when the Dresden office started destroying its archives, but it was probably not before mid December, since Putin mentioned that one of the reasons he felt it was imperative to stop the KGB office being overrun on December 5 was to safeguard its files, which contained the names of agents.

120. *Voenno-promyshlenny kurer*, Dec. 14, 2005.

121. Bezrukov, interview with ZDF (2016). This is no doubt why the Stasi archives, while they contain millions of files on the surveillance of East Germany's citizens, have relatively little on foreign intelligence or on such sensitive topics as East German support for the Red Army Faction and other terrorist groups.

122. Putin, *First Person*, p. 76.

123. The following is taken from the accounts Zuchold gave to David Crawford (author's interview, Berlin, May 5, 2017), Michael Renz (author's interview, Wiesbaden, June 8, 2017) and *Die Welt*, March 25, 2000. See also CORRECT!V, May 30, 2015. According to Crawford, Zuchold approached the BfV in December 1990. Zuchold afterwards worked as a security guard for ZDF and later for a firm in Mannheim.

124. Bezrukov, *supra*.

125. Lyudmila said they travelled to Leningrad by train, arriving on February 3, 1990 (Blotsky, Vol. 2, p. 271). Putin thought they left at the end of January (*First Person*, p. 86). Agartanov, who resigned from the KGB in March 1989, claimed that Putin was still in Dresden in the summer of 1990, but he apparently confused the dates (Usoltsev, *Sosluzhivets*, pp. 239 & 241–2).

126. Bragin, Strana.ru, March 9, 2004. Mylnikov worked in Dresden from 1980 to 1985, Agartanov from 1982 to 1987 and Chemezov from 1983 to 1988.

127. It was said that Werner Grossmann, Markus Wolf's successor at the head of the HVA, the foreign espionage arm of the Stasi, had complained about Putin to the KGB (Crawford, author's interview, *supra*). Although it is true that there had been friction between Böhm and the Dresden office over the KGB's attempts to poach active Stasi agents, that had nothing to do with Grossmann's service, which in January 1990 had far more important things to worry about than the activities of a middle-ranking KGB officer in Dresden.

128. Yury Shutov, who was briefly an assistant to Anatoly Sobchak and later became a member of the St Petersburg Duma, where he was one of Putin's fiercest critics, was the source of many of these claims.

129. Oleg Blotsky promoted this idea, which almost certainly came from Putin himself, apparently as a red herring (Blotsky, Vol. 2, p. 280).

130. Rodric Braithwaite, private diary, May 31, 1989.

131. Richard Bridge, author's interview, London, May 12, 2017.

132. Natalya Chaplina, who edited the Leningrad newspaper, *Chas pik*, in 1990, called him the embodiment of change (Kseniya Sobchak and Vera Krichevskaya, *Delo Sobchaka* [documentary film], 2018).

133. Ibid.

134. Kokh, Alfred, and Svinarenko, Igor, *A Crate of Vodka*, Enigma Books, New York, 2009, pp. 199–200.

135. Orttung, Robert, *From Leningrad to St. Petersburg*, St. Martin's Press, New York, 1995, pp. 67–71; Sobchak, Anatoly, *For a New Russia*, HarperCollins, London, 1992, pp. 94–9.

136. 'Findings of the Commission of the USSR Congress of People's Deputies to Investigate the Events which Occurred in the City of Tbilisi on 9 April 1989' at digitalarchive.wilsoncenter.org/document/117183

137. The following account is drawn from *Delo Sobchaka*.

138. Oleg Kalugin described a successful attempt to implant a KGB informer in the Democratic movement in Omsk. The agent, Sergei Baburin, rose to become a member of the Russian Supreme Soviet (*Chas pik*, March 10, 1993).

139. Valery Pavlov, author's interview, St Petersburg, Nov. 27, 2019.

140. Matveyev said later, 'When I looked through his file, I was attracted by his legal education. As a lawyer myself, I knew the value of a law degree from Leningrad University' (Blotsky, Vol. 2, p. 230).

141. Many different sources have stated publicly that Putin was offered a position in Moscow. They include Putin himself and Sergei Roldugin (Putin, *First Person*, pp. 85–6); Lyudmila (who was keen to move to Moscow); Matveyev; and another colleague from the Red Banner Institute (Blotsky, Vol. 2, pp. 273 & 280–83). See also Sobchak, *For a New Russia*, p. 94. Lyudmila said 'the position [in Moscow] and the rank corresponding to it were higher than he was offered in Leningrad'. Some, if not all, of these accounts appear to have been intended to muddy the waters.

142. When Putin returned from Dresden, Matveyev was working at the FCD headquarters at Yasenevo.

143. *Chas pik*, Nov. 25, 1991.

144. In his own account of his return to Leningrad, Putin stressed his frustration at working for an intelligence service whose reports were ignored by the political leadership. 'The work we did was no longer necessary,' he said. 'Nobody at Moscow Centre was reading our reports. Didn't we warn them about what was coming? . . . Who wants to work for nothing? To spend years of your life – for what – just to get paid?' (*First Person*, pp. 85–6). Many

other ex-KGB officers made similar complaints. But that was from the standpoint of ten years later, after the Soviet Union had collapsed and the consequences had become clear. In February 1990, when Putin left Dresden, all that still lay ahead.

5: Back in the USSR

1. Blotsky, Vol. 2, p. 271.
2. Smolyak, *Sobchak*, p. 76. See also Boulmer, Leningrad, TD 74, May 16, 1989 and Moscow TD 2229, March 23, 1990, CADN.
3. Putin, *First Person*, p. 87.
4. Blotsky, Vol. 2, pp. 271–2 & 274.
5. Ministère des Affaires Étrangères, Direction d'Europe, 886/EU, March 29, 1990, CADN. Those terms were used by the Soviet first deputy Prime Minister, Lev Voronin, to the French Finance Minister, Pierre Bérégovoy, on March 26, 1990. The following year an opinion survey in Leningrad found that more than half of those questioned expected 'civil war, famine or armed conflict' (*Smena*, Nov. 27, 1991).
6. CADN, 886/EU, *supra*.
7. Ministère des Affaires Étrangères, Direction d'Europe, 1802/EU-URSS, June 27, 1990, CADN.
8. Claude Arnaud, French Ambassador in Moscow, 13/EU, Jan. 8, 1985, CADN. Despite Gorbachev's anti-alcohol programme, the situation was not much better five years later.
9. Barbara Hay, author's interview, London, Sept. 21, 2016.
10. The film's title was taken from a line by the nineteenth-century poet, Arseny Golenishchev-Kutuzov, which became a popular saying during the February Revolution in 1917. Gorbachev used a very similar phrase – 'We cannot go on living as we have been' – on the eve of his election as Soviet leader in March 1985 (*Pravda*, Dec. 1, 1990).
11. *Smena*, Jan. 16, March 8, April 6 and June 7, 1990.
12. Gurevich, *Putin*, p. 103.
13. Pyotr Kotov, author's interview, St Petersburg, May 28, 2019 ('an old building') and Barbara Hay, *supra* ('run-down').
14. Charles Ryan, author's interview, Conshohocken, Pa., March 14 2019.
15. Blotsky, Vol. 2, pp. 273–4.
16. Usoltsev, *Sosluzhivets*, pp. 76 & 231–2, Blotsky, Vol. 2, p. 289 and *Argumenty i Fakty*, Oct. 23, 2006. General Shirokov also noted Putin's passion for cars (*Voenno-promyshlenny kurer*, Dec. 14, 2005).
17. This account is drawn from Golovko's book, a privately printed memoir entitled *Zhizn byla interesnoi*, Litera, St Petersburg, 2002, Vol. 1, pp. 345–50. A copy is held by the Russian National Library in St Petersburg.
18. Richard Miles, the then US Consul General in Leningrad, met Putin in that capacity in the spring of 1990 to arrange for his daughter to spend a semester studying at the university (author's interview, Fort Hunt, Va., Dec. 11, 2018). He later made it sound even more impressive, claiming falsely that he had been Vice Rector himself ('Interview with ABC', Nov. 7, 2001, *supra*).
19. Lempert, *Daily Life in a Crumbling Empire*, Vol. 1, pp. 461–3.
20. Pepper, John, *Russian Tide*, privately published, 2012, pp. 20–21, author's interview, Jan. 24, and private communication, Jan. 28, 2019.
21. Blotsky, Vol. 2, p. 273.

22. Ibid., pp. 287-8.

23. Putin, *First Person*, p. 88.

24. Unless otherwise indicated, the following section is drawn from Smolyak, *Sobchak*, pp. 19, 31–4 & 52–5, and Orttung, *From Leningrad to St. Petersburg*, pp. 26–7 & 291–2 n. 24.

25. Sobchak, *For a New Russia*, p. 28; Garcelon, Marc, *Revolutionary Passage: From Soviet to Post-Soviet Russia, 1995–2000*, Temple University Press, Philadelphia, 2005, pp. 69–70; and Shutov, Yury, *Krestnyi otets 'piterskikh'*, Algoritm, Moscow, 2015, pp. 21–2 & 24.

26. Sobchak had supported Professor Olimpiad Ioffe when he had been dismissed from the Law Faculty, a stance which required considerable courage. He had afterwards been at daggers drawn with Ioffe's successor, Yury Tolstoi, who had retaliated by getting Sobchak's doctorate delayed and later trying to block his candidature as a deputy (Valery Pavlov, author's interview, Nov. 27, 2019). See also *Zvezda*, no. 5, 2008, which gives an account of Sobchak's speech in defence of Ioffe before his expulsion. According to Sobchak's elder brother, Aleksandr, Tolstoi had had an affair with Sobchak's first wife, Nonna, which, if true, would help to explain the enmity between them. See flb.ru/infoprint/42858.html

27. Sobchak, *For a New Russia*, pp. 107–10. It is possible that the KGB's decision to base Putin in Leningrad rather than Moscow was taken in anticipation of Sobchak re-establishing his base there. His defeat by Lukyanov was predictable and the KGB might well have picked up other signals that he was becoming disenchanted with Moscow. The timing appears to fit. It is not known when Putin took up his position as Molchanov's deputy, but it may not have been until the end of February or the beginning of March.

28. Orttung, *From Leningrad to St. Petersburg*, p. 132.

29. Marcel Roux, Leningrad, 71/AMB, July 17, 1990, CADN.

30. The analogy was drawn by Aleksandr Belyaev, who stood in as acting Chairman while Filippov and Salye quarrelled (author's interview, St Petersburg, June 3, 2019).

31. Orttung (*supra*, p. 130) writes that nearly 200 Lensoviet deputies signed the petition requesting Sobchak to stand. Smolyak says 100 deputies signed (*Sobchak*, p. 56).

32. The following draws on Smolyak, ibid., pp. 56–9. An opinion poll in mid April found that 68 per cent of those questioned favoured Sobchak as Lensoviet Chairman, 7 per cent Filippov and 4 per cent Salye (*Smena*, April 18, 1990).

33. Sobchak was elected on May 13 with 75 per cent of the votes cast (*Smena*, May 16, 1990).

34. *Chas pik*, Nov. 25, 1991.

35. Sobchak's widow, Lyudmila Narusova, said: 'By chance they met again in the corridors of the university. Sobchak asked him, what are you doing these days? He replied, "I am working as an assistant to the [Vice] Rector, dealing with the foreign students." Sobchak said, "I remember you when you were studying in the Law Faculty. You were a good student and you were good at languages. I need someone to work in the team I am putting together"' (author's interview, Moscow, Nov. 21, 2019). An almost identical account is given in Smolyak, *supra*, p. 84. Putin himself, however, said – truthfully, on this occasion – that 'I did not actually know him'. He had never been Sobchak's 'favourite student', as others had claimed, he said. 'I didn't have any personal connexions to him . . . He was just one of our lecturers' (*First Person*, p. 88).

36. Putin, *First Person*, pp. 88–9 (translation amended).

37. It is usually stated that Putin became Sobchak's assistant in May 1990. If he indeed met Sobchak after he became Lensoviet Chairman, it cannot have been before the beginning of June since, immediately after becoming Chairman, Sobchak left for America. But since

Putin's account of their meeting in the Mariinsky Palace was fiction, it may well have been earlier – perhaps even before Sobchak's election as a deputy on May 13. The chronology is difficult to establish. Leonid Polokhov spoke of meeting Putin at the Mariinsky Palace in May, but it must have been at least two months later (Blotsky, Vol. 2, p. 287). Barbara Hay, who was then with the British Embassy in Moscow, thought she saw Putin with Valery Pavlov outside Sobchak's office when she visited Leningrad in June. But Pavlov was sure he did not meet Putin until the autumn. He thought Hay must have confused Putin with Viktor Kochygin, another ex-KGB officer in Sobchak's entourage (Barbara Hay, author's interview, London, Sept. 21 & 25, 2016; Valery Pavlov, author's interview, Nov. 27, 2019). Whatever the precise timing, Putin did not officially take up his post until several months later.

38.   In his initial account, Putin himself said: 'Anatoly Aleksandrovich [Sobchak] knew in which service I had been employed previously' (*Chas pik*, Nov. 25, 1991).

39.   In *First Person*, pp. 87–8, Putin identified the intermediary as one of 'my old friends from the Law Faculty [who had] become . . . [a] professor'. In Blotsky, Vol. 2, pp. 296–7, he spoke of 'a fellow student', who had 'covered all this [background] already, so I just had to repeat it'. The only fellow student who had become a professor was Yegorov.

40.   *New York Times*, April 27, 1992.

41.   Oleg Kalugin, author's interview, Oct. 30, 2018.

42.   Ruslan Linkov and Yuly Rybakov, author's interviews, St Petersburg, June 2 & 3, 2019.

43.   Orttung, *From Leningrad to St. Petersburg*, p. 134; Roux, Leningrad, TD 140, June 19, 1990, CADN.

44.   Sergei Baluyev, 'Anatoly Sobchak podderzhivayet programmu Mikhaila Gorbacheva', in *Smena* [date unrecorded, summer 1990]. The approval rating of the Lensoviet fell from 48 per cent in June to 30 per cent in October 1990, while Sobchak's rating was stable at above 60 per cent (Orttung, *supra*, pp. 135–6).

45.   Savisaar, Edgar, *Peaminister*, Kleio, Tartu, 2004, pp. 291–7.

46.   Unless otherwise indicated, the following is drawn from Shutov, *Krestnyi otets*, pp. 119–20, 124–6, 128 & 130.

47.   Valery Pavlov, author's interview, Nov. 27, 2019.

48.   Ibid.; Dmitry Zapolsky, author's interview, Nov. 26, 2019; Golovko, *Zhizn byla interesnoi*, Vol. 2, pp. 263–71.

49.   *Smena*, Oct. 10, 1991 & April 22, 1992. See also Konstantinov, Andrei, *Banditsky Peterburg*, Vol. 2, Amfora, St Petersburg, 2009, pp. 51–3. Shutov wrote that he began working for Sobchak in March 1990 and continued until at least the middle of September, which appears to be correct (*Krestnyi otets*, pp. 15 & 110). Valery Pavlov remembered first meeting him in May 1990. *Chas pik* wrote that 'in urban mythology, he was the connecting link between the mafia and the city authorities' (April 6, 1992).

50.   Roux, Leningrad, 85/AMB, Sept 18, 1990, CADN; Orttung, *From Leningrad to St. Petersburg*, p. 274.

51.   Roux, Leningrad, TD 093, April 9, and TD 098, April 18, 1990, CADN.

52.   *Chas pik*, Oct. 12, 1994.

53.   Putin, *First Person*, p. 88.

54.   Ibid., p. 91.

55.   Linkov has described Putin's help to Starovoitova on multiple occasions (Meier, Andrew, *Black Earth*, W. W. Norton, New York, 2003, p. 347; Linkov, Ruslan, *Zapiski nedobitka*, Amfora, St Petersburg, 2007, p. 73; Linkov, author's interview, June 2, 2019), and has

maintained his account despite denials by Putin's spokesman, Dmitry Peskov. Yuly Rybakov and Andrei Illarionov, both fierce critics of Putin, have given a different version.
Rybakov said that when Putin approached Starovoitova, offering to help with her campaign, she refused, and he started working for Sobchak shortly afterwards (Rybakov,
author's interview, June 3, 2019). Andrei Illarionov claimed to have heard the same story
from Starovoitova herself, shortly before her death in 1998 ('Smertelnaya oshibka Ana-
toliya Sobchaka', June 13, 2012, at aillarionov.livejournal.com/?skip=10&tag=%D0%9F%D
0%B8%D1%82%D0%B5%D1%80). The common point in all their accounts is that Putin
did approach her, whether she accepted his offer or not.

56. *Smena*, June 17, 1990.

57. Valery Pavlov said he first met Putin 'at the end of August or perhaps even the beginning
of September' (author's interview, *supra*). Dmitry Medvedev said that Sobchak invited him
to work as his adviser at the end of August and Putin arrived 'about a month later' (Svanidze, Nikolai and Marina, *Medvedev*, Amfora, St Petersburg, 2008, pp. 210–11). When
Ronald Reagan arrived in Leningrad on September 18, Pavlov and Shutov accompanied
Sobchak to the airport to greet him but Putin was not mentioned as being present (Shutov,
Krestnyi otets, p. 110). His appointment became official when Sobchak issued Decree No.
13-r, dated October 12, 1990 (Pavel Tsyplenkov, *20 let parlamentarizma v Sankt-Peterburge*, 2nd
edition, 2010, available online at www.litmir.me/br/?b=140104&p=5).

58. Sobchak and Krichevskaya, *Delo Sobchaka*.

59. Pavlov, author's interview, *supra*. Shutov claimed that he resigned after discovering that
Sobchak was allegedly salting away money in California, but that appears to be a fiction
(*Krestnyi otets*, pp. 103–6). The most intriguing aspect of Shutov's account is that he makes
no criticism of Putin, to whom he refers only in passing. Sobchak maintained that Shutov
worked for him only 'for two or three months' (*Vechernyi Peterburg*, Oct. 10, 1991) and that
he was never an official assistant but merely a volunteer. Other sources say that he was
finally given an official post a week before he was dismissed.

60. *Smena*, Oct. 10, 1991 & April 22, 1992; Konstantinov, *Banditsky Peterburg*, Vol. 2, pp. 51–3.

61. Roux, 97/AMB, Oct. 9, 1990, CADN.

62. *Smena*, Oct. 10, 1991 & Jan. 29, 1992. Putin may have suggested that Shutov had a financial
interest in the arrangement. Sobchak's wife, Lyudmila Narusova, said later that her husband broke with him after discovering that Shutov had started to abuse his position.

63. A photograph in *Pravda vostoka* on Oct. 9, 1991, shows Putin with Sobchak in Tashkent,
carrying his master's briefcase, a respectful distance behind (fergananews.com/article.
php?id=5517=).

64. Pavlov, author's interview, *supra*.

65. Barbara Hay, who had been appointed British Consul General, noted in her diary on October 16, 1991: 'Valery Pavlov is working in Sobchak's constituency office. He refuses to join
the staff at the Mayor's office. Wise man!'

66. Pavlov, author's interview, *supra*.

67. Putin, *First Person*, p. 89 (translation amended).

68. Putin's disparaging reference to the 'traditions of the Komsomol' made clear that he was
aiming his remarks not just at Shuto, but at Pavlov as well.

69. Linkov, author's interview, June 2, 2019.

70. 'Draft Proposal for the Lensoviet', attached to Roux, Leningrad, 132/AMB, Dec. 3, 1990,
CADN.

71. Savisaar, *Peaminister*, p. 286. The French Ambassador, Jean-Marie Mérillon, wrote the same

year that 'Leningrad in many respects appears to be a fourth Baltic State' (Mérillon, Moscow, 197 EU-URSS, June 13, 1990, CADN).

72.   Estonia had been a province of the Russian Empire since 1710, and before that had been part of the Livonian and Swedish empires. The Tartu treaty marked the first *de jure* recognition of Estonian statehood and its legacy would remain a point of contention in Estonian–Russian relations for decades after independence was finally restored. It was not, however, the only issue. In 1990 and early 1991, Arnold Rüütel, the Chairman of the Estonian Supreme Council and thus *de facto* President, campaigned unsuccessfully for the creation of an Ingerman State to be established in the disputed territory east of Narva, as a buffer between north-east Estonia and Russia. Rüütel imagined it as a homeland for the Ingrian people, the descendants of the original inhabitants of north-west Russia, but the idea was stillborn. Much more significant was an attempt by Russian settlers, shortly after the Komarovka incident, to declare a separatist republic in north-east Estonia with Narva as its capital. It, too, was prevented, but a few years later would re-emerge as a major problem for the Estonian government in which Putin would be closely involved.

73.   Ibid., pp. 287 & 959; Laar, Mart, *Pööre*, Read OÜ, Tallinn, p. 232. A similar venture in Pechory district, adjoining Estonia's southern border, was rebuffed by Soviet troops.

74.   Savisaar, *supra*, pp. 290–91 & 344–9.

75.   Laar, *Pööre*, p. 232, and author's interview, Tallinn, May 27, 2017.

76.   von Wistinghausen, Henning, *Im freien Estland*, Böhlau-Verlag, Vienna, 2004, p. 52, and Örjan Berner, author's interview, Stockholm, Feb. 26, 2017.

77.   Accounts of the events in Vilnius and their aftermath may be found in Aron, Leon, *Boris Yeltsin: A Revolutionary Life*, HarperCollins, London, 2000, pp. 410–17, and Taubman, William, *Gorbachev: His Life and Times*, Simon and Schuster, New York, 2017, pp. 575–7.

78.   von Wistinghausen, *supra*, pp. 54–5; Orttung, *From Leningrad to St. Petersburg*, p. 156; Roux, Leningrad, 009/AMB, Jan. 22, 1991, CADN.

79.   Taubman, *supra*, pp. 532 & 535.

80.   See ibid., pp. 500–538.

81.   von Wistinghausen, *supra*.

82.   Until August 25, 1991, Belarus was officially named Byelorussia. For simplicity it is here referred to throughout by its post-independence name, as are Moldova (formerly Moldavia), Kyrgyzstan (Kirghizia) and Turkmenistan (Turkmenia).

83.   *Nezavisimaya gazeta*, July 31, 1998.

84.   Smolyak, *Sobchak*, pp. 61–2 & 116.

85.   Ibid., pp. 63–4.

86.   *Chas pik*, Oct. 7, 1991.

87.   Orttung, *supra*, pp. 137–9.

88.   Matlock, Jack, *Autopsy on an Empire*, Random House, New York, 1995, pp. 540–54.

89.   Sobchak, *For a New Russia*, p. 175.

90.   This account is drawn from Sobchak, ibid., pp. 176–82. Sobchak said the phone call came at 6.30 a.m., but it must have been earlier. By 6.30 a.m. there was no need for a message from Kazakhstan, as the emergency decree had already been broadcast on Moscow Radio. See also Aron, *Yeltsin*, pp. 440–43, and Veritin, A., Miloserdova, N., and Petrov, G., *Protivostoyanie*, Ekopolis i Kultura, St Petersburg, 1992, pp. 12–13.

91.   Sobchak's account was at times exaggerated. He claimed, for instance, that paratroopers arrived at Yeltsin's dacha to arrest them '10 minutes after we left', and that three KGB officers at the airport, who had been instructed to arrest him, not only refused to do so but

assured his security until his plane took off' (*For a New Russia*, pp. 177–8). That was poetic licence. But on the essentials, his recollection was accurate, as was confirmed not only by French diplomatic reports (Delumeau, Leningrad, TD 174, 177, 178 and 181, August 20, 21, 22 and 26, 1991, CADN; Peissik, Moscow, TD 3740, August 20, 1991, CADN) but also by a conversation immediately after the coup between the British Ambassador, Rodric Braithwaite, and Sobchak's assistant, Valery Pavlov (Braithwaite, private diary, August 22, 1991).

92. Unless otherwise indicated, the following is drawn from Veritin et al., *Protivostoyanie*, pp. 14–18.

93. Ibid., pp. 26–7. See also Smolyak, *Sobchak*, pp. 70–71.

94. Blotsky, Vol. 2, p. 332.

95. Putin, *First Person*, p. 93.

96. Blotsky, Vol. 2, p. 319; von Wistinghausen, *Im freien Estland*, p. 106. Lyudmila's account (in Putin, *First Person*, pp. 92–3) confuses the chronology.

97. Putin, ibid., p. 92.

98. Veritin et al., *supra*, pp. 20 & 52–4. Sobchak's wife, Lyudmila Narusova, maintained that Putin had organised a security detachment to meet him at the airport. So did Franz Sedelmayer, a young German businessman in Leningrad, who remembered being told about the mission a few days after the putsch by one of the special forces officers who had been sent to the airport to provide an escort (Narusova, author's interview, Nov. 21, 2019; Sedelmayer, author's interview, Spotsylvania, Va., Oct. 30, 2018 and Sedelmayer, Franz, *Welcome to Putingrad*, privately published, 2017, p. 76). Sedelmayer had assumed that Putin must have organised it but Sobchak himself later confirmed that he had spoken to Kramarev directly (Sobchak, *For a New Russia*, p. 178). Four bodyguards flew with Sobchak from Moscow (*Chas pik*, Sept. 9, 1991).

99. Sobchak, *For a New Russia*, pp. 178–9.

100. Veritin et al., *supra*, p. 54.

101. Ibid., p. 63.

102. Sobchak, *For a New Russia*, pp. 178–81; Smolyak, *Sobchak*, p. 72.

103. Belyaev, author's interview, June 3, 2019.

104. 'I had experienced what had happened at Tbilisi,' Samsonov said later. 'What I learnt from that was that we in the army should not play political games' (Veritin et al., *supra*, p. 129).

105. Smolyak, *supra*, p. 70. Afterwards Lyudmila Narusova claimed that Putin had begged Sobchak to wear a bulletproof jacket, as, framed in the window, he would make a perfect target for a sniper. Sobchak, she said, refused, protesting that if he showed fear, how could he expect others not to (Sobchak and Krichevskaya, *Delo Sobchaka*). Unfortunately for the veracity of this moving tale, Putin was then still stuck in Vilnius. Narusova was even further away, on holiday on the Black Sea coast in Georgia.

106. Veritin et al., *supra*, pp. 70–73, Smolyak, *supra*, pp. 71–2 and Sobchak, *supra*, pp. 179-80.

107. Smolyak, *supra*, p. 73.

108. Both Samsonov and Shcherbakov had at the back of their minds the tragedy that had occurred on the same spot almost a century before, when the imperial guard opened fire on crowds converging on Palace Square to try to deliver a petition to the Tsar. 'Bloody Sunday', as it came to be called, triggered the 1905 revolution, which led indirectly to the Tsar's abdication and the Bolshevik revolution twelve years later.

109. John Pepper, author's interview, Jan. 24, 2019.

110. Yuly Rybakov, author's interview, St Petersburg, June 3 2019. Putin wrote later that they passed out pistols, but he left his own service revolver in a safe (*First Person*, p. 93. See also Golovko, *Zhizn byla interesnoi*, Vol. 1, p. 346).

111. Belyaev, author's interview, June 3, 2019; Veritin et al., *supra*, p. 112; 'Iz stenogrammy vystupleniya na soveschanii pravookhranitelnykh organov ... Arkadiya Kramareva', *Smena*, Aug. 23, 1991.

112. Veritin et al., *supra*, pp. 117–22; Smolyak., *supra*, p. 74. Sobchak later sought to minimise the time he had spent in the bunker, but the official report drawn up for the Petrosoviet said he had left the Mariinsky Palace at 12.40 a.m. and returned at 6.30 a.m. (*Vechernyi Peterburg*, Oct. 11, 1991).

113. Cited in Colton, Timothy, *Yeltsin: A Life*, Basic Books, New York, 2008, p. 194.

114. *Australian Financial Review*, Oct. 4, 1991.

115. Braithwaite, private diary, Aug. 22, 1991; see also *New York Times*, Sept. 11, 1991. Anatoly Chubais thought that, notwithstanding his denials, Sobchak was open to the possibility of a presidential career (Sobchak and Krichevskaya, *Delo Sobchaka*).

116. *Moskovskie novosti*, Sept. 1, 1991.

117. Narusova, author's interview, Nov. 21, 2019; Juhani Leppä, author's interview, Turku, March 4, 2017.

118. Soviet GDP fell by between 2.4 and 5 per cent in 1990 and by a further 5 per cent in 1991 (Goldman, Marshall, *The Piratization of Russia*, Routledge, London and New York, 2003, p. 13).

119. Roux, Leningrad/St Petersburg, 135/AMB, Dec. 4, 1990, 106/AMB, Oct. 8 and TD 243, Oct. 29, 1991, CADN.

120. Sobchak and Belyaev, letter to Jacques Delors, undated but Sept. 11, 1991, CADN.

121. Roux, 106/AMB, Oct. 8 and Delumeau, St Petersburg, TD 270, Nov. 25, 1991, CADN.

122. Barbara Hay, author's interview, Sept. 21, 2016.

123. Note ... sur l'approvisionnement, Nov. 12, 1991, CADN.

124. Ministère des Affaires Étrangères [MAE], Division médicale, Paris, 92/297/DV/CP (Dinah Vernant), March 4, 1992, CADN.

125. Jack Gosnell, author's interview, Falls Church, Va., Oct. 30–31, 2018. Gosnell maintained that the decision to take the food convoy through the city centre was made not by him but by the Soviet military. Nonetheless, it was his decision to lead the way, flying the American flag. The Europeans were furious at what they saw as US grandstanding, when, as the French put it, America had sent 'microscopic amounts' of aid (MAE, Division médicale, *supra*). The largest portion of aid came from the European Community, in particular from Germany

126. Hay, author's interview, Sept. 21, 2016. 'They all did it!', she said.

127. Delumeau, St Petersburg, TD 271, Nov. 26, 1991, CADN; MAE, Division médicale, *supra*. On BSE, see *Sankt-Peterburgskie vedomosti*, Jan. 11, 1992 and Braithwaite, private diary, Jan. 2–8 & 10, 1992.

128. Matlock, Jack, *Superpower Illusions*, Yale University Press, New Haven and London, 2011, pp. 107–9.

129. 'Note pour le Ministre', Ministère de l'Industrie, Paris [a series of four notes from Irène Commeau, all dated April 29, 1991], CADN.

130. Maly Sovet, 'Reshenie ob otchete deputatskoi gruppy po voprosu realizatsii Komitetom vneshnikh svyazei pri mere kvot na syr'e i materialy', May 8, 1992, online at libking.ru/books/nonf-/nonfiction/189647-9-marina-sale-doklad-o-deyatelnosti-v-v-putina-na-postu-glavy-komiteta-po-vneshnim-svyazyam-merii-sankt-peterburga.html#book. See also *Kommersant*, April 27, 1992. *Smena*, April 14, 1992, and some other sources put the total value at 124 million US dollars. Marina Salye's archive of documents related to the Maly Sovet investigation is online at www.facebook.com/photo/?fbid=384738471550788&set=a.384728321551803.94156.273762169315086

131. Vladimir Pribylovsky, *Pereklichka Vladimira Putina*, p. 35. Ilham's brother, Dzhangir Ragimov, was the director general of Dzhikop, which was a Russian–German joint venture.

132. Felipe Turover Chudinov, the son of a Spanish Civil War veteran who lived in Moscow, told Catherine Belton that 'he had been sent to St Petersburg to help Putin set up the oil-for-food scheme' and that the profits from it were to be used to repay debts to foreign front organisations incurred by the KGB and the Communist Party in Soviet times to finance influence operations abroad (Belton, *Putin's People*, pp. 92–3). The claim makes no sense. Soviet front organisations abroad had no funds of their own and were entirely financed from Moscow. Even if there had been debts, no one in Russia in the early 1990s would have dreamt of repaying them, nor would anyone have sent Turover to advise Putin on how to set up a scheme to do so. Turover, who held Spanish, Russian and Israeli passports, was the subject of a scathing investigative report by the leading Spanish newspaper, *El Pais* (Aug. 29, 1999), which called into question many aspects of his past. In Moscow, he worked in finance and cultivated the rich and powerful, becoming close in the late 1990s to the Prosecutor General, Yuri Skuratov. He fled Russia in 1999 during the Mabetex affair and afterwards blamed Putin for his troubles there. Belton does not go into that, describing him, incorrectly, as 'a former senior officer of the Foreign Intelligence Directorate of the KGB' and a scion of the elite of the intelligence service. Turover may well have been a *seksot*, a secret collaborator of the KGB, but his family background – he is Jewish – and his biography during the years he spent in Russia rule out his ever having been an officer in the security services, let alone for the First Chief Directorate or the SVR. Belton and others have suggested that the 'oil-for-food' scheme may have been intended to finance the Mayor's 'slush fund'. It is certainly true that Sobchak, like every other regional leader, established an off-the-books fund for what might euphemistically be called discretionary spending. But there is no evidence that the 'oil-for-food' deals were intended to finance it, let alone that they did so.

133. Pribylovsky, *supra*. Anikin was still listed as deputy head of the FRC in mid July 1992 but left shortly afterwards.

134. Aleksandr Belyaev, who was no friend of Putin, said that in fairness it had to be remembered that import–export business had always been handled by Moscow (Belyaev, 'O piterskoi karere Putina', interview with Radio Liberty, March 23, 2010, www.svoboda.org/a/1990526.html).

135. Not only did Khizha's barter deals fail, but in November 1991, he approved an 'oil-for-food' deal very similar to those which Putin later attempted (Maly Sovet, *supra*). 100,000 tons of diesel oil from the Kirishnefteorgsintez refinery in Leningrad oblast were exported on the basis that the proceeds would be used to buy foodstuffs. No food arrived in that case either. According to Andrei Nechayev, who was then first deputy Minister of Economic Affairs, the deal was handled through a company in Finland owned by Gennady Timchenko (Nechayev, author's interview, Moscow, Nov. 18, 2019).

136. Belyaev, *supra*.

137. Nechayev, *supra*. Vladimir Ivanidze, 'Spasaya podpolkovnika Putina: vtoraya popytka', March 16, 2010, www.svoboda.org/a/1983851.html

138. Putin said afterwards that the companies had approached the FRC, not the other way around, and that 'we agreed to their offer' (*First Person*, p. 98). According to Andrei Nechayev, companies all over Russia were keen to obtain export quotas because of the money that could be made from them, so in principle the claim was plausible (Nechayev, *supra*). On the other hand, many of the companies which Putin approved appeared to have

728 NOTES TO PAGES 154–58

been set up solely to undertake the import–export deals the committee licensed and several were run by his friends.

139. Cited in Michael Rieger, www.libertarianism.org/columns/world-without-prices-economic-calculation-soviet-union, Aug. 1, 2017.

140. Hay, author's interview, Sept. 21, 2016; Braithwaite, private diary, Feb. 22 and April 4, 1992.

141. Robert Sasson, author's interview, Moscow, June 13, 2019.

142. Belyaev, *supra*.

143. Putin, *First Person*, pp. 98–9.

144. Dawisha, Karen, *Putin's Kleptocracy: Who Owns Russia?*, Simon and Schuster, New York, 2014, pp. 117–18.

145. The British Ambassador, Rodric Braithwaite, was told by Tomas Alibegov, the first deputy chairman of the Russian Foreign Trade Bank, in January 1992: 'They are all at it: the chemical industry, the oil products industry, the car industry. The only industry which is not so far salting its money away abroad is the timber industry.' He added that the authorities were unable, or unwilling, to enforce penalties. The previous year Braithwaite had been told that billions of US dollars were being held illegally by state firms in foreign bank accounts (private diary, Jan. 9, 1991 and Jan. 8, 1992).

146. *Smena*, April 1, and *Kommersant*, April 27, 1992.

147. Aven issued a decree to this effect on March 25, 1992 (gdb.rferl.org/0476FAA5-7927-4B80-9827-A5A6B1E07DD5.jpg).

148. According to Putin, 'the customs office people, and first and foremost the *chinovniks* of the Ministry of Foreign Economic Relations [in St Petersburg], saw the licences slipping through their fingers', as a result of which they would lose control of significant financial flows (*Vechernyi Peterburg*, May 11, 1992). See also Ivanidze, 'Spasaya podpolkovnika Putina', *supra*.

149. Belyaev, *supra*; Putin, *First Person*, p. 98.

150. *Smena*, Jan. 16, 1992.

151. Boris Vishnevsky, author's interview, St Petersburg, May 31, 2019. See also Belyaev, *supra*.

152. The working group claimed that Putin's committee 'set the [purchase] prices' of the rare metals which were to be exported (Maly Sovet, 'Reshenie', May 8, 1992, and Pribylovsky, *supra*). That was no doubt what would have happened in Soviet times, but it was not how a free market worked. Dzhikop negotiated the price it paid for the rare earth metals with the state-owned companies which provided them, not with City Hall.

153. *Nevskoe vremya*, March 24, 1992; *Kommersant*, July 6, 1992.

154. Maly Sovet, 'Reshenie', May 8, 1992, *supra*. The report was forwarded to the Main Control Directorate in the last week of March (Yuri Boldyrev, author's interview, Moscow, Nov. 20, 2019).

155. *Smena*, March 31, 1992; 'Pochemu Marina Salye molchala o Putine 10 let?', March 2, 2010, www.svoboda.org/a/1972366.html

156. Alfred Kokh, author's interview, Rosenheim, Germany, Oct. 9, 2019.

157. Boldyrev, author's interview, Nov. 20, 2019. See also 'Kak Sobchak i Putin khodili na kover', March 9, 2010, at www.svoboda.org/a/1978453.html

158. *Sankt-Peterburgskie vedomosti*, Jan. 19, 1994. One company sold 10.4 million dollars' worth of copper in the West and imported 398,000 US dollars' worth of foodstuffs, banking the remaining 10 million abroad.

159. Gavriil Popov in Sobchak and Krichevskaya, *Delo Sobchaka*.

160. 'Kak Sobchak i Putin . . .', *supra*. Boldyrev issued his recommendation on March 30, five days after Aven's decree transferring Pakhomov's responsibilities to Putin's committee. He

said later that the Main Control Directorate had dealt with about 40 cases comparable to Putin's in the 18 months he spent there, and that 'four or five governors were dismissed as well as a number of deputy governors'. In certain cases, he added, Yeltsin refused to allow an investigation to proceed in order to protect the individual concerned.

161. *Smena*, March 3, *Sankt-Peterburgskie vedomosti*, March 5 and *Kommersant*, March 9, 1992. The end of rationing, which had begun in Leningrad with sugar in 1989, was announced at the end of April and took effect in June (*Sankt-Peterburgskie vedomosti*, April 25 and June 5, 1992).

162. The 'food scandal' has been discussed at length by Masha Gessen in *The Man Without a Face*, and by Karen Dawisha in *Putin's Kleptocracy*. Both accepted at face value the account of Marina Salye, whom Gessen (p. 104) called 'the city's most trusted politician', a description at odds with opinion polls at the time, which found that she was trusted by only 4 per cent of respondents. It was Salye who gave Gessen (p. 123) the fantasist figure of one billion dollars for the total value of goods exported, which Dawisha also quoted. Dawisha misunderstood the terms of the licensing agreements, writing that the 25 to 50 per cent commission on the proceeds of the export sales was to go to the Foreign Relations Committee, when in fact it went to the intermediary companies. She then stated, without citing any source or explaining how this might have happened, that 'it is clear that some of it went into the Mayor's Contingency Fund, which Putin had access to . . . thus making it another vehicle for corruption and capital flight' (pp. 109–10). Neither book pretends to be a balanced account. Gessen's chapter titles include 'The Autobiography of a Thug' and 'Insatiable Greed'. Dawisha wrote that, despite 'a huge effort to find concrete evidence of Putin's bribetaking', none was found, which proved not that he was innocent but merely how good he was at covering his tracks (p. 125). Sadly, Dawisha was already ill with cancer when her book was completed, and it contains errors which, had she been well, she would certainly not have let pass. As a scholar of Russian affairs, it is probably not the book she would have most wished to be remembered for.

163. *Smena*, Jan. 16, March 31, April 1 and May 9, 1992. A longer and much more critical inside-page article, echoing many of the points Salye had made, appeared in the paper on April 14, but it was an outlier. The main St Petersburg newspaper, *Sankt-Peterburgskie vedomosti*, carried on March 24 a factual account of Salye's report and noted on July 1 that Putin had been absolved of blame but gave no other details.

164. *Kommersant*, April 27 & July 6, 1992. See also *Nevskoe vremya*, April 1, 1992.

165. 'Pochemu Marina Salye molchala o Putine 10 let?', March 2, 2010, *supra*. Dmitry Lenkov, another leader of the 'DemRossiya' faction in the City Council which was in principle hostile to Putin, said afterwards that, compared with what had followed, the food scandal was 'innocent trifles' (*Nezavisimaya gazeta*, July 31, 1998).

166. *Sankt-Peterburgskie vedomosti*, July 1, 1992.

167. *Australian Financial Review*, Oct. 4, 1991.

168. Charles Ryan, author's interview, Jan. 19, 2019.

169. Delumeau, TD 181, August 26, 1991, CADN.

170. *Obozrevatel*, Jan. 1, 1993.

171. Author's interviews, Franz Sedelmayer, Oct. 30, 2018; Jack Gosnell, Oct. 30–31, 2018; Richard Miles, Dec. 11, 2018; John Pepper, Jan. 24, 2019; and Sedelmayer, *Putingrad*, pp. 12 & 37–8.

172. *Sankt-Peterburgskie vedomosti*, Sept. 14, 1991. Humanitarian aid was initially the responsibility of the Committee for Social Affairs, but was soon transferred to Putin's FRC. On the expansion of Pulkovo, see ibid., March 24 & May 12, 1994; on the FRC's role in the setting

up of the Foreign Currency Exchange, *Kommersant*, May 25, 1992; on the Oil Port, author's interviews, Charles Ryan, March 14, 2019, and Raivo Vare, Tallinn, March 1, 2017; on foreign television broadcasts, *Sankt-Peterburgskie vedomosti*, May 26, 1993; and on Crédit Lyonnais and BNP–Dresdner Bank, Marlène Julien, author's interview, Dana Point, California, Feb. 22, 2019, and *St. Petersburg Press*, Sept. 21–27, 1993.

173. *Kommersant*, May 25, 1992.
174. 'This is something which people don't know – Putin was put in charge of the property and funds of the Communist Party after it was banned . . . They discovered there a black treasury – money for campaigns, and offshore accounts' (Aleksandr Belyaev, author's interview, June 3, 2019). A partial list of Party property in the Leningrad Region is given in *Chas pik*, June 18, 1990 & May 12, 1992.
175. On Oct. 11, 1991, *Vechernyi Peterburg* reported that, in order to create an 'overall concept of tourist development in St Petersburg', any gambling project would henceforth require FRC approval. Two months later Putin was appointed head of the city's Gambling Commission (*Smena*, Jan. 4, 1992).
176. According to Aleksandr Belyaev (*supra*), Putin never had his own office at Mariinsky. Barbara Hay visited him at Smolny on October 31 (author's interview, Sept. 21, 2016). Sobchak himself apparently moved to Smolny in mid November.
177. George Handy, author's interview, Nov. 30, 2018.
178. Sedelmayer, author's interview, Dec. 12, 2018.
179. Dmitry Zapolsky, *Putinburg*, PVL Consulting (UK), 2019, pp. 300–301.
180. Hay, *supra*.
181. Yentaltseva worked for Putin from 1991 to 1996 (*First Person*, p. 96). Belton writes that Sechin had links with the KGB and, while a student at Leningrad University, had acted as an informer (*Putin's People*, p. 185). That may well be correct, but during his time in Africa he worked for military intelligence.
182. *Smena*, April 23, 1992.
183. Gurevich, *Putin*, p. 94.
184. Tom Adshead, a British banker who has worked in Russia for almost 30 years, described the typical modus operandi: 'It's a Russian management style . . . [At most] Russian organisations – there's a weekly meeting, and at each weekly meeting someone gets fired [or comes close to it]. That has to happen. The middle managers know this, so it's all prepared in advance. Someone has to be the sacrificial lamb . . . It's something that annoys me about a lot of Western Russian experts, because you get a completely different view of Russia when you've actually worked in a Russian organisation . . . [Even] most Westernised Russians would say that if you have a Russian organisation with Russians working in it, you can't manage it like you would a Western company. You have to be the very type of an aggressive boss, a *khozyain* . . . It just doesn't work otherwise . . . Most successful Russian organisations work in the Russian way and it's very despotic' (author's interview, Moscow, May 21, 2019).
185. Putin, *First Person*, p. 96.
186. *Smena*, April 23, 1992.
187. Belyaev, author's interview, June 3, 2019.
188. Pavlov, author's interview, Nov. 27, 2019.
189. Sven Hirdman, author's interview, Stockholm, Feb. 26, 2017. That reaction was not limited to foreigners. Dmitry Trenin, the head of the Carnegie Center in Moscow, took part in a small discussion group co-chaired by Sobchak and the French President, Jacques Chirac, in

St Petersburg in October 1994. 'Putin must have been there,' he said. 'But I have no recollection of him. Zero' (author's interview, Moscow, June 11, 2019).

190. Jaakko Kalela, author's interview, Helsinki, March 2, 2017. Hirdman said: 'He melted into the wall.'

191. Cited by Hay in author's interview, Sept. 21, 2016.

192. David Pepper, author's interview, Jan. 28, 2019.

193. Golovko, *Zhizn byla interesnoi*, Vol. 1, p. 347.

194. Blotsky, Vol. 2, p. 322.

195. Sture Stiernlöf, 'Vladimir Putin, en förslagen operator', for the Swedish Foreign Ministry, Jan. 17, 2000.

196. Märt Volmer, the Estonian Consul General, also remembered him speaking extremely quietly (Volmer, author's interview, Copenhagen, Oct. 10, 2017).

197. Stiernlöf, *supra*.

198. Gosnell, author's interview, Oct. 30, 2018.

199. Tom Pickering, author's interview, Washington, D.C., Feb. 15, 2019.

200. Sedelmayer, *Putingrad*, pp. 10–13.

201. Ibid., pp. 136–8; Sedelmayer, author's interview, Oct. 30, 2019.

202. Sedelmayer, *Putingrad*, pp. 122–4.

203. Ibid., and John Evans, author's interview, Washington, D.C., March 10, 2017.

204. Sedelmayer, author's interview, *supra*.

205. Usoltsev, *Sosluzhivets*, p. 216.

206. Sedelmayer, author's interview, *supra*. According to Vera Gurevich, as a child, Putin had been reluctant to speak at class meetings (*Putin*, p. 47). In Dresden, he disliked speaking in public and avoided it whenever possible (Usoltsev, *supra*, pp. 171–2). When he received a large French delegation visiting St Petersburg in the autumn of 1992, they came away feeling that they had been fobbed off with a second-rank official (Blatmann, TD 625, Sept. 14, 1992, CADN).

207. According to Belyaev, this was not the meeting where Putin was asked to explain the 'oil for food' affair but an earlier occasion (author's interview, June 3, 2019).

208. Putin, *First Person*, p. 39.

209. Ibid., p. 103. Among the foreigners, only Sture Stiernlöf wondered whether Putin's quiet demeanour did not conceal an innate shyness (Stiernlöf, *supra*, Jan. 17, 2000).

210. Stiernlöf, 'The Man Who Knew Putin', Dec. 17, 2014, published on the now defunct site, elderlywriter.blogspot.fr

211. A contemporary photograph shows Putin so attired. See also Kelly, *St Petersburg: Shadows of the Past*, pp. 274 & 410, n. 164. Years later these sartorial eccentricities continued. Andrei Illarionov, who later became Putin's economic adviser, remembered that when he was introduced to him in 1998, he was wearing a lime-green suit (author's interview, Washington, D.C., Feb. 16, 2019).

212. Gunnar Lund, author's interview, Stockholm, Feb. 26, 2017.

213. Blotsky, Vol. 2, pp. 275–6 & 321 (lessons). Lyudmila Narusova, author's interview, Nov. 21, 2019 (Piterschule). In her interviews with Blotsky, Lyudmila Putin dropped heavy hints that her marriage was not entirely happy, and later both she and Putin were more explicit in conversations with Lyudmila's German friend, Irene Pietsch, recounted in her book, *Heikle Freundschaften*.

214. Author's interviews in Paris with Marek Halter, June 24, 2016, and Elizabeth Guigou, Oct. 14, 2016.

215. Putin, *First Person*, pp. 100–101; *Business Standard*, New Delhi, Aug. 29, 2013 (www.business-standard.com/article/international/putin-filmmaker-says-lonely-leader-scared-to-loosen-grip-113082900011_1.html).

216. Irene Pietsch, *Heikle Freundschaften*, p. 377.

217. *Hufvudstadsbladet*, Helsinki, Sept. 22, 2016. The match took place in 1994.

218. Leppä, author's interview, March 4, 2017; *Helsingin Sanomat*, Jan. 9, 2000.

219. Putin, *First Person*, p. 150.

220. *Vechernyi Peterburg*, Aug. 5, 1991. Like most newspaper interviews at that time, the text was submitted to Putin for correction before publication (Pyotr Kotov, author's interview, St Petersburg, May 28, 2019).

221. *Sankt-Peterburgskie vedomosti*, Sept. 14, 1991.

222. *Vechernyi Peterburg, supra.*

223. Charles Ryan, author's interview, March 3, 2019.

224. Alfred Kokh wrote that Chubais was dismissed (Kokh and Svinarenko, *A Crate of Vodka*, p. 201). Chubais himself denied that (Delumeau, TD 266, Nov. 20, 1991, CADN). However, his relationship with Sobchak was difficult. The projected Free Enterprise Zone, which he had championed, was going nowhere and Sobchak, very conscious of his status as a full professor, had been reluctant to take advice from a younger man who was merely an associate professor (Kokh, author's interview, Oct. 9, 2019).

225. Charles Ryan, *supra*. Putin maintained later that he 'never had any direct interaction with Chubais' when they were in St Petersburg (*First Person*, p. 193).

226. *Smena*, April 23, 1992. The former Property Committee head, Aleksandr Utevsky, left the City Hall in December, 1991.

227. Kokh, author's interview, *supra*.

228. Ryan, *supra*.

229. *Sankt-Peterburgskie vedomosti*, Oct. 26 and Nov. 5, 1993.

230. *Smena*, March 3 and *Chas pik*, April 6, 1992. The *New York Times* concurred. In a rare report from St Petersburg, the newspaper's Moscow correspondent, Steven Erlanger, wrote: 'It is Mr. Khizha who . . . is now Mr. Sobchak's chief deputy, managing the city while the Mayor thinks, speaks and travels abroad' (April 27, 1992).

231. *Chas pik*, ibid.

232. *Smena*, May 22, 1992. As a former 'red director', Khizha was brought into the government in an attempt to mollify the Russian Supreme Soviet, which opposed Yeltsin's market reforms (Aron, *Yeltsin*, p. 499).

233. *Sankt-Peterburgskie vedomosti*, Feb. 19, 1992.

234. *Chas pik*, June 27, 1992. Sobchak was prone to act on impulse. While there is no evidence that Putin counselled caution, the subtle, drawn-out manner in which Shcherbakov was edged aside resembles Putin's way of doing things rather than the Mayor's full-frontal approach.

235. *Smena*, Nov. 17, 1992.

236. Ibid. and *Nevskoe vremya*, Nov. 17, 1992.

237. *Sankt-Peterburgskie vedomosti*, Nov. 28, 1992, and Jan. 16 & 26, 1993.

238. Vatanyar Yagya, whom Sobchak appointed to succeed Chubais as his Chief Adviser on Economic Affairs, and subsequently on International Relations as well, might also have been seen as a rival. However Putin treated him differently. Yagya was an academic and had previously chaired the International Affairs Commission of the Lensoviet. At the end of 1991, he spent two months working as Putin's deputy in the newly formed FRC. He had

little political ambition. When he became Sobchak's Chief Adviser, he was careful not to encroach on Putin's territory. They worked together, apparently without friction, for the next five years (*Smena*, July 25, 1991 & Jan. 10, 1992).

239. Cited in Aron, *Yeltsin*, p. 507.

240. See, for example, *Kommersant*, Feb. 9, and *Sankt-Peterburgskie vedomosti*, April 15, 1993.

241. Blatmann, TD 222, March 10, 1992, CADN. Although Belyaev and other leading figures in the Petrosoviet supported Yeltsin, they were not indifferent to Khasbulatov's call for local soviets to 'intensify supervision' of executive bodies (*RFE/RL Daily Report*, June 2, 1993).

242. *Izvestia*, Sept. 22, 1992.

243. Ibid., Sept. 25 & 28, 1993. Shcherbakov's position was less clear-cut than that might make it appear. He refused Rutskoi's offer to appoint him Mayor in Sobchak's place and, despite the rift, appeared regularly with Putin at briefings for the consuls.

244. Blatmann, TD 770, Oct. 5, 1993, CADN. This section is drawn from Blatmann's handwritten notes on Putin's daily briefings, conserved in the French Diplomatic Archives at Nantes (CADN), and from his despatches, TD 730, Sept. 25 and TD 743, Sept. 27 (on Shcherbakov); TD 722, Sept. 22; TD 726, Sept. 23; TD 729, Sept. 25; TD 742, Sept. 27; TD 753, Sept. 29; and TD 759, Sept 30; as well as from *Sankt-Peterburgskie vedomosti*, *Nevskoe vremya* and *Vechernyi Peterburg*, Sept. 22–Oct. 5, 1992.

245. Cited in Aron, *Yeltsin*, p. 537.

246. Ibid., p. 544.

247. Sture Stiernlöf, 'Vladimir Putin, en förslagen operator', *supra*.

248. This and the following section are drawn from Orttung, *From Leningrad to St. Petersburg*, pp. 208–15 & 271–2.

249. The first published reference to Yakovlev's appointment appears to have been in *Sankt-Petersburgskie vedomosti* (Feb. 20, 1993), which described him as deputy Mayor responsible for Urban Economy.

250. If both Sobchak and Putin were away, either Yakovlev or the head of the city administration, Valery Malyshev, acted in Sobchak's place. For the July, 1994, Bastille Day reception at the French consulate, Putin was guest of honour, followed by Yakovlev and Kudrin in that order (CADN).

251. Sergeyev, who had previously been Khizha's first deputy and also represented the defence industry, had been appointed in May 1992 (*Chas pik*, May 25, 1992).

252. Kudrin, Vitaly Mutko, the deputy Mayor responsible for Social Affairs, and Mikhail Manevich, deputy Mayor in charge of the Property Committee, were all friends. So were Oleg Kharchenko, the City Architect, and Vladimir Yakovlev, the chairman of the Cultural Committee (no relation to his homonym), who were also deputy mayors. Valery Malyshev, another deputy (later, first deputy) Mayor and Andrei Stepanov who headed the Food Supply Committee, were uncommitted. Besides Sobchak and his nine deputies, the City Government had three other members responsible for the police, human rights and justice.

253. *Nevskoe vremya*, May 8, 1996.

6: The Grey Cardinal

1. Belyaev, author's interview, June 3, 2019.

2. *Chas pik*, Nov. 25, 1991. Ten years later, in an interview with Oleg Blotsky, Putin gave a long, rambling account of the purported attempts to blackmail him, in which he claimed that

those incidents had made him ask himself whether he should resign from the KGB (Blotsky, Vol. 2, pp. 328–9). Others, including Roldugin (*First Person*, p. 85), Bragin (Strana. ru, March 9, 2004, at www.flb.ru/info/26023.html) and Agartanov (Usoltsev, *Sosluzhivets*, p. 239), remembered him wondering aloud whether he should continue working for the KGB as early as 1990. Bragin thought Putin was frustrated that his career was not making progress. That, too, appears to have been an attempt to divert attention from his mission to cultivate Sobchak.

3.   Putin later claimed that a television interview he gave that winter was in response to the purported 'blackmail' attempts (*First Person*, p. 92). That interview, lasting 45 minutes and filmed by the well-known Russian director, Igor Shadkhan, was broadcast under the title, *Vlast'* ['Powerholders'] on March 2, 1992. There was no pre-publicity and almost no one remembers watching it (*Chas pik*, March 2, and *Smena*, March 3, 1992; Natalya Shadkhan, author's interview, St Petersburg, May 31, 2019). In fact, in *Vlast'*, he referred to his KGB career only very briefly (transcript, privately held). The programme had been commissioned by Sobchak for quite different reasons. It was to publicise the work of the Mayor's Office at a time when the Petrosoviet was criticising the administration in general and Putin in particular for the failed 'oil-for-food' deal (Dmitry Yezhkov and Lyudmila Narusova, author's interviews, May 30 and Nov. 21, 2019).

4.   Blotsky, Vol. 2, pp. 300–301.

5.   In August 1991, Sobchak had appointed Colonel Pavel Koshelev, who had previously worked in the 2nd and 5th Departments in Leningrad, as Head of Administration in the Petrograd district of the city. Unlike Putin, Koshelev did not hide the fact that he was still a member of the KGB's active reserve (*Chas pik*, Dec. 9, 1991). Later Viktor Ivanov was appointed directly from the KGB's successor organisation, the FSK, to become Chief of the Administrative Organs Department of the City Administration. Other ex-KGB recruits included Ivanov's predecessor, Anatoly Smirnov; Viktor Kochyrev; and Viktor Zolotov, who headed Sobchak's bodyguard service.

6.   In the interview, Putin deliberately blurred the distinction between his initial meeting with Sobchak in 1990 and Sobchak's invitation to him to head the FRC a year later, merely stating that he had resigned 'by the summer of the present year' (*nyneshnim letom*).

7.   Usoltsev, *Sosluzhivets*, p. 239.

8.   Putin had written an undergraduate thesis on international trade law in his last year at the Law Faculty. There is nothing to suggest that he intended to write a dissertation on this or any other topic after his return from Germany. When, in 1996, he did embark on a thesis, it was on a very different subject – natural resources – and for quite different reasons.

9.   Putin, *First Person*, pp. 92–4. See also Blotsky, Vol. 2, pp. 330–32.

10. Sobchak and Krichevskaya, *Delo Sobchaka*.

11. Blotsky, Vol. 2, pp. 330–32. The new version also had the advantage of portraying Vladimir Kryuchkov, who had been amnestied in 1994, in a positive light. By then Putin had come round to the view that although Kryuchkov and the other putschists had been mistaken, their motives had been honourable.

12. Ibid.

13. Putin, *First Person*, p. 96.

14. Catherine Belton quotes an unnamed colleague of Putin as saying that he continued to be paid by the KGB as a member of the active reserve for at least a year after the putsch (*Putin's People*, p. 24).

15. Putin told an interviewer in 1999 that he had 'recently' been promoted to 'full colonel in

the reserves' (*Komsomolskaya pravda*, July 8, 1999; see also *First Person*, p. 133) – a promotion which would not have been possible had he left the service, as he claimed, eight years earlier. Further evidence that he continued to serve was furnished by his income declarations for 2004 and 2011, in which he stated that he was receiving a military pension as a retired KGB officer (*Moscow Times*, Dec. 23, 2012). To be eligible for a pension, an officer had to have served a minimum of 20 years.

16. On the uncertain future of the security services in the winter of 1993, see Voronov, *Sluzhba*, pp. 140–57, and *Chas pik*, Dec. 29, 1993.

17. Sedelmayer, author's interview, Dec. 12, 2018. The same uncertainty about where Putin stood is suggested by his account of a meeting with some KGB colleagues, who supposedly asked him if he could obtain Sobchak's signature on a document they needed. To show them the trust the Mayor placed in him, he brought out some blank sheets with Sobchak's signature. At that, he said, they desisted (*First Person*, p. 90). The story is implausible, but if an incident of this kind occurred, it must have been in late 1993 or early 1994 – in other words, at about the same time Sedelmayer was told that no one knew where Putin's loyalties lay any more – because until then Sobchak had delegated his signature not to Putin but to Vice Admiral Shcherbakov.

18. There is a view among western intelligence services that it would have made no difference whether Putin had resigned or not – he would still have been able to work with his former KGB colleagues. That would certainly have been true had he left to work in the private sector, as many KGB officers did in the early 1990s. But to have switched sides after being assigned to work with Sobchak – an avowed opponent of the KGB and its successors – would not have been seen in the same way.

19. Decree No. 1192-r, Nov. 23, 1994, in *Sankt-Peterburgskie vedomosti*, Feb. 28, 1995.

20. Ibid., July 2, 1994.

21. Tom Pickering and Strobe Talbott, author's interviews, Washington, D.C., Feb. 15, 2019. *Sankt-Peterburgskie vedomosti* commented sourly that it hoped that 'in Moscow, [Clinton] will be in a better mood' (April 20, 1996).

22. Ivan Lavrentjev, '1993. aasta Narva autonoomia referendumi, läbiviimine ja-kukkumine', Bachelor's Degree Dissertation, Tallinna Ülikool, Ajaloo Instituut, Tallinn, 2015.

23. Sedelmayer, *Putingrad*, pp. 65–6, 135–40 & 162; *Sankt-Peterburgskie vedomosti*, Aug. 3, 1994; Svetlana Gavrilina, author's interview, Nov. 25, 2019.

24. Blotsky, Vol. 2, p. 320.

25. Putin, *First Person*, p. 94.

26. Ibid., p. 85.

27. See 'Soratniki po borbe', Dec. 21, 2015, at putinism.wordpress.com/2015/12/21/soratniki and antimonstrs.livejournal.com/80016.html

28. This account draws on the memories of Dmitry Potapenko (author's interview, Moscow, Nov. 22, 2019). See also Volkov, Vadim, *Violent Entrepreneurs*, Cornell University Press, Ithaca, N.Y., 2002.

29. Ibid., pp. 100–101.

30. *Sankt-Peterburgskie vedomosti*, Feb. 3, 1994.

31. That year there were 1,330 murders in St Petersburg, with a population of 5 million, compared to 1,177 murders in New York, with a population 40 per cent bigger. See also the crime statistics in ibid., Jan. 11, 1994.

32. Klebnikov, Paul, *Godfather of the Kremlin: Boris Berezovsky and the Looting of Russia*, Harcourt, New York, 2000, p. 32.

33. *Chas pik*, March 3, 1995. The official figure was 8 per cent, but the police estimated the true rate to be four or five times more.

34. *Sankt-Peterburgskie vedomosti*, Feb. 2, and *Chas pik*, March 16, 1994.

35. Golovko, *Zhizn byla interesnoi*, Vol. 1, pp. 346–50.

36. *Chas pik*, Aug. 15, 1994. The survey was undertaken at a school in Kharkiv, in Ukraine, but there is no reason to think that the results in St Petersburg would have been very different.

37. Ibid., April 4, 1996.

38. Dmitry Potapenko, author's interview, Nov. 22, 2019.

39. *Sankt-Peterburgskie vedomosti*, May 13, 1994.

40. Cited in ibid., June 17, 1994.

41. Yevgeny Vyshenkov, author's interview, June 1, 2019.

42. *Chas pik*, March 30, 1992.

43. Ibid., Aug. 24, 1994.

44. *Sankt-Peterburgskie vedomosti*, Sept. 16, 1994.

45. Ibid., Aug. 4, 1993.

46. Ibid., June 16, 1995.

47. Sedelmayer, *Putingrad*, pp. 191–3. It was officially named the 'Fund for the Security of Enterprises and Persons' (*Sankt-Peterburgskie vedomosti*, Oct. 8, 1993). Anatoly Smirnov went on to become First Vice President of the Baltic College of Lawyers.

48. Dmitry Zapolsky, *Putinburg*, pp. 142–3, 155–6 & 327; *Chas pik*, Sept. 14. 1995.

49. Volkov, *Violent Entrepreneurs*, pp. 108–14 & 124.

50. John Evans, author's interview, March 10, 2017. For details of the Subway dispute, see *St. Petersburg Times*, July 11 and Aug. 15 & 29, and *Chas pik*, Aug. 30, 1995.

51. Sedelmayer, author's interview, Dec. 12, 2018.

52. The following is drawn from the *St. Petersburg Times*, April 7, 1997; March 9 & 16, April 24, May 1 & 12, June 26 & 30, 1998; April 30, 1999; May 28, 2002; Aug. 29 & Oct. 3, 2003; April 30, 2004; and from *Vedomosti*, Moscow, Oct. 5, 2001.

53. *Sankt-Peterburgskie vedomosti*, April 29, 1994.

54. *Chas pik*, Nov. 17, 1995.

55. Vyshenkov, author's interview, June 1, 2019.

56. This account is drawn from *Chas pik*, Jan. 12, March 22 & May 25, and *Sankt-Peterburgskie vedomosti*, Jan. 17, 19 & 27 and May 16, 1995.

57. Kumarin became a PFC Vice President in 1998, by which time Sobchak was no longer Mayor. He was later forced to give up the post but continued to control the company until he was arrested in 2007. See also Volkov, *Violent Entrepreneurs*, pp. 112–15 & 124.

58. Vyshenkov, author's interview, June 1, 2019. According to Dmitry Yezhkov (author's interview, May 30, 2019), Traber had protection from the security services and, by employing Chechen enforcers, soon acquired a monopoly on the antiques trade in the city.

59. *Sankt-Peterburgskie vedomosti*, Oct. 20, 1994. The British Consul, Barbara Hay, remembered Lyudmila Narusova trying to take Mrs Thatcher to antique shops when she visited in October 1991, and wondering what lay behind it. There seemed to be something 'not straight' going on, she thought. 'Maybe people did have [real antiques] in their attics, but maybe they came from somewhere else . . .' (Hay, author's interview, Sept. 25, 2016).

60. Robert Sasson, author's interview, June 13, 2019.

61. Thirty years later, Kumarin would be in prison and Petrov in exile. Through holding companies in Cyprus, Traber then controlled not only the Oil Port and the St Petersburg Sea Port, but also the new ports at Primorsk and Ust-Luga (see 'Terminal v portu Ust-Luga

perekhodit pod control Ilyi Trabera', Jan. 22, 2018, www.dp.ru/a/2018/01/22/SMI_ terminal_v_portu_Ust; Anastasia Kirilenko, '4% Putina: Kak blizkie k Kremlyu kriminalnye avtoritety otmyvayut neftyanye dengi v Monako', Dec. 19, 2017, theins.ru/korrupciya/ 85048; and Roman Anin, 'Zavody, tsisterny, ofshory, sosedi', in *Novaya gazeta*, April 19, 2011.

62. Vyshenkov, author's interview, June 1, 2019. Kumarin had used his influence with the Mayor's Office to get the City Administration to finance a flyover at Avtovo, allowing freight trains carrying oil to go directly to the port. In 2016, he was sentenced to an additional 23 years in a penal colony for the attempted murder of Vasiliev.

63. This account comes from the former Estonian Minister of State, Raivo Vare (author's interview, Tallinn, March 1, 2017). Vare represented Estonia in Royal Pakhoed's development of the Tallinn port. His Dutch colleague, Franz Nobel, had negotiated the agreement in St Petersburg and was present at the meeting where Putin spoke. Royal Pakhoed subsequently became part of the Royal Vopal Group.

64. According to Aleksandr Gorshkov, when Putin was deputy Mayor he used to meet Traber at the PFC office near Liteiny Prospekt. Traber was already sufficiently powerful that he felt able not only to require the deputy Mayor to come to him, rather than the other way round, but he often kept Putin waiting (author's interview, St Petersburg, Nov. 27, 2019). Traber's bodyguard, Sergei Kosyrev, also remembered Putin's visits (Anastasia Kirilenko, '4% Putina', *supra*). There have been frequent claims that, at some point in the discussions concerning the oil port, threats were made against Putin's family and he sent his daughters to Germany for safety – by some accounts as wards of the Dresdner Bank representative, Matthias Warnig. The most credible testimony to that effect comes from a Western banker, a colleague of Warnig, who insists on anonymity. The claims have proved impossible to verify and Yevgeny Vyshenkov, whose contacts in St Petersburg criminal circles are unrivalled, doubts that they are true (author's interview, June 1, 2019).

65. The following account is drawn from Sedelmayer, *Putingrad*, pp. 205–28; Sedelmayer, author's interview, Oct. 30, 2018; *Nevskoe vremya*, Oct. 19, 1995; *Sankt-Peterburgskie vedomosti*, Oct. 11 & 24, 1995; and *St. Petersburg Times*, Oct. 24, 1995, Jan. 30, 1996, Dec. 19, 2008 & Oct. 19, 2010.

66. Gleb Pavlovsky, who would go on to become Yeltsin's, and later, Putin's spin doctor, said: 'St Petersburg was unique at that time . . . in having two different worlds, criminal . . . and political, right next to each other. Somewhere in between these two spheres were Putin and his colleagues . . . [They] straddled the frontier between the two.' (Sobchak and Krichevskaya, *Delo Sobchaka*).

67. The quotation is from Vladimir Yakovlev (Sergei Shelin, author's interview, St Petersburg, May 29, 2019). Yakovlev was speaking of his own administration, but it was true of Sobchak's time as well.

68. *Sankt-Peterburgskie vedomosti*, Oct. 6, 1993.

69. Ibid., Oct. 8, 1993.

70. *Kommersant*, Moscow, Dec. 2, 1995.

71. From an interview published in *Nevskoe vremya*, March 17, 1994.

72. *Kommersant*, Sept. 12, 1996. The Kharchenko case was reported at length in *Chas pik*, Aug. 8, Oct. 20 & Dec. 29, 1993; Oct. 12 & 19 and Dec. 21, 1994; and June 6, 1995. Officers in the Transport Department of the FSB had been angered by Kharchenko's decision to end the Soviet-era practice of having FSB officers attached to each merchant ship, which provided them with opportunities not only for travel but for obtaining foreign currency.

73. Konstantinov, Andrei, *Korrumpirovannyi Peterburg*, Folio, Moscow, 1997, Part 4, 'Levkina ikra', www.e-reading.club/bookreader.php/29224/Konstantinov_-_Korrumpirovannyii_ Peterburg.html; *Izvestia*, Feb. 2 and *Kommersant*, Sept. 2, 1995; *Ogonyok*, Nov. 4, 1996.

74. *Kommersant*, June 24, 1997.

75. See *Nezavisimaya gazeta*, July 31, 1998.

76. Sergei Baluyev, author's interview, St Petersburg, May 29, 2018.

77. Vyshenkov, author's interview, June 1, 2019.

78. *Kommersant*, Dec. 5, 1992 and *Sankt-Peterburgskie vedomosti*, April 13 & June 9, 1993.

79. *Sankt-Peterburgskie vedomosti*, Aug. 27, 1993. See also ibid., Feb 24 & April 22, 1994.

80. Pribylovsky, *Pereklichka Vladimira Putina*, pp. 46–7.

81. *Chas pik*, Oct. 12, 1994.

82. *Kommersant*, March 31, 2000.

83. According to Dmitry Zapolsky, it was built by the Turkish construction company, ATA, which was then active in St Petersburg (*Putinburg*, p. 339). Another plausible source of finance was Twentieth Trust, a construction company headed by a member of the Legislative Assembly, Sergei Nikeshin, who was close to Sobchak and had been granted contracts by the city authorities on exceptionally favourable terms. Karen Dawisha, relying on the testimony of Andrei Zykov, a one-time investigator in the Russian prosecutor's office with a penchant for conspiracy theories, claimed incorrectly that Twentieth Trust built villas in Spain for Putin, Sobchak and others. Nikeshin's firm did indeed build an apartment complex in the Spanish town of Torrevieja, but it did not build villas there for Putin or anyone else (*Putin's Kleptocracy*, pp. 146–7). Putin and his wife, Lyudmila, both claimed later that they had been building the dacha in Karelia since 1991 (*First Person*, pp. 119 & 121–2; also p. 115). That was presumably intended to disguise the fact that it had been paid for by others.

84. In 1992, when Putin was appointed deputy Mayor, he said his salary was ten times the minimum wage, or 3,420 roubles, equivalent to 100 US dollars a month at the official exchange rate (*Sankt-Peterburgskie vedomosti*, Feb. 29, 1992). In 1995, President Yeltsin's official salary was said to be 25 million roubles a year (with the rampant inflation of the time, then worth 400 US dollars a month); the Mayor of Moscow, Luzhkov, claimed that he earned 12 million roubles (200 dollars a month), which at that time was barely enough to keep a family of three alive; Sobchak declared 800 dollars a month, including book royalties and lecture fees abroad (*Nevskoe vremya*, April 16, 1996). None of these figures bore any relation to the real income of those concerned.

85. It is possible that Putin's dacha was discreetly financed by his neighbours, the other members of what would later be known as the *Ozero* cooperative, all of whom were wealthy and who may well have wished to express their appreciation to a highly placed city official.

86. Dmitry Travin, author's interview, St Petersburg, June 4, 2019.

87. *Vlast'*, transcript, privately held.

88. *Smena*, April 23, 1992.

89. Pyotr Aven, *Vremya Berezovskogo*, AST, Moscow, 2019, pp. 123–4. The fact that Aven went out of his way to protect Putin during the food scandal, six months later, may well have been in part to make up for this episode.

90. Gessen, *Man Without a Face*, pp. 15–16. Gessen dates this to 1990. It must have been several years later.

91. Aven, pp. 353–4.

92. Natalya Gevorkyan, author's interview, Paris, March 31, 2016. In a Western context, that story might sound far-fetched. In Russia, it is exactly how people behave.

93. Charles Ryan, author's interview, March 14, 2019.

94. John Scarlett, who was MI6 Moscow Station Chief from 1991 to 1994 and later head of MI6 from 2004 to 2009, spoke of Putin's attitude in very similar terms. He said he knew of one case where Putin took 'quite a large sum', adding: 'I can't give you the details – but I am sure of what I say. I wouldn't blame him for that, it's not a condemnation – I might have acted the same way in those circumstances: everyone was taking what they could get when there was an opportunity' (Scarlett, author's interview, London, Sept. 26, 2016).

95. This is the case made by Karen Dawisha in *Putin's Kleptocracy* (Ch. 3, 'Accusations of Illicit Activities', esp. pp. 126–45), in which she also addressed Putin's relations with the private security service, Baltik-Eskort, and his association with Leonid Reiman, who later became Russia's Telecommunications Minister. This is not the place to analyse her charges in detail, but in each case, she failed to find a 'smoking gun' proving that Putin personally profited from those connections. While she wrote with justification of 'the list of Putin's close allies who were mired in one corruption scandal after another' (p. 154), propinquity is not the same as guilt. Vladimir Pribylovsky dealt with the same issues in *Pereklichka Vladimira Putina* (esp. pp. 24–41), but was more cautious about drawing sweeping conclusions. The following account is drawn mainly from contemporary reports in *Sankt-Peterburgskie vedomosti*, *Kommersant*, *Chas pik* and *Nevskoe vremya*.

96. Not everyone approved. The police chief, Arkady Kramarev, complained that it was immoral for the city to use gambling revenues to pay its way (*Smena*, March 28, 1992).

97. In 1993, there were 26 registered casinos, 180 betting parlours and 1,600 slot machines in the city.

98. Putin, *First Person*, pp. 101–2.

99. *Sankt-Peterburgskie vedomosti*, Dec. 21, 1994.

100. Kudrin replaced Putin as Chairman on October 15, 1992 (*Sankt-Peterburgskie vedomosti*, Sept. 7, 1993, and Pribylovsky, *supra*, pp. 24–5). The Mayor's Office did not begin issuing licences to gambling establishments until February 1994 (ibid., Feb. 9, 1994).

101. Dmitry Zapolsky, *Putinburg*, pp. 49–51, 61, 69 & 89; Smolyak, *Sobchak*, p. 135. Mirilashvili later served an eight-year sentence in a labour camp on a trumped-up charge of having created 'a criminal group' to free his elderly father who had been kidnapped for ransom (*Vestnik*, June 25, 2003).

102. The above is taken from *Turun Sanomat*, Jan. 6 and *Sankt-Peterburgskie vedomosti*, Jan. 10 & June 6, 1995; Leppä, author's interview, March 4, 2017; and Anders Blom, author's interview, March 5, 2017. According to Leppä, Elia and Putin have remained in touch ever since.

103. Osmo Lipponen, author's interview, Helsinki, May 30, 2017. For a somewhat exaggerated account, see also Åslund, Anders, *Russia's Capitalist Revolution*, Peterson Institute, Washington, D.C., 2007, p. 201.

104. An extract from the speech is available at www.youtube.com/watch/?v=vGP99cz35HI

105. Blotsky, Vol. 2, p. 354.

106. *Chas pik*, Oct. 12, 1994.

107. The following account is from Svetlana Gavrilina, who worked for *Smena* in the mid 1990s (author's interview, Nov. 25, 2019).

108. Ibid. Putin had evidently taken to heart Roldugin's reproach that he gabbled. He may have learnt from Sobchak, who, as Aleksandr Gorshkov recalled, was also capable of giving an

animated interview and saying absolutely nothing (Gorshkov, author's interview, Nov. 27, 2019).

109. Gavrilina, *supra*.

110. *Chas pik*, Oct. 12, 1994.

111. The apartment, at 17–24 Line 2, Vasilyevsky Ostrov, comprised 1,200 square feet (112.8 sq. m.), including a 170-square-foot (16 sq. m.) kitchen (Yevgeny Vyshenkov, private communication, June 22, 2019). The family moved in at the end of 1993.

112. See for instance Dawisha, *Putin's Kleptocracy*, p. 95.

113. Blotsky, Vol. 2, p. 379.

114. Andrei Illarionov argues that there was probably a much larger sum in the briefcase and that, in any case, Putin would have kept the bulk of his savings at his apartment in St Petersburg (author's interview, Washington, D.C., March 13, 2019). There is no evidence for this, however, and given the risk of burglary from an empty flat, he might well have preferred to keep his money with him. Lyudmila told Irene Pietsch that the family had lost all their savings in the fire (*Heikle Freundschaften*, p. 237).

115. Blotsky, Vol. 2, p. 321.

116. Charles Ryan, author's interview, March 14, 2019.

117. Lyudmila Narusova, author's interview, Nov. 21, 2019.

118. This account is drawn from Putin, *First Person*, pp. 104–10 and Blotsky, Vol. 2, pp. 352–3.

119. *Chas pik* stated: 'To get ill in St Petersburg is life-threatening. There is no medicine and operations are not being done' (Oct. 26, 1994).

120. Putin said later that he went to the Emergency Room at the hospital but left after the chief doctor assured him that all was well (*First Person*, p. 104). That may have been so, though it is at odds with Turner's account. His secretary, Marina Yentaltseva, who looked after the children until Lyudmila's mother arrived from Kaliningrad, said Putin had had meetings all that evening and 'got free of Ted Turner' only in the early hours of the morning (ibid., p. 108).

121. Eberhard von Puttkamer, author's interview, May 6, 2017.

122. Putin, *First Person*, p. 100.

123. ORT, Feb. 8, 2000.

124. Putin, *First Person*, p. 110.

125. Von Wistinghausen, *Im freien Estland*, p. 489.

126. Irene Pietsch, *Heikle Freundschaften*, pp. 236–7.

127. This was what Warnig told Uwe Müller and Dirk Banse, who have written extensively about his relationship with Putin for *Die Welt* (Müller and Banse, author's interview, Berlin, June 13, 2017). Putin himself also said they first met in St Petersburg ('Interview with ARD', Jan. 15, 2009, archive.premier.gov.ru/events/news/3001/).

128. The *Wall Street Journal* (Feb. 23, 2005) reported that, after working for the Stasi in Düsseldorf, under cover of being a member of the East German Trade Mission there, Warnig moved to Dresden in October 1989 and was recruited by Putin as an agent shortly afterwards. Putin's wife, Lyudmila, was also quoted as saying that Warnig and Putin had known each other in Dresden (Pietsch, p. 271). Müller and Banse (*supra*) say that after leaving Düsseldorf, Warnig he did not go to Dresden but joined the East German Ministry of Economic Affairs in Berlin, and that in a group photograph, purporting to show Putin and Warnig attending a celebration in Dresden in December 1989, marking the 71st anniversary of the founding of the *Cheka*, he is misidentified.

129. Pietsch, pp. 217, 253 & 313.

130. Ibid., p. 366.

131. Ibid., pp. 221 & 317.

132. Ibid., pp. 223–4 & 290.

133. Ibid., p. 388.

134. Ibid., p. 274.

135. Marlène Julien, author's interview, Feb. 22, 2019.

136. Aleksandr Belyaev, author's interview, June 3, 2019.

137. This account is taken from *Smena*, Oct. 8, 1991 and March 31, 1992; Konstantinov, *Banditsky Peterburg*, Vol. 2, pp. 51–6; and Aleksandr Gorshkov, author's interview, Nov. 27, 2019. The version given by Yuri Felshtinsky and Vladimir Pribylovsky in *The Corporation*, pp. 250–54) should be treated with caution.

138. It might be argued that Sobchak could have mentioned his problems with Shutov to Ilya Traber, who would have been perfectly capable of organising the attack. But in that case it would have been carried out by gang members, not by off-duty policemen.

139. This does not necessarily mean that Putin or anybody else gave orders for Shutov's skull to be broken. He may have disturbed the intruders as they were searching his apartment. On the other hand, the use of hammers to bludgeon a victim's head was a well-known method of intimidation which sometimes had fatal consequences. Six years later a local journalist, Anatoly Levin-Utkin, was killed in this way.

140. Carl Bildt, author's interview, Stockholm, Oct. 13, 2017; Gunnar Lund and Michael Sohlman, author's interviews, Stockholm, Feb. 26, 2017; Sture Stiernlöf, 'Vladimir Putin, en förslagen operator', *supra*.

141. Stiernlöf, ibid.

142. The following is drawn from Stiernlöf, ibid. and Lund, *supra*. See also *Sankt-Peterburgskie vedomosti*, May 5 and June 30, 1994.

143. Both Carl Bildt and Stiernlöf were convinced that Putin was also responsible for forcing out the Swedish co-owners of the Grand Europe Hotel, which was taken over by the German Kempinski Group. But on this issue, the memories of the participants differ. Carl-Henrik Victorin, the Managing Director of Reso, the Swedish group managing the hotel, insisted that Reso had been reluctant to give up its management contract. Kaj Hober, the lawyer who had represented Reso, said that, on the contrary, the group wanted to quit the hotel business. Victorin accompanied Putin to Frankfurt for the negotiations with Kempinski and said he assumed that there had been a kickback to the Mayor's Office, because 'that was the way business was done in Germany at that time' (author's interviews with Victorin and Hober, Stockholm, Oct. 11 & 12, 2017; Bildt and Stiernlöf, *supra*). The change of ownership was triggered by a 24-million-dollar fine, imposed by the Tax Inspectorate, then headed by Dmitry Filippov, because Reso had banked their profits in a Swedish, rather than a Russian, bank, and the law had been changed retroactively to make that illegal. Filippov acted independently and there is nothing to prove that the Mayor's Office deliberately engineered the tax bill to force the Swedes to leave (*Sankt-Peterburgskie vedomosti*, May 11, 1994 and Nov. 2, 1995; *Chas pik* and *Nevskoe vremya*, Nov. 2, 1995; and *St. Petersburg Press*, Feb. 8–14 & Aug. 16–22, 1994). There was also a long-running dispute over the privatisation of the city's other five-star hotel, the Astoria, which had been seized illegally by its Russian director. In that case, Putin was not involved.

144. Sergei Baluyev, author's interview, May 29, 2019.

145. Two of the biggest projects were the restoration of Austrian Square and a plan to redevelop New Holland Island. The latter, in particular, was controversial on aesthetic as well as

financial grounds, and there was constant sniping from the Legislative Assembly, whose members claimed that both schemes were marred by corruption. That was no doubt so but, as usual, there was no proof.

146. Fabritsky recounted the incident to Franz Sedelmayer (author's interview, Dec. 12, 2018).

147. Sobchak and Krichevskaya, *Delo Sobchaka*.

148. The following account is drawn from Konstantinov, *Korrumpirovannyi Peterburg*, Ch. 1, 'V koridorakh vlasti', and Sobchak and Krichevskaya, *supra*.

149. Narusova claimed in *Delo Sobchaka* that the whole of the cost of purchasing the neighbouring apartment came from the family's own resources. If true, that raises the question of where the money came from, for Sobchak could never have saved that much from his officially declared income.

150. *Sankt-Peterburgskie vedomosti*, Feb. 8, 1995.

151. Charles Ryan, author's interview, March 14, 2019. The Swedish ambassador, Örjan Berner, remembered Sobchak speaking at inordinate length at a ceremony on the 50th anniversary of the lifting of the Leningrad Blockade, oblivious to the growing irritation of the Armenian President, Levon Ter-Petrosyan, who was the guest of honour (author's interview, Feb. 26, 2017, and *Sankt-Peterburgskie vedomosti*, Jan. 28, 1994).

152. Zapolsky, *Putinburg*, p. 198.

153. Belyaev, author's interview, June 3, 2019. Lev Korsunsky also wrote of Sobchak's 'rare ability to make enemies of former allies' (*Chas pik*, Jan. 24, 1996).

154. *Chas pik*, Sept. 29, 1993.

155. Ibid., Feb. 2, 1994.

156. *New York Times*, April 27, 1992.

157. Kokh and Svinarenko, *A Crate of Vodka*, p. 201.

158. *Smena*, Oct. 4 & 5, 1991, and *Sankt-Peterburgskie vedomosti*, June 2, 1995.

159. Putin, *First Person*, pp. 115–16.

160. *Chas pik*, March 15 and April 8, 1995.

161. *Sankt-Peterburgskie vedomosti*, June 10, 1993.

162. *Chas pik*, June 29, 1992.

163. *Nevskoe vremya*, Feb. 16, 1995.

164. Ibid., Dec. 30, 1995 and *Chas pik*, July 20, 1994.

165. Ibid., Jan. 12, and *Sankt-Peterburgskie vedomosti*, April 4, 1995.

166. *Chas pik*, Aug. 24, 1994.

167. Ibid., Dec. 17, 1994.

168. *Sankt-Peterburgskie vedomosti*, March 1, 1995.

169. *Nevskoe vremya*, Feb. 21, 1996.

170. *Chas pik*, Feb. 15, 1996; *Sankt-Peterburgskie vedomosti* said that only 2,800 buses were still running, out of 5,000 two years earlier (Oct. 12, 1995).

171. *Sankt-Peterburgskie vedomosti*, Dec. 30, 1993, Dec. 22, 1994, Sept. 30, 1995 and Feb. 16, 1996.

172. Touraine, TD 23, Jan. 17 1996, CADN.

173. *Chas pik*, June 9, 1993.

174. Ibid., Aug. 24, 1994.

175. Cited in Medvedev, Roy, *Post-Soviet Russia: A Journey Through the Yeltsin Era*, Columbia University Press, New York, 2000, p. 89.

176. Putin, *First Person*, p. 192.

177. *Chas pik*, Jan. 26, 1996.

178. Ibid., Feb. 14, 1995.

179. *Smena*, Jan. 29 & March 27, 1992.

180. *Sankt-Peterburgskie vedomosti*, Dec. 17, 1993.

181. Anatoly Chubais in Sobchak and Krichevskaya, *Delo Sobchaka*.

182. *Chas pik*, Dec. 17 & 28, 1994.

183. Opinion polls showed that 66 per cent of those questioned opposed the war (*Sankt-Peterburgskie vedomosti*, Feb. 14, 1995).

184. The investigation started on May 17, 1995 and was halted five months later (Konstantinov, *Korrumpirovannyi Peterburg*, Ch. 1, 'V koridorakh vlasti').

185. An extract from a television interview in late 1995, where Sobchak discusses alternative candidates to Yeltsin, is included in Sobchak and Krichevskaya, *supra*. See also Touraine, TD 23, Jan. 17, 1996, CADN.

186. See Aron, *Yeltsin*, pp. 575–80.

187. Colton, *Yeltsin*, pp. 310–16. Another incident occurred in September, when he failed to appear for a meeting with the Irish Prime Minister, Albert Reynolds, at Shannon Airport on his way back from the United States. Korzhakov had feared that Yeltsin was too drunk to participate and persuaded him to let Soskovets take his place (*Irish Times*, March 28, 2008).

188. Sobchak and Krichevskaya, *supra*.

189. Korzhakov confirmed that Skuratov was his personal choice (ibid.).

190. Konstantinov, *supra*.

191. Kasyanov, Mikhail, *Bez Putina*, Izdatelstvo Novaya Gazeta, Moscow, 2009, pp. 58–64. Yeltsin sent Kasyanov and Pavel Borodin, the Head of the Kremlin's General Affairs Office, on a secret mission to Paris and Bonn to negotiate the loans, which were disbursed in May 1996, a month before the vote.

192. Unless otherwise specified, this and the following section are drawn from Aron, *Yeltsin*, pp. 580–633.

193. *Sankt-Peterburgskie vedomosti*, May 17, 1996. Galina Starovoitova also noted that a loss for Sobchak risked damaging Yeltsin's chances of re-election (*Vechernyi Peterburg*, May 24, 1996).

194. Neither Sobchak nor the Legislative Assembly was happy with this arrangement, but Sobchak eventually accepted it on the grounds that it would give his opponents less time to prepare their campaigns (*Sankt-Peterburgskie vedomosti*, March 13 & 14, *Chas pik*, March 14, 20 and April 5, *Nevskoe vremya*, March 19 & 27, 1996). As in the spring of 1991, Putin was sent to convince the deputies that the new date must be approved (*Nezavisimaya gazeta*, July 31, 1998). A further indication that the change of date was specifically aimed at Sobchak was the decision to allow Moscow to hold its election on the same day as the presidential poll.

195. *Chas pik*, Oct. 12, 1994.

196. In the interview Putin gave for the programme, *Vlast'*, in February 1992, he also said that he wished 'to emphasise that I am not a politician but only an employee of the administrative apparatus'.

197. *Sankt-Peterburgskie vedomosti*, May 6 and July 22, 1995.

198. *Chas pik*, Dec. 2, 1995.

199. *Sankt-Peterburgskie vedomosti*, July 22, 1995.

200. Ibid., Aug. 1, 1995. The cheapest Zhiguli cost 32 million roubles. An industrial worker then earned 500–550,000 roubles a month, a teacher 100–400,000 roubles (*Chas pik*, Dec. 15, 1995).

201. Touraine, TD 507, Dec 27 1995, CADN.

202. *Sankt-Peterburgskie vedomosti*, Jan. 19, *Chas pik*, Jan. 25, 1996.

203. *Chas pik*, Jan. 25 & April 17, 1996.

204. Ibid., March 13, 1996. Sobchak tried to prevent Boldyrev standing by claiming that he was not permanently resident in St Petersburg, but the courts rejected his plaint (ibid., April 4, 1996).

205. *Sankt-Peterburgskie vedomosti*, March 28, 1996.

206. Smolyak, *Sobchak*, pp. 117–18.

207. The following account is drawn from Sobchak and Krichevskaya, *Delo Sobchaka*; Smolyak, *Sobchak*, pp. 118-9; and Aleksandr Yershov, author's interview, St Petersburg, Nov. 26, 2019.

208. *Chas pik*, Jan. 18, 1995.

209. Putin, *First Person*, p. 111. Yuri Rydnik said that Sobchak's campaign probably had 'ten times less money' than Yakovlev's (Sobchak and Krichevskaya, *supra*), which lends further weight to the argument that whatever corrupt activities Sobchak was guilty of were on a relatively small scale.

210. Sobchak and Krichevskaya, ibid. In the first week in June, when expenditure on television was at its peak, Yeltsin's campaign spent 2.9 million US dollars (Aron, *Yeltsin*, pp. 623–4).

211. Yezhkov, Dmitry, *Putin: Pochemu on stal takim?*, Algoritm, Moscow, 2012, p. 16.

212. The chief suspect was Aleksandr Prokhorenko, a member of the Legislative Assembly who acted as Putin's deputy in the St Petersburg chapter of Nash Dom Rossiya and had been named by Sobchak to be deputy head of his campaign team. He stayed on after Narusova was appointed but disliked her intensely and, as soon as the election was over, switched sides (Smolyak, *Sobchak*, pp. 116 & 124).

213. Sobchak and Krichevskaya, *supra*. If Proshin is to be believed – and it is difficult to know how candid he was being – he was able to show that lower-level officials in the Mayor's Office had acted illegally but was unable to prove that Sobchak himself had knowingly accepted the work done in his apartment as a bribe. Putin claimed that Skuratov had been trying to prove that Sobchak had used money from the city budget to renovate his apartment, which was false (*First Person*, p. 111). According to Trubetskoi, Sobchak made repeated efforts to meet Yeltsin in the first 10 days of May, but Rogozin prevented it (Sobchak and Krichevskaya, ibid.).

214. *Sankt-Peterburgskie vedomosti*, May 28, 1996; Putin, *First Person*, p. 112. On Moscow's involvement in the campaign, see also *Smena*, May 24 and *Vechernyi Peterburg*, May 27, 1996. On May 30, Sobchak sent an open letter to Skuratov and Yeltsin, complaining that the Prosecutor's Office was interfering in the election (*Nevskoe vremya*, May 31, 1996). The same day, *Vechernyi Peterburg* accused Korzhakov of seeking to orchestrate a second 'Leningrad Affair', a reference to the intrigue launched from Moscow against the city's leaders in the 1940s.

215. Perhaps to minimise his role in Sobchak's defeat, Putin said he joined the campaign between the two rounds, which was untrue (*First Person*, pp. 112–13). According to Yezhkov, he started working on the campaign about a month before the first round (Yezhkov, *supra*, p. 17; see also Smolyak, *supra*, p. 121).

216. *Sankt-Peterburgskie vedomosti*, May 14, 1996.

217. Yezhkov, ibid.

218. 'St Petersburg governor election', www.oocities.org/capitolhill/2568/e_rre96r.html#spb

219. *Chas pik*, May 22, 1996. Pavel Sheremet, in his book, *Piterskie tainy Vladimira Yakovleva* (Partizan, Moscow, 2005), claimed that Putin had organised the demonstration. According to Yakovlev's 'image-maker', Aleksandr Yershov, that was untrue: indeed, it would make little

sense since Sobchak wanted Boldyrev to get through to the second round. Yershov declined to name the individual who planned the demonstration, but did not dispute that it was one of his colleagues from Trubetskoi's team (author's interview, St Petersburg, Nov. 26, 2019).

220. *Chas pik*, April 30, 1996; Smolyak, *Sobchak*, p. 116. The assailant was never found, but the likeliest explanation is that it was the work of Yakovlev's team or of one of his supporters.

221. This was taken sufficiently seriously that when Yakovlev visited the St Petersburg television centre, where he had to walk down a glass-walled corridor, vulnerable to a sniper in the building opposite, he was hidden behind a huge umbrella (Yershov, *supra*). There were also unfounded rumours that a bomb had been planted in a cemetery which Yakovlev was to visit (*Moskovsky komsomolets*, Feb. 2, 2000).

222. *Vechernyi Peterburg*, May 24, 28, 29 & 30, 1996.

223. Ibid., May 20 and *Sankt-Peterburgskie vedomosti*, May 17 & 18, 1996; Smolyak, *Sobchak*, p. 121. Putin sued for 200 million roubles (40,000 US dollars) for damage to his reputation. But it was all a game. Asked how he intended to use the money if he won the case, Putin replied: 'I shall carry out a search and find "my" villa on the French Atlantic coast.'

224. Belyaev confessed that the idea of accusing Sobchak of exporting foreign currency had come to him after he learnt that the Mayor was helping Viktor Kharchenko to take out money to pay port fees (author's interview, June 3, 2019). The story took on a life of its own, and 25 years later there were still foreigners who had worked in St Petersburg at that time who insisted that it was true. Russians, better attuned to the ways of election campaigns, tended to be more sceptical.

225. Yershov, author's interview, Nov. 26, 2019.

226. Anna Sharogradskaya, author's interview, St Petersburg, May 27, 2019.

227. Smolyak, *supra*, p. 121.

228. 'St Petersburg governor election', *supra*.

229. That is not to say that Putin would have stayed on with Sobchak indefinitely. But, had Sobchak won, Putin's life would certainly have taken a different course.

230. The American 'spin doctors' – three consultants who had worked with Governor Pete Wilson of California – were attached to Yeltsin's official campaign headquarters in the President Hotel (Gleb Pavlovsky, author's interview, Moscow, Nov. 21, 2019 and *New York Times*, July 9, 1996). According to Pavlovsky, they were invited by Oleg Soskovets and achieved very little. Their own accounts, published in *Time* and the *Los Angeles Times* (July 9, 1996) claimed that Yeltsin's victory was largely thanks to their efforts.

231. Aven, *Vremya Berezovskogo*, p. 309.

232. Ibid., pp. 308–9.

233. Ibid., p. 508.

7: *The View from the Neva*

1. Sobchak and Krichevskaya, *Delo Sobchaka*, and Blotsky, Vol. 2, p. 361.

2. Although most of Putin's comments quoted here were made with hindsight, they are consistent with Putin's attitude to Sobchak at the time. Anders Blom remembered flying to St Petersburg from Helsinki with the head of the Finnish Sinebrychoff Brewery Group to sign a joint venture agreement in 1993. Putin explained when they arrived that he would

sign on Sobchak's behalf. The brewery chief, however, insisted that Sobchak must represent the Russian side, to which Putin responded, with a sigh: 'As you wish. But you will not get home tonight.' And so it was. Sobchak held forth for three hours, Blom remembered, explaining to his bemused guest what a wonderful agreement it was. Putin signed. By then it was too late for the delegation to leave and they had to stay overnight (Blom, author's interview, March 5, 2017).

3.   Putin, *First Person*, pp. 115 & 119.

4.   Blotsky, Vol. 2, p. 383, and Sobchak and Krichevskaya, *supra*.

5.   Sobchak and Krichevskaya.

6.   *Sankt-Peterburgskie vedomosti*, Jan. 31, 1996.

7.   *Chas pik*, Nov. 25, 1991.

8.   *Vlast'*, transcript, privately held.

9.   In June, 1992, an opinion poll found that 44 per cent of Russians questioned thought that Yeltsin's signature of the Belovezha Accords had been a mistake (*Sankt-Peterburgskie vedomosti*, April 14, 1993).

10.   Ibid., April 27 and July 7, 1994.

11.   Yeltsin set out this policy in a speech at Kazan, the capital of Tatarstan, on August 8, 1990.

12.   *Sankt-Peterburgskie vedomosti*, May 3, 1995.

13.   *Vechernyi Peterburg*, Nov. 28, 1992. See also *Sankt-Peterburgskoe ekho*, Nov. 4, 1992.

14.   Rodric Braithwaite, author's interview, London, Sept. 27, 2016.

15.   Braithwaite, private diary, Nov. 5, 1991.

16.   *Eesti Ekspress*, Jan. 6, 2016.

17.   Savisaar, *Peaminister*, pp. 723, 842–3, & 977. According to *Eesti Ekspress*, the convention was also signed by the Lensoviet and Leningrad oblast leaders, Aleksandr Belyaev and Yuri Yarov. Gorbachev's chief adviser, Aleksandr Yakovlev, headed the Soviet delegation to Latvia, and the former Foreign Minister, Eduard Shevardnadze, the delegation to Lithuania.

18.   Ibid., p. 980. The treaty was initialled in 1999 and signed in 2014 but in 2022 had still not been ratified, largely because of differences over whether or not there should be a reference in the preamble to the 1920 Treaty of Tartu.

19.   Märt Volmer, author's interview, Oct. 10, 2017. Before the consulate opened, an official would come from the embassy in Moscow to issue visas one day a week (*Sankt-Peterburgskie vedomosti*, Aug. 8, 1992).

20.   Eberhard von Puttkamer, author's interview, May 6, 2017.

21.   Volmer, *supra*. Sobchak eventually agreed to receive him on February 29, 1996 (*Vechernyi Peterburg*, March 1, 1996).

22.   Volmer, *supra*.

23.   *Sankt-Peterburgskie vedomosti*, Dec. 29, 1995 and Feb. 2, 10 & 15, 1994.

24.   Volmer, *supra*.

25.   *Sankt-Peterburgskie vedomosti*, Feb. 26, 1994.

26.   Bildt, author's interview, Oct. 13, 2017.

27.   Ibid.

28.   Indrek Tarand, author's interview, Brussels, May 3, 2017; Juri Pihl, author's interview, Tallinn, May 24, 2017. According to Ivan Lavrantjev, no formally constituted Russian military units were involved, but a Russian regiment returning from Transnistria was directed to bivouac near Kingisepp, about 14 miles east of Narva (Lavrantjev, '1993. aasta Narva autonoomia referendumi . . .', *supra*). Russian irregulars also took up positions near the border. Mart Laar, Estonia's Prime Minister at the time, who refers in his book, *Pööre*, to a Cossack

presence on the Russian side, writes that more than once during the crisis he had to dissuade the Estonian military from intervening (pp. 244–5). The Russian moves were not intended to prepare for intervention but rather as a warning to Estonia to allow the referendum to proceed and not to take pre-emptive military action. However that was not clear at the time.

29. Laar, *Pööre*, pp. 241–2; *Sankt-Peterburgskie vedomosti*, July 7, 1993. Laar's version of Bildt's visit, in which he claimed that the Swedish Prime Minister fully supported the Estonian position, bears little relation to Bildt's account, which emphasised the need for compromise.

30. Mauno Koivisto, *Witness to History*, Hurst, London, 1997, pp. 275–7.

31. Meri related the story to Juri Pihl, his intelligence chief (Pihl, author's interview, May 24, 2017).

32. Bildt, *supra*.

33. Lavrantjev, *supra*.

34. Lennart Meri, 'Address . . . at a Matthiae-Supper in Hamburg', Feb. 25, 1994, vp1992-2001. president.ee/eng/k6ned/k6ne.asp?ID=9401.

35. Vladimir Churov, cited in Putin, *First Person*, p. 103. Putin also singled out Meri's accusation of Russian neo-imperialism and his criticism of the West for allowing Russia to station peacekeepers around Sarajevo – points underlined by the Russian Foreign Ministry in a formal protest note (*Sankt-Peterburgskie vedomosti*, March 11, 1994).

36. *Chas pik*, Aug. 30, and *Sankt-Peterburgskie vedomosti*, Sept. 5, Oct. 24 & Dec. 6, 1995, commenting on the improvement in relations after the election of Tiit Vahi as Estonian Prime Minister.

37. *Sankt-Peterburgskie vedomosti*, March 11, 1994.

38. Ibid., July 1, 1992 ('Nearer Abroad'); *Chas pik*, March 24, 1993 ('New Abroad'), April 13, 1994 ('Nearest Abroad'), April 26, 1995, ('Near Abroad').

39. *Sankt-Peterburgskie vedomosti*, May 3, 1995. Intriguingly, at that time, Putin thought Russia's priority should be to strengthen relations with the former Soviet Central Asian republics and Azerbaijan.

40. Ibid.

41. *Chas pik*, Nov. 16, 1992.

42. *Sankt-Peterburgskie vedomosti*, May 19, 1994.

43. Ibid., March 16, 1994.

44. Bildt, author's interview, Oct. 13, 2017.

45. This and the following section are taken from *Sankt-Peterburgskie vedomosti*, May 3, 1995.

46. Blatmann to Ministère des Affaires Étrangères, Paris, TD 941, Dec. 15, 1993, CADN.

47. *Vechernyi Peterburg*, Aug. 5, 1991.

48. *Smena*, April 7, 1992.

49. *Sankt-Peterburgskie vedomosti*, May 20, 1995.

50. Vladimir Voronov, who became a partner of Rupert Murdoch, cited in Aven, *Vremya Berezovskogo*, p. 319.

51. *Vechernyi Peterburg*, May 23, 1996.

52. *Smena*, March 27, 1992.

53. *Sankt-Peterburgskie vedomosti*, May 3, 1995.

54. *Smena*, March 27, 1992.

55. *Sankt-Peterburgskie vedomosti*, May 3, 1995.

56. Ibid., Jan. 31, 1996.

57. Ibid., May 3, 1995.

58. *Sankt-Peterburgskie vedomosti*, Jan. 31, 1996.

59. Blatmann to Ministère des Affaires Étrangères, Paris, TD 941, Dec. 15, 1993, CADN.

60. *Chas pik*, Oct. 12, 1994.

61. Ibid., Nov. 25, 1991.

62. Blotsky, Vol. 2, p. 332. These comments were made in 2002, but they appear to be an accurate reflection of Putin's views in the mid 1990s, for relations with the former 'geopolitical opponent' had, if anything, improved in the meantime.

63. *Chas pik*, March 30, 1994.

64. *Sankt-Peterburgskie vedomosti*, Dec. 22, 1993.

65. Ibid., Dec. 28, 1993.

66. The St Petersburg press attributed the explanation to Ambassador Pickering. He himself has no recollection of it and it seems more likely that it was concocted by the Russian side (Tom Pickering, author's interview, Feb. 15, 2019).

67. *Sankt-Peterburgskie vedomosti*, May 3, 1995 & Jan. 31, 1996.

68. John Guy, who met Putin in November 1995, felt that 'for him, this attachment to the Near Abroad was a fundamental principle' (author's interview, Jan. 16, 2020).

69. In June 1994, François Mitterrand told Clinton that Russia's place was in the European Community. The previous autumn, Prime Minister Viktor Chernomyrdin had said that Russia wished to join and become a full member (*Sankt-Peterburgskie vedomosti*, Nov. 6, 1993 and June 9, 1994).

70. 'Record of Conversation between Mikhail Gorbachev and James Baker in Moscow', Feb. 9, 1990, Gorbachev Foundation Archive, cited in Savranskaya, Svetlana, and Blanton, Tom, 'NATO expansion: What Gorbachev Heard', Dec. 12, 2017 at nsarchive.gwu.edu/briefing-book/russia-programs/2017-12-12/nato-expansion-what-gorbachev-heard-western-leaders-early. The redacted version released by the State Department also contains the phrase, 'no extension of NATO's jurisdiction . . . one inch to the East'.

71. Ibid., and Hill, William H., *No Place for Russia: European Security Institutions since 1989*, Columbia University Press, New York, 2018, pp. 45–6.

72. Shaun Byrnes, author's interview, Arlington, Va., March 11, 2019. The State Department's position was that 'discussion of expanding [NATO] membership is not on the agenda' (James F. Dobbins, 'Memorandum to National Security Council', Oct. 25, 1990, in Savranskaya and Blanton, *supra*).

73. Braithwaite, private diary, March 5, 1991. Later that month the British Foreign Secretary, Douglas Hurd, told his Soviet counterpart that there were 'no plans . . . to include the countries of Eastern and Central Europe in NATO' (cited in Savranskaya and Blanton, *supra*).

74. 'Memorandum to Boris Yeltsin from Russian Supreme Soviet Delegation', July 1, 1991, ibid.

75. Dobbins, 'Memorandum to National Security Council', Oct. 25, 1990, ibid.

76. Byrnes, *supra*.

77. 'Memorandum of Conversation between Vaclav Havel and President Bush in Washington', Feb. 20, 1990, in Savranskaya and Blanton, *supra*. Havel continued to have reservations about creating a new dividing line in Europe until at least the end of 1993 (*Sankt-Peterburgskie vedomosti*, Nov. 30, 1993).

78. Hill, *No Place for Russia*, pp. 110–11. The first three candidates for NATO membership were Poland, Hungary and the Czech Republic. Twenty years later, they had become the three most illiberal and least democratic European Union states.

79. The classic account of the Clinton administration's decision to open NATO to new members in East and Central Europe is James Goldgeier's *Not Whether But When: The U.S.
Decision to Enlarge NATO*, Brookings Institution Press, Washington, D.C., 1999, esp. pp. 1–5,
9–11 & 19–76, from which, unless otherwise specified, this and the following section are
largely taken. See also Hill, *supra*, pp. 112–16.

80. Michael Morell, author's interview, McLean, Va., March 11, 2019.

81. Clinton, 'News conference with Visegrad leaders', Prague, Jan. 12, 1994, at www.presidency.
ucsb.edu/documents/the-presidents-news-conference-with-visegrad-leaders-prague

82. *Sankt-Peterburgskie vedomosti*, Dec. 11, 1993.

83. This was first formally set out in a State Department telegram in 1996 (Savranskaya and
Blanton, *supra*).

84. Strobe Talbott, author's interview, Washington, D.C., Feb. 15, 2019. Bob Gates, who was
Deputy National Security Adviser at the time of Baker's visit to Moscow, and later Director of the CIA, said that 'Gorbachev and others were led to believe that [enlargement]
would not happen, at least no time soon', and that the breaking of that commitment 'not
only aggravated the relationship between the United States and Russia but made it much
more difficult to do constructive business with them' (University of Virginia, Miller
Center, Presidential Oral Histories, Robert M. Gates, July 23–4, 2000, at millercenter.org/
the-presidency/presidential-oral-histories/robert-m-gates-deputy-director-central).

85. Ibid.

86. 'Memorandum of Conversation between Helmut Kohl and George Bush at Camp David',
Feb. 24, 1990, in Savranskaya and Blanton, *supra*.

87. The expression is variously attributed to Clinton himself, to Strobe Talbott and to Talbott's
deputy, Victoria Nuland. Kozyrev's remark is cited by Dimitri Simes in 'Losing Russia',
Oct. 29, 2007, www.realclearpolitics.com/articles/2007/10/losing_russia.html

88. Francis Richards, author's interview, Stanton St Quintin, May 12, 2017.

89. Guy, author's interview, Jan. 16, 2020.

8: *Moscow Rules*

1. Anders Blom remembered a dinner with Putin and Yakovlev in 1994 where, in his words,
'they were like brothers' (author's interview, March 5, 2017).

2. Putin, *First Person*, pp. 113–14.

3. Pyotr Aven recounted a case where a British High Court judge refused to believe that Berezovsky had threatened to 'destroy' two Russians – an oligarch and a politician – over a
media deal because, shortly afterwards, they and their wives all had dinner together. He
'failed to understand the Russian mentality', Aven wrote. 'Yet that was the Russian way'
(*Vremya Berezovskogo*, pp. 147 & 595–6).

4. Smolyak, *Sobchak*, p. 125.

5. Putin, *First Person*, p. 114. He apparently told Yakovlev of his refusal within days of the election, for on June 11, Kudrin and Manevich attended a news conference given by the new
governor, but Putin was absent (*Chas pik*, June 13, 1996).

6. Ibid., Oct. 12, 1994.

7. Vishnevsky assumed, wrongly, that Putin was trying to persuade Yakovlev to allow him to
keep his post in the city government (author's interview, Nov. 25, 2019). In fact, he had
asked to be allowed to continue using his office in Smolny until the second round of the

presidential election on July 3, as he was working for Yeltsin's campaign in St Petersburg on behalf of Nash Dom Rossiya. To that, Yakovlev grudgingly agreed (Putin, *First Person*, p. 113).

8.   Ibid.

9.   Lipponen, author's interview, May 30, 2017.

10. See Blotsky, Vol. 2, p. 374. Steven Lee Myers, without citing a source, dates his enrolment to May, which is plausible (*New Tsar*, p. 114). It was certainly during the spring of 1996.

11. An English translation of the dissertation was published by Kaj Hober in *The Journal of Eurasian Law*, Vol, 2, No. 1, 2008. The three preliminary papers were 'Indicators of the Effectiveness of Investment Projects in Developing Deposits of Rare and Precious Metals', presented at an international symposium in St Petersburg, held on October 8–11, 1996; 'Raw Materials Potential of the [Leningrad] Region'; and 'Geopolitical Situation, Natural Resources and Economic Production Potential of St. Petersburg and Leningrad Region'. A fourth paper on 'The Formation of the Legal and Economic Foundations of the Market Mechanism in Natural Resources Management' was published in 1997. A fifth, and apparently final, paper, 'Mineral Resources in the Development Strategy of the Russian Economy', appeared in the Mining Institute's journal, *Zapiski Gornogo instituta*, Vol. 144, No. 1, pp. 3–9, 1999; a translation by Harley Balzer was published in *Problems of Post-Communism*, Vol. 53, No. 1, 2006, pp. 49–54.

12. Hill and Gaddy, *Mr. Putin: Operative in the Kremlin*, pp. 81–2; Julian Cooper, private communication, July 23, 2020. Hill and Gaddy speculated that Putin might have read the translation while at the Andropov Institute. That seems far-fetched. It is far more likely that it was available at the Mining Institute.

13. *New York Times*, March 1, 2012. In 1998, Igor Sechin submitted a Candidate of Science dissertation at the same institute. His topic was oil logistics. Litvinenko supervised both theses. PhosAgro was originally owned by Mikhail Khodorkovsky's Menatep Group. After Khodorkovsky's arrest, Sechin played a key role in the redistribution of his asserts. Litvinenko acquired shares in PhosAgro which were then worth 260 million US dollars. By 2019, he owned 20.98 per cent of the equity, worth just over one billion dollars.

14. One may assume that his choice of topic was dictated, at least in part, by assurances from the Institute that whatever dissertation was submitted in his name would be well received.

15. According to Litvinenko, the dissertation was based on a report which Putin had arranged to have drawn up at Sobchak's request a year earlier, evaluating the prospects for expanding St Petersburg's port facilities. There is no way to verify that.

16. The chronology is consistent with this interpretation. Sobchak began preparing his campaign in January, 1996 (Smolyak, *Sobchak*, p. 116). Putin evidently realised early on that he might have an uphill struggle (see his comments in *First Person*, p. 111). He may also have learnt from his contacts in the FSB that Sobchak's opponents were looking for a new candidate to stand against him. By February or early March, he might have concluded that there was a real risk that Sobchak would lose.

17. Blotsky, Vol. 2, p. 384.

18. Ibid., p. 386.

19. Unless otherwise indicated, the following account is drawn from ibid., pp. 385–94. Putin gave slightly different versions of the move to Moscow in *First Person*, pp. 125–8, and in an interview with St Petersburg television in September 1996.

20. Raivo Vare, author's interview, March 1, 2017; Baker, Peter, and Glasser, Susan, *Kremlin*

Rising: Vladimir Putin's Russia and the end of Revolution, Scribner, New York, 2005, p. 48. Sergei Pugachev, in an interview with Kseniya Sobchak (Dozhd TV, Nov. 19, 2015), said 'Putin helped [Borodin] solve some issues of a private nature in Leningrad.'

21.   Pietsch, *Heikle Freundschaften*, pp. 221–2. Pietsch quoted Lyudmila as saying that Putin discussed his situation not with her but with 'a faithful follower', whom she did not name but who was probably Igor Sechin. It appears to have been during this period that Putin's close relationship with Sechin was sealed.

22.   Blotsky, Vol. 2, p. 364.

23.   To Lyudmila, the fire at the dacha was a sign that the time had come for them to 'burn their bridges' and move on (ibid., pp. 367 & 383–4). Felshtinsky and Pribylovsky date the fire to August 12 (*The Corporation*, p. 106) but it was probably earlier than that as by mid August Putin was with Kudrin in Moscow.

24.   According to Pietsch (*supra*, p. 237), Lyudmila also felt that the post was completely unsuited to him.

25.   Von Puttkamer remembered seeing Putin at breakfast in the Grand Europa Hotel on the day they both left – he to return to Berlin at the end of his tour, Putin to take up his new post in Moscow (author's interview, May 6, 2017). Von Puttkamer's departure was recorded in *Nevskoe vremya* the same day.

26.   Blotsky, Vol. 2, p. 397.

27.   Ibid., pp. 367–8, and Pietsch, p. 327.

28.   Ibid., p. 350.

29.   Putin, *First Person*, p. 128 and Blotsky, Vol. 2, p. 367.

30.   Pietsch, pp. 362–3.

31.   Ruslan Linkov said that when he was working with Galina Starovoitova, who was a member of the State Duma from 1995 to 1998, he and Putin often took the same flight back to St Petersburg at weekends (author's interview, June 2, 2019).

32.   Putin, ibid.

33.   Sergei Chemezov, quoted in Felshtinsky and Pribylovsky, *The Corporation*, p. 112.

34.   Blotsky, Vol. 2, pp. 399–400; Aven, *Vremya Berezovskogo*, p. 423.

35.   Speaking on the programme, 'Obozrevatel', TV 6, July 26, 1997.

36.   'Prestupnost i bezopasnost' (*Argus-Inform*), Aug. 1, 1998, available on integrum.ru

37.   Aven, ibid.

38.   Transcript, privately held. See www.youtube.com/watch?v=RHeWMA6Ocqc

39.   Cited in Pietsch, p. 316.

40.   *Kommersant*, May 27, 1997.

41.   Ibid., and RTR 'Vesti', 20.00, May 24, 1997.

42.   Interfax, May 24, 1997.

43.   *Kommersant*, April 15, 1997.

44.   Myers, *New Tsar*, pp. 113–14. As head of the Control Directorate, Putin reported abuses but did not initiate criminal proceedings. He often found that frustrating, but in this case was evidently relieved to be able to leave the decision to a higher level.

45.   RIA Novosti, Sept. 15, 1997.

46.   TASS, June 3, 1997.

47.   *Kommersant*, June 5, 1998.

48.   Aron, *Yeltsin*, pp. 662–3.

49.   *Financial Times*, Nov. 1, 1996.

50.   Aven, *supra*, pp. 357–8.

51. The following is drawn from Pietsch, *Heikle Freundschaften*, pp. 238–9, 364–5, 367–9, 377–9.

52. In July 1998, Lyudmila arrived with the children in the South of France, planning to spend six weeks in a four-star hotel, where accommodation alone cost the equivalent of 4,000 euros a week (twitter.com/KevinRothrock/status/1351550320124583936/photo/1 and /photo/2).

53. Lyudmila's reaction when her daughters were teased by other children about coming to school in a chauffeur-driven car was revealing in that respect. 'I would have told them – even though it's not true,' she said, 'that we have five cars with government drivers at our disposal, and the others are far bigger and more expensive than this one.' In other words, flaunt your new-found wealth and pretend you are even richer than you are (Pietsch, p. 363).

54. Ibid., pp. 374–5 & 381.

55. Unless otherwise indicated, this and the following section is drawn from Smolyak, *Sobchak*, pp. 135–40.

56. When Yakovlev's advisers proposed that he send a letter of good wishes to Sobchak to mark his 60th birthday on August 10, 1997, he refused. They then tried to persuade him that it would be politically advisable, even if he did not want to do it, because it would help to reconcile him with that half of the electorate – primarily democrats and intellectuals – which had voted for Sobchak the previous summer. Again he refused. Finally, when they insisted, he agreed to send a letter, but on condition that it was not made public, which destroyed the whole point of the exercise (Yershov, author's interview, Nov. 26, 2019).

57. Smolyak, pp. 139–40; Sobchak and Krichevskaya, *Delo Sobchaka;* Boris Yeltsin, *Midnight Diaries*, Public Affairs, New York, 2000, pp. 232–4.

58. Narusova, author's interview, Nov. 21, 2019. The Estonian consul, Mart Piiskop, remembered issuing Narusova entry visas for herself and her husband. He assumed afterwards that she had been laying a false trail (Piiskop, author's interview, Tallinn, May 22, 2017). See also Jüri Raidla, author's interview, Tallinn, May 23, 2017 and Savisaar, *Peaminister*, p. 284.

59. Smolyak, *Sobchak*, p. 141.

60. The following is drawn from interviews with Putin, Yumashev and Lyudmila Narusova in Sobchak and Krichevskaya, *supra*. See also Putin, *First Person*, pp. 116–17 and Narusova, author's interview, *supra*.

61. According to Narusova (ibid.), Timchenko paid for the flight. Smolyak (*supra*, p. 141) wrote that the costs of the evacuation were paid by the cellist, Mstislav Rostropovich and his wife, Galina Vishnevskaya. It is not clear which version is correct.

62. Some Russian historians argue that Putin's motives in aiding Sobchak's flight to Paris were not as pure as he made out. He acted, they claim, out of fear that, if Sobchak were interrogated, he would reveal details of corrupt activities which would implicate Putin. Like most such theories, this is impossible to disprove. But there is no firm evidence to support it and on the face of it, it appears implausible. The fact that Sobchak had no money to pay for the Medevac plane which took him to France and had to rely on friends to help him does not fit the image of a man who practised large-scale corruption. During the 21 months he spent in Paris, he stayed with a Russian acquaintance, Vladimir Ren, in a small apartment in the 7th arrondissement and appeared to be short of money. Alfred Kokh, who had no particular sympathy for Sobchak, recalled: 'When I met him in Paris, he was very happy to be invited out to dinner. He was not a rich man. He lived there very modestly' (author's interview, Oct. 9, 2019). In short, apart from the refurbishment of his St Petersburg apartment and various other relatively minor misdemeanours, there is nothing to suggest that Sobchak was in a position to make revelations which would seriously embarrass Putin.

63. Sobchak and Krichevskaya, *supra*.

64. *Novaya gazeta*, Aug. 16, 1999 & Feb. 14–20, 2000. The incident is related in Satter, *Darkness at Dawn*, pp. 204–5.

65. Kazakov was fired on November 14. Yumashev started thinking about promoting Putin immediately afterwards (Aven, *Vremya Berezovskogo*, p. 423; Blotsky, Vol. 2, p. 400; *Izvestia*, Nov. 18, *Novye Izvestia*, Nov. 20, and *Kommersant*, Nov. 21, 1997).

66. *Kommersant*, ibid., and *Rossiisky kto yest kto*, Aug. 1, 1998.

67. *Moscow Times*, May 26, 1998.

68. Aven, p. 423. In *First Person* (p. 129), Putin said: 'It was not very creative work. It was important, it was necessary . . . But it simply wasn't interesting for me. I don't know what I would have done if I had left. I probably would have started a law firm.' Several years later, he again said that in the spring of 1998, 'I was about to leave the civil service and become a lawyer perhaps'. Both statements served to bolster his claim that he had no ambitions to higher office ('Meeting with Finalists of the Student Essay Competition', June, 5, 2003, www.kremlin.ru/events/president/transcripts/22021).

69. Blotsky, Vol. 2, p. 399.

70. Aven, p. 436.

71. 'Meeting with University Students', Jan. 25, 2021, www.kremlin.ru/events/president/transcripts/64922

72. In October 1994, he spoke of perhaps working as 'a lawyer, or a co-founder [of a project] or a manager', but then added that he was speaking of projects 'on behalf of the city of St Petersburg, where I would be trusted to represent the city' (*Chas pik*, Oct. 12, 1994). Seven years later, he told Oleg Blotsky: 'To be honest . . . I preferred to stay in the public service (at a certain level) rather than go into any business structure . . . Leaving the civil service to go into some private business or something related to it . . . requires a special attitude to life, activities and the law. Of course, if there were no alternative, then, probably, I would engage in some activity as an individual, most likely . . . legal consultancy' (Vol. 2, p. 397).

73. In 62nd place (*Nezavisimaya gazeta*, July 8, 1998).

74. Aven, *Vremya Berezovskogo*, p. 424.

75. *Novaoe vremya*, June 7, 1998.

76. *Kommersant*, June 2, 1998; Oleg Kalugin, author's interview, Oct. 30, 2018.

77. TASS, June 10, 1998.

78. Interfax, June 4, RIA Novosti, June 4 and TASS, June 5, 1998.

79. 'Prestupnost i bezopasnost' (*Argus-Inform*), Aug. 1, 1998, *supra*.

80. *Moskovskie novosti*, Feb. 17 and TASS, July 3, 1998.

81. Kate Horner, author's interview, London, Sept. 28, 2016.

82. *Kommersant*, July 17, 1998.

83. *Sankt-Peterburgskie vedomosti*, March 1, 1994.

84. *Nezavisimaya gazeta*, July 30, 1998.

85. *Argumenty i Fakty* reported on June 9, 1997, that either Putin or Yevgeny Savostyanov, a former deputy Chairman of the FSB who had become deputy head of the Presidential Administration for personnel matters, would replace Kovalyov. Fresh rumours that Putin would become FSB Chairman were reported by RIA Novosti on September 3 and denied by the FSB shortly afterwards (*Literaturnaya gazeta*, Sept. 17, 1997).

86. *Kommersant*, June 3, 1998. On July 19, Radio Mayak reported that Kovalyov would be replaced by Putin. On July 21, *Kommersant* published a similar story, which Kovalyov immediately denied (*Nezavisimaya gazeta*, July 22, 1998). See also Agenstvo MiK, July 24, 1998.

87. This section draws on Blotsky, Vol. 2, pp. 400–401; Putin, *First Person*, pp. 130–32; and Pietsch, *Heikle Freundschaften*, pp. 306–7 & 383.

88. TASS, July 25, 1998. Mikhail Poltoranin, *Vlast' v trotilovom ekvivalente*, Vol. 1, Algoritm, Moscow, 2011, p. 435.

89. *Moskovsky komsomolets*, July 28, 1998.

90. Interfax, July 29, *Obshchaya gazeta*, July 30 and TsPKR [Tsentr politicheskoi konyunktury Rossii], Aug. 2, 1998. Aleksandr Golts claims that the last straw was a letter sent by Kovalyov and 11 other senior officials from the security services, objecting to a proposal to give the Defence Ministry priority in the use of conscripts, some of which had until then been assigned to the border troops and other units of the security services (author's interview, Nov. 20, 2019).

91. Mikhail Poltoranin, who had earlier been one of Yeltsin's deputy prime ministers, accused Putin – whom he did not name, but described as a man in the Presidential Administration 'with cold eyes and a cold heart' – of having organised Rokhlin's murder, and speculated that he had been promoted as a result (*supra*, pp. 419–36). Poltoranin was a less than credible source but he was not alone in claiming that Rokhlin had been killed for political reasons (see Andrei Rogachevsky, 'The Murder of General Rokhlin', *Europe–Asia Studies*, Vol. 52, No. 1, Jan. 2000, pp. 95–110). Despite inconsistencies in the evidence, it appears that the Russian courts were correct in concluding that he had been killed by his wife and there was no political motive. When Oksana Baltina, the wife of Admiral Eduard Baltin, who was a close friend, visited Rokhlin's wife in prison two days after the drama, her first words were: 'Oksana, I killed Levushka', using a pet name for her husband (pereprava.org/society/3971-general-protiv-prezidenta.html, Oct. 9, 2017). Aleksandr Golts, who made an extensive investigation of the affair, was also convinced that Rokhlin's wife had killed him in a fit of insanity (Golts, *supra*).

92. TASS, July 27, 1998.

93. Yeltsin, *Midnight Diaries*, p. 327. He also wrote that Kovalyov had 'an enormous antipathy to business' and 'despised people with large amounts of money'. It is not clear what prompted that. It appears to have been unfounded.

94. Gleb Pavlovsky said that Yeltsin thought Kovalyov was too soft (author's interview, Nov. 21, 2019). Putin said later: 'For various reasons (some known to me and some not entirely known), [Yeltsin] was not particularly pleased with the work of the FSB. Gradually he began to seek a replacement for . . . Kovalyov' (Blotsky, Vol. 2, p. 400).

95. Lyudmila told Irene Pietsch that her husband had received a telephone call from Moscow on July 21 and had flown back the following day. They had been staying at the Royal Casino Hotel in La Napoule, near Cannes (twitter.com/KevinRothrock/status/1351550320124583936/photo/1 and /photo/2). Putin later concealed that fact, claiming that Lyudmila had been on holiday with the children on the Baltic sea coast.

96. Putin claimed afterwards that he had learnt the news from Kiriyenko on the latter's return from seeing Yeltsin in Karelia (*First Person*, p. 130, *Kommersant*, July 30, 1998). In fact, Yumashev had informed him on his return from France. He was able to warn Lyudmila, using a coded expression which at first she did not understand – 'I've gone back to the place where I began' – because he was speaking on an unsecured line. She telephoned Irene Pietsch to give her the news before the official announcement on Saturday evening (Pietsch, *supra*, pp. 382–3).

97. Ibid.

98. Ibid., and Tregubova, Yelena, *Baiki Kremlyovskogo diggera*, Ad Marginem, Moscow, 2003, Ch. 8.

99. RTR, July 27, 1998.

100. In Putin's words, 'I was greeted cautiously' (*First Person*, p. 133).

101. *Kommersant*, July 30; 'Prestupnost i bezopasnost' (*Argus-Inform*), Aug. 1, 1998, *supra*.

102. Myers, *New Tsar*, p. 126.

103. Gleb Pavlovsky, author's interview, Nov. 21, 2019.

104. Interfax, Aug. 26 & Oct. 6 and *Russky telegraf*, Aug. 29, 1998.

105. Putin, *First Person*, p. 133.

106. This and the following section are drawn from Putin's interview with *Kommersant*, July 30, 1998.

107. 'Prestupnost i bezopasnost' (*Argus-Inform*), Aug. 1, 1998, *supra*.

108. *Nezavisimaya gazeta*, Aug 1, 1998. The FSB also carried out discreet surveillance of the Finance Ministry, the Central Bank and other financial institutions.

109. Illarionov, author's interview, Feb. 16, 2019.

110. Yeltsin, *Midnight Diaries*, pp. 199–200.

111. Goldfarb, Alex, and Litvinenko, Marina, *Death of a Dissident*, Free Press, New York, 2007, pp. 129–34 & 136.

112. *Kommersant*, Nov. 13, 1998.

113. Tsentr obshchestvennykh svyazei FSB Rossii, Nov. 17, 1998.

114. *Nezavisimaya gazeta*, Nov. 18, 1998.

115. Monitoring Teleradioefira/ Politika [VPS], transcript from RTR, 'Podrobnosti', Nov. 19, 1998.

116. RTR, 'Vesti', Nov. 20, 1998.

117. Pietsch, *Heikle Freundschaften*, pp. 290 & 374–5.

118. Markus Lyra, author's interview, Helsinki, March 2, 2017.

119. *Helsingin Sanomat*, Jan. 9, 2000.

120. Lyra, *supra*.

121. Aven, *Vremya Berezovskogo*, p. 699; Goldfarb and Litvinenko, *supra*, p. 154.

122. Tatyana Yumasheva, 'Kak Primakov pytalsya uvolit Putina', March 15, 2010, t-yumasheva. livejournal.com/19015.html, and Putin, *First Person*, p. 133. See also Yeltsin, *Midnight Diaries*, pp. 203–4. According to Yumashev, Primakov twice demanded Putin's dismissal (www. vedomosti.ru/politics/articles/2019/11/22/816979-on-videl-cheloveka-prodolzhit). Rumours of bad relations between Putin and Primakov were beginning to appear in the press early in 1999 (TsPKR, Jan. 31, 1999).

123. According to Yuri Skuratov, the refurbishment cost 700 million US dollars (*Kremlyovskie podryady*, Alistorus, Moscow, 2014, p. 40).

124. The head of Mabetex, Behdjet Pacolli, said later that he had agreed, at Borodin's request, to act as guarantor for credit cards issued to Yeltsin's daughters and wife but not to the President himself. He also paid 2.7 million US dollars to an account in the Cayman Islands in the name of Tatyana Yeltsin's first husband, Leonid Dyachenko (Belton, *Putin's People*, pp. 123–5 & 148–9).

125. In an interview with Kseniya Sobchak, Pugachev claimed that he had been instrumental in advancing Putin's career, maintaining: 'I brought him to the Kremlin and introduced him to Tatyana.' He, Tatyana and Yumashev had made the key decisions about Yeltsin's succession, he said, and he had been the person who had first suggested Putin as Prime Minister (Dozhd TV, Nov. 19, 2015). He made the same claims to Catherine Belton in interviews in 2016 and 2018 (*Putin's People*, pp. 5, 131, 137–8, 144–7, 150–51 & 155). No one else in the Kremlin at that time has confirmed Pugachev's role.

126. Yeltsin wrote later that he was unaware of the investigation until the middle of March. It is true that he was ill for much of this period but his claim of ignorance is not easy to believe (*Midnight Diaries*, p. 224).

127. *Moskovsky komsomolets*, May 12, 1999.

128. Belton, *supra*, p. 127. In this case, Pugachev's story rings true. He named the man who gave him the tape as Nazir Khapsirokov, who later headed the Moscow National Bank. Khapsirokov had been working in the Prosecutor General's Office as head of the Financial Department when Skuratov dismissed him amid allegations that he had abused his office. He was subsequently rewarded with a post in the Presidential Administration (*Novaya gazeta*, April 9, 1999; Jan. 31, 2000 and Nov. 28, 2005; *ORT*, April 14, 1999; and *Moskovskie novosti*, Sept. 19, 2000).

129. Yeltsin, *supra*, pp. 223–4.

130. According to Jüri Pihl, then head of Estonian Intelligence, Putin's presence was attested by a source who was in the studio during the broadcast (Pihl, author's interview, May 24, 2017). Others say the cassette was provided anonymously to several Russian TV channels but only RTR chose to transmit it (*Kommersant*, March 19, 1999; see also Myers, *New Tsar*, p. 136).

131. Skuratov was not finally dismissed until April 19, 2000, but after his suspension, interest in the case waned and, apart from the Communists and the Mayor of Moscow, Yuri Luzhkov, who continued to try to use it to pressure Yeltsin, support for him in parliament also flagged.

132. Yeltsin, *supra*, pp. 225 & 236.

133. Ibid., pp. 269 & 271.

134. The three were Mikhail Monastyrsky, Vyacheslav Shevchenko and the ringleader, Mikhail Glushchenko. Shevchenko was murdered in Cyprus in 2004. Monastyrsky died in France in 2007. Glushchenko is serving a 17-year term in prison. To try to win a lighter sentence, he falsely accused Vladimir Kumarin of having masterminded Starovoitova's murder (Yevgeny Vyshenkov, author's interview, June 1, 2019).

135. Quoted in Yeltsin, *supra*, p. 209.

136. RTR, 'Vesti', and RIA Novosti, Nov. 13, 1998.

137. Yeltsin, *supra*, p. 210.

138. Ibid., pp. 218 & 285.

139. Ibid., p. 275.

140. Pavlovsky, author's interview, Nov. 21, 2019.

141. Moroz, Oleg, *Pochemu on vybral Putina*, Rus-Olymp, Moscow, 2009, p. 2.

142. Yeltsin, *supra*, p. 281.

143. Ibid., p. 285.

144. Ibid., pp. 79–80 & 281.

145. Ibid., p. 283; Aven, *Vremya Berezovskogo*, p. 447. Yeltsin wrote that before appointing Kiriyenko, he also considered Vladimir Bulgak, the Minister of Communications; Sergei Dubinin, the Central Bank Chairman; and Andrei Nikolayev, the former head of the border troops (Yeltsin, *supra*, pp. 209–10).

146. Ibid., pp. 109, 276 & 283.

147. The evidence that Yeltsin began considering Putin as a possible successor in the summer of 1998 is circumstantial but compelling. It cannot have been earlier, because it was only then that the President started having face-to-face contact with him. It is unlikely to have been much later, because by August 1998, his first choice, Kiriyenko, had been found

wanting. Primakov's appointment was never more than a holding operation, even if the Prime Minister himself began to have other ideas.

148. Ibid., p. 329.

149. Sobchak and Krichevskaya, *Delo Sobchaka*, and Aven, *supra*, p. 424.

150. Yeltsin, pp. 328–9.

151. Ibid. and pp. 226–8.

152. Ibid., p. 284.

153. Aven, *supra*, pp. 222–4 & 249–50.

154. Yeltsin, *supra*, pp. 98–9.

155. Interfax, June 3, 1998. The other two were Viktor Zorin, who was brought in to run the Special Programmes Department, responsible for contingency plans in wartime, and Aleksei Molyakov, who became deputy Secretary of the Security Council.

156. Yeltsin, *supra*, p. 213.

157. Yeltsin's reservations about Stepashin stemmed from his record as FSB chief during the First Chechen War, when he had painted far too rosy a picture of the situation and had failed to see the difficulties Russian forces would encounter. By March 1999, it was already clear that a resumption of hostilities could not be ruled out. In that case, Stepashin would not be the ideal candidate. See Voloshin's comments on Stepashin as essentially a peacetime Prime Minister (Aven, *supra*, p. 449).

158. Tregubova, *Baiki Kremlyovskogo diggera*, Ch. 8 and *Izvestia*, Dec. 19, 1998. Tregubova was a free spirit who kept breaking the rules and was eventually expelled from the Kremlin journalists' pool. Putin also tried to win over Natalya Gevorkyan, but she maintained her independence. Tregubova's role as his preferred interviewer was later taken over by Andrei Kolesnikov of *Kommersant*, not to be confused with the writer of the same name at the Moscow Carnegie Center.

159. Markus Lyra, author's interview, March 2, 2017. To spare his blushes, the former CIA officer shall remain anonymous, but the incident highlights a recurrent weakness of Western intelligence services' and journalists' reporting on Russia: events which do not fit an expected pattern are too readily dismissed as implausible. Anomalies can be revealing and usually merit closer examination.

160. *Kommersant*, May 28, 1997 & July 30, 1998.

161. Interfax, May 24, 1997.

162. Rossiya1, June 14, 2020.

163. According to Strobe Talbott, the Russian Defence Minister, Marshal Igor Sergeyev, was at first unaware of the deployment, which appeared to have been authorised at Kvashnin's level. It would therefore have been logical for the Chief of Staff to seek political cover by consulting Putin as Secretary of the Security Council. Talbott's conversations with Putin on June 11 and 12 are consistent with this version (Talbott, *Russia Hand*, Random House, New York, 2002, pp. 335–7 & 339–45).

164. Jackson, General Sir Mike, *Soldier*, Bantam Books, London, 2007, p. 268.

165. Pavlovsky, author's interview, Nov. 21, 2019.

166. Talbott, *supra*, pp. 335–6; author's interview, Feb. 15, 2019; private communication, July 29, 2019.

167. Jackson, *supra*, p. 272.

168. Talbott, *supra*, p. 344.

169. In an angry telephone call to Clinton on April 25, urging him to stop the bombing of Yugoslavia, Yeltsin made a transparent reference to the risk of nuclear conflict: 'Don't push

Russia into this war! You know what Russia is, you know what Russia has at its disposal!'
When Talbott met Stepashin in Moscow on June 10, he, too, started the meeting by referring to the Cuban crisis (ibid., pp. 311 & 334).

170. Ibid., p. 306.

171. Ibid., p. 301.

172. Ibid., p. 300.

173. The Swedish ambassador, Sven Hirdman, remembered attending a Kremlin reception in
February 1999 where Stepashin put his arm round Putin and told him, 'Mr Ambassador,
don't listen to the criticisms, this man is a very good fellow' (Hirdman, author's interview,
Stockholm, Feb. 26, 2017).

174. Pavlovsky, author's interview, Nov. 21, 2019.

175. *Nezavisimaya gazeta*, Jan. 14, 2000. Yeltsin wrote later that he deliberately led the Duma to
believe that he was considering naming Aksyonenko, whom many deputies disliked, to
make them confirm Stepashin the more readily as a preferable alternative (*Midnight Diaries*, p. 287).

176. On August 6, *Kommersant* named Putin as one of several possible candidates to replace
Stepashin if Yeltsin decided to change the government.

177. At a Carnegie Endowment symposium, attended by the cream of America's Russia experts
in Washington, D.C. on July 26, Aksyonenko, Aleksandr Lebed, Luzhkov, Primakov and
Stepashin were all cited as possible successors to Yeltsin. No one mentioned Putin.

178. One straw in the wind came at the beginning of that month, when Yeltsin publicly praised
Putin's work at the FSB and said that he had 'a great future' (NTV, July 6, 1999).

179. According to Yumashev, Stepashin exasperated Yeltsin by trying to persuade him that he
should come to terms with Luzhkov, whom most of the elite thought would be unbeat-
able when the elections were held (Aven, *Vremya Berezovskogo*, p. 429).

180. Berezovsky later recounted his meeting with Putin to Masha Gessen (*Man Without a Face*,
p. 19) and to Andrei Illarionov (author's interview, Feb. 16, 2019). His account was partially
confirmed by Yumashev (Aven, *supra*, p. 427), who learnt later that Berezovsky had indeed
gone to see Putin during his holiday to tell him that Yeltsin intended to appoint him Prime
Minister, and it is consistent with Putin's calendar of engagements, which shows that he
was on leave from July 10 to 24 (RIA Novosti, July 23). Berezovsky said the family were on
holiday in Biarritz, in 'very modest, condominium-type accommodation', consisting of a
couple of bedrooms and a kitchen in an apartment-hotel, and that he met Putin for a drink
in the Hôtel du Palais on July 14. That much may well be true. It is plausible and it is hard
to see why Berezovsky should have invented it. Timchenko's charter firm, Airfix, had landing rights in Biarritz, and although the Direction de la surveillance du territoire (DST) had
no record of Putin's presence in the city (Jean-François Clair, author's interview, June 23,
2016), he had travelled to France before without the DST knowing. Where Berezovsky's
account becomes pure invention is his claim that Yeltsin had asked him to find out whether
Putin would be willing to accept the post of Prime Minister. Putin, he told Gessen,
responded that he would 'give it a shot', and Berezovsky then flew to Antibes where Yumashev and Tatyana were waiting anxiously for news. None of that was true. It was typical
of Berezovsky's attempts to present himself as the mastermind behind every key
decision.

181. Aven, *supra*, p. 444.

182. TASS, Aug. 11, 1999.

183. Yeltsin, *Midnight Diaries*, pp. 330–31.

184. This and the following section are drawn from Aven, *supra*, pp. 424–7. Yeltsin, in *Midnight Diaries*, gives a slightly different version. Yumashev's account to Aven in *Vremya Berezovskogo* appears to be more reliable.

185. Yeltsin, *supra*, pp. 332 & 334.

186. ORT, Aug. 9, 1999.

187. NTV, Aug. 9, 1999. To 'sit' – *sidet*, in Russian – is slang for being in jail.

188. Ibid., Aug. 10, 1999.

189. Interfax, Aug. 13; TASS, Aug. 13, 1999.

190. *Kommersant*, Aug. 28, 1999.

191. *Nezavisimaya gazeta*, Aug. 27, 1999. It has been suggested that Basayev's men were allowed unhindered passage back to Chechnya to prevent them carrying the conflict deeper into Dagestani territory. That is plausible. Moscow feared that Chechnya would provide the spark which would set the rest of the North Caucasus on fire. It does not necessarily contradict the idea that Basayev was lured into Dagestan. A limited border incursion to justify a resumption of hostilities was one thing; a conflict spreading across the region would be quite another.

192. *Kommersant*, Aug. 28, 1999.

193. TASS, Aug. 27, 1999.

194. Ibid., Sept. 9 & 10, 1999.

195. Although Putin emphasised the link to al-Qaeda to try to gain western sympathy, it turned out later that he was not exaggerating. Bin Laden's deputy, Ayman al-Zawahiri, had visited Chechnya in December, 1996, to explore the possibility of establishing his headquarters there before deciding to base himself instead in Afghanistan. The Saudi jihadi, Khattab, who became one of the key field commanders in the second Chechen War, had close ties to bin Laden and arranged for hundreds of Chechen fighters to train at camps in Afghanistan. In 1999, at least 100 Arab combatants were fighting in Chechnya (Meier, *Black Earth*, pp. 129, 455 n. 26 & 457–8 n. 38; and 'Security Council Committee established pursuant to resolution 1267 (1999) concerning Al-Quaida . . .', QE.I.99.03. Islamic International Brigade (IIB), Sept. 7, 2010. See also *The 9/11 Commission Report*, Washington, D.C., 2004, which details al-Qaeda's links with the Chechen insurgency).

196. Memorandum of Conversation, 'Meeting with Prime Minister Vladimir Putin of Russia', Auckland, Sept. 12, 1999, Clinton Presidential Library, Doc. 0100117, Box 4180.

197. Memorandum of Telephone Conversation, Sept. 8, 1999, Clinton Presidential Library.

198. Andrew Weiss, author's interview, Washington, D.C., March 13, 2019.

199. RTR, Aug. 9, 1999.

200. Unless otherwise specified, the following is drawn from Memorandum of Conversation, Sept. 12, 1999, *supra*.

201. Steve Sestanovitch, author's interview, Washington, D.C., Feb. 8, 2019.

202. Talbott, *Russia Hand*, p. 201.

203. Telephone Conversation with British Prime Minister Tony Blair, Oct. 13, 1999, Clinton Presidential Library. This was apparently Clinton's first conversation with Blair after the Auckland meeting.

204. Memorandum of Conversation, Sept. 12, 1999, *supra*.

205. Yeltsin, *Midnight Diaries*, p. 330.

206. Pavlovsky, author's interview, Nov. 21, 2019.

207. Aven, *Vremya Berezovskogo*, pp. 401 & 427–8.

208. *Moscow Times*, Feb. 2, 1999.

209. ORT, Sept. 13, 1999.

210. Ibid., Sept. 14, 1999.

211. Pavlovsky, *supra*. Putin later confirmed that 'it was only after the explosions of the residential buildings in Moscow that we decided to liquidate the terrorist bases in Chechnya' ('Interview with Canadian [Journalists] and RTR', Dec. 14, 2000, www.kremlin.ru/events/president/transcripts/21139).

212. He appears to have made up his mind on September 14 or 15.

213. ORT, Interfax and TASS, Sept. 16, 1999.

214. RTR, Sept. 19, 1999.

215. Ekho Moskvy, Sept. 24, 1999.

216. TASS, Sept. 23, 1999 (at a news conference in Rostov-na-Donu).

217. Ibid., Sept 24, 1999 (at a news conference in Astana).

218. Pavlovsky, *supra*.

219. Ekho Moskvy, Sept. 24, 1999.

220. NTV, Sept. 24, 1999.

221. *Moskovskie novosti*, Sept. 27 and Interfax, Sept. 29, 1999.

222. Interfax, Sept. 28, 1999.

223. TASS, Oct. 5, and ORT, Oct. 9, 1999.

224. *Kommersant*, Oct. 16, 1999.

225. RTR, Oct. 17 and ORT, Oct. 21, 1999.

226. ORT, Oct. 22, 1999.

227. RTR, Oct. 20, 1999.

228. Memorandum of Conversation, 'Meeting with Russian Prime Minister Putin', Oslo, Nov. 2, 1999, Clinton Presidential Library, Doc. 9908099, Box 2578.

229. John Beyrle, author's interview, Washington, D.C., March 12, 2019.

230. Memorandum of Conversation, *supra*. Putin was not alone in thinking that Clinton was mistaken. Even Grigory Yavlinsky of Yabloko, the leading democrat in the Duma, said that 'Western leaders don't fully understand the threat posed by Chechen terrorism' (*Nezavisimaya gazeta*, Nov. 19, 1999).

231. *Izvestia*, Nov. 6, 1999.

232. Ekho Moskvy, Aug. 27 (2 per cent); RTR, Sept, 26 and TV6, Oct. 3 (7–8 per cent); NTV and TASS, Oct 15 (13–18 per cent); Interfax, Oct. 22 (Putin leads with 21 per cent); Interfax, Nov. 10 (31 per cent); ORT, Nov. 20 (41 per cent); TV6, Dec. 12, 1999 (48 per cent). Although different polls gave varying results, the overall trend was consistent.

233. *Moscow Times*, Oct. 5, 1999.

234. Aven, *Vremya Berezovskogo*, pp. 430–31.

235. TV6, Nov. 7, 1999.

236. Pavlovsky, author's interview, Nov. 21, 2019.

237. Aven, *supra*, p. 429.

238. Pavlovsky, *supra*.

239. Interfax, Nov. 24, 1999.

240. Ibid., Dec. 7, 1999.

241. The businessman, Paul Tatum, died in a contract killing in 1996 after a dispute with his Chechen business partner, Umar Dzhabrailov, over the ownership of the Slavyanskaya Radisson Hotel in Moscow. Afterwards the hotel was taken over by Dzhabrailov and the Moscow City government, which Luzhkov headed.

242. Putin said that Yeltsin's proposal was 'quite unexpected' (ORT, Jan. 4, 2000).

243. Yeltsin, *Midnight Diaries*, pp. 6–7.

244. Putin, *First Person*, pp. 204–5; *Kommersant*, March 10, 2000.

245. Interfax, Dec. 13, 1999.

246. Putin, *supra*, p. 205.

247. ORT, Dec. 31, 1999.

248. Ibid., Jan. 4, 2000.

9: The Cap of Monomakh

1.   Yeltsin, *Midnight Diaries*, pp. 364–6.

2.   Pavlovsky, author's interview, Nov. 21, 2019.

3.   Yeltsin, *supra*, p. 364.

4.   *Komsomolskaya pravda*, Jan. 26, 2000.

5.   ORT, Ibid.

6.   Jim Collins, author's interview, Washington, D.C., March 12, 2019.

7.   ORT, *supra*.

8.   This account is taken from Putin, *First Person*, pp. 144–5, and ORT, Jan. 1, 2000.

9.   TASS, March 20, and Interfax, March 22, 2000.

10.   Except where otherwise indicated, the following is taken from 'Russia on the Threshold of the New Millennium', *Nezavisimaya gazeta*, Dec. 30, 1999. The text was posted on the government website two days earlier. The GNP figures for 1999 appear deliberately understated. On a Purchasing Power Parity basis, they would have been higher.

11.   Pietsch, *Heikle Freundschaften*, p. 218.

12.   Aven, *Vremya Berezovskogo*, p. 348.

13.   Collins, author's interview, March 12, 2019.

14.   Treisman, Daniel, *The Return*, Free Press, New York, 2011, pp. 72–3.

15.   *Moscow News*, Dec. 8, 1999. Nearly 20 years later, in an interview with Dozhd TV on March 17, 2018, Kozhukhov's views were little changed.

16.   RTR, Oct. 10, 1999.

17.   Pavlovsky, author's interview, Nov. 21, 2019.

18.   Peter Clement, author's interview, New York, Feb. 7, 2019. One conclusion reached by CIA analysts was that Putin's story about being cornered by a rat when he was a child was not so much, as Putin himself viewed it, a lesson that no one should be forced into a corner without being given a way out, but it should rather be read as a warning that, if Putin were ever cornered, he would turn and fight. When that was put to Gleb Pavlovsky, who, as chief strategist for Putin's campaign, had vetted the book before it was released, he grimaced and said: 'The secret services have their own way of looking at things. It's what psychologists call over-interpretation' (Pavlovsky, *supra*).

19.   ORT, Feb. 7, 2000.

20.   Ibid.

21.   RTR, Jan. 23, 2000.

22.   Albright, Madeleine, *Madam Secretary*, Macmillan, London. 2003, p. 556.

23.   Ibid., pp. 556 & 558 and *Guardian*, Feb. 3, 2000.

24.   *Kommersant*, Feb. 24, 2000.

25.   Blair, Tony, *A Journey*, Hutchinson, London, 2010, p. 244.

26.   NTV, Feb. 4 and Europe 1, Feb. 5, 2000.

27. *Kommersant*, Feb. 9, 2000.

28. Putin, *First Person*, pp. 171–3.

29. Ibid., p. 173.

30. Radio Mayak, March 18, 2000.

31. TASS, Nov. 17, 1999.

32. Richard Dearlove, author's interview, June 24, 2016.

33. Blair, *A Journey*, pp. 343–4.

34. Campbell, Alastair, *The Blair Years*, Hutchinson, London, 2007, pp. 444–5.

35. Powell, Jonathan, *The New Machiavelli: How to Wield Power in the Modern World*, Vintage, London, 2010, p. 289.

36. Campbell, *supra*, p. 445.

37. RTR, Jan. 23, 2000.

38. Ibid., Feb. 15, 2000.

39. NTV, Feb. 16, 2000.

40. 'Interview for BBC Breakfast with Frost', March 5, 2000, www.kremlin.ru/events/president/transcripts/24194

41. *Nezavisimaya gazeta*, March 7, 2000.

42. TASS, March 8, 2000.

43. 'Interview for BBC', *supra*.

44. Putin, *First Person*, p. 174.

45. Campbell, Alastair, *The Burden of Power: Countdown to Iraq*, Hutchinson, London, 2012, p. 187.

46. BBC Monitoring, March 14, 2000.

47. Stephen White, 'The Russian Presidential Election, March 2000', *Electoral Studies*, Vol. 20, No. 3, pp. 484–9.

48. Radio Mayak, March 18, 2000.

49. Vitaly Mansky, *Putin's Witnesses*, 2018, transcript. The comparison with Tampax and Snickers was not fortuitous. In the early 1990s, not long after Putin's return to Leningrad, the first full-page advertisements for western products in the city's newspapers were for Tampax and Snickers. They evidently stuck in Putin's mind.

50. Yeltsin, *Midnight Diaries*, p. 286.

51. Blair, *supra*, p. 245.

52. 'Open Letter to Voters', *Izvestia*, Feb. 25, 2000.

53. 'Vystuplenie na uchreditelnom sezde obshcherossiskogo obshchestvenno-politicheskogo dvizheniya "Yedinstvo"', Feb. 27, 2000 at www.kremlin.ru/events/president/transcripts/24145

54. ORT, Sept. 18, 1998.

55. Kokh and Svinarenko, *A Crate of Vodka*, p. 203.

56. Putin liaised with Sobchak through Dmitry Medvedev after his return, having apparently decided that it was expedient politically to keep a certain distance (Sobchak and Krichevskaya, *Delo Sobchaka*, and Valery Pavlov, author's interview, Nov. 27, 2019).

57. *St. Petersburg Times*, Feb. 25, 2000 and teleprogramma.pro/news/1266899-sadalskiy-vspomnil-kak-20-let-nazad-podralsya-na-pohoronah-anatoliya-u3419

58. RTR, Feb. 24, 2000.

59. The case for Sobchak having been killed has been set out by Arkady Vaksberg in *Le Laboratoire des Poisons* (Gallimard, Paris, 2007, pp. 290–300). He speculated that a toxic powder was applied to the bulb of a lamp on Sobchak's bedside table, and that when he switched it on

to read before going to sleep, as was his habit, the poison vaporised and killed him. No evidence of such a poison was found and many of Vaksberg's other claims do not withstand close scrutiny. However, Sobchak's widow, Lyudmila, was convinced that he had been murdered (lenta.ru/news/2000/02/22/narusova/ and Valery Pavlov, author's interview, Nov. 27, 2019) and at her insistence an investigation was launched. It was closed three months later on the grounds that there was no evidence of a crime having been committed. While exonerating Putin, Narusova continued to maintain for more than a decade afterwards that her husband had been killed and that some of those involved were still in power (*Novaya gazeta*, Nov. 9, 2012). More recently, however, she has stated that Sobchak's death, although not caused by a heart attack, was 'not sensational and not criminal. It's not important except for me and my family' (Narusova, author's interview, Nov. 21, 2019).

60. Hans Olsson, author's interview, Stockholm, Oct. 13, 2017. In his recollection, only 30 or 40 people were present.

61. The following account is taken from Mansky, *Putin's Witnesses*.

62. Yeltsin, *Midnight Diaries*, p. 14. If Yeltsin's account is accurate, Clinton must have been awakened to be told of the resignation, for he called as Yeltsin was being driven home from the Kremlin, which was before 6 a.m. in Washington, D.C. Yeltsin finally took the call at 9 a.m. EST ('Telcon with Russian President Boris Yeltsin', Dec. 31, 1999, Clinton Presidential library).

10: *Power Vertical*

1. ORT, Jan. 4, 2000.

2. See for instance, Paul Starobin, 'The Accidental Autocrat', *The Atlantic*, March 2005.

3. *Nezavisimaya gazeta*, Aug. 12, 2000.

4. RTV, April 17 ('equal rules') and Interfax, May 6, 2000 ('more rigid').

5. NTV, May 7, 2000.

6. 'Inauguration Ceremony of Vladimir Putin as President of Russia', at www.kremlin.ru/events/president/transcripts/21410 and 'Speech at Inauguration Ceremony', at www.kremlin.ru/events/president/transcripts/21399. The official film of the ceremony is at www.youtube.com/watch?v=4kZ9C4PN88I

7. Seppo Tiitinen, author's interview, May 29, 2017.

8. NTV, July 21, 2000.

9. Diana Kachalova, author's interview, St Petersburg, June 3, 2019.

10. NTV, April 28, 2001.

11. Kachalova, *supra*.

12. It had been built for the Soviet Prime Minister, Georgy Malenkov, who had been Khrushchev's principal rival to succeed Stalin. Malenkov never lived there, having been demoted before it was completed. Later, Khrushchev exiled him to Kazakhstan, where he worked as the lowly manager of a hydroelectric plant.

13. Dozhd TV, Nov. 19, 2015.

14. *Moskovskie novosti*, Nov. 8, 2000 and *Komsomolskaya pravda*, Aug. 12, 2008.

15. Powell, *New Machiavelli*, pp. 309–10, and author's interview, London, Sept. 22, 2016.

16. Campbell, *The Blair Years*, p. 589.

17. Kalela, author's interview, March 2, 2017.

18. von Puttkamer, author's interview, May 6, 2017.

19.   Collins, author's interview, March 12, 2019.

20.   Illarionov, author's interview, Feb. 16, 2019. He gave a slightly different account in 'Slovo i delo', *Kontinent*, No. 134, 2007, available online at magazines.gorky.media/continent/2007/134/slovo-i-delo.html

21.   Nonetheless, there were limits to his patience. After Putin had asked him three times to become his adviser, Illarionov wrote, 'I realised that there would not be a fourth invitation' ('Slovo i delo', *supra*).

22.   Mansky, *Putin's Witnesses*.

23.   Kendall said that for the first programme, entitled 'Talking Points' – the 'Direct Line' format came later – questions were submitted over the internet by foreign as well as Russian viewers and she personally selected those to be asked. The intention was to show Putin as a modern, switched-on young leader, addressing the rest of the world. The same pattern was followed in a later phone-in which she moderated in 2006. After that, the programmes became more stylised (author's interview, Cambridge, May 17–18, 2017).

24.   *Izvestia*, Oct. 19, 2000.

25.   *Nezavisimaya gazeta* (June 15, 2000) stated that the conflict had begun in the spring of 1999, when Primakov was ousted and replaced by Kiriyenko. Other evidence suggests it may have been even earlier, perhaps in the autumn of 1998, when the Prosecutor's Office began investigating NTV's takeover of Channel 11 in St Petersburg. In any event, it started during Yeltsin's presidency, not when Putin took power.

26.   Kasyanov, *Bez Putina*, pp. 71–3 & 101–5.

27.   Ibid, p. 103. Gleb Pavlovsky maintained that 'the idea did not come from Putin . . . Natalya Gevorkyan also argued that Tatyana, Yumashev and Voloshin 'were determined to kill NTV long before Putin came to power. He was presented with a fait accompli' (author's interview, March 31, 2016).

28.   ORT, Feb. 29, 2000. The decision was ostensibly aimed at ORT and at Centre TV, which was controlled by the Moscow Mayor's Office. But when their licences came up for renewal on May 24, both were extended in the normal way. It appears to have been a shot across the bows of NTV, to indicate what might lie in store if it did not mend its ways.

29.   'Interview with NBC', June 2, 2000, www.kremlin.ru/events/president/transcripts/24204

30.   Interfax reported on June 1 that NTV had been told in writing by the Kremlin that Zaches must go. Viktor Shenderovich, one of the main scriptwriters for 'Kukly', also said he had been warned that the character must disappear. Whatever the truth of the matter, Zaches was not seen again. The show continued until June, 2003, but Putin was represented by different puppets.

31.   *Sankt-Peterburgskie vedomosti*, Feb. 8, 2000. Mikhail Zygar remembered being told at the time that 'Kukly' was not the reason for the attack on NTV, 'it was just a little detail' (author's interview, Nov. 21, 2019. Putin himself said he had watched *Kukly* once or twice. 'It doesn't annoy me, but my friends take offense' (*First Person*, p. 158). He repeated that he had no complaints about the programme at a meeting with NTV journalists in January, 2001 (*Kommersant*, Jan. 30, 2001). See also Gleb Pavlovsky, 'The Putin Files', July 13, 2017, at www.pbs.org/wgbh/frontline/interview/gleb-pavlovsky

32.   Mikhail Zygar (*supra*) argues that the wider clampdown on the media was decided only later, after Berezovsky's Channel One incurred Putin's wrath by its coverage of the *Kursk* disaster in mid August. The chronology belies that. Talks on the sale of Berezovsky's shares to the state had already started at the beginning of August (Interfax, Aug. 2, 2000).

33. ORT, Feb. 8, 2000.

34. Pavlovsky, 'The Putin Files', *supra.*

35. Ibid.

36. *Vlast'*, transcript, privately held.

37. Mansky, *Putin's Witnesses.*

38. Kendall, author's interview, March 17, 2000.

39. The 'Russian State Information Doctrine', approved shortly after Putin took office, called for a strengthening of the state media and measures 'to protect society from distorted and inaccurate information' (*Segodnya*, Sept. 14, 2000).

40. Interfax, June 13, 2000.

41. NTV, June 13, 2000.

42. Interfax, June 14 & 15, 2000.

43. RTR, June 15, 2000.

44. *Nezavisimaya gazeta*, Sept. 20, 2000.

45. Ibid. Gorbachev quoted Putin as saying Lesin's behaviour had been 'intolerable' (Interfax, Sept. 26, 2000). He had earlier instructed Kasyanov to investigate Lesin's role (ibid., Sept. 21).

46. Putin was surrounded by 'all those old puppeteers', Gorbachev said. 'They have him in their grip' (Centre TV, May 20, 2000).

47. At a news conference at the White House on June 14, Clinton affirmed the principle of freedom of the press but was careful to add: 'I don't think we necessarily know all the facts'. There was pressure from individual congressmen, and a business delegation, led by the former US Ambassador, Robert Strauss, cancelled a visit, but that was as far as it went. Gusinsky had dual Russian–Israeli citizenship, and Prime Minister Ehud Barak's office sent the Russian government a message expressing the hope that the case would be treated 'with sensitivity' (Ekho Moskvy and Voice of Israel, June 16, 2000). European leaders generally kept silent.

48. Zygar, Mikhail, *All the Kremlin's Men*, Public Affairs, New York, 2016, p. 39.

49. *Nezavisimaya gazeta*, June 15, 2000.

50. ORT, June 15, 2000.

51. It also contained a grain of truth. The reason that NTV was so heavily in debt was that, after the August 1998 default, Gusinsky had been forced to take out 1.2 billion US dollars in loans to keep his business empire afloat (Kasyanov, *Bez Putina*, pp. 71–3).

52. *Izvestia*, Feb. 2, 2000.

53. Ekho Moskvy, July 12, 2000.

54. According to Yevgeny Kiselev, there had been an earlier meeting in May, before Gusinsky's arrest, when Putin had invited a smaller group of businessmen to his dacha for a shashlik barbecue, at which he had conveyed the same message in more general terms (Kasyanov, *Bez Putina*, p. 220). Catherine Belton, apparently citing Sergei Pugachev, has written that the barbecue took place the same day as the Kremlin meeting and not at Putin's dacha but, symbolically, at Stalin's former dacha at Kuntsevo (Belton, *Putin's People*, pp. 201–2). That appears to be untrue.

55. This and the following are taken from RTR and Interfax, July 28, 2000.

56. According to Interfax (July 24, 2000), Berezovsky and Roman Abramovich were not invited because of their 'excessive involvement in politics'.

57. Aven, *Vremya Berezovskogo*, pp. 406–7, 540, 580–1.

58. Ibid., p. 552.

59. Ibid., pp. 24 & 26.

60. Ibid., p. 639.

61. Ibid., p. 541.

62. *Kommersant*, March 31 and *Napi Magyarország*, Budapest, April 3, 2000.

63. TASS, May 13, 2000.

64. RTR, Aug. 31, 2000. This and the following section also draw on 'Remarks at a Meeting with Members of the Federation Council', May 17, www.kremlin.ru/events/president/transcripts/22307, 'Interview with German TV Channels ARD and ZDF', June 9, www.kremlin.ru/events/president/transcripts/24205 and 'Interview with the Newspaper, Izvestia', July 4, 2000, www.kremlin.ru/events/president/transcripts/24171; 'Excerpts from an Interview with the Chief Editors of the Newspapers, Komsomolskaya Pravda, Izvestia, Moskovsky Komsomolets and Trud, March 22, www.kremlin.ru/events/president/transcripts/21207; and 'Address to the Federal Assembly, April 3, 2001, www.kremlin.ru/events/president/transcripts/21216

65. TASS, Feb. 28, *Kommersant*, April 21 and NTV, May 6, 2000.

66. TASS, June 27, 2000.

67. Aven, *supra*, p. 553.

68. *Kommersant*, May 31, 2000.

69. TASS, May 31, 2000.

70. This and the following section are drawn from Aven, *supra*, pp. 541–2 & 553–4.

71. Ekho Moskvy, June 1, and RIA Novosti, July 7, 2000.

72. Berezovsky said he last met Putin at the beginning of July (NTV, July 17, 2000). According to Nikolai Kharitonov, a leading Communist deputy, by mid July Putin was avoiding him (RIA Novosti, July 17, 2000), hence the decision not to invite him to Putin's meeting with the business magnates on July 28.

73. Truscott, Peter, *Putin's Progress*, Simon and Schuster, London, 2004, p. 155 and TASS, Aug. 12, 2000. The following account is drawn mainly from contemporary Russian press coverage.

74. web.archive.org/web/20140220231704/http://www.militaryfactory.com/ships/detail.asp?ship_id=K141-Kursk

75. Truscott, *supra*, p. 156 and *Nezavisimaya gazeta*, Aug. 22, 2000.

76. *Novaya gazeta*, Oct. 23, 2012 and Pavlovsky, author's interview, Nov. 21, 2019.

77. TASS, at 11.01 am Moscow time – 48 hours after the accident occurred – on August 14, 2000.

78. RTR, Aug. 16, and *Komsomolskaya pravda*, Aug. 18, 2000.

79. *Segodnya*, Aug. 18, 2000.

80. Interfax, Aug 16 & 18, 2000.

81. Ibid., Aug. 16, 2000.

82. Marina Litvinovich, author's interview, Nov. 21, 2019.

83. *Segodnya*, Aug. 18, 2000.

84. Interfax, Aug. 16, 2000.

85. Ekho Moskvy, Aug. 16, and BBC Monitoring, Aug. 17, 2000.

86. *Nezavisimaya gazeta*, Aug. 18, 2000.

87. Ekho Moskvy, Aug. 18, and Interfax, Sept. 15, 2000.

88. NTV, Aug. 18, 2000.

89. Litvinovich, *supra*. See also Gessen, *Man Without a Face*, pp. 167–8.

90. At a meeting with Orthodox churchmen in the Kremlin on Sunday, Putin said: 'All of us, with pain in our hearts and – let me say without exaggeration – with tears in our eyes, are

following the tragedy that is now unfolding in the Barents Sea.' The NTV correspondent commented: 'As if regaining his senses, for the first time [Putin] has said something with real emotion' (NTV, Aug. 20, 2000).

91. Murmansk TV, Aug. 19, 2000. Truscott, in *Putin's Progress*, p. 160, gives a slightly different wording. See also *The Times*, Aug. 24, 2000.

92. Ekho Moskvy, Aug. 22, 2000.

93. Andrei Kolesnikov, *Putin: Chelovek s Ruchem*, Eksmo, Moscow, 2018, p. 26.

94. Ibid., p. 27.

95. The following extracts are collated from ibid., pp. 27–31 and *Kommersant-Vlast'* (Aug. 29, 2000), which obtained a recording of the meeting and published a transcript.

96. Interviewed for the TV documentary, 'Prezident', Rossiya 1, 2015.

97. By the end of November, Putin's approval rating, which had fallen to 65 per cent after the *Kursk* disaster, was back at 70 per cent, climbing to 72 per cent in December (Interfax, Nov. 29 and Dec. 25, 2000).

98. 'Interview with Tatyana Malkina', Republic.ru, Aug. 22, 2021.

99. CNN, Sept. 8, 2000.

100. Even in the West, uncertainty continued for at least a year afterwards as to the exact cause of the explosion. See, for instance, *Guardian*, Aug. 5, 2001.

101. *Kommersant-Vlast'*, *supra*.

102. On Putin's relations with Sergei Ivanov, see *First Person*, pp. 200–201.

103. *Obshchaya gazeta*, Dec. 6, 2001.

104. Putin told Larry King: 'I could have gone back to Moscow [at an earlier stage during the *Kursk* disaster]. But it would have been PR activity, since anywhere in Russia, or anywhere in the world, I always have communications links to the military . . . But from the point of view of PR, yes, that might have looked better' (CNN, Sept. 8, 2000).

105. He repeated the charges in an address to the nation the next day (RTR, Aug. 23, 2000).

106. Venediktov, interview with Dmitry Gordon, Aug. 19, 2019, at gordonua.com/publications/venediktov-putin-mne-skazal-tvoj-internet-sploshnaja-dezinformatsija-smotri-tam-lezhat-papki-kazhdaja-podpisana-generalom-esli-menja-obmanut-mogu-pogony-sorvat-1191705.html

107. Putin met Dorenko on August 29 (Ekho Moskvy, Sept. 9 & 10, and *Komsomolskaya pravda*, Sept. 12, 2000).

108. Gessen, *Man Without a Face*, pp. 171–2. The broadcast was on September 2.

109. Aven, *Vremya Berezovskogo*, p. 536.

110. Ibid., pp. 531–2. According to Goldfarb and Litvinenko, Berezovsky met Voloshin on August 19 and Putin on the morning of August 20 (*Death of a Dissident*, pp. 208–12), which places it before Putin's meeting at Vidyaevo on August 22. Aven (p. 631 n) also dated the meetings to August.

111. Gessen, *supra*, p. 174.

112. Interfax, Sept. 4, 2000.

113. Berezovsky claimed that he had agreed to the deal with Abramovich on the understanding that, after the sale, Nikolai Glushkov, a close friend and business colleague who had been arrested in December as part of the Aeroflot investigation, would be released. In the event, the promise, if there was one, was not honoured. In March 2004, Glushkov was acquitted and released. The Moscow City Court ordered a retrial and, in 2006, he was given a two-year suspended sentence.

114. The name change took place on September 2, 2002.

115. www.newsru.com/russia/30dec2001/elsin_interviu2.html. See also *Nezavisimaya gazeta*, Jan. 15 and *Kommersant*, Jan. 22 & 23, 2000.

116. RFE/Radio Liberty website, Dec. 29, 2005.

117. 'Answers to Questions at Columbia University', Sept. 26, 2003, www.kremlin.ru/events/president/transcripts/22129

118. Aven, *supra*, pp. 530–31.

119. Interview with Dmitry Gordon, Aug. 19, 2019, *supra*.

120. As in the case of the explosion in the underground shopping mall at Tverskaya Street on August 31, 1999, which was caused by a similar device packed with hexogen, it was never entirely clear whether it was the work of Chechens or of criminal origin. However, the authorities treated it as a terrorist attack (Interfax, Aug. 9; TASS, Aug 10; RTR and ORT, Aug. 2, 2000).

121. Putin started calling for a greater role for the Chechen police as early as July 2000. 'Local people should be trusted more boldly. We should gradually abandon the practice of sending in large contingents of OMON and special rapid reaction units from other territories,' he told Kadyrov, the Interior and Defence Ministers and the leaders of the neighbouring Caucasian republics ('Opening Remarks . . .' at Mozdok, North Ossetia, July 5, 2000, www.kremlin.ru/events/president/transcripts/21484). See also *Izvestia*, Oct. 19, 2001 and Channel One, Oct 12, 2002.

122. Interfax, Aug. 9, 2000.

123. *Kommersant*, July 13, 2002. See also Ahmad Kadyrov's remarks (TVS, July 29, 2002).

124. Ekho Moskvy, March 28, 2001.

125. Central TV, Aug. 2, 2001.

126. The hostage taking at the Dubrovka Theatre is described in detail in Baker and Glasser, *Kremlin Rising*, pp. 156–73.

127. Channel One, Oct. 24, 2002.

128. Al-Jazeera TV, in Arabic, Oct. 24, 2000.

129. *Sunday Times*, Oct. 27, 2002. No authoritative totals exist, either for the number of terrorists or the hostages. The figures given here are approximations.

130. *Moskovsky komsomolets*, Oct. 28, 2000.

131. Channel One, Oct. 28, 2002. Although those remarks were made two days afterwards, they reflected what Putin had been saying privately throughout the siege. From the outset of the war, three years earlier, he had insisted that Russia 'had no right to allow itself to be weak'. It was the same policy that the British Prime Minister, Margaret Thatcher, had followed when British hostages were seized in Lebanon. Any concession, she argued, would show that hostage-taking paid and encourage the terrorists to do the same again; in the long term, lives would be saved by being totally inflexible and refusing to negotiate.

132. *Moskovsky komsomolets*, Oct. 26, 2002.

133. Interfax, June 2, 2002.

134. Surviving hostages reported that Barayev's immediate reaction was to try to find an electrician to get the air-conditioning system switched off (Baker and Glasser, *supra*, p. 169).

135. Ibid., pp. 170–71.

136. The political scientist, Andrei Piontkovsky, commented that what happened at Dubrovka 'showed not even a Soviet-style indifference towards people's lives but a kind of centuries-old indifference, maybe from the time of the Tatar yoke . . . The saddest result of this tragedy is that, in this respect, the authorities have not changed one iota' (*Nezavisimaya gazeta*, Dec. 9, 2002).

137. Rossiya TV, Oct. 26, 2002.

138. Channel One, Nov. 5, 2002 and 'Meeting with French Regional Press and TV Channels', Feb. 12, 2003, www.kremlin.ru/events/president/transcripts/21874. See also Piontkovsky in *Nezavisimaya gazeta*, *supra*.

139. *Vremya novostei*, Nov. 5 and Channel One, Nov. 10, 2002.

140. 'Meeting with Representatives of the Chechen Public', Nov. 10, 2002, www.kremlin.ru/events/president/transcripts/21770

141. *Le Monde*, Nov. 13; see also Channel One and NTV, Nov. 11, 2002. That Putin stood by his words was made clear when the full transcript of that section was posted in Russian and English on the Kremlin website ('Excerpts from the Transcript of a News Conference following Russia-European Union Summit', Brussels, Nov. 11, at www.kremlin.ru/events/president/transcripts/21773).

142. Rossiya TV, Nov. 10, 2002.

143. *Izvestia* on October 30 quoted unnamed sources in the Kremlin as saying that Russia 'reserved the right to take preventive action, including on the territory of other countries'. *Vremya novostei*, on November 5, 2002, cited the Defence Minister, Sergei Ivanov, as saying that Putin had authorised 'adequate responses' to terrorists and their accomplices 'regardless of state borders'.

144. 'Address to the Residents of the Chechen Republic', March 16, 2003, www.kremlin.ru/events/president/transcripts/21939

145. *Rossiiskaya gazeta*, March 4, 2003.

146. Colonel Vladimir Plotnikov, cited by Interfax, Aug. 29, 2003.

147. *Nezavisimaya gazeta*, Jan. 17, 2005.

148. Baker and Glasser, *Kremlin Rising*, pp. 176–7; Ekho Moskvy, July 11, 2003.

149. 'Address to the Residents of the Chechen Republic', March 16, 2003, *supra*.

150. The independent newspaper, *Chechenskoe obshchestvo* (Grozny, Dec. 27, 2004), reported that 'there are changes for the better compared with, say, 2001, but it is still a long way to go to reach the level of 1991'.

151. 'Speech at a Meeting with Cabinet Ministers', May 11, 2004, www.kremlin.ru/events/president/transcripts/22457

152. Ren TV, Sept. 25, 2003.

153. Baker and Glasser, *supra*, pp. 300–301.

154. Ekho Moskvy, Oct. 4, 2003.

155. TASS, Oct. 7, 2003.

156. Rossiya TV, Feb. 9, 2004.

157. TASS, Feb. 6, 2004.

158. TASS and Interfax, May 9 and Rossiya TV and RIA Novosti, May 10, 2004.

159. *Moskovsky komsomolets*, May 11, 2004.

160. *Novye izvestia*, May 11, 2004.

161. Ekho Moskvy, July 6, 2004.

162. Except where otherwise indicated, the following account is drawn from Baker and Glasser, *supra*, pp. 15–37. Not only were they present throughout most of the siege themselves but they checked and cross-checked information obtained by others. Although there are a few errors, theirs is probably the most reliable and judicious account of what happened, neither exculpating the authorities nor minimising the incompetence and confusion which marked the entire episode.

163. Kavkaz-Tsentr News Agency, Sept. 17, 2004.

164. They demanded not only the withdrawal of Russian troops from Chechnya, but also the release of insurgents arrested during attacks in Ingushetia in June (TASS, Sept. 1, 2004).

165. The danger that this posed was immediately recognised in the Kremlin. Putin warned that it could 'explode the already shaky balance of interfaith and interethnic relations in the region' (Rossiya TV, Sept. 2, 2004).

166. Interfax and 'Interview with Turkish Media', Sept. 1, 2004, www.kremin.ru/events/president/transcripts/22585

167. Rossiya TV, Sept. 2, 2004.

168. *New York Times*, Sept. 13, 2004.

169. Channel One, Sept. 4, 2004, and www.kremlin.ru/events/president/transcripts/page/470

170. www.kremlin.ru/events/president/transcripts/22589

171. *New York Times*, March 31, 2010.

172. Radio Free Europe, Jan. 20, 2003, 'Russia: Moscow Media Boss Fired', www.rferl.org/a/1101954.html

173. 'Speech at a Meeting with the Media and State Duma Deputies', Nov. 25, 2002, at www.kremlin.ru/events/president/transcripts/21788

174. Radio Free Europe, Jan. 20, 2003.

175. RIA Novosti, June 13, 2001. See also Interfax, Jan. 25 & 29 and April 9, 2001. After Dubrovka, Putin repeated: 'No democratic government can exist without the publicity and openness provided by the media' ('Meeting with the Media and State Duma Deputies', Nov. 25, 2002, *supra*).

176. Interfax, Jan. 29, 2001.

177. Ekho Moskvy, April 5, 2001.

178. Ibid., Nov. 13, 2002.

179. Ibid., Oct. 4, 2002.

180. BBC Monitoring, Dec. 11, 2002.

181. See press releases from Radio Free Europe/Radio Liberty in Prague on Sept. 2 and 4, 2004.

182. Local officials said later they had minimised the numbers for fear of creating panic (Baker and Glasser, *Kremlin Rising*, p. 21). The first, tentative suggestions that more than a hundred hostages were being held were published on September 3, more than 48 hours after the siege had begun, by Ekho Moskvy, *Kommersant* and Gazeta.ru. The government refused to confirm the higher figure until after the school had been stormed.

183. North Ossetia FSB chief Valery Andreyev, cited by NTV, Sept. 3 and Ren TV, Sept. 4, 2004. The official inquiry found that no foreigners were involved (Ekho Moskvy, Oct. 18, 2004).

184. BBC Monitoring, Sept. 8, 2004. See also the *Guardian* of the same date.

185. Ekho Moskvy, Sept. 6 & 7, and *Kommersant*, Sept. 7, 2004.

186. During the debate on the media law, Aleksei Mitrofanov, a Duma deputy, argued that 'if the media don't talk about these things, 90 per cent of the terrorists' motivation will simply disappear' (*Kommersant*, Nov. 26, 2002).

187. *Moskovsky komsomolets* and *Novaya gazeta*, Sept. 6, 2004. See also *Vedomosti* of the same date.

188. 'Address by President Putin', Sept. 4, 2004, www.kremlin.ru/events/president/transcripts/22589

189. The following is drawn from Putin's speech on September 13, 2004 (www.kremlin.ru/events/president/transcripts/22592).

190. 'Press Conference with Russian and Foreign Media', June 20, 2003, www.kremlin.ru/events/president/transcripts/22028

191. See for instance, Putin's speech to a conference of the heads of regional legislatures on

May 12, 2002, in which he said that otherwise voters would always choose 'not between ideas but between persons they like and persons they like less' (www.kremlin.ru/events/president/transcripts/21599).

192. Speech at a meeting with leaders of *Yedinaya Rossiya* [United Russia], March 26, 2003 (www.kremlin.ru/events/president/transcripts/21946). Lenin used the term 'transmission belt' to describe the role of the trades unions, which should transmit the ideas of the Communist Party, the vanguard of the proletariat, to the working masses.

193. *Nezavisimaya gazeta*, Aug. 19, 2003.

194. www.kremlin.ru/events/president/transcripts/22589

195. Vladimir Petukhov, the Mayor of Nefteyugansk, in western Siberia, the major production centre for Yukos, was assassinated on June 26, 1998, which was Khodorkovsky's 35th birthday. Petukhov had accused Yukos of tax evasion. The company's security service was later accused of organising the murder (*Kommersant*, May 23, 2006). It seems more likely, however, that whoever was behind the murder had chosen that date to lay a false trail. The evidence produced at the subsequent trial was singularly unconvincing. Yukos, like most of the other major companies which emerged in Russia in the 1990s, had played fast and loose during its early days (Charles Ryan, author's interview, March 14, 2019), but in this particular case, the accusation was almost certainly untrue.

196. *Forbes*, March 18, 2002.

197. Mansky, author's interview, Nov. 29, 2019. From January, 2000, when Mansky started filming the documentary about Putin, to June 2001, when it was broadcast by RTR under the title, 'Red Tsars: Presidents of Russia. Putin – Leap Year', he had direct access to Putin and was a frequent visitor to the Kremlin. Earlier programmes in the series had been devoted to Gorbachev and Yeltsin.

198. Yezhkov, *Putin: Pochemu on stal takim?*, pp. 6–7.

199. Baker and Glasser, *Kremlin Rising*, p. 281.

200. Aven, *Vremya Berezovskogo*, p. 529.

201. Mikhail Khodorkovsky, *Tyurma i volya*, Alpina Didzhital, Moscow, 2012, p. 50.

202. Ibid. See also *Sunday Times*, May 18, 2008.

203. This and the following section are drawn from Kasyanov, *Bez Putina*, pp. 199–202 (where he says that Khodorkovsky approached him 'towards the end of 2002'); Khodorkovsky, *supra*, pp. 274–6 (where he dates the approach to February/March 2003); and Kasyanov, author's interview, Nov. 19, 2019. I have followed the chronology given in Khodorkovsky's book.

204. Khodorkovsky, *supra*, p. 275.

205. Kasyanov, author's interview, *supra*.

206. No complete transcript of the meeting has been published. Unless otherwise indicated, the following account is drawn from *Kommersant*, Feb. 20, 2003 and Khodorkovsky, *supra*, pp. 41, 282 & 285.

207. Kasyanov, *Bez Putina*, p. 218.

208. Yulia Latynina on TVS, May 29, 2003.

209. Khodorkovsky, *supra*, p. 282.

210. Interfax, Feb. 19, 2003.

211. Zygar, *All the Kremlin's Men*, p. 53, and author's interview, Nov. 21, 2019.

212. A contemporary report described it as 'a sharp exchange' but no more (*Kommersant*, Feb. 20, 2003).

213. *New York Times*, April 21, 2003.

214. Khodorkovsky, *supra*, pp. 49–51.

215. Khodorkovsky was widely quoted as having told Putin at the meeting on February 19: 'Vladimir Vladimirovich, you do not understand the importance of building relations with China.' He has repeatedly denied saying that and the story appears to be untrue.

216. utro.ru/articles/2003/05/26/201631.shtml

217. See Newsru.com, 'The report of Russian political scientists about the conspiracy of the oligarchs turned out to be fake', May 30; and Vladimir Pribylovsky, 'Oligarchs, True and False', June 10, 2003 (www.jamestown.org/program/oligarchs-true-and-false/).

218. Press Conference with Russian and Foreign Media, June 20, 2003, *supra*.

219. NTV, July 10, 2003.

220. *Argumenty i Fakty.* July 16, 2003.

221. Centre TV, July 20, 2003.

222. Ekho Moskvy, Aug. 14, 2003.

223. *Argumenty i Fakty, supra.* Putin made the remark at Voronezh on March 18, 2000. A month after his inauguration, he repeated, 'there will be no oligarchs in the sense [of] people who try to get close to the government to pursue their selfish ends' ('Interview with NBC', June 2, 2000, *supra*). Later he again said, 'there shall be no such group of people' ('Interview with ORT, RTR and Nezavisimaya Gazeta', Dec. 25, 2000, www.kremlin.ru/events/president/transcripts/21149).

224. John Browne, *Beyond Business*, Weidenfeld and Nicolson, London, 2010, p. 145. The quote is as given, but it is permissible to wonder whether Putin did not use a more colourful phrase.

225. Baker and Glasser, *Kremlin Rising*, pp. 286–7 & 292.

226. Aven, *Vremya Berezovskogo*, pp. 547–8.

11: A Bonfire of Illusions

1. Memorandum of Telephone Conversation with Acting President Putin, Jan. 1, 2000, Clinton Presidential Library, Box 4072, Doc. 0000008.

2. Memorandum of Telephone Conversation with Prime Minister Blair, Nov. 23, 2000, Clinton Presidential Library.

3. Ibid., April 19, 2000. The remark, which followed Clinton's own failed attempt at health-care reform in the United States, was apparently made without irony.

4. Memorandum of Telephone Conversation with President Putin, June 9, 2000, Box 4115, Doc. 0007645, ibid.

5. Memorandum of Conversation, New York, Sept. 6, 2000, ibid.

6. RTR, Nov. 9, 2000.

7. Memorandum of Conversation, New York, Sept. 6, 2000, *supra*.

8. Memorandum of Telephone Conversation, July 10, 2000 and Memorandum of Conversation, Brunei, Nov. 15, 2000, ibid.

9. Memorandum of Telephone Conversation, Dec. 27, 2000, ibid.

10. Memorandum of Telephone Conversation, Sept. 30, 2000, ibid.

11. Ukrainian TV, First National Channel, Kyiv, April 23, 2000.

12. TASS, Dec. 6, 2000.

13. Memorandum of Telephone Conversation, Dec. 27, 2000, *supra*.

14. Memorandum of Conversation with Russian President Yeltsin, Istanbul, Nov. 19, 1999, ibid.

15. Press conference in London, April 17, 2000, www.kremlin.ru/events/president/transcripts/21379 and 'Interview with Die Welt am Sonntag', June 11, 2000, www.kremlin.

ru/events/president/transcripts/24202. Putin first spoke publicly of the only foreseeable
threat coming from Scuds in June, 2001, after meeting George W. Bush in Ljubljana.

16. 'Interview with NBC', June 2, www.kremlin.ru/events/president/transcripts/24204; 'Press
statement following talks with Italian Prime Minister, Giuliano Amato, June 5, www.
kremlin.ru/events/president/transcripts/24210, and 'Press conference [after] G8 in
Okinawa', July 23, 2000, www.kremlin.ru/events/president/transcripts/21497

17. 'Interview with Larry King, CNN', Sept. 8, 2000, www.kremlin.ru/events/president/
transcripts/21558

18. The Clinton Presidential Library has not released the memcons of the President's meetings with Putin in Moscow on June 3 and 4, 2000, but the following week Putin summed
up the gist of the talks to a German correspondent ('Interview with Die Welt am Sonntag',
June 11, 2000, *supra*).

19. NTV, April 14, 2000.

20. Memorandum of Telephone Conversation with President-Elect Putin, April 15, 2000, Clinton Presidential Library.

21. Interfax, April 14. Putin gave Clinton a Russian proposal for START III at the G7 summit
in Okinawa (ibid., July 21). On November 13, he suggested that a ceiling of 1,500 warheads
could be achieved by 2008 and afterwards reduced further (*Segodnya* and RTR, Nov. 14,
2000).

22. 'Speech at a meeting of the State Duma . . .', April 14, 2000, www.kremlin.ru/events/
president/transcripts/21357

23. Xinhua and Interfax, July 18, 2000.

24. Memorandum of Telephone Conversation with Prime Minister Blair, May 27, 2000, Clinton Presidential Library.

25. Putin said later: 'We proceeded on the basis that to have a serious dialogue, we should wait
for his successor' ('Meeting with Moscow Bureau Chiefs of Leading US Media', Nov. 10,
2001, www.kremlin.ru/events/president/transcripts/21394).

26. 'Press conference . . . at Rostov na Donu', Nov. 8, 2000, www.kremlin.ru/events/president/
transcripts/21131

27. 'Interview with ORT, RTR and Nezavisimaya gazeta', Dec. 25, 2000, www.kremlin.ru/
events/president/transcripts/21149

28. RTR, Dec. 14, 2000.

29. 'Interview with India Today . . .', Sept. 29, 2000, www.kremlin.ru/events/president/
transcripts/24229

30. 'Press conference', May 4, 2001, www.kremlin.ru/events/president/transcripts/21230

31. 'Speech at a meeting of the leadership of the Armed Forces of the Russian Federation',
Nov. 20, 2000, www.kremlin.ru/events/president/transcripts/21119. Putin had made a
similar point about certain forces in the West being 'steeped in Cold War thinking' to
David Frost eight months earlier.

32. 'Statement and answers to journalists' questions', St Christoph, Austria, Feb. 9, 2001, www.
kremlin.ru/events/president/transcripts/21178

33. This citation is from an interview with *Corriere della Sera* on July 16, 2001 (www.kremlin.ru/
events/president/transcipts/21286). He had made the same point more succinctly several
months earlier ('Statement and answers', Feb. 9, 2001, *supra*).

34. 'Press Conference for Russian and Foreign Journalists', July 18, 2001, www.kremlin.ru/
events/president/transcripts/21291

35. John Scarlett, author's interview, Sept. 26, 2016.

36. John Beyrle, author's interview, March 12, 2019. Beyrle said that Bush spoke more loudly than usual when he was tense, and that was the case at Ljubljana.

37. Ibid.; Rice, Condoleezza, *No Higher Honor*, Crown, New York, 2011, p. 61; Bush, George W., *Decision Points*, Crown, New York, 2010, p. 195; and 'Speech at representatives of the US public and political leaders', Nov. 14, 2001, www.kremlin.ru/events/president/transcripts/21398. Putin had by then been Prime Minister or President for almost two years and had had many meetings with Western leaders. On this occasion, Bush, not Putin, was the neophyte. Yet Putin seemed to make a show of appearing tense, opening the meeting by reading from briefing cards – something he normally never did. It is fair to ask whether his nervousness was feigned, designed to draw Bush out, to make the American feel master of the occasion and himself non-threatening. If so, it was a remarkable success.

38. *New York Times*, June 17, 2001.

39. 'Press Conference by President Bush and Russian Federation President Putin', June 16 (White House, Office of the Press Secretary), georgewbush-whitehouse.archives.gov/news/releases/2001/06/20010618.html and 'Conversation with Heads of Local Bureaux of Leading US Media Outlets', June 18, 2000, www.kremlin.ru/events/president/transcripts/21269.

40. 'Press Conference', June 16, 2000, *supra*.

41. Rice, *supra*, p. 63.

42. Michael Morgan, author's interview, Dec. 29, 2018.

43. *New York Times*, June 18, 2001.

44. Reuters, Sept. 26, 2008.

45. John Evans and Alexander Vershbow, author's interviews, Washington, D.C., March 10, 2017 and Dec. 10, 2018.

46. Bush, *supra*, p. 196, and Rice, *supra*, p. 63.

47. Putin recounted the story of his baptism, the sanctification of the cross and the fire which engulfed the dacha in *First Person*, pp. 11–12 & 119–22 and in 'Interview with Larry King, CNN', Sept. 8, 2000, *supra*.

48. Rice, *supra*, .p. 63.

49. Bush, *supra*, p. 196.

50. 'Conversation with Heads of Local Bureaux', June 18, 2000, *supra*.

51. *Helsingin Sanomat*, Sept. 1, 2001.

52. 'Conversation with Heads of Local Bureaux', June 18, 2001, *supra*.

53. Fox News, June 17, 2001, www.acronym.org.uk/old/archive/textonly/dd/dd58/58docs1.htm#powell

54. 'Conversation with Heads of Local Bureaux', June 18, 2001, *supra*.

55. *Helsingin Sanomat*, Sept. 1, 2001.

56. 'Press Conference with President of Finland, Tarja Halonen', Helsinki, Sept. 3, 2001, www.kremlin.ru/events/president/transcripts/21319

57. 'Press conference [after] G8 in Okinawa', July 23, 2000, www.kremlin.ru/events/president/transcripts/21497. He made a similar statement at his meeting with Bush in Ljubljana, telling US journalists two days later: 'There are bases [in Afghanistan] for training terrorists who act not only against us but against you,' yet in America there was 'total silence' about the Taliban ('Conversation with Heads of Local Bureaux', June 18, 2001, *supra*).

58. 'Interview with Bild', Sept. 18, www.kremlin.ru/events/president/transcripts/21334; and Interfax, Sept. 11, 2001, at 18.25 Moscow Time.

59. Bush, *Decision Points*, p. 196, Rice, *No Higher Honor*, pp. 74–5 and Interfax, Sept. 11, at 20.40 Moscow Time. See also TASS, Sept. 11, 2001 at 19.48.

60. The two aircraft hit the World Trade Centre at 16.46 and 17.03 Moscow Time. Interfax reported at 18.17 and 18.24 that Putin had sent condolences, presumably a reference to his phone call to Rice. The follow-up telegram was reported by Interfax at 19.47 and the full text issued by TASS at 21.28.

61. NTV, Sept. 11, 2001, 19.00 Moscow Time. According to NTV, the meeting ended shortly before 20.00.

62. Bush, p. 196. Bush said later: 'America, and I in particular, will remember this act of friendship in a time of need' ('Press conference at Shanghai', Oct. 21, 2001, www.kremlin.ru/events/president/transcripts/21373).

63. NTV, Sept. 11, 2001, 16.50 Moscow Time.

64. Bush, *supra*, p.196.

65. Ibid., pp. 196–7.

66. 'Interview with ABC', Nov. 7, 2001, www.kremlin.ru/events/president/transcripts/21392

67. Rice, *supra*, p. 62.

68. Memorandum of Conversation, 'Meeting with Russian Prime Minister Putin', Oslo, Nov. 2, 1999, *supra*.

69. *The 9/11 Commission Report*, 2004, p. 274.

70. The links between al-Qaeda and the Chechen insurgency are pp. 58, 64, 125, 149, 160, 165–6, 233, 274, 496, nn. 90 & 96, 524, n. 97, 525, n. 103, 526–7, n. 107.

71. 'Interview with Bild', Sept. 18, 2001, *supra*. Condoleezza Rice wrote in her memoirs that 'Putin never let us forget it [the warning he had given Bush at Ljubljana], recalling that conversation time and time again' (*No Higher Honor*, p. 63). That is not borne out by any other source and appears to reflect the animosity that developed afterwards, when relations had soured, rather than the reality of the time.

72. 'Interview with Bild', Sept. 18, 2001, *supra*.

73. 'Speech to the Bundestag', Berlin, Sept. 25, 2001, www.kremlin.ru/events/president/transcripts/21340

74. 'Speech at a meeting with veterans . . .', May 8, 2001, www.kremlin.ru/events/president/transcripts/21233

75. 'Interview with ABC', Nov. 7, 2001, www.kremlin.ru/events/president/transcripts/21392

76. 'Interview with the Financial Times', Dec.17, 2001, www.kremlin.ru/events/president/transcripts/21447

77. Rice, *No Higher Honor*, p. 60.

78. 'Answers to Questions at a Joint Press Conference', Oct. 21, 2001, *supra*.

79. *Rossiiskaya gazeta*, Oct. 23, 2001.

80. 'Interview with the Financial Times', Dec.17, 2001, *supra*.

81. 'Answers to Questions at a Joint Press Conference', Oct. 21, 2001, *supra*.

82. 'Press conference after meeting George Robertson', www.kremlin.ru/events/president/transcripts/21350, and 'Statement and Answers to Questions Following the Russia-EU Summit', www.kremlin.ru/events/president/transcripts/21354, Brussels, Oct. 3, 2001.

83. RTR, Oct. 5, and 'Press conference with the British Prime Minister, Tony Blair', Chequers, Dec. 21, 2001, www.kremlin.ru/events/president/transcripts/21456

84. 'Questions at Rice University', Nov. 14, 2001, www.kremlin.ru/events/president/transcripts/21400

85. 'Interview with NPR', Nov. 16, 2001, www.kremlin.ru/events/president/transcripts/21402

86. 'Press conference', Dec 21, 2001, *supra*.

87. 'Joint News Conference with Ukrainian President Leonid Kuchma', Sochi, May 17, 2002, www.kremlin.ru/events/president/transcripts/21598

88. 'Joint Press Conference with US President George W. Bush', May 24, 2002, www.kremlin.ru/events/president/transcripts/21606

89. ORT, June 24, 2002. Putin restated this at a meeting with Chinese journalists on November 27 (www.kremlin.ru/events/president/transcripts/21793).

90. 'Joint News Conference', May 17, 2002, *supra*.

91. Francis Richards, author's interview, May 12, 2017.

92. Daniel Fried, author's interview, Washington, D.C., Dec. 10, 2018. Fried did not date the conversation but said it was early on in Bush's first term.

93. 'Interview with Al-Jazeera', Oct. 16, 2003, Kuala Lumpur, www.kremlin.ru/events/president/transcripts/22162

94. Richard Dearlove, author's interview, May 16, 2016.

95. 'Joint Press Conference with NATO Secretary General George Robertson', Nov. 11, 2002, www.kremlin.ru/events/president/transcripts/21774

96. 'Interview with Al-Jazeera', Oct. 16, 2003, *supra*.

97. Richards, *supra*.

98. NTV, Oct. 18, 2001.

99. *Izvestia*, July 10, 2002.

100. 'Interview with New York Times', Oct. 4, 2003, www.kremlin.ru/events/president/transcripts/22145

101. 'Excerpts from a talk with German and Russian Media', April 7, 2002, www.kremlin.ru/events/president/transcripts/21552

102. 'News Conference on the Results of the Russian-Spanish Negotiations', Madrid, June 14, 2000, www.kremlin.ru/events/president/transcripts/24214

103. 'Discussion at the Russian Rectors Congress', Dec. 6, 2002, www.kremlin.ru/events/president/transcripts/21803. The Defence Minister, Sergei Ivanov, used the same metaphor, but in a different sense. 'We are finally starting to live up to our coat of arms,' he said. 'We are looking with equal attention to both East and West' (*Izvestia*, Nov. 9, 2000).

104. 'Interview with the Financial Times', Dec. 17, 2001, *supra*.

105. Reuters, Sept. 18, 2001, and Suskind, Ron, *The One Percent Doctrine*, Simon and Schuster, New York, 2006, p. 23. There is no proof that Cheney was responsible for the original leak to the American media which made public the supposed Iraqi connection, but it is entirely plausible. The Vice President had been from the outset one of the leading Iraq hawks in the administration. Even after the intelligence community had expressed scepticism about the Iraq story, which had come from Czech sources, Cheney continued to cite it as evidence of Iraqi connivance with al-Qaeda. It was not the only occasion on which Cheney's entourage went to unusual lengths to support the case for going to war. Subsequently his Chief of Staff, Scooter Libby, attempted covertly to discredit a report casting doubt on Saddam's supposed endeavours to manufacture nuclear weapons. He was afterwards convicted of perjury.

106. 'Meet the Press', NBC, Dec. 9, 2001, georgewbush-whitehouse.archives.gov/vicepresident/news-speeches/speeches/print/vp20011209.html.

107. georgewbush-whitehouse.archives.gov/news/releases/2002/01/20020129-11.html

108. Bush, *Decision Points*, p. 233.

109. 'News Conference following the G8 Summit', Evian, June 3, 2003, www.kremlin.ru/events/president/transcripts/22019

110. 'Interview with the Wall Street Journal', Feb. 11, www.kremlin.ru/events/president/transcripts/21498 and 'Interview with the Hindu and Star TV', Dec. 2, 2002, www.kremlin.ru/events/president/transcripts/24683

111. 'Transcript of meeting with German and Russian media', April 7, 2002, www.kremlin.ru/events/president/transcripts/21552

112. 'Speech and Answers to Questions at . . . Kiev University', Jan. 28, 2003, www.kremlin.ru/events/president/transcripts/21852

113. 'Interview with TF1', Feb. 11, 2003, www.kremlin.ru/events/president/transcripts/21869

114. 'Interview with FR3', Feb. 9, 2003, www.kremlin.ru/events/president/transcripts/21864

115. 'Interview with TF1', Feb. 11, 2003, *supra*.

116. 'Interview with FR3', Feb. 9, 2003, *supra*, and 'Interview with Bulgarian Journalists', Feb. 28, 2003, www.kremlin.ru/events/president/transcripts/21891

117. 'Extracts from Press Conference with . . . Schroder and Chirac', April 11, 2003, www.kremlin.ru/events/president/transcripts/21964

118. 'Joint Press Conference with Tony Blair', April 29 2003, www.kremlin.ru/events/president/transcripts/21984

119. *Washington Post*, April 14, 2003.

120. 'Press Conference with Blair', *supra*.

121. 'Transcript of Press Conference for Russian and Foreign Journalists', June 20, www.kremlin.ru/events/president/transcripts/22028, and 'Interview with BBC', June 22, 2003, www.kremlin.ru/events/president/transcripts/22031

122. 'Interview with FR3', Feb. 9, *supra*, and 'Interview with French regional correspondents', Feb. 12, 2003, www.kremlin.ru/events/president/transcripts/21874

123. Jim Collins, author's interview, March 12, 2019.

124. 'Speech to a meeting of the leadership of the Russian Armed Forces', Nov. 20, 2000, www.kremlin.ru/events/president/transcripts/21119

125. 'Interview with Focus', Sept. 19, 2001, www.kremlin.ru/events/president/transcripts/21336

126. 'Interview with the Hindu', Dec. 3, 2004, www.kremlin.ru/events/president/transcripts/22716. Britain granted asylum to Akhmed Zakayev, then Maskhadov's Deputy Prime Minister and the rebel government's principal representative abroad, in November 2003. The Foreign Minister, Ilyas Akhmadov, was given asylum in the United States in August 2004.

127. *Guardian*, Sept. 8, 2004.

128. 'Statement to the Press [after] Russian-Azerbaijani Talks', Feb. 6, 2004, www.kremlin.ru/events/president/transcripts/22352

129. 'Address of the Russian President, Vladimir Putin', Sept. 4, 2004, www.kremlin.ru/events/president/transcripts/22589

130. *Guardian*, Sept. 8, 2004.

131. 'Speech at the World Congress of News Agencies'. Sept. 24, www.kremlin.ru/events/president/transcripts/22610 and 'Interview with Renmin Ribao', Oct. 13, 2004, www.kremlin.ru/events/president/transcripts/22633

132. 'Press conference for Russian and Foreign Journalists', Dec. 23, 2004, www.kremlin.ru/events/president/transcripts/22757

133. 'Speech at a conference', New Delhi, Dec. 3, 2004, www.kremlin.ru/events/president/transcripts/22720

134. 'Press conference . . .', Dec. 23, 2004, *supra*.

135. 'Direct Line with Readers of Komsomolskaya Pravda', Feb. 9, 2000, www.kremlin.ru/events/president/transcripts/24370

136. RIA Novosti, Oct. 12, 2000 and Belarusian Radio, Minsk, Aug. 29, 2001.

137. RTR, June 13, 2002.

138. Memorandum of Telephone Conversation with President Putin, Dec. 27, 2000, Clinton Presidential Library.

139. 'News Conference for Russian and Foreign Journalists', June 24, 2002, www.kremlin.ru/events/president/transcripts/21651

140. 'Questions at a Meeting with the Command of the Siberian Military District', Aug. 28, 2002, www.kremlin.ru/events/president/transcripts/21696

141. Rustavi 2 TV, Tbilisi, Feb. 12, 2004.

142. 'Meeting with Journalists', Sochi, March 27, 2004, www.kremlin.ru/events/president/transcripts/22400

143. Rossiya TV, Dec. 18, 2003.

144. Ekho Moskvy, Feb. 10, 2004.

145. Rustavi 2 TV; NTV; and 'Speech on Independence Day', May 26, 2004, www.saakashviliarchive.info/en/PressOffice/News/SpeechesAndStatements?p=2777&i=11

146. *Guardian*, Sept. 9, 2004.

147. Memorandum of Conversation, New York, Sept. 6, 2000, Clinton Presidential Library.

148. *Kommersant*, May 23, 2000.

149. Ekho Moskvy, June 19, 2003.

150. An opinion poll in which 2,000 respondents were questioned between August 19 and 26, gave Yushchenko 30 per cent in the first round and Yanukovych, 24 per cent (UNIAN, Kyiv, Sept. 1, 2004). If a second round were held, the opposition leader would have 40 per cent of voting intentions, Yanukovych, 34 per cent (*Ukrayinska pravda*, Sept. 10, 2004).

151. Rossiya TV and UT 1 TV, Kyiv, Oct. 9, 2004.

152. *Novaya gazeta*, Oct. 28, 2004.

153. 'Press Conference Following the Meeting with . . . Leonid Kuchma', Sochi, Aug. 19, 2004, www.kremlin.ru/events/president/transcripts/22571. In a phone-in programme on First TV on October 26, Putin said Yanukovych's government had made 'good progress and [is] an example to be followed'.

154. UT 1 TV, Kyiv, Oct. 9, 2004.

155. Ibid., Oct. 26, 2004.

156. *Ukrayinska pravda*, Kiev, Oct. 13, and Korrespondent.net, Kyiv, Oct. 15, 2004.

157. *Zerkalo nedeli*, Kiev, Nov. 6, 2004.

158. One Plus One TV, Kiev and 5 Kanal TV, Kyiv, Nov. 12, 2004. The videotape showing Putin's remarks was distributed to the Ukrainian media by Kuchma's press office.

159. *Izvestia*, Nov. 22, 2004.

160. 'Joint Press Conference with Portuguese Prime Minister Pedro Santana Lopes', Lisbon, Nov. 23. 2004, www.kremlin.ru/events/president/transcripts/22705

161. See *Kommersant*, Aug. 2 and Channel One, Nov. 24, 2004.

162. 'News Conference at the end of the Russia-EU Summit', The Hague, Nov. 25, www.kremlin.ru/events/president/transcripts/22707 and Rossiya TV, Dec. 23, 2004.

163. 'Responses to Questions from Russian Journalists', Ankara, Dec. 6, 2004, www.kremlin.ru/events/president/transcripts/22732

164. For example, Stanislas Belkovsky in *Nezavisimaya gazeta*, Nov. 24, 2004.

165. Cited by Alexander Vershbow (author's interview, Dec. 10, 2018).

166. *Komsomolskaya pravda*, Nov. 23, 2004.

167. 'President Bush's Second Inaugural Address', Jan. 20, 2005, www.npr.org/templates/story/story.php?storyId=4460172&t=1641837148914

168. Charles Krauthammer, who coined the phrase, 'the Bush Doctrine', wrote that democracy promotion was the final development of the doctrine, having been preceded by unilateral withdrawals from treaty commitments such as the ABM Treaty; the war against terror; and pre-emptive strikes, notably against Iraq (*Washington Post*, Sept. 13, 2008). It was inspired by a Defence Planning Guidance document drawn up in 1992 by the then Under Secretary for Defense for Policy, Paul Wolfowitz.

169. Alexander Vershbow, *supra*.

170. Interfax, Jan. 6 & 7, 2001, and *Guardian*, Aug. 18, 2004.

171. 'Joint interview with . . . Gerhard Schröder to Russian and German TV channels', St Petersburg, April 9, 2001, www.kremlin.ru/events/president/transcripts/24399

172. Hubert Vedrine, author's interview, Paris, Sept. 28, 2015.

173. Nigel Sheinwald, author's interview, London, May 17, 2017.

174. 'Press Conference with Polish President Aleksander Kwasniewski', Baltiisk, June 28, 2003, www.kremlin.ru/events/president/transcripts/22043

175. Interfax, April 18, 2000.

176. Anthony Brenton, author's interview, Cambridge, May 14, 2017.

177. Sheinwald, *supra*.

178. *Der Spiegel*, Oct. 26, 2006.

179. *St. Petersburg Times*, Aug. 9, 2002.

180. Richard Dearlove, author's interview, June 24, 2016.

181. Sheinwald, *supra*.

182. *Kommersant*, June 15, 2004.

183. Brenton, *supra*.

184. 'Beginning of Meeting with British Prime Minister Anthony Blair', June 13, 2005, www.kremlin.ru/events/president/transcripts/23023

185. Brenton, *supra*.

186. Sheinwald, *supra*.

187. *Nezavisimaya gazeta*, Oct. 6, 2005.

188. Sheinwald and Brenton, *supra*.

189. Brenton, *supra*.

190. 'Address to the Federal Assembly', May 26, 2004, www.kremlin.ru/events/president/transcripts/22494

191. Rossiya 1, Jan. 22, *New York Times*, Jan. 24 and NTV, Jan. 29, 2006.

192. See Anton Orekh's commentary on Ekho Moskvy, Jan. 25, 2006.

193. *Guardian*, Jan. 19, 2012.

194. Rossiya 1, Jan. 31, 2006.

195. Ibid. and 'Press Statement and Answers to Questions', Jan. 25, 2006, www.kremlin.ru/events/president/transcripts/23409

196. 'Meeting with Ella Pamfilova', Nov. 24, www.kremlin.ru/events/president/transcripts/23300, 'Meeting with the Cabinet', Dec. 5, www.kremlin.ru/events/president/transcripts/23316, and 'Meeting with Vladimir Lukin', Dec. 10, 2005, www.kremlin.ru/events/president/transcripts/23324

197. Interfax, Jan. 24, 2006. The Spanish counterpart of the Council, the Cervantes Institute in Moscow, was likewise accused of failing to pay taxes on 'fee-paying Spanish language

lessons', but in that case an amicable solution was reached ('Interview to the Spanish Media', Feb. 7, 2006, www.kremlin.ru/events/president/transcripts/23419).

198. Brenton, author's interview, *supra* and Powell, *The New Machiavelli*, p. 310.

199. Ren TV, July 11, 2006.

200. The following section is taken from Ekho Moskvy, July 21 and Dec. 14, Interfax, Sept. 4, Ren TV, Dec. 5, [Russian] Ministry of Foreign Affairs website, Dec. 12, 2006 and Yevgeny Finkel and Yitzhak M. Brudny, 'Russia and the Colour Revolutions', *Democratization*, Vol. 19, No. 1, pp. 15–36.

201. Ren TV, July 11, and *Kommersant*, July 12, 2006.

202. Alexander Vershbow, author's interview, Dec. 10, 2018.

203. This account is drawn largely from the recollections of Charles Ryan, who was then with Deutsche Bank in Moscow and organised the loan consortium (author's interview, Jan. 9, 2019).

204. Civil Action No. H-05-0714, in re: Yukos Oil Company, in the United States District Court for the Southern District of Texas, Houston Division, www.iiiglobal.org/sites/default/files/media/32h_Yukos_Order__Stay_18Mar05.pdf

205. Baikalfinansgrup was registered on December 6, four days before the board of Yukos-Moscow authorised the filing of the bankruptcy petition (see the account of the Yukos case at www.casetext.com/case/in-re-yukos-oil-co-1). According to Putin, there was a risk that Yukos's shareholders would sue to try to recover their investment in the company. If the purchaser was an intermediary company, the final owner – whether Rosneft or Gazprom – would be protected ('Interview to the Spanish Media', Feb. 7, 2006, *supra*).

206. 'Press Conference with Russian and Foreign Media', Dec. 23, 2004, www.kremlin.ru/events/president/transcripts/22757

207. 'Interview with Radio Slovensko and STV', Feb. 22, 2005, www.kremlin.ru/events/president/transcripts/22837

208. *Komsomolskaya pravda*, Feb. 22 and Ekho Moskvy, Feb. 23, 2005.

209. Xinhua, Feb. 25, 2005.

210. *Süddeutsche Zeitung*, Feb. 25, 2005.

211. 'Concluding Remarks at Meeting with Newly Promoted Senior Officers', March 9, 2007, www.kremlin.ru/events/president/transcripts/24078

212. *Komsomolskaya pravda*, April 20, 2005.

213. Ekho Moskvy, April 20, 2005.

214. 'Interview with . . . Al Ahram', April 25, www.kremlin.ru/events/president/transcripts/22930, and 'Joint Press Conference with President Hosni Mubarak', April 27, 2005, www.kremlin.ru/events/president/transcripts/22933

215. 'Interview with TF1', July 12, 2006, www.kremlin.ru/events/president/transcripts/23700

216. 'Press Conference following talks with George W. Bush', St Petersburg, July 15, 2006, www.kremlin.ru/events/president/transcripts/23708

217. 'Press Conference following talks with Tony Blair', June 13, 2005, www.kremlin.ru/events/president/transcripts/23024

218. Putin first expressed concern publicly about self-determination for Kosovo at a meeting with the Serbian President, Boris Tadić, in mid-November (Interfax, Radio Belgrade and Rossiya TV, Nov. 15, 2005), although several months earlier he had spoken of the 'fundamental' importance of 'preserving the principle of ensuring existing European frontiers' ('Press Conference following the Meeting with Gerhard Schröder and Jacques Chirac', Kaliningrad, July 3, 2005, www.kremlin.ru/events/president/transcripts/23075).

219. See, for example, 'Interview with ARD and ZDF', May 5, www.kremlin.ru/events/president/transcripts/22948, 'The Lessons of Victory over Nazism', in *Le Figaro*, May 7, www.kremlin.ru/events/president/transcripts/22949, and 'Interview with Mike Wallace', May 9, 2005, www.kremlin.ru/events/president/transcripts/22958. Putin's complaints were not new, but from mid 2005 onwards, they became more persistent.

220. 'Annual Address to the Federal Assembly', April 25, 2005, www.kremlin.ru/events/president/transcripts/22931. The English-language version on the Kremlin website, in an attempt to mitigate the damage, mistranslated the phrase as 'a major geopolitical catastrophe'. Putin sought to clarify the remark two weeks later in his interview with ARD and ZDF, *supra*; see also *Time*, Dec. 31, 2007. But the problem was his use of the word 'geopolitical', as he implicitly recognised six years later when he told the French television station, TF1: 'It was a huge humanitarian disaster. Not a political or ideological disaster, but a purely humanitarian upheaval' ('Interview', June 4, 2014, www.kremlin.ru/events/president/transcripts/45832).

221. 'Press Conference following the CIS Summit', Sept. 19, 2003, www.kremlin.ru/events/president/transcripts/22119

222. 'Meeting with Students', July 21, 2017, www.kremlin.ru/events/president/transcripts/55114, and 'Truth and Justice Forum', March 2, 2018, www.kremlin.ru/events/president/transcripts/56969

223. 'Answers to Questions during a Meeting with Election Campaign Representatives', Feb. 12, 2004, www.kremlin.ru/events/president/transcripts/24817 ('milch cow'), and Rossiya 1, Jan. 31, 2006 ('billions').

224. 'Press Conference with Angela Merkel', Jan. 21, 2007, www.kremlin.ru/events/president/transcripts/24008

225. Burns to Rice, 'Lavrov's Visit and Strategic Engagement with Russia' (Secret), Feb. 28, 2006, www.carnegieendowment.org/publications/interactive/back-channel

226. 'Speech to Vilnius Conference', May 4, 2006, georgewbush-whitehouse.archives.gov/news/releases/2006/05/20060504-1.html

227. *Daily Telegraph*, May 5, 2006.

228. 'Address to the Federal Assembly', May 10, 2006, *supra*. Putin told Russian journalists afterwards that his remarks had been extempore (www.kremlin.ru/events/president/transcripts/23579).

229. The United States, Putin said, gave 'exaggerated importance to the use of force in international relations' and foisted this approach on others ('Speech at Meeting with [Russian] Ambassadors', June 27, 2006, www.kremlin.ru/events/president/transcripts/23669)

230. 'Interview with NBC', July 12, 2006, www.kremlin.ru/events/president/transcripts/23699

231. 'Press Conference following Talks with Angela Merkel', Jan. 16, www.kremlin.ru/events/president/transcripts/23388, and 'Interactive Webcast', July 6, 2006, www.kremlin.ru/events/president/transcripts/23691

232. 'Speech to the Federal Assembly', May 10, www.kremlin.ru/events/president/transcripts/23577; 'Speech at Meeting with [Russian] Ambassadors', June 27, 2006, *supra*; and 'Speech at Energy Conference', June 26, 2003, www.kremlin.ru/events/president/transcripts/22040

233. Cowell, Alan, *The Terminal Spy*, Crown, New York, 2008, pp. 12 & 15.

234. Unless otherwise specified, the following account is drawn from *The Litvinenko Inquiry*, conducted by Robert Owen and published on January 21, 2016.

235. CNN, Nov. 24, 2006.

236. Interfax, Nov. 23, 2006.

237. Powell, author's interview, Sept. 22, 2016.

238. The existence of the source was reported by the *New York Times* on September 9, 2019, two years after his exfiltration from Moscow. The CIA had concluded that American press reports on Russian interference in the 2016 presidential election, which referred to information from 'deep within the Russian government', risked blowing his cover. He was resettled in the United States, where he and his family now live under new identities. The *Times* report made no mention of the Litvinenko operation. But others with knowledge of the evidence given in the Litvinenko Inquiry have confirmed that the crucial material indicating Putin's involvement came from 'HUMINT' [Human Intelligence] provided by the United States. The only US intelligence asset in Moscow capable of providing information at that level was the source referred to in the *Times* account.

239. *The Litvinenko Inquiry*, London, January, 2016, p. 246. A further consideration was the need to avoid endangering the CIA's source, then still in Moscow. It was partly for that reason that the British government had been reluctant to hold a public inquiry.

240. An American educationalist, Urie Bronfenbrenner, recounted an incident in Moscow in the 1960s when a group of teenagers, seeing a four-year-old boy approaching, with his parents walking behind, 'scooped him up, hugged him, kissed him resoundingly, and passed him on to the rest of the company, who did likewise, and then began a merry children's dance.' Such behaviour on the part of an American adolescent male, said Bronfenbrenner, 'would surely prompt his parents to consult a psychiatrist'. In Russia it was entirely normal (*Two Worlds of Childhood*, p. 9).

241. Sheinwald, author's interview, May 17, 2017.

242. Powell, *supra*, and AFP, June 10, 2007.

243. *New York Times*, June 23, 2007.

244. Interfax, Dec. 12, 2007.

245. The following account is taken from Burns, 'Memorandum for the Record' (Secret), Oct. 22, 2006, www.carnegieendowment.org/publications/interactive/back-channel. There is a much more colourful description of the meeting in Rice's memoir, *No Higher Honor* (pp. 530–33), which is largely repeated, with a few additional details, by Angus Roxburgh in *The Strongman* (2nd edition, I.B.Tauris, London, 2013, , pp. 170–73). By Rice's account, Putin kept her waiting for two hours at her hotel before summoning her to Meiendorf Castle, a nineteenth-century state residence near Barvikha, where she found the entire Security Council gathered to celebrate the birthdays of Igor Ivanov and Dmitry Medvedev. She eventually told Putin, 'this has been fun, but . . . could I talk to you alone?' whereupon he took her off to a side room for a tête-à-tête with only the Defence and Foreign Ministers present. Burns, in his memorandum – which was the official record of the discussion – made no mention of being kept waiting and described the invitation to Barvikha as 'a very unusual [i.e. friendly] gesture'. Rice wrote that she interpreted it as Putin trying to manipulate her. During the dinner, Burns wrote, there was 'substantial conversation punctuated by toasts'. Rice remembered 'crude jokes about Georgians'. Afterwards, according to Burns, Putin, not Rice, suggested that they continue the discussion in private. Although the two accounts broadly agree on the substance of the discussions, the tone is completely different. I have taken Burns's version as being more reliable as it was written at the time, whereas Rice's was four years later, after relations had soured. For the tête-à-tête with Putin, there was no American interpreter present, so Burns's record is the only contemporary account. There is

a further reason for doubting the reliability of Rice's version. She told Ron Asmus that during the tête-à-tête, she warned Putin that there would be serious consequences if Moscow intervened militarily in Georgia, at which point 'the Russian President became furious, stood up and walked out' (Ronald D. Asmus, *A Little War that Shook the World*, Palgrave Macmillan, New York, 2010, pp. 74 & 243 n. 11). That is not what she wrote in her memoir, nor does it appear in Burns's account. It appears to be untrue.

246. See, for instance, 'Press Conference for Russian and Foreign Media', Jan. 31, www.kremlin. ru/events/president/transcripts/23412, 'Meeting with Leaders of News Agencies of G8 Member Countries', June 2, www.kremlin.ru/events/president/transcripts/23613, and 'Meeting of Valdai Discussion Club', Sept. 9, 2006, www.kremlin.ru/events/president/transcripts/23789

247. Burns to Rice (Secret), Oct. 17, 2006, www.carnegieendowment.org/publications/interactive/back-channel

248. 'Speech at the Munich Conference', Feb. 10, 2007, www.kremlin.ru/events/president/transcripts/24034. The English translation of this speech on the Kremlin website is particularly poor and should not be relied on.

249. *Financial Times*, Feb. 11, 2007.

250. *New York Times*, Feb. 11, 2007.

251. Burns to Rice, 'Thoughts on Munich and Russian Government Reshuffle', Feb. 16, 2007, www.carnegieendowment.org/publications/interactive/back-channel

252. See Tatyana Stanovaya, Politkom.ru, Feb. 12, 2007.

253. Even Burns, arguably the most perceptive US Ambassador during Putin's tenure, reported to Rice that while 'Lavrov and the others talk a lot about multipolarity, Putin himself seems to understand that without the U.S. as a frame of reference, . . . Russia's own interests would suffer' (Burns to Rice, Oct. 17, 2006, *supra*). That was wishful thinking.

254. Putin used the expression to describe relations between the USSR and China in the late 1950s, when, behind the façade of eternal friendship there was 'tension and dissatisfaction beneath the surface'. The same, he said, had become true of Russia's relations with the United States ('Meeting of Valdai Discussion Club', Sept. 9, 2006, *supra*).

255. Burns to Rice, 'Thoughts on Munich and Russian Government Reshuffle' (Secret), Feb. 16, 2007, www.carnegieendowment.org/publications/interactive/back-channel

256. 'Answers to Questions from the Russian Media', Amman, Feb. 13, 2007, www.kremlin.ru/events/president/transcripts/24041

257. Burns to Bush and Rice, 'Your Meeting with Putin at the G8' (Secret), May 31, 2007, www.carnegieendowment.org/publications/interactive/back-channel

258. 'Annual Address to the Federal Assembly', April 26, 2007, www.kremlin.ru/events/president/transcripts/24203

259. 'Press Conference with Portuguese Prime Minister, José Sócrates', May 29, 2007, www.kremlin.ru/events/president/transcripts/24295

260. 'Press Statement and Answers following Talks with Greek President, Karolos Papoulias', May 31, 2007, www.kremlin.ru/events/president/transcripts/24311

261. 'Interview with Newspaper Journalists from G8 Member Countries', June 4, 2007, www.kremlin.ru/events/president/transcripts/24313

262. Ibid.

263. 'Press Statement and Answers to Questions following Meeting with George Bush', June 7, www.kremlin.ru/events/president/transcripts/24318, and 'Press Conference after G8', June 8, 2007, Heiligendamm, www.kremlin.ru/events/president/transcripts/24322

264. 'Press Conference with George Bush', Walker's Point, July 2, 2007, www.kremlin.ru/events/president/transcripts/24393, and 'Press Statement and Answers . . . on Russian-American Talks', Sochi, April 6, 2008, www.kremlin.ru/events/president/transcripts/24905. See also Rice, *No Higher Honor*, pp. 676–7.

265. See, for instance, Putin's interview with *Time* when the magazine named him its 'Person of the Year'. The full text is given on the Kremlin website, 'Interview with Time magazine', Dec. 19, 2007, www.kremlin.ru/events/president/transcripts/24735 [hereafter, *Time*, Dec. 31, 2007].

266. Rice, *supra*, p. 580.

267. 'Speech at the Munich Conference', Feb. 10, 2007, *supra*.

268. 'Press Statement . . . following Shanghai Cooperation Organisation Summit, Aug. 17, 2007, www.kremlin.ru/events/president/transcripts/24475

269. 'Press Statement and Answers following the 20th Russia-EU Summit', Oct. 26, 2007, www.kremlin.ru/events/president/transcripts/24624

270. *Time*, Dec. 31, 2007.

271. Rossiya 24, Feb. 14 and *Moskovskaya pravda*, Feb. 27, 2008.

272. Except where otherwise indicated, the following account is taken from Asmus (*A Little War that Shook the World*, pp. 105–7), who cites the Georgian transcript of the meeting.

273. *24 Saati*, Tbilisi, Jan. 19 & Feb. 27, 2008.

274. Asmus, *supra*, p. 107.

275. TASS, Feb. 21, 2008.

276. Asmus, ibid.

277. 'Press Conference with Viktor Yushchenko', Feb. 12, 2008, www.kremlin.ru/events/president/transcripts/24833

278. Burns to Rice, 'Russia Strategy' (Secret), Feb. 8, 2008, www.carnegieendowment.org/publications/interactive/back-channel

279. 'President Bush Visits Bucharest', April 2, 2008, georgewbush-whitehouse.archives.gov/news/releases/2008/04/20080402-2.html

280. Stephen Hadley, author's interview, Washington, D.C., March 11, 2019.

281. *Komsomolskaya pravda*, Nov. 18, 2004. Rice had taken a summer course at Moscow State University 30 years earlier but, apart from that one brief stay, had never lived in Russia. American colleagues, who asked not to be quoted, also said her Russian was not fluent. She always used an interpreter during negotiations.

282. Hadley, *supra*. Ron Asmus, who provides a detailed account of the haggling over the declaration (*supra*, pp. 131–4), states that the crucial input came from the Lithuanian, Polish and Romanian leaders and from Merkel. Rice gives a somewhat different account in *No Higher Honor*, pp. 674–5.

283. 'Bucharest Summit Declaration', April 3, 2008, www.nato.int/cps/en/natolive/official_texts_8443.htm?mode=pressrelease

284. Hadley, *supra* and Asmus, *supra*, p. 134.

285. *Financial Times*, April 2, 2008.

286. MZE TV, Tbilisi, April 3, 2008.

287. Interfax-Ukraine, April 3, 2008.

288. Hadley, *supra*.

289. Asmus, *supra*, p. 128.

290. Unusually, the text of Putin's speech was not published, perhaps because the Kremlin felt

its moderate tone was misleading. Extracts are available at www.unian.info/world/111033-text-of-putin-s-speech-at-nato-summit-bucharest-april-2-2008.html

291. *Nezavisimaya gazeta*, April 11, 2008 and Zygar, *All the Kremlin's Men*, pp. 153–4. Putin's remarks to Bush at Sochi were leaked by the Russians and published in the Ukrainian press, where they drew predictable outrage. The intention was apparently to correct the impression that Moscow had accepted the outcome at Bucharest. In most accounts they are confused with Putin's speech to the NATO–Russia summit.

292. Hadley, *supra*.

293. Ibid. See also Asmus, p. 107, where Putin is quoted angrily complaining about the US failure to follow through on promises to allow Russian inspectors access to the proposed radar stations in Eastern Europe.

294. 'Press Conference following the Russian-US Talks', Sochi, April 6, 2008, www.kremlin.ru/events/president/transcripts/24905

295. Hadley, *supra*.

296. Ekho Moskvy, April 8, 2008.

297. *New Yorker*, March 19, 2019.

298. Three months after the 9/11 attacks, Putin said the understanding between Russia and the United States was that 'the US does not intend to stay there [in the bases] long-term' (Reuters, Dec. 5, 2001). US forces remained at the base at Manas, Kyrgyzstan, until June, 2014.

299. 'Meeting of Valdai Discussion Club', Sept. 9, 2006, *supra*, and *Time*, Dec. 31, 2007.

12: *The Russian Idea*

1. 'Meeting of Valdai Discussion Club', Sept. 9, 2006, *supra*.

2. 'Interview with India Today . . .', Sept. 29, 2000, *supra*.

3. 'Interview with the Turkish Media', Sept 1, 2004, *supra*.

4. 'Interview for ORT, Reuters and NHK', July 11, 2000, www.kremlin.ru/events/president/transcripts/21149

5. *Nezavisimaya gazeta*, July 13, 1996.

6. *Rossiiskaya gazeta*, July 30, 1996.

7. See Colton, *Yeltsin: A Life*, pp. 389–90.

8. 'Opening Address at a Meeting with Campaign Workers', Feb. 28, 2000, www.kremlin.ru/events/president/transcripts/24146

9. 'Interview with Izvestia', July 14, 2000, www.kremlin.ru/events/president/transcripts/24171

10. 'Interview with Gazeta Wyborcza and Polish TVP', Jan. 15, 2002, *supra*.

11. Putin, *First Person*, pp. 169 & 194, and 'Interview with Fuji TV'. July 4, 2000, www.kremlin.ru/events/president/transcripts/24181

12. 'Interview with India Today . . .', Sept. 29, 2000, *supra*.

13. 'Interview with NBC', June 2, 2000, *supra*.

14. Usoltsev, *Sosluzhivets*, pp. 184–6.

15. Joseph Pearce, 'Putin and Solzhenitsyn', *The Imaginative Conservative*, Aug. 20, 2018.

16. Burns to State Department, April 4, 2008, www.wikileaks.org/plusd/cables/08MOSCOW932_a.html

17. While not attacking Putin's decision to restore the State symbols per se, Solzhenitsyn said

the timing was 'completely inappropriate'. There were other much more urgent tasks, notably the struggle to alleviate poverty (Rossiya TV, Dec. 13, 2000).

18.   Interfax, Nov. 21, 2000.

19.   TASS and ORT, Dec. 4, 2000.

20.   *Komsomolskaya pravda*, Dec. 8, 2000.

21.   Cited in Banerji, Arup, *Writing History in the Soviet Union*, Routledge, Abingdon and New York, 2018, p. 275.

22.   Interfax, Dec. 5, 2000.

23.   ORT, Dec. 4, 2000.

24.   15 years later the United States would find itself caught up in a very similar debate, which would have significant echoes in Britain and elsewhere in Western Europe, over 'cancel culture', what to do with Confederate monuments and how to treat the historical memory of slavery.

25.   Rossiya TV, Dec. 30, 2000.

26.   At his inauguration, in May 2000, Putin said: 'We must not forget anything, . . . we must know our history as it really was and draw lessons from it . . . We shall hand down to our descendants all that is best in it' ('Speech at the Inauguration Ceremony', May 7, 2000, *supra*).

27.   Mansky, *Putin's Witnesses*, 2018.

28.   From an opinion survey in 2007 (BBC Monitoring, June 9, 2008).

29.   'Press Conference for Russian and Foreign Journalists', July 18, 2001, *supra*.

30.   Rossiya TV, Dec. 7, 2000.

31.   TASS, Oct. 2 & 3, 2005.

32.   'Meeting with Patriarch Aleksei II', April 2, 2007, www.kremlin.ru/events/president/transcripts/24133

33.   'Interview with Mike Wallace', May 9, 2005, *supra*.

34.   Interfax, Feb. 23, 2000 and Channel One, March 17, 2003.

35.   Ekho Moskvy, May 6, 2005.

36.   Rossiya TV, Feb. 22, 2005.

37.   'Talking with the Press after visiting the Butovo Memorial Site', Oct. 30, 2007, transcript and video recording, www.kremlin.ru/events/president/transcripts/24627. See also *New York Times*, Oct. 31, 2007.

38.   Rossiya TV, Oct. 30, 2007.

39.   Andrei Kolesnikov in *Kommersant*, Oct. 31, 2007.

40.   'Interview with New York Times', Oct. 4, 2003, *supra*.

41.   Interfax, Sept. 13, 2001.

42.   Ibid., March 5, 2008.

43.   Chornomorska teleradiokompaniya, Simferopol, Jan. 26, 2005.

44.   *Izvestia*, April 11, 2005.

45.   ASTV, Yuzhno-Sakhalinsk, March 30, 2006.

46.   Sakh.com, April 5, 2006.

47.   Rossiya TV, Oct. 18, 2007.

48.   'Talking with the Press after visiting the Butovo Memorial Site', Oct. 30, 2007, *supra*.

49.   This and the following section, unless otherwise indicated, are drawn from *Kommersant*, Dec. 27, 2007 and BBC Monitoring, June 9, 2008.

50.   *Diena*, Riga, Sept. 21, 2007.

51.   Centre TV, Dec. 24, 2007.

52. *Time*, Dec. 31, 2007.

53. 'Joint Interview with Gerhard Schröder for Bild', May 7, 2005, www.kremlin.ru/events/president/transcripts/22950. He had made essentially the same point after a meeting with the Polish President, Aleksandr Kwasniewski, three years earlier (TASS, Jan. 16, 2002).

54. See Interfax, Jan. 16, 2014 and *Moscow Times*, May 8, 2017. Japan, a member of the G7 and a leading ally of the West, still refuses to acknowledge the atrocities it committed in China during the Pacific War, including the massacre of hundreds of thousands of civilians in Nanjing in 1937 and 1938, and the work of Unit 731, in Manchuria, which conducted biological experiments on Chinese prisoners far exceeding in horror anything that Josef Mengele did at Auschwitz. The Japanese scientists who worked at Unit 731 were protected by the United States after the war to gain access to the knowledge they had acquired. That does not appear in American or Japanese history textbooks. Less egregiously, Britain, France, Spain and most other west European countries also have dark pages in their pasts – the slave trade; the trade in opium with China; colonial massacres – which they, too, long preferred to pass over in silence. It may be argued that there is an important difference. Scholars in these countries – even in Japan, where discussion of wartime atrocities attracts noisy protests from nationalist groups – are not prevented by their governments from researching these topics, as is increasingly now the case in Russia. But that does little to alter public awareness. How many Americans today know that the waterboarding of prisoners was first practised on a large scale by the US Army in the Philippines 120 years ago and that it provoked an outcry from liberals, among them Mark Twain, when the facts became known? Unless they are taught in school history classes, such episodes are in practice expunged from public memory.

55. Hansard, House of Commons, Aug. 2, 1944.

56. *Time*, Dec. 31, 2007.

57. 'Interview with Le Figaro', Oct. 26, 2000, *supra*.

58. When Putin was head of the Kremlin's Main Control Directorate in 1997, he was involved in discussions concerning the relations between the Orthodox Church and other religious denominations. However, according to Irene Pietsch, who visited the Putins that summer, he kept his distance from the Church hierarchy (Pietsch, *Heikle Freundschaften*, pp. 350, 353 & 355–7).

59. 'Interview with Paris Match', July 6, 2000, *supra*.

60. 'Interview with NBC', June 6 and 'Interview with Larry King', Sept. 8, 2000, *supra*. A year later he repeated, 'As for faith, I prefer never to discuss it publicly' ('Interview with ARD', Sept. 19, 2001, *supra*).

61. 'Interview with Le Figaro', Oct. 26, 2000, *supra*.

62. 'Interview with Corriere della Sera', July 16, 2001, *supra*.

63. Bill Clinton was shown the chapel in the Kremlin in June, 2000 (Talbott, *Russia Hand*, p. 394), as was Eberhard von Puttkamer a year or two later (von Puttkamer, author's interview, May 6, 2017).

64. Gleb Pavlovsky, 'The Putin Files', July 13, 2017, at www.pbs.org/wgbh/frontline/interview/gleb-pavlovsky

65. Dozhd TV, Nov. 19, 2015.

66. Ibid., and Johan Molander, author's interview, Stockholm, Oct. 12, 2017. Molander, who later became Swedish Ambassador to Moscow, remembered watching him at church services. 'It was very obvious that he didn't really know how. He was very awkward.'

67. Zygar, *All the Kremlin's Men*, p. 234.

68. 'Press Conference with Russian and Foreign Media', Feb. 1, 2007, www.kremlin.ru/events/president/transcripts/24026; see also 'Interview with ARD', Sept. 19, 2001, and 'Meeting of Valdai Discussion Club', Sept. 9, 2006, *supra*.

69. 'Conversation with Reporters', Aug. 20, 2001, www.kremlin.ru/events/president/transcripts/21314; 'Meeting with . . . Participants in the Second Global Conference on Justice', July 9, 2001, www.kremlin.ru/events/president/transcripts/21280; *Vesti TV News*, Feb. 14, 2008.

70. *Time*, Dec. 31, 2007.

71. Zygar, author's interview, Nov. 21, 2019.

72. Dozhd TV, Nov. 19, 2015.

73. *The Atlantic*, March, 2005.

74. 'Interview with the New Straits Times, Malaysia', July 3, 2003, www.kremlin.ru/events/president/transcripts/22049

75. 'Answers to Participants at the APEC Business Meeting', Oct. 19, 2001, www.kremlin.ru/events/president/transcripts/21371

76. See, for example, 'News Conference for Russian and Foreign Journalists', June 24, 2002, *supra*.

77. Rossiya TV, June 27, 2001.

78. 'Remarks at the Presidential Council for Culture and the Arts', May 30, 2007, www.kremlin.ru/events/president/transcripts/24298

79. Walter Laqueur, in *Putinism: Russia and its Future with the West*, St. Martin's Press, New York, 2015, p. 179, wrote that Ilyin's institute was part of the Ministry of Propaganda headed by Josef Goebbels. It is true that, from 1933 to 1934, it was financed by the Propaganda Ministry, but Ilyin had been working there since 1923, ten years before the Nazis came to power. During most of that time it was financed by the Foreign Ministry of the Weimar Republic.

80. Ilyin, 'O fashizme', 1948, www.web.archive.org/web/20050214142008/http://ru-contra.nm.ru/pi/2.html

81. Ilyin, 'Natsional-sotsializm. Novy dukh. 1', *Vozrozhdeniye*, Paris, May 17, 1933, www.iljinru.tsygankov.ru/works/vozr170533full.html. This article was Ilyin's strongest defence of National Socialism. He never wrote the planned second part, perhaps reflecting disillusionment.

82. 'Chto yest gosudarstvo – korporatsiya ilu uchrezhdeniye?' ['What is the State – a Corporation or an Institution?'] 10–17 January 1949, www.hrono.ru/statii/2009/ilin_gosudar.php

83. Nikolai Berdyaev, *The Russian Idea*, Macmillan, New York, 1948, pp. 1–2.

84. Daniel Treisman, 'Inequality: the Russian Experience', *Current History*, Oct. 2012. In the United States, the combined wealth of the 10 richest men in 2021 amounted to just under 5 per cent of GDP.

85. Berdyaev, *supra*, p. 2.

86. Xinhua, July 16, 2000, and 'Speech to the Islamic Conference', Putrajaya, Malaysia, Oct. 16, 2003, www.kremlin.ru/events/president/transcripts/24298

87. This idea was developed by Vladislav Surkov in his article 'Russkaya politicheskaya kultura. Vzglyad iz utopii' ['Russian Political Culture: The View from Utopia'], *Nezavisimaya gazeta*, June 22, 2007.

88. 'Press Conference for the Russian and Foreign Media', Jan. 31, 2006, www.kremlin.ru/events/president/transcripts/23412

89. See, for example, the annual report of the Prosecutor General, Vladimir Ustinov (Channel One, Feb. 3, 2006).

90. Cited in Laqueur, *Putinism*, p. 178, which refers to 'Ivan Ilyich', presumably a printing error. Ilyin's patronymic was Aleksandrovich.

91. Nikita Mikhalkov said later that he had urged Putin to do so because the lease on Ilyin's grave near Zürich was about to expire (Rossiya 1, April 26, 2015).

92. *Kommersant*, May 29, 2006.

93. 'Interview with ZDF', July 13, 2006, www.kremlin.ru/events/president/transcripts/23703. The term, 'managed democracy', had been around since the start of Putin's first term but had never won widespread acceptance (Yevgeny Kiselev on Ekho Moskvy, June 20, 2000).

94. 'Meeting of Valdai Discussion Club', Sept. 14, 2007, www.kremlin.ru/events/president/transcripts/24537

95. 'Interview with Radio Slovensko and STV', Feb. 22, 2005, *supra*.

96. 'Meeting of Valdai Discussion Club', Sept. 14, 2007, *supra*.

97. Ibid. and 'Speech of Expanded Meeting of the State Council', Feb. 8, 2008, www.kremlin.ru/events/president/transcripts/24825

98. 'Interview with Paris Match', July 6, www.kremlin.ru/events/president/transcripts/24166 and 'Annual Address to the Federal Assembly', July 8, 2000, www.kremlin.ru/events/president/transcripts/21480

99. 'Address to the Federal Assembly', May 26, 2004, *supra*.

100. 'Interview with New York Times', Oct. 4, 2003, *supra*.

101. 'Interview with NBC', July 12, 2006, *supra*.

102. *Izvestia*, July 14, 2000. See also 'Interview with CTV', July 12, 2006, www.kremlin.ru/events/president/transcripts/23702

103. 'Press Conference for Russian and Foreign Media', Jan. 31, 2006, *supra*.

104. 'Annual Address to the Federal Assembly', April 26, 2007, www.kremlin.ru/events/president/transcripts/24203

13: *Body Politic*

1. 'Meeting with British Businessmen', April 17, 2000, www.kremlin.ru/events/president/transcripts/21368

2. In Putin's words, 'In the first stage, we focused on establishing the so-called vertical power structures . . . After that job was completed, we switched to the problems themselves' ('Meeting with . . . Participants in the Second Global Conference on Justice', July 9, 2001, *supra*). See also 'Interview with Xinhua and RTR', July 16, 2000, www.kremlin.ru/events/president/transcripts/24168

3. RIA Novosti, March 31, 2000.

4. Clifford Gaddy and Barry Ickes, 'Russia after the Global Financial Crisis', in *Eurasian Geography and Economics*, 2010, Vol. 51, No. 3, p. 288.

5. NTV International, June 15, Radio Rossiya, June 18, and 'Conversation with Heads of Local Bureaux of Leading US Media Outlets', June 18, 2001, *supra*.

6. This section draws on Mark Galeotti's useful study, *The Vory: Russia's Super Mafia* (Yale University Press, New Haven and London, 2018), esp. pp. 207–43.

7. 'Interview with Channel One, NTV and Rossiya TV', Nov. 11, 2004, www.kremlin.ru/events/president/transcripts/22690

8. 'Opening Address to the Council for Priority National Projects and Demographic Policy', Oct. 5, 2006, www.kremlin.ru/events/president/transcripts/23827

9. Galeotti, *supra*, p. 208.

10. 'Speech at Congress of Yedinstvo', May 27, 2000, *supra*.

11. 'Press Conference at Election Headquarters', March 15, 2004, www.kremlin.ru/events/president/transcripts/22383

12. Rossiya TV, Feb. 16, 2000. See also 'Questions from the Media', Irkutsk, Feb. 18, 2000, www.kremlin.ru/events/president/transcripts/24138

13. According to *Novaya gazeta* (April 27, 2000), the Accounts Chamber discovered in 1999 that more than 30 million US dollars were missing from the accounts of a Russian–Vietnamese joint venture, Vietsovpetro, for which Kalyuzhny was responsible. See also NTV, May 20, 2000 and *Baltic Times,* Jan. 27, 2005.

14. Ekho Moskvy, Feb. 24, 2001.

15. Nazdratenko's governance of Primorye is discussed in David Satter's book, *Darkness at Dawn*, pp. 165–81 & 278–80, nn. 3–10 & 13–14.

16. Interfax, June 16, 2003.

17. ORT, Feb. 8, 2000.

18. *Kommersant*, Nov. 16 and TV6, Nov. 28, 2001.

19. Interfax, Jan. 3, 2002, and Kasyanov, *Bez Putina*, pp. 154–5.

20. *Komsomolskaya pravda*, March 12, 2003.

21. 'Address to Nationwide Conference of Small Businesses', March 15, 2000, www.kremlin.ru/events/president/transcripts/21234

22. 'Interview with Chief Editors of Komsomolskaya Pravda, Izvestia, Moskovsky Komsomolets and Trud', March 22, 2001, www.kremlin.ru/events/president/transcripts/21207

23. 'Address to Nationwide Conference of Small Businesses', March 15, 2000, *supra*, and 'Address to the Chernozemye Association', March 18, 2000, www.kremlin.ru/events/president/transcripts/21254

24. 'Address to the Chernozemye Association', *supra*.

25. 'Speech at National Congress of Municipalities', Oct. 23, 2007, www.kremlin.ru/events/president/transcripts/24617. See also 'Speech to Meeting of State Council on Russia's Development Strategy to 2020', Feb. 8, 2008, www.kremlin.ru/events/president/transcripts/24825

26. 'Opening Remarks at Yedinaya Rossiya [United Russia] Congress', Oct. 1, 2007, www.kremlin.ru/events/president/transcripts/24562

27. 'Address to Nationwide Conference of Small Businesses', March 15, 2000, *supra*; 'Interview with Bulgarian TV and Trud', Feb. 28, 2003, www.kremlin.ru/events/president/transcripts/21891; 'Interview with Paris Match', July 6, 2000, *supra*; 'Webcast with the President of Russia', July 6, 2006, www.kremlin.ru/events/president/transcripts/23691; and 'Press Conference with Russian and Foreign Media', Feb. 1, 2007, 1, 2007, *supra*.

28. 'Address to a Justice Ministry Board Meeting', Jan. 31, 2000, www.kremlin.ru/events/president/transcripts/21574. Elaborating later, he said that he 'meant only that the law should be interpreted in a uniform way by everyone everywhere in Russia' ('Interview with ARD and ZDF', June 9, 2000, *supra*).

29. 'Address to the All-Union Meeting of Prosecutors', cited in *Smena*, Feb. 21, 1991. The full text was issued by TASS on February 13 and is reprinted in Zvyagintsev, Aleksandr, and Orlov, Yuri, *Neizvestnaya Femida*, Olma-Press, Moscow, 2003, pp. 450–54.

30. Rossiya TV, Feb. 12, 2004.

31. Channel One, March 5, 2004.

32. TASS, April 1, *Kommersant*, April 19 & 22 and TASS, May 24, 2004.

33. *Vedomosti*, Dec. 30, 2004. See also Gazeta.ru, Dec. 31, 2004.

34. 'Press Conference with Russian and Foreign Media', Dec. 23, 2004, *supra*.

35. *New York Times*, Dec. 1, 2010.

36. Sergei Ivanov, speaking on Ren TV, March 28, 2009.

37. According to the ILO, in 2011, public-sector employment in Russia was 40.6 per cent of total employment, which the World Bank calculated as just over 70 million that year. More recent figures are not available. In OECD member states, on average 22 per cent of the workforce hold public-sector jobs.

38. 'Meeting of State Council on Russia's Development Strategy', Feb. 2, 2008, *supra*.

39. 'Annual Address to the Federal Assembly', April 25, 2005, *supra*.

40. TASS, May 25, Interfax and Rossiya TV, June 4, 2005.

41. *Time*, Dec. 31, 2007 and 'Annual Press Conference', Feb. 14, 2008, www.kremlin.ru/events/president/transcripts/24835

42. See Treisman, Daniel, *The Return*, Free Press, 2011, pp. 232–5.

43. When Vyakhirev eventually stepped down, *Forbes* put his net worth at 1.3 billion US dollars (Forbes.ru, Sept. 10, 2012, www.forbes.ru/sobytiya/lyudi/116519-istoriya-ottsa-gazproma-rema-vyahireva-ot-bezgranichnoi-vlasti-do-zabveniya-na).

44. Unless otherwise indicated, this and the following section are drawn from Charles Ryan, author's interview, March 14, 2019.

45. Ekho Moskvy, June 30, 2000.

46. In his book, *Red Notice* (Bantam Press, London, 2015, pp. 148–56), Browder gives a rather different account, in which he suggests that the Hermitage Fund's activism was the key factor leading to reforms at Gazprom. He makes no mention of the behind-the-scenes negotiations involving Fyodorov and appears not to have known about them, for he describes the outcome in May 2001 as a complete surprise.

47. *Izvestia*, May 31, 2001.

48. Browder, *supra*, p. 156 and Rossiya TV, May 30, 2001.

49. Kasyanov, *Bez Putina*, pp. 133–4.

50. 'Meeting of Valdai Discussion Club', Sept. 9, 2006, *supra* and Kasyanov, *Bez Putina*, pp. 230–32.

51. *Izvestia*, July 14, 2000.

52. Aven, *Vremya Berezovskogo*, p. 439.

53. *Kommersant*, Oct. 29, and *Kommersant-Vlast'*, Nov. 10, 2003.

54. *Kommersant*, Oct. 9, 2007. Cherkesov had first raised the problem of internecine struggles among the security services three years earlier in an article for *Komsomolskaya pravda* on December 29, 2004.

55. See www.youtube.com/watch?v=PD3ufaenico, Kasyanov, *Bez Putina*, p. 165 and author's interview, Nov. 19, 2019. In many sources these remarks are dated incorrectly to 1999. Kasyanov insists that they were made in December 2000, which must be correct, for otherwise he could not have been present in his capacity as Prime Minister.

56. 'Address at a Gala Function [for] State Security Employees' Day', Dec. 20, 2000, www.kremlin.ru/events/president/transcripts/24270

57. Interfax, June 20 and *Segodnya*, June 21, 2000.

58. These are drawn from entries on the presidential website, www.kremlin.ru, for the period from October to December, 2005.

59. Illarionov, author's interview, Feb. 16 and Kasyanov, author's interview, Nov. 19, 2019.

60. See for example his schedule on December 20, 2000. After flying back overnight from

Canada, he worked all day in the Kremlin and addressed a meeting of FSB officers in the evening.

61. 'Transcript of Internet Conference', March 6, 2000 and 'Interview with Turkish Media', Sept. 1, 2004, *supra* (work-outs); 'Press Conference following G8 Summit', Sea Island, Georgia, June 11, 2004, www.kremlin.ru/events/president/transcripts/22501 (kasha); and Talbott, *Russia Hand*, p. 394 (gym).

62. *Time*, Dec. 31, 2007

63. Strana.ru, March 9, 2004, www.flb.ru/info/26023.html

64. Stone, *The Putin Interviews*, p. 23. Putin claimed that he never read 'abstracts', i.e. intelligence summaries, but that cannot have been true. There were not enough hours in the day for him to read raw intelligence reports on all the subjects he had to deal with.

65. *Izvestia*, June 2, 2000. See also Kasyanov, author's interview, Nov. 19, 2019.

66. 'Interview with Mike Wallace', May 9, 2005, *supra*.

67. Putin's wife, Lyudmila, told Crown Princess Viktoria of Sweden when she visited Moscow in April, 2001, that he spent an hour every evening working on his English (Sven Hirdman, author's interview, Feb. 26, 2017). See also *Rossiiskaya gazeta*, Dec. 6, 2000.

68. *Chas pik*, Nov. 11, 1991 and David Pepper, author's interview, Jan. 28, 2019.

69. *Rossiiskaya gazeta*, *supra*.

70. Aven, *Vremya Berezovskogo*, p. 522.

71. *Time*, Dec. 31, 2007.

72. 'Interview with Paris Match', July 6, 2000, *supra*; 'Transcript of Internet Conference', March 6, 2001, *supra*; and 'Interview for NPR', Nov. 16, 2001, *supra*.

73. Ibid. See also 'Meeting with Cadets', Nov. 4, 2007, www.kremlin.ru/events/president/transcripts/24647

74. Ibid.

75. 'Press Conference for the Russian and Foreign Media', Jan. 31, 2006, *supra*.

76. *Time*, Dec. 31, 2007.

77. 'Interview with Leaders Magazine', Nov. 14, 2001, www.kremlin.ru/events/president/transcripts/23350

78. *Kommersant*, Nov. 16, Rossiya TV, Nov 18, TV6, Dec. 28 and Channel Three TV, Dec. 29, 2001.

79. Pavlovsky, author's interview, Nov. 21, 2019.

80. Interfax and ORT, July 12 and *Segodnya*, July 13 & 15, 2000.

81. Ibid., July 15 and *Kommersant*, Aug. 1, 2000. The following spring, when Sergeyev retired, he was appointed Putin's assistant for strategic stability issues (RIA Novosti, March 28, 2001).

82. 'Interview with CBC and CTV . . .', Dec. 14, 2000, www.kremlin.ru/events/president/transcripts/21139

83. TASS, Dec. 28, 2004 and Interfax, Jan. 3, 2005. German Gref, the Economic Development Minister, also criticised the Yuganskneftegaz sale, a rare occasion when the two men agreed (*Kommersant*, Jan. 11, 2005).

84. Ekho Moskvy, Dec. 30, 2004.

85. Interfax, Jan. 3, 2005.

86. Kasyanov, author's interview, Nov. 19, 2019. Putin also said that at the weekly cabinet meetings, 'our conversations often become quite sharp' ('Press Conference with Russian and Foreign Media', June 20, 2003, *supra*).

87. Kasyanov, ibid.

88. Aven, *Vremya Berezovskogo*, p. 534 (see also p. 524).

89. *Time*, Dec. 31, 2019.

90. Natalya Gevorkyan, author's interview, March 31, 2016.

91. 'Speech at the Munich Conference', Feb. 10, 2007, *supra*.

92. TASS, Oct 16, 2000.

93. Yonhap, Seoul, July 5 and Radio Rossiya, July 19, 2000; Rossiya TV, Feb. 27, 2001.

94. 'News Conference [in] Novosibirsk', Nov. 17, 2000, www.kremlin.ru/events/president/transcripts/21121

95. 'Interview with CBC and CTV . . .', Dec. 14, 2000, *supra*.

96. 'Meeting with Finalists of Student Essay Competition', June 5, 2003, www.kremlin.ru/events/president/transcripts/22021

97. Molander, author's interview, Oct. 12, 2017.

98. Brenton, author's interview, May 14, 2017.

99. Hirdman, author's interview, Feb. 26, 2017.

100. Persson, author's interview, Stockholm, Feb. 27, 2017.

101. Hans-Friedrich von Ploetz, author's interview, Berlin, May 5, 2017.

102. Persson, *supra*.

103. Ibid. and Måns Lönnroth, private communication, Sept. 20, 2017.

104. Brenton, *supra*.

105. 'Interview with American TV Channels', Sept 20, 2003, www.kremlin.ru/events/president/transcripts/22125

106. 'Opening Remarks at the United Russia Party's Third Congress', Sept. 20, 2003, www.kremlin.ru/events/president/transcripts/22120

107. Gleb Pavlovsky on Ekho Moskvy, Dec. 18, 2003.

108. Interfax, Dec. 8, 2003.

109. 'Interview with New York Times', Oct. 4, 2003, *supra*.

110. Rossiya TV, Dec. 8, 2003.

111. The story of Rybkin's alleged abduction is taken from Goldfarb and Litvinenko, *Death of a Dissident*, pp. 306–9. See also Interfax, Feb. 7 & 11, Ekho Moskvy, Feb. 8, 10 & 11, *Nezavisimaya gazeta* and Interfax, Feb. 10, TASS, Feb. 12, and BBC News, Feb. 13 (news.bbc.co.uk/1/hi/world/europe/3485971.stm) & March 5, 2004 (news.bbc.co.uk/2/hi/europe/3536215.stm).

112. Unless otherwise indicated, the following account is drawn from Kasyanov, *Bez Putina*, pp. 239–51 & 261 and author's interview, Nov. 19, 2019.

113. NTV World, Feb. 24, 2004.

114. *Izvestia*, March 2, and Ren TV, March 15, 2004.

115. Utro.ru, Sept. 13, 2007.

116. Kasyanov, *supra*, pp. 247–51.

117. OSCE, *Russian Federation Presidential Election, Observation Mission Report*, March 14, 2004, www.osce.org/odihr/elections/russia/33101; *Moscow Times*, March 15, 2004.

118. 'Annual Address to the Federal Assembly', May 16, 2003, www.kremlin.ru/events/president/transcripts/21998

119. 'Annual Address to the Federal Assembly', May 10, 2006, www.kremlin.ru/events/president/transcripts/22120

120. See Putin's remarks to a joint meeting of the ministries of Finance and Economic Development, NTV World, March 19, 2004.

121. Rossiya TV, March 14, 2004.

122. Interview with deputy Prime Minister Aleksandr Zhukov, ibid., March 24, 2004.

123. Rossiya TV, March 14, 2004.

124. Centre TV, April 27, 2004.

125. RIA Novosti, April 29, 2004.

126. *Nezavisimaya gazeta*, April 22, 2004.

127. TASS, June 16, 2004.

128. Ibid., July 26, and Rossiya TV, Dec. 23, 2004.

129. Deputy Prime Minister Zhukov initially stated that there were 12 million recipients of benefits (ibid., May 29, 2004). Later that year the figure was recalculated as 12.8 million (TASS, Oct. 20, 2004).

130. NTV World, July 2, 2004.

131. Ekho Moskvy, July 29 and Aug. 2, 2004.

132. *Izvestia, Komsomolskaya pravda, Trud* and *Moskovsky komsomolets*, Jan. 12, 2005.

133. *Moskovsky komsomolets* and Tribuna.ru, Jan. 12, 2005.

134. 'The Duma has distanced itself from them with police lines and the President with silence' (*Kommersant-Vlast'*, Aug. 9, 2004).

135. In his annual phone-in on September 27, 2005, Putin cited the example of St Petersburg, where, he said, half the population had the right to free transport (www.kremlin.ru/events/president/transcripts/23190). When he was deputy Mayor, he had already started calling for an end to the system.

136. 'Interview with Newspaper Journalists from G8 Member Countries', June 4, 2007, *supra*.

137. 'Interview with Chief Editors of Komsomolskaya Pravda, Izvestia, Moskovsky Komsomolets and Trud', March 22, 2001, *supra*.

138. *Izvestia*, Jan. 12, 2005.

139. The Chairman of the Duma Labour Committee, Andrei Isayev, claimed that agitators were 'trying to use pensioners as gunpowder for an Orange Revolution in a Russian way' (Ekho Moskvy, Jan. 14, 2005). Two days later, protesters in St Petersburg compared their action to what was happening in Kyiv (Ren TV, Jan. 16, 2004).

140. Kasyanov, *Bez Putina*, pp. 136–8.

141. 'Meeting with Moscow Bureau Chiefs of Leading US Media', Nov. 10, 2001, *supra*.

142. 'Answers to Questions at Columbia University', Sept. 26, 2003 and 'Press Conference for the Russian and Foreign Media', Jan. 31, 2006, *supra*.

143. 'Questions at the World Economic Forum in Moscow', Oct. 3, 2003, www.kremlin.ru/events/president/transcripts/22141

144. Bill Burns referred repeatedly to 'Russia's swaggering and pugnacious behaviour' in his despatches to Washington (see, for example, Burns to President Bush (Secret), June 1, 2007, www.carnegieendowment.org/publications/interactive/back-channel).

145. Bush, *Decision Points*, pp. 431–3.

146. 'Report to the President and the Federal Assembly', Strana.ru, April 30, 2002.

147. TASS, Dec. 27, 2005.

148. The following is drawn from Joshua Yaffa, 'Oligarchy 2.0', in the *New Yorker*, May 29, 2017.

149. Mikhail Korchemkin, cited in ibid.

150. The Rotenbergs' companies built parts of the infrastructure for the Sochi Olympics in 2014, as well as the bridge over the Kerch Straits linking Crimea with the rest of Russia.

151. 'Putin's Secret Riches', BBC One, Jan. 25, 2016.

152. *Washington Post*, Dec. 23, 2010 and *Novaya gazeta*, Feb. 14, 2011.

153. *Guardian*, Dec. 21, 2007.

154. Ibid, Dec. 22, 2007 and 'Transcript of Annual Press Conference', Feb. 14, 2008, www.kremlin.ru/events/president/transcripts/24835. In the English-language version of his remarks on the Kremlin website, that phrase was bowdlerised.

155. In a series of interviews with Ekho Moskvy, Belkovsky argued that Medvedev would not succeed Putin as President (Feb. 23, 2007); that when Putin stepped down as President, he would not stay in Russia but take up a position with an international organisation (April 6, 2007); that Putin would not become Prime Minister under Medvedev (Oct. 6, 2007), and much more of the same kind. More often than not, his predictions were mistaken.

156. 'Putin's Secret Riches', *supra*.

157. *Washington Post*, Oct. 20, 2021.

158. Michael Morell, author's interview, March 11, 2019.

159. Favier, Pierre, and Martin-Roland, Michel, *La Décennie Mitterrand*, Vol. 3, *Les Défis, 1988–1991*, Le Seuil, Paris, 1996 p. 377.

160. *Novaya gazeta*, Nov. 23, 2011.

161. Morell, *supra*.

162. In Morell's words: 'This is my personal judgement, maybe informed by what I have read over the years' (ibid.).

163. 'Interview with Mike Wallace', May 9, 2005, *supra*.

164. 'Meeting with Students', July 21, 2017, www.kremlin.ru/events/president/transcripts/55114

165. Illarionov, author's interview, Feb. 16, 2019.

166. NTV World, Jan. 11, 2005.

167. 'Meeting of State Council on Russia's Development Strategy', Feb. 2, 2008, *supra*.

168. 'Annual Address to the Federal Assembly', April 25, 2005, *supra*.

169. One such public dressing-down was given to Aleksei Kudrin, after delays in paying a wage increase ('Meeting with the Cabinet', April 14, 2008, www.kremlin.ru/events/president/transcripts/24917). Another concerned delays in improving border security.

170. 'Press Conference with Russian and Foreign Media', Dec. 23, 2004, *supra*.

171. Viktor Yerofeyev, author's interview, Moscow, Nov. 20, 2019. The incident involved the Minister of Culture, Mikhail Shvydkoi, and occurred in late 2002 or early 2003. The change in Putin's attitude to his colleagues did not come suddenly, at the beginning of his second term. It developed gradually. Shvydkoi's experience was an early example.

172. Sheinwald, author's interview, May 17, 2017.

173. Ren TV, Dec. 18 and NTV, Dec. 20, 2003.

174. See *Izvestia*, Sept. 28, 2005. In contrast, the annual news conference, in which foreign journalists participated and which was also broadcast live, had no such constraints.

175. Except where otherwise indicated, the following is drawn from Christoph Heusgen, author's interview, New York, March 14, 2019.

176. *Deutsche Welle*, Jan. 18, 2006.

177. 'Beginning of Meeting with German Chancellor Angela Merkel', Sochi, Jan. 21, 2007, www.kremlin.ru/events/president/transcripts/24007

178. Heusgen, *supra*.

179. 'The Astonishing Rise of Angela Merkel', *New Yorker*, Dec. 1, 2014. Putin later claimed falsely that he had not known Merkel was afraid of dogs and had never intended to frighten her (*Bild*, Jan. 11, 2016).

180. Ekho Moskvy, April 14, 2000.

181. *Segodnya*, April 15, 2000.

182. 'Meeting of Valdai Discussion Club', Sept. 14, 2007, *supra*.

183. 'Meeting with Members of Russian Youth Organisations', July 24, 2007, www.kremlin.ru/events/president/transcripts/24433. See also 'Press Statement and Answers to Questions',

Nov. 6, 2003, www.kremlin.ru/events/president/transcripts/22190, and *Time*, Dec. 31, 2007.

184. 'Interview with Mike Wallace', May 9, 2005, *supra*.

185. 'The Madeleine Albright Declaration', *Novaya gazeta*, June 24 and *Forbes*, July 16, 2015.

186. *Rossiiskaya gazeta*, Dec. 22, 2006.

187. 'Direct Line with President Putin', Oct. 18, 2007, www.kremlin.ru/events/president/transcripts/24606

188. *Moscow Times*, Nov. 7, 2007.

189. *Kommersant*, June 22, 2015.

190. A classic example was the civil war in Cambodia in the 1980s, when China (openly) and the United States (covertly) supported the Khmer Rouge in an unwinnable war against the Vietnamese-backed regime in Phnom Penh in order to weaken Vietnam and its patron, the Soviet Union. Later Putin himself stoked conflict in eastern Ukraine to weaken the regime in Kyiv. Russia also maintained frozen conflicts in Abkhazia and South Ossetia to put pressure on Georgia.

191. 'Interview with NBC', July 12, 2006, *supra*.

192. Bloomberg, Aug. 27, 2013, www.business-standard.com/article/international/putin-filmmaker-says-lonely-leader-scared-to-loosen-grip-113082900011_1.html

193. TVS, Aug. 30, 2002.

194. NTV World, Oct. 30, 2003.

195. www.youtube.com/watch?v=zk_VszbZa_s

196. 'News Conference for Russian and Foreign Journalists', ORT, June 24, 2002. This section was omitted from the official transcript on the Kremlin website.

197. Alexander Vershbow, author's interview, Dec. 10, 2018.

198. In November 2005, she backed out of a trip to Japan at the last moment (Kyodo, Nov. 19, 2005). After that, she accompanied Putin on only one other foreign visit, to Luxemburg in the spring of 2007 (Interfax, May 24, 2007). The Bulgarian news agency, BTA, reported on January 7, 2008, that she would participate in a visit to Sofia that month, but Dmitry Medvedev accompanied Putin instead.

199. *Kommersant*, March 14, 2000.

200. The *Moskovsky korrespondent* report, published on April 12, 2008, claimed that Putin and his wife had divorced and that he and Kabayeva would marry that summer. The newspaper was shut down by its owner, Aleksandr Lebedev, supposedly for financial reasons, a week later. Alina Kabayeva had been engaged to a police officer but broke off the engagement in 2005 (Segodnya.ru, Feb. 14, 2006). By then Putin and Lyudmila were living largely separate lives. They continued to appear together occasionally in public – at a meeting with Patriarch Kirill in May, 2009, and at a jazz concert in Sochi three months later – but it was essentially for show. A decade later, a Russian website, Proekt, reported that, after moving to Moscow in 1996, Putin had had a relationship with another young woman, Svetlana Krivonogikh, who allegedly bore him a daughter in 2003 ('Zheleznye Maski', Nov. 24, 2020, www.maski-proekt.media/tainaya-semya-zolotova, www.maski-proekt.media/tainaya-semya-putina and www.maski-proekt.media/yuri-koval chuk). Krivonogikh evidently had a wealthy patron from among Putin's circle but there are reasons to doubt that it was Putin himself. Had they had a relationship, one might have expected that he would keep her and her daughter better hidden. Eight months after the story appeared, Proekt was banned, ostensibly in retaliation for an investigation into the hidden wealth of the Interior Minister, Vladimir Kolokoltsev (*Moscow Times*, July 16, 2021).

201. 'Answers to Journalists' Questions', April 18, 2008, *supra*.

202. Rossiya TV, Jan. 31, 2006.

203. A prime example was François Mitterrand, whose political career took on a new lease of life after he fell in love with a woman half his age, with whom he set up a second household which he maintained, parallel to his official family, until his death 30 years later (Short, Philip, *Mitterrand: A Study in Ambiguity*, Bodley Head, London, 2013, pp. 213–14 & 240–41).

204. Sven Hirdman noticed that that was the case when Putin gave lunch in the Kremlin for the King of Sweden (author's interview, Feb. 26, 2017).

205. *Ekspress-K*, Almaty, Oct. 10, 2000, quoting the Kazakh Public Health Ministry on preparations for Putin's visit to Kazakhstan later that month.

206. A summary of the report was obtained by ZDF (Michael Renz, author's interview, Wiesbaden, June 8, and Erich Schmidt-Eenboom, author's interview, June 9, 2017).

207. RIA Novosti, Feb. 23, 2000.

208. Novy Kanal TV, Kyiv, and Interfax, Sept. 12, 2000.

209. TASS, Oct. 16, RIA Novosti, Oct. 28, and Rossiya TV, Oct. 28 and Nov. 4, 2001.

210. *Sunday Times*, Oct. 19, 2003.

211. *Voice of Iran*, Oct. 15, 2007.

212. *Nezavisimaya gazeta*, Feb. 25, 2000.

213. Another alleged attempt, not mentioned in the BND report, was supposedly foiled when two Chechens were arrested in Odessa in 2012 (ibid., Feb. 28, 2012).

214. Stone, *The Putin Interviews*, pp. 21–2.

215. On April 17, 2003, a veteran liberal deputy in the Duma, Sergei Yushenkov, was shot dead outside his apartment block in Moscow. He had been investigating the 1999 apartment bombings and the Dubrovka theatre siege, which led to widespread speculation that he had been killed by the FSB. Four men were convicted of his murder but the motive was never convincingly established.

216. The article, which was unfinished, was published in *Novaya gazeta* on October 12, 2006. It described a young man, handcuffed and suspended from a metal pipe, being repeatedly beaten unconscious and threatened with rape by Kadyrovtsy at an interrogation centre in Grozny in order to make him confess to murders he had not committed.

217. Rossiya 24 and 'Joint Press Conference with Angela Merkel', Dresden, Oct. 10, 2006, *supra*.

218. 'Speech at the St Petersburg Dialogue Social Forum', Dresden, Oct. 10, 2006, www.kremlin.ru/events/president/transcripts/23839

219. Yuri Felshtinsky and Vladimir Pribylovsky (*The Corporation*, p. 482) have suggested that the murder was organised by Khozh-Ahmed Nukhayev, an opaque figure with links to Kadyrov, to the FSB and to organised crime, perhaps on behalf of Umar Dzhabrailov, a Chechen businessman in Moscow, 'as a favour to Kadyrov'. Dzhabrailov was suspected of ordering the murder of his American business partner, Paul Tatum, in 1996. Nukhayev had been the subject of a book by the American journalist, Paul Klebnikov, *Razgovor s varvarom [Conversation with a Barbarian]* (Detektiv-Press, Moscow, 2003). A year after its publication, Klebnikov was also killed, it was suspected on Nukhayev's orders. The connection is significant because Putin drew a parallel between Politkovskaya's killing and that of Klebnikov, a possible indication that he, too, believed that Nukhayev was implicated ('Interview with Suddeutsche Zeitung', Oct. 10, 2006, www.kremlin.ru/events/president/transcripts/23834). It was the closest he ever came to linking Kadyrov to her murder.

220. *New York Times*, Dec. 27, 2010.

221. 'Interview with Suddeutsche Zeitung', *supra*.

222. After Browder asked Dmitry Medvedev to intervene on his behalf, he was again denied an entry visa. 'I don't know why that particular individual was denied entry,' Putin told journalists a few months later. 'I imagine that that person may have violated our country's laws' ('Briefing for Journalists', July 17, 2006, www.kremlin.ru/events/president/transcripts/23715; see also Browder, *Red Notice*, pp. 183–92).

223. Ibid., pp. 203–5 & 218–24.

224. NTV World, June 16, 2006.

225. *Kommersant*, Sept. 14, 2006.

226. *Russky Newsweek*, Nov. 13, 2006.

227. *Yezhednevny zhurnal*. Oct. 4 and *Kommersant*, Oct. 9, 2007.

228. *Novye izvestia*, Aug. 3, 2020.

229. Mikhail Zygar, author's interview, Nov. 21, 2019.

230. NTV World, Nov. 14, 2005.

231. Burns to Rice, Oct. 17, 2006, www.carnegieendowment.org/publications/interactive/back-channel

232. These figures are for 2002 (Interfax, Feb. 21, 2003), but there is no reason to think they diminished over the next five years.

233. Ibid., Jan. 25, *Moskovsky komsomolets*, Jan. 26 and *Izvestia*, Jan. 31, 2006.

234. Radio Rossiya and TASS, Jan. 15, NTV and TASS, Jan. 16, and *Kommersant*, Jan. 26, 2004.

235. *Rossiiskaya gazeta*, Jan. 27, 2006.

236. Ren TV, Jan. 28, 2006 and Zygar, *All the Kremlin's Men*, p. 133.

237. *Komsomolskaya pravda*, Feb. 17, 2006.

238. Zygar, p. 136.

239. Ibid., p. 137.

240. Ibid., p. 135.

241. *New York Times*, Sept. 13 and *Kommersant*, Sept. 14, 2007. Mikhail Zygar wrote that Putin rapped Zubkov over the knuckles for hinting at presidential ambitions (ibid., pp. 144–5), but Putin's own comments suggested that Zubkov spoke with his approval in order to muddy the waters (RTR Planeta TV, Sept. 14, 2007).

242. Zygar, p. 146.

243. Rossiya 24, Feb. 14, 2008.

244. Charles Ryan, author's interview, March 14, 2019.

245. NTV World, Feb. 15, 2006.

246. 'Concluding Remarks at United Russia Party Congress', Oct. 1, 2007, www.kremlin.ru/events/president/transcripts/24561

247. 'Transcript of Meeting with Road Workers', Nov. 13, 2007, www.kremlin.ru/events/president/transcripts/24676

248. 'Speech to a Gathering of Supporters', Nov. 21, 2007, www.kremlin.ru/events/president/transcripts/24713

249. Zygar, *supra*, p. 210, and Putin, 'Press Conference with Russian and Foreign Media', Feb. 1, 2007, *supra*.

250. 'Excerpts from Transcript of United Russia's Party Congress', Dec. 17, 2007, www.kremlin.ru/events/president/transcripts/24729. Putin had earlier said that it was a 'realistic' possibility that he would head the government, but it was too early to talk about ('Concluding Remarks at United Russia Party Congress', Oct. 1, 2007, *supra*).

251. Zygar, *supra*, p. 146.

252. *Daily Telegraph*, March 3, 2008.

253. *Kommersant* and *Novaya gazeta*, March 3, 2008.

254. *Le Monde*, May 31, 2008, lemonde.fr/europe/article/2008/05/31/la-version-integrale-de-l-interview-de-vladimir-poutine_1052321_3214.html. The Russian text is at archive.premier.gov.ru/visits/world/6048/events/1708/

255. Rossiya 24, Feb. 14, 2008.

256. *Time*, Dec. 31, 2007.

257. 'Meeting of Valdai Discussion Club', Sept. 14, 2007, www.kremlin.ru/events/president/transcripts/24729

258. *Nezavisimaya gazeta*, April 16, 2008.

14: *Tandemocracy*

1. *New York Times*, Nov. 7, 2008.

2. Ibid.

3. Ibid.

4. 'Meeting of Valdai Club', Sept. 11, 2008, archive.premier.gov.ru/events/news/1897/. In the opening days of the conflict, the fact that Georgia had attacked first was noted in the Western media. But after the Russians intervened, that was soon forgotten. Thereafter both Western governments and the press spoke of 'the Russian invasion of Georgia' with no mention of the way it had started.

5. 'U.S. Watched as a Squabble Turned into a Showdown', *New York Times*, Aug. 18, 2008.

6. John Beyrle, author's interview, March 12, 2019.

7. Pavel Felgenhauer, cited by RFE/Radio Liberty, Aug. 16; see also *Novaya gazeta*, Aug. 14, 2008.

8. Aleksandr Golts, *Military Reform and Militarism in Russia*, Jamestown Foundation, Washington, D.C., 2018, pp. 106–7.

9. Putin discussed the background to the invasion at a news conference after a meeting in Moscow with the Armenian President, Serzh Sargsyan (Rossiya 24, Aug. 8, 2012). See also *Eurasia Daily Monitor*, Jamestown Foundation, Aug. 9, 2012.

10. Bush did not refer to this conversation in his memoir, but Putin mentioned it to journalists after the luncheon (Interfax and TASS, Aug. 8, 2008).

11. Bush, *Decision Points*, pp. 434–5.

12. John Beyrle, *supra*. Beyrle was present at the principals' meeting which Bush called on his return.

13. Rice, *No Higher Honor*, pp. 687–8. Rice wrote that the conversation took place on Monday, August 11. It was in fact the previous afternoon (Russian Ministry of Foreign Affairs website and Interfax, Aug. 10, 2008).

14. 'Meeting of Valdai Club', Sept. 11, 2008, *supra*.

15. Nicolas Sarkozy's account of his mediation mission is given in his memoir, *Le Temps des Tempêtes*, Vol. 1, Editions de l'Observatoire, Paris, 2020, pp. 470–82.

16. Asked during his annual phone-in whether had really said that, Putin replied: 'And why not?' (Dec. 4, 2008, archive.premier.gov.ru/events/news/2638/). The line was omitted from Sarkozy's account of the conversation (*supra.*, pp. 475–6), but was reported in the French press at the time (see Vincent Jauvert, 'Sarko le russe: histoire secrète d'un revirement', in *Le Nouvel Observateur*, Nov. 13, 2008 and Asmus, *Little War that Shook the World*, p. 248 n. 5).

17. *L'Express*, Feb. 24, 2011.

18. Asmus, *supra*, p. 108.

19. *Financial Times*, Aug. 27, 2008.

20. Asmus, *supra*, p. 109.

21. Channel One and Rossiya 24, Aug. 9, 2008.

22. AFP, May 15, 2008.

23. 'Annual Address to the Federal Assembly', May 10, 2006, *supra*.

24. 'Interview with ORT, RTR and Nezavisimaya gazeta', Dec. 25, 2000, *supra*.

25. Unless otherwise indicated, the following account of the military reforms is drawn from Golts, *supra*, pp. 87–177.

26. Ibid., pp. 106–7.

27. AVN Military News Agency, Jan. 15, 2002, *Kommersant*, April 11, 2003 and Ekho Moskvy, July 27, 2004.

28. General Nikolai Makarov, cited by Interfax, Dec. 30, 2008.

29. 'Meeting with Finalists of Student Essay Competition', June 5, 2003, *supra*.

30. Ruslan Pukhov, 'Serdyukov Cleans Up the Arbat', *Moscow Defense Brief*, No. 1, 2008.

31. Rossiya TV, Dec 4, 2008.

32. Aleksandr Golts, author's interview, Nov. 20, 2019.

33. Gil Barndollar, 'The Best or Worst of Both Worlds? Russia's Mixed Military Manpower System', Center for Strategic and International Studies, Sept. 23, 2020.

34. *New York Times*, Sept. 5, 2008.

35. *Washington Post*, Sept. 2, 2008.

36. *New York Times*, Aug. 16, 2008.

37. 'Speech to the 7th International Investment Forum', Sochi, Sept. 19, 2008, archive.premier.gov.ru/events/news/1953/

38. 'Address to Cabinet Meeting', Oct. 1, 2008, archive.premier.gov.ru/events/news/2023/

39. 'Meeting with KPRF Deputies in the State Duma', Oct. 9, 2008, archive.premier.gov.ru/events/news/2091/

40. *Washington Post*, Oct. 25, 2008.

41. Gazeta.ru, Oct. 17, 2008.

42. This account is drawn from his 'Speech to Meeting of State Council on Russia's Development Strategy to 2020', Feb. 8, 2008, *supra*, and 'Annual Press Conference', Feb. 14, 2008, *supra*.

43. 'Address to the Federal Assembly', Nov. 5, 2008, www.kremlin.ru/events/president/transcripts/1968

44. *New York Times*, Feb. 8, 2009.

45. An early sign of a change in Russia's attitude came shortly after Medvedev was sworn in, when Putin told *Le Monde* on May 31, 2008, that while Tehran had the right to enrich uranium, 'Iran does not exist in a vacuum. It is located in a very complicated, explosive, region of the world.'

46. John Beyrle, author's interview, March 12, 2019 and Barack Obama's account of his September, 2009, meeting with Medvedev in New York, in *A Promised Land*, Crown, New York, 2020, p. 471.

47. Ibid., pp. 337 & 341.

48. The following is drawn from ibid., pp. 462–5.

49. *Le Monde*, May 31, 2008.

50. Voice of America, Nov. 2, 2009.

51. Obama, *supra*, p. 484.

52. Ben Rhodes, author's interview, Venice Beach, Feb. 22, 2019.

53. *Yezhednevny zhurnal*, July 16, 2010.

54. According to Gazeta.ru, Aug. 9, 2010, in the second half of July, the death rate in Moscow averaged 700 people a day, compared with 360 to 380 deaths in normal years. The Health Ministry dismissed the figures, which came from the city health authorities, as 'unofficial'.

55. *Kommersant*, Aug. 11 and Interfax, Aug. 26, 2010.

56. *Moskovsky komsomolets*, Sept. 1 and *Rossiiskaya gazeta*, Sept. 6, 2010.

57. *Vedomosti*, Sept. 21, 2010.

58. TASS and www.bbc.com/news/world-europe-11424183, Sept. 28, 2010.

59. See, for instance, 'Interview with Journalists from G8 Countries', (June 4, 2007, *supra*), where Putin said that 'a term of five, six or seven years would be acceptable, but the number of consecutive terms should be limited'.

60. Politcom.ru, March 31, Interfax, April 2 and *Nezavisimaya gazeta*, April 3, 2011. Altogether 17 vice premiers and ministers were required to give up their directorships by July 1 and another group by October 1, but Sechin was seen as Medvedev's main target.

61. Andrei Illarionov, author's interview, March 13, 2019, and 'Slovo i delo' (part 2), *Kontinent*, No. 136, 2008, at www.magazines.gorky.media/continent/2008/136/slovo-i-delo-2.html

62. Gazeta.ru, Sept. 6, 2010.

63. During Medvedev's presidency, a 'stop list' was introduced, under which critics of the regime were banned from appearing on the state-owned TV channels (*New York Times*, June 3, 2008). Further restrictions were introduced after the Georgian war (*Washington Post*, Sept. 15, 2008).

64. *Novaya gazeta*, June 15, 2011.

65. *Financial Times*, Jan. 3, 2013.

66. Rossiya 24, Dec. 16, 2010.

67. Ibid., July 24 and Rossiya TV, July 28, 2008.

68. Ekho Moskvy, July 25, 2008.

69. Ren TV, July 31, 2008.

70. For the background to the Pikalyovo incident, see *New York Times*, June 4; Politkom.ru, June 5; *Eurasian Daily Monitor*, June 9, 2009, at www.jamestown.org/program/putin-resolves-protest-in-pikalevo/; and Stephen Fortescue, 'Putin in Pikalevo: PR or watershed?', *Australian Slavonic and East European Studies*, 2009, Vol. 23, Nos. 1–2, pp. 19–28.

71. See www.youtube.com/watch?v=48Kk7kobMQY

72. 'Conversation with Vladimir Putin', Dec. 3, 2009, archive.premier.gov.ru/events/news/8412/

73. Douglas Lund, author's interview, Prague, Dec. 27, 2018.

74. *Nezavisimaya gazeta*, Sept. 11, 2008.

75. Reuters, Sept. 2, 2008.

76. *Guardian*, March 15, 2012.

77. Ibid., Oct. 6, 2011.

78. NTV, Oct. 10, 2008.

79. *Guardian*, Aug. 6, 2009.

80. Ekho Moskvy, Nov. 14, 2009; Politkom.ru, Aug. 12 and Associated Press, Aug. 25, 2010; TASS, July 27, 2019.

81. Channel One, July 7, 2009. Putin also took part in a bikers' rally at Sevastopol in the

summer of 2010 and at Novorossiysk the following year (NTV, Channel One, Ren TV and Rossiya 1, Aug. 29, 2011). See also NTV World, Sept. 10, 2011.

82. Putin's performance is at www.npr.org/sections/thetwo-way/2010/12/13/132030597/video-russia-s-putin-sings-blueberry-hill-at-charity-dinner?t=1617552097887. See also Interfax, March 6 and *Moskovsky komsomolets*, March 9, 2011.

83. *Yezhednevny zhurnal*, Sept. 1, 2010.

84. Ibid.

85. *Zerkalo nedeli*, Jan. 24, 2009.

86. Zygar, *All the Kremlin's Men*, p. 166.

87. Ibid., pp. 124–7 and Zygar, author's interview, Nov. 21, 2019.

88. Tarja Halonen, author's interview, Helsinki, March 6, 2017.

89. Ben Rhodes, author's interview, Feb. 22, 2019.

90. Reuters, Jan. 7, 2008.

91. Vesti TV, Feb. 14, 2008.

92. Clinton, *Hard Choices*, pp. 213–14.

93. John Beyrle, author's interview, March 12, 2019. Clinton remembered it differently, writing: 'We engaged in a contentious debate about . . . the World Trade Organisation that kept going in circles' (*Hard Choices*, ibid.) She appears to have confused the occasion, for Washington and Moscow were by then in agreement about Russia's accession to the WTO.

94. Bill Clinton had undergone a medical procedure in February to insert two stents following heart surgery in 2004. But that did not prevent him following an active schedule for the rest of that year. There were clearly political considerations. Although relations with Russia had improved during Obama's first term, accompanying Putin to Franz Josef Land might have seemed a step too far. Ben Rhodes (author's interview, *supra*) felt that the invitation could have been accepted and that, had it been made to Clinton's successor, John Kerry, it probably would have been.

95. Channel One, Jan. 17, 2012, transcript at www.1tv.ru/news/leontiev/196647

96. Ben Rhodes, a close friend of McFaul, conceded that, with hindsight, 'perhaps we failed to recognise how Putin was likely to receive this person who had written so much on democracy and had so many contacts with [Russian] civil society' (author's interview, *supra*).

97. A correspondent of *Süddeutsche Zeitung*, interviewing Putin on October 10, 2006, recalled that he had said 'in a very small circle' that, although he could not stand for a third term, he could 'take a break . . . and then come back'. Putin did not dispute his account and the remark was included in the transcript posted on the Kremlin website (www.kremlin.ru/events/president/transcripts/23834). It briefly took on a new lease of life in the Russian press nine months later and was then picked up by the *Washington Post* (June 23, 2007).

98. Putin said repeatedly that he would hold the presidency only for a limited time. See, for instance, *inter alia*, 'Putin: Leap Year', Rossiya TV, June 12, 2001; 'Talk with German and Russian Media' April 7, 2002, *supra*; 'Interview with TF1', July 12, 2006, *supra*; 'Annual Press Conference', Feb. 14, 2008, *supra*.

99. Rhodes, *supra*.

100. The source, a member of the US National Security Council at the time, asked not to be quoted by name because he was referencing classified information.

101. 'The Great Reforms and Modernisation of Russia', March 3, 2011, St Petersburg, www.kremlin.ru/events/president/transcripts/10506

102. Ibid. and Zygar, *supra*, p. 196.

103. Ibid., p. 199. Sobyanin was succeeded by Vyacheslav Volodin, a Putin loyalist from United Russia, who would later become Chairman of the Duma.

104. 'Interview with Russia Today', Sept. 6, 2012, www.kremlin.ru/events/president/transcripts/16393

105. Rossiya 24, Feb. 24, 2011.

106. Ibid.

107. *Yezhednevny zhurnal*, Feb. 25, 2011.

108. Zygar, *supra*, p. 198, *Kommersant*, March 21, 2011 and Obama, *Promised Land*, p. 660.

109. Ibid., p. 655.

110. Interfax, March 21, 2011.

111. NTV, March 21, 2011.

112. Zygar, *supra*, p. 198.

113. Ibid., p. 199.

114. *New York Times*, Dec. 1, 2010.

115. Ekho Moskvy, Dec. 16, 2008.

116. Tarja Halonen, author's interview, March 6, 2017.

117. Zygar, *supra*, pp. 199–203.

118. Interfax, Aug. 16, 2011 and Zygar, pp. 204–5. Zygar gives what purports to be a detailed account of the conversation, but as only Putin and Medvedev were present and neither has spoken about it on the record, it appears to be based on the confidences of members of Medvedev's entourage. Since these may or may not be accurate, it is not cited here.

119. Seymour Hersh, writing in the *London Review of Books* (Jan. 7, 2016), quoted a senior diplomat from the US Embassy in Moscow as saying that he had been informed that Putin had watched the video three times. Operatives of the CIA, MI6 in Britain and Estonian intelligence all independently repeated claims that Putin kept a copy of the video which he watched from time to time (author's interviews, Washington, D.C., London and Tallinn).

120. 'A Conversation with Vladimir Putin: Continued', Dec. 15, 2011, archive.premier.gov.ru/events/news/17409/

121. 'Congress of United Russia', Sept. 24, 2011, www.kremlin.ru/events/president/news/12802

122. *Moscow Times*, Sept. 13, 2011.

123. Ibid., Dec. 5, 2011.

124. 'A Conversation with Vladimir Putin: Continued', Dec. 15, 2011, *supra*.

125. In February, 2011, Navalny announced a competition for a campaign poster for 'United Russia: The Party of Crooks and Thieves' (Politcom.ru, March 11, 2011). See also Zaks.ru, March 12, 2011, for an account of a Communist Party rally in St Petersburg where the slogan was used.

126. *Argumenty i Fakty*, July 3, 2006.

127. BBC Monitoring, Nov. 21, 2011.

128. www.youtube.com/watch?v=OkauBOKR2x0

129. www.youtube.com/watch?v=hQK2IsvoMFM

130. *New York Times*, Dec. 10, 2011.

131. Gazeta.ru, Dec. 25, 2007 and www.youtube.com/watch?v=hTotCSaWZ9Q

132. *New York Times*, Dec. 25, 2011.

133. Ibid., Feb. 5, 2012.

134. Ibid., Dec. 10, 2011.

135. Ibid. and *Washington Post*, Dec. 10, 2011.

136. *Kommersant*, Dec. 24, 2011.

137. 'A Conversation with Vladimir Putin: Continued', Dec. 15, 2011, *supra*.

138. Ibid.

139. Reuters, Dec. 6, 2011 and www.youtube.com/watch?v=Lv2X3dZdeyQ

140. *New York Times* and *Guardian*, Dec. 9, 2011.

141. In an interview with *Time* (Dec. 31, 2007), Putin accused Garry Kasparov, who then headed the opposition, of benefitting from 'very important financial support' from abroad, and complained that certain foreign countries, which he did not name, were using such methods to interfere in Russia's internal affairs.

142. *Guardian, supra*.

143. NTV, Dec. 11, 2011.

144. Rossiya 1, Dec. 15, 2011.

145. *Kommersant*, Feb. 20, 2012.

146. *Novaya gazeta*, Feb. 13, 2012.

147. Centre TV, Feb. 12, 2012.

148. Rossiya 24, Feb. 23, 2012.

149. Even the Russian election monitoring association, GOLOS, which had been at loggerheads with the government over election fraud, agreed that Putin had won more than 50 per cent of the vote and that there were therefore no grounds for contesting the result (*Nezavisimaya gazeta*, March 7, 2012).

150. Rossiya 1, March 4, 2012.

151. Rossiya 24, March 4, 2012.

152. 'Meeting of Valdai Club', Oct. 24, 2014, www.kremlin.ru/events/president/transcripts/46860, and 'Interview to TASS', Nov. 24, 2014, www.kremlin.ru/events/president/transcripts/47054

15: *The Staitjacket Tightens*

1. Gurevich, *Putin*, p. 52.

2. The quotation is from Lord Lugard, Governor General of Nigeria from 1914 to 1919 (*The Dual Mandate in British Tropical Africa*, William Blackwood, London, 1922). Putin had touched on the same idea in his phone-in the previous winter ('A Conversation with Vladimir Putin: Continued', Dec. 15, 2011, *supra*).

3. Cited by Maksim Trudolyubov in *New York Times*, Jan. 7, 2014.

4. A Conversation with Vladimir Putin: Continued', Dec. 15, 2011, *supra*.

5. *New York Times*, May 19, 2012.

6. Ibid.

7. *Nezavisimaya gazeta*, May 21, 2012.

8. Interfax, May 6, 7 & 8 and *New York Times*, May 7, 2012.

9. Interfax, June 5 & 7 and *Rossiiskaya gazeta*, June 9, 2012.

10. *Washington Post*, June 6, 2012.

11. *New York Times*, June 9 and 'Interview with Russia Today', Sept. 6, 2012, www.kremlin.ru/events/president/transcripts/16393

12. *New York Times*, June 12, 2012, citing a pro-Kremlin site, LifeNews.ru

13. A VTsIOM poll found that 47 per cent of those questioned felt the new fines were excessive while Levada recorded 38 per cent opposing the bill and 26 per cent finding the fines too high (Interfax, June 7 & 8, 2012).

14. Ibid., June 11 & 12, 2012.

15. *Moskovsky komsomolets*, June 13, 2012.

16. Interfax, July 21, 2012.

17. The following account draws on *New York Times*, July 31, 2012, and Gessen, Masha, *Words Will Break Cement*, Granta Books, London, 2014, esp. pp. 116–19 & 121.

18. 'Interview with Russia Today', Sept. 6, 2012, *supra*.

19. *Moscow Times*, March 28, Radio Free Europe / Radio Liberty, April 5 and *Financial Times*, April 14, 2012.

20. Interfax and RIA Novosti, March 24, 2012. These were Kirill's first public comments, but he had probably made his views known to Putin much earlier (see *Nezavisimaya gazeta*, March 12, 2012).

21. The three women were arrested on March 3, the eve of Election Day (Gessen, *supra*, pp. 130–33).

22. Mikhail Leontyev, a pro-Kremlin commentator on Channel One, warned that putting them in jail would be playing into the hands of those who wanted to make them martyrs (Channel One, July 2, 2012). The Church's spokesman, Vsevolod Chaplin, also called for leniency, arguing that 'there is no need to put them in jail' (Interfax, March 6, 2012). Chaplin frequently clashed with Kirill and was later fired.

23. Rossiya 24, Aug. 2, 2012.

24. RAPSI, Oct. 10, at www.rapsinews.com/judicial_news/20121010/264941012.html and *The Atlantic*, Oct. 23, 2012.

25. *Moscow Times*, Aug. 16, 2012 and Gessen, *supra*, pp. 185–6 & 194.

26. *Moskovsky komsomolets*, Aug. 18 and *Moscow Times*, Aug. 2, 2012.

27. Interfax, July 31, 2012.

28. For the following section, see *The Atlantic*, April 22, 2013 and 'An Analysis of the Russian Federation's Prosecutions of Alexei Navalny', Loeb and Loeb LLP, Chicago, April 1, 2013 (docs.google.com/file/d/0B_VQeHLcziV_VkkodlBSRTQ2Yjg/view?pli=1&resourcekey=0-v9un8H1kYopLU51NKQ4beA). Although not without error, the latter contains a detailed and generally reliable account of the initial investigation.

29. 'Interview for Channel One and Associated Press', Sept. 4, 2013, www.kremlin.ru/events/president/transcripts/19143

30. *New York Times*, Dec. 14, BBC News, Dec. 20, 2012 at www.bbc.com/news/world-europe-20798023, and BBC Russian Service, Dec. 29, 2014, at www.bbc.com/russian/russia/2014/12/141229_navalny_yves_rocher_background

31. Interfax, July 18 & 19, 2013.

32. Whether Putin encouraged Sobyanin to stand for re-election, or whether Sobyanin himself made that decision and Putin turned it to his advantage, is unclear. The pretext was that the Duma had restored direct elections for provincial leaders. But Sobyanin's term had two years to run and there was no obvious reason for him to seek a fresh mandate. None of the other governors did so.

33. Sobyanin later let slip that Putin had personally taken the decision to allow Navalny to take part (RIA Novosti, Oct. 20, 2013). Putin denied it, saying that they had not discussed 'concrete names' (Rossiya 1, Dec. 19, 2013).

34. All candidates were required to have the support of at least 110 district councillors representing at least three quarters of the city's districts. Since the district councils were dominated by members of United Russia, it would have been impossible for Navalny to obtain the required signatures without Sobyanin's intervention (see *Yezhednevny zhurnal*, July 17, 2013).

35. 10 per cent was the level of support shown by public opinion polls at that time (Interfax, July 23 and *Moscow Times*, Aug. 1, 2013), up from 5 per cent before the sentencing (Politcom.ru, July 22, 2013).

36. Rossiya 1, Dec. 19, 2013. Putin's remark, during his annual call-in, prompted titters among the audience, causing him to add: 'We would have done so not using administrative means, but legal and political ones'. In the same vein, he suggested elsewhere that Navalny's participation was his doing. 'All these people are partly the results of my actions,' he said. '[It] ensures that the public has the opportunity to get to know different people with different views' ('Seliger 2013 Youth Forum', Aug. 2, 2013, www.kremlin.ru/events/president/transcripts/18993).

37. Interfax, Sept. 9, 2013.

38. 'Meeting of Valdai Club', Sept. 19, 2013, www.kremlin.ru/events/president/transcripts/19243

39. BBC Monitoring, Sept. 11, 2013.

40. *Yezhednevny zhurnal*, Sept. 4, 2013.

41. *Kommersant*, Sept. 10, 2013.

42. Gazeta.ru and Politkom.ru, Oct. 16, 2013.

43. 'News Conference', Dec. 19, www.kremlin.ru/events/president/transcripts/19859 and *New York Times*, Dec. 21, 2013.

44. 'Speech at the 119th session of the International Olympic Committee', Guatemala, July 4, 2007, www.kremlin.ru/events/president/transcripts/24402

45. Radio Free Europe/Radio Liberty, Feb. 24 and *New York Times*, July 25, 2014.

46. 'News Conference', Dec. 19, 2013, *supra*.

47. *New York Times*, Feb. 26 & March 1, 2014.

48. See *Moscow Times*, Feb. 12 and *Novaya gazeta*, Nov. 1, 2013; *Vedomosti*, Feb. 13, 2014; and *Fashion Network*, Jan. 2, 2015 at fr.fashionnetwork.com/news/Russie-la-difficile-position-d-yves-rocher-dans-l-affaire-navalny,452821.html

49. RAPSI, Nov. 15, 2013 at www.rapsinews.com/judicial_news/20131115/269672881.html and *Interfax*, Dec. 30, 2014.

50. Dozhd TV, Jan. 5 and Ekho Moskvy, Jan. 6, 2015.

51. *New York Times*, Jan. 7, 2014.

52. *Washington Post*, Jan. 31, 2014.

53. BBC Monitoring, May 2, 2013.

54. 'Forum of Independent Regional and Local Media', April 24, 2014, www.kremlin.ru/events/president/transcripts/20858

55. *New York Times*, May 7, 2014.

56. RuNet Echo, April 21, 2014 at globalvoices.org/2014/04/21/so-long-mr-durov-and-thanks-for-all-the-fish; *Moscow Times*, Sept. 28, 2014; *New York Times*, Dec. 3, 2014; and *Washington Post*, Jan. 1, 2015.

57. *New York Times*, Sept. 22, 2012.

58. Vesti.ru, May 21, 2012.

59. Ekho Moskvy, May 21, 2012.

60. Pavlovsky, author's interview, Nov. 21, 2019.

61. 'Transcript of Meeting [in] Sakhalin Region', July 16, 2013, www.kremlin.ru/events/president/transcripts/18824

62. Aleksandr Golts cited a meeting at which the Defence Minister, Anatoly Serdyukov, publicly challenged Medvedev's instructions, apparently with Putin's backing.

63. 'Russian generals accuse Medvedev of hesitation in Russia-Georgia war', RFE/RL, Aug. 8, 2012. The documetary is available at www.youtube.com/watch?v=WWBVW U4bo4g. According to Ilya Zhegulyov, whose book, *Khod Tsarem* (Alpina, Moscow, 2021), discusses the rivalries within Putin's inner circle, it was compiled by journalists at Channel 5, owned by the Kovalchuk brothers (Republic.ru, Dec. 24, 2021). It is tempting to speculate, although there is no proof, that Igor Sechin was among those behind it.

64. 'Putin answered Journalists' Questions [in] Leningrad Oblast', Aug. 7, www.kremlin.ru/events/president/transcripts/16164 and 'Answers to Journalists' Questions following a Meeting with the President of Armenia', Aug. 8, 2012, www.kremlin.ru/events/president/transcripts/16776

65. Interfax, Aug. 8, 2012.

66. 'Direct Line with Vladimir Putin', April 25, 2013, www.kremlin.ru/events/president/transcripts/17976. Kudrin had resigned as Finance Minister in September 2011 citing differences with Medvedev over economic policy (see Putin, 'Visit to Russia Today', June 11, 2013, www.kremlin.ru/events/president/transcripts/18319).

67. Pavlovsky, *supra*.

68. 'Address to the Federal Assembly', Dec. 12, 2012. www.kremlin.ru/events/president/transcripts/17118

69. Interfax, Jan. 25, 2010.

70. Torrence recounted the story in a C-Span panel discussion on March 13, 2000 (www.c-span.org/video/?155985-1/perspectives-russian-president-putin&start=5271) and in an article, 'Social Life in St. Petersburg', in Reed, Joyce Lasky, and Ruble, Blair [eds], *St. Petersburg 1993–2003: The Dynamic Decade*, St Petersburg Conservancy, Washington, D.C., 2010, p. 58. John Evans remembered the lunch as having taken place a year later (author's interview, March 10, 2017). Torrence himself wrote of Sobchak's disapproval of his lifestyle but said Putin 'never struck me as even caring' ('Social Life', p. 58).

71. NTV World and Rossiya TV, April 4, 2006.

72. RIA Novosti, May 28, 2004. 58 members of the Duma voted in favour of criminalisation.

73. Gazeta.ru, May 10, 2012.

74. BBC Monitoring, Aug. 22, 2012.

75. Ibid., Interfax, June 11 and *Vedomosti*, June 13, 2013.

76. 'Answers to Journalists' Questions on the Results of the Russian-Dutch Talks', Amsterdam, April 8, 2013, www.kremlin.ru/events/president/transcripts/17850. He had made a similar point during a phone-in six years earlier. 'My attitude . . . is connected with the implementation of my official duties', he told a questioner. 'One of the main problems facing the country is demographic!' (Vesti TV, Feb. 1, 2007).

77. 'Interview with Channel One and Associated Press', Sept. 4, 2013, *supra*. According to Richard Torrence, people in St Petersburg used to joke in the 1990s, 'Oh, we love Tchaikovsky. Just not for that!' (John Evans, *supra*).

78. The following citations are drawn from 'Meeting of Valdai Club', Sept. 19, 2013, *supra*.

79. The Dutch PNVD was established by three self-described paedophiles in May 2006 and dissolved four years later. It might have been dismissed as an act of the lunatic fringe had a Dutch judge not defended, on free-speech grounds, its right to exist and contest elections. The ruling caused widespread consternation (BBC News, July 17 and *Guardian*, July 18, 2006).

80. An exception was Neil Buckley's report in the *Financial Times* (Sept. 20, 2013).

81. 'Direct Line with Vladimir Putin', April 17, 2014, www.kremlin.ru/events/president/transcripts/20796

82. 'Address to the Federal Assembly', Dec. 12, 2013, www.kremlin.ru/events/president/transcripts/19825

83. *Washington Post*, March 3, 2014.

84. Ivan Ilyin, 'Chto sulit miru raschleneniye Rossii' ['What the Dismembering of Russia Bodes for the World'], in *Natsionalnaya Rossiya: Nashi zadachi* [*Our Tasks*], Algoritm, Moscow, 2017, p. 112.

85. 'Direct Line . . .', April 17, 2014, *supra*.

86. 'Interview with TASS', Nov. 14, 2014, *supra*.

87. Ibid. and 'Direct Line . . .', *supra*. Putin spoke in similar terms in both interviews.

88. 'Direct Line . . .', *supra*.

89. Zygar, *All the Kremlin's Men*, p. 249. Zygar's source, a Russian official, was present during the meeting (author's interview, Nov. 21, 2019). Some years later, Putin would make similar statements publicly.

90. No one who has not lived in the Soviet Union in the 1960s or '70s can begin to imagine the mental disconnect between Westerners and Soviet citizens at that time. It was partly, though not entirely, due to the totalitarian system, which required all except overt dissidents to mould their behaviour and, to a large extent, their thinking to a standard pattern. Anatoly (now Natan) Sharansky, who spent nine years in Soviet prisons before emigrating to Israel, where he became a right-wing politician, used to say that the freest place in the Soviet Union in his day was a labour camp, because there, the *zeks*, the prisoners, although physically incarcerated, were free of the mental straitjacket worn by everyone else. Even absent totalitarian restraints, the lack of contact with the outside world meant that for most Soviet citizens, normal, human relations with Westerners only occurred if both sides were drunk or during a shouting match, when emotions took over and inhibitions were dulled. In Russia today, half a century later, that disconnect has almost entirely disappeared. The differences which remain are largely cultural, not unlike those between Germans and Spaniards.

91. 'Meeting with . . . history teachers', Nov. 5, 2014, www.kremlin.ru/events/president/transcripts/46951

92. 'Meeting with authors of the concept for a new history textbook', Jan. 16, 2014, www.kremlin.ru/events/president/transcripts/20071. 'Kontseptsiya novogo uchebnometodicheskogo kompleksa po otechestvennoi istorii' ['Concept of New Teaching Materials for National History'], as it was formally known, was published on October 28, 2013: studfile.net/preview/6023595/

93. 'Inauguration of a monument to the heroes of the First World War', Aug. 1, 2014, www.kremlin.ru/events/president/transcripts/46385

94. 'Kontseptsiya . . .', *supra*, p. 3.

95. 'Meeting . . . on patriotic education for young people', Sept. 12, 2012, www.kremlin.ru/events/president/transcripts/16470

96. Vladimir Karamurza, 'The Official Past. The New Conception of History Textbooks', Nov. 8, 2013, at echo.msk.ru/blog/karamurza/1193730-echo/

97. See 'The Official Policy of Memory and the "Blackening of History"', Republic.ru, Sept. 18, 2021.

98. For an analysis of the 'Kontseptsiya', see Michael Lovorn and Tatyana Tsyrlina-Spady,

'Nationalism and Ideology in Teaching Russian History', in *World Studies in Education*, Vol. 16, No. 1, 2015, pp. 31–52, and BBC Monitoring, Nov. 21, 2013.

16: *Payback*

1. The Russian vetoes, which were supported by China, came on October 4, 2011, February 4 and July 19, 2012. Russia blocked two other draft resolutions, in late January and early February 2012, before they could be brought to a vote.
2. 'News conference following Russian-Italian talks', July 23, 2012, www.kremlin.ru/events/president/transcripts/16047
3. 'Visit to Russia Today', June 11, 2013, *supra*.
4. 'News Conference', Dec. 20, 2012, www.kremlin.ru/events/president/transcripts/17173
5. 'Interview with Russia Today', Sept. 6, 2012, *supra*.
6. 'News Conference', Dec. 20, 2012, *supra*.
7. 'Answers to Journalists' Questions', Hanover, April 8, 2013, www.kremlin.ru/events/president/transcripts/17846
8. 'News Conference following Russia-EU summit', June 4, 2013, www.kremlin.ru/events/president/transcripts/18253
9. Ibid.
10. 'Visit to Russia Today', June 11, 2013, *supra*.
11. 'News Conference', Lough Erne, June 18, 2013, www.kremlin.ru/events/president/transcripts/18361
12. Rhodes, Ben, *The World as It Is*, Random House Penguin, 2018, pp. 232–7.
13. 'News Conference following G20 Summit', Sept. 6, 2013, www.kremlin.ru/events/president/transcripts/19168
14. According to Ben Rhodes (*supra*, p. 240), Obama had repeatedly proposed that the US and Russia work together 'to address the threat from Syria's chemical weapons stockpile [but] Russia had resisted'. In September, 2013, that changed (see *Washington Post*, Sept. 7, 2013).
15. *New York Times*, Sept. 12, 2013.
16. TASS, 'Russia on the Global Stage', March 11, 2020 [but recorded on Feb. 20], www.kremlin.ru/events/president/transcripts/62971
17. 'Answers to Journalists' Questions', Bali, Oct. 8, 2013, www.kremlin.ru/events/president/transcripts/19382
18. *Washington Post*, Feb. 17 & March 31, 2012.
19. BBC News, Sept. 19, 2012.
20. *Washington Post*, Jan. 4, 2013.
21. 'Interview with Michael McFaul', May 10, 2021, Monterey Initiative in Russian Studies, www.middlebury.edu/institute/sites/www.middlebury.edu.institute/files/2021-05/Ambassadorial%20Series%20Transcripts_v3.pdf?fv=1Q2Iu44- (at p. 73).
22. See 'Interview with Russia Today', Sept. 6, 2012, *supra*.
23. 'Address to the Federal Assembly', Dec. 12, 2013, *supra*.
24. 'Working Visit to France', News conference with President Hollande, June 1, 2012, www.kremlin.ru/events/president/transcripts/15525
25. 'Meeting of Valdai Club', Sept. 19, 2013, *supra*.
26. 'Interview with Russia Today', Sept. 6, 2012, *supra*. He did not use the term, 'deep state', on that occasion, though it was clearly what he had in mind. Six years later he explained: 'It's

not just the power of the President of the United States that counts, it's the power of the so-called deep state, the ruling class' ('News Conference', Sochi, Aug. 22, 2018, www.kremlin.ru/events/president/transcripts/58347)

27. Obama had been caught in front of an open microphone in Seoul on March 12, 2012, telling Medvedev: 'On all these issues, but particularly missile defence, this can be solved, but it's important for him [Putin] to give me space . . . After my election, I have more flexibility.'

28. Romney used the term in an interview with CNN on March 26, 2012.

29. 'News Conference', Sochi, Sept. 11, 2012, www.kremlin.ru/events/president/transcripts/16465

30. Hillary Clinton was initially supportive of the proposed legislation (*Washington Post*, July 26, 2011). She subsequently claimed that Russia was sending attack helicopters to Assad's forces in a move which would escalate the conflict in Syria (*New York Times*, June 13, 2012). In fact they were old helicopters which had been in Russia for routine maintenance. Pentagon officials had to walk back her remarks.

31. 'News Conference', Dec. 20, 2012, *supra*.

32. 'Visit to Russia Today', June 11, 2013, *supra*.

33. Interfax, Dec. 17 and *Kommersant*, Dec. 18, 2012.

34. BBC Monitoring, 'Russian TV and Radio Highlights', Dec. 25, 2012.

35. *Kommersant*, Dec. 19, 2012.

36. RIA Novosti, Dec. 18, 2012.

37. This was made clear by his statements to members of the Duma and the Federation Council on December 13 ('Meeting of the Council of Legislators', www.kremlin.ru/events/president/transcripts/17125). See also *Nezavisimaya gazeta*, Dec. 20, 2012.

38. 'News Conference', Dec. 20, 2012, *supra*. A week earlier, Putin had accused American judges of 'exculpating . . . and absolving their perpetrators of responsibility'. What was bad, he said, was the American authorities' 'self-justifying attitude'. Russia must look for a response which would be 'adequate but not go too far' ('Meeting of the Council of Legislators', Dec. 13, 2012, *supra*).

39. A Levada survey reported by Interfax on January 25, 2013, found that 47 per cent of respondents 'probably or definitely' supported the adoption ban while 31 per cent opposed it. A different poll found 56 per cent in favour (RIA Novosti, Dec. 28, 2012).

40. Ibid., Jan. 3, 2013 and *Moscow Times*, Oct. 8, 2014.

41. *Kommersant* (Aug. 26, 2013) reported that Snowden had spent several days staying at the Russian Consulate in Hong Kong before his departure for Moscow. Snowden's lawyers denied that and it appears to be untrue. However, according to Putin, Snowden did speak to Russian diplomats in Hong Kong.

42. Rossiya 24, June 25, 2013.

43. 'Visit to Russia Today', June 11, 2013, *supra*.

44. 'News Conference', July 1, 2013, www.kremlin.ru/events/president/transcripts/18441

45. Interfax, June 29, 2013, quoting a Kremlin source, said Yuri Chaika had given his US counterpart, Eric Holder, the text of a draft extradition treaty at a meeting in Washington on May 14, 2012. The Americans reportedly jibbed because Russia's constitution prevented the extradition of Russian citizens, although that had not stopped the United States reaching agreement with France, which also refused the extradition of its nationals. For Putin's comments, see 'Interview with Channel One and Associated Press', Sept. 4, 2013, *supra*.

46. NTV reported on June 26, three days after Snowden's arrival, that he had left the hotel for transit passengers at the airport where he was thought to have been staying. Rossiya 1

called him 'an invisible man' because, within the enclosed transit area, he seemed to have disappeared. It was widely assumed that the Russian special services had moved him to a safe house.

47. *Washington Post*, July 15, 2013.

48. A transcript of Obama's news conference was published in the *Washington Post*, Aug. 10, 2013.

49. Ibid.

50. 'Interview with Channel One and Associated Press', Sept. 4, 2013, *supra*.

51. 'Visit to Russia Today', June 11, 2013, *supra*.

52. This citation is taken from Putin's speech to the Valdai Club on October 24, 2014 (www.kremlin.ru/events/president/transcripts/18441), when he repeated that America had to have enemies and named Iran, China and Russia as suitable candidates for that role. He had made a similar, though less explicit, statement a year earlier.

53. *Washington Post*, Aug. 10, 2013.

54. Ibid., Feb. 24, 2014.

55. 'Meeting with Russian Ambassadors', July 9, 2012, www.kremlin.ru/events/president/transcripts/15902

56. Ibid.

57. Christoph Heusgen, author's interview, March 14, 2019.

58. Hans-Friedrich von Ploetz, author's interview, May 5, 2017.

59. The main problem was the EU's 'Third Energy Package', approved in September, 2009, which prohibited companies from both producing gas and controlling the pipeline systems though which it was delivered. Putin argued that it discriminated against Gazprom and was 'a direct violation of EU–Russia accords' ('News Conference following Russia-E.U. Summit', Dec. 21, 2012, www.kremlin.ru/events/president/transcripts/17178).

60. Heusgen, *supra*.

61. 'Meeting of Valdai Club', Sept. 19, 2013, *supra*.

62. Heusgen, *supra*.

63. Ibid.

64. 'Direct Line with Vladimir Putin', April 25, *supra*, and 'Answers to Journalists' Questions', Dec. 2, 2013, www.kremlin.ru/events/president/transcripts/19741

65. Ronald McIntosh, *Turbulent Times*, Biteback Publishing, London, 2014, p. 260.

66. www.youtube.com/watch?v=MSxaa-67yGM#t=89

67. *Washington Post*, Sept. 27, 2013.

68. *The Atlantic*, Aug. 2, 2021.

69. Presidential Website, Kyiv, Nov. 29, 2013.

70. 'News Conference', Nov. 22, www.kremlin.ru/events/president/transcripts/19677, 'News Conference', Dec. 19, 2013, *supra*, and 'Russia-E.U. Summit', Brussels, Jan. 28, 2014, www.kremlin.ru/events/president/transcripts/19741

71. Zygar, *All the Kremlin's Men*, p. 268.

72. *New York Times*, Feb. 24, 2014, and 'Vladimir Putin Answered Journalists' Questions on . . . Ukraine', March 4, 2014, www.kremlin.ru/events/president/transcripts/20366

73. *New York Times*, Feb. 25, 2014.

74. 'Vladimir Putin Answered Journalists' Questions on . . . Ukraine', ibid., and Putin's interview in 'Crimea: The Path to the Motherland', Rossiya 1, March 15, 2015.

75. Zygar, *supra*, p. 268, and 'Crimea', Rossiya 1, ibid.

76. *New York Times*, Feb. 24, 2014.

77. 'Crimea', Rossiya 1, *supra*.

78. *Washington Post*, Feb. 27, 2014.

79. 'Vladimir Putin Answered Journalists' Questions on . . . Ukraine', *supra*.

80. Zygar, *supra*, p. 268.

81. Putin said the meeting took place in the Kremlin ('Crimea', Rossiya 1, *supra*), Zygar (*supra*, pp. 276–9), who spoke to some of the participants, situated it at Novo-Ogaryovo. Except where otherwise indicated, the following account derives from these two sources.

82. 'News Conference', Dec. 19, 2013, *supra*.

83. 'Direct Line with Vladimir Putin', April 17, 2014, www.kremlin.ru/events/president/news/20796

84. *Washington Post*, Feb. 27 and *New York Times*, Feb. 28, 2014.

85. Aleksandr Golts, author's interview, Nov. 20, 2019.

86. *Nezavisimaya gazeta*, March 3, 2014, www.ng.ru/cis/2014-03-03/100_obzor030314.html

87. *Kyiv Post*, March 15, 2014.

88. *New York Times*, March 3, 2014.

89. 'Telephone Conversation', March 2, 2014, www.kremlin.ru/events/president/news/20359

90. Marvin Kalb, Brookings Institution, March 4, 2014, www.brookings.edu/blog/up-front/2014/03/04/is-putin-in-another-world. Merkel spoke to Putin on February 28, March 2, and again on March 5.

91. 'Vladimir Putin Answered Journalists' Questions on . . . Ukraine', March 4, 2014, *supra*.

92. Public Opinion Survey: Residents of the Autonomous Republic of Crimea, May 16–30, 2013, Baltic Surveys/Gallup Organisation, p. 39, pdf.usaid.gov/pdf_docs/pnaec705.pdf

93. 'Direct Line with Vladimir Putin', April 17, 2014, *supra*.

94. The text of Putin's speech is at www.kremlin.ru/events/president/news/20603. He used the phrase 'to return Crimea to be part of Russia' in the documentary, 'Crimea: Rossiya 1, *supra*.

95. 'Direct Line with Vladimir Putin', April 17, 2014, *supra*. In his speech to the Federal Assembly, he spoke of the danger of NATO acquiring a base at Sevastopol but did not make a direct connection between annexing Crimea and preventing Ukrainian membership of the alliance. That was spelt out a month later.

96. That point was made forcefully by Angela Merkel at Bucharest. North Macedonia was prevented from joining NATO for more than 10 years because it was involved not even in a territorial dispute but simply in an argument with Greece over its official name.

97. Politico, March 2, 2014.

98. *Guardian*, March 25, 2014.

99. At some point before the crisis over Crimea, probably in 2012 or 2013, Angela Merkel reminded Putin that, at Bucharest, Germany had blocked the United States' attempts to give Ukraine and Georgia Membership Action Plans. 'In the NATO treaty,' she told him, 'it says that new members have to contribute to the security of the whole system, and with both [Ukraine and Georgia] we get conflict, therefore no membership action plan.' Putin replied: 'Angela, I trust you. But one day you will not be there any more. Suppose then that the position changes' (Heusgen, author's interview, March 14, 2019).

100. Associated Press, July 5, 2014.

101. Kremlin officials cited by Aleksandr Golts (author's interview, Nov. 20, 2019).

102. 'Interview with Channel One and Associated Press', Sept. 4, and 'Answers to Journalists' Questions', Bali, Oct. 8, 2013, *supra*. See also 'News Conference', Dec. 19, 2013, *supra*.

103. In 1974, the United States imposed an arms embargo on Turkey, but it remained a member of NATO and the embargo was rescinded three years later.

104. For example, Putin's remark in May: 'I am sure this will soon become a thing of the past and we will be able to cooperate as we did before' ('Meeting with Heads of International News Agencies', May 24, 2014, www.kremlin.ru/events/president/news/21090).

105. According to Aleksandr Golts (*supra*), after the Crimean operation, Putin had a meeting with the Chiefs of Staff to see what was militarily feasible in Novorossiya. He was told that, from a military standpoint, the situation would be totally different from Crimea and the difficulties would be formidable.

106. 'Replies to Journalists' Questions', May 7, 2014, www.kremlin.ru/events/president/news/20973

107. 'Replies to Journalists' Questions', Shanghai, May 21, 2014, www.kremlin.ru/events/president/news/21064

108. Ibid., 'Replies to Journalists' Questions', May 7, *supra*, and 'Meeting with Heads of International News Agencies', May 24, 2014, *supra*.

109. 'Answers to Journalists' Questions', Ouistreham, June 6, 2014, www.kremlin.ru/events/president/transcripts/20973

110. BBC News, June 6, 2014.

111. 'Direct Line with Vladimir Putin', April 17, *supra*, and 'Answers to Journalists' Questions', April 29, 2014, www.kremlin.ru/events/president/news/20880

112. The Malaysian airliner had lost radio contact at 1.20 p.m. GMT. At 2.49 p.m. GMT, *Ukrainskaya pravda* reported that it had crashed and, linking the disaster to the earlier incident on July 14, speculated that the separatists had shot it down. Interfax reported the Malaysian crash at 3.01 p.m. GMT. It was officially confirmed by the Ukrainian agency, UNIAN, at 3.21 p.m. GMT. Interfax reported the separatist claim at 3.14 p.m. GMT. The likeliest explanation for the delay is that, until the news broke of the Malaysian crash, the news agencies did not regard the separatists' announcement as important.

113. Aleksandr Golts, *supra*.

114. *Novaya gazeta*, July 23, 2014.

115. Bellingcat, April 28, 2020, www.bellingcat.com/news/2020/04/28/burlaka

116. *Novaya gazeta*, July 23, 2014.

117. 'Address by the President of Russia', July 21, 2014, www.kremlin.ru/events/president/news/45262. Russian commentators suggested that it was broadcast at 1.30 a.m., Moscow time, because that was late afternoon in Washington, D.C. But it was not as if Russian TV was watched by large numbers of Americans. On Sunday evening Putin had spoken by telephone to Cameron and Merkel. Those discussions apparently convinced him that Russia was facing an unprecedented crisis and that he needed to address it publicly without further delay.

118. 'From Crimea to the Boeing', July 21, 2014, snob.ru/profile/25718/blog/78794

119. 'Frightened Putin', www.republic.ru/posts/1/1130645 (no longer accessible online) and *Yezhednevny zhurnal*, July 21, 2014.

120. Hollande, François, *Les Leçons du pouvoir*, Stock, Paris, 2018, p. 73.

121. A scan of the signed Russian text of the agreement can be found at www.osce.org/files/f/documents/5/b/140221.pdf

122. 'Transcript of Obama's Remarks on the Fight against ISIS', *New York Times*, Sept. 10, 2014.

123. 'Meeting of Valdai Club', Oct. 22, 2015, www.kremlin.ru/events/president/transcripts/50548

124. 'Plenary Session of the 19th St Petersburg International Economic Forum', June 19, 2015, www.kremlin.ru/events/president/transcripts/49733

125. 'Interview with Al Ahram', Feb. 9, 2015, www.kremlin.ru/events/president/transcripts/47643 and 'Interview with CBS and PBS', Sept. 29, 2015 (but broadcast on Sept. 27), www.kremlin.ru/events/president/transcripts/50380

126. 'Speech to UN General Assembly', Sept. 28, 2015, www.kremlin.ru/events/president/transcripts/50385

127. 'CSTO Summit', Dushanbe, Sept 15, 2015, www.kremlin.ru/events/president/transcripts/50291

128. 'Speech to U.N. General Assembly', Sept. 28, 2015, *supra*.

129. Ibid. and 'Interview with CBS and PBS', Sept. 29, 2015, *supra*. In his UN speech, Putin accused Washington of trying to use the jihadists to overthrow Assad, which the United States strongly denied. His underlying argument, that the US and ISIS and al-Qaeda had the same goal, albeit for quite different reasons, and that, if they succeeded, the result would be to reduce Syria to the same state as Libya or Iraq, was less easily dismissed.

130. 'Answers to Journalists' Questions', New York, Sept. 29, 2015, www.kremlin.ru/events/president/transcripts/50394

131. 'The Obama Doctrine', *The Atlantic*, March 10, 2016.

132. 'Meeting with Government Members', Sept. 30, 2015, www.kremlin.ru/events/president/transcripts/50401. See also 'Answers to Russian Journalists' Questions', Sept. 4, 2015, www.kremlin.ru/events/president/transcripts/50234

133. *Washington Post*, Oct. 23, 2015.

134. 'Meeting with Defence Minister', Dec. 8, 2015, www.kremlin.ru/events/president/transcripts/50892

135. 'The Kuznetsov Smokescreen', *Eurasia Daily Monitor*, Oct. 27, 2016.

136. 'News Conference', Tehran, Sept. 7, 2018, www.kremlin.ru/events/president/transcripts/58483

137. 'Meeting of Valdai Club', Oct. 27, 2016, www.kremlin.ru/events/president/transcripts/53151

138. *New York Times*, Nov. 26, 2015.

139. 'News Conference', May 3, 2017, www.kremlin.ru/events/president/transcripts/54444

140. Ibid.

141. 'Answers to Journalists' Questions', June 15, 2017, www.kremlin.ru/events/president/transcripts/54794

142. 'Meeting with Defence Minister', Oct. 7, www.kremlin.ru/events/president/transcripts/50458, and Anadolu News Agency, Nov. 20, 2015. See also *Zaman*, Nov. 22, BBC Monitoring, Nov. 23 & 24, and *Hürriyet*, Nov. 24, 2015.

143. 'Annual News Conference', Dec. 17, 2015, www.kremlin.ru/events/president/transcripts/50971

144. 'Meeting with King Abdullah', Nov. 24, 2015, www.kremlin.ru/events/president/transcripts/50775 and 'Address to the Federal Assembly', Dec. 3, 2015, www.kremlin.ru/events/president/transcripts/50864

145. Ibid. and 'Answers to Journalists' Questions', Paris, Nov. 30, 2015, www.kremlin.ru/events/president/transcripts/50850

146. 'Address to the Federal Assembly', *supra*.

147. Putin went on to claim that it was to protect this lucrative commerce that the Russian plane had been shot down ('Answers to Journalists' Questions', Nov. 30, 2015, *supra*).

148. Ibid. and 'Address to the Federal Assembly', *supra*.

149. 'Answers to Journalists' Questions', Nov. 25, www.kremlin.ru/events/president/transcripts/50777, and 'Annual News Conference', Dec. 17, 2015, *supra*.

150. Rossiya 24, Nov. 25, 2015.

151. 'Annual News Conference', *supra*.

152. Interfax, June 27, 2016.

153. 'News Conference', Aug. 9, 2016, www.kremlin.ru/events/president/transcripts/52673

154. Dmitry Bechaev, 'Turkey's Tightrope between Russia and the United States', Carnegie.ru, April 14, 2021.

155. 'Meeting of Valdai Club', Oct. 18, 2018, www.kremlin.ru/events/president/transcripts/58848

156. 'Interview with TF1', Oct. 12 (but recorded on Oct. 11), www.kremlin.ru/events/president/transcripts/53081 and 'Russia Calling Investment Forum', Oct. 12, 2016, www.kremlin.ru/events/president/transcripts/53077

157. 'Direct Line with Vladimir Putin', June 7, 2018, www.kremlin.ru/events/president/transcripts/57692 and BBC Monitoring, March 2, 2018.

158. 'Interview with Interfax and Anadolu', Nov. 13, 2015, www.kremlin.ru/events/president/transcripts/50682

159. 'Truth and Justice Forum', April 7, 2016, www.kremlin.ru/events/president/transcripts/51685

160. 'Meeting with John Kerry', March 24, www.kremlin.ru/events/president/transcripts/51562. Putin said that autumn that Kerry was doing 'tremendous work' on Syria ('Interview with Bloomberg', Sept. 5, 2016, www.kremlin.ru/events/president/transcripts/52830), and described him as 'a good guy' ('Meeting of Valdai Club', Dec, 2017, www.kremlin.ru/events/president/transcripts/55882).

161. 'Interview with TASS', Nov. 14, 2014, www.kremlin.ru/events/president/transcripts/47009

162. *New York Times*, July 29, 2016.

163. 'Interview with Europe 1 and TF1', June 4, 2014, *supra*.

164. *Izvestia*, Oct. 7, 1998.

165. The Internet Research Agency was registered in June 2013. The FBI dates the beginning of its attempts to interfere in the US elections to October 2013 ('Wanted by the FBI: Mikhail Leonidovich Burchik', www.fbi.gov/wanted/counterintelligence/mikhail-leonidovich-burchik). However, Burchik did not officially join the agency until the following March, and other sources indicate that it started work in earnest in April 2014 (*Washington Post*, February 16, 2018).

166. 'Visit to Russia Today', June 11, 2013, www.kremlin.ru/events/president/transcripts/18319

167. 'Media Forum', St Petersburg, April 24, 2014, www.kremlin.ru/events/president/transcripts/20858

168. James Dobbins, in a discussion at Hanover, N.H., Oct. 11, 2018, and *Washington Post*, Dec. 12, 2000.

169. *New York Times*, Dec. 18, 2016.

170. *Foreign Policy*, Jan. 10, 2017.

171. *Just Security*, Jan. 22, 2019. Thomas Carothers of the Carnegie Endowment has also argued against equating Russian and American efforts at election interference. Like Sipher, he claimed that American actions were usually in a good cause – to promote democracy, not

to undermine it – and that, in any case, since the end of the Cold War, the United States had interfered in other countries' elections much less than in the past ('Is the U.S. Hypocritical to Criticise Russian Election Meddling?', www.carnegieendowment.org, March 12, 2018).

172. More than a year after the election, Scott Shane noted that instances of US meddling had been 'largely missing from the flood of reporting' (*New York Times*, Feb. 18, 2018).

173. 'Interview with Bloomberg', Sept. 5, 2016, *supra*.

174. 'Russia Calling Investment Forum', Oct. 12 and 'Meeting of Valdai Club, Oct. 27, 2016, *supra*.

175. 'Meeting of Valdai Club', Oct. 27, 2016, *supra*.

176. 'St Petersburg International Economic Forum', June 17, 2016, www.kremlin.ru/events/president/transcripts/52178

177. Putin sent a congratulatory message on November 9, which he followed up with a phone call on November 14. He used the phrase, 'convincing victory', shortly before Trump's inauguration ('News Conference with Igor Dodon', Jan. 17, 2017, www.kremlin.ru/events/president/transcripts/53744).

178. 'Interview with Le Figaro', May 31, 2017, www.kremlin.ru/events/president/transcripts/54638

179. 'Meeting of Valdai Club', Oct. 27, 2016, *supra*.

180. Yahoo! News, July 21, 2017, news.yahoo.com/ex-cia-director-hayden-russia-election-meddling-successful-covert-operation-history-212056443.html

181. 'News Conference', Helsinki, July 16, 2018, www.kremlin.ru/events/president/transcripts/58017

182. CNN, July 18, 2018.

183. *USA Today*, Sept. 28, 2016. The hacker who went by the pseudonym, Plague, in Larsson's book, *The Girl who Kicked the Hornets' Nest* (MacLehose Press, London, 2009, p. 384) was described as 'a severely overweight and socially challenged thirty-year-old living on disability benefit'.

184. 'Interview with Bloomberg', Sept. 5, 2016, *supra*.

185. Buzzfeed, Jan. 10, 2017.

186. *New York Times*, Oct. 8, 2016.

187. Trump told the FBI Chief, James Comey, that he had arrived in Moscow in the morning and had left later the same day. The flight plan of his private jet showed that he had stayed one night and part of a second night there (*Time*, April 23, 2018).

188. 'News Conference with Igor Dodon', Jan. 17, 2017, *supra*.

189. text.npr.org/629554155, and nymag.com/intelligencer/2018/07/trumps-sad-weak-encounter-with-putin-in-helsinki.html, July 16, 2018

190. 'Russian Energy Week Forum', Oct. 4, 2017, www.kremlin.ru/events/president/transcripts/55767

191. 'Meeting of Valdai Club', Oct. 19, 2017, *supra*. Putin had first used the term, 'Russophobia', in June.

192. 'St Petersburg International Economic Forum', June 2, 2017, www.kremlin.ru/events/president/transcripts/54667

193. 'Interview with Michael McFaul', May 10, 2021, Monterey Initiative in Russian Studies, *supra*.

194. *New York Times*, June 19, 2021.

195. Ibid. and *Guardian*, Dec. 29, 2016.

196. John Sipher in *Foreign Policy*, Oct. 13, 2017.

197. 'News Conference', Dec. 20, 2018, www.kremlin.ru/events/president/transcripts/59445

198. 'Direct Line with Vladimir Putin', June 20, 2019, www.kremlin.ru/events/president/transcripts/60795

199. 'Meetings with Heads of International News Agencies', June 1, 2017, www.kremlin.ru/events/president/transcripts/54650

200. 'Interview with NBC', June 5, 2017, www.kremlin.ru/events/president/transcripts/54688

201. 'Russia Energy Week Forum', Oct. 2, 2019, www.kremlin.ru/events/president/transcripts/61704

202. 'Expanded Meeting of Defence Ministry Board', Dec. 22, 2017, www.kremlin.ru/events/president/transcripts/56472

203. Russia suspended its participation in the CFE Treaty in 2007 and formally withdrew in 2015.

204. In 2016, the Obama administration sought to change the terms of the Plutonium Management and Disposition Agreement, under which Russia and the US had agreed to convert excess weapons-grade plutonium into reactor fuel. The US justified its decision on the grounds of soaring costs: it was estimated that disposing of 34 tons of plutonium would cost up to 30 billion US dollars. Instead it proposed diluting and storing the plutonium, which was cheaper but left open the possibility that the stored plutonium could later be recovered. Russia, which by then was already operating its own conversion plant, accused the US of reneging on its obligations and the agreement collapsed (*World Nuclear News*, Feb. 10, and *Bulletin of the Atomic Scientists*, April 28, 2016). Moscow announced the destruction of its 38,000-ton chemical weapons stockpile in 2017. The United States, citing cost and technical reasons, was not expected to complete the destruction of its smaller stockpile, amounting to 23,000 tons, until 2023 ('Russia Destroys Last Chemical Weapons', Nov. 2017, www.armscontrol.org/act/2017-11/news/russia-destroys-last-chemical-weapons).

205. See, for instance, 'Meeting on Defence Industry Deployment', May 13, www.kremlin.ru/events/president/transcripts/51911 and 'News Conference with Alexis Tsipras', Athens, May 27, 2016, www.kremlin.ru/events/president/transcripts/52024

206. 'President Trump has broken all records,' Putin said ('Meeting with Heads of International News Agencies', June 6, 2019, www.kremlin.ru/events/president/transcripts/60675).

207. 'Meeting of Valdai Club', Oct. 19, 2017, *supra*.

208. 'Annual Address to the Federal Assembly', March 1, 2018, www.kremlin.ru/events/president/transcripts/56957

209. 'Russia Calling Investment Forum', Nov. 28, 2018, www.kremlin.ru/events/president/transcripts/59216

210. 'Annual Address to the Federal Assembly', March 1, 2018, *supra*.

211. American experts were sceptical of many of Putin's more detailed claims, particularly regarding the manoeuvrability of the Avangard glide vehicle. British officials were less dismissive. The Chief of Defence Intelligence, Lieutenant General Jim Hockenhull, said Russia was 'pushing the boundaries of science' and developing weapons which 'would have a global reach and allow attack from unexpected directions' (*Sunday Telegraph*, Sept. 13, 2020).

212. TASS, Aug. 10, *Novaya gazeta*, Aug. 12 & 21, 2019.

213. Aleksandr Golts, author's interview, Nov. 20, 2019.

214. 'Conversation with Gerbert Yefremov', Sept. 19, 2020, www.kremlin.ru/events/president/transcripts/64058

215. 'Annual Address to the Federal Assembly', March 1, 2018, *supra*.

216. *Guardian*, Oct. 22, 2018.

217. The phrase is from the Democratic Senator, Elizabeth Warren, on Twitter on September 10, 2019.

218. 'Meeting with John Bolton', Oct. 23, 2018, www.kremlin.ru/events/president/transcripts/58880

219. 'News Conference', Dec. 23, 2016, www.kremlin.ru/events/president/transcripts/53573

220. 'Interview with TF1', Oct. 12, 2016, *supra*.

221. 'We have become more persistent in asserting our interests,' Putin said. 'We follow an independent domestic and foreign policy and our sovereignty is not for sale. In some quarters, this does not go down well' ('Plenary Session of the 19th St Petersburg International Economic Forum', June 19, *supra*, and 'Security Council Meeting', July 3, 2015, www.kremlin.ru/events/president/transcripts/49862).

222. 'Address to the Federal Assembly', Dec. 1, 2016, www.kremlin.ru/events/president/transcripts/53379, and 'Meeting of Valdai Club', Oct. 19, 2017, *supra*. From 2014, after the annexation of Crimea, until January 2021, when Trump stepped down, the direction of Russian foreign policy remained essentially unchanged. The citations which follow are all drawn from the period 2014–2019 but are not in strict chronological order. They illustrate ideas to which Putin kept returning and which would continue to influence him in his fourth term, after Joe Biden became US President.

223. 'Interview with Bild', Jan. 11, 2016, www.kremlin.ru/events/president/transcripts/51154

224. 'Meeting of Valdai Club', Oct. 24, 2014, *supra*.

225. 'Interview with Bild', *supra*.

226. www.nato.int/cps/en/natolive/official_texts_17120.htm

227. 'Interview with NBC', March 10, 2018, www.kremlin.ru/events/president/transcripts/57027

228. 'Meeting of Valdai Club, Oct. 19, 2017, *supra*.

229. 'News Conference', Dec. 18, 2014, www.kremlin.ru/events/president/transcripts/47250

230. 'Direct Line with Vladimir Putin'. April 17, 2014, *supra*.

231. 'Address to the Federal Assembly', Dec. 4, 2014, www.kremlin.ru/events/president/transcripts/47173

232. 'News Conference', Dec. 20, 2018, *supra*.

233. 'Interview with TASS', Nov. 24, 2014 (but recorded on Nov. 13), www.kremlin.ru/events/president/transcripts/47054

234. 'Direct Line with Vladimir Putin', June 7, 2018, www.kremlin.ru/events/president/transcripts/57692

235. 'St Petersburg International Economic Forum', June 7, 2019, www.kremlin.ru/events/president/transcripts/60707

236. 'Answers to Journalists' Questions', Dushanbe, Sept. 12, 2014, www.kremlin.ru/events/president/transcripts/46612

237. 'Meeting of Valdai Club', Oct. 24, 2014, *supra*.

238. 'News Conference', Dec. 18, 2014, *supra*.

239. The thesis that hegemonic powers are never more dangerous than when their dominance is under threat is set out in Graham Allison's book, *Destined for War: Can America and China Escape Thucydides's Trap?*, Houghton Mifflin Harcourt, New York, 2017.

240. 'St Petersburg International Economic Forum', June 7, 2019, *supra*. Putin had already begun thinking in these terms much earlier. 'The traditional powerhouses of the global

economy – the US, the EU and Japan – are seeing their leadership erode', he told Russian diplomats in 2012 ('Meeting with Russian Ambassadors', July 9, 2012, *supra*).

241. Ibid.; 'Meeting of Valdai Club', Oct. 3, 2019, www.kremlin.ru/events/president/transcripts/61719 and 'Eastern Economic Forum', Sept. 5, 2019, *supra*.

242. Ibid.

243. 'Direct Line with Vladimir Putin', April 17, 2014, *supra*. See also 'Meeting of Supreme Eurasian Economic Council', Nur-Sultan [Astana], May 29, 2019, www.kremlin.ru/events/president/transcripts/60597

244. 'Interview with Mir TV and Radio', June 13, 2019, www.kremlin.ru/events/president/transcripts/60741

245. 'Speech to Davos Online Forum', Jan. 27, 2021, www.kremlin.ru/events/president/transcripts/64938 and 'News Conference with Italian Prime Minister', Rome, July 4, 2019, www.kremlin.ru/events/president/transcripts/60920

246. 'Meeting of Russian Federation Ambassadors', June 30, 2016, www.kremlin.ru/events/president/transcripts/52298

247. 'St Petersburg International Economic Forum', June 7, 2019, *supra*.

248. 'Meeting of Valdai Club', Oct. 18, 2018, *supra*.

249. 'Russian Energy Week Forum', Oct. 3, 2018, *supra*.

250. 'Interview with Le Figaro', May 31, 2017, *supra*.

17: *Nemtsov, Wild Boar Sausages and the End of Liberalism*

1. Putin had first used those terms in his address to parliament on March 18, 2014, after the annexation of Crimea. They had subsequently become a fixture in the pro-government media.

2. The case for Putin being responsible for Nemtsov's murder has been laid out by David Satter in the *National Review* (Oct. 31, 2017). Satter is a leading proponent of the theory that the FSB carried out the apartment bombings in Moscow in 1999 in order to bring Putin to power. The evidence he adduced to show that Putin had ordered Nemtsov's killing was entirely circumstantial. He wrote that in February 2012, the former Chechen minister, Akhmed Zakayev, warned Nemtsov in Oslo that the authorities were planning to kill him. Why an exiled Chechen, living in London, should have better intelligence about the Kremlin's intentions than Nemtsov, who lived in Moscow and retained influential contacts among the Russian elite, was not explained. He also referred to a broadcast, in which Putin allegedly warned that the opposition was planning to murder one of its leaders and blame it on the regime. There was no such broadcast. In 1997, it was Nemtsov who persuaded Yeltsin to halt the persecution of Putin's mentor, Sobchak. Putin knew that. It was not something he would forget.

3. An opinion poll by the Levada Centre, published the day of Nemtsov's murder, found that only 15 per cent of respondents sympathised with his views, while 68 per cent did not (*Moscow Times*, Feb. 28, 2015).

4. Interfax, March 8, 2015 and www.instagram.com/p/z-dKqICRua (no longer accessible).

5. After the Moscow radio station, Ekho Moskvy, had come out in support of *Charlie Hebdo* on freedom of speech grounds, Kadyrov had attacked its editor, Aleksei Venediktov, warning that, if the authorities did not intervene, 'someone else will settle accounts with [him]'. Nemtsov accused Kadyrov of making criminal threats, adding that he was becoming 'more brazen by the day' because he knew he had Putin's backing (BBC Monitoring, Jan. 9, 2015 and Nemtsov's Facebook page the same day, www.facebook.com/photo.php?fbid=

747515231984746&set=a.462364940499778.1073741826.100001788291627&type=1).   Commentary from Chechens and Daghestanis on Twitter and Facebook after Nemtsov's murder noted that he had a record of opposing the Chechen wars and was regarded by many Muslims in the Caucasus as an ally (BBC Monitoring, March 9, 2015).

6.   *Moskovsky komsomolets*, March 10 and *Novaya gazeta*, March 11, 2015. The following account is partly based on 'Kak ubivali Borisa Nemtsova: polnaya khronologiya . . .' [How they killed Boris Nemtsov: complete chronology], March 1, 2021, munscanner.com/2021/03/nemtsov/

7.   It later emerged that Nemtsov had been under intermittent surveillance for the previous ten months by a group of FSB operatives from the Directorate for the Protection of Constitutional Order, responsible for internal political security. However, on February 17, ten days before his death, the group switched its attention to another opposition figure, Viktor Kara-Murza. There is no evidence that they were involved in Nemtsov's murder – the FSB normally uses poison in such cases – but it raises the question of whether they were withdrawn and, if so, on whose orders, to leave the field clear for the Chechens to kill him (www.bellingcat.com/news/2022/03/28/boris-nemtsov-tailed-by-fsb-squad-prior-to-2015-murder/)

8.   Interfax, March 9, 2015.

9.   Dozhd TV, March 9, 2015.

10.   Zygar, *All the Kremlin's Men*, pp. 315–17 & 320.

11.   www.instagram.com/p/02r0HhCRly (no longer accessible).

12.   *Novaya gazeta*, March 13, 2015.

13.   Kadyrov gave an account of his reception at the Kremlin after his return at www.instagram.com/p/1L4_u6iRh1 (no longer accessible).

14.   'Kak ubivali Borisa Nemtsova', *supra*, and 'Neizvestnye ubiisy Nemtsova: Chto sledstvie upustilo . . .' ['Unknown Murderers of Nemtsov: What the investigation missed . . .'], Nov. 2, 2020, zona.media/article/2020/11/02/nemtsov. An English translation may be found at munscanner.com/2020/11/nemtsov-en/. The Russian investigators named Geremeyev's driver, Ruslan Mukhutdinov, as the organiser of the murder, apparently to try to divert attention from Geremeyev himself. Mukhutdinov also took refuge in Dzhalka. In 2020, he was photographed there with other members of the Geremeyev clan. That year, on February 27, the fifth anniversary of Nemtsov's death, Putin signed a decree awarding Senator Suleiman Geremeyev the Order of Merit of the Fatherland (2nd Class).

15.   'Direct Line with Vladimir Putin', April 16, 2015, www.kremlin.ru/events/president/transcripts/49261

16.   See Tatyana Felgenhauer's question and Putin's response in 'Annual News Conference', Dec. 14, 2017, www.kremlin.ru/events/president/transcripts/56378

17.   Zygar, *supra*, p. 323.

18.   Interfax, Jan. 12, Andrei Pertsev, 'Kadyrov's Calculated Provocation', Carnegie.ru, Jan. 27, and Tatia Lemondzhava, 'The Chechen Gambit', *Foreign Policy*, March 2, 2016.

19.   'Direct Line with Vladimir Putin', April 14, 2016, www.kremlin.ru/events/president/transcripts/51716

20.   *Christian Science Monitor*, Sept. 20, 2017.

21.   'Meeting with Ramzan Kadyrov', March 25, 2016, www.kremlin.ru/events/president/transcripts/51567

22.   *Novaya gazeta*, April 3, novayagazeta.ru/articles/2017/04/01/71983-ubiystvo-chesti; 'Answers to Journalists' Questions', May 2, www.kremlin.ru/events/president/transcripts/54439; and 'Joint News Conference with Macron', May 29, 2017, www.kremlin.ru/events/president/transcripts/54618. See also *Washington Post*, July 15, 2017.

23. Dozhd TV, Tass and Rossiya 1, Sept. 4, 2017.

24. 'News Conference', Xiamen, Sept. 5, 2017, www.kremlin.ru/events/president/transcripts/55535

25. Earley, Pete, *Comrade J*, p. 301.

26. In an interview with Chechen TV on August 23, 2011, Putin said, 'He's like a son to me', a phrase calculated to resonate in a region where family and clan loyalties dominate (cited in Zygar, *supra*, pp. 322 & 354 n. 8).

27. Cited in Amy Knight, 'The Kremlin's Chechen Dragon', *New York Review of Books*, May 27, 2010.

28. Lemondzhava, 'The Chechen Gambit', *supra*. To put that in context, the other Caucasian republics received between 55 and 83 per cent of their budgetary finance from Moscow, so Chechnya was not an exception (*Eurasia Daily Monitor*, Jan. 12, 2015).

29. Forbes.ru, April 19, 2010.

30. Leonid Bershidsky, 'Why Putin Sacrificed his Economy Minister', Bloomberg, Nov. 15, 2016.

31. 'Russia Calling Investment Forum', Oct. 12, 2016, *supra*.

32. *Financial Times*, Dec. 10, 2016.

33. *Vedomosti*, Nov. 15, 2016.

34. *Komsomolskaya pravda*, Nov. 16, 2016.

35. 'Vesti nedeli', Rossiya 1, Sept. 10, 2017.

36. *Novaya gazeta*, Nov. 29, 2017.

37. 'Annual News Conference', Dec. 14, 2017, *supra*.

38. Ibid.

39. 'Eastern Economic Forum', Sept. 12, 2018, www.kremlin.ru/events/president/transcripts/58537

40. *Financial Times*, June 27, 2019, and www.kremlin.ru/events/president/transcripts/60836

41. 'Russian Energy Week Forum', Oct. 3, 2018, www.kremlin.ru/events/president/transcripts/58701

42. 'Visit to Chelyabinsk Compressor Plant', Nov. 9, www.kremlin.ru/events/president/transcripts/56028, 'Annual News Conference', Dec. 14, 2017, *supra* and 'Annual News Conference', Dec. 19, 2019, www.kremlin.ru/events/president/transcripts/62366

43. 'Meeting With Gorky Automobile Plant Workers', Dec. 6, 2017, www.kremlin.ru/events/president/transcripts/56323 and 'News Conference with Austrian Chancellor', Feb. 28, 2018, www.kremlin.ru/events/president/transcripts/56952

44. 'Answers to Journalists' Questions', April 14, 2016, www.kremlin.ru/events/president/transcripts/51718

45. 'Truth and Justice Forum', April 7, 2016, *supra*.

46. *Independent*, May 30, 2019.

47. Interview with Ekho Moskvy, cited in the *Washington Post*, March 6, 2017.

48. Ibid.

49. Author's interview in St Petersburg, May, 2019.

50. This account was provided in October 2019 by the businessman's daughter.

51. A Levada poll published on November 7, 2017, found that 46 per cent of respondents were generally satisfied with the work of the police in their city (www.levada.ru/2017/11/07/otnoshenie-k-politsii/).

52. Putin's popularity remained above 80 per cent from March 2014, to April 2018 (www.levada.ru/indikatory/). Paradoxically, this was so even though more and more Russians

held him personally responsible for the failure to combat corruption (www.levada. ru/2017/03/28/vlasti-nelzya-narodu-mozhno/. See also *Vedomosti*, Nov. 21, 2018).

53. '20 Questions with Vladimir Putin', TASS, Feb. 20, 2020, Part 15, www.kremlin.ru/events/ president/transcripts/62997. See also Andreichuk, Stanislav, 'Parties as State Employees', April 3, 2019, www.ridl.io/ru/ partijnye-bjudzhetniki-kak-politicheskie-partii-zhivut-za-schet-rossijan/ and Denis Gudkov's article, 'We are returning to late Soviet times', Oct. 13, 2017, www.levada.ru/2017/10/13/ my-vozvrashchaemsya-v-pozdnesovetskie-vremena

54. 'Nazvanie partii Navalnogo . . .', May 27, 2019, zona.media/news/2019/05/27/russia-future

55. Cameron Ross, 'Regional Elections in Russia', June 26, 2018, nature.com/articles/ s41599-018-0137-1

56. Putin spoke at length about the dangers of extremist ideology at a meeting of the Security Council on November 20, 2014, www.kremlin.ru/events/president/transcripts/47045, and to the Interior Ministry Board on March 9, 2017, www.kremlin.ru/events/president/ transcripts/54014

57. See *Kommersant*, March 20, 2012. An early exception had been Eduard Limonov's National Bolshevik Party, a marginal extreme left-wing group which had been banned in 2007.

58. *Moscow Times*, May 24, 2017.

59. 'Answers to Journalists' Questions', June 15, 2017, *supra*.

60. *Novaya gazeta*, Aug. 23, 2017.

61. *Moskovsky komsomolets*, Aug. 23, 2017.

62. 'Direct Line with Vladimir Putin', June 15, 2017, www.kremlin.ru/events/president/ transcripts/54790 and BBC Monitoring, May 26 & July 20, 2017. Even Rossiya 1, the princi-pal state TV channel which always hewed to the official line, condemned the hounding of the film director, Aleksei Uchitel, by a conservative Duma deputy as 'an abuse of power' ('Sunday Night with Vladimir Solovyov', May 28, 2017).

63. 'Interview with Bloomberg', Sept. 5, 2016, *supra*.

64. 'Interview with Financial Times', June 27, 2019 [Russian-language text], www.kremlin.ru/ events/president/transcripts/60836

65. See, for instance, Republic.ru, Aug. 30, 2021.

66. 'Russia Energy Week Forum', Oct. 2, 2019, *supra*.

67. 'Ukaz prezidenta Rossiiskoi Federatsii o strategii natsionalnoi bezopasnosti Rossiiskoi Fed-eratsii', July 2, 2021.

68. 'Russia's National Security Strategy', Carnegie.ru, July 6, 2021.

69. *Rossiiskaya gazeta*, Dec. 12, 2019. See also 'Meeting with . . . History Teachers', Nov. 5, 2014, *supra*, and 'Meeting of Russian Popular Front', Jan. 25, 2016, www.kremlin.ru/events/ president/transcripts/51206

70. 'Annual News Conference', Dec. 19, 2019, *supra*.

71. 'Opening of Wall of Sorrow', Oct. 30, 2017, www.kremlin.ru/events/president/ transcripts/55948

72. 'Meeting with . . . History Teachers', Nov. 5, 2014, *supra*.

73. 'Annual News Conference', Dec. 19, 2019,

74. '20 Questions with Vladimir Putin', TASS, Feb. 20, 2020, Part 15, *supra*.

75. According to the Levada Institute, Navalny's ratings remained fairly constant at around 2 per cent.

18: *The Endgame*

1. Putin, *First Person*, p. 197.
2. Putin said this repeatedly over the years. See, for instance, 'Interview with NBC', March 10, 2018, *supra*.
3. 'Meeting with Members of the Federation Council' May 17, 2000, *supra*.
4. Rossiya 1, June 12, 2001.
5. 'Meeting with Finalists of Student Essay Competition', June 5, 2003, *supra*.
6. One of the very few exceptions was the resignation of the British Prime Minister, Harold Wilson, in March, 1976, three years before new elections were due. He said afterwards that he was exhausted and had decided not to continue in the post after he turned 60. In 2021, Anglea Merkel also retired voluntarily after 16 years as German Chancellor, Most other Western political leaders who have left office early have done so after political setbacks.
7. 'News Conference', Dec. 20, 2012, *supra*.
8. 'Interview with ARD', April 5, 2013, www.kremlin.ru/events/president/transcripts/17808, and 'Meeting with Students', July 21, 2017, www.kremlin.ru/events/president/transcripts/55114
9. 'Meeting with . . . History Teachers', Nov. 5, 2014, *supra*.
10. 'Meeting with members of the public in Ivanovo Region', March 6, 2020, www.kremlin.ru/events/president/transcripts/62953
11. '20 Questions with Vladimir Putin', TASS, Feb. 20, 2020, Part 17, www.kremlin.ru/events/president/transcripts/63034
12. Rossiya TV, Sept. 27, 2005.
13. 'Annual News Conference', Dec. 17, 2015, *supra*.
14. 'Meeting with Minister of Labour', April 26, 2017, www.kremlin.ru/events/president/transcripts/543823. The effects of the collapse of the birth rate in 1943 and 1944 were still being felt in Russia 70 years later.
15. According to Putin, the total pension bill in 2018 amounted to 7.3 trillion roubles, or more than 100 billion US dollars, of which 3.3 trillion came from the state budget ('Address to Russian Citizens', Aug. 29, 2018, www.kremlin.ru/events/president/transcripts/58405).
16. *Nezavisimaya gazeta*, May 21 and *Vedomosti*, June 19, 2018. Not coincidentally, Medvedev announced the proposed measures on June 14, the opening day of the World Cup.
17. BBC Monitoring, June 14, 2018.
18. Putin touched on this in numerous speeches. For a succinct summary, see Rossiya TV, Sept. 27, 2005.
19. OECD, 'Pensions at a Glance, 2017', doi.org/10.1787/pension_glance-2017-21-en. Putin cited Russian forecasts of a further 15 years for men aged 65 by 2030 and 24 years for women ('Conversation with . . . World Cup Volunteers', July 20, 2018, www.kremlin.ru/events/president/transcripts/58075).
20. 'Address to Russian Citizens', Aug. 29, 2018, *supra*.
21. www.levada.ru/indikatory/odobrenie-organov-vlasti/
22. *Vedomosti*, Sept. 4, 2018.
23. 'News Conference', Dec. 20, 2018, *supra*.
24. 'Address to Russian Citizens', *supra*.
25. Leonid Bershidsky, 'Putin Gets a Reminder to Turn His Attention Back Home', Bloomberg, July 20, 2018.
26. *Rossiiskaya gazeta*, Dec. 25, 2018.

27. *Kommersant*, Oct. 23, 2014.

28. *Vedomosti*, June 20, 2019.

29. 'A Living Constitution for Development', July 17, 2019, www.pnp.ru/politics/zhivaya-konstituciya-razvitiya.html

30. 'Annual News Conference', Dec. 19, 2019, *supra*.

31. Konstantin Kostin, formerly deputy Head of the Presidential Administration, in *Vedomosti*, Dec. 20, 2019.

32. He had first raised the question of whether the word 'consecutive' was appropriate at the start of his third term but had allowed the matter to drop. It was the subject of renewed discussion in the Russian media following Volodin's article in July 2019 (ibid., Aug. 6 & Dec. 20, 2019).

33. Suggestions that it could also be used to bar Aleksei Navalny appear to be incorrect. He spent four months at Yale in the autumn of 2010, but as a visiting fellow, meaning that he did not have residency.

34. *Financial Times*, July 29, 2019.

35. '20 Questions with Vladimir Putin', TASS, Feb. 20, 2020, Part 1, www.kremlin.ru/events/president/transcripts/62843

36. 'Direct Line with Vladimir Putin', June 7, 2018, *supra*.

37. 'Annual News Conference', Dec. 20, 2018, *supra*.

38. *Moskovsky komsomolets*, Jan. 24, 2020.

39. *Novaya gazeta*, Jan. 23, 2020.

40. *Kommersant*, Jan. 17, 2020.

41. Russian epidemiologists were told on December 31, 2019, to begin monitoring the Covid-19 situation in China ('Meeting on Coronavirus', April 7, 2020, www.kremlin.ru/events/president/transcripts/63173).

42. Both the Kremlin and Tereshkova herself denied that she had been encouraged to propose the amendment (*Komsomolskaya pravda*, www.kp.ru/daily/27103.4/4176371/ and Interfax, March 12, 2020). The chronology alone makes that extremely hard to believe. Tereshkova made her proposal at 10.51 a.m. GMT. Putin arrived at the Duma at 12.00 p.m. GMT with a lengthy written speech already prepared. The bill was passed on a second reading at 1.06 p.m. GMT (BBC Monitoring, March 16, 2020, citing timings given by TASS).

43. Interfax, March 10, 2020.

44. 'Plenary Session of State Duma', March 10, 2020, www.kremlin.ru/events/president/transcripts/62964

45. *Vedomosti*, March 11, 2020.

46. Putin himself gave the game away two years later when he protested that the measures supposedly intended to increase the powers of parliament were 'not some kind of cover, but something meaningful' ('Meeting with Deputies', June 21, 2021, www.kremlin.ru/events/president/transcripts/65894). See also *Nezavisimaya gazeta*, Feb. 19 and *Moskovsky komsomolets*, Feb. 20, 2020, and Noble, Ben, and Petrov, Nikolai, 'From Constitution to Law: Implementing the 2020 Russian Constitutional Changes', March 30, 2021, brill.com/view/journals/rupo/6/1/article-p130_8.xml?language=en

47. *Vedomosti*, March 13, and *Novaya gazeta*, March 14, 2020.

48. Opinion surveys taken from January 2020 onward consistently showed a majority in favour of the constitutional changes.

49. See, for instance, *New York Times*, July 2, 2020: 'Russia's national plebiscite, intended to keep President Vladimir V. Putin in power until at least 2036 . . .'

50. In an interview shown on Rossiya 1 on March 8, 2020, Putin said the purpose of the constitutional change was not 'to prolong my time in office'. Later he explained what he meant: 'Without it, people at very many levels of government will . . . start looking around in search of possible successors instead of working normally . . . I know this from personal experience' (ibid., June 21, 2020).

51. Aleksandr Ryklin, 'Pozhiznennoe dlya vozhdya', Republic.ru, Nov. 6, 2020.

52. 'Interview with NBC', June 14, 2021, *supra*.

53. A good account of the gradual expansion of Foreign Agent legislation is given in Rimma Polyak, 'Zolotoi yarlyk: kak menyalos ponyatie "inostranny agent" v rossiiskom zakonodatelstve' ['Golden Nametag: How the Concept of "Foreign Agent" Changed in Russian Legislation'] April 26, 2021, republic.ru/posts/100247?utm_source=republic.ru&utm_medium=email&utm_campaign=morning

54. Interfax, May 23, 2015 and www.rbc.ru/politics/23/05/2015/55609f719a794774b30bd2a7

55. '20 Questions with Vladimir Putin', TASS, Feb. 20, 2020, Part 7, www.kremlin.ru/events/president/transcripts/62924

56. This account is drawn from a Bellingcat investigation, published on December 14, 2020 (www.bellingcat.com/news/uk-and-europe/2020/12/14/fsb-team-of-chemical-weapon-experts-implicated-in-alexey-navalny-novichok-poisoning/). The same FSB team trailed Navalny in 2017, when he was planning to contest the following year's presidential election, but the surveillance stopped after he was prevented from registering as a candidate.

57. Navalny said he had called the specialist, Konstantin Kudryavtsev, on his mobile phone using special software to make it appear that he was speaking from FSB headquarters in Moscow. He identified himself as an aide to Nikolai Patrushev, the Security Council Secretary, and said he was gathering material for a high-level inquiry. In a recording of the call, posted on Navalny's YouTube channel, the man identified as Kudryavtsev said the plan had failed because they had not foreseen that the pilot would make an emergency landing at Omsk. (The original recording, at www.youtube.com/watch?v=ibqiet6bG38, has been removed. Re-edited versions with Russian and English subtitles are at www.youtube.com/watch?v=HlJbwUhIBxE and www.youtube.com/watch?v=gwvA49ZXnf8). Any doubts about its authenticity were laid to rest a year later when it was announced that three men had been arrested for selling Navalny's associates the phone numbers of Kudryavtsev and other operatives involved in the poisoning (TASS and the Telegram channel, Baza, Nov. 1, 2021).

58. RIA Novosti, Sept 3, Interfax, Sept. 9, Channel One, Sept. 11, and 'Comment by the Information and Press Department', Sept. 25, 2020, www.mid.ru/foreign_policy/news/-/asset_publisher/cKNonkJE02Bw/content/id/4350818?p_p_id=101_INSTANCE_cKNonkJE02Bw&_101_INSTANCE_cKNonkJE02Bw_languageId=ru_RU

59. *Le Monde*, Sept. 22, 2020.

60. Rossiya 1 and Rossiya 24, Dec. 17, 2020. The Russian phrase is ambiguous: it could mean 'if we had wanted', or 'if they had wanted'.

61. www.youtube.com/watch?v=HlJbwUhIBxE

62. 'Interview with Austrian ORF', June 4, 2018, www.kremlin.ru/events/president/transcripts/57675

63. 'Interview with NBC', June 14, 2021, www.kremlin.ru/events/president/transcripts/65861

64. In 2017, the *Washington Post* bureau chief in Moscow, David Filipov, compiled a list of ten critics of Putin's regime who had died suspicious deaths. Boris Nemtsov and Anna Politkovskaya

were victims of the Kadyrov regime in Chechnya. That may also have been the case with Stanislav Markelov and Anastasiya Baburova, a lawyer and a journalist for *Novaya gazeta*, shot in Moscow in 2009, although members of a neo-Nazi group were convicted of their murders. Natalia Estemirova, a human rights activist, was killed in Chechnya, probably by FSB officers whose activities she was investigating. Denis Voronenkov, a former Communist deputy who had become a fierce opponent of Putin's regime, was the victim of a contract hit ordered by business associates. Boris Berezovsky almost certainly committed suicide, although the British coroner recorded an open verdict. Sergei Magnitsky's death was brought about by corrupt Interior Ministry officials. Sergei Yushenkov, a former army colonel and veteran liberal member of the Duma who was investigating the 'Three Whales' scandal, was killed as part of an FSB cover-up. Another Duma deputy, Yuri Shchekochikhin, who was poisoned in 2003, probably died for the same reason. Of the 10 cases Filipov listed, only the death of Aleksandr Litvinenko can be laid firmly at Putin's door. All the others appear to have been killed for reasons unconnected with the Kremlin (*Washington Post*, March 24, 2017). That is not to exonerate Putin. The culpability of his regime is not in question. But making broad-brush accusations which, on closer examination, do not stand up, does not help us to understand either the man or the administration he heads.

65. The extent to which leaders should be held responsible for the ills of their societies is a vast subject which goes far beyond the compass of this book.

66. The classic examples were the murders of Stalin's rival, Kirov, in Leningrad in 1934, and of Trotsky in Mexico City in 1940. The execution of Lavrenty Beria in December, 1953, nine months after Stalin's death, was the last officially sanctioned killing of a political leader in Russia. But Beria had the blood of thousands on his hands.

67. 'Meeting with Students', July 21, 2017, *supra*.

68. Andrei Kolesnikov, 'Why Navalny Makes Many Russians Uncomfortable', Carnegie moscow.org, March 10, and *Moscow Times*, July 10, 2021.

69. See Rimma Polyak, 'Zolotoi Yarlik . . .', April 26, 2021, *supra*.

70. *Washington Post*, April 18, 2021.

71. *Novaya gazeta*, Dec. 11, 2020.

72. 'In Declaring Navalny Extremist, Russia has Crossed a New Rubicon', Carnegiemoscow. org, May 25, 2021.

73. Under Hong Kong's security laws, a man was sentenced to nine years' in jail for carrying a flag with the words, 'Liberate Hong Kong: Revolution of Our Times', which the court ruled was a call for secession. He could have been given a life sentence (*New York Times*, July 31, 2021).

74. *Kommersant*, *Vedomosti* and *RBK*, June 10, 2021.

75. Ivan Davydov in Republic.ru, Aug. 24, 2021.

76. Rimma Polyak in Republic.ru, Aug 16, 2021.

77. *New York Times*, Aug. 31, 2021.

78. 'Annual News Conference', Dec. 17, 2020, www.kremlin.ru/events/president/transcripts/ 64671

79. edition.cnn.com/videos/politics/2021/03/17/president-biden-vladimir-putin-russia-gma- newday-vpx.cnn/video/playlists/around-the-world/

80. *Washington Post*, Feb. 5, 2017.

81. edition.cnn.com/videos . . . , *supra*.

82. *Komsomolskaya pravda* and *Rossiiskaya gazeta*, March 18, 2021.

83. Rossiya 24, March 18, 2021.

84. The extension was agreed by Patrushev and Biden's National Security Adviser, Jake Sullivan, on January 25 and made public after Biden and Putin spoke the following day.

85. The White House spokesman, Jan Psaki, claimed that it was a Russian initiative, apparently to deflect criticism that, in the midst of the Navalny affair, Biden was not being tough enough.

86. 'Interview with NBC', June 14, 2021, *supra*.

87. Ibid.

88. Until the official US transcript of Biden's meeting with Putin is released, there is no way to be sure exactly what words were used. But Biden's account does raise a number of questions. When he met Putin, in March 2011, the Obama administration still hoped that its vaunted 'reset' with Russia might succeed. It is highly implausible that in those circumstances, Biden would have set out to taunt him. As Putin himself said, 'when leaders meet, they usually try to create the conditions for a positive result.' Moreover, Biden would have been well aware that, two years earlier, Hillary Clinton had made an almost identical comment – 'by definition, he doesn't have a soul' – which had irritated Putin greatly. The chronology is also telling. Biden first recounted the story to Evan Osnos at a moment when Russia and the US were at loggerheads over Ukraine ('The Biden Agenda', *New Yorker*, July 28, 2014). Then he repeated it in March 2021, at another moment when he wished to display a tough line towards Russia. On both occasions, he was clearly speaking, in Putin's words, for 'domestic political consumption'. That does not rule out the possibility that some such discussion may have occurred. But perhaps not in the form Biden claimed to remember.

89. *Independent*, April 9, *Guardian*, April 10, and *Washington Post*, April 11, 2021.

90. 'Russian-US Talks', Geneva, June 16, 2021, www.kremlin.ru/events/president/transcripts/65869

91. 'News Conference after U.S.-Russia Talks', Geneva, June 16, 2021, www.kremlin.ru/events/president/transcripts/65870

92. 'U.S.-Russia Presidential Joint Statement', June 16, 2021, www.kremlin.ru/supplement/5658. The first meeting, at deputy ministerial level, devoted mainly to cybersecurity, was held in Geneva on July 28.

93. 'Meeting of Valdai Club', Sochi, Oct. 21, 2021, www.kremlin.ru/events/president/transcripts/66975

94. 'Interview with CBS and PBS', Sept. 29, 2015, *supra*.

95. 'Speech to the Federal Assembly', April 21, 2021, www.kremlin.ru/events/president/transcripts/65418

96. 'Annual News Conference', Dec. 17, 2020, *supra*.

97. 'Annual News Conference', Dec. 20, 2018, *supra*.

98. Comments on Putin's introductory remarks at a meeting of the Valdai Club (Oct. 22, 2020, *supra*). Putin's speech to the World Economic Forum in Davos in January 2021 (*supra*) was another example.

99. 'The 75th Anniversary of the Great Victory: A Shared Responsibility to History', June 19, 2020, www.kremlin.ru/events/president/transcripts/63527 See also 'On the Historical Unity of Ukrainians and Russians', July 12, 2021, www.kremlin.ru/events/president/transcripts/66181

100. Ivan Davydov, 'The Unnatural Intelligence of Repression: Is there a domestic policy in Russia?', Republic.ru, Nov. 12, 2021.

101. Rossiya 1, Nov. 13, 2021.

102. Other possibilities include the chairmanship of a reconstituted State Council – a body which, as Aleksei Venediktov noted, is 'an empty, square frame which can be filled with

anything you want' – or, in theory at least, the presidency of a future Russia–Belarus Union State. The latter, however, would depend on Putin agreeing a division of powers with Aleksandr Lukashenko, a goal which has eluded successive Russian governments ('Putin is Building a Government Structure for 2024', Republic.ru, Oct. 25, 2021).

103. The citation is from the last of Putin's interviews with TASS, recorded on February 20, 2020, but not issued until October 7 because of the Covid-19 pandemic (www.putin.tass.ru/ru/o-detyakh-i-vnukakh).

104. Questions about his future intentions, which earlier he had been quite willing to discuss, were now systematically rebuffed ('Interview with CNBC', Oct. 14, 2021, www.kremlin.ru/events/president/transcripts/66920).

105. '20 Questions with Vladimir Putin', TASS, Feb. 20, 2020, Part 17, *supra*.

106. 'Putin's Labyrinth', Carnegiemoscow.org, Oct. 20, 2021.

107. 'Direct Line with Vladimir Putin', June 30, 2021, *supra*.

108. 'On the Historical Unity of Russians and Ukrainians', July 12, 2021, *supra*.

109. 'Vladimir Putin answered Questions . . .', July 13, 2021, www.kremlin.ru/events/president/news/66191

110. 'On the Historical Unity . . .', *supra*.

111. 'Expanded Meeting of the Foreign Ministry Board', Nov. 18, 2021, www.kremlin.ru/events/president/transcripts/67123

112. 'Ceremony for . . . Letters of Credence', Dec. 1, 2021, www.kremlin.ru/events/president/transcripts/67250

113. *Washington Post*, Jan. 7 and *New York Times*, Jan. 9, 2022.

114. BBC Monitoring, Feb. 4, 2022.

115. 'Address by the President', Feb. 21, www.kremlin.ru/events/president/transcripts/67825 and 'Vladimir Putin answered media questions', Feb. 22, 2022, www.kremlin.ru/events/president/transcripts/67838

116. BBC Monitoring, Feb. 25, 2022.

117. *Novaya gazeta*, Feb. 25, 2022.

118. 'Address by the President . . .', Feb. 24, 2022, www.kremlin.ru/events/president/transcripts/67843.

119. Proekt, Dec. 8, 2020 (www.proekt.media/article/kabinet-putina-v-sochi).

120. That seemed to be confirmed when, less than 10 days later, Putin was shown sitting in the midst of a group of Aeroflot personnel (www.kremlin.ru/events/president/news/67913/ photos on March 5, 2022). A series of in-person meetings with government officials followed, starting on March 9. In April, Putin held a meeting with members of a pro-government NGO in the Catherine Hall, where, in contrast to the Security Council meeting, he sat close to the other delegates and afterwards mingled with them (www.kremlin.ru/events/president/news/68250/photos/67884). After the declaration of war on February 24, the long table was not seen again.

121. 'Address by the President . . .', Feb. 24, supra; Interfax, Feb. 27; *Nezavisimaya gazeta*, March 4 and *New York Times*, March 23, 2022.

122. www.theintercept.com/2022/03/11/russia-putin-ukraine-invasion-us-intelligence/

123. Blinken's adviser, Derek Chollet, confirmed that, before the Russian invasion, the US told Moscow that the question of Ukraine's relationship with NATO was 'not on the table' (War on the Rocks, April 13, 2022. www.warontherocks.com/2022/04/a-conversation-with-the-counselor-derek-chollet-on-navigating-the-world/

124. Fiona Hill in *New York Times*, April 9, 2022.

125. Lavrov, interview transcript on Telegram channel Pul N3, March 16, 2022.

126. 'Joint Press Conference with President of Belarus', April 12, 2022, www.kremlin.r/events/president/transcripts/68182

127. There were signs early on in the conflict that this had not passed unnoticed. The Polish leader, Jaroslaw Kaczynski, called for 'a large NATO operational command headquarters [to be based] in Poland as a clear signal to Moscow that the leadership level of NATO now exists in the East as well' (*Welt am Sonntag*, April 3, 2022). In another, more explicit comment, the British politician, Lord Meghnad Desai, said NATO had been shown to be 'a paper tiger... When it is all over, European countries will have to re-examine their security strategies', March 23, 2022 (www.omfif.org/2022/03/war-has-shattered-illusions-of-the-west/)

128. *Washington Post*, April 17, 2022.

129. Reuters, April 21, 2022.

130. Defense Secretary Lloyd Austin, cited in *Washington Post*, April 25, 2022.

131. Republic.ru, March 17, 2022.

132. War crimes are an abomination but they are not genocide. To use such terms loosely devalues the specific horror of the Holocaust and other racial massacres like that in Rwanda. Whatever crimes Russia has committed in Ukraine, and there have been many, genocide – in the sense of a conscious attempt to exterminate in whole or in part the Ukrainian people – is not one of them. To claim otherwise is to descend to the same level as Russia when it alleges falsely that the Ukrainian government has been carrying out genocide against the inhabitants of Donetsk and Luhansk.

133. *New York Times*, May 4, 2022.

134. 'Meeting on socioeconomic support for the regions', March 16, 2022, www.kremlin.ru/events/president/transcripts/67996.

135. Andrei Movchan, Republic.ru, April 25, 2022.

Afterword

1. Dmitry Trenin, 'After Cop26', Carnegiemoscow.org, Nov. 16, 2021.

2. This is discussed at length by Dmitry Trenin in *Novy balans sil: Rossiya v poiskakh vneshnepoliticheskogo ravnovesiya*, Alpina, Moscow, 2021.

3. One of the first published reports to note this development was Aleksandr Golts, 'Sovmestnye rossiisko-kitaiskie ucheniya', Republic.ru, Aug. 30, 2021. See also *New York Times*, Nov. 3 and Nov. 29, 2021.

4. 'Meeting of Valdai Club', Oct. 21, 2021, *supra*.

Index